# NINTH EDITION

# AN INTRODUCTION TO MANAGEMENT SCIENCE

## QUANTITATIVE APPROACHES TO DECISION MAKING

**David R. Anderson**
University of Cincinnati

**Dennis J. Sweeney**
University of Cincinnati

**Thomas A. Williams**
Rochester Institute of Technology

**South-Western College Publishing**
*an International Thomson Publishing company*  I(T)P®

Cincinnati • Albany • Boston • Detroit • Johannesburg • London • Madrid • Melbourne • Mexico City
New York • Pacific Grove • San Francisco • Scottsdale • Singapore • Tokyo • Toronto

**Dedication:** To Our Parents

Acquisitions Editor: Charles E. McCormick, Jr.
Developmental Editor: Alice C. Denny
Marketing Manager: Joseph A. Sabatino
Production Editor: Deanna R. Quinn
Manufacturing Coordinator: Dana Began Schwartz
Internal Design: Michael H. Stratton
Cover Design: Michael H. Stratton
Cover Photographer: Mark Tomalty/Masterfile
Production House and Compositor: BookMasters, Inc.
Printer: World Color Book Services

Printed in the United States of America
1  2  3  4  5  6  7  8  9  10

International Thomson Publishing Europe
Berkshire House
168-173 High Holborn
London, WC1V7AA, United Kingdom

Nelson ITP, Australia
102 Dodds Street
South Melbourne
Victoria 3205 Australia

Nelson Canada
1120 Birchmount Road
Scarborough, Ontario
Canada M1K 5G4

International Thomson Publishing Southern Africa
Building 18, Constantia Square
138 Sixteenth Road, P.O. Box 2459
Halfway House, 1685 South Africa

International Thomson Editores
Seneca, 53
Colonia Polanco
11560 Mèxico D.F. Mèxico

International Thomson Publishing Asia
60 Alberta Street #15-01
Albert Complex
Singapore 189969

International Thomson Publishing Japan
Hirakawa-cho Kyowa Building, 3F
2-2-1 Hirakawa-cho, Chiyoda-ku
Tokyo 102, Japan

You can request permission to use material from this text through the following phone and fax numbers:
telephone: 1-800-730-2214     fax: 1-800-730-2215
Or you can visit our web site at http://www.thomsonrights.com

**Library of Congress Cataloging-in-Publication Data**

Anderson, David Ray
    Introduction to management science : quantitative approaches to decision making / David R. Anderson, Dennis J. Sweeney, Thomas A. Williams. — 9th ed.
        p.   cm.
    Includes bibliographical references and index.
    ISBN 0-324-00321-8 (hc. : alk. paper)
    1. Management science.   I. Sweeney, Dennis J.   II. Williams, Thomas Arthur.   III. Title.
    HD30.25.A63   2000
    658.4—dc21                                   99-27530

This book is printed on acid-free paper.

# CONTENTS IN BRIEF

# CONTENTS

**Chapter 3    Linear Programming:  Sensitivity Analysis and Interpretation
               of Solution   88**

**Chapter 4    Linear Programming Applications   146**

The purpose of the ninth edition, as with previous editions, is to provide undergraduate and graduate students with a sound conceptual understanding of the role that management science plays in the decision-making process. The text describes many applications in which management science has been used successfully. Former users of this text have told us that the applications we describe have led them to find new ways to use management science in their companies.

*An Introduction to Management Science* is applications oriented and continues to use the problem scenario approach that has been a hallmark of every edition of the text. Using the problem scenario approach, we describe a problem in conjunction with the management science technique being introduced. The development of the management science technique or model includes applying it to the problem to generate a solution or recommendation. We have found that this approach helps to motivate the student by demonstrating not only how the procedure works, but also how it can contribute to the decision-making process.

From the very first edition we have been committed to the challenge of writing a textbook that would help make the mathematical and technical concepts of management science understandable and useful to students of business and economics. Judging from the responses from our teaching colleagues and thousands of students, we have successfully met the challenge. Indeed, the comments and suggestions of many loyal users have helped to make the text successful.

Throughout the text we have utilized generally accepted notation so that students who pursue study beyond the level of this text might be comfortable reading more advanced material. To assist in further study, a references and bibliography section is included at the back of the book.

## CHANGES IN THE NINTH EDITION

In preparing the ninth edition, we have been careful to maintain the overall format and approach of the previous edition. However, based on our classroom experiences and suggestions from users of previous editions, a number of changes have been made to enhance the content, managerial orientation, and readability of the text.

## LINEAR PROGRAMMING

Chapter 2 has undergone a major revision that includes a step-by-step discussion of problem formulation or modeling. We emphasize the need for understanding the problem thoroughly, writing a verbal description of the objective and each constraint, defining the decision variables, writing the objective in terms of the decision variables, and writing the constraints in terms of the decision variables. We think this new approach will ease students' transition to modeling more complex problems in Chapters 3 and 4.

In the previous edition, the computer solution of a linear program was not introduced until Chapter 3. In the new edition we have moved this discussion to Chapter 2, immediately following the graphical solution procedure. In this section we show how *The Management Scientist* software package can be used to solve a linear program. Appendix A at the back of the book provides an overview of the features available with *The Management Scientist*. Step-by-step instructions for using the software to solve a linear program are provided in the appendix to Chapter 2. In addition, a new Appendix G has been added to illustrate the use of LINDO in solving linear programming problems.

In introducing both the maximization and minimization cases we have changed from using $x_1$ and $x_2$ notation for the decision variables to more descriptive notation. For example, in the Par, Inc., problem used to introduce linear programming, we now let $S$ denote the number of standard bags and $D$ the number of deluxe bags. However, because we believe it is important for students to be able to write a mathematical model using general linear programming notation, the final section in Chapter 2 shows the use of general notation.

Chapter 3 now focuses on sensitivity analysis and interpretation. It also offers additional practice in formulating, solving, and interpreting the solution for more complex problems.

## SIMULATION

Chapter 13 on simulation has undergone a major revision. The new edition provides simulation output for both one-channel and two-channel waiting line systems, and discusses the added service benefits of the two-channel system. The chapter also offers approximately 20 new problems, a revised spreadsheet appendix, and two new Management Science in Action vignettes.

## DECISION ANALYSIS

Chapter 14's coverage of decision analysis has been revised in order to provide more emphasis on the decision-making process and less on the technical details of computing revised probabilities. Use of Bayes Theorem and the detailed calculations of revised probabilities are now included in an optional section.

## MULTICRITERIA DECISON PROBLEMS

A new section on scoring models has been added to Chapter 15 as a quick and relatively easy way to identify a decision alternative for a multicriteria problem. The section on AHP has been restructured to better match the flow of the decision process for a car selection problem that now involves three alternatives with data for three automobiles: Accord, Saturn, and Cavalier. A Microsoft® Excel appendix showing how to implement the scoring model has also been added.

## SPREADSHEET APPENDIXES

Spreadsheet appendixes to show how Excel can be used to implement some of the methods explained in the text were first introduced in the previous edition. Based on our teaching experience using Excel, we have rewritten the previous spreadsheet appendixes and have added four new ones. The new edition offers spreadsheet appendixes for Chapter 1, Introduction; Chapter 2, Introduction to Linear Programming; Chapter 3, Linear Programming: Sensitivity Analysis and Interpretation of Solution; Chapter 7, Transportation, Assignment, and Transshipment Problems; Chapter 8, Integer Linear Programming; Chapter 11, Inventory Models; Chapter 12, Waiting Line Models; Chapter 13, Simulation; Chapter 14, Decision Analysis; Chapter 15, Multicriteria Decision Problems; and Chapter 16, Forecasting. For students and faculty who are comfortable with spreadsheets, these appendixes provide an alternative to the software tools provided by management science software packages.

## NEW PROBLEMS AND CASE PROBLEMS

We have updated approximately 10 percent of the problems in the book and have added new case problems in linear programming, linear programming applications, integer linear programming, and waiting line models.

## *THE MANAGEMENT SCIENTIST* SOFTWARE PACKAGE

The new version 5.0 of *The Management Scientist* is now available for Windows 95, Windows 98, and Windows NT operating systems. We have made a number of improvements in entering and editing data in several modules. For instance, in the forecasting module the user may now add and delete time series observations. The integer programming module has been reworked to provide a more stable and robust solution procedure, and the user interface has been enhanced to improve ease of use.

## FEATURES AND PEDAGOGY

We have continued many of the features from previous editions. Some of the important ones are noted here.

### Annotations

Annotations that highlight key points and provide additional insights for the student are a continuing feature of this edition. These annotations, which appear in the margins, are designed to provide emphasis and enhance understanding of the terms and concepts being presented in the text.

### Notes & Comments

At the end of many sections, we provide Notes & Comments designed to give the student additional insights about the quantitative methodology and its application. Notes & Comments include warnings about or limitations of the methodology, recommendations for application, brief descriptions of additional technical considerations, and other matters.

### Self-Test Exercises

Certain exercises are identified as self-test exercises. Completely worked-out solutions for those exercises are provided in an appendix at the end of the text. Students can attempt the self-test exercises and immediately check the solution to evaluate their understanding of the concepts presented in the chapter.

## ANCILLARY TEACHING AND LEARNING MATERIALS

As has always been the case, this new edition of *An Introduction to Management Science* has ancillaries that will increase the value of the text to both students and instructors.

- **Study Guide** (ISBN: 0-324-00324-2)   Prepared by John Loucks of St. Edward's University, the *Study Guide* will provide the student with significant supplementary study materials. It contains an outline, a review and a list of formulas for each text chapter, sample exercises with step-by-step solutions, exercises with answers, and a series of self-testing questions with answers. The *Study Guide* may be purchased at a special price when bundled with the textbook (Smartpak ISBN: 0-324-07946-X).
- *The Management Scientist,* version 5.0 (ISBN: 0-324-00890-2)   provides 12 computer modules for working through the problems in the course. The software is class tested to run with little or no instructor supervision. Thorough documentation, including examples of how to use the software on actual problems, accompanies the

CD-ROM. *The Management Scientist* software may also be purchased at a value price when bundled with the textbook (Smartpak ISBN: 0-538-50834-5).

- **LINDO® version 6.01**    The new Windows version of LINDO has been completely redesigned to make it more intuitive and easier to use. It has the familiar Windows graphical interface with pull-down menus, dialog boxes, and a tool bar for frequently used commands. An educational version of LINDO 6.01 software is sold at a discounted price when it is packaged with the text (Smartpak ISBN: 0-324-07944-3). In Appendix G we describe how to use the Windows version of LINDO by entering and solving the Par, Inc., problem introduced in Chapter 2.

The following support materials are available to adopters from the ITP Academic Resource Center at 800-423-0563 or through **www.swcollege.com:**

- **Solutions Manual**    The *Solutions Manual* (ISBN: 0-324-00323-4), prepared by the authors, includes solutions for all problems in the text. At the request of the instructor, the *Solutions Manual* can be packaged with the text for student purchase.
- **Instructor's Manual**    The *Instructor's Manual* (ISBN: 0-324-00322-6), also prepared by the authors, contains solutions to all case problems presented in the text. The manual also provides brief annotations for problems in the text. These annotations will help instructor's select homework problems designed to meet their course objectives.
- **Microsoft® PowerPoint™ Presentation Slides**    Also prepared by John Loucks, the presentation slides (ISBN: 0-324-00326-9) contain a teaching outline that incorporates graphics to help instructors create even more stimulating lectures. The PowerPoint 97 slides may be adapted using PowerPoint software to facilitate classroom use.
- **Test Bank**    Prepared by a new member of the ASW team, Kenneth Lawrence of New Jersey Institute of Technology, the Test Bank (ISBN: 0-324-00325-0) includes true/false, multiple choice, short answer questions, and problems for each chapter. South-Western's computerized testing software (ISBN: 0-324-00327-7) allows instructors to create, edit, store, and print exams.

## COURSE OUTLINE FLEXIBILITY

The text has been designed to enhance the instructor's flexibility in selecting topics to meet specific course needs. The single-semester and single-quarter outlines that follow are a sampling of the many options available.

### One-Semester Course
### Emphasis on Linear Programming, Model Development, and Applications

- Introduction (Chapter 1)
- Introduction to Linear Programming and Computer Solutions (Chapters 2 and 3)
- Linear Programming Applications (Chapter 4)
- Transportation, Assignment, and Transshipment Models (Chapter 7)
- Integer Programming (Chapter 8)
- Project Scheduling: Pert/CPM (Chapter 10)
- Inventory Models (Chapter 11)
- Waiting Lines (Chapter 12)
- Simulation (Chapter 13)
- Decision Analysis (Chapter 14)
- Multicriteria Decision Making (Chapter 15)

The instructor in a one-semester course who wants to focus on model development and other applications could either spend more time on the applications in Chapter 4 or cover additional topics.

### One-Quarter Course
### Emphasis on Linear Programming, Model Development, and Applications

- Introduction (Chapter 1)
- Introduction to Linear Programming and Computer Solutions (Chapters 2 and 3)
- Linear Programming Applications (selected portions of Chapters 4 and 7)
- Project Scheduling: Pert/CPM (Chapter 10)
- Waiting Lines (Chapter 12)
- Simulation (Chapter 13)
- Decison Analysis (Chapter 14)

## ACKNOWLEDGMENTS

We owe a debt to many of our colleagues and friends for their helpful comments and suggestions during the development of this and previous editions.

Robert L. Armacost, University of Central Florida

Uttarayan Bagchi, University of Texas at Austin

Edward Baker, University of Miami

Norman Baker, University of Cincinnati

Oded Berman, University of Toronto

Jeffrey Camm, University of Cincinnati

Ying Chien, University of Scranton

John Eatman, University of North Carolina-Greensboro

Ronald Ebert, University of Missouri-Columbia

Don Edwards, University of South Carolina

Ronald Ehresman, Baldwin-Wallace College

Peter Ellis, Utah State University

Lawrence Ettkin, Chattanooga

Jim Evans, University of Cincinnati

Michael Ford, Rochester Institute of Technology

Terri Friel, Eastern Kentucky University

Phil Fry, Boise State University

Robert Garfinkel, University of Connecticut

Nicholas G. Hall, The Ohio State University

Michael E. Hanna, University of Houston-Clear Lake

David Hott, Florida Institute of Technology

Barry Kadets, Bryant College

John Lawrence, Jr., California State University-Fullerton

Ka-sing Man, Georgetown University

William G. Marchal, University of Toledo

Kamlesh Mathur, Case Western Reserve University

Joseph Mazzola, Duke University

Patrick McKeown, University of Georgia

Constance McLaren, Indiana State University

Edward Minieka, University of Illinois-Chicago

Mario Miranda, The Ohio State University

Alan Neebe, University of North Carolina

David Pentico, Duquesne University

B. Madhusudan Rao, Bowling Green State University

Handanhal V. Ravinder, University of New Mexico

Donna Retzlaff-Roberts, University of Memphis

Don R. Robinson, Illinois State University

Richard Rosenthal, Naval Postgraduate School

Antoinette Somers, Wayne State University

Christopher S. Tang, University of California-Los Angeles

Giri Kumar Tayi, State University of New York-Albany

Willban Terpening, Gonzaga University

Edward P. Winkofsky, Mead Corporation

Sajjad Zahir, University of Lethbridge

Our associates from organizations who supplied the Management Science in Practice applications made a major contribution to the text. These individuals are cited in a credit line on the first page of each application.

We are also indebted to our acquisitions editor Charles McCormick, Jr., our senior developmental editor Alice Denny, our production editor Deanna Quinn, our designer Mike Stratton, our marketing manager Joe Sabatino, and others at South-Western College Publishing for their counsel and support during the preparation of this text.

*David R. Anderson*
*Dennis J. Sweeney*
*Thomas A. Williams*

**David R. Anderson.**  David R. Anderson is Professor of Quantitative Analysis in the College of Business Administration at the University of Cincinnati. Born in Grand Forks, North Dakota, he earned his B.S., M.S., and Ph.D. degrees from Purdue University. Professor Anderson has served as Head of the Department of Quantitative Analysis and Operations Management and as Associate Dean of the College of Business Administration. In addition, he was the coordinator of the College's first Executive Program.

At the University of Cincinnati, Professor Anderson has taught introductory statistics for business students as well as graduate-level courses in regression analysis, multivariate analysis, and management science. He has also taught statistical courses at the Department of Labor in Washington, D.C. He has been honored with nominations and awards for excellence in teaching and excellence in service to student organizations.

Professor Anderson has coauthored eight textbooks in the areas of statistics, management science, linear programming, and production and operations management. He is an active consultant in the field of sampling and statistical methods.

**Dennis J. Sweeney.**  Dennis J. Sweeney is Professor of Quantitative Analysis and Director of the Center for Productivity Improvement at the University of Cincinnati. Born in Des Moines, Iowa, he earned a B.S.B.A. degree from Drake University and his M.B.A. and D.B.A. degrees from Indiana University where he was an NDEA Fellow. During 1978–79, Professor Sweeney worked in the management science group at Procter & Gamble; during 1981–82, he was a visiting professor at Duke University. Professor Sweeney served as Head of the Department of Quantitative Analysis and as Associate Dean of the College of Business Administration at the University of Cincinnati.

Professor Sweeney has published more than 30 articles and monographs in the area of management science and statistics. The National Science Foundation, IBM, Procter & Gamble, Federated Department Stores, Kroger, and Cincinnati Gas & Electric have funded his research, which has been published in *Management Science, Operations Research, Mathematical Programming, Decision Sciences,* and other journals.

Professor Sweeney has coauthored eight textbooks in the areas of statistics, management science, linear programming, and production and operations management.

**Thomas A. Williams.**  Thomas A. Williams is Professor of Management Science in the College of Business at Rochester Institute of Technology. Born in Elmira, New York, he earned his B.S. degree at Clarkson University. He did his graduate work at Rensselaer Polytechnic Institute, where he received his M.S. and Ph.D. degrees.

Before joining the College of Business at RIT, Professor Williams served for seven years as a faculty member in the College of Business Administration at the University of Cincinnati, where he developed the undergraduate program in Information Systems and then served as its coordinator. At RIT he was the first chairman of the Decision Sciences Department. He teaches courses in management science and statistics, as well as graduate courses in regression and decision analysis.

Professor Williams is the coauthor of nine textbooks in the areas of management science, statistics, production and operations management, and mathematics. He has been a consultant for numerous *Fortune* 500 companies and has worked on projects ranging from the use of data analysis to the development of large-scale regression models.

# 1

# INTRODUCTION

## CONTENTS

Management science, an approach to decision making based on the scientific method, makes extensive use of quantitative analysis. A variety of names exists for the body of knowledge involving quantitative approaches to decision making; in addition to management science, two other widely known and accepted names are *operations research* and *decision science*. Today, many use the terms management science, operations research, and decision science interchangeably.

The scientific management revolution of the early 1900s, initiated by Frederic W. Taylor, provided the foundation for the use of quantitative methods in management. But modern management science research is generally considered to have originated during the World War II period, when teams were formed to deal with strategic and tactical problems faced by the military. These teams, which often consisted of people with diverse specialties (e.g., mathematicians, engineers, and behavioral scientists), were joined together to solve a common problem through the utilization of the scientific method. After the war, many of these team members continued their research in the field of management science.

Two developments that occurred during the post–World War II period led to the growth and use of management science in nonmilitary applications. First, continued research resulted in numerous methodological developments. Probably the most significant development was the discovery by George Dantzig, in 1947, of the simplex method for solving linear programming problems. Many more methodological developments followed, and in 1957 the first book on operations research was published by Churchman, Ackoff, and Arnoff.[1]

Concurrently with these methodological developments, there was a virtual explosion in computing power made available through digital computers. Computers enabled practitioners to use the methodological advances to solve a large variety of problems. The computer technology explosion continues; personal computers are now more powerful than earlier mainframe computers. Today, variants of the post–World War II methodological developments are being used on personal computers to solve problems larger than those solved on mainframe computers in the 1990s.

## I.I    PROBLEM SOLVING AND DECISION MAKING

**Problem solving** can be defined as the process of identifying a difference between the actual and the desired state of affairs and then taking action to resolve the difference. For problems important enough to justify the time and effort of careful analysis, the problem-solving process involves the following seven steps:

1. Identify and define the problem.
2. Determine the set of alternative solutions.
3. Determine the criterion or criteria that will be used to evaluate the alternatives.
4. Evaluate the alternatives.
5. Choose an alternative.
6. Implement the selected alternative.
7. Evaluate the results to determine whether a satisfactory solution has been obtained.

**Decision making** is the term generally associated with the first five steps of the problem-solving process. Thus, the first step of decision making is to identify and define the problem. Decision making ends with the choosing of an alternative, which is the act of making the decision.

---

[1] C. W. Churchman, R. L. Ackoff, and E. L. Arnoff, *Introduction to Operations Research* (New York: Wiley, 1957).

Let us consider the following example of the decision-making process. For the moment assume that you are currently unemployed and that you would like a position that will lead to a satisfying career. Suppose that your job search has resulted in offers from companies in Rochester, New York; Dallas, Texas; Greensboro, North Carolina; and Pittsburgh, Pennsylvania. Thus, the alternatives for your decision problem can be stated as follows:

1. Accept the position in Rochester.
2. Accept the position in Dallas.
3. Accept the position in Greensboro.
4. Accept the position in Pittsburgh.

The next step of the problem-solving process involves determining the criteria that will be used to evaluate the four alternatives. Obviously, the starting salary is a factor of some importance. If salary were the only criterion of importance to you, the alternative selected as "best" would be the one with the highest starting salary. Problems in which the objective is to find the best solution with respect to one criterion are referred to as **single-criterion decision problems.**

Suppose that you have also concluded that the potential for advancement and the location of the job are two other criteria of major importance. Thus, the three criteria in your decision problem are starting salary, potential for advancement, and location. Problems that involve more than one criterion are referred to as **multicriteria decision problems.**

The next step of the decision-making process is to evaluate each of the alternatives with respect to each criterion. For example, evaluating each alternative relative to the starting salary criterion is done simply by recording the starting salary for each job alternative. Evaluating each alternative with respect to the potential for advancement and the location of the job is more difficult to do, however, since these evaluations are based primarily on subjective factors that are often difficult to quantify. Suppose for now that you have decided to measure potential for advancement and job location by rating each of these criteria as poor, fair, average, good, or excellent. The data that you have compiled are shown in Table 1.1.

You are now ready to make a choice from the available alternatives. What makes this choice phase so difficult is that the criteria are probably not all equally important, and no one alternative is "best" with regard to all criteria. Although we will present a method for dealing with situations like this one later in the text, for now let us suppose that after a careful evaluation of the data in Table 1.1, you have decided to select alternative 3; alternative 3 is thus referred to as the **decision.**

At this point in time, the decision-making process is complete. In summary, we see that this process involves five steps:

1. Define the problem.
2. Identify the alternatives.

| Table 1.1 | DATA FOR THE JOB EVALUATION DECISION-MAKING PROBLEM | | |
|---|---|---|---|
| **Alternative** | **Starting Salary** | **Potential for Advancement** | **Job Location** |
| 1. Rochester | $38,500 | Average | Average |
| 2. Dallas | $36,000 | Excellent | Good |
| 3. Greensboro | $36,000 | Good | Excellent |
| 4. Pittsburgh | $37,000 | Average | Good |

3. Determine the criteria.
4. Evaluate the alternatives.
5. Choose an alternative.

Note that missing from this list are the last two steps in the problem-solving process: implementing the selected alternative and evaluating the results to determine whether a satisfactory solution has been obtained. This omission is not meant to diminish the importance of each of these activities, but to emphasize the more limited scope of the term *decision making* as compared to the term *problem solving*. Figure 1.1 summarizes the relationship between these two concepts.

*Figure* 1.1     **THE RELATIONSHIP BETWEEN PROBLEM SOLVING AND DECISION MAKING**

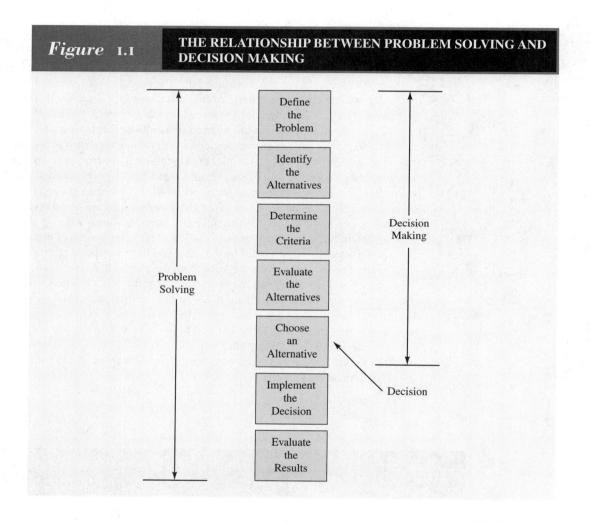

## I.2     QUANTITATIVE ANALYSIS AND DECISION MAKING

Consider the flowchart presented in Figure 1.2. Note that we have combined the first three steps of the decision-making process under the heading of "Structuring the Problem" and the latter two steps under the heading "Analyzing the Problem." Let us now

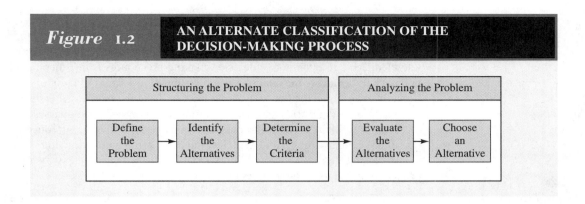

**Figure 1.2**    AN ALTERNATE CLASSIFICATION OF THE DECISION-MAKING PROCESS

consider in greater detail how to carry out the set of activities that make up the decision-making process.

Figure 1.3 shows that the analysis phase of the decision-making process may take two basic forms: qualitative and quantitative. Qualitative analysis is based primarily on the manager's judgment and experience; it includes the manager's intuitive "feel" for the problem and is more an art than a science. If the manager has had experience with similar problems, or if the problem is relatively simple, heavy emphasis may be placed upon a qualitative analysis. However, if the manager has had little experience with similar problems, or if the problem is sufficiently complex, then a quantitative analysis of the problem can be an especially important consideration in the manager's final decision.

When using the quantitative approach, an analyst will concentrate on the quantitative facts or data associated with the problem and develop mathematical expressions that describe the objectives, constraints, and other relationships that exist in the problem. Then, by using one or more quantitative methods, the analyst will make a recommendation based on the quantitative aspects of the problem.

Although skills in the qualitative approach are inherent in the manager and usually increase with experience, the skills of the quantitative approach can be learned only by

Quantitative methods are especially helpful with large, complex problems. For example, in the coordination of the thousands of tasks associated with landing the Apollo 11 safely on the moon, quantitative techniques helped to ensure that more than 300,000 pieces of work performed by more than 400,000 people were integrated smoothly.

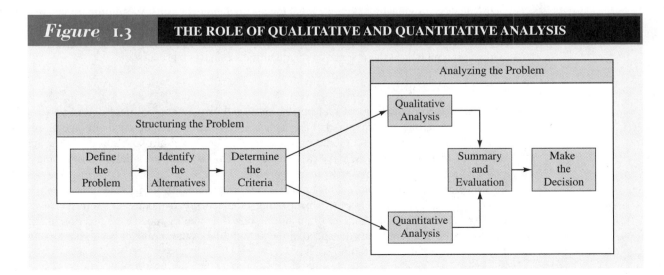

**Figure 1.3**    THE ROLE OF QUALITATIVE AND QUANTITATIVE ANALYSIS

studying the assumptions and methods of management science. A manager can increase decision-making effectiveness by learning more about quantitative methodology and by better understanding its contribution to the decision-making process. A manager who is knowledgeable in quantitative decision-making procedures is in a much better position to compare and evaluate the qualitative and quantitative sources of recommendations and ultimately to combine the two sources in order to make the best possible decision.

The box in Figure 1.3 entitled "Quantitative Analysis" encompasses most of the subject matter of this text. We will consider a managerial problem, introduce the appropriate quantitative methodology, and then develop the recommended decision.

In closing this section, let us briefly state some of the reasons why a quantitative approach might be used in the decision-making process:

Try Problem 4 to test your understanding of why quantitative approaches might be needed in a particular problem.

1.  The problem is complex, and the manager cannot develop a good solution without the aid of quantitative analysis.
2.  The problem is especially important (e.g., a great deal of money is involved), and the manager desires a thorough analysis before attempting to make a decision.
3.  The problem is new, and the manager has no previous experience from which to draw.
4.  The problem is repetitive, and the manager saves time and effort by relying on quantitative procedures to make routine decision recommendations.

## 1.3    QUANTITATIVE ANALYSIS

From Figure 1.3 we see that quantitative analysis begins once the problem has been structured. It usually takes imagination, teamwork, and considerable effort to transform a rather general problem description into a well-defined problem that can be approached via quantitative analysis. The more the analyst is involved in the process of structuring the problem, the more likely the ensuing quantitative analysis will make an important contribution to the decision-making process.

To successfully apply quantitative analysis to decision making, the management scientist must work closely with the manager or user of the results. When both the management scientist and the manager agree that the problem has been adequately structured, work can begin on developing a model to represent the problem mathematically. Solution procedures can then be employed to find the best solution for the model. This best solution for the model then becomes a recommendation to the decision maker. The process of developing and solving models is the essence of the quantitative analysis process.

### Model Development

**Models** are representations of real objects or situations and can be presented in various forms. For example, a scale model of an airplane is a representation of a real airplane. Similarly, a child's toy truck is a model of a real truck. The model airplane and toy truck are examples of models that are physical replicas of real objects. In modeling terminology, physical replicas are referred to as **iconic models.**

A second classification includes models that are physical in form but do not have the same physical appearance as the object being modeled. Such models are referred to as **analog models.** The speedometer of an automobile is an analog model; the position of the needle on the dial represents the speed of the automobile. A thermometer is another analog model representing temperature.

A third classification of models—the type we will primarily be studying—includes representations of a problem by a system of symbols and mathematical relationships or expressions. Such models are referred to as **mathematical models** and are a critical part of any quantitative approach to decision making. For example, the total profit from the sale of a product can be determined by multiplying the profit per unit by the quantity sold. If we let $x$ represent the number of units sold and $P$ the total profit, then, with a profit of \$10 per unit, the following mathematical model defines the total profit earned by selling $x$ units:

$$P = 10x \tag{1.1}$$

The purpose, or value, of any model is that it enables us to make inferences about the real situation by studying and analyzing the model. For example, an airplane designer might test an iconic model of a new airplane in a wind tunnel to learn about the potential flying characteristics of the full-size airplane. Similarly, a mathematical model may be used to make inferences about how much profit will be earned if a specified quantity of a particular product is sold. According to the mathematical model of equation (1.1), we would expect selling three units of the product ($x = 3$) would provide a profit of $P = 10(3) = \$30$.

In general, experimenting with models requires less time and is less expensive than experimenting with the real object or situation. A model airplane is certainly quicker and less expensive to build and study than the full-size airplane. Similarly, the mathematical model in equation (1.1) allows a quick identification of profit expectations without actually requiring the manager to produce and sell $x$ units. Models also have the advantage of reducing the risk associated with experimenting with the real situation. In particular, bad designs or bad decisions that cause the model airplane to crash or a mathematical model to project a \$10,000 loss can be avoided in the real situation.

Herbert A. Simon, a Nobel prize winner in economics and an expert in decision making, said that a mathematical model does not have to be exact; it just has to be close enough to provide better results than can be obtained by common sense.

The value of model-based conclusions and decisions is dependent on how well the model represents the real situation. The more closely the model airplane represents the real airplane, the more accurate the conclusions and predictions will be. Similarly, the more closely the mathematical model represents the company's true profit-volume relationship, the more accurate the profit projections will be.

Because this text deals with quantitative analysis based on mathematical models, let us look more closely at the mathematical modeling process. When initially considering a managerial problem, we usually find that the problem definition phase leads to a specific objective, such as maximization of profit or minimization of cost, and possibly a set of restrictions or **constraints,** such as production capacities. The success of the mathematical model and quantitative approach will depend heavily on how accurately the objective and constraints can be expressed in terms of mathematical equations or relationships.

A mathematical expression that describes the problem's objective is referred to as the **objective function.** For example, the profit equation $P = 10x$ would be an objective function for a firm attempting to maximize profit. A production capacity constraint would be necessary if, for instance, 5 hours are required to produce each unit and only 40 hours are available per week. Let $x$ indicate the number of units produced each week. The production time constraint is given by

$$5x \leq 40 \tag{1.2}$$

The value of $5x$ is the total time required to produce $x$ units; the symbol $\leq$ indicates that the production time required must be less than or equal to the 40 hours available.

The decision problem or question is the following: How many units of the product should be scheduled each week to maximize profit? A complete mathematical model for this simple production problem is

$$\text{Maximize} \qquad P = 10x \qquad \text{objective function}$$

subject to (s.t.)

$$\left. \begin{array}{r} 5x \leq 40 \\ x \geq 0 \end{array} \right\} \text{constraints}$$

The $x \geq 0$ constraint requires the production quantity $x$ to be greater than or equal to zero, which simply recognizes the fact that it is not possible to manufacture a negative number of units. The optimal solution to this model can be easily calculated and is given by $x = 8$, with an associated profit of \$80. This model is an example of a linear programming model. In subsequent chapters we will discuss more complicated mathematical models and learn how to solve them in situations where the answers are not nearly so obvious.

In the preceding mathematical model, the profit per unit (\$10), the production time per unit (5 hours), and the production capacity (40 hours) are environmental factors that are not under the control of the manager or decision maker. Such environmental factors, which can affect both the objective function and the constraints, are referred to as **uncontrollable inputs** to the model. Inputs that are controlled or determined by the decision maker are referred to as **controllable inputs** to the model. In the example given, the production quantity $x$ is the controllable input to the model. Controllable inputs are the decision alternatives specified by the manager and thus are also referred to as the **decision variables** of the model.

Once all controllable and uncontrollable inputs are specified, the objective function and constraints can be evaluated and the output of the model determined. In this sense, the output of the model is simply the projection of what would happen if those particular environmental factors and decisions occurred in the real situation. A flowchart of how controllable and uncontrollable inputs are transformed by the mathematical model into output is shown in Figure 1.4. A similar flowchart showing the specific details of the production model is shown in Figure 1.5.

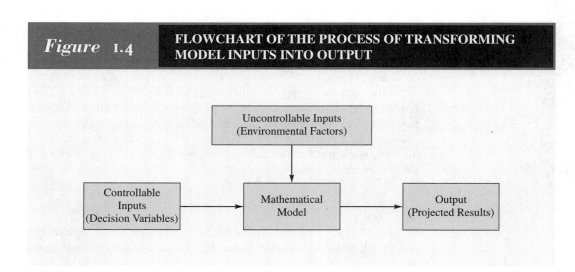

**Figure 1.4**   **FLOWCHART OF THE PROCESS OF TRANSFORMING MODEL INPUTS INTO OUTPUT**

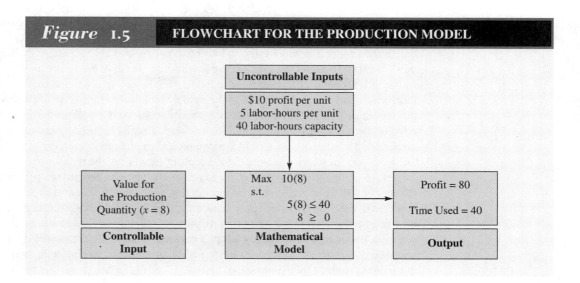

**Figure 1.5**          **FLOWCHART FOR THE PRODUCTION MODEL**

As stated earlier, the uncontrollable inputs are those the decision maker cannot influence. The specific controllable and uncontrollable inputs of a model depend on the particular problem or decision-making situation. In the production problem, the production time available (40), is an uncontrollable input. However, if it were possible to hire more employees or use overtime, the number of hours of production time would become a controllable input and therefore a decision variable in the model.

Uncontrollable inputs can either be known exactly or be uncertain and subject to variation. If all uncontrollable inputs to a model are known and cannot vary, the model is referred to as a **deterministic model.** Corporate income tax rates are not under the influence of the manager and thus constitute an uncontrollable input in many decision models. Since these rates are known and fixed (at least in the short run), a mathematical model with corporate income tax rates as the only uncontrollable input would be a deterministic model. The distinguishing feature of a deterministic model is that the uncontrollable input values are known in advance.

If any of the uncontrollable inputs are uncertain and subject to variation, the model is referred to as a **stochastic** or **probabilistic model.** An uncontrollable input to many production planning models is demand for the product. Since future demand may be any of a range of values, a mathematical model that treats demand with uncertainty would be called a stochastic model. In the production model, the number of hours of production time required per unit, the total hours available, and the unit profit were all uncontrollable inputs. Since the uncontrollable inputs were all known to take on fixed values, the model was deterministic. If, however, the number of hours of production time per unit could vary from 3 to 6 hours depending on the quality of the raw material, the model would be stochastic. The distinguishing feature of a stochastic model is that the value of the output cannot be determined even if the value of the controllable input is known because the specific values of the uncontrollable inputs are unknown. In this respect, stochastic models are often more difficult to analyze.

## Data Preparation

Another step in the quantitative analysis of a problem is the preparation of the data required by the model. Data in this sense refer to the values of the uncontrollable inputs to the model.

All uncontrollable inputs or data must be specified before we can analyze the model and recommend a decision or solution for the problem.

In the production model, the values of the uncontrollable inputs or data were $10 per unit for profit, 5 hours per unit for production time, and 40 hours for production capacity. In the development of the model, these data values were known and incorporated into the model as it was being developed. If the model is relatively small and the uncontrollable input values or data required are few, the quantitative analyst will probably combine model development and data preparation into one step. That is, in these situations the data values are inserted as the equations of the mathematical model are developed.

However, in many mathematical modeling situations, the data or uncontrollable input values are not readily available. In these situations the management scientist may know that the model will need profit per unit, production time, and production capacity data, but the values will not be known until the accounting, production, and engineering departments can be consulted. Rather than attempting to collect the required data as the model is being developed, the analyst will usually adopt a general notation for the model development step and then a separate data preparation step will be performed to obtain the uncontrollable input values required by the model.

Using the general notation

$$c = \text{profit per unit}$$
$$a = \text{production time in hours per unit}$$
$$b = \text{production capacity in hours}$$

the model development step of the production problem would result in the following general model:

$$\text{Max} \quad cx$$
$$\text{s.t.}$$
$$ax \leq b$$
$$x \geq 0$$

A separate data preparation step to identify the values for $c$, $a$, and $b$ would then be necessary to complete the model.

Many inexperienced quantitative analysts assume that once the problem has been defined and a general model developed, the problem is essentially solved. These individuals tend to believe that data preparation is a trivial step in the process and can be easily handled by clerical staff. Actually, this assumption could not be farther from the truth, especially with large-scale models that have numerous data input values. For example, a moderate-size linear programming model with 50 decision variables and 25 constraints could have over 1300 data elements that must be identified in the data preparation step. The time required to prepare these data and the possibility of data collection errors will make the data preparation step a critical part of the quantitative analysis process. Often, a fairly large database is needed to support a mathematical model, and information systems specialists also become involved in the data preparation step.

## Model Solution

Once the model development and data preparation steps have been completed, we can proceed to the model solution step. In this step, the analyst will attempt to identify the values of the decision variables that provide the "best" output for the model. The specific decision-variable value or values providing the "best" output will be referred to as the **optimal solution** for the model. For the production problem, the model solution step involves finding the value of the production quantity decision variable $x$ that maximizes profit while not causing a violation of the production capacity constraint.

One procedure that might be used in the model solution step involves a trial-and-error approach in which the model is used to test and evaluate various decision alternatives. In the production model, this procedure would mean testing and evaluating the model under various production quantities or values of $x$. Referring to Figure 1.5, note that we could input trial values for $x$ and check the corresponding output for projected profit and satisfaction of the production capacity constraint. If a particular decision alternative does not satisfy one or more of the model constraints, the decision alternative is rejected as being **infeasible,** regardless of the objective function value. If all constraints are satisfied, the decision alternative is **feasible** and a candidate for the "best" solution or recommended decision. Through this trial-and-error process of evaluating selected decision alternatives, a decision maker can identify a good—and possibly the best—feasible solution to the problem. This solution would then be the recommended decision for the problem.

Table 1.2 shows the results of a trial-and-error approach to solving the production model of Figure 1.5. The recommended decision is a production quantity of 8 since the feasible solution with the highest projected profit occurs at $x = 8$.

Although the trial-and-error solution process is often acceptable and can provide valuable information for the manager, it has the drawbacks of not necessarily providing the best solution and of being inefficient in terms of requiring numerous calculations if many decision alternatives are tried. Thus, quantitative analysts have developed special solution procedures for many models that are much more efficient than the trial-and-error approach. Throughout this text, you will be introduced to solution procedures that are applicable to the specific mathematical models that will be formulated. Some relatively small models or problems can be solved by hand computations, but most practical applications require the use of a computer.

Model development and model solution steps are not completely separable. An analyst will want both to develop an accurate model or representation of the actual problem situation and to be able to find a solution to the model. If we approach the model development step by attempting to find the most accurate and realistic mathematical model, we may find

| Table 1.2 | TRIAL-AND-ERROR SOLUTION FOR THE PRODUCTION MODEL OF FIGURE 1.5 | | |
|---|---|---|---|
| **Decision Alternative (Production Quantity)** $x$ | **Projected Profit** | **Total Hours of Production** | **Feasible Solution?** (Hours Used ≤ 40) |
| 0 | 0 | 0 | Yes |
| 2 | 20 | 10 | Yes |
| 4 | 40 | 20 | Yes |
| 6 | 60 | 30 | Yes |
| 8 | 80 | 40 | Yes |
| 10 | 100 | 50 | No |
| 12 | 120 | 60 | No |

the model so large and complex that it is impossible to obtain a solution. In this case, a simpler and perhaps more easily understood model with a readily available solution procedure is preferred even if the recommended solution is only a rough approximation of the best decision. As you learn more about quantitative solution procedures, you will have a better idea of the types of mathematical models that can be developed and solved.

Try Problem 8 to test your understanding of the concept of a mathematical model and what is referred to as the optimal solution to the model.

After a model solution has been obtained, both the management scientist and the manager will be interested in determining how good the solution really is. Even though the analyst has undoubtedly taken many precautions to develop a realistic model, often the goodness or accuracy of the model cannot be assessed until model solutions are generated. Model testing and validation are frequently conducted with relatively small "test" problems that have known or at least expected solutions. If the model generates the expected solutions, and if other output information appears correct, the go-ahead may be given to use the model on the full-scale problem. However, if the model test and validation identify potential problems or inaccuracies inherent in the model, corrective action, such as model modification and/or collection of more accurate input data, may be taken. Whatever the corrective action, the model solution will not be used in practice until the model has satisfactorily passed testing and validation.

## Report Generation

An important part of the quantitative analysis process is the preparation of managerial reports based on the model's solution. Referring to Figure 1.3, we see that the solution based on the quantitative analysis of a problem is one of the inputs the manager considers before making a final decision. Thus, the results of the model must appear in a managerial report that can be easily understood by the decision maker. The report includes the recommended decision and other pertinent information about the results that may be helpful to the decision maker.

## A Note Regarding Implementation

As discussed in Section 1.2, the manager is responsible for integrating the quantitative solution with qualitative considerations in order to make the best possible decision. After completing the decision-making process, the manager must oversee the implementation and follow-up evaluation of the decision. During the implementation and follow-up, the manager should continue to monitor the contribution of the model. At times, this process may lead to requests for model expansion or refinement that will cause the management scientist to return to an earlier step of the quantitative analysis process.

Successful implementation of results is of critical importance to the management scientist as well as the manager. If the results of the quantitative analysis process are not correctly implemented, the entire effort may be of no value. It doesn't take too many unsuccessful implementations before the management scientist is out of work. Because implementation often requires people to do things differently, it often meets with resistance. People want to know, "What's wrong with the way we've been doing it?" and so on. One of the most effective ways to ensure successful implementation is to include users throughout the modeling process. A user who feels a part of identifying the problem and developing the solution is much more likely to enthusiastically implement the results. The success rate for implementing the results of a management science project is much greater for those projects in which there has been extensive user involvement.

1. Developments in computer technology have increased the availability of management science techniques to decision makers. A variety of software packages are now available for personal computers. Versions of The Management Scientist, Microsoft Excel, and LINDO are widely used in management science courses.
2. The Management Scientist is a software package developed by the authors of this text. Version 5.0 is now available for Windows 95, Windows 98, and Windows NT operating systems. This software can be used to solve problems in the text as well as small-scale problems encountered in practice. Appendix A provides an overview of the features and use of The Management Scientist.
3. Various chapter appendixes provide step-by-step instructions for using The Management Scientist and Excel to solve problems in the text.

## 1.4 MODELS OF COST, REVENUE, AND PROFIT

Some of the most basic quantitative models arising in business and economic applications are those involving the relationship between a volume variable—such as production volume or sales volume—and cost, revenue, and profit. Through the use of these models, a manager can determine the projected cost, revenue, and/or profit associated with an established production quantity or a forecasted sales volume. Financial planning, production planning, sales quotas, and other areas of decision making can benefit from such cost, revenue, and profit models.

### Cost and Volume Models

The cost of manufacturing or producing a product is a function of the volume produced. This cost can usually be defined as a sum of two costs: fixed cost and variable cost. **Fixed cost** is the portion of the total cost that does not depend on the production volume; this cost remains the same no matter how much is produced. **Variable cost,** on the other hand, is the portion of the total cost that is dependent on and varies with the production volume. To illustrate how cost and volume models can be developed, we will consider a manufacturing problem faced by Nowlin Plastics.

Nowlin Plastics produces a variety of compact disc (CD) storage cases. Nowlin's best selling product is the CD-50, a slim, plastic CD holder with a specially designed lining that protects the optical surface of the disk. Several products are produced on the same manufacturing line, and a setup cost is incurred each time a changeover is made for a new product. Suppose that the setup cost for the CD-50 is $3000. This setup cost is a fixed cost that is incurred regardless of the number of units eventually produced. In addition, suppose that variable labor and material costs are $2 for each unit produced. The cost-volume model for producing $x$ units of the CD-50 can be written as

$$C(x) = 3000 + 2x \qquad (1.3)$$

where

$$x = \text{production volume in units}$$
$$C(x) = \text{total cost of producing } x \text{ units}$$

Once a production volume is established, the model in equation (1.3) can be used to compute the total production cost. For example, the decision to produce $x = 1200$ units would result in a total cost of $C(1200) = 3000 + 2(1200) = \$5400$.

**Marginal cost** is defined as the rate of change of the total cost with represent to production volume. That is, it is the cost increase associated with a one-unit increase in the production volume. In the cost model of equation (1.3), we see that the total cost $C(x)$ will increase by \$2 for each unit increase in the production volume. Thus, the marginal cost is \$2. With more complex total cost models, marginal cost may depend on the production volume. In such cases, we could have marginal cost increasing or decreasing with the production volume $x$.

### Revenue and Volume Models

Management of Nowlin Plastics will also want information on the projected revenue associated with selling a specified number of units. Thus, a model of the relationship between revenue and volume is also needed. Suppose that each CD-50 storage unit sells for \$5. The model for total revenue can be written as

$$R(x) = 5x \tag{1.4}$$

where

$$x = \text{sales volume in units}$$
$$R(x) = \text{total revenue associated with selling } x \text{ units}$$

**Marginal revenue** is defined as the rate of change of total revenue with respect to sales volume. That is, it is the increase in total revenue resulting from a one-unit increase in sales volume. In the model of equation (1.4), we see that the marginal revenue is \$5. In this case, marginal revenue is constant and does not vary with the sales volume. With more complex models, we may find that marginal revenue increases or decreases as the sales volume $x$ increases.

### Profit and Volume Models

One of the most important criteria for management decision making is profit. Managers need to be able to know the profit implications of their decisions. If we assume that we will only produce what can be sold, the production volume and sales volume will be equal. We can combine equations (1.3) and (1.4) to develop a profit-volume model that will determine profit associated with a specified production-sales volume. Since total profit is total revenue minus total cost, the following model provides the profit associated with producing and selling $x$ units:

$$\begin{aligned} P(x) &= R(x) - C(x) \\ &= 5x - (3000 + 2x) = -3000 + 3x \end{aligned} \tag{1.5}$$

Thus, the model for profit $P(x)$ can be derived from the models of the revenue-volume and cost-volume relationships.

### Breakeven Analysis

Using equation (1.5), we can now determine the profit associated with any production volume $x$. For example, suppose that a demand forecast indicates that 500 units of the product can be sold. The decision to produce and sell the 500 units results in a projected profit of

$$P(500) = -3000 + 3(500) = -1500$$

In other words, a loss of $1500 is predicted. If sales are expected to be 500 units, the manager may decide against producing the product. However, a demand forecast of 1800 units would show a projected profit of

$$P(1800) = -3000 + 3(1800) = 2400$$

This profit may be enough to justify proceeding with the production and sale of the product.

We see that a volume of 500 units will yield a loss, whereas a volume of 1800 provides a profit. The volume that results in total revenue equaling total cost (providing $0 profit) is called the **breakeven point.** If the breakeven point is known, a manager can quickly infer that a volume above the breakeven point will result in a profit, while a volume below the breakeven point will result in a loss. Thus, the breakeven point for a product provides valuable information for a manager who must make a yes/no decision concerning production of the product.

Let us now return to the Nowlin Plastics example and show how the profit model in equation (1.5) can be used to compute the breakeven point. The breakeven point can be found by setting the profit expression equal to zero and solving for the production volume. Using equation (1.5), we have

$$P(x) = -3000 + 3x = 0$$
$$3x = 3000$$
$$x = 1000$$

Try Problem 15 to test your ability to determine the breakeven point for a quantitative model.

With this information, we know that production and sales of the product must be at least 1000 units before a profit can be expected. The graphs of the total cost model, the total revenue model, and the location of the breakeven point are shown in Figure 1.6. In this chapter's appendix we also show how Excel can be used to perform a breakeven analysis for the Nowlin Plastics production example.

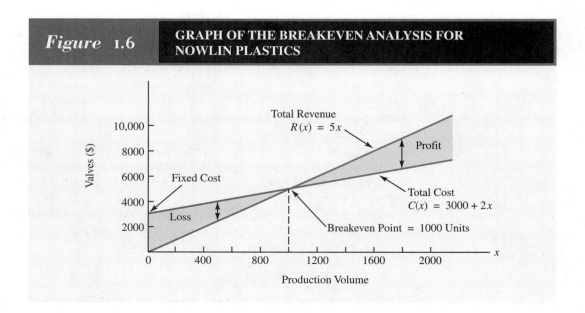

**Figure 1.6**    **GRAPH OF THE BREAKEVEN ANALYSIS FOR NOWLIN PLASTICS**

## 1.5    MANAGEMENT SCIENCE TECHNIQUES

In this section we present a brief overview of the management science techniques covered in this text. Over the years, practitioners have found numerous applications for the following:

**Linear Programming.**    Linear programming is a problem-solving approach that has been developed for situations involving maximizing or minimizing a linear function subject to linear constraints that limit the degree to which the objective can be pursued. The production model developed in Section 1.3 (see Figure 1.5) is an example of a simple linear programming model.

**Integer Linear Programming.**    Integer linear programming is an approach used for problems that can be set up as linear programs with the additional requirement that some or all of the decision recommendations be integer values.

**Network Models.**    A network is a graphical description of a problem consisting of circles called nodes that are interconnected by lines called arcs. Specialized solution procedures exist for these types of problems, enabling us to quickly solve problems in such areas as transportation system design, information system design, and project scheduling.

**Project Scheduling: PERT/CPM.**    In many situations, managers are responsible for planning, scheduling, and controlling projects that consist of numerous separate jobs or tasks performed by a variety of departments, individuals, and so forth. The PERT (Program Evaluation and Review Technique) and CPM (Critical Path Method) techniques help managers carry out their project scheduling responsibilities.

**Inventory Models.**    Inventory models are used by managers faced with the dual problems of maintaining sufficient inventories to meet demand for goods and, at the same time, incurring the lowest possible inventory holding costs.

**Waiting-Line or Queueing Models.**    Waiting-line or queueing models have been developed to help managers understand and make better decisions concerning the operation of systems involving waiting lines.

**Simulation.**    Simulation is a technique used to model the operation of a system. This technique employs a computer program to model the operation and perform simulation computations.

**Decision Analysis.**    Decision analysis can be used to determine optimal strategies in situations involving several decision alternatives and an uncertain or risk-filled pattern of events.

**Goal Programming.**    Goal programming is a technique for solving multicriteria decision problems, usually within the framework of linear programming.

**Analytic Hierarchy Process.**    This multicriteria decision-making technique permits the inclusion of subjective factors in arriving at a recommended decision.

**Forecasting.**    Forecasting methods are techniques that can be used to predict future aspects of a business operation.

**Markov-Process Models.**    Markov-process models are useful in studying the evolution of certain systems over repeated trials. For example, Markov processes have been used to describe the probability that a machine, functioning in one period, will function or break down in another period.

**Dynamic Programming.**    Dynamic programming is an approach that allows us to break up a large problem in such a fashion that once all the smaller problems have been solved, we are left with an optimal solution to the large problem.

### Methods Used Most Frequently

Our experience as both practitioners and educators has been that the most frequently used management science techniques are linear programming, integer programming, network models (including transportation and transshipment models), and simulation. Depending upon the industry, the other methods in the preceding list are used more or less frequently.

Helping to bridge the gap between the manager and the management scientist is a major focus of the text. We believe that the barriers to the use of management science can best be removed by increasing the manager's understanding of how management science can be applied. The text will help you develop an understanding of which management science techniques are most useful, how they are used, and, most importantly, how they can assist managers in making better decisions.

The Management Science in Action: Taco Bell's SMART Labor Management System shows how Taco Bell was able to use management science to ensure that the maximum time customers wait in line is between three and five minutes. The SMART system consists of three models: a forecasting model, a simulation model, and an integer programming model. This system has provided Taco Bell with a major competitive advantage, and is typical of the widespread role of management science in service industries. Throughout the text we will illustrate the applications of management science with Management Science in Action vignettes.

## N O T E S and Comments

1. Operations research analyst is listed by the Bureau of Labor Statistics as one of the fastest growing occupations for careers requiring a bachelor's degree. The predicted growth is from 57,000 jobs in 1990 to 100,000 jobs in 2005, an increase of 73%.

2. The Institute for Operations Research and the Management Sciences (INFORMS) and the Decision Sciences Institute (DSI) are two professional societies that publish journals and newsletters dealing with current research and applications of operations research and management science techniques.

# MANAGEMENT SCIENCE IN ACTION

## TACO BELL'S SMART LABOR MANAGEMENT SYSTEM*

Taco Bell turned to management science in order to develop methods for better handling customer demand while still keeping labor costs down. The company created the SMART (Scheduling Management and Restaurant Tool) Labor Management System (LMS) in order to determine a method of scheduling employees that will ensure that the maximum time customers wait in line is between three and five minutes. The SMART LMS consists of three integrated models: a forecasting model, a simulation model, and an integer programming model.

The forecasting model determines how many dollars worth of business each store will generate each day. Unlike a manufacturing plant, which makes forecasts in terms of years, months, or weeks, Taco Bell needs to develop predictions of customer arrivals based on 15-minute intervals. Then, using the predictions of how much business a store will generate the following day, a simulation model determines how many employees will be needed and how they should be positioned throughout the facility. To determine the labor table for the next day, the simulation model must take into account the differences

in Taco Bell facilities, the build-to-order food preparation approach used by Taco Bell, and the randomness associated with customer demand. Using the labor table generated by the simulation model, the integer programming model determines how many people are needed on the schedule for a particular day and what their shifts should be so that payroll costs are minimized. The integer programming model also takes into account all of the customer-service responsibilities and provides Taco Bell managers with the ability to schedule other tasks such as cleaning and maintenance.

The system is used in all company-owned stores, and by 1996 had been adopted by 70 percent of franchisees. From 1993–1996, the new system resulted in labor costs savings of $40.34 million. Employee feedback is positive, and other fast food companies have indicated that the new system has provided Taco Bell with a major competitive advantage.

*Based on Nancy Bistritz, "Taco Bell Finds Recipe For Success," *OR/MS Today*, (October 1997): 20–21.

·····················································································/ /·············

## SUMMARY

This text is about how management science may be used to help managers make better decisions. The focus of this text is on the decision-making process and on the role of management science in that process. We have discussed the problem orientation of this process and in an overview have shown how mathematical models can be used in this type of analysis.

The difference between the model and the situation or managerial problem it represents is an important point. Mathematical models are abstractions of real-world situations and, as such, cannot capture all the aspects of the real situation. However, if a model can capture the major relevant aspects of the problem and can then provide a solution recommendation, it can be a valuable aid to decision making.

One of the characteristics of management science that will become increasingly apparent as we proceed through the text is the search for a best solution to the problem. In carrying out the quantitative analysis, we shall be attempting to develop procedures for finding the "best" or optimal solution.

·····················································································/ /·············

## GLOSSARY

**Problem solving**   The process of identifying a difference between the actual and the desired state of affairs and then taking action to resolve the difference.

**Decision making**   The process of defining the problem, identifying the alternatives, determining the criteria, evaluating the alternatives, and choosing an alternative.

**Single-criterion decision problem**   A problem in which the objective is to find the "best" solution with respect to just one criterion.

**Multicriteria decision problem**   A problem that involves more than one criterion; the objective is to find the "best" solution, taking into account all the criteria.

**Decision**   The alternative selected.

**Model**   A representation of a real object or situation.

**Iconic model**   A physical replica, or representation, of a real object.

**Analog model**   While physical in form, an analog model does not have a physical appearance similar to the real object or situation it represents.

**Mathematical model**   Mathematical symbols and expressions used to represent a real situation.

**Constraints**   Restrictions or limitations imposed on a problem.

**Objective function**   A mathematical expression used to represent the criterion for evaluating solutions to a problem.

**Controllable input**   The decision alternatives or inputs that can be specified by the decision maker.

**Decision variable**   Another term for controllable input.

**Uncontrollable input**  The environmental factors or inputs that cannot be controlled by the decision maker.

**Deterministic model**  A model in which all uncontrollable inputs are known and cannot vary.

**Stochastic model**  A model in which at least one uncontrollable input is uncertain and subject to variation; stochastic models are also referred to as probabilistic models.

**Optimal solution**  The specific decision variable value or values that provide the "best" output for the model.

**Feasible solution**  A decision alternative or solution that satisfies all constraints.

**Infeasible solution**  A decision alternative or solution that violates one or more constraints.

**Fixed cost**  The portion of the total cost that does not depend on the volume; this cost remains the same no matter how much is produced.

**Variable cost**  The portion of the total cost that is dependent on and varies with the volume.

**Marginal cost**  The rate of change of the total cost with respect to volume.

**Marginal revenue**  The rate of change of total revenue with respect to volume.

**Breakeven point**  The volume at which total revenue equals total cost.

............................................................................................../ /............

## PROBLEMS

1.  Define the terms *management science* and *operations research.*

2.  Describe the major reasons for the growth in the use of management science since World War II.

3.  Discuss the different roles played by the qualitative and quantitative approaches to managerial decision making. Why is it important for a manager or decision maker to have a good understanding of both of these approaches to decision making?

**SELF TEST**

4.  A firm has just completed a new plant that will produce more than 500 different products, using more than 50 different production lines and machines. The production scheduling decisions are critical in that sales will be lost if customer demands are not met on time. If no individual in the firm has had experience with this production operation, and if new production schedules must be generated each week, why should the firm consider a quantitative approach to the production scheduling problem?

5.  List and discuss the steps of the decision-making process.

6.  Give an example of each of the three types of models discussed in this chapter: iconic, analog, and mathematical.

7.  What are the advantages of analyzing and experimenting with a model as opposed to a real object or situation?

**SELF TEST**

8.  Recall the production model from Section 1.3:

$$\text{Max} \quad 10x$$
$$\text{s.t.}$$
$$5x \leq 40$$
$$x \geq 0$$

Suppose the firm in this example considers a second product that has a unit profit of $5 and requires 2 hours for each unit produced. Use $y$ as the number of units of product 2 produced.

a. Show the mathematical model when both products are considered simultaneously.

b. Identify the controllable and uncontrollable inputs for this model.

c. Draw the flowchart of the input-output process for this model (see Figure 1.5).

d. What are the optimal solution values of $x$ and $y$?

9. Is the model developed in Problem 8 a deterministic or a stochastic model? Explain.

10. Suppose we modify the model in Problem 8 to obtain the following mathematical model:

$$\text{Max} \quad 10x$$

$$\text{s.t.}$$

$$ax \leq 40$$

$$x \geq 0$$

where $a$ is the number of hours required for each unit produced. With $a = 5$, the optimal solution $x = 8$. If we have a stochastic model with $a = 3$, $a = 4$, $a = 5$, or $a = 6$ as the possible values for the number of hours required per unit, what is the optimal value for $x$? What problems does this stochastic model cause?

11. A retail store in Des Moines, Iowa, receives shipments of a particular product from Kansas City and Minneapolis. Let

$$x = \text{units of product received from Kansas City}$$

$$y = \text{units of product received from Minneapolis}$$

a. Write an expression for the total units of product received by the retail store in Des Moines.

b. Shipments from Kansas City cost $0.20 per unit, and shipments from Minneapolis cost $0.25 per unit. Develop an objective function representing the total cost of shipments to Des Moines.

c. Assuming the monthly demand at the retail store is 5000 units, develop a constraint that requires 5000 units to be shipped to Des Moines.

d. No more than 4000 units can be shipped from Kansas City, and no more than 3000 units can be shipped from Minneapolis in a month. Develop constraints to model this situation.

e. Of course, negative amounts cannot be shipped. Combine the objective function and constraints developed to state a mathematical model for satisfying the demand at the Des Moines retail store at minimum cost.

12. Suppose you are going on a weekend trip to a city that is $d$ miles away. Develop a model that determines your round-trip gasoline costs. What assumptions or approximations are necessary to treat this model as a deterministic model? Are these assumptions or approximations acceptable to you?

13. For most products, higher prices result in a decreased demand, whereas lower prices result in an increased demand. Let

$$d = \text{annual demand for a product in units}$$

$$p = \text{price per unit}$$

Assume that a firm accepts the following price-demand relationship as being realistic:

$$d = 800 - 10p$$

where $p$ must be between \$20 and \$70.

a.   How many units can the firm sell at the \$20 per-unit price? At the \$70 per-unit price?

b.   Show the mathematical model for the total revenue (TR), which is the annual demand multiplied by the unit price.

c.   Based on other considerations, the firm's management will only consider price alternatives of \$30, \$40, and \$50. Use your model from part (b) to determine the price alternative that will maximize the total revenue.

d.   What are the expected annual demand and the total revenue according to your recommended price?

14.   Suppose that a manager has a choice between the following two mathematical models of a given situation: (a) a relatively simple model that is a reasonable approximation of the real situation and (b) a thorough and complex model that is the most accurate mathematical representation of the real situation possible. Why might the model described in part (a) be preferred by the manager?

**SELF TEST**

15.   The O'Neill Shoe Manufacturing Company will produce a special-style shoe if the order size is large enough to provide a reasonable profit. For each special-style order, the company incurs a fixed cost of \$1000 for the production setup. The variable cost is \$30 per pair, and each pair sells for \$40.

a.   Let $x$ indicate the number of pairs of shoes produced. Develop a mathematical model for the total cost of producing $x$ pairs of shoes.

b.   Let $P$ indicate the total profit. Develop a mathematical model for the total profit realized from an order for $x$ pairs of shoes.

c.   How large must the shoe order be before O'Neill will break even?

16.   Eastman Publishing Company is considering publishing a paperback textbook on spreadsheet applications for business. The fixed cost of manuscript preparation, textbook design, and production setup is estimated to be \$80,000. Variable production and material costs are estimated to be \$3 per book. Demand over the life of the book is estimated to be 4000 copies. The publisher plans to sell the text to college and university bookstores for \$20 each.

a.   What is the breakeven point?

b.   What profit or loss can be anticipated with a demand of 4000 copies?

c.   With a demand of 4000 copies, what is the minimum price per copy that the publisher must charge to break even?

d.   If the publisher believes that the price per copy could be increased to \$25.95 and not affect the anticipated demand of 4000 copies, what action would you recommend? What profit or loss can be anticipated?

17.   Preliminary plans are underway for the construction of a new stadium for a major league baseball team. City officials have questioned the number and profitability of the luxury corporate boxes planned for the upper deck of the stadium. Corporations and selected individuals may buy the boxes for \$100,000 each. The fixed construction cost for the upper-deck area is estimated to be \$1,500,000, with a variable cost of \$50,000 for each box constructed.

a.   What is the breakeven point for the number of luxury boxes in the new stadium?

b.   Preliminary drawings for the stadium show that space is available for the construction of up to 50 luxury boxes. Promoters indicate that buyers are available and that all 50 could be sold if constructed. What is your recommendation concerning the construction of luxury boxes? What profit is anticipated?

18. Financial Analysts, Inc., is an investment firm that manages stock portfolios for a number of clients. A new client has just requested that the firm handle an $80,000 portfolio. As an initial investment strategy, the client would like to restrict the portfolio to a mix of the following two stocks:

| Stock | Price/ Share | Estimated Annual Return/Share | Maximum Possible Investment |
|---|---|---|---|
| Oil Alaska | $50 | $6 | $50,000 |
| Southwest Petroleum | $30 | $4 | $45,000 |

Let

$$x = \text{number of shares of Oil Alaska}$$
$$y = \text{number of shares of Southwest Petroleum}$$

a. Develop the objective function, assuming that the client desires to maximize the total annual return.
b. Show the mathematical expression for each of the following three constraints:
   (1) Total investment funds available are $80,000.
   (2) Maximum Oil Alaska investment is $50,000.
   (3) Maximum Southwest Petroleum investment is $45,000.

*Note:* Adding the $x \geq 0$ and $y \geq 0$ constraints provides a linear programming model for the investment problem. A solution procedure for this model will be discussed in Chapter 2.

19. Models of inventory systems frequently consider the relationships among a beginning inventory, a production quantity, a demand or sales, and an ending inventory. For a given production period $j$, let

$$s_{j-1} = \text{ending inventory from the previous period (beginning inventory for period } j)$$
$$x_j = \text{production quantity in period } j$$
$$d_j = \text{demand in period } j$$
$$s_j = \text{ending inventory for period } j$$

a. Write the mathematical relationship or model that describes how these four variables are related.
b. What constraint should be added if production capacity for period $j$ is given by $C_j$?
c. What constraint should be added if inventory requirements for period $j$ mandate an ending inventory of at least $I_j$?

## Appendix 1.1   USING SPREADSHEETS FOR BREAKEVEN ANALYSIS

In Section 1.4 we introduced the Nowlin Plastics production example to illustrate how quantitative models can be used to help a manager determine the projected cost, revenue, and/or profit associated with an established production quantity or a forecasted sales volume. In this appendix we introduce spreadsheet applications by showing how to use Excel to perform a quantitative analysis of the Nowlin Plastics example.

Refer to the spreadsheet shown in Figure 1.7. We begin by entering the problem data into the top portion of the spreadsheet. The value of 3000 in cell B3 is the setup cost, the value of 2 in cell B5 is the variable labor and material costs per unit, and the value of 5 in cell B7 is the selling price per unit. In general, whenever we perform a quantitative analysis using a spreadsheet, we will enter the problem data in the top portion of the spreadsheet and reserve the bottom portion for model development. The label "Models" in cell B10 helps to provide a visual reminder of this convention.

Cell B12 in the models portion of the spreadsheet contains the proposed production volume in units. Because the values for total cost, total revenue, and total profit depend upon the value of this decision variable, we have placed a border around cell B12 and screened the cell for emphasis. Based upon the value in cell B12, the cell formulas in cells B14, B16, and B18 are used to compute values for total cost, total revenue, and total profit (loss), respectively. First, recall that the value of total cost is the sum of the fixed cost (cell B3) and the total variable cost. Since the total variable cost is the product of the variable cost per unit (cell B5) and the production volume (cell B12), it is given by B5*B12. Thus, to compute the value of total cost we entered the formula =B3+B5*B12 in cell B14. Next, since total revenue is the product of the selling price per unit (cell B7) and the number of units produced (cell B12), in cell B16 we have entered the formula =B7*B12. Finally, the total profit (or loss) is the difference between the total revenue (cell B16) and the total cost (cell B14). Thus, in cell B18 we have entered the formula =B16−B14. The spreadsheet shown in Figure 1.7 shows the formulas used to make these computations; we refer to it as a formula spreadsheet.

**Figure 1.7    FORMULA SPREADSHEET FOR THE NOWLIN PLASTICS PRODUCTION EXAMPLE**

|  | A | B |
|---|---|---|
| 1 | **Nowlin Plastics** | |
| 2 | | |
| 3 | **Fixed Cost** | 3000 |
| 4 | | |
| 5 | **Variable Cost Per Unit** | 2 |
| 6 | | |
| 7 | **Selling Price Per Unit** | 5 |
| 8 | | |
| 9 | | |
| 10 | **Models** | |
| 11 | | |
| 12 | **Production Volume** | 800 |
| 13 | | |
| 14 | **Total Cost** | =B3+B5*B12 |
| 15 | | |
| 16 | **Total Revenue** | =B7*B12 |
| 17 | | |
| 18 | **Total Profit (Loss)** | =B16-B14 |

To examine the effect of selecting a particular value for the production volume, we have entered a value of 800 in cell B12. The spreadsheet shown in Figure 1.8 shows the values obtained by the formulas; a production volume of 800 units results in a total cost of $4600, a total revenue of $4000, and a loss of $600. To examine the effect of other production volumes, we only need to enter a different value into cell B12. To examine the effect of different costs and selling prices, we simply enter the appropriate values in the data portion of the spreadsheet; the results will be displayed in the model section of the spreadsheet.

In Section 1.4 we illustrated breakeven analysis. Let us now see how a spreadsheet can be used to compute the breakeven point for the Nowlin Plastics production example. We begin by considering a trial-and-error approach using Excel's Table command.

## Determining the Breakeven Point Using Excel's Table Command

The breakeven point is the production volume that results in total revenue equal to total cost and hence a profit of $0. One way to determine the breakeven point is to use a trial-and-error approach. For example, in Figure 1.8 we saw that a trial production volume of 800 units resulted in a loss of $600. Since this trial solution resulted in a loss, a production volume of 800 units cannot be the breakeven point. We could continue to experiment with other production volumes by simply entering different values into cell B12 and observing

| Figure 1.8 | SPREADSHEET SOLUTION USING A PRODUCTION VOLUME OF 800 UNITS FOR THE NOWLIN PLASTICS PRODUCTION EXAMPLE |
|---|---|

|   | A | B |
|---|---|---|
| 1 | **Nowlin Plastics** | |
| 2 | | |
| 3 | **Fixed Cost** | $3,000 |
| 4 | | |
| 5 | **Variable Cost Per Unit** | $2 |
| 6 | | |
| 7 | **Selling Price Per Unit** | $5 |
| 8 | | |
| 9 | | |
| 10 | **Models** | |
| 11 | | |
| 12 | **Production Volume** | 800 |
| 13 | | |
| 14 | **Total Cost** | $4,600 |
| 15 | | |
| 16 | **Total Revenue** | $4,000 |
| 17 | | |
| 18 | **Total Profit (Loss)** | -$600 |

the resulting profit or loss in cell B18. A better approach is to use Excel's Table command for doing this type of what-if analysis.

Suppose that we wanted to compute the profit or loss associated with production quantities ranging in value from 200 units to 2000 units, in increments of 200. We begin by entering these trial production values into a row or column of the spreadsheet. Note that we have entered these values into cells D13:D22 of the spreadsheet shown in Figure 1.9. Next, we enter the formula for profit into cell E12. Since the formula for profit has already been entered into cell B18, we entered the formula =B18 into cell E12. The following steps used Excel's Table command to compute profit and loss projections for each trial production value.

Step 1  Select cells D12:E22
Step 2  Select the **Data** pull-down menu
Step 3  Choose the **Table** option
Step 4  When the **Table** dialog box appears
          Enter B12 in the **Column Input Cell**
          Select **OK**

The profit and loss values corresponding to each of the trial production values are displayed in cells E13:E22. Thus, we see that a production quantity of 200 units results in a loss of

| | | | USING EXCEL'S TABLE COMMAND TO COMPUTE THE |
|---|---|---|---|
| *Figure* | 1.9 | | BREAKEVEN POINT FOR THE NOWLIN PLASTICS PRODUCTION EXAMPLE |

| | A | B | C | D | E |
|---|---|---|---|---|---|
| 1 | **Nowlin Plastics** | | | | |
| 2 | | | | | |
| 3 | **Fixed Cost** | $3,000 | | | |
| 4 | | | | | |
| 5 | **Variable Cost Per Unit** | $2 | | | |
| 6 | | | | | |
| 7 | **Selling Price Per Unit** | $5 | | | |
| 8 | | | | | |
| 9 | | | | | |
| 10 | **Models** | | | | |
| 11 | | | | | |
| 12 | **Production Volume** | 800 | | | -$600 |
| 13 | | | | 200 | -$2,400 |
| 14 | **Total Cost** | $4,600 | | 400 | -$1,800 |
| 15 | | | | 600 | -$1,200 |
| 16 | **Total Revenue** | $4,000 | | 800 | -$600 |
| 17 | | | | 1000 | $0 |
| 18 | **Total Profit (Loss)** | -$600 | | 1200 | $600 |
| 19 | | | | 1400 | $1,200 |
| 20 | | | | 1600 | $1,800 |
| 21 | | | | 1800 | $2,400 |
| 22 | | | | 2000 | $3,000 |

$2,400, a production quantity of 400 results in a loss of $1,800, and so on. Since a production quantity of 1000 results in a profit of $0, it is the breakeven point for Nowlin Plastics.

### Determining the Breakeven Point Using Goal Seek

Another way to find a breakeven point using a spreadsheet is to use the Goal Seek tool. The Goal Seek tool in Microsoft Excel allows the user to determine the value for an input cell that will cause the value of a related output cell to equal some specified value (called the *goal*). In the case of breakeven analysis, the "goal" is to set Total Profit to zero by "seeking" an appropriate value for Production Volume. Goal Seek will allow us to find the value of production volume that will set Nowlin Plastics' total profit to zero. The following steps describe how to use Goal Seek to find the breakeven point for Nowlin Plastics:

Step 1  Select the **Tools** pull-down menu
Step 2  Choose the **Goal Seek** option
Step 3  When the **Goal Seek dialog box** appears:
      Enter B18 in the **Set cell** box
      Enter 0 in the **To value** box
      Enter B12 in the **By changing cell** box
      Select **OK**

The completed **Goal Seek dialog box** is shown in Figure 1.10, and the spreadsheet obtained after selecting **OK** is shown in Figure 1.11. The Total Profit in cell B18 is zero, and the Production Volume in cell B12 has been set to the breakeven point of 1000.

**Figure 1.10    GOAL SEEK DIALOG BOX FOR THE NOWLIN PLASTICS PRODUCITON EXAMPLE**

## MANAGEMENT SCIENCE IN PRACTICE FEATURE

Management Science in Practice write-ups prepared by practitioners are presented at the end of 15 chapters. We feel these articles provide a meaningful extension to the text material. The purpose of these application write-ups is to provide the reader with a better appreciation for the types of companies that use management science and the types of problems these companies are able to solve.

| Figure | I.II | BREAKEVEN POINT FOUND USING GOAL SEEK FOR THE NOWLIN PLASTICS PRODUCTION EXAMPLE |
|--------|------|------------------------------------------------------------------------------|

|    | A | B |
|----|---|---|
| 1  | **Nowlin Plastics** | |
| 2  | | |
| 3  | **Fixed Cost** | $3,000 |
| 4  | | |
| 5  | **Variable Cost Per Unit** | $2 |
| 6  | | |
| 7  | **Selling Price Per Unit** | $5 |
| 8  | | |
| 9  | | |
| 10 | **Models** | |
| 11 | | |
| 12 | **Production Volume** | 1000 |
| 13 | | |
| 14 | **Total Cost** | 5000 |
| 15 | | |
| 16 | **Total Revenue** | 5000 |
| 17 | | |
| 18 | **Total Profit (Loss)** | 0 |

Each Management Science in Practice write-up begins with a description of the company and continues with a discussion of the areas in which the company has successfully applied management science. The remainder of the write-up deals with an application that is closely related to the preceding chapter. An effort has been made to avoid unnecessary technical detail and to focus on the managerial aspects and the value of the results to the company.

Because Chapter 1 is designed to provide an introduction to management science, we have not emphasized any particular solution methodology. Thus, we have placed the Mead Corporation write-up at the end of this first chapter because it provides an overview of several areas in which management science can be used effectively. It is evidence of the impact management science is having at some companies.

# MEAD CORPORATION*

## DAYTON, OHIO

Mead is a major producer of papers for premium periodicals, books, commercial printing, and business forms, with special expertise in coating technologies. The company and its affiliates also produce pulp and lumber, a variety of specialty papers, and converted wood and paper products. Mead is a leader in the design and manufacture of packaging systems for beverage and other consumables markets. The company is a world leader in the production of coated board, and manufactures shipping containers and corrugating medium. Mead is a major manufacturer of paper-based school and office products, and operates a nationwide network of distribution centers for paper, packaging, and supplies.

## Management Science at Mead Corporation

Management science applications at Mead are developed and implemented by the company's Decision Analysis (DA) Department. The DA Department provides timely, efficient internal consulting services to the operating groups and corporate staff in the functional areas of operations, finance, marketing, and human resources. The department assists decision makers by providing them with analytical tools of management science as well as personal analysis and recommendations. Through conversations and observations, the department recognizes needs where management science techniques are applicable, and it then recommends appropriate projects. In addition, the department provides a resource reservoir for information and assistance on quantitative methodology and assumes responsibility for keeping current in management science techniques

that could produce efficiencies at Mead. This charter results in a variety of projects and applications that span the corporation. Four examples of management science applications at Mead are described here.

## A Corporate Planning System

The DA Department built and maintains a corporate planning system. This system allows business units to create and evaluate their five-year plans in an interactive computer environment.

Once the individual business units have finished their planning, the system consolidates the information at a group level. The assumptions of the units and the group are evaluated and reconciled. The use of this computer model facilitates the process by ensuring uniformity of calculations and reporting by all the planning units. Ultimately, the information is consolidated and evaluated at a corporate level.

## A Timberland Financing Model

Another example of a management science application involves the development of a timberland financing model. Working directly with financial management, analysts assisted in the creation of a deterministic model that considered the major factors in a timberland financing arrangement. The model was used to examine the liability and profitability of timberland acquisition under various assumptions concerning forest growth rates, the inflation rate, and other financial considerations. By using the model, management was able to examine fully the acquisition and modify the financial arrangement as operating conditions warranted. The model is currently operated and modified by financial management and is considered a major tool in the examination of timberland financing.

*The authors are indebted to Dr. Edward P. Winkofsky, Mead Corporation, Dayton, Ohio, for providing this application.

## Inventory Analysis

Inventory analysis is an area in which more sophisticated tools of management science have been used. Simulation models have been used to describe the major factors (e.g., demand or usage rates, lead times, and production rates) in an inventory system. Typically, an inventory model includes purchase, storage, ordering, stockout, and degradation costs. The simulation model is used to evaluate reorder points, safety stocks, customer service levels, review periods, and the response time of the inventory system to extraordinary events.

Once developed and in place, the model can be updated as economic and operating conditions change. Thus, the model can be used by management to evaluate its inventory system on an ongoing basis and to ensure that it is operating in a cost-efficient manner. These inventory simulation models are user friendly and can be operated and maintained by management with little formal computer training.

## A Timber Harvesting Model

Mead also uses models to assist with the long-range management of the company's timberland. Through the use of large-scale linear programs, timber harvesting plans have been developed to cover a substantial time horizon. These models consider wood market conditions, mill pulpwood requirements, harvesting capacities, and general forest management principles. Within these constraints, the model develops an optimal harvesting and purchasing schedule based on discounted cash flow. Alternative schedules are developed to reflect various assumptions concerning forest growth, wood availability, and general economic conditions.

Quantitative methods are also used in the development of the inputs for the linear programming models already described. Timber prices and supplies as well as mill requirements must be forecast over the time horizon. Advanced sampling techniques are used to evaluate land holdings and to project forest growth. The harvest schedule is developed through the use of a number of management science techniques.

## Summary

The applications briefly described here—although only a few of the many management science projects at Mead—convey the breadth of the activities currently in use within the company. The management scientist at Mead must be able to work in a number of different environments and be proficient in a wide range of quantitative methods. In addition, the analyst must possess exceptional oral and written communication skills. Only with this background will the analyst be able to achieve the major objective of management science at Mead— the development and implementation of user-friendly quantitative models that will support and enhance management decision making throughout the organization.

## Questions

1. Which techniques listed in Section 1.5 are being used in the four management science applications described at the Mead Corporation?
2. Which of the Mead applications use a deterministic model, and which use a stochastic model? What conditions in the applications indicate a stochastic model is necessary?
3. Discuss how quantitative analysis described in Section 1.3 occurs in Mead's inventory analysis application.
4. Discuss the benefits associated with the management science applications at Mead.

# 2

# AN INTRODUCTION TO LINEAR PROGRAMMING

## CONTENTS

Linear programming is a problem-solving approach that has been developed to help managers make decisions. The following situations describe some typical applications of linear programming:

Linear programming was initially referred to as "programming in a linear structure." In 1948 Tjalling Koopmans suggested to George Dantzig that the name was much too long; Koopman's suggestion was to shorten it to linear programming. George Dantzig agreed and the field we now know as linear programming was named.

1. A manufacturer wants to develop a production schedule and an inventory policy that will satisfy sales demand in future periods. Ideally, the schedule and policy will enable the company to satisfy demand and at the same time *minimize* the total production and inventory costs.

2. A financial analyst must select an investment portfolio from a variety of stock and bond investment alternatives. The analyst would like to establish the portfolio that *maximizes* the return on investment.

3. A marketing manager wants to determine how best to allocate a fixed advertising budget among alternative advertising media such as radio, television, newspaper, and magazine. The manager would like to determine the media mix that *maximizes* advertising effectiveness.

4. A company has warehouses in a number of locations throughout the United States. For a set of customer demands, the company would like to determine how much each warehouse should ship to each customer so that total transportation costs are *minimized*.

These examples are only a few of the situations in which linear programming has been used successfully, but they illustrate the diversity of linear programming applications. A close scrutiny reveals one basic property they all have in common. In each example, we were concerned with *maximizing* or *minimizing* some quantity. In example 1, the manufacturer wanted to minimize costs; in example 2, the financial analyst wanted to maximize return on investment; in example 3, the marketing manager wanted to maximize advertising effectiveness; and in example 4, the company wanted to minimize total transportation costs. *In all linear programming problems, the maximization or minimization of some quantity is the objective.*

All linear programming problems also have a second property: restrictions or **constraints** that limit the degree to which the objective can be pursued. In example 1, the manufacturer is restricted by constraints requiring product demand to be satisfied and by the constraints limiting production capacity. The financial analyst's portfolio problem is constrained by the total amount of investment funds available and the maximum amounts that can be invested in each stock or bond. The marketing manager's media selection decision is constrained by a fixed advertising budget and the availability of the various media. In the transportation problem, the minimum-cost shipping schedule is constrained by the supply of product available at each warehouse. *Thus, constraints are another general feature of every linear programming problem.*

## 2.1    A SIMPLE MAXIMIZATION PROBLEM

Par, Inc., is a small manufacturer of golf equipment and supplies whose management has decided to move into the market for medium- and high-priced golf bags. Par's distributor is enthusiastic about the new product line and has agreed to buy all the golf bags Par produces over the next 3 months.

After a thorough investigation of the steps involved in manufacturing a golf bag, management has determined that each golf bag produced will require the following operations:

1. Cutting and dyeing the material
2. Sewing
3. Finishing (inserting umbrella holder, club separators, etc.)
4. Inspection and packaging

The director of manufacturing has analyzed each of the operations and concluded that if the company produces a medium-priced standard model, each bag will require $7/10$ hour in the cutting and dyeing department, $1/2$ hour in the sewing department, 1 hour in the finishing department, and $1/10$ hour in the inspection and packaging department. The more expensive deluxe model will require 1 hour for cutting and dyeing, $5/6$ hour for sewing, $2/3$ hour for finishing, and $1/4$ hour for inspection and packaging. This production information is summarized in Table 2.1.

Par's production is constrained by a limited number of hours available in each department. After studying departmental work load projections, the director of manufacturing estimates that 630 hours for cutting and dyeing, 600 hours for sewing, 708 hours for finishing, and 135 hours for inspection and packaging will be available for the production of golf bags during the next 3 months.

The accounting department has analyzed the production data, assigned all relevant variable costs, and arrived at prices for both bags that will result in a profit contribution[1] of $10 for every standard bag and $9 for every deluxe bag produced. Let us now develop a mathematical model of the Par, Inc., problem that can be used to determine the number of standard bags and the number of deluxe bags to produce in order to maximize total profit contribution.

*It is important to understand that we are maximizing profit contribution, not profit. Overhead and other shared costs must be deducted before arriving at a profit figure.*

## Problem Formulation

**Problem formulation** or **modeling** is the process of translating the verbal statement of a problem into a mathematical statement. Formulating models is an art that can only be mastered with practice and experience. Even though every problem has some unique features, most problems also have common features. As a result, *some* general guidelines for model formulation can be helpful, especially for beginners. We will illustrate these general guidelines by developing a mathematical model for the Par, Inc., problem.

| *Table* 2.1 | PRODUCTION REQUIREMENTS PER GOLF BAG | |
|---|---|---|
| | **Production Time (hours)** | |
| **Department** | **Standard Bag** | **Deluxe Bag** |
| Cutting and Dyeing | $7/10$ | 1 |
| Sewing | $1/2$ | $5/6$ |
| Finishing | 1 | $2/3$ |
| Inspection and Packaging | $1/10$ | $1/4$ |

---

[1] From an accounting perspective, profit contribution is more correctly described as the contribution margin per bag; for example, overhead and other shared costs have not been allocated.

**Understand the Problem Thoroughly.**   We selected the Par, Inc., problem to introduce linear programming because it is easy to understand. However, more complex problems will require much more thinking in order to identify the items that need to be included in the model. In such cases, read the problem description quickly to get a feel for what is involved. Taking notes will help you focus on the key issues and facts.

**Describe the Objective.**   The objective is to maximize the total contribution to profit.

**Describe Each Constraint.**   Four constraints relate to the number of hours of manufacturing time available; they restrict the number of standard bags and the number of deluxe bags that can be produced.

**Constraint 1**   Number of hours of cutting and dyeing time used must be less than or equal to the number of hours of cutting and dyeing time available.

**Constraint 2**   Number of hours of sewing time used must be less than or equal to the number of hours of sewing time available.

**Constraint 3**   Number of hours of finishing time used must be less than or equal to the number of hours of finishing time available.

**Constraint 4**   Number of hours of inspection and packaging time used must be less than or equal to the number of hours of inspection and packaging time available.

**Define the Decision Variables.**   The controllable inputs for Par, Inc., are (1) the number of standard bags produced, and (2) the number of deluxe bags produced. Let

$$S = \text{number of standard bags}$$
$$D = \text{number of deluxe bags}$$

In linear programming terminology, $S$ and $D$ are referred to as the **decision variables.**

**Write the Objective in Terms of the Decision Variables.**   Par's profit contribution comes from two sources: (1) the profit contribution made by producing $S$ standard bags, and (2) the profit contribution made by producing $D$ deluxe bags. Since Par makes $10 for every standard bag, the company will make $10S$ if $S$ standard bags are produced. Also, since Par makes $9 for every deluxe bag, the company will make $9D$ if $D$ deluxe bags are produced. Thus, we have

$$\text{Total Profit Contribution} = 10S + 9D$$

Since the objective—maximize total profit contribution—is a function of the decision variables $S$ and $D$, we refer to $10S + 9D$ as the *objective function.* Using "Max" as an abbreviation for maximize, we write Par's objective as follows:

$$\text{Max } 10S + 9D$$

**Write the Constraints in Terms of the Decision Variables**

Constraint 1:

$$\begin{pmatrix}\text{Hours of cutting and}\\ \text{dyeing time used}\end{pmatrix} \le \begin{pmatrix}\text{Hours of cutting and}\\ \text{dyeing time available}\end{pmatrix}$$

Every standard bag Par produces will use $\frac{7}{10}$ hour cutting and dyeing time, therefore the total number of hours of cutting and dyeing time used in the manufacture of $S$ standard bags is $\frac{7}{10}S$. In addition, because every deluxe bag produced uses 1 hour of cutting and dyeing time, the production of $D$ deluxe bags will use $1D$ hours of cutting and dyeing time. Thus, the total cutting and dyeing time required for the production of $S$ standard bags and $D$ deluxe bags is given by

$$\text{Total hours of cutting and dyeing time used} = \frac{7}{10}S + 1D$$

The director of manufacturing has stated that Par has at most 630 hours of cutting and dyeing time available. Therefore, the production combination we select must satisfy the requirement

$$\frac{7}{10}S + 1D \leq 630 \tag{2.1}$$

Constraint 2:

The units of measurement on the left-hand side of the constraint must match the units of measurement on the right-hand side.

$$\left(\begin{array}{c}\text{Hours of sewing} \\ \text{time used}\end{array}\right) \leq \left(\begin{array}{c}\text{Hours of sewing} \\ \text{time available}\end{array}\right)$$

From Table 2.1 we see that every standard bag manufactured will require $\frac{1}{2}$ hour for sewing, and every deluxe bag will require $\frac{5}{6}$ hour for sewing. Because 600 hours of sewing time are available, it follows that

$$\frac{1}{2}S + \frac{5}{6}D \leq 600 \tag{2.2}$$

Constraint 3:

$$\left(\begin{array}{c}\text{Hours of finishing} \\ \text{time used}\end{array}\right) \leq \left(\begin{array}{c}\text{Hours of finishing} \\ \text{time available}\end{array}\right)$$

Every standard bag manufactured will require 1 hour for finishing, and every deluxe bag will require $\frac{2}{3}$ hour for finishing. With 708 hours of finishing time available, it follows that

$$1S + \frac{2}{3}D \leq 708 \tag{2.3}$$

Constraint 4:

$$\left(\begin{array}{c}\text{Hours of inspection and} \\ \text{packaging time used}\end{array}\right) \leq \left(\begin{array}{c}\text{Hours of inspection and} \\ \text{packaging time available}\end{array}\right)$$

Every standard bag manufactured will require $\frac{1}{10}$ hour for inspection and packaging, and every deluxe bag will require $\frac{1}{4}$ hour for inspection and packaging. Because 135 hours of inspection and packaging time are available, it follows that

$$\frac{1}{10}S + \frac{1}{4}D \leq 135 \tag{2.4}$$

We have now specified the mathematical relationships for the constraints associated with the four departments. Have we forgotten any other constraints? Can Par produce a negative number of standard or deluxe bags? Clearly, the answer is no. Thus, to prevent the decision variables $S$ and $D$ from having negative values, two constraints,

$$S \geq 0 \quad \text{and} \quad D \geq 0 \tag{2.5}$$

must be added. These constraints ensure that the solution to the problem will contain non-negative values for the decision variables and are thus referred to as the **nonnegativity constraints.** Nonnegativity constraints are a general feature of all liner programming problems and may be written in the abbreviated form:

$$S, D \geq 0$$

## Mathematical Statement of the Par, Inc., Problem

Try Problem 22(a) to test your ability to formulate a mathematical model for a maximization linear programming problem with less-than-or-equal-to constraints.

The mathematical statement or mathematical formulation of the Par, Inc., problem is now complete. We have succeeded in translating the objective and constraints of the problem into a set of mathematical relationships referred to as a **mathematical model.** The complete mathematical model for the Par problem is as follows:

$$\text{Max} \quad 10S + 9D \tag{2.6}$$

subject to (s.t.)

$$\frac{7}{10}S + 1D \leq 630 \quad \text{Cutting and dyeing}$$
$$\frac{1}{2}S + \frac{5}{6}D \leq 600 \quad \text{Sewing}$$
$$1S + \frac{2}{3}D \leq 708 \quad \text{Finishing}$$
$$\frac{1}{10}S + \frac{1}{4}D \leq 135 \quad \text{Inspection and packaging}$$
$$S, D \geq 0$$

Our job now is to find the product mix (i.e., the combination of $S$ and $D$) that satisfies all the constraints and, at the same time, yields a value for the objective function that is greater than or equal to the value given by any other feasible solution. Once these values are calculated, we will have found the optimal solution to the problem.

This mathematical model of the Par problem is a **linear program.** The problem has the objective and constraints that, as we said earlier, are common properties of all *linear* programs. But what is the special feature of this mathematical model that makes it a linear program? The special feature that makes it a linear program is that the objective function and all constraint functions (the left-hand sides of the constraint inequalities) are linear functions of the decision variables.

Mathematical functions in which each variable appears in a separate term and is raised to the first power are called **linear functions.** The objective function ($10S + 9D$) is linear because each decision variable appears in a separate term and has an exponent of 1. The amount of production time required in the cutting and dyeing department ($\frac{7}{10}S + 1D$) is also a linear function of the decision variables for the same reason. Similarly, the functions on the left-hand side of all the constraint inequalities (the constraint functions) are linear functions. Thus, the mathematical formulation of this problem is referred to as a linear program.

Try Problem 1 to test your ability to recognize the types of mathematical relationships that can be found in a linear program.

Linear *programming* has nothing to do with computer programming. The use of the word *programming* here means "choosing a course of action." Linear programming involves choosing a course of action when the mathematical model of the problem contains only linear functions.

| N O T E S *and Comments* | 1. The three assumptions necessary for a linear programming model to be appropriate are proportionality, additivity, and divisibility. *Proportionality* means that the contribution to the objective function and the amount of resources used in each constraint are proportional to the value of each decision variable. *Additivity* means that the value of the objective function and the total resources used can be found by summing the objective function contribution and the resources used for all decision variables. *Divisibility* means that the decision variables are continuous. The divisibility assumption plus the nonnegativity constraints mean that decision variables can take on any value greater than or equal to zero. |
|---|---|

2. Management scientists formulate and solve a variety of mathematical models that contain an objective function and a set of constraints. Models of this type are referred to as *mathematical programming models.* Linear programming models are a special type of mathematical programming model in that the objective function and all constraint functions are linear.

## 2.2     GRAPHICAL SOLUTION PROCEDURE

A linear programming problem involving only two decision variables can be solved using a graphical solution procedure. Let us begin the graphical solution procedure by developing a graph that displays the possible solutions ($S$ and $D$ values) for the Par problem. The graph (Figure 2.1) will have values of $S$ on the horizontal axis and values of $D$ on the vertical axis. Any point on the graph can be identified by the $S$ and $D$ values, which indicate the position of the point along the horizontal and vertical axes, respectively. Since every point $(S, D)$ corresponds to a possible solution, every point on the graph is called a *solution point.* The solution point where $S = 0$ and $D = 0$ is referred to as the origin. Because $S$ and $D$ must be nonnegative, the graph in Figure 2.1 only displays solutions where $S \geq 0$ and $D \geq 0$.

Earlier, we saw that the inequality representing the cutting and dyeing constraint is

$$\tfrac{7}{10}S + 1D \leq 630$$

To show all solution points that satisfy this relationship, we start by graphing the solution points satisfying the constraint as an equality. That is, the points where $\tfrac{7}{10}S + 1D = 630$. Because the graph of this equation is a line, it can be obtained by identifying two points that satisfy the equation and then drawing a line through the points. Setting $S = 0$ and solving for $D$, we see that the point ($S = 0$, $D = 630$) satisfies the equation. To find a second point satisfying this equation, we set $D = 0$ and solve for $S$. By doing so, we obtain $\tfrac{7}{10}S + 1(0) = 630$, or $S = 900$. Thus, a second point satisfying the equation is ($S = 900$, $D = 0$). Given these two points, we can now graph the line corresponding to the equation

$$\tfrac{7}{10}S + 1D = 630$$

This line, which will be called the cutting and dyeing *constraint line,* is shown in Figure 2.2. We have labeled this line "C & D" to indicate that it represents the cutting and dyeing constraint line.

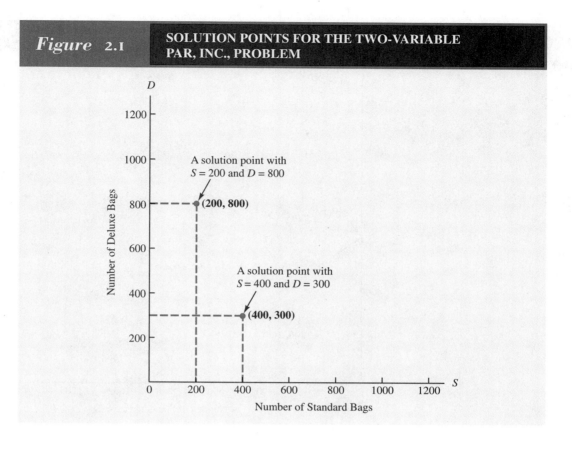

**Figure 2.1    SOLUTION POINTS FOR THE TWO-VARIABLE PAR, INC., PROBLEM**

Recall that the inequality representing the cutting and dyeing constraint is

$$\tfrac{7}{10}S + 1D \leq 630$$

Can you identify all of the solution points that satisfy this constraint? Because all points on the line satisfy $\tfrac{7}{10}S + 1D = 630$, we know any point on this line must satisfy the constraint. But where are the solution points satisfying $\tfrac{7}{10}S + 1D < 630$? Consider two solution points: $(S = 200, D = 200)$ and $(S = 600, D = 500)$. You can see from Figure 2.2 that the first solution point is below the constraint line and the second is above the constraint line. Which of these solutions will satisfy the cutting and dyeing constraint? For the point $(S = 200, D = 200)$, we see that

$$\tfrac{7}{10}S + 1D = \tfrac{7}{10}(200) + 1(200) = 340$$

Since the 340 hours is less than the 630 hours available, the $(S = 200, D = 200)$ production combination, or solution point, satisfies the constraint. For the point $(S = 600, D = 500)$, we have

$$\tfrac{7}{10}S + 1D = \tfrac{7}{10}(600) + 1(500) = 920$$

The 920 hours is greater than the 630 hours available, so the $(S = 600, D = 500)$ solution point does not satisfy the constraint and is thus not feasible.

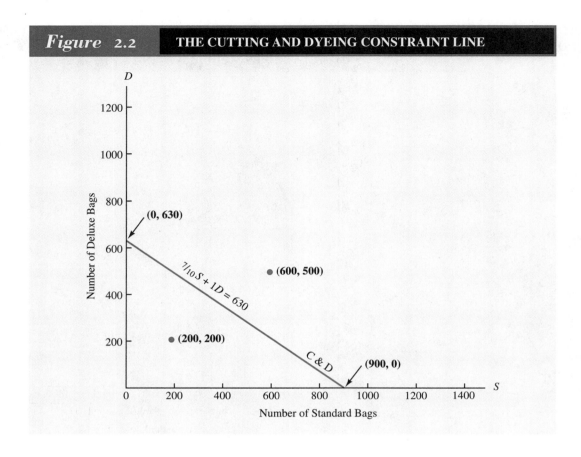

**Figure 2.2**     THE CUTTING AND DYEING CONSTRAINT LINE

Can you graph a constraint line and find the solution points that are feasible? Try Problem 2.

If a solution point is not feasible for a particular constraint, then all other solution points on the same side of that constraint line are not feasible. If a solution point is feasible for a particular constraint, then all other solution points on the same side of the constraint line are feasible for that constraint. Thus, one needs to evaluate the constraint function for only one solution point to determine which side of a constraint line is feasible. In Figure 2.3 we indicate all points satisfying the cutting and dyeing constraint by the shaded region.

We continue by identifying the solution points satisfying each of the other three constraints. The solutions that are feasible for each of these constraints are shown in Figure 2.4.

We now have four separate graphs showing the feasible solution points for each of the four constraints. In a linear programming problem, we need to identify the solution points that satisfy *all* the constraints *simultaneously*. To find these solution points, we can draw all four constraints on one graph and observe the region containing the points that do in fact satisfy all the constraints simultaneously.

Try Problem 7 to test your ability to find the feasible region given several constraints.

The graphs in Figures 2.3 and 2.4 can be superimposed to obtain one graph with all four constraints. This combined-constraint graph is shown in Figure 2.5. The shaded region in this figure includes every solution point that satisfies all the constraints simultaneously. Since solutions that satisfy all the constraints are termed **feasible solutions,** the shaded region is called the feasible solution region, or simply the **feasible region.** Any solution point on the boundary of the feasible region or within the feasible region is a *feasible solution point.*

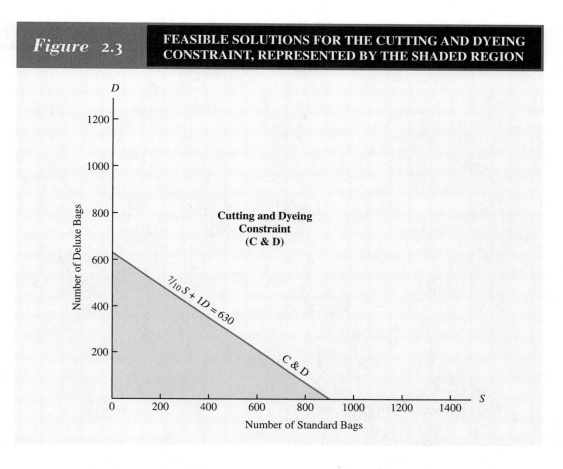

**Figure 2.3**    **FEASIBLE SOLUTIONS FOR THE CUTTING AND DYEING CONSTRAINT, REPRESENTED BY THE SHADED REGION**

Now that we have identified the feasible region, we are ready to proceed with the graphical solution procedure and find the optimal solution to the Par, Inc., problem. Recall that the optimal solution for a linear programming problem is the feasible solution that provides the best possible value of the objective function. Let us start the optimizing step of the graphical solution procedure by redrawing the feasible region on a separate graph. The graph is shown in Figure 2.6.

One approach to finding the optimal solution would be to evaluate the objective function for each feasible solution; the optimal solution would then be the one yielding the largest value. The difficulty with this approach is that there are an infinite number of feasible solutions; thus, because one cannot possibly evaluate an infinity of feasible solutions, this trial-and-error procedure cannot be used to identify the optimal solution.

Rather than trying to compute the profit contribution for each feasible solution, we select an arbitrary value for profit contribution and identify all the feasible solutions $(S, D)$ that yield the selected value. For example, what feasible solutions provide a profit contribution of $1800? These solutions are given by the values of $S$ and $D$ in the feasible region that will make the objective function

$$10S + 9D = 1800$$

This expression is simply the equation of a line. Thus, all feasible solution points $(S, D)$ yielding a profit contribution of $1800 must be on the line. We learned earlier in this section

| **Figure** 2.4 | **FEASIBLE SOLUTIONS FOR THE SEWING, FINISHING, AND INSPECTION AND PACKAGING CONSTRAINTS, REPRESENTED BY THE SHADED REGIONS** |

how to graph a constraint line. The procedure for graphing the profit or objective function line is the same. Letting $S = 0$, we see that $D$ must be 200; thus, the solution point ($S = 0$, $D = 200$) is on the line. Similarly, by letting $D = 0$, we see that the solution point ($S = 180$, $D = 0$) is also on the line. Drawing the line through these two points identifies all the solutions that have a profit contribution of $1800. A graph of this profit line is presented in Figure 2.7.

Because the objective is to find the feasible solution yielding the largest profit contribution, let us proceed by selecting higher profit contributions and finding the solutions yielding the selected values. For instance, let us find all solutions yielding profit contribu-

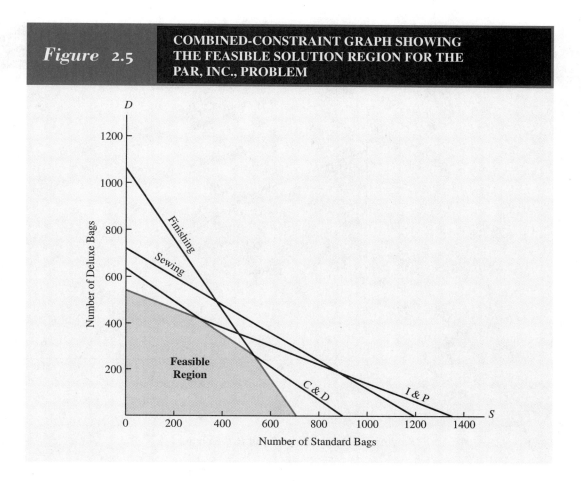

**Figure 2.5**   COMBINED-CONSTRAINT GRAPH SHOWING THE FEASIBLE SOLUTION REGION FOR THE PAR, INC., PROBLEM

tions of \$3600 and \$5400. To do so, we must find the $S$ and $D$ values that are on the following lines:

$$10S + 9D = 3600$$

and

$$10S + 9D = 5400$$

Using the previous procedure for graphing profit and constraint lines, we have drawn the \$3600 and \$5400 profit lines on the graph in Figure 2.8. Although not all solution points on the \$5400 profit line are in the feasible region, at least some points on the line are, and it is therefore possible to obtain a feasible solution that provides a \$5400 profit contribution.

Can we find a feasible solution yielding an even higher profit contribution? Look at Figure 2.8, and see what general observations you can make about the profit lines already drawn. Note the following: (1) the profit lines are *parallel* to each other, and (2) higher profit lines are obtained as we move farther from the origin. These observations can also be expressed algebraically. Let $P$ represent total profit contribution. The objective function is

$$P = 10S + 9D$$

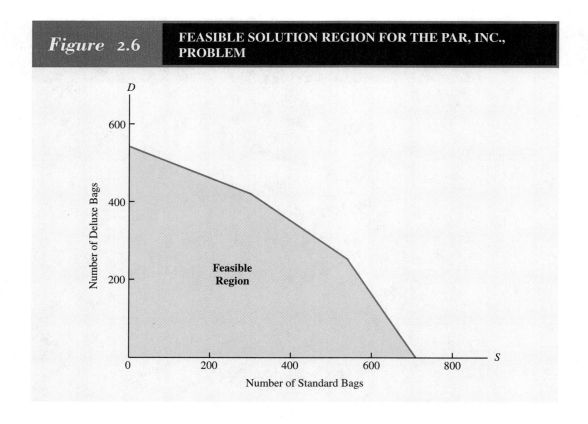

**Figure 2.6**       FEASIBLE SOLUTION REGION FOR THE PAR, INC., PROBLEM

Solving for $D$ in terms of $S$ and $P$, we obtain

$$9D = -10S + P$$
$$D = -\tfrac{10}{9}S + \tfrac{1}{9}P \qquad (2.7)$$

Equation (2.7) is the *slope-intercept form* of the linear equation relating $S$ and $D$. The co-efficient of $S$, $-\tfrac{10}{9}$, is the slope of the line, and the term $\tfrac{1}{9}P$ is the $D$ intercept (i.e., the value of $D$ where the graph of equation (2.7) crosses the $D$ axis). Substituting the profit contributions of $P = 1800$, $P = 3600$, and $P = 5400$ into equation (2.7) yields the following slope-intercept equations for the profit lines shown in Figure 2.8:

For $P = 1800$,

$$D = -\tfrac{10}{9}S + 200$$

For $P = 3600$,

$$D = -\tfrac{10}{9}S + 400$$

For $P = 5400$,

$$D = -\tfrac{10}{9}S + 600$$

Can you graph the profit line for a linear program? Try Problem 6.

The slope $(-\tfrac{10}{9})$ is the same for each profit line since the profit lines are parallel. Further, we see that the $D$ intercept increases with larger profit contributions. Thus, higher profit lines are farther from the origin.

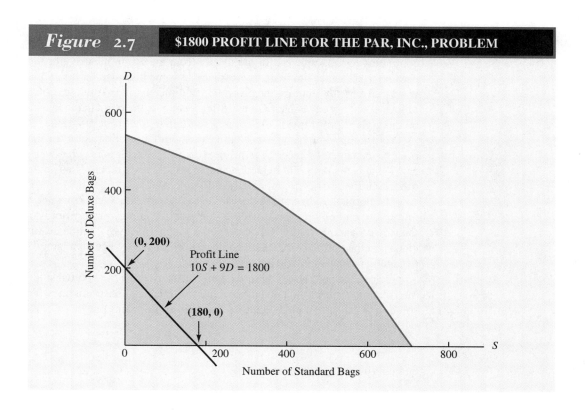

**Figure  2.7**    **$1800 PROFIT LINE FOR THE PAR, INC., PROBLEM**

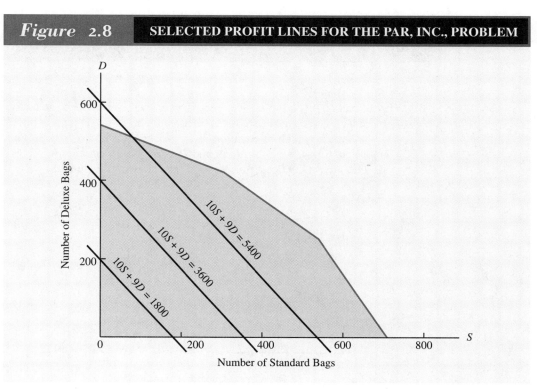

**Figure  2.8**    **SELECTED PROFIT LINES FOR THE PAR, INC., PROBLEM**

Because the profit lines are parallel and higher profit lines are farther from the origin, we can obtain solutions that yield increasingly larger values for the objective function by continuing to move the profit line farther from the origin in such a fashion that it remains parallel to the other profit lines. However, at some point we will find that any further outward movement will place the profit line completely outside the feasible region. Since solutions outside the feasible region are unacceptable, the point in the feasible region that lies on the highest profit line is the optimal solution to the linear program.

You should now be able to identify the optimal solution point for this problem. Use a ruler or the edge of a piece of paper, and move the profit line as far from the origin as you can. What is the last point in the feasible region that you reach? This point, which is the optimal solution, is shown graphically in Figure 2.9.

The optimal values of the decision variables are the $S$ and $D$ values at the optimal solution. Depending on the accuracy of the graph, you may or may not be able to determine the *exact* $S$ and $D$ values. Referring to the graph in Figure 2.9, the best we can do is conclude that the optimal production combination consists of approximately 550 standard bags ($S$) and approximately 250 deluxe bags ($D$).

A closer inspection of Figures 2.5 and 2.9 shows that the optimal solution point is at the intersection of the cutting and dyeing and the finishing constraint lines. That is, the optimal solution point is on both the cutting and dyeing constraint line

$$\frac{7}{10}S + 1D = 630 \tag{2.8}$$

and the finishing constraint line

$$1S + \frac{2}{3}D = 708 \tag{2.9}$$

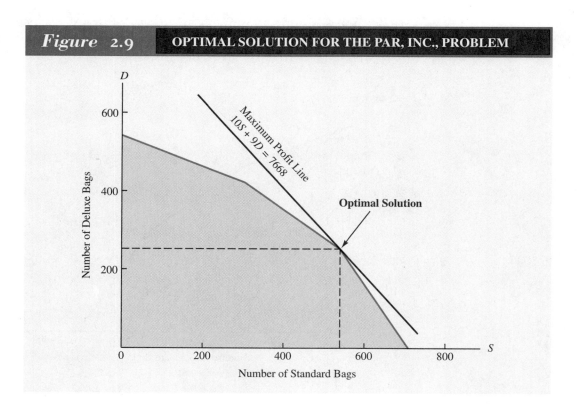

**Figure 2.9    OPTIMAL SOLUTION FOR THE PAR, INC., PROBLEM**

Thus, the optimal values of the decision variables $S$ and $D$ must satisfy both equations (2.8) and (2.9) simultaneously. Using equation (2.8) and solving for $S$ gives

$$\tfrac{7}{10}S = 630 - 1D$$

or

$$S = 900 - \tfrac{10}{7}D \tag{2.10}$$

Substituting this expression for $S$ into equation (2.9) and solving for $D$ provides the following:

$$1(900 - \tfrac{10}{7}D) + \tfrac{2}{3}D = 708$$
$$900 - \tfrac{10}{7}D + \tfrac{2}{3}D = 708$$
$$900 - \tfrac{30}{21}D + \tfrac{14}{21}D = 708$$
$$-\tfrac{16}{21}D = -192$$
$$D = \frac{192}{\tfrac{16}{21}} = 252$$

Using $D = 252$ in equation (2.10) and solving for $S$, we obtain

$$S = 900 - \tfrac{10}{7}(252)$$
$$= 900 - 360 = 540$$

*Although the optimal solution to the Par, Inc., problem consists of integer values for the decision variables, this result will not always be the case.*

The exact location of the optimal solution point is $S = 540$ and $D = 252$. Hence, the optimal production quantities for Par, Inc., are 540 standard bags and 252 deluxe bags, with a resulting profit contribution of $10(540) + 9(252) = \$7668$.

For a linear programming problem with two decision variables, the exact values of the decision variables can be determined by first using the graphical solution procedure to identify the optimal solution point and then solving the two simultaneous constraint equations associated with it.

*Try Problem 10 to test your ability to use the graphical solution procedure to identify the optimal solution and find the exact values of the decision variables at the optimal solution.*

## A Note on Graphing Lines

An important aspect of the graphical method is the ability to graph lines showing the constraints and the objective function of the linear program. The procedure we have used for graphing the equation of a line is to find any two points satisfying the equation and then draw the line through the two points. For the Par, Inc., constraints, the two points were easily found by the setting $S = 0$ and solving the constraint equation for $D$. Then we set $D = 0$ and solved for $S$. For the cutting and dyeing constraint line

$$\tfrac{7}{10}S + 1D = 630$$

this procedure identified the two points ($S = 0$, $D = 630$) and ($S = 900$, $D = 0$). The cutting and dyeing constraint line was then graphed by drawing a line through these two points.

All constraints and objective function lines in two-variable linear programs can be graphed if two points on the line can be identified. However, finding the two points on the line is not always as easy as shown in the Par, Inc., problem. For example, suppose a company manufactures two models of a small hand-held computer: the Assistant ($A$) and the Professional ($P$). Management needs 50 units of the Professional model for its own salesforce, and expects sales of the Professional to be at most one-half of the sales of the Assistant. A constraint enforcing this requirement is

$$P - 50 \leq \tfrac{1}{2}A$$

or

$$2P - 100 \leq A$$

or

$$2P - A \leq 100$$

Using the equality form and setting $P = 0$, we find the point $(P = 0, A = -100)$ is on the constraint line. Setting $A = 0$, we find a second point $(P = 50, A = 0)$ on the constraint line. If we have drawn only the nonnegative $(P \geq 0, A \geq 0)$ portion of the graph, the first point $(P = 0, A = -100)$ cannot be plotted because $A = -100$ is not on the graph. Whenever we have two points on the line, but one or both of the points cannot be plotted in the nonnegative portion of the graph, the simplest approach is to enlarge the graph. In this example, the point $(P = 0, A = -100)$ can be plotted by extending the graph to include the negative $A$ axis. Once both points satisfying the constraint equation have been located, the line can be drawn. The constraint line and the feasible solutions for the constraint $2P - A \leq 100$ are shown in Figure 2.10.

As another example, consider a problem involving two decision variables, $R$ and $T$. Suppose that the number of units of $R$ produced had to be at least equal to the number of units of $T$ produced. A constraint enforcing this requirement is

$$R \geq T$$

or

$$R - T \geq 0$$

Can you graph a constraint line when the origin is on the constraint line? Try Problem 5.

To find all solutions satisfying the constraint as an equality, we first set $R = 0$ and solve for $T$. This result shows that the origin $(T = 0, R = 0)$ is on the constraint line. Setting $T = 0$ and solving for $R$ provides the same point. However, we can obtain a second point on the line by setting $T$ equal to any value other than zero and then solving for $R$. For instance, setting $T = 100$ and solving for $R$, we find that the point $(T = 100, R = 100)$ is on the line. With the two points $(R = 0, T = 0)$ and $(R = 100, T = 100)$, the constraint line $R - T = 0$ and the feasible solutions for $R - T \geq 0$ can be plotted as shown in Figure 2.11.

## Summary of the Graphical Solution Procedure for Maximization Problems

For additional practice in using the graphical solution procedure, try Problem 22(b), 22(c), and 22(d).

As we have seen, the graphical solution procedure is a method for solving two-variable linear programming problems such as the Par, Inc., problem. The steps of the graphical solution procedure for a maximization problem are summarized here:

1. Prepare a graph of the feasible solutions for each of the constraints.
2. Determine the feasible region by identifying the solutions that satisfy all the constraints simultaneously.
3. Draw an objective function line showing the values of the decision variables that yield a specified value of the objective function.

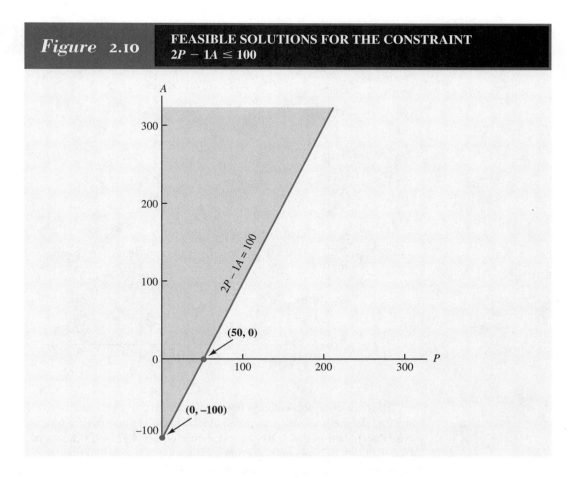

**Figure  2.10    FEASIBLE SOLUTIONS FOR THE CONSTRAINT 2P − 1A ≤ 100**

4. Move parallel objective function lines toward larger objective function values until further movement would take the line completely outside the feasible region.
5. Any feasible solution on the objective function line with the largest value is an optimal solution.

## Slack Variables

In addition to the optimal solution and its associated profit contribution. Par's management will probably want information about the production time requirements for each production operation. We can determine this information by substituting the optimal solution values ($S = 540$, $D = 252$) into the constraints of the linear program.

| Constraint | Hours Required for $S = 540$ and $D = 252$ | Hours Available | Unused Hours |
|---|---|---|---|
| Cutting and dyeing | $\frac{7}{10}(540) + 1(252) = 630$ | 630 | 0 |
| Sewing | $\frac{1}{2}(540) + \frac{5}{6}(252) = 480$ | 600 | 120 |
| Finishing | $1(540) + \frac{2}{3}(252) = 708$ | 708 | 0 |
| Inspection and packaging | $\frac{1}{10}(540) + \frac{1}{4}(252) = 117$ | 135 | 18 |

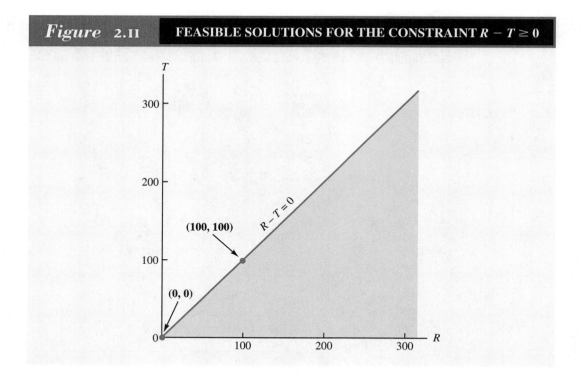

**Figure 2.11    FEASIBLE SOLUTIONS FOR THE CONSTRAINT $R - T \geq 0$**

Thus, the complete solution tells management that the production of 540 standard bags and 252 deluxe bags will require all available cutting and dyeing time (630 hours) and all available finishing time (708 hours), while $600 - 480 = 120$ hours of sewing time and $135 - 117 = 18$ hours of inspection and packaging time will remain unused. The 120 hours of unused sewing time and 18 hours of unused inspection and packaging time are referred to as *slack* for the two departments. In linear programming terminology, any unused capacity for a $\leq$ constraint is referred to as the *slack* associated with the constraint.

Can you identify the slack associated with a constraint? Try Problem 22(e).

Often variables, called **slack variables,** are added to the formulation of a linear programming problem to represent the slack, or idle capacity. Unused capacity makes no contribution to profit; thus, slack variables have coefficients of zero in the objective function. After the addition of four slack variables, denoted $S_1$, $S_2$, $S_3$, and $S_4$ the mathematical model of the Par, Inc., problem becomes

$$\text{Max} \quad 10S + 9D + 0S_1 + 0S_2 + 0S_3 + 0S_4$$
$$\text{s.t.}$$
$$\tfrac{7}{10}S + 1D + 1S_1 \qquad\qquad\qquad\qquad = 630$$
$$\tfrac{1}{2}S + \tfrac{5}{6}D \qquad + 1S_2 \qquad\qquad\qquad = 600$$
$$1S + \tfrac{2}{3}D \qquad\qquad + 1S_3 \qquad\qquad = 708$$
$$\tfrac{1}{10}S + \tfrac{1}{4}D \qquad\qquad\qquad + 1S_4 = 135$$
$$S, D, S_1, S_2, S_3, S_4 \geq 0$$

Whenever a linear program is written in a form with all constraints expressed as equalities, it is said to be written in **standard form.**

Can you write a linear
program in standard form?
Try Problem 18.

Referring to the standard form of the Par, Inc., problem, we see that at the optimal solution ($S = 540$ and $D = 252$), the values for the slack variables are

| Constraint | Value of Slack Variable |
|---|---|
| Cutting and dyeing | $S_1 = 0$ |
| Sewing | $S_2 = 120$ |
| Finishing | $S_3 = 0$ |
| Inspection and packaging | $S_4 = 18$ |

Could we have used the graphical solution to provide some of this information? The answer is yes. By finding the optimal solution point on Figure 2.5, we can see that the cutting and dyeing and the finishing constraints restrict, or *bind*, the feasible region at this point. Thus, this solution requires the use of all available time for these two operations. In other words, the graph shows us that the cutting and dyeing and the finishing departments will have zero slack. On the other hand, since the sewing and the inspection and packaging constraints are not binding the feasible region at the optimal solution, we can expect some unused time or slack for these two operations.

As a final comment on the graphical analysis of this problem, we call your attention to the sewing capacity constraint as shown in Figure 2.5. Note, in particular, that this constraint did not affect the feasible region. That is, the feasible region would be the same whether the sewing capacity constraint were included or not. This tells us that there is enough sewing time available to accommodate any production level that can be achieved by the other three departments. Since the sewing constraint does not affect the feasible region and thus cannot affect the optimal solution, it is called a **redundant constraint.**

## N O T E S  and *Comments*

1. In the standard-form representation of a linear programming model, the objective function coefficients for slack variables are zero. This zero coefficient implies that slack variables, which represent unused resources, do not affect the value of the objective function. However, in some applications, unused resources can be sold and contribute to profit. In such cases, the corresponding slack variables become decision variables representing the amount of resources to be sold. For each of these variables, a nonzero coefficient in the objective function would reflect the profit associated with selling a unit of the corresponding resource.

2. Redundant constraints do not affect the feasible region; as a result, they can be removed from a linear programming model without affecting the optimal solution. However, if the linear programming model is to be resolved later, changes in some of the data might make a previously redundant constraint a binding constraint. Thus, we recommend keeping all constraints in the linear programming model even though at some point in time one or more of the constraints may be redundant.

## 2.3   EXTREME POINTS AND THE OPTIMAL SOLUTION

Suppose that the profit contribution for Par's standard golf bag is reduced from $10 to $5 per bag, while the profit contribution for the deluxe golf bag and all the constraints remain unchanged. The complete linear programming model of this new problem is identical to the mathematical model in Section 2.1, except for the revised objective function:

$$\text{Max } 5S + 9D$$

How does this change in the objective function affect the optimal solution to the Par, Inc., problem? Figure 2.12 shows the graphical solution of this new problem with the revised objective function. Note that since the constraints have not changed, the feasible region has not changed. However, the profit lines have been altered to reflect the new objective function.

By moving the profit line in a parallel manner toward higher profit values, we find the optimal solution as shown in Figure 2.12. The values of the decision variables at this point are $S = 300$ and $D = 420$. The reduced profit contribution for the standard bag has caused a change in the optimal solution. In fact, as you may have suspected, we are cutting back the production of the lower-profit standard bags and increasing the production of the higher-profit deluxe bags.

What have you observed about the location of the optimal solutions in the two linear programming problems that we have solved thus far? Look closely at the graphical solu-

**Figure 2.12**   OPTIMAL SOLUTION FOR THE PAR, INC., PROBLEM WITH AN OBJECTIVE FUNCTION OF $5S + 9D$

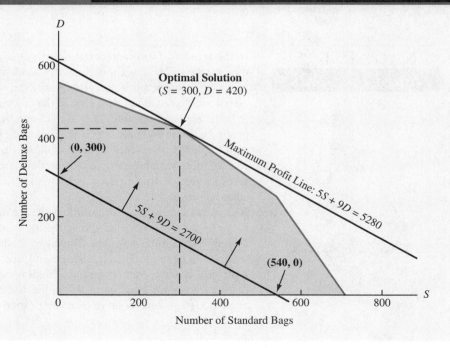

tions in Figures 2.9 and 2.12. Notice that the optimal solutions occur at once of the vertices or "corners" of the feasible region. In linear programming terminology, these vertices are referred to as the **extreme points** of the feasible region. The Par, Inc., problem has five vertices, or five extreme points, for its feasible region (see Figure 2.13). We can now formally state our observation about the location of optimal solutions as follows:

Try Problem 14 to test your ability to identify the extreme points of the feasible region and determine the optimal solution by computing and comparing the objective function value at each extreme point.

An optimal solution to a linear programming problem can be found at an extreme point of the feasible region for the problem.[2]

This property means that if you are looking for the optimal solution to a linear programming problem, you do not have to evaluate all feasible solution points. In fact, you have to consider *only* the feasible solutions that occur at the extreme points of the feasible region. Thus, for the Par, Inc., problem, instead of computing and comparing the profit contributions for all feasible solutions, we can find the optimal solution by evaluating the five extreme-point solutions and selecting the one that provides the largest profit contribution. Actually, the graphical solution procedure is nothing more than a convenient way of identifying an optimal extreme point for two-variable problems.

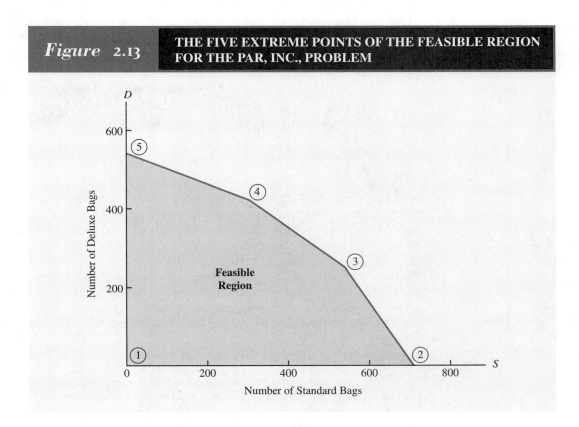

**Figure 2.13    THE FIVE EXTREME POINTS OF THE FEASIBLE REGION FOR THE PAR, INC., PROBLEM**

---

[2] We will discuss in Section 2.5 the two special cases (infeasibility and unboundedness) in linear programming which have no optimal solution, and this statement does not apply.

........................................................................................../  /.............

## 2.4    COMPUTER SOLUTION OF THE PAR, INC., PROBLEM

In January 1952 the first successful computer solution of a linear programming problem was performed on the SEAC (Standards Eastern Automatic Computer). The SEAC, the first digital computer built by the National Bureau of Standards under U.S. Air Force sponsorship, had a 512-word memory and magnetic tape for external storage.

Computer programs designed to solve linear programming problems are now widely available. Most companies and universities have access to these computer programs. After a short period of familiarization with the specific features of the package, users are able to solve linear programming problems with few difficulties. Problems involving thousands of variables and thousands of constraints are now routinely solved with computer packages. Most large linear programs can be solved with just a few minutes of computer time; small linear programs usually require only a few seconds.

More recently, with the virtual explosion of software for personal computers, a large number of user-friendly computer programs that can solve linear programs have become available. These programs, developed by academicians and small software companies, are almost all easy to use. Most of these programs are designed to solve smaller linear programs (a few hundred variables). But, some can be used to solve problems involving thousands of variables and constraints. Linear programming solvers are now part of many spreadsheet packages. In Appendix 2.2, we show how to use the solver available with Microsoft Excel.

The Management Scientist, a software package developed by the authors of this text, contains a linear programming module. Let us demonstrate its usage by solving the Par, Inc., problem we introduced in Section 2.1. Since computer input must utilize decimal rather than fractional data values, we restate the problem with decimal coefficients:

$$\text{Max} \quad 10S + 9D$$

$$\text{s.t.}$$

$$
\begin{array}{llll}
0.7S + & 1D \leq 630 & \text{Cutting and dyeing} \\
0.5S + 0.83333D \leq 600 & \text{Sewing} \\
1.0S + 0.66667D \leq 708 & \text{Finishing} \\
0.1S + & 0.25D \leq 135 & \text{Inspection and packaging} \\
S, D \geq 0
\end{array}
$$

Note that in the preceding form, the coefficient of $D$ in the sewing constraint is written as 0.83333, which is the closest five-place decimal value to the fraction $\frac{5}{6}$. A similar rounding occurs for the $D$ coefficient in the finishing constraint, where the decimal 0.66667 is used as the closest five-place decimal value to the fraction $\frac{2}{3}$. When this rounding of the input data is required, we may expect the computer solution to be slightly different from the hand-calculated solution based on the exact fractional values. However, as you will see, the two solutions are extremely close, and the slight rounding of the input data causes no serious problem. The solution generated by the Management Scientist is shown in Figure 2.14. The steps required to generate this solution are described in Appendix 2.1.

### Interpretation of Computer Output

Let us look more closely at The Management Scientist output in Figure 2.14 and interpret the computer solution provided for the Par, Inc., problem. First, note the number 7667.99463, which appears to the right of Objective Function Value. Rounding this value, we can conclude that the optimal solution to this problem will provide a profit of $7668. Directly below the objective function value, we find the values of the decision variables at the optimal solution. After rounding we have $S = 540$ standard bags and $D = 252$ deluxe bags as the optimal production quantities.

---

**Figure 2.14**  THE MANAGEMENT SCIENTIST SOLUTION FOR THE PAR, INC., PROBLEM

```
Objective Function Value =        7667.99463

        Variable              Value              Reduced Costs
       ----------          ------------         --------------
           S                539.99841              0.00000
           D                252.00113              0.00000

        Constraint         Slack/Surplus          Dual Prices
       ----------          ------------         --------------
           1                  0.00000               4.37496
           2                120.00070               0.00000
           3                  0.00000               6.93753
           4                 17.99988               0.00000

OBJECTIVE COEFFICIENT RANGES

        Variable       Lower Limit     Current Value     Upper Limit
       ----------      -----------     -------------     -----------
           S             6.30000         10.00000          13.49993
           D             6.66670          9.00000          14.28572

RIGHT HAND SIDE RANGES

        Constraint     Lower Limit     Current Value     Upper Limit
       ----------      -----------     -------------     -----------
           1            495.59998        630.00000        682.36316
           2            479.99930        600.00000      No Upper Limit
           3            580.00146        708.00000        900.00000
           4            117.00012        135.00000      No Upper Limit
```

The information in the Reduced Costs column indicates how much the objective function coefficient of each decision variable would have to improve[3] before it would be possible for that variable to assume a positive value in the optimal solution. If a decision variable is already positive in the optimal solution, its reduced cost is zero. For the Par, Inc., problem, the optimal solution is $S = 540$ and $D = 252$. Since both variables already have positive values, their corresponding reduced costs are zero. In Chapter 3 we will interpret the reduced cost for a decision variable that does not have a positive value in the optimal solution.

Immediately following the optimal $S$ and $D$ values and the reduced cost information, the computer output provides information about the status of the constraints. Recall that the Par, Inc., problem had four less-than-or-equal-to constraints corresponding to the hours available in each of four production departments. The information shown in the Slack/Surplus column

---

[3] For a maximization problem, improve means get bigger; for a minimization problem, improve means get smaller.

provides the value of the slack variable for each of the departments. This information (after rounding) is summarized here:

| Constraint Number | Constraint Name | Slack |
|:---:|:---|:---:|
| 1 | Cutting and dyeing | 0 |
| 2 | Sewing | 120 |
| 3 | Finishing | 0 |
| 4 | Inspection and packaging | 18 |

From this information, we see that the binding constraints (the cutting and dyeing and the finishing constraints) have zero slack at the optimal solution. The sewing department has 120 hours of slack, or unused capacity, and the inspection and packaging department has 18 hours of slack or unused capacity.

The rest of the output in Figure 2.14 can be used to determine how a change in a coefficient of the objective function or a change in the right-hand-side value of a constraint will affect the optimal solution. We will discuss the use of this information in Chapter 3 when we study the topic of sensitivity analysis.

| N O T E S | Linear programming solvers are now a standard feature of most spread- |
|:---|:---|
| *and Comments* | sheet packages. Excel, Lotus 1-2-3, and Quattro Pro all come with built-in solvers capable of solving optimization problems, including linear programs. The solver in each of these spreadsheet packages was developed by Frontline Systems and provides a similar user interface. In Appendix 2.2 we show how spreadsheets can be used to solve linear programs by using Excel to solve the Par, Inc., problem. |

## 2.5 A SIMPLE MINIMIZATION PROBLEM

M&D Chemicals produces two products that are sold as raw materials to companies manufacturing bath soaps and laundry detergents. Based on an analysis of current inventory levels and potential demand for the coming month, M&D's management has specified that the combined production for products A and B must total at least 350 gallons. Separately, a major customer's order for 125 gallons of product A must also be satisfied. Product A requires 2 hours of processing time per gallon while product B requires 1 hour of processing time per gallon, and for the coming month, 600 hours of processing time are available. M&D's objective is to satisfy these requirements at a minimum total production cost. Production costs are $2 per gallon for product A and $3 per gallon for product B.

To find the minimum-cost production schedule, we will formulate the M&D Chemicals problem as a linear program. Following a procedure similar to the one used for Par, Inc., we first define the decision variables and the objective function for the problem. Let

$$A = \text{number of gallons of product A}$$
$$B = \text{number of gallons of product B}$$

Since the production costs are $2 per gallon for product A and $3 per gallon for product B, the objective function that corresponds to the minimization of the total production cost can be written as

$$\text{Min } 2A + 3B$$

Next consider the constraints placed on the M&D Chemicals problem. To satisfy the major customer's demand for 125 gallons of product A, we know $A$ must be at least 125. Thus, we write the constraint

$$1A \geq 125$$

Since the combined production for both products must total at least 350 gallons, we can write the constraint

$$1A + 1B \geq 350$$

Finally, since the limitation on available processing time is 600 hours, we add the constraint

$$2A + 1B \leq 600$$

After adding the nonnegativity constraints ($A, B \geq 0$), we have the following linear program for the M&D Chemicals problem:

$$
\begin{aligned}
\text{Min} \quad & 2A + 3B \\
\text{s.t.} \quad & \\
& 1A \quad\quad\; \geq 125 \quad \text{Demand for product A} \\
& 1A + 1B \geq 350 \quad \text{Total production} \\
& 2A + 1B \leq 600 \quad \text{Processing time} \\
& A, B \geq 0
\end{aligned}
$$

Because the linear programming model has only two decision variables, the graphical solution procedure can be used to find the optimal production quantities. The graphical method for this problem, just as in the Par problem, requires us to first graph the constraint lines to find the feasible region. By graphing each constraint line separately and then checking points on either side of the constraint line, the feasible solutions for each constraint can be identified. By combining the feasible solutions for each constraint on the same graph, we obtain the feasible region shown in Figure 2.15.

To find the minimum-cost solution, we now draw the objective function line corresponding to a particular total cost value. For example, we might start by drawing the line $2A + 3B = 1200$. This line is shown in Figure 2.16. Clearly some points in the feasible region would provide a total cost of $1200. To find the values of $A$ and $B$ that provide smaller total cost values, we move the objective function line in a lower left direction until, if we moved it any farther, it would be entirely outside the feasible region. Note that the objective function line $2A + 3B = 800$ intersects the feasible region at the extreme point $A = 250$ and $B = 100$. This extreme point provides the minimum-cost solution with an objective function value of 800. From Figures 2.15 and 2.16, we can see that the total production constraint and the processing time constraint are binding. Just as in every linear programming problem, the optimal solution occurs at an extreme point of the feasible region.

**Figure 2.15**     **THE FEASIBLE REGION FOR THE M&D CHEMICALS PROBLEM**

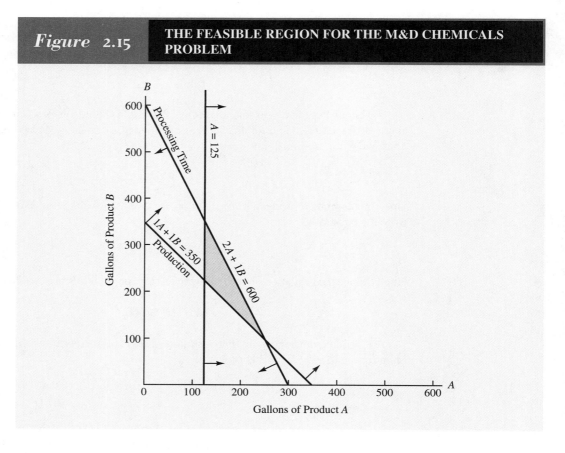

## Summary of the Graphical Solution Procedure for Minimization Problems

Can you use the graphical solution procedure to determine the optimal solution for a minimization problem? Try Problem 29.

The steps of the graphical solution procedure for a minimization problem are summarized here:

1. Prepare a graph of the feasible solutions for each of the constraints.
2. Determine the feasible region by identifying the solutions that satisfy all the constraints simultaneously.
3. Draw an objective function line showing the values of the decision variables that yield a specified value of the objective function.
4. Move parallel objective function lines toward smaller objective function values until further movement would take the line completely outside the feasible region.
5. Any feasible solution on the objective function line with the smallest value is an optimal solution.

## Surplus Variables

The optimal solution to the M&D Chemicals problem shows that the desired total production of $A + B = 350$ gallons has been achieved by using all available processing time of $2A + 1B = 2(250) + 1(100) = 600$ hours. In addition, note that the constraint

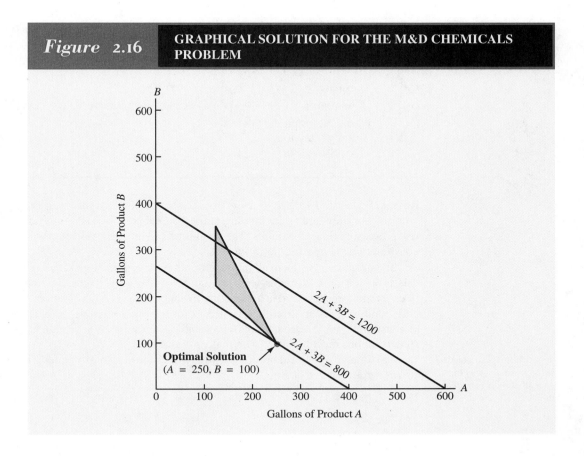

**Figure 2.16    GRAPHICAL SOLUTION FOR THE M&D CHEMICALS PROBLEM**

requiring that product A demand be met has been satisfied with $A = 250$ gallons. In fact, the production of product A exceeds its minimum level by $250 - 125 = 125$ gallons. This excess production for product A is referred to as *surplus*. In linear programming terminology, any excess quantity corresponding to a $\geq$ constraint is referred to as surplus.

Recall that with a $\leq$ constraint, a slack variable can be added to the left-hand side of the inequality to convert the constraint to equality form. With a $\geq$ constraint, a **surplus variable** can be subtracted from the left-hand side of the inequality to convert the constraint to equality form. Just as with slack variables, surplus variables are given a coefficient of zero in the objective function because they have no effect on its value. After including two surplus variables, $S_1$ and $S_2$, for the $\geq$ constraints and one slack variable, $S_3$, for the $\leq$ constraint, the linear programming model of the M&D Chemicals problem becomes

$$\text{Min} \quad 2A + 3B + 0S_1 + 0S_2 + 0S_3$$
$$\text{s.t.}$$
$$1A \qquad\quad - 1S_1 \qquad\qquad\qquad = 125$$
$$1A + 1B \qquad\quad - 1S_2 \qquad\qquad = 350$$
$$2A + 1B \qquad\qquad\qquad + 1S_3 = 600$$
$$A, B, S_1, S_2, S_3 \geq 0$$

Try Problem 33 to test your ability to use slack and surplus variables to write a linear program in standard form.

All the constraints are now equalities. Hence, the preceding formulation is the standard-form representation of the M&D Chemicals problem. At the optimal solution of $A = 250$ and $B = 100$, the values of the surplus and slack variables are as follows:

| Constraint | Value of Surplus or Slack Variables |
|---|---|
| Demand for product $A$ | $S_1 = 125$ |
| Total production | $S_2 = 0$ |
| Processing time | $S_3 = 0$ |

Refer to Figures 2.15 and 2.16. Note that the zero surplus and slack variables are associated with the constraints that are binding at the optimal solution—that is, the total production and processing time constraints. The surplus of 125 units is associated with the nonbinding constraint on the demand for product $A$.

In the Par, Inc., problem all the constraints were of the $\leq$ type, and in the M&D Chemicals problem the constraints were a mixture of $\geq$ and $\leq$ types. The number and types of constraints encountered in a particular linear programming problem depends on the specific conditions existing in the problem. Linear programming problems may have some $\leq$ constraints, some $\geq$ constraints, and some $=$ constraints. For an equality constraint, feasible solutions must lie directly on the constraint line.

Try Problem 32 to practice solving a linear program with all three constraint forms.

An example of a linear program with two decision variables, $G$ and $H$, and all three constraint forms is given here:

$$\text{Min} \quad 2G + 2H$$
$$\text{s.t.}$$
$$1G + 3H \leq 12$$
$$3G + 1H \geq 13$$
$$1G - 1H = 3$$
$$G, H \geq 0$$

The standard-form representation of this problem is

$$\text{Min} \quad 2G + 2H + 0S_1 + 0S_2$$
$$\text{s.t.}$$
$$1G + 3H + 1S_1 \qquad = 12$$
$$3G + 1H \qquad - 1S_2 = 13$$
$$1G - 1H \qquad = 3$$
$$G, H, S_1, S_2 \geq 0$$

The standard form requires a slack variable for the $\leq$ constraint and a surplus variable for the $\geq$ constraint. However, neither a slack nor a surplus variable is required for the third constraint since it is already in equality form.

When solving linear programs graphically, it is not necessary to write the problem in its standard form. Nevertheless, you should be able to compute the values of the slack and surplus variables and understand what they mean, since the values of slack and surplus variables are included in the computer solution of linear programs. In Chapter 5 we will introduce an algebraic solution procedure, the simplex method, which can be used to find optimal extreme-point solutions for linear programming problems with as many as several thousand decision variables. The mathematical steps of the simplex method involve solving simultaneous equations that represent the constraints of the linear program. Thus, in setting up a linear program for solution by the simplex method, we must have one linear equation for each constraint in the problem; therefore, the problem must be in its standard form.

A final point: The standard form of the linear programming problem is equivalent to the original formulation of the problem. That is, the optimal solution to any linear programming problem is the same as the optimal solution to the standard form of the problem. The standard form has not changed the basic problem; it has only changed how we write the constraints for the problem.

### Computer Solution of the M&D Chemicals Problem

The solution obtained using The Management Scientist is presented in Figure 2.17. The computer output shows that the minimum-cost solution yields an objective function value

**Figure 2.17  THE MANAGEMENT SCIENTIST SOLUTION FOR THE M&D CHEMICALS PROBLEM**

```
Objective Function Value =          800.000

        Variable            Value            Reduced Costs
        --------            -----            -------------
           A              250.000                0.000
           B              100.000                0.000

       Constraint       Slack/Surplus         Dual Prices
       ----------       -------------         -----------
           1              125.000                0.000
           2                0.000               -4.000
           3                0.000                1.000

OBJECTIVE COEFFICIENT RANGES

   Variable      Lower Limit      Current Value      Upper Limit
   --------      -----------      -------------      -----------
      A        No Lower Limit         2.000             3.000
      B             2.000             3.000         No Upper Limit

RIGHT HAND SIDE RANGES

  Constraint     Lower Limit      Current Value      Upper Limit
  ----------     -----------      -------------      -----------
      1        No Lower Limit        125.000           250.000
      2            300.000           350.000           475.000
      3            475.000           600.000           700.000
```

of $800. The values of the decision variables show that 250 gallons of product A and 100 gallons of product B provide the minimum-cost solution.

The Slack/Surplus column shows that the $\geq$ constraint corresponding to the demand for product A (see constraint 1) has a surplus of 125 units. This column tells us that production of product A in the optimal solution exceeds demand by 125 gallons. The Slack/Surplus values are zero for the total production requirement (constraint 2) and the processing time limitation (constraint 3), which indicates that these constraints are binding at the optimal solution. We will discuss the rest of the computer output in Figure 2.17 in Chapter 3 when we study the topic of sensitivity analysis.

## 2.6    SPECIAL CASES

In this section we discuss three special situations that can arise when we attempt to solve linear programming problems.

### Alternative Optimal Solutions

From the discussion of the graphical solution procedure, we know that optimal solutions can be found at the extreme points of the feasible region. Now let us consider the special case in which the optimal objective function line coincides with one of the binding constraint lines on the boundary of the feasible region. We will see that this can lead to the case of **alternative optimal solutions;** in such cases, more than one solution provides the optimal value for the objective function.

To illustrate the case of alternative optimal solutions, we return to the Par, Inc., problem. However, let us assume that the profit for the standard golf bag ($S$) has been decreased to $6.30. The revised objective function becomes $6.3S + 9D$. The graphical solution of this problem is shown in Figure 2.18. Note that the optimal solution still occurs at an extreme point. In fact, it occurs at two extreme points: extreme point ④ ($S = 300, D = 420$) and extreme point ③ ($S = 540, D = 252$).

The objective function values at these two extreme points are identical; that is,

$$6.3S + 9D = 6.3(300) + 9(420) = 5670$$

and

$$6.3S + 9D = 6.3(540) + 9(252) = 5670$$

Furthermore, any point on the line connecting the two optimal extreme points also provides an optimal solution. For example, the solution point ($S = 420, D = 336$), which is halfway between the two extreme points, also provides the optimal objective function value of

$$6.3S + 9D = 6.3(420) + 9(336) = 5670$$

A linear programming problem with alternative optimal solutions is generally a good situation for the manager or decision maker. It means that several combinations of the decision variables are optimal and that the manager can select the most desirable optimal solution. Unfortunately, determining whether a problem has alternative optimal solutions is not a simple matter.

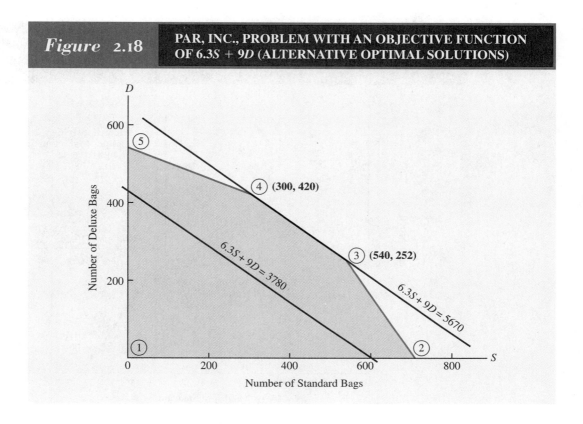

**Figure 2.18    PAR, INC., PROBLEM WITH AN OBJECTIVE FUNCTION OF 6.3S + 9D (ALTERNATIVE OPTIMAL SOLUTIONS)**

## Infeasibility

Problems with no feasible solution do arise in practice, most often because management's expectations are too high or because too many restrictions have been placed on the problem.

**Infeasibility** means that no solution to the linear programming problem satisfies all the constraints, including the nonnegativity conditions. Graphically, infeasibility means that a feasible region does not exist; that is, no points satisfy all the constraints and the nonnegativity conditions simultaneously. To illustrate this situation, let us look again at the problem faced by Par, Inc.

Suppose that management had specified that at least 500 of the standard bags and at least 360 of the deluxe bags must be manufactured. The graph of the solution region may now be constructed to reflect these new requirements (see Figure 2.19). The shaded area in the lower left-hand portion of the graph depicts those points satisfying the departmental constraints on the availability of time. The shaded area in the upper right-hand portion depicts those points satisfying the minimum production requirements of 500 standard and 360 deluxe bags. But no points satisfy both sets of constraints. Thus, we see that if management imposes these minimum production requirements, no feasible solution can result in the linear programming model.

How should we interpret infeasibility in terms of this current problem? First, we should tell management that given the resources available (i.e., production time for cutting and dyeing, sewing, finishing, and inspection and packaging), it is not possible to make 500 standard bags and 360 deluxe bags. Moreover, we can tell management exactly how much of each resource must be expended to make it possible to manufacture 500 standard and 360 deluxe bags. Table 2.2 shows the minimum amounts of resources that must be available, the amounts currently available, and additional amounts that would be required to

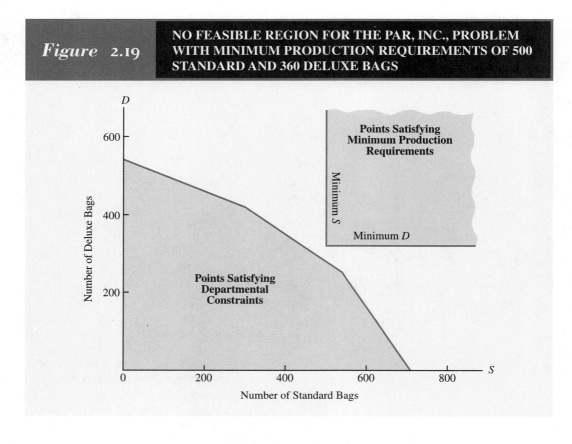

**Figure 2.19**     NO FEASIBLE REGION FOR THE PAR, INC., PROBLEM WITH MINIMUM PRODUCTION REQUIREMENTS OF 500 STANDARD AND 360 DELUXE BAGS

accomplish this. Thus, we need 80 more hours for cutting and dyeing, 32 more hours for finishing, and 5 more hours for inspection and packaging to meet management's minimum production requirements.

If, after reviewing this information, management still wants to manufacture 500 standard and 360 deluxe bags, additional resources must be provided. Perhaps by hiring another person to work in the cutting and dyeing department, transferring a person from elsewhere in the plant to work part-time in the finishing department, or having the sewing people help out periodically with the inspection and packaging, the resource requirements can be met.

**Table 2.2**     RESOURCES NEEDED TO MANUFACTURE 500 STANDARD BAGS AND 360 DELUXE BAGS

| Operation | Minimum Required Resources (hours) | Available Resources (hours) | Additional Resources Needed (hours) |
|---|---|---|---|
| Cutting and dyeing | $\frac{7}{10}(500) + 1(360) = 710$ | 630 | 80 |
| Sewing | $\frac{1}{2}(500) + \frac{5}{6}(360) = 550$ | 600 | None |
| Finishing | $1(500) + \frac{2}{3}(360) = 740$ | 708 | 32 |
| Inspection and packaging | $\frac{1}{10}(500) + \frac{1}{4}(360) = 140$ | 135 | 5 |

As you can see, many possibilities are available for corrective management action, once we discover the lack of a feasible solution. The important thing to realize is that linear programming analysis can help determine whether management's plans are feasible. By analyzing the problem using linear programming, we are often able to point out infeasible conditions and initiate corrective action.

Whenever you attempt to solve a problem that is infeasible using The Management Scientist, you will obtain a message that says "No Feasible Solution." In this case you know that no solution to the linear programming problem will satisfy all constraints, including the nonnegativity conditions. Careful inspection of your formulation is necessary to try to identify why the problem is infeasible. In some situations, the only reasonable approach is to drop one or more constraints and resolve the problem. If you are able to find an optimal solution for this revised problem, you will know that the constraint(s) that were omitted, in conjunction with the others, are causing the problem to be infeasible.

### Unbounded

The solution to a maximization linear programming problem is **unbounded** if the value of the solution may be made infinitely large without violating any of the constraints; for a minimization problem, the solution is unbounded if the value may be made infinitely small. This condition might be termed *managerial utopia;* for example, if this condition were to occur in a profit maximization problem, the manager could achieve an unlimited profit.

However, in linear programming models of real problems, the occurrence of an unbounded solution means that the problem has been improperly formulated. We know it is not possible to increase profits indefinitely. Therefore, we must conclude that if a profit maximization problem results in an unbounded solution, the mathematical model doesn't represent the real-world problem sufficiently. Usually, what has happened is that a constraint has been inadvertently omitted during problem formulation.

As an illustration, consider the following linear program with two decision variables, $X$ and $Y$.

$$\text{Max} \quad 20X + 10Y$$
$$\text{s.t.}$$
$$1X \qquad \geq 2$$
$$1Y \leq 5$$
$$X, Y \geq 0$$

In Figure 2.20 we have graphed the feasible region associated with this problem. Note that we can only indicate part of the feasible region since the feasible region extends indefinitely in the direction of the $X$ axis. Looking at the objective function lines in Figure 2.20, we see that the solution to this problem may be made as large as we desire. That is, no matter what solution we pick, we will always be able to reach some feasible solution with a larger value. Thus, we say that the solution to this linear program is *unbounded.*

Can you recognize whether a linear program involves alternative optimal solutions, infeasibility, or is unbounded? Try Problems 40 and 41.

Whenever you attempt to solve a problem that is unbounded using The Management Scientist, you will obtain a message that says, "Problem is Unbounded." Because unbounded solutions cannot occur in real problems, the first thing you should do is to review your model to determine whether you have incorrectly formulated the problem. In many cases, this error is the result of inadvertently omitting a constraint during problem formulation.

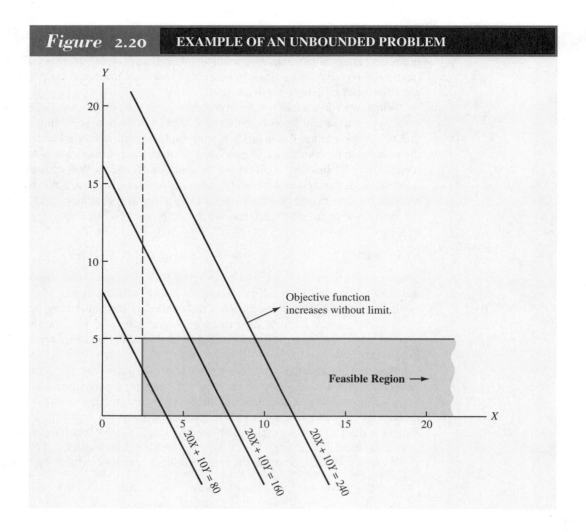

**Figure 2.20**    **EXAMPLE OF AN UNBOUNDED PROBLEM**

N O T E S
*and Comments*

1. Infeasibility is independent of the objective function. It exists because the constraints are so restrictive that they allow no feasible region for the linear programming model. Thus, when you encounter infeasibility, making changes in the coefficients of the objective function will not help; the problem will remain infeasible.

2. The occurrence of an unbounded solution is often the result of a missing constraint. However, a change in the objective function may cause a previously unbounded problem to become bounded with an optimal solution. For example, the graph in Figure 2.20 shows an unbounded solution for the objective function Max $20X + 10Y$. However, changing the objective function to Max $-20X - 10Y$ will provide the optimal solution $X = 2$ and $Y = 0$ even though no changes have been made in the constraints.

........................................................................................................./  /............

## 2.7    GENERAL LINEAR PROGRAMMING NOTATION

In this chapter we showed how to formulate mathematical models for the Par, Inc., and M&D Chemicals linear programming problems. To formulate a mathematical model of the Par, Inc., problem we began by defining two decision variables: $S$ = number of standard bags, and $D$ = number of deluxe bags. In the M&D Chemicals problem, the two decision variables were defined as $A$ = number of gallons of product A, and $B$ = number of gallons of product B. We selected decision variable names of $S$ and $D$ in the Par, Inc., problem and $A$ and $B$ in the M&D Chemicals problem to make it easier to recall what these decision variables represented in the problem. Although this approach works well for linear programs involving a small number of decision variables, it can become difficult when dealing with problems involving a large number of decision variables.

A more general notation that is often used for linear programs uses the letter $x$ with a subscript. For instance, in the Par, Inc., problem, we could have defined the decision variables as follows:

$$x_1 = \text{number of standard bags}$$
$$x_2 = \text{number of deluxe bags}$$

In the M&D Chemicals problem, the same variable names would be used, but their definitions would change:

$$x_1 = \text{number of gallons of product A}$$
$$x_2 = \text{number of gallons of product B}$$

A disadvantage of using general notation for decision variable is that we are no longer able to easily identify what the decision variables actually represent in the mathematical model. However, the advantage of general notation is that formulating a mathematical model for a problem that involves a large number of decision variables is much easier. For instance, for a linear programming problem with three decision variables, we would use variable names of $x_1$, $x_2$, and $x_3$; for a problem with four decision variables, we would use variable names of $x_1$, $x_2$, $x_3$, and $x_4$, and so on. Clearly, if a problem involved 1000 decision variables, trying to identify 1000 unique names would be difficult. However, using the general linear programming notation, the decision variables would be defined as $x_1, x_2, x_3, \ldots, x_{1000}$.

To illustrate the graphical solution procedure for a linear program written using general linear programming notation, consider the following mathematical model for a maximization problem involving two decision variables:

$$\text{Max} \quad 3x_1 + 2x_2$$
$$\text{s.t.}$$
$$2x_1 + 2x_2 \leq 8$$
$$1x_1 + 0.5x_2 \leq 3$$
$$x_1, x_2 \geq 0$$

We must first develop a graph that displays the possible solutions ($x_1$ and $x_2$ values) for the problem. The usual convention is to plot values of $x_1$ along the horizontal axis and values of $x_2$ along the vertical axis. Figure 2.21 shows the graphical solution for this two-variable problem. Note that for this problem the optimal solution is $x_1 = 2$ and $x_2 = 2$, with an objective function value of 10.

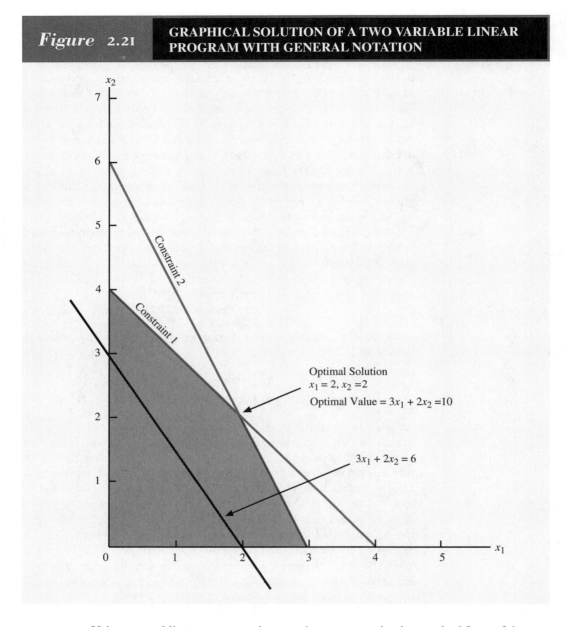

| **Figure** 2.21 | **GRAPHICAL SOLUTION OF A TWO VARIABLE LINEAR PROGRAM WITH GENERAL NOTATION** |

Using general linear programming notation we can write the standard form of the preceding problem as follows:

$$\text{Max} \quad 3x_1 + 2x_2 + 0s_1 + 0s_2$$

s.t.

$$2x_1 + 2x_2 + 1s_1 \qquad = 8$$
$$1x_1 + 0.5x_2 + \qquad 1s_2 = 3$$
$$x_1, x_2, s_1, s_2 \geq 0$$

Thus, at the optimal solution $x_1 = 2$ and $x_2 = 2$; the values of the slack variables are $s_1 = s_2 = 0$.

.................................................................................................../  /.............

## SUMMARY

We formulated mathematical models for two linear programming problems: the Par, Inc., maximization problem and the M&D Chemicals minimization problem. For both problems we showed how a graphical solution procedure and The Management Scientist software package can be used to identify an optimal solution. In formulating a mathematical model of these problems, we developed a general definition of a linear program.

A linear program is a mathematical model that has

1. a linear objective function that is to be maximized or minimized,
2. a set of linear constraints, and
3. variables that are all restricted to nonnegative values.

Slack variables may be used to write less-than-or-equal-to constraints in equality form and surplus variables may be used to write greater-than-or-equal-to constraints in equality form. The value of a slack variable can usually be interpreted as the amount of unused resource, while the value of a surplus variable indicates the amount over and above some stated minimum requirement. When all constraints have been written as equalities, the linear program has been written in its standard form.

If the solution to a linear program is infeasible or unbounded, no optimal solution to the problem can be found. In the case of infeasibility, no feasible solutions are possible; whereas, in the case of an unbounded solution, the objective function can be made infinitely large for a maximization problem and infinitely small for a minimization problem. In the case of alternative optimal solutions, two or more optimal extreme points exist, and all the points on the line segment connecting them are also optimal.

The chapter concluded with a section showing how to write a mathematical model using general linear programming notation.

.................................................................................................../  /.............

## GLOSSARY

**Decision variable**  A controllable input for a linear programming model.

**Constraint**  An equation or inequality that rules out certain combinations of decision variables as feasible solutions.

**Problem formulation**  The process of translating the verbal statement of a problem into a mathematical statement called the *mathematical model.*

**Nonnegativity constraints**  A set of constraints that requires all variables to be nonnegative.

**Mathematical model**  A representation of a problem where the objective and all constraint conditions are described by mathematical expressions.

**Linear program**  A mathematical model with a linear objective function, a set of linear constraints, and nonnegative variables.

**Linear functions**  Mathematical expressions in which the variables appear in separate terms and are raised to the first power.

**Feasible solution**  A solution that satisfies all the constraints.

**Feasible region**  The set of all feasible solutions.

**Slack variable** A variable added to the left-hand side of a less-than-or-equal-to constraint to convert the constraint into an equality. The value of this variable can usually be interpreted as the amount of unused resource.

**Standard form** A linear program in which all the constraints are written as equalities. The optimal solution of the standard form of a linear program is the same as the optimal solution of the original formulation of the linear program.

**Redundant constraint** A constraint that does not affect the feasible region. If a constraint is redundant, it can be removed from the problem without affecting the feasible region.

**Extreme point** Graphically speaking, extreme points are the feasible solution points occurring at the vertices or "corners" of the feasible region. With two-variable problems, extreme points are determined by the intersection of the constraint lines.

**Surplus variable** A variable subtracted from the left-hand side of a greater-than-or-equal-to constraint to convert the constraint into an equality. The value of this variable can usually be interpreted as the amount over and above some required minimum level.

**Alternative optimal solutions** The case in which more than one solution provides the optimal value for the objective function.

**Infeasibility** The situation in which no solution to the linear programming problem satisfies all the constraints.

**Unbounded** If the value of the solution may be made infinitely large in a maximization linear programming problem or infinitely small in a minimization problem without violating any of the constraints the problem is said to be unbounded.

## PROBLEMS

**SELF TEST**

1. Which of the following mathematical relationships could be found in a linear programming model, and which could not? For the relationships that are unacceptable for linear programs, state why.
   a. $-1x_1 + 2x_2 - 1x_3 \leq 70$
   b. $2x_1 - 2x_3 = 50$
   c. $1x_1 - 22x_2^2 + 4x_3 \leq 10$
   d. $3\sqrt{x_1} + 2x_2 - 1x_3 \geq 15$
   e. $1x_1 + 1x_2 + 1x_3 = 6$
   f. $2x_1 + 5x_2 + 1x_1x_2 \leq 25$

**SELF TEST**

2. Find the feasible solution points for the following constraints:
   a. $4x_1 + 2x_2 \leq 16$
   b. $4x_1 + 2x_2 \geq 16$
   c. $4x_1 + 2x_2 = 16$

3. Show a separate graph of the constraint lines and feasible solutions for each of the following constraints:
   a. $3x_1 + 2x_2 \leq 18$
   b. $12x_1 + 8x_2 \geq 480$
   c. $5x_1 + 10x_2 = 200$

4. Show a separate graph of the constraint lines and feasible solutions for each of the following constraints:
   a. $3x_1 - 4x_2 \geq 60$
   b. $-6x_1 + 5x_2 \leq 60$
   c. $5x_1 - 2x_2 \leq 0$

5. Show a separate graph of the constraint lines and feasible solutions for each of the following constraints:
   a. $x_1 \geq 0.25 (x_1 + x_2)$
   b. $x_2 \leq 0.10 (x_1 + x_2)$
   c. $x_1 \leq 0.50 (x_1 + x_2)$

6. Three objective functions for linear programming problems are $7x_1 + 10x_2$, $6x_1 + 4x_2$, and $-4x_1 + 7x_2$. Determine the slope of each objective function. Show the graph of each for objective function values equal to 420.

**SELF TEST**

7. Identify the feasible region for the following set of constraints:

$$\tfrac{1}{2}x_1 + \tfrac{1}{4}x_2 \geq 30$$
$$1x_1 + 5x_2 \geq 250$$
$$\tfrac{1}{4}x_1 + \tfrac{1}{2}x_2 \leq 50$$
$$x_1, x_2 \geq 0$$

**SELF TEST**

8. Identify the feasible region for the following set of constraints:

$$2x_1 - 1x_2 \leq 0$$
$$-1x_1 + 1.5x_2 \leq 200$$
$$x_1, x_2 \geq 0$$

9. Identify the feasible region for the following set of constraints:

$$3x_1 - 2x_2 \geq 0$$
$$2x_1 - 1x_2 \leq 200$$
$$1x_1 \leq 150$$
$$x_1, x_2 \geq 0$$

10. For the linear program

$$\text{Max} \quad 2x_1 + 3x_2$$
$$\text{s.t.}$$
$$1x_1 + 2x_2 \leq 6$$
$$5x_1 + 3x_2 \leq 15$$
$$x_1, x_2 \geq 0$$

**SELF TEST**

find the optimal solution using the graphical solution procedure. What is the value of the objective function at the optimal solution?

11. Solve the following linear program using the graphical solution procedure.

$$\text{Max} \quad 5x_1 + 5x_2$$
$$\text{s.t.}$$
$$1x_1 \qquad \leq 100$$
$$1x_2 \leq 80$$
$$2x_1 + 4x_2 \leq 400$$
$$x_1, x_2 \geq 0$$

12. Consider the following linear programming problem:

$$\text{Max} \quad 3x_1 + 3x_2$$
$$\text{s.t.}$$
$$2x_1 + 4x_2 \leq 12$$
$$6x_1 + 4x_2 \leq 24$$
$$x_1, x_2 \geq 0$$

a.  Find the optimal solution using the graphical solution procedure.
b.  If the objective function is changed to $2x_1 + 6x_2$, what will the optimal solution be?
c.  How many extreme points are there? What are the values of $x_1$ and $x_2$ at each extreme point?

13. Consider the following linear programming problem:

$$\text{Max} \quad 3x_1 + 2x_2$$

s.t.

$$2x_1 + 2x_2 \le 8$$
$$3x_1 + 2x_2 \le 12$$
$$1x_1 + 0.5x_2 \le 3$$
$$x_1, x_2 \ge 0$$

a.  Find the optimal solution using the graphical solution procedure. What is the value of the objective function?
b.  Does this problem have a redundant constraint? If so, what is it? Does the solution change if the redundant constraint is removed from the problem? Explain.

**SELF TEST**

14. Consider the following linear program:

$$\text{Max} \quad 1x_1 + 2x_2$$

s.t.

$$1x_1 \qquad \le 5$$
$$\qquad 1x_2 \le 4$$
$$2x_1 + 2x_2 = 12$$
$$x_1, x_2 \ge 0$$

a.  Show the feasible region.
b.  What are the extreme points of the feasible region?
c.  Find the optimal solution using the graphical procedure.

15. What constraint lines combine to form extreme point ④ of the Par, Inc., problem (see Figures 2.5 and 2.13)? Solve the simultaneous linear equations to show that the exact values of $S$ and $D$ at this extreme point are $S = 300$ and $D = 420$.

16. Suppose that Par's management encounters each of the following situations:
a.  The accounting department revises its estimate of the profit contribution for the deluxe bag to $18 per bag.
b.  A new low-cost material is available for the standard bag, and the profit contribution per standard bag can be increased to $20 per bag. (Assume the profit contribution of the deluxe bag is the original $9 value.)
c.  New sewing equipment is available that would increase the sewing operation capacity to 750 hours. (Assume $10S + 9D$ is the appropriate objective function.)
    If each of these conditions is encountered separately, what are the optimal solution and the total profit contribution for each situation?

17. Refer to the feasible region for the Par, Inc., problem in Figure 2.13.
a.  Develop an objective function that will make extreme point ⑤ the optimal extreme point.
b.  What is the optimal solution using the objective function you selected in part (a)?
c.  What are the values of the slack variables associated with this solution?

**SELF TEST**

18. Write the following linear program in standard form:

$$\text{Max} \quad 5x_1 + 2x_2 + 8x_3$$

s.t.

$$1x_1 - 2x_2 + \tfrac{1}{2}x_3 \le 420$$
$$2x_1 + 3x_2 - 1x_3 \le 610$$
$$6x_1 - 1x_2 + 3x_3 \le 125$$
$$x_1, x_2, x_3 \ge 0$$

19. For the linear program

$$\text{Max} \quad 4x_1 + 1x_2$$

s.t.

$$10x_1 + 2x_2 \le 30$$
$$3x_1 + 2x_2 \le 12$$
$$2x_1 + 2x_2 \le 10$$
$$x_1, x_2 \ge 0$$

    a. Write this problem in standard form.
    b. Solve the problem using the graphical solution procedure.
    c. What are the values of the three slack variables at the optimal solution?

20. Given the linear program

$$\text{Max} \quad 3x_1 + 4x_2$$

s.t.

$$-1x_1 + 2x_2 \le 8$$
$$1x_1 + 2x_2 \le 12$$
$$2x_1 + 1x_2 \le 16$$
$$x_1, x_2 \ge 0$$

    a. Write the problem in standard form.
    b. Solve the problem using the graphical solution procedure.
    c. What are the values of the three slack variables at the optimal solution?

21. RMC, Inc., is a small firm that produces a variety of chemical products. In a particular production process, three raw materials are blended (mixed together) to produce two products: a fuel additive and a solvent base. Each ton of fuel additive is a mixture of $\tfrac{2}{5}$ ton of material 1 and $\tfrac{3}{5}$ of material 3. A ton of solvent base is a mixture of $\tfrac{1}{2}$ ton of material 1, $\tfrac{1}{5}$ ton of material 2, and $\tfrac{3}{10}$ ton of material 3. After deducting relevant costs, the profit contribution is $40 for every ton of fuel additive produced and $30 for every ton of solvent base produced.

    RMC's production is constrained by a limited availability of the three raw materials. For the current production period, RMC has available the following quantities of each raw material:

| Raw Material | Amount Available for Production |
|---|---|
| Material 1 | 20 tons |
| Material 2 | 5 tons |
| Material 3 | 21 tons |

Assuming that RMC is interested in maximizing the total profit contribution, answer the following:

    a. What is the linear programming model for this problem?
    b. Find the optimal solution using the graphical solution procedure. How many tons of each product should be produced, and what is the projected total profit contribution?
    c. Is there any unused material? If so, how much?
    d. Are there any redundant constraints? If so, which ones?

22. Kelson Sporting Equipment, Inc., makes two different types of baseball gloves: a regular model and a catcher's model. The firm has 900 hours of production time available in its cutting and sewing department, 300 hours available in its finishing department, and 100 hours available in its packaging and shipping department. The production time requirements and the profit contribution per glove are given in the following table.

SELF TEST

| Model | Production Time (hours) | | | Profit/Glove |
| | Cutting and Sewing | Finishing | Packaging and Shipping | |
| --- | --- | --- | --- | --- |
| Regular model | 1 | $\frac{1}{2}$ | $\frac{1}{8}$ | $5 |
| Catcher's model | $\frac{3}{2}$ | $\frac{1}{3}$ | $\frac{1}{4}$ | $8 |

Assuming that the company is interested in maximizing the total profit contribution, answer the following:

a. What is the linear programming model for this problem?

b. Find the optimal solution using the graphical solution procedure. How many gloves of each model should Kelson manufacture?

c. What is the total profit contribution Kelson can earn with the above production quantities?

d. How many hours of production time will be scheduled in each department?

e. What is the slack time in each department?

23. George Johnson recently inherited a large sum of money; he wants to use a portion of this money to set up a trust fund for his two children. The trust fund has two investment options: (1) a bond fund and (2) a stock fund. The projected returns over the life of the investments are 6% for the bond fund and 10% for the stock fund. Whatever portion of the inheritance he finally decides to commit to the trust fund, he wants to invest at least 30% of that amount in the bond fund. In addition, he wants to select a mix that will enable him to obtain a total return of at least 7.5%.

a. Formulate a linear programming model that can be used to determine the percentage that should be allocated to each of the possible investment alternatives.

b. Solve the problem using the graphical solution procedure.

24. The Sea Wharf Restaurant would like to determine the best way to allocate a monthly advertising budget of $1000 between newspaper advertising and radio advertising. Management has decided that at least 25% of the budget must be spent on each type of media, and that the amount of money spent on local newspaper advertising must be at least twice the amount spent on radio advertising. A marketing consultant has developed an index that measures audience exposure per dollar of advertising on a scale from 0 to 100, with higher values implying greater audience exposure. If the value of the index for local newspaper advertising is 50 and the value of the index for spot radio advertising is 80, how should the restaurant allocate its advertising budget in order to maximize the value of total audience exposure?

a. Formulate a linear programming model that can be used to determine how the restaurant should allocate its advertising budget in order to maximize the value of total audience exposure.

b. Solve the problem using the graphical solution procedure.

25. Investment Advisors, Inc., is a brokerage firm that manages stock portfolios for a number of clients. A new client has requested that the firm handle an $80,000 investment portfolio. As an initial investment strategy, the client would like to restrict the portfolio to a mix of the following stocks:

| Stock | Price/Share | Estimated Annual Return/Share | Risk Index/Share |
| --- | --- | --- | --- |
| U.S. Oil | $25 | $3 | 0.50 |
| Hub Properties | $50 | $5 | 0.25 |

The risk index for the stock is a rating of the relative risk of the two investment alternatives. For the data given, U.S. Oil is judged to be the riskier investment. By constraining the total risk for the portfolio, the investment firm avoids placing excessive amounts of the portfolio in potentially high-return, but also high-risk, investments. For the current portfolio, an upper limit of 700 has been set for the total risk index of all investments. The firm has also set an upper limit of 1000 shares for the more risky U.S. Oil stock. How many shares of each stock should be purchased to maximize the total annual return?

26. Tom's, Inc., produces various Mexican food products and sells them to Western Foods, a chain of grocery stores located in Texas and New Mexico. Tom's Inc., makes two salsa products: Western Foods Salsa and Mexico City Salsa. Essentially, the two products have different blends of whole tomatoes, tomato sauce, and tomato paste. The Western Foods Salsa is a blend of 50% whole tomatoes, 30% tomato sauce, and 20% tomato paste. The Mexico City Salsa, which has a thicker and chunkier consistency, consists of 70% whole tomatoes, 10% tomato sauce, and 20% tomato paste. Each jar of salsa produced weighs 10 ounces. For the current production period Tom's, Inc., can purchase up to 280 pounds of whole tomatoes, 130 pounds of tomato sauce, and 100 pounds of tomato paste; the price per pound for these ingredients is $0.96, $0.64, and $0.56, respectively. The cost of the spices and the other ingredients is approximately $0.10 per jar. Tom's, Inc., buys empty glass jars for $0.02 each, and labeling and filling costs are estimated to be $0.03 for each jar of salsa produced. Tom's contract with Western Foods results in sales revenue of $1.64 for each jar of Western Foods Salsa and $1.93 for each jar of Mexico City Salsa.
    a. Develop a linear programming model that will enable Tom's to determine the mix of salsa products that will maximize the total profit contribution.
    b. Find the optimal solution.

27. The production editor for Rayburn Publishing Company has 1800 pages of manuscript that must be copyedited. Because of the short time frame involved, only two copyeditors are available: Erhan Mergen and Sue Smith. Erhan has 10 days available and Sue has 12 days available. Erhan can process 100 pages of manuscript per day and Sue can process 150 pages of manuscript per day. Rayburn Publishing has developed an index used to measure the overall quality of a copyeditor on a scale from 1 (worst) to 10 (best). Erhan's quality rating is 9 and Sue's quality rating is 6. In addition, Erhan charges $3 per page of copyedited manuscript and Sue charges $2 per page. If a budget of $4800 has been allocated for copyediting, how many pages should be assigned to each copyeditor in order to complete the project with the highest possible quality?

28. A financial advisor at Diehl Investments has identified two companies that are likely candidates for a takeover in the near future. Eastern Cable is a leading manufacturer of flexible cable systems used in the construction industry and ComSwitch is a new firm specializing in digital switching systems. Eastern Cable is currently trading for $40 per share and ComSwitch is currently trading for $25 per share. If the takeovers occur, the financial advisor estimates that the price of Eastern Cable will go to $55 per share and ComSwitch will go to $43 per share. At this point in time, the financial advisor has identified ComSwitch as the higher risk alternative. Assume that a client has indicated a willingness to invest a maximum of $50,000 in the two companies. The client wants to invest at least $15,000 in Eastern Cable and at least $10,000 in ComSwitch. Because of the higher risk associated with ComSwitch, the financial advisor has recommended that at most $25,000 should be invested in ComSwitch.
    a. Formulate a linear programming model that can be used to determine the number of shares of Eastern Cable and the number of shares of ComSwitch that will meet the investment constraints and maximize the total return for the investment.
    b. Graph the feasible region.
    c. Determine the coordinates of each extreme point.
    d. Find the optimal solution.

29.  Consider the following linear program:

$$\text{Min} \quad 3x_1 + 4x_2$$

s.t.

$$1x_1 + 3x_2 \geq 6$$
$$1x_1 + 1x_2 \geq 4$$
$$x_1, x_2 \geq 0$$

Identify the feasible region and find the optimal solution using the graphical solution procedure. What is the value of the objective function?

30.  Identify the three extreme-point solutions for the M&D Chemicals problem (see Section 2.5). Identify the value of the objective function and the values of the slack and surplus variables at each extreme point.

31.  Consider the following linear programming problem:

$$\text{Min} \quad x_1 + 2x_2$$

s.t.

$$x_1 + 4x_2 \leq 21$$
$$2x_1 + x_2 \geq 7$$
$$3x_1 + 1.5x_2 \leq 21$$
$$-2x_1 + 6x_2 \geq 0$$
$$x_1, x_2 \geq 0$$

a.  Find the optimal solution using the graphical solution procedure and the value of the objective function.

b.  Determine the amount of slack or surplus for each constraint.

c.  Suppose the objective function is changed to max $5x_1 + 2x_2$. Find the optimal solution and the value of the objective function.

32.  Consider the following linear program:

$$\text{Min} \quad 2x_1 + 2x_2$$

s.t.

$$1x_1 + 3x_2 \leq 12$$
$$3x_1 + 1x_2 \geq 13$$
$$1x_1 - 1x_2 = 3$$
$$x_1, x_2 \geq 0$$

a.  Show the feasible region.

b.  What are the extreme points of the feasible region?

c.  Find the optimal solution using the graphical solution procedure.

33.  For the linear program

$$\text{Min} \quad 6x_1 + 4x_2$$

s.t.

$$2x_1 + 1x_2 \geq 12$$
$$1x_1 + 1x_2 \geq 10$$
$$1x_2 \leq 4$$
$$x_1, x_2 \geq 0$$

   a.  Write the problem in standard form.
   b.  Solve the problem using the graphical solution procedure.
   c.  What are the values of the slack and surplus variables?

34.  As part of a quality improvement initiative, Consolidated Electronics employees complete a three-day training program on teaming and a two-day training program on problem solving. The manager of quality improvement has requested that at least 8 training programs on teaming and at least 10 training programs on problem solving be offered during the next six months. In addition, senior-level management has specified that at least 25 training programs must be offered during this period. Consolidated Electronics uses a consultant to teach the training programs. During the next quarter, the consultant has 84 days of training time available. Each training program on teaming costs $10,000 and each training program on problem solving costs $8,000.
   a.  Formulate a linear programming model that can be used to determine the number of training programs on teaming and the number of training programs on problem solving that should be offered in order to minimize total cost.
   b.  Graph the feasible region.
   c.  Determine the coordinates of each extreme point.
   d.  Solve for the minimum-cost solution.

35.  The New England Cheese Company produces two cheese spreads by blending mild cheddar cheese with extra sharp cheddar cheese. The cheese spreads are packaged in 12-ounce containers, which are then sold to distributors throughout the Northeast. The Regular blend contains 80% mild cheddar and 20% extra sharp, and the Zesty blend contains 60% mild cheddar and 40% extra sharp. This year, a local dairy cooperative has offered to provide up to 8100 pounds of mild cheddar cheese for $1.20 per pound and up to 3000 pounds of extra sharp cheddar cheese for $1.40 per pound. The cost to blend and package the cheese spreads, excluding the cost of the cheese, is $0.20 per container. If each container of Regular is sold for $1.95 and each container of Zesty is sold for $2.20, how many containers of Regular and Zesty should New England Cheese produce?

36.  Healthtech Food Products is considering developing a new low-fat snack food. It is to be a blend of two types of cereals, each of which has different fiber, fat, and protein characteristics. The following table shows these nutrition characteristics for one ounce of each type of cereal.

| Cereal | Dietary Fiber (grams) | Fat (grams) | Protein (grams) |
|--------|-----------------------|-------------|-----------------|
| A      | 2                     | 2           | 4               |
| B      | 1.5                   | 3           | 3               |

Note that each ounce of cereal A provides 2 grams of dietary fiber and that each ounce of cereal B provides 1.5 grams of dietary fiber. Thus, if Healthtech were to develop the new product using a mix consisting of 50% of cereal A and 50% cereal B, 1 ounce of the snack food would contain 1.75 grams of dietary fiber. Healthtech's nutrition requirements call for each ounce of the new food to have at least 1.7 grams of dietary fiber, no more than 2.8 grams of fat, and no more than 3.6 grams of protein. The cost of cereal A is $0.02 per ounce and the cost of cereal B is $0.025 per ounce. Healthtech wants to determine how much of each cereal is needed to produce 1 ounce of the new food product at the lowest possible cost.
   a.  Formulate a linear programming model for this situation.
   b.  Solve the problem using the graphical solution procedure.
   c.  What are the values of the slack and surplus variables?
   d.  If Healthtech markets the new snack food in an 8-ounce package, what is the cost per package?

37. Innis Investments manages funds for a number of companies and wealthy clients. The investment strategy is tailored to each client's needs. For a new client, Innis has been authorized to invest up to $1.2 million in two investment funds: a stock fund and a money market fund. Each unit of the stock fund costs $50 and provides an annual rate of return of 10%; each unit of the money market fund costs $100 and provides an annual rate of return of 4%.

    The client wants to minimize risk subject to the requirement that the annual income from the investment be at least $60,000. According to Innis's risk measurement system, each unit invested in the stock fund has a risk index of 8, and each unit invested in the money market fund has a risk index of 3; the higher risk index associated with the stock fund simply indicates that it is the riskier investment. Innis's client has also specified that at least $300,000 be invested in the money market fund.

    a. Determine how many units of each fund Innis should purchase for the client to minimize the total risk index for the portfolio.
    b. How much annual income will this investment strategy generate?
    c. Suppose the client desires to maximize annual return. How should the funds be invested?

38. Photo Chemicals produces two types of photographic developing fluids. Both products cost Photo Chemicals $1 per gallon to produce. Based on an analysis of current inventory levels and outstanding orders for the next month, Photo Chemicals' management has specified that at least 30 gallons of product 1 and at least 20 gallons of product 2 must be produced during the next 2 weeks. Management has also stated that an existing inventory of highly perishable raw material required in the production of both fluids must be used within the next 2 weeks. The current inventory of the perishable raw material is 80 pounds. While more of this raw material can be ordered if necessary, any of the current inventory that is not used within the next 2 weeks will spoil—hence, the management requirement that at least 80 pounds be used in the next 2 weeks. Furthermore, it is known that product 1 requires 1 pound of this perishable raw material per gallon and product 2 requires 2 pounds of the raw material per gallon. Since Photo Chemicals' objective is to keep its production costs at the minimum possible level, the firm's management is looking for a minimum-cost production plan that uses all the 80 pounds of perishable raw material and provides at least 30 gallons of product 1 and at least 20 gallons of product 2. What is the minimum-cost solution?

39. Bryant's Pizza, Inc., is a producer of frozen pizza products. The company makes a profit of $1.00 for each regular pizza it produces and $1.50 for each deluxe pizza produced. Each pizza includes a combination of dough mix and topping mix. The firm currently has 150 pounds of dough mix and 50 pounds of topping mix. Each regular pizza uses 1 pound of dough mix and 4 ounces of topping mix. Each deluxe pizza uses 1 pound of dough mix and 8 ounces of topping mix. Based on past demand, Bryant can sell at least 50 regular pizzas and at least 25 deluxe pizzas. How many regular and deluxe pizzas should the company make to maximize profits?

    a. What is the linear programming model for this problem in standard form?
    b. Find the optimal solution.
    c. What are the values and interpretations of all slack and surplus variables?
    d. Which constraints are binding?

40. Does the following linear program involve infeasibility, unbounded, and/or alternative optimal solutions? Explain.

$$\text{Max} \quad 4x_1 + 8x_2$$
$$\text{s.t.}$$
$$2x_1 + 2x_2 \leq 10$$
$$-1x_1 + 1x_2 \geq 8$$
$$x_1, x_2 \geq 0$$

**41.** Does the following linear program involve infeasibility, unbounded, and/or alternative optimal solutions? Explain.

$$\text{Max} \quad 1x_1 + 1x_2$$

s.t.

$$8x_1 + 6x_2 \geq 24$$
$$4x_1 + 6x_2 \geq -12$$
$$2x_2 \geq 4$$
$$x_1, x_2 \geq 0$$

**42.** Consider the following linear program:

$$\text{Max} \quad 1x_1 + 1x_2$$

s.t.

$$5x_1 + 3x_2 \leq 15$$
$$3x_1 + 5x_2 \leq 15$$
$$x_1, x_2 \geq 0$$

a. What is the optimal solution for this problem?
b. Suppose that the objective function is changed to $1x_1 + 2x_2$. Find the new optimal solution.
c. By adjusting the coefficient of $x_2$ in the objective function, develop a new objective function that will make the solutions found in parts (a) and (b) alternative optimal solutions.

**43.** Consider the following linear program:

$$\text{Max} \quad 1x_1 - 2x_2$$

s.t.

$$-4x_1 + 3x_2 \leq 3$$
$$1x_1 - 1x_2 \leq 3$$
$$x_1, x_2 \geq 0$$

a. Graph the feasible region for the problem.
b. Is the feasible region unbounded? Explain.
c. Find the optimal solution.
d. Does an unbounded feasible region imply that the optimal solution to the linear program will be unbounded?

**44.** The manager of a small independent grocery store is trying to determine the best use of her shelf space for soft drinks. The store carries national and generic brands and currently has 200 square feet of shelf space available. The manager wants to allocate at least 60% of the space to the national brands and, regardless of the profitability, allocate at least 10% of the space to the generic brands. How many square feet of space should the manager allocate to the national brands and the generic brands if
a. The national brands are more profitable than the generic brands?
b. Both brands are equally profitable?
c. The generic brand is more profitable than the national brand?

**45.** Discuss what happens to the M&D Chemicals problem (see Section 2.5) if the cost per gallon for product A is increased to $3.00 per gallon. What would you recommend? Explain.

**46.** For the M&D Chemicals problem in Section 2.5, discuss the effect of management's requiring total production of 500 gallons for the two products. List two or three actions M&D should consider to correct the situation you encounter.

47. Reconsider the RMC situation in Problem 21.
    a. Identify all the extreme points of the feasible region.
    b. Suppose RMC discovers a way to increase the profit of its solvent base to $60 per ton. Does this profit increase change the optimal solution? If so, how?
    c. Suppose the profit for the solvent base is $50 per ton. What is the optimal solution now? Comment on any special characteristics that may exist with this profit for the solvent base.

48. Reconsider the RMC situation in Problem 21. Suppose that management adds the requirements that at least 30 tons of fuel additive and at least 15 tons of solvent base must be produced.
    a. Graph the constraints for this revised RMC problem. What happens to the feasible region? Explain.
    b. If there are no feasible solutions, explain what is needed to produce 30 tons of fuel additive and 15 tons of solvent base.

49. Reconsider the Kelson Sporting Equipment, Inc., production example in Problem 22. Discuss the concepts of infeasibility, unbounded solutions, and alternative optimal solutions as they occur in each of the following situations:
    a. Management has requested that the production of baseball gloves (regular model plus catcher's model) be such that the total number of gloves produced is at least 750.
    b. The original problem has to be solved again because the profit contribution for the regular model is adjusted downward to $4 per glove.
    c. What would have to happen for this problem to be unbounded?

50. Expedition Outfitters manufactures a variety of specialty clothing for hiking, skiing, and mountain climbing. They have decided to begin production on two new parkas designed for use in extremely cold weather; the names selected for the two models are the Mount Everest Parka and the Rocky Mountain Parka. Their manufacturing plant has 120 hours of cutting time and 120 hours of sewing time available for producing these two parkas. Each Mount Everest Parka requires 30 minutes of cutting time and 45 minutes of sewing time, and each Rocky Mountain Parka requires 20 minutes of cutting time and 15 minutes of sewing time. The labor and material cost is $150 for each Mount Everest Parka and $50 for each Rocky Mountain Parka, and the retail prices through the firm's mail order catalog are $250 for the Mount Everest Parka and $200 for the Rocky Mountain Parka. Because management believes that the Mount Everest Parka is a unique coat that will enhance the image of the firm, they have specified that at least 20% of the total production must consist of this model. Assuming that Expedition Outfitters can sell as many coats of each type as they can produce, how many units of each model should they manufacture to maximize the total profit contribution?

51. English Motors, Ltd. (EML), has developed a new all-wheel-drive sports utility vehicle. As part of the marketing campaign, EML has developed a video tape sales presentation to send to both owners of current EML four-wheel-drive vehicles as well as to owners of four-wheel-drive sports utility vehicles offered by competitors; EML refers to these two target markets as the current customer market and the new customer market. Individuals who receive the new promotion video will also receive a coupon for a test drive of the new EML model for one weekend. A key factor in the success of the new promotion is the response rate, the percentage of individuals that receives the new promotion and test drives the new model. EML estimates that the response rate for the current customer market is 25% and the response rate for the new customer market is 20%. For the customers who test drive the new model the sales rate is the percentage of individuals that makes a purchase. Marketing research studies indicate that the sales rate is 12% for the current customer market and 20% for the new customer market. The cost for each promotion, excluding the test drive costs, are $4 for each promotion sent to the current customer market and $6 for each promotion sent to the new customer market. Management has also specified that a minimum of 30,000 current customers should test drive the new model and a minimum of 10,000 new customers should test drive the new model. In addition, the number of current customers that test drives the new vehicle must be at least twice the number of new cus-

tomers that test drives the new vehicle. If the marketing budget, excluding test drive costs, is $1,200,000, how many promotions should be sent to each group of customers in order to maximize total sales?

52. Creative Sports Design (CSD) manufactures a standard-size racket and an oversize racket. The firm's rackets are extremely light due to the use of a magnesium-graphite alloy that was invented by the firm's founder. Each standard-size racket uses 0.125 kilograms of the alloy and each over-size racket uses 0.4 kilograms; over the next two-week production period only 80 kilograms of the alloy are available. Each standard-size racket uses 10 minutes of manufacturing time and each oversize racket uses 12 minutes. The profit contributions are $10 for each standard-size racket and $15 for each oversize racket, and 40 hours of manufacturing time are available each week. Management has specified that at least 20% of the total production must be the standard-size racket. How many rackets of each type should CSD manufacture over the next two weeks to maximize the total profit contribution? Assume that because of the unique nature of their products, CSD can sell as many rackets as they can produce.

53. Management of High Tech Services (HTS) would like to develop a model that will help allocate their technicians' time between service calls to regular contract customers and new customers. A maximum of 80 hours of technician time is available over the two-week planning period. To satisfy cash flow requirements, at least $800 in revenue (per technician) must be generated during the two-week period. Technician time for regular customers generates $25 per hour. However, technician time for new customers only generates an average of $8 per hour because in many cases a new customer contact does not provide billable services. To ensure that new customer contacts are being maintained, the technician time spent on new customer contacts must be at least 60% of the time spent on regular customer contacts. Given these revenue and policy requirements, HTS would like to determine how to allocate technician time between regular customers and new customers so that the total number of customers contacted during the two-week period will be maximized. Technicians require an average of 50 minutes for each regular customer contact and 1 hour for each new customer contact.
    a. Develop a linear programming model that will enable HTS to allocate technician time between regular customers and new customers.
    b. Find the optimal solution.

54. Jackson Hole Manufacturing is a small manufacturer of plastic products used in the automotive and computer industries. One of its major contracts is with a large computer company and involves the production of plastic printer cases for the computer company's portable printers. The printer cases are produced on two injection molding machines. The M-100 machine has a production capacity of 25 printer cases per hour, and the M-200 machine has a production capacity of 40 cases per hour. Both machines use the same chemical material to produce the printer cases; the M-100 uses 40 pounds of the raw material per hour and the M-200 uses 50 pounds per hour. The computer company has asked Jackson Hole to produce as many of the cases during the upcoming week as possible and has said that it will pay $18 for each case Jackson Hole can deliver. However, next week is a regularly scheduled vacation period for most of Jackson Hole's production employees; during this time, annual maintenance is performed for all equipment in the plant. Because of the downtime for maintenance, the M-100 will be available for no more than 15 hours, and the M-200 will be available for no more than 10 hours. However, because of the high setup cost involved with both machines, management has a requirement that, if production is scheduled on either machine, the machine must be operated for at least 5 hours. The supplier of the chemical material used in the production process has informed Jackson Hole that a maximum of 1000 pounds of the chemical material will be available for next week's production; the cost for this raw material is $6 per pound. In addition to the raw material cost, Jackson Hole estimates that the hourly cost of operating the M-100 and the M-200 are $50 and $75, respectively.
    a. Formulate a linear programming model that can be used to maximize the contribution to profit.
    b. Find the optimal solution.

........................................................................................................................./  /...........

## Case Problem     ADVERTISING STRATEGY

Midtown Motors, Inc., has hired a marketing services firm to develop an advertising strategy for promoting Midtown's used-car sales. The marketing firm has recommended that Midtown use spot announcements on both television and radio as the advertising media for the proposed promotional campaign. Advertising strategy guidelines are expressed as follows:

1. Use at least 30 announcements for combined television and radio coverage.
2. Do not use more than 25 radio announcements.
3. The number of radio announcements cannot be less than the number of television announcements.

The television station has quoted a cost of $1200 per spot announcement, and the radio station has quoted a cost of $300 per spot announcement. Midtown's advertising budget has been set at $25,500. The marketing services firm has rated the various advertising media in terms of audience coverage and recall power of the advertisement. For Midtown's media alternatives, the television announcement is rated at 600, and the radio announcement is rated at 200. Midtown's president would like to know how many television and how many radio spot announcements should be used to maximize the overall rating of the advertising campaign.

Midtown's president believes the television station will consider running the Midtown spot announcement on its highly rated evening news program (at the same cost) if Midtown will consider using additional television announcements.

### Managerial Report

Perform an analysis of advertising strategy for Midtown Motors, and prepare a report to Midtown's president presenting your findings and recommendations. Include (but do not limit your discussion to) a consideration of the following:

1. The recommended number of television and radio spot announcements
2. The relative merits of each advertising medium
3. The news program rating that would be necessary before it would make sense to increase the number of television spots
4. The number of television spots that should be purchased if the news program is rated highly enough to make increasing the number of television spots advisable
5. The restrictions placed on the advertising strategy that Midtown might want to consider relaxing or altering
6. The best use of any possible increase in the advertising budget
7. Any other information that may help Midtown's president make the advertising strategy decision

Include a copy of your linear programming model and graphical solution in the appendix to your report.

........................................................................................................................./  /...........

## Case Problem     PRODUCTION STRATEGY

Better Fitness, Inc. (BFI), manufactures exercise equipment at its plant in Freeport, Long Island. It recently designed two universal weight machines for the home exercise market. Both machines use BFI-patented technology that provides the user with an extremely wide range of motion capability for each type of exercise performed. Until now, such capabilities have been available only on expensive weight machines used primarily by physical therapists.

At a recent trade show, demonstrations of the machines resulted in significant dealer interest. In fact, the number of orders that BFI received at the trade show far exceeded its manufacturing capabilities for the current production period. As a result, management decided to begin production of the two machines. The two machines, which BFI has named the BodyPlus 100 and the BodyPlus 200, require different amounts of resources to produce.

The BodyPlus 100 consists of a frame unit, a press station, and a pec-dec station. Each frame produced uses 4 hours of machining and welding time and 2 hours of painting and finishing time. Each press station requires 2 hours of machining and welding time and 1 hour of painting and finishing time, and each pec-dec station uses 2 hours of machining and welding time and 2 hours of painting and finishing time. In addition, 2 hours are spent assembling, testing, and packaging each BodyPlus 100. The raw material costs are $450 for each frame, $300 for each press station, and $250 for each pec-dec station; packaging costs are estimated to be $50 per unit.

The BodyPlus 200 consists of a frame unit, a press station, a pec-dec station, and a leg-press station. Each frame produced uses 5 hours of machining and welding time and 4 hours of painting and finishing time. Each press station requires 3 hours machining and welding time and 2 hours of painting and finishing time, each pec-dec station uses 2 hours of machining and welding time and 2 hours of painting and finishing time, and each leg-press station requires 2 hours of machining and welding time and 2 hours of painting and finishing time. In addition, 2 hours are spent assembling, testing, and packaging each BodyPlus 200. The raw material costs are $650 for each frame, $400 for each press station, $250 for each pec-dec station, and $200 for each leg-press station; packaging costs are estimated to be $75 per unit.

For the next production period, management estimates that 600 hours of machining and welding time, 450 hours of painting and finishing time, and 140 hours of assembly, testing, and packaging time will be available. Current labor costs are $20 per hour for machining and welding time, $15 per hour for painting and finishing time, and $12 per hour for assembly, testing, and packaging time. The market in which the two machines must compete suggests a retail price of $2400 for the BodyPlus 100 and $3500 for the BodyPlus 200, although some flexibility may be available to BFI because of the unique capabilities of the new machines. Authorized BFI dealers can purchase machines for 70% of the suggested retail price.

BFI's president believes that the unique capabilities of the BodyPlus 200 can help position BFI as one of the leaders in high-end exercise equipment. Consequently, he has stated that the number of units of the BodyPlus 200 produced must be at least 25% of the total production.

## Managerial Report

Analyze the production problem at Better Fitness, Inc., and prepare a report for BFI's president presenting your findings and recommendations. Include (but do not limit your discussion to) a consideration of the following items:

1. The recommended number of BodyPlus 100 and BodyPlus 200 machines to produce
2. The effect on profits of the requirement that the number of units of the BodyPlus 200 produced must be at least 25% of the total production
3. Where efforts should be expended in order to increase profits

Include a copy of your linear programming model and graphical solution in an appendix to your report.

............................................................................................../   /............

## Case Problem     HART VENTURE CAPITAL

Hart Venture Capital (HVC) specializes in providing venture capital for software development and Internet applications. Currently HVC has two investment opportunities: (1) Security Systems, a firm that needs additional capital to develop an Internet security software package; (2) Market Analysis, a market research company that needs additional capital to develop a software package for conducting customer satisfaction surveys. In exchange for Security Systems stock, the firm has asked HVC to provide $600,000 in year 1, $600,000 in year 2, and $250,000 in year 3 over the coming three-year period. In exchange for their stock, Market Analysis has asked HVC to provide $500,000 in year 1, $350,000 in year 2, and $400,000 in year 3 over the same three-year period. HVC believes that both investment opportunities are worth pursuing. However, because of other investments, they are willing to commit at most $800,000 for both projects in the first year, at most $700,000 in the second year, and $500,000 in the third year.

HVC's financial analysis team has reviewed both projects and has recommended that the company's objective should be to maximize the net present value of the total investment in Security Systems and Market Analysis. The net present value takes into account the estimated value of the stock at the end of the three-year period as well as the capital outflows that are necessary during each of the three years. Using an 8% rate of return, HVC's financial analysis team estimates that 100% funding of the Security Systems project has a net present value of $1,800,000 and 100% funding of the Market Analysis project has a net present value of $1,600,000.

HVC has the option to fund any percentage of the Security Systems and Market Analysis projects. For example, if HVC decides to fund 40% of the Security Systems project, investments of 0.40($600,000) = $240,000 would be required in year 1, 0.40($600,000) = $240,000 would be required in year 2, and 0.40($250,000) = $100,000 would be required in year 3. In this case, the net present value of the Security Systems project would be 0.40($1,800,000) = $720,000. The investment amounts and the net present value for partial funding of the Market Analysis project would be computed in the same manner.

### Managerial Report

Perform an analysis of HVC's investment problem and prepare a report that presents your findings and recommendations. Be sure to include information on the following:

1. The recommended percentage of each project that HVC should fund and the net present value of the total investment
2. A capital allocation plan for Security Systems and Market Analysis for the coming three-year period and the total HVC investment each year
3. The effect, if any, on the recommended percentage of each project that HVC should fund if HVC is willing to commit an additional $100,000 during the first year
4. A capital allocation plan if an additional $100,000 is made available
5. Your recommendation as to whether HVC should commit the additional $100,000 in the first year

Provide model details and relevant computer output in a report appendix.

## Appendix 2.1    SOLVING LINEAR PROGRAMS WITH THE MANAGEMENT SCIENTIST

In this appendix we describe how The Management Scientist software package can be used to solve the Par, Inc., linear programming problem. After starting The Management Scientist, execute the following steps.

Step 1    Select the **Linear Programming** module
Step 2    Choose **New** from the **File Menu**
Step 3    When the **Problem Features** dialog box appears:
        Enter 2 for **Number of Decision Variables**
        Enter 4 for **Number of Constraints**
        Select Maximize for **Optimization Type**
        Select **OK**
Step 4    When the data input worksheet appears (see Figure 2.22):
        Change the variable name X1 to S and the variable name X2 to D.
        Enter the objective function coefficients
        For each constraint:
            Enter the variable coefficients
            Enter the relation type ($<$, $=$, $>$)
            Enter the right-hand-side value
Step 5    Choose **Solve** from the **Solution menu**

The user entries in the data input worksheet are shown in color in Figure 2.22. The output from the Management Scientist is shown in Figure 2.14. In general, when entering the problem data, zero coefficients do not have to be entered. In addition, changes to the problem can be easily made by selecting the appropriate option from the Edit menu, and printed output can be obtained by selecting the Print Solution option from the Solution menu.

**Figure 2.22    DATA INPUT FOR THE PAR, INC., PROBLEM USING THE MANAGEMENT SCIENTIST**

| Optimization Type: Maximize | | | | |
|---|---|---|---|---|
| Variable Names: [Change if Desired] | S | D | | |
| Objective Function Coefficients | 10 | 9 | | |

| | Coefficients | | | |
|---|---|---|---|---|
| Subject To: | S | D | Relation (<, =, >) | Right Hand Side |
| Constraint 1 | 0.7 | 1 | < | 630 |
| Constraint 2 | 0.5 | 0.83333 | < | 600 |
| Constraint 3 | 1 | 0.66667 | < | 708 |
| Constraint 4 | 0.1 | 0.25 | < | 135 |

## Appendix 2.2    SPREADSHEET SOLUTION OF LINEAR PROGRAMS

In this appendix, we show how spreadsheets can be used to solve linear programs by using Excel to solve the Par, Inc., linear programming problem. In the spreadsheet layout for a linear program we enter the problem data in the top part of the spreadsheet and develop the linear programming model in the bottom part. There are four components or key elements in the spreadsheet model of a linear program: the decision variables, the objective function, the left-hand sides of the constraints, and the right-hand sides of the constraints. Thus, to formulate a spreadsheet model of a linear program we must reserve a set of cells for the decision variables, a cell for the objective function, a set of cells for the left-hand-side functions, and a set of cells for the right-hand sides of the constraints. To highlight these key elements each of these cells are screened. In addition to screening, the decision variable cells are also enclosed in a boldface line. Descriptive labels are used to make the spreadsheet easier for a user to read.

## Spreadsheet Formulation

When we formulate a spreadsheet model of a linear program, we perform the following steps:

1. Enter the problem data into the top part of the spreadsheet.
2. Specify cell locations for all decision variables.
3. Select a cell and enter a formula for computing the value of the objective function.
4. Select a cell and enter a formula for computing the left-hand side of each constraint.
5. Select a cell and enter a formula for computing the value of the right-hand side of each constraint.

The formula spreadsheet shown in Figure 2.23 was developed using the preceding five-step procedure. Note that the spreadsheet consists of two sections: a data section and a model section. Note that the four components of the model are screened and that the cells reserved for the decision variables are enclosed in a boldface line. Figure 2.23 is called a formula spreadsheet because it displays the formulas we have entered and not the values that are computed from those formulas.

In a moment we will see how Excel's solver is used to find the optimal solution to the Par problem. But, first let's review the steps taken to develop this spreadsheet formulation.

1. **Enter the problem data.** The production requirements for each product are shown in cells B5:C8, the number of hours available in each department is shown in cells D5:D8, and the profit contribution for each product is shown in cells B9:C9.
2. **Specify cell locations for all decision variables.** Cell B16 is reserved for the number of standard bags produced, and cell C16 is reserved for the number of deluxe bags produced. Note that no values are currently present in these cells; we will see in a moment how to use Solver to compute the optimal values for these cells.
3. **Select a cell and enter a formula for computing the value of the objective function.** Cell B18 contains the formula for computing the value of the objective function. It multiplies the objective function coefficients by the values of the decision variables and sums the results.
4. **Select a cell and enter a formula for computing the left-hand side of each constraint.** Cells B21:B24 contain formulas for computing the amount of hours used in each department—the left-hand sides of the constraints. For example, the formula in cell B21 multiplies the number of hours used in the cutting and dyeing department by the values of the decision variables.
5. **Select a cell and enter a formula for computing the value of the right-hand side of each constraint.** Cells D21:D24 contain the formulas for computing the right-hand-side values. The data for the right-hand sides is in cells D5:D8 and no further computation is necessary to compute their values as used in the Par linear pro-

gramming model. Thus, the formulas in cells D21:D24 simply reference the appropriate cells in the data section of the spreadsheet.

Note that we have also added some descriptive labels to make the model easier to read and understand. We have entered the text "Maximize Total Profit" into cell A18 to indicate that the objective function for the Par problem is to maximize total profit. We have entered "<=" into cells C21:C24 to show the relationship that exists between the left-hand-side cells and the right-hand-side cells. Although these descriptive labels are not necessary to use Excel Solver to find a solution, the labels make it easier for the user of the spreadsheet to understand the underlying structure of the problem.

After the spreadsheet formulation is complete, Excel Solver must be accessed to obtain the optimal solution. We now describe how Solver is used.

## Spreadsheet Solution

Excel Solver is a general optimization and resource allocation tool. The following steps describe how to use it to solve the linear programming model of the Par problem as presented in Figure 2.23.

### Figure 2.23    FORMULA SPREADSHEET FOR THE PAR, INC., PROBLEM

| | A | B | C | D |
|---|---|---|---|---|
| 1 | Par, Inc. | | | |
| 2 | | | | |
| 3 | | **Production Time** | | |
| 4 | **Operation** | **Standard** | **Deluxe** | **Time Available** |
| 5 | Cutting and Dyeing | 0.7 | 1 | 630 |
| 6 | Sewing | 0.5 | 0.83333 | 600 |
| 7 | Finishing | 1 | 0.66667 | 708 |
| 8 | Inspection and Packaging | 0.1 | 0.25 | 135 |
| 9 | **Profit Per Bag** | 10 | 9 | |
| 10 | | | | |
| 11 | | | | |
| 12 | **Model** | | | |
| 13 | | | | |
| 14 | | **Decision Variables** | | |
| 15 | | **Standard** | **Deluxe** | |
| 16 | **Bags Produced** | | | |
| 17 | | | | |
| 18 | **Maximize Total Profit** | =SUMPRODUCT(B9:C9,B16:C16) | | |
| 19 | | | | |
| 20 | **Constraints** | **Hours Used (LHS)** | | **Hours Available (RHS)** |
| 21 | Cutting and Dyeing | =SUMPRODUCT(B5:C5,$B$16:$C$16) | <= | =D5 |
| 22 | Sewing | =SUMPRODUCT(B6:C6,$B$16:$C$16) | <= | =D6 |
| 23 | Finishing | =SUMPRODUCT(B7:C7,$B$16:$C$16) | <= | =D7 |
| 24 | Inspection and Packaging | =SUMPRODUCT(B8:C8,$B$16:$C$16) | <= | =D8 |

Step 1 Select the **Tools** pull-down menu
Step 2 Select the **Solver** option
Step 3 When the **Solver Parameters** dialog box appears
    Enter B18 into the **Set Target Cell** box
    Select the **Max** option
    Enter B16:C16 into the **By Changing Cells** box
    Choose **Add**
Step 4 When the **Add Constraint** dialog box appears
    Enter B21:B24 in the **Cell Reference** box
    Select <=
    Enter D21:D24 into the **Constraint** box
    Choose **OK**
Step 5 When the **Solver Parameters** dialog box reappears
    Choose **Options**
Step 6 When the **Solver Options** dialog box appears
    Select **Assume Linear Model**
    Select **Assume Non-Negative**
    Choose **OK**
Step 7 When the **Solver Parameters** dialog box reappears
    Choose **Solve**
Step 8 When the **Solver Results** dialog box appears
    Select **Keep Solver Solution**
    Choose **OK** to produce the optimal solution output

Figure 2.24 shows the completed **Solver Parameters** dialog box, and Figure 2.25 shows the optimal solution in the spreadsheet. Note that after rounding, the optimal solution of 540 standard bags and 252 deluxe bags is the same as we obtained using the graphical solution procedure. In addition to the output information shown in Figure 2.25, Solver

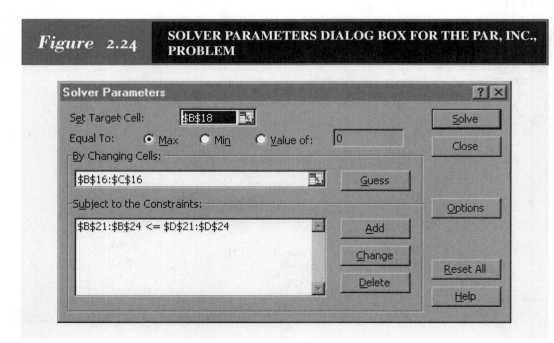

**Figure 2.24** SOLVER PARAMETERS DIALOG BOX FOR THE PAR, INC., PROBLEM

| *Figure* 2.25 | SPREADSHEET SOLUTION FOR THE PAR, INC., PROBLEM |
|---|---|

|  | A | B | C | D |
|---|---|---|---|---|
| 1 | Par, Inc. | | | |
| 2 | | | | |
| 3 | | Production Time | | |
| 4 | Operation | Standard | Deluxe | Time Available |
| 5 | Cutting and Dyeing | 0.7 | 1 | 630 |
| 6 | Sewing | 0.5 | 0.83333 | 600 |
| 7 | Finishing | 1 | 0.66667 | 708 |
| 8 | Inspection and Packaging | 0.1 | 0.25 | 135 |
| 9 | **Profit Per Bag** | 10 | 9 | |
| 10 | | | | |
| 11 | | | | |
| 12 | **Model** | | | |
| 13 | | | | |
| 14 | | Decision Variables | | |
| 15 | | Standard | Deluxe | |
| 16 | **Bags Produced** | 539.998425 | 252.0011025 | |
| 17 | | | | |
| 18 | **Maximize Total Profit** | 7668 | | |
| 19 | | | | |
| 20 | **Constraints** | **Hours Used (LHS)** | | **Hours Available (RHS)** |
| 21 | Cutting and Dyeing | 630 | <= | 630 |
| 22 | Sewing | 479.9992912 | <= | 600 |
| 23 | Finishing | 708 | <= | 708 |
| 24 | Inspection and Packaging | 117.0001181 | <= | 135 |

has an option to provide sensitivity analysis information. We discuss sensitivity analysis in Chapter 3.

In Step 6 we selected the **Assume Non-Negative** option in the **Solver Options** dialog box. We did this to avoid having to enter nonnegativity constraints for the decision variables. In general, whenever we want to solve a linear programming model in which the decision variables are all restricted to be nonnegative, we will select this option. In addition, in Step 4 we entered all four less-than-or-equal-to constraints simultaneously by entering B21:B24 into the **Cell Reference** box, selecting <=, and entering D21:D24 into the **Constraint** box. Alternatively, we could have entered the four constraints in a one-at-a-time fashion.

# 3

# LINEAR PROGRAMMING: SENSITIVITY

# ANALYSIS AND INTERPRETATION OF SOLUTION

## CONTENTS

**Sensitivity analysis** is the study of how the changes in the coefficients of a linear program affect the optimal solution. Using sensitivity analysis, we can answer questions such as the following:

1. How will a change *in a coefficient of the objective function* affect the optimal solution?
2. How will a change in the *right-hand-side value for a constraint* affect the optimal solution?

Because sensitivity analysis is concerned with how these changes affect the optimal solution, the analysis does not begin until the optimal solution to the original linear programming problem has been obtained. For that reason, sensitivity analysis is often referred to as *postoptimality analysis.*

Our approach to sensitivity analysis parallels the approach used to introduce linear programming in Chapter 2. We begin by showing how a graphical method can be used to perform sensitivity analysis for linear programming problems with two decision variables. Then, we show how The Management Scientist provides sensitivity analysis information.

We extend the discussion of problem formulation started in Chapter 2 by formulating and solving two slightly larger problems with three decision variables. In discussing the spreadsheet solution for each of these problems, we focus on managerial interpretation of the optimal solution and sensitivity analysis information. The final section of the chapter provides further practice in the formulation, solution, and interpretation of output for a larger problem involving four decision variables and various types of constraints.

## 3.1    INTRODUCTION TO SENSITIVITY ANALYSIS

Sensitivity analysis is important to decision makers because real-world problems exist in a changing environment. Prices of raw materials change, product demand changes, companies purchase new machinery, stock prices fluctuate, employee turnover occurs, and so on. If a linear programming model has been used in such an environment, we can expect some of the coefficients to change over time. We will then want to determine how these changes affect the optimal solution to the original linear programming problem. Sensitivity analysis provides us with the information needed to respond to such changes without requiring the complete solution of a revised linear program.

Recall the Par, Inc., problem:

$$\text{Max} \quad 10S + 9D$$

subject to (s.t.)

$$
\begin{array}{ll}
\tfrac{7}{10}S + 1D \le 630 & \text{Cutting and dyeing} \\
\tfrac{1}{2}S + \tfrac{5}{6}D \le 600 & \text{Sewing} \\
1S + \tfrac{2}{3}D \le 708 & \text{Finishing} \\
\tfrac{1}{10}S + \tfrac{1}{4}D \le 135 & \text{Inspection and packaging} \\
S, D \ge 0 &
\end{array}
$$

The optimal solution, $S = 540$ standard bags and $D = 252$ deluxe bags, was based on profit contribution figures of $10 per standard bag and $9 per deluxe bag. Suppose we later learn that a price reduction causes the profit contribution for the standard bag to fall from $10 to

$8.50. Sensitivity analysis can be used to determine whether the production schedule calling for 540 standard bags and 252 deluxe bags is still best. If it is, solving a modified linear programming problem with $8.50S + 9D$ as the new objective function will not be necessary.

Sensitivity analysis can also be used to determine which coefficients in a linear programming model are crucial. For example, suppose that management believes the $9 profit contribution for the deluxe bag is only a rough estimate of the profit contribution that will actually be obtained. If sensitivity analysis shows that 540 standard bags and 252 deluxe bags will be the optimal solution as long as the profit contribution for the deluxe bag is between $6.67 and $14.29, management should feel comfortable with the $9 per bag estimate and the recommended production quantities. However, if sensitivity analysis shows that 540 standard bags and 252 deluxe bags will be the optimal solution only if the profit contribution for the deluxe bags is between $8.90 and $9.25, management may want to review the accuracy of the $9 per bag estimate. Management would especially want to consider how the optimal production quantities should be revised if the profit contribution per deluxe bag were to drop.

Another aspect of sensitivity analysis concerns changes in the right-hand-side values of the constraints. Recall that in the Par, Inc., problem the optimal solution used all available time in the cutting and dyeing department and the finishing department. What would happen to the optimal solution and total profit contribution if Par could obtain additional quantities of either of these resources? Sensitivity analysis can help determine how much each added hour of production time is worth and how many hours can be added before diminishing returns set in.

## 3.2    GRAPHICAL SENSITIVITY ANALYSIS

For linear programming problems with two decision variables, graphical solution methods can be used to perform sensitivity analysis on the objective function coefficients and the right-hand-side values for the constraints.

### Objective Function Coefficients

Let us consider how changes in the objective function coefficients might affect the optimal solution to the Par, Inc., problem. The current contribution to profit is $10 per unit for the standard bag and $9 per unit for the deluxe bag. It seems obvious that an increase in the profit contribution for one of the bags might lead management to increase production of that bag, and a decrease in the profit contribution for one of the bags might lead management to decrease production of that bag. But it is not as obvious how much the profit contribution would have to change before management would want to change the production quantities.

The current optimal solution to this problem calls for producing 540 standard golf bags and 252 deluxe golf bags. The **range of optimality** for each objective function coefficient provides the range of values over which the current solution will remain optimal. Managerial attention needs to be focused on those objective function coefficients that have a narrow range of optimality and coefficients near the endpoints of the range. With these coefficients, a small change can necessitate modifying the optimal solution. Let us now compute the ranges of optimality for this problem.

Figure 3.1 shows the graphical solution. A careful inspection of this graph shows that as long as the slope of the objective function is between the slope of line A (which coincides with the cutting and dyeing constraint line) and the slope of line B (which coincides with

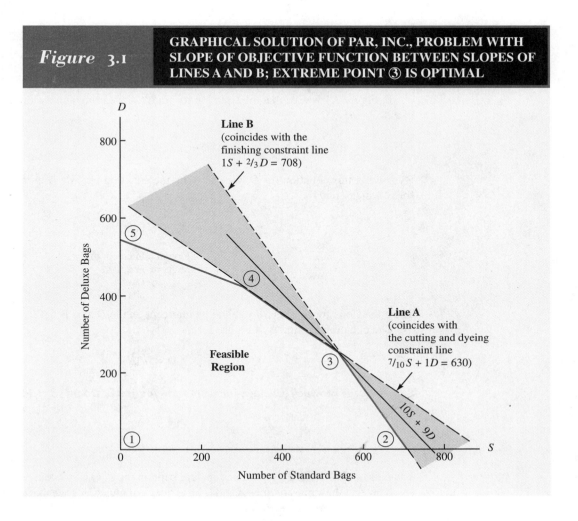

**Figure 3.1**    GRAPHICAL SOLUTION OF PAR, INC., PROBLEM WITH SLOPE OF OBJECTIVE FUNCTION BETWEEN SLOPES OF LINES A AND B; EXTREME POINT ③ IS OPTIMAL

the finishing constraint line), extreme point ③ with $S = 540$ and $D = 252$ will be optimal. Changing an objective function coefficient for $S$ or $D$ will cause the slope of the objective function to change. In Figure 3.1 we see that such changes cause the objective function line to rotate around extreme point ③. However, as long as the objective function line stays within the shaded region, extreme point ③ will remain optimal.

> The slope of the objective function line usually is negative; hence, rotating the objective function line clockwise makes the line steeper even though the slope is getting smaller (more negative).

Rotating the objective function line *counterclockwise* causes the slope to become less negative, and the slope increases. When the objective function line has been rotated counterclockwise (slope increased) enough to coincide with line A, we obtain alternative optimal solutions between extreme points ③ and ④. Any further counterclockwise rotation of the objective function line will cause extreme point ③ to be nonoptimal. Hence, the slope of line A provides an upper limit for the slope of the objective function line.

Rotating the objective function line *clockwise* causes the slope to become more negative, and the slope decreases. When the objective function line has been rotated clockwise (slope decreased) enough to coincide with line B, we obtain alternative optimal solutions between extreme points ③ and ②. Any further clockwise rotation of the objective function line will cause extreme point ③ to be nonoptimal. Hence, the slope of line B provides a lower limit for the slope of the objective function line.

Thus, extreme point ③ will be the optimal solution as long as

Slope of line B ≤ slope of the objective function line ≤ slope of line A

In Figure 3.1 we see that the equation for line A, the cutting and dyeing constraint line, is as follows:

$$^{7}/_{10}S + 1D = 630$$

By solving this equation for $D$, we can write the equation for line A in its slope-intercept form, which yields

$$D = -^{7}/_{10}S + 630$$

Slope of    Intercept of
line A      line A on
         $D$ axis

Thus, the slope for line A is $-^{7}/_{10}$, and its intercept on the $D$ axis is 630.

The equation for line B in Figure 3.1 is

$$1S + ^{2}/_{3}D = 708$$

Solving for $D$ provides the slope-intercept form for line B. Doing so yields

$$^{2}/_{3}D = -1S + 708$$
$$D = -^{3}/_{2}S + 1062$$

Thus, the slope of line B is $-^{3}/_{2}$, and its intercept on the $D$ axis is 1062.

Now that the slopes of lines A and B have been computed, we see that for extreme point ③ to remain optimal we must have

$$-^{3}/_{2} \leq \text{slope of objective function} \leq -^{7}/_{10} \tag{3.1}$$

Let us now consider the general form of the slope of the objective function. Let $C_S$ denote the profit of a standard bag, $C_D$ denote the profit of a deluxe bag, and $P$ denote the value of the objective function. Using this notation, the objective function can be written as

$$P = C_S S + C_D D$$

Writing this equation in slope-intercept form, we obtain

$$C_D D = -C_S S + P$$

and

$$D = -\frac{C_S}{C_D}S + \frac{P}{C_D}$$

Thus, we see that the slope of the objective function is given by $-C_S/C_D$. Substituting $-C_S/C_D$ into expression (3.1), we see that extreme point ③ will be optimal as long as the following expression is satisfied:

$$-\tfrac{3}{2} \le -\frac{C_S}{C_D} \le -\tfrac{7}{10} \qquad\qquad (3.2)$$

To compute the range of optimality for the standard-bag profit contribution, we hold the profit contribution for the deluxe bag fixed at its initial value $C_D = 9$. Doing so in expression (3.2), we obtain

$$-\tfrac{3}{2} \le -\frac{C_S}{9} \le -\tfrac{7}{10}$$

From the left-hand inequality, we have

$$-\tfrac{3}{2} \le -\frac{C_S}{9} \qquad \text{or} \qquad \tfrac{3}{2} \ge \frac{C_S}{9}$$

Thus,

$$\tfrac{27}{2} \ge C_S \qquad \text{or} \qquad C_S \le \tfrac{27}{2} = 13.5$$

From the right-hand inequality, we have

$$-\frac{C_S}{9} \le -\tfrac{7}{10} \qquad \text{or} \qquad \frac{C_S}{9} \ge \tfrac{7}{10}$$

Thus,

Can you compute the
range of optimality using
the graphical solution
procedure? Try Problem 3.

$$C_S \ge \tfrac{63}{10} \qquad \text{or} \qquad C_S \ge 6.3$$

Combining the calculated limits for $C_S$ provides the following range of optimality for the standard-bag profit contribution:

$$6.3 \le C_S \le 13.5$$

In the original problem for Par, Inc., the standard bag had a profit contribution of $10. The resulting optimal solution was 540 standard bags and 252 deluxe bags. The range of optimality for $C_S$ tells Par's management that, with other coefficients unchanged, the profit contribution for the standard bag can be anywhere between $6.30 and $13.50 and the production quantities of 540 standard bags and 252 deluxe bags will remain optimal. Note, however, that while the production quantities will not change, the total profit contribution (value of objective function) will change due to the change in profit contribution per standard bag.

These computations can be repeated, holding the profit contribution for standard bags constant at $C_S = 10$. In this case, the range of optimality for the deluxe-bag profit contribution can be determined. Check to see that this range is $6.67 \le C_D \le 14.29$.

In cases where the rotation of the objective function line about an optimal extreme point causes the objective function line to become *vertical,* there will be either no upper limit or no lower limit for the slope as it appears in the form of expression (3.2). To show how this special situation can occur, suppose that the objective function for the Par, Inc., problem is $18C_S + 9C_D$; in this case, extreme point ② in Figure 3.2 provides the optimal solution. Rotating the objective function line counterclockwise around extreme point ② provides an upper limit for the slope when the objective function line coincides with line B. Since we have previously seen that the slope of line B is $-\frac{3}{2}$, the upper limit for the slope of the objective function line must be $-\frac{3}{2}$. However, rotating the objective function line clockwise results in the slope becoming more and more negative, approaching a value of minus infinity as the objective function line becomes vertical; in this case, the slope of the objective function has no lower limit. Using the upper limit of $-\frac{3}{2}$, we can write

$$-\frac{C_S}{C_D} \le -\frac{3}{2}$$

Slope of the
objective function line

Following the previous procedure of holding $C_D$ constant at its original value, $C_D = 9$, we have

$$-\frac{C_S}{9} \le -\frac{3}{2} \qquad \text{or} \qquad \frac{C_S}{9} \ge \frac{3}{2}$$

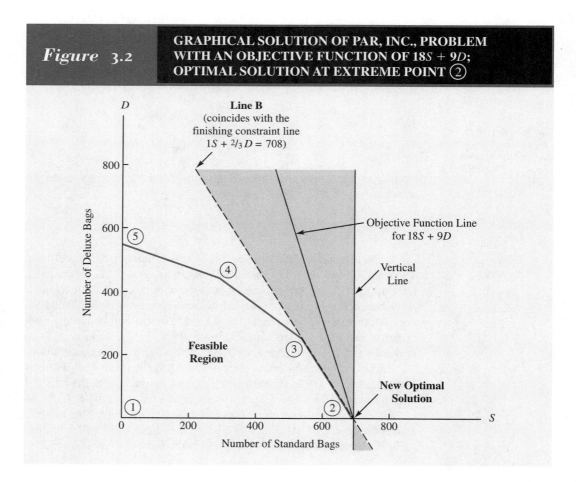

*Figure* **3.2**     **GRAPHICAL SOLUTION OF PAR, INC., PROBLEM WITH AN OBJECTIVE FUNCTION OF 18S + 9D; OPTIMAL SOLUTION AT EXTREME POINT ②**

Solving for $C_S$ provides the following result:

$$C_S \geq {}^{27}\!/_2 = 13.5$$

In reviewing Figure 3.2 we note that extreme point ② remains optimal for all values of $C_S$ above 13.5. Thus, we obtain the following range of optimality for $C_S$ at extreme point ②:

$$13.5 \leq C_S < \infty$$

**Simultaneous Changes.**   The range of optimality for objective function coefficients is only applicable for changes made to one coefficient at a time. All other coefficients are assumed to be fixed at their initial values. If two or more objective function coefficients are changed simultaneously, further analysis is necessary to determine whether the optimal solution will change. However, when solving two-variable problems graphically, expression (3.2) suggests an easy way to determine whether simultaneous changes in both objective function coefficients will cause a change in the optimal solution. Simply compute the slope of the objective function $(-C_S/C_D)$ for the new coefficient values. If this ratio is greater than or equal to the lower limit on the slope of the objective function and less than or equal to the upper limit, then the changes made will not cause a change in the optimal solution.

Consider changes in both of the objective function coefficients for the Par, Inc., problem. Suppose the profit contribution per standard bag is increased to $13 and the profit contribution per deluxe bag is simultaneously reduced to $8. Recall that the ranges of optimality for $C_S$ and $C_D$ (both computed in a one-at-a-time manner) are

$$6.3 \leq C_S \leq 13.5 \tag{3.3}$$
$$6.67 \leq C_D \leq 14.29 \tag{3.4}$$

For these ranges of optimality, we can conclude that changing either $C_S$ to $13 or $C_D$ to $8 (but not both) would not cause a change in the optimal solution of $S = 540$ and $D = 252$. But we cannot conclude from the ranges of optimality that changing both coefficients simultaneously would not result in a change in the optimal solution.

In expression (3.2) we showed that extreme point ③ remains optimal as long as

$$-{}^{3}\!/_2 \leq -\frac{C_S}{C_D} \leq -{}^{7}\!/_{10}$$

If $C_S$ is changed to 13 and simultaneously $C_D$ is changed to 8, the new objective function slope will be given by

$$-\frac{C_S}{C_D} = -\frac{13}{8} = -1.625$$

Since this value is less than the lower limit of $-{}^{3}\!/_2$, the current solution of $S = 540$ and $D = 252$ will no longer be optimal. By resolving the problem with $C_S = 13$ and $C_D = 8$ we will find that extreme point ② is the new optimal solution.

Looking at the ranges of optimality, we concluded that changing either $C_S$ to $13 or $C_D$ to $8 (but not both) would not cause a change in the optimal solution. But in recomputing the slope of the objective function with simultaneous changes for both $C_S$ and $C_D$, we saw that the optimal solution did change. This result emphasizes the fact that a range of optimality, by itself, can only be used to draw a conclusion about changes made to *one objective function coefficient at a time.*

## Right-Hand Sides

Let us now consider how a change in the right-hand side for a constraint may affect the feasible region and perhaps cause a change in the optimal solution to the problem. To illustrate this aspect of sensitivity analysis, let us consider what happens if an additional 10 hours of production time become available in the cutting and dyeing department of Par, Inc. The right-hand side of the cutting and dyeing constraint is changed from 630 to 640, and the constraint is rewritten as

$$\tfrac{7}{10}S + D \le 640$$

By obtaining an additional 10 hours of cutting and dyeing time, we have expanded the feasible region for the problem, as shown in Figure 3.3. Since the feasible region has been enlarged, we now want to determine whether one of the new feasible solutions provides an improvement in the value of the objective function. Application of the graphical solution procedure to the problem with the enlarged feasible region shows that the extreme point

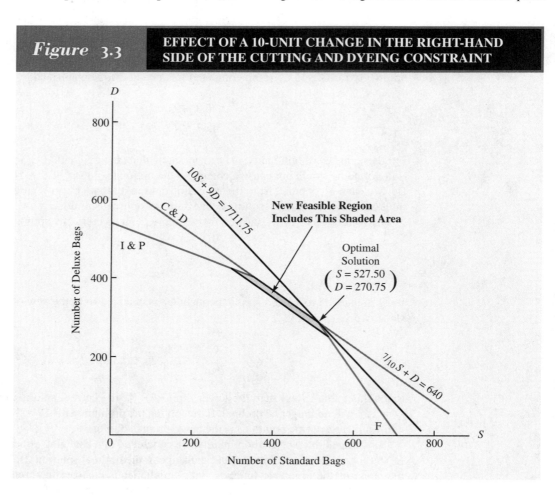

**Figure 3.3**  **EFFECT OF A 10-UNIT CHANGE IN THE RIGHT-HAND SIDE OF THE CUTTING AND DYEING CONSTRAINT**

with $S = 527.5$ and $D = 270.75$ now provides the optimal solution. The new value for the objective function is $10(527.5) + 9(270.75) = \$7711.75$; this provides an increase in profit of $\$7711.75 - \$7668.00 = \$43.75$. Thus, the increased profit occurs at a rate of $\$43.75/10$ hours $= \$4.375$ per hour added.

The *improvement* in the value of the optimal solution per unit increase in the right-hand side of the constraint is called the **dual price.** Here, the dual price for cutting and dyeing and production time is $\$4.375$ per hour; in other words, if we increase the right-hand side of the production and dyeing time constraint by 1 hour, the value of the objective function will improve by $\$4.375$. Conversely, if the right-hand side of the production and dyeing time constraint were to decrease by 1 hour, the objective function would get worse by $\$4.375$. The dual price can generally be used to determine what will happen to the value of the objective function when we make a one-unit change in the right-hand side of a constraint.

We caution here that the value of the dual price may be applicable only for small changes in the right-hand side. As more and more resources are obtained and the right-hand-side value continues to increase, other constraints will become binding and limit the change in the value of the objective function. For example, in the problem for Par, Inc., we would eventually reach a point where more cutting and dyeing time would be of no value; it would occur at the point where the cutting and dyeing constraint becomes non-binding. At this point, the dual price would equal zero. In the next section we will show how to determine the range of values for a right-hand side over which the dual price will accurately predict the improvement in the objective function. Finally, we note that the dual price for any nonbinding constraint will be zero because an increase in the right-hand side of such a constraint will affect only the value of the slack or surplus variable for that constraint.

To illustrate the correct interpretation of dual prices for a minimization problem, suppose we had solved a problem involving the minimization of total cost and that the value of the optimal solution was $\$100$. Furthermore, suppose that the dual price for a particular constraint was $-\$10$. The *negative dual price* tells us that the objective function *will not improve* if the value of the right-hand side is increased by one unit. Thus, if the right-hand side of this constraint is increased by one unit, the value of the objective function will get worse by the amount of $\$10$. Since becoming worse means an increase in the total cost, the value of the objective function will become $\$110$ if the right-hand side is increased by one unit. Conversely, a decrease in the right-hand side of one unit will decrease the total cost by $\$10$.

*Can you compute and interpret the dual price for a constraint? Try Problem 4.*

## N O T E S
### and Comments

1. If two objective function coefficients change simultaneously, both may move outside their respective ranges of optimality and not affect the optimal solution. For instance, in a two-variable linear program, the slope of the objective function will not change at all if both coefficients are changed by the same percentage.

2. Some texts associate the term *shadow price* with each constraint. The concept of a shadow price is closely related to the concept of a dual price. The shadow price associated with a constraint is the *change* in the value of the optimal solution per-unit increase in the right-hand side of the constraint. In general, the dual price and the shadow price are the *same* for all *maximization* linear programs. In *minimization* linear programs, the shadow price is the *negative* of the corresponding dual price.

## 3.3    SENSITIVITY ANALYSIS: COMPUTER SOLUTION

In Section 2.4 we showed how The Management Scientist can be used to solve the Par, Inc., linear program. Recall that in order to use The Management Scientist, we must use decimal rather than fractional values. The Par, Inc., problem with decimal coefficients is restated here:

$$\text{Max} \quad 10S + 9D$$

s.t.

$$
\begin{array}{rll}
0.7S + & 1D \le 630 & \text{Cutting and dyeing} \\
0.5S + 0.83333D \le 600 & & \text{Sewing} \\
1.0S + 0.66667D \le 708 & & \text{Finishing} \\
0.1S + & 0.25D \le 135 & \text{Inspection and packaging} \\
S, D \ge 0 &
\end{array}
$$

Let us demonstrate the use of The Management Scientist in performing sensitivity analysis by considering the solution to the Par, Inc., linear program shown in Figure 3.4.

### Interpretation of Computer Output

In Section 2.4 we discussed the output in the top portion of Figure 3.4. Thus, after rounding, we see that the optimal solution is $S = 540$ standard bags and $D = 252$ deluxe bags; the value of the optimal solution is $7668. As we discussed in Section 2.4, the **reduced costs** indicate how much the objective function coefficient of each decision variable would have to improve before that variable could assume a positive value in the optimal solution. For the Par, Inc., problem, both variables already have positive values, and thus their corresponding reduced costs are zero. In Section 3.4 we will interpret the reduced cost for a decision variable that does not have a positive value in the optimal solution.

Immediately following the optimal $S$ and $D$ values and the reduced cost information, the computer output provides information about the status of the constraints. Recall that the Par, Inc., problem had four less-than-or-equal-to constraints corresponding to the hours available in each of four production departments. The information shown in the Slack/Surplus column provides the value of the slack variable for each of the departments. This information (after rounding) is summarized here:

| Constraint Number | Constraint Name | Slack |
|---|---|---|
| 1 | Cutting and dyeing | 0 |
| 2 | Sewing | 120 |
| 3 | Finishing | 0 |
| 4 | Inspection and packaging | 18 |

From this information, we see that the binding constraints (the cutting and dyeing and the finishing constraints) have zero slack at the optimal solution. The sewing department has 120 hours of slack, or unused capacity, and the inspection and packaging department has 18 hours of slack or unused capacity.

---

**Figure 3.4**   THE MANAGEMENT SCIENTIST SOLUTION FOR THE PAR, INC., PROBLEM

```
Objective Function Value =          7667.99463

       Variable              Value              Reduced Costs
     -------------       ---------------      -----------------
          S                539.99841              0.00000
          D                252.00113              0.00000

      Constraint         Slack/Surplus            Dual Prices
     -------------       ---------------      -----------------
          1                  0.00000              4.37496
          2                120.00070              0.00000
          3                  0.00000              6.93753
          4                 17.99988              0.00000

OBJECTIVE COEFFICIENT RANGES

      Variable          Lower Limit        Current Value        Upper Limit
    -------------      ---------------     ---------------      ---------------
          S               6.30000            10.00000             13.49993
          D               6.66670             9.00000             14.28572

RIGHT HAND SIDE RANGES

     Constraint         Lower Limit        Current Value        Upper Limit
    -------------      ---------------     ---------------      ---------------
          1              495.59998           630.00000            682.36316
          2              479.99930           600.00000         No Upper Limit
          3              580.00146           708.00000            900.00000
          4              117.00012           135.00000         No Upper Limit
```

The Dual Prices column contains information about the marginal value of each of the four resources at the optimal solution. In Section 3.2 we defined the *dual price* as follows.

---

The dual price associated with a constraint is the *improvement* in the value of the solution per-unit increase in the right-hand side of the constraint.

---

Try Problem 11 to test your ability to use computer output to determine the optimal solution, and to interpret the values of the dual prices.

Thus, the nonzero dual prices of 4.37496 for constraint 1 (cutting and dyeing constraint) and 6.93753 for constraint 3 (finishing constraint) tell us that an additional hour of cutting and dyeing time improves (increases) the value of the optimal solution by $4.37 and an additional hour of finishing time improves (increases) the value of the optimal solution by $6.94. Thus, if the cutting and dyeing time were increased from 630 to 631 hours, with all other coefficients in the problem remaining the same, Par's profit would be increased by $4.37 from $7668 to $7668 + $4.37 = $7672.37. A similar interpretation for the finishing constraint implies that an increase from 708 to 709 hours of available finishing time, with all other coefficients in the problem remaining the same, would increase Par's profit to $7668 + $6.94 = $7674.94. Since the sewing and the inspection and packaging constraints both have slack or unused capacity available, the dual prices of zero show that additional hours of these two resources will not improve the value of the objective function.

Referring again to the computer output in Figure 3.4, we see that after providing the constraint information on slack/surplus variables and dual prices, The Management Scientist provides ranges for the objective function coefficients and the right-hand sides of the constraints.

Considering the information provided under the computer output heading labeled OBJECTIVE COEFFICIENT RANGES, we see that variable $S$, which has a current profit coefficient of 10, has the following *range of optimality* for $C_S$:

$$6.30 \le C_S \le 13.50$$

Therefore, as long as the profit contribution associated with the standard bag is between $6.30 and $13.50, the production of $S = 540$ standard bags and $D = 252$ deluxe bags will remain the optimal solution. Note that the range of optimality is the same as obtained by performing graphical sensitivity analysis for $C_S$ in Section 3.2.

Using the objective function coefficient range information for deluxe bags, we see that The Management Scientist has computed the following range of optimality:

$$6.67 \le C_D \le 14.29$$

This result tells us that as long as the profit contribution associated with the deluxe bag is between $6.67 and $14.29, the production of $S = 540$ standard bags and $D = 252$ deluxe bags will remain the optimal solution.

Try Problem 12 to test your ability to use computer output to determine the ranges of optimality and the ranges of feasibility.

The final section of the computer printout (RIGHT HAND SIDE RANGES) contains a range of information for the constraint right-hand sides. As long as the constraint right-hand side stays within this range, the associated dual price gives the improvement in the value of the optimal solution per-unit increase in the right-hand side. For example, let us consider the cutting and dyeing constraint with a current right-hand-side value of 630. Because the dual price for this constraint is $4.37, we can conclude that additional hours will increase the objective function by $4.37 per hour. It is also true that a reduction in the hours available will reduce the value of the objective function by $4.37 per hour. From the range information given, we see that the dual price of $4.37 is valid for increases up to 682.36316 and decreases down to 495.59998. A similar interpretation for the finishing constraint's right-hand side (constraint 3) shows that the dual price of $6.94 is applicable for increases up to 900 hours and decreases down to 580.00146 hours.

As mentioned, the right-hand-side ranges provide limits within which the dual prices are applicable. For changes outside the range, the problem must be resolved to find the new optimal solution and the new dual price. We shall call the range over which the dual price is applicable the **range of feasibility.** The ranges of feasibility for the Par, Inc., problem are summarized here:

| Constraint | Min RHS | Max RHS |
|---|---|---|
| Cutting and dyeing | 495.6 | 682.4 |
| Sewing | 480.0 | No upper limit |
| Finishing | 580.0 | 900.0 |
| Inspection and packaging | 117.0 | No upper limit |

As long as the values of the right-hand sides are within these ranges, the dual prices shown on the computer output will not change. Right-hand-side values outside these limits will result in changes in the dual price information.

## Simultaneous Changes

The sensitivity analysis information in computer output is based on the assumption that only one coefficient changes; it is assumed that all other coefficients will remain as stated in the original problem. Thus, the ranges for the objective function coefficients and the constraint right-hand sides are only applicable for changes in a single coefficient. In many cases, however, we may be interested in what would happen if two or more coefficients are changed simultaneously. As we will demonstrate, some analysis of simultaneous changes is possible with the help of the **100 percent rule**.[1] We begin by showing how the 100 percent rule applies to simultaneous changes in the objective function coefficients.

Suppose that in the Par, Inc., problem the accounting department concluded that the original profit contributions of $10 and $9 for the standard and deluxe bags, respectively, were incorrectly computed; the correct values should have been $11.50 and $8.25. To determine what effect, if any, these simultaneous changes have on the optimal solution, we need to first define the terms "allowable increase" and "allowable decrease." For an objective function coefficient, the *allowable increase* is the maximum amount the coefficient may be increased without exceeding the upper limit of the range of optimality; the *allowable decrease* is the maximum amount the coefficient may be decreased without dropping below the lower limit of the range of optimality.

From Figure 3.4 we see that the upper limit for the objective function coefficient of $S$ is 13.49993; thus, the allowable increase is $3.49993 = 13.49993 - 10$. In terms of percentage change, the increase of $1.50 in the objective function coefficient (from 10 to 11.50) for the standard bags is $(1.50/3.49993)(100) = 42.86\%$ of the allowable increase. Given the lower limit of 6.66670 for $D$, the allowable decrease for $D$ is $2.33330 = 9 - 6.66670$. In terms of percentage change, the decrease of $0.75 in the objective function coefficient (from 9 to 8.25) for the deluxe bags is $(0.75/2.33330)(100) = 32.14\%$ of the allowable decrease. The sum of the percentage change of the allowable increase (42.86%) and the percentage change of the allowable decrease (32.14%) is 75.00%.

Let us now state the 100 percent rule as it applies to simultaneous changes in the objective function coefficients.

### 100 Percent Rule for Objective Function Coefficients

For all objective function coefficients that are changed, sum the percentages of the allowable increases and the allowable decreases represented by the changes. If the sum of the percentage changes does not exceed 100%, the optimal solution will not change.

Thus, since the sum of the two percentage changes in the objective function coefficients for the Par, Inc., problem is 75%, these simultaneous changes will not affect the optimal solution. Note, however, that although the optimal solution is still $S = 539.99841$ and $D = 252.00113$, the value of the optimal solution will change since the profit contribution for the standard bags has increased to $11.50 and the profit contribution of the deluxe bags has decreased to $8.25.

[1] See S. P. Bradley, A. C. Hax, and T. L. Magnanti, *Applied Mathematical Programming* (Reading, Mass.: Addison-Wesley, 1977).

The 100 percent rule does not, however, say that the optimal solution will change if the sum of the percentage changes exceeds 100%. It is possible that the optimal solution will not change even though the sum of the percentage changes exceeds 100%. When the 100 percent rule is not satisfied, we must resolve the problem to determine what affect such changes will have on the optimal solution.

A similar version of the 100 percent rule also applies to simultaneous changes in the constraint right-hand sides.

---

### 100 Percent Rule for Constraint Right-Hand Sides

For all right-hand sides that are changed, sum the percentages of allowable increases and allowable decreases. If the sum of percentages does not exceed 100%, then the dual prices will not change.

---

Let us illustrate the 100 percent rule for constraint right-hand sides by considering simultaneous changes in the right-hand sides for the Par, Inc., problem. Suppose, for instance, that in this problem we could obtain 20 additional hours of cutting and dyeing time and 100 additional hours of finishing time. The allowable increase for cutting and dyeing time is $682.36316 - 630.0 = 52.36316$, and the allowable increase for finishing time is $900.0 - 708.0 = 192.0$ (see Figure 3.4). The 20 additional hours of cutting and dyeing time are $(20/52.36316)(100) = 38.19\%$ of the allowable increase in the constraint's right-hand side. The 100 additional hours of finishing time are $(100/192)(100) = 52.08\%$ of the allowable increase in the finishing time constraint's right-hand side. The sum of the percentage changes is $38.19\% + 52.08\% = 90.27\%$. Since the sum of the percentage changes does not exceed 100%, we can conclude that the dual prices are applicable and that the objective function will improve by $(20)(4.37) + (100)(6.94) = 781.40$.

### Interpretation of Computer Output—A Second Example

As another example of interpreting computer output, let us reconsider the M&D Chemicals minimization problem introduced in Section 2.5. The linear programming model for this problem is restated as follows, where $A$ = number of gallons of product A and $B$ = number of gallons of product B and it is desired to minimize production cost.

$$\text{Min} \quad 2A + 3B$$

s.t.

$$1A \geq 125 \quad \text{Demand for product A}$$
$$1A + 1B \geq 350 \quad \text{Total production}$$
$$2A + 1B \leq 600 \quad \text{Processing time}$$
$$A, B \geq 0$$

The solution obtained using The Management Scientist is presented in Figure 3.5. The computer output shows that the minimum-cost solution yields an objective function value of $800. The values of the decision variables show that 250 gallons of product A and 100 gallons of product B provide the minimum-cost solution.

The Slack/Surplus column shows that the $\geq$ constraint corresponding to the demand for product A (see constraint 1) has a surplus of 125 units. It tells us that production of prod-

## Figure 3.5    THE MANAGEMENT SCIENTIST SOLUTION FOR THE M&D CHEMICALS PROBLEM

```
Objective Function Value =              800.000

      Variable              Value              Reduced Costs
      --------           ----------           -------------
         A                 250.000                0.000
         B                 100.000                0.000

     Constraint         Slack/Surplus           Dual Prices
     ----------         -------------           -----------
         1                 125.000                0.000
         2                   0.000               -4.000
         3                   0.000                1.000

OBJECTIVE COEFFICIENT RANGES

    Variable         Lower Limit        Current Value       Upper Limit
    --------         -----------        -------------       -----------
       A          No Lower Limit           2.000              3.000
       B                2.000              3.000          No Upper Limit

RIGHT HAND SIDE RANGES

   Constraint        Lower Limit        Current Value       Upper Limit
   ----------        -----------        -------------       -----------
       1          No Lower Limit          125.000            250.000
       2              300.000             350.000            475.000
       3              475.000             600.000            700.000
```

uct A in the optimal solution exceeds demand by 125 gallons. The Slack/Surplus values are zero for the total production requirement (constraint 2) and the processing time limitation (constraint 3), which indicates that these constraints are binding at the optimal solution.

The Dual Prices column again shows us the *improvement* in the value of the optimal solution per-unit increase in the right-hand side of the constraint. Focusing first on the dual price of 1.00 for the processing time constraint (constraint 3), we see that if we can increase the processing time from 600 to 601 hours, the objective function value will *improve* by $1. Since the objective is to minimize costs, improvement in this case means a lowering of costs. Thus, if 601 hours of processing time are available, the value of the optimal solution will improve to $800 − $1 = $799. The RIGHT HAND SIDE RANGES section of the output shows that the upper limit for the processing time constraint (constraint 3) is 700 hours. Thus, the dual price of $1 per unit would be applicable for every additional hour of processing time up to a total of 700 hours.

Let us again return to the Dual Prices section of the output and consider the dual price for the total production constraint (constraint 2). The *negative dual price* tells us that the value of the optimal solution *will not improve* if the value of the right-hand side is increased by one unit. In fact, the dual price of $-4.00$ tells us that if the right-hand side of the total production constraint is increased from 350 to 351 units, the value of the optimal solution will worsen by the amount of $4. Since worsening means an increase in cost, the value of the optimal solution will become $800 + $4 = $804 if the one-unit increase in the total production requirement is made.

   Because the dual price refers to improvement in the value of the optimal solution per-unit increase in the right-hand side, a constraint with a negative dual price should not have its right-hand side increased. In fact, if the dual price is negative, efforts should be made to reduce the right-hand side of the constraint. If the right-hand side of the total production constraint were decreased from 350 to 349 units, the dual price tells us the total cost could be lowered by $4 to $800 − $4 = $796.

   Even though the dual price is the improvement in the value of the optimal solution per-unit increase in the right-hand side of a constraint, the interpretation of an *improvement* in the value of an objective function depends on whether we are solving a maximization or a minimization problem. The dual price for a $\leq$ constraint will always be greater than or equal to zero because increasing the right-hand side cannot make the value of the objective function worse. Similarly, the dual price for a $\geq$ constraint will always be less than or equal to zero because increasing the right-hand side cannot improve the value of the optimal solution.

   Finally, consider the right-hand-side ranges provided in Figure 3.5. The ranges of feasibility for the M&D Chemicals problem are summarized here:

| Constraint | Min RHS | Max RHS |
|---|---|---|
| Product A demand | No lower limit | 250 |
| Total production | 300 | 475 |
| Processing time | 475 | 700 |

Try Problem 16 to test your ability to interpret the computer output for a minimization problem.

As long as the right-hand sides are within these ranges, the dual prices shown on the computer printout are applicable.

## Cautionary Note on the Interpretation of Dual Prices

As stated previously, the dual price is the improvement in the value of the optimal solution per-unit increase in the right-hand side of a constraint. When the right-hand side of the constraint represents the amount of a resource available, the associated dual price is often interpreted as the maximum amount one should be willing to pay for one additional unit of the resource. However, such an interpretation is not always correct. To see why, we need to understand the difference between sunk and relevant costs. A **sunk cost** is one that is not affected by the decision made. It will be incurred no matter what values the decision variables assume. A **relevant cost** is one that depends on the decision made. The amount of a relevant cost will vary depending on the values of the decision variables.

   Let us reconsider the Par, Inc., problem. The amount of cutting and dyeing time available is 630 hours. The cost of the time available is a sunk cost if it must be paid regardless of the number of standard and deluxe golf bags produced. It would be a relevant cost if Par only had to pay for the number of hours of cutting and dyeing time actually used to produce golf bags. All relevant costs should be reflected in the objective function of a linear program. Sunk costs should not be reflected in the objective function. For Par, Inc., we have been assuming that the company must pay its employees' wages whether or not their time on the job is completely utilized. Therefore, the cost of the labor-hours resource for Par, Inc., is a sunk cost and has not been reflected in the objective function.

When the cost of a resource is *sunk,* the dual price can be interpreted as the maximum amount the company should be willing to pay for one additional unit of the resource. When the cost of a resource used is relevant, the dual price can be interpreted as the amount by which the value of the resource exceeds its cost. Thus, when the resource cost is relevant, the dual price can be interpreted as the maximum premium over the normal cost that the company should be willing to pay for one unit of the resource.

*Only relevant costs should be included in the objective function.*

## N O T E S  and Comments

1. Computer software packages for solving linear programs are readily available. Most of these provide the optimal solution, dual or shadow price information, the range of optimality for the objective function coefficients, and the range of feasibility for the right-hand sides. The labels used for the ranges of optimality and feasibility may vary, but the meaning is the same as what we have described here.

2. Whenever one of the right-hand sides is at an end point of its range of feasibility, the dual and shadow prices only provide one-sided information. In this case, they only predict the change in the optimal value of the objective function for changes toward the interior of the range.

3. A condition called *degeneracy* can cause a subtle difference in how we interpret changes in the objective function coefficients beyond the end points of the range of optimality. Degeneracy occurs when the dual price equals zero for one of the binding constraints. Degeneracy does not affect the interpretation of changes toward the interior of the range of optimality. However, when degeneracy is present, changes beyond the end points of the range do not necessarily mean a different solution will be optimal. From a practical point of view, changes beyond the end points of the range of optimality necessitate resolving the problem.

4. The 100 percent rule permits an analysis of multiple changes in the right-hand sides or multiple changes in the objective function coefficients. But the 100 percent rule cannot be applied to changes in both objective function coefficients *and* right-hand sides at the same time. In order to consider simultaneous changes for *both* right-hand-side values and objective function coefficients, the problem must be resolved.

5. Managers are frequently called on to provide an economic justification for new technology. Often the new technology is developed, or purchased, in order to conserve resources. The dual price can be helpful in such cases because it can be used to determine the savings attributable to the new technology by showing the savings per unit of resource conserved.

## 3.4     MORE THAN TWO DECISION VARIABLES

The graphical solution procedure is useful only for linear programs involving two decision variables. Computer software packages are designed to handle linear programs involving large numbers of variables and constraints. In this section we discuss the formulation and computer solution for two linear programs with three decision variables. In doing so, we will show how to interpret the reduced-cost portion of the computer output and will also illustrate the interpretation of dual prices for constraints that involve percentages.

## The Modified Par, Inc., Problem

The original Par, Inc., problem is restated as follows:

$$\text{Max} \quad 10S + 9D$$

s.t.

$$
\begin{array}{llll}
0.7S + & 1D \leq 630 & \text{Cutting and dyeing} \\
0.5S + 0.83333D \leq 600 & \text{Sewing} \\
1S + 0.66667D \leq 708 & \text{Finishing} \\
0.1S + 0.25D \leq 135 & \text{Inspection and packaging} \\
S, D \geq 0
\end{array}
$$

Recall that $S$ is the number of standard golf bags produced and $D$ is the number of deluxe golf bags produced. Suppose that management is also considering producing a lightweight model designed specifically for golfers who prefer to carry their bags. The design department estimates that each new lightweight model will require 0.8 hours for cutting and dyeing, 1 hour for sewing, 1 hour for finishing, and 0.25 hours for inspection and packaging. Because of the unique capabilities designed into the new model, Par's management feels they will realize a profit contribution of $12.85 for each lightweight model produced during the current production period.

Let us consider the modifications in the original linear programming model that are needed to incorporate the effect of this additional decision variable. We will let $L$ denote the number of lightweight bags produced. After adding $L$ to the objective function and to each of the four constraints, we obtain the following linear program for the modified problem:

$$\text{Max} \quad 10S + 9D + 12.85L$$

s.t.

$$
\begin{array}{llll}
0.7S + & 1D + & 0.8L \leq 630 & \text{Cutting and dyeing} \\
0.5S + 0.83333D + & 1L \leq 600 & \text{Sewing} \\
1S + 0.66667D + & 1L \leq 708 & \text{Finishing} \\
0.1S + & 0.25D + & 0.25L \leq 135 & \text{Inspection and packaging} \\
S, D, L \geq 0
\end{array}
$$

Figure 3.6 shows the solution to the modified problem using The Management Scientist. We see that the optimal solution calls for the production of 280 standard bags, 0 deluxe bags, and 428 of the new lightweight bags; the value of the optimal solution after rounding is $8299.80.

Let us now look at the information contained in the Reduced Costs column. Recall that the reduced costs indicate how much each objective function coefficient would have to improve before the corresponding decision variable could assume a positive value in the optimal solution. As the computer output shows, the reduced costs for $S$ and $L$ are zero because the corresponding decision variables already have positive values in the optimal solution. The reduced cost of 1.15003 for decision variable $D$ tells us that the profit contribution for the deluxe bag would have to increase to at least $9 + $1.15003 = $10.15003

| Figure 3.6 | THE MANAGEMENT SCIENTIST SOLUTION FOR THE MODIFIED PAR, INC., PROBLEM |
|---|---|

```
Objective Function Value =          8299.80078

        Variable              Value              Reduced Costs
     --------------      ---------------      ------------------
          S                 280.00000                0.00000
          D                   0.00000                1.15003
          L                 428.00000                0.00000


      Constraint          Slack/Surplus            Dual Prices
     --------------      ---------------      ------------------
          1                  91.60001                0.00000
          2                  32.00000                0.00000
          3                   0.00000                8.10000
          4                   0.00000               19.00000


OBJECTIVE COEFFICIENT RANGES

     Variable        Lower Limit        Current Value        Upper Limit
    -----------     ---------------     ---------------     ---------------
        S                5.14000            10.00000            12.07007
        D          No Lower Limit           9.00000            10.15003
        L               11.90907            12.85000            25.00000


RIGHT HAND SIDE RANGES

    Constraint       Lower Limit        Current Value        Upper Limit
    -----------     ---------------     ---------------     ---------------
        1              538.40002           630.00000        No Upper Limit
        2              568.00000           600.00000        No Upper Limit
        3              540.00000           708.00000           852.63159
        4               70.80000           135.00000           144.60001
```

before *D could* assume a positive value in the optimal solution.[2] In other words, unless the profit contribution for *D* increases by at least \$1.15 the value of *D* will remain at zero in the optimal solution.

   Suppose we increase the coefficient of *D* by exactly \$1.15003 and then resolve the problem using The Management Scientist. Figure 3.7 shows the new solution. Note that although *D* assumes a positive value in the new solution, the value of the optimal solution has not changed. In other words, increasing the profit contribution of *D* by *exactly* the amount of the reduced cost has resulted in alternative optimal solutions. Using a different

---

[2] In the case of degeneracy, a variable may not assume a positive value in the optimal solution even when the improvement in the profit contribution exceeds the value of the reduced cost. Our definition of reduced costs, stated as " . . . *could* assume a positive value . . . ," provides for such special cases. More advanced texts on mathematical programming discuss these special types of situations.

**Figure 3.7    THE MANAGEMENT SCIENTIST SOLUTION FOR THE MODIFIED PAR, INC., PROBLEM WITH THE COEFFICIENT OF D INCREASED BY $1.15003**

```
Objective Function Value =          8299.80078

     Variable            Value            Reduced Costs
  --------------     --------------     ------------------
        S               403.78317            0.00000
        D               222.81198            0.00000
        L               155.67476            0.00000


     Constraint        Slack/Surplus         Dual Prices
  --------------     --------------     ------------------
        1                 0.00000             0.00000
        2                56.75776             0.00000
        3                 0.00000             8.10000
        4                 0.00000            19.00000


OBJECTIVE COEFFICIENT RANGES

   Variable       Lower Limit      Current Value      Upper Limit
 ------------    -------------    ---------------    -------------
      S            10.00000          10.00000          12.51072
      D            10.15003          10.15003          15.40790
      L            10.65313          12.85000          12.85000


RIGHT HAND SIDE RANGES

  Constraint      Lower Limit      Current Value      Upper Limit
 ------------    -------------    ---------------    -------------
      1           538.40002         630.00000         682.36316
      2           543.24225         600.00000      No Upper Limit
      3           580.00140         708.00000         852.63159
      4           117.00012         135.00000         151.15410
```

computer software package, you may not see $D$ assume a positive value if you resolve the problem with an objective function coefficient of exactly 10.15003 for $D$—that is, the software package may show a different alternative optimal solution. However, if the profit contribution of $D$ is increased by *more than* $1.15003, then $D$ will not remain at zero in the optimal solution.

We also note from Figure 3.6 that the dual prices for constraints 3 and 4 are 8.1 and 19, respectively, indicating that these two constraints are binding in the optimal solution. Thus, each additional labor-hour in the finishing department would increase the value of the optimal solution by $8.10 and each additional labor-hour in the inspection and packaging department would increase the value of the optimal solution by $19.00. Because of a slack of 91.6 hours in the cutting and dyeing department and 32 hours in the sewing department (see Figure 3.6), management might want to consider the possibility of utilizing these unused labor-hours in the finishing or inspection and packaging departments. For example, some of the employees in the cutting and dyeing department could be used to perform certain operations in either the finishing department or the inspection and packaging department. In the future, Par's management may want to explore the possibility of cross-training employees so that unused capacity in one department could be shifted to other departments. In the next chapter we will consider similar modeling situations.

Suppose that after reviewing the solution shown in Figure 3.6, management states that they will not consider any solution that does not include the production of some deluxe bags. Management then decides to add the requirement that the number of deluxe bags produced must be at least 30% of the number of standard bags produced. Writing this requirement using the decision variables $S$ and $D$, we obtain

$$D \geq 0.3S$$

or

$$-0.3S + D \geq 0$$

Adding this new constraint to the modified Par, Inc., linear program and resolving the problem using The Management Scientist, we obtain the optimal solution shown in Figure 3.8.

Let us consider the interpretation of the dual price for constraint 5, the requirement that the number of deluxe bags produced must be at least 30% of the number of standard bags produced. The dual price of $-1.38$ indicates that a one-unit increase in the right-hand side of the constraint will lower profits by \$1.38. Thus, what the dual price of $-1.38$ is really telling us is what will happen to the value of the optimal solution if the constraint is changed to

$$D \geq 0.3S + 1$$

The correct interpretation of the dual price of $-1.38$ can now be stated as follows: If we are forced to produce one deluxe bag over and above the minimum 30% requirement, total profits will decrease by \$1.38. Conversely, if we relax the minimum 30% requirement by one bag ($D \geq 0.3S - 1$), total profits will increase by \$1.38.

The dual price for similar percentage (or ratio) constraints will not directly provide answers to questions concerning a percentage increase or decrease in the right-hand side of the constraint. For example, we might wonder what would happen to the value of the optimal solution if the number of deluxe bags has to be at least 31% of the number of standard bags. To answer such a question, we would resolve the problem using the constraint $-0.31S + D \geq 0$.

Because percentage (or ratio) constraints frequently occur in linear programming models, let us consider another example. For instance, suppose that Par's management states that the number of lightweight bags produced may not exceed 20% of the total golf bag production. Since the total production of golf bags is $S + D + L$, we can write this constraint as

$$L \leq 0.2(S + D + L)$$
$$L \leq 0.2S + 0.2D + 0.2L$$
$$-0.2S - 0.2D + 0.8L \leq 0$$

The solution obtained using The Management Scientist for the model that incorporates both the effects of this new percentage requirement and the previous requirement

| Figure 3.8 | THE MANAGEMENT SCIENTIST SOLUTION FOR THE MODIFIED PAR, INC., PROBLEM WITH THE 30% DELUXE-BAG REQUIREMENT |
|---|---|

```
Objective Function Value =            8183.87793

        Variable              Value              Reduced Costs
    --------------        --------------        -----------------
           S                335.99933               0.00000
           D                100.79980               0.00000
           L                304.80048               0.00000


      Constraint          Slack/Surplus             Dual Prices
    --------------        --------------        -----------------
           1                 50.16031               0.00000
           2                 43.20037               0.00000
           3                  0.00000               7.40998
           4                  0.00000              21.76006
           5                  0.00000              -1.38003


OBJECTIVE COEFFICIENT RANGES

     Variable        Lower Limit        Current Value        Upper Limit
   ------------     -------------      ---------------     --------------
        S              6.29500            10.00000            12.07007
        D             -3.35000             9.00000            10.15003
        L             11.90907            12.85000            18.14286


RIGHT HAND SIDE RANGES

   Constraint        Lower Limit        Current Value        Upper Limit
   ------------     -------------      ---------------     --------------
        1             579.83972           630.00000       No Upper Limit
        2             556.79962           600.00000       No Upper Limit
        3             540.00000           708.00000           765.00049
        4             103.24991           135.00000           147.00008
        5             -84.00000             0.00000           101.67704
```

$(-0.3S + D \geq 0)$ is shown in Figure 3.9. After rounding, the dual price corresponding to the new constraint (constraint 6) is 0.89. Thus, every additional lightweight bag we are allowed to produce over the current 20% limit will increase the value of the objective function by \$0.89; moreover, the right-hand-side range for this constraint shows that this interpretation is valid for increases of up to 156 units.

## The Bluegrass Farms Problem

To provide additional practice in formulating and interpreting the computer solution for linear programs involving more than two decision variables, we consider a minimization problem involving three decision variables. Bluegrass Farms, located in Lexington, Kentucky,

| Figure 3.9 | THE MANAGEMENT SCIENTIST SOLUTION FOR THE MODIFIED PAR, INC., PROBLEM INCORPORATING THE 20% LIGHTWEIGHT BAG REQUIREMENT AND THE 30% DELUXE BAG REQUIREMENT |
|---|---|

```
Objective Function Value =          8044.25488


      Variable              Value            Reduced Costs
   --------------     ---------------     ------------------
        S                403.44730              0.00000
        D                222.20738              0.00000
        L                156.41367              0.00000


     Constraint        Slack/Surplus          Dual Prices
   --------------     ---------------     ------------------
        1                  0.24859              0.00000
        2                 56.69057              0.00000
        3                  0.00000              8.87330
        4                  0.00000             13.05157
        5                101.17319              0.00000
        6                  0.00000              0.89226


OBJECTIVE COEFFICIENT RANGES

    Variable         Lower Limit       Current Value      Upper Limit
  ------------     ---------------    ---------------    ---------------
        S               3.13800          10.00000           12.07007
        D               6.47670           9.00000           10.15003
        L              11.90907          12.85000        No Upper Limit


RIGHT HAND SIDE RANGES

   Constraint        Lower Limit       Current Value      Upper Limit
  ------------     ---------------    ---------------    ---------------
       1             629.75140          630.00000        No Upper Limit
       2             543.30945          600.00000        No Upper Limit
       3             396.00146          708.00000          708.69653
       4             118.96714          135.00000          135.08900
       5          No Lower Limit          0.00000          101.17319
       6              -0.77936            0.00000          156.48053
```

has been experimenting with a special diet for its racehorses. The feed components available for the diet are a standard horse feed product, a vitamin-enriched oat product, and a new vitamin and mineral feed additive. The nutritional values in units per pound and the costs for the three feed components are summarized in Table 3.1; for example, each pound of the standard feed component contains 0.8 unit of ingredient A, 1 unit of ingredient B, and 0.1 units of ingredient C. The minimum daily diet requirements for each horse are three units of ingredient A, six units of ingredient B, and four units of ingredient C. In addition,

| Table 3.1 | NUTRITIONAL VALUE AND COST DATA FOR THE BLUEGRASS FARMS PROBLEM | | |
|---|---|---|---|
| Feed Component | Standard | Enriched Oat | Additive |
| Ingredient A | 0.8 | 0.2 | 0.0 |
| Ingredient B | 1.0 | 1.5 | 3.0 |
| Ingredient C | 0.1 | 0.6 | 2.0 |
| Cost per pound | $0.25 | $0.50 | $3.00 |

to control the weight of the horses, the total daily feed for a horse should not exceed 6 pounds. Bluegrass Farms would like to determine the minimum-cost mix that will satisfy the daily diet requirements.

## Formulation of the Bluegrass Farms Problem

To formulate a linear programming model for the Bluegrass Farms problem, we introduce the following three decision variables:

$$S = \text{number of pounds of the standard horse feed product}$$
$$E = \text{number of pounds of the enriched oat product}$$
$$A = \text{number of pounds of the vitamin and mineral feed additive}$$

Using the data in Table 3.1, the objective function for minimizing the total cost associated with the daily feed can be written as follows:

$$\min 0.25S + 0.50E + 3A$$

Since the minimum daily requirement for ingredient A is three units, we obtain the constraint

$$0.8S + 0.2E \geq 3$$

The constraint for ingredient B is

$$1.0S + 1.5E + 3.0A \geq 6$$

and the constraint for ingredient C is

$$0.1S + 0.6E + 2.0A \geq 4$$

Finally, the constraint that restricts the mix to at most 6 pounds is

$$S + E + A \leq 6$$

Combining all the constraints with the nonnegativity requirements enables us to write the complete linear programming model for the Bluegrass Farms problem as follows:

$$\text{Min} \quad 0.25S + 0.50E + 3A$$

s.t.

$$
\begin{array}{rll}
0.8S + 0.2E & \geq 3 & \text{Ingredient A} \\
1.0S + 1.5E + 3.0A & \geq 6 & \text{Ingredient B} \\
0.1S + 0.6E + 2.0A & \geq 4 & \text{Ingredient C} \\
S + E + A & \leq 6 & \text{Weight} \\
S, E, A \geq 0 &
\end{array}
$$

## Computer Solution and Interpretation for the Bluegrass Farms Problem

The output obtained using The Management Scientist to solve the Bluegrass Farms problem is shown in Figure 3.10. After rounding, we see that the optimal solution calls for a daily diet consisting of 3.51 pounds of the standard horse feed product, 0.95 pound of the enriched oat product, and 1.54 pounds of the vitamin and mineral feed additive. Thus, with feed component costs of $0.25, $0.50, and $3.00, the total cost of the optimal diet is

$$
\begin{aligned}
3.51 \text{ pounds @ } \$0.25 \text{ per pound} &= \$0.88 \\
0.95 \text{ pound @ } \$0.50 \text{ per pound} &= 0.47 \\
1.54 \text{ pounds @ } \$3.00 \text{ per pound} &= \underline{4.62} \\
\text{Total cost} &= \$5.97
\end{aligned}
$$

Note that after rounding, this result is the same as the objective function value in the computer output (Figure 3.10).

Looking at the Slack/Surplus section of the computer output, we find a value of 3.554 for constraint 2. Since constraint 2 is a greater-than-or-equal-to constraint, 3.554 is the surplus; the optimal solution exceeds the minimum daily diet requirement for ingredient B (six units) by 3.554 units. Because the surplus values for constraints 1 and 3 are both zero, we see that the optimal diet just meets the minimum requirements for ingredients A and C; moreover, a slack value of zero for constraint 4 shows that the optimal solution provides a total daily feed weight of 6 pounds.

The dual price (after rounding) for the ingredient A constraint (constraint 1) is $-1.22$. To interpret this value properly, we first look at the sign; it is negative, and therefore we know that increasing the right-hand side of constraint 1 will cause the solution value to worsen. Since this is a minimization problem, "worsen" means that the total daily cost will increase. A one-unit increase in the right-hand side of constraint 1 will increase the total cost of the daily diet by $1.22. Conversely, it is also correct to conclude that a decrease of one unit in the right-hand side will decrease the total cost by $1.22. Looking at the RIGHT HAND SIDE RANGES section of the computer output, we see that these interpretations are correct as long as the right-hand side is between 1.143 and 3.368.

Suppose that the Bluegrass management is willing to reconsider their position regarding the maximum weight of the daily diet. The dual price of 0.92 (after rounding) for constraint 4 shows that a one-unit increase in the right-hand side of constraint 4 will reduce total cost by $0.92. The RIGHT HAND SIDE RANGES section of the output shows that this interpretation is correct for increases in the right-hand side up to a maximum of 8.478 pounds. Thus, the effect of increasing the right-hand side of constraint 4 from 6 to 8 pounds is a decrease in the total daily cost of $2 \times \$0.92$ or $1.84. Keep in mind that if this change were made, the feasible region would change, and we would obtain a new optimal solution.

**Figure 3.10    THE MANAGEMENT SCIENTIST SOLUTION FOR THE BLUEGRASS FARMS PROBLEM**

```
Objective Function Value =            5.973

        Variable              Value           Reduced Costs
     --------------      --------------      ------------------
           S                 3.514               0.000
           E                 0.946               0.000
           A                 1.541               0.000

       Constraint         Slack/Surplus          Dual Prices
     --------------      --------------      ------------------
           1                 0.000              -1.216
           2                 3.554               0.000
           3                 0.000              -1.959
           4                 0.000               0.919

OBJECTIVE COEFFICIENT RANGES

      Variable        Lower Limit      Current Value      Upper Limit
     ------------    --------------    --------------    --------------
          S              -0.393            0.250       No Upper Limit
          E          No Lower Limit        0.500            0.925
          A               1.522            3.000       No Upper Limit

RIGHT HAND SIDE RANGES

     Constraint       Lower Limit      Current Value      Upper Limit
     ------------    --------------    --------------    --------------
          1               1.143            3.000            3.368
          2          No Lower Limit        6.000            9.554
          3               2.100            4.000            4.875
          4               5.562            6.000            8.478
```

The OBJECTIVE COEFFICIENT RANGES section of the computer output shows a lower limit of −0.393 for S. Clearly, in a real problem, the objective function coefficient of S (the cost of the standard horse feed product) cannot take on a negative value. So, from a practical point of view, we can think of the lower limit for the objective function coefficient of S as being zero. We can thus conclude that no matter how much the cost of the standard mix were to decrease, the optimal solution would not change. Even if Bluegrass Farms could obtain the standard horse feed product for free, the optimal solution would still specify a daily diet of 3.51 pounds of the standard horse feed product, 0.95 pound of the enriched oat product, and 1.54 pounds of the vitamin and mineral feed additive. However, any decrease in the per-unit cost of the standard feed would result in a decrease in the total cost for the optimal daily diet.

Note that the objective function coefficient values for S and A have no upper limit. Even if the cost of A were to increase, for example, from $3.00 to $13.00 per pound, the optimal solution would not change; the total cost of the solution, however, would increase by $10 (the amount of the increase) times 1.541 or $15.41. You must always keep in mind that the interpretations we have made using the sensitivity analysis information in the computer output are only appropriate if all other coefficients in the problem do not change. To consider simultaneous changes we must use the 100 percent rule or resolve the problem after making the changes.

## 3.5    THE ELECTRONICS COMMUNICATION PROBLEM

The Electronic Communications problem introduced in this section is a maximization problem involving four decision variables, two less-than-or-equal-to constraints, one equality constraint, and one greater-than-or-equal-to constraint. Our objective is to provide a summary of the process of formulating a mathematical model, using The Management Scientist to obtain an optimal solution, and interpreting the solution and sensitivity report information. In the next chapter we will continue to illustrate how linear programming can be applied by showing additional examples from the areas of marketing, finance, and production management. The Management Science in Action: An Optimal Wood Procurement Policy illustrates the diversity of problem situations to which linear programming can be applied. In this application, Wellborn Cabinet, Inc., was able to reduce annual raw material costs for one of its production systems by $412,000 as a result of formulating and solving a linear programming model. Your ability to formulate, solve, and interpret the solution to problems like the Electronics Communication problem is critical to understanding how more complex problems, such as the one encountered by Wellborn Cabinet, Inc., can be modeled using linear programming.

# MANAGEMENT SCIENCE IN ACTION

### AN OPTIMAL WOOD PROCUREMENT POLICY*

Wellborn Cabinet, Inc., operates an integrated sawmill and cabinet manufacturing system in Alabama. Its manufacturing facility consists of a sawmill, four dry kilns, and a wood cabinet assembly plant; the assembly plant includes a rough mill for producing cabinet components that are referred to as blanks. Because of the pressure to market quality products at competitive prices, a major concern for Wellborn Cabinet is to maintain consistency in product quality. A key factor in maintaining this quality depends on controlling the quality and costs of raw materials.

To produce blanks, Wellborn Cabinet purchases #1 and #2 grade hardwood logs, as well as #1 and #2 dry or green common grade lumber. During a typical five-day week of operation, the sawmill can process up to 1550 logs with a small-end diameter from 9 to 22 inches. Usually, the lumber is purchased in bundles containing random sizes. Both the logs processed by the sawmill and the green lumber purchased from outside suppliers are dried at the kilns to an average moisture

content of 7%; the dried material is then planed and converted into about 130 different sizes of blanks at the rough mill.

Wellborn developed a linear programming model of the blank production system. The objective was to determine a procurement plan that would minimize the total cost of producing blanks for a five-day work week. Constraints included capacities of the sawmill and dry kilns, the demand for blanks at the manufacturing plant, and the available supply of raw materials. The initial results indicate that the company can minimize the total cost of producing blanks by purchasing only #2 grade logs and #2 common green lumber; approximately 88% of the rough mill dry lumber requirements should come from #2 grade logs and the rest from purchased #2 common green lumber. The projected annual savings in raw material costs were $412,000.

*Based on H. F. Carino and C. H. LeNoir, Jr., "Optimizing Wood Procurement in Cabinet Manufacturing," *Interfaces* (March–April 1988): 10–19

Electronic Communications manufactures portable radio systems that can be used for two-way communications. The company's new product, which has a range of up to 25 miles, is particularly suitable for use in a variety of business and personal applications. The distribution channels for the new radio are as follows:

1. Marine equipment distributors
2. Business equipment distributors
3. National chain of retail stores
4. Direct mail

Because of differing distribution and promotional costs, the profitability of the product will vary with the distribution channel. In addition, the advertising cost and the personal sales effort required will vary with the distribution channels. Table 3.2 summarizes the contribution to profit, advertising cost, and personal sales effort data pertaining to the Electronic Communications problem. The firm has set the advertising budget at $5000 and there is a maximum of 1800 hours of sales force time available for allocation to the sales effort. Management has also decided to produce exactly 600 units for the current production period. Finally, an ongoing contract with the national chain of retail stores requires that at least 150 units be distributed through this distribution channel.

Electronic Communications is now faced with the problem of establishing a strategy that will provide for the distribution of the radios in such a way that overall profitability of the new radio production will be maximized. Decisions must be made as to how many units should be allocated to each of the four distribution channels, as well as how to allocate the advertising budget and salesforce effort to each of the four distribution channels.

### Problem Formulation

We will now write the objective function and the constraints for the Electronic Communications problem. For the objective function, we can write

Objective function: Maximize profit

Four constraints appear necessary for this problem. They are necessary because of (1) a limited advertising budget, (2) limited salesforce availability, (3) a production requirement, and (4) a retail stores distribution requirement.

**Constraint 1**  Advertising expenditures ≤ Budget
**Constraint 2**  Sales time used ≤ Time available

**Table 3.2  PROFIT, ADVERTISING COST, AND PERSONAL SALES TIME DATA FOR THE ELECTRONIC COMMUNICATIONS PROBLEM**

| Distribution Channel | Profit per Unit Sold | Advertising Cost per Unit Sold | Personal Sales Effort per Unit Sold |
|---|---|---|---|
| Marine distributors | $90 | $10 | 2 hours |
| Business distributors | $84 | $8 | 3 hours |
| National retail stores | $70 | $9 | 3 hours |
| Direct mail | $60 | $15 | None |

**Constraint 3**   Radios produced = Management requirement

**Constraint 4**   Retail distribution ≥ Contract requirement

These expressions provide descriptions of the objective function and the constraints. We are now ready to define the decision variables that will represent the decisions the manager must make.

For the Electronic Communications problem, we introduce the following four decision variables:

$M$ = the number of units produced for the marine equipment distribution channel

$B$ = the number of units produced for the business equipment distribution channel

$R$ = the number of units produced for the national retail chain distribution channel

$D$ = the number of units produced for the direct mail distribution channel

Using the data in Table 3.2, the objective function for maximizing the total contribution to profit associated with the radios can be written as follows:

$$\text{Max } 90M + 84B + 70R + 60D$$

Let us now develop a mathematical statement of the constraints for the problem. Since the advertising budget has been set at \$5000, the constraint that limits the amount of advertising expenditure can be written as follows:

$$10M + 8B + 9R + 15D \leq 5000$$

Similarly, since the sales time is limited to 1800 hours, we obtain the constraint

$$2M + 3B + 3R \leq 1800$$

Management's decision to produce exactly 600 units during the current production period is expressed as

$$M + B + R + D = 600$$

Finally, to account for the fact that the number of units distributed by the national chain of retail stores must be at least 150, we add the constraint

$$R \geq 150$$

Combining all of the constraints with the nonnegativity requirements enables us to write the complete linear programming model for the Electronic Communications problem as follows:

$$
\begin{aligned}
\text{Max} \quad & 90M + 84B + 70R + 60D \\
\text{s.t.} \quad & \\
& 10M + 8B + 9R + 15D \leq 5000 \quad \text{Advertising budget} \\
& 2M + 3B + 3R \leq 1800 \quad \text{Salesforce availability} \\
& M + B + R + D = 600 \quad \text{Production level} \\
& R \geq 150 \quad \text{Retail stores requirement} \\
& M, B, R, D \geq 0
\end{aligned}
$$

## Computer Solution and Interpretation

A portion of the output obtained using The Management Scientist to solve the Electronic Communications problem is shown in Figure 3.11. The Objective Function Value section shows that the optimal solution to the problem will provide a maximum profit of $48,450. The optimal values of the decision variables are given by $M = 25$, $B = 425$, $R = 150$, and $D = 0$. Thus, the optimal strategy for Electronic Communications is to concentrate on the business equipment distribution channel with $B = 425$ units. In addition, the firm should allocate 25 units to the marine distribution channel ($M = 25$) and meet its 150-unit commitment to the national retail chain store distribution channel ($R = 150$). With $D = 0$, the optimal solution indicates that the firm should not use the direct mail distribution channel.

Now consider the information contained in the Reduced Costs column. Recall that the reduced costs indicate how much each objective function coefficient would have to improve before the corresponding decision variable could assume a positive value in the optimal solution. As the computer output shows, the first three reduced costs are zero because the corresponding decision variables already have positive values in the optimal solution. However, the reduced cost of 45 for decision variable $D$ tells us that the profit for the new radios distributed via the direct mail channel would have to increase from its current value of $60 per unit to at least $60 + $45 = $105 per unit before it would be profitable to use the direct mail distribution channel.

The computer output information for the slack/surplus variables and the dual prices is restated here:

| Constraint Number | Constraint Name | Type of Constraint | Slack or Surplus | Dual Price |
|---|---|---|---|---|
| 1 | Advertising budget | ≤ | 0 | 3 |
| 2 | Salesforce availability | ≤ | 25 | 0 |
| 3 | Production level | = | 0 | 60 |
| 4 | Retail stores requirement | ≥ | 0 | −17 |

The advertising budget constraint has a slack of zero, indicating that the entire budget of $5000 has been used. The corresponding dual price of 3 tells us that an additional dollar added to the advertising budget will improve the objective function (increase the profit) by $3. Thus, the possibility of increasing the advertising budget should be seriously considered by the firm. The slack of 25 hours for the salesforce availability constraint shows that the allocated 1800 hours of sales time are adequate to distribute the radios produced and that 25 hours of sales time will remain unused. Since the production level constraint is an equality, the zero slack/surplus shown on the output is expected. However, the dual price of 60 associated with this constraint shows that if the firm were to consider increasing the production level for the radios, the value of the objective function, or profit, would improve at the rate of $60 per radio produced. Finally, the surplus of zero associated with the retail store distribution channel commitment is a result of this constraint being binding. The negative dual price indicates that increasing the commitment from 150 to 151 units will actually decrease the profit by $17. Thus, Electronic Communications may want to consider reducing its commitment to the retail store distribution channel. A *decrease* in the commitment will actually improve profit at the rate of $17 per unit.

*Figure* **3.11**

**A PORTION OF THE MANAGEMENT SCIENTIST COMPUTER OUTPUT FOR THE ELECTRONIC COMMUNICATIONS PROBLEM**

```
Objective Function Value =            48450.000

        Variable              Value              Reduced Costs
    --------------        ---------------        ------------------
           M                  25.000                  0.000
           B                 425.000                  0.000
           R                 150.000                  0.000
           D                   0.000                 45.000


       Constraint         Slack/Surplus             Dual Prices
    --------------        ---------------        ------------------
           1                   0.000                  3.000
           2                  25.000                  0.000
           3                   0.000                 60.000
           4                   0.000                -17.000
```

We now consider the additional sensitivity analysis information provided by the computer output shown in Figure 3.12. The ranges of optimality for the objective function coefficients are

$$84 \leq C_M < \text{No upper limit}$$
$$50 \leq C_B \leq 90$$
$$\text{No lower limit} < C_R \leq 87$$
$$\text{No lower limit} < C_D \leq 105$$

The current solution, or strategy, remains optimal, provided that the objective function coefficients remain in the given ranges of optimality. Note in particular the range of optimality associated with the direct mail distribution channel coefficient, $C_D$. This information is consistent with the earlier observation for the Reduced Costs portion of the output. In both instances, we see that the per-unit profit would have to increase to $105 before the direct mail distribution channel could be in the optimal solution with a positive value.

Finally, the sensitivity analysis information on RIGHT HAND SIDE RANGES, as shown in Figure 3.12, provides the ranges of feasibility for the right-hand-side values.

| Constraint | Min RHS | Current Value | Max RHS |
|---|---|---|---|
| Advertising budget | 4950 | 5000 | 5850 |
| Salesforce | 1775 | 1800 | No upper limit |
| Production level | 515 | 600 | 603.57 |
| Retail stores requirement | 0 | 150 | 200 |

---

**Figure 3.12** — OBJECTIVE COEFFICIENT AND RIGHT-HAND-SIDE RANGES PROVIDED BY THE MANAGEMENT SCIENTIST FOR THE ELECTRONIC COMMUNICATIONS PROBLEM

OBJECTIVE COEFFICIENT RANGES

| Variable | Lower Limit | Current Value | Upper Limit |
|---|---|---|---|
| M | 84.000 | 90.000 | No Upper Limit |
| B | 50.000 | 84.000 | 90.000 |
| R | No Lower Limit | 70.000 | 87.000 |
| D | No Lower Limit | 60.000 | 105.000 |

RIGHT HAND SIDE RANGES

| Constraint | Lower Limit | Current Value | Upper Limit |
|---|---|---|---|
| 1 | 4950.000 | 5000.000 | 5850.000 |
| 2 | 1775.000 | 1800.000 | No Upper Limit |
| 3 | 515.000 | 600.000 | 603.571 |
| 4 | 0.000 | 150.000 | 200.000 |

Do you feel comfortable interpreting the computer output for problems involving more than two decision variables? Try Problems 8 and 9.

Several interpretations of these ranges are possible. In particular, recall that the dual price for the advertising budget enabled us to conclude that each $1 increase in the budget would improve the profit by $3. The range for the advertising budget shows that this statement about the value of increasing the budget is appropriate up to an advertising budget of $5850. Increases above this level would not necessarily be beneficial. Also note that the dual price of −17 for the retail stores requirement suggested the desirability of reducing this commitment. The range of feasibility for this constraint shows that the commitment could be reduced to zero and the value of the reduction would be at the rate of $17 per unit.

Again, the *sensitivity analysis* or *postoptimality analysis* provided by computer software packages for linear programming problems considers only *one change at a time,* with all other coefficients of the problem remaining as originally specified. As mentioned earlier, simultaneous changes can sometimes be analyzed without resolving the problem, provided that the cumulative changes are not large enough to violate the 100 percent rule.

Finally, recall that the complete solution to the Electronic Communications problem requested information not only on the number of units to be distributed over each channel, but also on the allocation of the advertising budget and the salesforce effort to each distribution channel. Since the optimal solution is $M = 25$, $B = 425$, $R = 150$, and $D = 0$, we can simply evaluate each term in a given constraint to determine how much of the constraint resource is allocated to each distribution channel. For example, the advertising budget constraint of

$$10M + 8B + 9R + 15D \leq 5000$$

# MANAGEMENT SCIENCE IN ACTION

## USING LINEAR PROGRAMMING FOR TRAFFIC CONTROL*

The Hanshin Expressway was the first urban toll expressway in Osaka, Japan. Although in 1964 its length was only 2.3 kilometers, today it is a large-scale urban expressway network of 200 kilometers. The Hanshin Expressway provides service for the Hanshin (Osaka-Kobe) area, the second-most populated area in Japan. An average of 828,000 vehicles use the expressway each day, with daily traffic sometimes exceeding 1,000,000 vehicles. In 1990, the Hanshin Expressway Public Corporation started using an automated traffic control system in order to maximize the number of vehicles flowing into the expressway network.

The automated traffic control system relies on two control methods: (1) limiting the number of cars that enter the expressway at each entrance ramp; and (2) providing drivers with up-to-date and accurate traffic information, including expected travel times and information about accidents. The approach used to limit the number of vehicles depends upon whether the expressway is in a normal or steady state of operation, or whether some type of unusual event, such as an accident or a breakdown, has occurred.

In the first phase of the steady-state case, the Hanshin system uses a linear programming model to maximize the total number of vehicles entering the system, while preventing traffic congestion and adverse effects on surrounding road networks. The data that drive the linear programming model are collected from detectors installed every 500 meters along the expressway and at all entrance and exit ramps. Every five minutes the real-time data collected from the detectors are used to update the model coefficients, and a new linear program computes the maximum number of vehicles the expressway can accommodate.

The automated traffic control system has been very successful. According to surveys, traffic control has decreased the length of congested portions of the expressway by 30 percent and the duration by 20 percent. It has proved to be extremely cost effective, and drivers consider it an indispensable service.

*Based on T. Yoshino, T. Sasaki, and T. Hasegawa, "The Traffic-Control System on the Hanshin Expressway," *Interfaces* (January–February 1995): 94–108.

---

shows that $10M = 10(25) = \$250$, $8B = 8(425) = \$3400$, $9R = 9(150) = \$1350$, and $15D = 15(0) = \$0$. Thus, the advertising budget allocations are, respectively, $250, $3400, $1350, and $0 for each of the four distribution channels. Making similar calculations for the salesforce constraint results in the managerial summary of the Electronic Communications optimal solution as shown in Table 3.3.

| *Table* 3.3 | PROFIT-MAXIMIZING STRATEGY FOR THE ELECTRONIC COMMUNICATIONS PROBLEM | | |
|---|---|---|---|
| Distribution Channel | Volume | Advertising Allocation | Salesforce Allocation (hours) |
| Marine distributors | 25 | $ 250 | 50 |
| Business distributors | 425 | 3400 | 1275 |
| National retail stores | 150 | 1350 | 450 |
| Direct mail | 0 | 0 | 0 |
| Totals | 600 | $5000 | 1775 |
| Projected total profit = $48,450 | | | |

......................................................................................................../  /..............

## SUMMARY

We began the chapter with a discussion of sensitivity analysis: The study of how changes in the coefficients of a linear program affect the optimal solution. First, we showed how a graphical method can be used to determine how a change in one of the objective function coefficients or a change in the right-hand-side value for a constraint will affect the optimal solution to the problem. Because graphical sensitivity analysis is limited to linear programs with two decision variables, we showed how The Management Scientist can be used to produce a sensitivity report containing the same information.

We continued our discussion of problem formulation, sensitivity analysis, and the interpretation of the solution by introducing several modifications of the Par, Inc., problem. They involved an additional decision variable and several types of percentage, or ratio, constraints. Then, in order to provide additional practice in formulating and interpreting the solution for linear programs involving more than two decision variables, we introduced the Bluegrass Farms problem, a minimization problem involving three decision variables. In the last section we summarized all the work to date using the Electronic Communications problem, a maximization problem with four decision variables, two less-than-or-equal-to constraints, one equality constraint, and one greater-than-or-equal-to constraint.

The Management Science in Action: Using Linear Programming for Traffic Control provides just one of many examples of the widespread use of linear programming. In the next chapter we will see many more applications of linear programming.

......................................................................................................../  /..............

## GLOSSARY

**Sensitivity analysis** The evaluation of how changes in the coefficients of a linear programming problem affect the optimal solution to the problem.

**Range of optimality** The range of values over which an objective function coefficient may vary without causing any change in the values of the decision variables in the optimal solution.

**Dual price** The improvement in the value of the objective function per-unit increase in a constraint right-hand side.

**Reduced cost** The amount by which an objective function coefficient would have to improve (increase for a maximization problem, decrease for a minimization problem) before it would be possible for the corresponding variable to assume a positive value in the optimal solution.

**Range of feasibility** The range of values over which a right-hand side may vary without changing the value and interpretation of the dual price.

**100 percent rule** A rule indicating when simultaneous changes in two or more objective function coefficients will not cause a change in the optimal values for the decision variables. It can also be applied to indicate when two or more right-hand-side changes will not cause a change in any of the dual prices.

**Sunk cost** A cost that is not affected by the decision made. It will be incurred no matter what values the decision variables assume.

**Relevant cost** A cost that depends upon the decision made. The amount of a relevant cost will vary depending on the values of the decision variables.

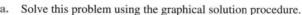

# PROBLEMS

1.  Recall the RMC problem (Chapter 2, Problem 21). Letting

$$F = \text{tons of fuel additive}$$
$$S = \text{tons of solvent base}$$

leads to the formulation

$$\text{Max} \quad 40F + 30S$$

s.t.

$$\tfrac{2}{5}F + \tfrac{1}{2}S \leq 20 \quad \text{Material 1}$$
$$\tfrac{1}{5}S \leq 5 \quad \text{Material 2}$$
$$\tfrac{3}{5}F + \tfrac{3}{10}S \leq 21 \quad \text{Material 3}$$
$$F, S \geq 0$$

Use the graphical sensitivity analysis approach to determine the range of optimality for the objective function coefficients.

2.  For Problem 1 use the graphical sensitivity approach to determine what happens if an additional 3 tons of material 3 become available. What is the corresponding dual price for the constraint?

**SELF TEST**

3.  Consider the following linear program:

$$\text{Max} \quad 2x_1 + 3x_2$$

s.t.

$$x_1 + x_2 \leq 10$$
$$2x_1 + x_2 \geq 4$$
$$x_1 + 3x_2 \leq 24$$
$$2x_1 + x_2 \leq 16$$
$$x_1, x_2 \geq 0$$

   a.  Solve this problem using the graphical solution procedure.
   b.  Compute the range of optimality for the objective function coefficient of $x_1$.
   c.  Compute the range of optimality for the objective function coefficient $x_2$.
   d.  Suppose the objective function coefficient of $x_1$ is increased from 2 to 2.5. What is the new optimal solution?
   e.  Suppose the objective function coefficient of $x_2$ is decreased from 3 to 1. What is the new optimal solution?

4.  Refer to Problem 3. Compute the dual prices for constraints 1 and 2 and interpret them.

**SELF TEST**
**(PROBLEM 4)**

5.  Consider the following linear program:

$$\text{Min} \quad x_1 + x_2$$

s.t.

$$x_1 + 2x_2 \geq 7$$
$$2x_1 + x_2 \geq 5$$
$$x_1 + 6x_2 \geq 11$$
$$x_1, x_2 \geq 0$$

a.  Solve this problem using the graphical solution procedure.
b.  Compute the range of optimality for the objective function coefficient of $x_1$.
c.  Compute the range of optimality for the objective function coefficient of $x_2$.
d.  Suppose the objective function coefficient of $x_1$ is increased to 1.5. Find the new optimal solution.
e.  Suppose the objective function coefficient of $x_2$ is decreased to $\frac{1}{3}$. Find the new optimal solution.

6.  Refer to Problem 5. Compute and interpret the dual prices for the constraints.

7.  Consider the following linear program:

$$\text{Max} \quad 5x_1 + 7x_2$$

s.t.

$$2x_1 + x_2 \geq 3$$
$$-x_1 + 5x_2 \geq 4$$
$$2x_1 - 3x_2 \leq 6$$
$$3x_1 + 2x_2 \leq 35$$
$$\tfrac{3}{7}x_1 + x_2 \leq 10$$
$$x_1, x_2 \geq 0$$

a.  Solve this problem using the graphical solution procedure.
b.  Compute the range of optimality for the objective function coefficient of $x_1$.
c.  Compute the range of optimality for the objective function coefficient $x_2$.
d.  Suppose the objective function coefficient of $x_1$ is decreased to 2. What is the new optimal solution?
e.  Suppose the objective function coefficient of $x_2$ is increased to 10. What is the new optimal solution?

8.  Refer to Problem 7. Suppose that the objective function coefficient for $x_2$ is reduced to 3.
a.  Resolve using the graphical solution procedure.
b.  Compute the dual prices for constraints 2 and 3.

9.  Refer again to Problem 3.
a.  Suppose the objective function coefficient of $x_1$ is increased to 3 and the objective function coefficient of $x_2$ is increased to 4. Find the new optimal solution.
b.  Suppose the objective function coefficient of $x_1$ is increased to 3 and the objective function coefficient of $x_2$ is decreased to 2. Find the new optimal solution.

10. Refer again to Problem 7.
a.  Suppose the objective function coefficient of $x_1$ is decreased to 4 and the objective function coefficient of $x_2$ is increased to 10. Find the new optimal solution.
b.  Suppose the objective function coefficient of $x_1$ is decreased to 4 and the objective function coefficient of $x_2$ is increased to 8. Find the new optimal solution.

**SELF TEST**

11. Recall the Kelson Sporting Equipment problem (Chapter 2, Problem 22). Letting

$$R = \text{number of regular gloves}$$
$$C = \text{number of catcher's mitts}$$

leads to the following formulation:

$$\text{Max} \quad 5R + 8C$$

s.t.

| | | |
|---|---|---|
| $R + \frac{3}{2}C \leq 900$ | Cutting and sewing |
| $\frac{1}{2}R + \frac{1}{3}C \leq 300$ | Finishing |
| $\frac{1}{8}R + \frac{1}{4}C \leq 100$ | Packaging and shipping |
| $R, C \geq 0$ | |

The computer solution obtained using The Management Scientist is shown in Figure 3.13.
   a.   What is the optimal solution, and what is the value of the total profit contribution?
   b.   Which constraints are binding?
   c.   What are the dual prices for the resources? Interpret each.
   d.   If overtime can be scheduled in one of the departments, where would you recommend doing so?

12.   Refer to the computer solution of the Kelson Sporting Equipment problem in Figure 3.13 (see Problem 11).
   a.   Compute the ranges of optimality for the objective function coefficients.
   b.   Interpret the ranges in part (a).
   c.   Interpret the range of feasibility for the right-hand sides.
   d.   How much will the value of the optimal solution improve if 20 extra hours of packaging and shipping time are made available?

13.   Recall the Investment Advisors problem (Chapter 2, Problem 25). Letting

$$U = \text{shares of U.S. Oil}$$
$$H = \text{shares of Hub Properties}$$

---

**Figure 3.13**     **THE MANAGEMENT SCIENTIST SOLUTION FOR THE KELSON SPORTING EQUIPMENT PROBLEM**

```
Objective Function Value =          3700.00146

        Variable              Value              Reduced Costs
     --------------      --------------        ------------------
          R                500.00153                0.00000
          C                149.99924                0.00000

       Constraint         Slack/Surplus             Dual Prices
     --------------      --------------        ------------------
          1                174.99962                0.00000
          2                  0.00000                2.99999
          3                  0.00000               28.00006

OBJECTIVE COEFFICIENT RANGES

     Variable          Lower Limit        Current Value        Upper Limit
   ------------      --------------      --------------      --------------
        R                4.00000             5.00000            12.00012
        C                3.33330             8.00000            10.00000

RIGHT HAND SIDE RANGES

    Constraint         Lower Limit        Current Value        Upper Limit
   ------------      --------------      --------------      --------------
        1              725.00037           900.00000        No Upper Limit
        2              133.33199           300.00000           400.00000
        3               75.00000           100.00000           134.99982
```

leads to the following formulation:

$$\text{Max} \quad 3U + 5H \qquad\qquad \text{Maximize total annual return}$$

s.t.

$$25U + 50H \le 80{,}000 \quad \text{Funds available}$$
$$0.50U + 0.25H \le \quad 700 \quad \text{Risk maximum}$$
$$1U \qquad\quad \le \quad 1000 \quad \text{U.S. Oil maximum}$$
$$U, H \ge 0$$

The computer solution of this problem is shown in Figure 3.14.

a.    What is the optimal solution, and what is the value of the total estimated annual return?

b.    Which constraints are binding? What is your interpretation of these constraints in terms of the problem?

c.    What are the dual prices for the constraints? Interpret each.

d.    Would it be beneficial to relax the constraint on the amount invested in U.S. Oil? Why or why not?

---

**Figure 3.14    THE MANAGEMENT SCIENTIST SOLUTION FOR THE INVESTMENT ADVISORS PROBLEM**

```
Objective Function Value =          8400.000

        Variable              Value              Reduced Costs
        --------              -----              -------------
          U                 800.000                 0.000
          H                1200.000                 0.000

       Constraint        Slack/Surplus             Dual Prices
       ----------        -------------             -----------
          1                 0.000                   0.093
          2                 0.000                   1.333
          3               200.000                   0.000
```

OBJECTIVE COEFFICIENT RANGES

| Variable | Lower Limit | Current Value | Upper Limit |
|----------|-------------|---------------|-------------|
| U | 2.500 | 3.000 | 10.000 |
| H | 1.500 | 5.000 | 6.000 |

RIGHT HAND SIDE RANGES

| Constraint | Lower Limit | Current Value | Upper Limit |
|------------|-------------|---------------|-------------|
| 1 | 65000.000 | 80000.000 | 140000.000 |
| 2 | 400.000 | 700.000 | 775.000 |
| 3 | 800.000 | 1000.000 | No Upper Limit |

14. Refer to Figure 3.14, which shows the computer solution of Problem 13.
   a. How much would the estimated per-share return for U.S. Oil have to increase before it would be beneficial to increase the investment in this stock?
   b. How much would the estimated per-share return for Hub Properties have to decrease before it would be beneficial to reduce the investment in this stock?
   c. How much would the total annual return be reduced if the U.S. Oil maximum were reduced to 900 shares?

15. Recall the Tom's Inc., problem (Chapter 2, Problem 26). Letting

$$W = \text{jars of Western Foods Salsa}$$
$$M = \text{jars of Mexico City Salsa}$$

leads to the formulation:

$$\text{Max} \quad 1W + 1.25M$$

s.t.

| | | | |
|---|---|---|---|
| $5W +$ | $7M \leq 4480$ | Whole tomatoes |
| $3W +$ | $1M \leq 2080$ | Tomato sauce |
| $2W +$ | $2M \leq 1600$ | Tomato paste |
| $W, M \geq 0$ | | |

The Management Scientist solution is shown in Figure 3.15.
   a. What is the optimal solution, and what are the optimal production quantities?
   b. Specify the range of optimality for the objective function coefficients.
   c. What are the dual prices for each constraint? Interpret each.
   d. Identify the range of feasibility for each of the right-hand-side values.

**SELF TEST**

16. Recall the Innis Investments problem (Chapter 2, Problem 37). Letting

$$S = \text{units purchased in the stock fund}$$
$$M = \text{units purchased in the money market fund}$$

leads to the following formulation:

$$\text{Min} \quad 8S + 3M$$

s.t.

| | | | |
|---|---|---|---|
| $50S + 100M \leq 1{,}200{,}000$ | Funds available |
| $5S + 4M \geq 60{,}000$ | Annual income |
| $M \geq 3{,}000$ | Units in money market |
| $S, M \geq 0$ | |

The computer solution is shown in Figure 3.16.
   a. What is the optimal solution, and what is the minimum total risk?
   b. Specify the range of optimality for the objective function coefficients.
   c. How much annual income will be earned by the portfolio?
   d. What is the rate of return for the portfolio?
   e. What is the dual price for the funds available constraint?
   f. What is the marginal rate of return on extra funds added to the portfolio?

**Figure 3.15**  THE MANAGEMENT SCIENTIST SOLUTION FOR THE TOM'S, INC., PROBLEM

```
OPTIMAL SOLUTION

Objective Function Value =          860.000

        Variable              Value              Reduced Costs
     --------------      ---------------      ------------------
           W                  560.000                  0.000
           M                  240.000                  0.000

       Constraint         Slack/Surplus            Dual Prices
     --------------      ---------------      ------------------
            1                  0.000                   0.125
            2                160.000                   0.000
            3                  0.000                   0.187

OBJECTIVE COEFFICIENT RANGES

     Variable       Lower Limit      Current Value       Upper Limit
   ------------   --------------   ---------------    ----------------
        W              0.893            1.000              1.250
        M              1.000            1.250              1.400

RIGHT HAND SIDE RANGES

   Constraint      Lower Limit      Current Value       Upper Limit
   ------------   --------------   ---------------    ----------------
        1            4320.000          4480.000           5600.000
        2            1920.000          2080.000       No Upper Limit
        3            1280.000          1600.000           1640.000
```

17. Refer to Problem 16 and the computer solution shown in Figure 3.16.
    a. Suppose the risk index for the stock fund (the value of $C_S$) increases from its current value of 8 to 12. How does the optimal solution change, if at all?
    b. Suppose the risk index for the money market fund (the value of $C_M$) increases from its current value of 3 to 3.5. How does the optimal solution change, if at all?
    c. Suppose $C_S$ increases to 12 and $C_M$ increases to 3.3. How does the optimal solution change, if at all?

**SELF TEST**

18. Suppose that in a product-mix problem $x_1$, $x_2$, $x_3$, and $x_4$ indicate the units of products 1, 2, 3, and 4, respectively, and the linear program is

$$\text{Max} \quad 4x_1 + 6x_2 + 3x_3 + 1x_4$$

s.t.

$$1.5x_1 + 2x_2 + 4x_3 + 3x_4 \leq 550 \quad \text{Machine A hours}$$
$$4x_1 + 1x_2 + 2x_3 + 1x_4 \leq 700 \quad \text{Machine B hours}$$
$$2x_1 + 3x_2 + 1x_3 + 2x_4 \leq 200 \quad \text{Machine C hours}$$
$$x_1, x_2, x_3, x_4 \geq 0$$

| Figure 3.16 | THE MANAGEMENT SCIENTIST SOLUTION FOR THE INNIS INVESTMENTS PROBLEM |
|---|---|

```
Objective Function Value =            62000.000

       Variable              Value              Reduced Costs
     ------------       ---------------       -----------------
          S                 4000.000                0.000
          M                10000.000                0.000

      Constraint         Slack/Surplus            Dual Prices
     ------------       ---------------       -----------------
          1                    0.000                0.057
          2                    0.000               -2.167
          3                 7000.000                0.000

OBJECTIVE COEFFICIENT RANGES

     Variable          Lower Limit        Current Value        Upper Limit
   ------------      ---------------     ---------------     ---------------
        S                     3.750             8.000         No Upper Limit
        M             No Lower Limit            3.000                 6.400

RIGHT HAND SIDE RANGES

   Constraint          Lower Limit        Current Value        Upper Limit
  ------------       ---------------     ---------------     ---------------
        1                780000.000         1200000.000         1500000.000
        2                 48000.000           60000.000          102000.000
        3             No Lower Limit            3000.000           10000.000
```

The computer solution developed using The Management Scientist is shown in Figure 3.17.
a. What is the optimal solution, and what is the value of the objective function?
b. Which constraints are binding?
c. Which machines have excess capacity available? How much?
d. If the objective function coefficient of $x_1$ is increased by 0.50, will the optimal solution change?

**SELF TEST**

19. Refer to the computer solution of Problem 18 in Figure 3.17.
a. Identify the range of optimality for each objective function coefficient.
b. Suppose the objective function coefficient for $x_1$ is decreased by 3, the objective function coefficient of $x_2$ is increased by 1.5, and the objective function coefficient for $x_4$ is increased by 1. What will the new optimal solution be?
c. Identify the range of feasibility for the right-hand-side values.
d. If the number of hours available on machine A is increased by 300, will the dual price for that constraint change?

**Figure 3.17      THE MANAGEMENT SCIENTIST SOLUTION FOR PROBLEM 18**

```
Objective Function Value =              525.000

     Variable              Value              Reduced Costs
   -------------        ------------        ----------------
        X1                  0.000                 0.050
        X2                 25.000                 0.000
        X3                125.000                 0.000
        X4                  0.000                 3.500

    Constraint          Slack/Surplus          Dual Prices
   -------------        -------------        ----------------
        1                   0.000                 0.300
        2                 425.000                 0.000
        3                   0.000                 1.800


OBJECTIVE COEFFICIENT RANGES

    Variable       Lower Limit      Current Value      Upper Limit
   ----------     ------------     --------------     ------------
        X1       No Lower Limit          4.000             4.050
        X2            5.923              6.000             9.000
        X3            2.000              3.000            12.000
        X4       No Lower Limit          1.000             4.500


RIGHT HAND SIDE RANGES

   Constraint      Lower Limit      Current Value      Upper Limit
   ----------     ------------     --------------     ------------
        1            133.333           550.000           800.000
        2            275.000           700.000       No Upper Limit
        3            137.500           200.000           825.000
```

20.  Consider the following linear program and computer solution shown in Figure 3.18.

$$\text{Min} \quad 15x_1 + 15x_2 + 16x_3$$
$$\text{s.t.}$$
$$1x_1 + \phantom{1x_2 +} 1x_3 \le 30$$
$$0.5x_1 - 1x_2 + 6x_3 \ge 15$$
$$3x_1 + 4x_2 - 1x_3 \ge 20$$
$$x_1, x_2, x_3 \ge 0$$

a.  What is the optimal solution, and what is the optimal value for the objective function?

b.  Which constraints are binding?

| Figure 3.18 | THE MANAGEMENT SCIENTIST SOLUTION FOR PROBLEM 20 |
|---|---|

```
Objective Function Value =            139.730

        Variable              Value              Reduced Costs
      --------------      --------------        ------------------
          X1                  7.297                    0.000
          X2                  0.000                    0.676
          X3                  1.892                    0.000


      Constraint          Slack/Surplus             Dual Prices
      --------------      --------------        ------------------
          1                 20.811                    0.000
          2                  0.000                   -3.405
          3                  0.000                   -4.432


OBJECTIVE COEFFICIENT RANGES

     Variable        Lower Limit        Current Value        Upper Limit
   ------------     -------------      ---------------      --------------
        X1               1.333             15.000               15.543
        X2              14.324             15.000          No Upper Limit
        X3              13.500             16.000              180.000


RIGHT HAND SIDE RANGES

   Constraint        Lower Limit        Current Value        Upper Limit
   ------------     -------------      ---------------      --------------
        1                9.189             30.000          No Upper Limit
        2                3.333             15.000              111.250
        3               -2.500             20.000               90.000
```

    c.   What are the dual prices? Interpret each.

    d.   If you could change the right-hand side of one constraint by one unit, which one would you choose? What would be the new value of the right-hand side?

21.  Refer to the computer solution of Problem 20 in Figure 3.18.

    a.   Interpret the ranges of optimality for the objective function coefficients.

    b.   Suppose the objective function coefficient of $x_1$ is increased by 0.25. What is the new optimal solution?

    c.   Suppose the objective function coefficient of $x_1$ is increased by 0.25 and the objective function coefficient of $x_2$ is decreased by 0.25. What is the new optimal solution?

22.  Supersport Footballs, Inc., has to determine the best number of All-Pro ($A$), College ($C$), and High School ($H$) models of footballs to produce in order to maximize profits. Constraints include production capacity limitations (time available in minutes) in each of three departments (cutting and dyeing, sewing, and inspection and packaging) as well as a constraint that requires the production of at least 1000 All-Pro footballs. The linear programming model of Supersport's problem is shown here:

$$\text{Max} \quad 3A + 5C + 4H$$
$$\text{s.t.}$$

$$12A + 10C + 8H \le 18{,}000 \quad \text{Cutting and dyeing}$$
$$15A + 15C + 12H \le 18{,}000 \quad \text{Sewing}$$
$$3A + 4C + 2H \le 9{,}000 \quad \text{Inspection and packaging}$$
$$1A \qquad\qquad \ge 1{,}000 \quad \text{All-Pro model}$$
$$A, C, H \ge 0$$

The computer solution to the Supersport problem is shown in Figure 3.19.

a. How many footballs of each type should Supersport produce to maximize the total profit contribution?

b. Which constraints are binding?

| Figure 3.19 | THE MANAGEMENT SCIENTIST SOLUTION FOR THE SUPERSPORT FOOTBALLS PROBLEM |
|---|---|

Objective Function Value =            4000.000

| Variable | Value | Reduced Costs |
|---|---|---|
| A | 1000.000 | 0.000 |
| C | 200.000 | 0.000 |
| H | 0.000 | 0.000 |

| Constraint | Slack/Surplus | Dual Prices |
|---|---|---|
| 1 | 4000.000 | 0.000 |
| 2 | 0.000 | 0.333 |
| 3 | 5200.000 | 0.000 |
| 4 | 0.000 | -2.000 |

OBJECTIVE COEFFICIENT RANGES

| Variable | Lower Limit | Current Value | Upper Limit |
|---|---|---|---|
| A | No Lower Limit | 3.000 | 5.000 |
| C | 5.000 | 5.000 | No Upper Limit |
| H | No Lower Limit | 4.000 | 4.000 |

RIGHT HAND SIDE RANGES

| Constraint | Lower Limit | Current Value | Upper Limit |
|---|---|---|---|
| 1 | 14000.000 | 18000.000 | No Upper Limit |
| 2 | 15000.000 | 18000.000 | 24000.000 |
| 3 | 3800.000 | 9000.000 | No Upper Limit |
| 4 | 0.000 | 1000.000 | 1200.000 |

    c.  Interpret the slack and/or surplus in each constraint.
    d.  Interpret the ranges of optimality for the profit contributions of the three footballs.

23.  Refer to the computer solution of Problem 22 (see Figure 3.19).
    a.  Overtime rates in the sewing department are $12 per hour. Would you recommend that the company consider using overtime in that department? Explain.
    b.  What is the dual price for the fourth constraint? Interpret its value for management.
    c.  Note that the reduced cost for $H$, the High-School football, is zero, but $H$ is not in the solution at a positive value. What is your interpretation of this value?
    d.  Suppose that the profit contribution of the College ball is increased by $1. How do you expect the solution to change?

24.  Adirondack Savings Bank (ASB) has $1,000,000 in new funds that must be allocated to home loans, personal loans, and automobile loans. The annual rates of return for the three types of loans are 7% for home loans, 12% for personal loans, and 9% for automobile loans. The bank's planning committee has decided that at least 40% of the new funds must be allocated to home loans. In addition, the planning committee has specified that the amount allocated to personal loans cannot exceed 60% of the amount allocated to automobile loans.
    a.  Formulate a linear programming model that can be used to determine the amount of funds ASB should allocate to each type of loan in order to maximize the total annual return for the new funds.
    b.  How much should be allocated to each type of loan? What is the total annual return? What is the annual percentage return?
    c.  If the interest rate on home loans increased to 9%, would the amount allocated to each type of loan change? Explain.
    d.  Suppose the total amount of new funds available was increased by $10,000. What effect would this have on the total annual return? Explain.
    e.  Assume that ASB has the original $1,000,000 in new funds available and that the planning committee has agreed to relax the requirement that at least 40% of the new funds must be allocated to home loans by 1%. How much would the annual return change? How much would the annual percentage return change?

*Note:* **Problems 25–32 and the case problems require computer solution and interpretation of the results.**

25.  Better Products, Inc., manufactures three products on two machines. In a typical week, 40 hours are available on each machine. The profit contribution and production time in hours per unit are as follows:

| Category | Product 1 | Product 2 | Product 3 |
|---|---|---|---|
| Profit/unit | $30 | $50 | $20 |
| Machine 1 time/unit | 0.5 | 2.0 | 0.75 |
| Machine 2 time/unit | 1.0 | 1.0 | 0.5 |

Two operators are required for machine 1; thus, 2 hours of labor must be scheduled for each hour of machine 1 time. Only one operator is required for machine 2. A maximum of 100 labor-hours is available for assignment to the machines during the coming week. Other production requirements are that product 1 cannot account for more than 50% of the units produced and that product 3 must account for at least 20% of the units produced.
    a.  How many units of each product should be produced to maximize the total profit contribution? What is the projected weekly profit associated with your solution?
    b.  How many hours of production time will be scheduled on each machine?

c. What is the value of an additional hour of labor?

d. Assume that labor capacity can be increased to 120 hours. Would you be interested in using the additional 20 hours available for this resource? Develop the optimal product mix assuming the extra hours are made available.

26. Industrial Designs has been awarded a contract to design a label for a new wine produced by Lake View Winery. The company estimates that 150 hours will be required to complete the project. Three of the firm's graphics designers are available for assignment to this project: Lisa, a senior designer and team leader; David, a senior designer; and Sarah, a junior designer. Because Lisa has worked on several projects for Lake View Winery, management has specified that Lisa must be assigned at least 40% of the total number of hours that are assigned to the two senior designers. To provide label-designing experience for Sarah, Sarah must be assigned at least 15% of the total project time. However, the number of hours assigned to Sarah must not exceed 25% of the total number of hours that are assigned to the two senior designers. Due to other project commitments, Lisa has a maximum of 50 hours available to work on this project. Hourly wage rates are $30 for Lisa, $25 for David, and $18 for Sarah.

a. Formulate a linear program that can be used to determine the number of hours each graphic designer should be assigned to the project in order to minimize total cost.

b. How many hours should each graphic designer be assigned to the project? What is the total cost?

c. Suppose Lisa could be assigned more than 50 hours. What effect would this have on the optimal solution? Explain.

d. If Sarah were not required to work a minimum number of hours on this project, would the optimal solution change? Explain.

27. Vollmer Manufacturing makes three components for sale to refrigeration companies. The components are processed on two machines: a shaper and a grinder. The times (in minutes) required on each machine are as follows:

| | Machine | |
|---|---|---|
| Component | Shaper | Grinder |
| 1 | 6 | 4 |
| 2 | 4 | 5 |
| 3 | 4 | 2 |

The shaper is available for 120 hours, and the grinder is available for 110 hours. No more than 200 units of component 3 can be sold, but up to 1000 units of each of the other components can be sold. In fact, the company already has orders for 600 units of component 1 that must be satisfied. The profit contributions for components 1, 2, and 3 are $8, $6, and $9, respectively.

a. Formulate and solve for the recommended production quantities.

b. What are the ranges of optimality for the profit contributions of the three components? Interpret these ranges for company management.

c. What are the ranges of feasibility for the right-hand sides? Interpret these ranges for company management.

d. If more time could be made available on the grinder, how much would it be worth?

e. If more units of component 3 can be sold by reducing the sales price by $4, should the company reduce the price?

28. National Insurance Associates carries an investment portfolio of stocks, bonds, and other investment alternatives. Currently $200,000 of funds are available and must be considered for new investment opportunities. The four stock options National is considering and the relevant financial data are as follows:

|  | Stock | | | |
|---|---|---|---|---|
|  | **A** | **B** | **C** | **D** |
| Price per share | $100 | $50 | $80 | $40 |
| Annual rate of return | 0.12 | 0.08 | 0.06 | 0.10 |
| Risk measure per dollar invested | 0.10 | 0.07 | 0.05 | 0.08 |

The risk measure indicates the relative uncertainty associated with the stock in terms of its realizing the projected annual return; higher values indicate greater risk. The risk measures are provided by the firm's top financial advisor.

National's top management has stipulated the following investment guidelines: the annual rate of return for the portfolio must be at least 9% and no one stock can account for more than 50% of the total dollar investment.

a. Use linear programming to develop an investment portfolio that minimizes risk.

b. If the firm ignores risk and uses a maximum return-on-investment strategy, what is the investment portfolio?

c. What is the dollar difference between the portfolios in parts (a) and (b)? Why might the company prefer the solution developed in part (a)?

29. Georgia Cabinets manufactures kitchen cabinets that are sold to local dealers throughout the Southeast. The company has a large backlog of orders for oak and cherry cabinets and has decided to contract with three smaller cabinetmakers to do the final finishing operation. For the three cabinetmakers, the number of hours required to complete all the oak cabinets, the number of hours required to complete all the cherry cabinets, the number of hours available for the final finishing operation, and the cost per hour to perform the work are shown here.

|  | **Cabinetmaker 1** | **Cabinetmaker 2** | **Cabinetmaker 3** |
|---|---|---|---|
| Hours required to complete all the oak cabinets | 50 | 42 | 30 |
| Hours required to complete all the cherry cabinets | 60 | 48 | 35 |
| Hours available | 40 | 30 | 35 |
| Cost per hour | $36 | $42 | $55 |

For example, Cabinetmaker 1 estimates it will take 50 hours to complete all the oak cabinets and 60 hours to complete all the cherry cabinets. However, Cabinetmaker 1 only has 40 hours available for the final finishing operation. Thus, Cabinetmaker 1 can only complete 40/50 = 0.80 or 80% of the oak cabinets if it worked only on oak cabinets. Similarly, Cabinetmaker 1 can only complete 40/60 = 0.67 or 67% of the cherry cabinets if it worked only on cherry cabinets.

a. Formulate a linear programming model that can be used to determine the percentage of the oak cabinets and the percentage of the cherry cabinets that should be given to each of the three cabinetmakers in order to minimize the total cost of completing both projects.

b. Solve the model formulated in part (a). What percentage of the oak cabinets and what percentage of the cherry cabinets should be assigned to each cabinetmaker? What is the total cost of completing both projects?

   c. If Cabinetmaker 1 has additional hours available, would the optimal solution change? Explain.

   d. If Cabinetmaker 2 has additional hours available, would the optimal solution change? Explain.

   e. Suppose Cabinetmaker 2 reduced its cost to $38 per hour. What effect would this have on the optimal solution? Explain.

30. The Management of Carson Stapler Manufacturing Company forecasts a 5000-unit demand for its Sure-Hold model during the next quarter. This stapler is assembled from three major components: base, staple cartridge, and handle. Until now Carson has manufactured all three components. However, the forecast of 5000 units is a new high in sales volume, and the firm may not have sufficient production capacity to make all the components. The company is considering contracting with a local firm to produce at least some of the components. The production time requirements per unit are as follows:

| | | Production Time (hours) | | |
|---|---|---|---|---|
| Department | Base | Cartridge | Handle | Time Available (hours) |
| A | 0.03 | 0.02 | 0.05 | 400 |
| B | 0.04 | 0.02 | 0.04 | 400 |
| C | 0.02 | 0.03 | 0.01 | 400 |

Note that each component manufactured by Carson uses manufacturing time in each of three departments.

    After considering the firm's overhead, material, and labor costs, the accounting department has determined the unit manufacturing cost for each component. These data, along with the purchase price quotations by the contracting firm, are as follows:

| Component | Manufacturing Cost | Purchase Cost |
|---|---|---|
| Base | $0.75 | $0.95 |
| Cartridge | $0.40 | $0.55 |
| Handle | $1.10 | $1.40 |

   a. Determine the make-or-buy decision for Carson that will meet the 5000-unit demand at a minimum total cost. How many units of each component should be made and how many purchased?

   b. Which departments are limiting the manufacturing volume? If overtime could be considered at the additional cost of $3 per hour, which department(s) should be allocated the overtime? Explain.

   c. Suppose that up to 80 hours of overtime could be scheduled in department A. What would you recommend?

31. Golf Shafts, Inc. (GSI), produces graphite shafts for several manufacturers of golf clubs. Two GSI manufacturing facilities, one located in San Diego and the other in Tampa, have the capability to produce shafts in varying degrees of stiffness, ranging from regular models used primarily by average golfers to extra stiff models used primarily by low-handicap and professional golfers. GSI has just received a contract for the production of 200,000 regular shafts and 75,000

stiff shafts. Since both plants are currently producing shafts for previous orders, neither plant has sufficient capacity by itself to fill the new order. The San Diego plant can produce up to a total of 120,000 shafts and the Tampa plant can produce up to a total of 180,000 shafts. Because of equipment differences at each of the plants and differing labor costs, the per-unit production costs vary as shown here:

|                | San Diego Cost | Tampa Cost |
|----------------|----------------|------------|
| Regular Shaft  | $5.25          | $4.95      |
| Stiff Shaft    | $5.45          | $5.70      |

a. Formulate a linear programming model to determine how GSI should schedule production for the new order in order to minimize the total production cost.
b. Solve the model that you developed in part (a).
c. Suppose that some of the previous orders at the Tampa plant could be rescheduled in order to free up additional capacity for the new order. Would this option be worthwhile? Explain.
d. Suppose that the cost to produce a stiff shaft in Tampa had been incorrectly computed, and that the correct cost is $5.30 per shaft. What effect, if any, would this have on the optimal solution developed in part (b)? What effect would this have on total production cost?

32. The Pfeiffer Company manages approximately $15 million for clients. For each client, Pfeiffer chooses a mix of three investment vehicles: a growth stock fund, an income fund, and a money market fund. Each client has different investment objectives and different tolerances for risk. To accommodate these differences, Pfeiffer places limits on the percentage of each portfolio that may be invested in the three funds and assigns a portfolio risk index to each client.

Here's how the system works for Dennis Hartmann, one of Pfeiffer's clients. Based on an evaluation of Hartmann's risk tolerance, Pfeiffer has assigned Hartmann's portfolio a risk index of 0.05. Furthermore, to maintain diversity, the fraction of Hartmann's portfolio invested in the growth and income funds must be at least 10% for each, and at least 20% must be in the money market fund.

The risk ratings for the growth, income, and money market funds are 0.10, 0.05, and 0.01, respectively. A portfolio risk index is computed as a weighted average of the risk ratings for the three funds where the weights are the fraction of the portfolio invested in each of the funds. Hartmann has given Pfeiffer $300,000 to manage. Pfeiffer is currently forecasting a yield of 20% on the growth fund, 10% on the income fund, and 6% on the money market fund.

a. Develop a linear programming model to select the best mix of investments for Hartmann's portfolio.
b. Solve the model you developed in part (a).
c. How much may the yields on the three funds vary before it will be necessary for Pfeiffer to modify Hartmann's portfolio?
d. If Hartmann were more risk tolerant, how much of a yield increase could he expect? For instance, what if his portfolio risk index is increased to 0.06?
e. If Pfeiffer revised the yield estimate for the growth fund downward to 0.10, how would you recommend modifying Hartmann's portfolio?
f. What information must Pfeiffer maintain on each client in order to use this system to manage client portfolios?
g. On a weekly basis Pfeiffer revises the yield estimates for the three funds. Suppose Pfeiffer has 50 clients. Describe how you would envision Pfeiffer making weekly modifications in each client's portfolio and allocating the total funds managed among the three investment funds.

33. La Jolla Beverage Products is considering producing a wine cooler that would be a blend of a white wine, a rosé wine, and fruit juice. To meet taste specifications, the wine cooler must

consist of at least 50% white wine, at least 20% and no more than 30% rosé, and exactly 20% fruit juice. La Jolla purchases the wine from local wineries and the fruit juice from a processing plant in San Francisco. For the current production period, 10,000 gallons of white wine and 8000 gallons of rosé wine can be purchased; there is no limit on the amount of fruit juice that can be ordered. The costs for the wine are $1.00 per gallon for the white and $1.50 per gallon for the rosé; the fruit juice can be purchased for $0.50 per gallon. La Jolla Beverage Products can sell all of the wine cooler they can produce for $2.50 per gallon.

a. Is the cost of the wine and fruit juice a sunk cost or a relevant cost in this situation? Explain.

b. Formulate a linear program to determine the blend of the three ingredients that will maximize the total profit contribution. Solve the linear program to determine the number of gallons of each ingredient La Jolla should purchase and the total profit contribution they will realize from this blend.

c. If La Jolla could obtain additional amounts of the white wine, should they do so? If so, how much should they be willing to pay for each additional gallon, and how many additional gallons would they want to purchase?

d. If La Jolla Beverage Products could obtain additional amounts of the rosé wine, should they do so? If so, how much should they be willing to pay for each additional gallon, and how many additional gallons would they want to purchase?

e. Interpret the dual price for the constraint corresponding to the requirement that the wine cooler must contain at least 50% white wine. What is your advice to management given this dual price?

f. Interpret the dual price for the constraint corresponding to the requirement that the wine cooler must contain exactly 20% fruit juice. What is your advice to management given this dual price?

34. The program manager for Channel 10 would like to determine the best way to allocate the time for the 11:00–11:30 evening news broadcast. Specifically, she would like to determine the number of minutes of broadcast time to devote to local news, national news, weather, and sports. Over the 30-minute broadcast, 10 minutes are set aside for advertising. The station's broadcast policy states that at least 15% of the time available should be devoted to local news coverage; the time devoted to local news or national news must be at least 50% of the total broadcast time; the time devoted to the weather segment must be less than or equal to the time devoted to the sports segment; the time devoted to the sports segment should be no longer than the total time spent on the local and national news; and at least 20% of the time should be devoted to the weather segment. The production costs per minute are $300 for local news, $200 for national news, $100 for weather, and $100 for sports.

a. Formulate and solve a linear program that can determine how the 20 available minutes should be used to minimize the total cost of producing the program.

b. Interpret the dual price for the constraint corresponding to the available time. What advice would you give the station manager given this dual price?

c. Interpret the dual price for the constraint corresponding to the requirement that at least 15% of the available time should be devoted to local coverage. What advice would you give the station manager given this dual price?

d. Interpret the dual price for the constraint corresponding to the requirement that the time devoted to the local and the national news must be at least 50% of the total broadcast time. What advice would you give the station manager given this dual price?

e. Interpret the dual price for the constraint corresponding to the requirement that the time devoted to the weather segment must be less than or equal to the time devoted to the sports segment. What advice would you give the station manager given this dual price?

35. Golf Coast Electronics is ready to award contracts for printing their annual report. For the past several years, the four-color annual report has been printed by Johnson Printing and Lakeside Litho. A new firm, Benson Printing, has inquired into the possibility of doing a portion of the printing. The quality and service level provided by Lakeside Litho has been extremely high; in fact, only 0.5% of their reports have had to be discarded because of quality problems. Johnson Printing has also had a high quality level historically, producing an average of only 1% unacceptable reports. Since Gulf Coast Electronics has had no experience with Benson Printing,

they have estimated their defective rate to be 10%. Gulf Coast would like to determine how many reports should be printed by each firm to obtain 75,000 acceptable-quality reports. To ensure that Benson Printing will receive some of the contract, management has specified that the number of reports awarded to Benson Printing must be at least 10% of the volume given to Johnson Printing. In addition, the total volume assigned to Benson Printing, Johnson Printing, and Lakeside Litho should not exceed 30,000, 50,000, and 50,000 copies, respectively. Because of the long-term relationship that has developed with Lakeside Litho, management has also specified that at least 30,000 reports should be awarded to Lakeside Litho. The cost per copy is $2.45 for Benson Printing, $2.50 for Johnson Printing, and $2.75 for Lakeside Litho.

a.  Formulate and solve a linear program for determining how many copies should be assigned to each printing firm to minimize the total cost of obtaining 75,000 acceptable-quality reports.

b.  Suppose that the quality level for Benson Printing is much better than estimated. What effect, if any, would this quality level have?

c.  Suppose that management is willing to reconsider their requirement that Lakeside Litho be awarded at least 30,000 reports. What effect, if any, would this consideration have?

........................................................................................../  /.............

## Case Problem    PRODUCT MIX

TJ's, Inc., makes three nut mixes for sale to grocery chains located in the Southeast. The three mixes, referred to as the Regular Mix, the Deluxe Mix, and the Holiday Mix, are made by mixing different percentages of five types of nuts.

In preparation for the fall season, TJ's has just purchased the following shipments of nuts at the prices shown:

| Type of Nut | Shipment Amount (pounds) | Cost per Shipment |
|-------------|--------------------------|-------------------|
| Almond      | 6000                     | $7500             |
| Brazil      | 7500                     | $7125             |
| Filbert     | 7500                     | $6750             |
| Pecan       | 6000                     | $7200             |
| Walnut      | 7500                     | $7875             |

The Regular Mix consists of 15% almonds, 25% Brazil nuts, 25% filberts, 10% pecans, and 25% walnuts. The Deluxe Mix consists of 20% of each type of nut, and the Holiday Mix consists of 25% almonds, 15% Brazil nuts, 15% filberts, 25% pecans, and 20% walnuts.

TJ's accountant has analyzed the cost of packaging materials, sales price per pound, and so forth, and has determined that the profit contribution per pound is $1.65 for the Regular Mix, $2.00 for the Deluxe Mix, and $2.25 for the Holiday Mix. These figures do not include the cost of specific types of nuts in the different mixes because that cost can vary greatly in the commodity markets.

Customer orders already received are summarized here:

| Type of Mix | Orders (pounds) |
|-------------|-----------------|
| Regular     | 10,000          |
| Deluxe      | 3,000           |
| Holiday     | 5,000           |

Because demand is running high, it is expected that TJ's will receive many more orders than can be satisfied.

TJ's is committed to using the available nuts to maximize profit over the fall season; nuts not used will be given to the Free Store. But even if it is not profitable to do so, TJ's president has indicated that the orders already received must be satisfied.

## Managerial Report

Perform an analysis of TJ's product-mix problem, and prepare a report for TJ's president that summarizes your findings. Be sure to include information and analysis on the following:

1. The cost per pound of the nuts included in the Regular, Deluxe, and Holiday mixes
2. The optimal product mix and the total profit contribution
3. Recommendations regarding how the total profit contribution can be increased if additional quantities of nuts can be purchased
4. A recommendation as to whether TJ's should purchase an additional 1000 pounds of almonds for $1000 from a supplier who overbought
5. Recommendations on how profit contribution could be increased (if at all) if TJ's does not satisfy all existing orders

## Case Problem    INVESTMENT STRATEGY

J. D. Williams, Inc., is an investment advisory firm that manages more than $120 million in funds for its numerous clients. The company uses an asset allocation model that recommends the portion of each client's portfolio to be invested in a growth stock fund, an income fund, and a money market fund. To maintain diversity in each client's portfolio, the firm places limits on the percentage of each portfolio that may be invested in each of the three funds. General guidelines indicate that the amount invested in the growth fund must be between 20% and 40% of the total portfolio value. Similar percentages for the other two funds stipulate that between 20% and 50% of the total portfolio value must be in the income fund and at least 30% of the total portfolio value must be in the money market fund.

In addition, the company attempts to assess the risk tolerance of each client and adjust the portfolio to meet the needs of the individual investor. For example, Williams has just contracted with a new client who has $800,000 to invest. Based on an evaluation of the client's risk tolerance, Williams has assigned a maximum risk index of 0.05 for the client. The firm's risk indicators show the risk of the growth fund at 0.10, the income fund at 0.07, and the money market fund at 0.01. An overall portfolio risk index is computed as a weighted average of the risk rating for the three funds where the weights are the fraction of the client's portfolio invested in each of the funds.

Additionally, Williams is currently forecasting annual yields of 18% for the growth fund, 12.5% for the income fund, and 7.5% for the money market fund. Based on the information provided, how should the new client be advised to allocate the $800,000 among the growth, income, and money market funds? Develop a linear programming model that will provide the maximum yield for the portfolio. Use your model to develop a managerial report.

## Managerial Report

1. Recommend how much of the $800,000 should be invested in each of the three funds. What is the annual yield you anticipate for the investment recommendation?

2. Assume that the client's risk index could be increased to 0.055. How much would the yield increase and how would the investment recommendation change?
3. Refer again to the original situation where the client's risk index was assessed to be 0.05. How would your investment recommendation change if the annual yield for the growth fund were revised downward to 16% or even to 14%?
4. Assume that the client has expressed some concern about having too much money in the growth fund. How would the original recommendation change if the amount invested in the growth fund is not allowed to exceed the amount invested in the income fund?
5. The asset allocation model you have developed may be useful in modifying the portfolios for all of the firm's clients whenever the anticipated yields for the three funds are periodically revised. What is your recommendation as to whether use of this model is possible?

## Appendix 3.1    SENSITIVITY ANALYSIS WITH SPREADSHEETS

In Appendix 2.2 we showed how Excel Solver can be used to solve the spreadsheet model of a linear program by using it to solve the Par, Inc., problem. Let us now see how it can be used to provide sensitivity analysis.

When Excel Solver has found the optimal solution to a linear program the **Solver Results** dialog box (see Figure 3.20) will appear on the screen. If only the solution is desired you simply select **OK.** To obtain the optimal solution and the sensitivity analysis output, you must select **Sensitivity** in the **Reports** box before selecting **OK;** the sensitivity report is created on another worksheet in the same Excel workbook. Following this procedure for the Par problem, we obtained the optimal solution shown in Figure 3.21 and the sensitivity report shown in Figure 3.22.

### Interpretation of Excel Sensitivity Report

In the Adjustable Cells section of the Sensitivity Report, the column labeled Final Value contains the optimal values of the decision variables. For the Par problem the optimal solution is 540 standard bags and 252 deluxe bags. Next, let us consider the values in the Reduced

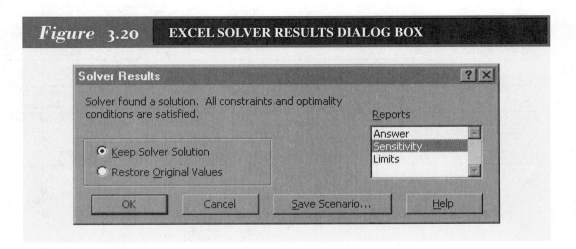

**Figure  3.20          EXCEL SOLVER RESULTS DIALOG BOX**

## Figure 3.21    SPREADSHEET SOLUTION FOR THE PAR, INC., PROBLEM

| | A | B | C | D |
|---|---|---|---|---|
| 1 | **Par, Inc.** | | | |
| 2 | | | | |
| 3 | | **Production Time** | | |
| 4 | **Operation** | **Standard** | **Deluxe** | **Time Available** |
| 5 | Cutting and Dyeing | 0.7 | 1 | 630 |
| 6 | Sewing | 0.5 | 0.83333 | 600 |
| 7 | Finishing | 1 | 0.66667 | 708 |
| 8 | Inspection and Packaging | 0.1 | 0.25 | 135 |
| 9 | **Profit Per Bag** | 10 | 9 | |
| 10 | | | | |
| 11 | | | | |
| 12 | **Model** | | | |
| 13 | | | | |
| 14 | | **Decision Variables** | | |
| 15 | | **Standard** | **Deluxe** | |
| 16 | **Bags Produced** | 539.998425 | 252.0011025 | |
| 17 | | | | |
| 18 | **Maximize Total Profit** | 7668 | | |
| 19 | | | | |
| 20 | **Constraints** | **Hours Used (LHS)** | | **Hours Available (RHS)** |
| 21 | Cutting and Dyeing | 630 | <= | 630 |
| 22 | Sewing | 479.9992912 | <= | 600 |
| 23 | Finishing | 708 | <= | 708 |
| 24 | Inspection and Packaging | 117.0001181 | <= | 135 |

## Figure 3.22    SENSITIVITY REPORT FOR THE PAR, INC., PROBLEM

Adjustable Cells

| Cell | Name | Final Value | Reduced Cost | Objective Coefficient | Allowable Increase | Allowable Decrease |
|---|---|---|---|---|---|---|
| $B$16 | Bags Produced Standard | 539.998425 | 0 | 10 | 3.4999325 | 3.7 |
| $C$16 | Bags Produced Deluxe | 252.0011025 | 0 | 9 | 5.285714286 | 2.3333 |

Constraints

| Cell | Name | Final Value | Shadow Price | Constraint R.H. Side | Allowable Increase | Allowable Decrease |
|---|---|---|---|---|---|---|
| $B$21 | Cutting and Dyeing Hours Used (LHS) | 630 | 4.37495664 | 630 | 52.36315884 | 134.4 |
| $B$22 | Sewing Hours Used (LHS) | 479.9992912 | 0 | 600 | 1E+30 | 120.0007088 |
| $B$23 | Finishing Hours Used (LHS) | 708 | 6.937530352 | 708 | 192 | 127.9986 |
| $B$24 | Inspection and Packaging Hours Used (LHS) | 117.0001181 | 0 | 135 | 1E+30 | 17.99988187 |

Cost column. In Excel, the absolute value of the reduced cost indicates how much the objective function coefficient of each decision variable would have to improve* before that variable could assume a positive value in the optimal solution. For the Par, Inc., problem, both decision variables already have positive values; thus, their reduced costs are zero.

To the right of the Reduced Cost column in Figure 3.19, we find three columns labeled Objective Coefficient, Allowable Increase, and Allowable Decrease. Note that for the standard bag decision variable, the objective function coefficient value is 10, the allowable increase value is 3.5, and the allowable decrease value is 3.7. Adding 3.5 to and subtracting 3.7 from the current coefficient of 10 provides the range of optimality for $C_S$.

$$6.3 \leq C_S \leq 13.5$$

Similarly, the range of optimality for $C_D$ is

$$6.67 \leq C_D \leq 14.29$$

Next, consider the information in the Constraints section of the report. The entries in the Final Value column are the number of hours needed in each department to produce the optimal production quantities of 540 standard bags and 252 deluxe bags. Thus, at the optimal solution, 630 hours of cutting and dyeing time, 480 hours of sewing time, 708 hours of finishing time, and 117 hours of inspection and packaging time are required. The values in the Constraint R.H. Side column are just the original right-hand-side values: 630 hours of cutting and dyeing time, 600 hours of sewing time, 708 hours of finishing time, and 135 hours of inspection and packaging time. Note that for the Par problem, the values of the slack variables for each constraint are simply the differences between the entries in the Constraint R.H. Side column and the corresponding entries in the Final Value column.

The entries in the Shadow Price column provide the *shadow price* for each constraint. The shadow price is the *change* in the value of the solution per-unit increase in the right-hand side of the constraint. The Management Scientist uses the term *dual price* to describe the *improvement* in the value of the solution per-unit increase in the right-hand side of a constraint. The shadow price and dual price are the same for maximization problems because improvement is an increase in value. For minimization problems, improvement is a decrease in value; thus, for minimization problems, the shadow price and dual price have opposite signs.

The last two columns of the Sensitivity Report contain the range of feasibility information for the constraint right-hand sides. For example, consider the cutting and dyeing constraint with an allowable increase value of 52.4 and an allowable decrease value of 134.4. The values in the Allowable Increase and Allowable Decrease columns indicate that the shadow price of $4.375 is valid for increases up to 52.4 hours and decreases to 134.4 hours. Thus, the shadow price of $4.375 is applicable for increases up to 630 + 52.4 = 682.4 and decreases down to 630 − 134.4 = 495.6 hours.

In summary, the range of feasibility information provides the limits where the shadow prices are applicable. For changes outside the range, the problem must be resolved to find the new optimal solution and the new shadow price.

---

*For a maximization problem, *improve* means get bigger; for a minimization problem, *improve* means get smaller.

# EASTMAN KODAK*

## ROCHESTER, NEW YORK

In 1881 entrepreneur/inventor George Eastman formed the Eastman Dry Plate Company with a vision that it would become a worldwide manufacturer and marketer of photographic goods. Today, Eastman Kodak is a $20-billion enterprise with manufacturing operations on four continents, and customers in more than 150 countries. Headquartered in Rochester, New York, Kodak's imaging products include amateur roll film, photographic paper, medical and industrial X-ray film, motion picture film, and graphic arts materials. In addition, Kodak is a manufacturer of imaging equipment and chemicals.

## Management Science at Kodak

Management science applications at Kodak can be traced back to pioneering efforts in the 1950s. Since then, management science has been employed to solve a variety of problems involving most of the operational areas of the company. Today, the majority of management science work is conducted by the Management Services Division, while a small group called Distribution Operations Research focuses on applying management science to worldwide logistics issues.

## Assigning Products to Worldwide Facilities

The sensitizing operation is the heart of the manufacturing process for photographic paper and film. In this operation, a light-sensitive emulsion is coated on a base to produce a sensitized master roll. The sensitized master rolls are then sent to a finishing operation where they are cut into proper dimensions. The sensitizing operation, by virtue of its centrality to the overall process and the

peculiarity of the manufacturing technologies required, receives a great deal of managerial attention, both at the operational and strategic levels.

One of Kodak's major planning issues involves the allocation of product to the various sensitizing facilities located throughout the world. The assignment of product to facilities is called the "world load." In determining the world load, Kodak is confronted with a number of interesting trade-offs. For instance, in terms of manufacturing costs, not all sensitizing facilities are equally efficient for all products. Some facilities tend to be more cost efficient over a broad range of products, but the margins by which they are better varies from product to product. However, many product-facility combinations are essentially impossible because of unique product specifications and machine capabilities. Nonetheless, there is a choice of facilities for practically every product.

The product-facility manufacturing costs are only part of the picture. The cheapest place to sensitize a particular product might, for example, be Australia. But, if most of the customers for that product are in Europe, then Australia becomes less favorable because of the high transportation costs involved. Transportation costs are therefore among the costs considered in determining the world load.

Another cost that must be considered involves the duties and duty drawbacks for the various countries throughout the world. Duty drawback is the "forgiving" of duty for a manufacturer who brings a semifinished product into a country, adds value to it, and then ships it out of that country. The effects of duty and duty drawback can significantly affect the allocation decision.

To assist in determining the world load, Kodak developed a linear programming model that accounts for the physical nature of the distribution problem and the

*The authors are indebted to Greg Sampson of Eastman Kodak for providing this application.

various cost elements already described. More specifically, the program's objective is to minimize total cost (manufacturing, transportation, and duties) subject to "natural" constraints such as satisfying demand and capacity constraints for each facility.

## Sensitivity Analysis and Interpretation

The linear programming model is a static representation of the problem situation, and the real world is always changing. Thus, Kodak cannot simply solve the linear program and implement the optimal solution; the static linear programming model must be used in a dynamic way. For instance, when demand expectations change, the model can be used to determine the effect the change will have on the world load. Or, suppose that country A and country B tear down duty barriers between them; what effect will it have on the world load? Suppose that the currency of country A rises compared to the currency of country B; how should the world load be modified? These are but a few of the situations of how the world load must be reevaluated based on the impact of external stimuli.

In addition to using the linear programming model in a "how-to-react" mode, the model is useful in a more active mode by considering questions such as the following: Is it worthwhile for facility F to spend $D$ dollars to lower the unit manufacturing cost of product $P$ from $X$ to $Y$? If such an investment is made, the effect may go well beyond the simple first-order impact at facility F; in fact, it is likely that the change at facility F will result in a reshuffling of the world load. The linear programming model helps evaluate the overall effect of possible changes at any facility.

## Managerial Use

The world-load model gives excellent directional advice and integrates the complex interaction of many factors, but many aspects of the world-load problem do not fall neatly into specific cost categories. Although it might be possible to construct a model that would account for almost every aspect of the real-world situation, the time and cost needed to develop it would be prohibitive. Kodak has chosen to use a simpler world-load model; sensitivity analysis is then used to explore many of the questions that management may want to address. In the final analysis, managers recognize that they cannot use the model by simply turning it on, reading the results, and executing the solution. The model's recommendations combined with managerial judgment provide the final decisions and actions for world-load allocation.

## Questions

1. What are some of the trade-offs associated with allocating the products to the various sensitizing facilities?
2. What costs are included in the objective function of the world-load model?
3. Briefly describe the role of sensitivity analysis in this application.
4. The world-load model does not account for all the various issues involved in assigning products to sensitizing facilities. What reason did Kodak have for not addressing *all* the issues, and what implications does this have for management?

# 4

# LINEAR PROGRAMMING APPLICATIONS

## CONTENTS

Linear programming has proven to be one of the most successful quantitative approaches to decision making. Applications have been reported in almost every industry. Problems studied include production scheduling, media selection, financial planning, capital budgeting, transportation, distribution system design, product mix, staffing, blending, and many others. As the variety of applications suggests, linear programming is a flexible problem-solving tool. In this chapter we present a variety of applications, including several from the traditional business areas of marketing, finance, and operations management. Modeling, computer solution, and interpretation of output are emphasized.

A mathematical model is developed for each problem studied. These models can be solved using a variety of computer packages including The Management Scientist, LINDO, and Excel Solver. In the chapter, computer solutions obtained using The Management Scientist are presented for most of the applications. The solution output for LINDO is similar; in the chapter appendix we illustrate the use of Excel Solver by solving a financial planning problem.

## 4.1    MARKETING APPLICATIONS

Applications of linear programming in marketing are numerous. In this section we discuss applications in media selection and marketing research.

### Media Selection

In Section 2.1 we provided some general guidelines for modeling linear programming problems. You may want to review Section 2.1 before proceeding with the linear programming applications in this chapter.

Media selection applications of linear programming are designed to help marketing managers allocate a fixed advertising budget to various advertising media. Potential media include newspapers, magazines, radio, television, and direct mail. In these applications, the objective is to maximize reach, frequency, and quality of exposure. Restrictions on the allowable allocation usually arise during consideration of company policy, contract requirements, and media availability. In the application that follows, we illustrate how a media selection problem might be formulated and solved using a linear programming model.

Relax-and-Enjoy Lake Development Corporation is developing a lakeside community at a privately owned lake. The primary market for the lakeside lots and homes includes all middle- and upper-income families within approximately 100 miles of the development. Relax-and-Enjoy has employed the advertising firm of Boone, Phillips and Jackson (BP&J) to design the promotional campaign.

After considering possible advertising media and the market to be covered, BP&J has recommended that the first month's advertising be restricted to five media. At the end of the month, BP&J will then reevaluate its strategy based on the month's results. BP&J has collected data on the number of potential customers reached, the cost per advertisement, the maximum number of times each medium is available, and the exposure quality rating for each of the five media. The quality rating is measured in terms of an exposure quality unit, a measure of the relative value of one advertisement in each of the media. This measure, based on BP&J's experience in the advertising business, takes into account factors such as audience demographics (age, income, and education of the audience reached), image presented, and quality of the advertisement. The information collected is presented in Table 4.1.

| *Table* 4.1 | ADVERTISING MEDIA ALTERNATIVES FOR THE RELAX-AND-ENJOY LAKE DEVELOPMENT CORPORATION | | | | |
|---|---|---|---|---|---|
| Advertising Media | Number of Potential Customers Reached | Cost ($) Per Advertisement | Maximum Times Available Per Month* | Exposure Quality Units |
| 1. Daytime TV (1 min), station WKLA | 1000 | 1500 | 15 | 65 |
| 2. Evening TV (30 sec), station WKLA | 2000 | 3000 | 10 | 90 |
| 3. Daily newspaper (full page), *The Morning Journal* | 1500 | 400 | 25 | 40 |
| 4. Sunday newspaper magazine (½ page color), *The Sunday Press* | 2500 | 1000 | 4 | 60 |
| 5. Radio, 8:00 A.M. or 5:00 P.M. news (30 sec), station KNOP | 300 | 100 | 30 | 20 |

*The maximum number of times the medium is available is either the maximum number of times the advertising medium occurs (e.g., four Sundays per month or the maximum number of times BP&J recommends that the medium be used).

Relax-and-Enjoy provided BP&J with an advertising budget of $30,000 for the first month's campaign. In addition, Relax-and-Enjoy imposed the following restrictions on how BP&J may allocate these funds: At least 10 television commercials must be used, at least 50,000 potential customers must be reached, and no more than $18,000 may be spent on television advertisements. What advertising media selection plan should be recommended?

The decision to be made is how many times to use each medium. We begin by defining the decision variables:

$$DTV = \text{number of times daytime TV is used}$$
$$ETV = \text{number of times evening TV is used}$$
$$DN = \text{number of times daily newspaper is used}$$
$$SN = \text{number of times Sunday newspaper is used}$$
$$R = \text{number of times radio is used}$$

The data on quality of exposure in Table 4.1 show that each daytime TV ($DTV$) advertisement is rated at 65 exposure quality units. Thus, an advertising plan with $DTV$ advertisements will provide a total of $65DTV$ exposure quality units. Continuing with the data in Table 4.1, we find evening TV ($ETV$) rated at 90 exposure quality units, daily newspaper ($DN$) rated at 40 exposure quality units, Sunday newspaper ($SN$) rated at 60 exposure quality units, and radio ($R$) rated at 20 exposure quality units. With the objective of maximizing the total exposure quality units for the overall media selection plan, the objective function becomes

$$\text{Max} \quad 65DTV + 90ETV + 40DN + 60SN + 20R \qquad \text{Exposure quality}$$

We now formulate the constraints for the model from the information given:

Care must be taken to ensure the linear programming model accurately reflects the real problem. Always review your formulation thoroughly before attempting to solve the model.

$$
\left.
\begin{aligned}
DTV &\leq 15 \\
ETV &\leq 10 \\
DN &\leq 25 \\
SN &\leq 4 \\
R &\leq 30
\end{aligned}
\right\} \begin{aligned} \text{Availability} \\ \text{of media} \end{aligned}
$$

$$1500DTV + 3000ETV + 400DN + 1000SN + 100R \leq 30{,}000 \ \text{Budget}$$

$$
\left.
\begin{aligned}
DTV + ETV &\geq 10 \\
1500DTV + 3000ETV &\leq 18{,}000
\end{aligned}
\right\} \begin{aligned} \text{Television} \\ \text{restrictions} \end{aligned}
$$

$$1000DTV + 2000ETV + 1500DN + 2500SN + 300R \geq 50{,}000 \ \text{Customers reached}$$

$$DTV, ETV, DN, SN, R \geq 0$$

Problem 1 provides practice at formulating a similar media selection model.

The computer solution to this five-variable, nine-constraint linear programming model is shown in Figure 4.1; a summary is presented in Table 4.2.

The optimal solution calls for advertisements to be distributed among daytime TV, daily newspaper, Sunday newspaper, and radio. The maximum number of exposure quality units is 2370, and the total number of customers reached is 61,500. The reduced costs column in Figure 4.1 indicates that the number of exposure quality units for evening TV would have to increase by at least 65 before this media alternative could appear in the optimal solution.

## Figure 4.1    THE MANAGEMENT SCIENTIST SOLUTION FOR THE RELAX-AND-ENJOY LAKE DEVELOPMENT CORPORATION PROBLEM

```
Objective Function Value =          2370.000

      Variable              Value            Reduced Costs
   --------------        ------------       ----------------
        DTV                10.000                0.000
        ETV                 0.000               65.000
        DN                 25.000                0.000
        SN                  2.000                0.000
        R                  30.000                0.000


     Constraint         Slack/Surplus           Dual Prices
   --------------        ------------       ----------------
         1                  5.000                0.000
         2                 10.000                0.000
         3                  0.000               16.000
         4                  2.000                0.000
         5                  0.000               14.000
         6                  0.000                0.060
         7                  0.000              -25.000
         8               3000.000                0.000
         9              11500.003                0.000
```

Media Availability

Budget

Television Restrictions

Audience Coverage

| Table 4.2 | ADVERTISING PLAN FOR THE RELAX-AND-ENJOY LAKE DEVELOPMENT CORPORATION | |
|---|---|---|

| Media | Frequency | Budget |
|---|---|---|
| Daytime TV | 10 | $15,000 |
| Daily newspaper | 25 | 10,000 |
| Sunday newspaper | 2 | 2,000 |
| Radio | 30 | 3,000 |
| | | $30,000 |

Exposure quality units = 2,370
Total customers reached = 61,500

Note that the budget constraint (constraint 6) has a dual price of 0.060. That is, a $1.00 increase in the advertising budget will lead to an increase of 0.06 exposure quality units. The dual price of $-25.000$ for constraint 7 indicates that reducing the number of television commercials by 1 will increase the exposure quality of the advertising plan by 25 units. Thus, Relax-and-Enjoy should consider reducing the requirement of having at least 10 television commercials.

A possible shortcoming of this model is that, even if the exposure quality measure were not subject to error, there is no guarantee that maximization of total exposure quality will lead to a maximization of profit or of sales (a common surrogate for profit). However, this issue is not a shortcoming of linear programming; rather, it is a shortcoming of the use of exposure quality as a criterion. If we could directly measure the effect of an advertisement on profit, we could use total profit as the objective to be maximized.

More complex media selection models may include considerations such as the reduced exposure quality value for repeat media usage, cost discounts for repeat media usage, audience overlap by different media, and/or timing recommendations for the advertisements.

## N O T E S and Comments

1. The media selection model required subjective evaluations of the exposure quality for the media alternatives. Marketing managers may have substantial data concerning exposure quality, but the final coefficients used in the objective function may also include considerations based primarily on managerial judgment. Judgment is an acceptable way of obtaining input for a linear programming model.

2. The media selection model presented in this section uses exposure quality as the objective function and places a constraint on the number of customers reached. An alternative formulation of this problem would be to use the number of customers reached as the objective function and add a constraint indicating the minimum total exposure quality required for the media plan.

## Marketing Research

An organization conducts marketing research to learn about consumer characteristics, attitudes, and preferences. Marketing research firms that specialize in providing such information often do the actual research for client organizations. Typical services offered by a marketing research firm include designing the study, conducting market surveys, analyzing the data collected, and providing summary reports and recommendations for the client. In the research design phase, targets or quotas may be established for the number and types of respondents to be surveyed. The marketing research firm's objective is to conduct the survey so as to meet the client's needs at a minimum cost.

Market Survey, Inc. (MSI), specializes in evaluating consumer reaction to new products, services, and advertising campaigns. A client firm has requested MSI's assistance in ascertaining consumer reaction to a recently marketed household product. During meetings with the client, MSI agreed to conduct door-to-door personal interviews to obtain responses from households with children and households without children. In addition, MSI agreed to conduct both day and evening interviews. Specifically, the client's contract called for MSI to conduct 1000 interviews under the following quota guidelines.

1. Interview at least 400 households with children.
2. Interview at least 400 households without children.
3. The total number of households interviewed during the evening must be at least as great as the number of households interviewed during the day.
4. At least 40% of the interviews for households with children must be conducted during the evening.
5. At least 60% of the interviews for households without children must be conducted during the evening.

Because the interviews for households with children take additional interviewer time and because evening interviewers are paid more than daytime interviewers, the cost varies with the type of interview. Based on previous research studies, estimates of the interview costs are as follows:

| | Interview Cost | |
| --- | --- | --- |
| **Household** | **Day** | **Evening** |
| Children | $20 | $25 |
| No children | $18 | $20 |

What is the household, time-of-day interview plan that will satisfy the contract requirements at a minimum total interviewing cost?

In formulating the linear programming model for the MSI problem, we utilize the following decision-variable notation:

$DC$ = the number of daytime interviews of households with children
$EC$ = the number of evening interviews of households with children
$DNC$ = the number of daytime interviews of households without children
$ENC$ = the number of evening interviews of households without children

We begin the linear programming model formulation by using the cost-per-interview data to develop the objective function:

$$\text{Min} \quad 20DC + 25EC + 18DNC + 20ENC$$

The constraint requiring a total of 1000 interviews is

$$DC + EC + DNC + ENC = 1000$$

The five specifications concerning the types of interviews are as follows.

- Households with children:

$$DC + EC \geq 400$$

- Households without children:

$$DNC + ENC \geq 400$$

- At least as many evening interviews as day interviews:

$$EC + ENC \geq DC + DNC$$

The usual format for linear programming model formulation and computer input places all decision variables on the left side of the inequality and a constant (possibly zero) on the right side. Thus, we rewrite this constraint as

$$-DC + EC - DNC + ENC \geq 0$$

- At least 40% of interviews of households with children during the evening:

$$EC \geq 0.4(DC + EC) \quad \text{or} \quad -0.4DC + 0.6EC \geq 0$$

- At least 60% of interviews of households without children during the evening:

$$ENC \geq 0.6(DNC + ENC) \quad \text{or} \quad -0.6DNC + 0.4ENC \geq 0$$

When we add the nonnegativity requirements, the four-variable and six-constraint linear programming model becomes

$$
\begin{aligned}
\text{Min} \quad & 20DC + 25EC + 18DNC + 20ENC \\
\text{s.t.} \quad &
\end{aligned}
$$

| | | | | | |
|---|---|---|---|---|---|
| $DC +$ | $EC +$ | $DNC +$ | $ENC = 1000$ | Total interviews |
| $DC +$ | $EC$ | | $\geq\ 400$ | Households with children |
| | | $DNC +$ | $ENC \geq\ 400$ | Households without children |
| $-DC +$ | $EC -$ | $DNC +$ | $ENC \geq\ \ \ 0$ | Evening interviews |
| $-0.4DC +$ | $0.6EC$ | | $\geq\ \ \ 0$ | Evening interviews in households with children |
| | | $-\ 0.6DNC +$ | $0.4ENC \geq\ \ \ 0$ | Evening interviews in households without children |

$$DC, EC, DNC, ENC \geq 0$$

The computer solution for this linear program is shown in Figure 4.2. The solution reveals that the minimum cost of $20,320 occurs with the following interview schedule.

| | **Number of Interviews** | | |
|---|---|---|---|
| **Household** | **Day** | **Evening** | **Totals** |
| Children | 240 | 160 | 400 |
| No children | 240 | 360 | 600 |
| Totals | 480 | 520 | 1000 |

Hence, 480 interviews will be scheduled during the day and 520 during the evening. Households with children will be covered by 400 interviews, and households without children will be covered by 600 interviews.

Selected sensitivity analysis information from Figure 4.2 shows a dual price of $-19.200$ for constraint 1. In other words, the objective function will get worse (the total interviewing cost will increase) by $19.20 if the number of interviews is increased from 1000 to 1001. Thus, $19.20 is the incremental cost of obtaining additional interviews. It also is the savings that could be realized by reducing the number of interviews from 1000 to 999.

The surplus variable, with a value of 200.000, for constraint 3 shows that 200 more households without children will be interviewed than required. Similarly, the surplus variable, with a value of 40.000, for constraint 4 shows that the number of evening interviews exceeds the number of daytime interviews by 40. The zero values for the surplus variables in constraints 5 and 6 indicate that the more expensive evening interviews are being held at a minimum. Indeed, the dual price of $-5.000$ for constraint 5 indicates that if one more household (with children) than the minimum requirement must be interviewed during the evening, the total interviewing cost will go up by $5.00. Similarly, constraint 6 shows that requiring one more household (without children) to be interviewed during the evening will increase costs by $2.00.

**Figure 4.2    THE MANAGEMENT SCIENTIST SOLUTION FOR THE MARKET SURVEY PROBLEM**

```
Objective Function Value =          20320.000

      Variable              Value            Reduced Costs
    --------------      --------------      ------------------
          DC              240.000                 0.000
          EC              160.000                 0.000
          DNC             240.000                 0.000
          ENC             360.000                 0.000

    Constraint          Slack/Surplus          Dual Prices
    --------------      --------------      ------------------
          1                 0.000                -19.200
          2                 0.000                 -2.800
          3               200.000                  0.000
          4                40.000                  0.000
          5                 0.000                 -5.000
          6                 0.000                 -2.000
```

## 4.2    FINANCIAL APPLICATIONS

In finance, linear programming has been applied in problem situations involving capital budgeting, make-or-buy decisions, asset allocation, portfolio selection, financial planning, and many more. In this section, we describe a portfolio selection problem and a problem involving funding of an early retirement program.

### Portfolio Selection

Portfolio selection problems involve situations in which a financial manager must select specific investments—for example, stocks and bonds—from a variety of investment alternatives. Managers of mutual funds, credit unions, insurance companies, and banks frequently encounter this type of problem. The objective function for portfolio selection problems usually is maximization of expected return or minimization of risk. The constraints usually take the form of restrictions on the type of permissible investments, state laws, company policy, maximum permissible risk, and so on. Problems of this type have been formulated and solved using a variety of mathematical programming techniques. In this section we formulate and solve a portfolio selection problem as a linear program.

Consider the case of Welte Mutual Funds, Inc., located in New York City. Welte has just obtained $100,000 by converting industrial bonds to cash and is now looking for other investment opportunities for these funds. Based on Welte's current investments, the firm's top financial analyst recommends that all new investments be made in the oil industry, steel industry, or in government bonds. Specifically, the analyst has identified five investment opportunities and projected their annual rates of return. The investments and rates of return are shown in Table 4.3.

Management of Welte has imposed the following investment guidelines.

1. Neither industry (oil or steel) should receive more than $50,000.
2. Government bonds should be at least 25% of the steel industry investments.
3. The investment in Pacific Oil, the high-return but high-risk investment, cannot be more than 60% of the total oil industry investment.

What portfolio recommendations—investments and amounts—should be made for the available $100,000? Given the objective of maximizing projected return subject to the budgetary and managerially imposed constraints, we can answer this question by formulating and solving a linear programming model of the problem. The solution will provide investment recommendations for the management of Welte Mutual Funds.

| *Table* 4.3 | INVESTMENT OPPORTUNITIES FOR WELTE MUTUAL FUNDS |
|---|---|

| Investment | Projected Rate of Return (%) |
|---|---|
| Atlantic Oil | 7.3 |
| Pacific Oil | 10.3 |
| Midwest Steel | 6.4 |
| Huber Steel | 7.5 |
| Government bonds | 4.5 |

Let

$$A = \text{dollars invested in Atlantic Oil}$$
$$P = \text{dollars invested in Pacific Oil}$$
$$M = \text{dollars invested in Midwest Steel}$$
$$H = \text{dollars invested in Huber Steel}$$
$$G = \text{dollars invested in government bonds}$$

Using the projected rates of return shown in Table 4.3, we write the objective function for maximizing the total return for the portfolio as

$$\text{Max} \quad 0.073A + 0.103P + 0.064M + 0.075H + 0.045G$$

The constraint specifying investment of the available $100,000 is

$$A + P + M + H + G = 100{,}000$$

The requirements that neither the oil nor the steel industry should receive more than $50,000 are

$$A + P \leq 50{,}000$$
$$M + H \leq 50{,}000$$

The requirement that government bonds be at least 25% of the steel industry investment is expressed as

$$G \geq 0.25(M + H) \quad \text{or} \quad -0.25M - 0.25H + G \geq 0$$

Finally, the constraint that Pacific Oil cannot be more than 60% of the total oil industry investment is

$$P \leq 0.60(A + P) \quad \text{or} \quad -0.60A + 0.40P \leq 0$$

By adding the nonnegativity restrictions, we obtain the complete linear programming model for the Welte Mutual Fund investment problem:

Max   $0.073A + 0.103P + 0.064M + 0.075H + 0.045G$
s.t.

| | | | | | | | |
|---|---|---|---|---|---|---|---|
| $A +$ | $P +$ | $M +$ | $H +$ | $G =$ | 100,000 | Available funds |
| $A +$ | $P$ | | | $\leq$ | 50,000 | Oil industry maximum |
| | | $M +$ | $H$ | $\leq$ | 50,000 | Steel industry maximum |
| | | $- \ 0.25M -$ | $0.25H +$ | $G \geq$ | 0 | Government bonds maximum |
| $- \ 0.6A +$ | $0.4P$ | | | $\leq$ | 0 | Pacific Oil restriction |

$$A, P, M, H, G \geq 0$$

| Figure 4.3 | THE MANAGEMENT SCIENTIST SOLUTION FOR THE WELTE MUTUAL FUNDS PROBLEM |
| --- | --- |

```
Objective Function Value =              8000.000

        Variable              Value              Reduced Costs
    --------------      ---------------      ------------------
           A               20000.000                 0.000
           P               30000.000                 0.000
           M                   0.000                 0.011
           H               40000.000                 0.000
           G               10000.000                 0.000


      Constraint         Slack/Surplus           Dual Prices
    --------------      ---------------      ------------------
           1                   0.000                 0.069
           2                   0.000                 0.022
           3               10000.000                 0.000
           4                   0.000                -0.024
           5                   0.000                 0.030
```

We solved this problem using The Management Scientist; the output is shown in Figure 4.3. Table 4.4 shows how the funds are divided among the securities. Note that the optimal solution indicates that the portfolio should be diversified among all the investment opportunities except Midwest Steel. The projected annual return for this portfolio is $8000, which is an overall return of 8%.

The computer printout shows the dual price for constraint 3 is zero. The reason is that the steel industry maximum isn't a binding constraint; increases in the steel industry limit of $50,000 will not improve the value of the objective function. Indeed, the slack variable for this constraint

| Table 4.4 | OPTIMAL PORTFOLIO SELECTION FOR WELTE MUTUAL FUNDS |
| --- | --- |

| Investment | Amount | Expected Annual Return |
| --- | --- | --- |
| Atlantic Oil | $ 20,000 | $1,460 |
| Pacific Oil | 30,000 | 3,090 |
| Huber Steel | 40,000 | 3,000 |
| Government bonds | 10,000 | 450 |
| Totals | $100,000 | $8,000 |

Expected annual return of $8,000
Overall rate of return = 8%

shows that the current steel industry investment is $10,000 below its limit of $50,000. The dual prices for the other constraints are nonzero, indicating that these constraints are binding.

The dual price for the available funds constraint provides information on the rate of return from additional investment funds.

The dual price of 0.069 for constraint 1 shows that the objective function can be increased by 0.069 if one more dollar can be made available for the portfolio investment. If more funds can be obtained at a cost of less than 6.9%, management should consider obtaining them. However, if a return in excess of 6.9% can be obtained by investing funds elsewhere (other than in these five securities), management should question the wisdom of investing the entire $100,000 in this portfolio.

Similar interpretations can be given to the other dual prices. Note that the dual price for constraint 4 is negative at $-0.024$. This result indicates that increasing the value on the right-hand side of the constraint by one unit can be expected to worsen the objective function by 0.024. That is, in terms of the optimal portfolio, if Welte invests one more dollar in government bonds (beyond the minimum requirement), the total return will decrease by $0.024. To see why this decrease occurs, note again from the dual price for constraint 1 that the marginal return on the funds invested in the portfolio is 6.9% (the average return is 8%). The rate of return on government bonds is 4.5%. Thus, the cost of investing one more dollar in government bonds is the difference between the marginal return on the portfolio and the marginal return on government bonds: 6.9% − 4.5% = 2.4%.

Practice formulating a variation of the Welte problem by working Problem 9.

Note that the optimal solution shows that Midwest Steel should not be included in the portfolio ($M = 0$). The associated reduced cost for $M$ of 0.011 tells us that the objective function coefficient for Midwest Steel would have to increase by 0.011 before considering the Midwest Steel investment alternative would be advisable. With such an increase the Midwest Steel return would be $0.064 + 0.011 = 0.075$, making this investment just as desirable as the currently used Huber Steel investment alternative.

Finally, a simple modification of the Welte linear programming model permits determining the fraction of available funds invested in each security. That is, we divide each of the right-hand-side values by 100,000. Then the optimal values for the variables will give the fraction of funds that should be invested in each security for a portfolio of any size.

## N O T E S and Comments

1. The optimal solution to the Welte Mutual Funds problem indicates that $20,000 is to be spent on the Atlantic Oil stock. If Atlantic Oil sells for $75 per share, we would have to purchase exactly 266⅔ shares in order to spend exactly $20,000. The difficulty of purchasing fractional shares is usually handled by purchasing the largest possible integer number of shares with the allotted funds (e.g., 266 shares of Atlantic Oil). This approach guarantees that the budget constraint will not be violated. This approach, of course, introduces the possibility that the solution will no longer be optimal, but the danger is slight if a large number of securities are involved. In cases where the analyst believes that the decision variables *must* have integer values, the problem must be formulated as an integer linear programming model. Integer linear programming is the topic of Chapter 8.

2. Financial portfolio theory stresses obtaining a proper balance between risk and return. In the Welte problem, we explicitly considered return in the objective function. Risk is controlled by choosing constraints that ensure diversity among oil and steel stocks and a balance between government bonds and the steel industry investment.

## Financial Planning

Linear programming has been used for a variety of financial planning applications. The Management Science in Action: Using Linear Programming for Optimal Lease Structuring describes how GE Capital used linear programming to optimize the structure of a leveraged lease.

Hewlitt Corporation has established an early retirement program as part of its corporate restructuring. At the close of the voluntary sign-up period, 68 employees had elected early retirement. As a result of these early retirements, the company has incurred the following obligations over the next 8 years. Cash requirements (in thousands of dollars) are due at the beginning of each year.

| Year | 1 | 2 | 3 | 4 | 5 | 6 | 7 | 8 |
|------|---|---|---|---|---|---|---|---|
| **Cash Requirement** | 430 | 210 | 222 | 231 | 240 | 195 | 225 | 255 |

The corporate treasurer must determine how much money must be set aside today to meet the 8-year financial obligations as they come due. The financing plan for the retirement program includes investments in government bonds as well as savings. The investments in government bonds are limited to three choices:

| Bond | Price | Rate | Years to Maturity |
|------|-------|------|-------------------|
| 1 | $1150 | 8.875 | 5 |
| 2 | 1000 | 5.500 | 6 |
| 3 | 1350 | 11.750 | 7 |

# MANAGEMENT SCIENCE IN ACTION

## USING LINEAR PROGRAMMING FOR OPTIMAL LEASE STRUCTURING*

GE Capital is a $70-billion subsidiary of General Electric. As one of the nation's largest and most diverse financial services companies, GE Capital arranges leases in both domestic and international markets, including leases for telecommunications; data processing; construction; and fleets of cars, trucks, and commercial aircraft. To help allocate and schedule the rental and debt payments of a leveraged lease, GE Capital analysts have developed an optimization model, which is available as an optional component of the company's lease analysis proprietary software.

Leveraged leases are designed to provide financing for assets with economic lives of at least five years, which require large capital outlays. A leveraged lease represents an agreement among the lessor (the owner of the asset), the lessee (the user of the asset), and the lender who provides a nonrecourse loan of 50% to 80% of the lessor's purchase price. In a nonrecourse loan, the lenders cannot turn to the lessor for repayment in the event of default. As the lessor in such arrangements, GE Capital is able to claim ownership and realize income tax benefits such as depreciation and interest deductions. These deductions usually produce tax losses during the early years of the lease, which reduces the total tax liability. Approximately 85% of all financial leases in the United States are leveraged leases.

In its simplest form, the leveraged lease structuring problem can be formulated as a linear program. The linear program models the after-tax cash flow for the lessor, taking into consideration rental receipts, borrowing and repaying of the loan, and income taxes. Constraints are formulated to ensure compliance with IRS guidelines and to enable customizing of leases to meet lessee and lessor requirements. The objective function can be entered in a custom fashion or selected from a predefined list. Typically, the objective is to minimize the lessee's cost, expressed as the net present value of rental payments, or to maximize the lessor's after-tax yield.

GE Capital developed an optimization approach that could be applied to single-investor lease structuring. In a study with the department most involved with these transactions, the optimization approach yielded substantial benefits. The approach has helped GE Capital win some single-investor transactions ranging in size from $1 million to $20 million.

*Based on C. J. Litty, "Optimal Lease Structuring at GE Capital," *Interfaces* (May–June 1994) pp. 34–45

The government bonds have a par value of $1000, which means that even with different prices each bond pays $1000 at maturity. The rates shown are based on the par value. For purposes of planning, the treasurer has assumed that any funds not invested in bonds will be placed in savings and earn interest at an annual rate of 4%.

We define the decision variables as follows:

$F$ = total dollars required to meet the retirement plan's 8-year obligation

$B_1$ = units of bond 1 purchased at the beginning of year 1

$B_2$ = units of bond 2 purchased at the beginning of year 1

$B_3$ = units of bond 3 purchased at the beginning of year 1

$S_i$ = amount placed in savings at the beginning of the year $i$    for $i = 1, \ldots, 8$

The objective function is to minimize the total dollars needed to meet the retirement plan's 8-year obligation, or

$$\text{Min} \quad F$$

A key feature of this type of financial planning problem is that a constraint must be formulated for each year of the planning horizon. In general, each constraint takes the form:

$$\begin{pmatrix} \text{Funds available at} \\ \text{the beginning of the year} \end{pmatrix} - \begin{pmatrix} \text{Funds invested in bonds} \\ \text{and placed in savings} \end{pmatrix} = \begin{pmatrix} \text{Cash obligation for} \\ \text{the current year} \end{pmatrix}$$

The funds available at the beginning of year 1 is given by $F$. With a current price of $1150 for bond 1 and investments expressed in thousands of dollars, the total investment for $B_1$ units of bond 1 would be $1.15B_1$. Similarly, the total investment in bonds 2 and 3 would be $1B_2$ and $1.35B_3$, respectively. The investment in savings for year 1 is $S_1$. Using these results and the first-year obligation of 430, we obtain the constraint for year 1:

$$F - 1.15B_1 - 1B_2 - 1.35B_3 - S_1 = 430 \quad \text{Year 1}$$

We do not consider future investments in bonds because the future price of bonds depends on interest rates and cannot be known in advance.

Investments in bonds can take place only in this first year, and the bonds will be held until maturity.

The funds available at the beginning of year 2 include the investment returns of 8.875% on the par value of bond 1, 5.5% on the par value of bond 2, 11.75% on the par value of bond 3, and 4% on savings. The new amount to be invested in savings for year 2 is $S_2$. With an obligation of 210, the constraint for year 2 is

$$0.08875B_1 + 0.055B_2 + 0.1175B_3 + 1.04S_1 - S_2 = 210 \quad \text{Year 2}$$

Similarly, the constraints for years 3 to 8 are

$$0.08875B_1 + 0.055B_2 + 0.1175B_3 + 1.04S_2 - S_3 = 222 \quad \text{Year 3}$$
$$0.08875B_1 + 0.055B_2 + 0.1175B_3 + 1.04S_3 - S_4 = 231 \quad \text{Year 4}$$
$$0.08875B_1 + 0.055B_2 + 0.1175B_3 + 1.04S_4 - S_5 = 240 \quad \text{Year 5}$$
$$1.08875B_1 + 0.055B_2 + 0.1175B_3 + 1.04S_5 - S_6 = 195 \quad \text{Year 6}$$
$$1.055B_2 + 0.1175B_3 + 1.04S_6 - S_7 = 225 \quad \text{Year 7}$$
$$1.1175B_3 + 1.04S_7 - S_8 = 255 \quad \text{Year 8}$$

Note that the constraint for year 6 shows that funds available from bond 1 are $1.08875B_1$. The coefficient of 1.08875 reflects the fact that bond 1 matures at the end of year 5. As a result, the par value plus the interest from bond 1 during year 5 is available at the beginning of year 6. Also, because bond 1 matures in year 5 and becomes available for use at the beginning of year 6, the variable $B_1$ does not appear in the constraints for years 7 and 8. Note the similar interpretation for bond 2, which matures at the end of year 6 and has the par value plus interest available at the beginning of year 7. In addition, bond 3 matures at the end of year 7 and has the par value plus interest available at the beginning of year 8.

Finally, note that a variable $S_8$ appears in the constraint for year 8. The retirement fund obligation will be completed at the beginning of year 8, so we anticipate that $S_8$ will be zero and no funds will be put into savings. However, the formulation includes $S_8$ in the event that the bond income plus interest from the savings in year 7 exceed the 255 cash requirement for year 8. Thus, $S_8$ is a surplus variable that shows any funds remaining after the 8-year cash requirements have been satisfied.

The solution to the 12 variable, 8 constraint linear program is shown in Figure 4.4. With an objective function value of 1728.79385, the total investment required to meet the retirement plan's

**Figure 4.4   THE MANAGEMENT SCIENTIST SOLUTION FOR THE HEWLITT CORPORATION CASH REQUIREMENTS PROBLEM**

Objective Function Value =        1728.79385

| Variable | Value | Reduced Costs |
|---|---|---|
| F | 1728.79385 | 0.00000 |
| B1 | 144.98815 | 0.00000 |
| B2 | 187.85585 | 0.00000 |
| B3 | 228.18792 | 0.00000 |
| S1 | 636.14794 | 0.00000 |
| S2 | 501.60571 | 0.00000 |
| S3 | 349.68179 | 0.00000 |
| S4 | 182.68091 | 0.00000 |
| S5 | 0.00000 | 0.06403 |
| S6 | 0.00000 | 0.01261 |
| S7 | 0.00000 | 0.02132 |
| S8 | 0.00000 | 0.67084 |

| Constraint | Slack/Surplus | Dual Prices |
|---|---|---|
| 1 | 0.00000 | -1.00000 |
| 2 | 0.00000 | -0.96154 |
| 3 | 0.00000 | -0.92456 |
| 4 | 0.00000 | -0.88900 |
| 5 | 0.00000 | -0.85480 |
| 6 | 0.00000 | -0.76036 |
| 7 | 0.00000 | -0.71899 |
| 8 | 0.00000 | -0.67084 |

8-year obligation is $1,728,794. Using the current prices of $1150, $1000, and $1350 for each of the bonds respectively, we can summarize the initial investments in the three bonds as follows:

| Bond | Units Purchased | Investment Amount |
|------|-----------------|-------------------|
| 1 | $B_1 = 144.988$ | $1150(144.988) = $166,736 |
| 2 | $B_2 = 187.856$ | $1000(187.856) = $187,856 |
| 3 | $B_3 = 228.188$ | $1350(228.188) = $308,054 |

The solution also shows that $636,148 (see $S_1$) will be placed in savings at the beginning of the first year. By starting with $1,728,794, the company can make the specified bond and savings investments and have enough left over to meet the retirement program's first-year cash requirement of $430,000.

The optimal solution in Figure 4.4 shows that the decision variables $S_1$, $S_2$, $S_3$, and $S_4$ all are greater than zero, indicating investments in savings are required in each of the first four years. However, interest from the bonds plus the bond maturity incomes will be sufficient to cover the retirement program's cash requirements in years 6 through 8.

*In this application, the dual price can be thought of as the negative of the present value of each dollar in the cash requirement. For example, each dollar that must be paid in year 8 has a present value of $0.67084.*

The dual prices have an interesting interpretation in this application. Each right-hand-side value corresponds to the payment that must be made in that year. Note that the dual prices are negative, indicating that reducing the payment in any year would be beneficial because the total funds required for the retirement program's obligation would be less. Also note that the dual prices show that reductions are more beneficial in the early years, with decreasing benefits in subsequent years. As a result, Hewlitt would benefit by reducing cash requirements in the early years even if it had to make equivalently larger cash payments in later years.

## N O T E S and Comments

1. The optimal solution for the Hewlitt Corporation problem shows fractional numbers of government bonds at 144.988, 187.856, and 228.188 units, respectively. However, fractional bond units usually are not available. If we were conservative and rounded up to 145, 188, and 229 units, respectively, the total funds required for the 8-year retirement program obligation would be approximately $1254 more than the total funds indicated by the objective function. Because of the magnitude of the funds involved, rounding up probably would provide a workable solution. If an optimal integer solution were required, the methods of integer linear programming covered in Chapter 8 would have to be used.

2. We implicitly assumed that interest from the government bonds is paid annually. Investments such as treasury notes actually provide interest payments every 6 months. In such cases, the model can be reformulated with 6-month periods, with interest and/or cash payments occurring every 6 months.

## 4.3    PRODUCTION MANAGEMENT APPLICATIONS

Many linear programming applications have been developed for production and operations management, including scheduling, staffing, inventory control, and capacity planning. In this section we describe examples with make-or-buy decisions, production scheduling, and workforce assignments.

## A Make-or-Buy Decision

We illustrate the use of a linear programming model to determine how much of each of several component parts a company should manufacture and how much it should purchase from an outside supplier. Such a decision is referred to as a make-or-buy decision.

The Janders Company markets various business and engineering products. Currently, Janders is preparing to introduce two new calculators: one for the business market called the Financial Manager and one for the engineering market called the Technician. Each calculator has three components: a base, an electronic cartridge, and a face plate or top. The same base is used for both calculators, but the cartridges and tops are different. All components can be manufactured by the company or purchased from outside suppliers. The manufacturing costs and purchase prices for the components are summarized in Table 4.5.

Janders' forecasters indicate that 3000 Financial Manager calculators and 2000 Technician calculators will be needed. However, manufacturing capacity is limited. The company has 200 hours of regular manufacturing time and 50 hours of overtime that can be scheduled for the calculators. Overtime involves a premium at the additional cost of $9 per hour. Table 4.6 shows manufacturing times (in minutes) for the components.

The problem for Janders is to determine how many units of each component to manufacture and how many units of each component to purchase. We define the decision variables as follows:

$BM$ = number of bases manufactured

$BP$ = number of bases purchased

$FCM$ = number of Financial cartridges manufactured

$FCP$ = number of Financial cartridges purchased

$TCM$ = number of Technician cartridges manufactured

$TCP$ = number of Technician cartridges purchased

$FTM$ = number of Financial tops manufactured

$FTP$ = number of Financial tops purchased

$TTM$ = number of Technician tops manufactured

$TTP$ = number of Technician tops purchased

***Table 4.5*** — MANUFACTURING COSTS AND PURCHASE PRICES FOR JANDERS' CALCULATOR COMPONENTS

| | Cost Per Unit | |
|---|---|---|
| Component | Manufacture (Regular Time) | Purchase |
| Base | $0.50 | $0.60 |
| Financial cartridge | 3.75 | 4.00 |
| Technician cartridge | 3.30 | 3.90 |
| Financial top | 0.60 | 0.65 |
| Technician top | 0.75 | 0.78 |

| Table 4.6 | MANUFACTURING TIMES IN MINUTES PER UNIT FOR JANDERS' CALCULATOR COMPONENTS |

| Component | Manufacturing Time |
| --- | --- |
| Base | 1.0 |
| Financial cartridge | 3.0 |
| Technician cartridge | 2.5 |
| Financial top | 1.0 |
| Technician top | 1.5 |

One additional decision variable is needed to determine the hours of overtime that must be scheduled:

$$OT = \text{number of hours of overtime to be scheduled}$$

The objective function is to minimize the total cost, including manufacturing costs, purchase costs, and overtime costs. Using the cost-per-unit data in Table 4.5 and the overtime premium cost rate of $9 per hour, we write the objective function as

$$\text{Min} \quad 0.5BM + 0.6BP + 3.75FCM + 4FCP + 3.3TCM + 3.9TCP + 0.6FTM + 0.65FTP + 0.75TTM + 0.78TTP + 9OT$$

The first five constraints specify the number of each component needed to satisfy the demand for 3000 Financial Manager calculators and 2000 Technician calculators. A total of 5000 base components are needed, with the number of other components depending on the demand for the particular calculator. The five demand constraints are

$$BM + BP = 5000 \quad \text{Bases}$$
$$FCM + FCP = 3000 \quad \text{Financial cartridges}$$
$$TCM + TCP = 2000 \quad \text{Technician cartridges}$$
$$FTM + FTP = 3000 \quad \text{Financial tops}$$
$$TTM + TTP = 2000 \quad \text{Technician tops}$$

Two constraints are needed to guarantee that manufacturing capacities for regular time and overtime cannot be exceeded. The first constraint limits overtime capacity to 50 hours, or

$$OT \leq 50$$

The same units of measure must be used for both the left-hand side and right-hand side of the constraint. In this case, minutes are used.

The second constraint states that the total manufacturing time required for all components must be less than or equal to the total manufacturing capacity, including regular time plus overtime. The manufacturing times for the components are expressed in minutes so we state the total manufacturing capacity constraint in minutes, with the 200 hours of regular time capacity becoming $60(200) = 12,000$ minutes. The actual overtime required is unknown at this point, so we write the overtime as $60OT$ minutes. Using the manufacturing times from Table 4.6, we have

$$BM + 3FCM + 2.5TCM + FTM + 1.5TTM \leq 12,000 + 60OT$$

Moving the decision variable for overtime to the left-hand side of the constraint provides the manufacturing capacity constraint:

$$BM + 3FCM + 2.5TCM + FTM + 1.5TTM - 60OT \leq 12{,}000$$

The complete formulation of Janders' make-or-buy problem with all decision variables greater than or equal to zero is

Min    $0.5BM + 0.6BP + 3.75FCM + 4FCP + 3.3TCM + 3.9TCP$
       $+ 0.6FTM + 0.65FTP + 0.75TTM + 0.78TTP + 9OT$

s.t.

| | | | | | | | | |
|---|---|---|---|---|---|---|---|---|
| $BM$ | | | | | $+$ | $BP =$ | 5000 | Bases |
| | $FCM$ | | | | $+$ | $FCP =$ | 3000 | Financial cartridges |
| | | $TCM$ | | | $+$ | $TCP =$ | 2000 | Technician cartridges |
| | | | $FTM$ | | $+$ | $FTP =$ | 3000 | Financial tops |
| | | | | $TTM +$ | | $TTP =$ | 2000 | Technician tops |
| | | | | | | $OT \leq$ | 50 | Overtime hours |
| $BM + 3FCM + 2.5TCM + FTM + 1.5TTM - 60OT \leq 12{,}000$ | | | | | | | | Manufacturing capacity |

Try Problem 12 for practice with a variation of the Janders make-or-buy problem.

The computer solution to this 11-variable, 7-constraint linear program is shown in Figure 4.5. The optimal solution indicates that all 5000 bases ($BM$), 667 Financial Manager cartridges ($FCM$), and 2000 Technician cartridges ($TCM$) should be manufactured. The remaining 2333 Financial Manager cartridges ($FCP$), all the Financial Manager tops ($FTP$), and all Technician tops ($TTP$) should be purchased. No overtime manufacturing is necessary, and the total cost associated with the optimal make-or-buy plan is $24,443.33.

Sensitivity analysis provides some additional information about the unused overtime capacity. The Reduced Costs column shows that the overtime ($OT$) premium would have to decrease by $4 per hour before overtime production should be considered. That is, if the overtime premium is $9 − $4 = $5 or less, Janders may want to replace some of the purchased components with components manufactured on overtime. Problem 12 at the end of the chapter asks you to reconsider the Janders problem with a lower overtime premium to show how the optimal make-or-buy solution changes.

The dual price for the manufacturing capacity constraint 7 is 0.083. This price indicates that an additional hour of manufacturing capacity is worth $0.083 per minute or ($0.083)(60) = $5 per hour. The range of feasibility for constraint 7 shows that this conclusion is valid until the amount of regular time increases to 19,000 minutes, or 316.7 hours.

Sensitivity analysis also indicates that a change in prices charged by the outside suppliers can affect the optimal solution. For instance, the range of optimality for the objective function coefficient for $BP$ is 0.583 to no upper limit. If the purchase price for bases remains at $0.583 or more, the number of bases purchased ($BP$) will remain at zero. However, if the purchase price drops below $0.583, Janders should begin to purchase rather than manufacture the base component. Similar sensitivity analysis conclusions about the purchase price ranges can be drawn for the other components.

Objective Function Value =          24443.333

| Variable | Value | Reduced Costs |
|----------|-------|---------------|
| BM | 5000.000 | 0.000 |
| BP | 0.000 | 0.017 |
| FCM | 666.667 | 0.000 |
| FCP | 2333.333 | 0.000 |
| TCM | 2000.000 | 0.000 |
| TCP | 0.000 | 0.392 |
| FTM | 0.000 | 0.033 |
| FTP | 3000.000 | 0.000 |
| TTM | 0.000 | 0.095 |
| TTP | 2000.000 | 0.000 |
| OT | 0.000 | 4.000 |

| Constraint | Slack/Surplus | Dual Prices |
|------------|---------------|-------------|
| 1 | 0.000 | -0.583 |
| 2 | 0.000 | -4.000 |
| 3 | 0.000 | -3.508 |
| 4 | 0.000 | -0.650 |
| 5 | 0.000 | -0.780 |
| 6 | 50.000 | 0.000 |
| 7 | 0.000 | 0.083 |

OBJECTIVE COEFFICIENT RANGES

| Variable | Lower Limit | Current Value | Upper Limit |
|----------|-------------|---------------|-------------|
| BM | No Lower Limit | 0.500 | 0.517 |
| BP | 0.583 | 0.600 | No Upper Limit |
| FCM | 3.700 | 3.750 | 3.850 |
| FCP | 3.900 | 4.000 | 4.050 |
| TCM | No Lower Limit | 3.300 | 3.692 |
| TCP | 3.508 | 3.900 | No Upper Limit |
| FTM | 0.567 | 0.600 | No Upper Limit |
| FTP | No Lower Limit | 0.650 | 0.683 |
| TTM | 0.655 | 0.750 | No Upper Limit |
| TTP | No Lower Limit | 0.780 | 0.875 |
| OT | 5.000 | 9.000 | No Upper Limit |

RIGHT HAND SIDE RANGES

| Constraint | Lower Limit | Current Value | Upper Limit |
|------------|-------------|---------------|-------------|
| 1 | 0.000 | 5000.000 | 7000.000 |
| 2 | 666.667 | 3000.000 | No Upper Limit |
| 3 | 0.000 | 2000.000 | 2800.000 |
| 4 | 0.000 | 3000.000 | No Upper Limit |
| 5 | 0.000 | 2000.000 | No Upper Limit |
| 6 | 0.000 | 50.000 | No Upper Limit |
| 7 | 10000.000 | 12000.000 | 19000.000 |

| N O T E S | The proper interpretation of the dual price for manufacturing capacity (constraint 7) in the Janders problem is that an additional hour of manufacturing capacity is worth ($0.083)(60) = $5 per hour. Thus, the company should be willing to pay a premium of $5 per hour over and above the current regular time cost per hour, which is already included in the manufacturing cost of the product. Thus, if the regular time cost is $18 per hour, Janders should be willing to pay up to $18 + $5 = $23 per hour to obtain additional labor capacity. |
|---|---|
| *and Comments* | |

## Production Scheduling

One of the most important applications of linear programming deals with multiperiod planning such as production scheduling. The solution to a production scheduling problem enables the manager to establish an efficient low-cost production schedule for one or more products over several time periods (weeks or months). Essentially, a production scheduling problem can be viewed as a product-mix problem for each of several periods in the future. The manager must determine the production levels that will allow the company to meet product demand requirements, given limitations on production capacity, labor capacity, and storage space, while minimizing total production costs.

One advantage of using linear programming for production scheduling problems is that they recur. A production schedule must be established for the current month, then again for the next month, for the month after that, and so on. When looking at the problem each month, the production manager will find that, although demand for the products has changed, production times, production capacities, storage space limitations, and so on are roughly the same. Thus, the production manager is basically resolving the same problem handled in previous months, and a general linear programming model of the production scheduling procedure may be frequently applied. Once the model has been formulated, the manager can simply supply the data—demand, capacities, and so on—for the given production period and use the linear programming model repeatedly to develop the production schedule.

Let us consider the case of the Bollinger Electronics Company, which produces two different electronic components for a major airplane engine manufacturer. The airplane engine manufacturer notifies the Bollinger sales office each quarter of its monthly requirements for components for each of the next 3 months. The monthly requirements for the components may vary considerably, depending on the type of engine the airplane engine manufacturer is producing. The order shown in Table 4.7 has just been received for the next 3-month period.

After the order is processed, a demand statement is sent to the production control department. The production control department must then develop a 3-month production plan

| *Table* 4.7 | THREE-MONTH DEMAND SCHEDULE FOR BOLLINGER ELECTRONICS COMPANY | | |
|---|---|---|---|
| Component | April | May | June |
| 322A | 1000 | 3000 | 5000 |
| 802B | 1000 | 500 | 3000 |

for the components. In arriving at the desired schedule, the production manager will want to identify

1. total production cost,
2. inventory holding cost, and
3. change-in-production-level costs.

In the remainder of this section, we show how to formulate a linear programming model of the production and inventory process for Bollinger Electronics to minimize the total cost.

To develop the model, we let $x_{im}$ denote the production volume in units for product $i$ in month $m$. Here $i = 1, 2$, and $m = 1, 2, 3$; $i = 1$ refers to component 322A, $i = 2$ refers to component 802B, $m = 1$ refers to April, $m = 2$ refers to May, and $m = 3$ refers to June. The purpose of the double subscript is to provide a more descriptive notation. We could simply use $x_6$ to represent the number of units of product 2 produced in month 3, but $x_{23}$ is more descriptive, identifying directly the product and month represented by the variable.

If component 322A costs \$20 per unit produced and component 802B costs \$10 per unit produced, the total production cost part of the objective function is

$$\text{Total production cost} = 20x_{11} + 20x_{12} + 20x_{13} + 10x_{21} + 10x_{22} + 10x_{23}$$

Since the production cost per unit is the same each month, we don't need to include the production costs in the objective function; that is, regardless of the production schedule selected, the total production cost will remain the same. In other words, production costs are not relevant costs for the production scheduling decision under consideration. In cases in which the production cost per unit is expected to change each month, the variable production costs per unit per month must be included in the objective function. Since the solution for the Bollinger Electronics problem will be the same whether or not these costs are included, we included them so that the value of the linear programming objective function will include all the costs associated with the problem.

To incorporate the relevant inventory holding costs into the model, we let $s_{im}$ denote the inventory level for product $i$ at the end of month $m$. Bollinger has determined that on a monthly basis inventory holding costs are 1.5% of the cost of the product; that is, $(0.015)(\$20) = \$0.30$ per unit for component 322A and $(0.015)(\$10) = \$0.15$ per unit for component 802B. A common assumption made in using the linear programming approach to production scheduling is that monthly ending inventories are an acceptable approximation to the average inventory levels throughout the month. Making this assumption, we write the inventory holding cost portion of the objective function as

$$\text{Inventory holding cost} = 0.30s_{11} + 0.30s_{12} + 0.30s_{13} + 0.15s_{21} + 0.15s_{22} + 0.15s_{23}$$

To incorporate the costs of fluctuations in production levels from month to month, we need to define two additional variables:

$$I_m = \text{increase in the total production level necessary during month } m$$
$$D_m = \text{decrease in the total production level necessary during month } m$$

After estimating the effects of employee layoffs, turnovers, reassignment training costs, and other costs associated with fluctuating production levels, Bollinger estimates that the cost associated with increasing the production level for any month is \$0.50 per unit increase. A similar cost associated with decreasing the production level for any month is \$0.20 per unit. Thus, we write the third portion of the objective function as

$$\text{Change-in-production-level costs} = 0.50I_1 + 0.50I_2 + 0.50I_3$$
$$+ 0.20D_1 + 0.20D_2 + 0.20D_3$$

Note that the cost associated with changes in production level is a function of the change in the total number of units produced in month $m$ compared to the total number of units produced in month $m - 1$. In other production scheduling applications, fluctuations in production level might be measured in terms of machine hours or labor-hours required rather than in terms of the total number of units produced.

Combining all three costs, the complete objective function becomes

$$\begin{aligned} \text{Min} \quad &20x_{11} + 20x_{12} + 20x_{13} + 10x_{21} + 10x_{22} + 10x_{23} + 0.30s_{11} \\ &+ 0.30s_{12} + 0.30s_{13} + 0.15s_{21} + 0.15s_{22} + 0.15s_{23} + 0.50I_1 \\ &+ 0.50I_2 + 0.50I_3 + 0.20D_1 + 0.20D_2 + 0.20D_3 \end{aligned}$$

We now consider the constraints. First, we must guarantee that the schedule meets customer demand. Since the units shipped can come from the current month's production or from inventory carried over from previous months, the demand requirement takes the form

$$\left(\begin{array}{c}\text{Ending}\\\text{inventory}\\\text{from previous}\\\text{month}\end{array}\right) + \left(\begin{array}{c}\text{Current}\\\text{production}\end{array}\right) - \left(\begin{array}{c}\text{Ending}\\\text{inventory}\\\text{for this}\\\text{month}\end{array}\right) = \left(\begin{array}{c}\text{This month's}\\\text{demand}\end{array}\right)$$

Suppose that the inventories at the beginning of the 3-month scheduling period were 500 units for component 322A and 200 units for component 802B. The demand for both products in the first month (April) was 1000 units, so the constraints for meeting demand in the first month become

$$500 + x_{11} - s_{11} = 1000$$
$$200 + x_{21} - s_{21} = 1000$$

Moving the constants to the right-hand side, we have

$$x_{11} - s_{11} = 500$$
$$x_{21} - s_{21} = 800$$

Similarly, we need demand constraints for both products in the second and third months. We write them as follows.

**Month 2**

$$s_{11} + x_{12} - s_{12} = 3000$$
$$s_{21} + x_{22} - s_{22} = 500$$

**Month 3**

$$s_{12} + x_{13} - s_{13} = 5000$$
$$s_{22} + x_{23} - s_{23} = 3000$$

If the company specifies a minimum inventory level at the end of the 3-month period of at least 400 units of component 322A and at least 200 units of component 802B, we can add the constraints

$$s_{13} \geq 400$$
$$s_{23} \geq 200$$

Suppose that we have the additional information on machine, labor, and storage capacity shown in Table 4.8. Machine, labor, and storage space requirements are given in Table 4.9. To reflect these limitations, the following constraints are necessary.

**Machine Capacity**

$$0.10x_{11} + 0.08x_{21} \leq 400 \quad \text{Month 1}$$
$$0.10x_{12} + 0.08x_{22} \leq 500 \quad \text{Month 2}$$
$$0.10x_{13} + 0.08x_{23} \leq 600 \quad \text{Month 3}$$

**Labor Capacity**

$$0.05x_{11} + 0.07x_{21} \leq 300 \quad \text{Month 1}$$
$$0.05x_{12} + 0.07x_{22} \leq 300 \quad \text{Month 2}$$
$$0.05x_{13} + 0.07x_{23} \leq 300 \quad \text{Month 3}$$

**Storage Capacity**

$$2s_{11} + 3s_{21} \leq 10,000 \quad \text{Month 1}$$
$$2s_{12} + 3s_{22} \leq 10,000 \quad \text{Month 2}$$
$$2s_{13} + 3s_{23} \leq 10,000 \quad \text{Month 3}$$

One final set of constraints must be added to guarantee that $I_m$ and $D_m$ will reflect the increase or decrease in the total production level for month $m$. Suppose that the production

| Table 4.8 | MACHINE, LABOR, AND STORAGE CAPACITIES FOR BOLLINGER ELECTRONICS | | |
|---|---|---|---|
| Month | Machine Capacity (hours) | Labor Capacity (hours) | Storage Capacity (square feet) |
| April | 400 | 300 | 10,000 |
| May | 500 | 300 | 10,000 |
| June | 600 | 300 | 10,000 |

| Table 4.9 | MACHINE, LABOR, AND STORAGE REQUIREMENTS FOR COMPONENTS 322A AND 802B | | |
|-----------|------------|---------|---------|
| Component | Machine (hours/unit) | Labor (hours/unit) | Storage (square feet/unit) |
| 322A | 0.10 | 0.05 | 2 |
| 802B | 0.08 | 0.07 | 3 |

levels for March, the month before the start of the current production scheduling period, had been 1500 units of component 322A and 1000 units of component 802B for a total production level of $1500 + 1000 = 2500$ units. We can find the amount of the change in production for April from the relationship

$$\text{April production} - \text{March production} = \text{Change}$$

Using the April production variables, $x_{11}$ and $x_{21}$, the March production of 2500 units, we have

$$(x_{11} + x_{21}) - 2500 = \text{Change}$$

Note that the change can be positive or negative. A positive change reflects an increase in the total production level, and a negative change reflects a decrease in the total production level. We can use the increase in production for April, $I_1$, and the decrease in production for April, $D_1$, to specify the constraint for the change in total production for the month of April:

$$(x_{11} + x_{21}) - 2500 = I_1 - D_1$$

Of course, we cannot have an increase in production and a decrease in production during the same 1-month period; thus, either, $I_1$ or $D_1$ will be zero. If April requires 3000 units of production, $I_1 = 500$ and $D_1 = 0$. If April requires 2200 units of production, $I_1 = 0$ and $D_1 = 300$. This approach of denoting the change in production level as the difference between two nonnegative variables, $I_1$ and $D_1$, permits both positive and negative changes in the total production level. If a single variable (say, $c_m$) had been used to represent the change in production level, only positive changes would be possible because of the non-negativity requirement.

Using the same approach in May and June (always subtracting the previous month's total production from the current month's total production), we obtain the constraints for the second and third months of the production scheduling period:

$$(x_{12} + x_{22}) - (x_{11} + x_{21}) = I_2 - D_2$$
$$(x_{13} + x_{23}) - (x_{12} + x_{22}) = I_3 - D_3$$

Placing the variables on the left-hand side and the constants on the right-hand side yields the complete set of what are commonly referred to as production-smoothing constraints:

$$
\begin{aligned}
x_{11} + x_{21} \qquad\qquad\qquad\quad - I_1 + D_1 &= 2500 \\
-x_{11} - x_{21} + x_{12} + x_{22} \qquad\qquad - I_2 + D_2 &= 0 \\
-x_{12} - x_{22} + x_{13} + x_{23} - I_3 + D_3 &= 0
\end{aligned}
$$

Problem 19 involves a
production scheduling
application with labor-
smoothing constraints.

The initially rather small, 2-product, 3-month scheduling problem has now developed into an 18-variable, 20-constraint linear programming problem. Note that in this problem we were concerned only with one type of machine process, one type of labor, and one type of storage area. Actual production scheduling problems usually involve several machine types, several labor grades, and/or several storage areas, requiring large-scale linear programs. For instance, a problem involving 100 products over a 12-month period could have more than 1000 variables and constraints.

Figure 4.6 shows the computer solution to the Bollinger Electronics production scheduling problem. Table 4.10 contains a portion of the managerial report based on the computer solution.

Consider the monthly variation in the production and inventory schedule shown in Table 4.10. Recall that the inventory cost for component 802B is one-half the inventory cost for component 322A. Therefore, as might be expected, component 802B is produced heavily in the first month (April) and then held in inventory for the demand that will occur in future months. Component 322A tends to be produced when needed, and only small amounts are carried in inventory.

The costs of increasing and decreasing the total production volume tend to smooth the monthly variations. In fact, the minimum-cost schedule calls for a 500-unit increase in total production in April and a 2200-unit increase in total production in May. The May production level of 5200 units is then maintained during June.

The machine usage section of the report shows ample machine capacity in all 3 months. However, labor capacity is at full utilization (slack = 0 for constraint 13 in Figure 4.6) in the month of May. The dual price shows that an additional hour of labor capacity in May will improve the objective function (lower cost) by approximately $1.11.

A linear programming model of a 2-product, 3-month production system can provide valuable information in terms of identifying a minimum-cost production schedule. In larger production systems, where the number of variables and constraints is too large to track manually, linear programming models can provide a significant advantage in developing cost-saving production schedules. The Management Science in Action: Libbey-Owens-Ford shows just how large linear programming models can be for applications involving production scheduling.

Linear programming
models for production
scheduling are often very
large. Thousands of
decision variables and
constraints are necessary
when the problem involves
numerous products,
machines, and time periods.
Data collection for large-
scale models can be more
time-consuming than either
the formulation of the
model or the development
of the computer solution.

## Workforce Assignment

Workforce assignment problems frequently occur when production managers must make decisions involving staffing requirements for a given planning period. Workforce assignments often have some flexibility, and at least some personnel can be assigned to more than one department or work center. Such is the case when employees have been cross-trained on two or more jobs or, for instance, when sales personnel can be transferred between stores. In the following application, we show how linear programming can be used to determine not only an optimal product mix, but also an optimal workforce assignment.

McCormick Manufacturing Company produces two products with contributions to profit per unit of $10 and $9, respectively. The labor requirements per unit produced and the total hours of labor available from personnel assigned to each of four departments are shown in Table 4.11. Assuming that the number of hours available in each department is fixed, we can formulate McCormick's problem as a standard product-mix linear program with the following decision variables:

$$P_1 = \text{units of product 1}$$
$$P_2 = \text{units of product 2}$$

| Figure 4.6 | THE MANAGEMENT SCIENTIST SOLUTION FOR THE BOLLINGER ELECTRONICS PROBLEM |
|---|---|

Objective Function Value =        225295.000

| Variable | Value | Reduced Costs |
|---|---|---|
| X11 | 500.000 | 0.000 |
| X12 | 3200.000 | 0.000 |
| X13 | 5200.000 | 0.000 |
| X21 | 2500.000 | 0.000 |
| X22 | 2000.000 | 0.000 |
| X23 | 0.000 | 0.128 |
| S11 | 0.000 | 0.172 |
| S12 | 200.000 | 0.000 |
| S13 | 400.000 | 0.000 |
| S21 | 1700.000 | 0.000 |
| S22 | 3200.000 | 0.000 |
| S23 | 200.000 | 0.000 |
| I1 | 500.000 | 0.000 |
| I2 | 2200.000 | 0.000 |
| I3 | 0.000 | 0.072 |
| D1 | 0.000 | 0.700 |
| D2 | 0.000 | 0.700 |
| D3 | 0.000 | 0.628 |

| Constraint | Slack/Surplus | Dual Prices |
|---|---|---|
| 1 | 0.000 | -20.000 |
| 2 | 0.000 | -10.000 |
| 3 | 0.000 | -20.128 |
| 4 | 0.000 | -10.150 |
| 5 | 0.000 | -20.428 |
| 6 | 0.000 | -10.300 |
| 7 | 0.000 | -20.728 |
| 8 | 0.000 | -10.450 |
| 9 | 150.000 | 0.000 |
| 10 | 20.000 | 0.000 |
| 11 | 80.000 | 0.000 |
| 12 | 100.000 | 0.000 |
| 13 | 0.000 | 1.111 |
| 14 | 40.000 | 0.000 |
| 15 | 4900.000 | 0.000 |
| 16 | 0.000 | 0.000 |
| 17 | 8600.000 | 0.000 |
| 18 | 0.000 | 0.500 |
| 19 | 0.000 | 0.500 |
| 20 | 0.000 | 0.428 |

| Table 4.10 | MINIMUM-COST PRODUCTION SCHEDULE INFORMATION FOR THE BOLLINGER ELECTRONICS PROBLEM | | |
|---|---|---|---|
| **Activity** | **April** | **May** | **June** |
| Production | | | |
| Component 322A | 500 | 3,200 | 5,200 |
| Component 802B | 2,500 | 2,000 | 0 |
| Totals | 3,000 | 5,200 | 5,200 |
| Ending inventory | | | |
| Component 322A | 0 | 200 | 400 |
| Component 802B | 1,700 | 3,200 | 200 |
| Machine usage | | | |
| Scheduled hours | 250 | 480 | 520 |
| Slack capacity hours | 150 | 20 | 80 |
| Labor usage | | | |
| Scheduled hours | 200 | 300 | 260 |
| Slack capacity hours | 100 | 0 | 40 |
| Storage usage | | | |
| Scheduled storage | 5,100 | 10,000 | 1,400 |
| Slack capacity | 4,900 | 0 | 8,600 |
| Total production, inventory, and production-smoothing cost = $225,295 | | | |

# MANAGEMENT SCIENCE IN ACTION

## LIBBEY-OWENS-FORD*

Libbey-Owens-Ford utilizes a large-scale linear programming model to achieve integrated production, distribution, and inventory planning for its flat glass products. The linear programming model is called FLAGPOL. Schedulers and planners in the flat-glass products group must coordinate production schedules for more than 200 different glass products. The products are made in 4 colors (clear, gray, bronze, and blue-green) and 26 thicknesses. Other options include 3 quality levels, 2 cutting classifications, 4 packaging modes, and various fabrication methods, including tempered glass and/or coated glass.

To integrate production, distribution, and inventory planning, company analysts developed a linear programming model that optimizes operations for all products over a 12-month planning horizon. The model is applied monthly, and its output helps planners react to unexpected changes in the operating environment and deal with strategic issues such as adding new plants and expanding capacity. A typical linear programming model has approximately 100,000 variables and 26,000 constraints. The company estimates that the FLAGPOL model provides an annual savings of more than $2 million.

*Based on Clarence H. Martin, Denver C. Dent, and James C. Eckhart, "Integrated Production, Distribution and Inventory Planning at Libbey-Owens-Ford," *Interfaces* (May–June 1993): 68–78.

| Table 4.11 | DEPARTMENTAL LABOR-HOURS PER UNIT AND TOTAL HOURS AVAILABLE FOR THE McCORMICK MANUFACTURING COMPANY | | |
|---|---|---|---|

| Department | Labor-Hours Per Unit | | Total Hours Available |
|---|---|---|---|
| | **Product 1** | **Product 2** | |
| 1 | 0.65 | 0.95 | 6500 |
| 2 | 0.45 | 0.85 | 6000 |
| 3 | 1.00 | 0.70 | 7000 |
| 4 | 0.15 | 0.30 | 1400 |

The linear program is

$$\text{Max} \quad 10P_1 + 9P_2$$
$$\text{s.t.}$$
$$0.65P_1 + 0.95P_2 \leq 6500$$
$$0.45P_1 + 0.85P_2 \leq 6000$$
$$1.00P_1 + 0.70P_2 \leq 7000$$
$$0.15P_1 + 0.30P_2 \leq 1400$$
$$P_1, P_2 \geq 0$$

The optimal solution to the linear programming model is shown in Figure 4.7. After rounding, it calls for 5744 units of product 1, 1795 units of product 2, and a total profit of

| Figure 4.7 | THE MANAGEMENT SCIENTIST SOLUTION FOR THE McCORMICK MANUFACTURING COMPANY PROBLEM WITH NO WORKFORCE TRANSFERS PERMITTED |
|---|---|

```
Objective Function Value =            73589.744

      Variable            Value           Reduced Costs
    --------------     --------------     ------------------
         P1               5743.590             0.000
         P2               1794.872             0.000

     Constraint        Slack/Surplus        Dual Prices
    --------------     --------------     ------------------
         1               1061.538             0.000
         2               1889.744             0.000
         3                  0.000             8.462
         4                  0.000            10.256
```

$73,590. With this optimal solution, departments 3 and 4 are operating at capacity, and departments 1 and 2 have a slack of approximately 1062 and 1890 hours, respectively. We would anticipate that the product mix would change and that the total profit would increase if the workforce assignment could be revised so that the slack, or unused hours, in departments 1 and 2 could be transferred to the departments currently working at capacity. However, the production manager may be uncertain as to how the workforce should be reallocated among the four departments. Let us expand the linear programming model to include decision variables that will help determine the optimal workforce assignment in addition to the profit-maximizing product mix.

Suppose that McCormick has a cross-training program that enables some employees to be transferred between departments. By taking advantage of the cross-training skills, a limited number of employees and labor-hours may be transferred from one department to another. For example, suppose that the cross-training permits transfers as shown in Table 4.12. Row 1 of this table shows that some employees assigned to department 1 have cross-training skills that permit them to be transferred to department 2 or 3. The right-hand column shows that, for the current production planning period, a maximum of 400 hours can be transferred from department 1. Similar cross-training transfer capabilities and capacities are shown for departments 2, 3, and 4.

When workforce assignments are flexible, we do not automatically know how many hours of labor should be assigned to or be transferred from each department. We need to add decision variables to the linear programming model to account for such changes.

$$b_i = \text{the labor-hours allocated to department } i \text{ for } i = 1, 2, 3, \text{ and } 4$$

$$t_{ij} = \text{the labor-hours transferred from department } i \text{ to department } j$$

*The right-hand sides are now treated as decision variables.*

With the addition of decision variables $b_1$, $b_2$, $b_3$, and $b_4$, we write the capacity restrictions for the four departments as follows:

$$0.65P_1 + 0.95P_2 \leq b_1$$
$$0.45P_1 + 0.85P_2 \leq b_2$$
$$1.00P_1 + 0.70P_2 \leq b_3$$
$$0.15P_1 + 0.30P_2 \leq b_4$$

| *Table* 4.12 | CROSS-TRAINING ABILITY AND CAPACITY INFORMATION | | | | |
|---|---|---|---|---|---|
| **From Department** | **Cross-Training Transfers Permitted to Department** | | | | **Maximum Hours Transferable** |
| | **1** | **2** | **3** | **4** | |
| 1 | — | yes | yes | — | 400 |
| 2 | — | — | yes | yes | 800 |
| 3 | — | — | — | yes | 100 |
| 4 | yes | yes | — | — | 200 |

Since $b_1$, $b_2$, $b_3$, and $b_4$ are now decision variables, we follow the standard practice of placing these variables on the left side of the inequalities, and the first four constraints of the linear programming model become

$$
\begin{aligned}
0.65P_1 + 0.95P_2 - b_1 & \quad & \le 0 \\
0.45P_1 + 0.85P_2 \quad - b_2 & \quad & \le 0 \\
1.00P_1 + 0.70P_2 \quad\quad - b_3 & \quad & \le 0 \\
0.15P_1 + 0.30P_2 \quad\quad\quad - b_4 & \le 0
\end{aligned}
$$

The labor-hours ultimately allocated to each department must be determined by a series of labor balance equations, or constraints, that include the number of hours initially assigned to each department plus the number of hours transferred into the department minus the number of hours transferred out of the department. Using department 1 as an example, we determine the workforce allocation as follows:

$$
b_1 = \left( \begin{array}{c} \text{Hours} \\ \text{initially in} \\ \text{department 1} \end{array} \right) + \left( \begin{array}{c} \text{Hours} \\ \text{transferred into} \\ \text{department 1} \end{array} \right) - \left( \begin{array}{c} \text{Hours} \\ \text{transferred out of} \\ \text{department 1} \end{array} \right)
$$

Table 4.11 shows 6500 hours initially assigned to department 1. We use the transfer decision variables $t_{i1}$ to denote transfers into department 1 and $t_{1j}$ to denote transfers from department 1. Table 4.12 shows that the cross-training capabilities involving department 1 are restricted to transfers from department 4 (variable $t_{41}$) and transfers to either department 2 or department 3 (variables $t_{12}$ and $t_{13}$). Thus, we can express the total workforce allocation for department 1 as

$$
b_1 = 6500 + t_{41} - t_{12} - t_{13}
$$

Moving the decision variables for the workforce transfers to the left-hand side, we have the labor balance equation or constraint

$$
b_1 - t_{41} + t_{12} + t_{13} = 6500
$$

This form of constraint will be needed for each of the four departments. Thus, the following labor balance constraints for departments 2, 3, and 4 would be added to the model.

$$
\begin{aligned}
b_2 - t_{12} - t_{42} + t_{23} + t_{24} &= 6000 \\
b_3 - t_{13} - t_{23} + t_{34} &= 7000 \\
b_4 - t_{24} - t_{34} + t_{41} + t_{42} &= 1400
\end{aligned}
$$

Finally, since Table 4.12 shows that the number of hours that may be transferred from each department is limited, a transfer capacity constraint must be added for each of the four departments. The additional constraints are

$$
\begin{aligned}
t_{12} + t_{13} &\le 400 \\
t_{23} + t_{24} &\le 800 \\
t_{34} &\le 100 \\
t_{41} + t_{42} &\le 200
\end{aligned}
$$

The complete linear programming model has 2 product decision variables ($P_1$ and $P_2$), 4 department workforce assignment variables ($b_1$, $b_2$, $b_3$, and $b_4$), 7 transfer variables $t_{12}$, $t_{13}$, $t_{23}$, $t_{24}$, $t_{34}$, $t_{41}$, and $t_{42}$), and 12 constraints. Figure 4.8 shows the optimal solution to this linear program provided by The Management Scientist.

McCormick's profit can be increased by \$10,421 to \$84,011 by taking advantage of crosstraining and workforce transfers. The optimal product mix of 6825 units of product 1 and 1751 units of product 2 can be achieved if $t_{13} = 400$ hours are transferred from department 1 to department 3; $t_{23} = 651$ hours are transferred from department 2 to department 3; and $t_{24} = 149$ hours are transferred from department 2 to department 4. The resulting workforce assignments for departments 1–4 would provide 6100, 5200, 8051, and 1549 hours, respectively.

Variations in the workforce assignment model could be used in situations such as allocating raw material resources to products, allocating machine time to products, and allocating salesforce time to stores or sales territories.

**Figure 4.8    THE MANAGEMENT SCIENTIST SOLUTION FOR THE McCORMICK MANUFACTURING COMPANY PROBLEM**

```
Objective Function Value =           84011.299

        Variable            Value          Reduced Costs
        --------            -----          -------------
           P1            6824.859             0.000
           P2            1751.412             0.000
           B1            6100.000             0.000
           B2            5200.000             0.000
           B3            8050.847             0.000
           B4            1549.153             0.000
          T12               0.000             8.249
          T13             400.000             0.000
          T23             650.847             0.000
          T24             149.153             0.000
          T34               0.000             0.000
          T41               0.000             7.458
          T42               0.000             8.249

       Constraint       Slack/Surplus        Dual Prices
       ----------       -------------        -----------
            1                0.000               0.791
            2              640.113               0.000
            3                0.000               8.249
            4                0.000               8.249
            5                0.000               0.791
            6                0.000               0.000
            7                0.000               8.249
            8                0.000               8.249
            9                0.000               7.458
           10                0.000               8.249
           11              100.000               0.000
           12              200.000               0.000
```

If a manager has the flexibility to assign personnel to different departments, reduced workforce idle time, improved workforce utilization, and improved profit should result. The linear programming model in this section automatically assigns employees and labor-hours to the departments in the most profitable manner.

## 4.4 BLENDING PROBLEMS

Blending problems arise whenever a manager must decide how to blend two or more resources to produce one or more products. In these situations, the resources contain one or more essential ingredients that must be blended into final products that will contain specific percentages of each. In most of these applications, then, management must decide how much of each resource to purchase to satisfy product specifications and product demands at minimum cost.

Blending problems occur frequently in the petroleum industry (e.g., blending crude oil to produce different octane gasolines), chemical industry (e.g., blending chemicals to produce fertilizers and weed killers), and food industry (e.g., blending ingredients to produce soft drinks and soups). In this section we illustrate how to apply linear programming to a blending problem in the petroleum industry.

The Grand Strand Oil Company produces regular and premium gasoline for independent service stations in the southeastern United States. The Grand Strand refinery manufactures the gasoline products by blending three petroleum components. The gasolines are sold at different prices, and the petroleum components have different costs. The firm wants to determine how to mix or blend the three components into the two gasoline products and maximize profits.

Data available show that regular gasoline can be sold for $1.00 per gallon and premium gasoline for $1.08 per gallon. For the current production planning period, Grand Strand can obtain the three petroleum components at the cost per gallon and in the quantities shown in Table 4.13.

Product specifications for the regular and premium gasolines restrict the amounts of each component that can be used in each gasoline product. Table 4.14 lists the product specifications. Current commitments to distributors require Grand Strand to produce at least 10,000 gallons of regular gasoline.

The Grand Strand blending problem is to determine how many gallons of each component should be used in the regular gasoline blend and how many should be used in the premium gasoline blend. The optimal blending solution should maximize the firm's profit, subject to the constraints on the available petroleum supplies shown in Table 4.13, the product specifications shown in Table 4.14, and the required 10,000 gallons of regular gasoline.

**Table 4.13   PETROLEUM COST AND SUPPLY FOR THE GRAND STRAND BLENDING PROBLEM**

| Petroleum Component | Cost/Gallon | Maximum Available |
|---|---|---|
| 1 | $0.50 | 5,000 gallons |
| 2 | $0.60 | 10,000 gallons |
| 3 | $0.84 | 10,000 gallons |

| Table 4.14 | PRODUCT SPECIFICATIONS FOR THE GRAND STRAND BLENDING PROBLEM |
|---|---|

| Product | Specifications |
|---|---|
| Regular gasoline | At most 30% component 1 |
| | At least 40% component 2 |
| | At most 20% component 3 |
| Premium gasoline | At least 25% component 1 |
| | At most 40% component 2 |
| | At least 30% component 3 |

We define the decision variables as

$$x_{ij} = \text{gallons of component } i \text{ used in gasoline } j,$$
where $i = 1, 2,$ or $3$ for components 1, 2, or 3,
and $j = r$ if regular or $j = p$ if premium

The six decision variables are

$$x_{1r} = \text{gallons of component 1 in regular gasoline}$$
$$x_{2r} = \text{gallons of component 2 in regular gasoline}$$
$$x_{3r} = \text{gallons of component 3 in regular gasoline}$$
$$x_{1p} = \text{gallons of component 1 in premium gasoline}$$
$$x_{2p} = \text{gallons of component 2 in premium gasoline}$$
$$x_{3p} = \text{gallons of component 3 in premium gasoline}$$

The total number of gallons of each type of gasoline produced is the sum of the number of gallons produced using each of the three petroleum components.

**Total Gallons Produced**

$$\text{Regular gasoline} = x_{1r} + x_{2r} + x_{3r}$$
$$\text{Premium gasoline} = x_{1p} + x_{2p} + x_{3p}$$

The total gallons of each petroleum component are computed in a similar fashion.

**Total Petroleum Component Use**

$$\text{Component 1} = x_{1r} + x_{1p}$$
$$\text{Component 2} = x_{2r} + x_{2p}$$
$$\text{Component 3} = x_{3r} + x_{3p}$$

We develop the objective function of maximizing the profit contribution by identifying the difference between the total revenue from both gasolines and the total cost of the three petroleum components. By multiplying the $1.00 per gallon price by the total gallons of regular gasoline, the $1.08 per gallon price by the total gallons of premium gasoline, and the component cost per gallon figures in Table 4.13 by the total gallons of each component used, we obtain the objective function:

$$\text{Max}\quad 1.00(x_{1r} + x_{2r} + x_{3r}) + 1.08(x_{1p} + x_{2p} + x_{3p})$$
$$- 0.50(x_{1r} + x_{1p}) - 0.60(x_{2r} + x_{2p}) - 0.84(x_{3r} + x_{3p})$$

When we combine terms, the objective function becomes

$$\text{Max}\quad 0.50x_{1r} + 0.40x_{2r} + 0.16x_{3r} + 0.58x_{1p} + 0.48x_{2p} + 0.24x_{3p}$$

The limitations on the availability of the three petroleum components are

$$
\begin{array}{lll}
x_{1r} + x_{1p} &\leq 5,000 & \text{Component 1} \\
x_{2r} + x_{2p} &\leq 10,000 & \text{Component 2} \\
x_{3r} + x_{3p} &\leq 10,000 & \text{Component 3}
\end{array}
$$

Six constraints are now required to meet the product specifications stated in Table 4.14. The first specification states that component 1 can account for no more than 30% of the total gallons of regular gasoline produced. That is,

$$x_{1r} \leq 0.30(x_{1r} + x_{2r} + x_{3r})$$

Rewriting this constraint with the variables on the left-hand side and a constant on the right-hand side yields

$$0.70x_{1r} - 0.30x_{2r} - 0.30x_{3r} \leq 0$$

The second product specification listed in Table 4.14 becomes

$$x_{2r} \geq 0.40(x_{1r} + x_{2r} + x_{3r})$$

and thus,

$$-0.40x_{1r} + 0.60x_{2r} - 0.40x_{3r} \geq 0$$

Similarly, we write the four remaining blending specifications listed in Table 4.14 as

$$
\begin{array}{l}
-0.20x_{1r} - 0.20x_{2r} + 0.80x_{3r} \leq 0 \\
+0.75x_{1p} - 0.25x_{2p} - 0.25x_{3p} \geq 0 \\
-0.40x_{1p} + 0.60x_{2p} - 0.40x_{3p} \leq 0 \\
-0.30x_{1p} - 0.30x_{2p} + 0.70x_{3p} \geq 0
\end{array}
$$

The constraint for at least 10,000 gallons of regular gasoline is

$$x_{1r} + x_{2r} + x_{3r} \geq 10,000$$

The complete linear programming model with 6 decision variables and 10 constraints is

$$\text{Max} \quad 0.50x_{1r} + 0.40x_{2r} + 0.16x_{3r} + 0.58x_{1p} + 0.48x_{2p} + 0.24x_{3p}$$

s.t.

$$
\begin{aligned}
x_{1r} \qquad\qquad\quad + \quad x_{1p} \qquad\qquad\qquad\quad &\leq 5{,}000 \\
x_{2r} \qquad\qquad\quad + \quad x_{2p} \qquad\qquad &\leq 10{,}000 \\
x_{3r} \qquad\qquad\qquad + \quad x_{3p} &\leq 10{,}000 \\
0.70x_{1r} - 0.30x_{2r} - 0.30x_{3r} \qquad\qquad\qquad\qquad &\leq \quad 0 \\
-0.40x_{1r} + 0.60x_{2r} - 0.40x_{3r} \qquad\qquad\qquad\qquad &\geq \quad 0 \\
-0.20x_{1r} - 0.20x_{2r} + 0.80x_{3r} \qquad\qquad\qquad\qquad &\leq \quad 0 \\
0.75x_{1p} - 0.25x_{2p} - 0.25x_{3p} &\geq \quad 0 \\
-0.40x_{1p} + 0.60x_{2p} - 0.40x_{3p} &\leq \quad 0 \\
-0.30x_{1p} - 0.30x_{2p} + 0.70x_{3p} &\geq \quad 0 \\
x_{1r} + \quad x_{2r} + \quad x_{3r} \qquad\qquad\qquad\qquad &\geq 10{,}000 \\
x_{1r}, x_{2r}, x_{3r}, x_{1p}, x_{2p}, x_{3p} &\geq 0
\end{aligned}
$$

*Try Problem 15 as another example of a blending model.*

The computer solution to the Grand Strand blending problem is shown in Figure 4.9. The optimal solution providing a profit of \$9300 is summarized in Table 4.15. The optimal

---

**Figure 4.9    THE MANAGEMENT SCIENTIST SOLUTION FOR THE GRAND STRAND BLENDING PROBLEM**

```
Objective Function Value =              9300.000

        Variable              Value           Reduced Costs
      ---------------    ---------------    -------------------
          X1R                  0.000               0.000
          X2R               8000.000               0.000
          X3R               2000.000               0.000
          X1P               5000.000               0.000
          X2P               2000.000               0.000
          X3P               8000.000               0.000


      Constraint          Slack/Surplus           Dual Prices
      ---------------    ---------------    -------------------
            1                  0.000               0.580
            2                  0.000               0.480
            3                  0.000               0.240
            4               3000.000               0.000
            5               4000.000               0.000
            6                  0.000               0.000
            7               1250.000               0.000
            8               4000.000               0.000
            9               3500.000               0.000
           10                  0.000              -0.080
```

| | **GRAND STRAND GASOLINE BLENDING SOLUTION** |
|---|---|

**Table 4.15**

**Gallons of Component (percentage)**

| Gasoline | Component 1 | Component 2 | Component 3 | Total |
|---|---|---|---|---|
| Regular | 0 (0%) | 8000 (80%) | 2000 (20%) | 10,000 |
| Premium | 5000 (33⅓%) | 2000 (13⅓%) | 8000 (53⅓%) | 15,000 |

blending strategy shows that 10,000 gallons of regular gasoline should be produced. The regular gasoline will be manufactured as a blend of 8000 gallons of component 2 and 2000 gallons of component 3. The 15,000 gallons of premium gasoline will be manufactured as a blend of 5000 gallons of component 1, 2000 gallons of component 2, and 8000 gallons of component 3.

The interpretation of the slack and surplus variables associated with the product specification constraints (constraints 4–9) in Figure 4.9 needs some clarification. If the constraint is a $\leq$ constraint, the value of the slack variable can be interpreted as the gallons of component use below the maximum amount of the component use specified by the constraint. For example, the slack of 3000.000 for constraint 4 shows that component 1 use is 3000 gallons below the maximum amount of component 1 that could have been used in the production of 10,000 gallons of regular gasoline. If the product specification constraint is a $\geq$ constraint, a surplus variable shows the gallons of component use above the minimum amount of component use specified by the blending constraint. For example, the surplus of 4000.000 for constraint 5 shows that component 2 use is 4000 gallons above the minimum amount of component 2 that must be used in the production of 10,000 gallons of regular gasoline.

**N O T E S**
**and Comments**

A convenient way to define the decision variables in a blending problem is to use a matrix in which the rows correspond to the raw materials and the columns correspond to the final products. For example, in the Grand Strand blending problem, we could define the decision variables as follows:

**Final Products**

| | | Regular Gasoline | Premium Gasoline |
|---|---|---|---|
| Raw Materials | Component 1 | $x_{1r}$ | $x_{1p}$ |
| | Component 2 | $x_{2r}$ | $x_{2p}$ |
| | Component 3 | $x_{3r}$ | $x_{3p}$ |

This approach has two advantages: (1) it provides a systematic way to define the decision variables for any blending problem; and (2) it provides a visual image of the decision variables in terms of how they are related to the raw materials, products, and each other.

## 4.5    DATA ENVELOPMENT ANALYSIS

**Data envelopment analysis (DEA)** is an application of linear programming that has been used to measure the relative efficiency of operating units with the same goals and objectives. For example, DEA has been used within individual fast-food outlets in the same chain. In this case, the goal of DEA was to identify the inefficient outlets that should be targeted for further study and, if necessary, corrective action. Other applications of DEA have measured the relative efficiencies of hospitals, banks, courts, schools, and so on. In these applications, the performance of each institution or organization was measured relative to the performance of all operating units in the same system. Management Science in Action: Managing Bank Productivity describes how a large northeastern bank used DEA to determine which branches were operating inefficiently.

The operating units of most organizations have multiple inputs such as staff size, salaries, hours of operation, and advertising budget, as well as multiple outputs such as profit, market share, and growth rate. In these situations, it is often difficult for a manager to determine which operating units are inefficient in converting their multiple inputs into multiple outputs. This particular area is where data envelopment analysis has proven to be a helpful managerial tool. We illustrate the application of data envelopment analysis by evaluating the performance of a group of four hospitals.

### Evaluating the Performance of Hospitals

The hospital administrators at General Hospital, University Hospital, County Hospital, and State Hospital have been meeting to discuss ways in which they can help one another

## MANAGEMENT SCIENCE IN ACTION

### MANAGING BANK PRODUCTIVITY*

Management of a large northeastern bank wanted to expand its existing 33-branch system to cover a wider geographic region. To help finance the expansion, management wanted to identify ways in which they could streamline existing operations to obtain substantial savings, but at the same time avoid sacrificing quality of service. As the first step in reviewing productivity of the branches, data envelopment analysis (DEA) was used to indicate which branches were operating inefficiently.

The DEA model they developed compared the actual operating results of each branch with those of all other branches in order to identify the less-productive branches. A less-productive branch is one that requires more resources to produce the same output as the best-practice branches. The best-practice branches are identified by a DEA productivity rating of 100 percent ($E = 1.00$), and the inefficient or less-productive branches are identified by a productivity rating of less than 100 percent ($E < 1.00$).

Five key resources used by each branch were determined, including the number of teller and manager personnel full-time equivalents (FTEs), branch operating expenses, and square feet of office space. In addition, 15 services that were performed by each branch were combined into five categories of service. For instance, the deposit, withdrawals, and checks cashed category was formed by treating each deposit, withdrawal, or check cashed as one transaction; for this service category, the output measure was the number of deposits, withdrawals, or checks cashed. Other service categories included measures of the number of bank checks, travelers checks, night deposits, and loans made by the branch. For each branch, data were collected for these resources and service measures for the previous year.

The solution to the DEA linear programming model using these data showed that 10 of the 33 branches had a DEA productivity rating of 100 percent and that 23 branches had a rating of less than 100 percent. In other words, there were 23 less-productive branches. For instance, one branch had a DEA rating of 37 percent, indicating that it was using about 63 percent excess resources. Overall, the findings indicated that the bank could make substantial productivity improvements and realize significant cost reductions by improving performance at the 23 less-productive branches.

Focusing on the less-productive branches, the bank was able to identify ways in which these branches could significantly reduce their resource requirement without reducing quality of service and while maintaining or even increasing the volume of services provided. The total potential savings were determined to be approximately $9 million. However, some changes required square feet reductions at certain branches, something that could not be done in the short run. For the next year, management concluded and reported to the board of directors that savings of over $6 million of the $30 million operating costs for these less-productive branches could be realized.

*Based on H. David Sherman, and George Ladino, "Managing Bank Productivity Using Data Envelopment Analysis (DEA)," *Interfaces* (March-April 1995); 60–73.

improve the performance at each of their hospitals. A consultant has suggested that they consider using DEA to measure the performance of each hospital relative to the performance of all four hospitals. In discussing how this could be done, the following three input measures and four output measures were identified:

### Input Measures

1. The number of full-time equivalent (FTE) nonphysician personnel
2. The amount spent on supplies
3. The number of bed-days available

Problem 26 asks you to formulate and solve a linear program to assess the relative efficiency of General Hospital.

### Output Measures

1. Patient-days of service under Medicare
2. Patient-days of service not under Medicare
3. Number of nurses trained
4. Number of interns trained

Summaries of the input and output measures for a one-year period at each of the four hospitals are shown in Tables 4.16 and 4.17. Let us show how DEA can use these data to identify relatively inefficient hospitals.

### An Overview of the DEA Approach

In this application of DEA, a linear programming model will be developed for each hospital whose efficiency is to be evaluated. To illustrate the modeling process, we will formulate a linear program that can be used to determine the relative efficiency of County Hospital.

**Table 4.16 — ANNUAL RESOURCES CONSUMED (INPUTS) BY THE FOUR HOSPITALS**

| Input Measure | General | University | County | State |
|---|---|---|---|---|
| Full-time equivalent nonphysicians | 285.20 | 162.30 | 275.70 | 210.40 |
| Supply expense ($1000s) | 123.80 | 128.70 | 348.50 | 154.10 |
| Bed-days available (1000s) | 106.72 | 64.21 | 104.10 | 104.04 |

**Table 4.17 — ANNUAL SERVICES PROVIDED (OUTPUTS) BY THE FOUR HOSPITALS**

| Output Measure | General | University | County | State |
|---|---|---|---|---|
| Medicare patient-days (1000s) | 48.14 | 34.62 | 36.72 | 33.16 |
| Non-Medicare patient-days (1000s) | 43.10 | 27.11 | 45.98 | 56.46 |
| Nurses trained | 253 | 148 | 175 | 160 |
| Interns trained | 41 | 27 | 23 | 84 |

First, using a linear programming model, we construct a **hypothetical composite,** in this case a composite hospital, based on the outputs and inputs for all operating units with the same goals. For each of the four hospitals' output measures, the output for the composite hospital is determined by computing a weighted average of the corresponding outputs for all four hospitals. For each of the three input measures, the input for the composite hospital is determined by using the same weights to compute a weighted average of the corresponding inputs for all four hospitals. Constraints in the linear programming model require all outputs for the composite hospital to be *greater than or equal to* the outputs of County Hospital, the hospital being evaluated. If the inputs for the composite unit can be shown to be *less than* the inputs for County Hospital, the composite hospital is shown to have the same, or more, output for *less input.* In this case, the model shows that the composite hospital is more efficient than County Hospital. In other words, the hospital being evaluated is *less efficient* than the composite hospital. Because the composite hospital is based on all four hospitals, the hospital being evaluated can be judged *relatively inefficient* when compared to the other hospitals in the group.

## The DEA Linear Programming Model

To determine the weight that each hospital will have in computing the outputs and inputs for the composite hospital, we use the following decision variables:

$$wg = \text{weight applied to inputs and outputs for General Hospital}$$
$$wu = \text{weight applied to inputs and outputs for University Hospital}$$
$$wc = \text{weight applied to inputs and outputs for County Hospital}$$
$$ws = \text{weight applied to inputs and outputs for State Hospital}$$

The DEA approach requires that the sum of these weights equal 1. Thus, the first constraint is

$$wg + wu + wc + ws = 1$$

In general, every DEA linear programming model will include a constraint that requires the weights for the operating units to sum to 1.

As we stated previously, for each output measure, the output for the composite hospital is determined by computing a weighted average of the corresponding outputs for all four hospitals. For instance, for output measure 1, the number of patient days of service under Medicare, the output for the composite hospital is

$$\begin{array}{l}\text{Medicare patient-days} \\ \text{for Composite Hospital}\end{array} = \left(\begin{array}{l}\text{Medicare patient-days} \\ \text{for General Hospital}\end{array}\right)wg + \left(\begin{array}{l}\text{Medicare patient-days} \\ \text{for University Hospital}\end{array}\right)wu$$

$$+ \left(\begin{array}{l}\text{Medicare patient-days} \\ \text{for County Hospital}\end{array}\right)wc + \left(\begin{array}{l}\text{Medicare patient-days} \\ \text{for State Hospital}\end{array}\right)ws$$

Substituting the number of medicare patient-days for each hospital as shown in Table 4.17, we obtain the following expression:

$$\begin{array}{l}\text{Medicare patient-days} \\ \text{for Composite Hospital}\end{array} = 48.14wg + 34.62wu + 36.72wc + 33.16ws$$

The other output measures for the composite hospital are computed in a similar fashion. Figure 4.10 provides a summary of the results.

For each of the four output measures, we need to write a constraint that requires the output for the composite hospital to be greater than or equal to the output for County Hospital. Thus, the general form of the output constraints is

$$\text{Output for the Composite Hospital} \geq \text{Output for County Hospital}$$

Since the number of medicare patient-days for County Hospital is 36.72, the output constraint corresponding to the number of medicare patient-days is

$$48.14wg + 34.62wu + 36.72wc + 33.16ws \geq 36.72$$

In a similar fashion, we formulated a constraint for each of the other three output measures, with the results as shown:

$$43.10wg + 27.11wu + 45.98wc + 56.46ws \geq 45.98 \quad \text{Non-Medicare}$$
$$253wg + 148wu + 175wc + 160ws \geq 175 \quad \text{Nurses}$$
$$41wg + 27wu + 23wc + 84ws \geq 23 \quad \text{Interns}$$

The four output constraints require the linear programming solution to provide weights that will make each output measure for the composite hospital greater than or equal to the corresponding output measure for County Hospital. Thus, if a solution satisfying the output constraints can be found, the composite hospital will have produced at least as much of each output as County Hospital.

---

**Figure 4.10   RELATIONSHIP BETWEEN THE OUTPUT MEASURES FOR THE FOUR HOSPITALS AND THE OUTPUT MEASURES FOR THE COMPOSITE HOSPITAL**

$wg$
**General**

| Medicare | 48.14 |
| Non-Medicare | 43.10 |
| Nurses | 253 |
| Interns | 41 |

$wu$
**University**

| Medicare | 34.62 |
| Non-Medicare | 27.11 |
| Nurses | 148 |
| Interns | 27 |

$wc$
**County**

| Medicare | 36.72 |
| Non-Medicare | 45.98 |
| Nurses | 175 |
| Interns | 23 |

$ws$
**State**

| Medicare | 33.16 |
| Non-Medicare | 56.46 |
| Nurses | 160 |
| Interns | 84 |

**Composite**

| Medicare | $48.14wg + 34.62wu + 36.72wc + 33.16ws$ |
| Non-Medicare | $43.10wg + 27.11wu + 45.98wc + 56.46ws$ |
| Nurses | $253wg + 148wu + 175wc + 160ws$ |
| Interns | $41wg + 27wu + 23wc + 84ws$ |

Next, we need to consider the constraints needed to model the relationship between the inputs for the composite hospital and the resources available to the composite hospital. A constraint is required for each of the three input measures. The general form for the input constraints is as follows:

$$\begin{array}{cc}\text{Input for the} \\ \text{Composite Hospital}\end{array} \leq \begin{array}{cc}\text{Resources available to} \\ \text{the Composite Hospital}\end{array}$$

For each input measure, the input for the composite hospital is a weighted average of the corresponding input for each of the four hospitals. Thus, for input measure 1, the number of full-time equivalent nonphysicians, the input for the composite hospital is

$$\begin{array}{c}\text{FTE nonphysicians} \\ \text{for Composite Hospital}\end{array} = \left(\begin{array}{c}\text{FTE nonphysicians} \\ \text{for General Hospital}\end{array}\right)wg + \left(\begin{array}{c}\text{FTE nonphysicians} \\ \text{for University Hospital}\end{array}\right)wu$$
$$+ \left(\begin{array}{c}\text{FTE nonphysicians} \\ \text{for County Hospital}\end{array}\right)wc + \left(\begin{array}{c}\text{FTE nonphysicians} \\ \text{for State Hospital}\end{array}\right)ws$$

Substituting the values for the number of full-time equivalent nonphysicians for each hospital as shown in Table 4.16, we obtain the following expression for the number of full-time equivalent nonphysicians for the composite hospital:

$$285.20wg + 162.30wu + 275.70wc + 210.40ws$$

In a similar manner, we can write expressions for each of the other two input measures as shown in Figure 4.11.

To complete the formulation of the input constraints, we must write expressions for the right-hand-side values for each constraint. First, note that the right-hand-side values are the resources available to the composite hospital. In the DEA approach, these right-hand-side

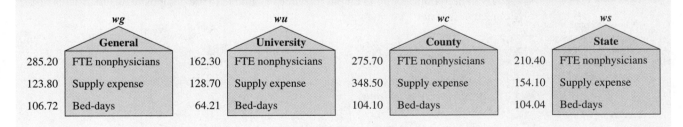

**Figure 4.11    RELATIONSHIP BETWEEN THE INPUT MEASURES FOR THE FOUR HOSPITALS AND THE INPUT MEASURES FOR THE COMPOSITE HOSPITAL**

values are a percentage of the input values for County Hospital. Thus, we must introduce the following decision variables:

$$E = \text{the fraction of County Hospital's input available to the composite hospital}$$

To illustrate the important role that $E$ plays in the DEA approach, we show how to write the expression for the number of FTE nonphysicians available to the composite hospital. Table 4.16 shows that the number of FTE nonphysicians used by County Hospital was 275.70; thus, $275.70E$ is the number of FTE nonphysicians available to the composite hospital. If $E = 1$, the number of FTE nonphysicians available to the composite hospital is 275.70, the same as the number of FTE nonphysicians used by County Hospital. However, if $E$ is greater than 1, the composite hospital would have available proportionally more non-physicians, while if $E$ is less than 1, the composite hospital would have available proportionally fewer FTE nonphysicians. Because of the effect that $E$ has in determining the resources available to the composite hospital, $E$ is referred to as the **efficiency index.**

We can now write the input constraint corresponding to the number of FTE nonphysicians available to the composite hospital:

$$285.20wg + 162.30wu + 275.70wc + 210.40ws \leq 275.70E$$

In a similar manner, we can write the input constraints for the supplies and bed-days available to the composite hospital. First, using the data in Table 4.16, we note that for each of these resources, the amount that is available to the composite hospital is $348.50E$ and $104.10E$, respectively. Thus, the input constraints for the supplies and bed-days are written as follows:

$$123.80wg + 128.70wu + 348.50wc + 154.10ws \leq 348.50E \quad \text{Supplies}$$
$$106.72wg + 64.21wu + 104.10wc + 104.04ws \leq 104.10E \quad \text{Bed-days}$$

If a solution with $E < 1$ can be found, the composite hospital does not need as many resources as County Hospital needs to produce the same level of output.

The objective function for the DEA model is to minimize the value of $E$, which is equivalent to minimizing the input resources available to the composite hospital. Thus, the objective function is written as

$$\text{Min } E$$

The DEA efficiency conclusion is based on the optimal objective function value for $E$. The decision rule is as follows:

If $E = 1$, the composite hospital requires *as much input* as County Hospital does. There is no evidence that County Hospital is inefficient.

If $E < 1$, the composite hospital requires *less input* to obtain the output achieved by County Hospital. The composite hospital is more efficient; thus, County Hospital can be judged relatively inefficient.

The DEA linear programming model for the efficiency evaluation of County Hospital has five decision variables and eight constraints. The complete model is rewritten as follows:

The logic of a DEA model is to determine whether a composite facility can achieve the *same or more output while requiring less input.* If more output with less input can be achieved, the facility being evaluated is judged to be relatively inefficient.

The objective function in a DEA model is always Min E. The facility being evaluated (County Hospital in this example) can be judged relatively inefficient if the optimal solution provides E less than 1, indicating that the composite facility requires less input resources.

Min $\quad E$

s.t.

$$wg + \quad wu + \quad wc + \quad ws = \quad 1$$
$$48.14wg + 34.62wu + 36.72wc + 33.16ws \geq 36.72$$
$$43.10wg + 27.11wu + 45.98wc + 56.46ws \geq 45.98$$
$$253wg + \quad 148wu + \quad 175wc + \quad 160ws \geq \quad 175$$
$$41wg + \quad 27wu + \quad 23wc + \quad 84ws \geq \quad 23$$
$$-275.70E + 285.20wg + 162.30wu + 275.70wc + 210.40ws \leq \quad 0$$
$$-348.50E + 123.80wg + 128.70wu + 348.50wc + 154.10ws \leq \quad 0$$
$$-104.10E + 106.72wg + 64.21wu + 104.10wc + 104.04ws \leq \quad 0$$
$$E, wg, wu, wc, ws \geq 0$$

Note that in this formulation of the model, we have moved the terms involving $E$ to the left side of the three input constraints because $E$ is a decision variable. This linear program was solved using The Management Scientist software package. The computer solution is shown in Figure 4.12.

We first note that the objective function shows that the efficiency score for County Hospital is 0.905. This score tells us that the composite hospital can obtain at least the

**Figure 4.12    THE MANAGEMENT SCIENTIST SOLUTION FOR THE DATA ENVELOPMENT ANALYSIS COUNTY HOSPITAL PROBLEM**

```
Objective Function Value =            0.905

       Variable            Value          Reduced Costs
       --------            -----          -------------
          E                0.905             0.000
          WG               0.212             0.000
          WU               0.260             0.000
          WC               0.000             0.095
          WS               0.527             0.000

      Constraint       Slack/Surplus        Dual Prices
      ----------       -------------        -----------
          1               0.000               0.239
          2               0.000              -0.014
          3               0.000              -0.014
          4               1.615               0.000
          5              37.027               0.000
          6              35.824               0.000
          7             174.422               0.000
          8               0.000               0.010
```

level of each output that County Hospital obtains by having available no more than 90.5% of the input resources required by County Hospital. Thus, the composite hospital is more efficient, and the DEA analysis has identified County Hospital as being relatively inefficient.

From the solution in Figure 4.12, we see that the composite hospital is formed from the weighted average of General Hospital ($wg = 0.212$), University Hospital ($wu = 0.260$), and State Hospital ($ws = 0.527$). Each input and output of the composite hospital is determined by the same weighted average of the inputs and outputs of these three hospitals.

The Slack/Surplus column provides some additional information about the efficiency of County Hospital compared to the composite hospital. Specifically, the composite hospital has at least as much of each output as County Hospital has (constraints 2–5) and provides 1.6 more nurses trained (surplus for constraint 4) and 37 more interns trained (surplus for constraint 5). The slack of zero from constraint 8 shows that the composite hospital uses approximately 90.5% of the bed-days used by County Hospital. The slack values for constraints 6 and 7 show that less than 90.5% of the FTE nonphysician and the supplies expense resources used at County Hospital are used by the composite hospital.

Clearly, the composite hospital is more efficient than County Hospital, and we are justified in concluding that County Hospital is relatively inefficient compared to the other hospitals in the group. Given the results of the DEA analysis, hospital administrators should examine operations to determine how County Hospital resources can be more effectively utilized.

### Summary of the DEA Approach

To use data envelopment analysis to measure the relative efficiency of County Hospital, we used a linear programming model to construct a hypothetical composite hospital based on the outputs and inputs for the four hospitals in the problem. The approach to solving other types of problems using DEA is similar. That is, for each operating unit that we want to measure the efficiency of, we must formulate and solve a linear programming model similar to the linear program we solved to measure the relative efficiency of County Hospital. The following step-by-step procedure should help you in formulating a linear programming model for other types of DEA applications. Note that the operating unit that we want to measure the relative efficiency of is referred to as the $j$th operating unit.

Step 1  Define decision variables or weights (one for each operating unit) that can be used to determine the inputs and outputs for the composite operating unit.

Step 2  Write a constraint that requires the weights to sum to 1.

Step 3  For each output measure, write a constraint that requires the output for the composite operating unit to be greater than or equal to the corresponding output for the $j$th operating unit.

Step 4  Define a decision variable, $E$, which determines the fraction of the $j$th operating unit's input available to the composite operating unit.

Step 5  For each input measure, write a constraint that requires the input for the composite operating unit to be less than or equal to the resources available to the composite operating unit.

Step 6  Write the objective function as Min $E$.

<table>
<tr>
<td>

**N O T E S**
**and Comments**

</td>
<td>

1. Remember that the goal of data envelopment analysis is to identify operating units that are relatively inefficient. The method *does not* necessarily identify the operating units that are *relatively efficient*. Just because the efficiency index is $E = 1$, we cannot conclude that the unit being analyzed is relatively efficient. Indeed, any unit that has the largest output on any one of the output measures cannot be judged relatively inefficient.

2. It is possible for DEA to show all but one unit to be relatively inefficient. Such would be the case if a unit producing the most of every output also consumes the least of every input. Such cases are extremely rare in practice.

3. In applying data envelopment analysis to problems involving a large group of operating units, practitioners have found that roughly 50% of the operating units can be identified as inefficient. Comparing each relatively inefficient unit to the units contributing to the composite unit may be helpful in understanding how the operation of each relatively inefficient unit can be improved.

</td>
</tr>
</table>

## SUMMARY

In this chapter we presented a broad range of applications that demonstrate how to use linear programming to assist in the decision-making process. We formulated and solved problems from marketing, finance, and production management, and illustrated how linear programming can be applied to blending problems and data envelopment analysis.

Many of the illustrations presented in this chapter are scaled-down versions of actual situations in which linear programming has been applied. In real-world applications, the problem may not be so concisely stated, the data for the problem may not be as readily available, and the problem most likely will involve numerous decision variables and/or constraints. However, a thorough study of the applications in this chapter is a good place to begin in applying linear programming to real problems.

## GLOSSARY

**Data envelopment analysis (DEA)** A linear programming application used to measure the relative efficiency of operating units with the same goals and objectives.

**Hypothetical composite** A weighted average of outputs and inputs of all operating units with similar goals.

**Efficiency index** Percentage of an individual operating unit's resources that are available to the composite operating unit.

## PROBLEMS

Note: The following problems have been designed to give you an understanding and appreciation of the broad range of problems that can be formulated as linear programs. You should be able to formulate a linear programming model for each of the problems. However, you will need access to a linear programming computer package to develop the solutions and make the requested interpretations.

**SELF TEST**

1. The Westchester Chamber of Commerce periodically sponsors public service seminars and programs. Currently, promotional plans are under way for this year's program. Advertising alternatives include television, radio, and newspaper. Audience estimates, costs, and maximum media usage limitations are as shown.

| Constraint | Television | Radio | Newspaper |
|---|---|---|---|
| Audience per advertisement | 100,000 | 18,000 | 40,000 |
| Cost per advertisement | $2,000 | $300 | $600 |
| Maximum media usage | 10 | 20 | 10 |

To ensure a balanced use of advertising media, radio advertisements must not exceed 50% of the total number of advertisements authorized. In addition, television should account for at least 10% of the total number of advertisements authorized.

a. If the promotional budget is limited to $18,200, how many commercial messages should be run on each medium to maximize total audience contact? What is the allocation of the budget among the three media, and what is the total audience reached?

b. By how much would audience contact increase if an extra $100 were allocated to the promotional budget?

2. The management of Hartman Company is trying to determine the amount of each of two products to produce over the coming planning period. The following information concerns labor availability, labor utilization, and product profitability.

| Department | Product (hours/unit) | | Labor-Hours Available |
|---|---|---|---|
| | 1 | 2 | |
| A | 1.00 | 0.35 | 100 |
| B | 0.30 | 0.20 | 36 |
| C | 0.20 | 0.50 | 50 |
| Profit contribution/unit | $30.00 | $15.00 | |

a. Develop a linear programming model of the Hartman Company problem. Solve the model to determine the optimal production quantities of products 1 and 2.

b. In computing the profit contribution per unit, management doesn't deduct labor costs because they are considered fixed for the upcoming planning period. However, suppose that overtime can be scheduled in some of the departments. Which departments would you recommend scheduling for overtime? How much would you be willing to pay per hour of overtime in each department?

c. Suppose that 10, 6, and 8 hours of overtime may be scheduled in departments A, B, and C, respectively. The cost per hour of overtime is $18 in department A, $22.50 in department B, and $12 in department C. Formulate a linear programming model that can be used to determine the optimal production quantities if overtime is made available. What are the optimal production quantities, and what is the revised total contribution to profit? How much overtime do you recommend using in each department? What is the increase in the total contribution to profit if overtime is used?

3.  The employee credit union at State University is planning the allocation of funds for the coming year. The credit union makes four types of loans to its members. In addition, the credit union invests in risk-free securities to stabilize income. The various revenue-producing investments together with annual rates of return are as follows:

| Type of Loan/Investment | Annual Rate of Return (%) |
|---|---|
| Automobile loans | 8 |
| Furniture loans | 10 |
| Other secured loans | 11 |
| Signature loans | 12 |
| Risk-free securities | 9 |

The credit union will have $2,000,000 available for investment during the coming year. State laws and credit union policies impose the following restrictions on the composition of the loans and investments.

- Risk-free securities may not exceed 30% of the total funds available for investment.
- Signature loans may not exceed 10% of the funds invested in all loans (automobile, furniture, other secured, and signature loans).
- Furniture loans plus other secured loans may not exceed the automobile loans.
- Other secured loans plus signature loans may not exceed the funds invested in risk-free securities.

How should the $2,000,000 be allocated to each of the loan/investment alternatives to maximize total annual return? What is the projected total annual return?

4.  Hilltop Coffee manufactures a coffee product by blending three types of coffee beans. The cost per pound and the available pounds of each bean are as follows:

| Bean | Cost Per Pound | Available Pounds |
|---|---|---|
| 1 | $0.50 | 500 |
| 2 | $0.70 | 600 |
| 3 | $0.45 | 400 |

Consumer tests with coffee products were used to provide ratings on a scale of 0–100, with higher ratings indicating higher quality. Product quality standards for the blended coffee require a consumer rating for aroma to be at least 75 and a consumer rating for taste to be at least 80. The individual ratings of the aroma and taste for coffee made from 100% of each bean are as follows.

| Bean | Aroma Rating | Taste Rating |
|---|---|---|
| 1 | 75 | 86 |
| 2 | 85 | 88 |
| 3 | 60 | 75 |

Assume that the aroma and taste attributes of the coffee blend will be a weighted average of the attributes of the beans used in the blend.

   a. What is the minimum-cost blend that will meet the quality standards and provide 1000 pounds of the blended coffee product?

   b. What is the cost per pound for the coffee blend?

   c. Determine the aroma and taste ratings for the coffee blend.

   d. If additional coffee were to be produced, what would be the expected cost per pound?

5. Ajax Fuels, Inc., is developing a new additive for airplane fuels. The additive is a mixture of three ingredients: A, B, and C. For proper performance, the total amount of additive (amount of A + amount of B + amount of C) must be at least 10 ounces per gallon of fuel. However, because of safety reasons, the amount of additive must not exceed 15 ounces per gallon of fuel. The mix or blend of the three ingredients is critical. At least 1 ounce of ingredient A must be used for every ounce of ingredient B. The amount of ingredient C must be greater than one-half the amount of ingredient A. If the costs per ounce for ingredients A, B, and C are $0.10, $0.03, and $0.09, respectively. find the minimum-cost mixture of A, B, and C for each gallon of airplane fuel.

6. G. Kunz and Sons, Inc., manufactures two products used in the heavy equipment industry. Both products require manufacturing operations in two departments. The following are the production time (in hours) and profit contribution figures for the two products.

| Product | Profit Per Unit | Labor-Hours Dept. A | Labor-Hours Dept. B |
|---------|-----------------|---------------------|---------------------|
| 1 | $25 | 6 | 12 |
| 2 | $20 | 8 | 10 |

For the coming production period, Kunz has available a total of 900 hours of labor that can be allocated to either of the two departments. Find the production plan and labor allocation (hours assigned in each department) that will maximize the total contribution to profit.

7. As part of the settlement for a class action lawsuit, Hoxworth Corporation must provide sufficient cash to make the following annual payments (in thousands of dollars).

| Year | 1 | 2 | 3 | 4 | 5 | 6 |
|------|-----|-----|-----|-----|-----|-----|
| Payment | 190 | 215 | 240 | 285 | 315 | 460 |

The annual payments must be made at the beginning of each year. The judge will approve an amount that, along with earnings on its investment, will cover the annual payments. Investment of the funds will be limited to savings (at 4% annually) and government securities, at prices and rates currently quoted in *The Wall Street Journal.*

   Hoxworth wants to develop a plan for making the annual payments by investing in the following securities (par value = $1000). Funds not invested in these securities will be placed in savings.

| Security | Current Price | Rate (%) | Years to Maturity |
|----------|---------------|----------|-------------------|
| 1 | $1055 | 6.750 | 3 |
| 2 | $1000 | 5.125 | 4 |

Assume that interest is paid annually. The plan will be submitted to the judge and, if approved, Hoxworth will be required to pay a trustee the amount that will be required to fund the plan.

    a. Use linear programming to find the minimum cash settlement necessary to fund the annual payments.

    b. Use the dual price to determine how much more Hoxworth should be willing to pay now to reduce the payment at the beginning of year 6 to $400,000.

    c. Use the dual price to determine how much more Hoxworth should be willing to pay to reduce the year 1 payment to $150,000?

    d. Suppose that the annual payments are to be made at the end of each year. Reformulate the model to accommodate this change. How much would Hoxworth save if this change could be negotiated?

8. The Clark County Sheriff's Department schedules police officers for 8-hour shifts. The beginning times for the shifts are 8:00 A.M., noon, 4:00 P.M., 8:00 P.M., midnight, and 4:00 A.M. An officer beginning a shift at one of these times works for the next 8 hours. During normal weekday operations, the number of officers needed varies depending on the time of day. The department staffing guidelines require the following minimum number of officers on duty:

| Time of Day | Minimum Officers on Duty |
|---|---|
| 8:00 A.M.–noon | 5 |
| Noon–4:00 P.M. | 6 |
| 4:00 P.M.–8:00 P.M. | 10 |
| 8:00 P.M.–MIDNIGHT | 7 |
| MIDNIGHT–4:00 A.M. | 4 |
| 4:00 A.M.–8:00 A.M. | 6 |

Determine the number of police officers that should be scheduled to begin the 8-hour shifts at each of the six times (8:00 A.M., noon, 4:00 P.M., 8:00 P.M., midnight, and 4:00 A.M.) to minimize the total number of officers required. (Hint: Let $x_1$ = the number of officers beginning work at 8:00 A.M., $x_2$ = the number of officers beginning work at noon, and so on.)

**SELF TEST**

9. Reconsider the Welte Mutual Funds problem from Section 4.2. Define your decision variables as the fraction of funds invested in each security. Also, modify the constraints limiting investments in the oil and steel industries as follows: No more than 50% of the total funds invested in stock (oil and steel) may be invested in the oil industry, and no more than 50% of the funds invested in stock (oil and steel) may be invested in the steel industry.

    a. Solve the revised linear programming model. What fraction of the portfolio should be invested in each type of security?

    b. How much should be invested in each type of security?

    c. What are the total earnings for the portfolio?

    d. What is the marginal rate of return on the portfolio? That is, how much more could be earned by investing one more dollar in the portfolio?

10. Lurix Electronics manufactures two products that can be produced on two different production lines. Both products have their lowest production costs when produced on the more modern of the two production lines. However, the modern production line does not have the capacity to handle the total production. As a result, some production will have to be routed to the older production line. The following data show total production requirements, production line capacities, and production costs.

| Product | Production Cost/Unit | | Minimum Production Requirements |
|---|---|---|---|
| | Modern Line | Old Line | |
| 1 | $ 3.00 | $ 5.00 | 500 units |
| 2 | $ 2.50 | $ 4.00 | 700 units |
| Production line capacities | 800 | 600 | |

Formulate a linear programming model that can be used to make the production routing decision. What is the recommended decision and the total cost?

11. Edwards Manufacturing Company purchases two component parts from three different suppliers. The suppliers have limited capacity, and no one supplier can meet all the company's needs. In addition, the suppliers charge different prices for the components. Component price data (in price per unit) are as follows:

| | Supplier | | |
|---|---|---|---|
| Component | 1 | 2 | 3 |
| 1 | $12 | $13 | $14 |
| 2 | $10 | $11 | $10 |

Each supplier has a limited capacity in terms of the total number of components it can supply. However, as long as Edwards provides sufficient advance orders, each supplier can devote its capacity to component 1, component 2, or any combination of the two components, if the total number of units ordered is within its capacity. Supplier capacities are as follows.

| Supplier | 1 | 2 | 3 |
|---|---|---|---|
| Capacity | 600 | 1000 | 800 |

If the Edwards production plan for the next period includes 1000 units of component 1 and 800 units of component 2, what purchases do you recommend? That is, how many units of each component should be ordered from each supplier? What is the total purchase cost for the components?

**SELF TEST**

12. Refer to the Janders application in Section 4.3. Consider each of the following variations of the original problem separately.
   a. Suppose that Janders' supplier lowers the price for the bases to $0.55 per unit. What is the new optimal solution and its value?
   b. Suppose that the supplier of the tops for the Technician calculator raises the unit price to $0.82. What is the new optimal solution and its value?
   c. If Janders' employees were willing to work overtime for an overtime premium of only $2 per hour, should Janders schedule overtime? Why or why not? What is the new optimal solution and its value?

13. Reconsider the McCormick Manufacturing Company problem in Section 4.3. Each of the following parts presents a variation of the original problem. Consider each question separately.
   a. Suppose that no more than 600 hours can be transferred from department 2. Based on the dual price information, how does the value of the optimal solution change?
   b. Modify the linear programming model to reflect the change described in part (a). Solve the revised formulation to verify your conclusion in part (a). What transfers are recommended?

c.  Suppose that the employees transferred from department 1 to department 3 are only 80% as productive in department 3 as the employees originally assigned to that department. Reformulate the original model in Section 4.3 accordingly and solve. What is the new optimal solution? (Hint: Modify the labor balance equation for department 3.)

14.  The production manager for the Classic Boat Corporation must determine how many units of the Classic 21 model to produce over the next four quarters. The company has a beginning inventory of 100 Classic 21 boats, and demand for the four quarters is 2000 units in quarter 1, 4000 units in quarter 2, 3000 units in quarter 3, and 1500 units in quarter 4. The firm has limited production capacity in each quarter. That is, up to 4000 units can be produced in quarter 1, 3000 units in quarter 2, 2000 units in quarter 3, and 4000 units in quarter 4. Each boat held in inventory in quarters 1 and 2 incurs an inventory holding cost of $250 per unit; the holding cost for quarters 3 and 4 is $300 per unit. The production costs for the first quarter are $10,000 per unit; these costs are expected to increase by 10% each quarter because of increases in labor and material costs. Management has specified that the ending inventory for quarter 4 must be at least 500 boats.

a.  Formulate a linear programming model that can be used to determine the production schedule that will minimize the total cost of meeting demand in each quarter subject to the production capacities in each quarter and also to the required ending inventory in quarter 4.

b.  Solve the linear program formulated in part (a). Then develop a table that will show for each quarter the number of units to manufacture, the ending inventory, and the costs incurred.

c.  Interpret each of the dual prices corresponding to the constraints developed to meet demand in each quarter. Based on these dual prices what advice would you give the production manager?

d.  Interpret each of the dual prices corresponding to the production capacity in each quarter. Based on each of these dual prices what advice would you give the production manager?

15.  Seastrand  Oil Company produces two grades of gasoline: regular and high octane. Both gasolines are produced by blending two types of crude oil. Although both types of crude oil contain the two important ingredients required to produce both gasolines, the percentage of important ingredients in each type of crude oil differs, as does the cost per gallon. The percentage of ingredients A and B in each type of crude oil and the cost per gallon are shown.

SELF TEST

| Crude Oil | Cost | Ingredient A | Ingredient B | |
|-----------|-------|--------------|--------------|------------------------------|
| 1 | $0.10 | 20% | 60% | Crude oil 1 is 60% ingredient B |
| 2 | $0.15 | 50% | 30% | |

Each gallon of regular gasoline must contain at least 40% of ingredient A, whereas each gallon of high octane can contain at most 50% of ingredient B. Daily demand for regular and high-octane gasoline is 800,000 and 500,000 gallons, respectively. How many gallons of each type of crude oil should be used in the two gasolines to satisfy daily demand at a minimum cost?

16.  The Ferguson Paper Company produces rolls of paper for use in adding machines, desk calculators, and cash registers. The rolls, which are 200 feet long, are produced in widths of $1\frac{1}{2}$, $2\frac{1}{2}$, and $3\frac{1}{2}$ inches. The production process provides 200-foot rolls in 10-inch widths only. The firm must therefore cut the rolls to the desired final product sizes. The seven cutting alternatives and the amount of waste generated by each are as follows.

| Cutting Alternative | Number of Rolls 1½ in. | 2½ in. | 3½ in. | Waste (inches) |
|---|---|---|---|---|
| 1 | 6 | 0 | 0 | 1 |
| 2 | 0 | 4 | 0 | 0 |
| 3 | 2 | 0 | 2 | 0 |
| 4 | 0 | 1 | 2 | ½ |
| 5 | 1 | 3 | 0 | 1 |
| 6 | 1 | 2 | 1 | 0 |
| 7 | 4 | 0 | 1 | ½ |

The minimum requirements for the three products are

| Roll Width (inches) | 1½ | 2½ | 3½ |
|---|---|---|---|
| Units | 1000 | 2000 | 4000 |

a. If the company wants to minimize the number of 10-inch rolls that must be manufactured, how many 10-inch rolls will be processed on each cutting alternative? How many rolls are required, and what is the total waste (inches)?

b. If the company wants to minimize the waste generated, how many 10-inch units will be processed on each cutting alternative? How many rolls are required, and what is the total waste (inches)?

c. What are the differences in approaches (a) and (b) to this problem? In this case, which objective do you prefer? Explain. What types of situations would make the other objective more desirable?

17. Frandec Company manufactures, assembles, and rebuilds material handling equipment used in warehouses and distribution centers. One product, called a Liftmaster, is assembled from four components: a frame, a motor, two supports, and a metal strap. Frandec's production schedule calls for 5000 Liftmasters to be made next month. Frandec purchases the motors from an outside supplier, but the frames, supports, and straps may either be manufactured by the company or purchased from an outside supplier. Manufacturing and purchase costs per unit are shown.

| Component | Manufacturing Cost | Purchase Cost |
|---|---|---|
| Frame | $38.00 | $51.00 |
| Support | 11.50 | 15.00 |
| Strap | 6.50 | 7.50 |

Three departments are involved in the production of these components. The time (in minutes per unit) required to process each component in each department and the available capacity (in hours) for the three departments are as follows.

| Component | Department Cutting | Milling | Shaping |
|---|---|---|---|
| Frame | 3.5 | 2.2 | 3.1 |
| Support | 1.3 | 1.7 | 2.6 |
| Strap | 0.8 | — | 1.7 |
| Capacity (hours) | 350 | 420 | 680 |

a. Formulate and solve a linear programming model for this make-or-buy application. How many of each component should be manufactured and how many should be purchased?
b. What is the total cost of the manufacturing and purchasing plan?
c. How many hours of production time are used in each department?
d. How much should Frandec be willing to pay for an additional hour of time in the shaping department?
e. Another manufacturer has offered to sell frames to Frandec for $45 each. Could Frandec improve its position by pursuing this opportunity? Why or why not?

18. The Two-Rivers Oil Company near Pittsburgh transports gasoline to its distributors by truck. The company has recently contracted to supply gasoline distributors in southern Ohio, and it has $600,000 available to spend on the necessary expansion of its fleet of gasoline tank trucks. Three models of gasoline tank trucks are available.

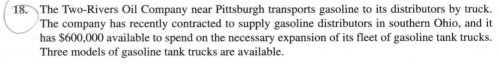

| Truck Model | Capacity (gallons) | Purchase Cost | Monthly Operating Cost, Including Depreciation |
|---|---|---|---|
| Super Tanker | 5000 | $67,000 | $550 |
| Regular Line | 2500 | $55,000 | $425 |
| Econo-Tanker | 1000 | $46,000 | $350 |

The company estimates that the monthly demand for the region will be 550,000 gallons of gasoline. Because of the size and speed differences of the trucks, the number of deliveries or round trips possible per month for each truck model will vary. Trip capacities are estimated at 15 trips per month for the Super Tanker, 20 trips per month for the Regular Line, and 25 trips per month for the Econo-Tanker. Based on maintenance and driver availability, the firm does not want to add more than 15 new vehicles to its fleet. In addition, the company has decided to purchase at least three of the new Econo-Tankers for use on short-run, low-demand routes. As a final constraint, the company does not want more than half the new models to be Super Tankers.
a. If the company wishes to satisfy the gasoline demand with a minimum monthly operating expense, how many models of each truck should be purchased?
b. If the company did not require at least three Econo-Tankers and did not limit the number of Super Tankers to at most half the new models, how many models of each truck should be purchased?

SELF TEST

19. The Silver Star Bicycle Company will be manufacturing both men's and women's models for its Easy-Pedal 10-speed bicycles during the next 2 months. Management wants to develop a production schedule indicating how many bicycles of each model should be produced in each month. Current demand forecasts call for 150 men's and 125 women's models to be shipped during the first month and 200 men's and 150 women's models to be shipped during the second month. Additional data are shown.

| Model | Production Costs | Labor Requirements (hours) | | Current Inventory |
|---|---|---|---|---|
| | | **Manufacturing** | **Assembly** | |
| Men's | $120 | 2.0 | 1.5 | 20 |
| Women's | $ 90 | 1.6 | 1.0 | 30 |

Last month the company used a total of 1000 hours of labor. The company's labor relations policy will not allow the combined total hours of labor (manufacturing plus assembly) to increase or decrease by more than 100 hours from month to month. In addition, the company charges monthly inventory at the rate of 2% of the production cost based on the inventory levels at the end of the month. The company would like to have at least 25 units of each model in inventory at the end of the 2 months.

    a.  Establish a production schedule that minimizes production and inventory costs and satisfies the labor-smoothing, demand, and inventory requirements. What inventories will be maintained and what are the monthly labor requirements?

    b.  If the company changed the constraints so that monthly labor increases and decreases could not exceed 50 hours, what would happen to the production schedule? How much will the cost increase? What would you recommend?

20. Filtron Corporation produces filtration containers used in water treatment systems. Although business has been growing, the demand each month varies considerably. As a result, the company utilizes a mix of part-time and full-time employees to meet production demands. Although this approach provides Filtron with great flexibility, it has resulted in increased costs and morale problems among employees. For instance, if Filtron needs to increase production from one month to the next, additional part-time employees have to be hired and trained, and costs go up. If Filtron has to decrease production, the workforce has to be reduced and Filtron incurs additional costs in terms of unemployment benefits and decreased morale. Best estimates are that increasing the number of units produced from one month to the next will increase production costs by $1.25 per unit, and that decreasing the number of units produced will increase production costs by $1.00 per unit. In February Filtron produced 10,000 filtration containers but only sold 7500 units; 2500 units are currently in inventory. The sales forecasts for March, April, and May are for 12,000 units, 8,000 units, and 15,000 units, respectively. In addition, Filtron has the capacity to store up to 3000 filtration containers at the end of any month. Management would like to determine the number of units to be produced in March, April, and May that will minimize the total cost of the monthly production increases and decreases.

21. Greenville Cabinets has received a contract to produce speaker cabinets for a major speaker manufacturer. The contract calls for the production of 3300 bookshelf speakers and 4100 floor speakers over the next two months, with the following delivery schedule.

| Model | Month 1 | Month 2 |
|---|---|---|
| Bookshelf | 2100 | 1200 |
| Floor | 1500 | 2600 |

Greenville estimates that the production time for each bookshelf model is 0.7 hour and the production time for each floor model is 1 hour. The raw material costs are $10 for each bookshelf model and $12 for each floor model. Labor costs are $22 per hour using regular production time and $33 using overtime. Greenville has up to 2400 hours of regular production time available each month and up to 1000 additional hours of overtime available each month. If production for either cabinet exceeds demand in month 1, the cabinets can be stored at a cost of $5 per cabinet. For each product, determine the number of units that should be manufactured each month on regular time and on overtime to minimize total production and storage costs.

22. TriCity Manufacturing (TCM) makes Styrofoam cups, plates, and sandwich and meal containers. Next week's schedule calls for the production of 80,000 small sandwich containers, 80,000 large sandwich containers, and 65,000 meal containers. To make these containers, Styrofoam sheets are melted and formed into final products using three machines: M1, M2, and M3. Machine M1 can process Styrofoam sheets with a maximum width of 12 inches. The width capacity of machine M2 is 16 inches, and the width capacity of machine M3 is 20 inches. The small sandwich containers require 10-inch wide Styrofoam sheets; thus, these containers can be produced on each of the three machines. The large sandwich containers require 12-inch wide sheets;

thus, these containers can also be produced on each of the three machines. However, the meal containers require 16-inch wide Styrofoam sheets, so the meal containers cannot be produced on machine M1. Waste is incurred in the production of all three containers because Styrofoam is lost in the heating and forming process as well as in the final trimming of the product. The amount of waste generated varies depending upon the container produced and the machine used. The following table shows the waste in square inches for each machine and product combination. The waste material is recycled for future use.

| Machine | Small Sandwich | Large Sandwich | Meal |
|---|---|---|---|
| M1 | 20 | 15 | — |
| M2 | 24 | 28 | 18 |
| M3 | 32 | 35 | 36 |

Production rates also depend upon the container produced and the machine used. The following table shows the production rates in units per minute for each machine and product combination. Machine capacities are limited for the next week. Time available is 35 hours for machine M1, 35 hours for machine M2, and 40 hours for machine M3.

| Machine | Small Sandwich | Large Sandwich | Meal |
|---|---|---|---|
| M1 | 30 | 25 | — |
| M2 | 45 | 40 | 30 |
| M3 | 60 | 52 | 44 |

a.  Costs associated with reprocessing the waste material have been increasing. Thus, TCM would like to minimize the amount of waste generated in meeting next week's production schedule. Formulate a linear programming model that can be used to determine the best production schedule.

b.  Solve the linear program formulated in part (a) to determine the production schedule. How much waste is generated? Which machines, if any, have idle capacity?

23. Multiperiod production and inventory planning models determine a production schedule and an ending inventory schedule for each of several periods that will maximize profit or minimize cost. Considering selling price, regular production costs, overtime costs, inventory carrying costs, and lost sales costs, develop a three-period production and inventory planning model for Allen Manufacturing Company. Use the following relevant information.

| Period | Selling Price Per Unit | Production Cost Per Unit | Demand | Ending Inventory Cost Per Unit |
|---|---|---|---|---|
| 1 | $5.00 | $2.80 | 500 | $0.50 |
| 2 | $5.00 | $2.90 | 300 | $0.50 |
| 3 | $5.50 | $3.00 | 400 | $0.55 |

| Period | Production Capacity (units) | |
| --- | --- | --- |
| | Regular | Overtime |
| 1 | 250 | 100 |
| 2 | 300 | 100 |
| 3 | 300 | 125 |

The overtime cost per unit in each period is 20% greater than the production cost per unit shown. The lost sales cost, which is $4 per unit in any period, accounts for lost customer goodwill, but does not account for the cost associated with the lost revenue. The beginning inventory for period 1 is 100 units. In addition, the firm wants to have at least 50 units in ending inventory for period 3 to prepare for period 4.

To account for the multiperiod aspects of the problem, each period $t$ will require balance equations or constraints based on two relationships:

$$\text{Lost sales } (t) = \text{demand } (t) - \text{sales } (t)$$

$$\text{Ending inventory } (t) = \text{beginning inventory } (t) + \text{production } (t) - \text{sales } (t)$$

Develop a linear program that can be used to determine the optimal production and inventory schedule for Allen Manufacturing. Determine the sales, regular production, overtime production, ending inventory, and lost sales for each of the three periods. What is the net profit associated with your solution?

24. Morton Financial must decide on the percentage of available funds to commit to each of two investments, referred to as A and B, over the next four periods. The following table shows the amount of new funds available for each of the four periods, as well as the cash expenditure required for each investment (negative values) or the cash income from the investment (positive values). The data shown (in thousands of dollars) reflect the amount of expenditure or income if 100% of the funds available in any period are invested in either A or B. For example, if Morton decides to invest 100% of the funds available in any period in investment A, it will incur cash expenditures of $1000 in period 1, $800 in period 2, $200 in period 3, and income of $200 in period 4. Note, however, if Morton made the decision to invest 80% in investment A, the cash expenditures or income would be 80% of the values shown.

| Period | New Investment Funds Available | Investment | |
| --- | --- | --- | --- |
| | | A | B |
| 1 | 1500 | −1000 | −800 |
| 2 | 400 | −800 | −500 |
| 3 | 500 | −200 | −300 |
| 4 | 100 | 200 | 300 |

The amount of funds available in any period is the sum of the new investment funds for the period, the new loan funds, the savings from the previous period, the cash income from investment A, and the cash income from investment B. The funds available in any period can be used to pay the loan and interest from the previous period, placed in savings, used to pay the cash expenditures for investment A, or used to pay the cash expenditures for investment B.

Assume an interest rate of 10% per period for savings and an interest rate of 18% per period on borrowed funds. Let

$$S(t) = \text{the savings for period } t$$
$$L(t) = \text{the new loan funds for period } t$$

Then, in any period $t$, the savings income from the previous period is $1.1S(t-1)$ and the loan and interest expenditure from the previous period is $1.18L(t-1)$.

At the end of period 4, investment A is expected to have a cash value of $3200 (assuming a 100% investment in A), and investment B is expected to have a cash value of $2500 (assuming a 100% investment in B). Additional income and expenses at the end of period 4 will be income from savings in period 4 less the repayment of the period 4 loan plus interest.

Suppose that the decision variables are defined as

$$x_1 = \text{the proportion of investment A undertaken}$$
$$x_2 = \text{the proportion of investment B undertaken}$$

For example, if $x_1 = 0.5$, $500 would be invested in investment A during the first period, and all remaining cash flows and ending investment A values would be multiplied by 0.5. The same holds for investment B. The model must include constraints $x_1 \leq 1$ and $x_2 \leq 1$ to make sure that no more than 100% of the investments can be undertaken.

If no more than $200 can be borrowed in any period, determine the proportions of investments A and B and the amount of savings and borrowing in each period that will maximize the cash value for the firm at the end of the four periods.

25. Western Family Steakhouse offers a variety of low-cost meals and quick service. Other than management, the steakhouse operates with two full-time employees who work 8 hours per day. The rest of the employees are part-time employees who are scheduled for 4-hour shifts during peak meal times. On Saturdays the steakhouse is open from 11:00 A.M. to 10:00 P.M. Management wants to develop a schedule for part-time employees that will minimize labor costs and still provide excellent customer service. The average wage rate for the part-time employees is $4.60 per hour. The total number of full-time and part-time employees needed varies with the time of day as shown.

| Time | Total Number of Employees Needed |
|------|:---:|
| 11:00 A.M.–noon | 9 |
| Noon–1:00 P.M. | 9 |
| 1:00 P.M.–2:00 P.M. | 9 |
| 2:00 P.M.–3:00 P.M. | 3 |
| 3:00 P.M.–4:00 P.M. | 3 |
| 4:00 P.M.–5:00 P.M. | 3 |
| 5:00 P.M.–6:00 P.M. | 6 |
| 6:00 P.M.–7:00 P.M. | 12 |
| 7:00 P.M.–8:00 P.M. | 12 |
| 8:00 P.M.–9:00 P.M. | 7 |
| 9:00 P.M.–10:00 P.M. | 7 |

One full-time employee comes on duty at 11:00 A.M., works 4 hours, takes an hour off, and returns for another 4 hours. The other full-time employee comes to work at 1:00 P.M. and works the same 4-hours-on, 1-hour-off, 4-hours-on pattern.

a. Develop a minimum-cost schedule for part-time employees.

b. What is the total payroll for the part-time employees? How many part-time shifts are needed? Use the surplus variables to comment on the desirability of scheduling at least some of the part-time employees for 3-hour shifts.

c. Assume that part-time employees can be assigned either a 3-hour or 4-hour shift. Develop a minimum-cost schedule for the part-time employees. How many part-time shifts are needed and what is the cost savings compared to the previous schedule?

26. In Section 4.5 data envelopment analysis was used to evaluate the relative efficiencies of four hospitals. Data for three input measures and four output measures were provided in Tables 4.16 and 4.17.

a. Use these data to develop a linear programming model that could be used to evaluate the performance of General Hospital.

b. The following computer solution was obtained using The Management Scientist. Does the solution indicate that General Hospital is relatively inefficient?

```
Objective Function Value = 1.000000

        Variable      Value        Reduced Costs
           E          1.000            0.000
           WG         1.000            0.000
           WU         0.000            0.000
           WC         0.000            0.331
           WS         0.000            0.215
```

c. Explain which hospital or hospitals make up the composite unit used to evaluate General Hospital and why.

27. Data envelopment analysis has been used to measure the relative efficiency of a group of hospitals (H. David Sherman, "Hospital Efficiency Measurement and Evaluation," *Medical Care*, October 1984). Sherman's study involved seven teaching hospitals; data on three input measures and four output measures are contained in the following tables.

| | Input Measures | | |
| Hospital | Full-Time Equivalent Nonphysicians | Supply Expense ($000s) | Bed-Days Available ($000s) |
|---|---|---|---|
| A | 310.0 | 134.60 | 116.00 |
| B | 278.5 | 114.30 | 106.80 |
| C | 165.6 | 131.30 | 65.52 |
| D | 250.0 | 316.00 | 94.40 |
| E | 206.4 | 151.20 | 102.10 |
| F | 384.0 | 217.00 | 153.70 |
| G | 530.1 | 770.80 | 215.00 |

| | Output Measures | | | |
| Hospital | Patient-Days (65 or older) (000s) | Patient-Days (under 65) (000s) | Nurses Trained | Interns Trained |
|---|---|---|---|---|
| A | 55.31 | 49.52 | 291 | 47 |
| B | 37.64 | 55.63 | 156 | 3 |
| C | 32.91 | 25.77 | 141 | 26 |
| D | 33.53 | 41.99 | 160 | 21 |
| E | 32.48 | 55.30 | 157 | 82 |
| F | 48.78 | 81.92 | 285 | 92 |
| G | 58.41 | 119.70 | 111 | 89 |

a. Formulate a linear programming model so that data envelopment analysis can be used to evaluate the performance of hospital D.
b. Solve the model.
c. Is hospital D relatively inefficient? What is the interpretation of the value of the objective function?
d. How many patient-days of each type are produced by the composite hospital?
e. Which hospitals would you recommend hospital D consider emulating to improve the efficiency of its operation?

28. Refer again to the data presented in Problem 27.
a. Formulate a linear programming model that can be used to perform data envelopment analysis for hospital E.
b. Solve the model.
c. Is hospital E relatively inefficient? What is the interpretation of the value of the objective function?
d. Which hospitals are involved in making up the composite hospital? Can you make a general statement about which hospitals will make up the composite unit associated with a unit that is not inefficient?

29. The Ranch House, Inc., operates five fast-food restaurants. Input measures for the restaurants include weekly hours of operation, full-time equivalent staff, and weekly supply expenses. Output measures of performance include average weekly contribution to profit, market share, and annual growth rate. Data for the input and output measures are shown in the following tables.

| | Input Measures | | |
| Restaurant | Hours of Operation | FTE Staff | Supplies ($) |
|---|---|---|---|
| Bardstown | 96 | 16 | 850 |
| Clarksville | 110 | 22 | 1400 |
| Jeffersonville | 100 | 18 | 1200 |
| New Albany | 125 | 25 | 1500 |
| St. Matthews | 120 | 24 | 1600 |

|  | | Output Measures | |
| Restaurant | Weekly Profit | Market Share (%) | Growth Rate (%) |
| --- | --- | --- | --- |
| Bardstown | $3800 | 25 | 8.0 |
| Clarksville | $4600 | 32 | 8.5 |
| Jeffersonville | $4400 | 35 | 8.0 |
| New Albany | $6500 | 30 | 10.0 |
| St. Matthews | $6000 | 28 | 9.0 |

a. Develop a linear programming model that can be used to evaluate the performance of the Clarksville Ranch House restaurant.
b. Solve the model.
c. Is the Clarksville Ranch House restaurant relatively inefficient? Discuss.
d. Where does the composite restaurant have more output than the Clarksville restaurant? How much less of each input resource does the composite restaurant require when compared to the Clarksville restaurant?
e. What other restaurants should be studied to find suggested ways for the Clarksville restaurant to improve its efficiency?

## Case Problem ENVIRONMENTAL PROTECTION

Skillings Industrial Chemicals, Inc., operates a refinery in southwestern Ohio near the Ohio River. The company's primary product is manufactured from a chemical process that requires the use of two raw materials—material A and material B. The production of 1 pound of the primary product requires the use of 1 pound of material A and 2 pounds of material B. The output of the chemical process is 1 pound of the primary product, 1 pound of liquid waste material, and 1 pound of solid waste by-product. The solid waste by-product is given to a local fertilizer plant as payment for picking it up and disposing of it. The liquid waste material has no market value, so the refinery has been dumping it directly into the Ohio River. The company's manufacturing process is shown schematically in Figure 4.13.

Government pollution guidelines established by the Environmental Protection Agency will no longer permit disposal of the liquid waste directly into the river. The refinery's research group has developed the following set of alternative uses for the liquid waste material.

1. Produce a secondary product K by adding 1 pound of raw material A to every pound of liquid waste.
2. Produce a secondary product M by adding 1 pound of raw material B to every pound of liquid waste.
3. Specially treat the liquid waste so that it meets pollution standards before dumping it into the river.

These three alternatives are depicted in Figure 4.14.

The company's management knows that the secondary products will be low in quality and may not be very profitable. However, management also recognizes that the special treatment alternative will be a relatively expensive operation. The company's problem is to determine how to satisfy the pollution regulations and still maintain the highest possible profit. How should the liquid waste material be handled? Should Skillings produce product K, produce product M, use the special treatment, or employ some combination of the three alternatives?

| Figure 4.13 | MANUFACTURING PROCESS AT SKILLINGS INDUSTRIAL CHEMICALS, INC. |
|---|---|

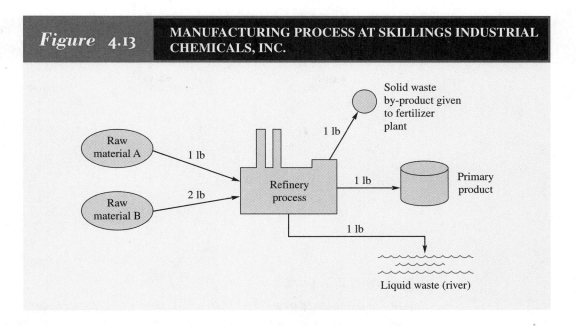

Last month 10,000 pounds of the company's primary product were produced. The accounting department has prepared a cost report showing the breakdown of fixed and variable expenses that were incurred during the month.

**Cost Analysis for 10,000 Pounds
of Primary Product**

| | |
|---|---|
| Fixed costs | |
| Administrative expenses | $12,000 |
| Refinery overhead | 4,000 |
| Variable costs | |
| Raw material A | 15,000 |
| Raw material B | 16,000 |
| Direct labor | 5,000 |
| Total | $52,000 |

In this cost analysis, the fixed-cost portion of the expenses is the same every month regardless of production level. Direct labor costs are expected to run $0.20 per pound for product K and $0.10 per pound for product M.

The company's primary product sells for $5.70 per pound. Secondary products K and M sell for $0.85 and $0.65 per pound, respectively. The special treatment of the liquid waste will cost $0.25 per pound.

A company accountant believes that product K is too expensive to manufacture and cannot be sold at a price that recovers its material and labor cost. The accountant's recommendation is to eliminate product K as an alternative.

For the upcoming production period, 5000 pounds of raw material A and 7000 pounds of raw material B will be available.

**Figure 4.14    ALTERNATIVES FOR HANDLING THE REFINERY LIQUID WASTE**

## Managerial Report

Develop an approach to the problem that will allow the company to determine how much primary product to produce, given the limitations on the amounts of the raw material available. Include recommendations as to how the company should dispose of the liquid waste to satisfy the environmental protection guidelines. How many pounds of product K should be produced? How many pounds of product M should be produced? How many pounds of liquid waste should be specially treated and dumped into the river? Include a discussion and analysis of the following in your report:

1. A cost analysis showing the profit contribution per pound for the primary product, product K, and product M
2. The optimal production quantities and waste disposal plan, including the projected profit
3. A discussion of the value of additional pounds of each raw material
4. A discussion of the sensitivity analysis of the objective function coefficients
5. Comments on the accountant's recommendation to eliminate product K as an alternative: Does the recommendation appear reasonable? What is your reaction to the recommendation? How would the optimal solution change if product K were eliminated?

## Case Problem    TRUCK LEASING STRATEGY

Reep Construction has recently won a contract for the excavation and site preparation of a new rest area on the Pennsylvania turnpike. In preparing his bid for the job, Bob Reep, founder and president of Reep Construction, estimated that it would take 4 months to perform the work and that 10, 12, 14, and 8 trucks would be needed in months 1 through 4, respectively.

The firm currently has 20 trucks of the type needed to perform the work on the new project. These trucks were obtained last year when Bob signed a long-term lease with PennState Leasing. Although most of these trucks are currently being used on existing jobs, Bob estimates that one truck will be available for use on the new project in month 1, two trucks will be available in month 2, three trucks will be available in month 3, and one truck will be available in month 4. Thus, to complete the project, Bob will have to lease additional trucks.

The long-term leasing contract with PennState has a monthly cost of $600 per truck. Reep Construction pays its truck drivers $20 an hour, and daily fuel costs are approximately $100 per truck. All maintenance costs are paid by PennState Leasing. For planning purposes, Bob estimates that each truck used on the new project will be operating 8 hours a day, 5 days a week for approximately 4 weeks each month.

Bob does not believe that current business conditions justify committing the firm to additional long-term leases. In discussing the short-term leasing possibilities with PennState Leasing, Bob has learned that he can obtain short-term leases of 1–4 months. Short-term leases differ from long-term leases in that the short-term leasing plans include the cost of both a truck and a driver. Maintenance costs for short-term leases also are paid by PennState Leasing. The following costs for each of the 4 months cover the lease of a truck and driver.

| Length of Lease | Cost per Month |
|:---------------:|:--------------:|
| 1 | $4000 |
| 2 | $3700 |
| 3 | $3225 |
| 4 | $3040 |

Bob Reep would like to acquire a lease that would minimize the cost of meeting the monthly trucking requirements for his new project, but he also takes great pride in the fact that his company has never laid off employees. Bob is committed to maintaining his no-layoff policy; that is, he will use his own drivers even if costs are higher.

## Managerial Report

Perform an analysis of Reep Construction's leasing problem and prepare a report for Bob Reep that summarizes your findings. Be sure to include information on and analysis of the following items

1.  The optimal leasing plan
2.  The costs associated with the optimal leasing plan
3.  The cost for Reep Construction to maintain its current policy of no layoffs

## Case Problem    PHOENIX COMPUTER

Phoenix Computer manufactures and sells personal computers directly to customers. Orders are accepted by phone and through the company's web site. Phoenix will be introducing several new laptop models over the next few months and management has recognized a need to develop technical support personnel to specialize in the new laptop systems. One option being considered is to hire new employees and put them through a 3-month training program. Another option is to put current customer service specialists through a 2-month training program on the new laptop models. Phoenix estimates that the need for laptop specialists will grow from 0 to 100 during the months of May through September as follows: May—20; June—30; July—85; August—85; and September—100. After September, Phoenix expects that maintaining a staff of 100 laptop specialists will be sufficient.

The annual salary for a new employee is estimated to be $27,000 whether the person is hired to enter the training program or to replace a current employee who is entering the training program. The annual salary for the current Phoenix employees who are being considered for the training program is approximately $36,000. The cost of the 3-month training program is $1500 per person, and the cost of the 2-month training program is $1000 per person. Note that the length of the training program means that a lag will occur between the time when a new person is hired and the time a new laptop specialist is available. The number of current employees who will be available for training is limited. Phoenix estimates that the following numbers can be made available in the coming months: March—15; April—20; May—0; June—5; and July—10. The training center has the capacity to start new 3-month and 2-month training classes each month; however, the total number of students (new and current employees) that begin training each month can not exceed 25.

Phoenix needs to determine the number of new hires that should begin the 3-month training program each month and the number of current employees that should begin the 2-month training program each month. The objective is to satisfy staffing needs during May through September at the lowest possible total cost; that is, minimize the incremental salary cost and the total training cost.

It is currently January, and Phoenix Computer would like to develop a plan for hiring new employees and determining the mix of new hires and current employees to place in the training program.

## Managerial Report

Perform an analysis of the Phoenix Computer problem and prepare a report that summarizes your findings. Be sure to include information on and analysis of the following items.

1. The incremental salary and training cost associated with hiring a new employee and training him/her to be a laptop specialist
2. The incremental salary and training cost associated with putting a current employee through the training program. Don't forget that a replacement must be hired when the current employee enters the program
3. Recommendations regarding the hiring and training plan that will minimize the salary and training costs over the February through August period as well as answers to these questions: What is the total cost of providing technical support for the new laptop models? How much higher will monthly payroll costs be in September than in January?

## Case Problem    TEXTILE MILL SCHEDULING

The Scottsville Textile Mill* produces five different fabrics. Each fabric can be woven on one or more of the mill's 38 looms. The sales department has forecast demand for the next month. The demand data are shown in Table 4.18, along with data on the selling price per yard, variable cost per yard, and purchase price per yard. The mill operates 24 hours a day and is scheduled for 30 days during the coming month.

The mill has two types of looms: dobbie and regular. The dobbie looms are more versatile and can be used for all five fabrics. The regular looms can produce only three of the fab-

---

*This case is based on the Calhoun Textile Mill Case by Jeffrey D. Camm, P. M. Dearing, and Suresh K. Tadisnia, 1987.

| | MONTHLY DEMAND, SELLING PRICE, VARIABLE COST, AND PURCHASE PRICE DATA FOR SCOTTSVILLE TEXTILE MILL FABRICS | | | |
|---|---|---|---|---|
| *Table* 4.18 | | | | |

| Fabric | Demand (yards) | Selling Price ($/yard) | Variable Cost ($/yard) | Purchase Price ($/yard) |
|---|---|---|---|---|
| 1 | 16,500 | 0.99 | 0.66 | 0.80 |
| 2 | 22,000 | 0.86 | 0.55 | 0.70 |
| 3 | 62,000 | 1.10 | 0.49 | 0.60 |
| 4 | 7,500 | 1.24 | 0.51 | 0.70 |
| 5 | 62,000 | 0.70 | 0.50 | 0.70 |

rics. The mill has a total of 38 looms, 8 are dobbie and 30 are regular. The rate of production for each fabric on each type of loom is given in Table 4.19. The time required to change over from producing one fabric to another is negligible and does not have to be considered.

The Scottsville Textile Mill satisfies all demand with either its own fabric or fabric purchased from another mill. That is, fabrics that cannot be woven at the Scottsville Mill because of limited loom capacity will be purchased from another mill. The purchase price of each fabric is also shown in Table 4.18.

## Managerial Report

Develop a model that can be used to schedule production for the Scottsville Textile Mill, and at the same time, determine how many yards of each fabric must be purchased from another mill. Include a discussion and analysis of the following items in your report.

1. The final production schedule and loom assignments for each fabric
2. The projected total contribution to profit
3. A discussion of the value of additional loom time (The mill is considering purchasing a ninth dobbie loom. What is your estimate of the monthly profit contribution of this additional loom?)

| | LOOM PRODUCTION RATES FOR THE SCOTTSVILLE TEXTILE MILL | |
|---|---|---|
| *Table* 4.19 | | |

| | Loom Rate (yards/hour) | |
|---|---|---|
| Fabric | Dobbie | Regular |
| 1 | 4.63 | — |
| 2 | 4.63 | — |
| 3 | 5.23 | 5.23 |
| 4 | 5.23 | 5.23 |
| 5 | 4.17 | 4.17 |

Note: Fabrics 1 and 2 can be manufactured only on the dobbie loom.

4. A discussion of the ranges for the objective function coefficients
5. A discussion of how the objective of minimizing total costs would provide a different model than the objective of maximizing total profit contribution: How would the interpretation of the ranges for the objective function coefficients differ for these two models?

## Appendix 4.1 SPREADSHEET SOLUTION OF HEWLITT CORPORATION FINANCIAL PLANNING PROBLEM

In Appendix 2.2 we showed how Excel can be used to solve the Par, Inc. linear programming problem. To illustrate the use of Excel in solving a more complex linear programming problem, we show the solution to the Hewlitt Corporation financial planning problem presented in Section 4.2.

The spreadsheet formulation and solution of the Hewlitt Corporation problem are shown in Figure 4.15. As described in Appendix 2.2, our practice is to put the data required for the problem in the top part of the spreadsheet and build the model in the bottom part of the spreadsheet. The model consists of a set of cells for the decision variables, a cell for the objective function, a set of cells for the left-hand-side functions, and a set of cells for the right-hand sides of the constraints. The cells for each of these model components are screened; the cells for the decision variables are also enclosed by a boldface line. Descriptive labels are used to make the spreadsheet easy to read.

### Figure 4.15 SPREADSHEET SOLUTION FOR THE HEWLITT CORPORATION PROBLEM

| | A | B | C | D | E | F | G | H | I | J | K | L |
|---|---|---|---|---|---|---|---|---|---|---|---|---|
| 1 | **Hewlitt Corporation Cash Requirements** | | | | | | | | | | | |
| 2 | | | | | | | | | | | | |
| 3 | | **Cash** | | | | | | | | | | |
| 4 | **Year** | **Rqmt.** | | | | **Bond** | | | | | | |
| 5 | 1 | 430 | | | 1 | 2 | 3 | | | | | |
| 6 | 2 | 210 | | **Price ($1000)** | 1.15 | 1 | 1.35 | | | | | |
| 7 | 3 | 222 | | **Rate** | 0.08875 | 0.055 | 0.1175 | | | | | |
| 8 | 4 | 231 | | **Years to Maturity** | 5 | 6 | 7 | | | | | |
| 9 | 5 | 240 | | | | | | | | | | |
| 10 | 6 | 195 | | **Annual Savings Multiple** | 1.04 | | | | | | | |
| 11 | 7 | 225 | | | | | | | | | | |
| 12 | 8 | 255 | | | | | | | | | | |
| 13 | | | | | | | | | | | | |
| 14 | **Model** | | | | | | | | | | | |
| 15 | | | | | | | | | | | | |
| 16 | F | B1 | B2 | B3 | S1 | S2 | S3 | S4 | S5 | S6 | S7 | S8 |
| 17 | 1728.79385 | 144.9881 | 187.8558 | 228.1879195 | 636.1479 | 501.6057 | 349.68179 | 182.6809 | 0 | 0 | 0 | 0 |
| 18 | | | | | | | | | | | | |
| 19 | | | | | **Cash Flow** | | **Net Cash** | | **Cash** | | | |
| 20 | **Min Funds** | 1728.794 | | **Constraints** | In | Out | **Flow** | | **Rqmt.** | | | |
| 21 | | | | Year 1 | 1728.794 | 1298.794 | 430 | = | 430 | | | |
| 22 | | | | Year 2 | 711.6057 | 501.6057 | 210 | = | 210 | | | |
| 23 | | | | Year 3 | 571.6818 | 349.6818 | 222 | = | 222 | | | |
| 24 | | | | Year 4 | 413.6809 | 182.6809 | 231 | = | 231 | | | |
| 25 | | | | Year 5 | 240 | 0 | 240 | = | 240 | | | |
| 26 | | | | Year 6 | 195 | 0 | 195 | = | 195 | | | |
| 27 | | | | Year 7 | 225 | 0 | 225 | = | 225 | | | |
| 28 | | | | Year 8 | 255 | 0 | 255 | = | 255 | | | |

## Spreadsheet Formulation

The data and descriptive labels are contained in cells A1:G12. The screened cells in the bottom portion of the spreadsheet contain the key elements of the model required by the Excel Solver.

Decision Variables
: Cells A17:L17 are reserved for the decision variables. The optimal values, (rounded to 3 places) are shown to be $F = 1728.794$, $B_1 = 144.988$, $B_2 = 187.856$, $B_3 = 228.188$, $S_1 = 636.148$, $S_2 = 501.606$, $S_3 = 349.682$, $S_4 = 182.681$, and $S_5 = S_6 = S_7 = S_8 = 0$.

Objective Function
: The formula =A17 has been placed into cell B20 to reflect the total funds required. It is simply the value of the decision variable, $F$. The total funds required by the optimal solution is shown to be $1,728,794.

Left-Hand Sides
: The left-hand sides for the 8 constraints represent the annual net cash flow. They are placed into cells G21:G28.
  Cell G21 =E21 − F21    (Copy to G22:G28)

For this problem, some of the above left-hand-side cells reference other cells that contain formulas. These referenced cells provide Hewlitt's cash flow in and cash flow out for each of the eight years.* The cells and their formulas are as follows:

Cell E21 =A17
Cell E22 =SUMPRODUCT($E$7:$G$7,$B$17:$D$17) + $F$10*E17
Cell E23 =SUMPRODUCT($E$7:$G$7,$B$17:$D$17) + $F$10*F17
Cell E24 =SUMPRODUCT($E$7:$G$7,$B$17:$D$17) + $F$10*G17
Cell E25 =SUMPRODUCT($E$7:$G$7,$B$17:$D$17) + $F$10*H17
Cell E26 =(1 + E7)*B17 + F7*C17 + G7*D17 + F10*I17
Cell E27 =(1 + F7)*C17 + G7*D17 + F10*J17
Cell E28 =(1 + G7)*D17 + F10*K17
Cell F21 =SUMPRODUCT(E6:G6,B17:D17) + E17
Cell F22 =F17
Cell F23 =G17
Cell F24 =H17
Cell F25 =I17
Cell F26 =J17
Cell F27 =K17
Cell F28 =L17

Right-Hand Sides
: The right-hand sides for the 8 constraints represent the annual cash requirements. They are placed into cells I21:I28.
  Cell I21   =B5    (Copy to I22:I28)

## Spreadsheet Solution

The solution can be obtained by selecting **Solver** from the **Tools** menu, entering the proper values into the **Solver Parameters** dialog box and specifying the options **Assume Linear Model** and **Assume Non-Negative.** The information entered into the **Solver Parameters** dialog box is shown in Figure 4.16. After solving, we requested the sensitivity report shown in Figure 4.17.

---

*The cash flow in is the sum of the positive terms in each constraint equation in the mathematical model, and the cash flow out is the sum of the negative terms in each constraint equation.

| Figure 4.16 | SOLVER PARAMETERS DIALOG BOX FOR THE HEWLITT CORPORATION PROBLEM |
| --- | --- |

## Discussion

Figures 4.15 and 4.17 contain essentially the same information as that provided by The Management Scientist solution in Figure 4.4. Recall that the Excel sensitivity report uses the term *shadow price* to describe the *change* in value of the solution per-unit increase in the right-hand side of a constraint. The Management Scientist and LINDO use the term *dual price* to describe the *improvement* in value of the solution per-unit increase in the right-hand side of a constraint. For maximization problems, the shadow price and dual price are the same; for minimization problems, the shadow price and dual price have opposite signs. Because the Hewlitt financial planning problem involves minimization, the shadow prices in the Excel sensitivity report (Figure 4.17) are the negative of the dual prices in The Management Scientist solution (Figure 4.4).

| Figure 4.17 | CONSTRAINTS SECTION OF THE SENSITIVITY REPORT FOR THE HEWLITT CORPORATION PROBLEM |
| --- | --- |

Constraints

| Cell | Name | Final Value | Shadow Price | Constraint R.H. Side | Allowable Increase | Allowable Decrease |
| --- | --- | --- | --- | --- | --- | --- |
| $G$21 | Year 1 Flow | 430 | 1 | 430 | 1E+30 | 1728.793855 |
| $G$22 | Year 2 Flow | 210 | 0.961538462 | 210 | 1E+30 | 661.5938616 |
| $G$23 | Year 3 Flow | 222 | 0.924556213 | 222 | 1E+30 | 521.6699405 |
| $G$24 | Year 4 Flow | 231 | 0.888996359 | 231 | 1E+30 | 363.6690626 |
| $G$25 | Year 5 Flow | 240 | 0.854804191 | 240 | 1E+30 | 189.9881496 |
| $G$26 | Year 6 Flow | 195 | 0.760364454 | 195 | 2149.927647 | 157.8558478 |
| $G$27 | Year 7 Flow | 225 | 0.718991202 | 225 | 3027.962172 | 198.1879195 |
| $G$28 | Year 8 Flow | 255 | 0.670839393 | 255 | 1583.881915 | 255 |

# MARATHON OIL COMPANY*

## FINDLAY, OHIO

Marathon Oil Company was founded in 1887 when 14 oilmen pooled their properties to organize an oil-producing company in the Trenton Rock oil fields of Ohio. In 1924 Marathon entered the refining and marketing phase of the petroleum industry. Today Marathon is a fully integrated oil company with significant international operations. In the United States the company markets petroleum products in 21 states, primarily in the Midwest and Southeast.

## Quantitative Methods at Marathon Oil Company

Marathon Oil's Operations Research Department was formed in 1963 in order to aid problem solving and decision making in all areas of the company. Approximately 50% of the applications involve linear programming. Typical problems include refinery models, distribution models, gasoline and fuel oil blending models, and crude oil evaluation studies. Another 30% of the applications involve complex chemical engineering simulation models of process operations. The remaining applications involve solution techniques using nonlinear programming, network flow algorithms, and statistical techniques such as regression analysis.

## A Marketing Planning Model

Marathon Oil Company has four refineries within the United States, operates 50 light products terminals, and has product demand at more than 95 locations. The Sup-

ply and Transportation Division is faced with the problem of determining which refinery should supply which terminal and, at the same time, determining which products should be transported via which pipeline, barge, or tanker to minimize cost. Product demand must be satisfied, and the supply capability of each refinery must not be exceeded. To help solve this difficult problem. Marathon's Operations Research Department developed a marketing planning model for the Operations Planning Department.

The marketing planning model is a large-scale linear programming model that takes into account sales not only at Marathon product terminals but also at all exchange locations. An exchange contract is an agreement with other oil product marketers that involves exchanging or trading Marathon's products for theirs at different locations. Thus, some geographic imbalance between supply and demand can be reduced. Both sides of the exchanges are represented since the results not only affect the net requirements at a demand location, but in addition have important financial implications. All pipelines, barges, and tankers within Marathon's marketing area are also represented in the linear programming model. The objective of the linear programming model is to minimize the cost of meeting a given demand structure, taking into account sales price, pipeline tariffs, exchange contract costs, product demand, terminal operating costs, refining costs, and product purchases.

The marketing planning model is used to solve a wide variety of planning problems. These vary from evaluating gasoline blending economics to analyzing the economics of a new terminal or pipeline. Although the types of problems that can be solved are almost unlimited, the model is most effective in handling the following:

*The authors are indebted to Robert W. Wernert of Marathon Oil Company, Findlay, Ohio, for providing this application.

1. Evaluating additional product demand locations, pipelines, and exchange contracts
2. Determining profitability of shifting sales from one product demand location to another
3. Determining the effects on supply and distribution when a pipeline increases its tariff
4. Optimizing production of the grades at the five refineries based on distribution

The linear programming model not only solves these problems, but also gives the financial impact of each solution.

## Benefits

With daily sales of about 10 million gallons of refined light product, a savings of even one-thousandth of a cent per gallon can result in significant long-term savings. At the same time, what may appear to be a savings in one area, such as refining or transportation, may actually add to overall costs when the effects are fully realized throughout the system. The marketing planning model allows a simultaneous examination of this total effect.

## Questions

1. What is the primary objective of Marathon's marketing planning model?
2. Describe the types of problems the marketing planning model is most effective in handling.
3. If daily savings using the model are one-tenth of a cent per gallon sold, what is the projected daily savings?

# 5

# LINEAR PROGRAMMING: THE SIMPLEX METHOD

## CONTENTS

In Chapter 2 we showed how the graphical solution procedure can be used to solve linear programming problems involving two decision variables. However, most linear programming problems are too large to be solved graphically, and an algebraic solution procedure must be employed. The most widely used algebraic procedure for solving linear programming problems is called the **simplex method.**[1] Computer programs based on this method can routinely solve linear programming problems with thousands of variables and constraints. The Management Science in Action: Fleet Assignment at Delta Airlines describes solving a linear program involving 60,000 variables and 40,000 constraints on a daily basis.

## 5.1    AN ALGEBRAIC OVERVIEW OF THE SIMPLEX METHOD

Let us introduce the problem we will use to demonstrate the simplex method. HighTech Industries imports electronic components that are used to assemble two different models of personal computers. One model is called the Deskpro, and the other model is called the Portable. HighTech's management is currently interested in developing a weekly production schedule for both products.

The Deskpro generates a profit contribution of $50 per unit, and the Portable generates a profit contribution of $40 per unit. For next week's production, a maximum of 150 hours of assembly time can be made available. Each unit of the Deskpro requires 3 hours of assembly time, and each unit of the Portable requires 5 hours of assembly time. In addition, HighTech currently has only 20 Portable display components in inventory; thus, no more than 20 units of the Portable may be assembled. Finally, only 300 square feet of warehouse space can be made available for new production. Assembly of each Deskpro requires 8 square feet of warehouse space; similarly, each Portable requires 5 square feet.

# MANAGEMENT SCIENCE IN ACTION

## FLEET ASSIGNMENT AT DELTA AIR LINES*

Delta Air Lines uses linear and integer programming in its Coldstart project to solve its fleet assignment problem. The problem is to match aircraft to flight legs and fill seats with paying passengers. Airline profitability depends on being able to assign the right size of aircraft to the right leg at the right time of day. An airline seat is a perishable commodity; once a flight takes off with an empty seat the profit potential of that seat is gone forever. Primary objectives of the fleet assignment model are to minimize operating costs and lost passenger revenue. Constraints are aircraft availability, balancing arrivals and departures at airports, and maintenance requirements.

The successful implementation of the Coldstart model for assigning fleet types to flight legs shows the size of linear programs that can be solved today. The typical size of the daily Coldstart model is about 60,000 variables and 40,000 constraints. The first step in solving the fleet assignment problem is to solve the model as a linear program. The model developers report successfully solving these problems on a daily basis and contend that use of the Coldstart model will save Delta Air Lines $300 million over the next three years.

*Based on R. Subramanian, R. P. Scheff, Jr., J. D. Quillinan, D. S. Wiper, and R. E. Marsten, "Coldstart: Fleet Assignment at Delta Air Lines," *Interfaces* (January–February 1994): 104–120.

[1] Several computer codes also employ what are called interior point solution procedures. These appear to work well on many problems but, at this time, the simplex method is by far the most widely used.

To develop a linear programming model for the HighTech problem, we will use the following decision variables:

$$x_1 = \text{number of units of the Deskpro}$$
$$x_2 = \text{number of units of the Portable}$$

The complete mathematical model for this problem is presented here.

$$\text{Max} \quad 50x_1 + 40x_2$$

s.t.

$$3x_1 + 5x_2 \leq 150 \quad \text{Assembly time}$$
$$1x_2 \leq 20 \quad \text{Portable display}$$
$$8x_1 + 5x_2 \leq 300 \quad \text{Warehouse capacity}$$
$$x_1, x_2 \geq 0$$

Adding a slack variable to each of the constraints permits us to write the problem in standard form.

$$\text{Max} \quad 50x_1 + 40x_2 + 0s_1 + 0s_2 + 0s_3 \tag{5.1}$$

s.t.

$$3x_1 + 5x_2 + 1s_1 \qquad\qquad = 150 \tag{5.2}$$
$$1x_2 \quad + 1s_2 \quad = 20 \tag{5.3}$$
$$8x_1 + 5x_2 \qquad\qquad + 1s_3 = 300 \tag{5.4}$$
$$x_1, x_2, s_1, s_2, s_3 \geq 0 \tag{5.5}$$

The simplex method was developed by George Dantzig while working for the U.S. Air Force. It was first published in 1949.

## Algebraic Properties of the Simplex Method

Constraint equations (5.2) to (5.4) form a system of three simultaneous linear equations with five variables. Whenever a system of simultaneous linear equations has more variables than equations, we can expect an infinite number of solutions. The simplex method can be viewed as an algebraic procedure for finding the best solution to such a system of equations. In the preceding example, the best solution is the solution to equations (5.2) to (5.4) that maximizes the objective function (5.1) and satisfies the nonnegativity conditions given by (5.5).

## Determining a Basic Solution

Since the HighTech Industries constraint equations have more variables (five) than equations (three), the simplex method finds solutions for these equations by assigning zero values to two of the variables and then solving for the values of the remaining three variables. For example, if we set $x_2 = 0$ and $s_1 = 0$, the system of constraint equations becomes

$$3x_1 \qquad\qquad = 150 \tag{5.6}$$
$$1s_2 \quad = 20 \tag{5.7}$$
$$8x_1 \quad + 1s_3 = 300 \tag{5.8}$$

Using equation (5.6) to solve for $x_1$, we have

$$3x_1 = 150$$

A basic solution is obtained by setting two of the five variables equal to zero and solving the three equations simultaneously for the values of the other three variables. Mathematically we are guaranteed a solution only if the resulting three equations are linearly independent. Fortunately, the simplex method is designed to guarantee that a solution exists for the basic variables at each iteration.

and hence $x_1 = 150/3 = 50$. Equation (5.7) provides $s_2 = 20$. Finally, substituting $x_1 = 50$ into equation (5.8) results in

$$8(50) + 1s_3 = 300$$

Solving for $s_3$, we obtain $s_3 = -100$.

Thus, we have obtained the following solution to the three-equation, five-variable set of linear equations:

$$
\begin{aligned}
x_1 &= & 50 \\
x_2 &= & 0 \\
s_1 &= & 0 \\
s_2 &= & 20 \\
s_3 &= & -100
\end{aligned}
$$

This solution is referred to as a **basic solution** for the HighTech linear programming problem. To state a general procedure for determining a basic solution, we must consider a standard-form linear programming problem consisting of $n$ variables and $m$ linear equations, where $n$ is greater than $m$.

---

### Basic Solution

To determine a basic solution, set $n - m$ of the variables equal to zero, and solve the $m$ linear constraint equations for the remaining $m$ variables.[2]

---

In terms of the HighTech problem, a basic solution can be obtained by setting any two variables equal to zero and then solving the system of three linear equations for the remaining three variables. We shall refer to the $n - m$ variables set equal to zero as the **nonbasic variables** and the remaining $m$ variables as the **basic variables.** Thus, in the preceding example, $x_2$ and $s_1$ are the nonbasic variables, and $x_1$, $s_2$, and $s_3$ are the basic variables.

## Basic Feasible Solutions

A basic solution can be either feasible or infeasible. A **basic feasible solution** is a basic solution that also satisfies the nonnegativity conditions. The basic solution found by setting $x_2$ and $s_1$ equal to zero and then solving for $x_1$, $s_2$, and $s_3$ is not a basic feasible solution because $s_3 = -100$. However, suppose that we had chosen to make $x_1$ and $x_2$ nonbasic vari-

---

[2] There are cases where a unique solution cannot be found for a system of $m$ equations and $m$ variables. However, these cases will never be encountered when using the simplex method.

ables by setting, $x_1 = 0$ and $x_2 = 0$. Solving for the corresponding basic solution is easy because with $x_1 = x_2 = 0$, the three constraint equations reduce to

$$1s_1 \qquad\qquad = 150$$
$$\qquad 1s_2 \qquad = \phantom{0}20$$
$$\qquad\qquad 1s_3 = 300$$

The complete solution with $x_1 = 0$ and $x_2 = 0$ is

$$x_1 = \phantom{00}0$$
$$x_2 = \phantom{00}0$$
$$s_1 = 150$$
$$s_2 = \phantom{0}20$$
$$s_3 = 300$$

This solution is a basic feasible solution since all of the variables satisfy the nonnegativity conditions.

The graph below shows all the constraint equations and basic solutions for the HighTech problem. Circled points ①–⑤ are basic feasible solutions; circled points ⑥–⑨ are basic solutions that are not feasible. The basic solution found by setting $x_2 = 0$ and $s_1 = 0$ corresponds to point ⑨; the basic feasible solution found by setting $x_1 = 0$ and $x_2 = 0$ corresponds to point ① in the feasible region.

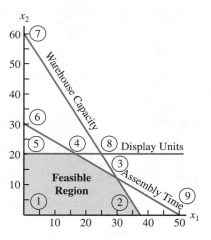

Can you find basic and basic feasible solutions to a system of equations at this point? Try Problem 1.

Figure 5.1 is a graph showing only the basic feasible solutions; note that each of these is an extreme point of the feasible region. In Chapter 2 we showed that the optimal solution to a linear programming problem can be found at an extreme point. At every extreme point is a corresponding basic feasible solution, so we can now conclude that there is an optimal basic feasible solution.[3] The simplex method is an iterative procedure for moving from one basic feasible solution (extreme point) to another until the optimal solution is reached.

---

[3] We are only considering cases where there is an optimal solution. That is, in the cases of infeasibility and unboundedness, there is no optimal solution, so there cannot be an optimal basic feasible solution.

**Figure 5.1**   FEASIBLE REGION AND EXTREME POINTS FOR THE HIGHTECH INDUSTRIES PROBLEM

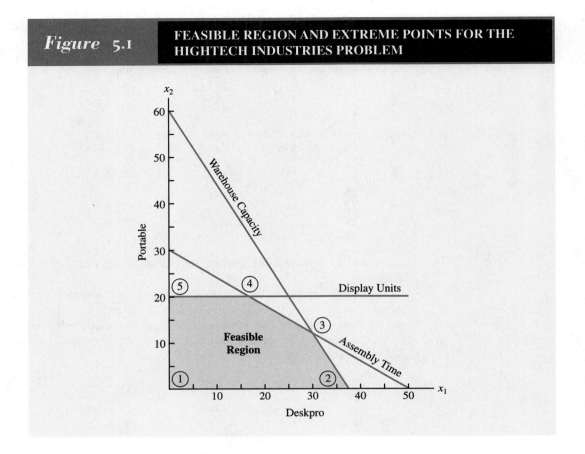

## 5.2   TABLEAU FORM

A basic feasible solution to the system of $m$ linear constraint equations and $n$ variables is required as a starting point for the simplex method. The purpose of tableau form is to provide an initial basic feasible solution.

Recall that for the HighTech problem, the standard-form representation is

$$\text{Max} \quad 50x_1 + 40x_2 + 0s_1 + 0s_2 + 0s_3$$

$$\text{s.t.}$$

$$3x_1 + 5x_2 + 1s_1 \qquad\qquad = 150$$
$$1x_2 \qquad + 1s_2 \qquad = 20$$
$$8x_1 + 5x_2 \qquad\qquad + 1s_3 = 300$$

$$x_1, x_2, s_1, s_2, s_3 \geq 0$$

When a linear programming problem with all less-than-or-equal-to constraints is written in standard form, it is easy to find a basic feasible solution. We simply set the decision variables equal to zero and solve for the values of the slack variables. Note that doing this sets the values of the slack variables equal to the right-hand-side values of the constraint equations. For the HighTech problem, this yields $x_1 = 0, x_2 = 0, s_1 = 150, s_2 = 20,$ and $s_3 = 300$ as the initial basic feasible solution.

If we study the standard-form representation of the HighTech constraint equations closely, we can identify two properties that make it possible to find an initial basic feasible solution. The first property requires that the following conditions be satisfied:

a.  For each constraint equation, the coefficient of one of the $m$ basic variables in that equation must be 1, and the coefficients for all the remaining basic variables in that equation must be 0.
b.  The coefficient for each basic variable must be 1 in only one constraint equation.

When these conditions are satisfied, exactly one basic variable with a coefficient of 1 is associated with each constraint equation, and for each of the $m$ constraint equations, it is a different basic variable. Thus, if the $n - m$ nonbasic variables are set equal to zero, the values of the basic variables are the values of the right-hand sides of the constraint equations.

The second property that enables us to find a basic feasible solution requires the values of the right-hand sides of the constraint equations be nonnegative. This nonnegativity ensures that the basic solution obtained by setting the basic variables equal to the values of the right-hand sides will be feasible.

*For linear programs with less-than-or-equal-to constraints, the slack variables provide the initial basic feasible solution identified in tableau form.*

If a linear programming problem satisfies these two properties, it is said to be in **tableau form.** Thus, we see that the standard-form representation of the HighTech problem is already in tableau form. In fact, standard form and tableau form for linear programs that have all less-than-or-equal-to constraints and nonnegative right-hand-side values are the same. Later in this chapter we will show how to set up the tableau form for linear programming problems where the standard form and the tableau form are not the same.

*In the HighTech problem, tableau form and standard form are the same, which is true for all LPs with only less-than-or-equal-to constraints and nonnegative right-hand sides.*

To summarize, the following three steps are necessary to prepare a linear programming problem for solution using the simplex method:

Step 1  Formulate the problem.
Step 2  Set up the standard form by adding slack and/or subtracting surplus variables.
Step 3  Set up the tableau form.

## 5.3   SETTING UP THE INITIAL SIMPLEX TABLEAU

After a linear programming problem has been converted to tableau form, we have an initial basic feasible solution that can be used to begin the simplex method. To provide a convenient means for performing the calculations required by the simplex solution procedure, we will first develop what is referred to as the initial **simplex tableau.**

Part of the initial simplex tableau is a table containing all the coefficients shown in the tableau form of a linear program. If we adopt the general notation

$$c_j = \text{objective function coefficient for variable } j$$
$$b_i = \text{right-hand-side value for constraint } i$$
$$a_{ij} = \text{coefficient associated with variable } j \text{ in constraint } i$$

we can show this portion of the initial simplex tableau as follows:

| $c_1$ | $c_2$ | $\ldots c_n$ | |
|---|---|---|---|
| $a_{11}$ | $a_{12}$ | $\ldots a_{1n}$ | $b_1$ |
| $a_{21}$ | $a_{22}$ | $\ldots a_{2n}$ | $b_2$ |
| . | . | . . . . | . |
| . | . | . . . . | . |
| $a_{m1}$ | $a_{m2}$ | $\ldots a_{mn}$ | $b_m$ |

Thus, for the HighTech problem we obtain the following partial initial simplex tableau:

| 50 | 40 | 0 | 0 | 0 | |
|---|---|---|---|---|---|
| 3 | 5 | 1 | 0 | 0 | **150** |
| 0 | 1 | 0 | 1 | 0 | **20** |
| 8 | 5 | 0 | 0 | 1 | **300** |

Later we may want to refer to the objective function coefficients, all the right-hand-side values, or all the coefficients in the constraints as a group. For such groupings, we will find the following general notation helpful:

$c$ row = row of objective function coefficients

$b$ column = column of right-hand-side values of the constraint equations

$A$ matrix = $m$ rows and $n$ columns of coefficients of the variables in the constraint equations

Using this notation, we can show these portions of the initial simplex tableau as follows:

| $c$ row | |
|---|---|
| $A$ matrix | $b$ column |

To help us recall that each of the columns contains the coefficients for one of the variables, we write the variable associated with each column directly above the column. By adding the variables we obtain

To practice setting up the portion of the simplex tableau corresponding to the objective function and constraints at this point, try Problem 4.

| $x_1$ | $x_2$ | $s_1$ | $s_2$ | $s_3$ | |
|---|---|---|---|---|---|
| 50 | 40 | 0 | 0 | 0 | |
| 3 | 5 | 1 | 0 | 0 | **150** |
| 0 | 1 | 0 | 1 | 0 | **20** |
| 8 | 5 | 0 | 0 | 1 | **300** |

The simplex tableau is
nothing more than a table
that helps keep track of the
simplex method calculations
and the equivalent system
of constraint equations
at each iteration.
Reconstructing the
original problem can be
accomplished from
the initial simplex tableau.

This portion of the initial simplex tableau contains the tableau-form representation of the problem; thus, it is easy to identify the initial basic feasible solution. First, we note that for each basic variable, there is a corresponding column that has a 1 in the only nonzero position. Such columns are known as **unit columns** or **unit vectors.** Second, a row of the tableau is associated with each basic variable. This row has a 1 in the unit column corresponding to the basic variable. The value of each basic variable is then given by the $b_i$ value in the row associated with the basic variable. In the example, row 1 is associated with basic variable $s_1$ since this row has a 1 in the unit column corresponding to $s_1$. Thus, the value of $s_1$ is given by the right-hand side value $b_1$: $s_1 = b_1 = 150$. In a similar fashion, $s_2 = b_2 = 20$, and $s_3 = b_3 = 300$.

To move from an initial basic feasible solution to a better basic feasible solution, the simplex method must generate a new basic feasible solution that yields a better value for the objective function. To do so requires changing the set of basic variables: we select one of the current nonbasic variables to be made basic and one of the current basic variables to be made nonbasic.

For computational convenience, we will add two new columns to the simplex tableau. One column is labeled "*Basis*" and the other column is labeled "$c_B$." In the **Basis** column, we list the current basic variables, and in the $c_B$ column, we list the corresponding objective function coefficient for each of the basic variables. For the HighTech problem, this results in the following:

| Basis | $c_B$ | $x_1$ | $x_2$ | $s_1$ | $s_2$ | $s_3$ | |
|-------|-------|-------|-------|-------|-------|-------|-----|
|       |       | 50    | 40    | 0     | 0     | 0     |     |
| $s_1$ | 0     | 3     | 5     | 1     | 0     | 0     | **150** |
| $s_2$ | 0     | 0     | 1     | 0     | 1     | 0     | **20** |
| $s_3$ | 0     | 8     | 5     | 0     | 0     | 1     | **300** |

Note that in the column labeled *Basis,* $s_1$ is listed as the first basic variable since its value is given by the right-hand-side value for the first equation. With $s_2$ listed second and $s_3$ listed third, the *Basis* column and right-hand-side values show the initial basic feasible solution has $s_1 = 150$, $s_2 = 20$, and $s_3 = 300$.

Can we improve the value of the objective function by moving to a new basic feasible solution? To find out whether it is possible, we add two rows to the bottom of the tableau. The first row, labeled $z_j$, represents the decrease in the value of the objective function that will result if one unit of the variable corresponding to the $j$th column of the $A$ matrix is brought into the basis. The second row, labeled $c_j - z_j$, represents the net change in the value of the objective function if one unit of the variable corresponding to the $j$th column of the $A$ matrix is brought into the solution. We refer to the $c_j - z_j$ row as the **net evaluation row.**

Let us first see how the entries in the $z_j$ row are computed. Suppose that we consider increasing the value of the nonbasic variable $x_1$ by one unit—that is, from $x_1 = 0$ to $x_1 = 1$. In order to make this change and at the same time continue to satisfy the constraint equations, the values of some of the other variables will have to be changed. As we will show, the simplex method requires that the necessary changes be made to basic variables only. For example, in the first constraint we have

$$3x_1 + 5x_2 + 1s_1 = 150$$

The current basic variable in this constraint equation is $s_1$. Assuming that $x_2$ remains a nonbasic variable with a value of 0, if $x_1$ is increased in value by 1, then $s_1$ must be decreased by 3 for the constraint to be satisfied. Similarly, if we were to increase the value of $x_1$ by 1 (and keep $x_2 = 0$), we can see from the second and third equations that although $s_2$ would not decrease, $s_3$ would decrease by 8.

From analyzing all the constraint equations, we see that the coefficients in the $x_1$ column indicate the amount of decrease in the current basic variables when the nonbasic variable $x_1$ is increased from 0 to 1. In general, all the column coefficients can be interpreted this way. For instance, if we make $x_2$ a basic variable at a value of 1, $s_1$ will decrease by 5, $s_2$ will decrease by 1, and $s_3$ will decrease by 5.

Recall that the values in the $c_B$ column of the simplex tableau are the objective function coefficients for the current basic variables. Hence, to compute the values in the $z_j$ row (the decrease in value of the objective function when $x_j$ is increased by one), we form the sum of the products obtained by multiplying the elements in the $c_B$ column by the corresponding elements in the $j$th column of the $A$ matrix. Doing these calculations we obtain

$$z_1 = 0(3) + 0(0) + 0(8) = 0$$
$$z_2 = 0(5) + 0(1) + 0(5) = 0$$
$$z_3 = 0(1) + 0(0) + 0(0) = 0$$
$$z_4 = 0(0) + 0(1) + 0(0) = 0$$
$$z_5 = 0(0) + 0(0) + 0(1) = 0$$

Because the objective function coefficient of $x_1$ is $c_1 = 50$, the value of $c_1 - z_1$ is $50 - 0 = 50$. Then the net result of bringing one unit of $x_1$ into the current basis will be an increase in profit of $50. Hence, in the net evaluation row corresponding to $x_1$, we enter 50. In the same manner, we can calculate the $c_j - z_j$ values for the remaining variables. The result is the following initial simplex tableau:

| Basis | $c_B$ | $x_1$ 50 | $x_2$ 40 | $s_1$ 0 | $s_2$ 0 | $s_3$ 0 | |
|---|---|---|---|---|---|---|---|
| $s_1$ | 0 | 3 | 5 | 1 | 0 | 0 | 150 |
| $s_2$ | 0 | 0 | 1 | 0 | 1 | 0 | 20 |
| $s_3$ | 0 | 8 | 5 | 0 | 0 | 1 | 300 |
| $z_j$ | | 0 | 0 | 0 | 0 | 0 | 0 |
| $c_j - z_j$ | | 50 | 40 | 0 | 0 | 0 | |

Value of the
Objective Function

In this tableau we also see a boldfaced 0 in the $z_j$ row in the last column. This zero is the value of the objective function associated with the current basic feasible solution. It was computed by multiplying the objective function coefficients in the $c_B$ column by the corresponding values of the basic variables shown in the last column of the tableau—that is, $0(150) + 0(20) + 0(300) = 0$.

Try Problem 5(a) for practice in setting up the complete initial simplex tableau for a problem with less-than-or-equal constraints.

The initial simplex tableau is now complete. It shows that the initial basic feasible solution ($x_1 = 0$, $x_2 = 0$, $s_1 = 150$, $s_2 = 20$, and $s_3 = 300$) has an objective function value, or profit, of \$0. In addition, the $c_j - z_j$ or net evaluation row has values that will guide us in improving the solution by moving to a better basic feasible solution.

......................................................................................./ /............

## 5.4    IMPROVING THE SOLUTION

From the net evaluation row, we see that each unit of the Deskpro ($x_1$) increases the value of the objective function by 50 and each unit of the Portable ($x_2$) increases the value of the objective function by 40. Since $x_1$ causes the largest per-unit increase, we choose it as the variable to bring into the basis. We must next determine which of the current basic variables to make nonbasic.

In discussing how to compute the $z_j$ values, we noted that each of the coefficients in the $x_1$ column indicates the amount of decrease in the corresponding basic variable that would result from increasing $x_1$ by one unit. Considering the first row, we see that every unit of the Deskpro produced will use 3 hours of assembly time, reducing $s_1$ by 3. In the current solution, $s_1 = 150$ and $x_1 = 0$. Thus—considering this row only—the maximum possible value of $x_1$ can be calculated by solving

$$3x_1 = 150$$

which provides

$$x_1 = 50$$

If $x_1$ is 50 (and $x_2$ remains a nonbasic variable with a value of 0), $s_1$ will have to be reduced to zero in order to satisfy the first constraint:

$$3x_1 + 5x_2 + 1s_1 = 150$$

Considering the second row, $0x_1 + 1x_2 + 1s_2 = 20$, we see that the coefficient of $x_1$ is 0. Thus, increasing $x_1$ will not have any effect on $s_2$; that is, increasing $x_1$ cannot drive the basic variable in the second row ($s_2$) to zero. Indeed, increases in $x_1$ will leave $s_2$ unchanged.

Finally, since the coefficient of $x_1$ is 8 in the third row, every unit that we increase $x_1$ will cause a decrease of eight units in $s_3$. Since the value of $s_3$ is currently 300, we can solve

$$8x_1 = 300$$

to find the maximum possible increase in $x_1$ before $s_3$ will become nonbasic at a value of zero; thus, we see that $x_1$ cannot be any larger than $^{300}\!/_8 = 37.5$.

Considering the three rows (constraints) simultaneously, we see that row 3 is the most restrictive. That is, producing 37.5 units of the Deskpro will force the corresponding slack variable to become nonbasic at a value of $s_3 = 0$.

In making the decision to produce as many Deskpro units as possible, we must change the set of variables in the basic feasible solution, which means obtaining a new basis. The simplex method moves from one basic feasible solution to another by selecting a nonbasic variable to replace one of the current basic variables. This process of moving from one basic feasible solution to another is called an **iteration.** We now summarize the rules for selecting a nonbasic variable to be made basic and for selecting a current basic variable to be made nonbasic.

---

### Criterion for Entering a New Variable into the Basis

Look at the net evaluation row $(c_j - z_j)$, and select the variable to enter the basis that will cause the largest per-unit improvement in the value of the objective function. In the case of a tie, follow the convention of selecting the variable to enter the basis that corresponds to the leftmost of the columns.

---

---

### Criterion for Removing a Variable from the Current Basis (Minimum Ratio Test)

To determine which basic variable will become nonbasic, only the positive coefficients in the incoming column correspond to basic variables that will decrease in value when the new basic variable enters.

Suppose the incoming basic variable corresponds to column $j$ in the $A$ portion of the simplex tableau. For each row $i$, compute the ratio $b_i/a_{ij}$ for each $a_{ij}$ greater than zero. The basic variable that will be removed from the basis corresponds to the minimum of these ratios. In case of a tie, we follow the convention of selecting the variable that corresponds to the uppermost of the tied rows.

---

To illustrate the computations involved, we add an extra column to the right of the tableau showing the $b_i/a_{ij}$ ratios.

| Basis | $c_B$ | $x_1$ 50 | $x_2$ 40 | $s_1$ 0 | $s_2$ 0 | $s_3$ 0 | | $\dfrac{b_i}{a_{i1}}$ |
|-------|-------|------|------|------|------|------|-----|------------------------|
| $s_1$ | 0 | 3 | 5 | 1 | 0 | 0 | 150 | $\dfrac{150}{3} = 50$ |
| $s_2$ | 0 | 0 | 1 | 0 | 1 | 0 | 20 | — |
| $s_3$ | 0 | ⑧ | 5 | 0 | 0 | 1 | 300 | $\dfrac{300}{8} = 37.5$ |
| $z_j$ | | 0 | 0 | 0 | 0 | 0 | 0 | |
| $c_j - z_j$ | | 50 | 40 | 0 | 0 | 0 | | |

We see that $c_1 - z_1 = 50$ is the largest positive value in the $c_j - z_j$ row. Hence, $x_1$ is selected to become the new basic variable. Checking the ratios $b_i/a_{i1}$ for values of $a_{i1}$ greater than zero, we see that $b_3/a_{31} = 300/8 = 37.5$ is the minimum of these ratios. Thus, the current basic variable associated with row 3 $(s_3)$ is the variable selected to leave the basis. In the tableau we have circled $a_{31} = 8$ to indicate that the variable corresponding to the first column is to enter the basis and that the basic variable corresponding to the third row is to leave the basis. Adopting the usual linear programming terminology, we refer to this circled element as the **pivot element.** The column and the row containing the pivot element are called the **pivot column** and the **pivot row,** respectively.

The circled value is the pivot element; the corresponding column and row are called the pivot column and pivot row.

To improve the current solution of $x_1 = 0$, $x_2 = 0$, $s_1 = 150$, $s_2 = 20$, and $s_3 = 300$, we should increase $x_1$ to 37.5. The production of 37.5 units of the Deskpro results in a profit of $50(37.5) = 1875$. In producing 37.5 units of the Deskpro, $s_3$ will be reduced to zero. Hence, $x_1$ will become the new basic variable, replacing $s_3$ in the previous basis.

## 5.5    CALCULATING THE NEXT TABLEAU

We now want to update the simplex tableau in such a fashion that the column associated with the new basic variable is a unit column; in this way its value will be given by the right-hand-side value of the corresponding row. We would like the column in the new tableau corresponding to $x_1$ to look just like the column corresponding to $s_3$ in the original tableau, so our goal is to make the column in the $A$ matrix corresponding to $x_1$ appear as

$$0$$
$$0$$
$$1$$

The way in which we transform the simplex tableau so that it still represents an equivalent system of constraint equations is to use the following **elementary row operations.**

---

### Elementery Row Operations

1. Multiply any row (equation) by a nonzero number.
2. Replace any row (equation) by the result of adding or subtracting a multiple of another row (equation) to it.

---

The application of these elementary row operations to a system of simultaneous linear equations will not change the solution to the system of equations; however, the elementary row operations will change the coefficients of the variables and the values of the right-hand sides.

The objective in performing elementary row operations is to transform the system of constraint equations into a form that makes it easy to identify the new basic feasible solution. Consequently, we must perform the elementary row operations in such a manner that we transform the column for the variable entering the basis into a unit column. We emphasize that the feasible solutions to the original constraint equations are the same as the feasible solutions to the modified constraint equations obtained by performing elementary row operations. However, many of the numerical values in the simplex tableau will change as the result of performing these row operations. Thus, the present method of referring to elements in the simplex tableau may lead to confusion.

Up to now we have made no distinction between the $A$ matrix and $b$ column coefficients in the tableau form of the problem and the corresponding coefficients in the simplex tableau. Indeed, we showed that the initial simplex tableau is formed by properly placing the $a_{ij}$, $c_j$, and $b_i$ elements as given in the tableau form of the problem into the simplex tableau. To avoid confusion in subsequent simplex tableaus, we will refer to the portion of the simplex tableau that initially contained the $a_{ij}$ values with the symbol $\bar{A}$, and the portion of the tableau that initially contained the $b_i$ values with the symbol $\bar{b}$. In terms of the simplex tableau, elements in $\bar{A}$ will be denoted by $\bar{a}_{ij}$, and elements in $\bar{b}$ will be denoted by $\bar{b}_i$. In subsequent simplex tableaus, elementary row operations will change the tableau elements. The overbar notation should avoid any confusion when we wish to distinguish between (1) the original constraint coefficient values $a_{ij}$ and right-hand-side values $b_i$ of the tableau form, and (2) the simplex tableau elements $\bar{a}_{ij}$ and $\bar{b}_i$.

Now let us see how elementary row operations are used to create the next simplex tableau for the HighTech problem. Recall that the goal is to transform the column in the $\bar{A}$ portion of the simplex tableau corresponding to $x_1$ to a unit column; that is,

$$\bar{a}_{11} = 0$$
$$\bar{a}_{21} = 0$$
$$\bar{a}_{31} = 1$$

To set $\bar{a}_{31} = 1$, we perform the first elementary row operation by multiplying the pivot row (row 3) by $\frac{1}{8}$ to obtain the equivalent equation

$$\tfrac{1}{8}(8x_1 + 5x_2 + 0s_1 + 0s_2 + 1s_3) = \tfrac{1}{8}(300)$$

or

$$1x_1 + \tfrac{5}{8}x_2 + 0s_1 + 0s_2 + \tfrac{1}{8}s_3 = \tfrac{75}{2} \tag{5.9}$$

We refer to equation (5.9) in the updated simplex tableau as the *new pivot row*.

To set $\bar{a}_{11} = 0$, we perform the second elementary row operation by first multiplying the new pivot row by 3 to obtain the equivalent equation

$$3(1x_1 + \tfrac{5}{8}x_2 + 0s_1 + 0s_2 + \tfrac{1}{8}s_3) = 3(\tfrac{75}{2})$$

or

$$3x_1 + \tfrac{15}{8}x_2 + 0s_1 + 0s_2 + \tfrac{3}{8}s_3 = \tfrac{225}{2} \tag{5.10}$$

Subtracting equation (5.10) from the equation represented by row 1 of the simplex tableau completes the application of the second elementary row operation; thus, after dropping the terms with zero coefficients, we obtain

$$(3x_1 + 5x_2 + 1s_1) - (3x_1 + \tfrac{15}{8}x_2 + \tfrac{3}{8}s_3) = 150 - \tfrac{225}{2}$$

or

$$0x_1 + \tfrac{25}{8}x_2 + 1s_1 - \tfrac{3}{8}s_3 = \tfrac{75}{2} \tag{5.11}$$

Since $\bar{a}_{21} = 0$, no row operations need be performed on the second row of the simplex tableau. Replacing rows 1 and 3 with the coefficients in equations (5.11) and (5.9), respectively, we obtain the new simplex tableau

| Basis | $c_B$ | $x_1$ 50 | $x_2$ 40 | $s_1$ 0 | $s_2$ 0 | $s_3$ 0 | |
|---|---|---|---|---|---|---|---|
| $s_1$ | 0 | 0 | $\tfrac{25}{8}$ | 1 | 0 | $-\tfrac{3}{8}$ | $\tfrac{75}{2}$ |
| $s_2$ | 0 | 0 | 1 | 0 | 1 | 0 | 20 |
| $x_1$ | 50 | 1 | $\tfrac{5}{8}$ | 0 | 0 | $\tfrac{1}{8}$ | $\tfrac{75}{2}$ |
| $z_j$ | | | | | | | **1875** |
| $c_j - z_j$ | | | | | | | |

Assigning zero values to the nonbasic variables $x_2$ and $s_3$ permits us to identify the following new basic feasible solution:

$$s_1 = {}^{75}\!/_2$$
$$s_2 = 20$$
$$x_1 = {}^{75}\!/_2$$

This solution is also provided by the last column in the new simplex tableau. The profit associated with this solution is obtained by multiplying the solution values for the basic variables as given in the $\bar{b}$ column by their corresponding objective function coefficients as given in the $c_B$ column; that is,

$$0({}^{75}\!/_2) + 0(20) + 50({}^{75}\!/_2) = 1875$$

## Interpreting the Results of an Iteration

In our example, the initial basic feasible solution was

$$x_1 = \quad 0$$
$$x_2 = \quad 0$$
$$s_1 = 150$$
$$s_2 = \quad 20$$
$$s_3 = 300$$

with a corresponding profit of \$0. One iteration of the simplex method moved us to another basic feasible solution with an objective function value of \$1875. This new basic feasible solution is

$$x_1 = {}^{75}\!/_2$$
$$x_2 = \quad 0$$
$$s_1 = {}^{75}\!/_2$$
$$s_2 = 20$$
$$s_3 = \quad 0$$

*The first iteration moves us from the origin in Figure 5.2 to extreme point 2.*

In Figure 5.2 we see that the initial basic feasible solution corresponds to extreme point ①. The first iteration moved us in the direction of the greatest increase per unit in profit— that is, along the $x_1$ axis. We moved away from extreme point ① in the $x_1$ direction until we could not move farther without violating one of the constraints. The tableau we calculated after one iteration is the basic feasible solution corresponding to extreme point ②.

We note from Figure 5.2 that at extreme point ② the warehouse capacity constraint is binding with $s_3 = 0$ and that the other two constraints contain slack. From the simplex tableau, we see that the amount of slack for these two constraints is given by $s_1 = {}^{75}\!/_2$ and $s_2 = 20$.

## Moving Toward a Better Solution

To see if a better basic feasible solution can be found, we need to calculate the $z_j$ and $c_j - z_j$ rows for the new simplex tableau. Recall that the elements in the $z_j$ row are the sum of the

**Figure 5.2** FEASIBLE REGION AND EXTREME POINTS FOR THE HIGHTECH INDUSTRIES PROBLEM

products obtained by multiplying the elements in the $c_B$ column of the simplex tableau by the corresponding elements in the columns of the $\bar{A}$ matrix. Thus, we obtain

$$z_1 = 0(0) \quad + 0(0) + 50(1) \ = 50$$
$$z_2 = 0(^{25}\!/_8) \quad + 0(1) + 50(^5\!/_8) = {}^{250}\!/_8$$
$$z_3 = 0(1) \quad + 0(0) + 50(0) \ = 0$$
$$z_4 + 0(0) \quad + 0(1) + 50(0) \ = 0$$
$$z_5 = 0(-^3\!/_8) + 0(0) + 50(^1\!/_8) = {}^{50}\!/_8$$

Subtracting $z_j$ from $c_j$ to compute the new net evaluation row, we obtain the following simplex tableau:

|  |  | $x_1$ | $x_2$ | $s_1$ | $s_2$ | $s_3$ |  |
|---|---|---|---|---|---|---|---|
| *Basis* | $c_B$ | 50 | 40 | 0 | 0 | 0 |  |
| $s_1$ | 0 | 0 | $^{25}\!/_8$ | 1 | 0 | $-^3\!/_8$ | $^{75}\!/_2$ |
| $s_2$ | 0 | 0 | 1 | 0 | 1 | 0 | **20** |
| $x_1$ | 50 | 1 | $^5\!/_8$ | 0 | 0 | $^1\!/_8$ | $^{75}\!/_2$ |
| $z_j$ |  | 50 | $^{250}\!/_8$ | 0 | 0 | $^{50}\!/_8$ | **1875** |
| $c_j - z_j$ |  | 0 | $^{70}\!/_8$ | 0 | 0 | $-^{50}\!/_8$ |  |

Let us now analyze the $c_j - z_j$ row to see whether we can introduce a new variable into the basis and continue to improve the value of the objective function. Using the rule for determining which variable should enter the basis next, we select $x_2$ since it has the highest positive coefficient in the $c_j - z_j$ row.

To determine which variable will be removed from the basis when $x_2$ enters, we must compute for each row $i$ the ratio $\bar{b}_i/\bar{a}_{i2}$ (remember, though, that we should compute this ratio only if $\bar{a}_{i2}$ is greater than zero); then we select the variable to leave the basis that corresponds to the minimum ratio. As before, we will show these ratios in an extra column of the simplex tableau:

| | | $x_1$ | $x_2$ | $s_1$ | $s_2$ | $s_3$ | | $\dfrac{\bar{b}_i}{\bar{a}_{i2}}$ |
|---|---|---|---|---|---|---|---|---|
| Basis | $c_B$ | 50 | 40 | 0 | 0 | 0 | | |
| $s_1$ | 0 | 0 | $\textcircled{$\tfrac{25}{8}$}$ | 1 | 0 | $-\tfrac{3}{8}$ | $\tfrac{75}{2}$ | $\dfrac{75/2}{25/8} = 12$ |
| $s_2$ | 0 | 0 | 1 | 0 | 1 | 0 | 20 | $\dfrac{20}{1} = 20$ |
| $x_1$ | 50 | 1 | $\tfrac{5}{8}$ | 0 | 0 | $\tfrac{1}{8}$ | $\tfrac{75}{2}$ | $\dfrac{75/2}{5/8} = 60$ |
| $z_j$ | | 50 | $\tfrac{250}{8}$ | 0 | 0 | $\tfrac{50}{8}$ | 1875 | |
| $c_j - z_j$ | | 0 | $\tfrac{70}{8}$ | 0 | 0 | $-\tfrac{50}{8}$ | | |

Since 12 is the minimum ratio, $s_1$ will leave the basis. The pivot element is $\bar{a}_{12} = \tfrac{25}{8}$, which is circled in the preceding tableau. The nonbasic variable $x_2$ must now be made a basic variable in row 1. This requirement means that we must perform the elementary row operations that will convert the $x_2$ column into a unit column with a 1 in row 1; that is, we will have to transform the second column in the tableau to the form

$$1$$
$$0$$
$$0$$

We can make this change by performing the following elementary row operations:

Step 1   Multiply every element in row 1 (the pivot row) by $\tfrac{8}{25}$ in order to make $\bar{a}_{12} = 1$.
Step 2   Subtract the new row 1 (the new pivot row) from row 2 to make $\bar{a}_{22} = 0$.
Step 3   Multiply the new pivot row by $\tfrac{5}{8}$, and subtract the result from row 3 to make $\bar{a}_{32} = 0$.

The new simplex tableau resulting from these row operations is as follows:

| | | $x_1$ | $x_2$ | $s_1$ | $s_2$ | $s_3$ | |
|---|---|---|---|---|---|---|---|
| Basis | $c_B$ | 50 | 40 | 0 | 0 | 0 | |
| $x_2$ | 40 | 0 | 1 | $\tfrac{8}{25}$ | 0 | $-\tfrac{3}{25}$ | 12 |
| $s_2$ | 0 | 0 | 0 | $-\tfrac{8}{25}$ | 1 | $\tfrac{3}{25}$ | 8 |
| $x_1$ | 50 | 1 | 0 | $-\tfrac{5}{25}$ | 0 | $\tfrac{5}{25}$ | 30 |
| $z_j$ | | 50 | 40 | $\tfrac{14}{5}$ | 0 | $\tfrac{26}{5}$ | 1980 |
| $c_j - z_j$ | | 0 | 0 | $-\tfrac{14}{5}$ | 0 | $-\tfrac{26}{5}$ | |

Note that the values of the basic variables are $x_2 = 12$, $s_2 = 8$, and $x_1 = 30$, and the corresponding profit is $40(12) + 0(8) + 50(30) = 1980$.

We must now determine whether to bring any other variable into the basis and thereby move to another basic feasible solution. Looking at the net evaluation row, we see that every element is zero or negative. Since $c_j - z_j$ is less than or equal to zero for both of the nonbasic variables $s_1$ and $s_3$, any attempt to bring a nonbasic variable into the basis at this point will result in a lowering of the current value of the objective function. Hence, this tableau represents the optimal solution. In general, the simplex method uses the following criterion to determine when the optimal solution has been obtained.

---

## Optimality Criterion

The optimal solution to a linear programming problem has been reached when all of the entries in the net evaluation row $(c_j - z_j)$ are zero or negative. In such cases, the optimal solution is the current basic feasible solution.

---

Referring to Figure 5.2, we can see graphically the process that the simplex method used to determine an optimal solution. The initial basic feasible solution corresponds to the origin ($x_1 = 0$, $x_2 = 0$, $s_1 = 150$, $s_2 = 20$, $s_3 = 300$). The first iteration caused $x_1$ to enter the basis and $s_3$ to leave. The second basic feasible solution corresponds to extreme point ② ($x_1 = {}^{75}\!/_2$, $x_2 = 0$, $s_1 = {}^{75}\!/_2$, $s_2 = 20$, $s_3 = 0$). At the next iteration, $x_2$ entered the basis and $s_1$ left. This iteration brought us to extreme point ③ and the optimal solution ($x_1 = 30$, $x_2 = 12$, $s_1 = 0$, $s_2 = 8$, $s_3 = 0$).

For the HighTech problem with only two decision variables, we had a choice of using the graphical or simplex method. For problems with more than two variables, we shall always use the simplex method.

## Interpreting the Optimal Solution

Using the final simplex tableau, we find the optimal solution to the HighTech problem consists of the basic variables $x_1$, $x_2$, and $s_2$ and nonbasic variables $s_1$ and $s_3$ with:

$$x_1 = 30$$
$$x_2 = 12$$
$$s_1 = 0$$
$$s_2 = 8$$
$$s_3 = 0$$

The value of the objective function is $1980. If management wants to maximize the total profit contribution, HighTech should produce 30 units of the Deskpro and 12 units of the Portable. Since $s_2 = 8$, management should note that there will be eight unused Portable display units. Moreover, since $s_1 = 0$ and $s_3 = 0$, no slack is associated with the assembly time constraint and the warehouse capacity constraint; in other words, these constraints are both binding. Consequently, if it is possible to obtain additional assembly time and/or additional warehouse space, management should consider doing so.

Figure 5.3 shows the computer solution to the HighTech problem using The Management Scientist software package. The optimal solution with $x_1 = 30$ and $x_2 = 12$ is shown to have an objective function value of $1980. The values of the slack variables complete the optimal solution with $s_1 = 0$, $s_2 = 8$ and $s_3 = 0$. The values in the reduced costs column are from the net evaluation row of the final simplex tableau. Note that the $c_j - z_j$ values in columns corresponding to $x_1$ and $x_2$ are both 0. The dual prices are the $z_j$ values for the three slack variables in the final simplex tableau. Referring to the final tableau, we see that the dual price for constraint 1 is the $z_j$ value corresponding to $s_1$ where $^{14}/_5 = 2.8$. Similarly, the dual price for constraint 2 is 0, and the dual price for constraint 3 is $^{26}/_5 = 5.2$. The use of the simplex method to compute dual prices will be discussed further when we cover sensitivity analysis in Chapter 6.

## Summary of the Simplex Method

Let us now summarize the steps followed to solve a linear program using the simplex method. We assume that the problem has all less-than-or-equal-to constraints and involves maximization.

Step 1  Formulate a linear programming model of the problem.
Step 2  Add slack variables to each constraint to obtain standard form. This is also the tableau form necessary to identify an initial basic feasible solution for problems involving all less-than-or-equal-to constraints.
Step 3  Set up the initial simplex tableau.
Step 4  Choose the nonbasic variable with the largest entry in the net evaluation row to bring into the basis. This variable identifies the pivot column: the column associated with the incoming variable.
Step 5  Choose as the pivot row that row with the smallest ratio of $\bar{b}_i / \bar{a}_{ij}$ for $\bar{a}_{ij} > 0$ where $j$ is the pivot column. This figure identifies the pivot row: the row of the variable leaving the basis when variable $j$ enters.
Step 6  Perform the necessary elementary row operations to convert the column for the incoming variable to a unit column with a 1 in the pivot row.
  a. Divide each element of the pivot row by the pivot element (the element in the pivot row and pivot column).

---

**Figure 5.3    THE MANAGEMENT SCIENTIST SOLUTION FOR THE HIGHTECH INDUSTRIES PROBLEM**

```
OPTIMAL SOLUTION

Objective Function Value =              1980.000

        Variable            Value              Reduced Costs
     --------------     --------------       ------------------
           X1               30.000                 0.000
           X2               12.000                 0.000


       Constraint        Slack/Surplus            Dual Prices
     --------------     --------------       ------------------
           1                0.000                  2.800
           2                8.000                  0.000
           3                0.000                  5.200
```

b. Obtain zeroes in all other positions of the pivot column by adding or subtracting an appropriate multiple of the new pivot row. Once the row operations have been completed, the value of the new basic feasible solution can be read from the $\bar{b}$ column of the tableau.

Step 7    Test for optimality. If $c_j - z_j \leq 0$ for all columns, we have the optimal solution. If not, return to step 4.

> **To test your ability to solve a problem employing the simplex method, try Problem 6.**

The algorithm is basically the same for problems with equality and greater-than-or-equal-to constraints except that setting up tableau form requires a little more work. We discuss what is involved in Section 5.6. The simple modification necessary for minimization problems is covered in Section 5.7.

---

| N O T E S *and Comments* | The entries in the net evaluation row provide the reduced costs that appear in the computer solution to a linear program. Recall that in Chapter 3 we defined the reduced cost as the amount by which an objective function coefficient would have to improve before it would be possible for the corresponding variable to assume a positive value in the optimal solution. In general, the reduced costs are the absolute values of the entries in the net evaluation row. |
|---|---|

---

## 5.6    TABLEAU FORM: THE GENERAL CASE

> **This section explains how to get started with the simplex method for problems with greater-than-or-equal-to and equality constraints.**

When a linear program contains all less-than-or-equal-to constraints with nonnegative right-hand-side values, it is easy to set up the tableau form; we simply add a slack variable to each constraint. However, obtaining tableau form is somewhat more complex if the linear program contains greater-than-or-equal-to constraints, equality constraints, and/or negative right-hand-side values. In this section we describe how to develop tableau form for each of these situations and also how to solve linear programs involving equality and greater-than-or-equal-to constraints using the simplex method.

### Greater-Than-or-Equal-to Constraints

Suppose that in the HighTech Industries problem, management wanted to ensure that the combined total production for both models would be at least 25 units. This requirement means that the following constraint must be added to the current linear program:

$$1x_1 + 1x_2 \geq 25$$

Adding this constraint results in the following modified problem:

$$\text{Max} \quad 50x_1 + 40x_2$$

s.t.

$$
\begin{aligned}
3x_1 + 5x_2 &\leq 150 \quad \text{Assembly time} \\
1x_2 &\leq 20 \quad \text{Portable display} \\
8x_1 + 5x_2 &\leq 300 \quad \text{Warehouse space} \\
1x_1 + 1x_2 &\geq 25 \quad \text{Minimum total production} \\
x_1, x_2 &\geq 0
\end{aligned}
$$

First, we use three slack variables and one surplus variable to write the problem in standard form. This provides the following:

$$\text{Max} \quad 50x_1 + 40x_2 + 0s_1 + 0s_2 + 0s_3 + 0s_4$$

s.t.

$$
\begin{aligned}
3x_1 + 5x_2 + 1s_1 \qquad\qquad\qquad\qquad &= 150 \qquad &(5.12)\\
1x_2 \qquad + 1s_2 \qquad\qquad\qquad &= 20 \qquad &(5.13)\\
8x_1 + 5x_2 \qquad\qquad + 1s_3 \qquad &= 300 \qquad &(5.14)\\
1x_1 + 1x_2 \qquad\qquad\qquad - 1s_4 &= 25 \qquad &(5.15)
\end{aligned}
$$

$$x_1, x_2, s_1, s_2, s_3, s_4 \geq 0$$

Now let us consider how we obtain an initial basic feasible solution to start the simplex method. Previously, we set $x_1 = 0$ and $x_2 = 0$ and selected the slack variables as the initial basic variables. The extension of this notion to the modified HighTech problem would suggest setting $x_1 = 0$ and $x_2 = 0$ and selecting the slack and surplus variables as the initial basic variables. Doing so results in the basic solution

$$
\begin{aligned}
x_1 &= \quad 0\\
x_2 &= \quad 0\\
s_1 &= 150\\
s_2 &= \quad 20\\
s_3 &= 300\\
s_4 &= -25
\end{aligned}
$$

Clearly this solution cannot be a basic feasible solution since $s_4 = -25$ violates the nonnegativity requirement. The difficulty is that the standard form and the tableau form are not equivalent when the problem contains greater-than-or-equal-to constraints.

To set up the tableau form, we shall resort to a mathematical "trick" that will enable us to find an initial basic feasible solution in terms of the slack variables $s_1$, $s_2$, and $s_3$ and a new variable we shall denote $a_4$. The new variable constitutes the mathematical trick. Variable $a_4$ really has nothing to do with the HighTech problem; it merely enables us to set up the tableau form and thus obtain an initial basic feasible solution. Since this new variable has been artificially created to start the simplex method, we will refer to it as an **artificial variable.**

> Artificial variables are appropriately named; they have no physical meaning in the real problem.

The notation for artificial variables is similar to the notation used to refer to the elements of the $A$ matrix. To avoid any confusion between the two, recall that the elements of the $A$ matrix (constraint coefficients) always have two subscripts, whereas artificial variables only one subscript.

With the addition of an artificial variable, we can convert the standard form of the problem into tableau form. We add artificial variable $a_4$ to constraint equation (5.15) to obtain the following representation of the system of equations in tableau form:

$$
\begin{aligned}
3x_1 + 5x_2 + 1s_1 \qquad\qquad\qquad\qquad\qquad &= 150\\
1x_2 \qquad + 1s_2 \qquad\qquad\qquad\qquad &= 20\\
8x_1 + 5x_2 \qquad\qquad + 1s_3 \qquad\qquad &= 300\\
1x_1 + 1x_2 \qquad\qquad\qquad - 1s_4 + 1a_4 &= 25
\end{aligned}
$$

Note that the subscript on the artificial variable identifies the constraint with which it is associated. Thus, $a_4$ is the artificial variable associated with the fourth constraint.

Since the variables $s_1$, $s_2$, $s_3$, and $a_4$ each appear in a different constraint with a coefficient of 1, and since the right-hand-side values are nonnegative, both requirements of the tableau form have been satisfied. We can now obtain an initial basic feasible solution by setting $x_1 = x_2 = s_4 = 0$. The complete solution is

$$
\begin{aligned}
x_1 &= & 0 \\
x_2 &= & 0 \\
s_1 &= & 150 \\
s_2 &= & 20 \\
s_3 &= & 300 \\
s_4 &= & 0 \\
a_4 &= & 25
\end{aligned}
$$

A basic feasible solution containing one or more artificial variables at positive values is not feasible for the real problem.

Is this solution feasible in terms of the real HighTech problem? No, it is not. It does not satisfy the constraint 4 combined total production requirement of 25 units. We must make an important distinction between a basic feasible solution for the tableau form and a feasible solution for the real problem. A basic feasible solution for the tableau form of a linear programming problem is not always a feasible solution for the real problem.

The reason for creating the tableau form is to obtain the initial basic feasible solution that is required to start the simplex method. Thus, we see that whenever it is necessary to introduce artificial variables, the initial simplex solution will not in general be feasible for the real problem. This situation is not as difficult as it might seem, however, since the only time we must have a feasible solution for the real problem is at the last iteration of the simplex method. Thus, devising a way to guarantee that any artificial variable would be eliminated from the basic feasible solution before the optimal solution is reached would eliminate the difficulty.

The way in which we guarantee that artificial variables will be eliminated before the optimal solution is reached is to assign each artificial variable a very large cost in the objective function. For example, in the modified HighTech problem, we could assign a very large negative number as the profit coefficient for artificial variable $a_4$. Hence, if this variable is in the basis, it will substantially reduce profits. As a result, this variable will be eliminated from the basis as soon as possible, which is precisely what we want to happen.

As an alternative to picking a large negative number such as $-100{,}000$ for the profit coefficient, we will denote the profit coefficient of each artificial variable by $-M$. Here it is assumed that $M$ represents a very large number—in other words, a number of large magnitude and hence, the letter $M$. This notation will make it easier to keep track of the elements of the simplex tableau that depend on the profit coefficients of the artificial variables. Using $-M$ as the profit coefficient for artificial variable $a_4$ in the modified HighTech problem, we can write the objective function for the tableau form of the problem as follows:

$$
\text{Max} \quad 50x_1 + 40x_2 + 0s_1 + 0s_2 + 0s_3 + 0s_4 - Ma_4
$$

The initial simplex tableau for the problem is shown here.

| Basis | $c_B$ | $x_1$ 50 | $x_2$ 40 | $s_1$ 0 | $s_2$ 0 | $s_3$ 0 | $s_4$ 0 | $a_4$ $-M$ | |
|-------|-------|----|----|---|---|---|---|-----|------|
| $s_1$ | 0 | 3 | 5 | 1 | 0 | 0 | 0 | 0 | 150 |
| $s_2$ | 0 | 0 | 1 | 0 | 1 | 0 | 0 | 0 | 20 |
| $s_3$ | 0 | 8 | 5 | 0 | 0 | 1 | 0 | 0 | 300 |
| $a_4$ | $-M$ | ① | 1 | 0 | 0 | 0 | $-1$ | 1 | 25 |
| $z_j$ | | $-M$ | $-M$ | 0 | 0 | 0 | $M$ | $-M$ | $-25M$ |
| $c_j - z_j$ | | $50 + M$ | $40 + M$ | 0 | 0 | 0 | $-M$ | 0 | |

This tableau corresponds to the solution $s_1 = 150$, $s_2 = 20$, $s_3 = 300$, $a_4 = 25$, and $x_1 = x_2 = s_4 = 0$. In terms of the simplex tableau, this solution is a basic feasible solution since all the variables are greater than or equal to zero and $n - m = 7 - 4 = 3$ of the variables are equal to zero.

Since $c_1 - z_1 = 50 + M$ is the largest value in the net evaluation row, we see that $x_1$ will become a basic variable during the first iteration of the simplex method. Further calculations with the simplex method show that $x_1$ will replace $a_4$ in the basic solution. The following simplex tableau is the result of the first iteration.

**Result of Iteration 1**

| Basis | $c_B$ | $x_1$ 50 | $x_2$ 40 | $s_1$ 0 | $s_2$ 0 | $s_3$ 0 | $s_4$ 0 | $a_4$ $-M$ | |
|-------|-------|----|-----|---|---|---|-----|--------|------|
| $s_1$ | 0 | 0 | 2 | 1 | 0 | 0 | 3 | $-3$ | 75 |
| $s_2$ | 0 | 0 | 1 | 0 | 1 | 0 | 0 | 0 | 20 |
| $s_3$ | 0 | 0 | $-3$ | 0 | 0 | 1 | 8 | $-8$ | 100 |
| $x_1$ | 50 | 1 | 1 | 0 | 0 | 0 | $-1$ | 1 | 25 |
| $z_j$ | | 50 | 50 | 0 | 0 | 0 | $-50$ | 50 | 1250 |
| $c_j - z_j$ | | 0 | $-10$ | 0 | 0 | 0 | 50 | $-M - 50$ | |

Since the artificial variable $a_4 = 0$, we now have a situation in which the basic feasible solution contained in the simplex tableau is also a feasible solution to the real HighTech problem. In addition, since $a_4$ is an artificial variable that was added simply to obtain an initial basic feasible solution, we can now drop its associated column from the simplex tableau. Indeed, whenever artificial variables are used, they can be dropped from the simplex tableau as soon as they have been eliminated from the basic feasible solution.

When artificial variables are required to obtain an initial basic feasible solution, the iterations required to eliminate the artificial variables are referred to as **phase I** of the simplex method. When all the artificial variables have been eliminated from the basis, phase I is complete, and a basic feasible solution to the real problem has been obtained. Thus, by dropping the column associated with $a_4$ from the current tableau, we obtain the following simplex tableau at the end of phase I.

Artificial variables can be dropped from the tableau once they leave the basis. Leaving them in will not lead to the wrong solution, but it will cause more work at each iteration.

|        |       | $x_1$ | $x_2$ | $s_1$ | $s_2$ | $s_3$ | $s_4$ |      |
|--------|-------|-------|-------|-------|-------|-------|-------|------|
| Basis  | $c_B$ | 50    | 40    | 0     | 0     | 0     | 0     |      |
| $s_1$  | 0     | 0     | 2     | 1     | 0     | 0     | 3     | 75   |
| $s_2$  | 0     | 0     | 1     | 0     | 1     | 0     | 0     | 20   |
| $s_3$  | 0     | 0     | −3    | 0     | 0     | 1     | ⑧     | 100  |
| $x_1$  | 50    | 1     | 1     | 0     | 0     | 0     | −1    | 25   |
| $z_j$       |   | 50    | 50    | 0     | 0     | 0     | −50   | 1250 |
| $c_j - z_j$ |   | 0     | −10   | 0     | 0     | 0     | 50    |      |

We are now ready to begin phase II of the simplex method. This phase simply continues the simplex method computations after all artificial variables have been removed. At the next iteration, variable $s_4$ with $c_j - z_j = 50$ is entered into the solution and variable $s_3$ is eliminated. The simplex tableau after this iteration is:

|        |       | $x_1$ | $x_2$   | $s_1$ | $s_2$ | $s_3$    | $s_4$ |          |
|--------|-------|-------|---------|-------|-------|----------|-------|----------|
| Basis  | $c_B$ | 50    | 40      | 0     | 0     | 0        | 0     |          |
| $s_1$  | 0     | 0     | ㉕⁄₈     | 1     | 0     | $-3/8$   | 0     | $75/2$   |
| $s_2$  | 0     | 0     | 1       | 0     | 1     | 0        | 0     | 20       |
| $s_4$  | 0     | 0     | $-3/8$  | 0     | 0     | $1/8$    | 1     | $25/2$   |
| $x_1$  | 50    | 1     | $5/8$   | 0     | 0     | $1/8$    | 0     | $75/2$   |
| $z_j$       |   | 50    | $250/8$ | 0     | 0     | $50/8$   | 0     | 1875     |
| $c_j - z_j$ |   | 0     | $70/8$  | 0     | 0     | $-50/8$  | 0     |          |

One more iteration is required. This time $x_2$ comes into the solution, and $s_1$ is eliminated. After performing this iteration, the following simplex tableau shows that the optimal solution has been reached.

|        |       | $x_1$ | $x_2$ | $s_1$     | $s_2$ | $s_3$     | $s_4$ |      |
|--------|-------|-------|-------|-----------|-------|-----------|-------|------|
| Basis  | $c_B$ | 50    | 40    | 0         | 0     | 0         | 0     |      |
| $x_2$  | 40    | 0     | 1     | $8/25$    | 0     | $-3/25$   | 0     | 12   |
| $s_2$  | 0     | 0     | 0     | $-8/25$   | 1     | $3/25$    | 0     | 8    |
| $s_4$  | 0     | 0     | 0     | $3/25$    | 0     | $2/25$    | 1     | 17   |
| $x_1$  | 50    | 1     | 0     | $-5/25$   | 0     | $5/25$    | 0     | 30   |
| $z_j$       |   | 50    | 40    | $14/5$    | 0     | $26/5$    | 0     | 1980 |
| $c_j - z_j$ |   | 0     | 0     | $-14/5$   | 0     | $-26/5$   | 0     |      |

It turns out that the optimal solution to the modified HighTech problem is the same as the solution for the original problem. However, the simplex method required more iterations to reach this extreme point, because an extra iteration was needed to eliminate the artificial variable ($a_4$) in phase I.

Fortunately, once we obtain an initial simplex tableau using artificial variables, we need not concern ourselves with whether the basic solution at a particular iteration is feasible for the real problem. We need only follow the rules for the simplex method. If we reach the optimality criterion (all $c_j - z_j \leq 0$) and all the artificial variables have been eliminated from the solution, then we have found the optimal solution. On the other hand, if we reach the optimality criterion and one or more of the artificial variables remain in solution at a positive value, then there is no feasible solution to the problem. This special case will be discussed further in Section 5.8.

## Equality Constraints

When an equality constraint occurs in a linear programming problem, we need to add an artificial variable to obtain tableau form and an initial basic feasible solution. For example, if constraint 1 is

$$6x_1 + 4x_2 - 5x_3 = 30$$

we would simply add an artificial variable $a_1$ to create a basic feasible solution in the initial simplex tableau. With the artificial variable, the constraint equation becomes

$$6x_1 + 4x_2 - 5x_3 + 1a_1 = 30$$

Now $a_1$ can be selected as the basic variable for this row, and its value is given by the right-hand side. Once we have created tableau form by adding an artificial variable to each equality constraint, the simplex method proceeds exactly as before.

## Eliminating Negative Right-Hand Side Values

One of the properties of the tableau form of a linear program is that the values on the right-hand sides of the constraints have to be nonnegative. In formulating a linear programming problem, we may find one or more of the constraints have negative right-hand-side values. To see how this might happen, suppose that the management of HighTech has specified that the number of units of the Portable model, $x_2$, has to be less than or equal to the number of units of the Deskpro model, $x_1$, after setting aside five units of the Deskpro for internal company use. We could formulate this constraint as

$$x_2 \leq x_1 - 5 \qquad (5.16)$$

Subtracting $x_1$ from both sides of the inequality places both variables on the left-hand side of the inequality. Thus,

$$-x_1 + x_2 \leq -5 \qquad (5.17)$$

Since this constraint has a negative right-hand-side value, we can develop an equivalent constraint with a nonnegative right-hand-side value by multiplying both sides of the constraint by $-1$. In doing so, we recognize that multiplying an inequality constraint by $-1$ changes the direction of the inequality.

Thus, to convert inequality (5.17) to an equivalent constraint with a nonnegative right-hand-side value, we multiply by $-1$ to obtain

$$x_1 - x_2 \geq 5 \qquad (5.18)$$

We now have an acceptable nonnegative right-hand-side value. Tableau form for this constraint can now be obtained by subtracting a surplus variable and adding an artificial variable.

For a greater-than-or-equal-to constraint, multiplying by $-1$ creates an equivalent less-than-or-equal-to constraint. For example, suppose we had the following greater-than-or-equal-to constraint:

$$6x_1 + 3x_2 - 4x_3 \geq -20$$

Multiplying by $-1$ to obtain an equivalent constraint with a nonnegative right-hand-side value leads to the following less-than-or-equal-to constraint

$$-6x_1 - 3x_2 + 4x_3 \leq 20$$

Tableau form can be created for this constraint by adding a slack variable.

For an equality constraint with a negative right-hand-side value, we simply multiply by $-1$ to obtain an equivalent constraint with a nonnegative right-hand-side value. An artificial variable can then be added to create the tableau form.

## Summary of the Steps to Create Tableau Form

Step 1  If the original formulation of the linear programming problem contains one or more constraints with negative right-hand-side values, multiply each of these constraints by $-1$. Multiplying by $-1$ will change the direction of the inequalities. This step will provide an equivalent linear program with nonnegative right-hand-side values.

Step 2  For $\leq$ constraints, add a slack variable to obtain an equality constraint. The coefficient of the slack variable in the objective function is assigned a value of zero. It provides the tableau form for the constraint, and the slack variable becomes one of the basic variables in the initial basic feasible solution.

Step 3  For $\geq$ constraints, subtract a surplus variable to obtain an equality constraint, and then add an artificial variable to obtain the tableau form. The coefficient of the surplus variable in the objective function is assigned a value of zero. The coefficient of the artificial variable in the objective function is assigned a value of $-M$. The artificial variable becomes one of the basic variables in the initial basic feasible solution.

Step 4  For equality constraints, add an artificial variable to obtain the tableau form. The coefficient of the artificial variable in the objective function is assigned a value of $-M$. The artificial variable becomes one of the basic variables in the initial basic feasible solution.

To obtain some practice in applying these steps, convert the following example problem into tableau form, and then set up the initial simplex tableau:

$$\text{Max} \quad 6x_1 + 3x_2 + 4x_3 + 1x_4$$
$$\text{s.t.}$$
$$-2x_1 - \tfrac{1}{2}x_2 + 1x_3 - 6x_4 = -60$$
$$1x_1 \qquad + 1x_3 + \tfrac{2}{3}x_4 \leq 20$$
$$- 1x_2 - 5x_3 \qquad \leq -50$$
$$x_1, x_2, x_3, x_4 \geq 0$$

To eliminate the negative right-hand-side values in constraints 1 and 3, we apply step 1. Multiplying both constraints by $-1$, we obtain the following equivalent linear program:

$$\text{Max}\quad 6x_1 + 3x_2 + 4x_3 + 1x_4$$

s.t.

$$2x_1 + \tfrac{1}{2}x_2 - 1x_3 + 6x_4 = 60$$
$$1x_1 \qquad + 1x_3 + \tfrac{2}{3}x_4 \le 20$$
$$1x_2 + 5x_3 \qquad \ge 50$$
$$x_1, x_2, x_3, x_4 \ge 0$$

Note that the direction of the $\le$ inequality in constraint 3 has been reversed as a result of multiplying the constraint by $-1$. By applying step 4 for constraint 1, step 2 for constraint 2, and step 3 for constraint 3, we obtain the following tableau form:

$$\text{Max}\quad 6x_1 + 3x_2 + 4x_3 + 1x_4 + 0s_2 + 0s_3 - Ma_1 - Ma_3$$

s.t.

$$2x_1 + \tfrac{1}{2}x_2 - 1x_3 + 6x_4 \qquad + 1a_1 \qquad = 60$$
$$1x_1 \qquad + 1x_3 + \tfrac{2}{3}x_4 + 1s_2 \qquad = 20$$
$$1x_2 + 5x_3 \qquad - 1s_3 \qquad + 1a_3 = 50$$
$$x_1, x_2, x_3, x_4, s_2, s_3, a_1, a_3 \ge 0$$

The initial simplex tableau corresponding to this tableau form is

| | | $x_1$ | $x_2$ | $x_3$ | $x_4$ | $s_2$ | $s_3$ | $a_1$ | $a_3$ | |
|---|---|---|---|---|---|---|---|---|---|---|
| Basis | $c_B$ | 6 | 3 | 4 | 1 | 0 | 0 | $-M$ | $-M$ | |
| $a_1$ | $-M$ | 2 | ½ | $-1$ | ⑥ | 0 | 0 | 1 | 0 | 60 |
| $s_2$ | 0 | 1 | 0 | 1 | ⅔ | 1 | 0 | 0 | 0 | 20 |
| $a_3$ | $-M$ | 0 | 1 | 5 | 0 | 0 | $-1$ | 0 | 1 | 50 |
| $z_j$ | | $-2M$ | $-\tfrac{3}{2}M$ | $-4M$ | $-6M$ | 0 | $M$ | $-M$ | $-M$ | $-110M$ |
| $c_j - z_j$ | | $6+2M$ | $3+\tfrac{3}{2}M$ | $4+4M$ | $1+6M$ | 0 | $-M$ | 0 | 0 | |

Note that we have circled the pivot element indicating that $x_4$ will enter and $a_1$ will leave the basis at the first iteration.

For practice setting up tableau form and developing the initial simplex tableau for problems with any constraint form, try Problem 15.

**N O T E S and Comments**

We have shown how to convert constraints with negative right-hand sides to equivalent constraints with positive right-hand sides. Actually, nothing is wrong with formulating a linear program and including negative right-hand sides. But if you want to use the ordinary simplex method to solve the linear program, you must first alter the constraints to eliminate the negative right-hand sides.

## 5.7    SOLVING A MINIMIZATION PROBLEM

We can use the simplex method to solve a minimization problem in two ways. The first approach requires that we change the rule used to introduce a variable into the basis. Recall that in the maximization case, we select the variable with the largest positive $c_j - z_j$ as the variable to introduce next into the basis, because the value of $c_j - z_j$ tells us the amount the objective function will increase if one unit of the variable in column $j$ is brought into solution. To solve the minimization problem, we simply reverse this rule. That is, we select the variable with the most negative $c_j - z_j$ as the one to introduce next. Of course, this approach means the stopping rule for the optimal solution will also have to be changed. Using this approach to solve a minimization problem, we would stop when every value in the net evaluation row is zero or positive.

The second approach to solving a minimization problem is the one we shall employ in this book. It is based on the fact that any minimization problem can be converted to an equivalent maximization problem by multiplying the objective function by $-1$. Solving the resulting maximization problem will provide the optimal solution to the minimization problem.

Let us illustrate this second approach by using the simplex method to solve the M&D Chemicals problem introduced in Chapter 2. Recall that in this problem, management wanted to minimize the cost of producing two products subject to a demand constraint for product *A*, a minimum total production quantity requirement, and a constraint on available processing time. The mathematical statement of the M&D Chemicals problem is shown here.

> *In keeping with the general notation of this chapter, we are using $x_1$ and $x_2$ to represent units of product A and product B.*

$$\text{Min} \quad 2x_1 + 3x_2$$

s.t.

$$
\begin{aligned}
1x_1 && &\geq 125 & &\text{Demand for product } A \\
1x_1 &+ 1x_2 & &\geq 350 & &\text{Total production} \\
2x_1 &+ 1x_2 & &\leq 600 & &\text{Processing time} \\
&& x_1, x_2 &\geq 0
\end{aligned}
$$

> *We convert a minimization problem to a maximization problem by multiplying the objective function by $-1$.*

To solve this problem using the simplex method, we first multiply the objective function by $-1$ to convert the minimization problem into the following equivalent maximization problem:

$$\text{Max} \quad -2x_1 - 3x_2$$

s.t.

$$
\begin{aligned}
1x_1 && &\geq 125 & &\text{Demand for product } A \\
1x_1 &+ 1x_2 & &\geq 350 & &\text{Total production} \\
2x_1 &+ 1x_2 & &\leq 600 & &\text{Processing time} \\
&& x_1, x_2 &\geq 0
\end{aligned}
$$

The tableau form for this problem is as follows:

$$\text{Max} \quad -2x_1 - 3x_2 + 0s_1 + 0s_2 + 0s_3 - Ma_1 - Ma_2$$

s.t.

$$
\begin{aligned}
1x_1 && &- 1s_1 && &+ 1a_1 && &= 125 \\
1x_1 &+ 1x_2 && &- 1s_2 && && + 1a_2 &= 350 \\
2x_1 &+ 1x_2 && && + 1s_3 && && &= 600 \\
\end{aligned}
$$

$$x_1, x_2, s_1, s_2, s_3, a_1, a_2 \geq 0$$

The initial simplex tableau is shown here:

| Basis | $c_B$ | $x_1$ $-2$ | $x_2$ $-3$ | $s_1$ $0$ | $s_2$ $0$ | $s_3$ $0$ | $a_1$ $-M$ | $a_2$ $-M$ | |
|---|---|---|---|---|---|---|---|---|---|
| $a_1$ | $-M$ | ① | 0 | $-1$ | 0 | 0 | 1 | 0 | 125 |
| $a_2$ | $-M$ | 1 | 1 | 0 | $-1$ | 0 | 0 | 1 | 350 |
| $s_3$ | 0 | 2 | 1 | 0 | 0 | 1 | 0 | 0 | 600 |
| $z_j$ | | $-2M$ | $-M$ | $M$ | $M$ | 0 | $-M$ | $-M$ | $-475M$ |
| $c_j - z_j$ | | $-2 + 2M$ | $-3 + M$ | $-M$ | $-M$ | 0 | 0 | 0 | |

At the first iteration, $x_1$ is brought into the basis and $a_1$ is removed. After dropping the $a_1$ column from the tableau, the result of the first iteration is as follows:

| Basis | $c_B$ | $x_1$ $-2$ | $x_2$ $-3$ | $s_1$ $0$ | $s_2$ $0$ | $s_3$ $0$ | $a_2$ $-M$ | |
|---|---|---|---|---|---|---|---|---|
| $x_1$ | $-2$ | 1 | 0 | $-1$ | 0 | 0 | 0 | 125 |
| $a_2$ | $-M$ | 0 | 1 | 1 | $-1$ | 0 | 1 | 225 |
| $s_3$ | 0 | 0 | 1 | ② | 0 | 1 | 0 | 350 |
| $z_j$ | | $-2$ | $-M$ | $2 - M$ | $M$ | 0 | $-M$ | $-250 - 225M$ |
| $c_j - z_j$ | | 0 | $-3 + M$ | $-2 + M$ | $-M$ | 0 | 0 | |

Continuing with two more iterations of the simplex method provides the following final simplex tableau:

| Basis | $c_B$ | $x_1$ $-2$ | $x_2$ $-3$ | $s_1$ $0$ | $s_2$ $0$ | $s_3$ $0$ | |
|---|---|---|---|---|---|---|---|
| $x_1$ | $-2$ | 1 | 0 | 0 | 1 | 1 | 250 |
| $x_2$ | $-3$ | 0 | 1 | 0 | $-2$ | $-1$ | 100 |
| $s_1$ | 0 | 0 | 0 | 1 | 1 | 1 | 125 |
| $z_j$ | | $-2$ | $-3$ | 0 | 4 | 1 | $-800$ |
| $c_j - z_j$ | | 0 | 0 | 0 | $-4$ | $-1$ | |

The value of the objective function $-800$ must be multiplied by $-1$ to obtain the value of the objective function for the original minimization problem. Thus, the minimum total cost of the optimal solution is $800.

In the next section we shall discuss some important special cases that may occur when trying to solve any linear programming problem. We will only consider the case for maximization problems, recognizing that all minimization problems may be placed into this form by multiplying the objective function by $-1$.

Try Problem 17 for practice solving a minimization problem with the simplex method.

## 5.8    SPECIAL CASES

In Chapter 2 we discussed how infeasibility, unboundedness, and alternative optimal solutions could occur when solving linear programming problems using the graphical solution procedure. These special cases can also arise when using the simplex method. In addition, a special case referred to as *degeneracy* can theoretically cause difficulties for the simplex method. In this section we show how these special cases can be recognized and handled when the simplex method is used.

### Infeasibility

Infeasibility occurs whenever no solution to the linear program can be found that satisfies all the constraints, including the nonnegativity constraints. Let us now see how infeasibility is recognized when the simplex method is used.

In Section 5.6, when discussing artificial variables, we mentioned that infeasibility can be recognized when the optimality criterion indicates that an optimal solution has been obtained and one or more of the artificial variables remain in the solution at a positive value. As an illustration of this situation, let us consider another modification of the HighTech Industries problem. Suppose management had imposed a minimum combined total production requirement of 50 units. The revised problem formulation is shown as follows.

$$\text{Max} \quad 50x_1 + 40x_2$$
$$\text{s.t.}$$

$$
\begin{aligned}
3x_1 + 5x_2 &\le 150 && \text{Assembly time} \\
1x_2 &\le 20 && \text{Portable display} \\
8x_1 + 5x_2 &\le 300 && \text{Warehouse space} \\
1x_1 + 1x_2 &\ge 50 && \text{Minimum total production} \\
x_1, x_2 &\ge 0
\end{aligned}
$$

Two iterations of the simplex method will provide the following tableau:

| Basis | $c_B$ | $x_1$ 50 | $x_2$ 40 | $s_1$ 0 | $s_2$ 0 | $s_3$ 0 | $s_4$ 0 | $a_4$ $-M$ | |
|---|---|---|---|---|---|---|---|---|---|
| $x_2$ | 40 | 0 | 1 | $8/25$ | 0 | $-3/25$ | 0 | 0 | 12 |
| $s_2$ | 0 | 0 | 0 | $-8/25$ | 1 | $3/25$ | 0 | 0 | 8 |
| $x_1$ | 50 | 1 | 0 | $-5/25$ | 0 | $5/25$ | 0 | 0 | 30 |
| $a_4$ | $-M$ | 0 | 0 | $-3/25$ | 0 | $-2/25$ | $-1$ | 1 | 8 |
| $z_j$ | | 50 | 40 | $\dfrac{70 + 3M}{25}$ | 0 | $\dfrac{130 + 2M}{25}$ | $M$ | $-M$ | $1980 - 8M$ |
| $c_j - z_j$ | | 0 | 0 | $\dfrac{-70 - 3M}{25}$ | 0 | $\dfrac{-130 - 2M}{25}$ | $-M$ | 0 | |

If an artificial variable is positive, the solution is not feasible for the real problem.

Note that $c_j - z_j \leq 0$ for all the variables; therefore, according to the optimality criterion, it should be the optimal solution. But this solution is *not feasible* for the modified HighTech problem because the artificial variable $a_4 = 8$ appears in the solution. The solution $x_1 = 30$ and $x_2 = 12$ results in a combined total production of 42 units instead of the constraint 4 requirement of at least 50 units. The fact that the artificial variable is in solution at a value of $a_4 = 8$ tells us that the final solution violates the fourth constraint $(1x_1 + 1x_2 \geq 50)$ by eight units.

If management is interested in knowing which of the first three constraints is preventing us from satisfying the total production requirement, a partial answer can be obtained from the final simplex tableau. Note that $s_2 = 8$, but that $s_1$ and $s_3$ are zero. This tells us that the assembly time and warehouse capacity constraints are binding. Since there are not enough assembly time and warehouse space available, we cannot satisfy the minimum combined total production requirement.

The management implications here are that additional assembly time and/or warehouse space must be made available to satisfy the total production requirement. If more time and/or space cannot be made available, management will have to relax the total production requirement by at least eight units.

Try Problem 23 to practice recognizing when there is no feasible solution to a problem using the simplex method.

In summary, a linear program is infeasible if no solution satisfies all the constraints simultaneously. We *recognize infeasibility when one or more of the artificial variables remain in the final solution at a positive value.* In closing, we note that linear programming problems with all $\leq$ constraints and nonnegative right-hand sides will always have a feasible solution. Because it is not necessary to introduce artificial variables to set up the initial simplex tableau for these types of problems, the final solution cannot possibly contain an artificial variable.

## Unboundedness

For maximization problems, we say that a linear program is unbounded if the value of the solution may be made infinitely large without violating any constraints. Thus, when unboundedness occurs, we can generally look for an error in the formulation of the problem.

Usually a constraint has been overlooked if unboundedness occurs.

The coefficients in the column of the $\bar{A}$ matrix associated with the incoming variable indicate how much each of the current basic variables will decrease if one unit of the incoming variable is brought into solution. Suppose then, that for a particular linear programming problem, we reach a point where the rule for determining which variable should enter the basis results in the decision to enter variable $x_2$. Assume that for this variable, $c_2 - z_2 = 5$, and that all $\bar{a}_{i2}$ in column 2 are $\leq 0$. Thus, each unit of $x_2$ brought into solution increases the objective function by five units. Furthermore, because $\bar{a}_{i2} \leq 0$ for all $i$, none of the current basic variables will be driven to zero, no matter how many units of $x_2$ we introduce. Thus, we can introduce an infinite amount of $x_2$ into solution and still maintain feasibility. Since each unit of $x_2$ increases the objective function by 5, we will have an unbounded solution. Hence, *the way we recognize the unbounded situation is that all the $\bar{a}_{ij}$ are less than or equal to zero in the column associated with the incoming variable.*

To illustrate this concept, let us consider the following example of an unbounded problem.

$$\text{Max} \quad 20x_1 + 10x_2$$
$$\text{s.t.} \quad 1x_1 \qquad \geq 2$$
$$1x_2 \leq 5$$
$$x_1, x_2 \geq 0$$

We subtract a surplus variable $s_1$ from the first constraint equation and add a slack variable $s_2$ to the second constraint equation to obtain the standard-form representation. We then add an artificial variable $a_1$ to the first constraint equation to obtain the tableau form and to set up the initial simplex tableau in terms of the basic variables $a_1$ and $s_2$. After bringing in $x_1$ and removing $a_1$ at the first iteration, the simplex tableau is as follows:

|  |  | $x_1$ | $x_2$ | $s_1$ | $s_2$ |  |
|---|---|---|---|---|---|---|
| Basis | $c_B$ | 20 | 10 | 0 | 0 |  |
| $x_1$ | 20 | 1 | 0 | −1 | 0 | 2 |
| $s_2$ | 0 | 0 | 1 | 0 | 1 | 5 |
| $z_j$ |  | 20 | 0 | −20 | 0 | 40 |
| $c_j - z_j$ |  | 0 | 10 | 20 | 0 |  |

Since $s_1$ has the largest positive $c_j - z_j$, we know we can increase the value of the objective function most rapidly by bringing $s_1$ into the basis. But $\bar{a}_{13} = -1$ and $\bar{a}_{23} = 0$; hence, we cannot form the ratio $\bar{b}_i/\bar{a}_{i3}$ for any $\bar{a}_{i3} > 0$; there are no values of $\bar{a}_{i3}$ that are greater than zero. This result indicates that the solution to the linear program is unbounded. The reason the solution is unbounded is that each unit of $s_1$ that is brought into solution drives zero units of $s_2$ out of solution (since $\bar{a}_{23} = 0$) and provides one extra unit of $x_1$ (since $\bar{a}_{13} = -1$). The reason is that $s_1$ is a surplus variable and can be interpreted as the amount of $x_1$ over the minimum amount required. The simplex tableau indicates we can introduce as much of $s_1$ as we desire without violating any constraints; the interpretation is that we can make as much as we want above the minimum amount of $x_1$ required. Because the objective function coefficient associated with $x_1$ is positive, there will be no upper bound on the value of the objective function.

In summary, a maximization linear program is unbounded if it is possible to make the value of the optimal solution as large as desired without violating any of the constraints. When employing the simplex solution procedure, an unbounded linear program exists if *at some iteration, the simplex method tells us to introduce variable j into the solution and all the $\bar{a}_{ij}$ are less than or equal to zero in the jth column.*

Try Problem 25 for another example of an unbounded problem.

We emphasize that the case of an unbounded solution will never occur in real cost minimization or profit maximization problems because it is not possible to reduce costs to minus infinity or to increase profits to plus infinity. Thus, if we encounter an unbounded solution to a linear programming problem, we should carefully reexamine the formulation of the problem to determine if a formulation error has occurred.

## Alternative Optimal Solutions

A linear program with two or more optimal solutions is said to have alternative optimal solutions. When using the simplex method, we cannot recognize that a linear program has alternative optimal solutions until the final simplex tableau is reached. Then if the linear program has alternative optimal solutions, $c_j - z_j$ will equal zero for one or more nonbasic variables.

To illustrate the case of alternative optimal solutions when using the simplex method, consider changing the objective function for the HighTech problem from $50x_1 + 40x_2$ to $30x_1 + 50x_2$; in doing so, we obtain the revised linear program:

$$\text{Max} \quad 30x_1 + 50x_2$$

s.t.

$$3x_1 + 5x_2 \le 150$$
$$1x_2 \le 20$$
$$8x_1 + 5x_2 \le 300$$
$$x_1, x_2 \ge 0$$

The final simplex tableau for this problem is shown here:

| | | $x_1$ | $x_2$ | $s_1$ | $s_2$ | $s_3$ | |
|---|---|---|---|---|---|---|---|
| Basis | $c_B$ | 30 | 50 | 0 | 0 | 0 | |
| $x_2$ | 50 | 0 | 1 | 0 | 1 | 0 | **20** |
| $s_3$ | 0 | 0 | 0 | $-\frac{8}{3}$ | $\frac{25}{3}$ | 1 | $\frac{200}{3}$ |
| $x_1$ | 30 | 1 | 0 | $\frac{1}{3}$ | $-\frac{5}{3}$ | 0 | $\frac{50}{3}$ |
| | $z_j$ | 30 | 50 | 10 | 0 | 0 | **1500** |
| | $c_j - z_j$ | 0 | 0 | $-10$ | 0 | 0 | |

All values in the net evaluation row are less than or equal to zero, indicating that an optimal solution has been found. This solution is given by $x_1 = \frac{50}{3}$, $x_2 = 20$, $s_1 = 0$, $s_2 = 0$, and $s_3 = \frac{200}{3}$. The value of the objective function is 1500.

In looking at the net evaluation row in the optimal simplex tableau, we see that the $c_j - z_j$ value for nonbasic variable $s_2$ is equal to zero. It indicates that the linear program may have alternative optimal solutions. In other words, because the net evaluation row entry for $s_2$ is zero, we can introduce $s_2$ into the basis without changing the value of the solution. The tableau obtained after introducing $s_2$ follows:

| | | $x_1$ | $x_2$ | $s_1$ | $s_2$ | $s_3$ | |
|---|---|---|---|---|---|---|---|
| Basis | $c_B$ | 30 | 50 | 0 | 0 | 0 | |
| $x_2$ | 50 | 0 | 1 | $\frac{8}{25}$ | 0 | $-\frac{3}{25}$ | **12** |
| $s_2$ | 0 | 0 | 0 | $-\frac{8}{25}$ | 1 | $\frac{3}{25}$ | **8** |
| $x_1$ | 30 | 1 | 0 | $-\frac{5}{25}$ | 0 | $\frac{5}{25}$ | **30** |
| | $z_j$ | 30 | 50 | 10 | 0 | 0 | **1500** |
| | $c_j - z_j$ | 0 | 0 | $-10$ | 0 | 0 | |

As shown, we have a different basic feasible solution: $x_1 = 30$, $x_2 = 12$, $s_1 = 0$, $s_2 = 8$, and $s_3 = 0$. However, this new solution is also optimal since $c_j - z_j \le 0$ for all $j$. Another way to confirm that this solution is still optimal is to note that the value of the solution has remained equal to 1500.

In summary, *when using the simplex method, we can recognize the possibility of alternative optimal solutions if $c_j - z_j$ equals zero for one or more of the nonbasic variables in the final simplex tableau.*

Try Problem 24 for another example of alternative optimal solutions.

### Degeneracy

A linear program is said to be **degenerate** if one or more of the basic variables have a value of zero. Degeneracy does not cause any particular difficulties for the graphical solution procedure; however, degeneracy can theoretically cause difficulties when the simplex method is used to solve a linear programming problem.

To see how a degenerate linear program could occur, consider a change in the right-hand-side value of the assembly time constraint for the HighTech problem. For example, what if the number of hours available had been 175 instead of 150? The modified linear program is shown below.

$$\text{Max} \quad 50x_1 + 40x_2$$

s.t.

$$3x_1 + 5x_2 \leq 175 \quad \text{Assembly time increased to 175 hours}$$
$$1x_2 \leq 20 \quad \text{Portable display}$$
$$8x_1 + 5x_2 \leq 300 \quad \text{Warehouse space}$$
$$x_1, x_2 \geq 0$$

The simplex tableau after one iteration is as follows:

| | | $x_1$ | $x_2$ | $s_1$ | $s_2$ | $s_3$ | |
|---|---|---|---|---|---|---|---|
| Basis | $c_B$ | 50 | 40 | 0 | 0 | 0 | |
| $s_1$ | 0 | 0 | $25/8$ | 1 | 0 | $-3/8$ | $125/2$ |
| $s_2$ | 0 | 0 | 1 | 0 | 1 | 0 | 20 |
| $x_1$ | 50 | 1 | $5/8$ | 0 | 0 | $1/8$ | $75/2$ |
| $z_j$ | | 50 | $250/8$ | 0 | 0 | $50/8$ | 1875 |
| $c_j - z_j$ | | 0 | $70/8$ | 0 | 0 | $-50/8$ | |

The entries in the net evaluation row indicate that $x_2$ should enter the basis. By calculating the appropriate ratios to determine the pivot row, we obtain

$$\frac{\bar{b}_1}{\bar{a}_{12}} = \frac{125/2}{25/8} = 20$$

$$\frac{\bar{b}_2}{\bar{a}_{22}} = \frac{20}{1} = 20$$

$$\frac{\bar{b}_3}{\bar{a}_{32}} = \frac{75/2}{5/8} = 60$$

We see that the first and second rows tie, which indicates that we will have a degenerate basic feasible solution at the next iteration. Recall that in the case of a tie, we follow the convention of selecting the uppermost row as the pivot row. Here, it means that $s_1$ will leave the basis. But from the tie for the minimum ratio we see that the basic variable in row 2, $s_2$, will also be driven to zero. Because it does not leave the basis, we will have a basic variable with a value of zero after performing this iteration. The simplex tableau after this iteration is as follows:

| Basis | $c_B$ | $x_1$ 50 | $x_2$ 40 | $s_1$ 0 | $s_2$ 0 | $s_3$ 0 | |
|-------|-------|-----|-----|-----|-----|-----|------|
| $x_2$ | 40 | 0 | 1 | $\frac{8}{25}$ | 0 | $-\frac{3}{25}$ | 20 |
| $s_2$ | 0 | 0 | 0 | $-\frac{8}{25}$ | 1 | $\frac{3}{25}$ | 0 |
| $x_1$ | 50 | 1 | 0 | $-\frac{5}{25}$ | 0 | $\frac{5}{25}$ | 25 |
| $z_j$ | | 50 | 40 | $\frac{70}{25}$ | 0 | $\frac{130}{25}$ | 2050 |
| $c_j - z_j$ | | 0 | 0 | $-\frac{70}{25}$ | 0 | $-\frac{130}{25}$ | |

As expected, we have a basic feasible solution with one of the basic variables, $s_2$, equal to zero. Whenever we have a tie in the minimum $\bar{b}_i/\bar{a}_{ij}$ ratio, there will always be a basic variable equal to zero in the next tableau. Because we are at the optimal solution in the preceding case, we do not care that $s_2$ is in solution at a zero value. However, if degeneracy occurs at some iteration prior to reaching the optimal solution, it is theoretically possible for the simplex method to cycle; that is, the procedure could possibly alternate between the same set of nonoptimal basic feasible solutions and never reach the optimal solution. Cycling has not proven to be a significant difficulty in practice. Therefore, we do not recommend introducing any special steps into the simplex method to eliminate the possibility that degeneracy will occur. If while performing the iterations of the simplex algorithm a tie occurs for the minimum $\bar{b}_i/\bar{a}_{ij}$ ratio, then we recommend simply selecting the upper row as the pivot row.

## N O T E S
## *and Comments*

1. We have stated that infeasibility is recognized when the stopping rule is encountered but one or more artificial variables are in solution at a positive value. This requirement does not necessarily mean that all artificial variables must be nonbasic to have a feasible solution. An artificial variable could be in solution at a zero value.
2. An unbounded feasible region must exist for a problem to be unbounded, but this does not guarantee that a problem will be unbounded. A minimization problem may be bounded whereas a maximization problem is unbounded with the same feasible region.

## SUMMARY

In this chapter the simplex method was introduced as an algebraic procedure for solving linear programming problems. Although the simplex method can be used to solve small linear programs by hand calculations, it becomes too cumbersome as problems get larger. As a result, we must utilize a computer if we want to solve large linear programs in any reasonable length of time. The computational procedures of most computer software packages are based on the simplex method.

We described how developing the tableau form of a linear program is a necessary step in the simplex solution procedure, including how to convert greater-than-or-equal-to constraints, equality constraints, and constraints with negative right-hand-side values into tableau form.

For linear programs with greater-than-or-equal-to constraints and/or equality constraints, artificial variables are used to obtain tableau form. An objective function coefficient of $-M$, where $M$ is a very large number, is assigned to each artificial variable. If there is a feasible solution to the real problem, all artificial variables will be driven out of solution (or to zero) before the simplex method reaches its optimality criterion. The iterations required to remove the artificial variables from solution constitute what is called phase I of the simplex method.

Two techniques were mentioned for solving minimization problems. The first approach involved changing the rule for introducing a variable into solution (choose the most negative $c_j - z_j$) and changing the optimality criterion (all $c_j - z_j \geq 0$). The second approach involved multiplying the objective function by $-1$ to obtain an equivalent maximization problem. With this change, any minimization problem can be solved using the steps required for a maximization problem, but the value of the optimal solution must be multiplied by $(-1)$ to obtain the optimal value of the original minimization problem.

As a review of the material in this chapter we now present a detailed step-by-step procedure for solving linear programs using the simplex method.

Step 1  Formulate a linear programming model of the problem.
Step 2  Define an equivalent linear program by performing the following operations:
   a. Multiply each constraint with a negative right-hand-side value by $-1$, and change the direction of the constraint inequality.
   b. For a minimization problem, convert the problem to an equivalent maximization problem by multiplying the objective function by $-1$.
Step 3  Set up the standard form of the linear program by adding appropriate slack and surplus variables.
Step 4  Set up the tableau form of the linear program to obtain an initial basic feasible solution. All linear programs must be set up this way before the initial simplex tableau can be obtained.
Step 5  Set up the initial simplex tableau to keep track of the calculations required by the simplex method.
Step 6  Choose the nonbasic variable with the largest $c_j - z_j$ to bring into the basis. The column associated with that variable is the pivot column.
Step 7  Choose as the pivot row that row with the smallest ratio of $\bar{b}_i/\bar{a}_{ij}$ for $\bar{a}_{ij} > 0$. This ratio is used to determine which variable will leave the basis when variable $j$ enters the basis. This ratio also indicates how many units of variable $j$ can be introduced into solution before the basic variable in the $i$th row equals zero.
Step 8  Perform the necessary elementary row operations to convert the pivot column to a unit column.
   a. Divide each element in the pivot row by the pivot element. The result is a new pivot row containing a 1 in the pivot column.
   b. Obtain zeroes in all other positions of the pivot column by adding or subtracting an appropriate multiple of the new pivot row.
Step 9  Test for optimality. If $c_j - z_j \leq 0$ for all columns, we have the optimal solution. If not, return to step 6.

In Section 5.8 we discussed how the special cases of infeasibility, unboundedness, alternative optimal solutions, and degeneracy can occur when solving linear programming problems with the simplex method.

........................................................................................................../  /..............

# GLOSSARY

**Simplex method**  An algebraic procedure for solving linear programming problems. The simplex method uses elementary row operations to iterate from one basic feasible solution (extreme point) to another until the optimal solution is reached.

**Basic solution**  Given a linear program in standard form, with $n$ variables and $m$ constraints, a basic solution is a solution obtained by setting $n - m$ of the variables equal to zero and solving the constraint equations for the values of the other $m$ variables. If a unique solution exists, it is a basic solution.

**Nonbasic variable**  One of $n - m$ variables set equal to zero in a basic solution.

**Basic variable**  One of the $m$ variables not required to equal zero in a basic solution.

**Basic feasible solution**  A basic solution that is also feasible; that is, it satisfies the non-negativity constraints. A basic feasible solution corresponds to an extreme point.

**Tableau form**  The form in which a linear program must be written before setting up the initial simplex tableau. When a linear program is written in tableau form, its $A$ matrix contains $m$ unit columns corresponding to the basic variables, and the values of these basic variables are given by the values in the $b$ column. A further requirement is that the entries in the $b$ column be greater than or equal to zero.

**Simplex tableau**  A table used to keep track of the calculations made when the simplex method is employed.

**Unit vector or unit column**  A vector or column of a matrix that has a zero in every position except one. In the nonzero position there is a 1. There is a unit column in the simplex tableau for each basic variable.

**Basis**  The set of variables that are not restricted to equal zero in the current basic solution. The variables that make up the basis are termed basic variables, and the remaining variables are called nonbasic variables.

**Net evaluation row**  The row in the simplex tableau that contains the value of $c_j - z_j$ for every variable (column).

**Elementary row operations**  Operations that may be performed on a system of simultaneous equations without changing the solution to the system of equations.

**Iteration**  An iteration of the simplex method consists of the sequence of elementary row operations performed in moving from one basic feasible solution to another.

**Pivot column**  The column in the simplex tableau corresponding to the nonbasic variable that is about to be introduced into solution.

**Pivot row**  The row in the simplex tableau corresponding to the basic variable that will leave the solution.

**Pivot element**  The element of the simplex tableau that is in both the pivot row and the pivot column.

**Artificial variable**  A variable that has no physical meaning in terms of the original linear programming problem, but serves merely to enable a basic feasible solution to be created for starting the simplex method. Artificial variables are assigned an objective function co-efficient of $-M$, where $M$ is a very large number.

**Phase I**  When artificial variables are present in the initial simplex tableau, phase I refers to the iterations of the simplex method that are used to drive the artificial variables out of solution. At the end of phase I, the basic feasible solution in the simplex tableau is also feasible for the real problem.

**Degeneracy**  When one or more of the basic variables has a value of zero.

········································································································ / /···········

## PROBLEMS

**SELF TEST**

1. Consider the following system of linear equations:

$$3x_1 + x_2 \quad\;\; = 6$$
$$2x_1 + 4x_2 + x_3 = 12$$

   a. Find the basic solution with $x_1 = 0$.
   b. Find the basic solution with $x_2 = 0$.
   c. Find the basic solution with $x_3 = 0$.
   d. Which of the above would be basic feasible solutions for a linear program?

2. Consider the following linear program:

$$\text{Max} \quad x_1 + 2x_2$$

   s.t.

$$x_1 + 5x_2 \le 10$$
$$2x_1 + 6x_2 \le 16$$
$$x_1, x_2 \ge 0$$

   a. Write the problem in standard form.
   b. How many variables will be set equal to zero in a basic solution for this problem?
   c. Find all the basic solutions, and indicate which are also feasible.
   d. Find the optimal solution by computing the value of each basic feasible solution.

3. Consider the following linear program:

$$\text{Max} \quad 5x_1 + 9x_2$$

   s.t.

$$\tfrac{1}{2}x_1 + 1x_2 \le 8$$
$$1x_1 + 1x_2 \ge 10$$
$$\tfrac{1}{4}x_1 + \tfrac{3}{2}x_2 \ge 6$$
$$x_1, x_2 \ge 0$$

   a. Write the problem in standard form.
   b. How many variables will be set equal to zero in a basic solution for this problem? Explain.
   c. Find the basic solution that corresponds to $s_1$ and $s_2$ equal to zero.
   d. Find the basic solution that corresponds to $x_1$ and $s_3$ equal to zero.
   e. Are your solutions for part (c) and/or (d) basic feasible solutions? Extreme-point solutions? Explain.
   f. Use the graphical approach to identify the solutions found in parts (c) and (d). Do the graphical results agree with your answer to part (e)? Explain.

**SELF TEST**

4.  Consider the following linear programming problem:

$$\text{Max}\quad 60x_1 + 90x_2$$

s.t.

$$15x_1 + 45x_2 \le 90$$
$$5x_1 + 5x_2 \le 20$$
$$x_1, x_2 \ge 0$$

a.  Write the problem in standard form.
b.  Develop the portion of the simplex tableau involving the objective function coefficients, the coefficients of the variables in the constraints, and the constants for the right-hand sides.

5.  A partially completed initial simplex tableau is given:

**SELF TEST**

|         |       | $x_1$ | $x_2$ | $s_1$ | $s_2$ |     |
|---------|-------|-------|-------|-------|-------|-----|
| Basis   | $c_B$ | 5     | 9     | 0     | 0     |     |
| $s_1$   | 0     | 10    | 9     | 1     | 0     | 90  |
| $s_2$   | 0     | −5    | 3     | 0     | 1     | 15  |
| $z_j$   |       |       |       |       |       |     |
| $c_j - z_j$ |   |       |       |       |       |     |

a.  Complete the initial tableau.
b.  Which variable would be brought into solution at the first iteration?
c.  Write the original linear program.

6.  The following partial initial simplex tableau is given:
a.  Complete the initial tableau.
b.  Write the problem in tableau form.
c.  What is the initial basis? Does this correspond to the origin? Explain.
d.  What is the value of the objective function at this initial solution?
e.  For the next iteration, which variable should enter the basis, and which variable should leave the basis?
f.  How many units of the entering variable will be in the next solution? Before making this first iteration, what do you think will be the value of the objective function after the first iteration?

|         |       | $x_1$ | $x_2$ | $x_3$ | $s_1$ | $s_2$ | $s_3$ |     |
|---------|-------|-------|-------|-------|-------|-------|-------|-----|
| Basis   | $c_B$ | 5     | 20    | 25    | 0     | 0     | 0     |     |
|         |       | 2     | 1     | 0     | 1     | 0     | 0     | 40  |
|         |       | 0     | 2     | 1     | 0     | 1     | 0     | 30  |
|         |       | 3     | 0     | −½    | 0     | 0     | 1     | 15  |
| $z_j$   |       |       |       |       |       |       |       |     |
| $c_j - z_j$ |   |       |       |       |       |       |       |     |

g.  Find the optimal solution using the simplex method.

7. Solve the following linear program using the graphical approach:

$$\text{Max} \quad 4x_1 + 5x_2$$

s.t.

$$2x_1 + 2x_2 \leq 20$$
$$3x_1 + 7x_2 \leq 42$$
$$x_1, x_2 \geq 0$$

Put the linear program in tableau form, and solve using the simplex method. Show the sequence of extreme points generated by the simplex method on your graph.

8. Recall the problem for Par, Inc., introduced in Section 2.1. The mathematical model for this problem, is restated as follows:

$$\text{Max} \quad 10x_1 + 9x_2$$

s.t.

$$\tfrac{7}{10}x_1 + 1x_2 \leq 630 \quad \text{Cutting and dyeing}$$
$$\tfrac{1}{2}x_1 + \tfrac{5}{6}x_2 \leq 600 \quad \text{Sewing}$$
$$1x_1 + \tfrac{2}{3}x_2 \leq 708 \quad \text{Finishing}$$
$$\tfrac{1}{10}x_1 + \tfrac{1}{4}x_2 \leq 135 \quad \text{Inspection and packaging}$$
$$x_1, x_2 \geq 0$$

where

$$x_1 = \text{number of standard bags produced}$$
$$x_2 = \text{number of deluxe bags produced}$$

a. Use the simplex method to determine how many bags of each model Par should manufacture.
b. What is the profit Par can earn with these production quantities?
c. How many hours of production time will be scheduled for each operation?
d. What is the slack time in each operation?

9. Solve the RMC problem (Chapter 2, Problem 21) using the simplex method. At each iteration, locate the basic feasible solution found by the simplex method on the graph of the feasible region. The problem formulation is shown here:

$$\text{Max} \quad 40x_1 + 30x_2$$

s.t.

$$\tfrac{2}{5}x_1 + \tfrac{1}{2}x_2 \leq 20 \quad \text{Material 1}$$
$$\tfrac{1}{5}x_2 \leq 5 \quad \text{Material 2}$$
$$\tfrac{3}{5}x_1 + \tfrac{3}{10}x_2 \leq 21 \quad \text{Material 3}$$
$$x_1, x_2 \geq 0$$

where

$$x_1 = \text{tons of fuel additive produced}$$
$$x_2 = \text{tons of solvent base produced}$$

10. Solve the following linear program:

$$\text{Max} \quad 5x_1 + 5x_2 + 24x_3$$

s.t.

$$15x_1 + 4x_2 + 12x_3 \leq 2800$$
$$15x_1 + 8x_2 \qquad\quad \leq 6000$$
$$x_1 \qquad\quad + 8x_3 \leq 1200$$
$$x_1, x_2, x_3 \geq 0$$

11. Solve the following linear program using both the graphical and the simplex methods:

$$\text{Max} \quad 2x_1 + 8x_2$$

s.t.

$$3x_1 + 9x_2 \leq 45$$
$$2x_1 + 1x_2 \geq 12$$
$$x_1, x_2 \geq 0$$

Show graphically how the simplex method moves from one basic feasible solution to another. Find the coordinates of all extreme points of the feasible region.

12. Suppose a company manufactures three products from two raw materials. The amount of raw material in each unit of each product is given.

| Raw Material | Product A | Product B | Product C |
|---|---|---|---|
| I | 7 lb | 6 lb | 3 lb |
| II | 5 lb | 4 lb | 2 lb |

If the company has available 100 pounds of material I and 200 pounds of material II, and if the profits for the three products are $20, $20, and $15 respectively, how much of each product should be produced to maximize profits?

13. Liva's Lumber, Inc., manufactures three types of plywood. The following table summarizes the production hours per unit in each of three production operations and other data for the problem.

| Plywood | Operations (hours) | | | Profit/Unit |
|---|---|---|---|---|
| | I | II | III | |
| Grade A | 2 | 2 | 4 | $40 |
| Grade B | 5 | 5 | 2 | $30 |
| Grade X | 10 | 3 | 2 | $20 |
| Maximum time available | 900 | 400 | 600 | |

How many units of each grade of lumber should be produced?

14. Ye Olde Cording Winery in Peoria, Illinois, makes three kinds of authentic German wine: Heidelberg Sweet, Heidelberg Regular, and Deutschland Extra Dry. The raw materials, labor, and profit for a gallon of each of these wines are summarized here:

| Wine | Grade A Grapes (bushels) | Grade B Grapes (bushels) | Sugar (pounds) | Labor (hours) | Profit/ Gallon |
|---|---|---|---|---|---|
| Heidelberg Sweet | 1 | 1 | 2 | 2 | $1.00 |
| Heidelberg Regular | 2 | 0 | 1 | 3 | $1.20 |
| Deutschland Extra Dry | 0 | 2 | 0 | 1 | $2.00 |

If the winery has 150 bushels of grade A grapes, 150 bushels of grade B grapes, 80 pounds of sugar, and 225 labor-hours available during the next week, what product mix of wines will maximize the company's profit?

a. Solve using the simplex method.

b. Interpret all slack variables.

c. An increase in which resources could improve the company's profit?

SELF TEST

15. Set up the tableau form for the following linear program (do not attempt to solve):

$$\text{Max} \quad 4x_1 + 2x_2 - 3x_3 + 5x_4$$

s.t.

$$2x_1 - 1x_2 + 1x_3 + 2x_4 \geq 50$$
$$3x_1 \quad\quad - 1x_3 + 2x_4 \leq 80$$
$$1x_1 + 1x_2 \quad\quad + 1x_4 = 60$$
$$x_1, x_2, x_3, x_4 \geq 0$$

16. Set up the tableau form for the following linear program (do not attempt to solve):

$$\text{Min} \quad 4x_1 + 5x_2 + 3x_3$$

s.t.

$$4x_1 \quad\quad + 2x_3 \geq 20$$
$$1x_2 - 1x_3 \leq -8$$
$$1x_1 - 2x_2 \quad\quad = -5$$
$$2x_1 + 1x_2 + 1x_3 \leq 12$$
$$x_1, x_2, x_3, \geq 0$$

SELF TEST

17. Solve the following linear program:

$$\text{Min} \quad 3x_1 + 4x_2 + 8x_3$$

s.t.

$$4x_1 + 2x_2 \quad\quad \geq 12$$
$$4x_2 + 8x_3 \geq 16$$
$$x_1, x_2, x_3 \geq 0$$

18. Solve the following linear program:

$$\text{Min} \quad 84x_1 + 4x_2 + 30x_3$$

s.t.

$$8x_1 + 1x_2 + 3x_3 \leq 240$$
$$16x_1 + 1x_2 + 7x_3 \geq 480$$
$$8x_1 - 1x_2 + 4x_3 \geq 160$$
$$x_1, x_2, x_3 \geq 0$$

19. Captain John's Yachts, Inc., located in Fort Lauderdale, Florida, rents three types of ocean-going boats: sailboats, cabin cruisers, and Captain John's favorite, the luxury yachts. Captain John advertises his boats with his famous "you rent—we pilot" slogan, which means that the company supplies the captain and crew for each rented boat. Each rented boat has one captain, of course, but the crew sizes (deck hands, galley hands, etc.) differ. The crew requirements, in addition to a captain, are one for sailboats, two for cabin cruisers, and three for yachts. Ten employees are captains, and an additional 18 employees fill the various crew positions. Currently, Captain John has rental requests for all of his boats: four sailboats, eight cabin cruisers, and three luxury yachts. If Captain John's daily profit contribution is $50 for sailboats, $70 for cruisers, and $100 for luxury yachts, how many boats of each type should he rent?

20. The Our-Bags-Don't-Break (OBDB) plastic bag company manufactures three plastic refuse bags for home use: a 20-gallon garbage bag, a 30-gallon garbage bag, and a 33-gallon leaf-and-grass bag. Using purchased plastic material, three operations are required to produce each end product: cutting, sealing, and packaging. The production time required to process each type of bag in every operation and the maximum production time available for each operation are shown (note that the production time figures in this table are per box of each type of bag).

| Type of Bag | Production Time (seconds/box) | | |
| --- | --- | --- | --- |
| | **Cutting** | **Sealing** | **Packaging** |
| 20 gallons | 2 | 2 | 3 |
| 30 gallons | 3 | 2 | 4 |
| 33 gallons | 3 | 3 | 5 |
| Time available | 2 hours | 3 hours | 4 hours |

If OBDB's profit contribution is $0.10 for each box of 20-gallon bags produced, $0.15 for each box of 30-gallon bags, and $0.20 for each box of 33-gallon bags, what is the optimal product mix?

21. Kirkman Brothers ice cream parlors sell three different flavors of Dairy Sweet ice milk: chocolate, vanilla, and banana. Due to extremely hot weather and a high demand for its products, Kirkman has run short of its supply of ingredients: milk, sugar, and cream. Hence, Kirkman will not be able to fill all the orders received from its retail outlets, the ice cream parlors. Due to these circumstances, Kirkman has decided to make the most profitable amounts of the three flavors, given the constraints on supply of the basic ingredients. The company will then ration the ice milk to the retail outlets.

Kirkman has collected the following data on profitability of the various flavors, availability of supplies, and amounts required for each flavor.

| Flavor | Profit/ Gallon | Usage/Gallon Milk (gallons) | Usage/Gallon Sugar (pounds) | Usage/Gallon Cream (gallons) |
|---|---|---|---|---|
| Chocolate | $1.00 | 0.45 | 0.50 | 0.10 |
| Vanilla | $0.90 | 0.50 | 0.40 | 0.15 |
| Banana | $0.95 | 0.40 | 0.40 | 0.20 |
| Maximum available | | 200 | 150 | 60 |

Determine the optimal product mix for Kirkman Brothers. What additional resources could be used profitably?

22.  Uforia Corporation sells two brands of perfume: Incentive and Temptation No. 1. Uforia sells exclusively through department stores and employs a three-person sales staff to call on its customers. The amount of time necessary for each sales representative to sell one case of each product varies with experience and ability. Data on the average time for each of Uforia's three sales representatives is presented here.

| Salesperson | Average Sales Time per Case (minutes) Incentive | Average Sales Time per Case (minutes) Temptation No. 1 |
|---|---|---|
| John | 10 | 15 |
| Brenda | 15 | 10 |
| Red | 12 | 6 |

Each sales representative spends approximately 80 hours per month in the actual selling of these two products. Cases of Incentive and Temptation No. 1 sell at profits of $30 and $25, respectively. How many cases of each perfume should each person sell during the next month to maximize the firm's profits? (Hint: Let $x_1$ = number of cases of Incentive sold by John, $x_2$ = number of cases of Temptation No. 1 sold by John, $x_3$ = number of cases of Incentive sold by Brenda, etc.)

   *Note:* In Problems 23–29, we provide examples of linear programs that result in one or more of the following situations:
   1. Optimal solution
   2. Infeasible solution
   3. Unbounded solution
   4. Alternative optimal solutions
   5. Degenerate solution

For each linear program, determine the solution situation that exists, and indicate how you identified each situation using the simplex method. For the problems with alternative optimal solutions, calculate at least two optimal solutions.

SELF TEST

23.

$$\text{Max} \quad 4x_1 + 8x_2$$
$$\text{s.t.}$$
$$2x_1 + 2x_2 \leq 10$$
$$-1x_1 + 1x_2 \geq 8$$
$$x_1, x_2 \geq 0$$

**24.**

$$\text{Min} \quad 3x_1 + 3x_2$$

s.t.

$$2x_1 + 0.5x_2 \geq 10$$
$$2x_1 \quad\quad \geq 4$$
$$4x_1 + 4x_2 \geq 32$$
$$x_1, x_2 \geq 0$$

**25.**

$$\text{Max} \quad 1x_1 + 1x_2$$

s.t.

$$8x_1 + 6x_2 \geq 24$$
$$4x_1 + 6x_2 \geq -12$$
$$2x_2 \geq 4$$
$$x_1, x_2 \geq 0$$

**26.**

$$\text{Max} \quad 2x_1 + 1x_2 + 1x_3$$

s.t.

$$4x_1 + 2x_2 + 2x_3 \geq 4$$
$$2x_1 + 4x_2 \quad\quad \leq 20$$
$$4x_1 + 8x_2 + 2x_3 \leq 16$$
$$x_1, x_2, x_3 \geq 0$$

**27.**

$$\text{Max} \quad 2x_1 + 4x_2$$

s.t.

$$1x_1 + \tfrac{1}{2}x_2 \leq 10$$
$$1x_1 + 1x_2 = 12$$
$$1x_1 + \tfrac{3}{2}x_2 \leq 18$$
$$x_1, x_2 \geq 0$$

**28.**

$$\text{Min} \quad -4x_1 + 5x_2 + 5x_3$$

s.t.

$$1x_2 + 1x_3 \geq 2$$
$$-1x_1 + 1x_2 + 1x_3 \geq 1$$
$$-1x_3 \geq 1$$
$$x_1, x_2, x_3 \geq 0$$

**29.** Solve the following linear program and identify any alternative optimal solutions.

$$\text{Max} \quad 120x_1 + 80x_2 + 14x_3$$

s.t.

$$4x_1 + 8x_2 + x_3 \leq 200$$
$$2x_2 + 1x_3 \leq 300$$
$$32x_1 + 4x_2 + 2x_3 = 400$$
$$x_1, x_2, x_3 \geq 0$$

**30.** Supersport Footballs, Inc., manufactures three kinds of football: an All-Pro model, a College model, and a High School model. All three footballs require operations in the following departments: cutting and dyeing, sewing, and inspection and packaging. The production times and maximum production availabilities are shown here.

| | Production Time (minutes) | | |
| Model | Cutting and Dyeing | Sewing | Inspection and Packaging |
| --- | --- | --- | --- |
| All-Pro | 12 | 15 | 3 |
| College | 10 | 15 | 4 |
| High School | 8 | 12 | 2 |
| Time available | 300 hours | 200 hours | 100 hours |

Current orders indicate that at least 1000 All-Pro footballs must be manufactured.

a.   If Supersport realizes a profit contribution of $3 for each All-Pro model, $5 for each College model, and $4 for each High School model, how many footballs of each type should be produced? What occurs in the solution of this problem? Why?

b.   If Supersport can increase sewing time to 300 hours and inspection and packaging time to 150 hours by using overtime, what is your recommendation?

# 6

## SIMPLEX-BASED SENSITIVITY ANALYSIS

## AND DUALITY

### CONTENTS

In Chapter 3 we defined sensitivity analysis as the study of how the optimal solution and the value of the optimal solution to a linear program change, given changes in the various coefficients of the problem. In this chapter we discuss how sensitivity analysis information such as the ranges for the objective function coefficients, dual prices, and the ranges for the right-hand-side values can be obtained from the final simplex tableau. The topic of duality is also introduced. We will see that associated with every linear programming problem is a dual problem that has an interesting economic interpretation.

## 6.1  SENSITIVITY ANALYSIS WITH THE SIMPLEX TABLEAU

The usual sensitivity analysis for linear programs involves computing ranges for the objective function coefficients and the right-hand-side values, as well as the dual prices.

### Objective Function Coefficients

Sensitivity analysis for an objective function coefficient involves placing a range on the coefficient's value. We call this range the **range of optimality.** As long as the actual value of the objective function coefficient is within the range of optimality, *the current basic feasible solution will remain optimal.* The range of optimality for a basic variable defines the objective function coefficient values for which that variable will remain part of the current optimal basic feasible solution. The range of optimality for a nonbasic variable defines the objective function coefficient values for which that variable will remain nonbasic.

In computing the range of optimality for an objective function coefficient, all other coefficients in the problem are assumed to remain at their original values; in other words, *only one coefficient is allowed to change at a time.* To illustrate the process of computing ranges for objective function coefficients, recall the HighTech Industries problem introduced in Chapter 5. The linear program for this problem is restated as follows:

$$\text{Max} \quad 50x_1 + 40x_2$$
s.t.
$$
\begin{aligned}
3x_1 + 5x_2 &\leq 150 \quad \text{Assembly time} \\
1x_2 &\leq 20 \quad \text{Portable display} \\
8x_1 + 5x_2 &\leq 300 \quad \text{Warehouse capacity} \\
x_1, x_2 &\geq 0
\end{aligned}
$$

where

$$x_1 = \text{number of units of the Deskpro}$$
$$x_2 = \text{number of units of the Portable}$$

The final simplex tableau for the HighTech problem is as follows.

|        |       | $x_1$ | $x_2$ | $s_1$ | $s_2$ | $s_3$ |      |
|--------|-------|-------|-------|-------|-------|-------|------|
| Basis  | $c_B$ | 50    | 40    | 0     | 0     | 0     |      |
| $x_2$  | 40    | 0     | 1     | $8/25$ | 0    | $-3/25$ | 12 |
| $s_2$  | 0     | 0     | 0     | $-8/25$ | 1   | $3/25$ | 8 |
| $x_1$  | 50    | 1     | 0     | $-5/25$ | 0   | $5/25$ | 30 |
| $z_j$      |  | 50 | 40 | $14/5$ | 0 | $26/5$ | 1980 |
| $c_j - z_j$ |  | 0 | 0 | $-14/5$ | 0 | $-26/5$ | |

Recall that when the simplex method is used to solve a linear program, an optimal solution is recognized when all entries in the net evaluation row ($c_j - z_j$) are $\le 0$. Because the preceding simplex tableau satisfies this criterion, the solution shown is optimal. However, if a change in one of the objective function coefficients were to cause one or more of the $c_j - z_j$ values to become positive, then the current solution would no longer be optimal; in such a case, one or more additional simplex iterations would be necessary to find the new optimal solution. *The range of optimality for an objective function coefficient, then, is determined by those coefficient values that maintain*

$$c_j - z_j \le 0 \tag{6.1}$$

*for all values of j.*

Let us illustrate this approach by computing the range of optimality for $c_1$, the profit contribution per unit of the Deskpro. Using $c_1$ (instead of 50) as the objective function coefficient of $x_1$, the final simplex tableau is as follows:

|        |       | $x_1$ | $x_2$ | $s_1$ | $s_2$ | $s_3$ |      |
|--------|-------|-------|-------|-------|-------|-------|------|
| Basis  | $c_B$ | $c_1$ | 40    | 0     | 0     | 0     |      |
| $x_2$  | 40    | 0     | 1     | $8/25$ | 0    | $-3/25$ | 12 |
| $s_2$  | 0     | 0     | 0     | $-8/25$ | 1   | $3/25$ | 8 |
| $x_1$  | $c_1$ | 1     | 0     | $-5/25$ | 0   | $5/25$ | 30 |
| $z_j$      |  | $c_1$ | 40 | $\frac{64-c_1}{5}$ | 0 | $\frac{c_1-24}{5}$ | $480+30c_1$ |
| $c_j - z_j$ |  | 0 | 0 | $\frac{c_1-64}{5}$ | 0 | $\frac{24-c_1}{5}$ | |

An objective function coefficient change causes changes in the $z_j$ and $c_j - z_j$ rows, but not in the variable values.

Note that this tableau is the same as the previous optimal tableau except that $c_1$ replaces 50. Thus, we have a $c_1$ in the objective function coefficient row and the $c_B$ column, and the $z_j$ and $c_j - z_j$ rows have been recomputed using $c_1$ instead of 50. The current solution will remain optimal as long as the value of $c_1$ results in all $c_j - z_j \le 0$. Hence, from the column for $s_1$ we must have

$$\frac{c_1 - 64}{5} \le 0$$

and from the column for $s_3$, we must have

$$\frac{24 - c_1}{5} \le 0$$

Using the first inequality, we obtain

$$c_1 - 64 \le 0$$

or

$$c_1 \le 64 \tag{6.2}$$

Similarly, from the second inequality, we obtain

$$24 - c_1 \le 0$$

or

$$24 \le c_1 \tag{6.3}$$

Since $c_1$ must satisfy both (6.2) and (6.3), the range of optimality for $c_1$ is given by

$$24 \le c_1 \le 64 \tag{6.4}$$

To see how management of HighTech can make use of this sensitivity analysis information, suppose an increase in material costs reduces the profit contribution per unit for the Deskpro to $30. The range of optimality indicates that the current solution ($x_1 = 30$, $x_2 = 12$, $s_1 = 0$, $s_2 = 8$, $s_3 = 0$) is still optimal. To verify this solution, let us recompute the final simplex tableau after reducing the value of $c_1$ to 30.

We have simply set $c_1 = 30$ everywhere it appears in the previous tableau.

|  |  | $x_1$ | $x_2$ | $s_1$ | $s_2$ | $s_3$ |  |
|---|---|---|---|---|---|---|---|
| Basis | $c_B$ | 30 | 40 | 0 | 0 | 0 |  |
| $x_2$ | 40 | 0 | 1 | $8/25$ | 0 | $-3/25$ | 12 |
| $s_2$ | 0 | 0 | 0 | $-8/25$ | 1 | $3/25$ | 8 |
| $x_1$ | 30 | 1 | 0 | $-5/25$ | 0 | $5/25$ | 30 |
| $z_j$ |  | 30 | 40 | $34/5$ | 0 | $6/5$ | 1380 |
| $c_j - z_j$ |  | 0 | 0 | $-34/5$ | 0 | $-6/5$ |  |

Since $c_j - z_j \le 0$ for all variables, the solution with $x_1 = 30$, $x_2 = 12$, $s_1 = 0$, $s_2 = 8$, and $s_3 = 0$ is still optimal. That is, the optimal solution with $c_1 = 30$ is the same as the optimal solution with $c_1 = 50$. Note, however, that the decrease in profit contribution per unit of the Deskpro has caused a reduction in total profit from $1980 to $1380.

What if the profit contribution per unit were reduced even further—say, to $20? Referring to the range of optimality for $c_1$ given by expression (6.4), we see that $c_1 = 20$

is outside the range; thus, we know that a change this large will cause a new basis to be optimal. To verify this new basis, we have modified the final simplex tableau by replacing $c_1$ by 20.

| Basis | $c_B$ | $x_1$ 20 | $x_2$ 40 | $s_1$ 0 | $s_2$ 0 | $s_3$ 0 | |
|---|---|---|---|---|---|---|---|
| $x_2$ | 40 | 0 | 1 | $8/25$ | 0 | $-3/25$ | 12 |
| $s_2$ | 0 | 0 | 0 | $-8/25$ | 1 | $3/25$ | 8 |
| $x_1$ | 20 | 1 | 0 | $-5/25$ | 0 | $5/25$ | 30 |
| $z_j$ | | 20 | 40 | $44/5$ | 0 | $-4/5$ | 1080 |
| $c_j - z_j$ | | 0 | 0 | $-44/5$ | 0 | $4/5$ | |

As expected, the current solution ($x_1 = 30$, $x_2 = 12$, $s_1 = 0$, $s_2 = 8$, and $s_3 = 0$) is no longer optimal since the entry in the $s_3$ column of the net evaluation row is greater than zero. This result implies that at least one more simplex iteration must be performed to reach the optimal solution. Continue to perform the simplex iterations in the previous tableau to verify that the new optimal solution will require the production of $16\frac{2}{3}$ units of the Deskpro and 20 units of the Portable.

The procedure we used to compute the range of optimality for $c_1$ can be used for any basic variable. The procedure for computing the range of optimality for nonbasic variables is even easier since a change in the objective function coefficient for a nonbasic variable causes only the corresponding $c_j - z_j$ entry to change in the final simplex tableau. To illustrate the approach, we show the following final simplex tableau for the original HighTech problem after replacing 0, the objective function coefficient for $s_1$, with the coefficient $c_{s_1}$:

> At the end points of the range, the corresponding variable is a candidate for entering the basis if it is currently out or for leaving the basis if it is currently in.

| Basis | $c_B$ | $x_1$ 50 | $x_2$ 40 | $s_1$ $c_{s_1}$ | $s_2$ 0 | $s_3$ 0 | |
|---|---|---|---|---|---|---|---|
| $x_2$ | 40 | 0 | 1 | $8/25$ | 0 | $-3/25$ | 12 |
| $s_2$ | 0 | 0 | 0 | $-8/25$ | 1 | $3/25$ | 8 |
| $x_1$ | 50 | 1 | 0 | $-5/25$ | 0 | $5/25$ | 30 |
| $z_j$ | | 50 | 40 | $14/5$ | 0 | $26/5$ | 1980 |
| $c_j - z_j$ | | 0 | 0 | $c_{s_1} - 14/5$ | 0 | $-26/5$ | |

Note that the only changes in the tableau are in the $s_1$ column. In applying inequality (6.1) to compute the range of optimality, we get

$$c_{s_1} - 14/5 \leq 0$$

and hence

$$c_{s_1} \leq 14/5$$

Therefore, as long as the objective function coefficient for $s_1$ is less than or equal to $^{14}/_5$, the current solution will be optimal. With no lower bound on how much the coefficient may be decreased, we write the range of optimality for $c_{s_1}$ as

$$c_{s_1} \leq 14/5$$

The same approach works for all nonbasic variables. In a maximization problem, there is no lower limit on the range of optimality, and the upper limit is given by $z_j$. Thus, the range of optimality for the objective function coefficient of any nonbasic variable is given by

$$c_j \leq z_j \qquad\qquad (6.5)$$

Let us summarize the steps necessary to compute the range of optimality for objective function coefficients. In stating the following steps, we assume that computing the range of optimality for $c_k$, the coefficient of $x_k$, in a maximization problem is the desired goal. Keep in mind that $x_k$ in this context may refer to one of the original decision variables, a slack variable, or a surplus variable.

### Steps to Compute the Range of Optimality

Step 1   Replace the numerical value of the objective function coefficient for $x_k$ with $c_k$ everywhere it appears in the final simplex tableau.

Step 2   Recompute $c_j - z_j$ for each nonbasic variable (if $x_k$ is a nonbasic variable, it is only necessary to recompute $c_k - z_k$).

Step 3   Requiring that $c_j - z_j \leq 0$, solve each inequality for any upper or lower bounds on $c_k$. If there are two or more upper bounds on $c_k$, the smallest of these is the upper bound on the range of optimality. If there are two or more lower bounds, the largest of these is the lower bound on the range of optimality.

Step 4   If the original problem is a minimization problem that was converted to a maximization problem in order to apply the simplex method, multiply the inequalities obtained in step 3 by $-1$, and change the direction of the inequalities to obtain the ranges of optimality for the original minimization problem.

Can you compute the range of optimality for objective function coefficients by working with the final simplex tableau? Try Problem 1.

By using the range of optimality to determine whether a change in an objective function coefficient is large enough to cause a change in the optimal solution, we can often avoid the process of formulating and solving a modified linear programming problem.

## Right-Hand-Side Values

In many linear programming problems, we can interpret the right-hand-side values (the $b_i$'s) as the resources available. For instance, in the HighTech Industries problem, the right-hand side of constraint 1 represents the available assembly time, the right-hand side of constraint 2 represents the available Portable displays, and the right-hand side of constraint 3 represents the available warehouse space. Dual prices provide information on the value of additional resources in these cases; the ranges over which these dual prices are valid are given by the ranges for the right-hand-side values.

**Dual Prices.**    In Chapter 3 we stated that the improvement in value of the optimal solution per-unit increase in a constraint's right-hand-side value is called a **dual price**.[1] When

---

[1] The closely related term *shadow price* is used by some authors. The shadow price is the same as the dual price for maximization problems; for minimization problems, the dual and shadow prices are equal in absolute value but have opposite signs. LINDO/PC and The Management Scientist provide dual prices as part of the computer output. Some software packages provide shadow prices.

the simplex method is used to solve a linear programming problem, the values of the dual prices are easy to obtain. They are found in the $z_j$ row of the final simplex tableau. To illustrate this point, the final simplex tableau for the HighTech problem is again shown.

| Basis | $c_B$ | $x_1$ 50 | $x_2$ 40 | $s_1$ 0 | $s_2$ 0 | $s_3$ 0 | |
|---|---|---|---|---|---|---|---|
| $x_2$ | 40 | 0 | 1 | $8/25$ | 0 | $-3/25$ | 12 |
| $s_2$ | 0 | 0 | 0 | $-8/25$ | 1 | $3/25$ | 8 |
| $x_1$ | 50 | 1 | 0 | $-5/25$ | 0 | $5/25$ | 30 |
| $z_j$ | | 50 | 40 | $14/5$ | 0 | $26/5$ | 1980 |
| $c_j - z_j$ | | 0 | 0 | $-14/5$ | 0 | $-26/5$ | |

The $z_j$ values for the three slack variables are $14/5$, 0, and $26/5$, respectively. Thus, the dual prices for the assembly time constraint, Portable display constraint, and warehouse capacity constraint are respectively $14/5 = \$2.80, 0.00$, and $26/5 = \$5.20$. The dual price of $\$5.20$ shows that more warehouse space will have the biggest positive impact on HighTech's profit.

To see why the $z_j$ values for the slack variables in the final simplex tableau are the dual prices, let us first consider the case for slack variables that are part of the optimal basic feasible solution. Each of these slack variables will have a $z_j$ value of zero, implying a dual price of zero for the corresponding constraint. For example, consider slack variable $s_2$, a basic variable in the HighTech problem. Since $s_2 = 8$ in the optimal solution, HighTech will have eight Portable display units unused. Consequently, how much would management of HighTech Industries be willing to pay to obtain additional Portable display units? Clearly the answer is nothing since at the optimal solution HighTech has an excess of this particular component. Additional amounts of this resource are of no value to the company, and, consequently, the dual price for this constraint is zero. In general, if a slack variable is a basic variable in the optimal solution, the value of $z_j$—and hence, the dual price of the corresponding resource—is zero.

Consider now the nonbasic slack variables—for example, $s_1$. In the previous subsection we determined that the current solution will remain optimal as long as the objective function coefficient for $s_1$ (denoted $c_{s_1}$) stays in the following range:

$$c_{s_1} \leq 14/5$$

It implies that the variable $s_1$ should not be increased from its current value of zero unless it is worth more than $14/5 = \$2.80$ to do so. We can conclude then that $\$2.80$ is the marginal value to HighTech of 1 hour of assembly time used in the production of Deskpro and Portable computers. Thus, if additional time can be obtained, HighTech should be willing to pay up to $\$2.80$ per hour for it. A similar interpretation can be given to the $z_j$ value for each of the nonbasic slack variables.

With a greater-than-or-equal-to constraint, the value of the dual price will be less than or equal to zero because a one-unit increase in the value of the right-hand side cannot be helpful; a one-unit increase makes it more difficult to satisfy the constraint. For a maximization problem, then, the optimal value can be expected to decrease when the right-hand side of a greater-than-or-equal-to constraint is increased. The dual price gives the amount of the expected improvement—a negative number, since we expect a decrease. As a result, the dual price for a greater-than-or-equal-to constraint is given by the negative of the $z_j$ entry for the corresponding surplus variable in the optimal simplex tableau.

Finally, it is possible to compute dual prices for equality constraints. They are given by the $z_j$ values for the corresponding artificial variables. We will not develop this case in detail here since we have recommended dropping each artificial variable column from the simplex tableau as soon as the corresponding artificial variable leaves the basis.

To summarize, when the simplex method is used to solve a linear programming problem, the dual prices for the constraints are contained in the final simplex tableau. Table 6.1 summarizes the rules for determining the dual prices for the various constraint types in a maximization problem solved by the simplex method.

Recall that we convert a minimization problem to a maximization problem by multiplying the objective function by $-1$ before using the simplex method. Nevertheless, the dual price is given by the same $z_j$ values since improvement for a minimization problem is a decrease in the optimal value.

To illustrate the approach for computing dual prices for a minimization problem, recall the M&D Chemicals problem that we solved in Section 5.7 as an equivalent maximization problem by multiplying the objective function by $-1$. The linear programming model for this problem and the final simplex tableau are restated as follows, with $x_1$ and $x_2$ representing manufacturing quantities of products $A$ and $B$, respectively.

Try Problem 3, parts (a), (b), and (c) for practice at finding dual prices from the optimal simplex tableau.

$$\text{Min} \quad 2x_1 + 3x_2$$
s.t.
$$
\begin{aligned}
1x_1 & & \geq 125 & \quad \text{Demand for product } A\\
1x_1 + 1x_2 & & \geq 350 & \quad \text{Total production}\\
2x_1 + 1x_2 & & \leq 600 & \quad \text{Processing time}\\
x_1, x_2 & & \geq 0
\end{aligned}
$$

| Basis | $c_B$ | $x_1$ $-2$ | $x_2$ $-3$ | $s_1$ $0$ | $s_2$ $0$ | $s_3$ $0$ | |
|---|---|---|---|---|---|---|---|
| $x_1$ | $-2$ | 1 | 0 | 0 | 1 | 1 | 250 |
| $x_2$ | $-3$ | 0 | 1 | 0 | $-2$ | $-1$ | 100 |
| $s_1$ | 0 | 0 | 0 | 1 | 1 | 1 | 125 |
| $z_j$ | | $-2$ | $-3$ | 0 | 4 | 1 | $-800$ |
| $c_j - z_j$ | | 0 | 0 | 0 | $-4$ | $-1$ | |

| Table 6.1 | TABLEAU LOCATION OF DUAL PRICE BY CONSTRAINT TYPE |
|---|---|

| Constraint Type | Dual Price Given by |
|---|---|
| $\leq$ | $z_j$ value for the slack variable associated with the constraint |
| $\geq$ | Negative of the $z_j$ value for the surplus variable associated with the constraint |
| $=$ | $z_j$ value for the artificial variable associated with the constraint |

Following the rules in Table 6.1 for identifying the dual price for each constraint type, the dual prices for the constraints in the M&D Chemicals problem are given in Table 6.2. Since constraint 1 is not binding, its dual price is zero. The dual price for constraint 2 shows that the marginal cost of increasing the total production requirement is $4 per unit. Finally, the dual price of one for the third constraint shows that the per-unit value of additional processing time is $1.

**Range of Feasibility.**    As we have just seen, the $z_j$ row in the final simplex tableau can be used to determine the dual price and, as a result, predict the change in the value of the objective function corresponding to a unit change in a $b_i$. This interpretation is only valid, however, as long as the change in $b_i$ is not large enough to make the current basic solution infeasible. Thus, we will be interested in calculating a range of values over which a particular $b_i$ can vary without any of the current basic variables becoming infeasible (i.e., less than zero). This range of values will be referred to as the **range of feasibility.**

A change in $b_i$ does not affect optimality ($c_j - z_j$ is unchanged), but it does affect feasibility. One of the current basic variables may become negative.

To demonstrate the effect of changing a $b_i$, consider increasing the amount of assembly time available in the HighTech problem from 150 to 160 hours. Will the current basis still yield a feasible solution? If so, given the dual price of $2.80 for the assembly time constraint, we can expect an increase in the value of the solution of $10(2.80) = 28$. The final simplex tableau corresponding to an increase in the assembly time of 10 hours is shown here.

| Basis | $c_B$ | $x_1$ 50 | $x_2$ 40 | $s_1$ 0 | $s_2$ 0 | $s_3$ 0 | |
|---|---|---|---|---|---|---|---|
| $x_2$ | 40 | 0 | 1 | $8/25$ | 0 | $-3/25$ | 15.2 |
| $s_2$ | 0 | 0 | 0 | $-8/25$ | 1 | $3/25$ | 4.8 |
| $x_1$ | 50 | 1 | 0 | $-5/25$ | 0 | $5/25$ | 28.0 |
| $z_j$ | | 50 | 40 | $14/5$ | 0 | $26/5$ | 2008 |
| $c_j - z_j$ | | 0 | 0 | $-14/5$ | 0 | $-26/5$ | |

The same basis, consisting of the basic variables $x_2$, $s_2$, and $x_1$, is feasible since all the basic variables are nonnegative. Note also that, just as we predicted using the dual price, the value of the optimal solution has increased by $10($2.80) = $28$, from $1980 to $2008.

You may wonder whether we had to resolve the problem completely to find this new solution. The answer is no! The only changes in the final simplex tableau (as compared with the final simplex tableau with $b_1 = 150$) are the differences in the values of the basic variables and the value of the objective function. That is, only the last column of the simplex

| Table 6.2 | DUAL PRICES FOR M&D CHEMICALS PROBLEM | |
|---|---|---|
| **Constraint** | **Constraint Type** | **Dual Price** |
| Demand for product 1 | $\geq$ | 0 |
| Total production | $\geq$ | $-4$ |
| Processing time | $\leq$ | 1 |

tableau has changed. The entries in this new last column of the simplex tableau were obtained by adding 10 times the first four entries in the $s_1$ column to the last column in the previous tableau:

$$\text{New solution} = \begin{bmatrix} 12 \\ 8 \\ 30 \\ \hline 1980 \end{bmatrix} + 10 \begin{bmatrix} \frac{8}{25} \\ -\frac{8}{25} \\ -\frac{5}{25} \\ \hline \frac{14}{5} \end{bmatrix} = \begin{bmatrix} 15.2 \\ 4.8 \\ 28.0 \\ \hline 2008 \end{bmatrix}$$

where the columns from left to right are: Old solution, Change in $b_1$, $s_1$ column, New solution.

Let us now consider why this procedure can be used to find the new solution. First, recall that each of the coefficients in the $s_1$ column indicates the amount of decrease in a basic variable that would result from increasing $s_1$ by one unit. In other words, these coefficients tell us how many units of each of the current basic variables will be driven out of solution if one unit of variable $s_1$ is brought into solution. Bringing one unit of $s_1$ into solution, however, is the same as reducing the availability of assembly time (decreasing $b_1$) by one unit; increasing $b_1$, the available assembly time, by one unit has just the opposite effect. Therefore, the entries in the $s_1$ column can also be interpreted as the changes in the values of the current basic variables corresponding to a one-unit increase in $b_1$.

To practice finding the new solution after a change in a right-hand side without resolving the problem when the same basis remains feasible, try Problem 3, parts (d) and (e).

The change in the value of the objective function corresponding to a one-unit increase in $b_1$ is given by the value of $z_j$ in that column (the dual price). In the foregoing case, the availability of assembly time increased by 10 units; thus, we multiplied the first four entries in the $s_1$ column by 10 to obtain the change in the value of the basic variables and the optimal value.

How do we know when a change in $b_1$ is so large that the current basis will become infeasible? We shall first answer this question specifically for the HighTech Industries problem and then state the general procedure for less-than-or-equal-to constraints. The approach taken with greater-than-or-equal-to and equality constraints will then be discussed.

We begin by showing how to compute upper and lower bounds for the maximum amount that $b_1$ can be changed before the current optimal basis becomes infeasible. We have seen how to find the new basic feasible solution values, given a 10-unit increase in $b_1$. In general, given a change in $b_1$ of $\Delta b_1$, the new values for the basic variables in the HighTech problem are given by

$$\begin{bmatrix} x_2 \\ s_2 \\ x_1 \end{bmatrix} = \begin{bmatrix} 12 \\ 8 \\ 30 \end{bmatrix} + \Delta b_1 \begin{bmatrix} \frac{8}{25} \\ -\frac{8}{25} \\ -\frac{5}{25} \end{bmatrix} = \begin{bmatrix} 12 + \frac{8}{25}\Delta b_1 \\ 8 - \frac{8}{25}\Delta b_1 \\ 30 - \frac{5}{25}\Delta b_1 \end{bmatrix} \quad (6.6)$$

As long as the new value of each basic variable remains nonnegative, the current basis will remain feasible and therefore optimal. We can keep the basic variables nonnegative by limiting the change in $b_1$ (i.e., $\Delta b_1$) so that we satisfy each of the following conditions:

$$12 + \tfrac{8}{25}\Delta b_1 \geq 0 \quad (6.7)$$

$$8 - \tfrac{8}{25}\Delta b_1 \geq 0 \quad (6.8)$$

$$30 - \tfrac{5}{25}\Delta b_1 \geq 0 \quad (6.9)$$

The left-hand sides of these inequalities represent the new values of the basic variables after $b_1$ has been changed by $\Delta b_1$.

Solving for $\Delta b_1$ in inequalities (6.7), (6.8), and (6.9), we obtain

$$\Delta b_1 \geq (\phantom{-}{}^{25}\!/_{8})(-12) = -37.5$$
$$\Delta b_1 \leq (-{}^{25}\!/_{8})(-\phantom{0}8) = 25$$
$$\Delta b_1 \leq (-{}^{25}\!/_{5})(-30) = 150$$

Since all three inequalities must be satisfied, the most restrictive limits on $b_1$ must be satisfied for all the current basic variables to remain nonnegative. Therefore, $\Delta b_1$ must satisfy

$$-37.5 \leq \Delta b_1 \leq 25 \tag{6.10}$$

The initial amount of assembly time available was 150 hours. Therefore, $b_1 = 150 + \Delta b_1$, where $b_1$ is the amount of assembly time available. We add 150 to each of the three terms in expression (6.10) to obtain

$$150 - 37.5 \leq 150 + \Delta b_1 \leq 150 + 25 \tag{6.11}$$

Replacing $150 + \Delta b_1$ with $b_1$, we obtain the range of feasibility for $b_1$:

$$112.5 \leq b_1 \leq 175$$

This range of feasibility for $b_1$ indicates that as long as the available assembly time is between 112.5 and 175 hours, the current optimal basis will remain feasible, which is why we call this range the range of feasibility.

Because the dual price for $b_1$ (assembly time) is ${}^{14}\!/_{5}$, we know profit can be increased by \$2.80 by obtaining an additional hour of assembly time. Suppose then that we increase $b_1$ by 25; that is, we increase $b_1$ to the upper limit of its range of feasibility, 175. The profit will increase to \$1980 + (\$2.80)25 = \$2050, and the values of the optimal basic variables become

$$x_2 = 12 + 25({}^{8}\!/_{25}) \phantom{00} = 20$$
$$s_2 = \phantom{0}8 + 25(-{}^{8}\!/_{25}) = \phantom{0}0$$
$$x_1 = 30 + 25(-{}^{5}\!/_{25}) = 25$$

What has happened to the solution? The increased assembly time has caused a revision in the optimal production plan. HighTech should produce more of the Portable and less of the Deskpro. Overall, the profit will be increased by (\$2.80)(25) = \$70. Note that although the optimal solution has changed, the basic variables that were optimal before are still optimal.

The procedure for determining the range of feasibility has been illustrated with the assembly time constraint. The procedure for calculating the range of feasibility for the right-hand side of any less-than-or-equal-to constraint is the same. The first step for a general constraint $i$ is to calculate the range of values for $b_i$ that satisfy the following inequalities.

$$
\begin{bmatrix} \bar{b}_1 \\ \bar{b}_2 \\ \cdot \\ \cdot \\ \cdot \\ \bar{b}_m \end{bmatrix} + \Delta b_i \begin{bmatrix} \bar{a}_{1j} \\ \bar{a}_{2j} \\ \cdot \\ \cdot \\ \cdot \\ \bar{a}_{mj} \end{bmatrix} \geq \begin{bmatrix} 0 \\ 0 \\ \cdot \\ \cdot \\ \cdot \\ 0 \end{bmatrix} \tag{6.12}
$$

Current solution (last column of the final simplex tableau)

Column of the final simplex tableau corresponding to the slack variable associated with constraint $i$

The inequalities are used to identify lower and upper limits on $\Delta b_i$. The range of feasibility can then be established by the maximum of the lower limits and the minimum of the upper limits.

Similar arguments can be used to develop a procedure for determining the range of feasibility for the right-hand-side value of a greater-than-or-equal-to constraint. Essentially the procedure is the same, with the column corresponding to the surplus variable associated with the constraint playing the central role. For a general greater-than-or-equal-to constraint $i$, we first calculate the range of values for $\Delta b_i$ that satisfy the inequalities shown in equation (6.13).

$$
\begin{bmatrix} \bar{b}_1 \\ \bar{b}_2 \\ \cdot \\ \cdot \\ \cdot \\ \bar{b}_m \end{bmatrix} - \Delta b_i \begin{bmatrix} \bar{a}_{1j} \\ \bar{a}_{2j} \\ \cdot \\ \cdot \\ \cdot \\ \bar{a}_{mj} \end{bmatrix} \geq \begin{bmatrix} 0 \\ 0 \\ \cdot \\ \cdot \\ \cdot \\ 0 \end{bmatrix} \tag{6.13}
$$

Current solution (last column of the final simplex tableau)

Column of the final simplex tableau corresponding to the surplus variable associated with constraint $i$

Once again, these inequalities establish lower and upper limits on $\Delta b_i$. Given these limits, the range of feasibility is easily determined.

A range of feasibility for the right-hand side of an equality constraint can also be com-

*Try Problem 4 to make sure you can compute the range of feasibility by working with the final simplex tableau.*

puted. To do so for equality constraint $i$, one could use the column of the final simplex tableau corresponding to the artificial variable associated with constraint $i$ in equation (6.12). Since we have suggested dropping the artificial variable columns from the simplex tableau as soon as the artificial variable becomes nonbasic, these columns will not be available in the final tableau. Thus, more involved calculations are required to compute a range of feasibility for equality constraints. Details may be found in more advanced texts.

*Changes that force $b_i$ outside its range of feasibility are normally accompanied by changes in the dual prices.*

As long as the change in a right-hand-side value is such that $b_i$ stays within its range of feasibility, the same basis will remain feasible and optimal. Changes that force $b_i$ outside its range of feasibility will force us to resolve the problem to find the new optimal solution consisting of a different set of basic variables. (More advanced linear programming texts show how it can be done without completely resolving the problem.) In any case, the calculation of the range of feasibility for each $b_i$ is valuable management information and should be included as part of the management report on any linear programming project. The range of feasibility is typically made available as part of the computer solution to the problem.

### Simultaneous Changes

In reviewing the procedures for developing the range of optimality and the range of feasibility, we note that only one coefficient at a time was permitted to vary. Our statements concerning changes within these ranges were made with the understanding that no other coefficients are permitted to change. However, sometimes we can make the same statements when either two or more objective function coefficients or two or more right-hand sides are varied simultaneously. When the simultaneous changes satisfy the 100 percent rule, the same statements are applicable. The 100 percent rule was explained in Chapter 3, but we will briefly review it here.

Let us define allowable increase as the amount a coefficient can be increased before reaching the upper limit of its range, and allowable decrease as the amount a coefficient can be decreased before reaching the lower limit of its range. Now suppose simultaneous changes are made in two or more objective function coefficients. For each coefficient changed, we compute the percentage of the allowable increase, or allowable decrease, represented by the change. If the sum of the percentages for all changes does not exceed 100%, we say that the 100 percent rule is satisfied and that the simultaneous changes will not cause a change in the optimal solution. However, just as with a single objective function coefficient change, the value of the solution will change because of the change in the coefficients.

Similarly, if two or more changes in constraint right-hand-side values are made, we again compute the percentage of allowable increase or allowable decrease represented by each change. If the sum of the percentages for all changes does not exceed 100%, we say that the 100 percent rule is satisfied. The dual prices are then valid for determining the change in value of the objective function associated with the right-hand-side changes.

---

### N O T E S
### *and Comments*

1. Sometimes, interpreting dual prices and choosing the appropriate sign can be confusing. It often helps to think of this process as follows. Relaxing a $\geq$ constraint means decreasing its right-hand side, and relaxing a $\leq$ constraint means increasing its right-hand side. Relaxing a constraint permits improvement in value; restricting a constraint (decreasing the right-hand side of a $\leq$ constraint or increasing the right-hand side of a $\geq$ constraint) has the opposite effect. In every case, the absolute value of the dual price gives the improvement in the optimal value associated with relaxing the constraint.

2. The Notes & Comments in Chapter 3 concerning sensitivity analysis are also applicable here. In particular, recall that the 100 percent rule cannot be applied to simultaneous changes in the objective function *and* the right-hand sides; it applies only to simultaneous changes in one or the other. Also note that this rule *does not* mean that simultaneous changes that do not satisfy the rule will necessarily cause a change in the solution. For instance, any proportional change in *all* the objective function coefficients will leave the optimal solution unchanged, and any proportional change in *all* the right-hand sides will leave the dual prices unchanged.

........................................................................................................../  /...............

## 6.2    DUALITY

Every linear programming problem has an associated linear programming problem called the **dual.** Referring to the original formulation of the linear programming problem as the **primal,** we will see how the primal can be converted into its corresponding dual. Then we will solve the dual linear programming problem and interpret the results. A fundamental property of the primal-dual relationship is that the optimal solution to either the primal or the dual problem also provides the optimal solution to the other. In cases where the primal and the dual problems differ in terms of computational difficulty, we can choose the easier problem to solve.

Let us return to the HighTech Industries problem. The original formulation—the primal—is as follows:

$$\text{Max} \quad 50x_1 + 40x_2$$

s.t.

$$
\begin{array}{llll}
3x_1 + & 5x_2 \leq 150 & \text{Assembly time} \\
       & 1x_2 \leq \phantom{0}20 & \text{Portable display} \\
8x_1 + & 5x_2 \leq 300 & \text{Warehouse space} \\
x_1, x_2 \geq 0
\end{array}
$$

A maximization problem with all less-than-or-equal-to constraints and nonnegativity requirements for the variables is said to be in **canonical form.** For a maximization problem in canonical form, such as the HighTech Industries problem, the conversion to the associated dual linear program is relatively easy. Let us state the dual of the HighTech problem and then identify the steps taken to make the primal-dual conversion. The HighTech dual problem is as follows:

$$\text{Min} \quad 150u_1 + 20u_2 + 300u_3$$

s.t.

$$
\begin{array}{llll}
3u_1 & + & 8u_3 \geq 50 \\
5u_1 + & 1u_2 + & 5u_3 \geq 40 \\
u_1, u_2, u_3 \geq 0
\end{array}
$$

This **canonical form for a minimization problem** is a minimization problem with all greater-than-or-equal-to constraints and nonnegativity requirements for the variables. Thus, the dual of a maximization problem in canonical form is a minimization problem in canonical form. The variables $u_1$, $u_2$, and $u_3$ are referred to as **dual variables.**

With the preceding example in mind, we make the following general statements about the *dual of a maximization problem in canonical form.*

1. The dual is a minimization problem in canonical form.
2. When the primal has $n$ decision variables ($n = 2$ in the HighTech problem), the dual will have $n$ constraints. The first constraint of the dual is associated with variable $x_1$ in the primal, the second constraint in the dual is associated with variable $x_2$ in the primal, and so on.

3. When the primal has $m$ constraints ($m = 3$ in the HighTech problem), the dual will have $m$ decision variables. Dual variable $u_1$ is associated with the first primal constraint, dual variable $u_2$ is associated with the second primal constraint, and so on.
4. The right-hand sides of the primal constraints become the objective function coefficients in the dual.
5. The objective function coefficients of the primal become the right-hand sides of the dual constraints.
6. The constraint coefficients of the $i$th primal variable become the coefficients in the $i$th constraint of the dual.

Try part (a) of Problem 17 for practice in finding the dual of a maximization problem in canonical form.

These six statements are the general requirements that must be satisfied when converting a maximization problem in canonical form to its associated dual: a minimization problem in canonical form. Even though these requirements may seem cumbersome at first, practice with a few simple problems will show that the primal-dual conversion process is relatively easy to implement.

Since we have formulated the HighTech dual linear programming problem, let us now proceed to solve it. With three variables in the dual, we will use the simplex method. After subtracting surplus variables $s_1$ and $s_2$ to obtain the standard form, adding artificial variables $a_1$ and $a_2$ to obtain the tableau form, and multiplying the objective function by $-1$ to convert the dual problem to an equivalent maximization problem, we arrive at the following initial simplex tableau.

| Basis | $c_B$ | $u_1$ $-150$ | $u_2$ $-20$ | $u_3$ $-300$ | $s_1$ $0$ | $s_2$ $0$ | $a_1$ $-M$ | $a_2$ $-M$ | |
|---|---|---|---|---|---|---|---|---|---|
| $a_1$ | $-M$ | 3 | 0 | ⑧ | $-1$ | 0 | 1 | 0 | 50 |
| $a_2$ | $-M$ | 5 | 1 | 5 | 0 | $-1$ | 0 | 1 | 40 |
| $z_j$ | | $-8M$ | $-M$ | $-13M$ | $M$ | $M$ | $-M$ | $-M$ | $-90M$ |
| $c_j - z_j$ | | $-150+8M$ | $-20+M$ | $-300+13M$ | $-M$ | $-M$ | 0 | 0 | |

At the first iteration, $u_3$ is brought into the basis, and $a_1$ is removed. At the second iteration, $u_1$ is brought into the basis, and $a_2$ is removed. At this point, the simplex tableau appears as follows.

| Basis | $c_B$ | $u_1$ $-150$ | $u_2$ $-20$ | $u_3$ $-300$ | $s_1$ $0$ | $s_2$ $0$ | |
|---|---|---|---|---|---|---|---|
| $u_3$ | $-300$ | 0 | $-3/25$ | 1 | $-5/25$ | $3/25$ | $26/5$ |
| $u_1$ | $-150$ | 1 | $8/25$ | 0 | $5/25$ | $-8/25$ | $14/5$ |
| $z_j$ | | $-150$ | $-12$ | $-300$ | 30 | 12 | $-1980$ |
| $c_j - z_j$ | | 0 | $-8$ | 0 | $-30$ | $-12$ | |

Because all the entries in the net evaluation row are less than or equal to zero, the optimal solution has been reached; it is $u_1 = 14/5$, $u_2 = 0$, $u_3 = 26/5$, $s_1 = 0$, and $s_2 = 0$. Since we have been maximizing the negative of the dual objective function, the value of the objective function for the optimal dual solution must be $-(-1980) = 1980$.

The final simplex tableau for the original HighTech Industries problem is shown here.

| Basis | $c_B$ | $x_1$ 50 | $x_2$ 40 | $s_1$ 0 | $s_2$ 0 | $s_3$ 0 | |
|---|---|---|---|---|---|---|---|
| $x_2$ | 40 | 0 | 1 | $8/25$ | 0 | $-3/25$ | 12 |
| $s_2$ | 0 | 0 | 0 | $-8/25$ | 1 | $3/25$ | 8 |
| $x_1$ | 50 | 1 | 0 | $-5/25$ | 0 | $5/25$ | 30 |
| $z_j$ | | 50 | 40 | $14/5$ | 0 | $26/5$ | 1980 |
| $c_j - z_j$ | | 0 | 0 | $-14/5$ | 0 | $-26/5$ | |

The optimal solution to the primal problem is $x_1 = 30$, $x_2 = 12$, $s_1 = 0$, $s_2 = 8$, and $s_3 = 0$. The optimal value of the objective function is 1980.

What observation can we make about the relationship between the optimal value of the objective function in the primal and the optimal value in the dual for the HighTech problem? The optimal value of the objective function is the same (1980) for both. This relationship is true for all primal and dual linear programming problems and is stated as property 1.

---

### Property 1

If the dual problem has an optimal solution, the primal problem has an optimal solution, and vice versa. Furthermore, the values of the optimal solutions to the dual and primal problems are equal.

---

This property tells us that if we had solved only the dual problem, we would have known that HighTech could make a maximum of $1980.

## Economic Interpretation of the Dual Variables

Before making further observations about the relationship between the primal and the dual solutions, let us consider the meaning or interpretation of the dual variables $u_1$, $u_2$, and $u_3$. Remember that in setting up the dual problem, each dual variable is associated with one of the constraints in the primal. Specifically, $u_1$ is associated with the assembly time constraint, $u_2$ with the Portable display constraint, and $u_3$ with the warehouse space constraint.

To understand and interpret these dual variables, let us return to property 1 of the primal-dual relationship, which stated that the objective function values for the primal and dual problems must be equal. At the optimal solution, the primal objective function results in

$$50x_1 + 40x_2 = 1980 \qquad (6.14)$$

while the dual objective function is

$$150u_1 + 20u_2 + 300u_3 = 1980 \qquad (6.15)$$

Using equation (6.14), let us restrict our interest to the interpretation of the primal objective function. Since $x_1$ and $x_2$ are the number of units of the Deskpro and the Portable that are assembled respectively, we have

$$\begin{pmatrix} \text{Dollar value} \\ \text{per unit of} \\ \text{Deskpro} \end{pmatrix} \begin{pmatrix} \text{Number of} \\ \text{units of} \\ \text{Deskpro} \end{pmatrix} + \begin{pmatrix} \text{Dollar value} \\ \text{per unit of} \\ \text{Portable} \end{pmatrix} \begin{pmatrix} \text{Number of} \\ \text{units of} \\ \text{Portable} \end{pmatrix} = \begin{matrix} \text{Total dollar} \\ \text{value of} \\ \text{production} \end{matrix}$$

From equation (6.15), we see that the coefficients of the dual objective function (150, 20, and 300) can be interpreted as the number of units of resources available. Thus, because the primal and dual objective functions are equal at optimality, we have

$$\begin{pmatrix} \text{Units of} \\ \text{resource} \\ 1 \end{pmatrix} u_1 + \begin{pmatrix} \text{Units of} \\ \text{resource} \\ 2 \end{pmatrix} u_2 + \begin{pmatrix} \text{Units of} \\ \text{resource} \\ 3 \end{pmatrix} u_3 = \begin{matrix} \text{Total dollar value} \\ \text{of production} \end{matrix}$$

Thus, we see that the dual variables must carry the interpretations of being the value per unit of resource. For the HighTech problem,

$u_1$ = dollar value per hour of assembly time
$u_2$ = dollar value per unit of the Portable display
$u_3$ = dollar value per square foot of warehouse space

Have we attempted to identify the value of these resources previously? Recall that in Section 6.1, when we considered sensitivity analysis of the right-hand sides, we identified the value of an additional unit of each resource. These values were called dual prices and are helpful to the decision maker in determining whether additional units of the resources should be made available.

The analysis in Section 6.1 led to the following dual prices for the resources in the High-Tech problem.

| Resource | Value per Additional Unit (dual price) |
|---|---|
| Assembly time | $2.80 |
| Portable display | $0.00 |
| Warehouse space | $5.20 |

The dual variables are the shadow prices; but, in a maximization problem, they also equal the dual prices. For a minimization problem, the dual prices are the negative of the dual variables.

Let us now return to the optimal solution for the HighTech dual problem. The values of the dual variables at the optimal solution are $u_1 = {}^{14}\!/_5 = 2.80$, $u_2 = 0$, and $u_3 = {}^{26}\!/_5 = 5.20$. For this maximization problem, the values of the dual variables and the dual prices are the same. For a minimization problem, the dual prices and the dual variables are the same in absolute value but have opposite signs. Thus, the optimal values of the dual variables identify the dual prices of each additional resource or input unit at the optimal solution.

In light of the preceding discussion, the following interpretation of the primal and dual problems can be made when the primal is a product-mix problem.

**Primal Problem.**   Given a per-unit value of each product, determine how much of each should be produced to maximize the value of the total production. Constraints require the amount of each resource used to be less than or equal to the amount available.

**Dual Problem.**    Given the availability of each resource, determine the per-unit value such that the total value of the resources used is minimized. Constraints require the resource value per unit be greater than or equal to the value of each unit of output.

## Using the Dual to Identify the Primal Solution

At the beginning of this section, we mentioned that an important feature of the primal-dual relationship is that when an optimal solution is reached, the value of the optimal solution for the primal problem is the same as the value of the optimal solution for the dual problem; see property 1. However, the question remains: If we solve only the dual problem, can we identify the optimal values for the primal variables?

Recall that in Section 6.1 we showed that when a primal problem is solved by the simplex method, the optimal values of the primal variables appear in the right-most column of the final tableau, and the dual prices (values of the dual variables) are found in the $z_j$ row. Since the final simplex tableau of the dual problem provides the optimal values of the dual variables, the values of the primal variables should be found in the $z_j$ row of the optimal dual tableau. This result is, in fact, the case and is formally stated as property 2.

---

### Property 2

Given the simplex tableau corresponding to the optimal dual solution, the optimal values of the primal decision variables are given by the $z_j$ entries for the surplus variables; furthermore, the optimal values of the primal slack variables are given by the negative of the $c_j - z_j$ entries for the $u_j$ variables.

---

To test your ability to find the primal solution from the optimal simplex tableau for the dual and also be able to interpret the dual variables, try parts (b) and (c) of Problem 17.

This property enables us to use the final simplex tableau for the dual of the HighTech problem to determine the optimal primal solution of $x_1 = 30$ units of the Deskpro and $x_2 = 12$ units of the Portable. These optimal values of $x_1$ and $x_2$, as well as the values for all primal slack variables, are given in the $z_j$ and $c_j - z_j$ rows of the final simplex tableau of the dual problem, which is shown again here.

|        |        | $u_1$ | $u_2$ | $u_3$ | $s_1$ | $s_2$ |       |
|--------|--------|-------|-------|-------|-------|-------|-------|
| Basis  | $c_B$  | $-150$ | $-20$ | $-300$ | 0 | 0 |       |
| $u_3$  | $-300$ | 0 | $-3/25$ | 1 | $-5/25$ | $3/25$ | $26/5$ |
| $u_1$  | $-150$ | 1 | $8/25$ | 0 | $5/25$ | $-8/25$ | $14/5$ |
| $z_j$  |        | $-150$ | $-12$ | $-300$ | 30 | 12 | $-1980$ |
| $c_j - z_j$ |   | 0 | $-8$ | 0 | $-30$ | $-12$ |       |

## Finding the Dual of Any Primal Problem

The HighTech Industries primal problem provided a good introduction to the concept of duality since it was formulated as a maximization problem in canonical form. For this form of primal problem, we have seen that conversion to the dual problem is rather easy. If the primal problem is a minimization problem in canonical form, then the dual is a maximization problem in canonical form. Therefore, finding the dual of a minimization problem in canonical form is also easy. Consider the following linear program in canonical form for a minimization problem:

$$\text{Min} \quad 6x_1 + 2x_2$$
$$\text{s.t.}$$
$$5x_1 - 1x_2 \geq 13$$
$$3x_1 + 7x_2 \geq 9$$
$$x_1, x_2 \geq 0$$

The dual is the following maximization problem in canonical form:

$$\text{Max} \quad 13u_1 + 9u_2$$
$$\text{s.t.}$$
$$5u_1 + 3u_2 \leq 6$$
$$-1u_1 + 7u_2 \leq 2$$
$$u_1, u_2 \geq 0$$

Try Problem 18 for practice in finding the dual of a minimization problem in canonical form.

While we could state a special set of rules for converting each type of primal problem into its associated dual, we believe it is easier to first convert any primal problem into an equivalent problem in canonical form. Then, we follow the procedures already established for finding the dual of a maximization or minimization problem in canonical form.

Let us illustrate the procedure for finding the dual of any linear programming problem by finding the dual of the following minimization problem:

$$\text{Min} \quad 2x_1 - 3x_2$$
$$\text{s.t.}$$
$$1x_1 + 2x_2 \leq 12$$
$$4x_1 - 2x_2 \geq 3$$
$$6x_1 - 1x_2 = 10$$
$$x_1, x_2 \geq 0$$

Since it is a minimization problem, we obtain the canonical form by converting all constraints to greater-than-or-equal-to form. For this problem, the necessary steps are as follows:

1. Convert the first constraint to greater-than-or-equal-to form by multiplying both sides of the inequality by $(-1)$. Doing so yields

$$-x_1 - 2x_2 \geq -12$$

2. Constraint 3 is an equality constraint. For an equality constraint, we first create two inequalities: one with $\leq$ form, the other with $\geq$ form. Doing so yields

$$6x_1 - 1x_2 \geq 10$$
$$6x_1 - 1x_2 \leq 10$$

Then, we multiply the $\leq$ constraint by $(-1)$ to get two $\geq$ constraints.

$$6x_1 - 1x_2 \geq \quad 10$$
$$-6x_1 + 1x_2 \geq -10$$

Now the original primal problem has been restated in the following equivalent form:

$$\text{Min} \quad 2x_1 - 3x_2$$
$$\text{s.t.}$$
$$-1x_1 - 2x_2 \geq -12$$
$$4x_1 - 2x_2 \geq \quad 3$$
$$6x_1 - 1x_2 \geq \quad 10$$
$$-6x_1 + 1x_2 \geq -10$$
$$x_1, x_2 \geq 0$$

With the primal problem now in canonical form for a minimization problem, we can easily convert to the dual problem by the primal-dual procedure presented earlier in this section. The dual becomes[2]

$$\text{Max} \quad -12u_1 + 3u_2 + 10u_3' - 10u_3''$$
$$\text{s.t.}$$
$$-1u_1 + 4u_2 + 6u_3' - 6u_3'' \leq \quad 2$$
$$-2u_1 - 2u_2 - 1u_3' + 1u_3'' \leq -3$$
$$u_1, u_2, u_3', u_3'' \geq 0$$

Can you write the dual of any linear programming problem? Try Problem 19.

Since the equality constraint required two $\geq$ constraints, we denote the dual variables associated with these constraints as $u_3'$ and $u_3''$. This notation reminds us that $u_3'$ and $u_3''$ both refer to the third constraint in the initial primal problem. Because two dual variables are associated with an equality constraint, the interpretation of the dual variable must be modified slightly. The dual variable for the equality constraint $6x_1 - 1x_2 = 10$ is given by the value of $u_3' - u_3''$ in the optimal solution to the dual. Hence, the dual variable for an equality constraint can be negative.

· · · · · · · · · · · · · · · · · · · · · · · · · · · · · · · · · · · · · · · · · · · · · · · · · · · · · · · · · · · · · · · · · · ·/ /· · · · · · · · · ·

## SUMMARY

In this chapter we showed how sensitivity analysis can be performed using the information in the final simplex tableau. This sensitivity analysis includes computing the range of optimality for objective function coefficients, dual prices, and the range of feasibility for the right-hand sides. Sensitivity information is routinely made available as part of the solution report provided by most linear programming computer packages.

---

[2] Note that the right-hand side of the second constraint is negative. Thus, we must multiply both sides of the constraint by $-1$ to obtain a positive value for the right-hand side before attempting to solve the problem with the simplex method.

We stress here that sensitivity analysis is based on the assumption that only one coefficient is allowed to change at a time; all other coefficients are assumed to remain at their original values. It is possible to do some limited sensitivity analysis on the effect of changing more than one coefficient at a time; the 100 percent rule was mentioned as being useful in this context.

In studying duality, we saw how the original linear programming problem, called the primal, can be converted into its associated dual linear programming problem. Solving either the primal or the dual provides the solution to the other. We learned that the value of the dual variable identifies the economic contribution or value of additional resources in the primal problem.

································································································/ /············

## GLOSSARY

**Range of optimality**  The range of values over which an objective function coefficient may vary without causing any change in the optimal solution (i.e., the values of all the variables will remain the same, but the value of the objective function will change).

**Dual price**  The improvement in value of the optimal solution per-unit increase in the value of the right-hand side associated with a linear programming constraint.

**Range of feasibility**  The range of values over which a $b_i$ may vary without causing the current basic solution to become infeasible. The values of the variables in the solution will change, but the same variables will remain basic. The dual prices for constraints do not change within these ranges.

**Dual problem**  A linear programming problem related to the primal problem. Solution of the dual also provides the solution to the primal.

**Primal problem**  The original formulation of a linear programming problem.

**Canonical form for a maximization problem**  A maximization problem with all less-than-or-equal-to constraints and nonnegativity requirements for the decision variables.

**Canonical form for a minimization problem**  A minimization problem with all greater-than-or-equal-to constraints and nonnegativity requirements for the decision variables.

**Dual variable**  The variable in a dual linear programming problem. Its optimal value provides the dual price for the associated primal resource.

································································································/ /············

## PROBLEMS

**SELF TEST**

1.  Consider the following linear programming problem.

$$\text{Max} \quad 5x_1 + 6x_2 + 4x_3$$

s.t.

$$3x_1 + 4x_2 + 2x_3 \leq 120$$
$$x_1 + 2x_2 + x_3 \leq 50$$
$$x_1 + 2x_2 + 3x_3 \geq 30$$
$$x_1, x_2, x_3 \geq 0$$

The optimal simplex tableau is

|  |  | $x_1$ | $x_2$ | $x_3$ | $s_1$ | $s_2$ | $s_3$ |  |
|---|---|---|---|---|---|---|---|---|
| Basic | $c_B$ | 5 | 6 | 4 | 0 | 0 | 0 |  |
| $s_3$ | 0 | 0 | 4 | 0 | −2 | 7 | 1 | 80 |
| $x_3$ | 4 | 0 | 2 | 1 | −1 | 3 | 0 | 30 |
| $x_1$ | 5 | 1 | 0 | 0 | 1 | −2 | 0 | 20 |
| $z_j$ |  | 5 | 8 | 4 | 1 | 2 | 0 | 220 |
| $c_j - z_j$ |  | 0 | −2 | 0 | −1 | −2 | 0 |  |

a. Compute the range of optimality for $c_1$.
b. Compute the range of optimality for $c_2$.
c. Compute the range of optimality for $c_{s_1}$.

2. For the HighTech problem, we found the range of optimality for $c_1$, the profit contribution per unit of the Deskpro. The final simplex tableau is given in Section 6.1. Find the following:
a. The range of optimality for $c_2$.
b. The range of optimality for $c_{s_2}$.
c. The range of optimality for $c_{s_3}$.
d. Suppose the per-unit profit contribution of the Portable ($c_2$) dropped to $35. How would the optimal solution change? What is the new value for total profit?

3. Refer to the problem formulation and optimal simplex tableau given in Problem 1.
a. Find the dual price for the first constraint.
b. Find the dual price for the second constraint.
c. Find the dual price for the third constraint.
d. Suppose the right-hand side of the first constraint is increased from 120 to 125. Find the new optimal solution and its value.
e. Suppose the right-hand side of the first constraint is decreased from 120 to 110. Find the new optimal solution and its value.

**SELF TEST**

4. Refer again to the problem formulation and optimal simplex tableau given in Problem 1.
a. Find the range of feasibility for $b_1$.
b. Find the range of feasibility for $b_2$.
c. Find the range of feasibility for $b_3$.

**SELF TEST**

5. For the HighTech problem, we found the range of feasibility for $b_1$, the assembly time available (see Section 6.1).
a. Find the range of feasibility for $b_2$.
b. Find the range of feasibility for $b_3$.
c. How much will HighTech's profit increase if there is a 20-square-foot increase in the amount of warehouse space available ($b_3$)?

6. Recall the Par, Inc., problem introduced in Chapter 2. The linear program for this problem is

$$\text{Max} \quad 10x_1 + 9x_2$$

s.t.

$$\frac{7}{10}x_1 + 1x_2 \le 630 \quad \text{Cutting and dyeing time}$$
$$\frac{1}{2}x_1 + \frac{5}{6}x_2 \le 600 \quad \text{Sewing time}$$
$$1x_1 + \frac{2}{3}x_2 \le 708 \quad \text{Finishing time}$$
$$\frac{1}{10}x_1 + \frac{1}{4}x_2 \le 135 \quad \text{Inspection and packaging time}$$
$$x_1, x_2 \ge 0$$

where

$$x_1 = \text{number of standard bags produced}$$
$$x_2 = \text{number of deluxe bags produced}$$

The final simplex tableau is

| Basis | $c_B$ | $x_1$ 10 | $x_2$ 9 | $s_1$ 0 | $s_2$ 0 | $s_3$ 0 | $s_4$ 0 | |
|---|---|---|---|---|---|---|---|---|
| $x_2$ | 9 | 0 | 1 | $^{30}/_{16}$ | 0 | $-^{21}/_{16}$ | 0 | 252 |
| $s_2$ | 0 | 0 | 0 | $-^{15}/_{16}$ | 1 | $^{5}/_{32}$ | 0 | 120 |
| $x_1$ | 10 | 1 | 0 | $-^{20}/_{16}$ | 0 | $^{30}/_{16}$ | 0 | 540 |
| $s_4$ | 0 | 0 | 0 | $-^{11}/_{32}$ | 0 | $^{9}/_{64}$ | 1 | 18 |
| $z_j$ | | 10 | 9 | $^{70}/_{16}$ | 0 | $^{111}/_{16}$ | 0 | 7668 |
| $c_j - z_j$ | | 0 | 0 | $-^{70}/_{16}$ | 0 | $-^{111}/_{16}$ | 0 | |

a. Calculate the range of optimality for the profit contribution, $c_1$, of the standard bag.
b. Calculate the range of optimality for the profit contribution, $c_2$, of the deluxe bag.
c. If the profit contribution per deluxe bag drops to $7 per unit, how will the optimal solution be affected?
d. What unit profit contribution would be necessary for the deluxe bag before Par, Inc., would consider changing its current production plan?
e. If the profit contribution of the deluxe bags can be increased to $15 per unit, what is the optimal production plan? State what you think will happen before you compute the new optimal solution.

7. For the Par, Inc., problem (Problem 6):
   a. Calculate the range of feasibility for $b_1$ (cutting and dyeing capacity).
   b. Calculate the range of feasibility for $b_2$ (sewing capacity).
   c. Calculate the range of feasibility for $b_3$ (finishing capacity).
   d. Calculate the range of feasibility for $b_4$ (inspection and packaging capacity).
   e. Which of these four departments are you interested in scheduling for overtime? Explain.

8. a. Calculate the final simplex tableau for the Par, Inc., problem (Problem 6) after increasing $b_1$ from 630 to $682^2/_{11}$.
   b. Would the current basis be optimal if $b_1$ were increased further? If not, what would be the new optimal basis?

9. Also for the Par, Inc., problem (Problem 6):
   a. How much would profit increase if an additional 30 hours became available in the cutting and dyeing department (i.e., if $b_1$ were increased from 630 to 660)?
   b. How much would profit decrease if 40 hours were removed from the sewing department?
   c. How much would profit decrease if, because of an employee accident, there were only 570 hours instead of 630 available in the cutting and dyeing department?

10. The following are additional conditions encountered by Par, Inc. (Problem 6).
    a. Suppose because of some new machinery Par, Inc., was able to make a small reduction in the amount of time it took to do the cutting and dyeing (constraint 1) for a standard bag. What effect would this reduction have on the objective function?
    b. Management believes that by buying a new sewing machine, the sewing time for standard bags can be reduced from ½ to ⅓ hour. Do you think this machine would be a good investment? Why?

11.  Recall the RMC problem (Chapter 2, Problem 21). Letting

$$x_1 = \text{tons of fuel additive produced}$$
$$x_2 = \text{tons of solvent base produced}$$

leads to the following formulation of the RMC problem:

$$\text{Max} \quad 40x_1 + 30x_2$$

s.t.

$$\frac{2}{5}x_1 + \frac{1}{2}x_2 \leq 20 \quad \text{Material 1}$$
$$\frac{1}{5}x_2 \leq 5 \quad \text{Material 2}$$
$$\frac{3}{5}x_1 + \frac{3}{10}x_2 \leq 21 \quad \text{Material 3}$$
$$x_1, x_2 \geq 0$$

The final simplex tableau is shown here.

| Basis | $c_B$ | $x_1$ 40 | $x_2$ 30 | $s_1$ 0 | $s_2$ 0 | $s_3$ 0 | |
|---|---|---|---|---|---|---|---|
| $x_2$ | 30 | 0 | 1 | $\frac{10}{3}$ | 0 | $-\frac{20}{9}$ | 20 |
| $s_2$ | 0 | 0 | 0 | $-\frac{2}{3}$ | 1 | $\frac{4}{9}$ | 1 |
| $x_1$ | 40 | 1 | 0 | $-\frac{5}{3}$ | 0 | $\frac{25}{9}$ | 25 |
| $z_j$ | | 40 | 30 | $\frac{100}{3}$ | 0 | $\frac{400}{9}$ | 1600 |
| $c_j - z_j$ | | 0 | 0 | $-\frac{100}{3}$ | 0 | $-\frac{400}{9}$ | |

   a.  Compute the ranges of optimality for $c_1$ and $c_2$.
   b.  Suppose that because of an increase in production costs, the profit per ton on the fuel additive is reduced to $30 per ton. What effect will this change have on the optimal solution?
   c.  What is the dual price for the material 1 constraint? What is the interpretation?
   d.  If RMC had an opportunity to purchase additional materials, which material would be the most valuable? How much should the company be willing to pay for this material?

12.  Refer to Problem 11.
   a.  Compute the range of feasibility for $b_1$ (material 1 availability).
   b.  Compute the range of feasibility for $b_2$ (material 2 availability).
   c.  Compute the range of feasibility for $b_3$ (material 3 availability).
   d.  What is the dual price for material 3? Over what range of values for $b_3$ is this dual price valid?

13.  Consider the following linear program:

$$\text{Max} \quad 3x_1 + 1x_2 + 5x_3 + 3x_4$$

s.t.

$$3x_1 + 1x_2 + 2x_3 \qquad = 30$$
$$2x_1 + 1x_2 + 3x_3 + 1x_4 \geq 15$$
$$2x_2 \qquad + 3x_4 \leq 25$$
$$x_1, x_2, x_3, x_4 \geq 0$$

   a.  Find the optimal solution.
   b.  Calculate the range of optimality for $c_3$.
   c.  What would be the effect of a four-unit decrease in $c_3$ (from 5 to 1) on the optimal solution and the value of that solution?

d.  Calculate the range of optimality for $c_2$.
e.  What would be the effect of a three-unit increase in $c_2$ (from 1 to 4) on the optimal solution and the value of that solution?

14.  Consider the final simplex tableau shown here.

| Basis | $c_B$ | $x_1$ | $x_2$ | $x_3$ | $x_4$ | $s_1$ | $s_2$ | $s_3$ | |
|---|---|---|---|---|---|---|---|---|---|
| | | 4 | 6 | 3 | 1 | 0 | 0 | 0 | |
| $x_3$ | 3 | $3/60$ | 0 | 1 | $1/2$ | $3/10$ | 0 | $-6/30$ | 125 |
| $s_2$ | 0 | $195/60$ | 0 | 0 | $-1/2$ | $-5/10$ | 1 | $-1$ | 425 |
| $x_2$ | 6 | $39/60$ | 1 | 0 | $1/2$ | $-1/10$ | 0 | $12/30$ | 25 |
| $z_j$ | | $81/20$ | 6 | 3 | $9/2$ | $3/10$ | 0 | $54/30$ | 525 |
| $c_j - z_j$ | | $-1/20$ | 0 | 0 | $-7/2$ | $-3/10$ | 0 | $-54/30$ | |

The original right-hand-side values were $b_1 = 550$, $b_2 = 700$, and $b_3 = 200$.
a.  Calculate the range of feasibility for $b_1$.
b.  Calculate the range of feasibility for $b_2$.
c.  Calculate the range of feasibility for $b_3$.

15.  Consider the following linear program:

$$\text{Max} \quad 15x_1 + 30x_2 + 20x_3$$
$$\text{s.t.}$$
$$1x_1 \quad\quad + 1x_3 \leq 4$$
$$0.5x_1 + 2x_2 + 1x_3 \leq 3$$
$$1x_1 + 1x_2 + 2x_3 \leq 6$$
$$x_1, x_2, x_3 \geq 0$$

Solve using the simplex method, and answer the following questions:
a.  What is the optimal solution?
b.  What is the value of the objective function?
c.  Which constraints are the binding constraints?
d.  How much slack is available in the nonbinding constraints?
e.  What are the dual prices associated with the three constraints? Which right-hand-side value would have the greatest effect on the value of the objective function if it could be changed?
f.  Develop the appropriate ranges for the coefficients of the objective function. What is your interpretation of these ranges?
g.  Develop and interpret the ranges of feasibility for the right-hand-side values.

16.  Recall the Innis Investments problem (Chapter 2, Problem 37). Letting

$$x_1 = \text{units purchased in the stock fund}$$
$$x_2 = \text{units purchased in the money market fund}$$

leads to the following formulation:

$$\text{Min} \quad 8x_1 + 3x_2 \quad\quad\quad \text{Total risk}$$
$$\text{s.t.}$$
$$50x_1 + 100x_2 \leq 1{,}200{,}000 \quad \text{Funds available}$$
$$5x_1 + 4x_2 \geq 60{,}000 \quad \text{Annual income}$$
$$1x_2 \geq 3{,}000 \quad \text{Minimum units in money market}$$
$$x_1, x_2 \geq 0$$

a.  Solve this problem using the simplex method.
b.  The value of the optimal solution is a measure of the riskiness of the portfolio. What effect will increasing the annual income requirement have on the riskiness of the portfolio?
c.  Find the range of feasibility for $b_2$.
d.  How will the optimal solution and its value change if the annual income requirement is increased from \$60,000 to \$65,000?
e.  How will the optimal solution and its value change if the risk measure for the stock fund is increased from 8 to 9?

17. Suppose that in a product-mix problem $x_1$, $x_2$, $x_3$, and $x_4$ indicate the units of products 1, 2, 3, and 4, respectively, and we have

$$\text{Max} \quad 4x_1 + 6x_2 + 3x_3 + 1x_4$$
s.t.
$$1.5x_1 + 2x_2 + 4x_3 + 3x_4 \le 550 \quad \text{Machine A hours}$$
$$4x_1 + 1x_2 + 2x_3 + 1x_4 \le 700 \quad \text{Machine B hours}$$
$$2x_1 + 3x_2 + 1x_3 + 2x_4 \le 200 \quad \text{Machine C hours}$$
$$x_1, x_2, x_3, x_4 \ge 0$$

a.  Formulate the dual to this problem.
b.  Solve the dual. Use the dual solution to show that the profit-maximizing product mix is $x_1 = 0$, $x_2 = 25$, $x_3 = 125$, and $x_4 = 0$.
c.  Use the dual variables to identify the machine or machines that are producing at maximum capacity. If the manager can select one machine for additional production capacity, which machine should have priority? Why?

18. Find the dual for the following linear program:

$$\text{Min} \quad 2800x_1 + 6000x_2 + 1200x_3$$
s.t.
$$15x_1 + 15x_2 + 1x_3 \ge 5$$
$$4x_1 + 8x_2 \ge 5$$
$$12x_1 + 8x_3 \ge 24$$
$$x_1, x_2, x_3 \ge 0$$

19. Write the following primal problem in canonical form, and find its dual.

$$\text{Max} \quad 3x_1 + 1x_2 + 5x_3 + 3x_4$$
s.t.
$$3x_1 + 1x_2 + 2x_3 = 30$$
$$2x_1 + 1x_2 + 3x_3 + 1x_4 \ge 15$$
$$2x_2 + 3x_4 \le 25$$
$$x_1, x_2, x_3, x_4 \ge 0$$

20. Photo Chemicals produces two types of photograph-developing fluids at a cost of \$1.00 per gallon. Let

$$x_1 = \text{gallons of product 1}$$
$$x_2 = \text{gallons of product 2}$$

Photo Chemicals management has required that at least 30 gallons of product 1 and at least 20 gallons of product 2 be produced. They have also required that at least 80 pounds of a perishable raw material be used in production. A linear programming formulation of the problem is as follows:

$$\text{Min} \quad 1x_1 + 1x_2$$

s.t.

$$1x_1 \qquad\qquad \geq 30 \quad \text{Minimum product 1}$$
$$1x_2 \geq 20 \quad \text{Minimum product 2}$$
$$1x_1 + 2x_2 \geq 80 \quad \text{Minimum raw material}$$
$$x_1, x_2 \geq 0$$

a. Show the dual problem.
b. Solve the dual problem, and show from it that the optimal production plan is $x_1 = 30$ and $x_2 = 25$.
c. The third constraint involves a management request that the current 80 pounds of a perishable raw material be used. However, after learning that the optimal solution calls for an excess production of five units of product 2, management is reconsidering the raw material requirement. Specifically, you have been asked to identify the cost effect if this constraint is relaxed. Use the dual variable to indicate the change in the cost if only 79 pounds of raw material have to be used.

21. Consider the following linear programming problem:

$$\text{Min} \quad 4x_1 + 3x_2 + 6x_3$$

s.t.

$$1x_1 + 0.5x_2 + 1x_3 \geq 15$$
$$2x_2 + 1x_3 \geq 30$$
$$1x_1 + 1x_2 + 2x_3 \geq 20$$
$$x_1, x_2, x_3 \geq 0$$

a. Write the dual problem.
b. Solve the dual.
c. Use the dual solution to identify the optimal solution to the original primal problem.
d. Verify that the optimal values for the primal and dual problems are equal.

22. A sales representative who sells two products is trying to determine the number of sales calls that should be made during the next month to promote each product. Based on past experience, there is an average $10 commission for every call on product 1 and a $5 commission for every call on product 2. The company requires at least 20 calls per month for each product and not more than 100 calls per month on any one product. In addition, the sales representative spends about 3 hours on each call for product 1 and 1 hour on each call for product 2. If there are a total of 175 selling hours available next month, how many calls should be made for each of the two products to maximize the commission?
a. Formulate a linear program for this problem.
b. Formulate and solve the dual problem.
c. Use the final simplex tableau for the dual to determine the optimal number of calls for the products. What is the maximum commission?
d. Interpret the values of the dual variables.

23. Consider the linear program

$$\text{Max} \quad 3x_1 + 2x_2$$

s.t.

$$1x_1 + 2x_2 \leq 8$$
$$2x_1 + 1x_2 \leq 10$$
$$x_1, x_2 \geq 0$$

a.  Solve this problem using the simplex method. Keep a record of the value of the objective function at each extreme point.
b.  Formulate and solve the dual of this problem using the graphical procedure.
c.  Compute the value of the dual objective function for each extreme-point solution of the dual problem.
d.  Compare the values of the objective function for each primal and dual extreme-point solution.
e.  Can a dual feasible solution yield a value less than a primal feasible solution? Can you state a result concerning bounds on the value of the primal solution provided by any feasible solution to the dual problem?

24. Suppose the optimal solution to a three-variable linear programming problem has $x_1 = 10$, $x_2 = 30$, and $x_3 = 15$. It is later discovered that the following two constraints were inadvertently omitted when formulating the problem.

$$6x_1 + 4x_2 - 1x_3 \leq 170$$
$$\tfrac{1}{4}x_1 + 1x_2 \quad\;\; \geq 25$$

Find the new optimal solution if possible. If it is not possible, state that it is not possible and why.

# PERFORMANCE ANALYSIS CORPORATION*

## CHAPEL HILL, NORTH CAROLINA

Performance Analysis Corporation, founded in 1979, is a management consulting company that specializes in the use of management science to design more efficient and effective operations for a wide variety of chain stores. Performance Analysis Corporation has evaluated the operation of banks, savings and loans, and grocery chains. The company has also been involved in evaluating the efficiency of fast-food outlets. In the following application, we describe how linear programming methodology has been used to provide an evaluation model for a chain of fast-food restaurants.

### Fast-Food Business

The fast-food business for a chain such as McDonald's or Kentucky Fried Chicken is characterized by hundreds, or even thousands, of individual restaurants, some of which are company owned and some of which are franchised. A typical restaurant may gross close to a million dollars annually; thus, the impact of relatively minor improvements at a large proportion of the restaurants can have a substantial effect on a chain's profitability and market share.

Although each individual restaurant in a given chain usually offers the same type of menu (with some minor geographical variations), they must often deal with vastly different environments and competition. In addition, the age of the restaurant, facade used, ease of access and egress, hours of operation, scale of operation, and so on can vary substantially from restaurant to restaurant.

A major objective of company management in the fast-food industry involves the performance evaluations of managers of individual restaurants in the chain. These evaluations are the basis for awarding year-end bonuses and for personal advancement purposes. Unfortunately, no single measure of performance such as profit can be used as the basis for the evaluation because other measures such as market share and rate of growth are also important.

### A Linear Programming Evaluation Model

One approach to the store evaluation problem utilizes the concept of Pareto optimality. According to this concept, a restaurant in a given chain is *relatively* inefficient if other restaurants in the same chain have the following characteristics:

1. Have the same or worse environment.
2. Produce at least the same levels of *all* outputs.
3. Utilize no more of *any* resource and *less* of at least one of the resources.

The mechanism for discovering which of the restaurants are Pareto inefficient involves the development and solution of a linear programming model.** Constraints on the problem involve requirements concerning the minimum acceptable levels of output (e.g., profit and market share) and conditions imposed by uncontrollable elements in the environment. The objective function calls for the minimization of the resources necessary to produce the output. Solution of the model produces the following output for each restaurant:

1. A score that assesses the level of so-called relative technical efficiency achieved by the particular restaurant over the time period in question.

---

*The authors are indebted to Richard C. Morey for providing this application.

**The model used is the data envelopment analysis model discussed in Section 4.5.

2. The reduction in controllable resources and/or the augmentation of outputs over the time period in question for an inefficient restaurant to have been rated as efficient.

3. A peer group of other restaurants with which each restaurant can be compared in the future.

Sensitivity analysis, especially that concerning the dual prices, provides important managerial information. For each constraint concerning a minimum acceptable output level, the dual price tells the manager how much one more unit of output would increase his/her efficiency measure. Analysis of the ranges for each of the constraint coefficients (the $a_{ij}$ values) provides information concerning how much outputs could be reduced or inputs increased before the restaurant would become inefficient.

## Types of Factors Utilized

The approach is capable of handling three types of factors: quantitative controllable factors, such as salaries paid or local advertising expenditures; noncontrollable quantitative factors, such as the median income in the geographic area served by the restaurant or the unemployment rate; and qualitative factors, such as the degree of competition or appearance of restaurant. The outputs include total sales of various types (e.g., by time of day), profits, market share, rate of growth of sales, and so forth.

## Benefits

The analysis typically identifies 40–50% of the restaurants as underperforming, given the previously stated conditions concerning the inputs available and outputs produced. Performance Analysis Corporation has found that if all of the relative inefficiencies identified are eliminated simultaneously, the resulting increase in corporate profits is typically in the neighborhood of 5–10%. This increase is truly substantial given the large scale of operations involved.

The district manager has an objective score card for each restaurant manager that indicates areas (e.g., overtime salary) where improvements may be in order. The efficient restaurants can be used to generate a set of best practices that can be models for other restaurants. Of primary benefit are the reactions of restaurant managers who appreciate that the evaluation process they are subject to recognizes the environment they are forced to operate within; deals with noncommensurability of outputs involved; is theory based and nonpolitical; and is defensible, understandable, and equitable.

## Questions

1. State in your own words what it means for one restaurant in a chain to be relatively inefficient when compared to another restaurant in the same chain.

2. Suppose the evaluation model showed that for a particular restaurant the resource mix necessary to produce a given output mix was 90% of what another restaurant was using to produce that same mix of output. Would you conclude that the restaurant was relatively efficient or inefficient? Why?

# 7

## TRANSPORTATION, ASSIGNMENT, AND TRANSSHIPMENT PROBLEMS

### CONTENTS

Transportation, assignment, and transshipment problems belong to a special class of linear programming problems called *network flow problems.* A separate chapter is devoted to these problems for two reasons. First, a wide variety of applications can be modeled as transportation, assignment, or transshipment problems. Second, these problems have a mathematical structure that has enabled management scientists to develop efficient specialized solution procedures; as a result, large problems can usually be solved with just a few seconds of computer time.

We will approach the network flow problems by illustrating each problem with a specific application. We first develop a graphical representation, called a *network,* of the problem and then show how each can be formulated and solved as a linear program. We present special-purpose solution procedures for the transportation and assignment problems in the last two sections of the chapter.

An applications-oriented introduction to the transportation, assignment, and transshipment problems can be obtained by covering Sections 7.1–7.4. Sections 7.5 and 7.6, involving special-purpose algorithms, are optional and can be skipped without loss of continuity.

## 7.1 TRANSPORTATION PROBLEM: A NETWORK MODEL AND A LINEAR PROGRAMMING FORMULATION

The **transportation problem** arises frequently in planning for the distribution of goods and services from several supply locations to several demand locations. Typically, the quantity of goods available at each supply location (origin) is limited, and the quantity of goods needed at each of several demand locations (destinations) is known. The usual objective in a transportation problem is to minimize the cost of shipping goods from the origins to the destinations.

Let us illustrate by considering a transportation problem faced by Foster Generators. This problem involves the transportation of a product from three plants to four distribution centers. Foster Generators has plants in Cleveland, Ohio; Bedford, Indiana; and York, Pennsylvania. Production capacities over the next 3-month planning period for one particular type of generator are as follows:

| Origin | Plant | 3-Month Production Capacity (units) |
|--------|-------|:---:|
| 1 | Cleveland | 5000 |
| 2 | Bedford | 6000 |
| 3 | York | 2500 |
| | Total | 13,500 |

The firm distributes its generators through four regional distribution centers located in Boston, Chicago, St. Louis, and Lexington; the 3-month forecast of demand for the distribution centers is as follows:

| Destination | Distribution Center | 3-Month Demand Forecast (units) |
|---|---|---|
| 1 | Boston | 6000 |
| 2 | Chicago | 4000 |
| 3 | St. Louis | 2000 |
| 4 | Lexington | 1500 |
| | Total | 13,500 |

Management would like to determine how much of its production should be shipped from each plant to each distribution center. Figure 7.1 shows graphically the 12 distribution routes Foster can use. Such a graph is called a **network;** the circles are referred to as **nodes** and the lines connecting the nodes as **arcs.** Each origin and destination is represented by a node, and each possible shipping route is represented by an arc. The amount of the supply is written next to each origin node, and the amount of the demand is written next to each destination node. The goods shipped from the origins to the destinations represent the flow in the network. Note that the direction of flow (from origin to destination) is indicated by the arrows.

Try Problem I for practice in developing a network model of a transportation problem.

For Foster's transportation problem, the objective is to determine the routes to be used and the quantity to be shipped via each route that will provide the minimum total transportation cost. The cost for each unit shipped on each route is given in Table 7.1 and is shown on each arc in Figure 7.1.

The first subscript identifies the "from" node of the corresponding arc and the second subscript identifies the "to" node of the arc.

A linear programming model can be used to solve this transportation problem. We will use double-subscripted decision variables, with $x_{11}$ denoting the number of units shipped from origin 1 (Cleveland) to destination 1 (Boston), $x_{12}$ denoting the number of units shipped from origin 1 (Cleveland) to destination 2 (Chicago), and so on. In general, the decision variables for a transportation problem having $m$ origins and $n$ destinations are written as follows:

$$x_{ij} = \text{number of units shipped from origin } i \text{ to destination } j$$
$$\text{where } i = 1, 2, \ldots, m, \text{ and } j = 1, 2, \ldots, n$$

Because the objective of the transportation problem is to minimize the total transportation cost, we can use the cost data in Table 7.1 or on the arcs in Figure 7.1 to develop the following cost expressions:

Transportation costs for
units shipped from Cleveland $= 3x_{11} + 2x_{12} + 7x_{13} + 6x_{14}$

Transportation costs for
units shipped from Bedford $\ \ = 7x_{21} + 5x_{22} + 2x_{23} + 3x_{24}$

Transportation costs for
units shipped from York $\ \ \ \ \ = 2x_{31} + 5x_{32} + 4x_{33} + 5x_{34}$

The sum of these expressions provides the objective function showing the total transportation cost for Foster Generators.

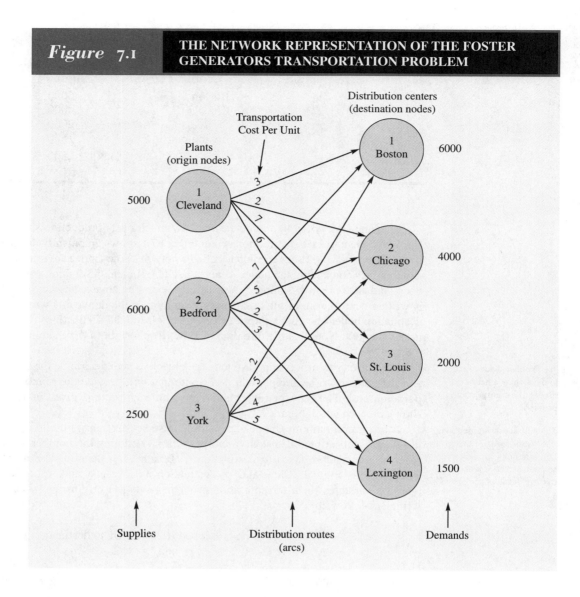

**Figure 7.1 — THE NETWORK REPRESENTATION OF THE FOSTER GENERATORS TRANSPORTATION PROBLEM**

**Table 7.1 — TRANSPORTATION COST PER UNIT FOR THE FOSTER GENERATORS TRANSPORTATION PROBLEM**

| | Destination | | | |
|---|---|---|---|---|
| **Origin** | **Boston** | **Chicago** | **St. Louis** | **Lexington** |
| Cleveland | 3 | 2 | 7 | 6 |
| Bedford | 7 | 5 | 2 | 3 |
| York | 2 | 5 | 4 | 5 |

Transportation problems need constraints because each origin has a limited supply and each destination has a specific demand. We will consider the supply constraints first. The capacity at the Cleveland plant is 5000 units. With the total number of units shipped from the Cleveland plant expressed as $x_{11} + x_{12} + x_{13} + x_{14}$, the supply constraint for the Cleveland plant is

$$x_{11} + x_{12} + x_{13} + x_{14} \leq 5000 \quad \text{Cleveland supply}$$

With three origins (plants), the Foster transportation problem has three supply constraints. Given the capacity of 6000 units at the Bedford plant and 2500 units at the York plant, the two additional supply constraints are

$$x_{21} + x_{22} + x_{23} + x_{24} \leq 6000 \quad \text{Bedford supply}$$
$$x_{31} + x_{32} + x_{33} + x_{34} \leq 2500 \quad \text{York supply}$$

With the four distribution centers as the destinations, four demand constraints are needed to ensure that destination demands will be satisfied:

To obtain a feasible solution, the total supply must be greater than or equal to the total demand.

$$x_{11} + x_{21} + x_{31} = 6000 \quad \text{Boston demand}$$
$$x_{12} + x_{22} + x_{32} = 4000 \quad \text{Chicago demand}$$
$$x_{13} + x_{23} + x_{33} = 2000 \quad \text{St. Louis demand}$$
$$x_{14} + x_{24} + x_{34} = 1500 \quad \text{Lexington demand}$$

Combining the objective function and constraints into one model provides a 12-variable, 7-constraint linear programming formulation of the Foster Generators transportation problem:

Min $3x_{11} + 2x_{12} + 7x_{13} + 6x_{14} + 7x_{21} + 5x_{22} + 2x_{23} + 3x_{24} + 2x_{31} + 5x_{32} + 4x_{33} + 5x_{34}$

s.t.

$$
\begin{array}{llll}
x_{11} + x_{12} + x_{13} + x_{14} & & & \leq 5000 \\
& x_{21} + x_{22} + x_{23} + x_{24} & & \leq 6000 \\
& & x_{31} + x_{32} + x_{33} + x_{34} & \leq 2500 \\
x_{11} & + x_{21} & + x_{31} & = 6000 \\
\quad x_{12} & + x_{22} & + x_{32} & = 4000 \\
\qquad x_{13} & + x_{23} & + x_{33} & = 2000 \\
\qquad\quad x_{14} & + x_{24} & + x_{34} & = 1500 \\
\end{array}
$$

$x_{ij} \geq 0 \quad$ for $i = 1, 2, 3; j = 1, 2, 3, 4$

Comparing the linear programming formulation to the network in Figure 7.1 leads to several observations. All the information needed for the linear programming formulation is on the network. Each node requires one constraint and each arc requires one variable. The sum of the variables corresponding to arcs from an origin node must be less than or equal to the origin's supply, and the sum of the variables corresponding to the arcs into a destination node must be equal to the destination's demand.

We solved the Foster Generators problem with the linear programming module of The Management Scientist. The computer solution (see Figure 7.2) shows that the minimum total transportation cost is $39,500. The values for the decision variables show the

| Figure 7.2 | THE MANAGEMENT SCIENTIST SOLUTION FOR THE FOSTER GENERATORS TRANSPORTATIONA PROBLEM |
| --- | --- |

```
Objective Function Value =           39500.000

       Variable              Value              Reduced Costs
     -------------       ---------------       ----------------
         X11               3500.000                0.000
         X12               1500.000                0.000
         X13                  0.000                8.000
         X14                  0.000                6.000
         X21                  0.000                1.000
         X22               2500.000                0.000
         X23               2000.000                0.000
         X24               1500.000                0.000
         X31               2500.000                0.000
         X32                  0.000                4.000
         X33                  0.000                6.000
         X34                  0.000                6.000
```

Try Problem 2 to test your ability to formulate and solve a linear programming model of a transportation problem.

optimal amounts to ship over each route. For example, with $x_{11} = 3500$, 3500 units should be shipped from Cleveland to Boston, and with $x_{12} = 1500$, 1500 units should be shipped from Cleveland to Chicago. Other values of the decision variables indicate the remaining shipping quantities and routes. Table 7.2 shows the minimum-cost transportation schedule and Figure 7.3 summarizes the optimal solution on the network.

## Problem Variations

The Foster Generators problem illustrates use of the basic transportation model. Variations of the basic transportation model may involve one or more of the following situations:

1. Total supply not equal to total demand
2. Maximization objective function
3. Route capacities or route minimums
4. Unacceptable routes

| Table 7.2 | OPTIMAL SOLUTION TO THE FOSTER GENERATORS TRANSPORTATION PROBLEM |
| --- | --- |

| Route | | Units | Cost | Total |
| From | To | Shipped | Per Unit | Cost |
| --- | --- | --- | --- | --- |
| Cleveland | Boston | 3500 | $3 | $10,500 |
| Cleveland | Chicago | 1500 | $2 | 3,000 |
| Bedford | Chicago | 2500 | $5 | 12,500 |
| Bedford | St. Louis | 2000 | $2 | 4,000 |
| Bedford | Lexington | 1500 | $3 | 4,500 |
| York | Boston | 2500 | $2 | 5,000 |
| | | | | $39,500 |

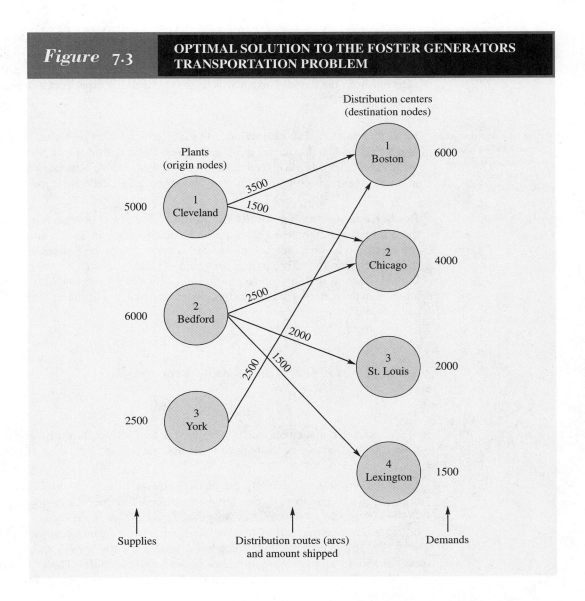

**Figure 7.3    OPTIMAL SOLUTION TO THE FOSTER GENERATORS TRANSPORTATION PROBLEM**

With slight modifications in the linear programming model, we can easily accommodate these situations.

**Total Supply Not Equal to Total Demand.**    Often *the total supply is not equal to the total demand.* If total supply exceeds total demand, no modification in the linear programming formulation is necessary. Excess supply will appear as slack in the linear programming solution. Slack for any particular origin can be interpreted as the unused supply or amount not shipped from the origin.

If total supply is less than total demand, the linear programming model of a transportation problem will not have a feasible solution. In this case, we modify the network representation by adding a *dummy origin* with a supply equal to the difference between the total demand and the total supply. With the addition of the dummy origin, and an arc from the dummy origin to each destination, the linear programming model will have a feasible solution. A zero cost per unit is assigned to each arc leaving the dummy origin so that the

Whenever total supply is less than total demand, the model does not determine how the unsatisfied demand is handled (e.g., backorders). The manager must handle this aspect of the problem.

value of the optimal solution for the revised problem will represent the shipping cost for the units actually shipped (no shipments actually will be made from the dummy origin). When the optimal solution is implemented, the destinations showing shipments being received from the dummy origin will be the destinations experiencing a shortfall or unsatisfied demand.

Try Problem 8 to test your ability to handle a case where demand is greater than supply with a maximization objective.

**Maximization Objective Function.** In some transportation problems, the objective is to find a solution that maximizes profit or revenue. Using the values for profit or revenue per unit as coefficients in the objective function, we simply solve a maximization rather than a minimization linear program. This change does not affect the constraints.

**Route Capacities and/or Route Minimums.** The linear programming formulation of the transportation problem also can accommodate capacities and/or minimum quantities for one or more of the routes. For example, suppose that in the Foster Generators problem the York-Boston route (origin 3 to destination 1) had a capacity of 1000 units because of limited space availability on its normal mode of transportation. With $x_{31}$ denoting the amount shipped from York to Boston, the route capacity constraint for the York-Boston route would be

$$x_{31} \leq 1000$$

Similarly, route minimums can be specified. For example,

$$x_{22} \geq 2000$$

would guarantee that a previously committed order for a Bedford-Chicago delivery of at least 2000 units would be maintained in the optimal solution.

**Unacceptable Routes.** Finally, establishing a route from every origin to every destination may not be possible. To handle this situation, we simply drop the corresponding arc from the network and remove the corresponding variable from the linear programming formulation. For example, if the Cleveland-St. Louis route were unacceptable or unusable, the arc from Cleveland to St. Louis could be dropped in Figure 7.1, and $x_{13}$ could be removed from the linear programming formulation. Solving the resulting 11-variable, 7-constraint model would provide the optimal solution while guaranteeing that the Cleveland-St. Louis route is not used.

## A General Linear Programming Model of the Transportation Problem

To show the general linear programming model of the transportation problem, we use the notation:

$$i = \text{index for origins, } i = 1, 2, \ldots, m$$
$$j = \text{index for destinations, } j = 1, 2, \ldots, n$$
$$x_{ij} = \text{number of units shipped from origin } i \text{ to destination } j$$
$$c_{ij} = \text{cost per unit of shipping from origin } i \text{ to destination } j$$
$$s_i = \text{supply or capacity in units at origin } i$$
$$d_j = \text{demand in units at destination } j$$

The general linear programming model of the $m$-origin, $n$-destination transportation problem is

$$\text{Min} \quad \sum_{i=1}^{m} \sum_{j=1}^{n} c_{ij} x_{ij}$$

s.t.

$$\sum_{j=1}^{n} x_{ij} \leq s_i \qquad i = 1, 2, \ldots, m \quad \text{Supply}$$

$$\sum_{i=1}^{m} x_{ij} = d_j \qquad j = 1, 2, \ldots, n \quad \text{Demand}$$

$$x_{ij} \geq 0 \qquad \text{for all } i \text{ and } j$$

As mentioned previously, we can add constraints of the form $x_{ij} \leq L_{ij}$ if the route from origin $i$ to destination $j$ has capacity $L_{ij}$. A transportation problem that includes constraints of this type is called a **capacitated transportation problem.** Similarly, we can add route minimum constraints of the form $x_{ij} \geq M_{ij}$ if the route from origin $i$ to destination $j$ must handle at least $M_{ij}$ units.

## N O T E S and Comments

1. Transportation problems encountered in practice usually lead to large linear programs. Transportation problems with 100 origins and 100 destinations are not unusual. Such a problem would involve $(100)(100) = 10,000$ variables. For such a problem, special-purpose solution procedures (see Section 7.5) are much more efficient than general-purpose linear programming codes. But if speed is not an issue, a general-purpose linear programming code that has the capability to solve large problems will solve most transportation problems.

2. To handle a situation in which some routes may be unacceptable, we stated that you could drop the corresponding arc from the network and remove the corresponding variable from the linear programming formulation. Another approach often used is to assign an extremely large objective function cost coefficient to any unacceptable arc. If the problem has already been formulated, another option is to add a constraint to the formulation that sets the variable you want to remove equal to zero.

3. The optimal solution to a transportation model will consist of integer values for the decision variables as long as all supply and demand values are integers. The reason is the special mathematical structure of the linear programming model. Each variable appears in exactly one supply and one demand constraint, and all coefficients in the constraint equations are 1s and 0s.

4. Although many transportation problems involve minimizing the cost of transporting goods between locations, many other applications of the transportation model exist. The Management Science in Action: Marine Corps Mobilization illustrates the use of a transportation model to send Marine Corps officers to billets.

# MANAGEMENT SCIENCE IN ACTION

## MARINE CORPS MOBILIZATION*

The U.S. Marine Corps has developed a network model for mobilizing its officers in the event of a world crisis or war. The problem is to send officers to billets (duty assignments) as quickly as possible. The model developed to solve this problem is a transportation model much like the ones discussed in this chapter, only much larger. The origins or supply nodes represent the officers available, and the destinations or demand nodes represent the billets. A realistic implementation might involve as many as 40,000 officers and 25,000 billets. If all officer-to-billets arc combinations are permitted, the transportation problem would have 1 billion arcs. To reduce the problem size, officers with similar qualifications are aggregated into the same supply node and similar duty assignments are aggregated into the same demand nodes. Using this approach and methods for eliminating infeasible arcs, the Marine Corps has solved problems involving 27,000 officers and 10,000 billets in 10 seconds on a personal computer.

Excellent results in sending officers of appropriate grade and job qualifications to the desired billets have been obtained. In a crisis, the availability and use of this system can make the difference between an appropriate response and disaster. The prior system required 2–4 days to produce a complete mobilization plan and provided a lower quality match between officer qualifications and billet needs. The Marine Corps is now using the mobilization model to enhance its peacetime capability.

*Based on D.O. Bausch, G.G. Brown, D.R. Hundley, S.H. Rapp, and R.E. Rosenthal, "Mobilizing Marine Corps Officers," *Interfaces* (July–August 1991); pp. 26–38.

## 7.2 ASSIGNMENT PROBLEM: THE NETWORK MODEL AND A LINEAR PROGRAMMING FORMULATION

The **assignment problem** arises in a variety of decision-making situations; typical assignment problems involve assigning jobs to machines, agents to tasks, sales personnel to sales territories, contracts to bidders, and so on. A distinguishing feature of the assignment problem is that *one* agent is assigned to *one and only one* task. Specifically, we look for the set of assignments that will optimize a stated objective, such as minimize cost, minimize time, or maximize profit.

To illustrate the assignment problem, let us consider the case of Fowle Marketing Research which has just received requests for market research studies from three new clients. The company faces the task of assigning a project leader (agent) to each client (task). Currently, three individuals have no other commitments and are available for the project leader assignments. Fowle's management realizes, however, that the time required to complete each study will depend on the experience and ability of the project leader assigned. The three projects have approximately the same priority, and the company wants to assign project leaders to minimize the total number of days required to complete all three projects. If a project leader is to be assigned to one client only, what assignments should be made?

To answer the assignment question, Fowle's management must first consider all possible project leader–client assignments and then estimate the corresponding project completion times. With three project leaders and three clients, nine assignment alternatives are possible. The alternatives and the estimated project completion times in days are summarized in Table 7.3.

Try part (a) of Problem 12 for practice in developing a network model for an assignment problem.

Figure 7.4 shows the network representation of Fowle's assignment problem. The nodes correspond to the project leaders and clients, and the arcs represent the possible assignments of project leaders to clients. The supply at each origin node and the demand at each destination node are 1; the cost of assigning a project leader to a client is the time it takes that project leader to complete the client's task. Note the similarity between the network mod-

| | | Client | |
|---|:---:|:---:|:---:|
| **Project Leader** | **1** | **2** | **3** |
| 1. Terry | 10 | 15 | 9 |
| 2. Carle | 9 | 18 | 5 |
| 3. McClymonds | 6 | 14 | 3 |

**Table 7.3** ESTIMATED PROJECT COMPLETION TIMES (DAYS) FOR THE FOWLE MARKETING RESEARCH ASSIGNMENT PROBLEM

els of the assignment problem (Figure 7.4) and the transportation problem (Figure 7.1). The assignment problem is a special case of the transportation problem in which all supply and demand values equal 1 and the amount shipped over each arc is either 0 or 1.

Since the assignment problem is a special case of the transportation problem, a linear programming formulation can be developed. Again, we need a constraint for each node and a variable for each arc. As in the transportation problem, we use double-subscripted

**Figure 7.4** A NETWORK MODEL OF THE FOWLE MARKETING RESEARCH ASSIGNMENT PROBLEM

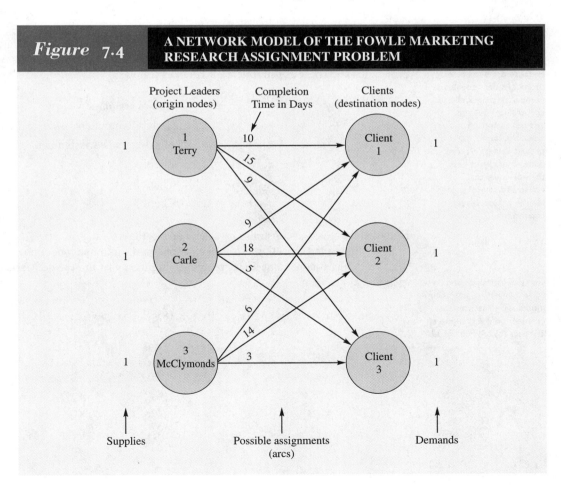

decision variables, with $x_{11}$ denoting the assignment of project leader 1 (Terry) to client 1, $x_{12}$ denoting the assignment of project leader 1 (Terry) to client 2, and so on. Thus, we define the decision variables for Fowle's assignment problem as

$$x_{ij} = \begin{cases} 1 \text{ if project leader } i \text{ is assigned to client } j \\ 0 \text{ otherwise} \end{cases}$$
$$\text{where } i = 1, 2, 3; j = 1, 2, 3$$

Using this notation and the completion time data in Table 7.3, we develop completion time expressions:

Days required for Terry's assignment $= 10x_{11} + 15x_{12} + 9x_{13}$
Days required for Carle's assignment $= 9x_{21} + 18x_{22} + 5x_{23}$
Days required for McClymonds's assignment $= 6x_{31} + 14x_{32} + 3x_{33}$

The sum of the completion times for the three project leaders will provide the total days required to complete the three assignments. Thus, the objective function is

$$\text{Min} \quad 10x_{11} + 15x_{12} + 9x_{13} + 9x_{21} + 18x_{22} + 5x_{23} + 6x_{31} + 14x_{32} + 3x_{33}$$

The constraints for the assignment problem reflect the conditions that each project leader can be assigned to at most one client and that each client must have one assigned project leader. These constraints are written as follows:

$x_{11} + x_{12} + x_{13} \le 1$   Terry's assignment
$x_{21} + x_{22} + x_{23} \le 1$   Carle's assignment
$x_{31} + x_{32} + x_{33} \le 1$   McClymonds's assignment
$x_{11} + x_{21} + x_{31} = 1$   Client 1
$x_{12} + x_{22} + x_{32} = 1$   Client 2
$x_{13} + x_{23} + x_{33} = 1$   Client 3

Because the number of project leaders equals the number of clients, all the constraints could be written as equalities. But when the number of project leaders exceeds the number of clients, less-than-or-equal-to constraints must be used for the project leader constraints.

Note that there is one constraint for each node in Figure 7.4.

Combining the objective function and constraints into one model provides the following 9-variable, 6-constraint linear programming model of the Fowle Marketing Research assignment problem.

Can you formulate and solve a linear programming model for an assignment problem on the computer? Try part (b) of Problem 12.

$$\text{Min} \quad 10x_{11} + 15x_{12} + 9x_{13} + 9x_{21} + 18x_{22} + 5x_{23} + 6x_{31} + 14x_{32} + 3x_{33}$$
s.t.

$$\begin{array}{llll}
x_{11} + x_{12} + x_{13} & & & \le 1 \\
& x_{21} + x_{22} + x_{23} & & \le 1 \\
& & x_{31} + x_{32} + x_{33} & \le 1 \\
x_{11} & + x_{21} & + x_{31} & = 1 \\
x_{12} & + x_{22} & + x_{32} & = 1 \\
x_{13} & + x_{23} & + x_{33} & = 1
\end{array}$$

$$x_{ij} \ge 0 \text{ for } i = 1, 2, 3; j = 1, 2, 3$$

**Figure 7.5**    THE MANAGEMENT SCIENTIST SOLUTION FOR THE FOWLE MARKETING RESEARCH ASSIGNMENT PROBLEM

```
Objective Function Value =              26.000

        Variable              Value              Reduced Costs
        --------------        --------------     ------------------
          X11                 0.000                  0.000
          X12                 1.000                  0.000
          X13                 0.000                  3.000
          X21                 0.000                  0.000
          X22                 0.000                  4.000
          X23                 1.000                  0.000
          X31                 1.000                  0.000
          X32                 0.000                  3.000
          X33                 0.000                  1.000
```

Figure 7.5 shows the computer solution for this model. Terry is assigned to client 2 ($x_{12} = 1$), Carle is assigned to client 3 ($x_{23} = 1$), and McClymonds is assigned to client 1 ($x_{31} = 1$). The total completion time required is 26 days. This solution is summarized in Table 7.4.

## Problem Variations

Because the assignment problem can be viewed as a special case of the transportation problem, the problem variations that may arise in an assignment problem parallel those for the transportation problem. Specifically, we can handle the following:

1. Total number of agents (supply) not equal to the total number of tasks (demand)
2. A maximization objective function
3. Unacceptable assignments

The situation in which the number of agents does not equal the number of tasks is analogous to total supply not equaling total demand in a transportation problem. If the number of agents exceeds the number of tasks, the extra agents simply remain unassigned in the linear programming model. If the number of tasks exceeds the number of agents, the linear

**Table 7.4**    OPTIMAL PROJECT LEADER ASSIGNMENTS FOR THE FOWLE MARKETING RESEARCH PROBLEM

| Project Leader | Assigned Client | Days |
|----------------|-----------------|------|
| Terry | 2 | 15 |
| Carle | 3 | 5 |
| McClymonds | 1 | 6 |
|  | Total | 26 |

programming model will not have a feasible solution. In this situation, a simple modification is to add enough dummy agents to equalize the number of agents and the number of tasks. For instance, in the Fowle problem we might have had five clients (tasks) and only three project leaders (agents). By adding two dummy project leaders, we can create a new assignment problem with the number of project leaders equal to the number of clients. The objective function coefficients for the assignment of dummy project leaders would be zero so that the value of the optimal solution would represent the total number of days required by the assignments actually made (no assignments will actually be made to the clients receiving dummy project leaders).

If the assignment alternatives are evaluated in terms of revenue or profit rather than time or cost, the linear programming formulation can be solved as a maximization rather than a minimization problem. In addition, if one or more assignments are unacceptable, the corresponding decision variable can be removed from the linear programming formulation. This scenario could happen, for example, if an agent did not have the experience necessary for one or more of the tasks.

## A General Linear Programming Model of the Assignment Problem

The general assignment problem involves $m$ agents and $n$ tasks. If we let $x_{ij} = 1$ or $0$ according to whether agent $i$ is assigned to task $j$, and if $c_{ij}$ denotes the cost of assigning agent $i$ to task $j$, we can write the general assignment model as

$$\text{Min} \quad \sum_{i=1}^{m} \sum_{j=1}^{n} c_{ij} x_{ij}$$

s.t.

$$\sum_{j=1}^{n} x_{ij} \leq 1 \qquad i = 1, 2, \ldots, m \quad \text{Agents}$$

$$\sum_{i=1}^{m} x_{ij} = 1 \qquad j = 1, 2, \ldots, n \quad \text{Tasks}$$

$$x_{ij} \geq 0 \qquad \text{for all } i \text{ and } j$$

## Multiple Assignments

At the beginning of this section, we indicated that a distinguishing feature of the assignment problem is that *one* agent is assigned to *one and only one* task. In generalizations of the assignment problem where one agent can be assigned to two or more tasks, the linear programming formulation of the problem can be easily modified. For example, let us assume that in the Fowle Marketing Research problem Terry could be assigned up to two clients; in this case, the constraint representing Terry's assignment would be $x_{11} + x_{12} + x_{13} \leq 2$. In general, if $a_i$ denotes the upper limit for the number of tasks to which agent $i$ can be assigned, we write the agent constraints as

If some tasks require more than one agent, the linear programming formulation can also accommodate the situation. Use the number of agents required as the right-hand side of the appropriate task constraint.

$$\sum_{j=1}^{n} x_{ij} \leq a_i \qquad i = 1, 2, \ldots, m$$

Thus, we see that one advantage of formulating and solving assignment problems as linear programs is that special cases such as the situation involving multiple assignments can be easily handled.

N O T E S
**and Comments**

1. As noted, the assignment model is a special case of the transportation model. We stated in the notes and comments at the end of the preceding section that the optimal solution to the transportation problem will consist of integer values for the decision variables as long as the supplies and demands are integers. For the assignment problem, all supplies and demands equal 1; thus, the optimal solution must be integer valued and the integer values must be 0 or 1.

2. Combining the method for handling multiple assignments with the notion of a dummy agent provides another means of dealing with situations when the number of tasks exceeds the number of agents. That is, we add one dummy agent, but provide the dummy agent with the capability to handle multiple tasks. The number of tasks the dummy agent can handle is equal to the difference between the number of tasks and the number of agents.

## 7.3    TRANSSHIPMENT PROBLEM: THE NETWORK MODEL AND A LINEAR PROGRAMMING FORMULATION

The **transshipment problem** is an extension of the transportation problem in which intermediate nodes, referred to as *transshipment nodes,* are added to account for locations such as warehouses. In this more general type of distribution problem, shipments may be made between any pair of the three general types of nodes: origin nodes, transshipment nodes, and destination nodes. For example, the transshipment problem permits shipments of goods from origins to transshipment nodes and on to destinations, from one origin to another origin, from one transshipment location to another, from one destination location to another, and directly from origins to destinations.

As was true for the transportation problem, the supply available at each origin is limited and the demand at each destination is specified. The objective in the transshipment problem is to determine how many units should be shipped over each arc in the network so that all destination demands are satisfied with the minimum possible transportation cost.

Try part (a) of Problem 23 for practice in developing a network representation of a transshipment problem.

Let us consider the transshipment problem faced by Ryan Electronics. Ryan is an electronics company with production facilities in Denver and Atlanta. Components produced at either facility may be shipped to either of the firm's regional warehouses, which are located in Kansas City and Louisville. From the regional warehouses, the firm supplies retail outlets in Detroit, Miami, Dallas, and New Orleans. The key features of the problem are shown in the network model depicted in Figure 7.6. Note that the supply at each origin and demand at each destination are shown in the left and right margins, respectively. Nodes 1 and 2 are the origin nodes; nodes 3 and 4 are the transshipment nodes; and nodes 5, 6, 7, and 8 are the destination nodes. The transportation cost per unit for each distribution route is shown in Table 7.5 and on the arcs of the network model in Figure 7.6.

As with the transportation and assignment problems, we can formulate a linear programming model of the transshipment problem from a network representation. Again, we need a constraint for each node and a variable for each arc. Let $x_{ij}$ denote the number of units shipped from node $i$ to node $j$. For example, $x_{13}$ denotes the number of units shipped from the Denver plant to the Kansas City warehouse, $x_{14}$ denotes the number of units shipped from the Denver plant to the Louisville warehouse, and so on. Since the supply at

| Figure 7.6 | NETWORK REPRESENTATION OF THE RYAN ELECTRONICS TRANSSHIPMENT PROBLEM |

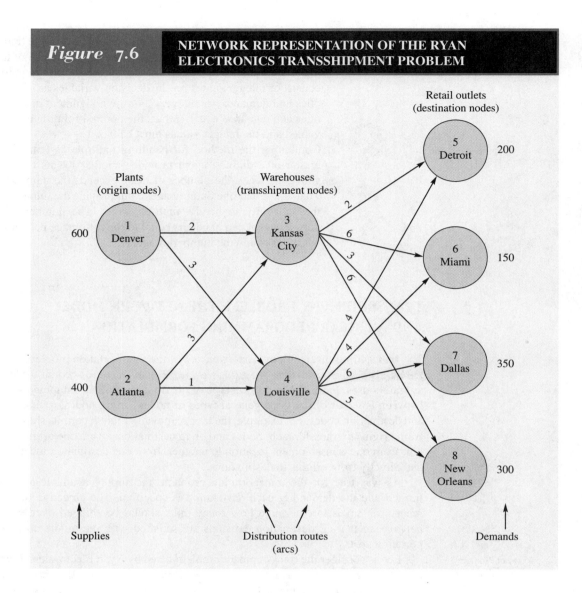

the Denver plant is 600 units, the amount shipped from the Denver plant must be less than or equal to 600. Mathematically, we write this supply constraint as

$$x_{13} + x_{14} \leq 600$$

Similarly, for the Atlanta plant we have

$$x_{23} + x_{24} \leq 400$$

We now consider how to write the constraints corresponding to the two transshipment nodes. For node 3 (the Kansas City warehouse), we must guarantee that the number of units shipped out must equal the number of units shipped into the warehouse. Since

| Table 7.5 | TRANSPORTATION COSTS PER UNIT FOR THE RYAN ELECTRONICS TRANSSHIPMENT PROBLEM | |
|-----------|-----------------------------------------------------------------------------|---|

| | Warehouse | |
|-------|-------------|------------|
| **Plant** | **Kansas City** | **Louisville** |
| Denver | 2 | 3 |
| Atlanta | 3 | 1 |

| | Retail Outlet | | | |
|-------------|-----------|-----------|------------|----------------|
| **Warehouse** | **Detroit** | **Miami** | **Dallas** | **New Orleans** |
| Kansas City | 2 | 6 | 3 | 6 |
| Louisville | 4 | 4 | 6 | 5 |

Number of units
shipped out of node $3 = x_{35} + x_{36} + x_{37} + x_{38}$

and

Number of units
shipped into node $3 = x_{13} + x_{23}$

we obtain

$$x_{35} + x_{36} + x_{37} + x_{38} = x_{13} + x_{23}$$

Placing all the variables on the left-hand side provides the constraint corresponding to node 3 as

$$-x_{13} - x_{23} + x_{35} + x_{36} + x_{37} + x_{38} = 0$$

Similarly, the constraint corresponding to node 4 is

$$-x_{14} - x_{24} + x_{45} + x_{46} + x_{47} + x_{48} = 0$$

To develop the constraints associated with the destination nodes, we recognize that for each node the amount shipped to the destination must equal the demand. For example, to satisfy the demand for 200 units at node 5 (the Detroit retail outlet), we write

$$x_{35} + x_{45} = 200$$

Similarly, for nodes 6, 7, and 8, we have

$$x_{36} + x_{46} = 150$$
$$x_{37} + x_{47} = 350$$
$$x_{38} + x_{48} = 300$$

Try parts (b) and (c) of
Problem 23 for practice
in developing the linear
programming model and
in solving a transshipment
problem.

As usual, the objective function reflects the total shipping cost over the 12 shipping routes. Combining the objective function and constraints leads to a 12-variable, 8-constraint linear programming model of the Ryan Electronics transshipment problem (see Figure 7.7). We used the linear programming module of The Management Scientist to obtain the optimal solution. Figure 7.8 shows the computer output, and Table 7.6 summarizes the optimal solution.

As mentioned at the beginning of this section, in the transshipment problem arcs may connect any pair of nodes. All such shipping patterns are possible in a transshipment problem. We still require only one constraint per node, but the constraint must include a vari-

**Figure 7.7  LINEAR PROGRAMMING FORMULATION OF THE RYAN ELECTRONICS TRANSSHIPMENT PROBLEM**

$$\text{Min } 2x_{13} + 3x_{14} + 3x_{23} + 1x_{24} + 2x_{35} + 6x_{36} + 3x_{37} + 6x_{38} + 4x_{45} + 4x_{46} + 6x_{47} + 5x_{48}$$
s.t.

$$
\begin{aligned}
x_{13} + x_{14} &\le 600 \quad \text{Origin node} \\
x_{23} + x_{24} &\le 400 \quad \text{constraints} \\
-x_{13} \quad - x_{23} \quad + x_{35} + x_{36} + x_{37} + x_{38} &= 0 \quad \text{Transshipment node} \\
- x_{14} \quad - x_{24} \quad + x_{45} + x_{46} + x_{47} + x_{48} &= 0 \quad \text{constraints} \\
x_{35} + x_{45} &= 200 \\
x_{36} + x_{46} &= 150 \quad \text{Destination node} \\
x_{37} + x_{47} &= 350 \quad \text{constraints} \\
x_{38} + x_{48} &= 300
\end{aligned}
$$

$$x_{ij} \ge 0 \text{ for all } i \text{ and } j$$

**Figure 7.8  THE MANAGEMENT SCIENTIST SOLUTION FOR THE RYAN ELECTRONICS TRANSSHIPMENT PROBLEM**

Objective Function Value =          5200.000

| Variable | Value | Reduced Costs |
|---|---|---|
| X13 | 550.000 | 0.000 |
| X14 | 50.000 | 0.000 |
| X23 | 0.000 | 3.000 |
| X24 | 400.000 | 0.000 |
| X35 | 200.000 | 0.000 |
| X36 | 0.000 | 1.000 |
| X37 | 350.000 | 0.000 |
| X38 | 0.000 | 0.000 |
| X45 | 0.000 | 3.000 |
| X46 | 150.000 | 0.000 |
| X47 | 0.000 | 4.000 |
| X48 | 300.000 | 0.000 |

| Table 7.6 | OPTIMAL SOLUTION TO THE RYAN ELECTRONICS TRANSSHIPMENT PROBLEM | | | |
|---|---|---|---|---|
| **Route** | | | **Cost** | |
| **From** | **To** | **Units Shipped** | **Per Unit** | **Total Cost** |
| Denver | Kansas City | 550 | $2 | $1100 |
| Denver | Louisville | 50 | $3 | 150 |
| Atlanta | Louisville | 400 | $1 | 400 |
| Kansas City | Detroit | 200 | $2 | 400 |
| Kansas City | Dallas | 350 | $3 | 1050 |
| Louisville | Miami | 150 | $4 | 600 |
| Louisville | New Orleans | 300 | $5 | 1500 |
| | | | | $5200 |

able for every arc entering or leaving the node. For origin nodes, the sum of the shipments out minus the sum of the shipments in must be less than or equal to the origin supply. For destination nodes, the sum of the shipments in minus the sum of the shipments out must equal demand. For transshipment nodes, the sum of the shipments out must equal the sum of the shipments in, as before.

For an illustration of this more general type of transshipment problem, let us modify the Ryan Electronics problem. Suppose that it is possible to ship directly from Atlanta to New Orleans at $4 per unit and from Dallas to New Orleans at $1 per unit. The network model corresponding to this modified Ryan Electronics problem is shown in Figure 7.9, the linear programming formulation is shown in Figure 7.10, and the computer solution is shown in Figure 7.11.

Try Problem 24 for practice working with transshipment problems with this more general structure.

In Figure 7.9 we added two new arcs to the network model. Thus, two new variables are necessary in the linear programming formulation. Figure 7.10 shows that the new variables $x_{28}$ and $x_{78}$, appear in the objective function and in the constraints corresponding to the nodes to which the new arcs are connected. Figure 7.11 shows that the value of the optimal solution has been reduced $600 by adding the two new shipping routes; $x_{28} = 250$ units are being shipped directly from Atlanta to New Orleans, and $x_{78} = 50$ units are being shipped from Dallas to New Orleans.

## Problem Variations

As with transportation and assignment problems, transshipment problems may be formulated with several variations, including the following:

1. Total supply not equal to total demand
2. Maximization objective function
3. Route capacities or route minimums
4. Unacceptable routes

The linear programming model modifications required to accommodate these variations are identical to the modifications required for the transportation problem described in Section 7.1. When we add one or more constraints of the form $x_{ij} \leq L_{ij}$ to show that the route from

**Figure 7.9**    NETWORK REPRESENTATION OF THE MODIFIED RYAN ELECTRONICS TRANSSHIPMENT PROBLEM

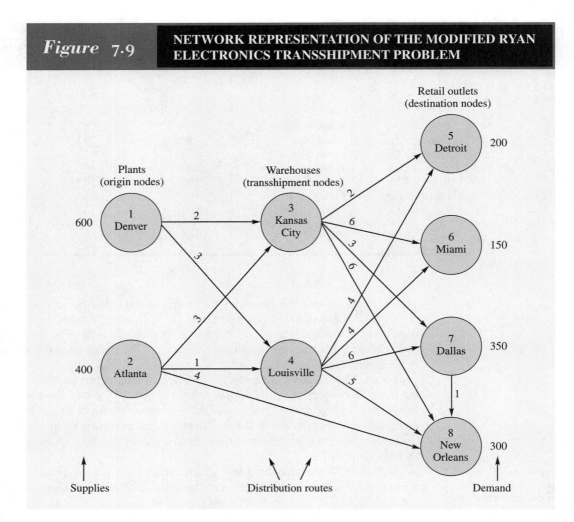

**Figure 7.10**    LINEAR PROGRAMMING FORMULATION OF THE MODIFIED RYAN ELECTRONICS TRANSSHIPMIENT PROBLEM

Min $\quad 2x_{13} + 3x_{14} + 3x_{23} + 1x_{24} + 2x_{35} + 6x_{36} + 3x_{37} + 6x_{38} + 4x_{45} + 4x_{46} + 6x_{47} + 5x_{48} + 4x_{28} + 1x_{78}$

s.t.

$$
\begin{array}{llll}
x_{13} + x_{14} & & & \leq 600 \\
\quad x_{23} + x_{24} & & + x_{28} & \leq 400 \\
-x_{13} \quad - x_{23} \quad + x_{35} + x_{36} + x_{37} + x_{38} & & & = 0 \\
\quad - x_{14} \quad - x_{24} \quad + x_{45} + x_{46} + x_{47} + x_{48} & & & = 0 \\
x_{35} \quad + x_{45} & & & = 200 \\
x_{36} \quad + x_{46} & & & = 150 \\
x_{37} \quad + x_{47} & - x_{78} & = 350 \\
x_{38} \quad + x_{48} + x_{28} + x_{78} & & = 300
\end{array}
$$

Origin node constraints

Transshipment node constraints

Destination node constraints

$x_{ij} \geq 0$  for all $i$ and $j$

```
                    THE MANAGEMENT SCIENTIST SOLUTION FOR THE
Figure  7.11        MODIFIED RYAN ELECTRONICS TRANSSHIPMENT
                    PROBLEM
```

```
Objective Function Value =            4600.000

        Variable            Value            Reduced Costs
     --------------     ---------------     ------------------
          X13              600.000              0.000
          X14                0.000              0.000
          X23                0.000              3.000
          X24              150.000              0.000
          X35              200.000              0.000
          X36                0.000              1.000
          X37              400.000              0.000
          X38                0.000              2.000
          X45                0.000              3.000
          X46              150.000              0.000
          X47                0.000              4.000
          X48                0.000              2.000
          X28              250.000              0.000
          X78               50.000              0.000
```

node $i$ to node $j$ has capacity $L_{ij}$, we refer to the transshipment problem as a **capacitated transshipment problem.**

## A General Linear Programming Model of the Transshipment Problem

The general linear programming model of the transshipment problem is

$$\text{Min} \quad \sum_{\text{all arcs}} c_{ij} x_{ij}$$

s.t.

$$\sum_{\text{arcs out}} x_{ij} - \sum_{\text{arcs in}} x_{ij} \leq s_i \qquad \text{Origin nodes } i$$

$$\sum_{\text{arcs out}} x_{ij} - \sum_{\text{arcs in}} x_{ij} = 0 \qquad \text{Transshipment nodes}$$

$$\sum_{\text{arcs in}} x_{ij} - \sum_{\text{arcs out}} x_{ij} = d_j \qquad \text{Destination nodes } j$$

$$x_{ij} \geq 0 \text{ for all } i \text{ and } j$$

where

$x_{ij} =$ number of units shipped from the node $i$ to node $j$

$c_{ij} =$ cost per unit of shipping from node $i$ to node $j$

$s_i =$ supply at origin node $i$

$d_j =$ demand at destination node $j$

1. In more advanced treatments of linear programming and network flow problems, the capacitated transshipment problem is called the pure network flow problem. Efficient special-purpose solution procedures are available for network flow problems and their special cases.

2. In the general linear programming formulation of the transshipment problem, the constraints for the destination nodes are often written as

$$\sum_{\text{arcs out}} x_{ij} - \sum_{\text{arcs in}} x_{ij} = -d_j$$

The advantage of writing the constraints this way is that the left-hand side of each constraint then represents the flow out of the node minus the flow in. But such constraints would then have to be multiplied by $-1$ to obtain nonnegative right-hand sides before solving the problem by many linear programming codes.

## 7.4 A PRODUCTION AND INVENTORY APPLICATION

The introduction to the transportation and transshipment problems in Sections 7.1 and 7.3 involved applications for the shipment of goods from several supply locations or origins to several demand sites or destinations. Although the shipment of goods is the subject of many transportation and transshipment problems, transportation and/or transshipment models can be developed for applications that have nothing to do with the physical shipment of goods from origins to destinations. In this section we show how to use a transshipment model to solve a production scheduling and inventory problem.

Contois Carpets is a small manufacturer of carpeting for home and office installations. Production capacity, demand, production cost per square yard, and inventory holding cost per square yard for the next four quarters are shown in Table 7.7. Note that production capacity, demand, and production costs vary by quarter, whereas the cost of carrying inventory from one quarter to the next is constant at $0.25 per yard. Contois wants to determine how many yards of carpeting to manufacture each quarter to minimize the total production and inventory cost for the four-quarter period.

We begin by developing a network representation of the problem. First, we create four nodes corresponding to the production in each quarter and four nodes corresponding to the demand in each quarter. Each production node is connected by an outgoing arc to the demand node for the same period. The flow on the arc represents the number of square yards

| *Table* 7.7 | PRODUCTION, DEMAND, AND COST ESTIMATES FOR CONTOIS CARPETS | | | |
|---|---|---|---|---|
| Quarter | Production Capacity (square yards) | Demand (square yards) | Production Cost ($/square yard) | Inventory Cost ($/square yard) |
| 1 | 600 | 400 | 2 | 0.25 |
| 2 | 300 | 500 | 5 | 0.25 |
| 3 | 500 | 400 | 3 | 0.25 |
| 4 | 400 | 400 | 3 | 0.25 |

The fact that the network shows flows into and out of demand nodes is what makes the model a transshipment model.

of carpet manufactured for the period. For each demand node, an outgoing arc represents the amount of inventory (square yards of carpet) carried over to the demand node for the next period. Figure 7.12 shows the network model. Note that nodes 1–4 represent the production for each quarter and that nodes 5–8 represent the demand for each quarter. The quarterly production capacities are shown in the left margin, and the quarterly demands are shown in the right margin.

The objective is to determine a production scheduling and inventory policy that will minimize the total production and inventory cost for the four quarters. Constraints involve production capacity and demand in each quarter. As usual, a linear programming model can be developed from the network by establishing a constraint for each node and a variable for each arc.

*Figure* 7.12   **NETWORK REPRESENTATION OF THE CONTOIS CARPETS PROBLEM**

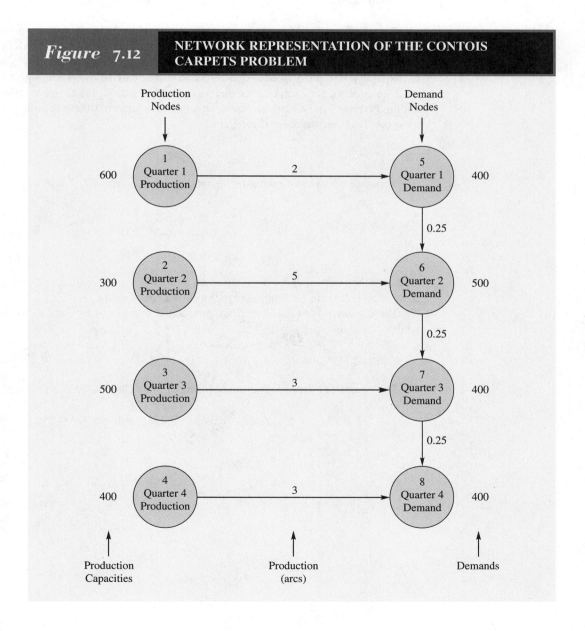

Let $x_{15}$ denote the number of square yards of carpet manufactured in quarter 1. The capacity of the facility is 600 square yards in quarter 1, so the production capacity constraint is

$$x_{15} \leq 600$$

Using similar decision variables, we obtain the production capacities for quarters 2–4:

$$x_{26} \leq 300$$
$$x_{37} \leq 500$$
$$x_{48} \leq 400$$

We now consider the development of the constraints for each of the demand nodes. For node 5, one arc enters the node, which represents the number of square yards of carpet produced in quarter 1, and one arc leaves the node, which represents the number of square yards of carpet that will not be sold in quarter 1 and will be carried over for possible sale in quarter 2. In general, for each quarter the beginning inventory plus the production minus the ending inventory must equal demand. However, for quarter 1 there is no beginning inventory; thus, the constraint for node 5 is

$$x_{15} - x_{56} = 400$$

The constraints associated with the demand nodes in quarters 2, 3, and 4 are

$$x_{56} + x_{26} - x_{67} = 500$$
$$x_{67} + x_{37} - x_{78} = 400$$
$$x_{78} + x_{48} = 400$$

Note that the constraints for node 8 (fourth-quarter demand) involves only two variables as there is no provision for holding inventory for a fifth quarter.

The objective is to minimize total production and inventory cost, so we write the objective function as

$$\underbrace{2x_{15} + 5x_{26} + 3x_{37} + 3x_{48}}_{\text{Production}} + \underbrace{0.25x_{56} + 0.25x_{67} + 0.25x_{78}}_{\text{Inventory}}$$

The complete linear programming formulation of the Contois Carpets problem is

$$\text{Min} \quad 2x_{15} + 5x_{26} + 3x_{37} + 3x_{48} + 0.25x_{56} + 0.25x_{67} + 0.25x_{78}$$

s.t.

$$
\begin{aligned}
x_{15} & & & & & & & & & \leq 600 \\
& x_{26} & & & & & & & & \leq 300 \\
& & x_{37} & & & & & & & \leq 500 \\
& & & x_{48} & & & & & & \leq 400 \\
x_{15} & & & & - x_{56} & & & & & = 400 \\
& x_{26} & & & + x_{56} & - x_{67} & & & & = 500 \\
& & x_{37} & & & + x_{67} & - x_{78} & & = 400 \\
& & & x_{48} & & & + x_{78} & & = 400
\end{aligned}
$$

$$x_{ij} \geq 0 \text{ for all } i \text{ and } j$$

We used the linear programming module of The Management Scientist to solve the Contois Carpets problem. Figure 7.13 shows the results: Contois Carpets should manufacture 600 square yards of carpet in quarter 1, 300 square yards in quarter 2, 400 square yards in quarter 3, and 400 square yards in quarter 4. Note also that 200 square yards will be carried over from quarter 1 to quarter 2. The total production and inventory cost is $5150.

---

N    O    T    E    S
*and Comments*

1. Often the same problem can be modeled in different ways. In this section we modeled the Contois Carpets problem as a transshipment problem. It also can be modeled as a transportation problem. In Problem 39 at the end of the chapter, we ask you to develop such a model.
2. In the network model we developed for the transshipment problem, the amount leaving the starting node for an arc is always equal to the amount entering the ending node for that arc. An extension of such a network model is the case where a gain or a loss occurs as an arc is traversed. The amount entering the destination node may be greater or smaller than the amount leaving the origin node. For instance, if cash is the commodity flowing across an arc, the cash earns interest from one period to the next. Thus, the amount of cash entering the next period is greater than the amount leaving the previous period by the amount of interest earned. Networks with gains or losses are treated in more advanced texts on network flow programming.

---

**Figure 7.13    THE MANAGEMENT SCIENTIST SOLUTION FOR THE CONTOIS CARPETS PROBLEM**

```
Objective Function Value =            5150.000

        Variable              Value            Reduced Costs
      --------------      --------------      ------------------
          X15               600.000                0.000
          X26               300.000                0.000
          X37               400.000                0.000
          X48               400.000                0.000
          X56               200.000                0.000
          X67                 0.000                2.250
          X78                 0.000                0.000
```

## 7.5    THE TRANSPORTATION SIMPLEX METHOD: A SPECIAL-PURPOSE SOLUTION PROCEDURE (OPTIONAL)

Solving transportation problems with a general-purpose linear programming code is fine for small- to medium-sized problems. However, these problems often grow very large (a problem with 100 origins and 1000 destinations would have 100,000 variables), and more efficient solution procedures are needed. The network structure of the transportation problem has enabled management scientists to develop special-purpose solution procedures that greatly simplify the computations.

In Section 7.1 we introduced the Foster Generators transportation problem and showed how to formulate and solve it as a linear program. The linear programming formulation involved 12 variables and 7 constraints. In this section we describe a special-purpose solution procedure, called the **transportation simplex method,** that takes advantage of the network structure of the transportation problem and makes possible the solution of large transportation problems efficiently on a computer and small transportation problems by hand.

The transportation simplex method, like the simplex method for linear programs, is a two-phase procedure; it involves first finding an initial feasible solution and then proceeding iteratively to make improvements in the solution until an optimal solution is reached. To summarize the data conveniently and to keep track of the calculations, we utilize a **transportation tableau.** The transportation tableau for the Foster Generators problem is presented in Table 7.8.

Note that the 12 *cells* in the tableau correspond to the 12 arcs shown in Figure 7.1; that is, each cell corresponds to the route from one origin to one destination. Thus, each cell in the transportation tableau corresponds to a variable in the linear programming formulation. The entries in the right-hand margin of the tableau indicate the supply at each origin, and the entries in the bottom margin indicate the demand at each destination. Each row corresponds to a supply node, and each column corresponds to a demand node in the network model of the problem. The number of rows plus the number of columns equals the number of constraints in the linear programming formulation of the problem. The entries in the upper right-hand corner of each cell show the transportation cost per unit shipped over the corresponding route. Note also that for the Foster Generators problem total supply equals total demand. The

| Table 7.8 | TRANSPORTATION TABLEAU FOR THE FOSTER GENERATORS TRANSPORTATION PROBLEM |
|-----------|---------------------------------------------------------------------------|

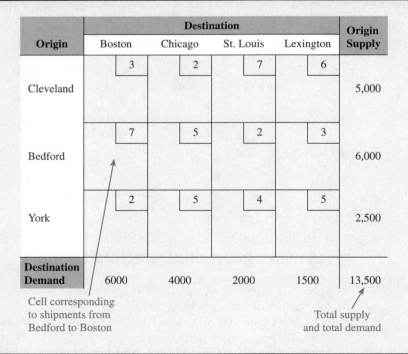

| | | Destination | | | | Origin |
|---|---|---|---|---|---|---|
| **Origin** | Boston | Chicago | St. Louis | Lexington | | **Supply** |
| Cleveland | 3 | 2 | 7 | 6 | | 5,000 |
| Bedford | 7 | 5 | 2 | 3 | | 6,000 |
| York | 2 | 5 | 4 | 5 | | 2,500 |
| **Destination Demand** | 6000 | 4000 | 2000 | 1500 | | 13,500 |

Cell corresponding
to shipments from
Bedford to Boston

Total supply
and total demand

transportation simplex method can be applied only to a balanced problem (total supply = total demand); if a problem is not balanced, a dummy origin or dummy destination must be added. The use of dummy origins and destinations will be discussed later in this section.

## Phase I: Finding an Initial Feasible Solution

The first phase of the transportation simplex method involves finding an initial feasible solution. Such a solution provides arc flows that satisfy each demand constraint without shipping more from any origin node than the supply available. The procedures most often used to find an initial feasible solution to a transportation problem are called heuristics. A **heuristic** is a commonsense procedure for quickly finding a solution to a problem.

Several heuristics have been developed to find an initial feasible solution to a transportation problem. Although some heuristics can find an initial feasible solution quickly, often the solution they find is not especially good in terms of minimizing total cost. Other heuristics may not find an initial feasible solution as quickly, but the solution they find is often good in terms of minimizing total cost. The heuristic we describe for finding an initial feasible solution to a transportation problem is called the **minimum-cost method.** This heuristic strikes a compromise between finding a feasible solution quickly and finding a feasible solution that is close to the optimal solution.

We begin by allocating as much flow as possible to the minimum-cost arc. In Table 7.8 we see that the Cleveland-Chicago, Bedford-St. Louis, and York-Boston routes each qualify as the minimum-cost arc since they each have a transportation cost of $2 per unit. When ties such as this occur, we follow the convention of selecting the arc to which the most flow can be allocated. In this case it corresponds to shipping 4000 units from Cleveland to Chicago, so we write 4000 in the Cleveland-Chicago cell of the transportation tableau. This selection reduces the supply at Cleveland from 5000 to 1000; hence, we cross out the 5000-unit supply value and replace it with the reduced value of 1000. In addition, allocating 4000 units to this arc satisfies the demand at Chicago, so we reduce the Chicago demand to zero and eliminate the corresponding column from further consideration by drawing a line through it. The transportation tableau now appears as shown in Table 7.9.

Now we look at the reduced tableau consisting of all unlined cells to identify the next minimum-cost arc. The routes between the Bedford-St. Louis and York-Boston tie with transportation cost of $2 per unit. More units of flow can be allocated to the York-Boston route, so we choose it for the next allocation. This step results in an allocation of 2500 units over the York-Boston route. To update the tableau, we reduce the Boston demand by 2500 units to 3500, reduce the York supply to zero, and eliminate this row from further consideration by lining through it. Continuing the process results in an allocation of 2000 units over the Bedford-St. Louis route and the elimination of the St. Louis column because its demand goes to zero. The transportation tableau obtained after carrying out the second and third iterations is shown in Table 7.10.

We now have two arcs that qualify for the minimum-cost arc with a value of 3: Cleveland-Boston and Bedford-Lexington. We can allocate a flow of 1000 units to the Cleveland-Boston route and a flow of 1500 to the Bedford-Lexington route, so we allocate 1500 units to the Bedford-Lexington route. Doing so results in a demand of zero at Lexington and eliminates this column. The next minimum-cost allocation is 1000 over the Cleveland-Boston route. After we make these two allocations, the transportation tableau appears as shown in Table 7.11.

The only remaining unlined cell is Bedford-Boston. Allocating 2500 units to the corresponding arc uses up the remaining supply at Bedford and satisfies all the demand at Boston. The resulting tableau is shown in Table 7.12.

**Table 7.9**  TRANSPORTATION TABLEAU AFTER ONE ITERATION OF THE MINIMUM-COST METHOD

| | Boston | Chicago | St. Louis | Lexington | Supply |
|---|---|---|---|---|---|
| Cleveland | 3 | 2<br>4000 | 7 | 6 | 1000<br>~~5000~~ |
| Bedford | 7 | 5 | 2 | 3 | 6000 |
| York | 2 | 5 | 4 | 5 | 2500 |
| **Demand** | 6000 | ~~4000~~<br>0 | 2000 | 1500 | |

**Table 7.10**  TRANSPORTATION TABLEAU AFTER THREE ITERATIONS OF THE MINIMUM-COST METHOD

| | Boston | Chicago | St. Louis | Lexington | Supply |
|---|---|---|---|---|---|
| Cleveland | 3 | 2<br>4000 | 7 | 6 | 1000<br>~~5000~~ |
| Bedford | 7 | 5 | 2<br>2000 | 3 | 4000<br>~~6000~~ |
| York | 2<br>~~2500~~ | 5 | 4 | 5 | 0<br>~~2500~~ |
| **Demand** | ~~6000~~<br>3500 | ~~4000~~<br>0 | ~~2000~~<br>0 | 1500 | |

| Table 7.11 | TRANSPORTATION TABLEAU AFTER FIVE ITERATIONS OF THE MINIMUM-COST METHOD |
|---|---|

|  | Boston | Chicago | St. Louis | Lexington | Supply |
|---|---|---|---|---|---|
| **Cleveland** | 3 / 1000 | 2 / 4000 | 7 | 6 | 0 / ~~1000~~ / ~~5000~~ |
| **Bedford** | 7 | 5 | 2 / 2000 | 3 / 1500 | 2500 / ~~4000~~ / ~~6000~~ |
| **York** | 2 / 2500 | 5 | 4 | 5 | 0 / ~~2500~~ |
| **Demand** | ~~6000~~ ~~3500~~ 2500 | ~~4000~~ 0 | ~~2000~~ 0 | ~~1500~~ 0 | |

| Table 7.12 | FINAL TABLEAU SHOWING THE INITIAL FEASIBLE SOLUTION OBTAINED USING THE MINIMUM-COST METHOD |
|---|---|

|  | Boston | Chicago | St. Louis | Lexington | Supply |
|---|---|---|---|---|---|
| **Cleveland** | 3 / 1000 | 2 / 4000 | 7 | 6 | 0 / ~~1000~~ / ~~5000~~ |
| **Bedford** | 7 / 2500 | 5 | 2 / 2000 | 3 / 1500 | 0 / ~~2500~~ / ~~4000~~ / ~~6000~~ |
| **York** | 2 / 2500 | 5 | 4 | 5 | 0 / ~~2500~~ |
| **Demand** | ~~6000~~ ~~3500~~ ~~2500~~ 0 | ~~4000~~ 0 | ~~2000~~ 0 | ~~1500~~ 0 | |

This solution is feasible because all the demand is satisfied and all the supply is used. The total transportation cost resulting from this initial feasible solution is calculated in Table 7.13. Phase I of the transportation simplex method is now complete; we have an initial feasible solution. The total transportation cost associated with this solution is $42,000.

**Summary of the Minimum-Cost Method.**   Before applying phase II of the transportation simplex method, let us summarize the steps for obtaining an initial feasible solution using the minimum-cost method.

To test your ability to use the minimum-cost method to find an initial feasible solution, try part (a) of Problem 34.

Step 1   Identify the cell in the transportation tableau with the lowest cost, and allocate as much flow as possible to this cell. In case of a tie, choose the cell corresponding to the arc over which the most units can be shipped. If ties still exist, choose any of the tied cells.

Step 2   Reduce the row supply and the column demand by the amount of flow allocated to the cell identified in step 1.

Step 3   If *all* row supplies and column demands have been exhausted, then stop; the allocations made will provide an initial feasible solution. Otherwise, continue with step 4.

Step 4   If the row supply is now zero, eliminate the row from further consideration by drawing a line through it. If the column demand is now zero, eliminate the column by drawing a line through it.

Step 5   Continue with step 1 for all unlined rows and columns.

## Phase II: Iterating to the Optimal Solution

Phase II of the transportation simplex method is a procedure for iterating from the initial feasible solution identified in phase I to the optimal solution. Recall that each cell in the transportation tableau corresponds to an arc (route) in the network model of the transportation problem. The first step at each iteration of phase II is to identify an incoming arc. The **incoming arc** is the currently unused route (unoccupied cell) where making a flow allocation will cause the largest per-unit reduction in total cost. Flow is then assigned to the incoming arc, and the amounts being shipped over all other arcs to which flow had previously been assigned (occupied cells) are adjusted as necessary to maintain a feasible solution. In the process of adjusting the flow assigned to the occupied cells, we identify and drop an **outgoing arc** from the solution. Thus, at each iteration in phase II, we bring a cur-

| *Table* 7.13 | | TOTAL COST OF THE INITIAL FEASIBLE SOLUTION OBTAINED USING THE MINIMUM-COST METHOD | | |
|---|---|---|---|---|
| **From** | Route **To** | Units **Shipped** | Cost **Per Unit** | **Total Cost** |
| Cleveland | Boston | 1000 | $3 | $ 3,000 |
| Cleveland | Chicago | 4000 | $2 | 8,000 |
| Bedford | Boston | 2500 | $7 | 17,500 |
| Bedford | St. Louis | 2000 | $2 | 4,000 |
| Bedford | Lexington | 1500 | $3 | 4,500 |
| York | Boston | 2500 | $2 | 5,000 |
| | | | | $42,000 |

rently unused arc (unoccupied cell) into the solution, and remove an arc to which flow had previously been assigned (occupied cell) from the solution.

To show how phase II of the transportation simplex method works, we must explain how to identify the incoming arc (cell), how to make the adjustments to the other occupied cells when flow is allocated to the incoming arc, and how to identify the outgoing arc (cell). We first consider identifying the incoming arc.

As mentioned, the incoming arc is the one that will cause the largest reduction per unit in the total cost of the current solution. To identify this arc, we must compute for each unused arc the amount by which total cost will be reduced by shipping one unit over that arc. The *mo*dified *dis*tribution or **MODI method** is a way to make this computation.

The MODI method requires that we define an index $u_i$ for each row of the tableau and an index $v_j$ for each column of the tableau. Computing these row and column indexes requires that the cost coefficient for each occupied cell equal $u_i + v_j$. Thus, since $c_{ij}$ is the cost per unit from origin $i$ to destination $j$, $u_i + v_j = c_{ij}$ for each occupied cell. Let us return to the initial feasible solution for the Foster Generators problem, which we found using the minimum-cost method (see Table 7.14), and use the MODI method to identify the incoming arc.

Requiring that $u_i + v_j = c_{ij}$ for all the occupied cells in the initial feasible solution leads to a system of six equations and seven indexes, or variables:

| Occupied Cell | $u_i + v_j = c_{ij}$ |
|---|---|
| Cleveland-Boston | $u_1 + v_1 = 3$ |
| Cleveland-Chicago | $u_1 + v_2 = 2$ |
| Bedford-Boston | $u_2 + v_1 = 7$ |
| Bedford-St. Louis | $u_2 + v_3 = 2$ |
| Bedford-Lexington | $u_2 + v_4 = 3$ |
| York-Boston | $u_3 + v_1 = 2$ |

**Table 7.14    INITIAL FEASIBLE SOLUTION TO THE FOSTER GENERATORS PROBLEM**

|  | Boston | Chicago | St. Louis | Lexington | Supply |
|---|---|---|---|---|---|
| Cleveland | 3 <br> 1000 | 2 <br> 4000 | 7 | 6 | 5000 |
| Bedford | 7 <br> 2500 | 5 | 2 <br> 2000 | 3 <br> 1500 | 6000 |
| York | 2 <br> 2500 | 5 | 4 | 5 | 2500 |
| Demand | 6000 | 4000 | 2000 | 1500 | |

With one more index (variable) than equation in this system, we can freely pick a value for one of the indexes and then solve for the others. We will always choose $u_1 = 0$ and then solve for the values of the other indexes. Setting $u_1 = 0$, we obtain

$$0 + v_1 = 3$$
$$0 + v_2 = 2$$
$$u_2 + v_1 = 7$$
$$u_2 + v_3 = 2$$
$$u_2 + v_4 = 3$$
$$u_3 + v_1 = 2$$

Solving these equations leads to the following values for $u_1$, $u_2$, $u_3$, $v_1$, $v_2$, $v_3$, and $v_4$:

$$u_1 = \phantom{-}0 \qquad v_1 = 3$$
$$u_2 = \phantom{-}4 \qquad v_2 = 2$$
$$u_3 = -1 \qquad v_3 = -2$$
$$v_4 = -1$$

Management scientists have shown that for each *unoccupied* cell, $e_{ij} = c_{ij} - u_i - v_j$ provides the change in total cost per unit that will be obtained by allocating one unit of flow to the corresponding arc. Thus, we will call $e_{ij}$ the **net evaluation index.** Because of the way $u_i$ and $v_j$ are computed, the net evaluation index for each occupied cell equals zero.

Rewriting the tableau containing the initial feasible solution for the Foster Generators problem and replacing the previous marginal information with the values of $u_i$ and $v_j$, we obtain Table 7.15. We computed the net evaluation index ($e_{ij}$) for each unoccupied cell, which is the circled number in the cell. Thus, shipping one unit over the route from origin 1 to destination 3 (Cleveland–St. Louis) will increase total cost by \$9; shipping one unit from origin 1 to destination 4 (Cleveland-Lexington) will increase total cost by \$7; shipping one unit from origin 2 to destination 2 (Bedford-Chicago) will decrease total cost by \$1; and so on.

On the basis of the net evaluation indexes, the best arc in terms of cost reduction (a net evaluation index of $-1$) is associated with the Bedford-Chicago route (origin 2–destination 2); thus, the cell in row 2 and column 2 is chosen as the incoming cell. Total cost decreases by \$1 for every unit of flow assigned to this arc. The question now is: How much flow should we assign to this arc? Because the total cost decreases by \$1 per unit assigned, we want to allocate the maximum possible flow. To find that maximum, we must recognize that, to maintain feasibility, each unit of flow assigned to this arc will require adjustments in the flow over the other currently used arcs. The **stepping-stone method** can be used to determine the adjustments necessary and to identify an outgoing arc.

**The Stepping-Stone Method.**    Suppose that we allocate one unit of flow to the incoming arc (the Bedford-Chicago route). To maintain feasibility—that is, not exceed the number of units to be shipped to Chicago—we would have to reduce the flow assigned to the Cleveland-Chicago arc to 3999. But then we would have to increase the flow on the Cleveland-Boston arc to 1001 so that the total Cleveland supply of 5000 units could be shipped. Finally, we would have to reduce the flow on the Bedford-Boston arc by 1 to satisfy the Boston demand. Table 7.16 summarizes this cycle of adjustments.

## Table 7.15 — NET EVALUATION INDEXES FOR THE INITIAL FEASIBLE SOLUTION TO THE FOSTER GENERATORS PROBLEM COMPUTED USING THE MODI METHOD

| $u_i$ | $v_j$ = 3 | 2 | −2 | −1 |
|---|---|---|---|---|
| 0 | 3 — 1000 | 2 — 4000 | 7 — ⑨ | 6 — ⑦ |
| 4 | 7 — 2500 | 5 — ⊝1 | 2 — 2000 | 3 — 1500 |
| −1 | 2 — 2500 | 5 — ④ | 4 — ⑦ | 5 — ⑦ |

## Table 7.16 — CYCLE OF ADJUSTMENTS IN OCCUPIED CELLS NECESSARY TO MAINTAIN FEASIBILITY WHEN SHIPPING ONE UNIT FROM BEDFORD TO CHICAGO

| | Boston | Chicago | St. Louis | Lexington | **Supply** |
|---|---|---|---|---|---|
| Cleveland | 3 — 1001 ~~1000~~ | 2 — 3999 ~~4000~~ | 7 | 6 | 5000 |
| Bedford | 7 — 2499 ~~2500~~ | 5 — 1 | 2 — 2000 | 3 — 1500 | 6000 |
| York | 2 — 2500 | 5 | 4 | 5 | 2500 |
| **Demand** | 6000 | 4000 | 2000 | 1500 | |

The cycle of adjustments needed in making an allocation to the Bedford-Chicago cell required changes in four cells: the incoming cell (Bedford-Chicago) and three currently occupied cells. We can view these four cells as forming a stepping-stone path in the tableau, where the corners of the path are currently occupied cells. The idea behind the stepping-stone path name is to view the tableau as a pond with the occupied cells as stones sticking up in it. To identify the stepping-stone path for an incoming cell, we start at the incoming cell and move horizontally and vertically using occupied cells as the stones at the corners of the path; the objective is to step from stone to stone and return to the incoming cell where we started. To focus attention on which occupied cells are part of the stepping-stone path, we draw each occupied cell in the stepping-stone path as a cylinder, which should reinforce the image of these cells as stone sticking up in the pond. Table 7.17 depicts the stepping-stone path associated with the incoming arc of the Bedford-Chicago route.

In Table 7.17 we placed a plus sign (+) or a minus sign (−) in each occupied cell on the stepping-stone path. A plus sign indicates that the allocation to that cell will increase by the same amount we allocate to the incoming cell. A minus sign indicates that the allocation to that cell will decrease by the amount allocated to the incoming cell. Thus, to determine the maximum amount that may be allocated to the incoming cell, we simply look to the cells on the stepping-stone path identified with a minus sign. Because no arc can have a negative flow, the minus-sign cell with the *smallest amount* allocated to it will determine the maximum amount that can be allocated to the incoming cell. After allocating this maximum amount to the incoming cell, we then make all the adjustments necessary on the stepping-stone path to maintain feasibility. The incoming cell becomes an occupied cell, and the outgoing cell is dropped from the current solution.

**Table 7.17**     **STEPPING-STONE PATH WITH THE BEDFORD-CHICAGO ROUTE AS THE INCOMING ARC**

| | Boston | Chicago | St. Louis | Lexington | Supply |
|---|---|---|---|---|---|
| Cleveland | +   3    1000 | −   2    4000 | 7 | 6 | 5000 |
| Bedford | −   7    2500 | 5 | 2    2000 | 3    1500 | 6000 |
| York | 2    2500 | 5 | 4 | 5 | 2500 |
| Demand | 6000 | 4000 | 2000 | 1500 | |

An occupied cell not on the stepping-stone path

An unoccupied cell

An occupied cell on the stepping-stone path

In the Foster Generators problem, the Bedford-Boston and Cleveland-Chicago cells are the ones where the allocation will decrease (the ones with a minus sign) as flow is allocated to the incoming arc (Bedford-Chicago). The 2500 units currently assigned to Bedford-Boston is less than the 4000 units assigned to Cleveland-Chicago, so we identify Bedford-Boston as the outgoing arc. We then obtain the new solution by allocating 2500 units to the Bedford-Chicago arc, making the appropriate adjustments on the stepping-stone path and dropping Bedford-Boston from the solution (its allocation has been driven to zero). Table 7.18 shows the tableau associated with the new solution. Note that the only changes from the previous tableau are located on the stepping-stone path originating in the Bedford-Chicago cell.

We now try to improve on the current solution. Again, the first step is to apply the MODI method to find the best incoming arc, so we recompute the row and column indexes by requiring that $u_i + v_j = c_{ij}$ for all occupied cells. The values of $u_i$ and $v_j$ can easily be computed directly on the tableau. Recall that we begin the MODI method by setting $u_1 = 0$. Thus, for the two occupied cells in row 1 of the table, $v_j = c_{1j}$; as a result, $v_1 = 3$ and $v_2 = 2$. Moving down the column associated with each newly computed column index, we compute the row index associated with each occupied cell in that column by subtracting $v_j$ from $c_{ij}$. Doing so for the newly found column indexes, $v_1$ and $v_2$, we find that $u_3 = 2 - 3 = -1$ and that $u_2 = 5 - 2 = 3$. Next, we use these row indexes to compute the column indexes for occupied cells in the associated rows, obtaining $v_3 = 2 - 3 = -1$ and $v_4 = 3 - 3 = 0$. Table 7.19 shows these new row and column indexes.

Also shown in Table 7.19 are the net changes (the circled numbers) in the value of the solution that will result from allocating one unit to each unoccupied cell. Recall that these are the net evaluation indexes given by $e_{ij} = c_{ij} - u_i - v_j$. Note that the net evaluation index for every unoccupied cell is now greater than or equal to zero. This condition shows that if current unoccupied cells are used, the cost will actually increase. Without an arc to which flow can be assigned to decrease the total cost, we have reached the optimal solution. Table 7.20 summarizes the optimal solution and shows its total cost. As expected, this

| Table 7.18 | NEW SOLUTION AFTER ONE ITERATION IN PHASE II OF THE TRANSPORTATION SIMPLEX METHOD | | | | |
|---|---|---|---|---|---|

| | Boston | Chicago | St. Louis | Lexington | Supply |
|---|---|---|---|---|---|
| **Cleveland** | 3<br>3500 | 2<br>1500 | 7 | 6 | 5000 |
| **Bedford** | 7 | 5<br>2500 | 2<br>2000 | 3<br>1500 | 6000 |
| **York** | 2<br>2500 | 5 | 4 | 5 | 2500 |
| **Demand** | 6000 | 4000 | 2000 | 1500 | |

## Table 7.19    MODI EVALUATION OF EACH CELL IN SOLUTION

| $u_i$ | $v_j$ = 3 | $v_j$ = 2 | $v_j$ = −1 | $v_j$ = 0 |
|---|---|---|---|---|
| 0 | 3 / 3500 | 2 / 1500 | 7 / ⑧ | 6 / ⑥ |
| 3 | 7 / ① | 5 / 2500 | 2 / 2000 | 3 / 1500 |
| −1 | 2 / 2500 | 5 / ④ | 4 / ⑥ | 5 / ⑥ |

solution is exactly the same as the one obtained using the linear programming solution approach (Figure 7.2).

**Maintaining $m + n - 1$ Occupied Cells.** Recall that $m$ represents the number of origins and $n$ represents the number of destinations. A solution to a transportation problem that has less than $m + n - 1$ cells with positive allocations is said to be **degenerate.** The solution to the Foster Generators problem is not degenerate; six cells are occupied and $m + n - 1 = 3 + 4 - 1 = 6$. The problem with degeneracy is that $m + n - 1$ occupied cells are required by the MODI method to compute all the row and column indexes. When degeneracy occurs, we must artificially create an occupied cell in order to compute the row and column indexes. Let us illustrate how degeneracy could occur and how to deal with it.

Table 7.21 shows the initial feasible solution obtained using the minimum-cost method for a transportation problem involving $m = 3$ origins and $n = 3$ destinations. To use the

## Table 7.20    OPTIMAL SOLUTION TO THE FOSTER GENERATORS TRANSPORTATION PROBLEM

| From | To | Units Shipped | Cost/Unit | Total Cost |
|---|---|---|---|---|
| Cleveland | Boston | 3500 | $3 | $10,500 |
| Cleveland | Chicago | 1500 | $2 | 3,000 |
| Bedford | Chicago | 2500 | $5 | 12,500 |
| Bedford | St. Louis | 2000 | $2 | 4,000 |
| Bedford | Lexington | 1500 | $3 | 4,500 |
| York | Boston | 2500 | $2 | 5,000 |
| | | | | $39,500 |

| Table 7.21 | TRANSPORTATION TABLEAU WITH A DEGENERATE INITIAL FEASIBLE SOLUTION |
|---|---|

| $u_i$ | $v_j$ 3 | 6 | | Supply |
|---|---|---|---|---|
| 0 | 3    35 | 6    25 | 7 | 60 |
| −1 | 8 | 5    30 | 7 | 30 |
| | 4 | 9 | 11    30 | 30 |
| **Demand** | 35 | 55 | 30 | |

MODI method for this problem, we must have $m + n - 1 = 3 + 3 - 1 = 5$ occupied cells. Since the initial feasible solution has only four occupied cells, the solution is degenerate.

Suppose that we try to use the MODI method to compute row and column indexes to begin phase II for this problem. Setting $u_1 = 0$ and computing the column indexes for each occupied cell in row 1, we obtain $v_1 = 3$ and $v_2 = 6$ (see Table 7.21). Continuing, we then compute the row indexes for all occupied cells in columns 1 and 2. Doing so yields $u_2 = 5 - 6 = -1$. At this point, we cannot compute any more row and column indexes because no cells in rows 1 or 2 of column 3 are occupied.

To compute all the row and column indexes when fewer than $m + n - 1$ cells are occupied, we must create one or more "artificially" occupied cells with a flow of zero. In Table 7.21 we must create one artificially occupied cell to have five occupied cells. Any currently unoccupied cell can be made an artificially occupied cell if doing so makes it possible to compute the remaining row and column indexes. For instance, treating the cell in row 2 and column 3 of Table 7.21 as an artificially occupied cell will enable us to compute $v_3$ and $u_3$, but placing it in row 2 and column 1 will not.

As we previously stated, whenever an artificially occupied cell is created, we assign a flow of zero to the corresponding arc. Table 7.22 shows the results of creating an artificially occupied cell in row 2 and column 3 of Table 7.21. Creation of the artificially occupied cell results in five occupied cells, so we can now compute the remaining row and column indexes. Using the row 2 index ($u_2 = -1$) and the artificially occupied cell in row 2, we compute the column index for column 3; thus, $v_3 = c_{23} - u_2 = 7 - (-1) = 8$. Then, using the column 3 index ($v_3 = 8$) and the occupied cell in row 3 and column 3 of the tableau, we compute the row 3 index: $u_3 = c_{33} - v_3 = 11 - 8 = 3$. Table 7.22 shows the complete set of row and column indexes and the net evaluation index for each unoccupied cell.

Reviewing the net evaluation indexes in Table 7.22, we identify the cell in row 3 and column 1 (net evaluation index $= -2$) as the incoming cell. The stepping-stone path and

**Table 7.22**　**TRANSPORTATION TABLEAU WITH AN ARTIFICIAL CELL IN ROW 2 AND COLUMN 3**

| $u_i$ | $v_j$ 3 | 6 | 8 | Supply |
|---|---|---|---|---|
| 0 | 3<br>35 | 6<br>25 | 7<br>⊝1 | 60 |
| −1 | 8<br>Ⓖ | 5<br>30 | 7<br>0 | 30 |
| 3 | 4<br>⊝2 | 9<br>⓪ | 11<br>30 | 30 |
| Demand | 35 | 55 | 30 | |

Artificially occupied cell

the adjustments necessary to maintain feasibility are shown in Table 7.23. Note that the stepping-stone path can be more complex than the simple one obtained for the incoming cell in the Foster Generators problem. The path in Table 7.23 requires adjustments in all five occupied cells to maintain feasibility. Again, the plus- and minus-sign labels simply show where increases and decreases in the allocation will occur as units of flow are added to the incoming cell. The smallest flow in a decreasing cell is a tie between the cell in row 2 and column 2 and the cell in row 3 and column 3.

Since the smallest amount in a decreasing cell is 30, the allocation we make to the incoming cell is 30 units. However, when 30 units are allocated to the incoming cell and the appropriate adjustments are made to the occupied cells on the stepping-stone path, the allocation to two cells goes to zero (row 2, column 2 and row 3, column 3). We may choose either one as the outgoing cell, but not both. One will be treated as unoccupied; the other will become an artificially occupied cell with a flow of zero allocated to it. The reason we cannot let both become unoccupied cells is that doing so would lead to a degenerate solution, and as before, we could not use the MODI method to compute the row and column indexes for the next iteration. When ties occur in choosing the outgoing cell, we can choose any one of the tied cells as the artificially occupied cell and then use the MODI method to recompute the row and column indexes. As long as no more than one cell is dropped at each iteration, the MODI method will work.

The solution obtained after allocating 30 units to the incoming cell in row 3 and column 1 and making the appropriate adjustments on the stepping-stone path leads to the tableau shown in Table 7.24. Note that we treated the cell in row 2 and column 2 as the artificially occupied cell. After computing the new row and column indexes, we see that the cell in row 1 and column 3 will be the next incoming cell. Each unit allocated to this cell will further decrease the value of the solution by 1. The stepping-stone path associated with this incoming cell is shown in Table 7.25. The cell in row 2 and column 3 is the outgoing

| Table 7.23 | STEPPING-STONE PATH FOR THE INCOMING CELL IN ROW 3 AND COLUMN 1 |

| $u_i$ | $v_j$ 3 | 6 | 8 | Supply |
|---|---|---|---|---|
| 0 | − 3 35 | + 6 25 | 7 | 60 |
| −1 | 8 | − 5 30 | + 7 0 | 30 |
| 3 | 4 | 9 | − 11 30 | 30 |
| Demand | 35 | 55 | 30 | |

| Table 7.24 | NEW ROW AND COLUMN INDEXES OBTAINED AFTER ALLOCATING 30 UNITS TO THE INCOMING CELL |

| $u_i$ | $v_j$ 3 | 6 | 8 | Supply |
|---|---|---|---|---|
| 0 | 3 5 | 6 55 | 7 (−1) | 60 |
| −1 | 8 (6) | 5 0 | 7 30 | 30 |
| 1 | 4 30 | 9 (2) | 11 (2) | 30 |
| Demand | 35 | 55 | 30 | |

**Table 7.25**  STEPPING-STONE PATH ASSOCIATED WITH THE INCOMING CELL IN ROW 1 AND COLUMN 3

| $u_i$ | $v_j$ = 3 | $v_j$ = 6 | $v_j$ = 8 | Supply |
|---|---|---|---|---|
| 0 | [3] | [6] − 55 | [7] → | 60 |
| −1 | [8] + | [5] − 0 | [7] 30 | 30 |
| 1 | [4] | [9] | [11] | 30 |
| Demand | 35 | 55 | 30 | |

cell; the tableau after this iteration is shown in Table 7.26. Note that we have found the optimal solution and that, even though several earlier iterations were degenerate, the final solution is not degenerate.

**Table 7.26**  OPTIMAL SOLUTION TO A PROBLEM WITH A DEGENERATE INITIAL FEASIBLE SOLUTION

| $u_i$ | $v_j$ = 3 | $v_j$ = 6 | $v_j$ = 7 | Supply |
|---|---|---|---|---|
| 0 | [3] 5 | [6] 25 | [7] 30 | 60 |
| −1 | [8] ⑥ | [5] 30 | [7] ① | 30 |
| 1 | [4] 30 | [9] ② | [11] ③ | 30 |
| Demand | 35 | 55 | 30 | |

## Summary of the Transportation Simplex Method

The transportation simplex method is a special-purpose solution procedure applicable to any network model having the special structure of the transportation problem. It is actually a clever implementation of the general simplex method for linear programming that takes advantage of the special mathematical structure of the transportation problem; but because of the special structure, the transportation simplex method is hundreds of times faster than the general simplex method.

Try part (b) of Problem 34 for practice using the transportation simplex method.

To apply the transportation simplex method, you must have a transportation problem with total supply equal to total demand; thus, for some problems you may need to add a dummy origin or dummy destination to put the problem in this form. The transportation simplex method takes the problem in this form and applies a two-phase solution procedure. In phase I, apply the minimum-cost method to find an initial feasible solution. In phase II, begin with the initial feasible solution and iterate until you reach an optimal solution. The steps of the transportation simplex method for a minimization problem are summarized as follows.

### Phase I

Find an initial feasible solution using the minimum-cost method.

### Phase II

Step 1   If the initial feasible solution is degenerate with less than $m + n - 1$ occupied cells, add an artificially occupied cell or cells so that $m + n - 1$ occupied cells exist in locations that enable use of the MODI method.

Step 2   Use the MODI method to compute row indexes, $u_i$, and column indexes, $v_j$.

Step 3   Compute the net evaluation index $e_{ij} = c_{ij} - u_i - v_j$ for each unoccupied cell.

Step 4   If $e_{ij} \geq 0$ for all unoccupied cells, stop; you have reached the optimal solution. Otherwise, proceed to step 5.

Step 5   Identify the unoccupied cell with the smallest (most negative) net evaluation index and select it as the incoming cell.

Step 6   Find the stepping-stone path associated with the incoming cell. Label each cell on the stepping-stone path whose flow will increase with a plus sign and each cell whose flow will decrease with a minus sign.

Step 7   Choose as the outgoing cell the minus-sign cell on the stepping-stone path with the smallest flow. If there is a tie, choose any one of the tied cells. The tied cells that are not chosen will be artificially occupied with a flow of zero at the next iteration.

Step 8   Allocate to the incoming cell the amount of flow currently given to the outgoing cell; make the appropriate adjustments to all cells on the stepping-stone path, and continue with step 2.

## Problem Variations

The following problem variations can be handled, with slight adaptations, by the transportation simplex method:

1. Total supply not equal to total demand
2. Maximization objective function
3. Unacceptable routes

The case where the total supply is not equal to the total demand can be handled easily by the transportation simplex method if we first introduce a dummy origin or a dummy destination. If total supply is greater than total demand, we introduce a **dummy destination** with demand equal to the excess of supply over demand. Similarly, if total demand is greater than total supply, we introduce a **dummy origin** with supply equal to the excess of demand over supply. In either case, the use of a dummy destination or a dummy origin will equalize total supply and total demand so that we can use the transportation simplex method. When a dummy destination or origin is present, we assign cost coefficients of zero to every arc into a dummy destination and to every arc out of a dummy origin. The reason is that no shipments will actually be made from a dummy origin or to a dummy destination when the solution is implemented and thus a zero cost per unit is appropriate.

The transportation simplex method also can be used to solve maximization problems. The only modification necessary involves the selection of an incoming cell. Instead of picking the cell with the smallest or most negative $e_{ij}$ value, we pick that cell for which $e_{ij}$ is largest. That is, we pick the cell that will cause the largest increase per unit in the objective function. If $e_{ij} \leq 0$ for all unoccupied cells, we stop; the maximization solution has been reached.

To handle unacceptable routes in a minimization problem, infeasible arcs must carry an extremely high cost, denoted $M$, to keep them out of the solution. Thus, if we have a route (arc) from an origin to a destination that for some reason cannot be used, we simply assign this arc a cost per unit of $M$, and it will not enter the solution. Unacceptable arcs would be assigned a profit per unit of $-M$ in a maximization problem.

## NOTES and Comments

1. Research devoted to developing efficient special-purpose solution procedures for network problems has shown that the transportation simplex method is one of the best. It is used in the transportation and assignment modules of The Management Scientist software package. A simple extension of this method also can be used to solve trans-shipment problems.

2. As we have previously noted, each cell in the transportation tableau corresponds to an arc (route) in the network model of the problem and a variable in the linear programming formulation. Phase II of the transportation simplex method is thus the same as phase II of the simplex method for linear programming. At each iteration, one variable is brought into solution and another variable is dropped from solution. The reason the method works so much better for transportation problems is that the special mathematical structure of the constraint equations means that only addition and subtraction operations are necessary. We can implement the entire procedure in a transportation tableau that has one row for each origin and one column for each destination. A simplex tableau for such a problem would require a row for each origin, a row for each destination, and a column for each arc; thus, the simplex tableau would be much larger.

## 7.6    THE ASSIGNMENT PROBLEM: A SPECIAL-PURPOSE SOLUTION PROCEDURE (OPTIONAL)

As mentioned previously, the assignment problem is a special case of the transportation problem. Thus, the transportation simplex method can be used to solve the assignment problem. However, the assignment problem has an even more special structure: All supplies and

| Table 7.27 | ESTIMATED PROJECT COMPLETION TIMES (DAYS) FOR THE FOWLE ASSIGNMENT PROBLEM | | |
|---|---|---|---|

| | | Client | |
|---|---|---|---|
| Project Leader | 1 | 2 | 3 |
| Terry | 10 | 15 | 9 |
| Carle | 9 | 18 | 5 |
| McClymonds | 6 | 14 | 3 |

demands equal 1. Because of this additional special structure, special-purpose solution procedures have been specifically designed to solve the assignment problem; one such procedure is called the **Hungarian method.** In this section we will show how the Hungarian method can be used to solve the Fowle Marketing Research problem.

Recall that the Fowle problem (see Section 7.2) involved assigning project leaders to clients; three project leaders were available and three research projects were to be completed for three clients. Fowle's assignment alternatives and estimated project completion times in days are restated in Table 7.27.

The Hungarian method involves what is called *matrix reduction*. Subtracting and adding appropriate values in the matrix yields an optimal solution to the assignment problem. Three major steps are associated with the procedure. Step 1 involves row and column reduction.

Step 1  Reduce the initial matrix by subtracting the smallest element in each row from every element in that row. Then, using the row-reduced matrix, subtract the smallest element in each column from every element in that column.

Thus, we first reduce the matrix in Table 7.27 by subtracting the minimum value in each row from each element in the row. With the minimum values of 9 for row 1, 5 for row 2, and 3 for row 3, the row-reduced matrix becomes

| | 1 | 2 | 3 |
|---|---|---|---|
| Terry | 1 | 6 | 0 |
| Carle | 4 | 13 | 0 |
| McClymonds | 3 | 11 | 0 |

The assignment problem represented by this reduced matrix is equivalent to the original assignment problem in the sense that the same solution will be optimal. To understand why, first note that the row 1 minimum element, 9, has been subtracted from every element in the first row. Since Terry must still be assigned to one of the clients, the only change is that in this revised problem the time for any assignment will be 9 days less. Similarly, Carle and McClymonds are shown with completion times requiring 5 and 3 fewer days, respectively.

Continuing with step 1 in the matrix reduction process, we now subtract the minimum element in each column of the row-reduced matrix from every element in the column. This operation also leads to an equivalent assignment problem; that is, the same solution will still be optimal, but the times required to complete each project are reduced. With the minimum values of 1 for column 1, 6 for column 2, and 0 for column 3, the reduced matrix becomes

|            | 1 | 2 | 3 |
|------------|---|---|---|
| Terry      | 0 | 0 | 0 |
| Carle      | 3 | 7 | 0 |
| McClymonds | 2 | 5 | 0 |

The goal of the Hungarian method is to continue reducing the matrix until the value of one of the solutions is zero—that is, until an assignment of project leaders to clients can be made that, in terms of the reduced matrix, requires a total time expenditure of zero days. Then, as long as there are no negative elements in the matrix, the zero-valued solution will be optimal. The way in which we perform this further reduction and recognize when we have reached an optimal solution is described in the following two steps.

Step 2   Find the minimum number of straight lines that must be drawn through the rows and the columns of the current matrix so that all the zeros in the matrix will be covered. If the minimum number of straight lines is the same as the number of rows (or equivalently, columns), an optimal assignment with a value of zero can be made. If the minimum number of lines is less than the number of rows, go to step 3.

Applying step 2, we see that the minimum number of lines required to cover all the zeros is 2. Thus, we must continue to step 3.

|            | 1 | 2 | 3 |                                  |
|------------|---|---|---|----------------------------------|
| Terry      | 0 | 0 | 0 | Two straight lines will cover    |
| Carle      | 3 | 7 | 0 | all the zeros (step 2)           |
| McClymonds | ② | 5 | 0 |                                  |

Step 3   Subtract the value of the smallest unlined element from every unlined element, and add this same value to every element at the intersection of two lines. All other elements remain unchanged. Return to step 2, and continue until the minimum number of lines necessary to cover all the zeros in the matrix is equal to the number of rows.

The minimum unlined element is 2. In the preceding matrix we circled this element. Subtracting 2 from all unlined elements and adding 2 to the intersection element for Terry and client 3 produces the new matrix:

|            | 1 | 2 | 3 |
|------------|---|---|---|
| Terry      | 0 | 0 | 2 |
| Carle      | 1 | 5 | 0 |
| McClymonds | 0 | 3 | 0 |

Returning to step 2, we find that the minimum number of straight lines required to cover all the zeros in the current matrix is 3. The following matrix illustrates the step 2 calculations.

|            | 1 | 2 | 3 |
|------------|---|---|---|
| Terry      | 0 | 0 | 2 |
| Carle      | 1 | 5 | 0 |
| McClymonds | 0 | 3 | 0 |

Three lines must be drawn to cover all zeros; therefore, the optimal solution has been reached

According to step 2, then, it must be possible to find an assignment with a value of zero. To do so we first locate any row or column that contains only one zero. If all have more than one zero, we choose the row or column with the fewest zeros. We draw a square around a zero in the chosen row or column, indicating an assignment, and eliminate that row and column from further consideration. Row 2 has only one zero in the Fowle problem, so we assign Carle to client 3 and eliminate row 2 and column 3 from further consideration. McClymonds must then be assigned to client 1 (the only remaining zero in row 3) and, finally, Terry to client 2. The solution to the Fowle problem, in terms of the reduced matrix, requires a time expenditure of zero days, as follows:

|            | 1  | 2  | 3  |
|------------|----|----|----|
| Terry      | 0  | [0]| 2  |
| Carle      | 1  | 5  | [0]|
| McClymonds | [0]| 3  | 0  |

We obtain the value of the optimal assignment by referring to the original assignment problem and summing the solution times associated with the optimal assignment—in this case, 15 for Terry to client 2, 5 for Carle to client 3, and 6 for McClymonds to client 1. Thus, we obtain the solution time of $15 + 5 + 6 = 26$ days.

### Finding the Minimum Number of Lines

Sometimes it is not obvious how the lines should be drawn through rows and columns of the matrix in order to cover all the zeros with the smallest number of lines. In these cases, the following heuristic works well. Choose any row or column with a single zero. If it is a row, draw a line through the column the zero is in; if it is a column, draw a line through the row the zero is in. Continue in this fashion until you cover all the zeros.

Can you solve an assignment problem using the Hungarian method? Try Problem 40.

If you make the mistake of drawing too many lines to cover the zeros in the reduced matrix and thus conclude incorrectly that you have reached an optimal solution, you will be unable to identify a zero-value assignment. Thus, if you think you have reached the optimal solution, but cannot find a set of zero-value assignments, go back to the preceding step and check to see if you can cover all the zeros with fewer lines.

### Problem Variations

We now discuss how to handle the following problem variations with the Hungarian method:

1. Number of agents not equal to number of tasks
2. Maximization objective function
3. Unacceptable assignments

**Number of Agents Not Equal to Number of Tasks.**    The Hungarian method requires that the number of rows (agents) equal the number of columns (tasks). Suppose that in the Fowle problem four project leaders (agents) had been available for assignment to the three new clients (tasks). Fowle still faces the same basic problem, namely, which project leaders should be assigned to which clients to minimize the total days required. Table 7.28 shows the project completion time estimates with a fourth project leader.

We know how to apply the Hungarian method when the number of rows and the number of columns are equal. We can apply the same procedure if we can add a new client. Since we do not have another client, we simply add a *dummy column,* or a dummy client. This dummy client is nonexistent, so the project leader assigned to the dummy client in the optimal assignment solution, in effect, will be the unassigned project leader.

What project completion time estimates should we show in this new dummy column? Since the dummy client assignment will not actually take place, a zero project completion time for all project leaders seems logical. Table 7.29 shows the Fowle assignment problem with a dummy client, labeled D. (Problem 42 at the end of the chapter asks you to use the Hungarian method to determine the optimal solution to this problem).

Note that if we had considered the case of four new clients and only three project leaders, we would have had to add a *dummy row* (dummy project leader) in order to apply the Hungarian method. The client receiving the dummy leader would not actually be assigned a project leader immediately and would have to wait until one becomes available. To obtain a problem form compatible with the solution algorithm, adding several dummy rows or dummy columns, but never both, may be necessary.

**Maximization Objective.**   To illustrate how maximization assignment problems can be handled, let us consider the problem facing management of Salisbury Discounts, Inc. Sup-

| Table 7.28 | ESTIMATED PROJECT COMPLETION TIME (DAYS) FOR THE FOWLE ASSIGNMENT PROBLEM WITH FOUR PROJECT LEADERS |
|---|---|

|  | | Client | |
|---|---|---|---|
| Project Leader | 1 | 2 | 3 |
| Terry | 10 | 15 | 9 |
| Carle | 9 | 18 | 5 |
| McClymonds | 6 | 14 | 3 |
| Higley | 8 | 16 | 6 |

| Table 7.29 | ESTIMATED PROJECT COMPLETION TIME (DAYS) FOR THE FOWLE ASSIGNMENT PROBLEM WITH A DUMMY CLIENT |
|---|---|

|  | | Client | | Dummy client → |
|---|---|---|---|---|
| Project Leader | 1 | 2 | 3 | D |
| Terry | 10 | 15 | 9 | 0 |
| Carle | 9 | 18 | 5 | 0 |
| McClymonds | 6 | 14 | 3 | 0 |
| Higley | 8 | 16 | 6 | 0 |

pose that Salisbury Discounts has just leased a new store and is attempting to determine where various departments should be located within the store. The store manager has four locations that have not yet been assigned a department and is considering five departments that might occupy the four locations. The departments under consideration are shoes, toys, auto parts, housewares, and videos. After a careful study of the layout of the remainder of the store, the store manager has made estimates of the expected annual profit for each department in each location. These are presented in Table 7.30.

This assignment problem requires a maximization objective. However, the problem also involves more rows than columns. Thus, we must first add a dummy column, corresponding to a dummy or fictitious location, in order to apply the Hungarian method. After adding a dummy column, we obtain the 5 × 5 Salisbury Discounts, Inc., assignment problem shown in Table 7.31.

We can obtain an equivalent minimization assignment problem by converting all the elements in the matrix to **opportunity losses.** We do so by subtracting every element in each column from the largest element in the column. Finding the assignment that minimizes opportunity loss leads to the same solution that maximizes the value of the assignment in the original problem. Thus, any maximization assignment problem can be converted to a minimization problem by converting the assignment matrix to one in which the elements represent opportunity losses. Hence, we begin the solution to this maximization assignment problem by developing an assignment matrix in which each element represents the opportunity loss for not making the "best" assignment. Table 7.32 presents the opportunity losses.

The opportunity loss from putting the shoe department in location 1 is $7000. That is, if we put the shoe department, instead of the best department (auto parts), in that location,

**Table 7.30** — ESTIMATED ANNUAL PROFIT ($000s) FOR EACH DEPARTMENT-LOCATION COMBINATION

| | Location | | | |
|---|---|---|---|---|
| Department | 1 | 2 | 3 | 4 |
| Shoe | 10 | 6 | 12 | 8 |
| Toy | 15 | 18 | 5 | 11 |
| Auto parts | 17 | 10 | 13 | 16 |
| Housewares | 14 | 12 | 13 | 10 |
| Video | 14 | 16 | 6 | 12 |

**Table 7.31** — ESTIMATED ANNUAL PROFIT ($000s) FOR EACH DEPARTMENT-LOCATION COMBINATION, INCLUDING A DUMMY LOCATION

| | Location | | | | Dummy location |
|---|---|---|---|---|---|
| Department | 1 | 2 | 3 | 4 | 5 |
| Shoe | 10 | 6 | 12 | 8 | 0 |
| Toy | 15 | 18 | 5 | 11 | 0 |
| Auto parts | 17 | 10 | 13 | 16 | 0 |
| Housewares | 14 | 12 | 13 | 10 | 0 |
| Video | 14 | 16 | 6 | 12 | 0 |

| Table 7.32 | OPPORTUNITY LOSS ($000s) FOR EACH DEPARTMENT-LOCATION COMBINATION | | | | |
|---|---|---|---|---|---|

| Department | 1 | 2 | 3 | 4 | 5 (Dummy location) |
|---|---|---|---|---|---|
| Shoe | 7 | 12 | 1 | 8 | 0 |
| Toy | 2 | 0 | 8 | 5 | 0 |
| Auto parts | 0 | 8 | 0 | 0 | 0 |
| Housewares | 3 | 6 | 0 | 6 | 0 |
| Video | 3 | 2 | 7 | 4 | 0 |

we forego the opportunity to make an additional $7000 in profit. The opportunity loss associated with putting the toy department in location 2 is zero because it yields the highest profit in that location. What about the opportunity losses associated with the dummy column? The assignment of a department to this dummy location means that the department will not be assigned a store location in the optimal solution. As all departments earn the same amount from this dummy location, zero, the opportunity loss for each department is zero.

Try Problem 43 for practice in using the Hungarian method for a maximization problem.

Following steps 1, 2, and 3 of the Hungarian method on Table 7.32 will minimize opportunity loss and determine the maximum profit assignment.

**Unacceptable Assignments.**   As an illustration of how we can handle unacceptable assignments, suppose that in the Salisbury Discounts, Inc., assignment problem the store manager believed that the toy department should not be considered for location 2 and that the auto parts department should not be considered for location 4. Essentially the store manager is saying that, based on other considerations, such as size of the area, adjacent departments, and so on, these two assignments are unacceptable alternatives.

Using the same approach for the assignment problem as we did for the transportation problem, we define a value of $M$ for unacceptable minimization assignments and a value of $-M$ for unacceptable maximization assignments, where $M$ is an arbitrarily large value. In fact, we assume $M$ to be so large that $M$ plus or minus any value is still extremely large. Thus, an $M$-valued cell in an assignment matrix retains its $M$ value throughout the matrix reduction calculations. An $M$-valued cell can never be zero, so it can never be an assignment in the final solution.

Problem 44 at the end of this chapter asks you to solve this assignment problem.

The Salisbury Discounts, Inc., assignment problem with the two unacceptable assignments is shown in Table 7.33. When this assignment matrix is converted to an opportunity loss matrix, the $-M$ profit value will be changed to $M$.

| Table 7.33 | ESTIMATED PROFIT FOR THE SALISBURY DEPARTMENT-LOCATION COMBINATIONS | | | | |
|---|---|---|---|---|---|

| Department | 1 | 2 | 3 | 4 | 5 |
|---|---|---|---|---|---|
| Shoe | 10 | 6 | 12 | 8 | 0 |
| Toy | 15 | $-M$ | 5 | 11 | 0 |
| Auto parts | 17 | 10 | 13 | $-M$ | 0 |
| Housewares | 14 | 12 | 13 | 10 | 0 |
| Video | 14 | 16 | 6 | 12 | 0 |

......................................................................................./  /............

# SUMMARY

In this chapter we introduced transportation, assignment, and transshipment problems. All three types of problems belong to the special category of linear programs called *network flow problems.* The network model of a transportation problem consists of nodes representing a set of origins and a set of destinations. In the basic model, an arc is used to represent the route from each origin to each destination. Each origin has a supply and each destination has a demand. The problem is to determine the optimal amount to ship from each origin to each destination.

The assignment model is a special case of the transportation model in which all supply and all demand values are equal to 1. We represent each agent as an origin node and each task as a destination node. The transshipment model is an extension of the transportation model to distribution problems involving transfer points referred to as transshipment nodes. In this more general model, we allow arcs between any pair of nodes. A variation of the transshipment problem allows for placing capacities on the arcs. This variation, called the *capacitated transshipment problem,* is also known in the network flow literature as the pure network problem.

We showed how each of these network flow problems could be modeled as a linear program, and we solved each using a general-purpose linear programming computer package. However, many practical applications of network flow models lead to large problems for which general-purpose linear programming codes are not efficient. The transportation simplex method was presented as an efficient special-purpose solution procedure for solving transportation problems. The procedure, and its extension to the transshipment problem, is hundreds of times faster than the general-purpose simplex method for large transportation and transshipment problems. The Hungarian method was presented as a special-purpose solution procedure for assignment problems.

In network flow problems, the optimal solution will be integral as long as all supplies and demands are integral. Therefore, when solving any transportation, assignment, or transshipment problem in which the supplies and demands are integral, we can expect to obtain an integer-valued solution.

......................................................................................./  /............

# GLOSSARY

**Transportation problem**  A network flow problem that often involves minimizing the cost of shipping goods from a set of origins to a set of destinations; it can be formulated and solved as a linear program by including a variable for each arc and a constraint for each node.

**Network**  A graphical representation of a problem consisting of numbered circles (nodes) interconnected by a series of lines (arcs); arrowheads on the arcs show the direction of flow. Transportation, assignment, and transshipment problems are network flow problems.

**Nodes**  The intersection or junction points of a network.

**Arcs**  The lines connecting the nodes in a network.

**Capacitated transportation problem**  A variation of the basic transportation problem in which these are capacities on some or all of the arcs.

**Assignment problem**  A network flow problem that often involves the assignment of agents to tasks; it can be formulated as a linear program and is a special case of the transportation problem.

**Transshipment problem** An extension of the transportation problem to distribution problems involving transfer points and possible shipments between any pair of nodes.

**Capacitated transshipment problem** A variation of the transshipment problem in which there are capacities on some or all of the arcs.

**Transportation simplex method** A special-purpose solution procedure for the transportation problem.

**Transportation tableau** A table representing a transportation problem in which each cell corresponds to a variable, or arc.

**Heuristic** A commonsense procedure for quickly finding a solution to a problem. Heuristics are used to find initial feasible solutions for the transportation simplex method and in other applications.

**Minimum-cost method** A heuristic used to find an initial feasible solution to a transportation problem; it is easy to use and usually provides a good (but no optimal) solution.

**Incoming arc** The unused arc (represented by an unoccupied cell in the transportation tableau) to which flow is assigned during an iteration of the transportation simplex method.

**Outgoing arc** The arc corresponding to an occupied cell that is dropped from solution during an iteration of the transportation simplex method.

**MODI method** The modified distribution method is a procedure for determining the net evaluation index for unused arcs in the transportation simplex method.

**Net evaluation index** The per-unit change in the objective function associated with assigning flow to an unused arc in the transportation simplex method.

**Stepping-stone path** The sequence of occupied cells that receive flow adjustments when flow is assigned to an unused arc in the transportation simplex method.

**Degenerate solution** A solution to a transportation problem in which fewer than $m + n - 1$ arcs (cells) have positive flow; $m$ is the number of origins and $n$ is the number of destinations.

**Dummy destination** A destination added to a transportation problem to make the total supply equal to the total demand. The demand assigned to the dummy destination is the difference between the total supply and the total demand.

**Dummy origin** An origin added to a transportation problem in order to make the total supply equal to the total demand. The supply assigned to the dummy origin is the difference between the total demand and the total supply.

**Hungarian method** A special-purpose solution procedure for solving an assignment problem.

**Opportunity loss** For each cell in an assignment matrix, the difference between the largest value in the column and the value in the cell. The entries in the cells of an assignment matrix must be converted to opportunity losses to solve maximization problems using the Hungarian method.

## PROBLEMS

Note: For Problems 1–32 a variety of solution methods can be used. In many cases, we ask you to formulate and solve the problem as a linear program. Where the solution method is not specified, you may also use the transportation or assignment modules of The Management Scientist or some other software package. Problems 33–45 are intended to be solved using the special-purpose algorithms of Sections 7.5 and 7.6. These special-purpose algorithms could also be used for many of the first 32 problems.

**SELF TEST**

1. A company imports goods at two ports: Philadelphia and New Orleans. Shipments of one of its products are made to customers in Atlanta, Dallas, Columbus, and Boston. For the next planning period, the supplies at each port, customer demands, and the shipping costs per case from each port to each customer are as follows:

| | | Customers | | | Port |
| Port | Atlanta | Dallas | Columbus | Boston | Supply |
| --- | --- | --- | --- | --- | --- |
| Philadelphia | 2 | 6 | 6 | 2 | 5000 |
| New Orleans | 1 | 2 | 5 | 7 | 3000 |
| **Demand** | 1400 | 3200 | 2000 | 1400 | |

Develop a network model of the distribution system for this problem.

**SELF TEST**

2. Consider the following network representation of a transportation problem:

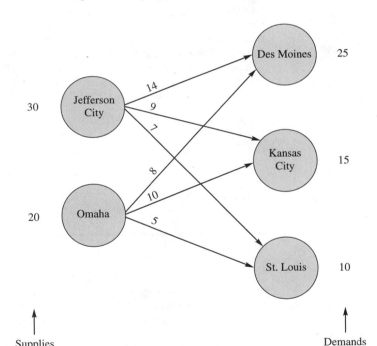

Supplies                                                        Demands

The supplies, demands, and transportation costs per unit are shown on the network.
   a. Develop a linear programming model for this problem; be sure to define the variables in your model.
   b. Solve the linear program to determine the optimal solution.

3. Reconsider the distribution system described in Problem 1.
   a. Develop a linear programming model for minimizing transportation costs.
   b. Solve the linear program to determine the minimum-cost shipping schedule.

4.  A product is produced at three plants and shipped to three warehouses (the transportation costs per unit are shown in the following table).

| Plant | Warehouse | | | Plant Capacity |
|---|---|---|---|---|
| | $W_1$ | $W_2$ | $W_3$ | |
| $P_1$ | 20 | 16 | 24 | 300 |
| $P_2$ | 10 | 10 | 8 | 500 |
| $P_3$ | 12 | 18 | 10 | 100 |
| **Warehouse demand** | 200 | 400 | 300 | |

a.  Show a network representation of the problem.
b.  Develop a linear programming model for minimizing transportation costs; solve this model to determine the minimum-cost solution.
c.  Suppose that the entries in the table represent profit per unit produced a plant $i$ and sold to warehouse $j$. How does the model change from that in part (b)?

5.  Tri-County Utilities, Inc., supplies natural gas to customers in a three-county area. The company purchases natural gas from two companies: Southern Gas and Northwest Gas. Demand forecasts for the coming winter season are Hamilton County, 400 units; Butler County, 200 units; and Clermont County, 300 units. Contracts to provide the following quantities have been written: Southern Gas, 500 units; and Northwest Gas, 400 units. Distribution costs for the counties vary, depending upon the location of the suppliers. The distribution costs per unit (in thousands of dollars) are as follows:

| From | To | | |
|---|---|---|---|
| | Hamilton | Butler | Clermont |
| Southern Gas | 10 | 20 | 15 |
| Northwest Gas | 12 | 15 | 18 |

a.  Develop a network representation of this problem.
b.  Develop a linear programming model that can be used to determine the plan that will minimize total distribution costs.
c.  Describe the distribution plan and show the total distribution cost.
d.  Recent residential and industrial growth in Butler County has the potential for increasing demand by as much as 100 units. Which supplier should Tri-County contract with to supply the additional capacity?:

6.  Arnoff Enterprises manufactures the central processing unit (CPU) for a line of personal computers. The CPUs are manufactured in Seattle, Columbus, and New York and shipped to warehouses in Pittsburgh, Mobile, Denver, Los Angeles, and Washington, D.C., for further distribution. The following transportation tableau shows the number of CPUs available at each plant and the number of CPUs required by each warehouse. The shipping costs (dollars per unit) are also shown in each cell.

| Plant | Warehouse | | | | | CPUs Available |
| | Pittsburgh | Mobile | Denver | Los Angeles | Washington | |
|---|---|---|---|---|---|---|
| Seattle | 10 | 20 | 5 | 9 | 10 | 9000 |
| Columbus | 2 | 10 | 8 | 30 | 6 | 4000 |
| New York | 1 | 20 | 7 | 10 | 4 | 8000 |
| CPUs Required | 3000 | 5000 | 4000 | 6000 | 3000 | 21,000 |

   **a.** Develop a network representation of this problem.
   **b.** Determine the amount that should be shipped from each plant to each warehouse to minimize the total shipping cost.
   **c.** The Pittsburgh warehouse has just increased its order by 1000 units, and Arnoff has authorized the Columbus plant to increase its production by 1000 units. Will this lead to an increase or decrease in total shipping costs? Solve for the new optimal solution.

**7.** Premier Consulting has two consultants, Avery and Baker, who can be scheduled to work for clients up to a maximum of 160 hours each over the next four weeks. A third consultant, Campbell, has some administrative assignments already planned and is available for clients up to a maximum of 140 hours over the next four weeks. The company has four clients with projects in process. The estimated hourly requirements for each of the clients over the four-week period are

| Client | Hours |
|---|---|
| A | 180 |
| B | 75 |
| C | 100 |
| D | 85 |

Hourly rates vary for the consultant-client combination and are based on several factors, including project type and the consultant's experience. The rates (dollars per hour) for each consultant-client combination are

| Consultant | Client A | Client B | Client C | Client D |
|---|---|---|---|---|
| Avery | 100 | 125 | 115 | 100 |
| Baker | 120 | 135 | 115 | 120 |
| Campbell | 155 | 150 | 140 | 130 |

a.  Develop a network representation of the problem.
b.  Formulate the problem as a linear program, with the optimal solution providing the hours each consultant should be scheduled for each client in order to maximize the consulting firm's billings. What is the schedule and what is the total billing?
c.  New information shows that Avery doesn't have the experience to be scheduled for client B. If this consulting assignment is not permitted, what impact does it have on total billings? What is the revised schedule?

**SELF TEST**

8.  Klein Chemicals, Inc., produces a special oil-base material that is currently in short supply. Four of Klein's customers have already placed orders that together exceed the combined capacity of Klein's two plants. Klein's management faces the problem of deciding how many units it should supply to each customer. Since the four customers are in different industries, different prices can be charged because of the various industry pricing structures. However, slightly different production costs at the two plants and varying transportation costs between the plants and customers make a "sell to the highest bidder" strategy unacceptable. After considering price, production costs, and transportation costs, Klein has established the following profit per unit for each plant-customer alternative.

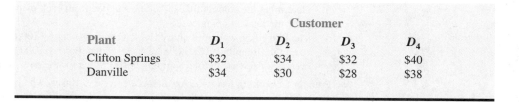

| Plant | Customer | | | |
|---|---|---|---|---|
| | $D_1$ | $D_2$ | $D_3$ | $D_4$ |
| Clifton Springs | $32 | $34 | $32 | $40 |
| Danville | $34 | $30 | $28 | $38 |

The plant capacities and customer orders are as follows:

| Plant Capacity (units) | | Distributor Orders (units) | |
|---|---|---|---|
| Clifton Springs | 5000 | $D_1$ | 2000 |
| | | $D_2$ | 5000 |
| Danville | 3000 | $D_3$ | 3000 |
| | | $D_4$ | 2000 |

How many units should each plant produce for each customer to maximize profits? Which customer demands will not be met? Show your network model and linear programming formulation.

9.  Sound Electronics, Inc., produces a battery-operated tape recorder at plants located in Martinsville, North Carolina; Plymouth, New York; and Franklin, Missouri. The unit transportation cost for shipments from the three plants to distribution centers in Chicago, Dallas, and New York are as follows:

|  | To | | |
|---|---|---|---|
| **From** | **Chicago** | **Dallas** | **New York** |
| Martinsville | 1.45 | 1.60 | 1.40 |
| Plymouth | 1.10 | 2.25 | 0.60 |
| Franklin | 1.20 | 1.20 | 1.80 |

After considering transportation costs, management has decided that under no circumstances will it use the Plymouth-Dallas route. The plant capacities and distributor orders for the next month are as follows:

| Plant | Capacity (units) |
|---|---|
| Martinsville | 400 |
| Plymouth | 600 |
| Franklin | 300 |

| Distributor | Orders (units) |
|---|---|
| Chicago | 400 |
| Dallas | 400 |
| New York | 400 |

Because of different wage scales at the three plants, the unit production cost varies from plant to plant. Assuming the costs are $29.50 per unit at Martinsville, $31.20 per unit at Plymouth, and $30.35 per unit at Franklin, find the production and distribution plan that minimizes production and transportation costs.

10. The Ace Manufacturing Company has orders for three similar products:

| Product | Orders (units) |
|---|---|
| A | 2000 |
| B | 500 |
| C | 1200 |

Three machines are available for the manufacturing operations. All three machines can produce all the products at the same production rate. However, due to varying defect percentages of each product on each machine, the unit costs of the products vary depending on the machine used. Machine capacities for the next week, and the unit costs, are as follows:

| Machine | Capacity (units) |
|---|---|
| 1 | 1500 |
| 2 | 1500 |
| 3 | 1000 |

| Machine | Product | | |
|---|---|---|---|
|  | **A** | **B** | **C** |
| 1 | $1.00 | $1.20 | $0.90 |
| 2 | $1.30 | $1.40 | $1.20 |
| 3 | $1.10 | $1.00 | $1.20 |

Formulate and solve a linear programming model that can be used to develop the minimum-cost production schedule for the products and machines.

11. Forbelt Corporation has a one-year contract to supply motors for all refrigerators produced by the Ice Age Corporation. Ice Age manufactures the refrigerators at four locations around the country: Boston, Dallas, Los Angeles, and St. Paul. Plans call for the following number (in thousands) of refrigerators to be produced at each location.

| | |
|---|---|
| Boston | 50 |
| Dallas | 70 |
| Los Angeles | 60 |
| St. Paul | 80 |

Forbelt has three plants that are capable of producing the motors. The plants and production capacities (in thousands) are

| | |
|---|---|
| Denver | 100 |
| Atlanta | 100 |
| Chicago | 150 |

Because of varying production and transportation costs, the profit that Forbelt earns on each lot of 1000 units depends on which plant produced the lot and which destination it was shipped to. The following table gives the accounting department estimates of the profit per unit (shipments will be made in lots of 1000 units).

| | Shipped To | | | |
|---|---|---|---|---|
| Produced At | Boston | Dallas | Los Angeles | St. Paul |
| Denver | 7 | 11 | 8 | 13 |
| Atlanta | 20 | 17 | 12 | 10 |
| Chicago | 8 | 18 | 13 | 16 |

With profit maximization as a criterion, Forbelt wants to determine how many motors should be produced at each plant and how many motors should be shipped from each plant to each destination.
a. Develop a network representation of this problem.
b. Find the optimal solution.

SELF TEST

12. Scott and Associates, Inc., is an accounting firm that has three new clients. Project leaders will be assigned to the three clients. Based on the different backgrounds and experiences of the leaders, the various leader-client assignments differ in terms of projected completion times. The possible assignments and the estimated completion times in days are

| Project Leader | Client | | |
|---|---|---|---|
| | 1 | 2 | 3 |
| Jackson | 10 | 16 | 32 |
| Ellis | 14 | 22 | 40 |
| Smith | 22 | 24 | 34 |

a. Develop a network representation of this problem.
b. Formulate the problem as a linear program, and solve. What is the total time required?

13. Assume that in Problem 12 an additional employee is available for possible assignment. The following table shows the assignment alternatives and the estimated completion times.

| Project Leader | Client | | |
|---|---|---|---|
| | 1 | 2 | 3 |
| Jackson | 10 | 16 | 32 |
| Ellis | 14 | 22 | 40 |
| Smith | 22 | 24 | 34 |
| Burton | 14 | 18 | 36 |

a. What is the optimal assignment?
b. How did the assignment change compared to the best assignment possible in Problem 12? Were any savings associated with considering Burton as one of the possible project leaders?
c. Which project leader remains unassigned?

14. Wilson Distributors, Inc., is opening two new sales territories in the western states. Three individuals currently selling in the Midwest and the East are being considered for promotion to regional sales manager positions in the new sales territories. Management has estimated total annual sales ($000s) for the assignment of each individual to each sales territory. The management sales projections are as follows:

| Regional Managers | Sales Region | |
|---|---|---|
| | Northwest | Southwest |
| Bostock | $100 | $95 |
| McMahon | $ 85 | $80 |
| Miller | $ 90 | $75 |

a. Develop a network representation of the problem.
b. Formulate and solve a linear programming model to obtain the optimal solution to this problem.

15. Fowle Marketing Research has four project leaders available for assignment to three clients. Find the assignment of project leaders to clients that will minimize the total time to complete all projects. The estimated project completion times in days are as follows:

| Project Leader | Client | | |
|---|---|---|---|
| | 1 | 2 | 3 |
| Terry | 10 | 15 | 9 |
| Carle | 9 | 18 | 5 |
| McClymonds | 6 | 14 | 3 |
| Higley | 8 | 16 | 6 |

16. a. Develop a network representation of the Salisbury Discount, Inc., department-location assignment problem using the estimated annual profit data provided in Table 7.30.
   b. Formulate a linear programming model, and solve for the department-location assignment that maximizes profit.

17. Consider the Salisbury Discount, Inc., assignment problem with two unacceptable assignments (see Table 7.33).
   a. Develop a network representation of the problem.
   b. Formulate and solve a linear programming model.

18. The U.S. Cable Company uses a distribution system with five distribution centers and eight customer zones. Each customer zone is assigned a sole source supplier and receives all of its cable products from the same distribution center. In an effort to balance demand and workload at the distribution centers, the company's vice-president of logistics has specified that distribution centers may not be assigned more than three customer zones. The following table shows the five distribution centers and cost of supplying each customer zone ($000s).
   a. Determine the assignment of customer zones to distribution centers that will minimize cost.
   b. Which distribution centers, if any, are not used?
   c. Suppose that each distribution center is limited to a maximum of two customer zones. How does this constraint change the assignment and the cost of supplying customer zones?

| Distribution Centers | Customer Zones | | | | | | | |
| --- | --- | --- | --- | --- | --- | --- | --- | --- |
| | Los Angeles | Chicago | Columbus | Atlanta | Newark | Kansas City | Denver | Dallas |
| Plano | 70 | 47 | 22 | 53 | 98 | 21 | 27 | 13 |
| Nashville | 75 | 38 | 19 | 58 | 90 | 34 | 40 | 26 |
| Flagstaff | 15 | 78 | 37 | 82 | 111 | 40 | 29 | 32 |
| Springfield | 60 | 23 | 8 | 39 | 82 | 36 | 32 | 45 |
| Boulder | 45 | 40 | 29 | 75 | 86 | 25 | 11 | 37 |

19. Mayfax Distributors, Inc., has four sales territories, each of which must be assigned a sales representative. From past experience the firm's sales manager has estimated the annual sales volume ($000s) for each sales representative in each sales territory. Find the sales representative-territory assignments that will maximize sales.

| Sales Representative | Sales Territory | | | |
| --- | --- | --- | --- | --- |
| | A | B | C | D |
| Washington | 44 | 80 | 52 | 60 |
| Benson | 60 | 56 | 40 | 72 |
| Fredricks | 36 | 60 | 48 | 48 |
| Hodson | 52 | 76 | 36 | 40 |

20. The department head of a management science department at a major midwestern university will be scheduling faculty to teach courses during the coming autumn term. Four core courses need to be covered. The four courses are at the UG, MBA, MS, and Ph.D. levels. Four professors will be assigned to the courses, with each professor receiving one of the courses. Student evaluations of professors are available from previous terms. Based on a rating scale of 4 (excellent), 3 (good), 2 (average), 1 (fair), and 0 (poor), the average student evaluations for each professor are shown. Professor D does not have a Ph.D. and cannot be assigned to teach the

Ph.D.-level course. If the department head makes teaching assignments based on maximizing the student evaluation ratings over all four courses, what staffing assignments should be made?

| | | Course | | |
|---|---|---|---|---|
| **Professor** | **UG** | **MBA** | **MS** | **Ph.D.** |
| A | 2.8 | 2.2 | 3.3 | 3.0 |
| B | 3.2 | 3.0 | 3.6 | 3.6 |
| C | 3.3 | 3.2 | 3.5 | 3.5 |
| D | 3.2 | 2.8 | 2.5 | — |

21. A market research firm has three clients who have each requested that the firm conduct a sample survey. Four available statisticians can be assigned to these three projects; however, all four statisticians are busy, and therefore each can handle only one of the clients. The following data show the number of hours required for each statistician to complete each job; the differences in time are based on experience and ability of the statisticians.

| | | Client | |
|---|---|---|---|
| **Statistician** | **A** | **B** | **C** |
| 1 | 150 | 210 | 270 |
| 2 | 170 | 230 | 220 |
| 3 | 180 | 230 | 225 |
| 4 | 160 | 240 | 230 |

   a.  Formulate and solve a linear programming model for this problem.
   b.  Suppose that the time it takes statistician 4 to complete the job for client A is increased from 160 to 165 hours. What effect will this have on the solution?
   c.  Suppose that the time it takes statistician 4 to complete the job for client A is decreased to 140 hours. What effect will this have on the solution?
   d.  Suppose that the time it takes statistician 3 to complete the job for client B increases to 250 hours. What effect will this have on the solution?

22. Hatcher Enterprises uses a chemical called Rbase in production operations at five divisions. There are only six suppliers of Rbase that meet Hatcher's quality control standards. All six of the suppliers can produce Rbase in sufficient quantities to accommodate the needs of each division. The quantity of Rbase needed by each of Hatcher's divisions and the price per gallon charged by each supplier are as follows:

| Division | Demand (1000s of gallons) |
|---|---|
| 1 | 40 |
| 2 | 45 |
| 3 | 50 |
| 4 | 35 |
| 5 | 45 |

| Supplier | Price Per Gallon ($) |
|---|---|
| 1 | 12.60 |
| 2 | 14.00 |
| 3 | 10.20 |
| 4 | 14.20 |
| 5 | 12.00 |
| 6 | 13.00 |

The cost per gallon ($) for shipping from each supplier to each division is provided in the following table.

| Division | Supplier | | | | | |
|---|---|---|---|---|---|---|
| | **1** | **2** | **3** | **4** | **5** | **6** |
| 1 | 2.75 | 2.50 | 3.15 | 2.80 | 2.75 | 2.75 |
| 2 | 0.80 | 0.20 | 5.40 | 1.20 | 3.40 | 1.00 |
| 3 | 4.70 | 2.60 | 5.30 | 2.80 | 6.00 | 5.60 |
| 4 | 2.60 | 1.80 | 4.40 | 2.40 | 5.00 | 2.80 |
| 5 | 3.40 | 0.40 | 5.00 | 1.20 | 2.60 | 3.60 |

Hatcher believes in spreading its business among suppliers so that the company will be less affected by supplier problems (e.g., labor strikes or resource availability). Company policy requires that each division have a separate supplier.

   a.   For each supplier-division combination, compute the total cost of supplying the division's demand.

   b.   Determine the optimal assignment of supplier to divisions.

**SELF TEST**

23.   The distribution system for the Herman Company consists of three plants, two warehouses, and four customers. Plant capacities and shipping costs ($) from each plant to each warehouse are

| Plant | Warehouse | | Capacity |
|---|---|---|---|
| | **1** | **2** | |
| 1 | 4 | 7 | 450 |
| 2 | 8 | 5 | 600 |
| 3 | 5 | 6 | 380 |

Customer demand and shipping costs per unit (in $) from each warehouse to each customer are

| Warehouse | Customer | | | |
|---|---|---|---|---|
| | **1** | **2** | **3** | **4** |
| 1 | 6 | 4 | 8 | 4 |
| 2 | 3 | 6 | 7 | 7 |
| **Demand** | 300 | 300 | 300 | 400 |

   a.   Develop a network model of this problem.

   b.   Formulate a linear programming model of the problem.

   c.   Use a computer code (e.g., The Management Scientist) to find the optimal shipping plan.

24.   Refer to Problem 23. Suppose that shipments between the two warehouses are permitted at $2 per unit and that direct shipments can be made from plant 3 to customer 4 at a cost of $7 per unit.

   a.   Develop a network model of this problem.

   b.   Formulate a linear programming model of this problem.

   c.   Find the optimal shipping plan.

25. CARD, Cleveland Area Rapid Delivery, operates a delivery service in the Cleveland metropolitan area. Most of CARD's business involves rapid delivery of documents and parcels between offices during the business day. CARD promotes its ability to make fast and on-time deliveries anywhere in the metropolitan area. When a customer calls with a delivery request, CARD quotes a guaranteed delivery time. The following network shows the street routes of seven pickup and delivery locations. The numbers above each arc indicate the travel time in minutes between the two locations.

    a.  Develop a linear programming model of a transshipment problem that can be used to find the minimum time required to make a delivery from location 1 to location 7.

    b.  How long does it take to make a delivery from location 1 to location 7.

    c.  Assume that it is now 1:00 P.M. CARD has just received a request for a pickup at location 1, and the closest CARD courier is 8 minutes away from location 1. If CARD provides a 20% safety margin in guaranteeing a delivery time, what is the guaranteed delivery time if the package picked up at location 1 is to be delivered to location 7?

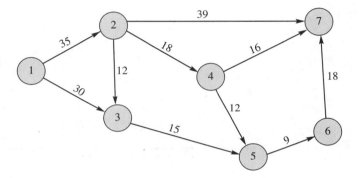

26. Adirondack Paper Mills, Inc., has paper plants in Augusta, Maine, and Tupper Lake, New York. Warehouse facilities are located in Albany, New York, and Portsmouth, New Hampshire. Distributors are located in Boston, New York, and Philadelphia. The plant capacities and distributor demands for the next month are as follows:

| Plant | Capacity (units) |
| --- | --- |
| Augusta | 300 |
| Tupper Lake | 100 |

| Distributor | Demand (units) |
| --- | --- |
| Boston | 150 |
| New York | 100 |
| Philadelphia | 150 |

The unit transportation costs ($) for shipments from the two plants to the two warehouses and from the two warehouses to the three distributors are as follows:

| | Warehouse | |
| --- | --- | --- |
| Plant | Albany | Portsmouth |
| Augusta | 7 | 5 |
| Tupper Lake | 3 | 4 |

|                | **Distributor** | | |
| **Warehouse** | **Boston** | **New York** | **Philadelphia** |
| Albany | 8 | 5 | 7 |
| Portsmouth | 5 | 6 | 10 |

a.  Draw the network representation of the Adirondack Paper Mills problem.
b.  Formulate the Adirondack Paper Mills problem as a linear programming problem.
c.  If you have access to a linear programming computer code, determine the minimum-cost shipping schedule for the problem.

27. Consider a transshipment problem consisting of three origin nodes, two transshipment nodes, and four destination nodes. The supplies at the origin nodes and the demands at the destination nodes are as follows:

| **Origin** | **Supply** |
| 1 | 400 |
| 2 | 450 |
| 3 | 350 |

| **Destination** | **Demand** |
| 1 | 200 |
| 2 | 500 |
| 3 | 300 |
| 4 | 200 |

The shipping costs per unit ($) are provided in the following table.

|  |  | | **To** | | | | |
| **From** | | **Transshipment** | | **Destination** | | | |
| | | 1 | 2 | 1 | 2 | 3 | 4 |
| **Origin** | 1 | 6 | 8 | — | — | — | — |
| | 2 | 8 | 12 | — | — | — | — |
| | 3 | 10 | 5 | — | — | — | — |
| **Transshipment** | 1 | — | — | 9 | 7 | 6 | 10 |
| | 2 | — | — | 7 | 9 | 6 | 8 |

a.  Draw the network representation of this problem.
b.  Formulate the appropriate linear programming problem.
c.  Solve for the optimal solution.

28. The Moore & Harman Company is in the business of buying and selling grain. An important aspect of the company's business is arranging for the purchased grain to be shipped to customers. If the company can keep freight costs low, profitability will be improved.

 Currently, the company has purchased three rail cars of grain at Muncie, Indiana; six rail cars at Brazil, Indiana; and five rail cars at Xenia, Ohio. Twelve carloads of grain have been sold. The locations and the amount sold at each location are as follows:

| Location | Number of Rail Car Loads |
|---|---|
| Macon, GA | 2 |
| Greenwood, SC | 4 |
| Concord, SC | 3 |
| Chatham, NC | 3 |

All shipments must be routed through either Louisville or Cincinnati. Shown are the shipping costs per bushel (in cents) from the origins to Louisville and Cincinnati and the costs per bushel to ship from Louisville and Cincinnati to the destinations.

| | To | | |
|---|---|---|---|
| From | Louisville | Cincinnati | |
| Muncie | 8 | 6 | ← Cost per bushel |
| Brazil | 3 | 8 | from Muncie to |
| Xenia | 9 | 3 | Cincinnati is 6¢ |

| | To | | | |
|---|---|---|---|---|
| From | Macon | Greenwood | Concord | Chatham |
| Louisville | 44 | 34 | 34 | 32 |
| Cincinnati | 57 | 35 | 28 | 24 |

Cost per bushel from
Cincinnati to Greenwood is 35¢

Determine a shipping schedule that will minimize the freight costs necessary to satisfy demand. Which (if any) rail cars of grain must be held at the origin until buyers can be found?

29. A rental car company has an imbalance of cars at seven of its locations. The following network shows the locations of concern (the nodes) and the cost to move a car between locations. A positive number by a node indicates an excess supply at the node, and a negative number indicates an excess demand.

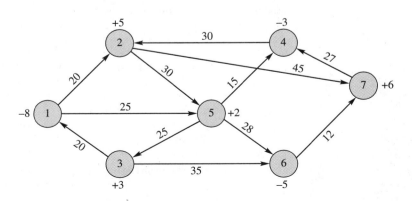

    a.  Develop a linear programming model for restoring the proper balance at the locations.

    b.  Solve the model formulated in part (a) to determine how the cars should be redistributed among the locations.

30.  The following linear programming formulations is for a transshipment problem.

$$\text{Min} \quad 11x_{13} + 12x_{14} + 10x_{21} + 8x_{34} + 10x_{35} + 11x_{42} + 9x_{45} + 12x_{52}$$

s.t.

$$
\begin{aligned}
x_{13} + x_{14} - x_{21} & & & & & & & \leq 5 \\
x_{21} & & - x_{42} & & - x_{52} & \leq 3 \\
x_{13} & - x_{34} - x_{35} & & & & = 6 \\
- x_{14} & - x_{34} & + x_{42} + x_{45} & & & \leq 2 \\
& x_{35} & + x_{45} - x_{52} & = 4
\end{aligned}
$$

$$x_{ij} \geq 0 \text{ for all } i, j$$

Show the network representation of this problem.

31.  Refer to the Contois Carpets problem for which the network representation is shown in Figure 7.12. Suppose that Contois has a beginning inventory of 50 yards of carpet and requires an inventory of 100 yards at the end of quarter 4.

    a.  Develop a network representation of this modified problem.

    b.  Develop a linear programming model, and solve for the optimal solution.

32.  Sanders Fishing Supply of Naples, Florida, manufactures a variety of fishing equipment, which it sells throughout the United States. For the next three months, Sanders estimates demand for a particular product at 150, 250, and 300 units, respectively. Sanders can supply this demand by producing on regular time or overtime. Because of other commitments and anticipated cost increases in month 3, the production capacities in units and the production costs per unit are as follows:

| Production | Capacity (units) | Cost Per Unit |
|---|---|---|
| Month 1—Regular | 275 | $ 50 |
| Month 1—Overtime | 100 | 80 |
| Month 2—Regular | 200 | 50 |
| Month 2—Overtime | 50 | 80 |
| Month 3—Regular | 100 | 60 |
| Month 3—Overtime | 50 | 100 |

Inventory may be carried from one month to the next, but the cost is $20 per unit per month. For example, regular production from month 1 used to meet demand in month 2 would cost Sanders $50 + $20 = $70 per unit. This same month 1 production used to meet demand in month 3 would cost Sanders $50 + 2($20) = $90 per unit.

    a.  Develop a network representation of this production scheduling problem as a transportation problem. (Hint: Use six origin nodes; the supply for origin node 1 is the maximum that can be produced in month 1 on regular time, and so on.)

    b.  Develop a linear programming model that can be used to schedule regular and overtime production for each of the three months.

    c.  What is the production schedule, how many units are carried in inventory each month, and what is the total cost?

    d.  Is there any unused production capacity? If so, where?

**Note:  The remaining problems involve the use of the special-purpose algorithms described in Sections 7.5 and 7.6 for solving transportation and assignment problems.**

33.  Consider the following transportation tableau with four origins and four destinations.

| Origin | Destination | | | | Supply |
|---|---|---|---|---|---|
| | $D_1$ | $D_2$ | $D_3$ | $D_4$ | |
| $O_1$ | 5 · 25 | 7 | 10 · 50 | 5 | 75 |
| $O_2$ | 6 | 5 | 8 · 100 | 2 · 75 | 175 |
| $O_3$ | 6 · 100 | 6 | 12 | 7 | 100 |
| $O_4$ | 8 | 5 · 100 | 14 | 4 · 50 | 150 |
| Demand | 125 | 100 | 150 | 125 | |

a.  Use the MODI method to determine whether this solution provides the minimum transportation cost. If it is not the minimum cost solution, find that solution. If it is the minimum cost solution, what is the total transportation cost?

b.  Does an alternative optimal solution exit? Explain. If so, find the alternative optimal solution. What is the total transportation cost associated with this solution?

34.  Consider the following minimum-cost transportation problem.

SELF TEST

| Origin | Destination | | | Supply |
|---|---|---|---|---|
| | Los Angeles | San Francisco | San Diego | |
| San Jose | 4 | 10 | 6 | 100 |
| Las Vegas | 8 | 16 | 6 | 300 |
| Tucson | 14 | 18 | 10 | 300 |
| Demand | 200 | 300 | 200 | 700 |

  a.  Use the minimum-cost method to find an initial feasible solution.
  b.  Use the transportation simplex method to find an optimal solution.
  c.  How would the optimal solution change if you must ship 100 units on the Tucson-San Diego route?
  d.  Because of road construction, the Las Vegas-San Diego route is now unacceptable. Resolve the initial problem.

35.  Refer to Problem 2.
  a.  Set up the transportation tableau for the problem.
  b.  Use the minimum-cost method to find an initial feasible solution.

36.  Refer to Problem 4. Use the transportation simplex method to find an optimal solution.

37.  Consider the following minimum-cost transportation problem.

| Origin | Destination | | | Supply |
|---|---|---|---|---|
| | $D_1$ | $D_2$ | $D_3$ | |
| $O_1$ | 6 | 8 | 8 | 250 |
| $O_2$ | 18 | 12 | 14 | 150 |
| $O_3$ | 8 | 12 | 10 | 100 |
| Demand | 150 | 200 | 150 | |

  a.  Use the minimum-cost method to find an initial feasible solution.
  b.  Use the transportation simplex method to find an optimal solution.
  c.  Using your solution to part (b), identify an alternative optimal solution.

38.  Use the per-unit cost changes for each unoccupied cell shown in Table 7.15 to do the following:
  a.  Consider the arc connecting Bedford and Chicago as a candidate for the incoming arc. Allocate 1 unit of flow, and make the necessary adjustments on the stepping-stone path to maintain feasibility. Compute the value of the new solution, and show that the change in value is exactly what has been indicated by the cost change per unit obtained using the MODI method.
  b.  Repeat part (a) for the arc connecting York and Lexington.

39.  Refer again to the Contois Carpets problem for which the network representation is shown in Figure 7.12. This problem can also be formulated and solved as a transportation problem.
  a.  Develop a network representation of it as a transportation problem. (Hint: Eliminate the inventory arcs, and add arcs showing that quarterly production can be used to satisfy demand in the current quarter and all future quarters.)
  b.  Solve the problem using the transportation simplex method.

40.  Refer to Problem 12. Using the Hungarian method, obtain the optimal solution.

41.  Refer to Problem 14. Use the Hungarian method to obtain the optimal solution.

SELF TEST

42.  Refer to Problem 15. Use the Hungarian method to obtain the optimal solution.

43. Use the Hungarian method to solve the Salisbury Discount, Inc., problem by using the profit data in Table 7.30.

44. Use the Hungarian method to solve the Salisbury Discount, Inc., problem as described in Problem 17.

45. Refer to Problem 19. Use the Hungarian method to find an optimal solution.

## Case Problem    DISTRIBUTION SYSTEM DESIGN

The Darby Company manufactures and distributes meters used to measure electric power consumption. The company started with a small production plant in El Paso and gradually built a customer base throughout Texas. A distribution center was established in Ft. Worth, Texas, and later, as business expanded to the north, a second distribution center was established in Santa Fe, New Mexico.

The El Paso plant was expanded when the company began marketing its meters in Arizona, California, Nevada, and Utah. With the growth of the West Coast business, the Darby Company opened a third distribution center in Las Vegas and just two years ago opened a second production plant in San Bernardino, California.

Manufacturing costs differ between the company's production plants. The cost of each meter produced at the El Paso plant is $10.50. The San Bernardino plant utilizes newer and more efficient equipment; as a result, manufacturing costs are $0.50 per meter less than at the El Paso plant.

Due to the company's rapid growth, not much attention had been paid to the efficiency of the distribution system, but Darby's management has decided that it is time to address this issue. The cost of shipping a meter from each of the two plants to each of the three distribution centers is shown in Table 7.34.

The quarterly production capacity is 30,000 meters at the older El Paso plant and 20,000 meters at the San Bernardino plant. Note that no shipments are allowed from the San Bernardino plant to the Ft. Worth distribution center.

The company serves nine customer zones from the three distribution centers. The forecast of the number of meters needed in each customer zone for the next quarter is shown in Table 7.35.

The cost per unit of shipping from each distribution center to each customer zone is given in Table 7.36; note that some of the distribution centers cannot serve certain customer zones.

In the current distribution system, demand at the Dallas, San Antonio, Wichita, and Kansas City customer zones is satisfied by shipments from the Ft. Worth distribution center. In a similar manner, the Denver, Salt Lake City, and Phoenix customer zones are served

| Table 7.34 | SHIPPING COST PER UNIT FROM PRODUCTION PLANTS TO DISTRIBUTION CENTERS ($) | | |
|---|---|---|---|
| | **Distribution Center** | | |
| **Plant** | **Ft. Worth** | **Santa Fe** | **Las Vegas** |
| El Paso | 3.20 | 2.20 | 4.20 |
| San Bernardino | — | 3.90 | 1.20 |

## Table 7.35 — QUARTERLY DEMAND FORECAST

| Customer Zone | Demand (meters) |
|---|---|
| Dallas | 6300 |
| San Antonio | 4880 |
| Wichita | 2130 |
| Kansas City | 1210 |
| Denver | 6120 |
| Salt Lake City | 4830 |
| Phoenix | 2750 |
| Los Angeles | 8580 |
| San Diego | 4460 |

by the Santa Fe distribution center, and the Los Angeles and San Diego customer zones are served by the Las Vegas distribution center. To determine how many units to ship from each plant, the quarterly customer demand forecasts are aggregated at the distribution centers, and a transportation model is used to minimize the cost of shipping from the production plants to the distribution centers.

## Managerial Report

You have been called in to make recommendations for improving the distribution system. Your report should address, but not be limited to, the following issues.

1. If the company does not change its current distribution strategy, what will its manufacturing and distribution costs be for the following quarter?
2. Suppose that the company is willing to consider dropping the distribution center limitations; that is, customers could be served by any of the distribution centers for which costs are available. Can costs be reduced? By how much?
3. The company wants to explore the possibility of satisfying some of the customer demand directly from the production plants. In particular, the shipping cost is $.30 per unit from San Bernardino to Los Angeles and $0.70 from San Bernardino to San Diego. The cost for direct shipments from El Paso to San Antonio is $3.50 per unit. Can distribution costs be further reduced by considering these direct plant-customer shipments?
4. Over the next five years, Darby is anticipating moderate growth (5000 meters) to the North and West. Would you recommend that they consider plant expansion at this time?

## Table 7.36 — SHIPPING COST FROM THE DISTRIBUTION CENTERS TO THE CUSTOMER ZONES ($)

| Distribution Center | Dallas | San Antonio | Wichita | Kansas City | Denver | Salt Lake City | Phoenix | Los Angeles | San Diego |
|---|---|---|---|---|---|---|---|---|---|
| Ft. Worth | 0.3 | 2.1 | 3.1 | 4.4 | 6.0 | — | — | — | — |
| Santa Fe | 5.2 | 5.4 | 4.5 | 6.0 | 2.7 | 4.7 | 3.4 | 3.3 | 2.7 |
| Las Vegas | — | — | — | — | 5.4 | 3.3 | 2.4 | 2.1 | 2.5 |

........................................................................................../  /..............

## Appendix 7.1    SPREADSHEET SOLUTION OF TRANSPORTATION AND ASSIGNMENT PROBLEMS

In this appendix we show how Excel Solver can be used to solve transportation and assignment problems. We start with the Foster Generators transportation problem.

### The Transportation Problem

The first step is to enter the data for the transportation costs, the origin supplies, and the destination demands in the top part of the spreadsheet. Then the linear programming model is developed in the bottom part of the spreadsheet. As with all linear programs the model has four key elements: the decision variables, the objective function, the constraint left-hand sides, and the constraint right-hand sides. For a transportation problem, the decision variables are the amounts shipped from each origin to each destination; the objective function is the total transportation cost; the left-hand sides are the number of units shipped from each origin and the number of units shipped into each destination; and the right-hand sides are the origin supplies and the destination demands.

The spreadsheet formulation and solution of the Foster Generators problem are shown in Figure 7.14. The data are in the top portion of the spreadsheet. The model appears in the bottom portion of the spreadsheet; the key elements are screened as usual.

**Figure 7.14    SPREADSHEET SOLUTION OF THE FOSTER GENERATORS PROBLEM**

| | A | B | C | D | E | F | G | H |
|---|---|---|---|---|---|---|---|---|
| 1 | **Foster Generators** | | | | | | | |
| 2 | | | | | | | | |
| 3 | | | | **Destination** | | | | |
| 4 | **Origin** | Boston | Chicago | St. Louis | Lexington | **Supply** | | |
| 5 | Cleveland | 3 | 2 | 7 | 6 | 5000 | | |
| 6 | Bedford | 7 | 5 | 2 | 3 | 6000 | | |
| 7 | York | 2 | 5 | 4 | 5 | 2500 | | |
| 8 | **Demand** | 6000 | 4000 | 2000 | 1500 | | | |
| 9 | | | | | | | | |
| 10 | | | | | | | | |
| 11 | **Model** | | | | | | | |
| 12 | | | | | | | | |
| 13 | | **Min Cost** | 39500 | | | | | |
| 14 | | | | | | | | |
| 15 | | | | **Destination** | | | | |
| 16 | **Origin** | Boston | Chicago | St. Louis | Lexington | **Total** | | |
| 17 | Cleveland | 3500 | 1500 | 0 | 0 | 5000 | <= | 5000 |
| 18 | Bedford | 0 | 2500 | 2000 | 1500 | 6000 | <= | 6000 |
| 19 | York | 2500 | 0 | 0 | 0 | 2500 | <= | 2500 |
| 20 | **Total** | 6000 | 4000 | 2000 | 1500 | | | |
| 21 | | = | = | = | = | | | |
| 22 | | 6000 | 4000 | 2000 | 1500 | | | |

## Spreadsheet Formulation

The data and descriptive labels are contained in cells A1:F8. The transportation costs are in cells B5:E7. The origin supplies are in cells F5:F7, and the destination demands are in cells B8:E8. The key elements of the model required by the Excel Solver are the decision variables, the objective function, the constraint left-hand sides, and the constraint right-hand sides. These cells are screened in the bottom portion of the spreadsheet.

Decision Variables Cells B17:E19 are reserved for the decision variables. The optimal values are shown to be $x_{11} = 3500$, $x_{12} = 1500$, $x_{22} = 2500$, $x_{23} = 2000$, $x_{24} = 1500$, and $x_{41} = 2500$. All other decision variables equal zero indicating nothing will be shipped over the corresponding routes.

Objective Function The formula =SUMPRODUCT(B5:E7,B17:E19) has been placed into cell C13 to reflect the cost of the solution. The minimum cost solution is shown to have a value of $39,500.

Left-Hand Sides Cells F17:F19 contain the left-hand sides for the supply constraints, and cells B20:E20 contain the left-hand sides for the demand constraints.
    Cell F17 =SUM(B17:E17)   (Copy to F18:F19)
    Cell B20 =SUM(B17:B19)   (Copy to C20:E20)

Right-Hand Sides Cells H17:H19 contain the right-hand sides for the supply constraints and Cells B22:E22 contain the right-hand sides for the demand constraints.
    Cell H17 =F5   (Copy to H18:H19)
    Cell B22 =B8   (Copy to C22:E22)

## Spreadsheet Solution

The solution shown in Figure 7.14 can be obtained by selecting **Solver** from the **Tools** menu, entering the proper values into the **Solver Parameters** dialog box, and specifying the options **Assume Linear Model** and **Assume Non-Negative.** The information entered into the **Solver Parameters** dialog box is shown in Figure 7.15.

## The Assignment Problem

The first step is to enter the data for the assignment costs in the top part of the spreadsheet. Even though the assignment model is a special case of the transportation model, it is not necessary to enter values for origin supplies and destination demands because they are always equal to one.

The linear programming model is developed in the bottom part of the spreadsheet. As with all linear programs the model has four key elements: the decision variables, the objective function, the constraint left-hand sides, and the constraint right-hand sides. For an assignment problem the decision variables indicate whether an agent is assigned to a task (with a 1 for yes or 0 for no); the objective function is the total cost of all assignments; the constraint left-hand sides are the number of tasks that are assigned to each agent and the number of agents that are assigned to each task; and the right-hand sides are the number of tasks each agent can handle (1) and the number of agents each task requires (1).

The spreadsheet formulation and solution are shown in Figure 7.16.

## Spreadsheet Formulation

The data and descriptive labels are contained in cells A1:D7. Note that we have not inserted supply and demand values since they are always equal to 1 in an assignment problem. The model appears in the bottom portion of the spreadsheet with the key elements screened.

**Figure 7.15**    SOLVER PARAMETERS DIALOG BOX FOR FOSTER GENERATORS PROBLEM

Solver Parameters

Set Target Cell:    $C$13

Equal To:    ○ Max    ● Min    ○ Value of:    0

By Changing Cells:

$B$17:$E$19    [Guess]

Subject to the Constraints:

$B$20:$E$20 = $B$22:$E$22
$F$17:$F$19 <= $H$17:$H$19

[Add]    [Change]    [Delete]

[Solve]    [Close]    [Options]    [Reset All]    [Help]

**Figure 7.16**    SPREADSHEET SOLUTION OF THE FOWLE MARKETING RESEARCH PROBLEM

| | A | B | C | D | E | F | G | H |
|---|---|---|---|---|---|---|---|---|
| 1 | **Fowle Marketing Research** | | | | | | | |
| 2 | | | | | | | | |
| 3 | | | **Client** | | | | | |
| 4 | **Project Leader** | 1 | 2 | 3 | | | | |
| 5 | Terry | 10 | 15 | 9 | | | | |
| 6 | Carle | 9 | 18 | 5 | | | | |
| 7 | McClymonds | 6 | 14 | 3 | | | | |
| 8 | | | | | | | | |
| 9 | | | | | | | | |
| 10 | **Model** | | | | | | | |
| 11 | | | | | | | | |
| 12 | | **Min Time** | 26 | | | | | |
| 13 | | | | | | | | |
| 14 | | | **Client** | | | | | |
| 15 | **Project Leader** | 1 | 2 | 3 | **Total** | | | |
| 16 | Terry | 0 | 1 | 0 | 1 | <= | 1 | |
| 17 | Carle | 0 | 0 | 1 | 1 | <= | 1 | |
| 18 | McClymonds | 1 | 0 | 0 | 1 | <= | 1 | |
| 19 | **Total** | 1 | 1 | 1 | | | | |
| 20 | | = | = | = | | | | |
| 21 | | 1 | 1 | 1 | | | | |

Decision Variables    Cells B16:D18 are reserved for the decision variables. The optimal values are shown to be $x_{12} = 1$, $x_{23} = 1$, and $x_{31} = 1$ with all other variables = 0.

Objective Function    The formula =SUMPRODUCT(B5:D7,B16:D18) has been placed into cell C12 to reflect the number of days required to complete all the jobs. The minimum time solution has a value of 26 days.

Left-Hand Sides    Cells E16:E18 contain the left-hand sides of the constraints for the number of clients each project leader can handle. Cells B19:D19 contain the left-hand sides of the constraints requiring that each client must be assigned a project leader.

      Cell E16 =SUM(B16:D16)    (Copy to E17:E18)
      Cell B19 =SUM(B16:B18)    (Copy to C19:D19)

Right-Hand Sides    Cells G16:G18 contain the right-hand sides for the project leader constraints and cells B21:D21 contain the right-hand sides for the client constraints. All right-hand side cell values are 1.

## Spreadsheet Solution

The solution shown in Figure 7.16 can be obtained by selecting **Solver** from the **Tools** menu, entering the proper values into the **Solver Parameters** dialog box, and specifying the options **Assume Linear Model** and **Assume Non-Negative.** The information entered into the **Solver Parameters** dialog box is shown in Figure 7.17.

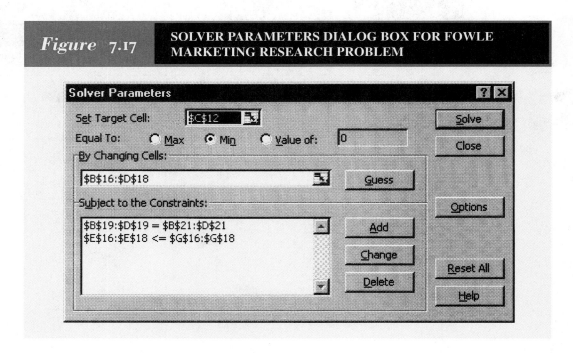

**Figure 7.17    SOLVER PARAMETERS DIALOG BOX FOR FOWLE MARKETING RESEARCH PROBLEM**

# PROCTER & GAMBLE*

## CINCINNATI, OHIO

Procter & Gamble (P&G) is in the consumer products business worldwide. P&G produces and markets such products as detergents, disposable diapers, coffee, over-the-counter pharmaceuticals, dentifrices, bar soaps, mouthwashes, and paper towels. It has the leading brand in more categories than any other consumer products company in the United States.

In order to maintain its leadership position in its many markets, P&G makes extensive use of management science. Some of the methodologies employed include probability and risk analysis, linear and integer programming, network flow analysis, and simulation. The individuals employing these methodologies are scattered throughout P&G's numerous divisions with perhaps the largest concentration being in the management systems division. P&G employs engineers, operations researchers, computer scientists, and businesspeople who are skilled in employing quantitative methodologies.

Recently P&G embarked on a major strategic planning initiative: the North American Product Sourcing Study. P&G was interested in consolidating its product sources and optimizing its distribution system design throughout North America. One of the decision support systems that proved to be a great aid in this project was called the Product Sourcing Heuristic (PSH). This heuristic was based on a transshipment model much like the ones described in this chapter.

In a preprocessing phase, the many P&G products were aggregated into groups that shared the same technology and could be made at the same plant. The PSH was used by product strategy teams that had responsibility for developing product sourcing options for the separate product groups. The various plants that could produce the product group were source nodes, the company's regional distribution centers were the transshipment nodes, and P&G's customer zones were the destinations. Direct shipments to customer zones as well as shipments through distribution centers were employed.

The product strategy teams used the heuristic interactively to explore a variety of questions concerning product sourcing and distribution. For instance, the team might be interested in the impact of closing two plants and consolidating production in three remaining plants. The product sourcing heuristic would then delete the source nodes corresponding to the two closed plants, make any capacity modifications recommended to the sources corresponding to the remaining three plants, and resolve the transshipment problem. The product strategy team could then examine the new solution, make some more modifications, solve again, and so on.

The Product Sourcing Heuristic was viewed as a valuable decision support system by all who used it. Probably the most valuable feature was that the model permitted a rapid evaluation of a variety of strategic options. A feature that was viewed as a big plus by all who used it was that solutions provided by the PSH were displayed on a map of North America using a geographic information system. This capability enabled strategic planners to review immediately the impact of their sourcing decisions across North America. The PSH has proven so successful that P&G is considering using it in other markets around the world.

*The authors are indebted to Mr. Franz Dill and Mr. Tom Chorman of Procter & Gamble for providing this application.

# 8

## INTEGER LINEAR PROGRAMMING

### CONTENTS

In this chapter we discuss a class of problems that are modeled as linear programs with the additional requirement that one or more variables must be integer. Such problems are called **integer linear programs.** If all variables must be integer, we have an all-integer linear program. If some, but not all, variables must be integer, we have a mixed-integer linear program. In many applications of integer linear programming, one or more integer variables are required to equal either 0 or 1. Such variables are called *0–1* or *binary variables.* If all variables are 0–1 variables, we have a 0–1 integer linear program.

Integer variables—especially 0–1 variables—provide substantial modeling flexibility. As a result, the number of applications that can be addressed with linear programming methodology is expanded. The cost of the added modeling flexibility is that problems involving integer variables are often much more difficult to solve. A linear programming problem with several thousand continuous variables can be solved with any of several commercial linear programming solvers. However, an all-integer linear programming problem with less than 100 variables can be extremely difficult to solve. Experienced management scientists can help identify the types of integer linear programs that are easy, or at least reasonable, to solve. Commercial computer software packages, such as MPSX-MIP®, OSL®, CPLEX®, and LINDO®, have extensive integer programming capability. The Management Scientist and spreadsheet packages, such as Excel, have the capability for solving smaller integer linear programs.

The objective of this chapter is to provide an applications-oriented introduction to integer linear programming. First, we discuss the different types of integer linear programming models. Then we show the formulation, graphical solution, and computer solution of an all-integer linear program. In Section 8.3, we discuss four applications of integer linear programming that make use of 0–1 variables: capital budgeting, fixed cost, distribution system design, and bank location problems. In Section 8.4, we provide additional illustrations of the modeling flexibility provided by 0–1 variables. A chapter appendix illustrates the use of Excel for solving integer programs.

## NOTES and Comments

1. Because integer linear programs are harder to solve than linear programs, one should not try to solve a problem as an integer program if simply rounding the linear programming solution is adequate. In many linear programming problems, such as those in previous chapters, rounding has little economic consequences on the objective function, and feasibility is not an issue. But, in problems such as determining how many jet engines to manufacture, the consequences of rounding can be substantial and integer programming methodology should be employed.

2. Some linear programming problems have a special structure, which guarantees that the variables will have integer values. The assignment, transportation, and transshipment problems of Chapter 7 have such structures. If the supply and the demand for transportation and transshipment problems are integer, the optimal linear programming solution will provide integer amounts shipped. For the assignment problem, the optimal linear programming solution will consist of 0s and 1s. So, for these specially structured problems linear programming methodology can be used to find optimal integer solutions. Integer linear programming algorithms are not necessary.

## 8.1     TYPES OF INTEGER LINEAR PROGRAMMING MODELS

The only difference between the problems studied in this chapter and the ones studied in earlier chapters on linear programming is that one, or more, variables are required to be integer. If all variables are required to be integer, we have an **all-integer linear program.** The following is a two-variable, all-integer linear programming model.

$$\text{Max} \quad 2x_1 + 3x_2$$
$$\text{s.t.}$$
$$3x_1 + 3x_2 \leq 12$$
$$\tfrac{2}{3}x_1 + 1x_2 \leq 4$$
$$1x_1 + 2x_2 \leq 6$$
$$x_1, x_2 \geq 0 \text{ and integer}$$

Note that if we drop the phrase "and integer" from this model, we have the familiar two-variable linear program. The linear program that results from dropping the integer requirements is called the **LP Relaxation** of the integer linear program.

If some, but not all, variables are required to be integer, we have a **mixed-integer linear program.** The following is a two-variable, mixed-integer linear program.

$$\text{Max} \quad 3x_1 + 4x_2$$
$$\text{s.t.}$$
$$-1x_1 + 2x_2 \leq 8$$
$$1x_1 + 2x_2 \leq 12$$
$$2x_1 + 1x_2 \leq 16$$
$$x_1, x_2 \geq 0 \text{ and } x_2 \text{ integer}$$

We obtain the LP Relaxation of this mixed-integer linear program by dropping the requirement that $x_2$ be integer.

In some applications, the integer variables may only take on the values 0 or 1. Then we have a **0–1 linear integer program.** As we see later in the chapter, 0–1 variables provide addition modeling capability. The Management Science in Action: Planning the Size of KLM's Aircraft Maintenance Teams describes how integer and 0–1 integer variables are used to determine the size of the engineering teams that perform maintenance on KLM's aircraft.

## 8.2     GRAPHICAL AND COMPUTER SOLUTIONS FOR AN ALL-INTEGER LINEAR PROGRAM

Eastborne Realty has $2,000,000 available for the purchase of new rental property. After an initial screening. Eastborne has reduced the investment alternatives to townhouses and apartment buildings. Each townhouse can be purchased for $282,000, and five are available. Each apartment building can be purchased for $400,000, and the developer will construct as many buildings as Eastborne wants to purchase.

# MANAGEMENT SCIENCE IN ACTION

## PLANNING THE SIZE OF KLM'S AIRCRAFT MAINTENANCE TEAMS*

KLM Royal Dutch Airlines has been the major Dutch carrier since 1919. Currently, KLM owns 90 aircraft of 8 different types and operates flights to 150 cities in 79 countries. To guarantee safety, KLM has a high-quality aircraft maintenance program with a workforce that includes 250 engineers and 150 nontechnical employees.

Preventive maintenance on an aircraft consists of both major and minor inspections. Major inspections require several hours to several months to complete. Minor inspections are conducted during the ground time between aircraft arrival and departure at an airport. Engineers from KLM's aircraft maintenance group are organized into teams that carry out the maintenance tasks.

The engineers are highly skilled and well trained. A governmental rule specifies that maintenance engineers are allowed to carry out inspections on a specific aircraft type only if licensed for that aircraft type. KLM's internal safety rules further limit engineers to licenses on at most two aircraft types. When licensed for a particular aircraft, an individual engineer's skills are certified as being mechanical, electrical, or radio.

KLM's management strives to develop a good match between workload requirements and the abilities of the assigned workforce.

Given a set of maintenance jobs, management attempts to minimize the number of engineers with appropriate license and skill combinations necessary to complete the jobs. An integer linear programming model helps with this task. The objective function is to minimize the number of engineers required per maintenance team. Integer decision variables are required because the number of engineers with each license and skill combination cannot be fractional. In addition, 0—1 integer variables are included in the model to guarantee that each maintenance job is carried out exactly once. Another integer programming model is used to determine the maximum number of maintenance jobs that can be scheduled given the size and composition of the maintenance workforce. KLM has found integer linear programming to be a valuable tool for solving problems dealing with personnel planning for aircraft maintenance.

* Based on M. C. Dijkstra, L. G. Kroon, M. Slomon, J. A. E. E. Van Nunen, and L. N. Van Wassenhove, "Planning the Size and Organization of KLM's Aircraft Maintenance Personnel," *Interfaces* (November—December 1994): 47—58.

---

Eastborne's property manager can devote up to 140 hours per month to these new properties; each townhouse is expected to require 4 hours per month, and each apartment building is expected to require 40 hours per month. The annual cash flow, after deducting mortgage payments and operating expenses, is estimated to be $10,000 per townhouse and $15,000 per apartment building. Eastborne's owner would like to determine the number of townhouses and the number of apartment buildings to purchase to maximize annual cash flow.

We begin by defining the decision variables as follows:

$$T = \text{number of townhouses}$$

$$A = \text{number of apartment buildings}$$

The objective function for cash flow ($1000s) is

$$\text{Max} \quad 10T + 15A$$

Three constraints must be satisfied:

$$282T + 400A \leq 2000 \quad \text{Funds available}$$
$$4T + 40A \leq 140 \quad \text{Manager's time}$$
$$T \leq 5 \quad \text{Townhouses available}$$

The variables $T$ and $A$ must be nonnegative. In addition, the purchase of a fractional number of townhouses and/or a fractional number of apartment buildings is unacceptable. Thus,

$T$ and $A$ must be integer. The model for the Eastborne Realty problem is the following all-integer linear program.

$$
\begin{aligned}
\text{Max} \quad & 10T + 15A \\
\text{s.t.} \quad & \\
& 282T + 400A \leq 2000 \\
& 4T + 40A \leq 140 \\
& T \qquad\quad \leq 5 \\
& T, A \geq 0 \text{ and integer}
\end{aligned}
$$

## Graphical Solution of the LP Relaxation

Suppose that we drop the integer requirements for $T$ and $A$ and solve the LP Relaxation of the Eastborne Realty Problem. Using the graphical solution procedure, as presented in Chapter 2, the optimal linear programming solution is shown in Figure 8.1. It is $T = 2.479$ townhouses and $A = 3.252$ apartment buildings. The optimal value of the objective function is 73.574, which indicates an annual cash flow of $73,574. Unfortunately, Eastborne cannot purchase fractional numbers of townhouses and apartment buildings; further analysis is necessary.

**Figure 8.1**   GRAPHICAL SOLUTION TO THE LP RELAXATION OF THE EASTBORNE REALTY PROBLEM

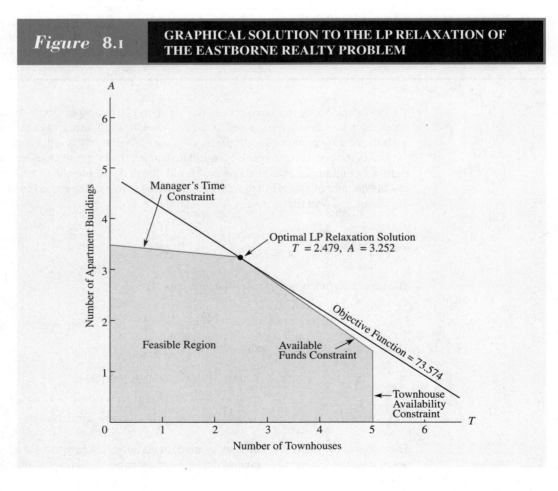

## Rounding to Obtain an Integer Solution

In many cases, a noninteger solution can be rounded to obtain an acceptable integer solution. For instance, a linear programming solution to a production scheduling problem might call for the production of 15,132.4 cases of breakfast cereal. The rounded integer solution of 15,132 cases would probably have minimal impact on the value of the objective function and the feasibility of the solution. Rounding would be a sensible approach. Indeed, whenever rounding has a minimal impact on the objective function and constraints, most managers find it acceptable. A near-optimal solution is fine.

However, rounding may not always be a good strategy. When the decision variables take on small values that have a major impact on the value of the objective function and/or feasibility, an optimal integer solution is needed. Let us return to the Eastborne Realty problem and examine the impact of rounding. The optimal solution to the LP Relaxation for Eastborne Realty resulted in $T = 2.479$ townhouses and $A = 3.252$ apartment buildings. Since each townhouse costs \$282,000 and each apartment building costs \$400,000, rounding to an integer solution can be expected to have a significant economic impact on the problem.

If a problem has only less-than-or-equal-to constraints with positive coefficients for the variables, rounding down will always provide a feasible integer solution.

Suppose that we round the solution to the LP Relaxation to obtain the integer solution $T = 2$ and $A = 3$, with an objective function value of $10(2) + 15(3) = 65$. The annual cash flow of \$65,000 is substantially less than the annual cash flow of \$73,574 provided by the solution to the LP Relaxation. Do other rounding possibilities exist? Exploring other rounding alternatives shows that the integer solution $T = 3$ and $A = 3$ is infeasible because it requires more funds than the \$2,000,000 Eastborne has available. The rounded solution of $T = 2$ and $A = 4$ is also infeasible for the same reason. At this point, rounding has led to two townhouses and three apartment buildings with an annual cash flow of \$65,000 as the best feasible integer solution to the problem. Unfortunately, we don't know whether this solution is the best integer solution to the problem.

Rounding to an integer solution is a trial-and-error approach. Each rounded solution must be evaluated for feasibility as well as for its impact on the value of the objective function. Even in cases where a rounded solution its feasible, we do not have a guarantee that we have found the optimal integer solution. We will see shortly that the rounded solution ($T = 2$ and $A = 3$) is not optimal for Eastborne Realty.

## Graphical Solution of the All-Integer Problem

Figure 8.2 shows the changes in the linear programming graphical solution procedure required to solve the Eastborne Realty integer linear programming problem. First, the graph of the feasible region is drawn exactly as in the LP Relaxation of the problem. Then, since the optimal solution must have integer values, we identify the feasible integer solutions with the dots shown in Figure 8.2. Finally, instead of moving the objective function line to the best extreme point in the feasible region, we move it in an improving direction as far as possible until reaching the dot (feasible integer point) providing the best value for the objective function. Viewing Figure 8.2, we see that the optimal integer solution occurs at $T = 4$ townhouses and $A = 2$ apartment buildings. The objective function value is $10(4) + 15(2) = 70$ providing an annual cash flow of \$70,000. This solution is significantly better than the best solution found by rounding: $T = 2$, $A = 3$ with an annual cash flow of \$65,000. Thus, we see that rounding would not have been the best strategy for Eastborne Realty.

Try Problem 2 for practice with the graphical solution of an integer program.

## Using the LP Relaxation to Establish Bounds

An important observation can be made from the analysis of the Eastborne Realty problem. It has to do with the relationship between the value of the optimal integer solution and the value of the optimal solution to the LP Relaxation.

**Figure 8.2**    GRAPHICAL SOLUTION OF THE EASTBORNE REALTY INTEGER PROBLEM

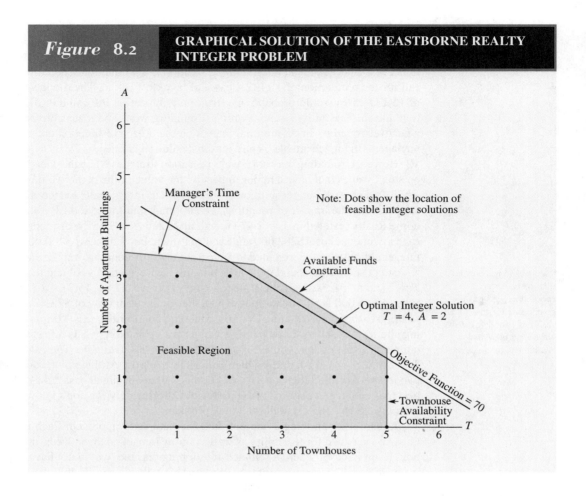

For integer linear programs involving maximization, the value of the optimal solution to the LP Relaxation provides an upper bound on the value of the optimal integer solution. For integer linear programs involving minimization, the value of the optimal solution to the LP Relaxation provides a lower bound on the value of the optimal integer solution.

This observation is valid for the Eastborne Realty problem. The value of the optimal integer solution is $70,000, and the value of the optimal solution to the LP Relaxation is $73,574. Thus, we know from the LP Relaxation solution that the upper bound for the value of the objective function is $73,574.

The bounding property of the LP Relaxation allows us to conclude that if, by chance, the solution to an LP Relaxation turns out to be an integer solution, it is also optimal for the integer linear program. This bounding property can also be helpful in determining if a rounded solution is "good enough." If a rounded LP Relaxation solution is feasible and provides a value of the objective function that is "almost as good as" the value of the objective function for the LP Relaxation, we know the rounded solution is a near-optimal integer solution. When this happens, we can avoid having to solve the problem as an integer linear program.

Try Problem 5 for the graphical solution of a mixed integer program.

## Computer Solution

As mentioned earlier, commercial software packages that can solve integer linear programs are widely available. Generally, these packages are reliable for problems having up to approximately 100 integer variables and may be used to solve specially structured problems with several thousand integer variables.

The Management Scientist can be used to solve the integer linear programs in this chapter. To use The Management Scientist to solve the Eastborne Realty problem, the data input worksheet is completed in the same way as for any linear program (see Appendix A). Then after instructing the computer to solve the problem, the user will be asked to indicate which of the variables are integer. Specifying both $T$ and $A$ as integers provides the optimal integer solution shown in Figure 8.3. The solution of $T = 4$ townhouses and $A = 2$ apartment buildings has a maximum annual cash flow of $70,000. The values of the slack variables tell us that the optimal solution has $72,000 of available funds unused, 44 hours of the manager's time still available and 1 of the available townhouses not purchased.

---

N O T E S
*and Comments*

In Appendix 8.1 we show the use of spreadsheets to solve integer programs by using Excel to solve the Eastborne Realty problem.

---

| *Figure* 8.3 | THE MANAGEMENT SCIENTIST SOLUTION FOR THE EASTBORNE REALTY PROBLEM |
|---|---|

```
Objective Function Value =                        70.000


      Variable                             Value
 _ _ _ _ _ _ _ _ _ _                   _ _ _ _ _ _ _ _ _
          T                                4.000
          A                                2.000


    Constraint                         Slack/Surplus
 _ _ _ _ _ _ _ _ _ _ _                _ _ _ _ _ _ _ _ _
          1                               72.000
          2                               44.000
          3                                1.000
```

## 8.3   APPLICATIONS INVOLVING 0–1 VARIABLES

Much of the modeling flexibility provided by integer linear programming is due to the use of 0–1 variables. In many applications, 0–1 variables provide selections or choices with the value of the variable equal to 1 if a corresponding activity is undertaken and equal to 0 if the corresponding activity is not undertaken. The capital budgeting, fixed cost, distribution system design, and bank location applications presented in this section make use of 0–1 variables.

## Capital Budgeting

The Ice-Cold Refrigerator Company is considering investing in several projects that have varying capital requirements over the next four years. Faced with limited capital each year, management would like to select the most profitable projects. The estimated net present value for each project,[1] the capital requirements, and the available capital over the four-year period are shown in Table 8.1.

The four 0–1 decision variables are as follows:

$P = 1$ if the plant expansion project is accepted; 0 if rejected

$W = 1$ if the warehouse expansion project is accepted; 0 if rejected

$M = 1$ if the new machinery project is accepted; 0 if rejected

$R = 1$ if the new product research project is accepted; 0 if rejected

The company's objective function is to maximize the net present value of the capital budgeting projects. The problem has four constraints: one for the funds available in each of the next four years.

A 0–1 integer linear programming model with dollars in thousands is as follows:

$$\text{Max} \quad 90P + 40W + 10M + 37R$$

s.t.

$$15P + 10W + 10M + 15R \leq 40 \quad \text{(Year 1 capital available)}$$
$$20P + 15W \qquad\quad\; + 10R \leq 50 \quad \text{(Year 2 capital available)}$$
$$20P + 20W \qquad\quad\; + 10R \leq 40 \quad \text{(Year 3 capital available)}$$
$$15P + \;\; 5W + \;\; 4M + 10R \leq 35 \quad \text{(Year 4 capital available)}$$
$$P, W, M, R = 0, 1$$

The integer programming solution from The Management Scientist is shown in Figure 8.4. The optimal solution is $P = 1$, $W = 1$, $M = 1$, $R = 0$, with a total estimated net present value of $140,000. Thus, the company should fund the plant expansion, the warehouse ex-

| Table 8.1 | PROJECT NET PRESENT VALUE, CAPITAL REQUIREMENTS, AND AVAILABLE CAPTIAL FOR THE ICE-COLD REFRIGERATOR COMPANY |
|---|---|

| | Project | | | | |
| | Plant Expansion | Warehouse Expansion | New Machinery | New Product Research | Total Capital Available |
|---|---|---|---|---|---|
| Present Value | $90,000 | $40,000 | $10,000 | $37,000 | |
| Year 1 Capital | $15,000 | $10,000 | $10,000 | $15,000 | $40,000 |
| Year 2 Capital | $20,000 | $15,000 | | $10,000 | $50,000 |
| Year 3 Capital | $20,000 | $20,000 | | $10,000 | $40,000 |
| Year 4 Capital | $15,000 | $ 5,000 | $ 4,000 | $10,000 | $35,000 |

[1] The estimated net present value is the net cash flow discounted back to the beginning of year 1.

| Figure 8.4 | THE MANAGEMENT SCIENTIST SOLUTION FOR THE ICE-COLD REFRIGERATOR COMPANY PROBLEM |
|---|---|

```
Objective Function Value =                    140.000

      __Variable__                          __ __Value__ __

           P                                    1.000

           W                                    1.000

           M                                    1.000

           R                                    0.000


      __Constraint__                        __Slack/Surplus__

           1                                    5.000

           2                                   15.000

           3                                    0.000

           4                                   11.000
```

pansion, and the new machinery projects. The new product research project should be put on hold unless additional capital funds become available. The values of the slack variables (see Figure 8.4) show that the company will have $5,000 remaining in year 1, $15,000 remaining in year 2, and $11,000 remaining in year 4. Checking the capital requirements for the new product research project, we see that enough funds are available for this project in year 2 and year 4. However, the company would have to find additional capital funds of $10,000 in year 1 and $10,000 in year 3 to fund the new product research project.

## Fixed Cost

In many applications, the cost of production has two components: a setup cost, which is a fixed cost, and a variable cost, which is directly related to the production quantity. The use of 0–1 variables makes including the setup cost possible in a model for a production application.

Consider the RMC problem. Three raw materials are used to produce 3 products: a fuel additive, a solvent base, and a carpet cleaning fluid. The following decision variables are used.

$$F = \text{tons of fuel additive produced}$$
$$S = \text{tons of solvent base produced}$$
$$C = \text{tons of carpet cleaning fluid produced}$$

The profit contributions are $40 per ton for the fuel additive, $30 per ton for the solvent base, and $50 per ton for the carpet cleaning fluid. Each ton of fuel additive is a blend of 0.4 tons of material 1 and 0.6 tons of material 3. Each ton of solvent base requires 0.5 tons of material 1, 0.2 tons of material 2, and 0.3 tons of material 3. Each ton of carpet cleaning fluid is a blend of 0.6 tons of material 1, 0.1 tons of material 2, and 0.3 tons of material 3. RMC has 20 tons of material 1, 5 tons of material 2, and 21 tons of material 3, and is interested in determining the optimal production quantities for the upcoming planning period.

A linear programming model of the RMC problem is shown.

$$\text{Max} \quad 40F + 30S + 50C$$

$$\text{s.t.}$$

$$0.4F + 0.5S + 0.6C \leq 20 \quad \text{Material 1}$$
$$0.2S + 0.1C \leq 5 \quad \text{Material 2}$$
$$0.6F + 0.3S + 0.3C \leq 21 \quad \text{Material 3}$$
$$F, S, C \geq 0$$

Using the linear programming module of The Management Scientist, we obtained an optimal solution consisting of 27.5 tons of fuel additive, 0 tons of solvent base, and 15 tons of carpet cleaning fluid, with a value of $1850. See Figure 8.5.

This linear programming formulation of the RMC problem does not include a fixed cost for production setup of the products. Suppose that the following data are available concerning the setup cost and the maximum production quantity for each of the 3 products.

| Product | Setup Cost | Maximum Production |
|---|---|---|
| Fuel additive | $200 | 50 tons |
| Solvent base | $ 50 | 25 tons |
| Carpet cleaning fluid | $400 | 40 tons |

The modeling flexibility provided by 0–1 variables can now be used to incorporate the fixed setup costs into the production model. The 0–1 variables are defined as follows:

$$SF = 1 \text{ if the fuel additive is produced; 0 if not}$$
$$SS = 1 \text{ if the solvent base is produced; 0 if not}$$
$$SC = 1 \text{ if the carpet cleaning fluid is produced; 0 if not}$$

Using these setup variables, the total setup cost is

$$200SF + 50SS + 400SC$$

**Figure 8.5   THE MANAGEMENT SCIENTIST SOLUTION TO THE RMC PROBLEM**

```
Objective Function Value =   1850.000

      Variable            Value            Reduced Costs
    ------------        ---------         ----------------
        F                27.500                  0.000
        S                 0.000                 12.500
        C                15.000                  0.000
```

We can now rewrite the objective function to include the setup cost. Thus, the net profit objective function becomes

$$\text{Max} \quad 40F + 30S + 50C - 200SF - 50SS - 400SC$$

Next, we must write production capacity constraints so that if a setup variable equals 0, production of the corresponding product is not permitted and, if a setup variable equals 1, production is permitted up to the maximum quantity. For the fuel additive, we do so by adding the following constraint:

$$F \leq 50SF$$

Note that, with this constraint present, production of the fuel additive is not permitted when $SF = 0$. When $SF = 1$, production of up to 50 tons of fuel additive is permitted. We can think of the setup variable as a switch. When it is off ($SF = 0$), production is not permitted; when it is on ($SF = 1$), production is permitted.

Similar production capacity constraints, using 0–1 variables, are added for the solvent base and carpet cleaning products

$$S \leq 25SS$$
$$C \leq 40SC$$

Moving all the variables to the left-hand side of the constraints provides the following fixed cost model for the RMC problem.

$$\text{Max} \quad 40F + 30S + 50C - 200SF - 50SS - 400SC$$

s.t.

| | | | | |
|---|---|---|---|---|
| $0.4F + 0.5S + 0.6C$ | | $\leq 20$ | Material 1 |
| $0.2S + 0.1C$ | | $\leq 5$ | Material 2 |
| $0.6F + 0.3S + 0.3C$ | | $\leq 21$ | Material 3 |
| $F$ | $- 50SF$ | $\leq 0$ | Maximum $F$ |
| $S$ | $- 25SS$ | $\leq 0$ | Maximum $S$ |
| $C$ | $- 40SC \leq 0$ | | Maximum C |

$$F, S, C \geq 0; \; SF, SS, SC = 0, 1$$

We solved the RMC problem with setup costs using The Management Scientist. As shown in Figure 8.6, the optimal solution shows 25 tons of fuel additive and 20 tons of solvent base. The value of the objective function after deducting the setup cost is $1,350. The setup cost for the fuel additive and the solvent base is $200 + $50 = $250. The optimal solution shows $SC = 0$, which indicates that the more expensive $400 setup cost for the carpet cleaning fluid should be avoided. Thus the carpet cleaning fluid is not produced.

The key to developing a fixed-cost model is the introduction of a 0–1 variable for each fixed cost and the specification of an upper bound for the corresponding production variable. For a production quantity $x$, a constraint of the form $x \leq My$ can then be used to allow production when the setup variable $y = 1$ and not to allow production when the setup variable $y = 0$. The value of the maximum production quantity $M$ should be large enough to allow for all reasonable levels of production. But, research has shown that choosing values of $M$ too large will slow the solution procedure.

| Figure 8.6 | THE MANAGEMENT SCIENTIST SOLUTION TO THE RMC PROBLEM WITH SETUP COSTS |
|---|---|

```
Objective Function Value = 1350.000

      Variable                    Value
      --------                   --------
         F                       25.000
         S                       20.000
         C                        0.000
        SF                        1.000
        SS                        1.000
        SC                        0.000
```

## Distribution System Design

The Martin-Beck Company operates a plant in St. Louis with an annual capacity of 30,000 units. Product is shipped to regional distribution centers located in Boston, Atlanta, and Houston. Because of an anticipated increase in demand, Martin-Beck plans to increase capacity by constructing a new plant in one or more of the following cities: Detroit, Toledo, Denver, or Kansas City. The estimated annual fixed cost and the annual capacity for the four proposed plants are as follows:

| Proposed Plant | Annual Fixed Cost | Annual Capacity |
|---|---|---|
| Detroit | $175,000 | 10,000 |
| Toledo | $300,000 | 20,000 |
| Denver | $375,000 | 30,000 |
| Kansas City | $500,000 | 40,000 |

The company's long-range planning group has developed forecasts of the anticipated annual demand at the distribution centers as follows:

| Distribution Center | Annual Demand |
|---|---|
| Boston | 30,000 |
| Atlanta | 20,000 |
| Houston | 20,000 |

The shipping cost per unit from each plant to each distribution center is shown in Table 8.2. A network representation of the potential Martin-Beck distribution system is shown in Figure 8.7. Each potential plant location is shown; capacities and demands are shown in thousands of units. This network representation is for a transportation problem with a plant at St. Louis and at all four proposed sites. However, the decision has not yet been made as to which new plant or plants will be constructed.

| Table 8.2 | SHIPPING COST PER UNIT FOR THE MARTIN-BECK DISTRIBUTION SYSTEM | | |
|---|---|---|---|

| | Distribution Centers | | |
| Plant Site | Boston | Atlanta | Houston |
|---|---|---|---|
| Detroit | 5 | 2 | 3 |
| Toledo | 4 | 3 | 4 |
| Denver | 9 | 7 | 5 |
| Kansas City | 10 | 4 | 2 |
| St. Louis | 8 | 4 | 3 |

| Figure 8.7 | THE NETWORK REPRESENTATION OF THE MARTIN-BECK COMPANY DISTRIBUTION SYSTEM PROBLEM |
|---|---|

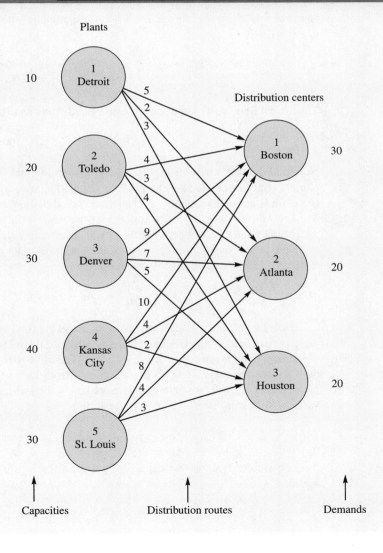

Let us now show how 0–1 variables can be used to develop a model for choosing the best plant locations and for determining how much to ship from each plant to each distribution center. We can use the following 0–1 variables to represent the plant construction decision.

$$y_1 = 1 \text{ if a plant is constructed in Detroit; 0 if not}$$
$$y_2 = 1 \text{ if a plant is constructed in Toledo; 0 if not}$$
$$y_3 = 1 \text{ if a plant is constructed in Denver; 0 if not}$$
$$y_4 = 1 \text{ if a plant is constructed in Kansas City; 0 if not}$$

The variables representing the amount shipped from each plant site to each distribution center are defined just as for a transportation problem.

$$x_{ij} = \text{the units shipped in thousands from plant } i \text{ to distribution center } j$$
$$i = 1, 2, 3, 4, 5 \quad \text{and} \quad j = 1, 2, 3$$

Using the shipping cost data in Table 8.2, the annual transportation cost in thousand of dollars is written

$$5x_{11} + 2x_{12} + 3x_{13} + 4x_{21} + 3x_{22} + 4x_{23} + 9x_{31} + 7x_{32} + 5x_{33}$$
$$+ 10x_{41} + 4x_{42} + 2x_{43} + 8x_{51} + 4x_{52} + 3x_{53}$$

The annual fixed cost of operating the new plant or plants in thousand of dollars is written as

$$175y_1 + 300y_2 + 375y_3 + 500y_4$$

Note that the 0–1 variables are defined so that the annual fixed cost of operating the new plants is only calculated for the plant or plants that are actually constructed (i.e., $y_i = 1$). If a plant is not constructed, $y_i = 0$ and the corresponding annual fixed cost is $0.

The Martin-Beck objective function is the sum of the annual transportation cost plus the annual fixed cost of operating the newly constructed plants.

Now let us consider the capacity constraints at the four proposed plants. Using Detroit as an example, we write the following constraint:

$$x_{11} + x_{12} + x_{13} \le 10y_1$$

If the Detroit plant is constructed, $y_1 = 1$ and the total amount shipped from Detroit to the three distribution centers must be less than or equal to Detroit's 10,000-unit capacity. If the Detroit plant is not constructed, $y_1 = 0$ will result in a 0 capacity at Detroit. In this case, the variables corresponding to the shipments from Detroit must all equal zero: $x_{11} = 0$, $x_{12} = 0$, and $x_{13} = 0$. By placing all variables on the left-hand side of the constraints, we have the following Detroit capacity constraint:

$$x_{11} + x_{12} + x_{13} - 10y_1 \le 0 \qquad \text{Detroit capacity}$$

In a similar fashion, the capacity constraint for the proposed plant in Toledo can be written

$$x_{21} + x_{22} + x_{23} - 20y_2 \le 0 \qquad \text{Toledo capacity}$$

Similar constraints can be written for the proposed plants in Denver and Kansas City. Note that since the plant already exists in St. Louis, we do not define a 0–1 variable for this plant. Its capacity constraint can be written as follows:

$$x_{51} + x_{52} + x_{53} \leq 30 \qquad \text{St. Louis capacity}$$

Three demand constraints will be needed, one for each of the three distribution centers. The demand constraint for the Boston distribution center with units in thousands is written as

$$x_{11} + x_{21} + x_{31} + x_{41} + x_{51} = 30 \qquad \text{Boston demand}$$

Similar constraints appear for the Atlanta and Houston distribution centers.

The complete model for the Martin-Beck distribution system design problem is as follows:

$$\begin{aligned}
\text{Min} \quad &5x_{11} + 2x_{12} + 3x_{13} + 4x_{21} + 3x_{22} + 4x_{23} + 9x_{31} + 7x_{32} + 5x_{33} + 10x_{41} + 4x_{42} \\
&+ 2x_{43} + 8x_{51} + 4x_{52} + 3x_{53} + 175y_1 + 300y_2 + 375y_3 + 500y_4
\end{aligned}$$

s.t.

| | | | |
|---|---|---|---|
| $x_{11} + x_{12} + x_{13} \quad - 10y_1$ | | $\leq 0$ | Detroit capacity |
| $x_{21} + x_{22} + x_{23} \quad - 20y_2$ | | $\leq 0$ | Toledo capacity |
| $x_{31} + x_{32} + x_{33} \quad - 30y_3$ | | $\leq 0$ | Denver capacity |
| $x_{41} + x_{42} + x_{43} \quad - 40y_4$ | | $\leq 0$ | Kansas City capacity |
| $x_{51} + x_{52} + x_{53}$ | | $\leq 30$ | St. Louis capacity |
| $x_{11} + x_{21} + x_{31} + x_{41} + x_{51}$ | | $= 30$ | Boston demand |
| $x_{12} + x_{22} + x_{32} + x_{42} + x_{52}$ | | $= 20$ | Atlanta demand |
| $x_{13} + x_{23} + x_{33} + x_{43} + x_{53}$ | | $= 20$ | Houston demand |

$$x_{ij} \geq \text{ for all } i \text{ and } j; \; y_1, y_2, y_3, y_4 = 0, 1$$

Using the integer linear programming module of The Management Scientist, we obtained the solution shown in Figure 8.8. The optimal solution calls for the construction of a plant in Kansas City ($y_4 = 1$); 20,000 units will be shipped from Kansas City to Atlanta ($x_{42} = 20$), 20,000 units will be shipped from Kansas City to Houston ($x_{43} = 20$), and 30,000 units will be shipped from St. Louis to Boston ($x_{51} = 30$). Note that the total cost of this solution including the fixed cost of $500,000 for the plant in Kansas City is $860,000.

This basic model can be expanded to accommodate distribution systems involving direct shipments from plants to warehouses, from plants to retail outlets, and of multiple products.[2] Using the special properties of 0–1 variables, the model can also be expanded to accommodate a variety of configuration constraints on the plant locations. For example, suppose in another problem, site 1 was in Dallas and site 2 was in Fort Worth. A company might not want to locate plants in both Dallas and Fort Worth because

---

[2] For computational reasons, it is usually preferable to replace the $m$ plant capacity constraints with $mn$ shipping route capacity constraints of the form $x_{ij} \leq \text{Min } \{s_i, d_j\} \, y_i$ for $i = 1, \ldots, m$, and $j = 1, \ldots, n$. The coefficient for $y_i$ in each of these constraints is the smaller of the origin capacity ($s_i$) or the destination demand ($d_j$). These additional constraints often cause the solution of the LP Relaxation to be integer.

**Figure 8.8** THE MANAGEMENT SCIENTIST SOLUTION FOR THE MARTIN-BECK COMPANY DISTRIBUTION SYSTEM PROBLEM

```
OPTIMAL SOLUTION

Objective Function Value =                         860.000

        Variable                                    Value
        X11                                         0.000
        X12                                         0.000
        X13                                         0.000
        X21                                         0.000
        X22                                         0.000
        X23                                         0.000
        X31                                         0.000
        X32                                         0.000
        X33                                         0.000
        X41                                         0.000
        X42                                        20.000
        X43                                        20.000
        X51                                        30.000
        X52                                         0.000
        X53                                         0.000
        Y1                                          0.000
        Y2                                          0.000
        Y3                                          0.000
        Y4                                          1.000

      Constraint                              Slack/Surplus
        1                                           0.000
        2                                           0.000
        3                                           0.000
        4                                           0.000
        5                                           0.000
        6                                           0.000
        7                                           0.000
        8                                           0.000
```

the cities are so close together. To prevent this from happening, the following constraint can be added to the model:

Problem 13, which is based on the Martin-Beck distribution system problem, provides additional practice involving 0–1 variables.

$$y_1 + y_2 \leq 1$$

This constraint allows either $y_1$ or $y_2$ to equal 1, but not both. If we had written the constraints as an equality, it would require that a plant be located in either Dallas or Fort Worth.

### Bank Location

The long-range planning department for the Ohio Trust Company is considering expanding its operation into a 20-county region in northeastern Ohio (see Figure 8.9). Currently, Ohio Trust does not have a principal place of business in any of the 20 counties. According to the banking laws in Ohio, if a bank establishes a principal place of business (PPB) in any

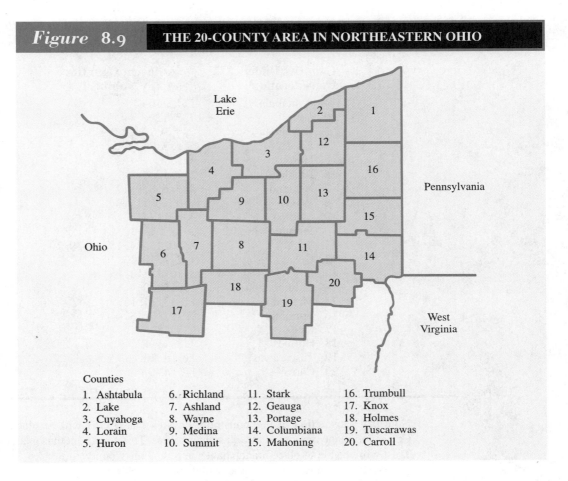

**Figure 8.9    THE 20-COUNTY AREA IN NORTHEASTERN OHIO**

Lake
Erie

Pennsylvania

Ohio

West
Virginia

**Counties**

| | | | |
|---|---|---|---|
| 1. Ashtabula | 6. Richland | 11. Stark | 16. Trumbull |
| 2. Lake | 7. Ashland | 12. Geauga | 17. Knox |
| 3. Cuyahoga | 8. Wayne | 13. Portage | 18. Holmes |
| 4. Lorain | 9. Medina | 14. Columbiana | 19. Tuscarawas |
| 5. Huron | 10. Summit | 15. Mahoning | 20. Carroll |

county, branch banks can be established in that county and in any adjacent county. However, to establish a new principal place of business, Ohio Trust must either obtain approval for a new bank from the state's superintendent of banks or purchase an existing bank.

Table 8.3 lists the 20 counties in the region and adjacent counties. For example, Ashtabula County is adjacent to Lake, Geauga, and Trumbull counties; Lake County is adjacent to Ashtabula, Cuyahoga, and Geauga counties; and so on.

As an initial step in its planning, Ohio Trust would like to determine the minimum number of PPBs necessary to do business throughout the 20-county region. A 0–1 integer programming model can be used to solve this problem for Ohio Trust. We define the variables as

$$x_i = 1 \text{ if a PPB is established in county } i; 0 \text{ otherwise}$$

To minimize the number of PPBs needed, we write the objective function as

$$\text{Min} \quad x_1 + x_2 + \cdots + x_{20}$$

The bank may locate branches in a county if the county contains a PPB or is adjacent to another county with a PPB. Thus, there will be one constraint for each county. For example, the constraint for Ashtabula County is

$$x_1 + x_2 + x_{12} + x_{16} \geq 1 \qquad \text{Ashtabula}$$

| Table 8.3 | COUNTIES IN THE OHIO TRUST EXPANSION REGION |
|---|---|

| Counties Under Consideration | Adjacent Counties (by Number) |
|---|---|
| 1. Ashtabula | 2, 12, 16 |
| 2. Lake | 1, 3, 12 |
| 3. Cuyahoga | 2, 4, 9, 10, 12, 13 |
| 4. Lorain | 3, 5, 7, 9 |
| 5. Huron | 4, 6, 7 |
| 6. Richland | 5, 7, 17 |
| 7. Ashland | 4, 5, 6, 8, 9, 17, 18 |
| 8. Wayne | 7, 9, 10, 11, 18 |
| 9. Medina | 3, 4, 7, 8, 10 |
| 10. Summit | 3, 8, 9, 11, 12, 13 |
| 11. Stark | 8, 10, 13, 14, 15, 18, 19, 20 |
| 12. Geauga | 1, 2, 3, 10, 13, 16 |
| 13. Portage | 3, 10, 11, 12, 15, 16 |
| 14. Columbiana | 11, 15, 20 |
| 15. Mahoning | 11, 13, 14, 16 |
| 16. Trumbull | 1, 12, 13, 15 |
| 17. Knox | 6, 7, 18 |
| 18. Holmes | 7, 8, 11, 17, 19 |
| 19. Tuscarawas | 11, 18, 20 |
| 20. Carroll | 11, 14, 19 |

Note that satisfaction of this constraint ensures that a PPB will be placed in Ashtabula County *or* in one or more of the adjacent counties. This constraint thus guarantees that Ohio Trust will be able to place branch banks in Ashtabula County.

The complete statement of the bank location problem is

$$\text{Min} \quad x_1 + x_2 + \quad \cdots \quad + x_{20}$$

s.t.

$$x_1 + x_2 \qquad + x_{12} + x_{16} \qquad \geq 1 \quad \text{Ashtabula}$$
$$x_1 + x_2 + x_3 + x_{12} \qquad \geq 1 \quad \text{Lake}$$
$$\vdots \qquad\qquad\qquad \vdots$$
$$x_{11} + x_{14} + x_{19} + x_{20} \geq 1 \quad \text{Carroll}$$
$$x_i = 0, 1 \quad i = 1, 2, \ldots, 20$$

We used The Management Scientist to solve this 20-variable, 20-constraint problem formulation. In Figure 8.10 we show a portion of the computer output. Note that the variable names correspond to the first four letters in the name of each county. Using the output, we see that the optimal solution calls for principal places of business in Ashland, Stark, and Geauga counties. With PPBs in these three counties, Ohio Trust can place branch banks in all 20 counties (see Figure 8.11). All other decision variables have an optimal value of zero, indicating that a PPB should not be placed in these counties. Clearly the integer programming model could be enlarged to allow for expansion into a larger area or throughout the entire state.

```
OPTIMAL SOLUTION

Objective Function Value = 3.000

    Variable                Value
  ------------            ----------
      ASHT                  0.000
      LAKE                  0.000
      CUYA                  0.000
      LORA                  0.000
      HURO                  0.000
      RICH                  0.000
      ASHL                  1.000
      WAYN                  0.000
      MEDI                  0.000
      SUMM                  0.000
      STAR                  1.000
      GEAU                  1.000
      PORT                  0.000
      COLU                  0.000
      MAHO                  0.000
      TRUM                  0.000
      KNOX                  0.000
      HOLM                  0.000
      TUSC                  0.000
      CARR                  0.000
```

## N O T E S
### and Comments

1. Most practical applications of integer linear programming involve only 0–1 integer variables. Indeed, some mixed-integer computer codes are designed to handle only integer variables with binary values. However, if a clever mathematical trick is employed, these codes can still be used for problems involving general integer variables. The trick is called *binary expansion* and requires that an upper bound be established for each integer variable. More advanced texts on integer programming show how this can be done.

2. The Management Science in Action: Analyzing Price Quotations Under Business Volume Discounts describes how 0–1 variables can be used in a model designed to take advantage of business volume discounts. Bellcore clients have saved millions of dollars by using a mixed-integer programming model.

3. General-purpose mixed-integer linear programming codes and some spreadsheet packages can be used for linear programming problems, all-integer problems, and problems involving some continuous and some integer variables. General-purpose codes are seldom the fastest for solving problems with special structure (such as the transportation, assignment, and transshipment problems); however, unless the problems are very large, speed is usually not a critical issue. Thus, most practitioners prefer to use one general-purpose computer package that can be used on a variety of problems rather than to maintain a variety of computer programs designed for special problems.

*Figure* 8.11 | **PRINCIPAL PLACE OF BUSINESS COUNTIES FOR OHIO TRUST**

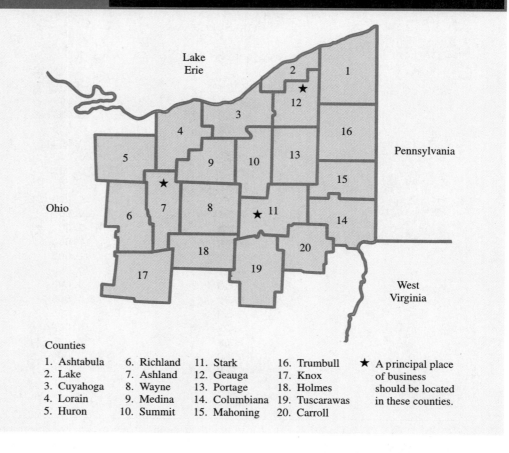

Counties

| | | | | |
|---|---|---|---|---|
| 1. Ashtabula | 6. Richland | 11. Stark | 16. Trumbull | ★ A principal place |
| 2. Lake | 7. Ashland | 12. Geauga | 17. Knox | of business |
| 3. Cuyahoga | 8. Wayne | 13. Portage | 18. Holmes | should be located |
| 4. Lorain | 9. Medina | 14. Columbiana | 19. Tuscarawas | in these counties. |
| 5. Huron | 10. Summit | 15. Mahoning | 20. Carroll | |

# MANAGEMENT SCIENCE IN ACTION

## ANALYZING PRICE QUOTATIONS UNDER BUSINESS VOLUME DISCOUNTS*

Bellcore was formed in 1984 to provide various support services for the regional Bell operating telephone companies. To reduce the cost of buying goods and services, Bellcore client companies are increasingly requesting business volume discounts from suppliers in place of traditional quantity discounts. With traditional quantity discounts, the price of each item purchased is discounted on the basis of the amount of the item purchased. Business volume discounts differ from single-item quantity discounts in that the supplier discounts the price of each item by a percentage that is based on the total dollar volume of business over all items awarded to the supplier; whatever this percentage, it remains the same for each item. In general, a firm can realize lower overall purchasing costs with business volume discounts and a supplier can increase total revenues by obtaining a large volume of that firm's business. However, business volume discounts greatly increase the complexity of the procurement process because the discount obtained depends on the purchase quantities and prices of all products purchased.

To assist Bellcore client companies in using business volume discounts, Bellcore developed the procurement decision support system (PDSS), a PC-based decision support program that uses a mixed-integer programming model to minimize the total cost of purchases. The model uses 0–1 integer variables to model the discount categories applicable to the problem and includes a variety of constraints involving factors such as supplier capacity and limits on the dollar amount awarded to a supplier. Since 1990, one Bellcore client company has reported two savings, one of $4.5 million and another of $15 million; these figures represent approximately 10% on the cost of purchases. Another client company has realized a reduction of approximately 80% in the cost of analyzing quotations, and users generally believe that PDSS is a useful tool in identifying opportunities in negotiations with suppliers.

*Based on P. Katz, A. Sadrian, and P. Tendick, "Telephone Companies Analyze Price Quotations with Bellcore's PDSS Software," *Interfaces* (January–February 1994): 50–63.

## 8.4    MODELING FLEXIBILITY PROVIDED BY 0–1 INTEGER VARIABLES

In Section 8.3 we presented four applications involving 0–1 integer variables. In this section we continue the discussion of the use of 0–1 integer variables in modeling. First, we show how 0–1 integer variables can be used to model multiple-choice and mutually exclusive constraints. Then, we show how 0–1 integer variables can be used to model situations in which $k$ projects out of a set of $n$ projects must be selected, as well as situations in which the acceptance of one project is conditional on the acceptance of another. We close the section with a cautionary note on the role of sensitivity analysis in integer linear programming.

### Multiple-Choice and Mutually Exclusive Constraints

Recall the Ice-Cold Refrigerator capital budgeting problem introduced in Section 8.3. The decision variables were defined as

$P = 1$ if the plant expansion project is accepted; 0 if rejected

$W = 1$ if the warehouse expansion project is accepted; 0 if rejected

$M = 1$ if the new machinery project is accepted; 0 if rejected

$R = 1$ if the new product research project is accepted; 0 if rejected

Suppose that, instead of one warehouse expansion project, the Ice-Cold Refrigerator Company actually has three warehouse expansion projects under consideration. One of the warehouses *must* be expanded because of increasing product demand, but new demand isn't sufficient to make expansion of more than one warehouse necessary. The following variable definitions and **multiple-choice constraint** could be incorporated into the previous 0–1 integer linear programming model to reflect this situation. Let

$W_1 = 1$ if the original warehouse expansion project is accepted; 0 if rejected

$W_2 = 1$ if the second warehouse expansion project is accepted; 0 if rejected

$W_3 = 1$ if the third warehouse expansion project is accepted; 0 if rejected

The multiple-choice constraint reflecting the requirement that exactly one of these projects must be selected is

$$W_1 + W_2 + W_3 = 1$$

Since $W_1$, $W_2$, and $W_3$ are allowed to assume only the values 0 or 1, one and only one of these projects must be selected from among the three choices.

If the requirement that one warehouse must be expanded did not exist, the multiple-choice constraint could be modified as follows:

$$W_1 + W_2 + W_3 \leq 1$$

This modification allows for the case of no warehouse expansion ($W_1 = W_2 = W_3 = 0$) but does not permit more than one warehouse to be expanded. This type of constraint is often called a **mutually exclusive constraint.**

### $k$ Out of $n$ Alternatives Constraint

An extension of the notion of a multiple-choice constraint can be used to model situations in which *k out of a set of n* projects must be selected—a *k* **out of** *n* **alternatives constraint.** Suppose that $W_1$, $W_2$, $W_3$, $W_4$, and $W_5$ represent five potential warehouse expansion projects and that two of the five projects must be accepted. The constraint that satisfies this new requirement is

$$W_1 + W_2 + W_3 + W_4 + W_5 = 2$$

If no more than two of the projects are to be selected, we would use the following less-than-or-equal-to constraint:

$$W_1 + W_2 + W_3 + W_4 + W_5 \leq 2$$

Again, each of these variables must be restricted to 0–1 values.

### Conditional and Corequisite Constraints

Sometimes the acceptance of one project is conditional on the acceptance of another. For example, suppose for the Ice-Cold Refrigerator Company that the warehouse expansion project was conditional on the plant expansion project. That is, management will not consider expanding the warehouse unless the plant is expanded. With $P$ representing plant expansion and $W$ representing warehouse expansion, a **conditional constraint** could be introduced to enforce this requirement:

$$W \leq P$$

As both $P$ and $W$ must be 0 or 1, whenever $P$ is 0, $W$ will be forced to 0. When $P$ is 1, $W$ is also allowed to be 1; thus, both the plant and the warehouse can be expanded. However, we note that the preceding constraint does not force the warehouse expansion project ($W$) to be accepted if the plant expansion project ($P$) is accepted.

If the warehouse expansion project had to be accepted whenever the plant expansion project was, and vice versa, we would say that $P$ and $W$ represented **corequisite constraint** projects. To model such a situation, we simply write the preceding constraint as an equality:

$$W = P$$

The constraint forces $P$ and $W$ to take on the same value.

*Try Problem 7 for practice with the modeling flexibility provided by 0–1 variables.*

### A Cautionary Note About Sensitivity Analysis

Sensitivity analysis often is more crucial for integer linear programming problems than for linear programming problems. A small change in one of the coefficients in the constraints can cause a relatively large change in the value of the optimal solution. To understand why, consider the following integer programming model of a simple capital budgeting problem involving four projects and a budgetary constraint for a single time period:

$$\text{Max} \quad 40x_1 + 60x_2 + 70x_3 + 160x_4$$
$$\text{s.t.}$$
$$16x_1 + 35x_2 + 45x_3 + 85x_4 \leq 100$$
$$x_1, x_2, x_3, x_4 = 0, 1$$

We obtain the optimal solution to this problem by enumerating the alternatives. It is $x_1 = 1$, $x_2 = 1$, $x_3 = 1$, and $x_4 = 0$, with an objective function value of $170. However, note that if the budget available is increased by $1 (from $100 to $101), the optimal solution changes to $x_1 = 1$, $x_2 = 0$, $x_3 = 0$, and $x_4 = 1$, with an objective function value of $200. That is, one additional dollar in the budget would lead to a $30 increase in the return. Surely management, when faced with such a situation, would increase the budget by $1. Because of the extreme sensitivity of the value of the optimal solution to the constraint coefficients, practitioners usually recommend resolving the integer linear program several times with slight variations in the coefficients before attempting to choose the best solution for implementation.

> Dual prices cannot be used for integer programming sensitivity analysis because they are designed for linear programs. Multiple computer runs usually are necessary for sensitivity analysis of integer linear programs.

## SUMMARY

In this chapter, we introduced the important extension of linear programming referred to as *integer linear programming*. The only difference between the integer linear programming problems discussed in this chapter and the linear programming problems studied in previous chapters is that one or more of the variables must be integer. If all variables must be integer, we have an all-integer linear program. If some, but not all, variables must be integer, we have a mixed-integer linear program. If all variables are 0–1 or binary variables, we have a 0–1 integer linear program.

Studying integer linear programming is important for two major reasons. First, integer linear programming may be helpful when fractional values for the variables are not permitted. Since rounding a linear programming solution may not provide an optimal integer solution, methods for finding optimal integer solutions are needed when the economic consequences of rounding are significant. A second reason for studying integer linear programming is the increased modeling flexibility provided through the use of 0–1 variables. We showed how 0–1 variables could be used to model important managerial considerations in capital budgeting, fixed cost, distribution system design, and bank location applications.

The number of applications of integer linear programming has been growing in recent years. This growth is due in part to the availability of commercial integer linear programming software packages. As researchers develop solution procedures capable of solving larger integer linear programs and as computer speed increases, a continuation of this growth of integer programming applications is expected.

## GLOSSARY

**Integer linear program**  A linear program with the additional requirement that at least one of the variables must be integer.

**All-integer linear program**  An integer linear program in which all variables are required to be integer.

**LP Relaxation**  The linear program that results from dropping the integer requirements for the variables in an integer linear program.

**Mixed-integer linear program**  An integer linear program in which some, but not all, variables are required to be integer.

**0–1 integer linear program**  An all-integer or mixed-integer linear program in which the integer variables are only permitted to assume the values 0 or 1. Also called *binary integer program*.

**Multiple-choice constraint**  A constraint requiring that the sum of two or more 0–1 variables equal 1. Thus, any feasible solution makes a choice of which variable to set equal to 1.

**Mutually exclusive constraint**  A constraint requiring that the sum of two or more 0–1 variables be less than or equal to 1. Thus, if one of the variables equals 1, the others must equal 0. However, all variables could equal 0.

**k out of n alternatives constraint**  An extension of the multiple-choice constraint. This constraint requires that the sum of $n$ 0–1 variables equal $k$.

**Conditional constraint**  A constraint involving 0–1 variables that does not allow certain variables to equal 1 unless certain other variables are equal to 1.

**Corequisite constraint**  A constraint requiring that two 0–1 variables be equal. Thus, they are both in or out of solution together.

## PROBLEMS

1. Indicate which of the following is an all-integer linear program and which is a mixed-integer linear program. Write the LP Relaxation for the problem but do not attempt to solve.

    a. Max   $30x_1 + 25x_2$

    s.t.

    $$3x_1 + 1.5x_2 \leq 400$$
    $$1.5x_1 + 2x_2 \leq 250$$
    $$1x_1 + 1x_2 \leq 150$$
    $$x_1, x_2 \geq 0 \text{ and } x_2 \text{ integer}$$

    b. Min   $3x_1 + 4x_2$

    s.t.

    $$2x_1 + 4x_2 \geq 8$$
    $$2x_1 + 6x_2 \geq 12$$
    $$x_1, x_2 \geq 0 \text{ and integer}$$

2. Consider the following all-integer linear program.

    $$\text{Max}\quad 5x_1 + 8x_2$$

    s.t.

    $$6x_1 + 5x_2 \leq 30$$
    $$9x_1 + 4x_2 \leq 36$$
    $$1x_1 + 2x_2 \leq 10$$
    $$x_1, x_2 \geq 0 \text{ and integer}$$

**SELF TEST**

    a. Graph the constraints for this problem. Use dots to indicate all feasible integer solutions.
    b. Find the optimal solution to the LP Relaxation. Round down to find a feasible integer solution.
    c. Find the optimal integer solution. Is it the same as the solution obtained in part (b) by rounding down?

3. Consider the following all-integer linear program.

$$\text{Max} \quad 1x_1 + 1x_2$$

s.t.

$$4x_1 + 6x_2 \le 22$$
$$1x_1 + 5x_2 \le 15$$
$$2x_1 + 1x_2 \le 9$$
$$x_1, x_2 \ge 0 \text{ and integer}$$

   a. Graph the constraints for this problem. Use dots to indicate all feasible integer solutions.
   b. Solve the LP Relaxation of this problem.
   c. Find the optimal integer solution.

4. Consider the following all-integer linear program.

$$\text{Max} \quad 10x_1 + 3x_2$$

s.t.

$$6x_1 + 7x_2 \le 40$$
$$3x_1 + 1x_2 \le 11$$
$$x_1, x_2 \ge 0 \text{ and integer}$$

   a. Formulate and solve the LP Relaxation of the problem. Solve it graphically, and round down to find a feasible solution. Specify an upper bound on the value of the optimal solution.
   b. Solve the integer linear program graphically. Compare the value of this solution with the solution obtained in part (a).
   c. Suppose the objective function changes to Max $3x_1 + 6x_2$. Repeat parts (a) and (b).

**SELF TEST**

5. Consider the following mixed-integer linear program.

$$\text{Max} \quad 2x_1 + 3x_2$$

s.t.

$$4x_1 + 9x_2 \le 36$$
$$7x_1 + 5x_2 \le 35$$
$$x_1, x_2 \ge 0 \text{ and } x_1 \text{ integer}$$

   a. Graph the constraints for this problem. Indicate on your graph all feasible mixed-integer solutions.
   b. Find the optimal solution to the LP Relaxation. Round the value of $x_1$ down to find a feasible mixed-integer solution. Is this solution optimal? Why or why not?
   c. Find the optimal solution for the mixed-integer linear program.

6. Consider the following mixed-integer linear program.

$$\text{Max} \quad 1x_1 + 1x_2$$

s.t.

$$7x_1 + 9x_2 \le 63$$
$$9x_1 + 5x_2 \le 45$$
$$3x_1 + 1x_2 \le 12$$
$$x_1, x_2 \ge 0 \text{ and } x_2 \text{ integer}$$

a. Graph the constraints for this problem. Indicate on your graph all feasible mixed-integer solutions.

b. Find the optimal solution to the LP Relaxation. Round the value of $x_2$ down to find a feasible mixed-integer solution. Specify upper and lower bounds on the value of the optimal solution to the mixed-integer linear program.

c. Find the optimal solution to the mixed-integer linear program.

**SELF TEST**

7. The following questions refer to a capital budgeting problem with six projects represented by 0–1 variables $x_1, x_2, x_3, x_4, x_5,$ and $x_6$.

   a. Write a constraint modeling a situation in which two of the projects 1, 3, 5, and 6 must be undertaken.

   b. Write a constraint modeling a situation in which, if projects 3 and 5 must be undertaken, they must be undertaken simultaneously.

   c. Write a constraint modeling a situation in which project 1 or 4 must be undertaken, but not both.

   d. Write constraints modeling a situation where project 4 cannot be undertaken unless projects 1 and 3 also are undertaken.

   e. Revise the requirement in part (d) to accommodate the case in which, when projects 1 and 3 are undertaken, project 4 also must be undertaken.

8. Spencer Enterprises is attempting to choose among a series of new investment alternatives. The potential investment alternatives, the net present value of the future stream of returns, the capital requirements, and the available capital funds over the next 3 years are summarized as follows:

| Alternative | Net-Present Value ($) | Capital Requirements ($) | | |
|---|---|---|---|---|
| | | Year I | Year 2 | Year 3 |
| 1 Limited warehouse expansion | 4,000 | 3,000 | 1,000 | 4,000 |
| 2 Extensive warehouse expansion | 6,000 | 2,500 | 3,500 | 3,500 |
| 3 Test market new product | 10,500 | 6,000 | 4,000 | 5,000 |
| 4 Advertising campaign | 4,000 | 2,000 | 1,500 | 1,800 |
| 5 Basic research | 8,000 | 5,000 | 1,000 | 4,000 |
| 6 Purchase new equipment | 3,000 | 1,000 | 500 | 900 |
| **Capital funds available** | | 10,500 | 7,000 | 8,750 |

a. Develop and solve an integer programming model for maximizing the net present value.

b. Assume that only one of the warehouse expansion projects can be implemented. Modify your model of part (a).

c. Suppose that, if test marketing of the new product is carried out, the advertising campaign also must be conducted. Modify your formulation of part (b) to reflect this new situation.

9. Hawkins Manufacturing Company produces connecting rods for 4- and 6-cylinder automobile engines using the same production line. The cost required to set up the production line to produce the 4-cylinder connecting rods is $2000, and the cost required to set up the production line for the 6-cylinder connecting rods is $3500. Manufacturing costs are $15 for each 4-cylinder connecting rod and $18 for each 6-cylinder connecting rod. Hawkins makes a decision at the end of each week as to which product will be manufactured the following week. If there is a production changeover from one week to the next, the weekend is used to reconfigure the production line. Once the line has been set up, the weekly production capacities are 6,000, 6-cylinder connecting rods and 8000 4-cylinder connecting rods. Let

$x_4$ = the number of 4-cylinder connecting rods produced next week

$x_6$ = the number of 6-cylinder connecting rods produced next week

$s_4$ = 1 if the production line is set up to produce the 4-cylinder connecting rods; 0 otherwise

$s_6$ = 1 if the production line is set up to produce the 6-cylinder connecting rods; 0 otherwise

**a.** Using the decision variables $x_4$ and $s_4$, write a constraint that limits next week's production of the 4-cylinder connecting rods to either 0 or 8000 units.

**b.** Using the decision variables $x_6$ and $s_6$, write a constraint that limits next week's production of the 6-cylinder connecting rods to either 0 or 6000 units.

**c.** Write 3 constraints that, taken together, limit the production of connecting rods for next week.

**d.** Write an objective function for minimizing the cost of production for next week.

10. Grave City is considering the relocation of several police substations to obtain better enforcement in high-crime areas. The locations under consideration together with the areas that can be covered from these locations are given in the following table.

| Potential Locations for Substations | Areas Covered |
|---|---|
| A | 1, 5, 7 |
| B | 1, 2, 5, 7 |
| C | 1, 3, 5 |
| D | 2, 4, 5 |
| E | 3, 4, 6 |
| F | 4, 5, 6 |
| G | 1, 5, 6, 7 |

**a.** Formulate an integer programming model that could be used to find the minimum number of locations necessary to provide coverage to all areas.

**b.** Solve the problem in part (a).

 11. Hart Manufacturing makes three products. Each product requires manufacturing operations in three departments: A, B, and C. The labor-hour requirements, by department, are

| Department | Product 1 | Product 2 | Product 3 |
|---|---|---|---|
| A | 1.50 | 3.00 | 2.00 |
| B | 2.00 | 1.00 | 2.50 |
| C | 0.25 | 0.25 | 0.25 |

During the next production period, the labor-hours available are 450 in department A, 350 in department B, and 50 in department C. The profit contributions per unit are $25 for product 1, $28 for product 2, and $30 for product 3.

**a.** Formulate a linear programming model for maximizing total profit contribution.

**b.** Solve the linear program formulated in part (a). How much of each product should be produced and what is the projected total profit contribution?

**c.** After evaluating the solution obtained in part (b), one of the production supervisors noted that production setup costs had not been taken into account. She noted that setup costs are $400 for product 1, $550 for product 2, and $600 for product 3. If the solution developed in part (b) is to be used, what is the total profit contribution after taking into account the setup costs?

**d.** Management realized that the optimal product mix, taking setup costs into account, might be different from the one recommended in part (b). Formulate a mixed-integer linear program that takes setup costs into account. Management has also stated that we should not consider making more than 175 units of product 1, 150 units of product 2, or 140 units of product 3.

**e.** Solve the mixed-integer linear program formulated in part (d). How much of each product should be produced and what is the projected total profit contribution? Compare this profit contribution to that obtained in part (c).

12. Yates Company supplies road salt to county highway departments. The company has three trucks, and the dispatcher is trying to schedule tomorrow's deliveries to Polk, Dallas, and Jasper counties. Two trucks have 15-ton capacities, and the third truck has a 30-ton capacity. Based on these truck capacities, two counties will receive 15 tons and the third will receive 30 tons of road salt. The dispatcher wants to determine how much to ship to each county. Let

$$x_1 = \text{amount shipped to Polk County}$$
$$x_2 = \text{amount shipped to Dallas County}$$
$$x_3 = \text{amount shipped to Jasper County}$$

and

$$y_i = \begin{cases} 1 \text{ if the 30-ton truck is assigned to county } i \\ 0 \text{ otherwise} \end{cases}$$

   a. Use these variable definitions and write constraints that appropriately restrict the amount shipped to each county.
   b. The cost of assigning the 30-ton truck to the three counties is $100 to Polk, $85 to Dallas, and $50 to Jasper. Formulate and solve a mixed-integer linear program to determine how much to ship to each county.

13. Recall the Martin-Beck Company distribution system problem in Section 8.3.
   a. Modify the formulation shown in Section 8.3 to account for the policy restriction that one plant, but not two, must be located either in Detroit or in Toledo.
   b. Modify the formulation shown in Section 8.3 to account for the policy restriction that no more than two plants can be located in Denver, Kansas City, and St. Louis.

SELF TEST

14. An automobile manufacturer has five outdated plants: one each in Michigan, Ohio, and California and two in New York. Management is considering modernizing these plants to manufacture engine blocks and transmissions for a new model car. The cost to modernize each plant and the manufacturing capacity after modernization are as follows:

| Plant | Cost ($ millions) | Engine Blocks (1000s) | Transmissions (1000s) |
|---|---|---|---|
| Michigan | 25 | 500 | 300 |
| New York | 35 | 800 | 400 |
| New York | 35 | 400 | 800 |
| Ohio | 40 | 900 | 600 |
| California | 20 | 200 | 300 |

The projected needs are for total capacities of 900,000 engine blocks and 900,000 transmissions. Management wants to determine which plants to modernize to meet projected manufacturing needs and, at the same time, minimize the total cost of modernization.
   a. Develop a table that lists every possible option available to management. As part of your table, indicate the total engine block capacity and transmission capacity for each possible option, whether the option is feasible based on the projected needs, and the total modernization cost for each option.
   b. Based on your analysis in part (a), what recommendation would you provide management?
   c. Formulate a 0–1 integer programming model that could be used to determine the optimal solution to the modernization question facing management.
   d. Solve the model formulated in part (c) to provide a recommendation for management.

15. CHB, Inc., is a bank holding company that is evaluating the potential for expanding into a 13-county region in the southwestern part of the state. State law permits establishing branches in

any county that is adjacent to a county in which a PPB (principal place of business) is located. The following map shows the 13-county region with the population of each county indicated.

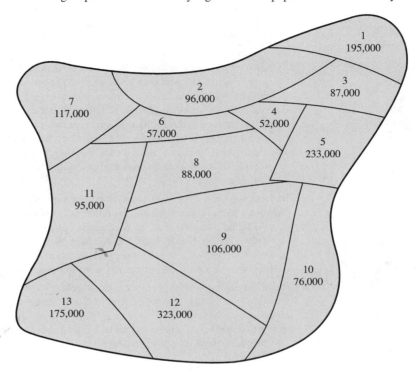

a.  Assume that only one PPB can be established in the region. Where should it be located to maximize the population served? (Hint: Review the Ohio Trust formulation in Section 8.3. Consider minimizing the population not served, and introduce variable $y_i = 1$ if it is not possible to establish a branch in county $i$, and $y_i = 0$ otherwise).

b.  Suppose that two PPBs can be established in the region. Where should they be located to maximize the population served?

c.  Management has learned that a bank located in county 5 is considering selling. If CHB purchases this bank, the requisite PPB will be established in county 5, and a base for beginning expansion in the region will also be established. What advice would you give the management of CHB?

16.  The Northshore Bank is working to develop an efficient work schedule for full-time and part-time tellers. The schedule must provide for efficient operation of the bank including adequate customer service, employee breaks, and so on. On Fridays the bank is open from 9:00 A.M. to 7:00 P.M. The number of tellers necessary to provide adequate customer service during each hour of operation is summarized here.

| Time | Number of Tellers | Time | Number of Tellers |
|---|---|---|---|
| 9:00 A.M.–10:00 A.M. | 6 | 2:00 P.M.–3:00 P.M. | 6 |
| 10:00 A.M.–11:00 A.M. | 4 | 3:00 P.M.–4:00 P.M. | 4 |
| 11:00 A.M.–Noon | 8 | 4:00 P.M.–5:00 P.M. | 7 |
| Noon–1:00 P.M. | 10 | 5:00 P.M.–6:00 P.M. | 6 |
| 1:00 P.M.–2:00 P.M. | 9 | 6:00 P.M.–7:00 P.M. | 6 |

Each full-time employee starts on the hour and works a four-hour shift, followed by one hour for lunch and then a three-hour shift. Part-time employees work one four-hour shift beginning on the hour. Considering salary and fringe benefits, full-time employees cost the bank $15 per hour ($105 a day), and part-time employees cost the bank $8 per hour ($32 per day).

    a.  Formulate an integer programming model that can be used to develop a schedule that will satisfy customer service needs at a minimum employee cost. (Hint: Let $x_i$ = number of full-time employees coming on duty at the beginning of hour $i$ and $y_i$ = number of part-time employees coming on duty at the beginning of hour $i$.)

    b.  Solve the LP Relaxation of your model in part (a).

    c.  Solve for the optimal schedule of tellers. Comment on the solution.

    d.  After reviewing the solution to part (c), the bank manager has realized that some additional requirements must be specified. Specifically, she wants to ensure that one full-time employee is on duty at all times and that there is a staff of at least five full-time employees. Revise your model to incorporate these additional requirements and solve for the optimal solution.

17.  Refer to the Ohio Trust bank location problem introduced in Section 8.3. Table 8.3 shows the counties under consideration and the adjacent counties.

    a.  Write the complete integer programming model for expansion into the following counties only: Loraine, Huron, Richland, Ashland, Wayne, Medina, and Knox.

    b.  Use trial and error to solve the problem in part (a).

    c.  If you have a computer program for integer programs, use it to solve the problem.

18.  Refer to Problem 14. Suppose that management determined that its cost estimates to modernize the New York plants were too low. Specifically, suppose that the actual cost is $40 million to modernize each plant.

    a.  What changes in your previous 0–1 integer linear programming model are needed to incorporate these changes in costs?

    b.  For these cost changes, what recommendations would you now provide management regarding the modernization plan?

    c.  Reconsider the solution obtained using the revised cost figures. Suppose that management decides that closing two plants in the same state is not acceptable. How could this policy restriction be added to your 0–1 integer programming model?

    d.  Based on the cost revision and the policy restriction presented in part (c), what recommendations would you now provide management regarding the modernization plan?

19.  The Bayside Art Gallery is considering installing a video camera security system to reduce its insurance premiums. A diagram of the eight display rooms that Bayside uses for exhibitions is shown in Figure 8.12; the openings between the rooms are numbered 1–13. A security firm has proposed that two-way cameras be installed at some room openings. Each camera has the ability to monitor the two rooms between which the camera is located. For example, if a camera were located at opening number 4, rooms 1 and 4 would be covered; if a camera were located at opening 11, rooms 7 and 8 would be covered; and so on. Management has decided not to locate a camera system at the entrance to the display rooms. The objective is to provide security coverage for all eight rooms using the minimum number of two-way cameras.

    a.  Formulate a 0–1 integer linear programming model that will enable Bayside's management to determine the locations for the camera systems.

    b.  Solve the model formulated in part (a) to determine how many two-way cameras to purchase and where they should be located.

    c.  Suppose that management wants to provide additional security coverage for room 7. Specifically, management wants room 7 to be covered by two cameras. How would your model formulated in part (a) have to change to accommodate this policy restriction?

    d.  With the policy restriction specified in part (c), determine how many two-way camera systems will need to be purchased and where they will be located.

20.  The Delta Group is a management consulting firm specializing in the health care industry. A team is being formed to study possible new markets, and a linear programming model has been

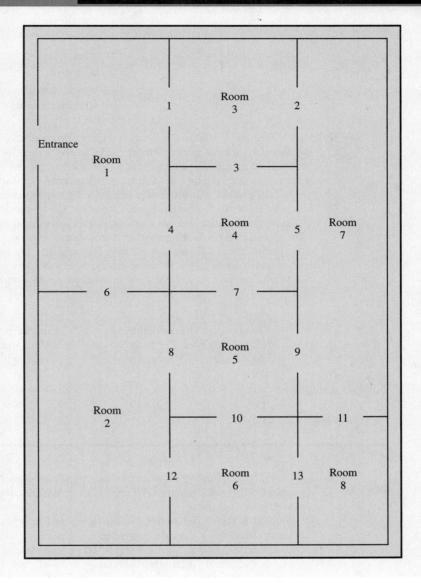

**Figure 8.12    DIAGRAM OF DISPLAY ROOMS FOR BAYSIDE ART GALLERY**

developed for selecting team members. However, one constraint the president has imposed is a team size of three, five, or seven members. The staff can't figure out how to incorporate this requirement in the model. The current model requires that team members be selected from three departments and uses the following variable definitions.

$$x_1 = \text{the number of employees selected from department 1}$$
$$x_2 = \text{the number of employees selected from department 2}$$
$$x_3 = \text{the number of employees selected from department 3}$$

Show the staff how to write constraints that will ensure that the team will consist of three, five, or seven employees. The following integer variables should be helpful.

$$y_1 = \begin{cases} 1 & \text{if team size is 3} \\ 0 & \text{otherwise} \end{cases}$$

$$y_2 = \begin{cases} 1 & \text{if team size is 5} \\ 0 & \text{otherwise} \end{cases}$$

$$y_3 = \begin{cases} 1 & \text{if team size is 7} \\ 0 & \text{otherwise} \end{cases}$$

 21. Roedel Electronics produces a variety of electrical components, including a remote controller for televisions and a remote controller for VCRs. Each controller consists of three subassemblies that are manufactured by Roedel: a base; a cartridge, and a keypad. Both controllers use the same base subassembly, but different cartridge and keypad subassemblies.

Roedel's sales forecast indicates that 7000 TV controllers and 5000 VCR controllers will be needed to satisfy demand during the upcoming Christmas season. Because only 500 hours of in-house manufacturing time are available, Roedel is considering purchasing some, or all, of the subassemblies from outside suppliers. If Roedel manufactures a subassembly in-house, it incurs a fixed setup cost as well as a variable manufacturing cost. The following table shows the setup cost, the manufacturing time per subassembly, the manufacturing cost per subassembly, and the cost to purchase each of the subassemblies from an outside supplier.

| Subassembly | Setup Cost ($) | Manufacturing Time Per Unit (min.) | Manufacturing Cost Per Unit ($) | Purchase Cost Per Unit ($) |
|---|---|---|---|---|
| Base | 1000 | 0.9 | 0.40 | 0.65 |
| TV cartridge | 1200 | 2.2 | 2.90 | 3.45 |
| VCR cartridge | 1900 | 3.0 | 3.15 | 3.70 |
| TV keypad | 1500 | 0.8 | 0.30 | 0.50 |
| VCR keypad | 1500 | 1.0 | 0.55 | 0.70 |

a. Determine how many units of each subassembly Roedel should manufacture and how many units Roedel should purchase. What is the total manufacturing and purchase cost associated with your recommendation?

b. Suppose Roedel is considering purchasing new machinery to produce VCR cartridges. For the new machinery, the setup cost is $3000; the manufacturing time is 2.5 minutes per cartridge, and the manufacturing cost is $2.60 per cartridge. Assuming that the new machinery is purchased, determine how many units of each subassembly Roedel should manufacture and how many units of each subassembly Roedel should purchase. What is the total manufacturing and purchase cost associated with your recommendation? Do you think the new machinery should be purchased? Explain.

## Case Problem    TEXTBOOK PUBLISHING

ASW Publishing, Inc., a small publisher of college textbooks, must make a decision regarding which books to publish next year. The books under consideration are listed in the following table, along with the projected three-year sales expected from each book.

| Book Subject | Type of Book | Projected Sales (000s) |
|---|---|---|
| Business calculus | New | 20 |
| Finite mathematics | Revision | 30 |
| General statistics | New | 15 |
| Mathematical statistics | New | 10 |
| Business statistics | Revision | 25 |
| Finance | New | 18 |
| Financial accounting | New | 25 |
| Managerial accounting | Revision | 50 |
| English literature | New | 20 |
| German | New | 30 |

The books that are listed as revisions are texts that ASW already has under contract; these texts are being considered for publication as new editions. The books that are listed as new have been reviewed by the company, but contracts have not yet been signed.

The company has three individuals who can be assigned to these projects, all of whom have varying amounts of time available; John has 60 days available, and Susan and Monica both have 40 days available. The days required by each person to complete each project are shown in the following table. For instance, if the business calculus book is published, it will require 30 days of John's time and 40 days of Susan's time. An "X" indicates that the person will not be used on the project. Note that at least two staff members will be assigned to each project except the finance book.

| Book Subject | John | Susan | Monica |
|---|---|---|---|
| Business calculus | 30 | 40 | X |
| Finite mathematics | 16 | 24 | X |
| General statistics | 24 | X | 30 |
| Mathematical statistics | 20 | X | 24 |
| Business statistics | 10 | X | 16 |
| Finance | X | X | 14 |
| Financial accounting | X | 24 | 26 |
| Managerial accounting | X | 28 | 30 |
| English literature | 40 | 34 | 30 |
| German | X | 50 | 36 |

ASW will not publish more than two statistics books or more than one accounting text in a single year. In addition, management has decided that one of the mathematics books (business calculus or finite math) must be published, but not both.

## Managerial Report

Prepare a report for the editorial director of ASW that describes your findings and recommendations regarding the best publication strategy for next year. In carrying out your analysis, assume that the fixed costs and the sales revenues per unit are approximately equal for all books; management is interested primarily in maximizing the total unit sales volume.

The editorial director has also asked that you include recommendations regarding the following possible changes.

1. If it would be advantageous to do so, Susan can be moved off another project to allow her to work 12 more days.
2. If it would be advantageous to do so, Monica can also be made available for another 10 days.
3. If one or more of the revisions could be postponed for another year, should they be? Clearly the company will risk losing market share by postponing a revision.

Include details of your analysis in an appendix to your report.

........................................................................................./ /............

## Case Problem    YEAGER NATIONAL BANK

Using aggressive mail promotion with low introductory interest rates, Yeager National Bank (YNB) has built a large base of credit card customers throughout the continental United States. Currently, all customers send their regular payments to the bank's corporate office located in Charlotte, North Carolina. Daily collections from customers making their regular payments are substantial, with an average of approximately $600,000. YNB estimates that it makes about 15% on its funds, and would like to ensure that customer payments are credited to the bank's account as soon as possible. For instance, if it takes 5 days for a customer's payment to be sent through the mail, processed, and credited to the bank's account, YNB has potentially lost 5 days worth of interest income. Although the time needed for this collection process cannot be completely eliminated, reducing it can be beneficial given the large amounts of money involved.

Instead of having all its credit card customers send their payments to Charlotte, YNB is considering having customers send their payments to one or more regional collection centers, referred to in the banking industry as lockboxes. Four lockbox locations have been proposed: Phoenix, Salt Lake City, Atlanta, and Boston. To determine which lockboxes to open and where lockbox customers should send their payments, YNB has divided its customer base into 5 geographical regions: Northwest, Southwest, Central, Northeast, and Southeast. Every customer in the same region will be instructed to send his or her payment to the same lockbox. The following table shows the average number of days it takes before a customer's payment is credited to the bank's account when the payment is sent from each of the regions to each of the potential lockboxes.

| Customer Zone | Location of Lockbox | | | | Daily Collection ($1000s) |
|---|---|---|---|---|---|
| | **Phoenix** | **Salt Lake City** | **Atlanta** | **Boston** | |
| Northwest | 4 | 2 | 4 | 4 | 80 |
| Southwest | 2 | 3 | 4 | 6 | 90 |
| Central | 5 | 3 | 3 | 4 | 150 |
| Northeast | 5 | 4 | 3 | 2 | 180 |
| Southeast | 4 | 6 | 2 | 3 | 100 |

## Managerial Report

Dave Wolff, the vice-president for cash management, has asked you to prepare a report containing your recommendations for the number of lockboxes and the best lockbox locations. Mr. Wolff is primarily concerned with minimizing lost interest income, but he wants you to also consider the effect of an annual fee charged for maintaining a lockbox at any location. Although the amount of the fee is unknown at this time, we can assume that the fees will be in the range of $20,000 to $30,000 per location. Once good potential locations have been selected, Mr. Wolff will inquire as to the annual fees.

.................................................................................../  /............

## Case Problem    PRODUCTION SCHEDULING WITH CHANGEOVER COSTS

Buckeye Manufacturing produces heads for engines used in the manufacture of trucks. The production line is highly complex, and it measures 900 feet in length. Two types of engine heads are produced on this line: the P-Head and the H-Head. The P-Head is used in heavy-duty trucks and the H-Head is used in smaller trucks. Because only one type of head can be produced at a time, the line is either set up to manufacture the P-Head or the H-Head, but not both. Changeovers are made over a weekend; costs are $500 in going from a setup for the P-Head to a setup for the H-Head, and vice-versa. When set up for the P-Head, the maximum production rate is 100 units per week and when set up for the H-Head, the maximum production rate is 80 units per week.

Buckeye has just shut down for the week; the line has been producing the P-Head. The manager wants to plan production and changeovers for the next eight weeks. Currently, Buckeye has an inventory of 125 P-Heads and 143 H-Heads. Inventory carrying costs are charged at an annual rate of 19.5% of the value of inventory. The production cost for the P-Head is $225, and the production cost for the H-Head is $310. The objective in developing a production schedule is to minimize the sum of production cost, plus inventory carrying cost, plus changeover cost.

Buckeye has received the following requirements schedule from its customer (an engine assembly plant) for the next nine weeks.

| Week | Product Demand | |
|------|:------:|:------:|
|      | P-Head | H-Head |
| 1 | 55 | 38 |
| 2 | 55 | 38 |
| 3 | 44 | 30 |
| 4 | 0  | 0  |
| 5 | 45 | 48 |
| 6 | 45 | 48 |
| 7 | 36 | 58 |
| 8 | 35 | 57 |
| 9 | 35 | 58 |

Safety stock requirements are such that week-ending inventory must provide for at least 80% of the next week's demand.

## Managerial Report

Prepare a report for Buckeye's management with a production and changeover schedule for the next eight weeks. Be sure to note how much of the total cost is due to production, how much is due to inventory, and how much is due to changeover.

## Appendix 8.1    SPREADSHEET SOLUTION OF INTEGER LINEAR PROGRAMS

Spreadsheet formulation and solution for integer linear programs is similar to that for linear programming problems. Actually the spreadsheet formulation is exactly the same. But some additional information must be provided when setting up the **Solver Parameters** and **Solver Options** dialog boxes. First, constraints must be added in the **Solver Parameters** dialog box to identify the integer variables. In addition, the value for **Tolerance** in the **Solver Options** dialog box may need to be adjusted to obtain a solution.

Let us demonstrate the spreadsheet solution of an integer linear program by showing how Excel can be used to solve the Eastborne Realty problem. The spreadsheet with the optimal solution is shown in Figure 8.13. We will describe the key elements of the spreadsheet, describe how to obtain the solution, and then interpret the solution.

### Spreadsheet Formulation

The data and descriptive labels appear in cells A1:G7 of the spreadsheet in Figure 8.13. The screened cells in the lower portion of the spreadsheet contain the information required by the Excel Solver (decision variables, objective function, constraint left-hand sides, and constraint right-hand sides).

**Figure 8.13**    **SPREADSHEET SOLUTION FOR THE EASTBORNE REALTY PROBLEM**

|  | A | B | C | D | E | F | G | H |
|---|---|---|---|---|---|---|---|---|
| 1 | **Eastborne Realty Problem** | | | | | | | |
| 2 | | | | | | | | |
| 3 | | **Townhouse** | **Apt. Bldg.** | | | | | |
| 4 | **Price($1000s)** | 282 | 400 | | **Funds Avl.($1000s)** | | 2000 | |
| 5 | **Mgr. Time** | 4 | 40 | | **Mgr. Time Avl.** | | 140 | |
| 6 | | | | | **Townhouses Avl.** | | 5 | |
| 7 | **Ann. Cash Flow ($1000s)** | 10 | 15 | | | | | |
| 8 | | | | | | | | |
| 9 | | | | | | | | |
| 10 | **Model** | | | | | | | |
| 11 | | | | | | | | |
| 12 | | | | | | | | |
| 13 | **Max Cash Flow** | 70 | | | | | | |
| 14 | | | | | **Constraints** | **LHS** | | **RHS** |
| 15 | | **Number of** | | | Funds | 1928 | <= | 2000 |
| 16 | | **Townhouses** | **Apt. Bldgs.** | | Time | 96 | <= | 140 |
| 17 | **Purchase Plan** | 4 | 2 | | Twnhses | 4 | <= | 5 |

Decision Variables    Cells B17:C17 are reserved for the decision variables. The optimal so-
                      lution is to purchase 4 townhouses and 2 apartment buildings.

Objective Function    The formula =SUMPRODUCT(B7:C7,B17:C17) has been placed
                      into cell B13 to reflect the annual cash flow associated with the solu-
                      tion. The optimal solution provides an annual cash flow of $70,000.

Left-Hand Sides       The left-hand sides for the 3 constraints are placed into cells F15:F17.
                        Cell F15 =SUMPRODUCT (B4:C4, $B$17:$C$17)
                              (Copy to sell F16)
                        Cell F17 =B17

Right-Hand Sides      The right-hand sides for the 3 constraints are placed into cells H15:H17.
                        Cell H15 =G4    (Copy to cells H16:H17)

## Spreadsheet Solution

Begin the solution procedure by selecting **Solver** from the **Tools** menu and entering the
proper values into the **Solver Parameters** dialog box as shown in Figure 8.14. The first
constraint shown is $B$17:$C$17 = integer. This constraint tells Solver that the decision
variables in cell B17 and cell C17 must be integer. The integer requirement is created by
using the **Add-Constraint** procedure. $B$17:$C17 is entered as the **Cell Reference** and
"**int**" rather than < =, = or = > is selected as the form of the constraint. When "**int**" is selected, the term integer automatically appears as the right-hand side of the constraint. Figure 8.14 shows the additional information required to complete the **Solver Parameters**
dialog box.

Next the **Options** button must be selected. As with linear programs, the options **Assume
Linear Model** and **Assume Non-Negative** must be checked. Finally, 0 can be entered into
the **Tolerance** box to replace the default setting of 5%. The tolerance of 5% means that
Solver will stop the search for the optimal integer solution whenever it finds an integer
solution that is within 5% of the value of the optimal solution (e.g., within 5% of the value
of the optimal solution to the LP Relaxation). To guarantee that Solver will keep searching

**Figure 8.14**    SOLVER PARAMETERS DIALOG BOX FOR THE EASTBORNE REALTY PROBLEM until an optimal integer solution is found, 0 must be entered into the **Tolerance** box. Figure 8.15 shows the completed **Solver Options** dialog box for the Eastborne Realty problem.[1] Selecting **OK** in the **Solver Options** dialog box and Selecting **Solve** in the **Solver Parameters** dialog box will instruct Solver to compute the optimal integer solution. The spreadsheet in Figure 8.13 shows the optimal solution is to purchase 4 townhouses and 2 apartment buildings. The annual cash flow is $70,000.

Zero–one variables are identified with the "**bin**" designation in the **Solver Parameters** dialog box.

If binary variables are present in an integer linear programming problem, you must select the designation "**bin**" instead of "**int**" when setting up the constraints in the **Solver Parameters** dialog box. With versions of Excel prior to Excel 97, handling 0–1 variables is a two-step procedure. First in the model development stage, a constraint requiring each 0–1 variable to be less than or equal to one must be added. Then, a constraint is added in the **Solver Parameters** dialog box requiring each 0–1 (binary) variable to equal "**int**". Together, these two requirements allow the variable to assume only the values 0 and 1.

**Figure  8.15**  SOLVER OPTIONS SELECTED FOR EASTBORNE REALTY PROBLEM. ASSUME LINEAR MODEL AND ASSUME NON-NEGATIVE BOXES ARE CHECKED AND TOLERANCE HAS BEEN SET TO ZERO

---

[1] The time required to obtain an optimal solution can be highly variable for integer linear programs. If an optimal solution has not been found within a reasonable amount of time, the tolerance can be reset to 5% or some other nonzero value so that the search procedure may stop when a near-optimal integer solution has been found.

# KETRON*

## ARLINGTON, VIRGINIA

Ketron Division of The Bionetics Corporation is an operations research organization with offices throughout the United States. An important part of Ketron's business involves work for local, state, and national governmental agencies.

The Ketron Management Science group is responsible for the development, enhancement, marketing, and support of MPSIII, a proprietary mathematical programming system that runs on a wide range of computers—from PCs to mainframes. Ketron Management Science provides consulting services for the design and implementation of mathematical programming applications. One such mixed-integer programming (MIP) application developed for a major sporting equipment company is outlined in the following sections.

## A Customer Order Allocation Model

A major sporting equipment company satisfies demand for its products by making shipments from its factories and other locations around the country where inventories are maintained. The company markets approximately 300 products and has about 30 sources of supply (factory and warehouse locations). The problem of interest is to determine how best to allocate customer orders to the various sources of supply such that the total manufacturing cost is minimized. Although transportation cost is not directly considered, it can be accounted for indirectly by not including variables corresponding to shipments from distant locations. Figure 8.16 provides a graphical representation of this problem. Note in

*The authors are indebted to J. A. Tomlin for providing this application.

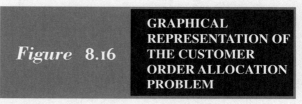

**Figure 8.16** — GRAPHICAL REPRESENTATION OF THE CUSTOMER ORDER ALLOCATION PROBLEM

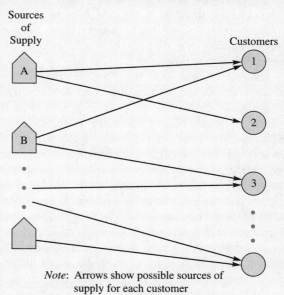

*Note*: Arrows show possible sources of supply for each customer

the figure that each customer can receive shipments from only a few of the various sources of supply. For example, we see that customer 1 may be supplied by source A or B, customer 2 may be supplied only by source A, and so on.

The customer order allocation problem is solved periodically. In a typical period, between 30 and 40 customers are to be supplied. Since most customers require several products, usually between 600 and 800 orders must be assigned to the sources of supply.

The sporting equipment company classifies each customer order as either a "guaranteed" or a "secondary" order. Guaranteed orders are single-source orders in that they must be filled by a single supplier to ensure that the complete order will be delivered to the customer at one time. This single-source requirement necessitates the use of integer variables in the model. Approximately 80% of the company's orders are guaranteed orders.

Secondary orders can be split among the various sources of supply. These orders are made by customers restocking inventory, and receiving partial shipments from different sources at different times is not a problem. The total of all secondary orders for a given product is treated as a goal or target in the model formulation. Deviations below the goal are permitted, but a penalty cost is associated with these deviations in the objective function. When deviations occur in the optimal solution, the secondary orders will not be completely satisfied; the shortfall is spread among customers in specified proportions.

Manufacturing considerations are such that raw material availability and the type of process used constrain the amount of production. In addition, groups of items that are similar may belong to a "model group" that must be jointly constrained at some factories. Several restrictions are also placed on international shipping. For various policy reasons, shipments between sources and customers in certain countries may not be made. This restriction reduces the number of variables in the model, but it necessitates extensive data checking to ensure that all guaranteed orders have a permissible source. If they do not, some means must be found to make the problem feasible before beginning to solve the mixed-integer programming model.

The primary objective of the model is to minimize the total manufacturing costs subject to the requirement that the guaranteed orders be met. As indicated previously, the deviations below the secondary demand goals are dealt with by defining variables that indicate the amount of any shortage. The cost associated with these variables represents a penalty for not having the item in inventory when it is required.

A description of the constraints and the objective function for the model follows.

## Constraints

- *Guaranteed orders:* Each customer's order for each product is assigned to a single supplier (a multiple-choice constraint).
- *Secondary orders:* For each product, the total amount of secondary demand assigned plus the shortfall must equal the total demand goal (target).
- *Raw material capacities:* The amount of each type of raw material used at a supply source cannot exceed the amount available.
- *Manufacturing capacities:* At each supply source, the capacity for each type of production process cannot be exceeded.
- *Individual product capacities:* The amount of product produced at a site cannot exceed that site's capacity for the product.
- *Group capacities:* The total production for a group of similar products at a site cannot exceed that site's capacity for the group of products.

## Objective Function

The objective is to minimize the sum of (1) the manufacturing cost for guaranteed orders, (2) the manufacturing cost for secondary orders, and (3) the penalty cost for unsatisfied secondary demand.

## Model Solution

Expecting to obtain an optimal solution for a problem of this complexity is unreasonable. Furthermore, the goal programming methodology for handling the secondary demand means that an "optimum" is of questionable interpretation. A "good" feasible mixed-integer solution is needed. If an integer solution is found whose value is within a few percent of the value of the LP Relaxation solution, the room for improvement is obviously small.

A fairly typical problem has about 800 constraints, 2000 0–1 assignment variables for the guaranteed orders, and 500 continuous variables associated with the secondary orders. This model is solved using Ketron's MPSIII system.

## Implementation Notes

In large-scale applications such as this one, considerable systems work is involved in generating the data for the model and the managerial reports. Special data processing languages are often available to ease the programming burden of these phases. The DATAFORM language facility of MPSIII is used to generate the data for this model and to prepare the reports.

In this application, making a completely separate preprocessing run is necessary to check for internal consistency and errors in the data. Only when the data appear logically error-free is the model generated and solved. Although tedious, this kind of preprocessing effort is critical for mixed-integer models since the cost of solving the wrong model can be significant. Furthermore, in some cases the data preprocessing step permits the size of the model to be reduced. Such a reduction is possible in this application when a demand for a product has only one legitimate source. The computational benefits of such reductions can be substantial.

## Questions

1. Discuss the relationship between the method for handling secondary orders and feasibility.
2. Discuss what is meant by the statement, an "optimum" is of questionable interpretation. Does it mean that any feasible solution is acceptable?

# 9

# NETWORK MODELS

## CONTENTS

Many managerial problems in areas such as transportation systems design, information systems design, and project scheduling have been successfully solved with the aid of network models and network analysis techniques. In Chapter 7 we showed how *networks* consisting of nodes and arcs can be used to provide graphical representations of transportation, assignment, and transshipment problems. In this chapter we present three additional network problems: the shortest-route problem, the minimal spanning tree problem, and the maximal flow problem. In each case, we will show how a network model can be developed and solved in order to provide an optimal solution to the problem.

## 9.1    THE SHORTEST-ROUTE PROBLEM

In this section we consider a network application in which the primary objective is to determine the **shortest route** or *path* between any pair of nodes in a network. Let us demonstrate the shortest-route problem by considering the situation facing the Gorman Construction Company. Gorman has several construction projects located throughout a three-county area. Construction sites are sometimes located as far as 50 miles from Gorman's main office. With multiple daily trips carrying personnel, equipment, and supplies to and from the construction locations, the costs associated with transportation activities are substantial. For any given construction site, the travel alternatives between the site and the office can be described by a network of roads, streets, and highways. The network shown in Figure 9.1 describes the travel alternatives to and from six of Gorman's newest construction sites. The circles or *nodes* of the network correspond to the site locations. The roads, streets, and highways appear as the *arcs* in the network. The distances between the sites are shown above the corresponding arcs. Gorman would like to determine the routes or paths that will minimize the total travel distance from the office to each site.

### A Shortest-Route Algorithm

To solve Gorman's problem, we need to determine the shortest route from Gorman's office, node 1, to each of the other nodes in the network. The algorithm we present uses a labeling procedure to find the shortest distance from node 1 to each of the other nodes. As we perform the steps of the labeling procedure, we will identify a *label* consisting of two numbers enclosed in brackets for each node. The first number in the label for a particular node indicates the distance from node 1 to that node, while the second number indicates the preceding node on the route from node 1 to that node. We will show the label for each node directly above or below the node in the network. For example, a label for a particular node might appear as shown in Figure 9.2.

At any step of the labeling procedure, a node is said to be either labeled or unlabeled. A labeled node is any node for which we have identified a path from node 1 to that node, and an unlabeled node is any node for which a path has not yet been identified. A labeled node is also said to be either permanently or tentatively labeled. That is, whenever the algorithm has determined the *shortest* distance from node 1 to a particular node, the node is said to have a *permanent* label. If, however, the shortest distance from node 1 to a particular labeled node has not yet been determined, the node is said to have a *tentative* label. Now let us show how labels are computed and how the labeling process can be used to determine the shortest route to each of the nodes in the network.

We begin the labeling process by giving node 1 the permanent label [0,S]. The 0 indicates that the distance from node 1 to itself is zero and the S identifies node 1 as the starting node. To distinguish between tentatively and permanently labeled nodes, we use dark shading for all permanently labeled nodes in the network. In addition, an arrow indicates the permanently

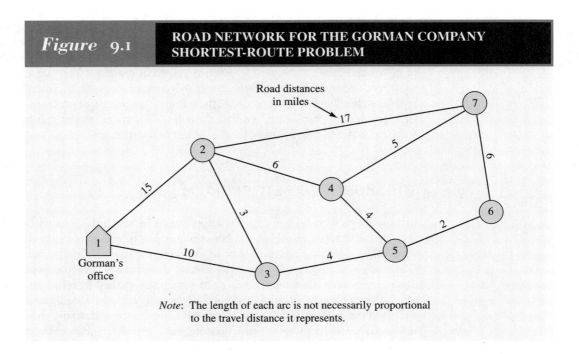

**Figure 9.1     ROAD NETWORK FOR THE GORMAN COMPANY SHORTEST-ROUTE PROBLEM**

*Note*: The length of each arc is not necessarily proportional to the travel distance it represents.

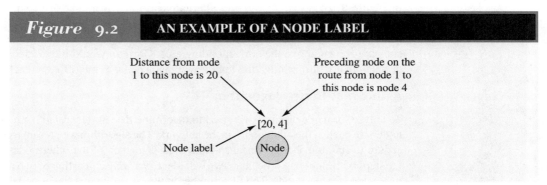

**Figure 9.2     AN EXAMPLE OF A NODE LABEL**

Distance from node 1 to this node is 20

Preceding node on the route from node 1 to this node is node 4

[20, 4]

Node label     Node

labeled node being investigated at each step of the labeling algorithm. The initial identification of Gorman's network is shown in Figure 9.3 when only node 1 is permanently labeled.

To perform the first step or iteration of the labeling procedure, we must consider every node that can be reached directly from node 1; hence, we look first at node 2 and then at node 3. We see that the direct distance from node 1 to node 2 is 15 miles. Thus, node 2 can be tentatively labeled [15,1], with the second number indicating that the preceding node on this route to node 2 is node 1. Next, we consider node 3 and find that the direct distance from node 1 to node 3 is 10 miles. Thus, the tentative label at node 3 is [10,1]. Figure 9.4 shows the results thus far with nodes 2 and 3 tentatively labeled.

Refer to Figure 9.4. We now consider all tentatively labeled nodes and identify the node with the smallest distance value in its label; thus, node 3 with a travel distance of 10 miles is selected. Could we get to node 3 following a shorter route? Because any other route to node 3 would require passing through other nodes, and because the distance from node 1 to all other nodes is greater than or equal to 10, a shorter route to node 3 cannot be found. Accordingly, node 3 is permanently labeled with a distance of 10 miles. Dark shading indicates

| Figure 9.3 | INITIAL NETWORK IDENTIFICATION FOR GORMAN'S SHORTEST-ROUTE PROBLEM |
| --- | --- |

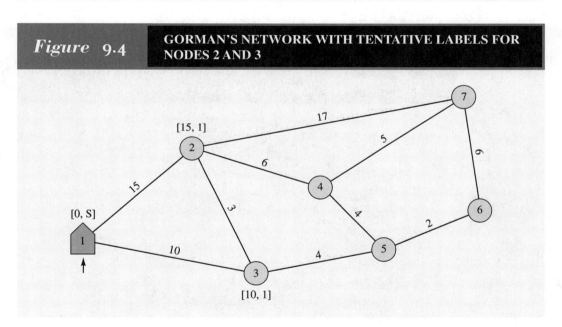

| Figure 9.4 | GORMAN'S NETWORK WITH TENTATIVE LABELS FOR NODES 2 AND 3 |
| --- | --- |

that node 3 is a permanently labeled node and the arrow indicates that node 3 will be used to start the next step of the labeling process; the result of these steps is shown in Figure 9.5.

We proceed by considering all nodes that are not permanently labeled and that can be reached directly from node 3; these are nodes 2 and 5. Note that the direct distance is 3 miles from node 3 to node 2 and it is 4 miles from node 3 to node 5. Because node 3's permanent label indicates that the shortest distance to node 3 is 10 miles, we see that we can reach node 2 in 10 + 3 = 13 miles and node 5 in 10 + 4 = 14 miles. Thus, the tentative label at node 2 is revised to [13,3] to indicate that we have now found a route from node 1 to node 2 that has a distance of 13 miles and passes through node 3. The tentative label for node 5 is set to [14,3]. Figure 9.6 shows the network computations up to this point.

| *Figure* 9.5 | **GORMAN'S NETWORK WITH NODE 3 IDENTIFIED AS A PERMANENTLY LABELED NODE** |
|---|---|

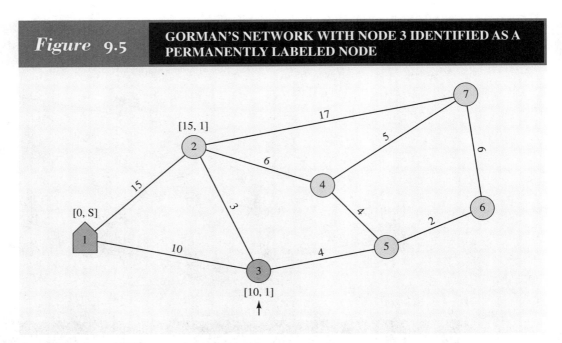

| *Figure* 9.6 | **GORMAN'S NETWORK WITH NEW TENTATIVE LABELS FOR NODES 2 AND 5** |
|---|---|

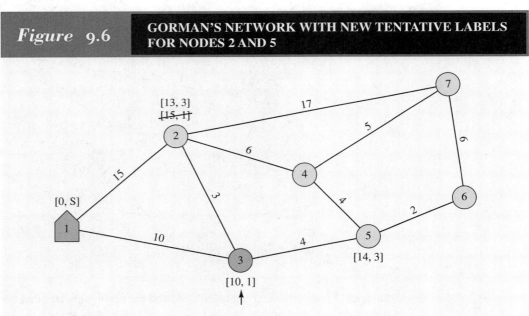

We next consider all tentatively labeled nodes in order to find the node with the smallest distance value in its label. From Figure 9.6 we see that this is node 2 with a distance of 13 miles. Node 2 is now permanently labeled because we know that it can be reached from node 1 in the shortest possible distance of 13 miles by going through node 3.

The next step or iteration begins at node 2, the most recently permanently labeled node. As before, we consider every nonpermanently labeled node that can be reached directly from node 2; that is, nodes 4 and 7. Starting with the distance value of 13 in the permanent label at node 2 and adding the direct distance from node 2 to both nodes 4 and 7, we see that node 4 can be reached in $13 + 6 = 19$ miles, while node 7 can be reached in $13 + 17 = 30$ miles. Thus, the tentative labels at nodes 4 and 7 are as shown in Figure 9.7.

From among the tentatively labeled nodes (nodes 4, 5, and 7), we select the node with the smallest distance value and declare that node permanently labeled. Thus node 5, with a distance of 14, becomes the new permanently labeled node. From node 5, then, we consider all nonpermanently labeled nodes that can be reached directly from node 5. Thus, the tentative label on node 4 is revised, and node 6 is tentatively labeled. Figure 9.8 depicts these calculations.

The smallest distance is again identified for the remaining tentatively labeled nodes, and this results in node 6 being permanently labeled. From node 6 we can determine a new tentative label with a distance value of 22 for node 7. After this step, the network appears as shown in Figure 9.9.

We now have only two remaining nonpermanently labeled nodes. Because the distance value at node 4 is smaller than that at node 7, node 4 becomes the new permanently labeled node. Because node 7 is the only nonpermanently labeled node that can be reached directly from node 4, we compare its distance value of 22 with the sum of the distance value at node 4 and the direct distance from node 4 to node 7, that is, $18 + 5 = 23$. Since the [22,6] tentative label at node 7 is smaller, it remains unchanged. Figure 9.10 shows the network at this point.

Because node 7 is the only remaining node with a tentative label, it is now permanently labeled. Figure 9.11 shows the final network with all nodes permanently labeled.

We can now use the information in the permanent labels to find the shortest route from node 1 to each node in the network. For example, node 7's permanent label tells us the shortest distance from node 1 to node 7 is 22 miles. To find the particular route that enables us to reach node 7 in 22 miles, we *start* at node 7 and work back to node 1. Node 7's label gives us the next direct link—node 6—and node 6's label indicates that node 5 is the next shortest-route link. Continuing this process, we note that we reach node 5 from node 3 and, finally, that we reach node 3 from node 1. Therefore, the shortest route from node 1

**Figure 9.7**    GORMAN'S NETWORK WITH A PERMANENT LABEL AT NODE 2 AND NEW TENTATIVE LABELS FOR NODES 4 AND 7

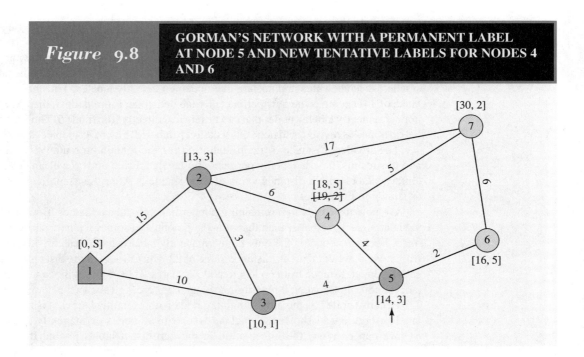

**Figure 9.8**  GORMAN'S NETWORK WITH A PERMANENT LABEL AT NODE 5 AND NEW TENTATIVE LABELS FOR NODES 4 AND 6

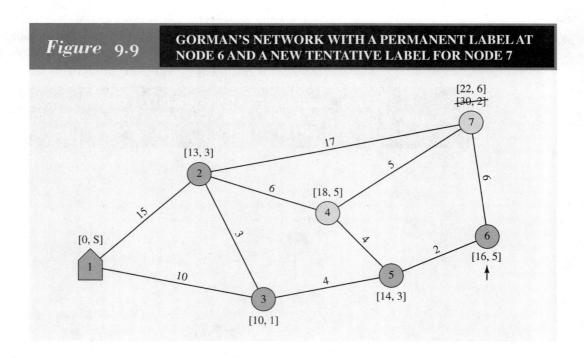

**Figure 9.9**  GORMAN'S NETWORK WITH A PERMANENT LABEL AT NODE 6 AND A NEW TENTATIVE LABEL FOR NODE 7

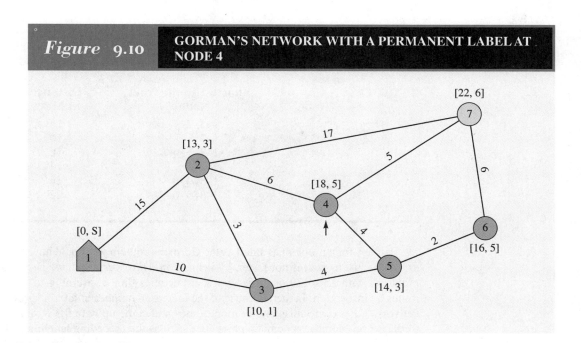

**Figure 9.10** — GORMAN'S NETWORK WITH A PERMANENT LABEL AT NODE 4

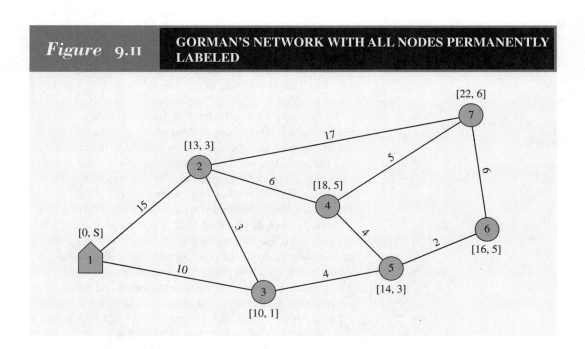

**Figure 9.11** — GORMAN'S NETWORK WITH ALL NODES PERMANENTLY LABELED

to node 7 is 1–3–5–6–7. Using this approach, the following shortest routes are identified for the Gorman transportation network:

| Node | Shortest Route from Node 1 | Distance in Miles |
|------|----------------------------|-------------------|
| 2 | 1–3–2 | 13 |
| 3 | 1–3 | 10 |
| 4 | 1–3–5–4 | 18 |
| 5 | 1–3–5 | 14 |
| 6 | 1–3–5–6 | 16 |
| 7 | 1–3–5–6–7 | 22 |

Perhaps for a problem as small as the Gorman problem you could have found the shortest routes just as fast, if not faster, by inspection. However, when we begin to investigate problems with 15 to 20 or more nodes, it becomes time-consuming to find the shortest routes by inspection. In fact, because of the increased number of alternate routes in a larger network, it is easy to miss one or more routes and come up with the wrong answer. Thus, for larger problems a systematic procedure such as the preceding labeling procedure is required. Even with the labeling method, we find that as the networks grow in size, it becomes necessary to implement the algorithm on a computer.

As we summarize the shortest-route algorithm, think of a network consisting of $N$ nodes. The following procedure can be used to find the shortest route from node 1 to each of the other nodes in the network.

Step 1  Assign node 1 the permanent label [0,S]. The 0 indicates that the distance from node 1 to itself is zero and the S indicates that node 1 is the starting node.

Step 2  Compute tentative labels for the nodes that can be reached directly from node 1. The first number in each label is the direct distance from node 1 to the node in question; we refer to this portion of the label as the distance value. The second number in each label, which we refer to as the preceding-node value, indicates the preceding node on the route from node 1 to the node in question; thus, in this step the preceding-node value is 1 because we are only considering nodes that can be directly reached from node 1.

Step 3  Identify the tentatively labeled node with the smallest distance value, and declare that node permanently labeled. If all nodes are permanently labeled, go to step 5.

Step 4  Consider the remaining nodes that are not permanently labeled and that can be reached directly from the new permanently labeled node identified in step 3. Compute new tentative labels for these nodes as follows:

a.  If the node in question has a tentative label, add the distance value at the new permanently labeled node to the direct distance from the new permanently labeled node to the node in question. If this sum is less than the distance value for the node in question, set the distance value for this node equal to this sum; in addition, set the preceding-node value equal to the new permanently labeled node that provided the smaller distance. Go to step 3.

b.  If the node in question is not yet labeled, create a tentative label by adding the distance value at the new permanently labeled node to the direct distance from the new permanently labeled node to the node in question. The preceding-node value is set equal to the new permanently labeled node. Go to step 3.

The shortest-route problem can also be formulated and solved as a transshipment problem. Simply set the supply at the start node and the demand at the end node equal to 1. However, unlike the labeling algorithm, this approach does not find the shortest route from the start node to every other node.

Step 5    The permanent labels identify both the shortest distance from node 1 to each node and the preceding node on the shortest route. The shortest route to a given node can be found by starting at the given node and moving to its preceding node. Continuing this backward movement through the network will provide the shortest route from node 1 to the node in question.

This algorithm will determine the shortest distance from node 1 to each of the other nodes in the network. Note that $N - 1$ iterations of the algorithm are required to find the shortest distance to all other nodes. If the shortest distance to every node is not needed, the algorithm can be stopped when those nodes of interest have been permanently labeled. The algorithm can also be easily modified to find the shortest distance from any node, say node $k$, to all other nodes in the network. To make such a change, we would merely begin by labeling node $k$ with the permanent label [0,S]. Then by applying the steps of the algorithm, we can find the shortest route from node $k$ to each of the other nodes in the network.

For practice in using the labeling algorithm to solve a shortest-route problem, try Problem 1.

The Management Scientist software package can be used to solve small shortest-route problems. Input for the program includes the number of nodes, the number of arcs, and the length of each arc. The output shown in Figure 9.12 provides the shortest route from node 1 to node 7 for the Gorman problem.

**Figure  9.12    THE MANAGEMENT SCIENTIST SOLUTION FOR THE GORMAN SHORTEST-ROUTE PROBLEM**

```
        ****   NETWORK DESCRIPTION   ****

              7 NODES AND 10 ARCS

    ARC      START NODE    END NODE     DISTANCE
    ---      ----------    --------     --------
     1            1            2            15
     2            1            3            10
     3            2            3             3
     4            2            4             6
     5            2            7            17
     6            3            5             4
     7            4            5             4
     8            4            7             5
     9            5            6             2
    10            6            7             6

    THE SHORTEST ROUTE FROM NODE 1 TO NODE 7
    ****************************************

    START NODE       END NODE        DISTANCE
    ----------       --------        --------
        1               3               10
        3               5                4
        5               6                2
        6               7                6

         TOTAL DISTANCE                  22
```

1. Many applications of the shortest-route algorithm involve criteria such as time or cost instead of distance. In these cases, the shortest-route algorithm provides the minimum-time or minimum-cost solution. However, since the shortest-route algorithm always identifies a minimum-value solution, it would not make sense to apply the algorithm to problems that involve a profit criterion.

2. In some applications, the value associated with an arc may be negative. For example, in situations where cost is the criterion, a negative arc value would denote a negative cost; in other words, a profit would be realized by traversing the arc. The shortest-route algorithm presented in this section can only be applied to networks with nonnegative arc values. More advanced texts discuss algorithms that can solve problems with negative arc values.

## 9.2    THE MINIMAL SPANNING TREE PROBLEM

In network terminology, the minimal spanning tree problem involves using the arcs of the network to reach *all* nodes of the network in such a fashion that the total length of all the arcs used in minimized. To better understand this problem, let us consider the communications system design problem encountered by a regional computer center.

The Southwestern Regional Computer Center must have special computer communications lines installed to connect five satellite users with a new central computer. The telephone company will install the new communications network. However, the installation is an expensive operation. To reduce costs, the center's management group wants the total length of the new communications lines to be as small as possible. While the central computer could be connected directly to each user, it appears to be more economical to install a direct line to some users and let other users tap into the system by linking them with users already connected to the system. The determination of this minimal length communications system design is an example of the **minimal spanning tree** problem. The network for this problem with possible connection alternatives and distances is shown in Figure 9.13. An algorithm that can be used to solve this network model is explained in the following subsection.

### A Minimal Spanning Tree Algorithm

For a network consisting of N nodes, a spanning tree will consist of N − 1 arcs.

A **spanning tree** for an $N$-node network is a set of $N - 1$ arcs that connects every node to every other node. A minimal spanning tree provides this set of arcs at minimal total arc cost, distance, etc. The network algorithm that can be used to solve the minimal spanning tree problem is simple. The steps of the algorithm are as follows:

Step 1  Arbitrarily begin at any node and connect it to the closest node in terms of the criterion being used (e.g., time, cost, or distance). The two nodes are referred to as *connected* nodes, and the remaining nodes are referred to as *unconnected* nodes.

**419**

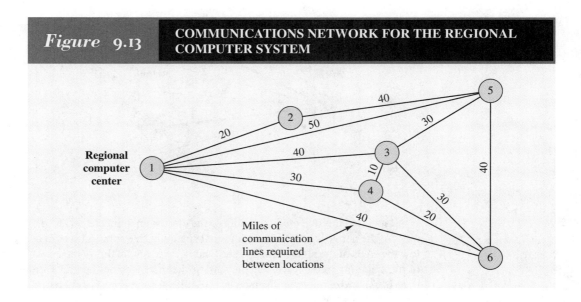

**Figure 9.13**

**COMMUNICATIONS NETWORK FOR THE REGIONAL COMPUTER SYSTEM**

**Step 2** Identify the unconnected node that is closest to one of the connected nodes. Break ties arbitrarily if two or more nodes qualify as the closest node. Add this new node to the set of connected nodes. Repeat this step until all nodes have been connected.

This network algorithm is easily implemented by making the connection decisions directly on the network.

Referring to the communications network for the regional computer center and arbitrarily beginning at node 1, we find the closest node is node 2 with a distance of 20. Using a bold line to connect nodes 1 and 2, step 1 of the algorithm provides the following result:

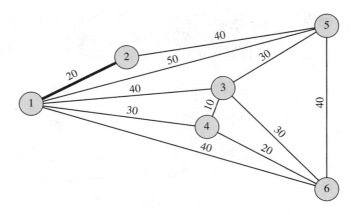

In step 2 of the algorithm, we find that the unconnected node closest to one of the connected nodes is node 4, with a distance of 30 miles from node 1. Adding node 4 to the set of connected nodes provides the following result:

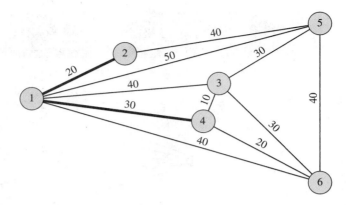

Repeating the step of always adding the closest unconnected node to the connected segment of the network provides the minimal spanning tree solution shown in Figure 9.14. Follow the steps of the algorithm, and see whether you obtain this solution. The minimal length of the spanning tree is given by the sum of the distances on the arcs forming the spanning tree. In this case, the total distance is 110 miles for the computer center's communications network. Note that while the computer center's network arcs were measured in distance, other network models may measure the arcs in terms of other criteria such as cost, time, and so on. In such cases, the minimal spanning tree algorithm will identify the optimal solution (minimal cost, minimal time, etc.) for the criterion being considered.

Can you now find a minimal spanning tree for a network? Try Problem 10.

The computer solution to the regional computer center's problem is shown in Figure 9.15. The Management Scientist was used to obtain the minimal spanning tree solution of 110 miles.

---

**N O T E S**
**and Comments**

The minimal spanning tree algorithm is considered a *greedy algorithm* since at each stage we can be "greedy" and take the best action available at that stage. Following this strategy at each successive stage will provide the overall optimal solution. Cases such as this, where a greedy algorithm provides the optimal solution, are rare. For many problems, however, greedy algorithms are excellent heuristics.

---

***Figure* 9.14    MINIMAL SPANNING TREE COMMUNICATIONS NETWORK FOR THE REGIONAL COMPUTER CENTER**

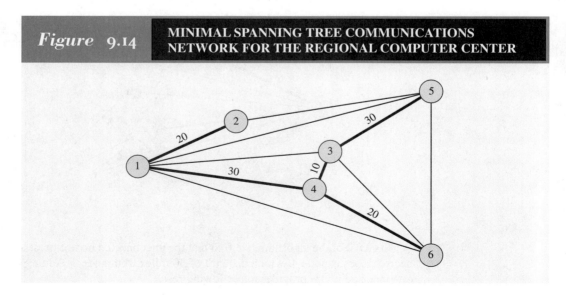

| | THE MANAGEMENT SCIENTIST SOLUTION FOR THE |
|---|---|
| **Figure** 9.15 | REGIONAL COMPUTER CENTER MINIMAL SPANNING TREE PROBLEM |

```
            ****   NETWORK DESCRIPTION  ****
                  6 NODES AND 11 ARCS
      ARC     START NODE      END NODE      DISTANCE
      ---     ----------      --------      --------
       1          1              2             20
       2          1              3             40
       3          1              4             30
       4          1              5             50
       5          1              6             40
       6          2              5             40
       7          3              4             10
       8          3              5             30
       9          3              6             30
      10          4              6             20
      11          5              6             40

                  MINIMAL SPANNING TREE
              *********************

      START NODE        END NODE        DISTANCE
      ----------        --------        --------
          1                2               20
          1                4               30
          4                3               10
          4                6               20
          3                5               30

              TOTAL LENGTH             110
```

## 9.3   THE MAXIMAL FLOW PROBLEM

Consider a network with one input or **source** node and one output or **sink** node. The **maximal flow** problem asks: What is the maximum amount of flow (vehicles, messages, fluid, etc.) that can enter and exit the network system in a given period of time? In this problem, we attempt to transmit flow through all arcs of the network as efficiently as possible. The amount of flow is limited due to capacity restrictions on the various arcs of the network. For example, highway types limit vehicle flow in a transportation system, while pipe sizes limit oil flow in an oil distribution system. The maximum or upper limit on the flow in an arc is referred to as the **flow capacity** of the arc. While we do not specify capacities for the nodes, we do assume that the flow out of a node is equal to the flow into the node.

As an example of the maximal flow problem, consider the north-south interstate highway system passing through Cincinnati, Ohio. The north-south vehicle flow reaches a level of 15,000 vehicles per hour at peak times. Due to a summer highway maintenance program, which calls for the temporary closing of lanes and lower speed limits, a network of alternate routes through Cincinnati has been proposed by a transportation planning committee. The alternate routes include other highways as well as city streets. Because of differences in speed limits and traffic patterns, flow capacities vary, depending on the particular streets and roads used. The proposed network with arc flow capacities is shown in Figure 9.16.

The flow capacities are based on the direction of the flow. For example, highway section or arc 1–2 shows a capacity of 5000 vehicles per hour in the 1–2 direction; however, a zero capacity exists in the 2–1 direction. This zero capacity means that the highway network planners do not want vehicles flowing from node 2 into node 1. Logically speaking, because node 1 is the input, or source, and a potential traffic jam location, it would be undesirable to permit traffic flow into the node 1 intersection from node 2. The directional capacities on arc 1–2 can also be interpreted as indicating a one-way street leading from the node 1 intersection. In any case, this example shows that the flow capacities of arcs can be dependent on the direction of the flow. Do you believe the highway system network shown in Figure 9.16 can accommodate the north-south maximum flow of 15,000 vehicles per hour? What is the maximal flow in vehicles per hour for the network? How much flow should go over each arc?

### A Maximal Flow Algorithm

As we shall see, the maximal flow algorithm presented in this section uses the following commonsense approach:

*The maximal flow problem can also be formulated and solved as a linear program.*

1. Find any path from the input (source) node to the output (sink) node that has flow capacities in the direction of the flow greater than zero for all arcs on the path.
2. Increase the flow along the path by as much as possible.
3. Continue looking for source-to-sink paths that have remaining flow capacities in the direction of the flow greater than zero for all arcs, and increase the flow along these paths as much as possible.
4. Stop when it is no longer possible to find a source-to-sink path with flow capacities in the direction of the flow greater than zero for all arcs on the path.

| *Figure* 9.16 | NETWORK OF HIGHWAY SYSTEM AND FLOW CAPACITIES (000S/HOUR) FOR CINCINNATI |
|---|---|

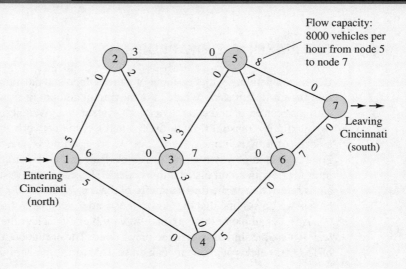

Before presenting the details of the maximal flow algorithm, let us briefly discuss a procedure that will ensure that these intuitive steps result in an optimal solution to this maximal flow problem.

The procedure permits previously assigned flow to take an alternate route by permitting fictional flows in the reverse direction. For example, consider the 3–6 arc:

Here we see that the initial flow capacity in the 3–6 direction is 7000 vehicles per hour, while no flow is permitted in the 6–3 direction.

If we choose to let 6000 vehicles per hour flow in the 3–6 direction, we will revise the flow capacities as follows:

Note that we have decreased the flow capacity in the 3–6 direction by 6000 vehicles per hour and simultaneously increased the flow capacity in the 6–3 direction by the same amount. The revised flow capacity of 1000 vehicles per hour in the 3–6 direction is readily interpreted as the remaining flow capacity for the arc. However, note that the 6–3 direction that had an initial flow capacity of zero now shows a revised flow capacity of 6000 vehicles per hour. This revised capacity in the 6–3 direction is actually indicating that a fictitious flow of up to 6000 vehicles per hour is permitted in this direction. Fictitious flow would not actually send vehicles in the 6–3 direction but would rather decrease the amount of flow originally committed to the 3–6 arc direction. In effect, fictitious flow in the 6–3 direction would result in diverting flow originally committed to the 3–6 direction to other arcs in the network.

This process of tracking flow capacities is an important part of the maximal flow algorithm. For example, in an earlier step of the algorithm, we might commit flow along a certain arc. Later, due to flows identified in other arcs, it may be desirable to decrease the flow along the original arc. The procedure will identify the extent to which our original decision to commit some flow needs to be revised in order to increase the total flow through the network.

Let us now look at the steps of the maximal flow algorithm.

Step 1  Find any path from the source (input) node to the sink (output) node that has flow capacities in the direction of the flow greater than zero for all arcs on the path. If no path is available, the optimal solution has been reached.

Step 2  Find the smallest arc capacity, $P_f$, on the path selected in step 1. Increase the flow through the network by sending an amount $P_f$ over the path selected in step 1.

Step 3  For the path selected in step 1, reduce all arc flow capacities in the direction of flow by $P_f$, and increase all arc flow capacities in the reverse direction by $P_f$. Go to step 1.

While the procedure will vary depending on the analyst's choice of paths in step 1, the algorithm will eventually provide the maximal flow solution. Our calculations for the highway flow network are as follows:

## Iteration 1

The path selected is 1–3–6–7; $P_j$, determined by arc 1–3, is 6. The revised network is as follows:

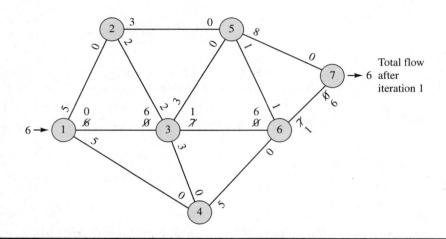

Total flow
6 after
iteration 1

## Iteration 2

The path selected is 1–2–5–7; $P_f$, determined by arc 2–5, is 3. The revised network is as follows:

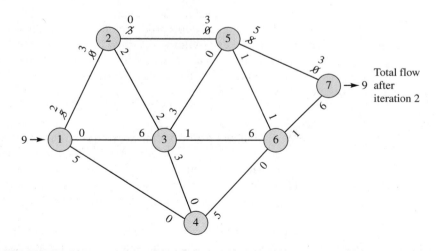

Total flow
9 after
iteration 2

The total flow through the network at each iteration can be found by summing the $P_f$ values from all iterations.

While we will not show the revised network after each iteration, you should attempt to update the network flow capacities as you follow the discussion. For example, what will this network look like after the following three iterations?

### Iteration 3

The path selected is 1–2–3–5–7; $P_f$, determined by arc 1–2 (or 2–3), is 2.

### Iteration 4

The path selected is 1–4–6–7; $P_f$, determined by arc 6–7, is 1.

### Iteration 5

The path selected is 1–4–6–5–7; $P_f$, determined by arc 6–5, is 1.

At this point, we have a total flow of 13,000 vehicles per hour, and the revised network capacities are as follows:

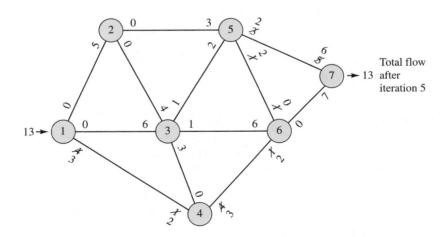

Are there any other paths from node 1 to node 7 that have flow capacities in the direction of the flow greater than zero? Try 1–4–6–3–5–7, with a flow of $P_f = 1$ determined by arc 3–5. This path increases the flow to 14,000 vehicles per hour. However, as you can see from the following revised network, no more paths from node 1 to node 7 have flow capacities greater than zero on all arcs of the path; thus, 14,000 vehicles per hour is the maximal flow for this network.

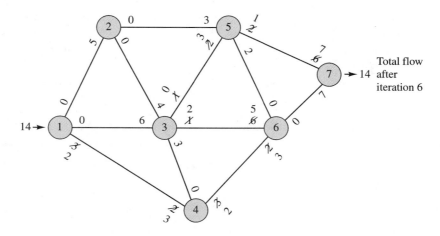

Total flow
14 after
iteration 6

Note that in iteration 6 a flow of 1000 vehicles per hour was permitted in the 6–3 direction. From the initial network, however, we know that the flow capacity in the 6–3 direction is zero; thus, the 1000 units of flow in the 6–3 direction represent a fictitious flow. The real effect of this flow is to divert 1000 units of flow originally committed to the 3–6 arc in iteration 1 along the 3–5 arc to enable us to get 1000 units more of flow through the network. Let us now determine the amount and direction of flow in each arc so that the total flow of 14,000 vehicles per hour can be attained.

Arc flows for the maximal flow solution can be found by comparing the final arc flow capacities with the initial arc flow capacities. If the final flow capacity is *less* than the initial flow capacity, flow is occurring over the arc with an amount equal to the difference between the initial and final flow capacities. For example, consider the 3–6 arc with initial and final flow capacities as follows.

### Initial Capacities

### Final Capacities

Since the final flow capacity in the 3–6 direction is less than the initial flow capacity, the arc has a flow of 7 − 2 = 5 in the 3–6 direction. This arc flow is summarized as follows:

Comparing final and initial arc flow capacities for all arcs in the network enables us to determine the final flow pattern as shown in Figure 9.17.

The results of the maximal flow analysis indicate that the planned highway network system will not handle the peak flow of 15,000 vehicles per hour. The transportation planners will have to expand the highway network, increase current arc flow capacities, or be prepared for serious traffic jam problems. If the network is extended or modified, another maximal flow analysis will determine the extent of any improved flow.

Try Problem 15 for practice in solving a maximal flow problem.

| Figure 9.17 | MAXIMAL FLOW PATTERN FOR THE HIGHWAY SYSTEM NETWORK |

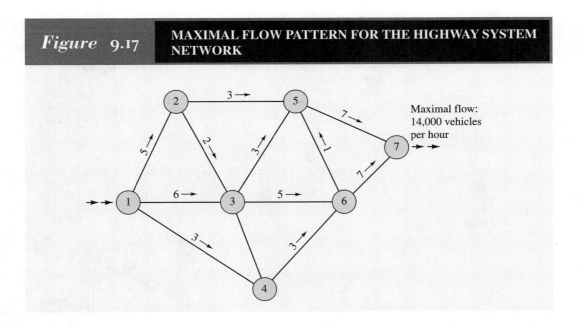

Maximal flow:
14,000 vehicles
per hour

Network models can be used to describe a variety of management science problems. Unfortunately, no one network solution algorithm can be used to solve every network problem. It is important to recognize the specific type of problem being modeled in order to select the correct specialized solution algorithm.

## SUMMARY

In this chapter we extended the discussion of the use of network models in managerial decision making. We introduced the shortest-route, minimal spanning tree, and maximal flow problems and presented specialized solution algorithms for each. The key to success in network approaches to problem solving is in seeing how the problem can be represented as a network model. While some network formulations are obvious, other problems may require substantial ingenuity to develop the appropriate network representation. In any case, once the network representation has been developed, specialized solution algorithms are available to solve the problem.

## GLOSSARY

**Shortest route**  Shortest path between two nodes in a network.

**Spanning tree**  A set of $N - 1$ arcs that connect every node in the network with all other nodes where $N$ is the number of nodes.

**Minimal spanning tree**  The spanning tree with the minimum length.

**Flow capacity**  The maximum flow for an arc of the network. The flow capacity in one direction may not equal the flow capacity in the reverse direction.

**Source**  A node that generates flow; flow can only move away from it and never into it.

**Sink**  A node that absorbs flow; flow can only move into it and never away from it.

**Maximal flow**  The maximum amount of flow that can enter and exit a network system during a given period of time.

······································································/ /············

## PROBLEMS

**SELF TEST**

1.  Find the shortest route from node 1 to each of the other nodes in the transportation network shown.

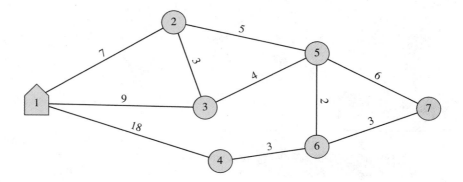

2.  For the Gorman Construction Company problem (see Figure 9.1), assume that node 7 is the company's warehouse and supply center. Several daily trips are commonly made from node 7 to the other nodes or construction sites. Using node 7 as the starting node, find the shortest route from this node to each of the other nodes in the network.

3.  In the original Gorman Construction Company problem, we found the shortest distance from the office (node 1) to each of the other nodes or construction sites. Because some of the roads are highways and others are city streets, the shortest-distance routes between the office and the construction sites may not necessarily provide the quickest or shortest-time routes. Shown here is the Gorman road network with travel time values rather than distance values. Find the shortest route from Gorman's office to each of the construction sites if the objective is to minimize travel time rather than distance.

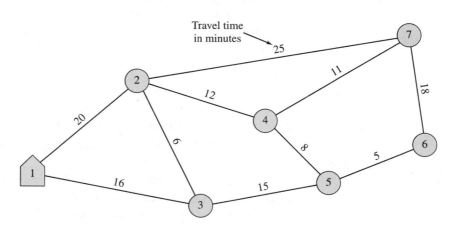

4.  Find the shortest route between nodes 1 and 8 in the following network:

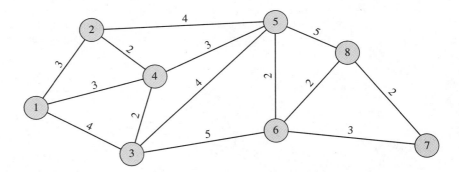

5.  Find the shortest route between nodes 1 and 10 in the following network:

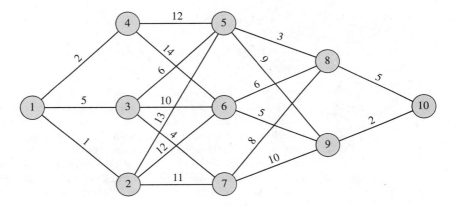

6.  Morgan Trucking Company operates a special fast-service pickup and delivery service between Chicago and 10 other cities located in a four-state area. When Morgan receives a request for service, it dispatches a truck from Chicago to the city requesting service as soon as possible. Since both fast service and minimum travel costs are objectives for Morgan, it is important that the dispatched truck take the shortest route from Chicago to the specified city. Assume that the following network (not drawn to scale) with distances given in miles represents the highway network for this problem. Find the shortest-route distances from Chicago to all 10 cites.

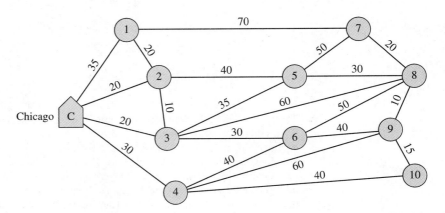

7. City Cab Company has identified 10 primary pickup and drop locations for cab riders in New York City. In an effort to minimize travel time and improve customer service and the utilization of the company's fleet of cabs, management would like the cab drivers to take the shortest route between locations whenever possible. Using the following network of roads and streets, what is the route a driver beginning at location 1 should take to reach location 10? The travel times in minutes are shown on the arcs of the network.

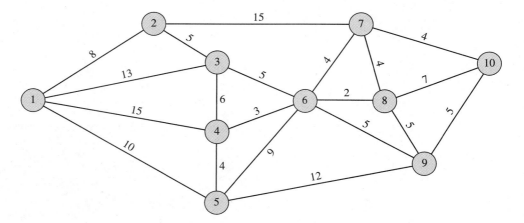

8. The Wisman Candy Company manufacturers a variety of candy products. Company trucks are used to deliver local orders directly to retail outlets. When the business was small, the drivers of the trucks were free to take routes of their choice as they made the delivery rounds to the retail outlets. However, as the business has grown, transportation and delivery costs have become significant. In an effort to improve the efficiency of the delivery operation, Wisman's management would like to determine the shortest delivery routes between retail outlets. For example, the following network shows the roads that may be taken between a retail outlet at node 1 and a retail outlet at node 11. Determine the shortest route for a truck that is currently at node 1 and must make a delivery to node 11.

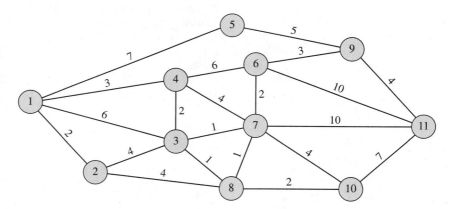

9. The five nodes in the following network represent points 1 year apart over a 4-year period. Each node indicates a time when a decision is made to keep or replace a firm's computer equipment. If a decision is made to replace the equipment, a decision must also be made as to how long the new equipment will be used. The arc from node 0 to node 1 represents the decision to keep the current equipment 1 year and replace it at the end of the year. The arc from node 0 to node 2 represents the decision to keep the current equipment 2 years and replace it at the end of year 2. The numbers above the arcs indicate the total cost associated with the equipment replacement decisions. These costs include discounted purchase price, trade-in value, op-

erating costs, and maintenance costs. Determine the minimum-cost equipment replacement policy for the 4-year period.

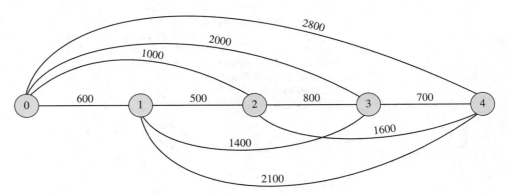

10. The State of Ohio recently purchased land for a new state park, and park planners have identified the ideal locations for the lodge, cabins, picnic groves, boat dock, and scenic points of interest. These locations are represented by the nodes of the following network. The arcs of the network represent possible road alternatives in the park. If the state park designers want to minimize the total road miles that must be constructed in the park and still permit access to all facilities (nodes), which road alternatives should be constructed?

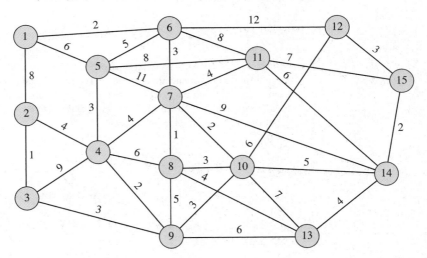

11. Develop the minimal spanning tree solution for the following emergency communication network.

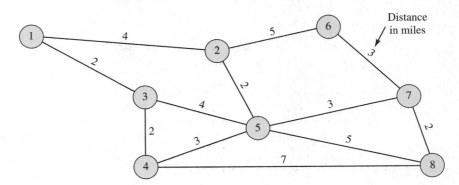

12. In a large soap products plant, quality control inspectors take samples of various products from the different production areas and deliver them to the lab for analysis. The inspection process is slow, and the inspectors spend substantial time transporting samples from the production areas to the lab. The company is considering installing a pneumatic tube conveyor system that could transport the samples between the production areas and the lab. The following network shows the location of the lab and the production areas (nodes) where the samples must be collected. The arcs are the alternatives being considered for the conveyor system. What is the minimum total length and layout of the conveyor system that will enable all production areas to send samples to the lab?

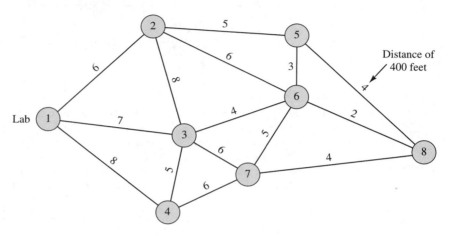

13. Midwest University is installing an electronic mail system. The following network shows the possible electronic connections among the offices. Distances between offices are shown in thousands of feet. Develop a design for the office communication system that will enable all offices to have access to the electronic mail service. Provide the design that minimizes the total length of connection among the eight offices.

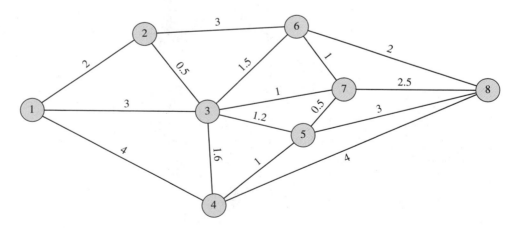

14. The Metrovision Cable Company has just received approval to begin providing cable television service to a suburb of Memphis, Tennessee. The nodes of the following network show the distribution points that must be reached by the company's primary cable lines. The arcs of the network show the number of miles between the distribution points. Determine the solution that will enable the company to reach all distribution points with the minimum length of primary cable line.

15. The north-south highway system passing through Albany, New York, can accommodate the capacities shown.

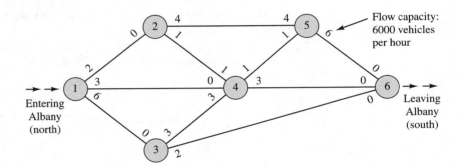

Can the highway system accommodate a north-south flow of 10,000 vehicles per hour?

16. If the Albany highway described in Problem 15 has revised flow capacities as shown in the following network, what is the maximal flow in vehicles per hour through the system? How many vehicles per hour must travel over each road (arc) to obtain this maximal flow?

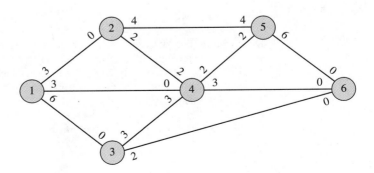

17. A long-distance telephone company uses an underground cable network of communication lines to provide high-quality audio communication between two major cities. Calls are carried through series cable lines and connecting nodes in the network as shown here.

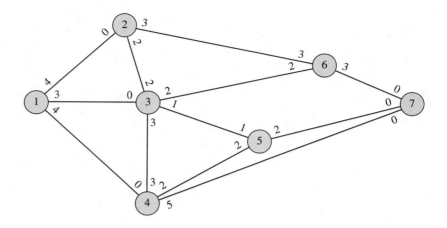

Also shown are the number of telephone calls (in thousands) that may occur simultaneously at any point in time. What is the maximum number of telephone calls that can be transmitted simultaneously between the two cities? What are the connecting nodes and cable flows when the system is operating at capacity?

18. The High-Price Oil Company owns a pipeline network that is used to convey oil from its source to several storage locations. A portion of the network is as follows:

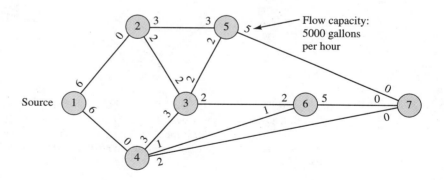

Due to the varying pipe sizes, the flow capacities also vary. By selectively opening and closing sections of the pipeline network, the firm can supply any of the storage locations.

a. If the firm wants to supply storage location 7 and fully utilize the system capacity, how long will it take to satisfy a location 7 demand of 100,000 gallons? What is the maximal flow for this pipeline system?

b. If a break occurs on line 2–3 and it is closed down, what is the maximal flow for the system? How long will it take to transmit 100,000 gallons to location 7?

19.  For the following highway network system, determine the maximal flow in vehicles per hour.

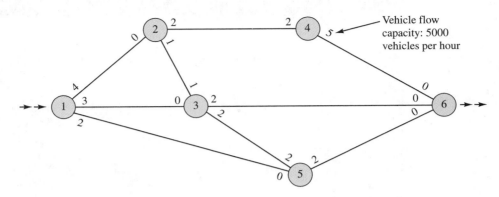

The highway commission is considering adding highway section 3–4 to permit a flow of 2000 vehicles per hour or, at an additional cost, a flow of 3000 vehicles per hour. What is your recommendation for the 3–4 arc of the network?

20.  A chemical processing plant has a network of pipes that are used to transfer liquid chemical products from one part of the plant to another. The following pipe network has pipe flow capacities in gallons per minute as shown. What is the maximum flow capacity for the system if the company wishes to transfer as much liquid chemical as possible from location 1 to location 9? How much of the chemical will flow through the section of pipe from node 3 to node 5?

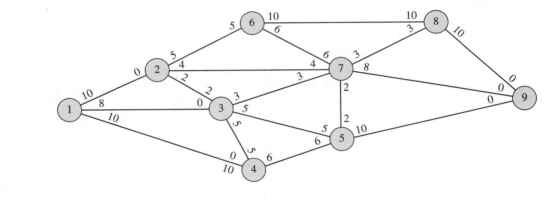

# Case Problem   AMBULANCE ROUTING

The city of Binghamton is served by two major hospitals: Western Medical and Binghamton General. Western Medical is located in the southwest part of the city, and Binghamton General is in the northeast.

Bob Jones, the hospital administrator at Western Medical, has been discussing the problem of scheduling and routing ambulances with Margaret Johnson, the hospital administrator at Binghamton General. Both administrators feel that some type of system needs to be developed to better coordinate the use of the ambulance services at the two hospitals so that together they can provide the fastest possible emergency service for the city.

**Figure 9.18     NETWORK FOR PROPOSED AMBULANCE SERVICE**

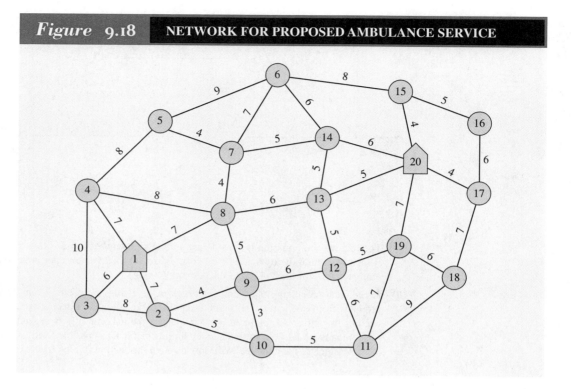

A proposal being considered is for all ambulance service calls to be handled through a central dispatcher, who would assign a call to the hospital capable of providing the fastest service. In studying this proposal, a project team consisting of employees from both hospitals met and decided that the best approach would be to divide the city into 20 service zones. In the proposed configuration, Western Medical would be located in zone 1 and Binghamton General in zone 20. A map showing the placement of the 20 zones and the travel time (in minutes) between adjacent zones is provided in Figure 9.18.

According to the proposed operating procedure, incoming emergency calls would be identified by zone number, and an ambulance from the hospital closest to that zone would be assigned the service call. However, if all ambulances from the closest hospital were occupied with other emergencies, the service call would be assigned to the other hospital. Regardless of which hospital responded to the service call, the individual or individuals requiring the emergency service would be taken to the closest hospital.

To make the coordinated service as efficient as possible, the ambulance drivers must know in advance the quickest route to take to each zone, which hospital the individual or individuals in that zone should be taken to, and the quickest route to that hospital.

## Managerial Report

Prepare a report for the two hospital administrators describing your analysis of the problem. Include in your report recommendations regarding the following items:

1. A chart for the dispatcher that identifies the primary hospital ambulance service for every zone in the city.
2. A chart for the Western Medical ambulance drivers that provides the minimum-time routes from Western Medical to every zone in the city, including Binghamton Gen-

eral. Include a chart that tells Western Medical drivers which hospital the individuals should be taken to and the route that should be followed.

3. A chart for the Binghamton General ambulance drivers that provides the minimum-time routes from Binghamton General to every zone in the city, including Western Medical. Include a chart that tells Binghamton General drivers which hospital the individuals should be taken to and the route that should be followed.

4. Include recommendations regarding how the system could be modified to take into account varying traffic conditions that occur throughout the day and/or changes in driving conditions resulting from temporary road construction projects.

# EDS

## PLANO, TEXAS*

EDS is a global leader in providing information technology services. For more than 30 years, the company has provided hardware, software, communications, and process solutions to companies and governments around the world. Headquartered in Plano, Texas, EDS helps customers become more competitive by focusing technology on business goals. Customers come from a variety of industries and include leaders in the automotive, government services, financial, insurance, communications, manufacturing, retail, energy, distribution, transportation, utilities, and health care industries. In 1984, EDS was acquired by the world's leading auto manufacturer, General Motors, and became an independently operated subsidiary.

## Minimal Spanning Tree Network Problem

EDS designs communication systems and information networks for many of its customers. In one application, a customer wanted to link together 64 locations for information flow, information processing, and communications. Interactive data including voice, video, and digital data had to be accommodated in the information flow between the various sites. The customer's locations included approximately 50 offices and information centers in the continental United States; they ranged from Connecticut to Florida to Michigan to Texas to California. Additional locations existed in Canada, Mexico, Hawaii, and Puerto Rico. The total of 64 company locations formed the nodes of the information network.

EDS's task was to span the network by finding the most cost-effective way to link 64 customer locations or nodes

* The authors are indebted to Greg A. Dennis of EDS for providing this application.

with the other customer locations as well as with existing EDS data centers. The arcs of the network were formed by connecting pairs of nodes in the network. In cases where land communication lines were available, the arcs consisted of fiber optic telephone lines. In other cases, the arcs were formed by satellite communication connections.

Using cost as the criterion, the information network developed by EDS was obtained by solving a minimal spanning tree problem. The ultimate goal was the development of a minimum-cost network design such that all locations (nodes) could communicate with all other locations (nodes). Figure 9.19 shows a portion of the information network developed by EDS. With a communication arc between the company's New Jersey center and the EDS center in Herndon, Virginia, the network enabled the company to communicate through Herndon with locations in Texas, Arizona, California, Hawaii, and Mexico by taking advantage of the existing EDS center in Plano, Texas. The use of the EDS centers in Herndon and Plano meant that the client could span its network without developing its own independent information network. An effective and economical communication system was developed for the customer.

## Questions

1. What were the nodes and the arcs of the information network?
2. Where does the minimal spanning tree problem enter into design of the information network?
3. Why were the number of nodes expanded to include existing EDS centers in addition to the 64 company locations? What advantages did this provide in developing the minimum-cost network design?

## Figure 9.19    A PORTION OF THE INFORMATION NETWORK DESIGNED BY EDS

# 10

## PROJECT SCHEDULING: PERT/CPM

### CONTENTS

In many situations, managers are responsible for planning, scheduling, and controlling projects that consist of numerous separate jobs or tasks performed by a variety of departments and individuals. Often these projects are so large and/or complex that the manager cannot possibly remember all the information pertaining to the plan, schedule, and progress of the project. In these situations the **program evaluation and review technique (PERT)** and the **critical path method (CPM)** have proven to be extremely valuable.

PERT and CPM have been used to plan, schedule, and control a wide variety of projects:

Henry L. Gantt developed the Gantt Chart as a graphical aid to scheduling jobs on machines in 1918. This application was the first of what has become known as *project scheduling techniques.*

1. Research and development of new products and processes
2. Construction of plants, buildings, and highways
3. Maintenance of large and complex equipment
4. Design and installation of new systems

In these types of projects, project managers must schedule and coordinate the various jobs or **activities** so that the entire project is completed on time. A complicating factor in carrying out this task is the interdependence of the activities; for example, some activities depend on the completion of other activities before they can be started. Projects may have as many as several thousand activities, so project managers look for procedures that will help them answer questions such as the following.

1. What is the total time to complete the project?
2. What are the scheduled start and finish dates for each specific activity?
3. Which activities are "critical" and must be completed *exactly* as scheduled to keep the project on schedule?
4. How long can "noncritical" activities be delayed before they cause an increase in the total project completion time?

PERT (Navy) and CPM (Du Pont and Remmington Rand) differ because they were developed by different people working on different projects. Today, the best aspects of each have been combined to provide a valuable project scheduling technique.

PERT and CPM can help answer these questions.

Although PERT and CPM have the same general purpose and utilize much of the same terminology, the techniques were developed independently. PERT was developed in the late 1950s specifically for the Polaris missile project. Many activities associated with this project had never been attempted previously, so PERT was developed to handle uncertain activity times. CPM was developed primarily for industrial projects for which activity times generally were known. CPM offered the option of reducing activity times by adding more workers and/or resources, usually at an increased cost. Thus, a distinguishing feature of CPM was that it identified trade-offs between time and cost for various project activities.

Today's computerized versions of PERT and CPM have combined the best features of both approaches. Thus, the distinction between the two techniques is no longer necessary. As a result, we refer to the project scheduling procedures covered in this chapter as PERT/CPM. We begin the discussion of PERT/CPM by considering a project for the expansion of the Western Hills Shopping Center.

## 10.1    PROJECT SCHEDULING WITH KNOWN ACTIVITY TIMES

The owner of the Western Hills Shopping Center is planning to modernize and expand the current 32-business shopping center complex. The project is expected to provide room for 8 to 10 new businesses. Financing has been arranged through a private investor. All that remains is for the owner of the shopping center to plan, schedule, and complete the expansion project. Let us show how PERT/CPM can help.

| Table 10.1 | LIST OF ACTIVITIES FOR THE WESTERN HILLS SHOPPING CENTER PROJECT | | |
|---|---|---|---|
| **Activity** | **Activity Description** | **Immediate Predecessor** | **Activity Time** |
| A | Prepare architectural drawings | — | 5 |
| B | Identify potential new tenants | — | 6 |
| C | Develop prospectus for tenants | A | 4 |
| D | Select contractor | A | 3 |
| E | Prepare building permits | A | 1 |
| F | Obtain approval for building permits | E | 4 |
| G | Perform construction | D, F | 14 |
| H | Finalize contracts with tenants | B, C | 12 |
| I | Tenants move in | G, H | 2 |
| | | Total | 51 |

The effort that goes into identifying activities, determining interrelationships among activities, and estimating activity times is crucial to the success of PERT/CPM. A significant amount of time may be needed to complete this initial phase of the project scheduling process.

Immediate predecessor information determines whether activities can be completed in parallel (worked on simultaneously) or in series (one completed before another begins). Generally, the more series relationships present in a project, the more time will be required to complete the project.

A project network is extremely helpful in visualizing the interrelationships among the activities. There are no rules for converting a list of activities and immediate predecessor information into a project network. The process of constructing a project network generally improves with practice and experience.

The first step in the PERT/CPM scheduling process is to develop a list of the activities that make up the project. Table 10.1 shows the list of activities for the Western Hills Shopping Center expansion project. Nine activities are described and denoted A through I for later reference. Table 10.1 also shows the immediate predecessor(s) and the activity time (in weeks) for each activity. For a given activity, the **immediate predecessor** column identifies the activities that must be completed *immediately prior* to the start of that activity. Activities A and B do not have immediate predecessors and can be started as soon as the project begins; thus, a dash is written in the immediate predecessor column for these activities. The other entries in the immediate predecessor column show that activities C, D, and E cannot be started until activity A has been completed; activity F cannot be started until activity E has been completed; activity G cannot be started until both activities D and F have been completed; activity H cannot be started until both activities B and C have been completed; and, finally, activity I cannot be started until both activities G and H have been completed. The project is finished when activity I is completed.

The last column in Table 10.1 shows the number of weeks required to complete each activity. For example, activity A takes 5 weeks, activity B takes 6 weeks, and so on. The sum of activity times is 51. As a result, you may think that the total time required to complete the project is 51 weeks. However, as we show, two or more activities often may be scheduled concurrently, thus shortening the completion time for the project. Ultimately, PERT/CPM will provide a detailed activity schedule for completing the project in the shortest time possible.

Using the immediate predecessor information in Table 10.1, we can construct a graphical representation of the project, or the **project network.** Figure 10.1 depicts the project network for Western Hills Shopping Center. The activities correspond to the *nodes* of the network (drawn as rectangles) and the *arcs* (the lines with arrows) show the precedence relationships among the activities. In addition, nodes have been added to the network to denote the start and the finish of the project. A project network will help a manager visualize the activity relationships and provide a basis for carrying out the PERT/CPM computations.

## The Concept of a Critical Path

To facilitate the PERT/CPM computations, we modified the project network as shown in Figure 10.2. Note that the upper left-hand corner of each node contains the corresponding activity letter. The activity time appears immediately below the letter.

## Figure 10.1    PROJECT NETWORK FOR THE WESTERN HILLS SHOPPING CENTER

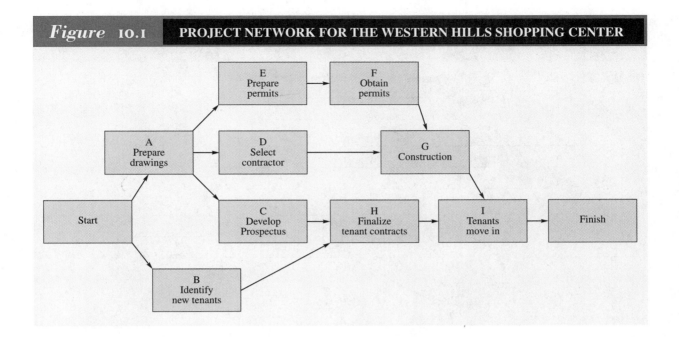

Try Problem 3. This problem provides the immediate predecessor information for a project with seven activities and asks you to develop the project network.

For convenience, we use the convention of referencing activities with letters. Generally, we assign the letters in approximate order as we move from left to right through the project network.

To determine the project completion time, we have to analyze the network and identify what is called the **critical path** for the network. However, before doing so, we need to define the concept of a path through the network. A **path** is a sequence of connected nodes that leads from the Start node to the Finish node. For instance, one path for the network in Figure 10.2 is defined by the sequence of nodes A-E-F-G-I. By inspection, we see that other paths are possible, such as A-D-G-I, A-C-H-I, and B-H-I. All paths in the network must be traversed in order to complete the project, so we will look for the path that requires the most time. Since all other paths are shorter in duration, this *longest* path determines the total time required to complete the project. If activities on the longest path are delayed, the entire project will be delayed. Thus, the longest path is the *critical path*. Activities on the critical path are referred to as the **critical activities** for the project. The following discussion presents a step-by-step algorithm for finding the critical path in a project network.

### Determining the Critical Path

We begin by finding the **earliest start time** and a **latest start time** for all activities in the network. Let

$$ES = \text{earliest start time for an activity}$$
$$EF = \text{earliest finish time for an activity}$$
$$t = \text{activity time}$$

The **earliest finish time** for any activity is

$$EF = ES + t \tag{10.1}$$

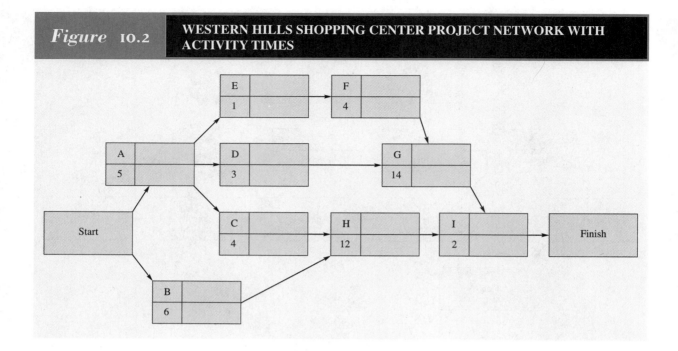

**Figure 10.2** WESTERN HILLS SHOPPING CENTER PROJECT NETWORK WITH ACTIVITY TIMES

Activity A can start as soon as the project starts, so we set the earliest start time for activity A equal to 0. With an activity time of 5 weeks, the earliest finish time for activity A is $EF = ES + t = 0 + 5 = 5$.

We will write the earliest start and earliest finish times in the node to the right of the activity letter. Using activity A as an example, we have

Earliest start time    Earliest finish time

| A | 0 | 5 |
|---|---|---|
| 5 | | |

Since an activity cannot be started until *all* immediately preceding activities have been finished, the following rule can be used to determine the earliest start time for each activity.

The earliest start time for an activity is equal to the *largest* of the earliest finish times for all its immediate predecessors.

Let us apply the earliest start time rule to the portion of the network involving nodes A, B, C, and H, as shown in Figure 10.3. With an earliest start time of 0 and an activity time of 6 for activity B, we show $ES = 0$ and $EF = ES + t = 0 + 6 = 6$ in the node for activity B. Looking at node C, we note that activity A is the only immediate predecessor for

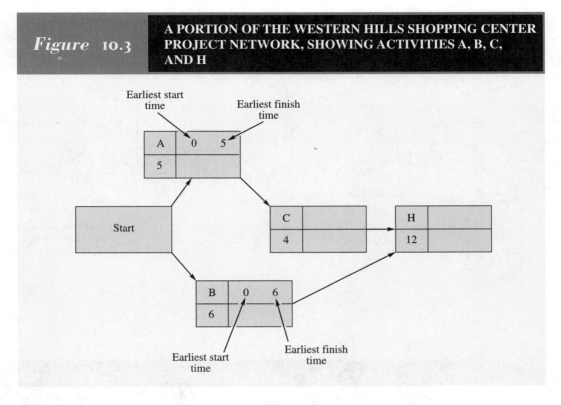

**Figure 10.3**

**A PORTION OF THE WESTERN HILLS SHOPPING CENTER PROJECT NETWORK, SHOWING ACTIVITIES A, B, C, AND H**

activity C. The earliest finish time for activity A is 5, so the earliest start time for activity C must be $ES = 5$. Thus, with an activity time of 4, the earliest finish time for activity C is $EF = ES + t = 5 + 4 = 9$. Both the earliest starting time and the earliest finish time can be shown in the node for activity C (see Figure 10.4).

Continuing with Figure 10.4, we move on to activity H and apply the earliest start time rule for this activity. With both activities B and C as immediate predecessors, the earliest start time for activity H must be equal to the largest of the earliest finish times for activities B and C. Thus, with $EF = 6$ for activity B and $EF = 9$ for activity C, we select the largest value, 9, as the earliest start time for activity H ($ES = 9$). With an activity time of 12 as shown in the node for activity H, the earliest finish time is $EF = ES + t = 9 + 12 = 21$. The $ES = 9$ and $EF = 21$ values can now be entered in the node for activity H in Figure 10.4.

Continuing with this **forward pass** through the network, we can establish the earliest start times and the earliest finish times for all activities in the network. Figure 10.5 shows the Western Hills Shopping Center project network with the $ES$ and $EF$ values for each activity. Note that the earliest finish time for activity I, the last activity in the project, is 26 weeks. Therefore, we now know that the total completion time for the project is 26 weeks.

We now continue the algorithm for finding the critical path by making a **backward pass** through the network. Since the project can be completed in 26 weeks, we begin the backward pass with a **latest finish time** of 26 for activity I. Once the latest finish time for an activity is known, the *latest start time* for an activity can be computed as follows. Let

$$LS = \text{latest start time for an activity}$$

$$LF = \text{latest finish time for an activity}$$

**Figure  10.4**   DETERMINING THE EARLIEST START TIME FOR ACTIVITY H

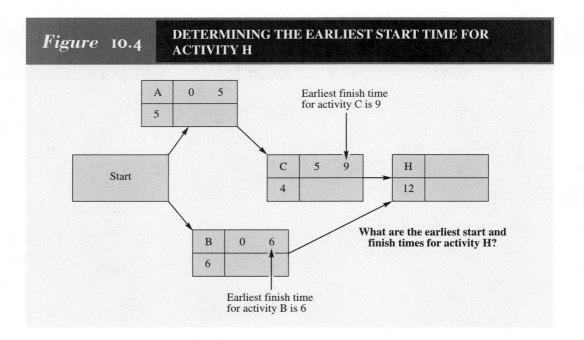

**Figure  10.5**   WESTERN HILLS SHOPPING CENTER PROJECT NETWORK WITH EARLIEST START AND EARLIEST FINISH TIMES SHOWN FOR ALL ACTIVITIES

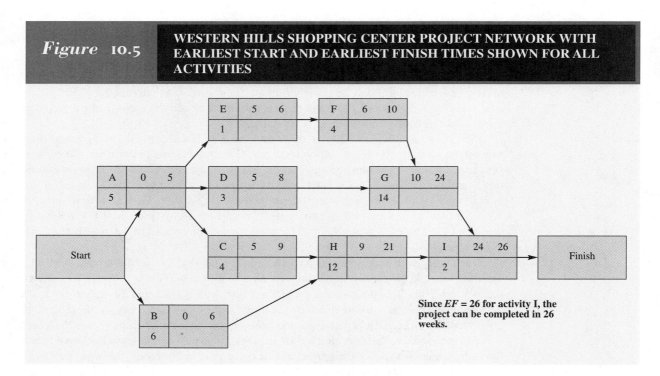

then

$$LS = LF - t \qquad (10.2)$$

Beginning the backward pass with activity I, we know that the latest finish time is $LF = 26$ and that the activity time is $t = 2$. Thus, the latest start time for activity I is $LS = LF - t = 26 - 2 = 24$. We will write the $LS$ and $LF$ values in the node directly below the earliest start ($ES$) and earliest finish ($EF$) times. Thus, for node I, we have

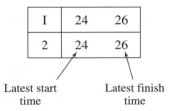

Latest start time          Latest finish time

The following rule can be used to determine the latest finish time for each activity in the network.

---

The latest finish time for an activity is the *smallest* of the latest start times for all activities that immediately follow the activity.

---

Logically, this rule states that the latest time an activity can be finished equals the earliest (smallest) value for the latest start time of following activities. Figure 10.6 shows the complete project network with the $LS$ and $LF$ backward pass results. We can use the latest finish time rule to verify the $LS$ and $LF$ values shown for activity H. The latest finish time for activity H must be the latest start time for activity I. Thus, we set $LF = 24$ for activity H. Using equation (10.2), we find that $LS = LF - t = 24 - 12 = 12$ as the latest start time for activity H. These values are shown in the node for activity H in Figure 10.6.

Activity A requires a more involved application of the latest start time rule. First, note that three activities (C, D, and E) immediately follow activity A. Figure 10.6 shows that the latest start times for activities C, D, and E are $LS = 8$, $LS = 7$, and $LS = 5$, respectively. The latest finish time rule for activity A states that the $LF$ for activity A is the smallest of the latest start times for activities C, D, and E. With the smallest value being 5 for activity E, we set the latest finish time for activity A to $LF = 5$. Verify this result and the other latest start times and latest finish times shown in the nodes in Figure 10.6.

The slack for each activity indicates the length of time the activity can be delayed without increasing the project completion time.

After we have completed the forward and backward passes, we can determine the amount of slack associated with each activity. **Slack** is the length of time an activity can be delayed without increasing the project completion time. The amount of slack for an activity is computed as follows:

$$Slack = LS - ES = LF - EF \qquad (10.3)$$

For example, the slack associated with activity C is $LS - ES = 8 - 5 = 3$ weeks. Hence, activity C can be delayed up to 3 weeks, and the entire project can still be completed in 26 weeks. In this sense, activity C is not critical to the completion of the entire project in 26 weeks. Next, we consider activity E. Using the information in Figure 10.6, we find that the

**Figure 10.6**    WESTERN HILLS SHOPPING CENTER PROJECT NETWORK WITH LATEST START AND LATEST FINISH TIMES SHOWN IN EACH NODE

slack is $LS - ES = 5 - 5 = 0$. Thus, activity E has zero, or no, slack. Thus, this activity cannot be delayed without increasing the completion time for the entire project. In other words, completing activity E exactly as scheduled is critical in terms of keeping the project on schedule. Thus, activity E is a critical activity. In general, the *critical activities* are the activities with zero slack.

> One of the primary contributions of PERT/CPM is the identification of the critical activities. The project manager will want to monitor critical activities closely because a delay in any one of these activities will lengthen the project completion time.

The start and finish times shown in Figure 10.6 can be used to develop a detailed start time and finish time schedule for all activities. Putting this information in tabular form provides the activity schedule shown in Table 10.2. Note that the slack column shows that activities A, E, F, G, and I have zero slack. Hence, these activities are the critical activities for the project. The path formed by nodes A-E-F-G-I is the *critical path* in the Western Hills Shopping Center project network. The detailed schedule shown in Table 10.2 indicates the slack or delay that can be tolerated for the noncritical activities before these activities will increase project completion time.

> The critical path algorithm is essentially a *longest path* algorithm. From the start node to the finish node, the critical path identifies the path that requires the most time.

## Contributions of PERT/CPM

Previously, we stated that project managers look for procedures that will help answer important questions regarding the planning, scheduling, and controlling of projects. Let us reconsider these questions in light of the information that the critical path calculations have given us.

1. How long will the project take to complete?
   *Answer:* The project can be completed in 26 weeks if each activity is completed on schedule.
2. What are the scheduled start and completion times for each activity?
   *Answer:* The activity schedule (see Table 10.2) shows the earliest start, latest start, earliest finish, and latest finish times for each activity.

| | Table 10.2 | | ACTIVITY SCHEDULE FOR THE WESTERN HILLS SHOPPING CENTER PROJECT | | | | |

| Activity | Earliest Start (*ES*) | Latest Start (*LS*) | Earliest Finish (*EF*) | Latest Finish (*LF*) | Slack (*LS* − *ES*) | Critical Path? |
|----------|------|------|------|------|------|------|
| A | 0 | 0 | 5 | 5 | 0 | Yes |
| B | 0 | 6 | 6 | 12 | 6 | |
| C | 5 | 8 | 9 | 12 | 3 | |
| D | 5 | 7 | 8 | 10 | 2 | |
| E | 5 | 5 | 6 | 6 | 0 | Yes |
| F | 6 | 6 | 10 | 10 | 0 | Yes |
| G | 10 | 10 | 24 | 24 | 0 | Yes |
| H | 9 | 12 | 21 | 24 | 3 | |
| I | 24 | 24 | 26 | 26 | 0 | Yes |

If the total time required to complete the project is too long, judgment about where and how to shorten the time of critical activities must be exercised. If any activity times are altered, the critical path calculations should be repeated to determine the impact on the activity schedule and the impact on total project completion time. In Section 10.3 we show how to use linear programming to find the least-cost way to shorten the project completion time.

Software packages such as The Management Scientist perform the critical path calculations quickly and efficiently. The project manager can modify any aspect of the project and quickly determine how the modification affects the activity schedule and the total time required to complete the project.

3. Which activities are critical and must be completed *exactly* as scheduled to keep the project on schedule?
   *Answer:* A, E, F, G, and I are the critical activities.
4. How long can noncritical activities be delayed before they cause an increase in the completion time for the project?
   *Answer:* The activity schedule (see Table 10.2) shows the slack associated with each activity.

Such information is valuable in managing any project. Although larger projects may increase substantially the time required to make the necessary calculations, the procedure and contributions of PERT/CPM to larger projects are identical to those for the shopping center expansion project. Furthermore, computer packages may be used to carry out the steps of the PERT/CPM procedure. Figure 10.7 shows the activity schedule for the shopping center expansion project developed by The Management Scientist software package. Input to the program included the activities, their immediate predecessors, and the expected activity times. Only a few minutes were required to input the information and generate the critical path and activity schedule. The Management Science in Action: Project Management on the PC describes the important role software packages play in the management of large projects.

## Summary of the PERT/CPM Critical Path Procedure

Before leaving this section, let us summarize the PERT/CPM critical path procedure.

Step 1 Develop a list of the activities that make up the project.
Step 2 Determine the immediate predecessor(s) for each activity in the project.
Step 3 Estimate the completion time for each activity.
Step 4 Draw a project network depicting the activities and immediate predecessors listed in steps 1 and 2.
Step 5 Use the project network and the activity time estimates to determine the earliest start and the earliest finish time for each activity by making a forward pass through the network. The earliest finish time for the last activity in the project identifies the total time required to complete the project.

**Figure 10.7 THE MANAGEMENT SCIENTIST ACTIVITY SCHEDULE FOR THE WESTERN HILLS SHOPPING CENTER PROJECT**

```
***    ACTIVITY SCHEDULE    ***

           EARLIEST  LATEST  EARLIEST  LATEST          CRITICAL
ACTIVITY    START    START    FINISH   FINISH  SLACK   ACTIVITY
-----------------------------------------------------------------
   A          0        0        5        5       0       YES
   B          0        6        6       12       6
   C          5        8        9       12       3
   D          5        7        8       10       2
   E          5        5        6        6       0       YES
   F          6        6       10       10       0       YES
   G         10       10       24       24       0       YES
   H          9       12       21       24       3
   I         24       24       26       26       0       YES
-----------------------------------------------------------------

     CRITICAL PATH:  A-E-F-G-I

     PROJECT COMPLETION TIME = 26
```

Step 6   Use the project completion time identified in step 5 as the latest finish time for the last activity and make a backward pass through the network to identify the latest start and latest finish time for each activity.

Step 7   Use the difference between the latest start time and the earliest start time for each activity to determine the slack for the activity.

Step 8   Find the activities with zero slack; these are the critical activities.

Step 9   Use the information from steps 5 and 6 to develop the activity schedule for the project.

# MANAGEMENT SCIENCE IN ACTION

## PROJECT MANAGEMENT ON THE PC*

More than 100 project management software packages are available for personal computers (PCs). A survey of users of well-known project management software packages for PCs identified applications such as the construction of a $20 million sawmill, the installation of a new software system in a hospital, the development of a communications satellite, the production of an electronic device, and the relocation of a facility. These projects ranged in size from 1000 activities for the sawmill construction project to 6500 activities for the facility relocation project.

At the low end of the market, packages generally cost less than $500. In this group, Harvard Total Project Manager®, Microsoft Project®, SuperProject Plus®, and Time Line® account for the majority of sales.

These packages have modest memory requirements, the ability to analyze projects with as many as 1000 activities, and can produce a wide range of reports. At the high end of the market, prices generally exceed $2000; this group includes packages such as OPEN®, PLAN®, PMS-II Professional®, Primavera Project Planner®, and PROMIS®. These more sophisticated systems are designed to handle projects with as many as 10,000 activities and have the ability to produce presentation-quality graphics.

*Based on E. Wasil, and A. A. Assad, "Project Management on the PC: Software, Applications, and Trends," Interfaces (March–April 1988): 75–84.

N O T E S
*and Comments*

If after analyzing a PERT/CPM network and finding that the project completion time is unacceptable (i.e., the project is going to take too long), a manager must take one or both of the following steps. First, review the original PERT/CPM network to see if the immediate predecessor relationships can be modified so that at least some of the critical path activities can be done simultaneously. Second, consider adding resources to critical path activities in an attempt to shorten the critical path; we discuss this alternative, referred to as *crashing,* in Section 10.3.

## 10.2    PROJECT SCHEDULING WITH UNCERTAIN ACTIVITY TIMES

In this section we consider the details of project scheduling for a problem involving new-product research and development. Because many of the activities in this project have never been attempted, the project manager wants to account for uncertainties in the activity times. Let us show how project scheduling can be conducted with uncertain activity times.

### The Daugherty Porta-Vac Project

The H. S. Daugherty Company has manufactured industrial vacuum cleaning systems for many years. Recently, a member of the company's new-product research team submitted a report suggesting that the company consider manufacturing a cordless vacuum cleaner. The new product, referred to as Porta-Vac, could contribute to Daugherty's expansion into the household market. Management hopes that it can be manufactured at a reasonable cost and that its portability and no-cord convenience will make it extremely attractive.

Daugherty's management wants to study the feasibility of manufacturing the Porta-Vac product. The feasibility study will recommend the action to be taken. To complete this study, information must be obtained from the firm's research and development (R&D), product testing, manufacturing, cost estimating, and market research groups. How long will this feasibility study take? In the following discussion, we show how to answer this question and provide an activity schedule for the project.

Again, the first step in the project scheduling process is to identify all activities that make up the project and then determine the immediate predecessor(s) for each activity. Table 10.3 shows these data for the Porta-Vac project.

| *Table* 10.3 | ACTIVITY LIST FOR THE PORTA-VAC PROJECT | |
|---|---|---|
| **Activity** | **Description** | **Immediate Predecessor** |
| A | Develop product design | — |
| B | Plan market research | — |
| C | Prepare routing (manufacturing engineering) | A |
| D | Build prototype model | A |
| E | Prepare marketing brochure | A |
| F | Prepare cost estimates (industrial engineering) | C |
| G | Do preliminary product testing | D |
| H | Complete market survey | B, E |
| I | Prepare pricing and forecast report | H |
| J | Prepare final report | F, G, I |

The Porta-Vac project network is shown in Figure 10.8. Verify that the network does in fact maintain the immediate predecessor relationships shown in Table 10.3.

## Uncertain Activity Times

Once we have developed the project network, we will need information on the time required to complete each activity. This information is used in the calculation of the total time required to complete the project and in the scheduling of specific activities. For repeat projects, such as construction and maintenance projects, managers may have the experience and historical data necessary to provide accurate activity time estimates. However, for new or unique projects, estimating the time for each activity may be quite difficult. In fact, in many cases, activity times are uncertain and are best described by a range of possible values rather than by one specific time estimate. In these instances, the uncertain activity times are treated as random variables with associated probability distributions. As a result, probability statements will be provided about the ability to meet a specific project completion date.

To incorporate uncertain activity times into the analysis, we need to obtain three time estimates for each activity:

**Optimistic time** $a$ = the minimum activity time if everything progresses ideally

**Most probable time** $m$ = the most probable activity time under normal conditions

**Pessimistic time** $b$ = the maximum activity time if significant delays are encountered

To illustrate the PERT/CPM procedure with uncertain activity times, let us consider the optimistic, most probable, and pessimistic time estimates for the Porta-Vac activities as presented in Table 10.4 Using activity A as an example, we see that the most probable time is

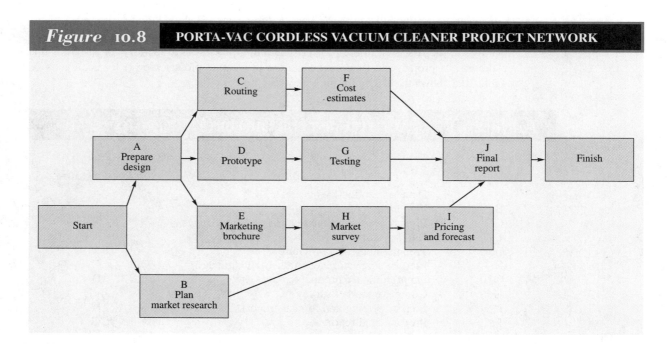

**Figure 10.8    PORTA-VAC CORDLESS VACUUM CLEANER PROJECT NETWORK**

| | Optimistic | Most Probable | Pessimistic |
|---|---|---|---|
| Activity | (*a*) | (*m*) | (*b*) |
| A | 4 | 5 | 12 |
| B | 1 | 1.5 | 5 |
| C | 2 | 3 | 4 |
| D | 3 | 4 | 11 |
| E | 2 | 3 | 4 |
| F | 1.5 | 2 | 2.5 |
| G | 1.5 | 3 | 4.5 |
| H | 2.5 | 3.5 | 7.5 |
| I | 1.5 | 2 | 2.5 |
| J | 1 | 2 | 3 |

**Table 10.4    OPTIMISTIC, MOST PROBABLE, AND PESSIMISTIC ACTIVITY TIME ESTIMATES (IN WEEKS) FOR THE PORTA-VAC PROJECT**

5 weeks with a range from 4 weeks (optimistic) to 12 weeks (pessimistic). If the activity could be repeated a large number of times, what is the average time for the activity? This average or **expected time** (*t*) is as follows:

$$t = \frac{a + 4m + b}{6} \tag{10.4}$$

For activity A we have an average or expected time of

$$t_A = \frac{4 + 4(5) + 12}{6} = \frac{36}{6} = 6 \text{ weeks}$$

With uncertain activity times, we can use the *variance* to describe the dispersion or variation in the activity time values. The variance of the activity time is given by the formula[1]

$$\sigma^2 = \left(\frac{b - a}{6}\right)^2 \tag{10.5}$$

The difference between the pessimistic (*b*) and optimistic (*a*) time estimates greatly affects the value of the variance. Large differences in these two values reflect a high degree of uncertainty in the activity time. Using equation (10.5), we obtain the measure of uncertainty—that is, the variance—of activity A, denoted $\sigma_A^2$:

$$\sigma_A^2 = \left(\frac{12 - 4}{6}\right)^2 = \left(\frac{8}{6}\right)^2 = 1.78$$

---

1. The variance equation is based on the notion that a standard deviation is approximately $\frac{1}{6}$ of the difference between the extreme values of the distribution: $(b - a)/6$. The variance is the square of the standard deviation.

Equations (10.4) and (10.5) are based on the assumption that the activity time distribution can be described by a **beta probability distribution**.[2] With this assumption, the probability distribution for the time to complete activity A is as shown in Figure 10.9. Using equations (10.4) and (10.5) and the data in Table 10.4, we calculated the expected times and variances for all Porta-Vac activities; the results are summarized in Table 10.5. The Porta-Vac project network with expected activity times is shown in Figure 10.10.

When uncertain activity times are used, the critical path calculations will determine only the expected or average time to complete the project. The actual time required to complete the project may differ. However, for planning purposes, the expected time should be valuable information for the project manager.

### The Critical Path

When we have the project network and the expected activity times, we are ready to proceed with the critical path calculations necessary to determine the expected time required to complete the project and determine the activity schedule. In these calculations, we treat the expected activity times (Table 10.5) as the fixed length or known duration of each activity. As a result, we can use the PERT/CPM critical path procedure introduced in Section 10.1 to find the critical path for the Porta-Vac project. After the critical activities and the expected time to complete the project have been determined, we analyze the effect of the activity time variability.

Activities that have larger variances show a greater degree of uncertainty. The project manager should monitor the progress of any activity with a large variance even if the expected times do not identify the activity as a critical activity.

Proceeding with a forward pass through the network shown in Figure 10.10, we can establish the earliest start (ES) and earliest finish (EF) times for each activity. Figure 10.11 shows the project network with the ES and EF values. Note that the earliest finish time for activity J, the last activity, is 17 weeks. Thus, the expected completion time for the project is 17 weeks. Next, we make a backward pass through the network. The backward pass provides the latest start (LS) and latest finish (LF) times shown in Figure 10.12.

The activity schedule for the Porta-Vac project is shown in Table 10.6. Note that the slack time (LS − ES) is also shown for each activity. The activities with zero slack (A, E, H, I, and J) form the critical path for the Porta-Vac project network.

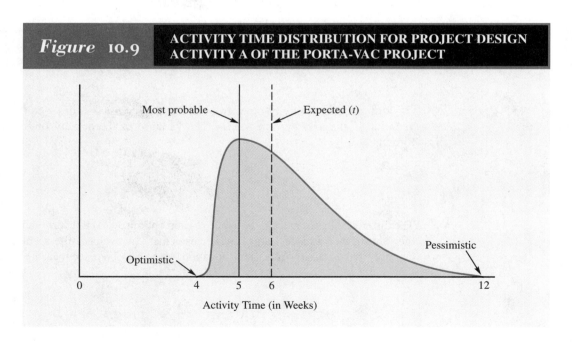

**Figure 10.9    ACTIVITY TIME DISTRIBUTION FOR PROJECT DESIGN ACTIVITY A OF THE PORTA-VAC PROJECT**

---

2. The equations for $t$ and $\sigma^2$ require additional assumptions about the parameters of the beta probability distribution. However, even when these additional assumptions are not made, the equations still provide good approximations of $t$ and $\sigma^2$.

| Table 10.5 | EXPECTED TIMES AND VARIANCES FOR THE PORTA-VAC PROJECT ACTIVITIES | |
|---|---|---|

| Activity | Expected Time (weeks) | Variance |
|---|---|---|
| A | 6 | 1.78 |
| B | 2 | 0.44 |
| C | 3 | 0.11 |
| D | 5 | 1.78 |
| E | 3 | 0.11 |
| F | 2 | 0.03 |
| G | 3 | 0.25 |
| H | 4 | 0.69 |
| I | 2 | 0.03 |
| J | 2 | 0.11 |
| Total | 32 | |

| Figure 10.10 | PORTA-VAC PROJECT NETWORK WITH EXPECTED ACTIVITY TIMES |
|---|---|

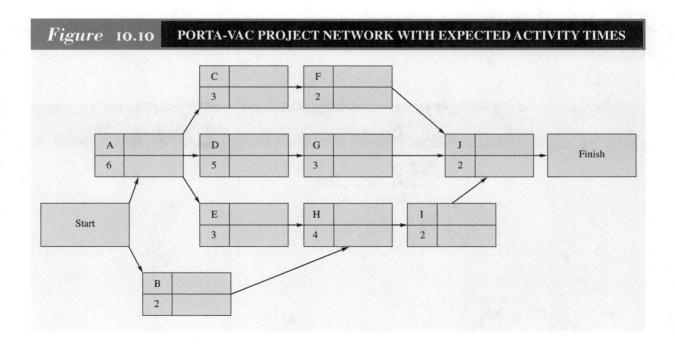

## Variability in Project Completion Time

We know that for the Porta-Vac project the critical path of A-E-H-I-J resulted in an expected total project completion time of 17 weeks. However, variation in critical activities can cause variation in the project completion time. Variation in noncritical activities ordinarily has no effect on the project completion time because of the slack time associated with these activities. However, if a noncritical activity is delayed long enough to expend its slack time, it

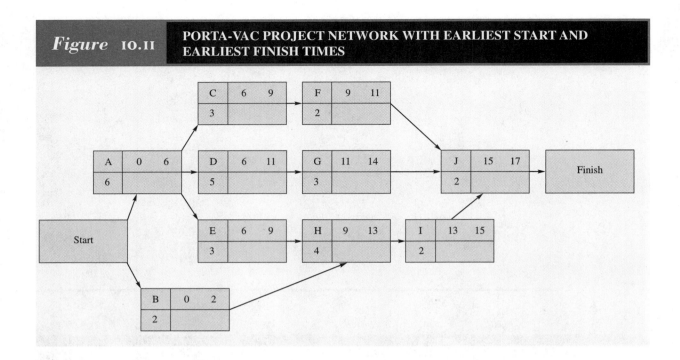

**Figure 10.11 — PORTA-VAC PROJECT NETWORK WITH EARLIEST START AND EARLIEST FINISH TIMES**

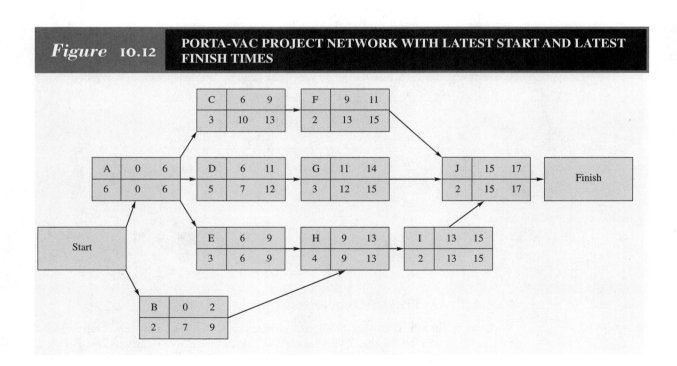

**Figure 10.12 — PORTA-VAC PROJECT NETWORK WITH LATEST START AND LATEST FINISH TIMES**

| | **Table 10.6** | | | **ACTIVITY SCHEDULE FOR THE PORTA-VAC PROJECT** | | | |
|---|---|---|---|---|---|---|---|

| Activity | Earliest Start (ES) | Latest Start (LS) | Earliest Finish (EF) | Latest Finish (LF) | Slack (LS − ES) | Critical Path? |
|---|---|---|---|---|---|---|
| A | 0 | 0 | 6 | 6 | 0 | Yes |
| B | 0 | 7 | 2 | 9 | 7 | |
| C | 6 | 10 | 9 | 13 | 4 | |
| D | 6 | 7 | 11 | 12 | 1 | |
| E | 6 | 6 | 9 | 9 | 0 | Yes |
| F | 9 | 13 | 11 | 15 | 4 | |
| G | 11 | 12 | 14 | 15 | 1 | |
| H | 9 | 9 | 13 | 13 | 0 | Yes |
| I | 13 | 13 | 15 | 15 | 0 | Yes |
| J | 15 | 15 | 17 | 17 | 0 | Yes |

becomes part of a new critical path and may affect the project completion time. Variability leading to a longer-than-expected total time for the critical activities will always extend the project completion time, and conversely, variability that results in a shorter-than-expected total time for the critical activities will reduce the project completion time, unless other activities become critical. Let us now use the variance in the critical activities to determine the variance in the project completion time.

Let $T$ denote the total time required to complete the project. The expected value of $T$, which is the sum of the expected times for the critical activities is

$$E(T) = t_A + t_E + t_H + t_I + t_J$$
$$= 6 + 3 + 4 + 2 + 2 = 17 \text{ weeks}$$

The variance in the project completion time is the sum of the variances of the critical path activities. Thus, the variance for the Porta-Vac project completion time is

$$\sigma^2 = \sigma_A^2 + \sigma_E^2 + \sigma_H^2 + \sigma_I^2 + \sigma_J^2$$
$$= 1.78 + 0.11 + 0.69 + 0.03 + 0.11 = 2.72$$

where $\sigma_A^2$, $\sigma_E^2$, $\sigma_H^2$, $\sigma_I^2$, and $\sigma_J^2$ are the variances of the critical activities.

*Problem 10 involves a project with uncertain activity times and asks you to compute the expected completion time and the variance for the project.*

The formula for $\sigma^2$ is based on the assumption that the activity times are independent. If two or more activities are dependent, the formula provides only an approximation to the variance of the project completion time. The closer the activities are to being independent, the better the approximation.

Knowing that the standard deviation is the square root of the variance, we compute the standard deviation $\sigma$ for the Porta-Vac project completion time as

$$\sigma = \sqrt{\sigma^2} = \sqrt{2.72} = 1.65$$

The normal distribution tends to be a better approximation of the distribution of total time for larger projects where the critical path has many activities.

Assuming that the distribution of the project completion time $T$ follows a normal or bell-shaped distribution[3] allows us to draw the distribution shown in Figure 10.13. With this distribution, we can compute the probability of meeting a specified project completion date. For example, suppose that management has allotted 20 weeks for the Porta-Vac project. What is the probability that we will meet the 20-week deadline? Using the normal probability distribution shown in Figure 10.14, we are asking for the probability that $T \leq 20$; this

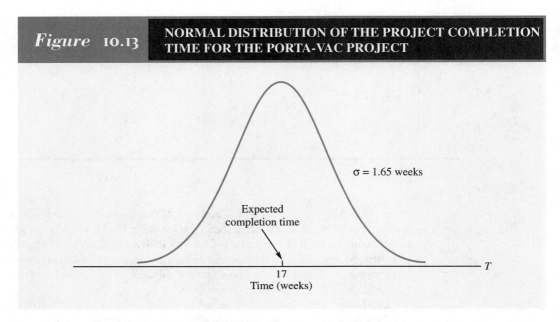

**Figure 10.13    NORMAL DISTRIBUTION OF THE PROJECT COMPLETION TIME FOR THE PORTA-VAC PROJECT**

$\sigma = 1.65$ weeks

Expected completion time

17
Time (weeks)

$T$

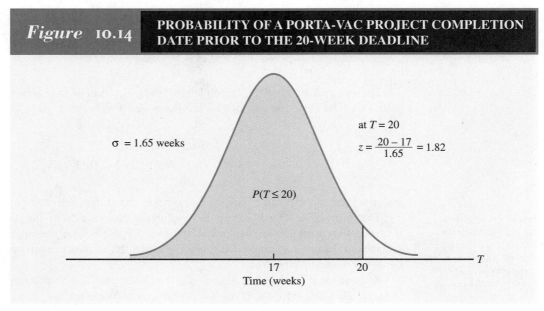

**Figure 10.14    PROBABILITY OF A PORTA-VAC PROJECT COMPLETION DATE PRIOR TO THE 20-WEEK DEADLINE**

$\sigma = 1.65$ weeks

at $T = 20$

$z = \dfrac{20 - 17}{1.65} = 1.82$

$P(T \leq 20)$

17        20
Time (weeks)

$T$

---

3. Use of the normal distribution as an approximation is based on the central limit theorem, which indicates that the sum of independent random variables (activity times) follows a normal distribution as the number of random variables becomes large.

probability is shown graphically as the shaded area in the figure. The $z$ value for the normal probability distribution at $T = 20$ is

$$z = \frac{20 - 17}{1.65} = 1.82$$

Using $z = 1.82$ and the table for the normal distribution (see Appendix B), we find that the probability of the project meeting the 20-week deadline is $0.4656 + 0.5000 = 0.9656$. Thus, even though activity time variability may cause the completion time to exceed 17 weeks, there is an excellent chance that the project will be completed before the 20-week deadline. Similar probability calculations can be made for other project deadline alternatives.

| N O T E S | For projects involving uncertain activity times, the probability that the project can be completed within a specified amount of time is helpful managerial information. However, remember that this probability estimate is based *only* on the critical activities. When uncertain activity times exist, longer-than-expected completion times for one or more noncritical activities may cause an original noncritical activity to become critical and hence increase the time required to complete the project. By frequently monitoring the progress of the project to make sure all activities are on schedule, the project manager will be better prepared to take corrective action if a noncritical activity begins to lengthen the duration of the project. |
|---|---|
| *and Comments* | |

## 10.3    CONSIDERING TIME-COST TRADE-OFFS

The original developers of CPM provided the project manager with the option of adding resources to selected activities to reduce project completion time. Added resources (such as more workers, overtime, and so on) generally increase project costs, so the decision to reduce activity times must take into consideration the additional cost involved. In effect, the project manager has to make a decision that involves trading reduced activity time for additional project cost.

Table 10.7 defines a two-machine maintenance project consisting of five activities. Since management has had substantial experience with similar projects, the times for

Using more resources to reduce activity times was proposed by the developers of CPM. The shortening of activity times is referred to as *crashing*.

| Table 10.7 | ACTIVITY LIST FOR THE TWO-MACHINE MAINTENANCE PROJECT |
|---|---|

| Activity | Description | Immediate Predecessor | Expected Time (days) |
|---|---|---|---|
| A | Overhaul machine I | — | 7 |
| B | Adjust machine I | A | 3 |
| C | Overhaul machine II | — | 6 |
| D | Adjust machine II | C | 3 |
| E | Test system | B, D | 2 |

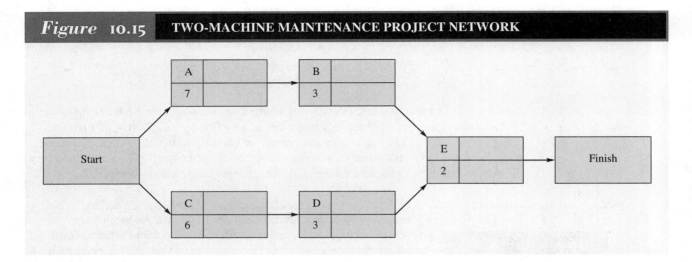

*Figure* 10.15  TWO-MACHINE MAINTENANCE PROJECT NETWORK

maintenance activities are considered to be known; hence, a single time estimate is given for each activity. The project network is shown in Figure 10.15.

The procedure for making critical path calculations for the maintenance project network is the same one used to find the critical path in the networks for both the Western Hills Shopping Center expansion project and the Porta-Vac project. Making the forward pass and backward pass calculations for the network in Figure 10.15, we obtained the activity schedule shown in Table 10.8. The zero slack times, and thus the critical path, are associated with activities A-B-E. The length of the critical path, and thus the total time required to complete the project, is 12 days.

## Crashing Activity Times

Now suppose that current production levels make completing the maintenance project within 10 days imperative. By looking at the length of the critical path of the network (12 days), we realize that meeting the desired project completion time is impossible unless we can shorten selected activity times. This shortening of activity times, which usually can be achieved by adding resources, is referred to as **crashing.** However, the added resources associated with crashing activity times usually result in added project costs, so we will want to identify the activities that cost the least to crash and then crash those activities only the amount necessary to meet the desired project completion time.

*Table* 10.8  ACTIVITY SCHEDULE FOR THE TWO-MACHINE MAINTENANCE

| Activity | Earliest Start (ES) | Latest Start (LS) | Earliest Finish (EF) | Latest Finish (LF) | Slack (LS − ES) | Critical Path? |
|---|---|---|---|---|---|---|
| A | 0 | 0 | 7 | 7 | 0 | Yes |
| B | 7 | 7 | 10 | 10 | 0 | Yes |
| C | 0 | 1 | 6 | 7 | 1 | |
| D | 6 | 7 | 9 | 10 | 1 | |
| E | 10 | 10 | 12 | 12 | 0 | Yes |

To determine just where and how much to crash activity times, we need information on how much each activity can be crashed and how much the crashing process costs. Hence, we must ask for the following information:

1. Activity cost under the normal or expected activity time
2. Time to complete the activity under maximum crashing (i.e., the shortest possible activity time)
3. Activity cost under maximum crashing

Let

$$\tau_i = \text{expected time for activity } i$$
$$\tau_i' = \text{time for activity } j \text{ under maximum crashing}$$
$$M_i = \text{maximum possible reduction in time for activity } i \text{ due to crashing}$$

Given $\tau_i$ and $\tau_i'$, we can compute $M_i$:

$$M_i = \tau_i - \tau_i' \tag{10.6}$$

Next, let $C_i$ denote the cost for activity $i$ under the normal or expected activity time and $C_i'$ denote the cost for activity $i$ under maximum crashing. Thus, per unit of time (e.g., per day), the crashing cost $K_i$ for each activity is given by

$$K_i = \frac{C_i' - C_i}{M_i} \tag{10.7}$$

For example, if the normal or expected time for activity A is 7 days at a cost of $C_A = \$500$ and the time under maximum crashing is 4 days at a cost of $C_A' = \$800$, equations (10.6) and (10.7) show that the maximum possible reduction in time for activity A is

$$M_A = 7 - 4 = 3 \text{ days}$$

with a crashing cost of

$$K_A = \frac{C_A' - C_A}{M_A} = \frac{800 - 500}{3} = \frac{300}{3} = \$100 \text{ per day}$$

We make the assumption that any portion or fraction of the activity crash time can be achieved for a corresponding portion of the activity crashing cost. For example, if we decided to crash activity A by only 1½ days, the added cost would be 1½($100) = $150, which results in a total activity cost of $500 + $150 = $650. Figure 10.16 shows the graph of the time-cost relationship for activity A. The complete normal and crash activity data for the two-machine maintenance project are given in Table 10.9.

Which activities should be crashed—and by how much—to meet the 10-day project completion deadline at minimum cost? Your first reaction to this question may be to consider crashing the critical activities—A, B, or E. Activity A has the lowest crashing cost per day of the three, and crashing this activity by 2 days will reduce the A-B-E path to the desired 10 days. Keep in mind, however, that as you crash the current critical activities, other paths may become critical. Thus, you will need to check the critical path in the revised network and perhaps either identify additional activities to crash or modify your initial crashing decision. For a small network, this trial-and-error approach can be used to make

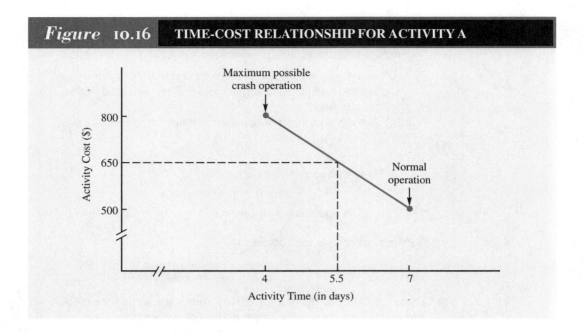

**Figure  10.16    TIME-COST RELATIONSHIP FOR ACTIVITY A**

**Table  10.9    NORMAL AND CRASH ACTIVITY DATA FOR THE TWO-MACHINE MAINTENANCE PROJECT**

| | Time (days) | | Total Cost | | Maximum Reduction in Time $(M_i)$ | Crash Cost Per day $\left(K_i = \dfrac{C_i' - C_i}{M_i}\right)$ |
|---|---|---|---|---|---|---|
| Activity | Normal | Crash | Normal ($C$) | Crash ($C_i'$) | | |
| A | 7 | 4 | $ 500 | $ 800 | 3 | $100 |
| B | 3 | 2 | 200 | 350 | 1 | 150 |
| C | 6 | 4 | 500 | 900 | 2 | 200 |
| D | 3 | 1 | 200 | 500 | 2 | 150 |
| E | 2 | 1 | 300 | 550 | 1 | 250 |
| | | | $1700 | $3100 | | |

crashing decisions; in larger networks, however, a mathematical procedure is required to determine the optimal crashing decisions. The following discussion shows how linear programming can be used to solve the network crashing problem.

## A Linear Programming Model for Crashing

In the PERT/CPM procedure, we used

$$EF = ES + t$$

to determine the earliest finish time for an activity. Note that if *ES*, the earliest start time for an activity, is known, the effect of crashing a particular activity will be to reduce *t* and hence *EF*, the earliest finish time. In essence, we use linear programming to determine which activities to crash and how much they should be crashed.

Consider activity A, which has an expected time of 7 days. Let $x_A$ = earliest finish time for activity A, and $y_A$ = amount of time activity A is crashed. If we assume that the project begins at time 0, the earliest start time for activity A is 0. Since the time for activity A is reduced by the amount of time that activity A is crashed, the earliest finish time for activity A is

$$x_A \geq 0 + (7 - y_A)$$

Moving $y_A$ to the left side,

$$x_A + y_A \geq 7$$

In general, let

$$x_i = \text{the earliest finish time for activity } i \qquad i = \text{A, B, C, D, E}$$
$$y_i = \text{the amount of time activity } i \text{ is crashed} \quad i = \text{A, B, C, D, E}$$

If we follow the same approach that we used for activity A, the constraint corresponding to the earliest finish time for activity C (expected time = 6 days) is

$$x_C \geq 0 + (6 - y_C) \quad \text{or} \quad x_C + y_C \geq 6$$

Continuing with the forward pass of the PERT/CPM procedure, we see that the earliest start time for activity B is $x_A$, the earliest finish time for activity A. Thus, the constraint corresponding to the earliest finish time for activity B is

$$x_B \geq x_A + (3 - y_B) \quad \text{or} \quad x_B + y_B - x_A \geq 3$$

Similarly, we obtain the constraint for the earliest finish time for activity D:

$$x_D \geq x_C + (3 - y_D) \quad \text{or} \quad x_D + y_D - x_C \geq 3$$

Finally, we consider activity E. The earliest start time for activity E equals the *largest* of the earliest finish times for activities B and D. Because the earliest finish times for both activities B and D will be determined by the crashing procedure, we must write two constraints for activity E, one based on the earliest finish time for activity B and one based upon the earliest finish time for activity D:

$$x_E + y_E - x_B \geq 2 \quad \text{and} \quad x_E + y_E - x_D \geq 2$$

Recall that current production levels made completing the maintenance project within 10 days imperative. Thus, the constraint for the earliest finish time for activity E is

$$x_E \leq 10$$

In addition, we must add the following five constraints corresponding to the maximum allowable crashing time for each activity:

$$y_A \leq 3, \qquad y_B \leq 1, \qquad y_C \leq 2, \qquad y_D \leq 2, \qquad \text{and} \qquad y_E \leq 1$$

As with all linear programs, we add the usual nonnegativity requirements for the decision variables.

All that remains is to develop an objective function for the model. Because the total project cost for a normal completion time is fixed at $1700 (see Table 10.9), we can minimize the total project cost (normal cost plus crashing cost) by minimizing the total crashing costs. Thus, the linear programming objective function becomes

$$\text{Min} \quad 100y_A + 150y_B + 200y_C + 150y_D + 250y_E$$

Thus, to determine the optimal crashing for each of the activities, we must solve a 10-variable, 12-constraint linear programming model. The linear programming module of The Management Scientist provides the optimal solution of crashing activity A by 1 day and activity E by 1 day, with a total crashing cost of $350. We can now develop a detailed activity schedule by using $7 - 1 = 6$ as the revised time for activity A and $2 - 1 = 1$ day as the revised time for activity E.

### NOTES and Comments

Note that the two-machine maintenance project network for the crashing illustration (see Figure 10.15) has only one activity, activity E, leading directly to the Finish node. As a result, the project completion time is equal to the completion time for activity E. Thus, the linear programming constraint requiring the project completion in 10 days or less could be written $x_E \le 10$.

If two or more activities lead directly to the Finish node of a project network, a slight modification is required in the linear programming model for crashing. Consider the following portion of a project network:

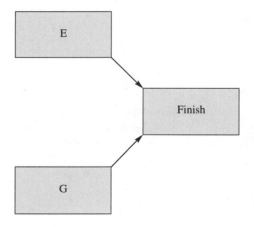

In this case, we suggest creating an additional variable, $x_{FIN}$, which indicates the finish or completion time for the entire project. The fact that the project cannot be finished until both activities E and G are completed can be modeled by the two constraints

$$x_{FIN} \ge x_E \quad \text{or} \quad x_{FIN} - x_E \ge 0$$
$$x_{FIN} \ge x_G \quad \text{or} \quad x_{FIN} - x_G \ge 0$$

The constraint that the project must be finished by time $T$ can be added as $x_{FIN} \le T$. Problem 22 gives you practice with this type of project network.

.................................................................................../  /..............

# SUMMARY

In this chapter we showed how PERT/CPM can be used to plan, schedule, and control a wide variety of projects. The key to this approach to project scheduling is the development of a PERT/CPM project network that depicts the activities and their precedence relationships. From this project network and activity time estimates, the critical path for the network and the associated critical activities can be identified. In the process, an activity schedule showing the earliest start and earliest finish times, the latest start and latest finish times, and the slack for each activity can be identified.

We showed how we can include capabilities for handling variable or uncertain activity times and how to use this information to provide a probability statement about the chances the project can be completed in a specified period of time. We introduced crashing as a procedure for reducing activity times to meet project completion deadlines, and showed how a linear programming model can be used to determine the crashing decisions that will minimize the cost of reducing the project completion time.

.................................................................................../  /..............

# GLOSSARY

**Program evaluation and review technique (PERT)**  A network-based project scheduling procedure.

**Critical path method (CPM)**  A network-based project scheduling procedure.

**Activities**  Specific jobs or tasks that are components of a project. Activities are represented by nodes in a project network.

**Immediate predecessors**  The activities that must be completed immediately prior to the start of a given activity.

**Project network**  A graphical representation of a project that depicts the activities and shows the predecessor relationships among the activities.

**Critical path**  The longest path in a project network.

**Path**  A sequence of connected nodes that leads from the Start node to the Finish node.

**Critical activities**  The activities on the critical path.

**Earliest start time**  The earliest time an activity may begin.

**Earliest finish time**  The earliest time an activity may be completed.

**Forward pass**  Part of the PERT/CPM procedure that involves moving forward through the project network to determine the earliest start and earliest finish times for each activity.

**Latest start time**  The latest time an activity may begin without increasing the project completion time.

**Latest finish time**  The latest time an activity may be completed without increasing the project completion time.

**Backward pass**  Part of the PERT/CPM procedure that involves moving backward through the network to determine the latest start and latest finish times for each activity.

**Optimistic time**  The minimum activity time if everything progresses ideally.

**Most probable time**  The most probable activity time under normal conditions.

**Pessimistic time**  The maximum activity time if significant delays are encountered.

**Expected time**  The average activity time.

**Beta probability distribution**  A probability distribution used to describe activity times.

**Slack**  The length of time an activity can be delayed without affecting the project completion time.

**Crashing**  The shortening of activity times by adding resources and hence usually increasing cost.

# PROBLEMS

1.  The Mohawk Discount Store is designing a management training program for individuals at its corporate headquarters. The company wants to design the program so that trainees can complete it as quickly as possible. Important precedence relationships must be maintained between assignments or activities in the program. For example, a trainee cannot serve as an assistant to the store manager until the trainee has obtained experience in the credit department and at least one sales department. The following activities are the assignments that must be completed by each trainee in the program. Construct a project network for this problem. Do not perform any further analysis.

| Activity | A | B | C | D | E | F | G | H |
|---|---|---|---|---|---|---|---|---|
| Immediate Predecessor | — | — | A | A, B | A, B | C | D, F | E, G |

2.  Bridge City Developers is coordinating the construction of an office complex. As part of the planning process, the company generated the following activity list. Draw a project network that can be used to assist in the scheduling of the project activities.

| Activity | A | B | C | D | E | F | G | H | I | J |
|---|---|---|---|---|---|---|---|---|---|---|
| Immediate Predecessor | — | — | — | A, B | A, B | D | E | C | C | F, G, H, I |

**SELF TEST**

3.  Construct a project network for the following project. The project is completed when activities F and G are both complete.

| Activity | A | B | C | D | E | F | G |
|---|---|---|---|---|---|---|---|
| Immediate Predecessor | — | — | A | A | C, B | C, B | D, E |

4.  Assume that the project in Problem 3 has the following activity times (in months).

| Activity | A | B | C | D | E | F | G |
|---|---|---|---|---|---|---|---|
| Time | 4 | 6 | 2 | 6 | 3 | 3 | 5 |

   a.  Find the critical path.
   b.  The project must be completed in $1\frac{1}{2}$ years. Do you anticipate difficulty in meeting the deadline? Explain.

5.  Management Decision Systems (MDS) is a consulting company that specializes in the development of decision support systems. MDS has just obtained a contract to develop a computer

system to assist the management of a large company in formulating its capital expenditure plan. The project leader has developed the following list of activities and immediate predecessors. Construct a project network for this problem.

| Activity | A | B | C | D | E | F | G | H | I | J |
|---|---|---|---|---|---|---|---|---|---|---|
| **Immediate Predecessor** | — | — | — | B | A | B | C, D | B, E | F, G | H |

**SELF TEST**

6.  Consider the following project network and activity times (in weeks).

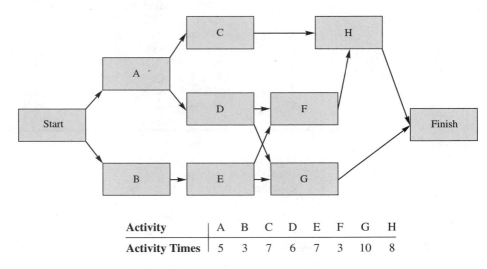

| Activity | A | B | C | D | E | F | G | H |
|---|---|---|---|---|---|---|---|---|
| **Activity Times** | 5 | 3 | 7 | 6 | 7 | 3 | 10 | 8 |

a.  Identify the critical path.
b.  How much time will be needed to complete this project?
c.  Can activity D be delayed without delaying the entire project? If so, by how many weeks?
d.  Can activity C be delayed without delaying the entire project? If so, by how many weeks?
e.  What is the schedule for activity E?

7.  A project involving the installation of a computer system comprises eight activities. The following table lists immediate predecessors and activity times (in weeks).

| Activity | Immediate Predecessor | Time |
|---|---|---|
| A | — | 3 |
| B | — | 6 |
| C | A | 2 |
| D | B, C | 5 |
| E | D | 4 |
| F | E | 3 |
| G | B, C | 9 |
| H | F, G | 3 |

a.  Draw a project network.
b.  What are the critical activities?
c.  What is the expected project completion time?

8. Colonial State College is considering building a new multipurpose athletic complex on campus. The complex would provide a new gymnasium for intercollegiate basketball games, expanded office space, classrooms, and intramural facilities. The following activities would have to be undertaken before construction can begin.

| Activity | Description | Immediate Predecessor | Time (weeks) |
|---|---|---|---|
| A | Survey building site | — | 6 |
| B | Develop initial design | — | 8 |
| C | Obtain board approval | A, B | 12 |
| D | Select architect | C | 4 |
| E | Establish budget | C | 6 |
| F | Finalize design | D, E | 15 |
| G | Obtain financing | E | 12 |
| H | Hire contractor | F, G | 8 |

a. Draw a project network.
b. Identify the critical path.
c. Develop the activity schedule for the project.
d. Does it appear reasonable that construction of the athletic complex could begin one year after the decision to begin the project with the site survey and initial design plans? What is the expected completion time for the project?

9. Hamilton County Parks is planning to develop a new park and recreational area on a recently purchased 100-acre tract. Project development activities include clearing playground and picnic areas, constructing roads, constructing a shelter house, purchasing picnic equipment, and so on. The following network and activity times (in weeks) are being used in the planning, scheduling, and controlling of this project.

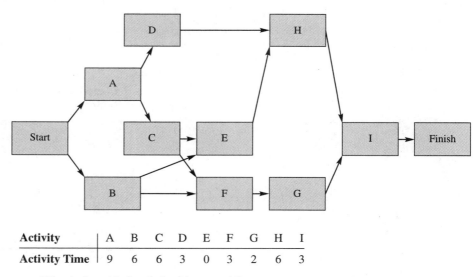

| Activity | A | B | C | D | E | F | G | H | I |
|---|---|---|---|---|---|---|---|---|---|
| Activity Time | 9 | 6 | 6 | 3 | 0 | 3 | 2 | 6 | 3 |

a. What is the critical path for this network?
b. Show the activity schedule for this project.
c. The park commissioner would like to open the park to the public within six months from the time the work on the project is started. Does this opening date appear to be feasible? Explain.

10. The following estimates of activity times (in days) are available for a small project.

| Activity | Optimistic | Most Probable | Pessimistic |
|----------|-----------|---------------|-------------|
| A | 4 | 5.0 | 6 |
| B | 8 | 9.0 | 10 |
| C | 7 | 7.5 | 11 |
| D | 7 | 9.0 | 10 |
| E | 6 | 7.0 | 9 |
| F | 5 | 6.0 | 7 |

a. Compute the expected activity completion times and the variance for each activity.
b. An analyst determined that the critical path consists of activities B–D–F. Compute the expected project completion time and the variance.

11. Building a backyard swimming pool consists of nine major activities. The activities and their immediate predecessors are shown. Develop the project network.

| Activity | A | B | C | D | E | F | G | H | I |
|----------|---|---|------|------|---|---|---|-----|---------|
| Immediate Predecessor | — | — | A, B | A, B | B | C | D | D, F | E, G, H |

12. Assume that the activity time estimates (in days) for the swimming pool construction project in Problem 11 are

| Activity | Optimistic | Most Probable | Pessimistic |
|----------|-----------|---------------|-------------|
| A | 3 | 5 | 6 |
| B | 2 | 4 | 6 |
| C | 5 | 6 | 7 |
| D | 7 | 9 | 10 |
| E | 2 | 4 | 6 |
| F | 1 | 2 | 3 |
| G | 5 | 8 | 10 |
| H | 6 | 8 | 10 |
| I | 3 | 4 | 5 |

a. What are the critical activities?
b. What is the expected time to complete the project?
c. What is the probability that the project can be completed in 25 or fewer days?

13. Suppose that the following estimates of activity times (in weeks) were provided for the network shown in Problem 6.

| Activity | Optimistic | Most Probable | Pessimistic |
|----------|-----------|---------------|-------------|
| A | 4.0 | 5.0 | 6.0 |
| B | 2.5 | 3.0 | 3.5 |
| C | 6.0 | 7.0 | 8.0 |
| D | 5.0 | 5.5 | 9.0 |
| E | 5.0 | 7.0 | 9.0 |
| F | 2.0 | 3.0 | 4.0 |
| G | 8.0 | 10.0 | 12.0 |
| H | 6.0 | 7.0 | 14.0 |

What is the probability that the project will be completed
a.   Within 21 weeks?
b.   Within 22 weeks?
c.   Within 25 weeks?

14.   Consider the following project network.

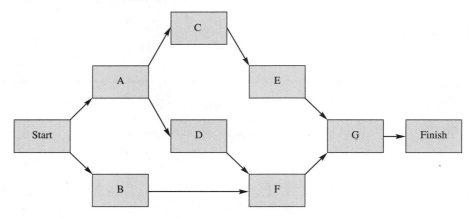

Estimates of the optimistic, most probable, and pessimistic times (in days) for the activities are

| Activity | Optimistic | Most Probable | Pessimistic |
|----------|-----------|---------------|-------------|
| A | 5 | 6 | 7 |
| B | 5 | 12 | 13 |
| C | 6 | 8 | 10 |
| D | 4 | 10 | 10 |
| E | 5 | 6 | 13 |
| F | 7 | 7 | 10 |
| G | 4 | 7 | 10 |

a.   Find the critical path.
b.   How much slack time, if any, is in activity C?
c.   Determine the expected project completion time and the variance.
d.   Find the probability that the project will be completed in 30 or fewer days.

15.   Doug Casey is in charge of planning and coordinating next spring's sales management training program for his company. Doug has listed the following activity information for this project.

| Activity | Description | Immediate Predecessor | Optimistic | Most Probable | Pessimistic |
|----------|-------------|-----------------------|------------|---------------|-------------|
| | | | | Time (weeks) | |
| A | Plain topic | — | 1.5 | 2.0 | 2.5 |
| B | Obtain speakers | A | 2.0 | 2.5 | 6.0 |
| C | List meeting locations | — | 1.0 | 2.0 | 3.0 |
| D | Select location | C | 1.5 | 2.0 | 2.5 |
| E | Finalize speaker travel plans | B, D | 0.5 | 1.0 | 1.5 |
| F | Make final check with speakers | E | 1.0 | 2.0 | 3.0 |
| G | Prepare and mail brochure | B, D | 3.0 | 3.5 | 7.0 |
| H | Take reservations | G | 3.0 | 4.0 | 5.0 |
| I | Handle last-minute details | F, H | 1.5 | 2.0 | 2.5 |

a.  Draw a project network.
b.  Prepare an activity schedule.
c.  What are the critical activities and what is the expected project completion time?
d.  If Doug wants a 0.99 probability of completing the project on time, how far ahead of the scheduled meeting date should he begin working on the project?

16. The Daugherty Porta-Vac project discussed in Section 10.2 had an expected project completion time of 17 weeks. The probability that the project could be completed in 20 weeks or less was 0.9656. The noncritical paths in the Porta-Vac project network are

A–D–G–J

A–C–F–J

B–H–I–J

a.  Use the information in Table 10.5 to compute the expected time and variance for each path shown.
b.  Compute the probability that each path will be completed in the desired 20-week period.
c.  Why is the computation of the probability of completing a project on time based on the analysis of the critical path? In what case, if any, would making the probability computation for a noncritical path be desirable?

17. The Porsche Shop, founded in 1985 by Dale Jensen, specializes in the restoration of vintage Porsche automobiles. One of Jensen's regular customers asked him to prepare an estimate for the restoration of a 1964 model 356SC Porsche. To estimate the time and cost to perform such a restoration, Jensen broke the restoration process into four separate activities: disassembly and initial preparation work (A), body restoration (B), engine restoration (C), and final assembly (D). Once activity A has been completed, activities B and C can be performed independently of each other; however, activity D can be started only if both activities B and C have been completed. Based on his inspection of the car, Jensen believes that the following time estimates (in days) are applicable.

| Activity | Optimistic | Most Probable | Pessimistic |
|----------|-----------|---------------|-------------|
| A        | 3         | 4             | 8           |
| B        | 5         | 8             | 11          |
| C        | 2         | 4             | 6           |
| D        | 4         | 5             | 12          |

Jensen estimates that the parts needed to restore the body will cost $3000 and that the parts needed to restore the engine will cost $5000. His current labor costs are $400 a day.
a.  Develop a project network.
b.  What is the expected project completion time?
c.  Jensen's business philosophy is based on making decisions using a best and worst case scenario. Develop cost estimates for completing the restoration based on both a best and worst case analysis. Assume that the total restoration cost is the sum of the labor cost plus the material cost.
d.  If Jensen obtains the job with a bid that is based on the costs associated with an expected completion time, what is the probability that he will lose money on the job?
e.  If Jensen obtains the job based on a bid of $16,800, what is the probability that he will lose money on the job?

18. The manager of the Oak Hills Swimming Club is planning the club's swimming team program. The first team practice is scheduled for May 1. The activities, their immediate predecessors, and the activity time estimates (in weeks) are as follows.

| Activity | Description | Immediate Predecessor | Time (weeks) Optimistic | Time (weeks) Most Probable | Time (weeks) Pessimistic |
|----------|-------------|-----------------------|------------|---------------|-------------|
| A | Meet with board | — | 1 | 1 | 2 |
| B | Hire coaches | A | 4 | 6 | 8 |
| C | Reserve pool | A | 2 | 4 | 6 |
| D | Announce program | B, C | 1 | 2 | 3 |
| E | Meet with coaches | B | 2 | 3 | 4 |
| F | Order team suits | A | 1 | 2 | 3 |
| G | Register swimmers | D | 1 | 2 | 3 |
| H | Collect fees | G | 1 | 2 | 3 |
| I | Plan first practice | E, H, F | 1 | 1 | 1 |

    a. Draw a project network.
    b. Develop an activity schedule.
    c. What are the critical activities and what is the expected project completion time?
    d. If the club manager plans to start the project on February 1, what is the probability the swimming program will be ready by the scheduled May 1 date (13 weeks)? Should the manager begin planning the swimming program before February 1?

19. The product development group at Landon Corporation has been working on a new computer software product that has the potential to capture a large market share. Through outside sources, Landon's management has learned that a competitor is working to introduce a similar product. As a result, Landon's top management has increased its pressure on the product development group. The group's leader has turned to PERT/CPM as an aid to scheduling the activities remaining before the new product can be brought to the market. The project network is as follows.

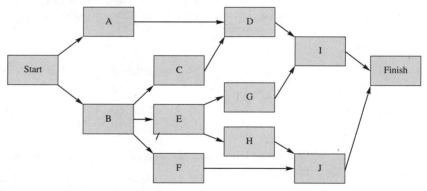

The activity time estimates (in weeks) are

| Activity | Optimistic | Most Probable | Pessimistic |
|----------|------------|---------------|-------------|
| A | 3.0 | 4.0 | 5.0 |
| B | 3.0 | 3.5 | 7.0 |
| C | 4.0 | 5.0 | 6.0 |
| D | 2.0 | 3.0 | 4.0 |
| E | 6.0 | 10.0 | 14.0 |
| F | 7.5 | 8.5 | 12.5 |
| G | 4.5 | 6.0 | 7.5 |
| H | 5.0 | 6.0 | 13.0 |
| I | 2.0 | 2.5 | 6.0 |
| J | 4.0 | 5.0 | 6.0 |

a. Develop an activity schedule for this project and identify the critical path activities.
b. What is the probability that the project will be completed so that Landon Corporation may introduce the new product within 25 weeks? Within 30 weeks?

20. Return to the computer installation project in Problem 7 and assume that the project has to be completed in 16 weeks. Crashing of the project is necessary. Use the following relevant information.

| | Time (weeks) | | Cost ($) | |
|---|---|---|---|---|
| Activity | Normal | Crash | Normal | Crash |
| A | 3 | 1 | 900 | 1700 |
| B | 6 | 3 | 2000 | 4000 |
| C | 2 | 1 | 500 | 1000 |
| D | 5 | 3 | 1800 | 2400 |
| E | 4 | 3 | 1500 | 1850 |
| F | 3 | 1 | 3000 | 3900 |
| G | 9 | 4 | 8000 | 9800 |
| H | 3 | 2 | 1000 | 2000 |

a. Formulate a linear programming model that can be used to make the crashing decisions for this project.
b. Solve the linear programming model and make the minimum-cost crashing decisions. What is the added cost of meeting the 16-week completion time?
c. Develop a complete activity schedule based on the crashed activity times.

21. Consider the following project network and activity times (in days).

SELF TEST

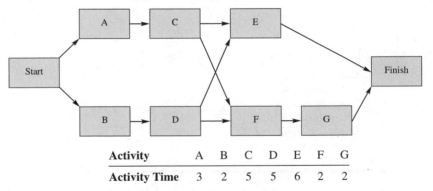

| Activity | A | B | C | D | E | F | G |
|---|---|---|---|---|---|---|---|
| Activity Time | 3 | 2 | 5 | 5 | 6 | 2 | 2 |

The crashing data for this project are as follows.

| | Time (days) | | Cost ($) | |
|---|---|---|---|---|
| Activity | Normal | Crash | Normal | Crash |
| A | 3 | 2 | 800 | 1400 |
| B | 2 | 1 | 1200 | 1900 |
| C | 5 | 3 | 2000 | 2800 |
| D | 5 | 3 | 1500 | 2300 |
| E | 6 | 4 | 1800 | 2800 |
| F | 2 | 1 | 600 | 1000 |
| G | 2 | 1 | 500 | 1000 |

a. Find the critical path and the expected project completion time.
b. What is the total project cost using the normal times?

**SELF TEST**

22. Refer to Problem 21. Assume that management desires a 12-day project completion time.
    a. Formulate a linear programming model that can be used to assist with the crashing decisions.
    b. What activities should be crashed?
    c. What is the total project cost for the 12-day completion time?

23. Consider the following project network. Note that the normal or expected activity times are denoted $\tau_i, i = A, B, \ldots, I$. Let $x_i$ = the earliest finish time for activity $i$. Formulate a linear programming model that can be used to determine the length of the critical path.

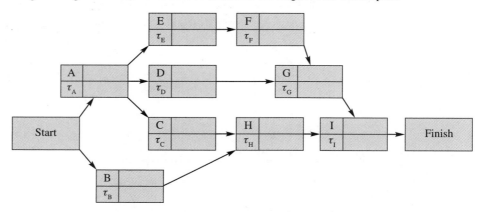

24. Office Automation, Inc., has developed a proposal for introducing a new computerized office system that will improve word processing and interoffice communications for a particular company. Contained in the proposal is a list of activities that must be accomplished to complete the new office system project. Use the following relevant information about the activities.

| Activity | Description | Immediate Predecessor | Time (weeks) | | Cost ($1000s) | |
|---|---|---|---|---|---|---|
| | | | **Normal** | **Crash** | **Normal** | **Crash** |
| A | Plan needs | — | 10 | 8 | 30 | 70 |
| B | Order equipment | A | 8 | 6 | 120 | 150 |
| C | Install equipment | B | 10 | 7 | 100 | 160 |
| D | Set up training lab | A | 7 | 6 | 40 | 50 |
| E | Conduct training course | D | 10 | 8 | 50 | 75 |
| F | Test system | C, E | 3 | 3 | 60 | — |

   a. Develop a project network.
   b. Develop an activity schedule.
   c. What are the critical activities and what is the expected project completion time?
   d. Assume that the company wants to complete the project in 6 months or 26 weeks. What crashing decisions do you recommend to meet the desired completion time at the least possible cost? Work through the network and attempt to make the crashing decisions by inspection.
   e. Develop an activity schedule for the crashed project.
   f. What added project cost is required to meet the 6-month completion time?

25. Because Landon Corporation (see Problem 19) is being pressured to complete the product development project at the earliest possible date, the project leader has requested that the possibility of crashing the project be evaluated.
   a. Formulate a linear programming model that could be used in making the crashing decisions.
   b. What information would have to be provided before the linear programming model could be implemented?

.................................................................................../  /...........

## Case Problem    WAREHOUSE EXPANSION

R. C. Coleman distributes a variety of food products that are sold through grocery store and supermarket outlets. The company receives orders directly from the individual outlets, with a typical order requesting the delivery of several cases of anywhere from 20 to 50 different products. Under the company's current warehouse operation, warehouse clerks dispatch order-picking personnel to fill each order and have the goods moved to the warehouse shipping area. Because of the high labor costs and relatively low productivity of hand order-picking, management has decided to automate the warehouse operation by installing a computer-controlled order-picking system, along with a conveyor system for moving goods from storage to the warehouse shipping area.

R. C. Coleman's director of material management has been named the project manager in charge of the automated warehouse system. After consulting with members of the engineering staff and warehouse management personnel, the director has compiled a list of activities associated with the project. The optimistic, most probable, and pessimistic times (in weeks) have also been provided for each activity.

| Activity | Description | Immediate Predecessor |
|---|---|---|
| A | Determine equipment needs | — |
| B | Obtain vendor proposals | — |
| C | Select vendor | A, B |
| D | Order system | C |
| E | Design new warehouse layout | C |
| F | Design warehouse | E |
| G | Design computer interface | C |
| H | Interface computer | D, F, G |
| I | Install system | D, F |
| J | Train system operators | H |
| K | Test system | I, J |

| | | Time | |
|---|---|---|---|
| Activity | Optimistic | Most Probable | Pessimistic |
| A | 4 | 6 | 8 |
| B | 6 | 8 | 16 |
| C | 2 | 4 | 6 |
| D | 8 | 10 | 24 |
| E | 7 | 10 | 13 |
| F | 4 | 6 | 8 |
| G | 4 | 6 | 20 |
| H | 4 | 6 | 8 |
| I | 4 | 6 | 14 |
| J | 3 | 4 | 5 |
| K | 2 | 4 | 6 |

## Managerial Report

Develop a report that presents the activity schedule and expected project completion time for the warehouse expansion project. Include a project network in the report. In addition, take into consideration the following issues.

1. R. C. Coleman's top management has established a required 40-week completion time for the project. Can this completion time be achieved? Include probability information in your discussion. What recommendations do you have if the 40-week completion time is required?

2. Suppose that management requests that activity times be shortened to provide an 80% chance of meeting the 40-week completion time. If the variance in the project completion time is the same as you found in part (a), how much should the expected project completion time be shortened to achieve the goal of an 80% chance of completion within 40 weeks?

3. Using the expected activity times as the normal times and the following crashing information, determine the activity crashing decisions and revised activity schedule for the warehouse expansion project.

| Activity | Crashed Activity Time (weeks) | Cost ($) Normal | Cost ($) Crashed |
|----------|------------------------------|--------|---------|
| A | 4 | 1,000 | 1,900 |
| B | 7 | 1,000 | 1,800 |
| C | 2 | 1,500 | 2,700 |
| D | 8 | 2,000 | 3,200 |
| E | 7 | 5,000 | 8,000 |
| F | 4 | 3,000 | 4,100 |
| G | 5 | 8,000 | 10,250 |
| H | 4 | 5,000 | 6,400 |
| I | 4 | 10,000 | 12,400 |
| J | 3 | 4,000 | 4,400 |
| K | 3 | 5,000 | 5,500 |

# SEASONGOOD & MAYER

## CINCINNATI, OHIO

Seasongood & Mayer, established in 1887, is an investment securities firm that engages in the following areas of municipal finance:

1. Underwriting new issues of municipal bonds
2. Trading—for example, acting as a market maker for the buying and selling of previously issued bonds
3. Investment banking—that is, the process of obtaining money from the capital markets at the lowest possible cost

The major applications of quantitative methods at Seasongood & Mayer are in the investment banking area. One particular application involved the use of PERT/CPM in the introduction of a $31 million hospital revenue bond issue.

## Scheduling the Introduction of a Bond Issue

Any major building project involves certain common steps:

1. Defining the project
2. Determining the cost of the project
3. Financing the project

The investment banker's role in building projects is to develop the method of financing that will result in the owner's receiving the necessary funds in a timely manner. In a hospital building project, the typical method of financing is tax-free hospital revenue bonds.

The construction cost for the building project is an important factor in determining the best approach to financing. Normally, the construction cost is based on a bid submitted by a contractor or a construction manager. However, this cost is usually guaranteed only for a specified period of time, such as 60–90 days. The major function of the hospital's investment banker is to arrange the timing of the financing in such a way that the proceeds of the bond issue can be made available within the time limit of the guaranteed-price construction bid. Since most hospitals must have the proceeds of their permanent long-term financing in hand prior to committing to major construction contracts, the investment banker's role is a significant one.

To arrange for the financing, the investment banker must coordinate the activities of hospital attorneys, the bond counsel, and so on. The cooperation of all parties and the coordination of project activities are best achieved if everyone recognizes the interdependency of the activities and the necessity of completing individual tasks in a timely manner. Seasongood & Mayer has found PERT/CPM to be useful in scheduling and coordinating such a project.

As managing underwriter for a $31,050,000 issue of Hospital Facilities Revenue Bonds for Providence Hospital in Hamilton County, Ohio, Seasongood & Mayer used the PERT/CPM critical path procedure to coordinate and schedule the project financing activities. Descriptions of the activities, times required, and immediate predecessors are given in Table 10.10. The project network is shown in Figure 10.17. The critical path activities K-L-M-N-P-Q-R-S-U-W resulted in a scheduled project completion time of 29.14 weeks. Specific schedules showing start and finish times for all activities were used to keep the entire project on track. The use of PERT/CPM was instrumental in helping Seasongood & Mayer obtain

| Table 10.10 | ACTIVITIES FOR THE SEASONGOOD & MAYER PROJECT |
| --- | --- |

| Activity | Time Required (weeks) | Description of Activity | Immediate Predecessor |
| --- | --- | --- | --- |
| A | 4 | Drafting and distribution of legal documents | — |
| B | 3 | Preparation and distribution of unaudited financial statements of hospital | — |
| C | 2 | Drafting and distribution of hospital history, description of services, and existing facilities for Preliminary Official Statement (POS) | — |
| D | 8 | Drafting and distribution of demand portion of feasibility study | — |
| E | 4 | Review (additions/deletions) and approval as to form of legal documents | A |
| F | 1 | Review (additions/deletions) and approval of history, etc., for POS | C |
| G | 4 | Review (additions/deletions) and approval of demand portion of feasibility study | D |
| H | 2 | Drafting and distribution of financial portion (as to form) of feasibility study | E, G |
| I | 2 | Drafting and distribution of plan of financing and all pertinent facts relevant to the bond transaction for POS | E |
| J | 0.5 | Review and approval of unaudited financial statements | B |
| K | 20 | Receipt of firm price for project | — |
| L | 1 | Review (additions/deletions), approval, and completion of financial portion of feasibility study | H, K |
| M | 1 | Drafting of POS completed | F, I, J, L |
| N | 0.14 | Distribution of all material to bond rating services | M |
| O | 0.28 | Printing and distribution of POS to all interested parties | M |
| P | 1 | Presentation to bond rating services (Standard & Poor's, Moody's) | N |
| Q | 1 | Receipt of bond rating | P |
| R | 2 | Marketing of bonds | O, Q |
| S | 0 | Execution of Purchase Contract | R |
| T | 0.14 | Authorization and completion of Final Official Statement, completion of legal documents | S |
| U | 3 | Fulfillment of all terms and conditions of Purchase Contract | S |
| V | 0 | Bond proceeds available to hospital | T, U |
| W | 0 | Hospital able to sign construction contract | T, U |

| Figure 10.17 | SEASONGOOD & MAYER PROJECT NETWORK |
| --- | --- |

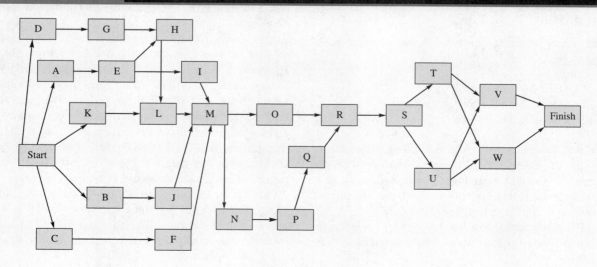

financing for this project within the time specified in the construction bid.

## Questions

1. What is the role of the investment banker in building projects?

2. For the hospital project described, what is the primary objective of the investment banker?

3. Perform the critical path calculations for the project network shown in Figure 10.17. Is there more than one critical path? Discuss.

# 11

# INVENTORY MODELS

## CONTENTS

Inventory refers to idle goods or materials that are held by an organization for use sometime in the future. Items carried in inventory include raw materials, purchased parts, components, subassemblies, work-in-process, finished goods, and supplies. One reason organizations maintain inventory is that it is rarely possible to predict sales levels, production times, demand, and usage needs exactly. Thus, inventory serves as a buffer against uncertain and fluctuating usage and keeps a supply of items available in case the items are needed by the organization or its customers. While inventory serves an important and essential role, the expense associated with financing and maintaining inventories is a substantial part of the cost of doing business. In large organizations, the cost associated with inventory can run into the millions of dollars.

Two important questions that must be answered in order to effectively manage inventories are as follows:

1. *How much* should be ordered when the inventory is replenished?
2. *When* should the inventory be replenished?

The purpose of this chapter is to show how quantitative models can assist in making these decisions.

We will first consider *deterministic* inventory models in which we assume that the rate of demand for the item is constant or nearly constant. Later we will consider *probabilistic* inventory models in which the demand for the item fluctuates and can be described only in probabilistic terms. In addition, we will describe an inventory management procedure referred to as *material requirements planning* (MRP); this approach is suited for managing inventories of raw materials, subassemblies, and components whose demand is directly dependent on the demand for the final products in the inventory system. Finally, in the last section of the chapter, we discuss a philosophy of material management and control known as *just-in-time* (JIT); the primary objective of JIT is to eliminate all sources of waste, including unnecessary inventory.

## 11.1 ECONOMIC ORDER QUANTITY (EOQ) MODEL

The cost associated with developing and maintaining inventory is larger than many people think. Models such as the ones presented in this chapter can be used to develop cost-effective inventory management decisions.

The **economic order quantity (EOQ) model** is applicable when the demand for an item has a constant, or nearly constant, rate and when the entire quantity ordered arrives in inventory at one point in time. The **constant demand rate** assumption means that the same number of units is taken from inventory each period of time such as 5 units every day, 25 units every week, 100 units every 4-week period, and so on.

To illustrate the EOQ model, let us consider the situation faced by the R & B Beverage Company. R & B Beverage is a distributor of beer, wine, and soft drink products. From a main warehouse located in Columbus, Ohio, R & B supplies nearly 1000 retail stores with beverage products. The beer inventory, which constitutes about 40% of the company's total inventory, averages approximately 50,000 cases. With an average cost per case of approximately $8, R & B estimates the value of its beer inventory to be $400,000.

The warehouse manager has decided to do a detailed study of the inventory costs associated with Bub Beer, the number-one-selling R & B beer. The purpose of the study is to establish the *how-much*-to-order and the *when*-to-order decisions for Bub Beer that will

One of the most criticized assumptions of the EOQ model is the constant demand rate. Obviously, the model would be inappropriate for items with widely fluctuating and variable demand rates. However, as this example attempts to show, the EOQ model can provide a realistic approximation of the optimal order quantity when demand is relatively stable and occurs at a nearly constant rate.

result in the lowest possible total cost. As the first step in the study, the warehouse manager has obtained the following demand data for the past 10 weeks:

| Week | Demand (cases) |
|---|---|
| 1 | 2,000 |
| 2 | 2,025 |
| 3 | 1,950 |
| 4 | 2,000 |
| 5 | 2,100 |
| 6 | 2,050 |
| 7 | 2,000 |
| 8 | 1,975 |
| 9 | 1,900 |
| 10 | 2,000 |
| Total cases | 20,000 |
| Average cases per week | 2,000 |

Strictly speaking, these weekly demand figures do not show a constant demand rate. However, given the relatively low variability exhibited by the weekly demand, inventory planning with a constant demand rate of 2000 cases per week appears acceptable. In practice, you will find that the actual inventory situation seldom, if ever, satisfies the assumptions of the model exactly. Thus, in any particular application, the manager must determine whether the model assumptions are close enough to reality for the model to be useful. In this situation, since demand varies from a low of 1900 cases to a high of 2100 cases, the assumption of constant demand of 2000 cases per week appears to be a reasonable approximation.

The how-much-to-order decision involves selecting an order quantity that draws a compromise between (1) keeping small inventories and ordering frequently and (2) keeping large inventories and ordering infrequently. The first alternative can result in undesirably high ordering costs, while the second alternative can result in undesirably high inventory holding costs. To find an optimal compromise between these conflicting alternatives, let us consider a mathematical model that shows the total cost as the sum of the holding cost and the ordering cost.[1]

**Holding costs** are the costs associated with maintaining or carrying a given level of inventory; these costs depend on the size of the inventory. The first holding cost to consider is the cost of financing the inventory investment. When a firm borrows money, it incurs an interest charge. If the firm uses its own money, it experiences an opportunity cost associated with not being able to use the money for other investments. In either case, an interest cost exists for the capital tied up in inventory. This **cost of capital** is usually expressed as a percentage of the amount invested. R & B estimates its cost of capital at an annual rate of 18%.

A number of other holding costs such as insurance, taxes, breakage, pilferage, and warehouse overhead also depend on the value of the inventory. R & B estimates these other costs at an annual rate of approximately 7% of the value of its inventory. Thus, the total holding cost for the R & B beer inventory is 25% of the value of the inventory.

As with other quantitative models, accurate estimates of cost parameters are critical. In the EOQ model, estimates of both the inventory holding cost and the ordering cost are needed. Also see footnote 1, which refers to *relevant* costs.

[1] While quantitative analysts typically refer to "total-cost" models for inventory systems, often these models describe only the total *variable* or total *relevant* costs for the decision being considered. Costs that are not affected by the how-much-to-order decision are considered fixed or constant and are not included in the model.

Assume that the cost of one case of Bub Beer is $8. Since R & B estimates its annual holding cost to be 25% of the value of its inventory, the cost of holding one case of Bub Beer in inventory for 1 year is 0.25($8) = $2.00. Note that defining the holding cost as a percentage of the value of the product is convenient because it is easily transferable to other products. For example, a case of Carle's Red Ribbon Beer, which costs $7.00 per case, would have an annual holding cost of 0.25($7.00) = $1.75 per case.

The next step in the inventory analysis is to determine the **ordering cost.** This cost, which is considered fixed regardless of the order quantity, covers the preparation of the voucher, the processing of the order including payment, postage, telephone, transportation, invoice verification, receiving, and so on. For R & B Beverage, the largest portion of the ordering cost involves the salaries of the purchasers. An analysis of the purchasing process showed that a purchaser spends approximately 45 minutes preparing and processing an order for Bub Beer. With a wage rate and fringe benefit cost for purchasers of $20 per hour, the labor portion of the ordering cost is $15. Making allowances for paper, postage, telephone, transportation, and receiving costs at $17 per order, the manager estimates that the ordering cost is $32 per order. That is, R & B is paying $32 per order regardless of the quantity requested in the order.

The holding cost, ordering cost, and demand information are the three data items that must be known prior to the use of the EOQ model. After developing these data for the R & B problem, we can look at how they are used to develop a total-cost model. We begin by defining $Q$ to be the order quantity. Thus, the how-much-to-order decision involves finding the value of $Q$ that will minimize the sum of holding and ordering costs.

The inventory level for Bub will have a maximum value of $Q$ units when an order of size $Q$ is received from the supplier. R & B will then satisfy customer demand from inventory until the inventory is depleted, at which time another shipment of $Q$ units will be received. Suppose that R & B is open 5 days each week. Thus, assuming a constant demand rate of 2000 cases per week or 400 cases per day, the graph of the inventory level for Bub Beer is as shown in Figure 11.1. Note that the graph indicates an average inventory level of $\frac{1}{2}Q$ for the period in question. This level should appear reasonable since the maximum

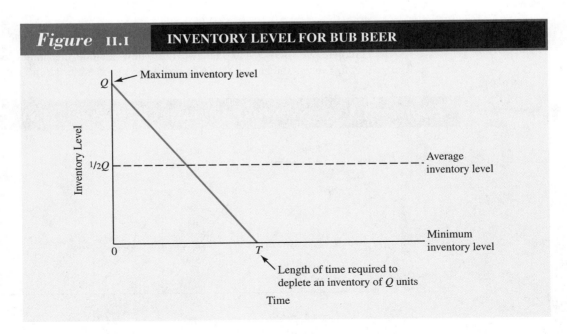

**Figure 11.1    INVENTORY LEVEL FOR BUB BEER**

inventory level is $Q$, the minimum is zero, and the inventory level declines at a constant rate over the period.

Figure 11.1 shows the inventory pattern during one order cycle of length $T$. As time goes on, this pattern will repeat. The complete inventory pattern is shown in Figure 11.2. If the average inventory during each cycle is $\frac{1}{2}Q$, the average inventory level over any number of cycles is also $\frac{1}{2}Q$.

The holding cost can be calculated using the average inventory level. That is, we can calculate the holding cost by multiplying the average inventory level by the cost of carrying one unit in inventory for the stated period. The period selected for the model is up to you; it could be 1 week, 1 month, 1 year, or more. However, since the holding cost for many industries and businesses is expressed as an *annual* percentage, most inventory models are developed on an *annual cost* basis.

Let

> Most inventory cost models use an *annual cost*. Thus, demand should be expressed in units per year and inventory holding cost should be based on an annual rate. The ordering cost should be expressed as a cost per order with the model providing the calculation of the total annual ordering cost.

$$I = \text{annual holding cost rate}$$
$$C = \text{unit cost of the inventory item}$$
$$C_h = \text{annual cost of holding one unit in inventory}$$

The annual cost of holding one unit in inventory is

$$C_h = IC \tag{11.1}$$

> $C_h$ is the cost of holding one unit in inventory for one year. Since smaller order quantities $Q$ will result in lower inventory levels, total annual holding cost can be reduced by using smaller order quantities.

The general equation for the annual holding cost for the average inventory of $\frac{1}{2}Q$ units is as follows:

$$\begin{pmatrix} \text{Annual} \\ \text{holding cost} \end{pmatrix} = \begin{pmatrix} \text{Average} \\ \text{inventory} \\ \text{level} \end{pmatrix}\begin{pmatrix} \text{Annual holding} \\ \text{cost} \\ \text{per unit} \end{pmatrix}$$
$$= \frac{1}{2}\,QC_h \tag{11.2}$$

To complete the total-cost model, we must now include the annual ordering cost. The goal is to express the annual ordering cost in terms of the order quantity $Q$. The first

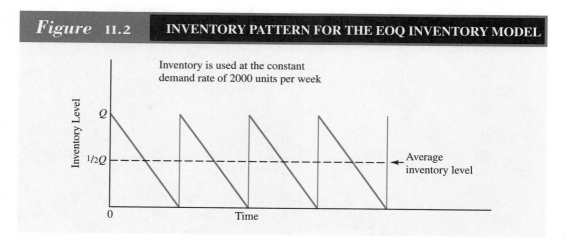

**Figure 11.2     INVENTORY PATTERN FOR THE EOQ INVENTORY MODEL**

question is, How many orders will be placed during the year? Let $D$ denote the annual demand for the product. For R & B Beverage, $D =$ (52 weeks)(2000 cases per week) $=$ 104,000 cases per year. We know that by ordering $Q$ units every time we order, we will have to place $D/Q$ orders per year. If $C_o$ is the cost of placing one order, the general equation for the annual ordering cost is as follows:

$$\begin{matrix} \text{Annual} \\ \text{ordering cost} \end{matrix} = \begin{pmatrix} \text{Number of} \\ \text{orders} \\ \text{per year} \end{pmatrix} \begin{pmatrix} \text{Cost} \\ \text{per} \\ \text{order} \end{pmatrix}$$

$$= \left(\frac{D}{Q}\right) C_o \qquad (11.3)$$

$C_o$ the fixed cost per order, is independent of the amount ordered. For a given annual demand of $D$ units, the total annual ordering cost can be reduced by using larger order quantities.

Thus, the total annual cost, denoted $TC$, can be expressed as follows:

$$\begin{matrix} \text{Total} \\ \text{annual} \\ \text{cost} \end{matrix} = \begin{matrix} \text{Annual} \\ \text{holding} \\ \text{cost} \end{matrix} + \begin{matrix} \text{Annual} \\ \text{ordering} \\ \text{cost} \end{matrix}$$

The cost of goods ($DC$) is not included in the total annual cost equation (11.4) because it is *not* a *relevant* cost for the EOQ model.

$$TC = \frac{1}{2} QC_h + \frac{D}{Q} C_o \qquad (11.4)$$

Using the Bub Beer data ($C_h = IC = (0.25)(\$8) = \$2$, $C_o = \$32$, and $D = 104,000$), the total annual cost model is

$$TC = \frac{1}{2} Q(\$2) + \frac{104,000}{Q}(\$32) = Q + \frac{3,328,000}{Q}$$

The development of the total-cost model has gone a long way toward solving the inventory problem. We now are able to express the total annual cost as a function of *how much* should be ordered. The development of a realistic total-cost model is perhaps the most important part of the application of quantitative methods to inventory decision making. Equation (11.4) is the general total-cost equation for inventory situations in which the assumptions of the economic order quantity model are valid.

### The How-Much-to-Order Decision

The next step is to find the order quantity $Q$ that will minimize the total annual cost for Bub Beer. Using a trial-and-error approach, we can compute the total annual cost for several possible order quantities. As a starting point, let us consider $Q = 8000$. The total annual cost for Bub Beer is

$$TC = Q + \frac{3,328,000}{Q}$$

$$= 8000 + \frac{3,328,000}{8000} = \$8416$$

A trial order quantity of 5000 gives

$$TC = 5000 + \frac{3,328,000}{5000} = \$5666$$

| Table 11.1 | ANNUAL HOLDING, ORDERING, AND TOTAL COSTS FOR VARIOUS ORDER QUANTITIES OF BUB BEER | | |
|---|---|---|---|
| | | **Annual Cost** | |
| **Order Quantity** | **Holding** | **Ordering** | **Total** |
| 5000 | $5000 | $ 666 | $5666 |
| 4000 | 4000 | 832 | 4832 |
| 3000 | 3000 | 1109 | 4109 |
| 2000 | 2000 | 1664 | 3664 |
| 1000 | 1000 | 3328 | 4328 |

The results of several other trial order quantities are shown in Table 11.1. As can be seen, the lowest cost solution is around 2000 cases. Graphs of the annual holding and ordering costs, and total annual costs are shown in Figure 11.3.

The advantage of the trial-and-error approach is that it is rather easy to do and provides the total annual cost for a number of possible order quantity decisions. In this case, the minimum-cost order quantity appears to be approximately 2000 cases. The disadvantage of this approach, however, is that it does not provide the exact minimum-cost order quantity.

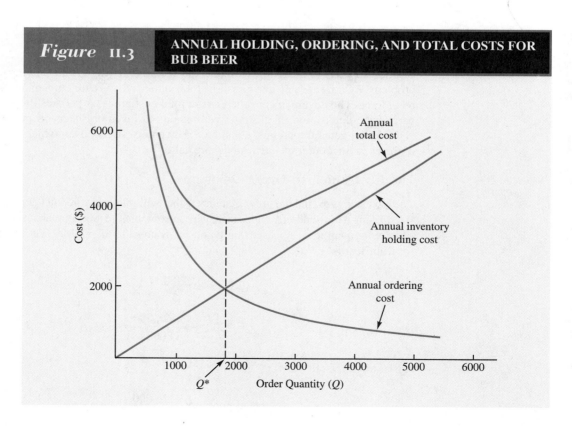

**Figure 11.3     ANNUAL HOLDING, ORDERING, AND TOTAL COSTS FOR BUB BEER**

The EOQ formula determines the optimal order quantity by balancing the annual holding cost and the annual ordering cost. Problem 2 at the end of the chapter will show that the optimal order quantity $Q*$ will provide an annual holding cost equal to the annual ordering cost.

Refer to Figure 11.3. The minimum total-cost order quantity is denoted by an order size of $Q*$. By using differential calculus, it can be shown (see Appendix 11.2) that the value of $Q*$ that minimizes the total annual cost is given by the formula

$$Q* = \sqrt{\frac{2DC_o}{C_h}} \tag{11.5}$$

This formula is referred to as the *economic order quantity (EOQ) formula.*

Using equation (11.5), the minimum total-annual-cost order quantity for Bub Beer is

$$Q* = \sqrt{\frac{2(104,000)32}{2}} = 1824 \text{ cases}$$

In 1915 F. W. Harris derived the mathematical formula for the economic order quantity. It was the first application of quantitative methods to the area of inventory management.

The use of an order quantity of 1824 in equation (11.4) shows that the minimum-cost inventory policy for Bub Beer has a total annual cost of $3649. Note that $Q* = 1824$ has balanced the holding and ordering costs. Check for yourself to see that these costs are equal.[2] (Problem 2 at the end of the chapter asks you to show that equal holding and ordering costs is a property of the EOQ model.)

### The When-to-Order Decision

Now that we know how much to order, we want to address the question of *when* to order. To answer this question, we need to introduce the concept of inventory position. The **inventory position** is defined as the amount of inventory on hand plus the amount of inventory on order. The when-to-order decision is expressed in terms of a **reorder point**—the inventory position at which a new order should be placed.

The reorder point is expressed in terms of *inventory position,* the amount of inventory on hand plus the amount on order. Some people think that the reorder point is expressed in terms of inventory on hand. With short lead times, inventory position is usually the same as the inventory on hand. However, with long lead times, inventory position may be larger than inventory on hand.

The manufacturer of Bub Beer guarantees a 2-day delivery on any order placed by R & B Beverage. Hence, assuming a constant demand rate of 2000 cases per week or 400 cases per day, we expect (2 days)(400 cases/day) = 800 cases of Bub to be sold during the 2 days it takes a new order to reach the R & B warehouse. In inventory terminology, the 2-day delivery period is referred to as the **lead time** for a new order, and the 800-case demand anticipated during this period is referred to as the **lead-time demand.** Thus, R & B should order a new shipment of Bub Beer from the manufacturer when the inventory level reaches 800 cases. For inventory systems using the constant demand rate assumption and a fixed lead time, the reorder point is the same as the lead-time demand. For these systems, the general expression for the reorder point is as follows:

$$r = dm \tag{11.6}$$

where

$$r = \text{reorder point}$$
$$d = \text{demand per day}$$
$$m = \text{lead time for a new order in days}$$

---

[2] Actually, $Q*$ from equation (11.5) is 1824.28, but since we cannot order fractional cases of beer, a $Q*$ of 1824 is shown. This value of $Q*$ may cause a few cents deviation between the two costs. If $Q*$ is used at its exact value, the holding and ordering costs will be exactly the same.

The cycle time can be expressed in years with $T = Q^*/D$. Because inventory managers may wish to think of cycle time in other units, $T$ can be adjusted to months by multiplying by 12; to weeks by multiplying by 52; or as we show, to days by multiplying by the number of working days per year, which may vary from firm to firm.

The question of how frequently the order will be placed can now be answered. The period between orders is referred to as the **cycle time.** Previously in equation (11.2), we defined $D/Q$ as the number of orders that will be placed in a year. Thus, $D/Q^* = 104,000/1824 = 57$ is the number of orders R & B Beverage will place for Bub Beer each year. If R & B places 57 orders over 250 working days, it will order approximately every $250/57 = 4.4$ working days. Thus, the cycle time is 4.4 working days. The general expression for a cycle time[3] of $T$ days is given by

$$T = \frac{250}{D/Q^*} = \frac{250Q^*}{D} \tag{11.7}$$

## Sensitivity Analysis in the EOQ Model

Even though substantial time may have been spent in arriving at the cost per order ($32) and the holding cost rate (25%), we should realize that these figures are at best good estimates. Thus, we may want to consider how much the recommended order quantity would change if the estimated ordering and holding costs had been different. To determine the effects of various cost scenarios, we can calculate the recommended order quantity under several different cost conditions. Table 11.2 shows the minimum total-cost order quantity for several cost possibilities. As you can see from the table, the value of $Q^*$ appears relatively stable, even with some variations in the cost estimates. Based on these results, the best order quantity for Bub Beer is somewhere around 1700–2000 cases. If operated properly, the total cost for the Bub Beer inventory system should be close to $3400–$3800 per year. We also note that little risk is associated with implementing the calculated order quantity of 1824. For example, if holding cost rate = 24%, $C_o$ = $34, and the true optimal order quantity $Q^*$ = 1919, R & B experiences only a $5 increase in the total annual cost; that is, $3690 − $3685 = $5, with $Q = 1824$.

From the preceding analysis, we would say that this EOQ model is insensitive to small variations or errors in the cost estimates. This insensitivity is a property of EOQ models in general, which indicates that if we have at least reasonable estimates of ordering cost and holding cost, we can expect to obtain a good approximation of the true minimum-cost order quantity.

| *Table* 11.2 | OPTIMAL ORDER QUANTITIES FOR SEVERAL COST POSSIBILITIES | | | |
|---|---|---|---|---|
| Possible Inventory Holding Cost (%) | Possible Cost Per Order | Optimal Order Quantity ($Q^*$) | Projected Total Annual Cost | |
| | | | Using $Q^*$ | Using $Q = 1824$ |
| 24 | $30 | 1803 | $3461 | $3462 |
| 24 | 34 | 1919 | 3685 | 3690 |
| 26 | 30 | 1732 | 3603 | 3607 |
| 26 | 34 | 1844 | 3835 | 3836 |

---

[3] This general expression for cycle time is based on 250 working days per year. If the firm operated 300 working days per year and wanted to express cycle time in terms of working days, the cycle time would be given by $T = 300Q^*/D$.

## The Manager's Use of the EOQ Model

The EOQ model results in a recommended order quantity of 1824 units. Is this quantity the final decision, or should the manager's judgment enter into the establishment of the final inventory policy? Although the model has provided a good order-quantity recommendation, it may not have taken into account all aspects of the inventory situation. As a result, the decision maker may want to modify the final order-quantity recommendation to meet the unique circumstances of the inventory situation. In this case, the warehouse manager felt that increasing the order quantity from 1824 cases to 2000 cases to have an order quantity equal to 5 working days' demand would be desirable. By doing so, R & B Beverage can maintain a weekly order cycle.

The warehouse manager also realized that the EOQ model was based on the constant demand rate assumption of 2000 cases per week. While this rate is a good approximation, we must also recognize that sometimes the demand exceeds 2000 cases per week. If a reorder point of 800 cases is used, we would be expecting an 800-case demand during the lead time and the new order to arrive exactly when the inventory level reached zero. Such close timing and the new order to arrive exactly when the inventory level reached zero. Such close timing would have little room for error, and the scheduling of arrivals would be critical if stockouts (shortages) were to be avoided. To protect against shortages due to higher-than-expected demands or slightly delayed incoming orders, the warehouse manager recommended a 1200-case reorder point. Thus, under normal conditions, R & B Beverage will order 2000 cases of Bub whenever the current inventory reaches 1200 cases. During the expected 2-day lead time, 800 cases should be demanded, and 400 cases should be in inventory when an order arrives. The extra 400 cases serve as a safety precaution against a higher-than-expected demand or a delayed incoming order. In general, the amount by which the reorder point exceeds the expected lead-time demand is referred to as **safety stock.**

The decisions to adjust the order quantity and reorder point were purely judgment decisions and were not necessarily made with a minimum-cost objective in mind. However, they are examples of how managerial judgment might interface with the inventory decision model to arrive at a sound inventory policy. The final decision of $Q = 2000$ with a 400-case safety stock resulted in a total annual cost of $4464.[4]

## How Has the EOQ Decision Model Helped?

The EOQ model has objectively included holding and ordering costs and, with the aid of some management judgment, has led to a low-cost inventory policy. In addition, the general optimal order-quantity model, equation (11.5), is applicable to other R & B products. For example, Red Ribbon Beer ($7/case), which has an ordering cost of $32, a constant demand rate of 1200 cases per week (62,400 cases/year), and a 2-day lead-time period, has a recommended order quantity of

$$Q^* = \sqrt{\frac{2(62,400)(32)}{(0.25)(7)}} = 1511 \text{ cases}$$

a cycle time of $T = [250(1511)]/62,400 = 6.05$ days, and a reorder point of $r = (240)(2) = 480$ cases.

_The total-cost curve in Figure 11.3 is relatively flat near the value of $Q^*$. Consequently, the inventory manager can adjust the EOQ slightly to a more convenient level without seriously affecting the total cost._

_Problem 1 provides practice in applying the EOQ model to another R & B product._

---

[4] A Q of 2000 units resulted in a total cost of $3664 (see Table 11.1). The additional safety stock inventory of 400 units increases the average inventory by 400 units because it is on hand all year long. Thus, the inventory carrying charge is increased by 2(400) = $800, the total cost of the revised policy is $3664 + $800 = $4464.

## A Summary of the EOQ Model Assumptions

To use the optimal order-quantity and reorder-point model described here, an analyst must make assumptions about how the inventory system operates. The EOQ model with its economic order quantity formula is based on some specific assumptions about the R & B inventory system. A summary of the assumptions for this model is provided in Table 11.3. Before using the EOQ formula, carefully review these assumptions to ensure that they are applicable to the inventory system being analyzed. If the assumptions are not reasonable, seek a different inventory model.

Various types of inventory systems are used in practice, and the inventory models presented in the following sections alter one or more of the EOQ model assumptions shown in Table 11.3 to meet the needs of the different systems. When the assumptions change, a different inventory model with different optimal operating policies becomes necessary.

**Table 11.3    SUMMARY OF THE EOQ MODEL ASSUMPTIONS**

1. Demand $D$ is deterministic and occurs at a constant rate.
2. The order quantity $Q$ is the same for each order. The inventory level increases by $Q$ units each time an order is received.
3. The cost per order, $C_o$, is constant and does not depend on the quantity ordered.
4. The purchase cost per unit, $C$, is constant and does not depend on the quantity ordered.
5. The inventory holding cost per unit per time period, $C_h$, is constant. The total inventory holding cost depends on both $C_h$ and the size of the inventory.
6. Shortages such as stockouts or backorders are not permitted.
7. The lead time for an order is constant.
8. The inventory position is reviewed continuously. As a result, an order is placed as soon as the inventory position reaches the reorder point.

### NOTES and Comments

With relatively long lead times, the lead-time demand and the resulting reorder point $r$, determined by equation (11.6), may exceed $Q^*$. If this condition occurs, at least one order will be outstanding when a new order is placed. For example, assume that Bub Beer has a lead time of $m = 6$ days. With a daily demand of $d = 400$ cases, equation (11.6) shows that the reorder point would be $r = dm = 6 \times 400 = 2400$ cases. Thus, a new order for Bub Beer should be placed whenever the inventory position (the amount of inventory on hand plus the amount of inventory on order) reaches 2400. With an order quantity of $Q = 2000$ cases, the inventory position of 2400 cases occurs when one order of 2000 cases is outstanding and $2400 - 2000 = 400$ cases are on hand.

## 11.2    ECONOMIC PRODUCTION LOT-SIZE MODEL

The inventory model presented in this section is similar to the EOQ model in that we are attempting to determine *how much* we should order and *when* the order should be placed. We again assume a constant demand rate. However, instead of assuming that the goods arrive in a shipment of size $Q^*$, as in the EOQ model, we assume that units are supplied

The inventory model in this section alters assumption 2 of the EOQ model (see Table 11.3). The assumption concerning the arrival of $Q$ units each time an order is received is changed to a constant production supply rate.

to inventory at a constant rate over several days or several weeks. The **constant supply rate** assumption implies that the same number of units is supplied to inventory each period of time (e.g., 10 units every day or 50 units every week). This model is designed for production situations in which, once an order is placed, production begins and a constant number of units is added to inventory each day until the production run has been completed.

If we have a production system that produces 50 units per day and we decide to schedule 10 days of production, we have a 50(10) = 500-unit production lot size. The **lot size** is the number of units in an order. In general, if we let $Q$ indicate the production lot size, the approach to the inventory decisions is similar to the EOQ model; that is, we build a holding and ordering cost model that expresses the total cost as a function of the production lot size. Then we attempt to find the production lot size that minimizes the total cost.

One other condition that should be mentioned at this time is that the model only applies to situations where the production rate is greater than the demand rate; the production system must be able to satisfy demand. For instance, if the constant demand rate is 2000 units per week, the production rate must be at least 2000 units per week to satisfy demand.

During the production run, demand will be reducing the inventory while production will be adding to inventory. Since we have assumed that the production rate exceeds the demand rate, each day during a production run we will be producing more units than are demanded. Thus, the excess production will cause a gradual inventory buildup during the production period. When the production run is completed, the continuing demand will cause the inventory to gradually decline until a new production run is started. The inventory pattern for this system is shown in Figure 11.4.

This model differs from the EOQ model in that a setup cost replaces the ordering cost and the saw-tooth inventory pattern shown in Figure 11.4 differs from the inventory pattern shown in Figure 11.2.

As in the EOQ model, we are now dealing with two costs, the holding cost and the ordering cost. While the holding cost is identical to the definition in the EOQ model, the interpretation of the ordering cost is slightly different. In fact, in a production situation the ordering cost is more correctly referred to as the production **setup cost.** This cost, which includes labor, material, and lost production costs incurred while preparing the production system for operation, is a fixed cost that occurs for every production run regardless of the production lot size.

## The Total-Cost Model

Let us begin building the production lot size model by writing the holding cost in terms of the production lot size $Q$. Again, the approach is to develop an expression for average

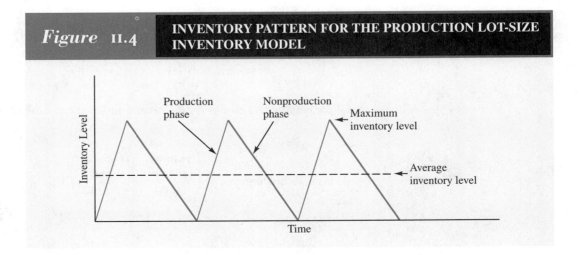

**Figure 11.4**    **INVENTORY PATTERN FOR THE PRODUCTION LOT-SIZE INVENTORY MODEL**

inventory and then establish the holding costs associated with the average inventory level. We use a 1-year time period and an annual cost for the model.

In the EOQ model the average inventory is one-half the maximum inventory or $\frac{1}{2}Q$. Figure 11.4 shows that for a production lot-size model a constant inventory buildup rate occurs during the production run and a constant inventory depletion rate occurs during the nonproduction period; thus, the average inventory will be one-half the maximum inventory level. However, in this inventory system the production lot size $Q$ does not go into inventory at one point in time, and thus the inventory level never reaches a level of $Q$ units.

To show how we can compute the maximum inventory level, let

$$d = \text{daily demand rate}$$

$$p = \text{daily production rate}$$

$$t = \text{number of days for a production run}$$

At this point, the logic of the production lot-size model is easier to follow using a daily demand rate $d$ and a daily production rate $p$. However, when the total annual cost model is eventually developed (see equation 11.15), we recommend that inputs to the model be expressed in terms of the annual demand rate $D$ and the annual production rate $P$.

Because we are assuming that $p$ will be larger than $d$, the daily inventory buildup rate during the production phase is $p - d$. If we run production for $t$ days and place $p - d$ units in inventory each day, the inventory level at the end of the production run will be $(p - d)t$. From Figure 11.4 we can see that the inventory level at the end of the production run is also the maximum inventory level. Thus

$$\text{Maximum inventory level} = (p - d)t \tag{11.8}$$

If we know we are producing a production lot size of $Q$ units at a daily production rate of $p$ units, then $Q = pt$, and the length of the production run $t$ must be

$$t = \frac{Q}{p} \text{ days} \tag{11.9}$$

Thus

$$\text{Maximum inventory level} = (p - d)t = (p - d)\left(\frac{Q}{p}\right)$$

$$= \left(1 - \frac{d}{p}\right)Q \tag{11.10}$$

The average inventory level, which is one-half the maximum inventory level, is given by

$$\text{Average inventory level} = \frac{1}{2}\left(1 - \frac{d}{p}\right)Q \tag{11.11}$$

With an annual per unit holding cost of $C_h$, the general equation for annual holding cost is as follows:

$$\begin{pmatrix} \text{Annual} \\ \text{holding cost} \end{pmatrix} = \begin{pmatrix} \text{Average} \\ \text{inventory} \\ \text{level} \end{pmatrix}\begin{pmatrix} \text{Annual} \\ \text{cost} \\ \text{per unit} \end{pmatrix}$$

$$= \frac{1}{2}\left(1 - \frac{d}{p}\right)QC_h \tag{11.12}$$

If $D$ is the annual demand for the product and $C_o$ is the setup cost for a production run, then the annual setup cost, which takes the place of the annual ordering cost in the EOQ model, is as follows:

$$\text{Annual setup cost} = \left(\begin{array}{c}\text{Number of production}\\ \text{runs per year}\end{array}\right)\left(\begin{array}{c}\text{Setup cost}\\ \text{per run}\end{array}\right)$$

$$= \frac{D}{Q}C_o \tag{11.13}$$

Thus, the total annual cost ($TC$) model is

$$TC = \frac{1}{2}\left(1 - \frac{d}{p}\right)QC_h + \frac{D}{Q}C_o \tag{11.14}$$

Suppose that a production facility operates 250 days per year; 115 days are idle due to weekends and holidays. Then we can write daily demand $d$ in terms of annual demand $D$ as follows:

$$d = \frac{D}{250}$$

Now let $P$ denote the annual production for the product if the product were produced every day. Then

$$P = 250p \qquad \text{and} \qquad p = \frac{P}{250}$$

Thus[5]

$$\frac{d}{p} = \frac{D/250}{P/250} = \frac{D}{P}$$

Therefore, we can write the total annual cost model as follows:

$$TC = \frac{1}{2}\left(1 - \frac{D}{P}\right)QC_h + \frac{D}{Q}C_o \tag{11.15}$$

Equations (11.14) and (11.15) are equivalent. However, equation (11.15) may be used more frequently since an *annual* cost model tends to make the analyst think in terms of collecting *annual* demand data ($D$) and *annual* production data ($P$) rather than daily data.

### Finding the Economic Production Lot Size

Given estimates of the holding cost ($C_h$), setup cost, ($C_o$), annual demand rate ($D$), and annual production rate ($P$), we could use a trial-and-error approach to compute the total annual cost for various production lot sizes ($Q$). However, this trial-and-error is not necessary;

---

[5] The ratio $d/p = D/P$ regardless of the number of days of operation; 250 days is used here merely as an illustration.

we can use the minimum-cost formula for $Q^*$ that has been developed using differential calculus (see Appendix 11.3). The equation is as follows:

As the production rate $P$ approaches infinity, $D/P$ approaches zero. In this case, equation (11.16) is equivalent to the EOQ model in equation (11.5).

$$Q^* = \sqrt{\frac{2DC_o}{(1 - D/P)C_h}} \qquad (11.16)$$

**An Example.**    Beauty Bar Soap is produced on a production line that has an annual capacity of 60,000 cases. The annual demand is estimated at 26,000 cases, with the demand rate essentially constant throughout the year. The cleaning, preparation, and setup of the production line cost approximately $135. The manufacturing cost per case is $4.50, and the annual holding cost is figured at a 24% rate. Thus, $C_h = IC = 0.24(\$4.50) = \$1.08$. What is the recommended production lot size?

Using equation (11.16), we have

$$Q^* = \sqrt{\frac{2(26,000)(135)}{(1 - 26,000/60,000)(1.08)}} = 3387$$

The total annual cost using equation (11.15) and $Q^* = 3387$ is $2073.

Work Problem 13 as an example of an economic production lot-size model.

Other relevant data include a 1-week lead time to schedule and set up a production run. Thus, the lead-time demand of $26,000/52 = 500$ cases is the reorder point. The cycle time is the time between production runs. Using equation (11.7), the cycle time is estimated to be $T = 250Q^*/D = [(250)(3387)]/26,000$, or about 33 working days. Thus, we should plan a production run of 3387 units about every 33 working days.

Certainly the manager will want to review the model recommendations. Adjusting the recommended $Q^* = 3387$ to a slightly different figure and/or adding safety stock may be desirable.

## 11.3    AN INVENTORY MODEL WITH PLANNED SHORTAGES

A shortage or stockout is a demand that cannot be supplied. In many situations, shortages are undesirable and should be avoided if at all possible. However, in other cases it may be desirable—from an economic point of view—to plan for and allow shortages. In practice, these types of situations are most commonly found where the value of the inventory per unit is high and hence the holding cost is high. An example of this type of situation is a new car dealer's inventory. Often a specific car that a customer wants may not be in stock. However, if the customer is willing to wait a few weeks, the dealer is usually able to order it.

The assumptions of the EOQ model in Table 11.3 apply to this inventory model with the exception that shortages, referred to as *backorders*, are now permitted.

The model developed in this section takes into account a type of shortage known as a **backorder.** In a backorder situation, we assume that when a customer places an order and discovers that the supplier is out of stock, the customer waits until the new shipment arrives, and then the order is filled. Frequently, the waiting period in backordering situations is relatively short. Thus, by promising the customer top priority and immediate delivery when the goods become available, companies may be able to convince the customer to wait until the order arrives. In these cases, the backorder assumption is valid.

The backorder model that we develop is an extension of the EOQ model presented in Section 11.1. We use the EOQ model in which all goods arrive in inventory at one time and are subject to a constant demand rate (see Table 11.3 for a summary of the EOQ model assumptions). If we let $S$ indicate the number of backorders that are accumulated when a new shipment of size $Q$ is received, then the inventory system for the backorder case has the following characteristics:

- If $S$ backorders exist when a new shipment of size $Q$ arrives, the $S$ backorders are shipped to the appropriate customers, and the remaining $Q - S$ units are placed in inventory. Therefore, $Q - S$ is the maximum inventory level.
- The inventory cycle of $T$ days is divided into two distinct phases; $t_1$ days when inventory is on hand and orders are filled as they occur, and $t_2$ days when stockouts occur and all new orders are placed on backorder.

The inventory pattern for the inventory model with backorders, where negative inventory represents the number of backorders, is shown in Figure 11.5.

With the inventory pattern now defined, we can proceed with the basic step of all inventory models—namely, the development of a total-cost model. For the inventory model with backorders, we encounter the usual holding costs and ordering costs. We also incur a backorder cost in terms of the labor and special delivery costs directly associated with the handling of the backorders. Another portion of the backorder cost accounts for the loss of goodwill because some customers will have to wait for their orders. Since the **goodwill cost** depends on how long a customer has to wait, it is customary to adopt the convention of expressing backorder cost in terms of the cost of having a unit on backorder for a stated period of time. This method of costing backorders on a time basis is similar to the method used to compute the inventory holding cost, and we can use it to compute a total annual cost of backorders once the average backorder level and the backorder cost per unit per period are known.

Let us begin the development of a total-cost model by calculating the average inventory level for a hypothetical problem. If we have an average inventory of two units for 3 days and no inventory on the fourth day, what is the average inventory level over the 4-day period? It is

$$\frac{2 \text{ units (3 days)} + 0 \text{ units (1 day)}}{4 \text{ days}} = \frac{6}{4} = 1.5 \text{ units}$$

**Figure 11.5    INVENTORY PATTERN FOR AN INVENTORY MODEL WITH BACKORDERS**

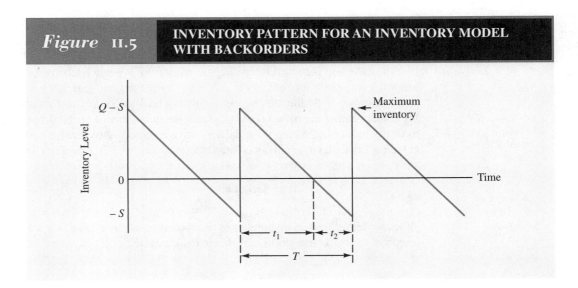

Refer to Figure 11.5. You can see that this situation is what happens in the backorder model. With a maximum inventory of $Q - S$ units, the $t_1$ days we have inventory on hand will have an average inventory of $(Q - S)/2$. No inventory is carried for the $t_2$ days in which we experience backorders. Thus, over the total cycle time of $T = t_1 + t_2$ days, we can compute the average inventory level as follows:

$$\text{Average inventory level} = \frac{\frac{1}{2}(Q - S)t_1 + 0t_2}{t_1 + t_2} = \frac{\frac{1}{2}(Q - S)t_1}{T} \qquad (11.17)$$

Can we find other ways of expressing $t_1$ and $T$? Because we know that the maximum inventory is $Q - S$ and that $d$ represents the constant daily demand, we have

$$t_1 = \frac{Q - S}{d} \text{ days} \qquad (11.18)$$

That is, the maximum inventory level of $Q - S$ units will be used up in $(Q - S)/d$ days. Since $Q$ units are ordered each cycle, we know the length of a cycle must be

$$T = \frac{Q}{d} \text{ days} \qquad (11.19)$$

Combining equations (11.18) and (11.19) with equation (11.17), we can compute the average inventory level as follows:

$$\text{Average inventory level} = \frac{\frac{1}{2}(Q - S)[(Q - S)/d]}{Q/d} = \frac{(Q - S)^2}{2Q} \qquad (11.20)$$

Thus, the average inventory level is expressed in terms of two inventory decisions: how much we will order ($Q$) and the maximum number of backorders we will allow ($S$).

The formula for the annual number of orders placed using this model is identical to that for the EOQ model. With $D$ representing the annual demand, we have

$$\text{Annual number of orders} = \frac{D}{Q} \qquad (11.21)$$

The next step is to develop an expression for the average backorder level. Because we know the maximum for backorders is $S$, we can use the same logic we used to establish average inventory in finding the average number of backorders. We have an average number of backorders during the period $t_2$ of $\frac{1}{2}$ the maximum number of backorders or $\frac{1}{2}S$. We do not have any backorders during the $t_1$ days we have inventory, therefore we can calculate the average backorder level in a manner similar to equation (11.17). Using this approach, we have

$$\text{Average backorder level} = \frac{0t_1 + (S/2)t_2}{T} = \frac{(S/2)t_2}{T} \qquad (11.22)$$

When we let the maximum number of backorders reach an amount $S$ at a daily rate of $d$, the length of the backorder portion of the inventory cycle is

$$t_2 = \frac{S}{d} \qquad (11.23)$$

Using equations (11.23) and (11.19) in equation (11.22), we have

$$\text{Average backorder level} = \frac{(S/2)(S/d)}{Q/d} = \frac{S^2}{2Q} \tag{11.24}$$

Let

$$C_h = \text{cost to maintain one unit in inventory for 1 year}$$
$$C_o = \text{cost per order}$$
$$C_b = \text{cost to maintain one unit on backorder for 1 year}$$

The total annual cost ($TC$) for the inventory model with backorders becomes

$$TC = \frac{(Q-S)^2}{2Q}\,C_h + \frac{D}{Q}\,C_o + \frac{S^2}{2Q}\,C_b \tag{11.25}$$

Given the cost estimates $C_h$, $C_o$, and $C_b$ and the annual demand $D$, the minimum-cost values for the order quantity $Q^*$ and the planned backorders $S^*$ are as follows (see Appendix 11.4):

$$Q^* = \sqrt{\frac{2DC_o}{C_h}\left(\frac{C_h + C_b}{C_b}\right)} \tag{11.26}$$

$$S^* = Q^*\left(\frac{C_h}{C_h + C_b}\right) \tag{11.27}$$

**An Example.**    Suppose that the Higley Radio Components Company has a product for which the assumptions of the inventory model with backorders are valid. Information obtained by the company is as follows:

$$D = 2000 \text{ units per year}$$
$$I = 0.20$$
$$C = \$50 \text{ per unit}$$
$$C_h = IC = (0.20)(\$50) = \$10 \text{ per unit per year}$$
$$C_o = \$25 \text{ per order}$$

The backorder cost $C_b$ is one of the most difficult costs to estimate in inventory models. The reason is that it attempts to measure the cost associated with the loss of goodwill when a customer must wait for an order. Expressing this cost on an annual basis adds to the difficulty.

The company is considering the possibility of allowing some backorders to occur for the product. The annual backorder cost has been estimated to be \$30 per unit per year. Using equations (11.26) and (11.27), we have

$$Q^* = \sqrt{\frac{2(2000)(25)}{10}\left(\frac{10 + 30}{30}\right)} = 115$$

and

$$S^* = 115\left(\frac{10}{10 + 30}\right) = 29$$

An inventory situation that incorporates backorder costs is considered in Problem 15.

If this solution is implemented, the system will operate with the following properties:

$$\text{Maximum inventory} = Q - S = 115 - 29 = 86$$

$$\text{Cycle time} = T = \frac{Q}{D}(250) = \frac{115}{2000}(250) = 14.4 \text{ working days}$$

The total annual cost is

If backorders can be tolerated, the total cost including the backordering cost will be less than the total cost of the EOQ model. Some people think the model with backordering will have a greater cost because it includes a backordering cost in addition to the usual inventory holding and ordering costs. You can point out the fallacy in this thinking by noting that the backorder model leads to lower inventory levels and hence lower inventory holding costs.

$$\text{Holding cost} = \frac{(86)^2}{2(115)}(10) = \$322$$

$$\text{Ordering cost} = \frac{2000}{115}(25) \;\;= \$435$$

$$\text{Backorder cost} = \frac{(29)^2}{2(115)}(30) = \$110$$

$$\text{Total cost} \;\;= \$867$$

If the company had chosen to prohibit backorders and had adopted the regular EOQ model, the recommended inventory decision would have been

$$Q^* = \sqrt{\frac{2(2000)(25)}{10}} = \sqrt{10,000} = 100$$

This order quantity would have resulted in a holding cost and an ordering cost of $500 each or a total annual cost of $1000. Thus, in this problem, allowing backorders is projecting a $1000 - \$867 = \$133$ or 13.3% savings in cost from the no-stockout EOQ model. The preceding comparison and conclusion are based on the assumption that the backorder model with an annual cost per backordered unit of $30 is a valid model for the actual inventory situation. If the company is concerned that stockouts might lead to lost sales, then the savings might not be enough to warrant switching to an inventory policy that allowed for planned shortages.

N O T E S
*and Comments*

Equation (11.27) shows that the optimal number of planned backorders $S^*$ is proportional to the ratio $C_h/(C_h + C_b)$, where $C_h$ is the annual holding cost per unit and $C_b$ if the annual backorder cost per unit. Whenever $C_h$ increases, this ratio becomes larger, and the number of planned backorders increases. This explains why items that have a high per-unit cost and a correspondingly high annual holding cost are more economically handled on a backorder basis. On the other hand, whenever the backorder cost $C_b$ increases, the ratio becomes smaller, and the number of planned backorders decreases. Thus, the model provides the intuitive result that items with high backordering costs will be handled with few backorders. In fact, with high backorder costs, the backorder model and the EOQ model with no backordering allowed provide similar inventory policies.

........................................................................................../  /...........

## 11.4    QUANTITY DISCOUNTS FOR THE EOQ MODEL

**Quantity discounts** occur in numerous situations in which suppliers provide an incentive for large order quantities by offering a lower purchase cost when items are ordered in larger quantities. In this section we show how the EOQ model can be used when quantity discounts are available.

*In the quantity discount model, assumption 4 of the EOQ model in Table 11.3 is altered. The cost per unit varies depending on the quantity ordered.*

Assume that we have a product in which the basic EOQ model (see Table 11.3) is applicable. Instead of a fixed unit cost, the supplier quotes the following discount schedule.

| Discount Category | Order Size | Discount (%) | Unit Cost |
|---|---|---|---|
| 1 | 0 to 999 | 0 | $5.00 |
| 2 | 1000 to 2499 | 3 | 4.85 |
| 3 | 2500 and over | 5 | 4.75 |

The 5% discount for the 2500-unit minimum order quantity looks tempting. However, realizing that higher order quantities result in higher inventory holding costs, we should prepare a thorough cost analysis before making a final ordering and inventory policy recommendation.

Suppose that the data and cost analyses show an annual holding cost rate of 20%, an ordering cost of $49 per order, and an annual demand of 5000 units; what order quantity should we select? The following three-step procedure shows the calculations necessary to make this decision. In the preliminary calculations, we use $Q_1$ to indicate the order quantity for discount category 1, $Q_2$ for discount category 2, and $Q_3$ for discount category 3.

Step 1   For each discount category, compute a $Q^*$ using the EOQ formula based on the unit cost associated with the discount category.

Recall that the EOQ model provides $Q^* = \sqrt{2DC_o/C_h}$, where $C_h = IC = (0.20)C$. With three discount categories providing three different unit costs $C$, we obtain

$$Q_1^* = \sqrt{\frac{2(5000)49}{(0.20)(5.00)}} = 700$$

$$Q_2^* = \sqrt{\frac{2(5000)49}{(0.20)(4.85)}} = 711$$

$$Q_3^* = \sqrt{\frac{2(5000)49}{(0.20)(4.75)}} = 718$$

Since the only differences in the EOQ formulas are slight differences in the holding cost, the economic order quantities resulting from this step will be approximately the same. However, these order quantities will usually not all be of the size necessary to qualify for the discount price assumed. In the preceding case, both $Q_2^*$ and $Q_3^*$ are insufficient order quantities to obtain their assumed discounted costs of $4.85 and $4.75, respectively. For those order quantities for which the assumed price cannot be obtained, the following procedure must be used.

Step 2  For the $Q^*$ that is too small to qualify for the assumed discount price, adjust the order quantity upward to the nearest order quantity that will allow the product to be purchased at the assumed price.

In our example, this adjustment causes us to set

$$Q_2^* = 1000$$

and

$$Q_3^* = 2500$$

In the EOQ model with quantity discounts, the annual purchase cost must be included because purchase cost depends on the order quantity. Thus, it is a relevant cost.

If a calculated $Q^*$ for a given discount price is large enough to qualify for a bigger discount, that value of $Q^*$ cannot lead to an optimal solution. Although the reason may not be obvious, it does turn out to be a property of the EOQ quantity discount model. Problem 23 at the end of the chapter asks you to show that this property is true.

In the previous inventory models considered, the annual purchase cost of the item was not included because it was constant and never affected by the inventory-order policy decision. However, in the quantity discount model, the annual purchase cost depends on the order-quantity and the associated unit cost. Thus, annual purchase cost (annual demand $D \times$ unit cost $C$) is included in the equation for total cost as shown here.

$$TC = \frac{Q}{2} C_h + \frac{D}{Q} C_o + DC \qquad (11.28)$$

Using this total-cost equation, we can determine the optimal order quantity for the EOQ discount model in step 3.

Step 3  For each order quantity resulting from steps 1 and 2, compute the total annual cost using the unit price from the appropriate discount category and equation (11.28). The order quantity yielding the minimum total annual cost is the optimal order quantity.

Problem 21 will give you practice in applying the EOQ model to situations with quantity discounts.

The step 3 calculations for the example problem are summarized in Table 11.4. As you can see, a decision to order 1000 units at the 3% discount rate yields the minimum-cost solution. While the 2500-unit order quantity would result in a 5% discount, its excessive holding cost makes it the second best solution. Figure 11.6 shows the total-cost curve for each of the three discount categories. Note that $Q^* = 1000$ provides the minimum-cost order quantity.

| *Table* 11.4 | | TOTAL ANNUAL COST CALCULATIONS FOR THE EOQ MODEL WITH QUANTITY DISCOUNTS | | | | |
|---|---|---|---|---|---|---|

| Discount Category | Unit Cost | Order Quantity | Annual Cost Holding | Annual Cost Ordering | Annual Cost Purchase | Total |
|---|---|---|---|---|---|---|
| 1 | $5.00 | 700 | $ 350 | $350 | $25,000 | $25,700 |
| 2 | 4.85 | 1000 | 485 | 245 | 24,250 | 24,980 |
| 3 | 4.75 | 2500 | 1188 | 98 | 23,750 | 25,036 |

**Figure 11.6**    **TOTAL-COST CURVES FOR THE THREE DISCOUNT CATEGORIES**

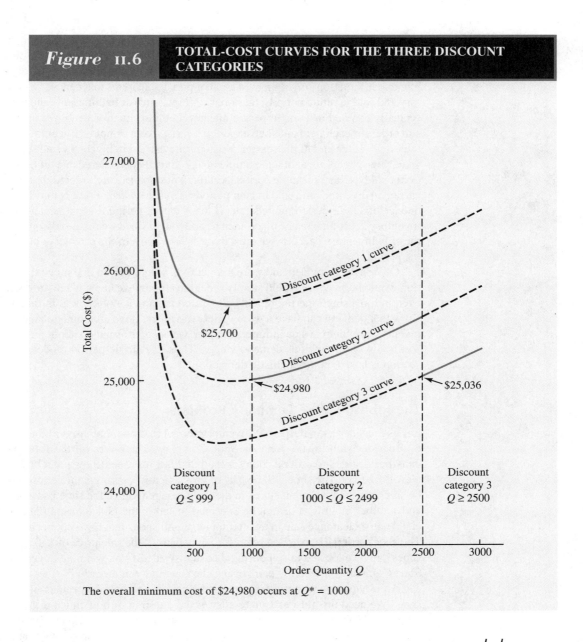

The overall minimum cost of $24,980 occurs at $Q^* = 1000$

## 11.5   A SINGLE-PERIOD INVENTORY MODEL WITH PROBABILISTIC DEMAND

This inventory model is the first in the chapter that explicitly treats probabilistic demand. Unlike the EOQ model, it is for a single period with unused inventory not carried over to future periods.

The inventory models that we have discussed thus far have been based on the assumption that the demand rate is constant and **deterministic** throughout the year. We developed minimum-cost order quantity and reorder-point policies based on this assumption. In situations in which the demand rate is not deterministic, models have been developed that treat demand as **probabilistic** and best described by a probability distribution. In this section we consider a **single-period inventory model** with probabilistic demand.

The single-period inventory model refers to inventory situations in which *one* order is placed for the product; at the end of the period, the product has either sold out, or a surplus of unsold items will be sold for a salvage value. The single-period inventory model is applicable in situations involving seasonal or perishable items that cannot be carried in inventory and sold in future periods. Seasonal clothing (such as bathing suits and winter coats) are typically handled in a single-period manner. In these situations, a buyer places one preseason order for each item and then experiences a stockout or holds a clearance sale on the surplus stock at the end of the season. No items are carried in inventory and sold the following year. Newspapers are another example of a product that is ordered one time and is either sold or not sold during the single period. Although newspapers are ordered daily, they cannot be carried in inventory and sold in later periods. Thus, newspaper orders may be treated as a sequence of single-period models; that is, each day or period is separate, and a single-period inventory decision must be made each period (day). Since we order only once for the period, the only inventory decision we must make is *how much* of the product to order at the start of the period.

Obviously, if the demand were known for a single-period inventory situation, the solution would be easy; we would simply order the amount we knew would be demanded. However, in most single-period models, the exact demand is not known. In fact, forecasts may show that demand can have a wide variety of values. If we are going to analyze this type of inventory problem in a quantitative manner, we need information about the probabilities associated with the various demand values. Thus, the single-period model presented in this section is based on probabilistic demand.

## The Johnson Shoe Company Problem

Let us consider a single-period inventory model that could be used to make a how-much-to-order decision for the Johnson Shoe Company. The buyer for the Johnson Shoe Company has decided to order a shoe for men that has just been shown at a buyers' meeting in New York City. The shoe will be part of the company's spring-summer promotion and will be sold through nine retail stores in the Chicago area. Since the shoe is designed for spring and summer months, it cannot be expected to sell in the fall. Johnson plans to hold a special August clearance sale in an attempt to sell all shoes that have not been sold by July 31. The shoes cost $40 a pair and retail for $60 a pair. At the sale price of $30 a pair, all surplus shoes can be expected to sell during the August sale. If you were the buyer for the Johnson Shoe Company, how many pairs of the shoes would you order?

An obvious question at this time is, What are the possible values of demand for the shoe? We need this information to answer the question of how much to order. Let us suppose that the uniform probability distribution shown in Figure 11.7 can be used to describe the demand for the size 10D shoes. In particular, note that the range of demand is from 350 to 650 pairs of shoes, with an average, or expected, demand of 500 pairs of shoes.

**Incremental analysis** is a method that can be used to determine the optimal order quantity for a single-period inventory model. Incremental analysis addresses the how-much-to-order question by comparing the cost or loss of *ordering one additional unit* with the cost or loss of *not ordering one additional unit*. The costs involved are defined as follows:

$c_o$ = cost per unit of *overestimating* demand. This cost represents the loss of ordering one additional unit and finding that it cannot be sold.

$c_u$ = cost per unit of *underestimating* demand. This cost represents the opportunity loss of not ordering one additional unit and finding that it could have been sold.

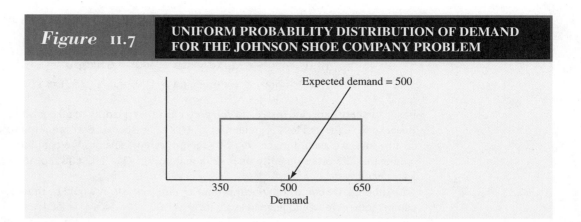

**Figure 11.7** UNIFORM PROBABILITY DISTRIBUTION OF DEMAND FOR THE JOHNSON SHOE COMPANY PROBLEM

The cost of underestimating demand is usually harder to determine than the cost of overestimating demand. The reason is that the cost of underestimating demand includes a lost profit and may include a customer goodwill cost because the customer is unable to purchase the item when desired.

In the Johnson Shoe Company problem, the company will incur the cost of overestimating demand whenever it orders too much and has to sell the extra shoes during the August sale. Thus, the cost per unit of overestimating demand is equal to the purchase cost per unit minus the August sales price per unit; that is, $c_o = \$40 - \$30 = \$10$. Therefore, Johnson will lose $10 for each pair of shoes that it orders over the quantity demanded. The cost of underestimating demand is the lost profit because a pair of shoes that could have been sold was not available in inventory. Thus, the per-unit cost of underestimating demand is the difference between the regular selling price per unit and the purchase cost per unit; that is, $c_u = \$60 - \$40 = \$20$.

Since the exact level of demand for the size 10D shoes is unknown, we have to consider the probability of demand and thus the probability of obtaining the associated costs or losses. For example, let us assume that Johnson Shoe Company management wishes to consider an order quantity equal to the average or expected demand for 500 pairs of shoes. In incremental analysis, we consider the possible losses associated with an order quantity of 501 (ordering one additional unit) and an order quantity of 500 (not ordering one additional unit). The order-quantity alternatives and the possible losses are summarized here.

| Order-Quantity Alternatives | Loss Occurs If | Possible Loss | Probability Loss Occurs |
|---|---|---|---|
| $Q = 501$ | Demand overestimated; the additional unit *cannot* be sold. | $c_o = \$10$ | $P(\text{demand} \leq 500)$ |
| $Q = 500$ | Demand underestimated; an additional unit *could have* been sold. | $c_u = \$20$ | $P(\text{demand} > 500)$ |

By looking at the demand probability distribution in Figure 11.7, we see that $P(\text{demand} \leq 500) = 0.50$ and that $P(\text{demand} > 500) = 0.50$. By multiplying the possible losses, $c_o = \$10$ and $c_u = \$20$, by the probability of obtaining the loss, we can compute the expected value of the loss, or simply the *expected loss* (EL), associated with the order-quantity alternatives. Thus

$$EL(Q = 501) = c_o P(\text{demand} \leq 500) = \$10(0.50) = \$5$$
$$EL(Q = 500) = c_u P(\text{demand} > 500) = \$20(0.50) = \$10$$

Based on these expected losses, do you prefer an order quantity of 501 or 500 pairs of shoes? Because the expected loss is greater for $Q = 500$, and because we want to avoid this higher cost or loss, we should make $Q = 501$ the preferred decision. We could now consider incrementing the order quantity one additional unit to $Q = 502$ and repeating the expected loss calculations.

Although we could continue this unit-by-unit analysis, it would be time-consuming and cumbersome. We would have to evaluate $Q = 502$, $Q = 503$, $Q = 504$, and so on, until we found the value of $Q$ where the expected loss of ordering one incremental unit is equal to the expected loss of not ordering one incremental unit; that is, the optimal order quantity $Q^*$ occurs when the incremental analysis shows that

$$EL(Q^* + 1) = EL(Q^*) \tag{11.29}$$

When this relationship holds, increasing the order quantity by one additional unit has no economic advantage. Using the logic with which we computed the expected losses for the order quantities of 501 and 500, the general expressions for $EL(Q^* + 1)$ and $EL(Q^*)$ can be written

$$EL(Q^* + 1) = c_o P(\text{demand} \leq Q^*) \tag{11.30}$$
$$EL(Q^*) = c_u P(\text{demand} > Q^*) \tag{11.31}$$

Because we know from basic probability that

$$P(\text{demand} \leq Q^*) + P(\text{demand} > Q^*) = 1 \tag{11.32}$$

we can write

$$P(\text{demand} > Q^*) = 1 - P(\text{demand} \leq Q^*) \tag{11.33}$$

Using this expression, equation (11.31) can be rewritten as

$$EL(Q^*) = c_u[1 - P(\text{demand} \leq Q^*)] \tag{11.34}$$

Equations (11.30) and (11.34) can be used to show that $EL(Q^* + 1) = EL(Q^*)$ whenever

$$c_o P(\text{demand} \leq Q^*) = c_u[1 - P(\text{demand} \leq Q^*)] \tag{11.35}$$

Solving for $P(\text{demand} \leq Q^*)$, we have

$$P(\text{demand} \leq Q^*) = \frac{c_u}{c_u + c_o} \tag{11.36}$$

This expression provides the general condition for the optimal order quantity $Q^*$ in the single-period inventory model.

In the Johnson Shoe Company problem $c_o = \$10$ and $c_u = \$20$. Thus, equation (11.36) shows that the optimal order size for Johnson shoes must satisfy the following condition:

$$P(\text{demand} \leq Q^*) = \frac{c_u}{c_u + c_o} = \frac{20}{20 + 10} = \frac{20}{30} = \frac{2}{3}$$

We can find the optimal order quantity $Q^*$ by referring to the assumed probability distribution shown in Figure 11.7 and finding the value of $Q$ that will provide $P(\text{demand} \leq Q^*) = \frac{2}{3}$. To find this solution, we note that in the uniform distribution the probability is evenly distributed over the entire range of 350–650 pairs of shoes. Thus, we can satisfy the expression for $Q^*$ by moving two-thirds of the way from 350 to 650. Since this range is $650 - 350 = 300$, we move 200 units from 350 toward 650. Doing so provides the optimal order quantity of 550 pairs of size 10D shoes.

In summary, the key to establishing an optimal order quantity for single-period inventory models is to identify the probability distribution that describes the demand for the item and the costs of overestimation and underestimation. Then, using the information for the costs of overestimation and underestimation, equation (11.36) can be used to find the location of $Q^*$ in the probability distribution.

### The Kremer Chemical Company Problem

As another example of a single-period inventory model with probabilistic demand, consider the situation faced by the Kremer Chemical Company. Kremer has a contract with one of its customers to supply a unique liquid chemical product. Historically, the customer places orders approximately every 6 months. Since a 2-month aging condition exists for the product, Kremer will have to make its production quantity decision before the customer places an order. Kremer's inventory problem is to determine the number of pounds of the chemical to produce in anticipation of the customer's order.

Kremer's manufacturing costs for the chemical are $15 per pound, and the product sells at the fixed contract price of $20 per pound. If Kremer underproduces, it will be unable to satisfy the customer's demand. If this condition occurs, Kremer has agreed to absorb the added cost of filling the order by purchasing a higher quality substitute product from another chemical firm. The substitute product, including additional transportation expenses, will cost Kremer $19 per pound. If Kremer overproduces, it will have more product in inventory than the customer requires. Because of the spoilage potential for the product, Kremer cannot store excess production until the customer's next order. As a result, Kremer reprocesses the excess production and sells the surplus for $5 per pound.

Based on previous experience with the customer's orders, Kremer believes that the normal probability distribution shown in Figure 11.8 best describes the possible demand. Note that the normal distribution shows an average or expected demand of $\mu = 1000$ pounds with a standard deviation of $\sigma = 100$ pounds. Using Kremer's price and cost data as well as the probability distribution of demand shown in Figure 11.8, how much production should Kremer plan for in anticipation of the customer's order for the liquid chemical?

Let us compute the cost of underestimation, $c_u$, and the cost of overestimation, $c_o$, as required for equation (11.36). First, if Kremer underproduces, it will have to purchase a substitute product at a higher cost per unit to satisfy the customer's demand for the product. Since the substitute product costs $19 per pound and Kremer could have manufactured the product for $15 per pound, a cost of $c_u = \$19 - \$15 = \$4$ exists for every pound of underestimated demand. If Kremer overestimates demand, the company incurs a cost of $15 per pound to manufacture the product and then sells the reprocessed excess product for

**Figure  11.8**    NORMAL PROBABILITY DISTRIBUTION OF DEMAND FOR THE KREMER CHEMICAL COMPANY PROBLEM

$5 per pound. Thus, Kremer has a per-unit cost of $c_o = \$15 - \$5 = \$10$ for overestimating demand.

Applying equation (11.36) indicates that the optimal order quantity must satisfy the following condition:

$$P(\text{demand} \le Q^*) = \frac{c_u}{c_u + c_o} = \frac{4}{4 + 10} = 0.29$$

We can use the normal probability distribution for demand as shown in Figure 11.9 to find the order quantity that satisfies the condition that $P(\text{demand} \le Q^*) = 0.29$. From Appendix B, we see that 0.29 of the area in the left tail of the curve of the normal probability distribution occurs at $z = 0.55$ standard deviations *below* the mean. Since the mean or expected demand is given by $\mu = 1000$ and the standard deviation is $\sigma = 100$, we have

> An example of a single-period inventory model with probabilistic demand described by a normal probability distribution is considered in Problem 25.

$$Q^* = \mu - 0.55\sigma$$
$$= 1000 - 0.55(100) = 945$$

**Figure  11.9**    PROBABILITY DISTRIBUTION OF DEMAND FOR THE KREMER CHEMICAL COMPANY PROBLEM SHOWING THE LOCATION OF THE OPTIMAL ORDER QUANTITY $Q^*$

Thus, with the assumed normal probability distribution of demand, the Kremer Chemical Company should produce 945 pounds of the chemical in anticipation of the customer's order. Note that in this case the cost of underestimation is less than the cost of overestimation. Thus, Kremer is willing to risk a higher probability of underestimation and hence a higher probability of a stockout. In fact, Kremer's optimal order quantity has a 0.29 probability of having a surplus and a $1 - 0.29 = 0.71$ probability of a stockout.

<table>
<tr><td>

N O T E S
***and Comments***

</td><td>

1. In any probabilistic inventory model, the assumption about the probability distribution for demand is critical and can affect the recommended inventory decision. In the problems presented in this section, we used the uniform and the normal probability distributions to describe demand. In some situations, other probability distributions may be more appropriate. In using probabilistic inventory models, we must exercise care in selecting the probability distribution that most realistically describes demand.

2. In the single-period inventory model, the value of $c_u/(c_u + c_o)$ plays a critical role in selecting the order quantity [see equation (11.36)]. Whenever $c_u = c_o$, $c_u/(c_u + c_o)$ equals 0.50; in this case, we should select an order quantity corresponding to the median demand. With this choice, a stockout is just as likely as a surplus because the two costs are equal. However, whenever $c_u < c_o$, a smaller order quantity will be recommended. In this case, the smaller order quantity will provide a higher probability of a stockout; however, the more expensive cost of overestimating demand and having a surplus will tend to be avoided. Finally, whenever $c_u > c_o$, a larger order quantity will be recommended. In this case, the larger order quantity provides a lower probability of a stockout in an attempt to avoid the more expensive cost of underestimating demand and experiencing a stockout.

</td></tr>
</table>

## 11.6    AN ORDER-QUANTITY, REORDER-POINT MODEL WITH PROBABILISTIC DEMAND

The inventory model in this section is based on the assumptions of the EOQ model shown in Table 11.3 with the exception that demand is probabilistic rather than deterministic. With probabilistic demand, occasional shortages may occur.

In the previous section we considered a single-period inventory model with probabilistic demand. In this section we extend our discussion to a multiperiod order-quantity, reorder-point inventory model with probabilistic demand. In the multiperiod model, the inventory system operates continuously with many repeating periods or cycles; inventory can be carried from one period to the next. Whenever the inventory position reaches the reorder point, an order for $Q$ units is placed. Since demand is probabilistic, the time the reorder point will be reached, the time between orders, and the time the order of $Q$ units will arrive in inventory cannot be determined in advance.

The inventory pattern for the order-quantity, reorder-point model with probabilistic demand will have the general appearance shown in Figure 11.10. Note that the increases or jumps in the inventory level occur whenever an order of $Q$ units arrives. The inventory level decreases at a nonconstant rate based on the probabilistic demand. A new order is placed whenever the reorder point is reached. At times, the order quantity of $Q$ units will arrive before inventory reaches zero. However, at other times, higher demand will cause a stockout

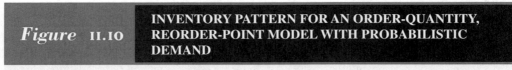

### Figure 11.10  INVENTORY PATTERN FOR AN ORDER-QUANTITY, REORDER-POINT MODEL WITH PROBABILISTIC DEMAND

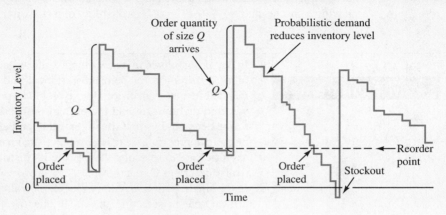

before a new order is received. As with other order-quantity, reorder-point models, the manager must determine the order quantity $Q$ and the reorder point $r$ for the inventory system.

The exact mathematical formulation of an order-quantity, reorder-point inventory model with probabilistic demand is beyond the scope of this text. However, we present a procedure that can be used to obtain good, workable order-quantity and reorder-point inventory policies. The solution procedure can be expected to provide only an approximation of the optimal solution, but it can yield good solutions in many practical situations.

Let us consider the inventory problem of Dabco Industrial Lighting Distributors. Dabco purchases a special high-intensity light bulb for industrial lighting systems from a well-known light bulb manufacturer. Dabco would like a recommendation on how much to order and when to order so that a low-cost inventory policy can be maintained. Pertinent facts are that the ordering cost is $12 per order, one bulb costs $6, and Dabco uses a 20% annual holding cost rate for its inventory ($C_h = IC = 0.20 \times \$6 = \$1.20$). Dabco, which has more than 1000 customers, experiences a probabilistic demand; in fact, the number of units demanded varies considerably from day to day and from week to week. The lead time for a new order of light bulbs is 1 week. Historical sales data indicate that demand during a 1-week lead time can be described by a normal probability distribution with a mean of 154 light bulbs and a standard deviation of 25 light bulbs. The normal distribution of demand during the lead time is shown in Figure 11.11. Because the mean demand during 1-week is 154 units, Dabco can anticipate a mean or expected annual demand of 154 units per week $\times$ 52 weeks per year = 8008 units per year.

### The How-Much-to-Order Decision

Although we are in a probabilistic demand situation, we have an estimate of the expected annual demand of 8008 units. We can apply the EOQ model from Section 11.1 as an approximation of the best order quantity, with the expected annual demand used for $D$. In Dabco's case

$$Q^* = \sqrt{\frac{2DC_o}{C_h}} = \sqrt{\frac{2(8008)(12)}{(1.20)}} = 400 \text{ units}$$

**Figure** 11.11    LEAD-TIME DEMAND PROBABILITY DISTRIBUTION FOR DABCO LIGHT BULBS

When we studied the sensitivity of the EOQ model, we learned that the total cost of operating an inventory system was relatively insensitive to order quantities that were in the neighborhood of $Q^*$. Using this knowledge, we expect 400 units per order to be a good approximation of the optimal order quantity. Even if annual demand were as low as 7000 units or as high as 9000 units, an order quantity of 400 units should be a relatively good low-cost order size. Thus, given our best estimate of annual demand at 8008 units, we will use $Q^* = 400$.

We have established the 400-unit order quantity by ignoring the fact that demand is probabilistic. Using $Q^* = 400$, Dabco can anticipate placing approximately $D/Q^* = 8008/400 = 20$ orders per year with an average of approximately $250/20 = 12.5$ working days between orders.

## The When-to-Order Decision

We now want to establish a when-to-order decision rule or reorder point that will trigger the ordering process. With a mean lead-time demand of 154 units, you might first suggest a 154-unit reorder point. However, considering the probability of demand now becomes extremely important. If 154 is the mean lead-time demand, and if demand is symmetrically distributed about 154, then the lead-time demand will be more than 154 units roughly 50% of the time. When the demand during the 1-week lead time exceeds 154 units, Dabco will experience a shortage or stockout. Thus, using a reorder point of 154 units, approximately 50% of the time (10 of the 20 orders a year) Dabco will be short of bulbs before the new supply arrives. This shortage rate would most likely be viewed as unacceptable.

The probability of a stockout during any one inventory cycle is easiest to estimate by first determining the number of orders that are expected during the year. The inventory manager can usually state a willingness to allow perhaps one, two, or three stockouts during the year. The allowable stockouts per year divided by the number of orders per year will provide the desired probability of a stockout.

Refer to the **lead-time demand distribution** shown in Figure 11.11. Given this distribution, we can now determine how the reorder point $r$ affects the probability of a stockout. Because stockouts occur whenever the demand during the lead time exceeds the reorder point, we can find the probability of a stockout by using the lead-time demand distribution to compute the probability that demand will exceed $r$.

We could now approach the when-to-order problem by defining a cost per stockout and then attempting to include this cost in a total-cost equation. Alternatively, we can ask management to specify the average number of stockouts that can be tolerated per year. If demand for a product is probabilistic, a manager who will never tolerate a stockout is being somewhat unrealistic because attempting to avoid stockouts completely will require high reorder points, high inventory levels, and an associated high holding cost.

Suppose in this case that Dabco management is willing to tolerate an average of one stockout per year. Since Dabco places 20 orders per year, this decision implies that management is willing to allow demand during lead time to exceed the reorder point one time in 20, or 5% of the time. The reorder point $r$ can be found by using the lead-time demand distribution to find the value of $r$ with a 5% chance of having a lead-time demand that will exceed it. This situation is shown graphically in Figure 11.12.

From the standard normal probability distribution table in Appendix B, we see that the $r$ value is 1.645 standard deviations above the mean. Therefore, for the assumed normal distribution for lead-time demand with $\mu = 154$ and $\sigma = 25$, the reorder point $r$ is

$$r = 154 + 1.645(25) = 195$$

If a normal distribution is used for lead-time demand, the general equation for $r$ is

$$r = \mu + z\sigma \qquad\qquad (11.37)$$

where $z$ is the number of standard deviations necessary to obtain the acceptable stockout probability.

Thus, the recommended inventory decision is to order 400 units whenever the inventory level reaches the reorder point of 195. Since the mean or expected demand during the lead time is 154 units, the $195 - 154 = 41$ units serve as a safety stock, which absorbs higher-than-usual demand during the lead time. Roughly 95% of the time, the 195 units will be able to satisfy demand during the lead time. The anticipated annual cost for this system is as follows:

| | | |
|---|---|---|
| Ordering cost | $(D/Q)C_o = (8008/400)12 =$ | $240.24 |
| Holding cost, normal inventory | $(Q/2)C_h = (400/2)(1.20) =$ | $240.00 |
| Holding cost, safety stock | $(41)C_h = \quad 41(1.20) \quad =$ | $ 49.20 |
| | Total | $529.44 |

*Try Problem 29 as an example of an order-quantity, reorder-point model with probabilistic demand.*

If Dabco could have assumed that a known, constant demand rate of 8008 units per year existed for the light bulbs, then $Q^* = 400$, $r = 154$, and a total annual cost of $240 + $240 = $480 would have been optimal. When demand is uncertain and can only

*Figure* **11.12**     **REORDER POINT $r$ THAT ALLOWS A 5% CHANCE OF A STOCKOUT FOR DABCO LIGHT BULBS**

be expressed in probabilistic terms, a larger total cost can be expected. The larger cost occurs in the form of larger holding costs because more inventory must be maintained to limit the number of stockouts. For Dabco, this additional inventory or safety stock was 41 units, with an additional annual holding cost of $49.20. The Management Science in Action: Information from a Netherlands Supplier Lowers Inventory Cost describes how a warehouser in the Netherlands has implemented an order-quantity, reorder-point system with probabilistic demand.

## MANAGEMENT SCIENCE IN ACTION

### INFORMATION FROM A NETHERLANDS SUPPLIER LOWERS INVENTORY COST*

In the Netherlands, companies such as Philips, Rank Xerox, and Fokker have followed the trend of developing closer relations between the firm and its suppliers. As teamwork, coordination, and information sharing improve, opportunities are available for better cost control in the operation of inventory systems.

One Dutch public warehouser has a contract with its supplier under which the supplier routinely provides information regarding the status and schedule of upcoming production runs. The warehouser's inventory system operates as an order-quantity, reorder-point system with probabilistic demand. When the order-quantity, $Q$ has been determined, the warehouser selects the desired reorder point for the product. The distribution of the lead-time demand is essential in determining the reorder point. Usually, the lead-time demand distribution is approx-

imated directly, taking into account both the probabilistic demand and the probabilistic length of the lead-time period.

The supplier's information concerning scheduled production runs provides the warehouser with a better understanding of the lead time involved for a product and the resulting lead-time demand distribution. With this information, the warehouse can modify the reorder point accordingly. Information sharing by the supplier thus enables the order-quantity, reorder-point system to operate with a lower inventory holding cost.

*Based on F. A. van der Duyn Schouten, M. J. G. van Eijs, and R. M. J. Heuts, "The Value of Supplier Information to Improve Management of a Retailer's Inventory," *Decision Sciences*, vol. 25, no. 1 (January–February 1994): 1–14.

### NOTES *and Comments*

The Dabco reorder point was based on a 5% probability of a stockout during the lead-time period. Thus, on 95% of all order cycles Dabco will be able to satisfy customer demand without experiencing a stockout. Defining *service level* as the percentage of all order cycles that do not experience a stockout, we would say that Dabco has a 95% service level. However, other definitions of service level may include the percentage of all customer demand that can be satisfied from inventory. Thus, when an inventory manager expresses a desired service level, clarify exactly what the manager means by the term *service level*.

## 11.7    A PERIODIC-REVIEW MODEL WITH PROBABILISTIC DEMAND

The order-quantity, reorder-point inventory models previously discussed require a **continuous-review** inventory system. In a continuous-review inventory system, the inventory position is monitored continuously so that an order can be placed whenever the reorder point is reached. Computerized inventory systems can easily provide the continuous review required by the order-quantity, reorder-point models.

An alternative to the continuous-review system is the **periodic-review inventory system.** With a periodic-review system, the inventory level is checked and reordering is done only at specified points in time. For example, inventory levels may be checked and orders placed on a weekly, biweekly, monthly, or some other periodic basis. When a firm or business handles multiple products, the periodic-review system has the advantage of requiring that orders for several items be placed at the same preset periodic-review time. With this type of inventory system, the shipping and receiving of orders for multiple products are easily coordinated. Under the previously discussed order-quantity, reorder-point systems, the reorder points for various products can be encountered at substantially different points in time, making the coordination of orders for multiple products more difficult.

To illustrate this system, let us consider Dollar Discounts, a firm with several retail stores that carry a wide variety of products for household use. The company operates its inventory system with a two-week periodic review. Under this system, a retail store manager may order any number of units of any product from the Dollar Discounts central warehouse every two weeks. Orders for all products going to a particular store are combined into one shipment. When making the order-quantity decision for each product at a given review period, the store manager knows that a reorder for the product cannot be made until the next review period.

Assuming that the lead time is less than the length of the review period, an order placed at a review period will be received prior to the next review period. In this case, the how-much-to-order decision at any review period is determined using the following:

$$Q = M - H \qquad\qquad (11.38)$$

where

$$Q = \text{the order quantity}$$
$$M = \text{the replenishment level}$$
$$H = \text{the inventory on hand at the review period}$$

Because the demand is probabilistic, the inventory on hand at the review period, $H$, will vary. Thus, the order quantity that must be sufficient to bring the inventory position back to its maximum or replenishment level $M$ can be expected to vary each period. For example, if the replenishment level for a particular product is 50 units, and the inventory on hand at the review period is $H = 12$ units, an order of $Q = M - H = 50 - 12 = 38$ units should be made. Thus, under the periodic-review model, enough units are ordered each review period to bring the inventory position back up to the replenishment level.

A typical inventory pattern for a periodic-review system with probabilistic demand is shown in Figure 11.13. Note that the time between periodic reviews is predetermined and fixed. The order quantity Q at each review period can vary and is shown to be the difference between the replenishment level and the inventory on hand. Finally, as with other probabilistic models, an unusually high demand can result in an occasional stockout.

The decision variable in the periodic-review model is the replenishment level $M$. To determine $M$, we could begin by developing a total-cost model, including holding, ordering, and stockout costs. Instead, we describe an approach that is often used in practice. In this approach, the objective is to determine a replenishment level that will meet a desired performance level, such as a reasonably low probability of stockout or a reasonably low number of stockouts per year.

In the Dollar Discounts problem, we assume that management's objective is to determine the replenishment level with only a 1% chance of a stockout. In the periodic-review

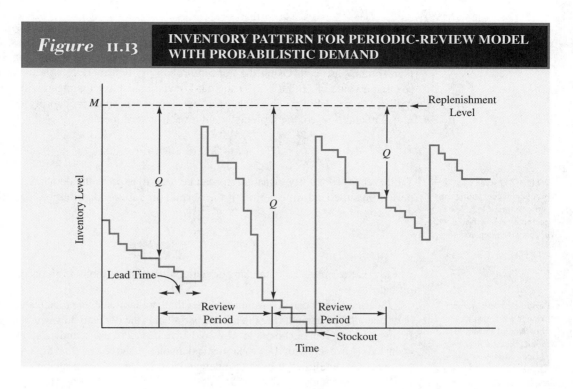

**Figure 11.13**  INVENTORY PATTERN FOR PERIODIC-REVIEW MODEL WITH PROBABILISTIC DEMAND

model, the order quantity at each review period must be sufficient to cover demand for the *review period plus the demand for the following lead time.* That is, the order quantity that brings the inventory position up to the replenishment level *M* must last until the order made at the next review period is received in inventory. The length of this time is equal to the review period plus the lead time. Figure 11.14 shows the normal probability distribution of demand during the review period plus the lead-time period for one of the Dollar Discounts products. The mean demand is 250 units, and the standard deviation of demand is 45 units. Given this situation, the logic used to establish *M* is similar to the logic used to establish

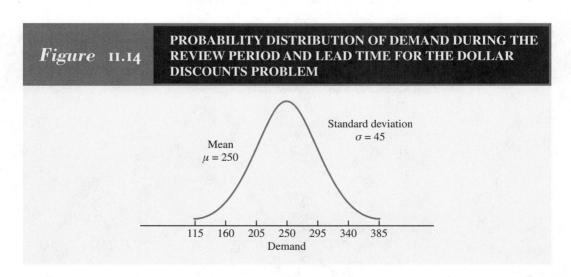

**Figure 11.14**  PROBABILITY DISTRIBUTION OF DEMAND DURING THE REVIEW PERIOD AND LEAD TIME FOR THE DOLLAR DISCOUNTS PROBLEM

the reorder point in Section 11.6. Figure 11.15 shows the replenishment level $M$ with a 1% chance that demand will exceed that replenishment level. In other words, Figure 11.15 shows the replenishment level that allows a 1% chance of a stockout associated with the replenishment decision. Using the normal probability distribution table in Appendix B, we see that a value of $M$ that is 2.33 standard deviations above the mean will allow stockouts with a 1% probability. Therefore, for the assumed normal probability distribution with $\mu = 250$ and $\sigma = 45$, the replenishment level is determined by

$$M = 250 + 2.33(45) = 355$$

Problem 33 gives you practice in computing the replenishment level for a periodic-review model with probabilistic demand.

While other probability distributions can be used to express the demand during the review period plus the lead-time period, if the normal probability distribution is used, the general expression for $M$ is

$$M = \mu + z\sigma \tag{11.39}$$

where $z$ is the number of standard deviations necessary to obtain the acceptable stockout probability.

Periodic-review systems provide advantages of coordinated orders for multiple items. However, periodic-review systems require larger safety stock levels than corresponding continuous-review systems.

If demand had been deterministic rather than probabilistic, the replenishment level would have been the demand during the review period plus the demand during the lead-time period. In this case, the replenishment level would have been 250 units, and no stockout would have occurred. However, with the probabilistic demand, we have seen that higher inventory levels are necessary to allow for uncertain demand and to control the probability of a stockout. In the Dollar Discounts problem, $355 - 250 = 105$ is the safety stock that is necessary to absorb any higher-than-usual demand during the review period plus the demand during the lead-time period. This safety stock limits the probability of a stockout to 1%. The Management Science in Action: Inventory Model Helps Hewlett-Packard's Product Design for Worldwide Markets describes a periodic-review inventory system at Hewlett-Packard.

### More Complex Periodic-Review Models

The periodic-review model that we have just discussed is one approach to determining a replenishment level for the periodic-review inventory system with probabilistic demand. More complex versions of the periodic-review model incorporate a reorder point as another deci-

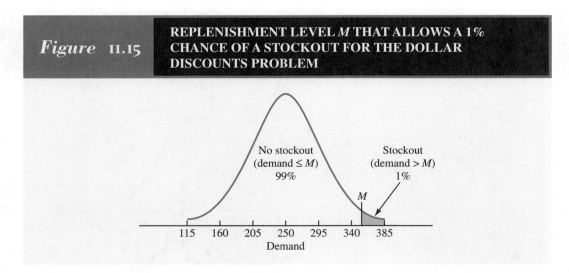

**Figure 11.15**    REPLENISHMENT LEVEL $M$ THAT ALLOWS A 1% CHANCE OF A STOCKOUT FOR THE DOLLAR DISCOUNTS PROBLEM

sion variable. That is, instead of ordering at every periodic review, a reorder point is established. If the inventory on hand at the periodic review is at or below the reorder point, a decision is made to order up to the replenishment level. However, if the inventory on hand at the periodic review is greater than the reorder level, such an order is not placed, and the system continues until the next periodic review. In this case, the cost of ordering is a relevant cost and can be included in a cost model along with holding and stockout costs. Optimal policies can be reached based on minimizing the expected total cost. Situations with lead times longer than the review period add to the complexity of the model. The mathematical level required to treat these more extensive periodic-review models is beyond the scope of this text.

## MANAGEMENT SCIENCE IN ACTION

### INVENTORY MODEL HELPS HEWLETT-PACKARD'S PRODUCT DESIGN FOR WORLDWIDE MARKETS*

Product design always affects the efficiency of manufacturing operations. At Hewlett-Packard's Vancouver, Washington, division, managers are also learning how product design affects product customization, distribution, and delivery to worldwide markets. In most cases, different markets require different product configurations because of language, environment, and/or government regulations. Should Hewlett-Packard design variations of each product to meet the unique requirements of each market, or should it design a more general product with product customization being completed in the local market area?

An inventory model was used to study the inventory levels and costs associated with the product design alternatives for the Hewlett-Packard Deskjet-Plus printer. Inventory levels for the printer are maintained on a periodic-review basis. Planners review the inventory position (on-hand inventory plus inventory in the pipeline) weekly. Orders are placed for quantities needed to return the inventory position to the target inventory level. Demand during the lead time is assumed to follow a normal probability distribution.

The inventory model projected the inventory cost associated with each product design alternative. As a result, Hewlett-Packard's Vancouver, Washington, division redesigned its products to support final customization of the product at the local distribution center level. The inventory model projected an 18% reduction in the total inventory investment, which saved millions of dollars.

*Based on H. L. Lee, C. Billington, and B. Carter, "Hewlett-Packard Gains Control of Inventory and Service through Design for Localization," *Interfaces*, vol. 23, no. 4 (July–August 1993): 1–11.

### NOTES
### *and Comments*

1. The periodic-review model presented in this section is based on the assumption that the lead time for an order is less than the periodic-review period. Most periodic-review systems operate under this condition. However, the case in which the lead time is longer than the review period can be handled by defining $H$ in equation (11.38) as the inventory position, where $H$ includes the inventory on hand plus the inventory on order. In this case, the order quantity at any review period is the amount needed for the inventory on hand plus *all* outstanding orders needed to reach the replenishment level.

2. In the order-quantity, reorder-point model discussed in Section 11.6, a continuous review was used to initiate an order whenever the reorder point was reached. The safety stock for this model was based on the probabilistic demand during the lead time. The periodic-review model presented in this section also determined a recommended safety stock. However, since the inventory review was only periodic, the safety stock was based on the probabilistic demand during the *review period plus the lead-time period*. This longer period for the safety stock computation means that periodic-review systems tend to require a larger safety stock than do continuous-review systems.

## II.8 MATERIAL REQUIREMENTS PLANNING

The inventory models we have discussed thus far have been found to be most appropriate for managing the inventories of finished goods. Finished goods are characterized as having **independent demands** that may be forecast. In this section we focus on the planning and controlling of manufacturing inventories such as raw materials, components, and subassemblies. The demand for these types of items is **dependent** on the amounts of finished goods that are scheduled to be produced and can be *calculated* from the forecasts and scheduled production of finished goods. A technique that can be used to manage dependent demand inventories is called **material requirements planning (MRP).**

### Dependent Demand and the MRP Concept

To illustrate dependent demand and the MRP concept, consider a finished product that is manufactured using a single component that is purchased from an outside supplier. The demand for the finished product consists of many independent demands from many customers. Because these demands occur somewhat randomly, the demand rate is often fairly constant, and the assumptions of the production lot size model are reasonable. The inventory level for the finished product is shown at the top of Figure 11.16. When produc-

**Figure 11.16 — FINISHED PRODUCT AND COMPONENT PART INVENTORY LEVELS WITHOUT AN MRP SYSTEM**

tion of the finished product is initiated (point A on the time axis), the component parts are withdrawn from inventory in order to meet the manufacturing needs. The inventory level of the component part is shown at the bottom of Figure 11.16. When the component inventory level falls below its reorder point, an order for the component is placed with the supplier. The shipment is received at point B, and the component inventory is replenished. However, note that the component is not needed again until the next production run for the finished product, which is scheduled to occur at point C. Clearly, the investment in the component inventory from points B to C is unnecessary. We can eliminate this unnecessary component inventory by "backing up" from point C according to the purchase lead time so that the components will arrive just at time C. This situation is illustrated in Figure 11.17. Note that the component inventory level and corresponding inventory investment are less in Figure 11.17 than in Figure 11.16.

The philosophy of basing component inventory orders on the demand and production needs of other items is the approach followed by MRP. When operating properly, the MRP system will reduce inventory investment, improve work flow, reduce the shortage of materials and components, and help achieve more reliable delivery schedules.

## Information System for MRP

What makes the MRP process difficult to implement is that many finished products consist of dozens or hundreds of parts, many of which are in turn dependent on other parts. Therefore, there must be accurate data and a reliable computer information system to perform the many calculations required for MRP.

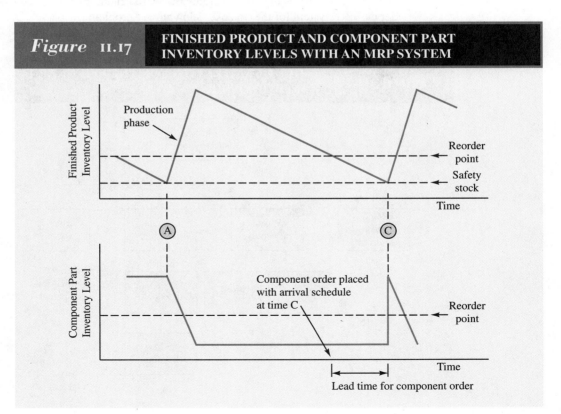

*Figure* 11.17   **FINISHED PRODUCT AND COMPONENT PART INVENTORY LEVELS WITH AN MRP SYSTEM**

Material requirements planning calculations begin with the **master production schedule,** which states the number of units of each finished product to be produced during each time period. With the information in the master production schedule, we can begin to determine when the various components that make up the final products must be available. Thus, the next step will be to identify the list of components that are required by the products. This information is available from the **bill of materials (BOM).**

The BOM is a structured parts list; however, it differs from an ordinary parts list in that it shows the hierarchical relationship between the finished product and its various components. An example of a BOM for the Spiecker Company is shown in Figure 11.18. This figure shows the bill of materials for a 14-inch snowblower. The finished product is shown at the top of the hierarchy (called level 0). It consists of one main housing assembly, one wheel assembly, one engine assembly, and one handle assembly. If we consider the BOM as a "family tree," then the 14-inch snowblower is the "parent" item for each of these assemblies. These assemblies, in turn, are parent items for all the components included in them. Thus, the wheel assembly is the parent item of one blade assembly and two wheels. In general, items at level $k$ are parent items for components at level $k + 1$. From the BOM, we can determine exactly how many components are needed to produce the quantity of finished products stated in the master production schedule.

A schematic diagram of an MRP information system is given in Figure 11.19. Forecasts and orders are used to develop the master production schedule. The master production schedule, BOM, and current inventory files are the inputs needed to begin the MRP computations. The outputs from the MRP system are the requirements for each item in the BOM along with the dates each item is needed. This information is used to plan order releases for production and purchasing. To illustrate how these calculations are performed, let us consider an MRP system for the Spiecker snowblower problem.

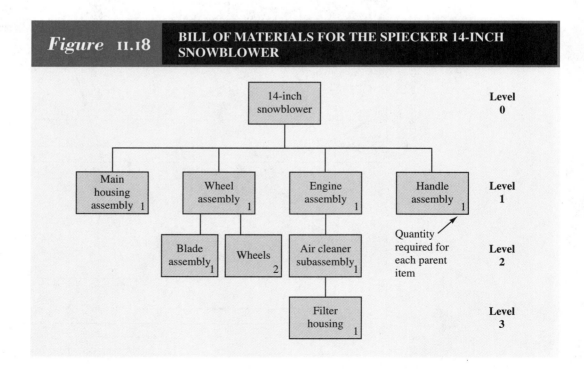

**Figure 11.18    BILL OF MATERIALS FOR THE SPIECKER 14-INCH SNOWBLOWER**

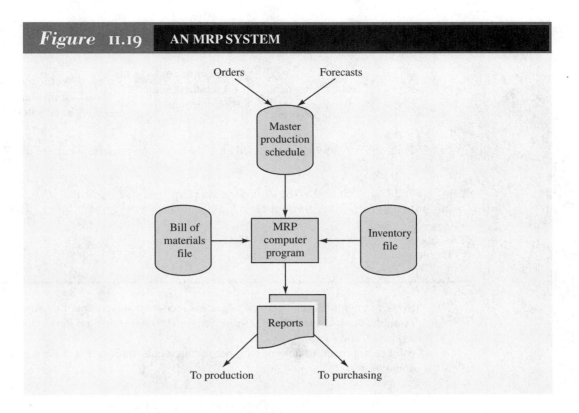

## Figure 11.19 — AN MRP SYSTEM

## MRP Calculations

In MRP terminology, the time periods, which are called *buckets,* are often 1 week in length. Buckets, such as 1 week, are good for scheduling production over a short time horizon but may be too precise for long-range planning; larger buckets are used as the planning horizon gets longer. However, for the Spiecker Manufacturing problem, we assume that all buckets are 1 week in length.

The master production schedule calls for the final assembly of 1250 units of the 14-inch snowblower during week 21 of the current planning period. The assembly lead time is 1 week; thus, to meet this schedule, the four main assemblies in the bill of materials must be completed no later than the end of week 20. We now examine the production and inventory control aspects for the engine assembly in detail, concentrating on how the MRP approach can be applied. Relevant data regarding the number of units in inventory and lead time are given in Table 11.5.

## Table 11.5 — INVENTORY ON HAND AND LEAD TIME FOR THE SPIECKER MANUFACTURING PROBLEM

| Component | Units in Inventory | Lead Time (weeks) |
|---|---|---|
| Engine assembly | 450 | 4 |
| Air cleaner subassembly | 250 | 1 |
| Filter housing | 500 | 2 |

Before the advent of MRP, the net requirement for each component was often found using the following formula:

$$\text{Net component requirement} = \left(\begin{array}{c}\text{Number of components}\\\text{required to meet}\\\text{demand for}\\\text{finished good}\end{array}\right) - \left(\begin{array}{c}\text{Number of}\\\text{components}\\\text{in inventory}\end{array}\right)$$

Thus, the net requirements, based on 1250 snowblowers, are calculated as follows:

| Components | Number of Components Required to Meet Demand for 1250 Snowblowers | Number in Inventory | Net Requirement |
|---|---|---|---|
| Engines | 1250 | 450 | 800 |
| Air cleaners | 1250 | 250 | 1000 |
| Filter housings | 1250 | 500 | 750 |

However, note that this approach does not recognize the nature of dependent demand; for example, the number of filter housings required is dependent on the number of air cleaners produced, and so on.

The approach to determining net requirements whenever a dependent demand situation exists is

$$\text{Net component requirement} = \left(\begin{array}{c}\text{Gross component}\\\text{requirement}\end{array}\right) - \left(\begin{array}{c}\text{Scheduled}\\\text{receipts}\end{array}\right) - \left(\begin{array}{c}\text{Number of}\\\text{components}\\\text{in inventory}\end{array}\right)$$

where the gross component requirement is the quantity of the component needed to support production at the next higher level of assembly. For example, the gross component requirement for the filter housing is the number of filter housings required to meet the net requirement for the air cleaner subassembly; the gross component requirement for the air cleaner subassembly is the number of air cleaners needed to meet the net requirement for the engine assembly; and so on. Let us see how these requirements can be computed for Spiecker Manufacturing. (We assume, for simplicity, that scheduled receipts are zero.)

The computation of MRP net requirements is the subject of Problem 37.

| | Units | |
|---|---|---|
| Quantity of snowblowers to be produced: | 1250 | |
| Gross requirements, engines: | 1250 | |
| Less engines in inventory: | 450 | |
| *Net requirements, engines:* | 800 | ← Engines |
| Gross requirements, air cleaners: | 800 | |
| Less air cleaners in inventory: | 250 | |
| *Net requirements, air cleaners:* | 550 | ← Air cleaners |
| Gross requirements, filter housings: | 550 | |
| Less filter housings in inventory: | 500 | |
| *Net requirements, filter housings:* | 50 | ← Filter housings |

A primary function of material requirements planning is to convert gross requirements into net requirements. Once the net requirements are established, shop orders and purchase orders can be issued to cover the net requirements.

While the net requirement for engines under the MRP approach is still 800 units, note how MRP has used the dependent-demand information to show that fewer air cleaners and filter housings will be needed. In addition to considering dependent demand in the determination of net requirements for components, an MRP system also determines when the net requirements are needed. MRP handles this aspect of production and inventory control using the **time-phasing** concept. By starting with the time that the finished product must be completed, we can work backward to determine when an order for each component must be placed. For example, the time-phasing calculations for the Spiecker snowblower problem might appear as follows:

|                                              | Week |                        |
|----------------------------------------------|------|------------------------|
| Complete order for engines:                  | 20   |                        |
| Minus lead time for engines:                 | 4    |                        |
| *Place an order for engines:*                | 16   | ← Order engines        |
| Complete order for air cleaners:             | 16   |                        |
| Minus lead time for air cleaners:            | 1    |                        |
| *Place an order for air cleaners:*           | 15   | ← Order air cleaners   |
| Complete order for filter housings:          | 15   |                        |
| Minus lead time for filter housings:         | 2    |                        |
| *Placing an order for filter housings:*      | 13   | ← Order filter housings|

The components are scheduled so that they are made available only when required for the next higher level of assembly. Similar calculations can be made for all the other components of the snowblower, and if the bill of materials is exploded into detailed part requirements, a complete schedule for shop orders and purchase requisitions is available.

Until the development of large-scale computers, the sheer volume of calculations prohibited the implementation of an MRP system. For example, even in our small illustration, you can begin to appreciate the complexity involved in keeping track of the production and inventory status for every component.

## 11.9   THE JUST-IN-TIME APPROACH TO INVENTORY MANAGEMENT

The Japanese have captured a sizable share of world markets for many products because of the progress they have made in manufacturing. Among the reasons for this success are the Japanese style of management, the development of new technologies, and the use of new methods of material management and control. One method that has received much attention is known as **just-in-time (JIT)**. JIT represents a philosophy whose objective is the elimination of all sources of waste including unnecessary inventory.

The fundamental principle of JIT is to produce the right units in the right quantity at the right time. With JIT, units are produced only when they are required. Inventories are not needed, or are at least minimized. For JIT to function effectively, fundamental changes in traditional production systems must take place. These changes require modifications in the production layout design and material flow process; in addition, setup times must be reduced.

Poor equipment layout is one of the major causes of inefficiencies in manufacturing. In a typical U.S. manufacturing environment, material is transported from the supplier to the warehouse and then to the plant. Within the plant, material may be transported from department to department. When production is completed, the finished goods may be returned to the warehouse, where they are stored until later distribution to the customer. Even with optimal inventory models, inventory and material handling costs can be substantial. The JIT approach helps reduce inventory and material handling costs by providing a flow of raw materials and finished goods in which material introduced at one end of the manufacturing process moves without delays into the finished products.

The driving force behind JIT production is the coordination of successive production activities. A key component of this coordination is an information system called a **kanban**—the Japanese word for *card*. The type and number of units required by the production process are written on kanbans, which are used to initiate the withdrawal and the production of units through the production process. By beginning at the final assembly, the kanban "pulls" parts and components from preceding work stations. Thus, the entire manufacturing operation is synchronized to the final assembly stage. In this fashion, JIT prohibits earlier sources of supply and production from "pushing" units forward and building unnecessary and excessive inventories.

It is important to realize that the total quality concept is critical in the implementation of the JIT philosophy. Because lot sizes are small and inventory levels are minimal, this method provides no safety stock to replace nonconforming or defective units. Any quality problems disrupt the flow of materials throughout the plant and can be disastrous to the JIT system.

Finally, the coordination of the materials flow from suppliers to the manufacturer is another critical component of JIT. The JIT philosophy does not permit the shipment of large lots from suppliers that would build unnecessarily high inventory levels and costs. To maintain the smooth flow required by JIT, suppliers must make just-in-time deliveries. Instead of the large shipments that must be counted, inspected, and stored, suppliers make smaller deliveries on a daily basis or even more frequently as necessary to accommodate the manufacturer's daily production schedule. JIT requires a close partnership between the suppliers and the manufacturer to enable materials to be obtained on time and with zero defects.

The benefits of JIT are improved profits, resulting from reduced inventory costs, and improved quality. In the area of inventory management, the more obvious benefits of JIT are the reduced inventory levels, the increased inventory turnover, and the overall lower holding costs.

## SUMMARY

In this chapter we presented some of the approaches management scientists use to assist managers in establishing low-cost inventory policies. We first considered cases where the demand rate for the product is constant. In analyzing these inventory systems, total-cost models were developed, which included ordering costs, holding costs, and, in some cases, backordering costs. Then minimum-cost formulas for the order quantity $Q$ were presented. A reorder point $r$ can be established by considering the lead-time demand.

In addition, we discussed inventory models where a deterministic and constant rate could not be assumed, and thus, demand was described by a probability distribution. A critical issue with these probabilistic inventory models is obtaining a probability distribution that most realistically approximates the demand distribution. We first described a single-period model where only one order is placed for the product and, at the end of the period, either the product has sold out or there is a surplus of unsold products that will be sold for a salvage value. Solution procedures were then presented for multiperiod models based on either an order-quantity, reorder-point, continuous-review system or a replenishment-level, periodic-review system.

We pointed out that the models presented in the earlier sections of the chapter are for independent-demand situations and are most applicable for managing finished goods inventory. For manufacturing inventories of subassemblies and component parts, where dependent demand exists, methods such as material requirements planning (MRP) offer significant advantages. Finally, we discussed the just-in-time philosophy that has evolved from the Japanese approach to material management and control. In inventory management, JIT is directed at reducing inventory levels and increasing inventory turnover.

In closing this chapter, we reemphasize that inventory and inventory systems can be an expensive phase of a firm's operation. It is of utmost economic importance for managers to be aware of the cost of inventory systems and to make the best possible operating policy decisions for the inventory system. Inventory models, as presented in this chapter, can help managers to develop good inventory policies.

## GLOSSARY

**Economic order quantity (EOQ)**  The order quantity that minimizes the annual holding cost plus the annual ordering cost.

**Constant demand rate**  An assumption of many inventory models that states that the same number of units are taken from inventory each period of time.

**Holding cost**  The cost associated with maintaining an inventory investment, including the cost of the capital investment in the inventory, insurance, taxes, warehouse overhead, and so on. This cost may be stated as a percentage of the inventory investment or as a cost per unit.

**Cost of capital**  The cost a firm incurs to obtain capital for investment. It may be stated as an annual percentage rate, and it is part of the holding cost associated with maintaining inventory levels.

**Ordering cost**  The fixed cost (salaries, paper, transportation, etc.) associated with placing an order for an item.

**Inventory position**  The inventory on hand plus the inventory on order.

**Reorder point**  The inventory position at which a new order should be placed.

**Lead time**  The time between the placing of an order and its receipt in the inventory system.

**Lead-time demand**  The number of units demanded during the lead-time period.

**Cycle time**  The length of time between the placing of two consecutive orders.

**Safety stock**  Inventory maintained in order to reduce the number of stockouts resulting from higher-than-expected demand.

**Constant supply rate**  A situation in which the inventory is built up at a constant rate over a period of time.

**Lot size**  The order quantity in the production inventory model.

**Setup cost**  The fixed cost (labor, materials, lost production) associated with preparing for a new production run.

**Backorder** The receipt of an order for a product when no units are in inventory. These backorders become shortages, which are eventually satisfied when a new supply of the product becomes available.

**Goodwill cost** A cost associated with a backorder, a lost sale, or any form of stockout or unsatisfied demand. This cost may be used to reflect the loss of future profits because a customer experienced an unsatisfied demand.

**Quantity discounts** Discounts or lower unit costs offered by the manufacturer when a customer purchases larger quantities of the product.

**Deterministic inventory model** A model where demand is considered known and not subject to uncertainty.

**Probabilistic inventory model** A model where demand is not known exactly; probabilities must be associated with the possible values for demand.

**Single-period inventory model** An inventory model in which only one order is placed for the product, and at the end of the period either the item has sold out, or a surplus of unsold items will be sold for a salvage value.

**Incremental analysis** A method used to determine an optimal order quantity by comparing the cost of ordering an additional unit with the cost of not ordering an additional unit.

**Lead-time demand distribution** The distribution of demand that occurs during the lead-time period.

**Continuous-review inventory system** A system in which the inventory position is monitored or reviewed on a continuous basis so that a new order can be placed as soon as the reorder point is reached.

**Periodic-review inventory system** A system in which the inventory position is checked or reviewed at predetermined periodic points in time. Reorders are placed only at periodic-review points.

**Independent demand** Demand for an item that is independent of the demand for other products or items. Usually independent demand is generated by customers placing orders for finished goods.

**Dependent demand** Demand for a product, component, subassembly, or item that is dependent on the demand for another product or item.

**Material requirements planning (MRP)** A computerized inventory management system whose functions are to schedule production and to control the level of inventory for components with dependent demand.

**Master production schedule** A statement of how many finished items are to be produced, and when.

**Bill of materials (BOM)** A structured parts list that shows the manner in which the product is put together.

**Time phasing** Adding the dimension of time to inventory status data in an MRP environment.

**Just-in-time** A philosophy that encourages the elimination of waste in time and resources. In inventory management, JIT works to reduce inventory levels and increase inventory turnover.

**Kanban** The Japanese word for *card,* which refers to the information system used for implementing JIT.

## PROBLEMS

**SELF TEST**

**1.** Suppose that the R & B Beverage Company has a soft drink product that has a constant annual demand rate of 3600 cases. A case of the soft drink costs R & B $3. Ordering costs are $20 per order and holding costs are 25% of the value of the inventory. R & B has 250 working days per year, and the lead time is 5 days. Identify the following aspects of the inventory policy.
   a. Economic order quantity
   b. Reorder point
   c. Cycle time
   d. Total annual cost

**2.** A general property of the EOQ inventory model is that total inventory holding and total ordering costs are equal at the optimal solution. Use the data in Problem 1 to show that this result is true. Use equations (11.1), (11.2), and (11.3) to show that, in general, total holding costs and total ordering costs are equal whenever $Q^*$ is used.

**3.** The reorder point [see equation (11.6)] is defined as the lead-time demand for an item. In cases of long lead times, the lead-time demand and thus the reorder point may exceed the economic order quantity $Q^*$. In such cases, the inventory position will not equal the inventory on hand when an order is placed, and the reorder point may be expressed in terms of either the inventory position or the inventory on hand. Consider the economic order quantity model with $D = 5000$, $C_o = \$32$, $C_h = \$2$, and 250 working days per year. Identify the reorder point in terms of the inventory position and in terms of the inventory on hand for each of the following lead times.
   a. 5 days
   b. 15 days
   c. 25 days
   d. 45 days

**4.** Westside Auto purchases a component used in the manufacture of automobile generators directly from the supplier. Westside's generator production operation, which is operated at a constant rate, will require 1000 components per month throughout the year (12,000 units annually). Assume that the ordering costs are $25 per order, the unit cost is $2.50 per component, and that annual holding costs are 20% of the value of the inventory. Westside has 250 working days per year, and the lead time is 5 days. Answer the following inventory policy questions.
   a. What is the EOQ for this component?
   b. What is the reorder point?
   c. What is the cycle time?
   d. What are the total annual holding and ordering costs associated with your recommended EOQ?

**5.** Suppose that Westside's management in Problem 4 likes the operational efficiency of ordering once each month and in quantities of 1000 units. How much more expensive would this policy be than your EOQ recommendation? Would you recommend in favor of the 1000-unit order quantity? Explain. What would the reorder point be if the 1000-unit quantity were acceptable?

**6.** Tele-Reco is a new specialty store that sells television sets, videotape recorders, video games, and other television-related products. A new Japanese-manufactured videotape recorder costs Tele-Reco $600 per unit. Tele-Reco's annual holding cost rate is 22%. Ordering costs are estimated to be $70 per order.
   a. If demand for the new videotape recorder is expected to be constant with a rate of 20 units per month, what is the recommended order quantity for the videotape recorder?
   b. What are the estimated annual inventory holding and ordering costs associated with this product?
   c. How many orders will be placed per year?
   d. With 250 working days per year, what is the cycle time for this product?

7. A large distributor of oil-well drilling equipment has operated over the past 2 years with EOQ policies based on an annual holding cost rate of 22%. Under the EOQ policy, a particular product has been ordered with a $Q^* = 80$. A recent evaluation of holding costs shows that because of an increase in the interest rate associated with bank loans, the annual holding cost rate should be 27%.
   a. What is the new economic order quantity for the product?
   b. Develop a general expression showing how the economic order quantity changes when the annual holding cost rate is changed from $I$ to $I'$.

8. Nation-Wide Bus Lines is proud of its 6-week bus driver training program that it conducts for all new Nation-Wide drivers. As long as the class size remains less than or equal to 35, a 6-week training program costs Nation-Wide $22,000 for instructors, equipment, and so on. The Nation-Wide training program must provide the company with approximately five new drivers per month. After completing the training program, new drivers are paid $1600 per month but do not work until a full-time driver position is open. Nation-Wide views the $1600 per month paid to each idle new driver as a holding cost necessary to maintain a supply of newly trained drivers available for immediate service. Viewing new drivers as inventory-type units, how large should the training classes be to minimize Nation-Wide's total annual training and new driver idle-time costs? How many training classes should the company hold each year? What is the total annual cost associated with your recommendation?

9. Cress Electronic Products manufactures components used in the automotive industry. Cress purchases parts for use in its manufacturing operation from a variety of different suppliers. One particular supplier provides a part where the assumptions of the EOQ model are realistic. The annual demand is 5000 units, the ordering cost is $80 per order, and the annual holding cost rate is 25%.
   a. If the cost of the part is $20 per unit, what is the economic order quantity?
   b. Assume 250 days of operation per year. If the lead time for an order is 12 days, what is the reorder point?
   c. If the lead time for the part is 7 weeks (35 days), what is the reorder point?
   d. What is the reorder point for part (c) if the reorder point is expressed in terms of the inventory on hand rather than the inventory position?

10. All-Star Bat Manufacturing, Inc., supplies baseball bats to major and minor league baseball teams. After an initial order in January, demand over the 6-month baseball season is approximately constant at 1000 bats per month. Assuming that the bat production process can handle up to 4000 bats per month, the bat production setup costs are $150 per setup, the production cost is $10 per bat, and that holding costs have a monthly rate of 2%, what production lot size would you recommend to meet the demand during the baseball season? If All-Star operates 20 days per month, how often will the production process operate, and what is the length of a production run?

11. Assume that a production line operates such that the production lot-size model of Section 11.2 is applicable. Given $D = 6400$ units per year, $C_o = \$100$, and $C_h = \$2$ per unit per year, compute the minimum-cost production lot size for each of the following production rates:
   a. 8000 units per year
   b. 10,000 units per year
   c. 32,000 units per year
   d. 100,000 units per year
   Compute the EOQ recommended lot size using equation (11.5). What two observations can you make about the relationship between the EOQ model and the production lot-size model?

12. Assume that you are reviewing the production lot-size decision associated with a production operation where $P = 8000$ units per year, $D = 2000$ units per year, $C_o = \$300$, and $C_h = \$1.60$ per unit per year. Also assume that current practice calls for production runs of 500 units every 3 months. Would you recommend changing the current production lot-size? Why or why not? How much could be saved by converting to your production lot-size recommendation?

13. Wilson Publishing Company produces books for the retail market. Demand for a current book is expected to occur at a constant annual rate of 7200 copies. The cost of one copy of the book is $14.50. The holding cost is based on an 18% annual rate, and production setup costs are $150 per setup. The equipment on which the book is produced has an annual production volume of 25,000 copies. Wilson has 250 working days per year, and the lead time for a production run is 15 days. Use the production lot-size model to compute the following values:
   a. Minimum-cost production lot-size
   b. Number of production runs per year
   c. Cycle time
   d. Length of a production run
   e. Maximum inventory level
   f. Total annual cost
   g. Reorder point

14. A well-known manufacturer of several brands of toothpaste uses the production lot-size model to determine production quantities for its various products. The product known as Extra White is currently being produced in production lot sizes of 5000 units. The length of the production run for this quantity is 10 days. Because of a recent shortage of a particular raw material, the supplier of the material has announced a cost increase that will be passed along to the manufacturer of Extra White. Current estimates are that the new raw material cost will increase the manufacturing cost of the toothpaste products by 23% per unit. What will be the effect of this price increase on the production lot sizes for Extra White?

15. Suppose that Westside Auto of Problem 4, with $D = 12{,}000$ units per year, $C_h = (2.50)(0.20) = \$0.50$, and $C_o = \$25$, decided to operate with a backorder inventory policy. Backorder costs are estimated to be $5 per unit per year. Identify the following:
   a. Minimum-cost order quantity
   b. Maximum number of backorders
   c. Maximum inventory level
   d. Cycle time
   e. Total annual cost

16. Assuming 250 days of operation per year and a lead time of 5 days, what is the reorder point for Westside Auto in Problem 15? Show the general formula for the reorder point for the EOQ model with backorders. In general, is the reorder point when backorders are allowed greater than or less than the reorder point when backorders are not allowed? Explain.

17. A manager of an inventory system believes that inventory models are important decision-making aids. While often using an EOQ policy, the manager has never considered a backorder model because of the assumption that backorders were "bad" and should be avoided. However, with upper management's continued pressure for cost reduction, you have been asked to analyze the economics of a backordering policy for some products that can possibly be backordered. For a specific product with $D = 800$ units per year, $C_o = \$150$, $C_h = \$3$, and $C_b = \$20$, what is the difference in total annual cost between the EOQ model and the planned shortage or backorder model? If the manager adds constraints that no more than 25% of the units can be backordered and that no customer will have to wait more than 15 days for an order, should the backorder inventory policy be adopted? Assume 250 working days per year.

18. If the lead time for new orders is 20 days for the inventory system discussed in Problem 17, find the reorder point for both the EOQ and the backorder models.

19. The A&M Hobby Shop carries a line of radio-controlled model racing cars. Demand for the cars is assumed to be constant at a rate of 40 cars per month. The cars cost $60 each, and ordering costs are approximately $15 per order, regardless of the order size. The annual holding cost rate is 20%.
   a. Determine the economic order quantity and total annual cost under the assumption that no backorders are permitted.
   b. Using a $45 per unit per year backorder cost, determine the minimum-cost inventory policy and total annual cost for the model racing cars.

c.  What is the maximum number of days a customer would have to wait for a backorder under the policy in part (b)? Assume that the Hobby Shop is open for business 30 days per year.

d.  Would you recommend a no-backorder or a backorder inventory policy for this product? Explain.

e.  If the lead time is 6 days, what is the reorder point for both the no-backorder and backorder inventory policies?

20.  Assume that the following quantity discount schedule is appropriate. If annual demand is 120 units, ordering costs are $20 per order, and the annual holding cost rate is 25%, what order quantity would you recommend?

| Order Size | Discount (%) | Unit Cost |
|---|---|---|
| 0 to 49 | 0 | $30.00 |
| 50 to 99 | 5 | 28.50 |
| 100 or more | 10 | 27.00 |

**SELF TEST**

21.  Apply the EOQ model to the following quantity discount situation in which $D = 500$ units per year, $C_o = \$40$, and the annual holding cost rate is 20%. What order quantity do you recommend?

| Discount Category | Order Size | Discount (%) | Unit Cost |
|---|---|---|---|
| 1 | 0 to 99 | 0 | $10.00 |
| 2 | 100 or more | 3 | 9.70 |

22.  Keith Shoe Stores carries a basic black dress shoe for men that sells at an approximate constant rate of 500 pairs of shoes every 3 months. Keith's current buying policy is to order 500 pairs each time an order is placed. It costs Keith $30 to place an order. The annual holding cost rate is 20%. With the order quantity of 500, Keith obtains the shoes at the lowest possible unit cost of $28 per pair. Other quantity discounts offered by the manufacturer are as follows. What is the minimum-cost order quantity for the shoes? What are the annual savings of your inventory policy over the policy currently being used by Keith?

| Order Quantity | Price Per Pair |
|---|---|
| 0–99 | $36 |
| 100–199 | 32 |
| 200–299 | 30 |
| 300 or more | 28 |

23.  In the EOQ model with quantity discounts, we stated that if the $Q^*$ for a price category is larger than necessary to qualify for the category price, the category cannot be optimal. Use the two discount categories in Problem 21 to show that this statement is true. That is, plot and total-cost curves for the two categories and show that if the category 2 minimum cost $Q$ is an acceptable solution, we do not have to consider category 1.

24. The J&B Card Shop sells calendars depicting a different Colonial scene each month. The once-a-year order for each year's calendar arrives in September. From past experience, the September-to-July demand for the calendars can be approximated by a normal probability distribution with $\mu = 500$ and $\sigma = 120$. The calendars cost $1.50 each, and J&B sells them for $3 each.
    a.  If J&B throws out all unsold calendars at the end of July (i.e., salvage value is zero), how many calendars should be ordered?
    b.  If J&B reduces the calendar price to $1 at the end of July and can sell all surplus calendars at this price, how many calendars should be ordered?

**SELF TEST**

25. The Gilbert Air-Conditioning Company is considering the purchase of a special shipment of portable air conditioners manufactured in Japan. Each unit will cost Gilbert $80, and it will be sold for $125. Gilbert does not want to carry surplus air conditioners over until the following year. Thus, all surplus air conditioners will be sold to a wholesaler for $50 per unit. Assume that the air conditioner demand follows a normal probability distribution with $\mu = 20$ and $\sigma = 8$.
    a.  What is the recommended order quantity?
    b.  What is the probability that Gilbert will sell all units it orders?

26. A popular newsstand is attempting to determine how many copies of the local newspaper it should purchase each day. Demand for the newspaper can be approximated by a normal probability distribution with $\mu = 450$ and $\sigma = 100$. The newspaper costs the newsstand 35¢ a copy and sells for 50¢ a copy. The newsstand does not receive any value from surplus papers and thus absorbs a 100% loss on all unsold papers.
    a.  How many copies of the newspaper paper should be purchased each day?
    b.  What is the probability that the newsstand will have a stockout?
    c.  The manager of the newsstand is concerned about the newsstand's image if the probability of stockout is high. Customers often purchase other items after coming to the newsstand. Frequent stockouts would cause customers to go to another newsstand. The manager agrees that a 50¢ goodwill cost should be assigned to any stockout. What is the new recommended order quantity and the new probability of a stockout?

27. A perishable dairy product is ordered daily at a particular supermarket. The product, which costs $1.19 per unit, sells for $1.65 per unit. If units are unsold at the end of the day, the supplier takes them back at a rebate of $1 per unit. Assume that daily demand is approximately normally distributed with $\mu = 150$ and $\sigma = 30$.
    a.  What is your recommended daily order quantity for the supermarket?
    b.  What is the probability that the supermarket will sell all the units it orders?
    c.  In problems such as these, why would the supplier offer a rebate as high as $1? For example, why not offer a nominal rebate of, say, 25¢ per unit? What happens to the supermarket order quantity as the rebate is reduced?

28. A retail outlet sells a seasonal product for $10 per unit. The cost of the product is $8 per unit. All units not sold during the regular season are sold for half the retail price in an end-of-season clearance sale. Assume that demand for the product is uniformly distributed between 200 and 800.
    a.  What is the recommended order quantity?
    b.  What is the probability that at least some customers will ask to purchase the product after the outlet is sold out? That is, what is the probability of a stockout using your order quantity in part (a)?
    c.  To keep customers happy and returning to the store later, the owner feels that stockouts should be avoided if at all possible. What is your recommended order quantity if the owner is willing to tolerate a 0.15 probability of a stockout?
    d.  Using your answer to part (c), what is the goodwill cost you are assigning to a stockout?

**SELF TEST**

29. Floyd Distributors, Inc., provides a variety of auto parts to small local garages. Floyd purchases parts from manufacturers according to the EOQ model and then ships the parts from a regional warehouse direct to its customers. For a particular type of muffler, Floyd's EOQ analysis

recommends orders with $Q^* = 25$ to satisfy an annual demand of 200 mufflers. Floyd's has 250 working days per year, and the lead time averages 15 days.
   a. What is the reorder point if Floyd assumes a constant demand rate?
   b. Suppose that an analysis of Floyd's muffler demand shows that the lead-time demand follows a normal probability distribution with $\mu = 12$ and $\sigma = 2.5$. If Floyd's management can tolerate one stockout per year, what is the revised reorder point?
   c. What is the safety stock for part (b)? If $C_h = \$5/\text{unit/year}$, what is the extra cost due to the uncertainty of demand?

30. For Floyd Distributors in Problem 29, we were given $Q^* = 25$, $D = 200$, $C_h = \$5$, and a normal lead-time demand distribution with $\mu = 12$ and $\sigma = 2.5$.
   a. What is Floyd's reorder point if the firm is willing to tolerate two stockouts during the year?
   b. What is Floyd's reorder point if the firm wants to restrict the probability of a stockout on any one cycle to at most 1%?
   c. What are the safety stock levels and the annual safety stock costs for the reorder points found in parts (a) and (b)?

31. A product with an annual demand of 1000 units has $C_o = \$25.50$ and $C_h = \$8$. The demand exhibits some variability such that the lead-time demand follows a normal probability distribution with $\mu = 25$ and $\sigma = 5$.
   a. What is the recommended order quantity?
   b. What are the reorder point and safety stock if the firm desires at most a 2% probability of stockout on any given order cycle?
   c. If a manager sets the reorder point at 30, what is the probability of a stockout on any given order cycle? How many times would you expect to stockout during the year if this reorder point were used?

32. The B&S Novelty and Craft Shop in Bennington, Vermont, sells a variety of quality handmade items to tourists. B&S will sell 300 hand-carved miniature replicas of a Colonial soldier each year, but the demand pattern during the year is uncertain. The replicas sell for $20 each, and B&S uses a 15% annual inventory holding cost rate. Ordering costs are $5 per order, and demand during the lead time follows a normal probability distribution with $\mu = 15$ and $\sigma = 6$.
   a. What is the recommended order quantity?
   b. If B&S is willing to accept a stockout roughly twice a year, what reorder point would you recommend? What is the probability that B&S will have a stockout in any one order-cycle?
   c. What are the safety stock and annual safety stock costs for this product?

**SELF TEST**

33. A firm uses a 1-week periodic review inventory system. A 2-day lead time is needed for any order, and the firm is willing to tolerate an average of one stockout per year.
   a. Using the firm's service guideline, what is the probability of a stockout associated with each replenishment decision?
   b. What is the replenishment level if demand during the review period plus lead-time period is normally distributed with a mean of 60 units and a standard deviation of 12 units?
   c. What is the replenishment level if demand during the review period plus lead-time period is uniformly distributed between 35 and 85 units?

34. Foster Drugs, Inc., handles a variety of health and beauty aid products. A particular hair conditioner product costs Foster Drugs $2.95 per unit. The annual holding cost rate is 20%. An order-quantity, reorder-point inventory model recommends an order quantity of 300 units per order.
   a. Lead time is one week and the lead-time demand is normally distributed with a mean of 150 units and a standard deviation of 40 units. What is the reorder point if the firm is willing to tolerate a 1% chance of stockout on any one cycle?
   b. What safety stock and annual safety stock cost are associated with your recommendation in part (a)?

c.   The order-quantity, reorder-point model requires a continuous-review system. Management is considering making a transition to a periodic-review system in an attempt to coordinate ordering for many of its products. The demand during the proposed two-week review period and the one-week lead-time period is normally distributed with a mean of 450 units and a standard deviation of 70 units. What is the recommended replenishment level for this periodic-review system if the firm is willing to tolerate the same 1% chance of stockout associated with any replenishment decision?

d.   What safety stock and annual safety stock cost are associated with your recommendation in part (c)?

e.   Compare your answers to parts (b) and (d). The company is seriously considering the periodic-review system. Would you support this decision? Explain.

f.   Would you tend to favor the continuous-review system for more expensive items? For example, assume that the product in the above example sold for $295 per unit. Explain.

35.   Statewide Auto Parts uses a 4-week periodic-review system to reorder parts for its inventory stock. A 1-week lead time is required to fill the order. Demand for one particular part during the 5-week replenishment period is normally distributed with a mean of 18 units and a standard deviation of 6 units.

a.   At a particular periodic review, 8 units are in inventory. The parts manager places an order for 16 units. What is the probability that this part will have a stockout before an order that is placed at the next 4-week review period arrives?

b.   Assume that the company is willing to tolerate a 2.5% chance of a stockout associated with a replenishment decision. How many parts should the manager have ordered in part (a)? What is the replenishment level for the 4-week periodic-review system?

36.   Rose Office Supplies, Inc., which is open 6 days a week, uses a 2-week periodic review for its store inventory. On alternating Monday mornings, the store manager fills out an order sheet requiring a shipment of various items from the company's warehouse. A particular three-ring notebook sells at an average rate of 16 notebooks per week. The standard deviation in sales is 5 notebooks per week. The lead time for a new shipment is 3 days. The mean lead-time demand is 8 notebooks with a standard deviation of 3.5.

a.   What is the mean or expected demand during the review period plus the lead-time period?

b.   Under the assumption of independent demand from week to week, the variances in demands are additive. Thus, the variance of the demand during the review period plus the lead-time period is equal to the variance of demand during the first week plus the variance of demand during the second week plus the variance of demand during the lead-time period. What is the variance of demand during the review period plus the lead-time period? What is the standard deviation of demand during the review period plus the lead-time period?

c.   Assuming that demand has a normal probability distribution, what is the replenishment level that will provide an expected stockout rate of one per year?

d.   On Monday, March 22, 18 notebooks remain in inventory at the store. How many notebooks should the store manager order?

**SELF TEST**

37.   Consider the Spiecker Manufacturing problem of Section 11.8. Determine the net requirements for the engine assembly, the air cleaner, subassembly, and the filter housing if the number of units in inventory were 2000, 1500, and 1000, respectively. Assume that 5000 units of the 14-inch snowblower are required in week 21.

38.   For the Spiecker Manufacturing problem of Section 11.8, determine the effect on time phasing if lead times were 10 for the engine assembly, 3 for the air cleaner subassembly, and 5 for the filter housing.

39.   C & D Lawn Products manufactures a rotary spreader for applying fertilizer. A portion of the bill of materials is shown as follows:

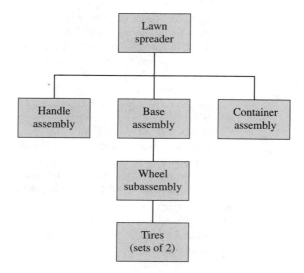

If 3000 lawn spreaders are needed to satisfy a customer's order, determine the net requirements for the base assembly, wheel subassembly, and tires (sets of two). Assume that 1000 base assemblies, 1500 wheel subassemblies, and 800 tires (sets of two) are currently in inventory.

40. In Problem 39, assume that the lead time for the base assembly, wheel subassembly, and tires are 2 weeks, 4 weeks, and 5 weeks, respectively. If all components must be completed no later than week 15 of the current production period, determine when orders must be placed to meet the production schedule.

## Case Problem    A MAKE-OR-BUY ANALYSIS

Managers at Wagner Fabricating Company are reviewing the economic feasibility of manufacturing a part that it currently purchases from a supplier. Forecasted annual demand for the part is 3200 units. Wagner operates 250 days per year.

Wagner's financial analysts have established a cost of capital of 14% for the use of funds for investments within the company. In addition, over the past year $600,000 has been the average investment in the company's inventory. Accounting information shows that a total of $24,000 was spent on taxes and insurance related to the company's inventory. In addition, an estimated $9000 was lost due to inventory shrinkage, which included damaged goods as well as pilferage. A remaining $15,000 was spent on warehouse overhead, including utility expenses for heating and lighting.

An analysis of the purchasing operation shows that approximately 2 hours are required to process and coordinate an order for the part regardless of the quantity ordered. Purchasing salaries average $28 per hour, including employee benefits. In addition, a detailed analysis of 125 orders showed that $2375 was spent on telephone, paper, and postage directly related to the ordering process.

A 1-week lead time is required to obtain the part from the supplier. An analysis of demand during the lead time shows that lead-time demand is approximately normally distributed with a mean of 64 units and a standard deviation of 10 units. Service level guidelines indicate that one stockout per year is acceptable.

Currently, the company has a contract to purchase the part from a supplier at a cost of $18 per unit. However, over the past few months, the company's production capacity has been expanded. As a result, excess capacity is now available in certain production depart-ments, and the company is considering the alternative of producing the parts itself.

Forecasted utilization of equipment shows that production capacity will be available for the part being considered. The production capacity is available at the rate of 1000 units per month, with up to 5 months of production time available. Management believes that with a 2-week lead time, schedules can be arranged so that the part can be produced whenever needed. The demand during the 2-week lead time is approximately normally distributed, with a mean of 128 units and a standard deviation of 20 units. Production costs are expected to be $17 per part.

A concern of management is that setup costs will be significant. The total cost of labor and lost production time is estimated to be $50 per hour, and a full 8-hour shift will be needed to set up the equipment for producing the part.

## Managerial Report

Develop a report for management of Wagner Fabricating that will address the question of whether the company should continue to purchase the part from the supplier or begin to pro-duce the part itself. Include the following factors in your report:

1. An analysis of the holding costs, including the appropriate annual holding cost rate.
2. An analysis of ordering costs, including the appropriate cost per order from the supplier.
3. An analysis of setup costs for the production operation.
4. A development of the inventory policy for the following two alternatives:
   a. Ordering a fixed quantity $Q$ from the supplier
   b. Ordering a fixed quantity $Q$ from in-plant production
5. Include the following in the policies of parts 4(a) and 4(b):
   a. Optimal quantity $Q^*$
   b. Number of order or production runs per year
   c. Cycle time
   d. Reorder point
   e. Amount of safety stock
   f. Expected maximum inventory level
   g. Average inventory level
   h. Annual holding cost
   i. Annual ordering cost
   j. Annual cost of the units purchased or manufactured
   k. Total annual cost of the purchase policy and the total annual cost of the produc-tion policy
6. Make a recommendation as to whether the company should purchase or manufac-ture the part. What is the saving associated with your recommendation as compared with the other alternative?

## Appendix 11.1    INVENTORY MODELS WITH SPREADSHEETS

In this appendix we show how a spreadsheet can be used to implement the economic order quantity (EOQ) model introduced in Section 11.1. The spreadsheet for the EOQ model can be modified to accommodate the other inventory models presented in this chapter.

Figure 11.20 shows the Excel spreadsheet for the Bub Beer economic order quan-tity model presented in Section 11.1. The annual demand, ordering cost, annual inventory

**Figure II.20**    **SPREADSHEET FOR THE BUB BEER EOQ INVENTORY MODEL**

| | A | B |
|---|---|---|
| 1 | **Bub Beer Economic Order Quantity** | |
| 2 | | |
| 3 | Annual Demand | 104,000 |
| 4 | Ordering Cost | $32.00 |
| 5 | Annual Inventory Holding Rate % | 25 |
| 6 | Cost Per Unit | $8.00 |
| 7 | Working Days Per Year | 250 |
| 8 | Lead Time (Days) | 2 |
| 9 | | |
| 10 | | |
| 11 | **Optimal Inventory Policy** | |
| 12 | | |
| 13 | Economic Order Quantity | 1824.28 |
| 14 | Total Annual Cost | $3,648.56 |
| 15 | | |
| 16 | **Requested Order Quantity** | 1824.28 |
| 17 | | |
| 18 | Annual Inventory Holding Cost | $1,824.28 |
| 19 | Annual Ordering Cost | $1,824.28 |
| 20 | Total Annual Cost | $3,648.56 |
| 21 | Maximum Inventory Level | 1,824.28 |
| 22 | Average Inventory Level | 912.14 |
| 23 | Reorder Point | 832.00 |
| 24 | Number of Orders Per Year | 57.01 |
| 25 | Cycle Time (Days) | 4.39 |
| 26 | | |
| 27 | Annual Cost Over EOQ | $0.00 |
| 28 | Percentage | 0.00% |

holding rate, cost per unit, working days per year, and lead time in days are entered into cells B3:B8. The cell formulas used to compute the optimal inventory policy are as follows:

| | |
|---|---|
| Cell B13 | =SQRT(2*B3*B4/(B6*B5/100)) |
| Cell B14 | =(B13/2)*(B6*B5/100)+B3*B4/B13 |
| Cell B16 | =B13 |
| Cell B18 | =(B16/2)*(B5*B6/100) |
| Cell B19 | =(B3/B16)*B4 |
| Cell B20 | =B18+B19 |

Cell B21    =B16
Cell B22    =B21/2
Cell B23    =(B3/B7)*B8
Cell B24    =B3/B16
Cell B25    =B7/B24
Cell B27    =B20-B14
Cell B28    =B27/B14

Using equation (11.5), the spreadsheet places the economic order quantity, $Q^*$, in cell B13. Cell B14 contains the total annual cost assuming the economic order quantity

---

**Figure II.21    SPREADSHEET FOR THE BUB BEER EOQ INVENTORY MODEL WITH $Q = 2000$**

|   | A | B |
|---|---|---|
| 1 | **Bub Beer Economic Order Quantity** | |
| 2 | | |
| 3 | Annual Demand | 104,000 |
| 4 | Ordering Cost | $32.00 |
| 5 | Annual Inventory Holding Rate % | 25 |
| 6 | Cost Per Unit | $8.00 |
| 7 | Working Days Per Year | 250 |
| 8 | Lead Time (Days) | 2 |
| 9 | | |
| 10 | | |
| 11 | **Optimal Inventory Policy** | |
| 12 | | |
| 13 | Economic Order Quantity | 1824.28 |
| 14 | Total Annual Cost | $3,648.56 |
| 15 | | |
| 16 | **Requested Order Quantity** | 2000.00 |
| 17 | | |
| 18 | Annual Inventory Holding Cost | $2,000.00 |
| 19 | Annual Ordering Cost | $1,664.00 |
| 20 | Total Annual Cost | $3,664.00 |
| 21 | Maximum Inventory Level | 2,000.00 |
| 22 | Average Inventory Level | 1000.00 |
| 23 | Reorder Point | 832.00 |
| 24 | Number of Orders Per Year | 52.00 |
| 25 | Cycle Time (Days) | 4.81 |
| 26 | | |
| 27 | Annual Cost Over EOQ | $15.44 |
| 28 | Percentage | 0.42% |

is implemented. The remaining spreadsheet cells provide additional information that will help the manager understand the inventory operation and determine the final order quantity to be used.

After viewing the spreadsheet solution in Figure 11.20, the manager can easily evaluate alternative order quantities. For example, assume that the manager believes that an order quantity of 2000 cases would be easier to implement than the economic order quantity model's recommendation of $Q^* = 1824.28$. In this case, the manager simply enters 2000 as the requested order quantity in cell B16. The spreadsheet will automatically revise the inventory policy information. Figure 11.21 shows the results based on the requested order quantity of 2000 cases. In particular, note that the last two entries on the spreadsheet, cells B27 and B28, show that the added cost with $Q = 2000$ is only \$15.44 per year, or only 0.42%. Other inventory order quantities can be evaluated by placing the requested economic order quantity in cell B16. In this case, the manager preferred the 2000-case order quantity with its slight cost increase over the economic order quantity model's recommendation of $Q^* = 1824.28$.

As with most other spreadsheet applications, the manager may change one or more of the models inputs and quickly learn how any change affects the optimal order quantity and the total annual cost. For example, changing the inventory holding cost rate and/or the order cost would show how sensitive the recommended economic order quantity and the total annual cost are to these input values.

## Appendix 11.2  DEVELOPMENT OF THE OPTIMAL ORDER-QUANTITY ($Q^*$) FORMULA FOR THE EOQ MODEL

Given equation (11.4) as the total annual cost for the EOQ model,

$$TC = \frac{1}{2}QC_h + \frac{D}{Q}C_o \tag{11.4}$$

we can find the order quantity $Q$ that minimizes the total cost by setting the derivative, $dTC/dQ$, equal to zero and solving for $Q^*$.

$$\frac{dTC}{dQ} = \frac{1}{2}C_h - \frac{D}{Q^2}C_o = 0$$

$$\frac{1}{2}C_h = \frac{D}{Q^2}C_o$$

$$C_hQ^2 = 2DC_o$$

$$Q^2 = \frac{2DC_o}{C_h}$$

Hence,

$$Q^* = \sqrt{\frac{2DC_o}{C_h}} \tag{11.5}$$

The second derivative is

$$\frac{d^2 TC}{dQ^2} = \frac{2D}{Q^3} C_o$$

Since the value of the second derivative is greater than zero for $D$, $C_o$, and $Q$ greater than zero, $Q^*$ from equation (11.5) is the minimum-cost solution.

## Appendix 11.3    DEVELOPMENT OF THE OPTIMAL LOT-SIZE ($Q^*$) FORMULA FOR THE PRODUCTION LOT-SIZE MODEL

Given equation (11.15) as the total annual cost for the production lot-size model,

$$TC = \frac{1}{2}\left(1 - \frac{D}{P}\right)QC_h + \frac{D}{Q}C_o \tag{11.15}$$

we can find the order quantity $Q$ that minimizes the total cost by setting the derivative, $dTC/dQ$, equal to zero and solving for $Q^*$.

$$\frac{dTC}{dQ} = \frac{1}{2}\left(1 - \frac{D}{P}\right)C_h + \frac{D}{Q^2}C_o = 0$$

Solving for $Q^*$, we have

$$\frac{1}{2}\left(1 - \frac{D}{P}\right)C_h = \frac{D}{Q^2}C_o$$

$$\left(1 - \frac{D}{P}\right)C_h Q^2 = 2DC_o$$

$$Q^2 = \frac{2DC_o}{(1 - D/P)C_h}$$

Hence,

$$Q^* = \sqrt{\frac{2DC_o}{(1 - D/P)C_h}} \tag{11.28}$$

The second derivative is

$$\frac{d^2 TC}{dQ^2} = \frac{2DC_o}{Q^3}$$

Since the value of the second derivative is greater than zero for $D$, $C_o$, and $Q$ greater than zero, $Q^*$ from equation (11.16) is a minimum-cost solution.

**Appendix 11.4**   DEVELOPMENT OF THE OPTIMAL ORDER-QUANTITY ($Q^*$) AND OPTIMAL BACKORDER ($S^*$) FORMULAS FOR THE PLANNED SHORTAGE MODEL

Given equation (11.25) as the total annual cost for the planned shortage model,

$$TC = \frac{(Q-S)^2}{2Q}\,C_h + \frac{D}{Q}\,C_o + \frac{S^2}{2Q}\,C_b \qquad (11.25)$$

we have two inventory decision variables, $Q$ and $S$. To find the $Q$ and $S$ values that minimize equation (11.25), we must set the two partial derivatives, $\partial TC/\partial Q$ and $\partial TC/\partial S$, equal to zero. First, let us rewrite equation (11.25) as follows:

$$TC = \left(\frac{Q^2 - 2QS + S^2}{2Q}\right)C_h + \frac{D}{Q}\,C_o + \frac{S^2}{2Q}\,C_b$$

$$= \frac{Q}{2}\,C_h - SC_h + \frac{C_h}{2Q}\,S^2 + \frac{DC_o}{Q} + \frac{C_b}{2Q}\,S^2$$

$$= \left(\frac{C_h + C_b}{2Q}\right)S^2 - SC_h + \frac{QC_h}{2} + \frac{DC_o}{Q}$$

Then setting $\partial TC/\partial S = 0$, we obtain

$$\frac{\partial TC}{\partial S} = \left(\frac{C_h + C_b}{Q}\right)S - C_h = 0$$

Solving for $S^*$, we have

$$\left(\frac{C_h - C_b}{Q}\right)S = C_h$$

Thus

$$S^* = Q\left(\frac{C_h}{C_h + C_b}\right) \qquad (11.27)$$

Setting $\partial TC/\partial Q = 0$, we obtain

$$\frac{\partial TC}{\partial Q} = \frac{-(C_h + C_b)S^2}{2Q^2} + \frac{C_h}{2} - \frac{DC_o}{Q^2} = 0$$

Substituting $S^*$ of equation (11.27), we have

$$\frac{\partial TC}{\partial Q} = \frac{-(C_h + C_b)Q^2(C_h)^2/(C_h + C_b)^2}{2Q^2} + \frac{C_h}{2} - \frac{DC_o}{Q^2} = 0$$

We can solve for $Q^*$ as follows:

$$\frac{-C_h^2}{2(C_h + C_b)} + \frac{C_h}{2} = \frac{DC_o}{Q^2}$$

$$\frac{-C_h^2 + C_h(C_h + C_b)}{2(C_h + C_b)} = \frac{DC_o}{Q^2}$$

$$Q^2 = \frac{2(C_h + C_b)DC_o}{C_h C_b}$$

$$Q^2 = \frac{2C_h DC_o}{C_h C_b} + \frac{2C_b DC_o}{C_h C_b}$$

$$Q^2 = \frac{2DC_o}{C_h}\left(\frac{C_h}{C_b} + \frac{C_b}{C_b}\right)$$

Hence

$$Q^* = \sqrt{\frac{2DC_o}{C_h}\left(\frac{C_h + C_b}{C_b}\right)} \qquad (11.26)$$

The second-order conditions will show that equations (11.26) and (11.27) are the minimum-cost solutions.

# CVS CORPORATION*

## WOONSOCKET, RHODE ISLAND

The first CVS store opened in Lowell, Massachusetts, in 1963, under the name "Consumer Value Store." In the 1990s, CVS mergers and acquisition included drugstore chains formerly known as Peoples, SuperRx, Revco, and Arbor Drugs. The Revco acquisition in 1997 and the Arbor Drugs acquisition in 1998 made CVS the largest drugstore chain in the United States with 4100 stores in 25 states. In 1998, CVS dispensed approximately 12% of all retail prescriptions in the United States.

General inventory management in the drugstore business involves several product categories: basic products carried on an everyday basis, seasonal products carried only during certain times of the year (such as fruitcakes during holidays), and special items bought on an in-and-out basis throughout the year.

By far the most critical inventory issue is the replenishment of basic products. At most retail drug chains, this type of product is ordered under a periodic-review inventory system, with the review period being one week. The weekly review uses electronic ordering equipment that scans an order label affixed to the shelf. Such a label is located on the shelf directly below each item. Among other information on this label is the "order-to-quantity." (*Note:* This replenishment level is referenced in the periodic-review inventory model of Section 11.7.) The store employee placing the order determines the quantity to order by subtracting the number of units of product on the shelf from the order-to quantity (OTQ). For example, if the OTQ is 6 and two units of product are on the shelf, the quantity ordered would be 4. The OTQ is the key factor in inventory control for basic products.

Several factors are considered in determining individual item OTQs. The most obvious is average weekly demand or movement. Suppose, for example, an item averages two units per week per store in warehouse deliveries. Setting the OTQ equal to 2 would not allow for sales fluctuations that exceeded the average of 2. To compensate for this, and to avoid stockouts, the OTQ is set equal to a 3-week demand or movement. Thus, in this example, the OTQ would become 6.

Another factor to consider is whether an item can be ordered in units or cases. In some instances, delivering in anything less than case quantities is not feasible for the warehouse. An example would be candy bars. Stores must order a minimum of one case (36 units), no matter what the movement indicates. Thus, the OTQ is 36 or a multiple of 36 to accommodate the case order restriction. Merchandising esthetics must also be considered when determining an OTQ. If an item has four facings or open positions on the shelf, but the optimum OTQ determined by movement is 3, one space would be without product. This vacancy would create an out-of-stock impression to the customer, and, thus, the OTQ would be increased to at least 4. Seasonal fluctuations in movement must be considered when OTQs are determined. For example, the OTQ for a cough and cold item would be significantly higher in January than it would be in July. Adhesive bandages would be just the opposite, with higher usage in the summer than in the winter.

Today, OTQs are based on average company warehouse movement into the stores. A computer program determines OTQs by item by individual store, based on that store's movement, rather than on the company movement.

Good inventory management does not occur in a vacuum, but must be interrelated with sales, gross mar-

---

*The authors are indebted to Bob Carver for providing this application. This inventory system was originally implemented in the CVS stores formerly known as SuperRx.

gin, and expense control objectives. This inventory management system allows merchandisers to act out "what if" scenarios relating to OTQs, product costs, retail sales prices, inventory carrying costs, sales, and other factors. As an example, optimum order-to quantities normally result in some percentage of missed sales because of individual item movement fluctuations. On the other hand, increasing the OTQs to maximize sales also increases inventory, decreases inventory turnover, and thus ties up capital that could otherwise be used for building new stores, remodeling existing locations, and so on. By using the new inventory management techniques, the company can maximize both sales and inventory turnover.

Rapidly becoming a necessity rather than a luxury, the use of this technology ensures the maximization of sales, profits, and inventory turnovers that ultimately determine the success or failure of a drug chain.

## Questions

1. Does the inventory system in this application use continuous-review or periodic-review? Why would this system be preferred for a retail business such as CVS?
2. What is the decision rule that is used to provide a safety stock and minimize stockouts?

# 12

## WAITING LINE MODELS

### CONTENTS

Recall the last time that you had to wait at a supermarket checkout counter, for a teller at your local bank, or to be served at a fast-food restaurant. In these and many other waiting line situations, the time spent waiting is undesirable. Adding more checkout clerks, bank tellers, or servers is not always the most economical strategy for improving service, so businesses need to determine ways to keep waiting times within tolerable limits.

Models have been developed to help managers understand and make better decisions concerning the operation of waiting lines. In management science terminology, a waiting line is also known as a **queue,** and the body of knowledge dealing with waiting lines is known as **queuing theory.** In the early 1900s A. K. Erlang, a Danish telephone engineer, began a study of the congestion and waiting times occurring in the completion of telephone calls. Since then, queuing theory has grown far more sophisticated and has been applied to a wide variety of waiting line situations.

Waiting line models consist of mathematical formulas and relationships that can be used to determine the **operating characteristics** (performance measures) for a waiting line. Some of the operating characteristics of interest include the following:

1. The probability that no units are in the system
2. The average number of units in the waiting line
3. The average number of units in the system (the number of units in the waiting line plus the number of units being served)
4. The average time a unit spends in the waiting line
5. The average time a unit spends in the system (the waiting time plus the service time)
6. The probability that an arriving unit has to wait for service

Managers who have such information are better able to make decisions that balance desirable service levels against the cost of providing the service.

## 12.1    THE STRUCTURE OF A WAITING LINE SYSTEM

To illustrate the basic features of a waiting line model, we consider the waiting line at the Burger Dome fast-food restaurant. Burger Dome sells hamburgers, cheeseburgers, french fries, soft drinks, and milk shakes, as well as a limited number of specialty items and dessert selections. Although Burger Dome would like to serve each customer immediately, at times more customers arrive than can be handled by the Burger Dome food-service staff. Thus, customers wait in line to place and receive their orders.

Burger Dome is concerned that the methods currently used to serve customers are resulting in excessive waiting times. Management has asked that a waiting line study be performed to help determine the best approach to reducing waiting times and improving service.

### The Single-Channel Waiting Line

In the current Burger Dome operation, a server takes a customer's order, determines the total cost of the order, takes the money from the customer, and then fills the order. Once the first customer's order is filled, the server takes the order of the next customer waiting for service. This operation is an example of a **single-channel waiting line.** By this, we mean that each customer entering the Burger Dome restaurant must pass through the *one* channel—one order-taking and order-filling station—to place an order, pay the bill, and receive the food. When more customers arrive than can be served immediately, they form a waiting line and wait for the order-taking and order-filling station to become available. A diagram of the Burger Dome single-channel waiting line is shown in Figure 12.1.

## The Distribution of Arrivals

Defining the arrival process for a waiting line involves determining the probability distribution for the number of arrivals in a given period of time. For many waiting line situations, the arrivals occur *randomly and independently* of other arrivals, and we cannot predict when an arrival will occur. In such cases, management scientists have found that the **Poisson probability distribution** provides a good description of the arrival pattern.

The Poisson probability function provides the probability of $x$ arrivals in a specific time period. The probability function is as follows.[1]

$$P(x) = \frac{\lambda^x e^{-\lambda}}{x!} \quad \text{for } x = 0, 1, 2, \ldots \tag{12.1}$$

where

$x =$ the number of arrivals in the time period

$\lambda =$ the mean number of arrivals per time period

$e = 2.71828$

Values of $e^{-\lambda}$ can be found using a calculator or by using Appendix C.

Suppose that Burger Dome has analyzed data on customer arrivals and has concluded that the mean arrival rate is 45 customers per hour. For a 1-minute period, the mean arrival rate would be $\lambda = 45$ customers/60 minutes $= 0.75$ customers per minute. Thus, we can use the following Poisson probability function to compute the probability of $x$ customer arrivals during a 1-minute period:

$$P(x) = \frac{\lambda^x e^{-\lambda}}{x!} = \frac{0.75^x e^{-0.75}}{x!} \tag{12.2}$$

Thus, the probabilities of 0, 1, and 2 customer arrivals during a 1-minute period are

$$P(0) = \frac{(0.75)^0 e^{-0.75}}{0!} = e^{-0.75} = 0.4724$$

$$P(1) = \frac{(0.75)^1 e^{-0.75}}{1!} = 0.75 e^{-0.75} = 0.75(0.4724) = 0.3543$$

$$P(2) = \frac{(0.75)^2 e^{-0.75}}{2!} = \frac{(0.75)^2 e^{-0.75}}{2!} = \frac{(0.5625)(0.4724)}{2} = 0.1329$$

---

1. The term *x!, x factorial,* is defined as $x! = x(x-1)(x-2)\ldots(2)(1)$. For example $4! = (4)(3)(2)(1) = 24$. For the special case of $x = 0, 0! = 1$ by definition.

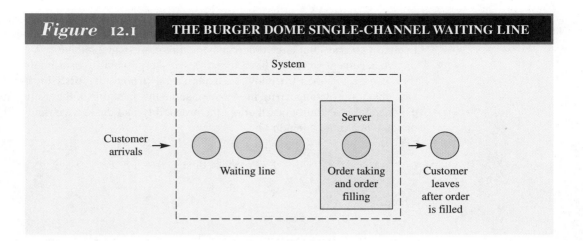

**Figure 12.1    THE BURGER DOME SINGLE-CHANNEL WAITING LINE**

The probability of no customers in a 1-minute period is 0.4724, the probability of 1 customer in a 1-minute period is 0.3543, and the probability of 2 customers in a 1-minute period is 0.1329. Table 12.1 shows the Poisson probabilities for customer arrivals during a 1-minute period.

The waiting line models that will be presented in Sections 12.2 and 12.3 use the Poisson probability distribution to describe the customer arrivals at Burger Dome. In practice, you should record the actual number of arrivals per time period for several days or weeks and compare the frequency distribution of the observed number of arrivals to the Poisson probability distribution to determine whether the Poisson probability distribution provides a reasonable approximation of the arrival distribution.

## The Distribution of Service Times

The service time is the time a customer spends at the service facility once the service has started. At Burger Dome, the service time starts when a customer begins to place the order with the food server and continues until the customer has received the order. Service times

**Table 12.1    POISSON PROBABILITIES FOR THE NUMBER OF CUSTOMER ARRIVALS AT A BURGER DOME RESTAURANT DURING A 1-MINUTE PERIOD ($\lambda = 0.75$)**

| Number of Arrivals | Probability |
|---|---|
| 0 | 0.4724 |
| 1 | 0.3543 |
| 2 | 0.1329 |
| 3 | 0.0332 |
| 4 | 0.0062 |
| 5 or more | 0.0010 |

are rarely constant. At Burger Dome, the number of times ordered and the mix of items ordered vary considerably from one customer to the next. Small orders can be handled in a matter of seconds, but large orders may require more than 2 minutes.

Management scientists have found that if the probability distribution for the service time can be assumed to follow an **exponential probability distribution,** formulas are available for providing useful information about the operation of the waiting line. Using an exponential probability distribution, the probability that the service time will be less than or equal to a time of length $t$ is

$$P(\text{service time} \leq t) = 1 - e^{-\mu t} \tag{12.3}$$

where

$\mu$ = the mean number of units that can be served per time period
$e = 2.71828$

Suppose that Burger Dome has studied the order-taking and order-filling process and has found that the single food server can process an average of 60 customer orders per hour. On a 1-minute basis, the mean service rate would be $\mu = 60$ customers/60 minutes = 1 customer per minute. For example, with $\mu = 1$, we can use equation (12.3) to compute probabilities such as the probability an order can be processed in $\frac{1}{2}$ minute or less, 1 minute or less, and 2 minutes or less. These computations are

$$P(\text{service time} \leq 0.5 \text{ min.}) = 1 - e^{-1(0.5)} = 1 - 0.6065 = 0.3935$$
$$P(\text{service time} \leq 1.0 \text{ min.}) = 1 - e^{-1(1.0)} = 1 - 0.3679 = 0.6321$$
$$P(\text{service time} \leq 2.0 \text{ min.}) = 1 - e^{-1(2.0)} = 1 - 0.1353 = 0.8647$$

Thus, we would conclude that there is a 0.3935 probability that an order can be processed in $\frac{1}{2}$ minute or less, a 0.6321 probability that it can be processed in 1 minute or less, and a 0.8647 probability that it can be processed in 2 minutes or less.

In several waiting line models presented in this chapter, we assume that the probability distribution for the service time follows an exponential probability distribution. In practice, you should collect data on actual service times to determine whether the exponential probability distribution is a reasonable approximation of the service times for your application.

> A property of the exponential probability distribution is that there is a 0.6321 probability that the random variable takes on a value less than its mean. In waiting line applications, the exponential probability distribution indicates that approximately 63% of the service times are less than the mean service time and approximately 37% of the service times are greater than the mean service time.

## Queue Discipline

In describing a waiting line system, we must define the manner in which the waiting units are arranged for service. For the Burger Dome waiting line, and in general for most customer-oriented waiting lines, the units waiting for service are arranged on a **first-come, first served** basis; this approach is referred to as an **FCFS** queue discipline. However, some situations call for different queue disciplines. For example, when people wait for an elevator, the last one on the elevator is often the first one to complete service (i.e., the first to leave the elevator). Other types of queue disciplines assign priorities to the waiting units and then serve the unit with the highest priority first. In this chapter we consider only waiting lines based on a first-come, first-served queue discipline.

## Steady-State Operation

When the Burger Dome restaurant opens in the morning, no customers are in the restaurant. Gradually, activity builds up to a normal or steady state. The beginning or start-up period is referred to as the **transient period.** The transient period ends when the system reaches the normal or **steady-state operation.** Waiting line models describe the steady-state operating characteristics of a waiting line.

**12.2  THE SINGLE-CHANNEL WAITING LINE MODEL WITH POISSON ARRIVALS AND EXPONENTIAL SERVICE TIMES**

Waiting line models are often based on assumptions such as Poisson arrivals and exponential service times. When applying any waiting line model, data should be collected on the actual system to ensure that the assumptions of the model are reasonable.

In this section we present formulas that can be used to determine the steady-state operating characteristics for a single-channel waiting line. The formulas are applicable if the arrivals follow a Poisson probability distribution and the service times follow an exponential probability distribution. As these assumptions apply to the Burger Dome waiting line problem introduced in Section 12.1, we show how formulas can be used to determine Burger Dome's operating characteristics and thus provide management with helpful decision-making information.

The mathematical methodology used to derive the formulas for the operating characteristics of waiting lines is rather complex. However, our purpose in this chapter is not to provide the theoretical development of waiting line models, but rather to show how the formulas that have been developed can provide information about operating characteristics of the waiting line. Readers interested in the mathematical development of the formulas can consult the specialized texts listed in the References and Bibliography appendix at the end of the text.

### The Operating Characteristics

The following formulas can be used to compute the steady-state operating characteristics for a single-channel waiting line with Poisson arrivals and exponential service times, where

$$\lambda = \text{the mean number of arrivals per time period (the mean arrival rate)}$$
$$\mu = \text{the mean number of services per time period (the mean service rate)}$$

Equations (12.4) through (12.10) do not provide formulas for *optimal* conditions. Rather, these equations provide information about the steady-state operating characteristics of a waiting line.

1. The probability that no units are in the system:

$$P_0 = 1 - \frac{\lambda}{\mu} \tag{12.4}$$

2. The average number of units in the waiting line:

$$L_q = \frac{\lambda^2}{\mu(\mu - \lambda)} \tag{12.5}$$

3. The average number of units in the system:

$$L = L_q + \frac{\lambda}{\mu} \tag{12.6}$$

4. The average time a unit spends in the waiting line:

$$W_q = \frac{L_q}{\lambda} \tag{12.7}$$

5. The average time a unit spends in the system:

$$W = W_q + \frac{1}{\mu} \tag{12.8}$$

6. The probability that an arriving unit has to wait for service:

$$P_w = \frac{\lambda}{\mu} \tag{12.9}$$

7. The probability of $n$ units in the system:

$$P_n = \left(\frac{\lambda}{\mu}\right)^n P_0 \tag{12.10}$$

The values of the **mean arrival rate** $\lambda$ and the **mean service rate** $\mu$ are clearly important components in determining the operating characteristics. Equation (12.9) shows that the ratio of the mean arrival rate to the mean service rate, $\lambda/\mu$, provides the probability that an arriving unit has to wait because the service facility is in use. Hence, $\lambda/\mu$ often is referred to as the *utilization factor* for the service facility.

The operating characteristics presented in equations (12.4) through (12.10) are applicable only when the mean service rate $\mu$ is *greater than* the mean arrival rate $\lambda$—in other words, when $\lambda/\mu < 1$. If this condition does not exist, the waiting line will continue to grow without limit because the service facility does not have sufficient capacity to handle the arriving units. Thus, in using equations (12.4) through (12.10), we must have $\mu > \lambda$.

## Operating Characteristics for the Burger Dome Problem

Recall that for the Burger Dome problem we had a mean arrival rate of $\lambda = 0.75$ customers per minute and a mean service rate of $\mu = 1$ customer per minute. Thus, with $\mu > \lambda$, equations (12.4) through (12.10) can be used to provide operating characteristics for the Burger Dome single-channel waiting line:

$$P_0 = 1 - \frac{\lambda}{\mu} = 1 - \frac{0.75}{1} = 0.25$$

$$L_q = \frac{\lambda^2}{\mu(\mu - \lambda)} = \frac{0.75^2}{1(1 - 0.75)} = 2.25 \text{ customers}$$

$$L = L_q = \frac{\lambda}{\mu} + 2.25 + \frac{0.75}{1} = 3 \text{ customers}$$

$$W_q = \frac{L_q}{\lambda} = \frac{2.25}{0.75} = 3 \text{ minutes}$$

$$W = W_q + \frac{1}{\mu} = 3 + \frac{1}{1} = 4 \text{ minutes}$$

$$P_w = \frac{\lambda}{\mu} = \frac{0.75}{1} = 0.75$$

Problem 5 asks you to compute the operating characteristics for a single-channel waiting line application.

Equation (12.10) can be used to determine the probability of any number of customers in the system. Applying it provides the probability information in Table 12.2.

## The Manager's Use of Waiting Line Models

The results of the single-channel waiting line for Burger Dome show several important things about the operation of the waiting line. In particular, customers wait an average of 3 minutes before beginning to place an order, which appears somewhat long for a business based on fast service. In addition, the facts that the average number of customers waiting in line is 2.25 and that 75% of the arriving customers have to wait for service are indicators that something should be done to improve the waiting line operation. Table 12.2 shows a 0.1335 probability that seven or more customers are in the Burger Dome system at one time. This condition indicates a fairly high probability that Burger Dome will experience some long waiting lines if it continues to use the single-channel operation.

If the operating characteristics are unsatisfactory in terms of meeting company standards for service, Burger Dome's management should consider alternative designs or plans for improving the waiting line operation.

## Improving the Waiting Line Operation

Waiting line models often indicate where improvements in operating characteristics are desirable. However, the decision of how to modify the waiting line configuration to improve the operating characteristics must be based on the insights and creativity of the analyst.

After reviewing the operating characteristics provided by the waiting line model, Burger Dome's management concluded that improvements designed to reduce waiting times are desirable. To make improvements in the waiting line operation, analysts often focus on ways to improve the service rate. Generally, service rate improvements are obtained by making either or both the following changes:

1. Increase the mean service rate $\mu$ by making a creative design change or by using new technology.
2. Add service channels so that more customers can be served simultaneously.

Assume that in considering alternative 1, Burger Dome's management decides to employ an order filler who will assist the order taker at the cash register. The customer begins the service process by placing the order with the order taker. As the order is placed, the order taker announces the order over an intercom system, and the order filler begins filling the order. When

| *Table* 12.2 | THE PROBABILITY OF $n$ CUSTOMERS IN THE SYSTEM FOR THE BURGER DOME WAITING LINE PROBLEM | |
|---|---|---|

| Number of Customers | Probability |
|---|---|
| 0 | 0.2500 |
| 1 | 0.1875 |
| 2 | 0.1406 |
| 3 | 0.1055 |
| 4 | 0.0791 |
| 5 | 0.0593 |
| 6 | 0.0445 |
| 7 or more | 0.1335 |

the order is completed, the order taker handles the money, while the order filler continues to fill the order. With this design, Burger Dome's management estimates the mean service rate can be increased from the current service rate of 60 customers per hour to 75 customers per hour. Thus, the mean service rate for the revised system is $\mu = 75$ customers/60 minutes $= 1.25$ customers per minute. For $\lambda = 0.75$ customers per minute and $\mu = 1.25$ customers per minute, equations (12.4) through (12.10) can be used to provide the new operating characteristics for the Burger Dome waiting line. These operating characteristics are summarized in Table 12.3.

The information in Table 12.3 indicates that all operating characteristics have improved because of the increased service rate. In particular, the average time a customer spends in the waiting line has been reduced from 3 to 1.2 minutes and the average time a customer spends in the system has been reduced from 4 to 2 minutes. Are any other alternatives available that Burger Dome can use to increase the service rate? If so, and if the mean service rate $\mu$ can be identified for each alternative, equations (12.4) through (12.10) can be used to determine the revised operating characteristics and any improvements in the waiting line system. The added cost of any proposed change can be compared to the corresponding service improvements to help the manager determine whether the proposed service improvements are worthwhile.

As mentioned previously, another option that is often available is to provide one or more additional service channels so that more than one customer may be served at the same time. The extension of the single-channel waiting line model to the multiple-channel waiting line model is the topic of the next section.

*Problem 11 asks you to determine whether a change in the mean service rate will meet the company's service guideline for its customers.*

**Table 12.3**    OPERATING CHARACTERISTICS FOR THE BURGER DOME SYSTEM WITH THE MEAN SERVICE RATE INCREASED TO $\mu = 1.25$ CUSTOMERS PER MINUTE

| | |
|---|---|
| Probability of no customers in the system | 0.400 |
| Average number of customers in the waiting line | 0.900 |
| Average number of customers in the system | 1.500 |
| Average time in the waiting line | 1.200 minutes |
| Average time in the system | 2.000 minutes |
| Probability that an arriving customer has to wait | 0.600 |
| Probability that seven or more customers are in the system | 0.028 |

**NOTES and Comments**

1. The assumption that arrivals follow a Poisson probability distribution is equivalent to the assumption that the time between arrivals has an exponential probability distribution. For example, if the arrivals for a waiting line follow a Poisson probability distribution with a mean of 20 arrivals per hour, the time between arrivals will follow an exponential probability distribution, with a mean time between arrivals of $\frac{1}{20}$ or 0.05 hour.

2. Many individuals believe that whenever the mean service rate $\mu$ is greater than the mean arrival rate $\lambda$, the system should be able to handle or serve all arrivals. However, as the Burger Dome example shows, the variability of arrival times and service times may result in long waiting times even when the mean service rate exceeds the mean arrival rate. A contribution of waiting line models is that they can point out undesirable waiting line operating characteristics even when the $\mu > \lambda$ condition appears satisfactory.

## 12.3 THE MULTIPLE-CHANNEL WAITING LINE MODEL WITH POISSON ARRIVALS AND EXPONENTIAL SERVICE TIMES

You may be familiar with multiple-channel systems that also have multiple waiting lines. The waiting line model in this section has multiple channels, but only a *single* waiting line. Operating characteristics for a multiple-channel system are better when a single waiting line, rather than multiple waiting lines, is used.

A **multiple-channel waiting line** consists of two or more service channels that are assumed to be identical in terms of service capability. In the multiple-channel system, arriving units wait in a single waiting line and then move to the first available channel to be served.

The single-channel Burger Dome operation can be expanded to a two-channel system by opening a second service channel. Figure 12.2 shows a diagram of the Burger Dome two-channel waiting line.

In this section we present formulas that can be used to determine the steady-state operating characteristics for a multiple-channel waiting line. These formulas are applicable if the following conditions exist.

1. The arrivals follow a Poisson probability distribution.
2. The service time for each channel follows an exponential probability distribution.
3. The means service rate $\mu$ is the same for each channel.
4. The arrivals wait in a single waiting line and then move to the first open channel for service.

### The Operating Characteristics

The following formulas can be used to compute the steady-state operating characteristics for multiple-channel waiting lines, where

$$\lambda = \text{the mean arrival rate for the system}$$
$$\mu = \text{the mean service rate for } each \text{ channel}$$
$$k = \text{the number of channels}$$

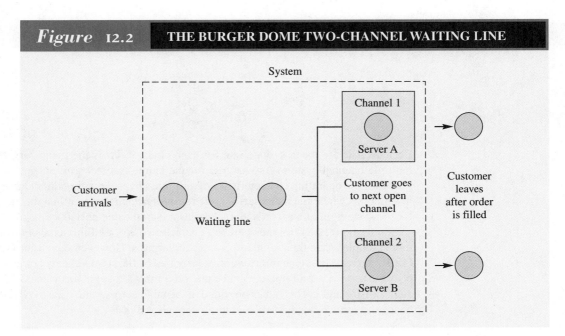

**Figure 12.2    THE BURGER DOME TWO-CHANNEL WAITING LINE**

1. The probability that no units are in the system:

$$P_0 = \frac{1}{\sum_{n=0}^{k-1} \dfrac{(\lambda/\mu)^n}{n!} + \dfrac{(\lambda/\mu)^k}{k!}\left(\dfrac{k\mu}{k\mu - \lambda}\right)} \qquad (12.11)$$

2. The average number of units in the waiting line:

$$L_q = \frac{(\lambda/\mu)^k \lambda \mu}{(k-1)!(k\mu - \lambda)^2} P_0 \qquad (12.12)$$

3. The average number of units in the system:

$$L = L_q + \frac{\lambda}{\mu} \qquad (12.13)$$

4. The average time a unit spends in the waiting line:

$$W_q = \frac{L_q}{\lambda} \qquad (12.14)$$

5. The average time a unit spends in the system:

$$W = W_q + \frac{1}{\mu} \qquad (12.15)$$

6. The probability that an arriving unit has to wait for service:

$$P_w = \frac{1}{k!}\left(\frac{\lambda}{\mu}\right)^k\left(\frac{k\mu}{k\mu - \lambda}\right)P_0 \qquad (12.16)$$

7. The probability of $n$ units in the system:

$$P_n = \frac{(\lambda/\mu)^n}{n!} P_0 \quad \text{for } n \le k \qquad (12.17)$$

$$P_n = \frac{(\lambda/\mu)^n}{k!k^{(n-k)}} P_0 \quad \text{for } n > k \qquad (12.18)$$

Because $\mu$ is the mean service rate for each channel, $k\mu$ is the mean service rate for the multiple-channel system. As was true for the single-channel waiting line model, the formulas for the operating characteristics of multiple-channel waiting lines can be applied only in situations where the mean service rate for the system is greater than the mean arrival rate for the system; in other words, the formulas are applicable only if $k\mu$ is greater than $\lambda$.

Some expressions for the operating characteristics of multiple-channel waiting lines are more complex than their single-channel counterparts. However, equations (12.11) through (12.18) provide the same information as provided by the single-channel model. To help simplify the use of the multiple-channel equations, Table 12.4 contains values of $P_0$ for selected values of $\lambda/\mu$ and $k$. The values provided in the table correspond to cases where $k\mu > \lambda$, and hence the service rate is sufficient to process all arrivals.

| Table 12.4 | VALUES OF $P_0$ FOR MULTIPLE-CHANNEL WAITING LINES WITH POISSON ARRIVALS AND EXPONENTIAL SERVICE TIMES |

| | Number of Channels ($k$) | | | |
| Ratio $\lambda/\mu$ | 2 | 3 | 4 | 5 |
|---|---|---|---|---|
| 0.15 | 0.8605 | 0.8607 | 0.8607 | 0.8607 |
| 0.20 | 0.8182 | 0.8187 | 0.8187 | 0.8187 |
| 0.25 | 0.7778 | 0.7788 | 0.7788 | 0.7788 |
| 0.30 | 0.7391 | 0.7407 | 0.7408 | 0.7408 |
| 0.35 | 0.7021 | 0.7046 | 0.7047 | 0.7047 |
| 0.40 | 0.6667 | 0.6701 | 0.6703 | 0.6703 |
| 0.45 | 0.6327 | 0.6373 | 0.6376 | 0.6376 |
| 0.50 | 0.6000 | 0.6061 | 0.6065 | 0.6065 |
| 0.55 | 0.5686 | 0.5763 | 0.5769 | 0.5769 |
| 0.60 | 0.5385 | 0.5479 | 0.5487 | 0.5488 |
| 0.65 | 0.5094 | 0.5209 | 0.5219 | 0.5220 |
| 0.70 | 0.4815 | 0.4952 | 0.4965 | 0.4966 |
| 0.75 | 0.4545 | 0.4706 | 0.4722 | 0.4724 |
| 0.80 | 0.4286 | 0.4472 | 0.4491 | 0.4493 |
| 0.85 | 0.4035 | 0.4248 | 0.4271 | 0.4274 |
| 0.90 | 0.3793 | 0.4035 | 0.4062 | 0.4065 |
| 0.95 | 0.3559 | 0.3831 | 0.3863 | 0.3867 |
| 1.00 | 0.3333 | 0.3636 | 0.3673 | 0.3678 |
| 1.20 | 0.2500 | 0.2941 | 0.3002 | 0.3011 |
| 1.40 | 0.1765 | 0.2360 | 0.2449 | 0.2463 |
| 1.60 | 0.1111 | 0.1872 | 0.1993 | 0.2014 |
| 1.80 | 0.0526 | 0.1460 | 0.1616 | 0.1646 |
| 2.00 | | 0.1111 | 0.1304 | 0.1343 |
| 2.20 | | 0.0815 | 0.1046 | 0.1094 |
| 2.40 | | 0.0562 | 0.0831 | 0.0889 |
| 2.60 | | 0.0345 | 0.0651 | 0.0721 |
| 2.80 | | 0.0160 | 0.0521 | 0.0581 |
| 3.00 | | | 0.0377 | 0.0466 |
| 3.20 | | | 0.0273 | 0.0372 |
| 3.40 | | | 0.0186 | 0.0293 |
| 3.60 | | | 0.0113 | 0.0228 |
| 3.80 | | | 0.0051 | 0.0174 |
| 4.00 | | | | 0.0130 |
| 4.20 | | | | 0.0093 |
| 4.40 | | | | 0.0063 |
| 4.60 | | | | 0.0038 |
| 4.80 | | | | 0.0017 |

## Operating Characteristics for the Burger Dome Problem

To illustrate the multiple-channel waiting line model, we return to the Burger Dome fast-food restaurant waiting line problem. Suppose that management wants to evaluate the desirability of opening a second order-processing station so that two customers can be served simultaneously. Assume a single waiting line with the first customer in line moving to the first available server. Let us evaluate the operating characteristics for this two-channel system.

We use equations (12.12) through (12.18) for the $k = 2$ channel system. For a mean arrival rate of $\lambda = 0.75$ customers per minute and mean service rate of $\mu = 1$ customer per minute for each channel, we obtain the operating characteristics:

$$P_0 = 0.4545 \quad \text{(from Table 12.4 with } \lambda/\mu = 0.75\text{)}$$

$$L_q = \frac{(0.75/1)^2(0.75)(1)}{(2 - 1)![2(1) - 0.75]^2}(0.4545) = 0.1227 \text{ customer}$$

$$L = L_q + \frac{\lambda}{\mu} = 0.1227 + \frac{0.75}{1} = 0.8727 \text{ customer}$$

$$W_q = \frac{L_q}{\lambda} = \frac{0.1227}{0.75} = 0.1636 \text{ minute}$$

$$W = W_q + \frac{1}{\mu} = 0.1636 + \frac{1}{1} = 1.1636 \text{ minutes}$$

$$P_w = \frac{1}{2!}\left(\frac{0.75}{1}\right)^2\left[\frac{2(1)}{2(1) - 0.75}\right](0.4545) = 0.2045$$

Try Problem 19, which will give you practice in determining the operating characteristics for a two-channel waiting line.

Using equations (12.17 and (12.18), we can compute the probabilities of $n$ customers in the system. The results from these computations are summarized in Table 12.5.

We can now compare the steady-state operating characteristics of the two-channel system to the operating characteristics of the original single-channel system discussed in Section 12.2.

1. The average time a customer spends in the system (waiting time plus service time) is reduced from $W = 4$ minutes to $W = 1.1636$ minutes.
2. The average number of customers in the waiting line is reduced from $L_q = 2.25$ customers to $L_q = 0.1227$ customers.
3. The average time a customer spends in the waiting line is reduced from $W_q = 3$ minutes to $W_q = 0.1636$ minutes.
4. The probability that a customer has to wait for service is reduced from $P_w = 0.75$ to $P_w = 0.2045$.

Clearly the two-channel system will significantly improve the operating characteristics of the waiting line. However, adding an order filler at each service station would further increase the mean service rate and improve the operating characteristics. The final decision

| Table 12.5 | THE PROBABILITY OF $n$ CUSTOMERS IN THE SYSTEM FOR THE BURGER DOME TWO-CHANNEL WAITING LINE |
|---|---|

| Number of Customers | Probability |
|---|---|
| 0 | 0.4545 |
| 1 | 0.3409 |
| 2 | 0.1278 |
| 3 | 0.0479 |
| 4 | 0.0180 |
| 5 or more | 0.0109 |

regarding the staffing policy at Burger Dome rests with the Burger Dome management. The waiting line study has simply provided the operating characteristics that can be anticipated under three configurations: a single-channel system with one employee, a single-channel system with two employees, and a two-channel system with an employee for each channel. After considering these results, what action would you recommend? In this case, Burger Dome adopted the following policy statement: For periods when customer arrivals are expected to average 45 customers per hour, Burger Dome will open two order-processing channels with one employee assigned to each.

By changing the mean arrival rate $\lambda$ to reflect arrival rates at different times of the day, and then computing the operating characteristics, Burger Dome's management can establish guidelines and policies that tell the store managers when they should schedule service operations with a single channel, two channels, or perhaps even three or more channels. The Management Science in Action article for Lourdes Hospital shows how a multiple-channel waiting line model has been used to help make hospital staffing decisions.

| N O T E S *and Comments* | The multiple-channel waiting line model is based on a single waiting line. You may have also encountered situations where each of the $k$ channels has its own waiting line. Management scientists have shown that the operating characteristics of multiple-channel systems are better if a single waiting line is used. People like them better also; no one who comes in after you can be served ahead of you. Thus, when possible, banks, airline reservation counters, food-service establishments, and other businesses frequently use a single waiting line for a multiple-channel system. |
| --- | --- |

# MANAGEMENT SCIENCE IN ACTION

## HOSPITAL STAFFING BASED ON A MULTIPLE-CHANNEL WAITING LINE MODEL*

Lourdes Hospital in Binghamton, New York, uses a centralized staff to schedule appointments for the hospital's outpatient, inpatient, and ambulance services. Physicians, their staffs, hospital personnel, and patients contact the centralized scheduling office by telephone to establish desired appointment times.

Efficiency of the scheduling process depends on the department's staff being able to process incoming telephone calls in a timely manner. Periodically, incoming requests for services overload the staff's ability to answer the telephone and process the appointments. As a result, users reported undesirable delays and lengthy waiting times. Management used a waiting line model to study the operation and suggest staffing changes that could improve the efficiency of the centralized scheduling process.

Data were collected on the number of telephone calls that arrived during each 15-minute period. The calls were random, not depending on the day of the week. A Poisson probability distribution was a good description of the random arrivals, with peak arrival times occurring between 9:00 A.M. and 11:30 A.M. and between 2:00 P.M. and 3:45 P.M. each

day. An investigation of service times found that, although service times were not exactly exponential, the exponential probability distribution provided a reasonable approximation.

In effect, the hospital's scheduling service was viewed as a multiple-channel waiting line with Poisson arrivals and exponential service times. The number of channels was simply the number of individuals on the scheduling staff. With the mean arrival rate adjusted for the different periods of the day, a waiting line model with $k$ channels was used to estimate the probability that an arriving call would have to wait for service. The staff size was determined by selecting the number of channels that kept the steady state probability of waiting to no more than 10%. Staff schedules and workloads were adjusted, efficiency improved, and the number of complaints about waiting for service declined.

*Based on S. R. Agnihothri and P. F. Taylor, "Staffing a Centralized Appointment Scheduling Department in Lourdes Hospital," *Interfaces* 21, no. 5 (September–October 1991): 1–11.

........................................................................................./  /............

## 12.4  SOME GENERAL RELATIONSHIPS FOR WAITING LINE MODELS

In Sections 12.2 and 12.3 we presented formulas for computing the operating characteristics for single-channel and multiple-channel waiting lines with Poisson arrivals and exponential service times. The operating characteristics of interest included

$L_q$ = the average number of units in the waiting line
$L$ = the average number of units in the system
$W_q$ = the average time a unit spends in the waiting line
$W$ = the average time a unit spends in the system

John D. C. Little showed that several relationships exist among these four characteristics and that these relationships apply to a variety of different waiting line systems. Two of the relationships, referred to as *Little's flow equations,* are

$$L = \lambda W \tag{12.19}$$
$$L_q = \lambda W_q \tag{12.20}$$

Equation (12.19) shows that the average number of units in the system, $L$, can be found by multiplying the mean arrival rate, $\lambda$, by the average time a unit spends in the system, $W$. Equation (12.20) shows that the same relationship holds between the average number of units in the waiting line, $L_q$, and the average time a unit spends in the waiting line, $W_q$.

Using equation (12.20) and solving for $W_q$, we obtain

$$W_q = \frac{L_q}{\lambda} \tag{12.21}$$

Equation (12.21) follows directly from Little's second flow equation. We used it for the single-channel waiting line model in Section 12.2 and the multiple-channel waiting line model in Section 12.3 [see equations (12.7) and (12.14)]. Once $L_q$ is computed for either of these models, equation (12.21) can then be used to compute $W_q$.

Another general expression that applies to waiting line models is that the average time in the system, $W$, is equal to the average time in the waiting line, $W_q$, plus the average service time. For a system with a mean service rate $\mu$, the mean service time is $1/\mu$. Thus, we have the general relationship

$$W = W_q + \frac{1}{\mu} \tag{12.22}$$

Recall that we used equation (12.22) to provide the average time in the system for both the single- and multiple-channel waiting line models [see equations (12.8) and (12.15)].

The importance of Little's flow equations is that they apply to *any waiting line model* regardless of whether arrivals follow the Poisson probability distribution and regardless of whether service times follow the exponential probability distribution. For example, in a study of the grocery checkout counters at Murphy's Foodliner, an analyst concluded that

The advantage of Little's flow equations is that they show how operating characteristics $L, L_q, W,$ and $W_q$ are related in any waiting line system. Arrivals and service times do not have to follow specific probability distributions for the flow equations to be applicable.

arrivals follow the Poisson probability distribution with the mean arrival rate of 24 customers per hour or $\lambda = 24/60 = 0.40$ customers per minute. However, the analyst found that service times follow a normal probability distribution rather than an exponential probability distribution. The mean service rate was found to be 30 customers per hour or $\mu = 30/60 = 0.50$ customers per minute. A time study of actual customer waiting times showed that, on average, a customer spends 4.5 minutes in the system (waiting time plus checkout time); that is, $W = 4.5$. Using the waiting line relationships discussed in this section, we can now compute other operating characteristics for this waiting line.

First, using equation (12.22) and solving for $W_q$, we have

$$W_q = W - \frac{1}{\mu} = 4.5 - \frac{1}{0.50} = 2.5 \text{ minutes}$$

The application of Little's flow equations is demonstrated in Problem 25.

With both $W$ and $W_q$ known, we can use Little's flow equations, (12.19) and (12.20), to compute

$$L = \lambda W = 0.40(4.5) = 1.8 \text{ customers}$$
$$L_q = \lambda W_q = 0.40(2.5) = 1 \text{ customer}$$

The manager of Murphy's Foodliner can now review these operating characteristics to see whether action should be taken to improve the service and to reduce the waiting time and the length of the waiting line.

---

### N O T E S  *and Comments*

In waiting line systems where the length of the waiting line is limited (e.g., a small waiting area), some arriving units will be blocked from joining the waiting line and will be lost. In this case, the blocked or lost arrivals will make the mean number of units entering the system something less than the mean arrival rate. By defining $\lambda$ as the mean number of units *joining the system,* rather than the mean arrival rate, the relationships discussed in this section can be used to determine $W, L, W_q,$ and $L_q$.

---

## 12.5    ECONOMIC ANALYSIS OF WAITING LINES

Frequently, decisions involving the design of waiting lines will be based on a subjective evaluation of the operating characteristics of the waiting line. For example, a manager may decide that an average waiting time of one minute or less and an average of two customers or less in the system are reasonable goals. The waiting line models presented in the preceding sections can be used to determine the number of channels that will meet the manager's waiting line performance goals.

On the other hand, a manager may want to identify the cost of operating the waiting line system and then base the decision regarding system design on a minimum hourly or daily operating cost. Before an economic analysis of a waiting line can be conducted, a total-cost model, which includes the cost of waiting and the cost of service, must be developed.

To develop a total-cost model for a waiting line, we begin by defining the notation to be used:

$$c_w = \text{the waiting cost per time period for each unit}$$
$$L = \text{the average number of units in the system}$$
$$c_s = \text{the service cost per time period for each channel}$$
$$k = \text{the number of channels}$$
$$TC = \text{the total cost per time period}$$

Waiting cost is based on average number of units in the system. It includes the time spent waiting in line plus the time spent being served.

The total cost is the sum of the waiting cost and the service cost; that is,

$$TC = c_w L + c_s k \qquad (12.23)$$

Adding more channels always improves the operating characteristics of the waiting line and reduces the waiting cost. However, additional channels increases the service cost. An economic analysis of waiting lines attempts to find the number of channels that will minimize total cost by balancing the waiting cost and the service cost.

To conduct an economic analysis of a waiting line, we must obtain reasonable estimates of the waiting cost and the service cost. Of these two costs, the waiting cost is usually the more difficult to evaluate. In the Burger Dome restaurant problem, the waiting cost would be the cost per minute for a customer waiting for service. This cost is not a direct cost to Burger Dome. However, if Burger Dome ignores this cost and allows long waiting lines, customers ultimately will take their business elsewhere. Thus, Burger Dome will experience lost sales and, in effect, incur a cost.

The service cost is generally easier to determine. This cost is the relevant cost associated with operating each service channel. In the Burger Dome problem, this cost would include the server's wages, benefits, and any other direct costs associated with operating the service channel. At Burger Dome, this cost is estimated to be $7 per hour.

To demonstrate the use of equation (12.23), we assume that Burger Dome is willing to assign a cost of $10 per hour for customer waiting time. We use the average number of units in the system, $L$, as computed in Sections 12.2 and 12.3 to obtain the total hourly cost for the single-channel and two-channel systems:

Single-channel system ($L = 3$ customers)

$$TC = c_w L + c_s k$$
$$= 10(3) + 7(1) = \$37.00 \text{ per hour}$$

Two-channel system ($L = 0.8727$ customer):

$$TC = c_w L + c_s k$$
$$= 10(0.8727) + 7(2) = \$22.73 \text{ per hour}$$

Problem 21 will test your ability to conduct an economic analysis of proposed single-channel and two-channel waiting line systems.

Thus, based on the cost data provided by Burger Dome, the two-channel system provides the most economical operation.

Figure 12.3 shows the general shapes of the cost curves in the economic analysis of waiting lines. The service cost increases as the number of channels is increased. However, with more channels, the service is better. As a result, waiting time and cost decrease as the number of channels is increased. The number of channels that will provide a good approximation of the minimum total-cost design can be found by evaluating the total cost for several design alternatives.

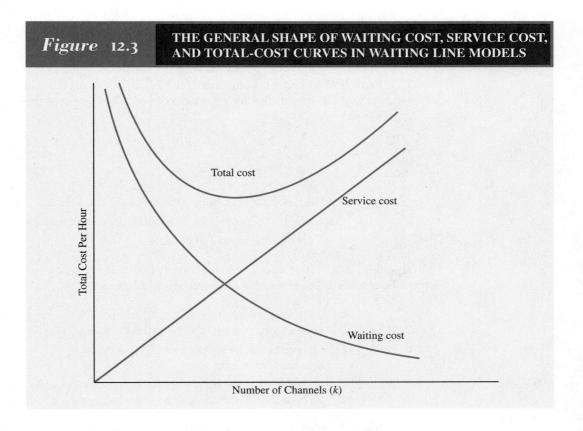

**Figure 12.3**   **THE GENERAL SHAPE OF WAITING COST, SERVICE COST, AND TOTAL-COST CURVES IN WAITING LINE MODELS**

| N O T E S *and Comments* |
| :--- |

1. In dealing with government agencies and utility companies, customers may not be able to take their business elsewhere. In these situations, no lost business occurs when long waiting times are encountered. This condition is one reason that service in such organizations may be poor and that customers in such situations may experience long waiting times.

2. In some instances, the organization providing the service also employs the units waiting for the service. For example, consider the case of a company that owns and operates the trucks used to deliver goods to and from its manufacturing plant. In addition to the costs associated with the trucks waiting to be loaded or unloaded, the firm also pays the wages of the truck loaders and unloaders who operate the service channel. In this case, the cost of having the trucks wait and the cost of operating the service channel are direct expenses to the firm. An economic analysis of the waiting line system is highly recommended for these types of situations.

........................................................................................................................../ /............

## 12.6 OTHER WAITING LINE MODELS

D. G. Kendall suggested a notation that is helpful in classifying the wide variety of different waiting line models that have been developed. The three-symbol Kendall notation is as follows:

$$A/B/k$$

where

| | |
|---|---|
| $A$ | denotes the probability distribution for the arrivals |
| $B$ | denotes the probability distribution for the service time |
| $k$ | denotes the number of channels |

Depending on the letter appearing in the $A$ or $B$ position, a variety of waiting line systems can be described. The letters that are commonly used are as follows:

| | |
|---|---|
| $M$ | designates a Poisson probability distribution for the arrivals or an exponential probability distribution for service time |
| $D$ | designates that the arrivals or the service time is deterministic or constant |
| $G$ | designates that the arrivals or the service time has a general probability distribution with a known mean and variance |

Using the Kendall notation, the single-channel waiting line model with Poisson arrivals and exponential service times is classified as an $M/M/1$ model. The 2-channel waiting line model with Poisson arrivals and exponential service times presented in Section 12.3 would be classified as an $M/M/2$ model.

---

**N O T E S**
**and Comments**

In some cases, the Kendall notation is extended to five symbols. The fourth symbol indicates the largest number of units that can be in the system, and the fifth symbol indicates the size of the population. The fourth symbol is used in situations where the waiting line can hold a finite or maximum number of units, and the fifth symbol is necessary when the population of arriving units or customers is finite. When the fourth and fifth symbols of the Kendall notation are omitted, the waiting line system is assumed to have infinite capacity, and the population is assumed to be infinite.

---

........................................................................................................................../ /............

## 12.7 THE SINGLE-CHANNEL WAITING LINE MODEL WITH POISSON ARRIVALS AND ARBITRARY SERVICE TIMES

Let us return to the single-channel waiting line model where arrivals are described by a Poisson probability distribution. However, we now assume that the probability distribution for the service times is not an exponential probability distribution. Thus, using the Kendall notation, the waiting line model that is appropriate is an $M/G/1$ model, where $G$ denotes a general or unspecified probability distribution.

## Operating Characteristics for the *M/G*/1 Model

The notation used to describe the operating characteristics for the *M/G*/1 model is

$$\lambda = \text{the mean arrival rate}$$
$$\mu = \text{the mean service rate}$$
$$\sigma = \text{the standard deviation of the service time}$$

Some of the steady-state operating characteristics of the *M/G*/1 waiting line model are as follows:

1. The probability that no units are in the system:

$$P_0 = 1 - \frac{\lambda}{\mu} \tag{12.24}$$

2. The average number of units in the waiting line:

$$L_q = \frac{\lambda^2\sigma^2 + (\lambda/\mu)^2}{2(1 - \lambda/\mu)} \tag{12.25}$$

3. The average number of units in the system:

$$L = L_q + \frac{\lambda}{\mu} \tag{12.26}$$

4. The average time a unit spends in the waiting line:

$$W_q = \frac{L_q}{\lambda} \tag{12.27}$$

5. The average time a unit spends in the system:

$$W = W_q + \frac{1}{\mu} \tag{12.28}$$

6. The probability that an arriving unit has to wait for service:

$$P_w = \frac{\lambda}{\mu} \tag{12.29}$$

Note that the relationships for *L*, $W_q$, and *W* are the same as the relationships used for the waiting line models in Sections 12.2 and 12.3. They are given by Little's flow equations.

**An Example.**   Retail sales at Hartlage's Seafood Supply are handled by one clerk. Customer arrivals are random, and the average arrival rate is 21 customers per hour or $\lambda = 21/60 = 0.35$ customers per minute. A study of the service process shows that the average or mean service time is 2 minutes per customer, with a standard deviation of $\sigma = 1.2$ minutes. The mean time of 2 minutes per customer shows that the clerk has a mean service

The sidebar note:
When providing input to the *M/G*/1 model, you should be consistent in terms of the time period. for example, if $\lambda$ and $\mu$ are expressed in terms of the number of units per *hour*, the standard deviation of the service time should be expressed in *hours*. The example that follows uses minutes as the time period for the arrival and service data.

Problem 27 provides another application of a single-channel waiting line with Poisson arrivals and arbitrary service times.

rate of $\mu = \frac{1}{2} = 0.50$ customers per minute. The operating characteristics of this $M/G/1$ waiting line system are

$$P_0 = 1 - \frac{\lambda}{\mu} = 1 - \frac{0.35}{0.50} = 0.30$$

$$L_q = \frac{(0.35)^2(1.2)^2 + (0.35/0.50)^2}{2(1 - 0.35/0.50)} = 1.1107 \text{ customers}$$

$$L = L_q + \frac{\lambda}{\mu} = 1.1107 + \frac{0.35}{0.50} = 1.8107 \text{ customers}$$

$$W_q = \frac{L_q}{\lambda} = \frac{1.1107}{0.35} = 3.1733 \text{ minutes}$$

$$W = W_q + \frac{1}{\mu} = 3.1733 + \frac{1}{0.50} = 5.1733 \text{ minutes}$$

$$P_w = \frac{\lambda}{\mu} = \frac{0.35}{0.50} = 0.70$$

Hartlage's manager can review these operating characteristics to determine whether scheduling a second clerk appears to be worthwhile.

## Constant Service Times

We want to comment briefly on the single-channel waiting line model that assumes random arrivals but constant service times. Such a waiting line can occur in production and manufacturing environments where machine-controlled service times are constant. This waiting line is described by the $M/D/1$ model, with the $D$ referring to the deterministic service times. With the $M/D/1$ model, the average number of units in the waiting line, $L_q$, can be found by using equation (12.25) with the condition that the standard deviation of the constant service time is $\sigma = 0$. Thus, the expression for the average number of units in the waiting line for the $M/D/1$ waiting line becomes

$$L_q = \frac{(\lambda/\mu)^2}{2(1 - \lambda/\mu)} \tag{12.30}$$

The other expressions presented earlier in this section can be used to determine additional operating characteristics of the $M/D/1$ system.

| N O T E S |
| :---: |
| *and Comments* |

Whenever the operating characteristics of a waiting line are unacceptable, managers often try to improve service by increasing the mean service rate $\mu$. This is a good idea, but equation (12.25) shows that the variation in the service times also affects the operating characteristics of the waiting line. Because the standard deviation of service times, $\sigma$, appears in the numerator of equation (12.25), a larger variation in service times results in a larger average number of units in the waiting line. Hence, another alternative for improving the service capabilities of a waiting line is to reduce the variation in the service times. Thus, even when the mean service rate of the service facility cannot be increased, a reduction in $\sigma$ will reduce the average number of units in the waiting line and improve the other operating characteristics of the system.

............................................................................................../  /.............

## 12.8    A MULTIPLE-CHANNEL MODEL WITH POISSON ARRIVALS, ARBITRARY SERVICE TIMES, AND NO WAITING LINE

An interesting variation of the waiting line models discussed so far involves a system in which no waiting is allowed. Arriving units or customers seek service from one of several service channels. If all channels are busy, arriving units are denied access to the system. In waiting line terminology, arrivals occurring when the system is full are **blocked** and are cleared from the system. Such customers may be lost or may attempt a return to the system later.

The specific model considered in this section is based on the following assumptions.

1.  The system has $k$ channels.
2.  The arrivals follow a Poisson probability distribution, with mean arrival rate $\lambda$.
3.  The service times for each channel may have any probability distribution.
4.  The mean service rate $\mu$ is the same for each channel.
5.  An arrival enters the system only if at least one channel is available. An arrival occurring when all channels are busy is blocked—that is, denied service and not allowed to enter the system.

With $G$ denoting a general or unspecified probability distribution for service times, the appropriate model for this situation is referred to as an *M/G/k* model with "blocked customers cleared." The question addressed in this type of situation is, How many channels or servers should be used?

A primary application of this model involves the design of telephone and other communication systems where the arrivals are the calls and the channels are the number of telephone or communication lines available. In such a system, the calls are made to one telephone number, with each call automatically switched to an open channel if possible. When all channels are busy, additional calls receive a busy signal and are denied access to the system.

### The Operating Characteristics for the *M/G/k* Model with Blocked Customers Cleared

We approach the problem of selecting the best number of channels by computing the steady-state probabilities that $j$ of the $k$ channels will be busy. These probabilities are

$$P_j = \frac{(\lambda/\mu)^j/j!}{\displaystyle\sum_{i=0}^{k} (\lambda/\mu)^i/i!} \tag{12.31}$$

where

$\lambda$ = the mean arrival rate

$\mu$ = the mean service rate for each channel

$k$ = the number of channels

$P_j$ = the probability that $j$ of the $k$ channels are busy
         for $j = 0, 1, 2, \ldots, k$

With no waiting allowed, operating characteristics $L_q$ and $W_q$ considered in previous waiting line models are automatically zero regardless of the number of service channels. In this situation, the more important design consideration involves determining how the percentage of blocked customers is affected by the number of service channels.

The most important probability value is $P_k$, which is the probability that all $k$ channels are busy. On a percentage basis, $P_k$ indicates the percentage of arrivals that are blocked and denied access to the system.

Another operating characteristic of interest is the average number of units in the system; note that this number is equivalent to the average number of channels in use. Letting $L$ denote the average number of units in the system, we have

$$L = \frac{\lambda}{\mu} (1 - P_k) \tag{12.32}$$

**An Example.** Microdata Software, Inc., uses a telephone ordering system for its computer software products. Callers place orders with Microdata by using the company's 800 telephone number. Assume that calls to this telephone number arrive at an average rate of $\lambda = 12$ calls per hour. The time required to process a telephone order varies considerably from order to order. However, each Microdata sales representative can be expected to handle an average of $\mu = 6$ calls per hour. Currently, the Microdata 800 telephone number has three internal lines or channels, each operated by a separate sales representative. Calls received on the 800 number are automatically transferred to an open line or channel if available.

Whenever all three lines are busy, callers receive a busy signal. In the past, Microdata's management has assumed that callers receiving a busy signal will call back later. However, recent research on telephone ordering has shown that a substantial number of callers who are denied access do not call back later. These lost calls represent lost revenues for the firm, so Microdata's management has requested an analysis of the telephone ordering system. Specifically, management wants to know the percentage of callers who are getting busy signals and are being blocked from the system. If management's goal is to provide sufficient capacity to handle 90% of the callers, how many telephone lines and sales representatives should Microdata use?

We can demonstrate the use of equation (12.31) by computing $P_3$, the probability that all three of the currently available telephone lines will be in use and additional callers will be blocked:

$$P_3 = \frac{(^{12}/_6)^3/3!}{(^{12}/_6)^0/0! + (^{12}/_6)^1/1! + (^{12}/_6)^2/2! + (^{12}/_6)^3/3!} = \frac{1.3333}{6.3333} = 0.2105$$

With $P_3 = 0.2105$, approximately 21% of the calls, or slightly more than one in five calls, are being blocked. Only 79% of the calls are being handled immediately by the 3-line system.

Let us assume that Microdata expands to a 4-line system. Then, the probability that all four channels will be in use and that callers will be blocked is

$$P_4 = \frac{(^{12}/_6)^4/4!}{(^{12}/_6)^0/0! + (^{12}/_6)^1/1! + (^{12}/_6)^2/2! + (^{12}/_6)^3/3! + (^{12}/_6)^4/4!} = \frac{0.6667}{7} = 0.0952$$

Try Problem 30 to obtain practice in multiple-channel systems with no waiting line.

With only 9.52% of the callers blocked, 90.48% of the callers will reach the Microdata sales representatives. Thus, Microdata should expand its order-processing operation to 4 lines to meet management's goal of providing sufficient capacity to handle at least 90% of the callers. The average number of calls in the 4-line system and thus the average number of lines and sales representatives that will be busy is

$$L = \frac{\lambda}{\mu} (1 - P_4) = \frac{12}{6} (1 - 0.0952) = 1.8095$$

Although an average of less than 2 lines will be busy, the 4-line system is necessary to provide the capacity to handle at least 90% of the callers. We used equation (12.31) to calculate the probability that 0, 1, 2, 3, or 4 lines will be busy. These probabilities are summarized in Table 12.6.

As we discussed in Section 12.5, an economic analysis of waiting lines can be used to guide system design decisions. In the Microdata system, the cost of the additional line and additional sales representative should be relatively easy to establish. This cost can be balanced against the cost of the blocked calls. With 9.52% of the calls blocked and $\lambda = 12$ calls per hour, an 8-hour day will have an average of $8(12)(0.0952) = 9.1$ blocked calls. If Microdata can estimate the cost of possible lost sales, the cost of these blocked calls can be established. The economic analysis based on the service cost and the blocked-call cost can assist in determining the optimal number of lines for the system.

| *Table* 12.6 | PROBABILITIES OF BUSY LINES FOR THE MICRODATA 4-LINE SYSTEM |
|---|---|

| Number of Busy Lines | Probability |
|---|---|
| 0 | 0.1429 |
| 1 | 0.2857 |
| 2 | 0.2857 |
| 3 | 0.1905 |
| 4 | 0.0952 |

**NOTES and Comments**

Many of the operating characteristics we have considered in previous sections are not relevant for the *M/G/k* model with blocked customers cleared. In particular, the average time in the waiting line, $W_q$, and the average number of units in the waiting line, $L_q$, are no longer considered because waiting is not permitted in this type of system.

## 12.9  WAITING LINE MODELS WITH FINITE CALLING POPULATIONS

For the waiting line models introduced so far, the population of units or customers arriving for service has been considered to be unlimited. In technical terms, when no limit is placed on how many units may seek service, the model is said to have an **infinite calling population.** Under this assumption, the mean arrival rate $\lambda$ remains constant regardless of how many units are in the waiting line system. This assumption of an infinite calling population is made in most waiting line models.

In other cases, the maximum number of units or customers that may seek service is assumed to be finite. In this situation, the mean arrival rate for the system changes, depending on the number of units in the waiting line, and the waiting line model is said to have a **finite calling population.** The formulas for the operating characteristics of the previous waiting line models must be modified to account for the effect of the finite calling population.

In previous waiting line models, the arrival rate was constant and independent of the number of units in the system. With a finite calling population, the arrival rate decreases as the number of units in the system increases because, with more units in the system, fewer units are available for arrivals.

The mean arrival rate $\lambda$ is defined differently for the finite calling population model. Specifically, $\lambda$ is defined in terms of the mean arrival rate for *each unit*.

The finite calling population model discussed in this section is based on the following assumptions.

1. The arrivals for *each unit* follow a Poisson probability distribution, with mean arrival rate $\lambda$.
2. The service times follow an exponential probability distribution, with mean service rate $\mu$.
3. The population of units that may seek service is finite.

With a single channel, the waiting line model is referred to as an *M/M/*1 model with a finite calling population.

The mean arrival rate for the *M/M/*1 model with a finite calling population is defined in terms of how often *each unit* arrives or seeks service. This situation differs from that for previous waiting line models in which $\lambda$ denoted the mean arrival rate for the system. With a finite calling population, the mean arrival rate for the system varies, depending on the number of units in the system. Instead of adjusting for the changing system arrival rate, in the finite calling population model $\lambda$ indicates the mean arrival rate for each unit.

### The Operating Characteristics for the *M/M/*1 Model with a Finite Calling Population

The following formulas are used to determine the steady-state operating characteristics for an *M/M/*1 model with a finite calling population, where

$$\lambda = \text{the mean arrival rate for each unit}$$
$$\mu = \text{the mean service rate}$$
$$N = \text{the size of the population}$$

1. The probability that no units are in the system:

$$P_0 = \frac{1}{\sum_{n=0}^{N} \frac{N!}{(N-n)!}\left(\frac{\lambda}{\mu}\right)^n} \tag{12.33}$$

2. The average number of units in the waiting line:

$$L_q = N - \frac{\lambda + \mu}{\lambda}(1 - P_0) \tag{12.34}$$

3. The average number of units in the system:

$$L = L_q + (1 - P_0) \tag{12.35}$$

4. The average time a unit spends in the waiting line:

$$W_q = \frac{L_q}{(N-L)\lambda} \tag{12.36}$$

5. The average time a unit spends in the system:

$$W = W_q + \frac{1}{\mu} \tag{12.37}$$

6. The probability an arriving unit has to wait for service:

$$P_w = 1 - P_0 \tag{12.38}$$

7. The probability of $n$ units in the system:

$$P_n = \frac{N!}{(N-n)!}\left(\frac{\lambda}{\mu}\right)^n P_0 \quad \text{for } n = 0, 1, \ldots, N \tag{12.39}$$

One of the primary applications of the $M/M/1$ model with a finite calling population is referred to as the *machine repair problem.* In this problem, a group of machines is considered to be the finite population of "customers" that may request repair service. Whenever a machine breaks down, an arrival occurs in the sense that a new repair request is initiated. If another machine breaks down before the repair work has been completed on the first machine, the second machine begins to form a "waiting line" for repair service. Additional breakdowns by other machines will add to the length of the waiting line. The assumption of first-come, first-served indicates that machines are repaired in the order they break down. The $M/M/1$ model shows that one person or one channel is available to perform the repair service. To return the machine to operation, each machine with a breakdown must be repaired by the single-channel operation.

**An Example.**    The Kolkmeyer Manufacturing Company has a group of six identical machines; each machine operates an average of 20 hours between breakdowns. Thus, the mean arrival rate or request for repair service for each machine is $\lambda = \frac{1}{20} = 0.05$ per hour. With randomly occurring breakdowns, the Poisson probability distribution is used to describe the machine breakdown arrival process. One person from the maintenance department provides the single-channel repair service for the six machines. The exponentially distributed service times have a mean of 2 hours per machine or a mean service rate of $\mu = \frac{1}{2} = 0.50$ machines per hour.

With $\lambda = 0.05$ and $\mu = 0.50$, we use equations (12.33) through (12.38) to compute the operating characteristics for this system. Note that the use of equation (12.33) makes the computations involved somewhat cumbersome. Confirm for yourself that equation (12.33) provides the value of $P_0 = 0.4845$. The computations for the other operating characteristics are

$$L_q = 6 - \left(\frac{0.05 + 0.50}{0.05}\right)(1 - 0.4845) = 0.3297 \text{ machine}$$

$$L = 0.3295 + (1 - 0.4845) = 0.8451 \text{ machine}$$

$$W_q = \frac{0.3295}{(6 - 0.845)0.05} = 1.279 \text{ hours}$$

$$W = 1.279 + \frac{1}{0.50} = 3.279 \text{ hours}$$

$$P_w = 1 - P_0 = 1 - 0.4845 = 0.5155$$

Finally, equation (12.39) can be used to compute the probabilities of any number of machines being in the repair system.

As with other waiting line models, the operating characteristics provide the manager with information about the waiting line operation. Whether these operating characteristics suggest that better repair service is needed depends on the cost of the idle machine waiting time compared to the cost of assigning an additional person to make the repair operation either a two-channel system or a faster one-channel system.

*Figure* 12.4 **THE MANAGEMENT SCIENTIST SOLUTION FOR THE KOLKMEYER TWO-CHANNEL MACHINE REPAIR PROBLEM**

```
WAITING LINE MODELS
*******************
     NUMBER OF CHANNELS = 2
     POISSON ARRIVALS WITH MEAN RATE = .05
     EXPONENTIAL SERVICE TIMES WITH MEAN RATE = .5 PER CHANNEL
     FINITE CALLING POPULATION OF SIZE = 6

OPERATING CHARACTERISTICS
--------------------------
THE PROBABILITY OF NO UNITS IN THE SYSTEM              0.5602
THE AVERAGE NUMBER OF UNITS IN THE WAITING LINE        0.0227
THE AVERAGE NUMBER OF UNITS IN THE SYSTEM              0.5661
THE AVERAGE TIME A UNIT SPENDS IN THE WAITING LINE     0.0834
THE AVERAGE TIME A UNIT SPENDS IN THE SYSTEM           2.0834
THE PROBABILITY THAT AN ARRIVING UNIT HAS TO WAIT      0.1036


Number of Units in the System          Probability
-----------------------------          -----------
              0                           0.5602
              1                           0.3361
              2                           0.0840
              3                           0.0168
              4                           0.0025
              5                           0.0003
              6                           0.0000
```

Operating characteristics of an *M/M/*1 waiting line with a finite calling population are considered in Problem 34.

Computations for the multiple-channel finite calling population model are more complex than those for the single-channel model. A computer solution is virtually mandatory in this case. The Management Scientist software package that accompanies this text has the capability of analyzing the finite calling population model. The computer output for the Kolkmeyer machine repair problem with a two-person, two-channel repair system is shown in Figure 12.4. By considering the cost of machine waiting or downtime and the cost of repair personnel, management can determine whether the two-channel system is cost effective.

## SUMMARY

In this chapter we presented a variety of waiting line models that have been developed to help managers make better decisions concerning the operation of waiting lines. For each model, we presented formulas that could be used to develop operating characteristics or performance measures for the system being studied. The operating characteristics presented include the following:

1. Probability that no units are in the system
2. Average number of units in the waiting line

3. Average number of units in the system
4. Average time a unit spends in the waiting line
5. Average time a unit spends in the system
6. Probability that arriving units will have to wait for service

We also showed how an economic analysis of the waiting line could be conducted by developing a total-cost model that includes the cost associated with units waiting for service and the cost required to operate the service facility.

As many of the examples in this chapter show, the most obvious applications of waiting line models are situations in which customers arrive for service such as at a grocery checkout counter, bank, or restaurant. However, with a little creativity, waiting line models can be applied to many different situations such as telephone calls waiting for connections, mail orders waiting for processing, machines waiting for repairs, manufacturing jobs waiting to be processed, and money waiting to be spent or invested. The Management Science in Action article describes how a waiting line model provided the basis for improving productivity of a fire department in New Haven, Connecticut.

The complexity and diversity of waiting line systems found in practice often prevents an analyst from finding an existing waiting line model that fits the specific application being studied. Simulation, the topic discussed in Chapter 13, provides an approach to determining the operating characteristics of such waiting line systems.

# MANAGEMENT SCIENCE IN ACTION

## IMPROVING FIRE DEPARTMENT PRODUCTIVITY*

The New Haven, Connecticut, Fire Department implemented a reorganization plan with cross-trained fire and medical personnel responding to both fire and medical emergencies. A waiting line model provided the basis for the reorganization by demonstrating that substantial improvements in emergency medical response time could be achieved with only a small reduction in fire protection. Annual savings were reported to be $1.4 million.

The model was based on Poisson arrivals and exponential service times for both fire and medical emergencies. It was used to estimate the average time that a person placing a call would have to wait for the appropriate emergency unit to arrive at the location. Waiting times were estimated by the model's prediction of the average travel time to reach each of the city's 28 census tracts.

The model was first applied to the original system of 16 fire units and 4 emergency medical units that operated independently. It was then applied to the proposed reorganization plan that involved cross-trained department personnel qualified to respond to both fire and medical emergencies. Results from the model demonstrated that average travel times could be reduced under the reorganization plan. Various facility location alternatives also were evaluated. When implemented, the reorganization plan reduced operating cost and improved public safety services.

*Based on A. J. Sweeney, L. Goldring, and E. D. Geyer, "Improving Fire Department Productivity: Merging Fire and Emergency Medical Units in New Haven," *Interfaces* 23, no. 1 (January–February 1993): 109–129.

# GLOSSARY

**Queue**  A waiting line.

**Queuing theory**  The body of knowledge dealing with waiting lines.

**Operating characteristics**  The performance measures for a waiting line including the probability that no units are in the system, the average number of units in the waiting line, the average waiting time, and so on.

**Single-channel waiting line**  A waiting line with only one service facility.

**Poisson probability distribution**  A probability distribution used to describe the arrival pattern for some waiting line models.

**Exponential probability distribution**  A probability distribution used to describe the service time for some waiting line models.

**First-come, first-served (FCFS)**  The queue discipline that serves waiting units on a first-come, first-served basis.

**Transient period**  The start-up period for a waiting line, occurring before the waiting line reaches a normal or steady-state operation.

**Steady-state operation**  The normal operation of the waiting line after it has gone through a start-up or transient period. The operating characteristics of waiting lines are computed for steady-state conditions.

**Mean arrival rate**  The average number of customers or units arriving in a given period of time.

**Mean service rate**  The average number of customers or units that can be served by one service facility in a given period of time.

**Multiple-channel waiting line**  A waiting line with two or more parallel service facilities.

**Blocked**  When arriving units cannot enter the waiting line because the system is full. Blocked units can occur when waiting lines are not allowed or when waiting lines have a finite capacity.

**Infinite calling population**  The population of customers or units who may seek service has no specified upper limit.

**Finite calling population**  The population of customers or units who may seek service has a fixed and finite value.

## PROBLEMS

1. Willow Brook National Bank operates a drive-up teller window that allows customers to complete bank transactions without getting out of their cars. On weekday mornings, arrivals to the drive-up teller window occur at random, with a mean arrival rate of 24 customers per hour or 0.4 customers per minute.
   a. What is the mean or expected number of customers that will arrive in a 5-minute period?
   b. Assume that the Poisson probability distribution can be used to describe the arrival process. Use the mean arrival rate in part (a) and compute the probabilities that exactly 0, 1, 2, and 3 customers will arrive during a 5-minute period.
   c. Delays are expected if more than 3 customers arrive during any 5-minute period. What is the probability that delays will occur?

2. In the Willow Brook National Bank waiting line system (see Problem 1), assume that the service times for the drive-up teller follow an exponential probability distribution with a mean service rate of 36 customers per hour or 0.6 customer per minute. Use the exponential probability distribution to answer the following questions.
   a. What is the probability the service time is 1 minute or less?
   b. What is the probability the service time is 2 minutes or less?
   c. What is the probability the service time is more than 2 minutes?

3. Use the single-channel drive-up bank teller operation referred to in Problems 1 and 2 to determine the following operating characteristics for the system.
   a. The probability that no customers are in the system
   b. The average number of customers waiting
   c. The average number of customers in the system
   d. The average time a customer spends waiting
   e. The average time a customer spends in the system
   f. The probability that arriving customers will have to wait for service

4. Use the single-channel drive-up bank teller operation referred to in Problems 1–3 to determine the probabilities of 0, 1, 2, and 3 customers in the system. What is the probability that more than 3 customers will be in the drive-up teller system at the same time?

**SELF TEST**

5. The reference desk of a university library receives requests for assistance. Assume that a Poisson probability distribution with a mean rate of 10 requests per hour can be used to describe the arrival pattern and that service times follow an exponential probability distribution with a mean service rate of 12 requests per hour.
   a. What is the probability that no requests for assistance are in the system?
   b. What is the average number of requests that will be waiting for service?
   c. What is the average waiting time in minutes before service begins?
   d. What is the average time at the reference desk in minutes (waiting time plus service time)?
   e. What is the probability that a new arrival has to wait for service?

6. Trucks using a single-channel loading dock arrive according to a Poisson probability distribution. The time required to load/unload follows an exponential probability distribution. The mean arrival rate is 12 trucks per day, and the mean service rate is 18 trucks per day.
   a. What is the probability that no trucks are in the system?
   b. What is the average number of trucks waiting for service?
   c. What is the average time a truck waits for the loading/unloading service to begin?
   d. What is the probability that an arriving truck will have to wait for service?

7. Speedy Oil provides a single-channel automobile oil change and lubrication service. New arrivals occur at the rate of 2.5 cars per hour and the mean service rate is 5 cars per hour. Assume that arrivals follow a Poisson probability distribution and that service times follow an exponential probability distribution.
   a. What is the average number of cars in the system?
   b. What is the average time that a car waits for the oil and lubrication service to begin?
   c. What is the average time a car spends in the system?
   d. What is the probability that an arrival has to wait for service?

8. For the Burger Dome single-channel waiting line in Section 12.2, assume that the arrival rate is increased to 1 customer per minute and that the mean service rate is increased to 1.25 customers per minute. Compute the following operating characteristics for the new system: $P_0$, $L_q$, $L$, $W_q$, $W$, and $P_w$. Does this system provide better or poorer service compared to the original system? Discuss any differences and the reason for these differences.

9. Marty's Barber Shop has one barber. Customers arrive at the rate of 2.2 customers per hour, and haircuts are given at the average rate of 5 per hour. Use the Poisson arrivals and exponential service times model to answer the following questions.
   a. What is the probability that no units are in the system?
   b. What is the probability that 1 customer is receiving a haircut and no one is waiting?
   c. What is the probability that 1 customer is receiving a haircut and 1 customer is waiting?
   d. What is the probability that 1 customer is receiving a haircut and 2 customers are waiting?
   e. What is the probability that more than 2 customers are waiting?
   f. What is the average time a customer waits for service?

10. Trosper Tire Company has decided to hire a new mechanic to handle all tire changes for customers ordering a new set of tires. Two mechanics have applied for the job. One mechanic has

limited experience, can be hired for $14 per hour, and can service an average of 3 customers per hour. The other mechanic has several years of experience, can service an average of 4 customers per hour, but must be paid $20 per hour. Assume that customers arrive at the Trosper garage at the rate of 2 customers per hour.

a. What are the waiting line operating characteristics using each mechanic, assuming Poisson arrivals and exponential service times?

b. If the company assigns a customer waiting cost of $30 per hour, which mechanic provides the lower operating cost?

SELF TEST

11. Agan Interior Design provides home and office decorating assistance to its customers. In normal operation, an average of 2.5 customers arrive each hour. One design consultant is available to answer customer questions and make product recommendations. The consultant averages 10 minutes with each customer.

a. Compute the operating characteristics of the customer waiting line, assuming Poisson arrivals and exponential service times.

b. Service goals dictate that an arriving customer should not wait for service more than an average of 5 minutes. Is this goal being met? If not, what action do you recommend?

c. If the consultant can reduce the average time spent per customer to 8 minutes, what is the mean service rate? Will the service goal be met?

12. Pete's Market is a small local grocery store with only one checkout counter. Assume that shoppers arrive at the checkout lane according to a Poisson probability distribution, with a mean arrival rate of 15 customers per hour. The checkout service times follow an exponential probability distribution, with a mean service rate of 20 customers per hour.

a. Compute the operating characteristics for this waiting line.

b. If the manager's service goal is to limit the waiting time prior to beginning the checkout process to no more than 5 minutes, what recommendations would you provide regarding the current checkout system?

13. After reviewing the waiting line analysis of Problem 12, the manager of Pete's Market wants to consider one of the following alternatives for improving service. What alternative would you recommend? Justify your recommendation.

a. Hire a second person to bag the groceries while the cash register operator is entering the cost data and collecting money from the customer. With this improved single-channel operation, the mean service rate could be increased to 30 customers per hour.

b. Hire a second person to operate a second checkout counter. The two-channel operation would have a mean service rate of 20 customers per hour for each channel.

14. Ocala Software Systems operates a technical support center for its software customers. If customers have installation and/or use problems with Ocala software products, they may telephone the technical support center and obtain free consultation. Currently, Ocala operates its support center with one consultant. If the consultant is busy when a new customer call arrives, the customer hears a recorded message stating that all consultants are currently busy with other customers. The customer is then asked to hold and a consultant will be available as soon as possible. The customer calls follow a Poisson probability distribution with a mean arrival rate of 5 calls per hour. On average, it takes 7.5 minutes for a consultant to answer a customer's questions. The service time follows an exponential probability distribution.

a. What is the mean service rate in terms of customers per hour?

b. What is the probability that no customers are in the system and the consultant is idle?

c. What is the average number of customers waiting for a consultant?

d. What is the average time a customer waits for a consultant?

e. What is the probability that a customer will have to wait for a consultant?

f. Ocala's customer service department has recently received several letters from customers complaining about the difficulty of obtaining technical support. If Ocala's customer service guidelines state that no more than 35% of all customers should have to wait for technical support and that the average waiting time should be 2 minutes or less, does your waiting line analysis indicate that Ocala is or is not meeting its customer service guidelines? What action, if any, would you recommend?

15. To improve customer service, Ocala Software Systems (see Problem 14) wants to investigate the effect of using a second consultant at its technical support center. What effect would the additional consultant have on customer service? Would two technical consultants enable Ocala to meet its service guidelines with no more than 35% of all customers having to wait for technical support and an average customer waiting time of 2 minutes or less? Discuss.

16. The new Fore and Aft Marina is to be located on the Ohio River near Madison, Indiana. Assume that Fore and Aft has decided to build a docking facility where one boat at a time can stop for gas and servicing. Assume that arrivals follow a Poisson probability distribution, with a mean of 5 boats per hour, and that service times follow an exponential probability distribution, with a mean of 10 boats per hour. Answer the following questions.
    a. What is the probability that no boats are in the system?
    b. What is the average number of boats that will be waiting for service?
    c. What is the average time a boat will spend waiting for service?
    d. What is the average time a boat will spend at the dock?
    e. If you were the manager of Fore and Aft Marina, would you be satisfied with the service level your system will be providing? Why or why not?

17. The manager of the Fore and Aft Marina in Problem 16 wants to investigate the possibility of enlarging the docking facility so that two boats can stop for gas and servicing simultaneously. Assume that the mean arrival rate is 5 boats per hour and that the mean service rate for each channel is 10 boats per hour.
    a. What is the probability that the boat dock will be idle?
    b. What is the average number of boats that will be waiting for service?
    c. What is the average time a boat will spend waiting for service?
    d. What is the average time a boat will spend at the dock?
    e. If you were the manager of Fore and Aft Marina, would you be satisfied with the service level your system will be providing? Why or why not?

18. The City Beverage Drive-Thru is considering a two-channel service system. Cars arrive according to the Poisson probability distribution, with a mean arrival rate of 6 cars per hour. The service times have an exponential probability distribution, with a mean service rate of 10 cars per hour for each channel.
    a. What is the probability that no cars are in the system?
    b. What is the average number of cars waiting for service?
    c. What is the average time waiting for service?
    d. What is the average time in the system?
    e. What is the probability that an arriving car will have to wait for service?

**SELF TEST**

19. Consider a two-channel waiting line with Poisson arrivals and exponential service times. The mean arrival rate is 14 units per hour, and the mean service rate is 10 units per hour for each channel.
    a. What is the probability that no units are in the system?
    b. What is the average number of units in the system?
    c. What is the average time a unit waits for service?
    d. What is the average time a unit is in the system?
    e. What is the probability of having to wait for service?

20. Refer to Problem 19. Assume that the system is expanded to a three-channel operation.
    a. Compute the operating characteristics for this waiting line system.
    b. If the service goal is to provide sufficient capacity so that no more than 25% of the customers have to wait for service, is the two- or three-channel system preferred?

**SELF TEST**

21. Refer to the Agan Interior Design situation in Problem 11. Agan's management would like to evaluate two alternatives:
    • Use one consultant with an average service time of 8 minutes per customer.
    • Expand to two consultants, each of whom has an average service time of 10 minutes per customer.
    If the consultants are paid $16 per hour and the customer waiting time is valued at $25 per hour for waiting time prior to service, should Agan expand to the two-consultant system? Explain.

22. A fast-food franchise is considering operating a drive-up window food-service operation. Assume that customer arrivals follow a Poisson probability distribution, with a mean arrival rate of 24 cars per hour, and that service times follow an exponential probability distribution. Arriving customers place orders at an intercom station at the back of the parking lot and then drive to the service window to pay for and receive their orders. The following three service alternatives are being considered.
    - A single-channel operation in which one employee fills the order and takes the money from the customer. The average service time for this alternative is 2 minutes.
    - A single-channel operation in which one employee fills the order while a second employee takes the money from the customer. The average service time for this alternative is 1.25 minutes.
    - A two-channel operation with two service windows and two employees. The employee stationed at each window fills the order and takes the money for customers arriving at the window. The average service time for this alternative is 2 minutes for each channel.

    Answer the following questions and recommend an alternative design for the fast-food franchise.
    a. What is the probability that no cars are in the system?
    b. What is the average number of cars waiting for service?
    c. What is the average number of cars in the system?
    d. What is the average time a car waits for service?
    e. What is the average time in the system?
    f. What is the probability that an arriving car will have to wait for service?

23. The following cost information is available for the fast-food franchise in Problem 22.
    - Customer waiting time is valued at $25 per hour to reflect the fact that waiting time is costly to the fast-food business.
    - The cost of each employee is $6.50 per hour.
    - To account for equipment and space, an additional cost of $20 per hour is attributable to each channel.

    What is the lowest-cost design for the fast-food business?

24. Patients arrive at a dentist's office at a mean rate of 2.8 patients per hour. The dentist can treat patients at the mean rate of 3 patients per hour. A study of patient waiting times shows that, on average, a patient waits 30 minutes before seeing the dentist.
    a. What are the mean arrival and treatment rates in terms of patients per minute?
    b. What is the average number of patients in the waiting room?
    c. If a patient arrives at 10:10 A.M., at what time is the patient expected to leave the office?

**SELF TEST**

25. A study of the multichannel food-service operation at the Red Birds' baseball park shows that the average time between the arrival of a customer at the food-service counter and his or her departure with a filled order is 10 minutes. During the game, customers arrive at the average rate of 4 per minute. The food-service operation requires an average of 2 minutes per customer order.
    a. What is the mean service rate per channel in terms of customers per minute?
    b. What is the average waiting time in the line prior to placing an order?
    c. On average, how many customers are in the food-service system?

26. Manning Autos operates an automotive service counter. While completing the repair work, Manning mechanics arrive at the company's parts department counter at the mean rate of 4 per hour. The parts coordinator spends an average of 6 minutes with each mechanic, discussing the parts the mechanic needs and retrieving the parts from inventory.
    a. Currently, Manning has one parts coordinator. On average, each mechanic waits 4 minutes before the parts coordinator is available to answer questions and/or retrieve parts from inventory. Find $L_q$, $W$, and $L$ for this single-channel parts operation.
    b. A trial period with a second parts coordinator showed that, on average, each mechanic waited only 1 minute before a parts coordinator was available. Find $L_q$, $W$, and $L$ for this two-channel parts operation.
    c. If the cost of each mechanic is $20 per hour and the cost of each parts coordinator is $12 per hour, is the one-channel or the two-channel system more economical?

**27.** Gubser Welding, Inc., operates a welding service for construction and automotive repair jobs. Assume that the arrival of jobs at the company's office can be described by a Poisson probability distribution with a mean arrival rate of 2 jobs per 8-hour day. The time required to complete the jobs follows a normal probability distribution with a mean time of 3.2 hours and a standard deviation of 2 hours. Answer the following questions, assuming that Gubser uses one welder to complete all jobs.

    **a.** What is the mean arrival rate in jobs per hour?

    **b.** What is the mean service rate in jobs per hour?

    **c.** What is the average number of jobs waiting for service?

    **d.** What is the average time a job waits before the welder can begin working on it?

    **e.** What is the average number of hours between when a job is received and when it is completed?

    **f.** What percentage of the time is Gubser's welder busy?

**28.** Jobs arrive randomly at a particular assembly plant; assume that the mean arrival rate is 5 jobs per hour. Service times (in minutes per job) do not follow the exponential probability distribution. Two proposed designs for the plant's assembly operation are shown.

|  | | Service Time |
| --- | --- | --- |
| **Design** | **Mean** | **Standard Deviation** |
| A | 6.0 | 3.0 |
| B | 6.25 | 0.6 |

    **a.** What is the mean service rate in jobs per hour for each design?

    **b.** For the mean service rates in part (a), what design appears to provide the best or fastest service rate?

    **c.** What are the standard deviations of the service times in hours?

    **d.** Use the $M/G/1$ model in Section 12.7 to compute the operating characteristics for each design.

    **e.** Which design provides the best operating characteristics? Why?

**29.** The Robotics Manufacturing Company operates an equipment repair business where emergency jobs arrive randomly at the rate of 3 jobs per 8-hour day. The company's repair facility is a single-channel system operated by a repair technician. The service time varies with a mean repair time of 2 hours and a standard deviation of 1.5 hours. The company's cost of the repair operation is $28 per hour. In the economic analysis of the waiting line system, Robotics uses $35 per hour cost for customers waiting during the repair process.

    **a.** What are the arrival rate and service rate in jobs per hour?

    **b.** Show the operating characteristics including the total cost per hour.

    **c.** The company is considering purchasing a computer-based equipment repair system that would enable a constant repair time of 2 hours. For practical purposes, the standard deviation is 0. Because of the computer-based equipment, the company's cost of the new operation would be $32 per hour. The firm's director of operations has said no to the request for new equipment because the hourly cost is $4 higher and the mean repair time is the same. Do you agree? What effect will the new system have on the waiting line characteristics of the repair service?

    **d.** Does paying for the computer-based system to reduce the variation in service time make economic sense? How much will the new system save the company during a 40-hour work week?

**30.** A large insurance company has a central computing system that contains a variety of information about customer accounts. Insurance agents in a six-state area use telephone lines to access the customer information database. Currently, the company's central computer system allows 3 users to access the central computer simultaneously. Agents who attempt to use the system when it is full are denied access; no waiting is allowed. Management realizes that with its expanding business, more requests will be made to the central information system. Being denied access to the system is inefficient as well as annoying for agents. Access requests follow a Poisson probability distribution, with a mean of 42 calls per hour. The mean service rate per line is 20 calls per hour.

a.  What is the probability that 0, 1, 2, and 3 access lines will be in use?
b.  What is the probability that an agent will be denied access to the system?
c.  What is the average number of access lines in use?
d.  In planning for the future, management wants to be able to handle $\lambda = 50$ calls per hour; in addition, the probability that an agent will be denied access to the system should be no greater than the value computed in part (b). How many access lines should this system have?

31.  Mid-West Publishing Company publishes college textbooks. The company operates an 800 telephone number whereby potential adopters can ask questions about forthcoming texts, request examination copies of texts, and place orders. Currently, two extension lines are used, with two representatives handling the telephone inquiries. Calls occurring when both extension lines are being used receive a busy signal; no waiting is allowed. Each representative can accommodate an average of 12 calls per hour. The mean arrival rate is 20 calls per hour.

a.  How many extension lines should be used if the company wants to handle 90% of the calls immediately?
b.  What is the average number of extension lines that will be busy if your recommendation in part (a) is used?
c.  What percentage of calls receive a busy signal for the current telephone system with two extension lines?

32.  City Cab, Inc., uses two dispatchers to handle requests for service and to dispatch the cabs. The telephone calls that are made to City Cab use a common telephone number. When both dispatchers are busy, the caller hears a busy signal; no waiting is allowed. Callers who receive a busy signal can call back later or call another cab service. Assume that the arrival of calls follows a Poisson probability distribution, with a mean of 40 calls per hour, and that each dispatcher can handle a mean of 30 calls per hour.

a.  What percentage of time are both dispatchers idle?
b.  What percentage of time are both dispatchers busy?
c.  What is the probability callers will receive a busy signal if 2, 3, or 4 dispatchers are used?
d.  If management wants no more than 12% of the callers to receive a busy signal, how many dispatchers should be used?

33.  Kolkmeyer Manufacturing Company (see Section 12.9) is considering adding 2 machines to its manufacturing operation. This addition will bring the number of machines to 8. Mr. Andrews, president of Kolkmeyer, has asked for a study of the need to add a second employee to the repair operation. The mean arrival rate is 0.05 machine per hour for each machine, and the mean service rate for each individual assigned to the repair operation is 0.50 machine per hour.

a.  Compute the operating characteristics if the company retains the single-employee repair operation.
b.  Compute the operating characteristics if a second employee is added to the machine repair operation.
c.  Each employee is paid $20 per hour. Machine downtime is valued at $80 per hour. From an economic point of view, should one or two employees handle the machine repair operation? Explain.

**SELF TEST**

34.  Five administrative assistants use an office copier. The average time between arrivals for each assistant is 40 minutes, which is equivalent to a mean arrival rate of $1/40 = 0.025$ arrivals per minute. The mean time each assistant spends at the copier is 5 minutes, which is equivalent to a mean service rate of $\frac{1}{5} = 0.20$ users per minute. Use the *M/M/1* model with a finite calling population to determine the following:

a.  The probability that the copier is idle
b.  The average number of administrative assistants in the waiting line
c.  The average number of administrative assistants at the copier

    **d.**  The average time an assistant spends waiting for the copier

    **e.**  The average time an assistant spends at the copier

    **f.**  During an 8-hour day, how many minutes does an assistant spend at the copier? How much of this time is waiting time?

    **g.**  Should management consider purchasing a second copier? Explain.

**35.**  Schips Department Store operates a fleet of 10 trucks. The trucks arrive at random times throughout the day at the store's truck dock to be loaded with new deliveries or to have incoming shipments from the regional warehouse unloaded. Each truck returns to the truck dock for service 2 times per 8-hour day. Thus, the mean arrival rate per truck is 0.25 trucks per hour. The mean service rate is 4 trucks per hour. Using the Poisson arrivals and exponential service times model with a finite calling population of 10 trucks, determine the following operating characteristics:

    **a.**  The probability no trucks are at the truck dock

    **b.**  The average number of trucks waiting for loading/unloading

    **c.**  The average number of trucks in the truck dock area

    **d.**  The average waiting time before loading/unloading begins

    **e.**  The average waiting time in the system

    **f.**  What is the hourly cost of operation if the cost is $50 per hour for each truck and $30 per hour for the truck dock?

    **g.**  Consider a two-channel truck dock operation where the second channel could be operated for an additional $30 per hour. How much would the average number of trucks waiting for loading/unloading have to be reduced to make the two-channel truck dock economically feasible?

    **h.**  Should the company consider expanding to the two-channel truck dock? Explain.

## Case Problem    AIRLINE RESERVATIONS

Regional Airlines is establishing a new telephone system for handling flight reservations. During the 10:00 A.M. to 11:00 A.M. time period, calls to the reservation agent occur randomly at an average of one call every 3.75 minutes. Historical service time data show that a reservation agent spends an average of 3 minutes with each customer. The waiting line model assumptions of Poisson arrivals and exponential service times appear reasonable for the telephone reservation system.

Regional Airlines' management believes that offering an efficient telephone reservation system is an important part of establishing an image as a service-oriented airline. If the system is properly implemented, Regional Airlines will establish good customer relations, which in the long run will increase business. However, if the telephone reservation system is frequently overloaded and customers have difficulty contacting an agent, a negative customer reaction may lead to an eventual loss of business. The cost of a ticket reservation agent is $20 per hour. Thus, management wants to provide good service, but it does not want to incur the cost of overstaffing the telephone reservation operation by using more agents than necessary.

At a planning meeting, Regional's management team agreed that an acceptable customer service goal is to answer at least 85% of the incoming calls immediately. During the planning meeting, Regional's vice president of administration pointed out that the data show that the average service rate for an agent is faster than the average arrival rate of the telephone calls. The vice president's conclusion was that personnel costs could be minimized by using one agent and that the single agent should be able to handle the telephone reservations and still have some idle time. The vice president of marketing restated the importance of customer service and expressed support for at least two reservation agents.

The current telephone reservation system design does not allow callers to wait. Callers who attempt to reach a reservation agent when all agents are occupied receive a busy signal and are blocked from the system. A representative from the telephone company suggested that Regional Airlines consider an expanded system that accommodates waiting. In the expanded system, when a customer calls and all agents are busy, a recorded message tells the customer that the call is being held in the order received and that an agent will be available shortly. The customer can stay on the line and listen to background music while waiting for an agent. Regional's management will need more information before switching to the expanded system.

## Managerial Report

Prepare a managerial report for Regional Airlines analyzing the telephone reservation system. Evaluate both the system that does not allow waiting and the expanded system that allows waiting. Include the following information in your report.

1. A detailed analysis of the operating characteristics of the reservation system with one agent as proposed by the vice president of administration. What is your recommendation concerning a single-agent system?
2. A detailed analysis of the operating characteristics of the reservation system based on your recommendation regarding the number of agents Regional should use.
3. What appear to be the advantages or disadvantages of the expanded system? Discuss the number of waiting callers the expanded system would need to accommodate.
4. The telephone arrival data presented are for the 10:00 A.M. to 11:00 A.M. time period; however, the arrival rate of incoming calls is expected to change from hour to hour. Describe how your waiting line analysis could be used to develop a ticket agent staffing plan that would enable the company to provide different levels of staffing for the ticket reservation system at different times during the day. Indicate the information that you would need to develop this staffing plan.

## Case Problem     OFFICE EQUIPMENT, INC.

Office Equipment, Inc. (OEI), leases automatic mailing machines to business customers in Fort Wayne, Indiana. The company's success has been built on establishing a reputation of providing timely maintenance and repair service. Each OEI service contract states that a service technician will arrive at a customer's business site within an average of 3 hours from the time that the customer notifies OEI of an equipment problem.

Currently, OEI has 10 customers with service contracts. One service technician is responsible for handling all service calls. A statistical analysis of historical service records indicates that a customer requests a service call at an average rate of 1 call per 50 hours of operation. If the service technician is available when a customer calls for service, it takes the technician an average of one hour of travel time to reach the customer's office and an average of 1.5 hours to complete the repair service. However, if the service technician is busy with another customer when a new customer calls for service, the technician completes the current service call and any other waiting service calls before responding to the new service call. In such cases, once the technician is free from all existing service commitments, the technician takes an average of one hour of travel time to reach the new customer's office and an average of 1.5 hours to complete the repair service. The cost of the service technician is $80 per hour. The downtime cost (wait time and service time) for customers is $100 per hour.

OEI is planning to expand its business. Within one year, OEI projects that it will have 20 customers, and within two years, OEI projects that it will have 30 customers. Although OEI is satisfied that one service technician can handle the 10 existing customers, management is concerned about the ability of one technician to meet the average 3-hour service call guarantee when the OEI customer base expands. In a recent planning meeting, the marketing manager made a proposal to add a second service technician when OEI reaches 20 customers and to add a third service technician when OEI reaches 30 customers. Before making a final decision, management has asked for an analysis of OEI service capabilities. OEI is particularly interested in meeting the average 3-hour waiting time guarantee at the lowest possible total cost.

## Managerial Report

Develop a managerial report summarizing your analysis of the OEI service capabilities. Make recommendations regarding the number of technicians to be used when OEI reaches 20 customers and when OEI reaches 30 customers. Include a discussion of the following in your report.

1. What is the mean arrival rate for each customer per hour?
2. What is the mean service rate in terms of the number of customers per hour? Note that the average travel time of one hour becomes part of the service time because the time that the service technician is busy handling a service call includes the travel time plus the time required to complete the repair.
3. Waiting line models generally assume that the arriving customers are in the same location as the service facility. Discuss the OEI situation in light of the fact that a service technician travels an average of one hour to reach each customer. How should the travel time and the waiting time predicted by the waiting line model be combined to determine the total customer waiting time?
4. OEI is satisfied that one service technician can handle the 10 existing customers. Use a waiting line model to determine the following information:
   - Probability that no customers are in the system
   - Average number of customers in the waiting line
   - Average number of customers in the system
   - Average time a customer waits until the service technician arrives
   - Average time a customer waits until the machine is back in operation
   - Probability that a customer will have to wait more than one hour for the service technician to arrive
   - The number of hours a week the technician is not making service calls
   - The total cost per hour for the service operation

   Do you agree with OEI management that one technician can meet the average 3-hour service call guarantee? Explain.
5. What is your recommendation for the number of service technicians to hire when OEI expands to 20 customers? Use the information that you developed in part 4 to justify your answer.
6. What is your recommendation for the number of service technicians to hire when OEI expands to 30 customers? Use the information that you developed in part 4 to justify your answer.
7. What are the annual savings of your recommendation in part 6 compared to the planning committee's proposal that 30 customers will require three service technicians? Assume 250 days of operation per year.

## Appendix 12.1  WAITING LINE MODELS WITH SPREADSHEETS

### Single-Channel Waiting Lines

Spreadsheets provide a fast and relatively easy way to compute the operating characteristics of a waiting line system. Figure 12.5 shows the Excel spreadsheet for the Burger Dome single-channel waiting line presented in Section 12.2. Note that we have listed the assumptions of Poisson arrivals and exponential service times in cells A4 and A5 as a reminder that these assumptions characterize the waiting line model being used to analyze the Burger Dome system.

Only two input values are required: the mean arrival rate, $\lambda = 0.75$ customers per minute, shown in cell B7; and the mean service rate, $\mu = 1$ customer per minute, shown in cell B8. The operating characteristics provided by equations (12.4) through (12.9) are computed using the following cell formulas:

| | |
|---|---|
| Cell C13 | Probability that no customers are in the system, $P_0$<br>$=1-B7/B8$ |
| Cell C14 | Average number of customers in the waiting line, $L_q$<br>$=B7^2/(B8*(B8-B7))$ |
| Cell C15 | Average number of customers in the system, $L$<br>$=C14+B7/B8$ |
| Cell C16 | Average time a customer spends in the waiting line, $W_q$<br>$=C14/B7$ |

**Figure 12.5  SPREADSHEET SOLUTION FOR THE BURGER DOME SINGLE-CHANNEL PROBLEM**

| | A | B | C |
|---|---|---|---|
| 1 | **Burger Dome Single-Channel Waiting Line** | | |
| 2 | | | |
| 3 | **Assumptions** | | |
| 4 | **Poisson Arrivals** | | |
| 5 | **Exponential Service Times** | | |
| 6 | | | |
| 7 | Mean Arrival Rate | 0.75 | |
| 8 | Mean Service Rate | 1 | |
| 9 | | | |
| 10 | | | |
| 11 | **Operating Characteristics** | | |
| 12 | | | |
| 13 | Probability that no customers are in the system, $P_o$ | | 0.2500 |
| 14 | Average number of customers in the waiting line, $L_q$ | | 2.2500 |
| 15 | Average number of customers in the system, $L$ | | 3.0000 |
| 16 | Average time a customer spends in the waiting line, $W_q$ | | 3.0000 |
| 17 | Average time a customer spends in the system, $W$ | | 4.0000 |
| 18 | Probability an arriving customer has to wait, $P_w$ | | 0.7500 |

Cell C17    Average time a customer spends in the system, $W$
 =C16+1/B8

Cell C18    Probability an arriving customer waits for service, $P_w$
 =B7/B8

By changing the mean arrival rate and/or mean service rate in cells B7 and B8, the spreadsheet will automatically calculate the operating characteristics for the modified single-channel waiting line.

## Multiple-Channel Waiting Lines

To show how a spreadsheet can be used to compute the operating characteristics of a multiple-channel waiting line with Poisson arrivals and exponential service times, we use the same spreadsheet format that we used for the single-channel waiting line model in Figure 12.5. The only differences are that we input the number of channels and that we use equations (12.11) through (12.16) for the computations. Figure 12.6 shows the spreadsheet for the Burger Dome multiple-channel waiting line system. The assumptions of Poisson arrivals and exponential service times are shown in cells A4 and A5. The three required inputs and their cell locations are as follows: the number of channels, $k = 2$, shown in cell B7; the mean arrival rate, $\lambda = 0.75$ customers per minute, shown in cell B8; and the mean service rate, $\mu = 1$ customer per minute, shown in cell B9. The six operating characteristics in Figure 12.6 are based upon the values of $k$, $\lambda$ and $\mu$.

In some cases, the equations used to compute the operating characteristics for a multiple-channel waiting line are more complex than the equations used for a single-channel waiting line. Note in particular equation (12.11), which provides the probability that no units are in the system, $P_0$. This equation is substantially more complex than the equation for $P_0$ shown in equation (12.4). In fact, equation (12.11) is so complex that we will develop a special Excel function to evaluate it.

The equation used to compute $P_0$ for the multiple-channel waiting line model in Section 12.3 is

$$P_0 = \frac{1}{\displaystyle\sum_{n=0}^{k-1} \frac{(\lambda/\mu)^n}{n!} + \frac{(\lambda/\mu)^k}{k!}\left(\frac{k\mu}{k\mu - \lambda}\right)}$$

Note that the number of channels, $k$, the mean arrival rate $\lambda$ (lambda), and the mean service rate $\mu$ (mu) must be known in order to compute $P_0$.

The steps required to create the $P_0$ function with Excel are as follows:

Step 1   Select the **Tools** pull-down menu
Step 2   Select the **Macro** option
Step 3   Choose the **Visual Basic Editor**
Step 4   When the Visual Basic Editor appears
       Select the **Insert** pull-down menu
       Choose the **Module** option
Step 5   When the Module sheet appears enter

Function Your_Function_Name(Arg1, Arg2, . . . )

where **Your_Function_Name** is any name you wish to use for the function and where **Arg1, Arg2,** etc., are the arguments of the function or the inputs that you

**Figure 12.6    SPREADSHEET SOLUTION FOR THE BURGER DOME MULTIPLE-CHANNEL PROBLEM**

| | A | B | C |
|---|---|---|---|
| 1 | **Burger Dome Multiple-Channel Waiting Line** | | |
| 2 | | | |
| 3 | **Assumptions** | | |
| 4 | **Poisson Arrivals** | | |
| 5 | **Exponential Service Times** | | |
| 6 | | | |
| 7 | Number of Channels | 2 | |
| 8 | Mean Arrival Rate | 0.75 | |
| 9 | Mean Service Rate Per Channel | 1 | |
| 10 | | | |
| 11 | | | |
| 12 | **Operating Characteristics** | | |
| 13 | | | |
| 14 | Probability that no customers are in the system, $P_0$ | | 0.4545 |
| 15 | Average number of customers in the waiting line, $L_q$ | | 0.1227 |
| 16 | Average number of customers in the system, $L$ | | 0.8727 |
| 17 | Average time a customer spends in the waiting line, $W_q$ | | 0.1636 |
| 18 | Average time a customer spends in the system, $W$ | | 1.1636 |
| 19 | Probability an arriving customer has to wait, $P_w$ | | 0.2045 |

will need to evaluate the function. For the multiple-channel waiting line model, we named the function $P0$ and listed the three arguments or inputs as k, lamda, and mu. Thus, we entered the following:

$$\text{Function } P0(k, lambda, mu)$$

Step 6   Next write a Visual Basic program to evaluate the function. The exact statement sequence may vary and depends upon the programming skills of the user. The Visual Basic program we entered for $P_0$ is shown in Figure 12.7. End Function appears as the last line of the program

Step 7   Select the **File** pull-down menu
Choose the **Close and Return to Microsoft Excel** option

You will be returned to the spreadsheet application. You can now choose the cell where the $P_0$ function is to appear. Using the spreadsheet in Figure 12.6, we can enter the newly created $P_0$ function in the spreadsheet as follows:

Cell C14    Probability that no customers are in the system, $P_0$
=P0(B7,B8,B9)

As shown in Figure 12.6, this function provides the probability of no customers in the system, $P_0 = 0.4545$.

**Figure 12.7** THE VISUAL BASIC PROGRAM FOR $P_0$ IN THE MULTIPLE-CHANNEL WAITING LINE MODEL IN SECTION 12.3

```
Function P0(k, lambda, mu)
Sum = 0
For n = 0 To k − 1
Sum = Sum + (lambda/mu)^n/Application.Fact(n)
Next
P0 = 1/(Sum + ((lambda/mu)^k/Application.Fact(k))*(k*mu(k*mu − lambda)))
End Function
```

The operating characteristics provided by equations (12.12) through (12.16) are computed using the following cell formulas:[2]

Cell C15  Average number of customers in the waiting line, $L_q$
=(((B8/B9)^B7\*B8\*B9)/(FACT (B7−1)\* (B7\*B9−B8)^2))\*C14

Cell C16  Average number of customers in the system, $L$
=C15+B8/B9

Cell C17  Average time a customer spends in the waiting line, $W_q$
=C15/B8

Cell C18  Average time a customer spends in the system, $W$
=C17+1/B9

Cell C19  Probability an arriving customer has to wait for service, $P_w$ =(1/FACT(B7))\*(B8/B9)^B7\* (B7\*B9/(B7\*B9−B8))\*C14

The spreadsheet shown in Figure 12.6 can be used to compute the operating characteristics for both single-channel and multiple-channel waiting lines with Poisson arrivals and exponential service times. For example, entering 1 for the number of channels into cell B7 will provide the Burger Dome single-channel operating characteristics shown previously in Figure 12.5. In fact, the spreadsheet in Figure 12.6 is a general spreadsheet that can be used for any waiting line where the assumptions of Poisson arrivals and exponential service times are appropriate. Entering the number of channels, the mean arrival rate and the mean service rate is all that is necessary to compute the desired operating characteristic information. Thus, the spreadsheet provides a quick and easy way to determine how alternative designs affect the operating characteristics of the waiting line.

## Other Waiting Line Models

Spreadsheets can be developed for all of the waiting line models presented in this chapter. The format of each spreadsheet will be similar to the spreadsheets shown in Figures 12.5 and 12.6. The cell formulas must be based on the equations for the operating characteristics presented for the corresponding waiting line model. The equations for the single-channel waiting line model with Poisson arrivals and arbitrary service times in Section 12.7

2. Cell formulas C15 and C19 use Excel's FACT worksheet function to compute the factorial of a number. For instance, FACT (B7 − 1) in cell formula C15 is used to compute the value of (k − 1)! in equation (12.12).

are relatively easily expressed with Excel cell formulas. The multiple-channel model with Poisson arrivals, arbitrary service times, and no waiting in Section 12.8 and the multiple-channel model with a finite calling population presented in Section 12.9 are more complex and require special Excel functions. For example, equation (12.31) for $P_j$ and equation (12.33) for $P_0$ require the special functions. The details of developing spreadsheets for these other waiting line models are presented in *Contemporary Management Science with Spreadsheets,* by D. R. Anderson, D. J. Sweeney, and T. A. Williams, South-Western College Publishing, 1999.

# CITIBANK*

## LONG ISLAND CITY, NEW YORK

Citibank, a major subsidiary of Citicorp, makes available a wide range of financial services, including checking and savings accounts, loans and mortgages, insurance, and investment services, within the framework of a unique strategy for delivering those services called Citibanking. Citibanking entails a consistent brand identity all over the world, consistent product offerings, and high-level customer service. Citibanking lets you manage your money anytime, anywhere, anyway you choose. Whether you need to save for the future or borrow for today, you can do it all at Citibank.

Citibanking's state-of-the-art automatic teller machines (ATMs) located in Citicard Banking Centers (CBCs), let customers do all their banking in one place with the touch of a finger, 24 hours a day, 7 days a week. More than 150 different banking functions from deposits to managing investments can be performed with ease. Citibanking ATMs are so much more than just cash machines that customers today use them for 80% of their transactions.

## A Waiting Line Application

The New York franchise of U.S. Citibanking operates approximately 250 CBCs. Each CBC provides customers with one or more ATMs, called customer activated terminals (or CATs), which are capable of performing a variety of banking transactions. Approximately 70% of the CBCs are located in Manhattan, the Bronx, Brooklyn, Queens, and Staten Island. The remaining 30% are suburban CBCs located in Nassau, Suffolk, Orange, Rockland, and Westchester counties. Measuring performance

---

*The authors are indebted to Stacey Karter, Citibank, for providing this application.

and service capacity at each CBC is an important part of Citibank's emphasis on providing superior access and convenience for its customers.

Each Citibank CBC operates as a waiting line system with randomly arriving customers seeking service at a CAT. Based on the use at each site, the number of CATs ranges from 1 to 20 with each site operating with a single queue. If 1 CAT is present, the system operates as a single-channel waiting line, with arriving customers waiting whenever the CAT is being used by another customer. At most CBC sites, multiple CATs provide a multiple-channel waiting line system.

A periodic CBC capacity study is used to determine the capacity needed at each center. The hardware supply at the center is measured in terms of the transactional volume (transactions per CAT per hour) the site is capable of supporting. Customer demand is measured in terms of the peak number of arrivals per hour at the site. Comparing supply and demand enables Citibank to classify each CBC as either

- Highly endangered—average peak hour waiting time exceeds 5 minutes.
- Borderline—average peak hour waiting time is 3–5 minutes.
- Sufficient—average peak hour waiting time is 3 minutes or less.

In a recent capacity study, demand data suggested approximately 6% of the CBCs should be classified as highly endangered and approximately 8% should be classified as borderline. In total, 34 sites were listed as candidates for possible capacity expansion with incremental CATs desired.

In order to make recommendations on the number of CATs to add at the selected sites, management needed additional information concerning the customer service levels at each site. Operating characteristics information provided by a waiting line model would be helpful in determining the number of CATs each center should have. Typical information provided by the model included:

- The average number of customers in the waiting line
- The average number of customers in the system
- The average time a customer spends in the waiting line
- The average time a customer spends in the system
- The probability that an arriving customer has to wait

In-house management information system (MIS) data on arrival rates and service times were collected to determine whether a multiple-channel waiting line model with Poisson arrivals and exponential service time could be used to model a CBC waiting line system. Customer arrivals were indeed random and adequately represented by a Poisson probability distribution. The mean arrival rate varied, depending on time of day and day of week. However, developing operating characteristic information for the peak or high demand periods was important. An average of the top 10 hourly demands was used to determine the mean arrival rate for each CBC site. Observed service times showed that the exponential probability distribution provided a reasonable approximation of the service time distribution.

For example, one midtown Manhattan branch site was classified as an endangered center operating with 5 CATs. Onsite observations were conducted to verify the MIS data and the peak arrival rate of 172 customers per hour. From the observed session times of 2 minutes per customer, the mean service rate per CAT was estimated to be 30 per hour. Five CATs were insufficient to meet this peak demand. A multiple-channel waiting line model with an expansion to 6 CATs showed that 88% of the customers would still have to wait and that the average waiting time would be 6 to 7 minutes. Expansion to 6 CATs still provided an unacceptable level of service. Expansion to 7 CATs provided acceptable service levels with an average of 2.4 customers in the waiting line. Hence, expansion to 8 CATs was not necessary at that time.

Even though peak demand periods were not always long enough to reach the steady-state conditions projected by the waiting line model, the operating characteristics indicated by the model provided general guidelines for capacity decisions. Use of the observed mean arrival and service rates unique to each site enabled the waiting line model to provide useful information for making the incremental CAT decisions at each CBC location.

## Questions

1. How did Citibank's CBCs operate as a waiting line system?
2. How did Citibank ensure appropriate arrival and service time rates for the CBC waiting line operation?
3. What information did the waiting line model provide? How was this information helpful in making the incremental CAT decisions for each site?

# 13

## SIMULATION

## CONTENTS

**Simulation** is one of the most widely used quantitative approaches to decision making. It is a method for learning about a real system by experimenting with a model that represents the system. The simulation model contains the mathematical expressions and logical relationships that describe how to compute the value of the outputs given the values of the inputs. Any simulation model has two inputs: controllable inputs and probabilistic inputs. Figure 13.1 shows a conceptual diagram of a simulation model.

In conducting a **simulation experiment,** an analyst selects the value, or values, for the **controllable inputs.** Then values for the **probability inputs** are randomly generated. The simulation model uses the values of the controllable inputs and the values of the probabilistic inputs to compute the value, or values, of the output. By conducting a series of experiments using a variety of values for the controllable inputs, the analyst learns how values of the controllable inputs affect or change the output of the simulation model. After reviewing the simulation results, the analyst is often able to make decision recommendations for the controllable inputs that will provide the desired output for the real system.

Simulation has been successfully applied in a variety of applications. The following examples are typical.

1. **New Product Development**   The objective of this simulation is to determine the probability that a new product will be profitable. A model is developed relating profit (the output measure) to various probabilistic inputs such as demand, parts cost, and labor cost. The only controllable input is whether to introduce the product. A variety of possible values will be generated for the probabilistic inputs, and the resulting profit will be computed. We develop a simulation model for this type of application in Section 13.1.

2. **Airline Overbooking**   The objective of this simulation is to determine the number of reservations an airline should accept for a particular flight. A simulation model is developed relating profit for the flight to a probabilistic input, the number of passengers with a reservation that show up and use their reservation, and a controllable input, the number of reservations accepted for the flight. For each selected value for the controllable input, a variety of possible values will be generated for the number of passengers that show up, and the resulting profit can be computed. Similar simulation models are applicable for hotel and car rental reservation systems.

3. **Inventory Policy**   The objective of this simulation is to choose an inventory policy that will provide good customer service at a reasonable cost. A model is developed relating two output measures, total inventory cost and the service level, to probabilistic inputs such as product demand and delivery lead time from vendors, and controllable inputs such as the order quantity and the reorder point. For each setting of the controllable inputs, a variety of possible values would be generated for the probabilistic inputs, and the resulting cost and service levels would be computed.

4. **Traffic Flow**   The objective of this simulation is to determine the effect of installing a left turn signal on the flow of traffic through a busy intersection. A model is developed relating waiting time for vehicles to get through the intersection to probabilistic inputs such as the number of vehicle arrivals and the fraction that want to make a left turn, and controllable inputs such as the length of time the left turn signal is on. For each setting of the controllable inputs, values would be generated for the probabilistic inputs, and the resulting vehicle waiting times would be computed.

5. **Waiting Lines**   The objective of this simulation is to determine the waiting times for customers at a bank's automated teller machine (ATM). A model is developed relating customer waiting times to probabilistic inputs such as customer arrivals and service times, and a controllable input, the number of ATM machines installed.

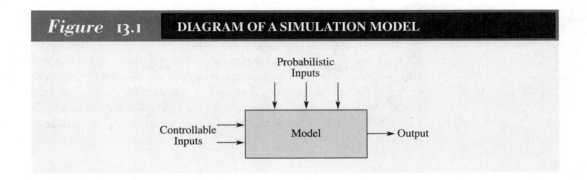

**Figure 13.1    DIAGRAM OF A SIMULATION MODEL**

For each value of the controllable input (the number of ATM machines), a variety of values would be generated for the probabilistic inputs and the customer waiting times would be computed. We develop a simulation model for this type of application in Section 13.3.

Simulation is not an optimization technique. It is a method that can be used to describe or predict how a system will operate given certain choices for the controllable inputs and randomly generated values for the probabilistic inputs. Management scientists often use simulation to determine values for the controllable inputs that are likely to lead to desirable system outputs. In this sense, simulation can be an effective tool in designing a system to provide good performance.

In this chapter we begin by showing how simulation can be used to study the financial risks associated with the development of a new product. We continue with illustrations showing how simulation can be used to establish an effective inventory policy and how simulation can be used to design waiting line systems. Other issues such as verifying the simulation program, validating the model, and selecting a simulation software package are discussed in Section 13.4.

## 13.1    RISK ANALYSIS

**Risk analysis** is the process of predicting the outcome of a decision in the face of uncertainty. In this section, we describe a problem that involves considerable uncertainty: the development of a new product. We first show how risk analysis can be conducted without using simulation; then, we show how a more comprehensive risk analysis can be conducted with the aid of simulation.

### The PortaCom Project

PortaCom manufactures personal computers and related equipment. PortaCom's product design group has developed a prototype for a new high-quality portable printer. The new printer has an innovative design and the potential to capture a significant share of the portable printer market. Preliminary marketing and financial analyses have provided the following selling price, first-year administrative cost and first-year advertising cost.

$$\text{Selling price} = \$249 \text{ per unit}$$
$$\text{Administrative cost} = \$400,000$$
$$\text{Advertising cost} = \$600,000$$

In the simulation model for the PortaCom problem, the preceding values are constants and are referred to as **parameters** of the model.

The cost of direct labor, the cost of parts, and the first-year demand for the printer are not known with certainty and are considered probabilistic inputs. At this stage of the planning process, PortaCom's best estimates of these inputs are $45 per unit for the direct labor cost, $90 per unit for the parts cost, and 15,000 units for the first-year demand. PortaCom would like an analysis of the first-year profit potential for the printer. Because of Porta-Com's tight cash flow situation, management is particularly concerned about the potential for a loss.

## What-If Analysis

One approach to risk analysis is called **what-if analysis.** A what-if analysis involves generating values for the probabilistic inputs (direct labor cost, parts cost, and first-year demand) and computing the resulting value for the output (profit). With a selling price of $249 per unit and administrative plus advertising costs equal to $400,000 + $600,000 = $1,000,000, the PortaCom profit model is

Profit = ($249 − Direct labor cost per unit − Parts cost per unit)(Demand) − $1,000,000

Letting

$$c_1 = \text{direct labor cost per unit}$$
$$c_2 = \text{parts cost per unit}$$

and

$$x = \text{first-year demand}$$

the profit model for the first year can be written as follows:

$$\text{Profit} = (249 - c_1 - c_2)x - 1,000,000 \qquad \textbf{(13.1)}$$

The PortaCom profit model can be depicted as shown in Figure 13.2.

Recall that PortaCom's best estimates of the direct labor cost per unit, the parts cost per unit, and first-year demand are $45, $90, and 15,000 units, respectively. These values constitute the **base-case scenario** for PortaCom. Substituting these values into equation (13.1) yields the following profit projection.

$$\text{Profit} = (249 - 45 - 90)(15,000) - 1,000,000 = 710,000$$

Thus, the base-case scenario leads to an anticipated profit of $710,000.

In risk analysis we are concerned with both the probability of a loss and the magnitude of a loss. Although the base-case scenario looks appealing, PortaCom might be interested in what happens if the estimates of the direct labor cost per unit, parts cost per unit, and first-year demand do not turn out to be as expected under the base-case scenario. For instance, suppose that PortaCom believes that direct labor costs could range from $43 to $47 per unit, parts cost could range from $80 to $100 per unit, and first-year demand could range from 1500 to 28,500 units. Using these ranges, what-if analysis can be used to evaluate a **worst-case scenario** and a **best-case scenario.**

**Figure 13.2    PORTACOM PROFIT MODEL**

The worst-case value for the direct labor cost is $47 (the highest value), the worst-case value for the parts cost is $100 (the highest value), and the worst-case value for demand is 1500 units (the lowest value). Thus, in the worst-case scenario, $c_1 = 47$, $c_2 = 100$, and $x = 1500$. Substituting these values into equation (13.1) leads to the following profit projection:

$$\text{Profit} = (249 - 47 - 100)(1500) - 1{,}000{,}000 = -847{,}000$$

So, the worst-case scenario leads to a projected loss of $847,000.

The best-case value for the direct labor cost is $c_1 = 43$ (the lowest value), the best-case value for the parts cost is 80 (the lowest value), and the best-case value for demand is 28,500 units (the highest value). Substituting these values into equation (13.1) leads to the following profit projection:

$$\text{Profit} = (249 - 43 - 80)(28{,}500) - 1{,}000{,}000 = 2{,}591{,}000$$

So, the best-case scenario leads to a projected profit is $2,591,000.

At this point the what-if analysis provides the conclusion that profits can range from a loss of $847,000 to a profit of $2,591,000 with a base-case scenario value of $710,000. Although the base-case profit of $710,000 is possible, the what-if analysis indicates that a substantial loss as well as a substantial profit is possible. Other scenarios that PortaCom might want to consider can also be evaluated. However, the difficulty with what-if analysis is that it does indicate the likelihood of the various profit or loss values. In particular, we do not know anything about the *probability* of a loss.

**Problem 2 will give you practice using what-if analysis.**

### Simulation

Using simulation to perform risk analysis for the PortaCom problem is like playing out many what-if scenarios by randomly generating values for the probabilistic inputs. The advantage of simulation is that it allows us to assess the probability of a profit and the probability of a loss.

Using the what-if approach to risk analysis, we selected values for the probabilistic inputs [direct labor cost per unit ($c_1$), parts cost per unit ($c_2$), and first-year demand ($x$)], and then computed the resulting profit. Applying simulation to the PortaCom problem requires generating values for the probabilistic inputs that are representative of what we might observe in practice. To generate such values, we must know the probability distribution for each probabilistic input. Further analysis by PortaCom has led to the following probability distributions for the direct labor cost per unit, the parts cost per unit and first-year demand:

One advantage of simulation is the ability to use probability distributions that are unique to the system being studied.

**Direct Labor Cost.**   PortaCom believes that the direct labor cost will range from $43 to $47 per unit and is described by the discrete probability distribution shown in Table 13.1. Thus, we see a 0.1 probability that the direct labor cost will be $43 per unit, a 0.2 probability that the direct labor cost will be $44 per unit, and so on. The highest probability of 0.4 is associated with a direct labor cost of $45 per unit.

**Parts Cost.**   This cost depends upon the general economy, the overall demand for parts, and the pricing policy of PortaCom's parts suppliers. PortaCom believes that the parts cost will range from $80 to $100 per unit and is described by the uniform probability distribution shown in Figure 13.3. Costs per unit between $80 and $100 are equally likely.

**First-year Demand.**   PortaCom believes that first-year demand is described by the normal probability distribution shown in Figure 13.4. The mean or expected value of first-year demand is 15,000 units. The standard deviation of 4500 units describes the variability in the first-year demand.

   To simulate the PortaCom problem, we must generate values for the three probabilistic inputs, and compute the resulting profit. Then, we generate another set of values for the

| Table 13.1 | PROBABILITY DISTRIBUTION FOR DIRECT LABOR COST PER UNIT |
|---|---|

| Direct Labor Cost Per Unit | Probability |
|---|---|
| $43 | 0.1 |
| $44 | 0.2 |
| $45 | 0.4 |
| $46 | 0.2 |
| $47 | 0.1 |

| Figure 13.3 | UNIFORM PROBABILITY DISTRIBUTION FOR THE PARTS COST PER UNIT |
|---|---|

Parts Cost Per Unit

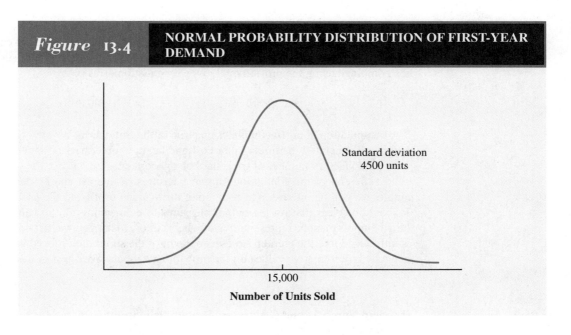

**Figure 13.4    NORMAL PROBABILITY DISTRIBUTION OF FIRST-YEAR DEMAND**

Standard deviation
4500 units

15,000

**Number of Units Sold**

probabilistic inputs, compute a second value for profit, and so on. We continue this process until we are satisfied that enough trials have been conducted to describe the probability distribution for profit. This process of generating probabilistic inputs and computing the value of the output is called *simulation*. The sequence of logical and mathematical operations required to conduct a simulation can be depicted with a flowchart. A flowchart for the PortaCom simulation is shown in Figure 13.5.

A flowchart provides a graphical representation that helps describe the logic of the simulation model.

Following the logic described by the flowchart we see that the model parameters— selling price, administrative cost, and advertising cost—are $249, $400,000, and $600,000, respectively. These values will remain fixed throughout the simulation.

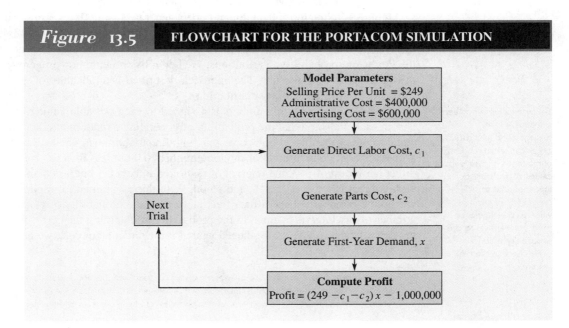

**Figure 13.5    FLOWCHART FOR THE PORTACOM SIMULATION**

**Model Parameters**
Selling Price Per Unit = $249
Administrative Cost = $400,000
Advertising Cost = $600,000

Generate Direct Labor Cost, $c_1$

Generate Parts Cost, $c_2$

Generate First-Year Demand, $x$

**Compute Profit**
Profit = $(249 - c_1 - c_2) x - 1,000,000$

Next Trial

The next three blocks depict the generation of values for the probabilistic inputs. First, a value for the direct labor cost ($c_1$) is generated. Then a value for the parts cost ($c_2$) is generated, followed by a value for the first-year demand ($x$). These probabilistic input values are combined using the profit model given by equation (13.1).

$$\text{Profit} = (249 - c_1 - c_2)x - 1{,}000{,}000$$

The computation of profit completes one trial of the simulation. We then return to the block where we generated the direct labor cost and begin another trial. This process is repeated until a satisfactory number of trials has been generated.

At the end of the simulation, output measures of interest can be developed. For example, we will be interested in computing the average profit and the probability of a loss. It should be clear that for the output measures to be meaningful, the values of the probabilistic inputs must be representative of what is likely to happen when the PortaCom printer is introduced into the market. An essential part of the simulation procedure is the ability to generate representative values for the probabilistic inputs. We now discuss how to generate these values.

**Random Numbers and Generating Probabilistic Input Values.**    In the PortaCom simulation, representative values must be generated for the direct labor cost per unit ($c_1$), the parts cost per unit ($c_2$), and the first-year demand ($x$). Random numbers and the probability distributions associated with each probabilistic input are used to generate representative values. To illustrate how to generate these values, we need to introduce the concept of *computer generated random numbers*.

Computer generated random numbers[1] are randomly selected decimal numbers from 0 up to, but not including, 1. The computer generated random number are equally likely and are uniformly distributed over the interval from 0 to 1. Computer generated random numbers can be obtained using built-in functions available in computer simulation packages and spreadsheets. For instance, placing = RAND() in a cell of an Excel spreadsheet will result in a random number between 0 and 1 being placed into that cell.

Table 13.2 contains 500 random numbers generated using Excel. These numbers can be viewed as a random sample of 500 values from a uniform probability distribution over the interval from 0 to 1. Let us show how random numbers can be used to generate values for the PortaCom probability distributions. We begin by showing how to generate a value for the direct labor cost per unit. The approach described is applicable for generating values from any discrete probability distribution.

An interval of random numbers is assigned to each possible value of the direct labor cost in such a fashion that the probability of generating a random number in the interval is equal to the probability of the corresponding direct labor cost. Table 13.3 shows how this process is done. The interval of random numbers 0.0 but less than 0.1 is associated with a direct labor cost of $43, the interval of random numbers 0.1 but less than 0.3 is associated with a direct labor cost of $44, and so on. With this assignment of random number intervals to the possible values of the direct labor cost, the probability of generating a random number in any interval is equal to the probability of obtaining the corresponding value for the direct labor cost. Thus, to select a value for the direct labor cost, we generate a random

Because random numbers are equally likely, management scientists can assign ranges of random numbers to corresponding values of probabilistic inputs so that the probability of any input value to the simulation model is identical to the probability of its occurrence in the real system.

[1]Computer generated random numbers are called *pseudorandom numbers*. Since they are generated through the use of mathematical formulas, they are not technically random. The difference between random numbers and pseudorandom numbers is primarily philosophical, and we use the term *random numbers* regardless of whether they are generated by a computer.

## Table 13.2    500 COMPUTER GENERATED RANDOM NUMBERS

| | | | | | | | | | |
|---|---|---|---|---|---|---|---|---|---|
| 0.6953 | 0.5247 | 0.1368 | 0.9850 | 0.7467 | 0.3813 | 0.5827 | 0.7893 | 0.7169 | 0.8166 |
| 0.0082 | 0.9925 | 0.6874 | 0.2122 | 0.6885 | 0.2159 | 0.4299 | 0.3467 | 0.2186 | 0.1033 |
| 0.6799 | 0.1241 | 0.3056 | 0.5590 | 0.0423 | 0.6515 | 0.2750 | 0.8156 | 0.2871 | 0.4680 |
| 0.8898 | 0.1514 | 0.1826 | 0.0004 | 0.5259 | 0.2425 | 0.8421 | 0.9248 | 0.9155 | 0.9518 |
| 0.6515 | 0.5027 | 0.9290 | 0.5177 | 0.3134 | 0.9177 | 0.2605 | 0.6668 | 0.1167 | 0.7870 |
| 0.3976 | 0.7790 | 0.0035 | 0.0064 | 0.0441 | 0.3437 | 0.1248 | 0.5442 | 0.9800 | 0.1857 |
| 0.0642 | 0.4086 | 0.6078 | 0.2044 | 0.0484 | 0.4691 | 0.7058 | 0.8552 | 0.5029 | 0.3288 |
| 0.0377 | 0.5250 | 0.7774 | 0.2390 | 0.9121 | 0.5345 | 0.8178 | 0.8443 | 0.4154 | 0.2526 |
| 0.5739 | 0.5181 | 0.0234 | 0.7305 | 0.0376 | 0.5169 | 0.5679 | 0.5495 | 0.7872 | 0.5321 |
| 0.5827 | 0.0341 | 0.7482 | 0.6351 | 0.9146 | 0.4700 | 0.7869 | 0.1337 | 0.0702 | 0.4219 |
| 0.0508 | 0.7905 | 0.2932 | 0.4971 | 0.0225 | 0.4466 | 0.5118 | 0.1200 | 0.0200 | 0.5445 |
| 0.4757 | 0.1399 | 0.5668 | 0.9569 | 0.7255 | 0.4650 | 0.4084 | 0.3701 | 0.9446 | 0.8064 |
| 0.6805 | 0.9931 | 0.4166 | 0.1091 | 0.7730 | 0.0691 | 0.9411 | 0.3468 | 0.0014 | 0.7379 |
| 0.2603 | 0.7507 | 0.6414 | 0.9907 | 0.2699 | 0.4571 | 0.9254 | 0.2371 | 0.8664 | 0.9553 |
| 0.8143 | 0.7625 | 0.1708 | 0.1900 | 0.2781 | 0.2830 | 0.6877 | 0.0488 | 0.8635 | 0.3155 |
| 0.5681 | 0.7854 | 0.5016 | 0.9403 | 0.1078 | 0.5255 | 0.8727 | 0.3815 | 0.5541 | 0.9833 |
| 0.1501 | 0.9363 | 0.3858 | 0.3545 | 0.5448 | 0.0643 | 0.3167 | 0.6732 | 0.6283 | 0.2631 |
| 0.8806 | 0.7989 | 0.7484 | 0.8083 | 0.2701 | 0.5039 | 0.9439 | 0.1027 | 0.9677 | 0.4597 |
| 0.4582 | 0.7590 | 0.4393 | 0.4704 | 0.6903 | 0.3732 | 0.6587 | 0.8675 | 0.2905 | 0.3058 |
| 0.0785 | 0.1467 | 0.3880 | 0.5274 | 0.8723 | 0.7517 | 0.9905 | 0.8904 | 0.8177 | 0.6660 |
| 0.1158 | 0.6635 | 0.4992 | 0.9070 | 0.2975 | 0.5686 | 0.8495 | 0.1652 | 0.2039 | 0.2553 |
| 0.2762 | 0.7018 | 0.6782 | 0.4013 | 0.2224 | 0.4672 | 0.5753 | 0.6219 | 0.6871 | 0.9255 |
| 0.9382 | 0.6411 | 0.7984 | 0.0608 | 0.5945 | 0.3977 | 0.4570 | 0.9924 | 0.8398 | 0.8361 |
| 0.5102 | 0.7021 | 0.4353 | 0.3398 | 0.8038 | 0.2260 | 0.1250 | 0.1884 | 0.3432 | 0.1192 |
| 0.2354 | 0.7410 | 0.7089 | 0.2579 | 0.1358 | 0.8446 | 0.1648 | 0.3889 | 0.5620 | 0.6555 |
| 0.9082 | 0.7906 | 0.7589 | 0.8870 | 0.1189 | 0.7125 | 0.6324 | 0.1096 | 0.5155 | 0.3449 |
| 0.6936 | 0.0702 | 0.9716 | 0.0374 | 0.0683 | 0.2397 | 0.7753 | 0.2029 | 0.1464 | 0.8000 |
| 0.4042 | 0.8158 | 0.3623 | 0.6614 | 0.7954 | 0.7516 | 0.6518 | 0.3638 | 0.3107 | 0.2718 |
| 0.9410 | 0.2201 | 0.6348 | 0.0367 | 0.0311 | 0.0688 | 0.2346 | 0.3927 | 0.7327 | 0.9994 |
| 0.0917 | 0.2504 | 0.2878 | 0.1735 | 0.3872 | 0.6816 | 0.2731 | 0.3846 | 0.6621 | 0.8983 |
| 0.8532 | 0.4869 | 0.2685 | 0.6349 | 0.9364 | 0.3451 | 0.4998 | 0.2842 | 0.0643 | 0.6656 |
| 0.8980 | 0.0455 | 0.8314 | 0.8189 | 0.6783 | 0.8086 | 0.1386 | 0.4442 | 0.9941 | 0.6812 |
| 0.8412 | 0.8792 | 0.2025 | 0.9320 | 0.7656 | 0.3815 | 0.5302 | 0.8744 | 0.4584 | 0.3585 |
| 0.5688 | 0.8633 | 0.5818 | 0.0692 | 0.2543 | 0.5453 | 0.9955 | 0.1237 | 0.7535 | 0.5993 |
| 0.5006 | 0.1215 | 0.8102 | 0.1026 | 0.9251 | 0.6851 | 0.1559 | 0.1214 | 0.2628 | 0.9374 |
| 0.5748 | 0.4164 | 0.3427 | 0.2809 | 0.8064 | 0.5855 | 0.2229 | 0.2805 | 0.9139 | 0.9013 |
| 0.1100 | 0.0873 | 0.9407 | 0.8747 | 0.0496 | 0.4380 | 0.5847 | 0.4183 | 0.5929 | 0.4863 |
| 0.5802 | 0.7747 | 0.1285 | 0.0074 | 0.6252 | 0.7747 | 0.0112 | 0.3958 | 0.3285 | 0.5389 |
| 0.1019 | 0.6628 | 0.8998 | 0.1334 | 0.2798 | 0.7351 | 0.7330 | 0.6723 | 0.6924 | 0.3963 |
| 0.9909 | 0.8991 | 0.2298 | 0.2603 | 0.6921 | 0.5573 | 0.8191 | 0.0384 | 0.2954 | 0.0636 |
| 0.6292 | 0.4923 | 0.0276 | 0.6734 | 0.6562 | 0.4231 | 0.1980 | 0.6551 | 0.3716 | 0.0507 |
| 0.9430 | 0.2579 | 0.7933 | 0.0945 | 0.3192 | 0.3195 | 0.7772 | 0.4672 | 0.7070 | 0.5925 |
| 0.9938 | 0.7098 | 0.7964 | 0.7952 | 0.8947 | 0.1214 | 0.8454 | 0.8294 | 0.5394 | 0.9413 |
| 0.4690 | 0.1395 | 0.0930 | 0.3189 | 0.6972 | 0.7291 | 0.8513 | 0.9256 | 0.7478 | 0.8124 |
| 0.2028 | 0.3774 | 0.0485 | 0.7718 | 0.9656 | 0.2444 | 0.0304 | 0.1395 | 0.1577 | 0.8625 |
| 0.6141 | 0.4131 | 0.2006 | 0.2329 | 0.6182 | 0.5151 | 0.6300 | 0.9311 | 0.3837 | 0.7828 |
| 0.2757 | 0.8479 | 0.7880 | 0.8492 | 0.6859 | 0.8947 | 0.6246 | 0.1574 | 0.4936 | 0.8077 |
| 0.0561 | 0.0126 | 0.6531 | 0.0378 | 0.4975 | 0.1133 | 0.3572 | 0.0071 | 0.4555 | 0.7563 |
| 0.1419 | 0.4308 | 0.8073 | 0.4681 | 0.0481 | 0.2918 | 0.2975 | 0.0685 | 0.6384 | 0.0812 |
| 0.3125 | 0.0053 | 0.9209 | 0.9768 | 0.3584 | 0.0390 | 0.2161 | 0.6333 | 0.4391 | 0.6991 |

| Table 13.3 | RANDOM NUMBER INTERVALS FOR GENERATING VALUES OF DIRECT LABOR COST PER UNIT | |
|---|---|---|
| Direct Labor Cost Per Unit | Probability | Interval of Random Numbers |
| $43 | 0.1 | 0.0 but less than 0.1 |
| $44 | 0.2 | 0.1 but less than 0.3 |
| $45 | 0.4 | 0.3 but less than 0.7 |
| $46 | 0.2 | 0.7 but less than 0.9 |
| $47 | 0.1 | 0.9 but less than 1.0 |

number between 0 and 1. If the random number is 0.0 but less than 0.1, we set the direct labor cost equal to $43. If the random number is 0.1 but less than 0.3, we set the direct labor cost equal to $44, and so on.

Problem 5 will give you the opportunity to establish intervals of random numbers and simulate demand from a discrete probability distribution.

Each trial of the simulation requires a value for the direct labor cost. Suppose that on the first trial the random number is 0.9109. From Table 13.3, the simulated value for the direct labor cost is $47 per unit. Suppose that on the second trial the random number is 0.2841. From Table 13.3, the simulated value for the direct labor cost is $44 per unit. Table 13.4 shows the results obtained for the first 10 simulation trials.

Each trial in the simulation requires a value of the direct labor cost, parts cost, and first-year demand. Let us now turn to the issue of generating values for the parts cost. The probability distribution for the parts cost per unit is the uniform distribution shown in Figure 13.3. Because this random variable has a different probability distribution than direct labor cost, we use random numbers in a slightly different way to generate values for parts cost. With a uniform probability distribution, the following relationship between the random number and the associated value of the parts cost is used.

$$\text{Parts Cost} = a + r(b - a) \tag{13.2}$$

| Table 13.4 | RANDOM GENERATION OF TEN VALUES FOR THE DIRECT LABOR COST PER UNIT | |
|---|---|---|
| Trial | Random Number | Direct Labor Cost ($) |
| 1 | 0.9109 | 47 |
| 2 | 0.2841 | 44 |
| 3 | 0.6531 | 45 |
| 4 | 0.0367 | 43 |
| 5 | 0.3451 | 45 |
| 6 | 0.2757 | 44 |
| 7 | 0.6859 | 45 |
| 8 | 0.6246 | 45 |
| 9 | 0.4936 | 45 |
| 10 | 0.8077 | 46 |

where

$$r = \text{random number between 0 and 1}$$
$$a = \text{smallest value for parts cost}$$
$$b = \text{largest value for parts cost}$$

For PortaCom, the smallest value for the parts cost is \$80, and the largest value is \$100. Applying equation (13.2) with $a = 80$ and $b = 100$ leads to the following formula for generating the parts cost given a random number, $r$.

$$\text{Parts Cost} = 80 + r(100 - 80) = 80 + r20 \qquad (13.3)$$

Let us use equation (13.3) to generate a value for the parts cost. Suppose that a random number of 0.2680 is obtained. The value for the parts cost is

$$\text{Parts Cost} = 80 + 0.2680(20) = 85.36 \text{ per unit}$$

Suppose that a random number of 0.5842 is generated on the next trial. The value for the parts cost is

$$\text{Parts Cost} = 80 + 0.5842(20) = 91.68 \text{ per unit}$$

With appropriate choices of $a$ and $b$, equation (13.2) can be used to generate values for any uniform probability distribution. Table 13.5 shows the generation of ten values for the parts cost per unit.

Finally, we need a random number procedure for generating the first-year demand. Since first-year demand is normally distributed with a mean of 15,000 units and a standard deviation of 4500 units (see Figure 13.4), we need a procedure for generating random values from a normal probability distribution. Because of the mathematical complexity, a detailed discussion of the procedure for generating random values from a normal probability distribution is omitted. However, computer simulation packages and spreadsheets include a built-in function that provides randomly generated values from a normal probability

| **Table** **13.5** | **RANDOM GENERATION OF TEN VALUES FOR THE PARTS COST PER UNIT** | |
|---|---|---|
| **Trial** | **Random Number** | **Parts Cost (\$)** |
| 1 | 0.2680 | 85.36 |
| 2 | 0.5842 | 91.68 |
| 3 | 0.6675 | 93.35 |
| 4 | 0.9280 | 98.56 |
| 5 | 0.4180 | 88.36 |
| 6 | 0.7342 | 94.68 |
| 7 | 0.4325 | 88.65 |
| 8 | 0.1186 | 82.37 |
| 9 | 0.6944 | 93.89 |
| 10 | 0.7869 | 95.74 |

distribution. In most cases the user only needs to provide the mean and standard deviation of the normal distribution. For example, using Excel the following formula can be placed into a cell to obtain a value for a probabilistic input that is normally distributed:

$$=NORMINV(RANDO(),Mean,Standard\ Deviation)$$

Because the mean for the first-year demand in the PortaCom problem is 15,000 and the standard deviation is 4500, the Excel statement

$$=NORMINV(RAND(),15000,4500) \qquad (13.4)$$

will provide a normally distributed value for first-year demand. For example, if Excel's RAND() function generates the random number 0.7005, the Excel function shown in equation (13.4) will provide a first-year demand of 17,366 units. If RAND() generates the random number 0.3204, equation (13.4) will provide a first-year demand of 12,900. Table 13.6 shows the results for the first ten randomly generated values for demand. Note that random numbers less than 0.5 generate first-year demand values below the mean and that random numbers greater than 0.5 generate first-year demand values greater than the mean.

**Running the Simulation Model.**   Running the simulation model means implementing the sequence of logical and mathematical operations described in the flowchart in Figure 13.5. The model parameters are $249 per unit for the selling price, $400,000 for the administrative cost, and $600,000 for the advertising cost. Each trial in the simulation involves randomly generating values for the probabilistic inputs (direct labor cost, parts cost, and first-year demand) and computing profit. The simulation is complete when a satisfactory number of trials have been conducted.

Let us compute the profit for the first trial assuming the following probabilistic inputs:

Direct Labor Cost:     $c_1 = 47$

Part Cost:               $c_2 = 85.36$

First-Year Demand:    $x = 17,366$

| Table 13.6 | RANDOM GENERATION OF TEN VALUES FOR FIRST-YEAR DEMAND |
|---|---|

| Trial | Random Number | Demand |
|---|---|---|
| 1 | 0.7005 | 17,366 |
| 2 | 0.3204 | 12,900 |
| 3 | 0.8968 | 20,686 |
| 4 | 0.1804 | 10,888 |
| 5 | 0.4346 | 14,259 |
| 6 | 0.9605 | 22,904 |
| 7 | 0.5646 | 15,732 |
| 8 | 0.7334 | 17,804 |
| 9 | 0.0216 | 5,902 |
| 10 | 0.3218 | 12,918 |

Spreadsheet packages such as Excel have built-in functions that make simulations based on probability distributions such as the normal probability distribution relatively easy.

Referring to the flowchart in Figure 13.5, we see that the profit obtained is

$$\text{Profit} = (249 - c_1 - c_2)x - 1,000,000$$
$$= (249 - 47 - 85.36)17,366 - 1,000,000 = 1,025,570$$

The first row of Table 13.7 shows the result of this trial of the PortaCom simulation.

The simulated profit for the PortaCom printer if the direct labor cost is $47 per unit, the parts cost is $85.36 per unit, and first-year demand is 17,366 units is $1,025,570. Of course, one simulation trial does not provide a complete understanding of the possible profit and loss. Because other values are possible for the probabilistic inputs, we can benefit from additional simulation trials.

Suppose that on a second simulation trial, random numbers of 0.2841, 0.5842, and 0.3204 are generated for the direct labor cost, the parts cost, and first-year demand, respectively. These random numbers will provide the probabilistic inputs of $44 for the direct labor cost, $91.68 for the parts cost, and 12,900 for first-year demand. These values provide a simulated profit of $461,828 on the second simulation trial (see the second row of Table 13.7).

Repetition of the simulation process with different values for the probabilistic inputs is an essential part of any simulation. Through the repeated trials, management will begin to understand what might happen when the product is introduced into the real world. We have shown the results of ten simulation trials in Table 13.7. For these 10 cases, we find a profit as high as $1,526,769 for the 6th trial and a loss of $350,131 for the 9th trial. Thus, we see both the possibility of a profit and a loss. Averages for the ten trials are presented at the bottom of the table. We see that the average profit for the ten trials is $713,743. The probability of a loss is 0.10, since one of the ten trials (the 9th) resulted in a loss. We note also that the average values for labor cost, parts cost, and first-year demand are fairly close to their means of $45, $90, and 15,000, respectively.

## Simulation of the PortaCom Problem

Using an Excel spreadsheet, we simulated the PortaCom project 500 times. The spreadsheet used to carry out the simulation is shown in Figure 13.6. Note that the simulation results for

| Table 13.7 | PORTACOM SIMULATION RESULTS FOR TEN TRIALS | | | |
|---|---|---|---|---|
| Trial | Direct Labor Cost Per Unit ($) | Parts Cost Per Unit ($) | Units Sold | Profit ($) |
| 1 | 47 | 85.36 | 17,366 | 1,025,570 |
| 2 | 44 | 91.68 | 12,900 | 461,828 |
| 3 | 45 | 93.35 | 20,686 | 1,288,906 |
| 4 | 43 | 98.56 | 10,888 | 169,807 |
| 5 | 45 | 88.36 | 14,259 | 648,911 |
| 6 | 44 | 94.68 | 22,904 | 1,526,769 |
| 7 | 45 | 88.65 | 15,732 | 814,686 |
| 8 | 45 | 82.37 | 17,804 | 1,165,501 |
| 9 | 45 | 93.89 | 5,902 | −350,131 |
| 10 | 46 | 95.74 | 12,918 | 385,585 |
| Total | 449 | 912.64 | 151,359 | 7,137,432 |
| Average | $44.90 | $91.26 | 15,136 | $713,743 |

*Figure* 13.6    SPREADSHEET SIMULATION FOR THE PORTACOM PROBLEM

| | A | B | C | D | E | F |
|---|---|---|---|---|---|---|
| 1 | **PortaCom Risk Analysis** | | | | | |
| 2 | | | | | | |
| 3 | Selling Price Per Unit | | $249 | | | |
| 4 | Administrative Cost | | $400,000 | | | |
| 5 | Advertising Cost | | $600,000 | | | |
| 6 | | | | | | |
| 7 | **Direct Labor Cost** | | | **Parts Cost (Uniform Distribution)** | | |
| 8 | Lower | Upper | | Smallest Value | $80 | |
| 9 | Random No. | Random No. | Cost Per Unit | Largest Value | $100 | |
| 10 | 0.0 | 0.1 | $43 | | | |
| 11 | 0.1 | 0.3 | $44 | | | |
| 12 | 0.3 | 0.7 | $45 | **Demand (Normal Distribution)** | | |
| 13 | 0.7 | 0.9 | $46 | Mean | 15000 | |
| 14 | 0.9 | 1.0 | $47 | Standard Dev | 4500 | |
| 15 | | | | | | |
| 16 | | | | | | |
| 17 | **Simulation Trials** | | | | | |
| 18 | | | | | | |
| 19 | | Direct Labor | Parts | First-Year | | |
| 20 | Trial | Cost Per Unit | Cost Per Unit | Demand | Profit | |
| 21 | 1 | 47 | $85.36 | 17,366 | $1,025,570 | |
| 22 | 2 | 44 | $91.68 | 12,900 | $461,828 | |
| 23 | 3 | 45 | $93.35 | 20,686 | $1,288,906 | |
| 24 | 4 | 43 | $98.56 | 10,888 | $169,807 | |
| 25 | 5 | 45 | $88.36 | 14,259 | $648,911 | |
| 516 | 496 | 44 | $98.67 | 8,730 | ($71,659) | |
| 517 | 497 | 45 | $94.38 | 19,257 | $1,110,841 | |
| 518 | 498 | 44 | $90.85 | 14,920 | $703,102 | |
| 519 | 499 | 43 | $90.37 | 13,471 | $557,662 | |
| 520 | 500 | 46 | $92.50 | 18,614 | $1,056,927 | |
| 521 | | | | | | |
| 522 | | | **Summary Statistics** | | | |
| 523 | | | Mean Profit | | $698,457 | |
| 524 | | | Standard Deviation | | $520,485 | |
| 525 | | | Minimum Profit | | ($785,234) | |
| 526 | | | Maximum Profit | | $2,367,058 | |
| 527 | | | Number of Losses | | 51 | |
| 528 | | | Probability of Loss | | 0.1020 | |

trials 6 through 495 have been hidden so that the results can be shown in a reasonably sized figure. If desired, the rows for these trials can be shown and the simulation results displayed for all 500 trials. The details of the Excel spreadsheet that provided the PortaCom simulation are described in Appendix 13.1.

The simulation summary statistics in Figure 13.6 provide information about the risk associated with PortaCom's new printer. The worst result obtained in a simulation of 500 trials is a loss of $785,234, and the best result is a profit of $2,367,058. The mean profit is $698,457. Fifty-one of the trials resulted in a loss; thus, the estimated probability of a loss is 51/500 = 0.1020.

*Simulation studies enable an objective estimate of the probability of a loss, which is an important aspect of risk analysis.*

A histogram of simulated profit values is shown in Figure 13.7. We note that the distribution of profit values is fairly symmetric with a large number of values in the range of $250,000 to $1,250,000. The probability of a large loss or a large gain is small. Only 3 trials resulted in a loss more than $500,000, and only 3 trials resulted in a profit greater than $2,000,000. However, the probability of a loss is significant. Forty-eight of the 500 trials resulted in a loss in the $0 to $500,000 range—almost 10%. The modal category, the one with the largest number of values, is the range of profits between $750,000 and $1,000,000.

In comparing the simulation approach to risk analysis to the what-if approach, we see that much more information is obtained by using simulation. With the what-if analysis, we learned that the base-case scenario projected a profit of $710,000. The worst-case scenario

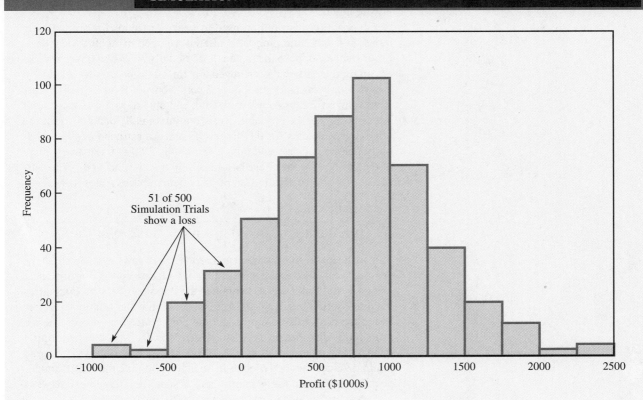

**Figure 13.7    HISTOGRAM OF SIMULATED PROFIT FOR 500 TRIALS OF THE PORTACOM SIMULATION**

projected a loss of $847,000, and the best-case scenario projected a profit of $2,591,000. From the 500 trials of the simulation run, we see that the worst- and best-case scenarios, although possible, are very unlikely. None of the 500 trials provided a loss as low as the worst-case or a profit as high as the best-case. Indeed, the advantage of simulation for risk analysis is the information it provides on the likely values of the output. We now know the probability of a loss, how the profit values are distributed over their range, and what profit values are most likely.

The simulation results help PortaCom's management better understand the profit/loss potential of the PortaCom portable printer. The 0.1020 probability of a loss may be acceptable to management given a probability of almost 0.80 (see Figure 13.7) that profit will exceed $250,000. On the other hand, PortaCom might want to conduct further market research before deciding whether to introduce the product. In any case, the simulation results should be helpful in reaching an appropriate decision.

For practice working through a simulation problem, try problems 9 and 14.

# N O T E S and Comments

1. The PortaCom simulation model is based on independent trials in which the results for one trial do not affect what happens in subsequent trials. Historically, simulation studies such as this were referred to as *Monte Carlo simulations.* The term *Monte Carlo simulation* was used because early practitioners of simulation saw similarities between the models they were developing and the gambling games played in the casinos of Monte Carlo. Today, many individuals interpret the term Monte Carlo simulation more broadly to mean any simulation that involves randomly generating values for the probabilistic inputs.

2. The probability distribution used to generate values for probabilistic inputs in a simulation model is often developed using historical data. For instance, suppose that an analysis of daily sales at a new car dealership for the past 50 days showed that on 2 days no cars were sold, on 5 days 1 car was sold, on 9 days 2 cars were sold, on 24 days 3 cars were sold, on 7 days 4 cars were sold, and on 3 days 5 cars were sold. We can estimate the probability distribution of daily demand using the relative frequencies for the observed data. An estimate of the probability that no cars are sold on a given day is $2/50 = 0.04$, an estimate of the probability that 1 car is sold is $5/50 = 0.10$ and so on. The estimated probability distribution of daily demand is as follows:

| Daily Sales | 0 | 1 | 2 | 3 | 4 | 5 |
|---|---|---|---|---|---|---|
| Probability | 0.04 | 0.10 | 0.18 | 0.48 | 0.14 | 0.06 |

3. Spreadsheet add-in packages such as @RISK® and Crystal Ball® have been developed to make spreadsheet simulation easier. For instance, using Crystal Ball we could simulate the PortaCom new product introduction by first entering the formulas showing the relationships between the probabilistic inputs and the output measure, profit. Then, a probability distribution type is selected for each probabilistic input from among a number of available choices. Crystal Ball will generate random values for each probabilistic input, compute the profit, and repeat the simulation for as many trials as specified. Graphical displays and a variety of descriptive statistics can be easily obtained.

······················································································/ /··········

## 13.2    AN INVENTORY SIMULATION

In this section we describe how simulation can be used to establish an inventory policy for a product that has an uncertain demand. The product is a home ventilation fan distributed by the Butler Electrical Supply Company. Each fan costs Butler $75 and sells for $125. Thus Butler realizes a gross profit of $125 − $75 = $50 for each fan sold. Monthly demand for the fan is described by a normal probability distribution with a mean of 100 units and a standard deviation of 20 units.

Butler receives monthly deliveries from its supplier and replenishes its inventory to a level of $Q$ at the beginning of each month. This beginning inventory level is referred to as the replenishment level. If monthly demand is less than the replenishment level, an inventory holding cost of $15 is charged for each unit that is not sold. However, if monthly demand is greater than the replenishment level, a stockout occurs and a shortage cost is incurred. Because Butler assigns a goodwill cost of $30 for each customer turned away, a shortage cost of $30 is charged for each unit of demand that cannot be satisfied. Management would like to use a simulation model to determine the average monthly net profit resulting from using a particular replenishment level. Management would also like information on the percentage of total demand that will be satisfied. This percentage is referred to as the *service level*.

The controllable input to the Butler simulation model is the replenishment level, $Q$. The probabilistic input is the monthly demand, $D$. There are two output measures: the average monthly net profit and the service level. Computation of the service level requires that we keep track of the number of fans sold each month and the total demand for fans for each month. The service level will be computed at the end of the simulation run as the ratio of total units sold to total demand. A diagram showing the relationship between the inputs and the outputs is shown in Figure 13.8.

When demand is less than or equal to the replenishment level ($D \leq Q$), $D$ units are sold, and an inventory holding cost of $15 is incurred for each of the $Q − D$ units that remain in inventory. Net profit for this case is computed as follows:

**Case 1: $D \leq Q$**

$$\text{Gross Profit} = \$50D$$
$$\text{Holding Cost} = \$15(Q − D)$$
$$\text{Net Profit} = \text{Gross Profit} − \text{Holding Cost} = \$50D − \$15(Q − D) \quad (13.5)$$

---

**Figure 13.8**    BUTLER INVENTORY SIMULATION MODEL

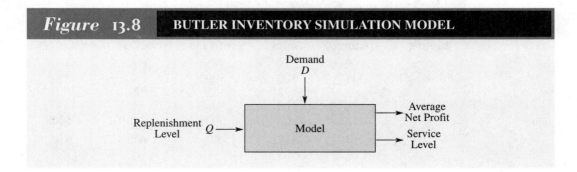

When demand is greater than the replenishment level ($D > Q$), $Q$ fans are sold, and a shortage cost of \$30 is imposed for each of the $D - Q$ units of demand not satisfied. Net profit for this case is computed as follows:

**Case 2: $D > Q$**

$$\text{Gross Profit} = \$50Q$$
$$\text{Shortage Cost} = \$30(D - Q)$$
$$\text{Net Profit} = \text{Gross Profit} - \text{Shortage Cost} = \$50Q - \$30(D - Q) \quad (13.6)$$

Figure 13.9 shows a flowchart that defines the sequence of logical and mathematical operations required to simulate the Butler inventory system. Each trial in the simulation represents one month of operation. The simulation is run for 300 months using a given replenishment level, $Q$. Then, the average profit and service level output measures are computed. Let us describe the steps involved in the simulation by illustrating the results for the first two months of a simulation run using a replenishment level of $Q = 100$.

The first block of the flowchart in Figure 13.9 sets the values of the model parameters: gross profit = \$50 per unit, holding cost = \$15 per unit, and shortage cost = \$30 per unit. The next block shows that a replenishment level of $Q$ is selected; in our illustration, $Q = 100$. Then, a value for monthly demand is generated. Since monthly demand is normally distributed with a mean of 100 units and a standard deviation of 20 units, we can use the Excel function = NORMINV(RAND(),100,20), as described in Section 13.1, to generate a value for monthly demand. Suppose that a value of $D = 79$ is generated on the first trial. This value of demand is then compared with the replenishment level, $Q$. With the replenishment level set at $Q = 100$, demand is less than the replenishment level, and the left branch of the flowchart is followed. Sales are set equal to demand (79), and gross profit, holding cost, and net profit are computed as follows:

$$\text{Gross Profit} = 50D = 50(79) = 3950$$
$$\text{Holding Cost} = 15(Q - D) = 15(100 - 79) = 315$$
$$\text{Net Profit} = \text{Gross Profit} - \text{Holding Cost} = 3950 - 315 = 3635$$

The values of demand, sales, gross profit, holding cost, and net profit are recorded for the first month. The first row of Table 13.8 summarizes the information for this first trial.

For the second month, suppose that a value of 111 is generated for monthly demand. Because demand is greater than the replenishment level, the right branch of the flowchart

| Table 13.8 | | BUTLER INVENTORY SIMULATION RESULTS FOR FIVE TRIALS WITH $Q = 100$ | | | | |
|---|---|---|---|---|---|---|
| Month | Demand | Sales | Gross Profit (\$) | Holding Cost (\$) | Shortage Cost (\$) | Net Profit (\$) |
| 1 | 79 | 79 | 3950 | 315 | 0 | 3635 |
| 2 | 111 | 100 | 5000 | 0 | 330 | 4670 |
| 3 | 93 | 93 | 4650 | 105 | 0 | 4545 |
| 4 | 100 | 100 | 5000 | 0 | 0 | 5000 |
| 5 | 118 | 100 | 5000 | 0 | 540 | 4460 |
| Totals | 501 | 472 | 23,600 | 420 | 870 | 22,310 |
| Average | 100 | 94 | \$4,720 | \$ 84 | \$174 | \$4,462 |

**Figure** 13.9    **FLOWCHART FOR THE BUTLER INVENTORY SIMULATION**

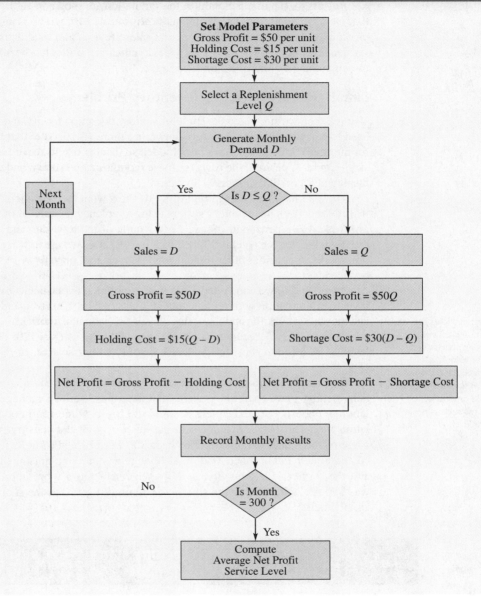

is followed. Sales are set equal to the replenishment level (100), and gross profit, shortage cost, and net profit are computed as follows:

$$\text{Gross Profit} = 50Q = 50(100) = 5000$$
$$\text{Shortage Cost} = 30(D - Q) = 30(111 - 100) = 330$$
$$\text{Net Profit} = \text{Gross Profit} - \text{Shortage Cost} = 5000 - 330 = 4670$$

The values of demand, sales, gross profit, holding cost, shortage cost, and net profit are recorded for the second month. The second row of Table 13.8 summarizes the information generated in the second trial.

Results for the first 5 months of the simulation are shown in Table 13.8. The totals show that we have an accumulated total net profit of $22,310, which is an average monthly net profit of $22,310/5 = $4,462. Total unit sales are 472, and total demand is 501. Thus, the service level is 472/501 = .942, or 94.2%, indicating Butler has been able to satisfy 94.2% of demand during the five month period.

### Simulation of the Butler Inventory Problem

Using Excel, we simulated the Butler inventory operation for 300 months. The spreadsheet used to carry out the simulation is shown in Figure 13.10. Note that the simulation results for months 6 through 295 have been hidden so that the results can be shown in a reasonably sized figure. If desired, the rows for these months can be shown and the simulation results displayed for all 300 months.

The summary statistics in Figure 13.10 show what can be anticipated over 300 months if Butler operates its inventory system using a replenishment level of 100. The average net profit is $4,293 per month. Since 27,917 units of the total demand of 30,181 units were satisfied, the service level is 27,917/30,181 = 92.5%. We are now ready to use the simulation model to consider other replenishment levels that may improve the net profit and the service level.

At this point, we conducted a series of simulation experiments by repeating the Butler inventory simulation with replenishment levels of 110, 120, 130, and 140 units. The average monthly net profits and the service levels are shown in Table 13.9. The highest monthly net profit of $4,575 occurs with a replenishment level of $Q = 120$. The associated service level is 98.6%. On the basis of these results, Butler selected a replenishment level of $Q = 120$.

Experimental simulation studies, such as this one for Butler's inventory policy, can help identify good operating policies and decisions. Butler's management has used simulation to choose a replenishment level of 120 for its home ventilation fan. With the simulation model in place, management can also explore the sensitivity of this decision to some of the model parameters. For instance, we assigned a shortage cost of $30 for any customer demand not met. With this shortage cost, the replenishment level was $Q = 120$ and the service level was 98.6%. If management felt a more appropriate shortage cost was $10 per unit, running the simulation again using $10 as the shortage cost would be a simple matter.

*Simulation allows the user to consider different operating policies and changes to model parameters and then to observe the impact of the changes on output measures such as profit or service level.*

| Table 13.9 | BUTLER INVENTORY SIMULATION RESULTS FOR 300 TRIALS | | |
|---|---|---|---|
| | Replenishment Level | Average Net Profit ($) | Service Level (%) |
| | 100 | 4293 | 92.5 |
| | 110 | 4524 | 96.5 |
| | 120 | 4575 | 98.6 |
| | 130 | 4519 | 99.6 |
| | 140 | 4399 | 99.9 |

**Figure 13.10**    **SPREADSHEET SIMULATION FOR THE BUTLER INVENTORY PROBLEM**

|     | A | B | C | D | E | F | G |
|-----|---|---|---|---|---|---|---|
| 1 | **Butler Inventory** | | | | | | |
| 2 | | | | | | | |
| 3 | Gross Profit Per Unit | | $50 | | | | |
| 4 | Holding Cost Per Unit | | $15 | | | | |
| 5 | Shortage Cost Per Unit | | $30 | | | | |
| 6 | | | | | | | |
| 7 | **Replenishment Level** | | 100 | | | | |
| 8 | | | | | | | |
| 9 | **Demand (Normal Distribution)** | | | | | | |
| 10 | Mean | 100 | | | | | |
| 11 | Standard Dev | 20 | | | | | |
| 12 | | | | | | | |
| 13 | | | | | | | |
| 14 | **Simulation** | | | | | | |
| 15 | | | | | | | |
| 16 | Month | Demand | Sales | Gross Profit | Holding Cost | Shortage Cost | Net Profit |
| 17 | 1 | 79 | 79 | $3,950 | $315 | $0 | $3,635 |
| 18 | 2 | 111 | 100 | $5,000 | $0 | $330 | $4,670 |
| 19 | 3 | 93 | 93 | $4,650 | $105 | $0 | $4,545 |
| 20 | 4 | 100 | 100 | $5,000 | $0 | $0 | $5,000 |
| 21 | 5 | 118 | 100 | $5,000 | $0 | $540 | $4,460 |
| 312 | 296 | 89 | 89 | $4,450 | $165 | $0 | $4,285 |
| 313 | 297 | 91 | 91 | $4,550 | $135 | $0 | $4,415 |
| 314 | 298 | 122 | 100 | $5,000 | $0 | $660 | $4,340 |
| 315 | 299 | 93 | 93 | $4,650 | $105 | $0 | $4,545 |
| 316 | 300 | 126 | 100 | $5,000 | $0 | $780 | $4,220 |
| 317 | | | | | | | |
| 318 | **Totals** | 30,181 | 27,917 | | **Summary Statistics** | | |
| 319 | | | | | Mean Profit | | $4,293 |
| 320 | | | | | Standard Deviation | | $658 |
| 321 | | | | | Minimum Profit | | ($206) |
| 322 | | | | | Maximum Profit | | $5,000 |
| 323 | | | | | Service Level | | 92.5% |

Problem 18 will give you a chance to develop a different simulation model.

We mentioned earlier that simulation is not an optimization technique. Even though we have used simulation to choose a replenishment level, we have no guarantee that this choice is optimal. All possible replenishment levels were not tested. Perhaps a manager would like to consider additional simulation runs with replenishment levels of $Q = 115$ and $Q = 125$ to search for an even better inventory policy. Also, we have no guarantee that with another set of 300 randomly generated demand values that the replenishment level with the highest profit would not change. However, with a large number of simulation trials, we should find a good and, at least, near optimal solution.

# MANAGEMENT SCIENCE IN ACTION

## SIMULATION HELPS PETROLEUM DISTRIBUTION IN THE GULF OF MEXICO*

Domestic suppliers who operate oil refineries along the Gulf Coast are helping to satisfy Florida's increasing demand for refined petroleum products. Barge fleets, operated either by independent shipping companies or by the petroleum companies themselves, are used to transport more than 20 different petroleum products to 15 Florida petroleum companies. The petroleum products are loaded at refineries in Texas, Louisiana, and Mississippi, and are discharged at tank terminals concentrated in Tampa, Port Everglades, and Jacksonville.

Barges operate under three types of contracts between the fleet operator and the client petroleum company:

- The client assumes total control of a barge and uses it for trips between its own refinery and one or more discharging ports.
- The client is guaranteed a certain volume will be moved during the contract period. Schedules vary considerably depending upon the customer's needs and the fleet operator's capabilities.
- The client hires a barge for a single trip.

A simulation model was developed to analyze the complex process of operating barge fleets in the Gulf of Mexico. An appropriate probability distribution was used to simulate requests for shipments by the petroleum companies. Additional probability distributions were used to simulate the travel times depending upon the size and type of barge. Using this information, the simulation model was used to track barge loading times, barge discharge times, barge utilization, and total cost.

Analysts used simulation runs with a variety of what-if scenarios to answer questions about the petroleum distribution system and to make recommendations for improving the efficiency of the operation. Simulation helped determine the following:

- The optimal trade-off between fleet utilization and on-time delivery
- The recommended fleet size
- The recommended barge capacities
- The best service contract structure to balance the trade-off between customer service and delivery cost

Implementation of the simulation-based recommendations demonstrated a significant improvement in the operation and a significant lowering of petroleum distribution costs.

*Based on E. D. Chajakis, "Sophisticated Crude Transportation," *OR/MS Today* (December 1997): 30–34.

---

## 13.3   A WAITING LINE SIMULATION

The simulation models discussed thus far have been based on independent trials in which the results for one trial do not affect what happens in subsequent trials. In this sense, the system being modeled does not change or evolve over time. Simulation models such as these are referred to as **static simulation models.** In this section, we develop a simulation model of a waiting line system where the state of the system, including the number of customers in the waiting line and whether the service facility is busy or idle, change or evolves over time. To incorporate time into the simulation model, we use a simulation clock to record the time that each customer arrives for service as well as the time that each customer completes service. Simulation models that must take into account how the system changes or evolves over time are referred to as **dynamic simulation models.** In situations where the arrivals and departures of customers are **events** that occur at *discrete* points in time, the simulation model is also referred to as a **discrete-event simulation model.**

In Chapter 12, we presented formulas that could be used to compute the steady-state operating characteristics of a waiting line, including the average waiting time, the average number of units in the waiting line, the probability of waiting, and so on. In most cases, the waiting line formulas were based on specific assumptions about the probability distribution for arrivals, the probability distribution for service times, the queue discipline, and so on. Simulation, as an alternative for studying waiting lines, is more flexible. In applications where the assumptions required by the waiting line formulas are not reasonable, simulation may be the only feasible approach to studying the waiting line system. In this section we discuss the simulation of the waiting line for the Hammondsport Savings Bank automated teller machine (ATM).

### The Hammondsport Savings Bank ATM Waiting Line

Hammondsport Savings Bank will open several new branch banks during the coming year. Each new branch is designed to have one automated teller machine (ATM). A concern is that during busy periods several customers may have to wait to use the ATM. This concern has led the bank to undertake a study of the ATM waiting line system. The bank's vice-president wants to determine whether one ATM will be sufficient. The bank has established service guidelines for its ATM system stating that the average customer waiting time for an ATM should be one minute or less. Let us show how a simulation model can be used to study the ATM waiting line at a particular branch.

### Customer Arrival Times

One probabilistic input to the ATM simulation model is the arrival times of customers who use the ATM. In waiting line simulations, arrival times are determined by randomly generating the time between two successive arrivals, referred to as *the interarrival time*. For the branch bank being studied, the customer interarrival times are assumed to be uniformly distributed between 0 and 5 minutes as shown in Figure 13.11. With $r$ denoting a random number between 0 and 1, an interarrival time for two successive customers can be simulated by using the formula for generating values from a uniform probability distribution.

$$\text{Interarrival Time} = a + r(b - a) \qquad (13.7)$$

where

$$r = \text{random number between 0 and 1}$$
$$a = \text{minimum interarrival time}$$
$$b = \text{maximum interarrival time}$$

A uniform probability distribution of interarrival times is used here to illustrate the simulation computations. Actually, any interarrival time probability distribution can be assumed, and the logic of the waiting line simulation model will not change.

For the Hammondsport ATM system, the minimum interarrival time is $a = 0$ minutes, and the maximum interarrival time is $b = 5$ minutes; therefore, the formula for generating an interarrival time is

$$\text{Interarrival Time} = 0 + r(5 - 0) = 5r \qquad (13.8)$$

Assume that the simulation run begins at time $= 0$. A random number of $r = 0.2804$ generates an interarrival time of $5(0.2804) = 1.4$ minutes for customer 1. Thus, customer 1 arrives 1.4 minutes after the simulation run begins. A second random number of $r = 0.2598$ generates an interarrival time of $5(0.2598) = 1.3$ minutes, indicating that customer 2 arrives 1.3 minutes after customer 1. Thus, customer 2 arrives $1.4 + 1.3 = 2.7$ minutes after the simulation begins. Continuing, a third random number of $r = 0.9802$ indicates that customer 3 arrives 4.9 minutes after customer 2, which is 7.6 minutes after the simulation begins.

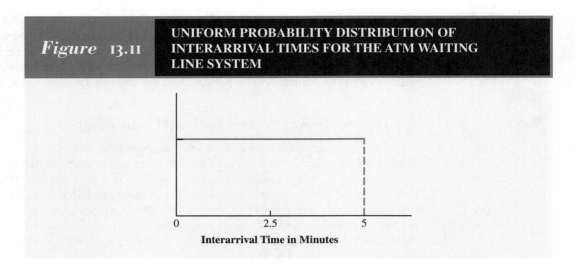

**Figure 13.11**

**UNIFORM PROBABILITY DISTRIBUTION OF INTERARRIVAL TIMES FOR THE ATM WAITING LINE SYSTEM**

## Customer Service Times

Another probabilistic input in the ATM simulation model is the service time, which is the time a customer spends using the ATM machine. Past data from similar ATMs indicates that a normal probability distribution with a mean of 2 minutes and a standard deviation of 0.5 minutes, as shown in Figure 13.12, can be used to describe service times. As discussed in Sections 13.1 and 13.2, values from a normal probability distribution with mean 2 and standard deviation 0.5 can be generated using the Excel function =NORMINV(RAND(),2,0.5). For example, the random number of 0.7257 generates a customer service time of 2.3 minutes.

## The Simulation Model

The probabilistic inputs to the Hammondsport Savings Bank ATM simulation model are the interarrival time and the service time. The controllable input is the number of ATMs used.

**Figure 13.12**

**NORMAL PROBABILITY DISTRIBUTION OF SERVICE TIMES FOR THE ATM WAITING LINE SYSTEM**

The output will consist of various operating characteristics such as the probability of waiting, the average waiting time, the maximum waiting time, and so on. We show a diagram of the ATM simulation model in Figure 13.13.

Figure 13.14 shows a flowchart that defines the sequence of logical and mathematical operations required to simulate the Hammondsport ATM system. The flowchart uses the following notation:

$$IAT = \text{Interarrival Time generated}$$
$$\text{Arrival Time } (i) = \text{Time at which customer } i \text{ arrives}$$
$$\text{Start Time } (i) = \text{Time at which customer } i \text{ starts service}$$
$$\text{Wait Time } (i) = \text{Waiting time for customer } i$$
$$ST = \text{Service Time generated}$$
$$\text{Completion Time } (i) = \text{Time at which customer } i \text{ completes service}$$
$$\text{System Time } (i) = \text{System time for customer } i \text{ (completion time } - \text{ arrival time)}$$

Referring to Figure 13.14, we see that the simulation is initialized in the first block of the flowchart. Then a new customer is created. An interarrival time is generated to determine the time since the preceding customer arrived.[2] The arrival time for the new customer is then computed by adding the interarrival time to the arrival time of the preceding customer.

The arrival time for the new customer must be compared to the completion time of the preceding customer to determine whether the ATM is idle or busy. If the arrival time of the new customer is greater than the completion time of the preceding customer, the preceding customer will have finished service prior to the arrival of the new customer. In this case, the ATM will be idle, and the new customer can begin service immediately. The service start time for the new customer is equal to the arrival time of the new customer. However, if the arrival time for the new customer is not greater than the completion time of the preceding customer, the new customer has arrived before the preceding customer has finished service. In this case, the ATM is busy; the new customer must wait to use the ATM until the preceding customer has completed service. The service start time for the new customer is equal to the completion time of the preceding customer.

Note that the time the new customer has to wait to use the ATM is the difference between the customer's service start time and the customer's arrival time. At this point, the customer is ready to use the ATM, and the simulation run continues with the generation

> The decision rule for deciding whether the ATM is idle or busy is the most difficult aspect of the logic in a waiting line simulation model.

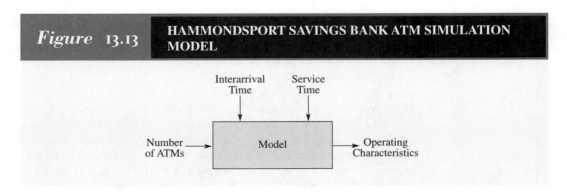

***Figure*** **13.13    HAMMONDSPORT SAVINGS BANK ATM SIMULATION MODEL**

---

[2] For the first customer, the interarrival time determines the time since the simulation started. Thus, the first interarrival time determines the time the first customer arrives.

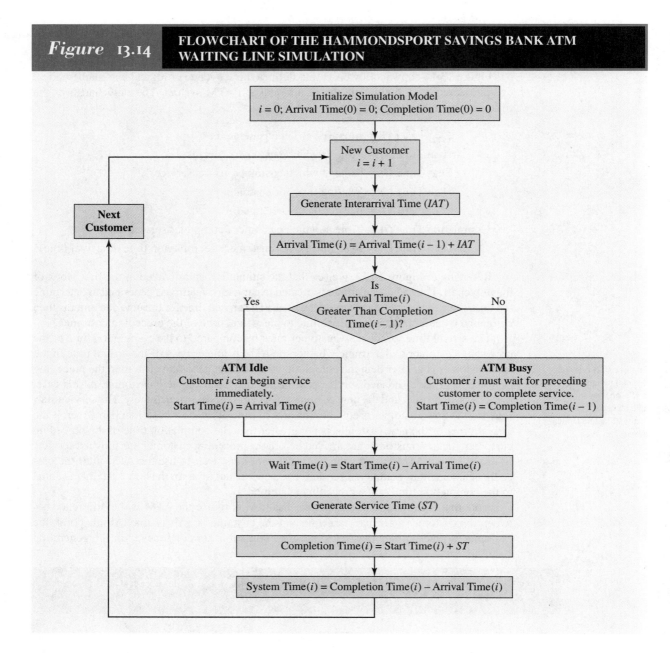

**Figure 13.14    FLOWCHART OF THE HAMMONDSPORT SAVINGS BANK ATM WAITING LINE SIMULATION**

of the customer's service time. The time at which the customer begins service plus the service time generated determine the customer's completion time. Finally, the total time the customer spends in the system is the difference between the customer's service completion time and the customer's arrival time. At this point, the computations are complete for the current customer, and the simulation continues with the next customer. The simulation is continued until a specified number of customers have been served by the ATM.

Simulation results for the first ten customers are shown in Table 13.10. We discuss the computations for the first 3 customers to illustrate the logic of the simulation model and to show how the information in Table 13.10 was developed.

| Table 13.10 | SIMULATION RESULTS FOR TEN ATM CUSTOMERS | | | | | | |
|---|---|---|---|---|---|---|---|
| Customer | Interarrival Time | Arrival Time | Service Start Time | Wait Time | Service Time | Completion Time | Time in System |
| 1 | 1.4 | 1.4 | 1.4 | 0.0 | 2.3 | 3.7 | 2.3 |
| 2 | 1.3 | 2.7 | 3.7 | 1.0 | 1.5 | 5.2 | 2.5 |
| 3 | 4.9 | 7.6 | 7.6 | 0.0 | 2.2 | 9.8 | 2.2 |
| 4 | 3.5 | 11.1 | 11.1 | 0.0 | 2.5 | 13.6 | 2.5 |
| 5 | 0.7 | 11.8 | 13.6 | 1.8 | 1.8 | 15.4 | 3.6 |
| 6 | 2.8 | 14.6 | 15.4 | 0.8 | 2.4 | 17.8 | 3.2 |
| 7 | 2.1 | 16.7 | 17.8 | 1.1 | 2.1 | 19.9 | 3.2 |
| 8 | 0.6 | 17.3 | 19.9 | 2.6 | 1.8 | 21.7 | 4.4 |
| 9 | 2.5 | 19.8 | 21.7 | 1.9 | 2.0 | 23.7 | 3.9 |
| 10 | 1.9 | 21.7 | 23.7 | 2.0 | 2.3 | 26.0 | 4.3 |
| Totals | 21.7 | | | 11.2 | 20.9 | | 32.1 |
| Averages | 2.17 | | | 1.12 | 2.09 | | 3.21 |

## Customer 1

- An interarrival time of $IAT = 1.4$ minutes is generated.
- Because the simulation run begins at time 0, the arrival time for customer 1 is $0 + 1.4 = 1.4$ minutes.
- Customer 1 may begin service immediately with a start time of 1.4 minutes.
- The waiting time for customer 1 is the start time minus the arrival time: $1.4 - 1.4 = 0$ minutes.
- A service time of $ST = 2.3$ minutes is generated for customer 1.
- The completion time for customer 1 is the start time plus the service time: $1.4 + 2.3 = 3.7$ minutes.
- The time in the system for customer 1 is the completion time minus the arrival time: $3.7 - 1.4 = 2.3$ minutes.

## Customer 2

- An interarrival time of $IAT = 1.3$ minutes is generated.
- Because the arrival time of customer 1 is 1.4, the arrival time for customer 2 is $1.4 + 1.3 = 2.7$ minutes.
- Because the completion time of customer 1 is 3.7 minutes, the arrival time of customer 2 is not greater than the completion time of customer 1; thus, the ATM is busy when customer 2 arrives.
- Customer 2 must wait for customer 1 to complete service before beginning service. Customer 1 completes service at 3.7 minutes, which becomes the start time for customer 2.
- The waiting time for customer 2 is the start time minus the arrival time: $3.7 - 2.7 = 1$ minute.
- A service time of $ST = 1.5$ minutes is generated for customer 2.
- The completion time for customer 2 is the start time plus the service time: $3.7 + 1.5 = 5.2$ minutes.
- The time in the system for customer 2 is the completion time minus the arrival time: $5.2 - 2.7 = 2.5$ minutes.

**Customer 3**

- An interarrival time of $IAT = 4.9$ minutes is generated.
- Because the arrival time of customer 2 was 2.7 minutes, the arrival time for customer 3 is $2.7 + 4.9 = 7.6$ minutes.
- The completion time of customer 2 is 5.2 minutes, so the arrival time for customer 3 is greater than the completion time of customer 2. Thus, the ATM is idle when customer 3 arrives.
- Customer 3 begins service immediately with a start time of 7.6 minutes.
- The waiting time for customer 3 is the start time minus the arrival time: $7.6 - 7.6 = 0$ minutes.
- A service time of $ST = 2.2$ minutes is generated for customer 3.
- The completion time for customer 3 is the start time plus the service time: $7.6 + 2.2 = 9.8$ minutes.
- The time in the system for customer 3 is the completion time minus the arrival time: $9.8 - 7.6 = 2.2$ minutes.

Using the totals in Table 13.10, we can compute an average waiting time for the 10 customers of $11.2/10 = 1.12$ minutes, and an average time in the system of $32.1/10 = 3.21$ minutes. Table 13.10 shows that seven of the ten customers had to wait. The total time for the ten-customer simulation is given by the completion time of the tenth customer: 26.0 minutes. However, at this point, we realize that a simulation for ten customers is much too short a period to draw any firm conclusions about the operation of the waiting line.

## Simulation of the Hammondsport Savings Bank ATM Problem

Using an Excel spreadsheet, we simulated the operation of the Hammondsport ATM waiting line system for 1000 customers. The spreadsheet used to carry out the simulation is shown in Figure 13.15. Note that the simulation results for customers 6 through 995 have been hidden so that the results can be shown in a reasonably sized figure. If desired, the rows for these customers can be shown and the simulation results displayed for all 1000 customers.

Ultimately, summary statistics will be collected in order to describe the results of 1000 customers. Before collecting the summary statistics, let us point out that most simulation studies of dynamic systems focus on the operation of the system during its long-run or steady-state operation. To ensure that the effect of start-up conditions are not included in the steady-state calculations, a dynamic simulation model is usually run for a specified period without collecting any data about the operation of the system. The length of the startup period can vary depending on the application. For the Hammondsport Savings Bank ATM simulation, we treated the results for the first 100 customers as the start-up period. Thus, the summary statistics shown in Figure 13.15 are for the 900 customers arriving during the steady-state period.

The summary statistics show that 549 of the 900 Hammondsport customers had to wait. This result provides a $549/900 = 0.61$ probability that a customer will have to wait for service. Or, in other words, approximately 61% of the customers will have to wait because the ATM is in use. The average waiting time is 1.59 minutes per customer with at least one customer waiting the maximum time of 13.5 minutes. The utilization rate of 0.7860 indicates that the ATM is in use 78.6% of the time. Finally, 393 of the 900 customers had to wait more than 1 minute (43.67% of all customers). A histogram of waiting times for the 900 customers is shown in Figure 13.16. This figure shows that 45 customers (5%) had a waiting time greater than six minutes.

**Figure 13.15**    SPREADSHEET SIMULATION OF THE HAMMONDSPORT SAVINGS BANK WITH ONE ATM

|  | A | B | C | D | E | F | G | H |
|---|---|---|---|---|---|---|---|---|
| 1 | **Hammondsport Savings Bank with One ATM** | | | | | | | |
| 2 | | | | | | | | |
| 3 | **Interarrival Times (Uniform Distribution)** | | | | | | | |
| 4 | Smallest Value | 0 | | | | | | |
| 5 | Largest Value | 5 | | | | | | |
| 6 | | | | | | | | |
| 7 | **Service Times (Normal Distribution)** | | | | | | | |
| 8 | Mean | 2 | | | | | | |
| 9 | Standard Dev | 0.5 | | | | | | |
| 10 | | | | | | | | |
| 11 | | | | | | | | |
| 12 | **Simulation** | | | | | | | |
| 13 | | | | | | | | |
| 14 | | Interarrival | Arrival | Service | Wait | Service | Completion | Time |
| 15 | Customer | Time | Time | Start Time | Time | Time | Time | in System |
| 16 | 1 | 1.4 | 1.4 | 1.4 | 0.0 | 2.3 | 3.7 | 2.3 |
| 17 | 2 | 1.3 | 2.7 | 3.7 | 1.0 | 1.5 | 5.2 | 2.5 |
| 18 | 3 | 4.9 | 7.6 | 7.6 | 0.0 | 2.2 | 9.8 | 2.2 |
| 19 | 4 | 3.5 | 11.1 | 11.1 | 0.0 | 2.5 | 13.6 | 2.5 |
| 20 | 5 | 0.7 | 11.8 | 13.6 | 1.8 | 1.8 | 15.4 | 3.6 |
| 1011 | 996 | 0.5 | 2496.8 | 2498.1 | 1.3 | 0.6 | 2498.7 | 1.9 |
| 1012 | 997 | 0.2 | 2497.0 | 2498.7 | 1.7 | 2.0 | 2500.7 | 3.7 |
| 1013 | 998 | 2.7 | 2499.7 | 2500.7 | 1.0 | 1.9 | 2502.5 | 2.8 |
| 1014 | 999 | 3.7 | 2503.4 | 2503.4 | 0.0 | 2.5 | 2505.8 | 2.5 |
| 1015 | 1000 | 4.1 | 2507.4 | 2507.4 | 0.0 | 1.9 | 2509.3 | 1.9 |
| 1016 | | | | | | | | |
| 1017 | | **Summary Statistics** | | | | | | |
| 1018 | | Number Waiting | | | 549 | | | |
| 1019 | | Probability of Waiting | | | 0.6100 | | | |
| 1020 | | Average Wait Time | | | 1.59 | | | |
| 1021 | | Maximum Wait Time | | | 13.5 | | | |
| 1022 | | Utilization of ATM | | | 0.7860 | | | |
| 1023 | | Number Waiting > 1 Min | | | 393 | | | |
| 1024 | | Probability of Waiting > 1 Min | | | 0.4367 | | | |

The simulation supports the conclusion that the branch will have a busy ATM system. With an average customer wait time of 1.59 minutes, the branch does not satisfy the bank's customer service guideline. This branch is a good candidate for installation of a second ATM.

### Simulation with Two ATMs

We extended the simulation model to the case of two ATMs. For the second ATM we also assume that the service time is normally distributed with a mean of 2 minutes and

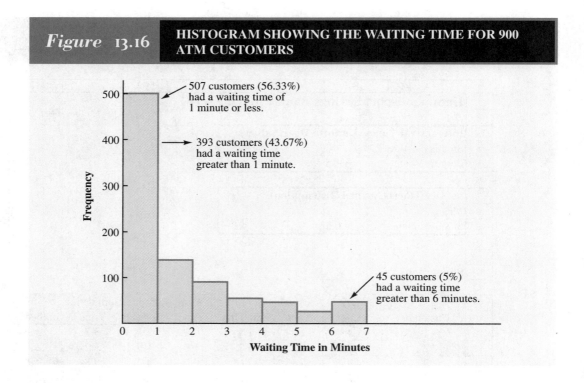

**Figure 13.16    HISTOGRAM SHOWING THE WAITING TIME FOR 900 ATM CUSTOMERS**

a standard deviation of 0.5 minutes. Table 13.11 shows the simulation results for the first ten customers. In comparing the 2-ATM system results in Table 13.11 with the single ATM simulation results shown in Table 13.10, we see that 2 additional columns are needed. These two columns show when each ATM becomes available for customer service. We assume that, when a new customer arrives, the customer will be served by the ATM that frees up first. When the simulation begins, the first customer is assigned to ATM 1.

**Table 13.11    SIMULATION RESULTS FOR TEN CUSTOMERS FOR A TWO-ATM SYSTEM**

| Customer | Interarrival Time | Arrival Time | Service Start Time | Wait Time | Service Time | Completion Time | Time in System | Time Available ATM 1 | Time Available ATM 2 |
|---|---|---|---|---|---|---|---|---|---|
| 1 | 1.7 | 1.7 | 1.7 | 0.0 | 2.1 | 3.8 | 2.1 | 3.8 | 0.0 |
| 2 | 0.7 | 2.4 | 2.4 | 0.0 | 2.0 | 4.4 | 2.0 | 3.8 | 4.4 |
| 3 | 2.0 | 4.4 | 4.4 | 0.0 | 1.4 | 5.8 | 1.4 | 5.8 | 4.4 |
| 4 | 0.1 | 4.5 | 4.5 | 0.0 | 0.9 | 5.4 | 0.9 | 5.8 | 5.4 |
| 5 | 4.6 | 9.1 | 9.1 | 0.0 | 2.2 | 11.3 | 2.2 | 5.8 | 11.3 |
| 6 | 1.3 | 10.4 | 10.4 | 0.0 | 1.6 | 12.0 | 1.6 | 12.0 | 11.3 |
| 7 | 0.6 | 11.0 | 11.3 | 0.3 | 1.7 | 13.0 | 2.0 | 12.0 | 13.0 |
| 8 | 0.3 | 11.3 | 12.0 | 0.7 | 2.2 | 14.2 | 2.9 | 14.2 | 13.0 |
| 9 | 3.4 | 14.7 | 14.7 | 0.0 | 2.9 | 17.6 | 2.9 | 14.2 | 17.6 |
| 10 | 0.1 | 14.8 | 14.8 | 0.0 | 2.8 | 17.6 | 2.8 | 17.6 | 17.6 |
| Totals | 14.8 | | | 1.0 | 19.8 | | 20.8 | | |
| Averages | 1.48 | | | 0.1 | 1.98 | | 2.08 | | |

Table 13.11 shows that customer 7 is the first customer that has to wait to use an ATM. We describe how customers 6, 7, 8 are processed to show how the logic of the simulation run for two ATMs differs from that with a single ATM.

### Customer 6

- An interarrival time of 1.3 minutes is generated, and customer 6 arrives $9.1 + 1.3 = 10.4$ minutes into the simulation.
- From the customer 5 row, we see that ATM 1 frees up at 5.8 minutes, and ATM 2 will free up at 11.3 minutes into the simulation. Because ATM 1 is free, customer 6 does not wait and begins service on ATM 1 at the arrival time of 10.4 minutes.
- A service time of 1.6 minutes is generated for customer 6. So customer 6 has a completion time of $10.4 + 1.6 = 12.0$ minutes.
- The time ATM 1 will next become available is set at 12.0 minutes; the time available for ATM 2 remains 11.3 minutes.

### Customer 7

- An interarrival time of 0.6 minutes is generated, and customer 7 arrives $10.4 + 0.6 = 11.0$ minutes into the simulation.
- From the previous row, we see that ATM 1 will not be available until 12.0 minutes, and ATM 2 will not be available until 11.3 minutes. So customer 7 must wait to use an ATM. Because ATM 2 will free up first, customer 7 begins service on that machine at a start time of 11.3 minutes. With an arrival time of 11.0 and a service start time of 11.3, customer 7 experiences a waiting time of $11.3 - 11.0 = 0.3$ minutes.
- A service time of 1.7 minutes is generated leading to a completion time of $11.3 + 1.7 = 13.0$ minutes.
- The time available for ATM 2 is updated to 13.0 minutes, and the time available for ATM 1 remains at 12.0 minutes.

### Customer 8

- An interarrival time of 0.3 minutes is generated, and customer 8 arrives $11.0 + 0.3 = 11.3$ minutes into the simulation.
- From the previous row, we see that ATM 1 will be the first available. Thus, customer 8 starts service on ATM 1 at 12.0 minutes resulting in a waiting time of $12.0 - 11.3 = 0.7$ minutes.
- A service time of 2.2 minutes is generated resulting in a completion time of $12.0 + 2.2 = 14.2$ minutes and a system time of $0.7 + 2.2 = 2.9$ minutes.
- The time available for ATM 1 is updated to 14.2 minutes, and the time available for ATM 2 remains at 13.0 minutes.

From the totals in Table 13.11, we see that the average waiting time for these ten customers is only $1.0/10 = 0.1$ minutes. Of course, a much longer simulation will be necessary before any conclusions can be drawn.

## Simulation Results with Two ATMs

The Excel spreadsheet that we used to conduct a simulation for 1000 customers is shown in Figure 13.17. Results for the first 100 customers were discarded to account for the start-up period. With 2 ATMs, the number of customers who had to wait was reduced from 549

**Figure 13.17**  SPREADSHEET SIMULATION OF THE HAMMONDSPORT SAVINGS BANK WITH 2 ATMs

| | A | B | C | D | E | F | G | H | I | J |
|---|---|---|---|---|---|---|---|---|---|---|
| 1 | **Hammondsport Savings Bank with Two ATMs** | | | | | | | | | |
| 2 | | | | | | | | | | |
| 3 | **Interarrival Times (Uniform Distribution)** | | | | | | | | | |
| 4 | Smallest Value | 0 | | | | | | | | |
| 5 | Largest Value | 5 | | | | | | | | |
| 6 | | | | | | | | | | |
| 7 | **Service Times (Normal Distribution)** | | | | | | | | | |
| 8 | Mean | 2 | | | | | | | | |
| 9 | Standard Dev | 0.5 | | | | | | | | |
| 10 | | | | | | | | | | |
| 11 | | | | | | | | | | |
| 12 | **Simulation** | | | | | | | | | |
| 13 | | | | | | | | | | |
| 14 | | Interarrival | Arrival | Service | Wait | Service | Completion | Time | Time Available | |
| 15 | Customer | Time | Time | Start Time | Time | Time | Time | in System | ATM 1 | ATM 2 |
| 16 | 1 | 1.7 | 1.7 | 1.7 | 0.0 | 2.1 | 3.8 | 2.1 | 3.8 | 0.0 |
| 17 | 2 | 0.7 | 2.4 | 2.4 | 0.0 | 2.0 | 4.4 | 2.0 | 3.8 | 4.4 |
| 18 | 3 | 2.0 | 4.4 | 4.4 | 0.0 | 1.4 | 5.8 | 1.4 | 5.8 | 4.4 |
| 19 | 4 | 0.1 | 4.5 | 4.5 | 0.0 | 0.9 | 5.4 | 0.9 | 5.8 | 5.4 |
| 20 | 5 | 4.6 | 9.1 | 9.1 | 0.0 | 2.2 | 11.3 | 2.2 | 5.8 | 11.3 |
| 1011 | 996 | 3.3 | 2483.2 | 2483.2 | 0.0 | 2.2 | 2485.4 | 2.2 | 2485.4 | 2482.1 |
| 1012 | 997 | 4.5 | 2487.7 | 2487.7 | 0.0 | 1.9 | 2489.6 | 1.9 | 2485.4 | 2489.6 |
| 1013 | 998 | 3.7 | 2491.5 | 2491.5 | 0.0 | 3.2 | 2494.7 | 3.2 | 2494.7 | 2489.6 |
| 1014 | 999 | 0.0 | 2491.5 | 2491.5 | 0.0 | 2.4 | 2493.9 | 2.4 | 2494.7 | 2493.9 |
| 1015 | 1000 | 2.6 | 2494.1 | 2494.1 | 0.0 | 2.8 | 2496.9 | 2.8 | 2494.7 | 2496.9 |
| 1016 | | | | | | | | | | |
| 1017 | | **Summary Statistics** | | | | | | | | |
| 1018 | | Number Waiting | | | 78 | | | | | |
| 1019 | | Probability of Waiting | | | 0.0867 | | | | | |
| 1020 | | Average Wait Time | | | 0.07 | | | | | |
| 1021 | | Maximum Wait Time | | | 2.9 | | | | | |
| 1022 | | Utilization of ATMs | | | 0.4084 | | | | | |
| 1023 | | Number Waiting > 1 Min | | | 23 | | | | | |
| 1024 | | Probability of Waiting > 1 Min | | | 0.0256 | | | | | |

to 78. This reduction provides a 78/900 = 0.0867 probability that a customer will have to wait for service when 2 ATMs are used. The 2-ATM system also reduced the average wait time to 0.07 minutes (4.2 seconds) per customer. The maximum wait time was reduced from 13.5 to 2.9 minutes, and each ATM was in use 40.84% of the time. Finally, only 23 of the 900 customers had to wait more than 1 minute for an ATM to become available. Thus, only 2.56% of customers had to wait more than one minute. The simulation results provide evidence that Hammondsport Savings Bank needs to expand to the 2-ATM system.

The simulation models that we have developed can now be used to study the ATM operation at other branch banks. In each case, assumptions must be made about the appropriate interarrival time and service time probability distributions. However, once appropriate assumptions have been made, the same simulation models can be used to determine the operating characteristics of the ATM waiting line system. The IBM and Air Canada simulation model described in the Management Science in Action possesses many of the same characteristics associated with the ATM simulation models that we developed in this section.

## N O T E S  and Comments

1. The ATM waiting line model was based on uniformly distributed interarrival times and normally distributed service times. One advantage of simulation is its flexibility in accommodating a variety of different probability distributions. For instance, if we believe an exponential distribution is more appropriate for interarrival times, the ATM simulation could be repeated by simply changing the way the interarrival times are generated.

2. At the beginning of this section, we defined *discrete-event simulation* as involving a dynamic system that evolves over time. The simulation computations focus on the sequence of events as they occur at discrete points in time. In the ATM waiting line example, customer arrivals and the customer service completions were the discrete events. Referring to the arrival times and completion times in Table 13.10, we see that the first 5 discrete events for the ATM waiting line simulation were as follows:

| Event | Description | Time Event Occurred |
|---|---|---|
| 1 | Customer 1 arrives | 1.4 |
| 2 | Customer 2 arrives | 2.7 |
| 3 | Customer 1 completes service | 3.7 |
| 4 | Customer 2 completes service | 5.2 |
| 5 | Customer 3 arrives | 7.6 |

3. We did not keep track of the number of customers in the ATM waiting line as we carried out the ATM simulation computations on a customer-by-customer basis. However, we can determine the average number of customers in the waiting line from other information in the simulation output. The following relationship is valid for any waiting line system:

$$\frac{\text{Average Number}}{\text{in Waiting Line}} = \frac{\text{Total Waiting Time}}{\text{Total Time of Simulation}}$$

For the system with 1 ATM, the 100th customer completed service at 247.8 minutes into the simulation. Thus, the total time of the simulation for the next 900 customers was $2509.3 - 247.8 = 2261.5$ minutes. The average wait time was 1.59 minutes. During the simulation, the 900 customers had a total wait time of $900(1.59) = 1431$ minutes. Therefore, the average number of customers in the waiting line is

Average Number in Waiting Line $= 1431/2261.5 = 0.63$ customers

# MANAGEMENT SCIENCE IN ACTION

## IBM SIMULATION MODEL HELPS IMPROVE CUSTOMER SERVICE FOR AIR CANADA*

IBM and Air Canada formed a partnership to develop a simulation model of Air Canada's domestic passenger process at the Toronto airport. Specifically, the simulation model is being used to track the flow of passengers from arrival at the airport terminal to final boarding. Simulated passengers move through activities including ticketing, coach passenger check-in, first-class passenger check-in, special assistance services (e.g., wheelchairs, unaccompanied minors, oversized baggage, pets), and the final boarding process at the gate.

The airline flight schedule is used to determine passenger arrivals at the airport. Each passenger entity is assigned an airport terminal appearance time based on the distribution of arrival times prior to the flight's scheduled departure. Based on appropriate statistical information about the percentage of passengers in each category, a passenger is identified as being business or leisure, domestic or regional, and originating or connecting. These passenger attributes vary with the time of day. Given the set of arriving passengers, the logic of the simulation model tracks flow of the passengers through the Air Canada system.

Multiple simulation runs have been used to forecast passenger service performance measures including peak and average wait times, peak

and average number of passengers waiting in line, and Air Canada's resource utilization. Simulation results have identified passenger flow bottlenecks during the ticketing process and during the coach check-in process. A detailed analysis showed that excessive wait times were occurring during a one-hour period in the morning. This information gave Air Canada a better understanding of its passenger flow process and identified areas where new technology and/or additional agents could be employed to improve the efficiency of the operation.

The simulation model is flexible in that it can be used to support what-if analysis. For example, what if a passenger self-ticketing booth were added, what if a passenger seat selection booth were added, what if advanced electronic ticketing were increased, and/or what if Air Canada agent schedules were modified? These what-if simulation runs help identify the best strategies for improving the passenger flow performance measures. In addition, the simulation model can be easily modified to simulate the passenger process at other airports.

*Based on P. Bitauld, K. Burch, S. El-Taji, E. Fanucchi, M. Montevecchi, J. Ohlsson, A. Palella, R. Rushmeier, and J. Snowdon, "Journey Management," OR/MS Today (October 1997): 30—33.

## 13.4 OTHER SIMULATION ISSUES

Because simulation is one of the most widely used management science techniques, a variety of software tools have been developed to help analysts implement a simulation model on a computer. In this section we comment on the software available and discuss some issues involved in verifying and validating a simulation model. We close the section with a discussion of some of the advantages and disadvantages of using simulation to study a real system.

### Computer Implementation

The use of spreadsheets for simulation has grown rapidly in recent years, and third-party software vendors have developed spreadsheet add-ins that make building simulation models on a spreadsheet much easier. These add-in packages provide an easy facility for generating random values from a variety of probability distributions and provide a rich array of statistics describing the simulation output. Two popular spreadsheet add-ins are Crystal Ball from Decisioneering and @RISK from Palisade Corporation. Although spreadsheets can be a valuable tool for some simulation studies, they are generally limited to smaller, less complex systems.

With the growth of simulation applications, both users of simulation and software developers began to realize that computer simulations have many common features: model development, generating values from probability distributions, maintaining a record of what happens during the simulation, and recording and summarizing the simulation output. A variety of special-purpose simulation packages are available, including GPSS®,

SIMSCRIPT®, SLAM®, and Arena®. These packages have built-in simulation clocks, simplified methods for generating probabilistic inputs, and procedures for collecting and summarizing the simulation output. Special-purpose simulation packages enable management scientists to simplify the process of developing and implementing the simulation model.

Simulation models can also be developed using general-purpose computer programming languages such as BASIC, FORTRAN, PASCAL, C, and C++. The disadvantage of using these languages is that special simulation procedures are not built in. One command in a special-purpose simulation package often performs the computations and record-keeping tasks that would require several BASIC, FORTRAN, PASCAL, C, or C++ statements to duplicate. The advantage of using a general-purpose programming language is that they offer greater flexibility in terms of being able to model more complex systems.

To decide which software to use, an analyst will have to consider the relative merits of a spreadsheet, a special-purpose simulation package, and a general-purpose computer programming language. The goal is to select the method that is easy to use while still providing an adequate representation of the system being studied.

## Verification and Validation

An important aspect of any simulation study involves confirming that the simulation model accurately describes the real system. Inaccurate simulation models cannot be expected to provide worthwhile information. Thus, before using simulation results to draw conclusions about a real system, one must take steps to verify and validate the simulation model.

**Verification** is the process of determining that the computer procedure that performs the simulation calculations is logically correct. Verification is largely a debugging task to make sure that no errors are in the computer procedure that implements the simulation. In some cases, an analyst may compare computer results for a limited number of events with independent hand calculations. In other cases, tests may be performed to verify that the probabilistic inputs are being generated correctly and that the output from the simulation model seems reasonable. The verification step is not complete until the user has developed a high degree of confidence that the computer procedure is error free.

**Validation** is the process of ensuring that the simulation model provides an accurate representation of a real system. Validation requires an agreement among analysts and managers that the logic and the assumptions used in the design of the simulation model accurately reflect how the real system operates. The first phase of the validation process is done prior to, or in conjunction with, the development of the computer procedure for the simulation process. Validation continues after the computer program has been developed with the analyst reviewing the simulation output to see whether the simulation results closely approximate the performance of the real system. If possible, the output of the simulation model is compared to the output of an existing real system to make sure that the simulation output closely approximates the performance of the real system. If this form of validation is not possible, an analyst can experiment with the simulation model and have one or more individuals experienced with the operation of the real system review the simulation output to determine whether it is a reasonable approximation to what would be obtained with the real system under similar conditions.

Verification and validation are not tasks to be taken lightly. They are key steps in any simulation study and are necessary to ensure that decisions and conclusions based on the simulation results are appropriate for the real system.

## Advantages and Disadvantages of Using Simulation

The primary advantages of simulation are that it is easy to understand and that the methodology can be used to model and learn about the behavior of complex systems that would be difficult, if not impossible, to deal with analytically. Simulation models are flexible; they can be used to describe systems without requiring the assumptions that are often required by mathematical models. In general, the larger the number of probabilistic inputs a system has, the more likely that a simulation model will provide the best approach for studying the system. Another advantage of simulation is that a simulation model provides a convenient experimental laboratory for the real system. Changing assumptions or operating policies in the simulation model and rerunning it can provide results that help predict how such changes will affect the operation of the real system. Experimenting directly with a real system is often not feasible.

Using simulation, we can ask what-if questions and project how the real system will behave. Although simulation does not guarantee optimality, it will usually provide near-optimal solutions. In addition, simulation models often warn against poor decision strategies by projecting disastrous outcomes such as system failures, large financial losses, and so on.

Simulation is not without some disadvantages. For complex systems, the process of developing, verifying, and validating a simulation model can be time-consuming and expensive. In addition, each simulation run only provides a sample of how the real system will operate. As such, the summary of the simulation data only provides estimates or approximations about the real system. Consequently, simulation does not guarantee an optimal solution. Nonetheless, the danger of obtaining poor solutions is slight if the analyst exercises good judgment in developing the simulation model and if the simulation process is run long enough under a wide variety of conditions so that the analyst has sufficient data to predict how the real system will operate.

# MANAGEMENT SCIENCE IN ACTION

## SIMULATION AT MEXICO'S VILPAC TRUCK COMPANY*

In increasing numbers, U.S. firms are joining diverse geographical and cultural partners in Western Europe, Asia, and Mexico to capitalize on each other's advantages and remain competitive in world markets. Mexico, the United States' third largest trading partner, offers a unique opportunity for integrating manufacturing operations. For example, Mexican and U.S. firms have been working together to turn the Mexican truck company, Vilpac, into a world-class manufacturing firm.

The selection of manufacturing configurations and the design of new plants at Vilpac is being guided by a simulation model of the firm's manufacturing operations. A network simulation language, SIMNET II®, has been used to model the manufacturing system that comprises some 95 machines and 1900 parts. Various simulation runs were used to validate the model. When applied to a plant that was producing 20 trucks per day, the simulation model accurately predicted production at 19.8 trucks per day.

The three interrelated modules of the simulation model include operations, corrective maintenance, and preventive maintenance. Various components of the model include capabilities for handling changes in customer demand, manufacturing cost, capacity, and work-in-process and inventory levels. Experimentation with the model investigated capacity requirements, product-mix effects, new products, inventory policies, product flow, setup times, production planning and control strategies, plant expansion, and new plant design. Tangible benefits include an increase in production of 260%, a reduction in work-in-process of 70%, and an increase in market share.

*Based on J. P. Nuno, D. L. Shunk, J. M. Padillo, and B. Beltran, "Mexico's Vilpac Truck Company Uses a CIM Implementation to Become a World Class Manufacturer," *Interfaces* no. 1 (January–February 1993): 59–75.

# SUMMARY

Simulation is a method for learning about a real system by experimenting with a model that represents the system. Some of the reasons simulation is frequently used are:

1. It can be used for a wide variety of practical problems.
2. The simulation approach is relatively easy to explain and understand. As a result, management confidence is increased, and acceptance of the results is more easily obtained.

3. Spreadsheet packages now provide another alternative for model implementation, and third-party vendors have developed add-ins that expand the capabilities of the spreadsheet packages.
4. Computer software developers have produced simulation packages that make it easier to develop and implement simulation models for more complex problems.

We first showed how simulation can be used for risk analysis by analyzing a situation involving the development of a new product: the PortaCom printer. We then showed how simulation can be used to select an inventory replenishment level that would provide both a good profit and a good customer service level. Finally, we developed a simulation model for the Hammondsport Savings Bank ATM waiting line system. This model is an example of a dynamic simulation model in which the state of the system changes or evolves over time.

Our approach was to develop a simulation model that contained both controllable inputs and probabilistic inputs. Procedures were developed for randomly generating values for the probabilistic inputs, and a flowchart was developed to show the sequence of logical and mathematical operations that describe the steps of the simulation process. Simulation results were obtained by running the simulation for a suitable number of trials or length of time. Simulation results were obtained and conclusions were drawn about the operation of the real system.

## GLOSSARY

**Simulation**  A method for learning about a real system by experimenting with a model that represents the system.

**Simulation experiment**  The generation of a sample of values for the probabilistic inputs of a simulation model and computing the resulting values of the model outputs.

**Controllable input**  Input to a simulation model that is selected by the decision maker.

**Probabilistic input**  Input to a simulation model that is subject to uncertainty. A probabilistic input is described by a probability distribution.

**Risk analysis**  The process of predicting the outcome of a decision in the face of uncertainty.

**Parameters**  Numerical values that appear in the mathematical relationships of a model. Parameters are considered known and remain constant over all trials of a simulation.

**What-if analysis**  A trial-and-error approach to learning about the range of possible outputs for a model. Trial values are chosen for the model inputs (these are the what-ifs) and the value of the output(s) is computed.

**Base-case scenario**  Determining the output given the most likely values for the probabilistic inputs of a model.

**Best-case scenario**  Determining the output given the best values that can be expected for the probabilistic inputs of a model.

**Worst-case scenario**  Determining the output given the worst values that can be expected for the probabilistic inputs of a model.

**Static simulation model**  A simulation model used in situations where the state of the system at one point in time does not affect the state of the system at future points in time. Each trial of the simulation is independent.

**Dynamic simulation model**  A simulation model used in situations where the state of the system affects how the system changes or evolves over time.

**Event**  An instantaneous occurrence that changes the state of the system in a simulation model.

**Discrete-event simulation model** A simulation model that describes how a system evolves over time by using events that occur at discrete points in time.

**Verification** The process of determining that a computer program implements a simulation model as it is intended.

**Validation** The process of determining that a simulation model provides an accurate representation of a real system.

......................................................................................../ /...........

## PROBLEMS

Note: Problems 1–12 are designed to give you practice in setting up a simulation model and demonstrating how random numbers can be used to generate values for the probabilistic inputs. These problems, which ask you to provide a small number of simulation trials, can be done with hand calculations. This approach should give you a good understanding of the simulation process, but the simulation results will not be sufficient for you to draw final conclusions or make decisions about the situation. Problems 13–24 are more realistic in that they ask you to generate simulation output(s) for a large number of trials and use the results to draw conclusions about the behavior of the system being studied. These problems require the use of a computer to carry out the simulation computations. The ability to use Excel or some other spreadsheet package will be necessary when you attempt Problems 13–24.

1. Consider the PortaCom project discussed in Section 13.1
    a. An engineer on the product development team believes that first-year sales for the new printer will be 20,000 units. Using estimates of $45 per unit for the direct labor cost and $90 per unit for the parts cost, what is the first-year profit using the engineer's sales estimate?
    b. The financial analyst on the product development team is more conservative, indicating that parts cost may well be $100 per unit. In addition, the analyst suggests that a sales volume of 10,000 units is more realistic. Using the most likely value of $45 per unit for the direct labor cost, what is the first-year profit using the financial analyst's estimates?
    c. Why is the simulation approach to risk analysis preferable to generating a variety of what-if scenarios such as those suggested by the engineer and the financial analyst?

SELF TEST

2. The management of Madeira Manufacturing Company is considering the introduction of a new product. The fixed cost to begin the production of the product is $30,000. The variable cost for the product is expected to be between $16 and $24 with a most likely value of $20 per unit. The product will sell for $50 per unit. Demand for the product is expected to range from 300 to 2100 units, with 1200 units the most likely demand.
    a. Develop the profit model for this product.
    b. Provide the base-case, worst-case, and best-case analyses.
    c. Discuss why simulation would be desirable.

3. Use the random numbers 0.3753, 0.9218, 0.0336, 0.5145, 0.7000 to generate 5 simulated values for the PortaCom direct labor cost per unit.

4. A retail store experiences the following probability distribution for sales of a product.

| Sales (units) | 0 | 1 | 2 | 3 | 4 | 5 | 6 |
|---|---|---|---|---|---|---|---|
| Probability | 0.08 | 0.12 | 0.28 | 0.24 | 0.14 | 0.10 | 0.04 |

    a. Set up intervals of random numbers that can be used to simulate sales.
    b. Random numbers generated for the first 10 days of a simulation are as follows: 0.4627, 0.8745, 0.4479, 0.6712, 0.4557, 0.8435, 0.2162, 0.1699, 0.1338, 0.2278. What is the sales value generated for each day?
    c. What are the total sales over the 10-day period?

**SELF TEST**

5.  The price of a share of a particular stock listed on the New York Stock Exchange is currently $39. The following probability distribution shows how the price per share is expected to change over a three-month period.

| Stock Price Change ($) | Probability |
|:---:|:---:|
| −2 | 0.05 |
| −1 | 0.10 |
| 0 | 0.25 |
| +1 | 0.20 |
| +2 | 0.20 |
| +3 | 0.10 |
| +4 | 0.10 |

a.  Set up intervals of random numbers that can be used to generate the change in stock price over a three-month period.
b.  With the current price of $39 per share and the random numbers 0.1091, 0.9407, 0.1941, and 0.8083, simulate the price per share for the next four 3-month periods. What is the ending simulated price per share?

6.  The Statewide Auto Insurance Company has developed the following probability distribution for automobile collision claims paid during the past year.

| Payment($) | Probability |
|:---:|:---:|
| 0 | 0.83 |
| 500 | 0.06 |
| 1,000 | 0.05 |
| 2,000 | 0.02 |
| 5,000 | 0.02 |
| 8,000 | 0.01 |
| 10,000 | 0.01 |

a.  Set up intervals of random numbers that can be used to generate automobile collision claim payments.
b.  Using the first 20 random numbers in column 4 of Table 13.2, simulate the payments for 20 policyholders. How many claims are paid and what is the total amount paid to the policyholders?

7.  A variety of routine maintenance checks are made on commercial airplanes prior to each take-off. A particular maintenance check of an airplane's landing gear requires between 10 and 18 minutes of a maintenance engineer's time. In fact, the exact time required is uniformly distributed over this interval. As part of a larger simulation model designed to determine total on-ground maintenance time for an airplane, we will need to simulate the actual time required to perform this maintenance check on the airplane's landing gear. Using random numbers of 0.1567, 0.9823, 0.3419, 0.5572, and 0.7758, compute the time required for each of five simulated maintenance checks of the airplane's landing gear.

8.  Baseball's World Series is a maximum of 7 games, with the winner being the first team to win 4 games. Assume that the Atlanta Braves are in the World Series and that the first 2 games are to be played in Atlanta; the next 3 games at the opponent's ball park; and the last 2 games, if

necessary, back in Atlanta. Taking into account the projected starting pitchers for each game and the homefield advantage, the probabilities of Atlanta winning each game are as follows:

| Game | 1 | 2 | 3 | 4 | 5 | 6 | 7 |
|---|---|---|---|---|---|---|---|
| **Probability of Win** | 0.60 | 0.55 | 0.48 | 0.45 | 0.48 | 0.55 | 0.50 |

a.   Set up random number intervals that can be used to determine the winner of each game. Let the smaller random numbers indicate that Atlanta wins the game. For example, the random number interval "0.00 but less than 0.60" corresponds to Atlanta winning game 1.

b.   Use the random numbers in column 6 of Table 13.2 beginning with 0.3813 to simulate the playing of the World Series. Do the Atlanta Braves win the series? How many games are played?

c.   Discuss how repeated simulation trials could be used to estimate the overall probability of Atlanta winning the series as well as the most likely number of games in the series.

9.   A project has four activities (A, B, C, and D) that must be performed sequentially. The probability distributions for the time required to complete each of the activities are as follows:

SELF TEST

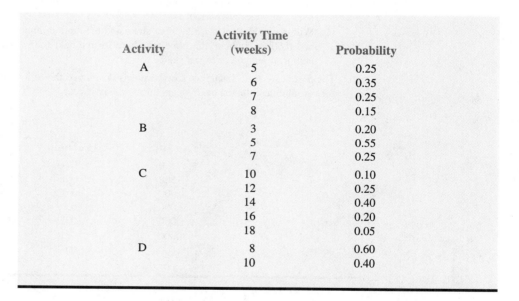

| Activity | Activity Time (weeks) | Probability |
|---|---|---|
| A | 5 | 0.25 |
|   | 6 | 0.35 |
|   | 7 | 0.25 |
|   | 8 | 0.15 |
| B | 3 | 0.20 |
|   | 5 | 0.55 |
|   | 7 | 0.25 |
| C | 10 | 0.10 |
|   | 12 | 0.25 |
|   | 14 | 0.40 |
|   | 16 | 0.20 |
|   | 18 | 0.05 |
| D | 8 | 0.60 |
|   | 10 | 0.40 |

a.   Provide the base-case, the worst-case, and best-case calculations for the time to complete the project.

b.   Use the random numbers 0.1778, 0.9617, 0.6849, and 0.4503 to simulate the completion time of the project in weeks.

c.   Discuss how simulation could be used to estimate the probability the project can be completed in 35 weeks or less.

10.   Larkin Corporation conducted a test designed to evaluate the effectiveness of a new television advertisement for one of its household products. The particular television advertisement was shown in a test market for a two-week period. In a follow-up study, randomly selected individuals were contacted by telephone and asked a series of questions to determine whether they could recall the message in the television advertisement and how likely they were to purchase the product. The test market study provided the following probabilities.

Individual could recall the message          0.40

Individual could not recall the message    0.60

Response to the question of how likely they were to purchase the product provided the following probabilities.

| Recall Response | Purchase Response | | |
|---|---|---|---|
| | Definitely No | Uncertain | Definitely Yes |
| Could recall message | 0.30 | 0.30 | 0.40 |
| Could not recall message | 0.50 | 0.40 | 0.10 |

a.  Set up intervals of random numbers that can be used to determine whether a sampled individual could recall the message and then how the individual responded to the purchase question.
b.  Use the following pairs of random numbers to simulate the results for three sampled individuals: individual 1 (0.5521, 0.6318), individual 2 (0.2189, 0.8432), individual 3 (0.3812, 0.1831). Which individual, if any, answered "definitely yes" to the purchase question?
c.  Discuss how a large number of simulation trials could be used to estimate the overall probability of an individual answering "definitely yes" to the likelihood of purchase question.

11.  A bowler has the following probability distribution for the number of pins knocked over on the first ball thrown.

| Number of Pins | Probability |
|---|---|
| 7 | 0.12 |
| 8 | 0.15 |
| 9 | 0.18 |
| 10 | 0.55 |

The probability distributions for the number of pins on the second ball are as follows:

| First-Ball Pins | Second-Ball Pins | | | |
|---|---|---|---|---|
| | 0 | 1 | 2 | 3 |
| 7 | 0.02 | 0.10 | 0.45 | 0.43 |
| 8 | 0.04 | 0.20 | 0.76 | |
| 9 | 0.06 | 0.94 | | |

a.  Set up intervals of random numbers that can be used to generate the number of pins knocked over on each ball.
b.  The first two random numbers in column 6 of Table 13.2 are 0.3813 and 0.2159. Use these to simulate what the bowler did on the first two balls rolled.
c.  Assume that the results in part (b) are for the first bowling frame. If you know how bowling scores are computed, continue to use the random numbers in Table 13.2 to compute the bowler's score for a full 10-frame game. The bowler's opponent rolled a 206 game. Did the simulated bowler beat the opponent?

12. The management of Brinkley Corporation is interested in using simulation to estimate the profit per unit for a new product. Probability distributions for the purchase cost, the labor cost, and the transportation cost are as follows:

| Purchase Cost ($) | Probability | Labor Cost ($) | Probability | Transportation Cost ($) | Probability |
|---|---|---|---|---|---|
| 10 | 0.25 | 20 | 0.10 | 3 | 0.75 |
| 11 | 0.45 | 22 | 0.25 | 5 | 0.25 |
| 12 | 0.30 | 24 | 0.35 | | |
| | | 25 | 0.30 | | |

Assume that these are the only costs and that the selling price for the product will be $45 per unit.
a. Provide the base-case, worst-case, and best-case calculations for the profit per unit.
b. Set up intervals of random numbers that can be used to randomly generate the three cost components.
c. Using the random numbers 0.3726, 0.5839 and 0.8275, calculate the profit per unit.
d. Using the random numbers 0.1862, 0.7466, and 0.6171, calculate the profit per unit.
e. Management believes the project may not be profitable if the profit per unit is less than $5. Explain how simulation can be used to estimate the probability the profit per unit will be less than $5.

13. Using the PortaCom Risk Analysis spreadsheet in Figure 13.6, develop your own spreadsheet for the PortaCom simulation model.
a. Compute the mean profit, the minimum profit, and the maximum profit.
b. What is your estimate of the probability of a loss?

**SELF TEST**

14. Develop a spreadsheet simulation for the following problem. The management of Madeira Manufacturing Company is considering the introduction of a new product. The fixed cost to begin the production of the product is $30,000. The variable cost for the product is uniformly distributed between $16 and $24 per unit. The product will sell for $50 per unit. Demand for the product is best described by a normal probability distribution with a mean of 1200 units and a standard deviation of 300 units. Use a spreadsheet simulation similar to Figure 13.6. Use 500 simulation trials to answer the following questions.
a. What is the mean profit for the simulation?
b. What is the probability the project will result in a loss?
c. What is your recommendation concerning the introduction of the product?

15. Use a spreadsheet to simulate the rolling of dice. Use the VLOOKUP function as described in Appendix 13.1 to select the outcome for each die. Place the number for the first die in column B and the number for the second die in column C. Show the sum in column D. Repeat the simulation for 1000 rolls of the dice. What is your simulation estimate of the probability of rolling a 7?

16. Based on experience, the time required to complete a college statistics exam is normally distributed with a mean of 42 minutes and a standard deviation of 8 minutes. A class has 70 students. Use a spreadsheet to simulate the exam completion times for 70 students. How many students are still working when the professor stops the exam at 50 minutes?

17. Grear Tire Company has produced a new tire with an estimated mean lifetime mileage of 36,500 miles. Management also believes that the standard deviation is 5000 miles and that tire mileage is normally distributed. Use a spreadsheet to simulate the miles obtained for a sample of 500 tires.
a. Use the Excel COUNTIF function to determine the number of tires that last longer than 40,000 miles. What is your estimate of the percentage of tires that will exceed 40,000 miles?

b.  Use COUNTIF to find the number of tires that obtain mileage less than 32,000 miles. Then, find the number with less than 30,000 miles and the number with less than 28,000 miles.

c.  If management would like to advertise a tire mileage guarantee such that approximately no more than 10% of the tires would obtain mileage low enough to qualify for the guarantee, what tire mileage considered in part (b) would you recommend for the guarantee?

**SELF TEST**

18. A building contractor is preparing a bid on a new construction project. Two other contractors will be submitting bids for the same project. Based on past bidding practices, bids from the other contractors can be described by the following probability distributions:

| Contractor | Probability Distribution of Bid |
|---|---|
| A | Uniform probability distribution between $600,000 and $800,000 |
| B | Normal probability distribution with a mean bid of $700,000 and a standard deviation of $50,000 |

a.  If the building contractor submits a bid of $750,000, what is the probability the building contractor will obtain the bid? Use a spreadsheet to simulate 1000 trials of the contract bidding process.

b.  The building contractor is also considering bids of $775,000 and $785,000. If the building contractor would like to bid such that the probability of winning the bid is about 0.80, what bid would you recommend? Repeat the simulation process with bids of $775,000 and $785,000 to justify your recommendation.

19. Develop your own spreadsheet for the Butler inventory simulation model shown in Figure 13.10. Suppose that management prefers not to charge for loss of goodwill. Run the Butler inventory simulation model with replenishment levels of 110, 115, 120, and 125. What is your recommendation?

20. In preparing for the upcoming holiday season, Mandrell Toy Company has designated a new doll called Freddy. The fixed cost to produce the doll is $100,000. The variable cost, which includes material, labor, and shipping costs, is $34 per doll. During the holiday selling season, Mandrell will sell the dolls for $42 each. If Mandrell overproduces the dolls, the excess dolls will be sold in January through a distributor who has agreed to pay Mandrell $10 per doll. Demand for new toys during the holiday selling season is extremely uncertain. Forecasts are for expected sales of 60,000 dolls with a standard deviation of 15,000. The normal probability distribution is assumed to be a good description of the demand.

a.  Create a spreadsheet similar to the inventory spreadsheet in Figure 13.10. Include columns showing demand, sales, revenue from sales, amount of surplus, revenue from sales of surplus, total cost, and net profit. Use your spreadsheet to simulate the sales of the Freddy doll using a production quantity of 60,000 units. Using 500 simulation trials, what is the estimate of the mean profit associated with the production quantity of 60,000 dolls?

b.  Before making a final decision on the production quantity, management has requested an analysis of a more aggressive 70,000 unit production quantity and a more conservative 50,000 unit production quantity. Run your simulation with these two production quantities. What is the mean profit associated with each? What is your recommendation on the production of the Freddy doll?

c.  Assuming that Mandrell's management adopts your recommendation, what is the probability of a stockout and a shortage of the Freddy dolls during the holiday season?

21. South Central Airlines operates a commuter flight between Atlanta and Charlotte. The plane holds 30 passengers, and the airline makes a $100 profit on each passenger on the flight. When South Central takes 30 reservations for the flight, experience has shown an average of 2 passengers do not show up. As a result, with 30 reservations, South Central is averaging 28 passengers with a profit of 28(100) = $2800 per flight. The airline operations office has asked for

an evaluation of an overbooking strategy where they would accept 32 reservations even though the airplane holds only 30 passengers. The probability distribution for the number of passengers showing up when 32 reservations are accepted is shown below.

| Passengers Showing Up | Probability |
| --- | --- |
| 28 | 0.05 |
| 29 | 0.25 |
| 30 | 0.50 |
| 31 | 0.15 |
| 32 | 0.05 |

The airline will receive a profit of $100 for each passenger on the flight up to the capacity of 30 passengers. The airline will incur a cost for any passenger denied seating on the flight. This cost covers added expenses of rescheduling the passenger as well as loss of goodwill, estimated to be $150 per passenger. Develop a spreadsheet model that will simulate the performance of the overbooking system. Simulate the number of passengers showing up for each of 500 flights by using the VLOOKUP function. Use the results to compute the profit for each flight.

a. Does your simulation recommend the overbooking strategy? What is the mean profit per flight if overbooking is implemented?

b. Explain how your simulation model can be used to evaluate other overbooking levels such as 31, 33, 34 and ultimately recommending a best overbooking strategy.

22. Develop your own waiting line simulation model for the Hammondsport Savings Bank problem (See Figure 13.15). Assume that a new branch is expected to open with interarrival times uniformly distributed between 0 and 4 minutes. The service times at this branch are anticipated to be normal with a mean of 2 minutes and a standard deviation of 0.5 minutes. Simulate the operation of this system for 600 customers using one ATM. What is your assessment of the ability to operate this branch with one ATM? What happens to the average wait time for customers near the end of the simulation period?

23. The Burger Dome waiting line model in Section 12.1 studies the wait time of customers at its fast-food restaurant. Burger Dome's single-channel waiting line system has a mean of 0.75 arrivals per minute and a service rate of 1 customer per minute.

a. Use a spreadsheet based on Figure 13.15 to simulate the operation of this waiting line. Assuming that customer arrivals follow a Poisson probability distribution, the interarrival times can be simulated with the cell formula $-(1/\lambda)*LN(RAND())$, where $\lambda = 0.75$. Assuming that the service time follows an exponential probability distribution, the service times can be simulated with the cell formula $-\mu*LN(RAND())$, where $\mu = 1$. Run the Burger Dome simulation for 500 customers. The analytical model in Chapter 12 indicates an average waiting time of 3 minutes per customer. What average waiting time does your simulation model show?

b. One advantage of using simulation is that a simulation model can be altered easily to reflect other assumptions about the probabilistic inputs. Assume that the service time is more accurately described by a normal probability distribution with a mean of 1 minute and a standard deviation of 0.2 minutes. This distribution has less service time variability than the exponential probability distribution used in part (a). What is the impact of this change on the average wait time?

24. Telephone calls come into an airline reservations office randomly at the mean rate of 15 calls per hour. The time between calls follows an exponential distribution with a mean of 4 minutes. When the two reservations agents are busy, a telephone message tells the caller that the call is important and to please wait on the line until the next reservation agent becomes available. The service time for each reservation agent is normally distributed with a mean of 4 minutes and a

standard deviation of 1 minute. Use a two-channel waiting line simulation model to evaluate this waiting line system. Use the spreadsheet design shown in Figure 13.17. The cell formula $=-4*LN(RAND())$ can be used to generate the interarrival times. Simulate the operation of the telephone reservation system for 600 customers. Discard the first 100 customers and collect data over the next 500 customers.

a.  Compute the mean interval arrival time and the mean service time. If your simulation model is operating correctly, both of these should have means of approximately 4 minutes.
b.  What is the mean customer wait time for this system?
c.  Use the =COUNTIF function to determine the number of customers who have to wait for a reservation agent. What percentage of the customers have to wait?

## Case Problem    COUNTY BEVERAGE DRIVE-THRU

County Beverage Drive-Thru, Inc., operates a chain of beverage supply stores in Northern Illinois. Each store has a single service lane; cars enter at one end of the store and exit at the other end. Customers pick up soft drinks, beer snacks, and party supplies without getting out of their cars. When a new customer arrives at the store, the customer waits until the preceding customer's order is complete and then drives into the store for service.

Typically, three employees operate each store during peak periods; two clerks take and fill orders; and a third clerk serves as cashier and store supervisor. County Beverage is considering a revised store design in which computerized order-taking and payment are integrated with specialized warehousing equipment. Management hopes that the new design will permit operating each store with one clerk. To determine whether the new design is beneficial, management has decided to build a new store using the revised design.

County Beverage's new store will be located near a major shopping center. Based on experience at other locations, management believes that during the peak late afternoon and evening hours, the time between arrivals follows an exponential probability distribution with a mean of 6 minutes. These peak hours are the most critical time period for the company; most of their profit is generated during these peak hours.

An extensive study of times required to fill orders with a single clerk has led to the following probability distribution of service times.

| Service Time (minutes) | Probability |
|:---:|:---:|
| 2 | 0.24 |
| 3 | 0.20 |
| 4 | 0.15 |
| 5 | 0.14 |
| 6 | 0.12 |
| 7 | 0.08 |
| 8 | 0.05 |
| 9 | 0.02 |
| Total | 1.00 |

In case customer wait times prove too long with just a single clerk, County Beverage's management is considering two alternatives: add a second clerk to help with bagging, taking orders, etc., or enlarge the drive-thru area so that two cars can be served at once (a two-channel system). With either of these options, two clerks will be needed. With the two-channel option, service times are expected to be the same for each channel. With the second clerk helping with a single channel, service times will be reduced. The following probability distribution describes service times given that option.

| Service Time (minutes) | Probability |
|:---:|:---:|
| 1 | 0.20 |
| 2 | 0.35 |
| 3 | 0.30 |
| 4 | 0.10 |
| 5 | 0.05 |
| Total | 1.00 |

County Beverage's management would like you to develop a spreadsheet simulation model of the new system and use it to compare the operation of the system using the following three designs:

**Design**

A   One channel, one clerk
B   One channel, two clerks
C   Two channels, each with one clerk

Management is especially concerned with how long customers have to wait for service. Research has shown that 30% of the customers will wait no longer than 6 minutes and that 90% will wait no longer than 10 minutes. As a guideline, management requires the average wait time to be less than 1.5 minutes.

## Managerial Report

Prepare a report that discusses the general development of the spreadsheet simulation model, and make any recommendations that you have regarding the best store design and staffing plan for County Beverage. One additional consideration is that the design allowing for a two-channel system will cost an additional $10,000 to build.

1.  List the information the spreadsheet simulation model should generate so that a decision can be made on the store design and the desired number of clerks.
2.  Run the simulation for 1000 customers for each alternative considered. You may want to consider making more than one run with each alternative. [*Note:* Values from an exponential probability distribution with mean $\mu$ can be generated in Excel using the following function: $=-\mu*\text{LN}(\text{RAND}())$]
3.  Be sure to note the number of customers County Beverage is likely to lose due to long customer wait times with each design alternative.

## Appendix 13.1    SIMULATION WITH SPREADSHEETS

Spreadsheets enable small and moderate-sized simulation models to be implemented relatively easily and quickly. In this appendix we show the Excel spreadsheets for the three simulation models presented in the chapter.

### The PortaCom Simulation Model

We simulated the PortaCom problem 500 times. The spreadsheet used to carry out the simulation is shown again in Figure 13.18. Note that the simulation results for trials 6 through 495 have been hidden so that the results can be shown in a reasonably sized figure. If desired, the rows for these trials can be shown and the simulation results displayed for all 500 trials. Let us describe the details of the Excel spreadsheet that provided the PortaCom simulation.

First, the PortaCom data are presented in the first 14 rows of the spreadsheet. The selling price per unit, administrative cost, and advertising cost parameters are entered directly into cells C3, C4, and C5. The discrete probability distribution for the direct labor cost per unit is shown in a tabular format. Note that the random number intervals are entered first followed by the corresponding cost per unit. For example, 0.0 in cell A10 and 0.1 in cell B10 show that a cost of $43 per unit will be assigned if the random number is in the interval 0.0 but less than 0.1. Thus, approximately 10% of the simulated direct labor costs will be $43 per unit. The uniform probability distribution with a smallest value of $80 in cell E8 and a largest value of $100 in cell E9 describes the parts cost per unit. Finally, a normal probability distribution with a mean of 15,000 units in cell E13 and a standard deviation of 4500 units in cell E14 describes the first-year demand distribution for the product. At this point we are ready to insert the Excel formulas that will carry out each simulation trial.

Simulation information for the first trial appears in row 21 of the spreadsheet. The cell formulas for row 21 are as follows:

| | |
|---|---|
| Cell A21 | Enter 1 for the first simulation trial |
| Cell B21 | Simulate the direct labor cost per unit[3] |
| | =VLOOKUP(RAND(),$A$10:$C$14,3) |
| Cell C21 | Simulate the parts cost per unit (uniform distribution) |
| | =$E$8+($E$9−$E$8)*RAND() |
| Cell D21 | Simulate the first-year demand (normal distribution) |
| | =NORMINV(RAND(),$E$13,$E$14) |
| Cell E21 | The profit obtained for the first trial |
| | =($C$3−B21−C21)*D21−$C$4−$C$5 |

Cells A21:E21 can be copied to A520:E520 in order to provide the 500 simulation trials.

Ultimately, summary statistics will be collected in order to describe the results of the 500 simulated trials. Using the standard Excel functions, the following summary statistics are computed for the 500 simulated profits appearing in cells E21 to E520.

---

[3] The VLOOKUP function generates a random number using the RAND() function. Then, using the table defined by the region from cells $A$10 to $C$14, the function identifies the row containing the RAND() random number and assigns the corresponding direct labor cost per unit shown in column C.

**Figure 13.18    SPREADSHEET SIMULATION FOR THE PORTACOM PROBLEM**

| | A | B | C | D | E | F |
|---|---|---|---|---|---|---|
| 1 | **PortaCom Risk Analysis** | | | | | |
| 2 | | | | | | |
| 3 | Selling Price Per Unit | | $249 | | | |
| 4 | Administrative Cost | | $400,000 | | | |
| 5 | Advertising Cost | | $600,000 | | | |
| 6 | | | | | | |
| 7 | **Direct Labor Cost** | | | **Parts Cost (Uniform Distribution)** | | |
| 8 | Lower | Upper | | Smallest Value | $80 | |
| 9 | Random No. | Random No. | Cost Per Unit | Largest Value | $100 | |
| 10 | 0.0 | 0.1 | $43 | | | |
| 11 | 0.1 | 0.3 | $44 | | | |
| 12 | 0.3 | 0.7 | $45 | **Demand (Normal Distribution)** | | |
| 13 | 0.7 | 0.9 | $46 | Mean | 15000 | |
| 14 | 0.9 | 1.0 | $47 | Standard Dev | 4500 | |
| 15 | | | | | | |
| 16 | | | | | | |
| 17 | **Simulation Trials** | | | | | |
| 18 | | | | | | |
| 19 | | Direct Labor | Parts | First-Year | | |
| 20 | Trial | Cost Per Unit | Cost Per Unit | Demand | Profit | |
| 21 | 1 | 47 | $85.36 | 17,366 | $1,025,570 | |
| 22 | 2 | 44 | $91.68 | 12,900 | $461,828 | |
| 23 | 3 | 45 | $93.35 | 20,686 | $1,288,906 | |
| 24 | 4 | 43 | $98.56 | 10,888 | $169,807 | |
| 25 | 5 | 45 | $88.36 | 14,259 | $648,911 | |
| 516 | 496 | 44 | $98.67 | 8,730 | ($71,659) | |
| 517 | 497 | 45 | $94.38 | 19,257 | $1,110,841 | |
| 518 | 498 | 44 | $90.85 | 14,920 | $703,102 | |
| 519 | 499 | 43 | $90.37 | 13,471 | $557,662 | |
| 520 | 500 | 46 | $92.50 | 18,614 | $1,056,927 | |
| 521 | | | | | | |
| 522 | | | **Summary Statistics** | | | |
| 523 | | | Mean Profit | | $698,457 | |
| 524 | | | Standard Deviation | | $520,485 | |
| 525 | | | Minimum Profit | | ($785,234) | |
| 526 | | | Maximum Profit | | $2,367,058 | |
| 527 | | | Number of Losses | | 51 | |
| 528 | | | Probability of Loss | | 0.1020 | |

Cell E523    The mean profit per trial =AVERAGE(E21:E520)
Cell E524    The standard deviation of profit =STDEV(E21:E520)
Cell E525    The minimum profit =MIN(E21:E520)
Cell E526    The maximum profit =MAX(E21:E520)
Cell E527    The count of the number of trials where a loss occurred
                (i.e., profit < \$0) =COUNTIF(E21:E520,"<0")
Cell E528    The percentage or probability of a loss based on the 500
                trials =E527/500

The F9 key can be used to perform another complete simulation of PortaCom. In this case, the entire spreadsheet will be recalculated and a set of new simulation results will be provided. Any data summaries, measures, or functions that have been built into the spreadsheet earlier will be updated automatically.

## The Butler Inventory Simulation Model

We simulated the Butler inventory operation for 300 months. The spreadsheet used to carry out the simulation is shown again in Figure 13.19. Note that the simulation results for months 6 through 295 have been hidden so that the results can be shown in a reasonably sized figure. If desired, the rows for these months can be shown and the simulation results displayed for all 300 months. Let us describe the details of the Excel spreadsheet that provided the Butler inventory simulation.

First, the Butler inventory data are presented in the first 11 rows of the spreadsheet. The gross profit per unit, holding cost per unit, and shortage cost per unit data are entered directly into cells C3, C4, and C5. The replenishment level is entered into cell C7, and the mean and standard deviation of the normal probability distribution for demand are entered into cells B10 and B11. At this point we are ready to insert Excel formulas that will carry out each simulation month or trial.

Simulation information for the first month or trial appears in row 17 of the spreadsheet. The cell formulas for row 17 are as follows:

Cell A17    Enter 1 for the first simulation month
Cell B17    Simulate demand (normal distribution)
                =NORMINV(RAND(),\$B\$10,\$B\$11)

Next compute the sales, which is equal to demand (cell B17) if demand is less than or equal to the replenishment level, or is equal to the replenishment level (cell C7) if demand is greater than the replenishment level.

Cell C17    Compute sales =IF(B17<=\$C\$7,B17,\$C\$7)
Cell D17    Calculate gross profit =\$C\$3*C17
Cell E17    Calculate the holding cost if demand is less than or equal
                to the replenishment level
                =IF(B17<=\$C\$7,\$C\$4*(\$C\$7−B17),0)
Cell F17    Calculate the shortage cost if demand is greater than the
                replenishment level
                =IF(B17>\$C\$7,\$C\$5*(B17−\$C\$7),0)
Cell G17    Calculate net profit =D17−E17−F17

**Figure 13.19** SPREADSHEET SIMULATION FOR THE BUTLER INVENTORY PROBLEM

| | A | B | C | D | E | F | G |
|---|---|---|---|---|---|---|---|
| 1 | **Butler Inventory** | | | | | | |
| 2 | | | | | | | |
| 3 | Gross Profit Per Unit | | $50 | | | | |
| 4 | Holding Cost Per Unit | | $15 | | | | |
| 5 | Shortage Cost Per Unit | | $30 | | | | |
| 6 | | | | | | | |
| 7 | **Replenishment Level** | | 100 | | | | |
| 8 | | | | | | | |
| 9 | **Demand (Normal Distribution)** | | | | | | |
| 10 | Mean | 100 | | | | | |
| 11 | Standard Dev | 20 | | | | | |
| 12 | | | | | | | |
| 13 | | | | | | | |
| 14 | **Simulation** | | | | | | |
| 15 | | | | | | | |
| 16 | Month | Demand | Sales | Gross Profit | Holding Cost | Shortage Cost | Net Profit |
| 17 | 1 | 79 | 79 | $3,950 | $315 | $0 | $3,635 |
| 18 | 2 | 111 | 100 | $5,000 | $0 | $330 | $4,670 |
| 19 | 3 | 93 | 93 | $4,650 | $105 | $0 | $4,545 |
| 20 | 4 | 100 | 100 | $5,000 | $0 | $0 | $5,000 |
| 21 | 5 | 118 | 100 | $5,000 | $0 | $540 | $4,460 |
| 312 | 296 | 89 | 89 | $4,450 | $165 | $0 | $4,285 |
| 313 | 297 | 91 | 91 | $4,550 | $135 | $0 | $4,415 |
| 314 | 298 | 122 | 100 | $5,000 | $0 | $660 | $4,340 |
| 315 | 299 | 93 | 93 | $4,650 | $105 | $0 | $4,545 |
| 316 | 300 | 126 | 100 | $5,000 | $0 | $780 | $4,220 |
| 317 | | | | | | | |
| 318 | **Totals** | 30,181 | 27,917 | | **Summary Statistics** | | |
| 319 | | | | | Mean Profit | | $4,293 |
| 320 | | | | | Standard Deviation | | $658 |
| 321 | | | | | Minimum Profit | | ($206) |
| 322 | | | | | Maximum Profit | | $5,000 |
| 323 | | | | | Service Level | | 92.5% |

Cells A17:G17 can be copied to cells A316:G316 in order to provide the 300 simulation months.

Finally, summary statistics will be collected in order to describe the results of the 300 simulated trials. Using the standard Excel functions, the following totals and summary statistics are computed for the 300 months.

| | |
|---|---|
| Cell B318 | Total Demand =SUM(B17:B316) |
| Cell C319 | Total Sales =SUM(C17:C316) |
| Cell G319 | The mean profit per month =AVERAGE(G17:G316) |

| Cell G320 | The standard deviation of net profit |
| | =STDEV(G17:G316) |
| Cell G321 | The minimum net profit =MIN(G17:G316) |
| Cell G322 | The maximum net profit =MAX(G17:G316) |
| Cell G323 | The service level =C318/B318 |

## The Hammondsport ATM Simulation Model

We simulated the operation of the Hammondsport ATM waiting line system for 1000 customers. The spreadsheet used to carry out the simulation is shown again in Figure 13.20. Note that the simulation results for customers 6 through 995 have been hidden so that the results can be shown in a reasonably sized figure. If desired, the rows for these customers can be shown and the simulation results displayed for all 1000 customers. Let us describe the details of the Excel spreadsheet that provided the Hammondsport ATM simulation.

The data are presented in the first 9 rows of the spreadsheet. The interarrival times are described by a uniform distribution with a smallest time of 0 minutes (cell B4) and a largest time of 5 minutes (cell B5). A normal probability distribution with a mean of 2 minutes (cell B8) and a standard deviation of 0.5 minutes (cell B9) describes the service time distribution.

Simulation information for the first customer appears in row 16 of the spreadsheet. The cell formulas for row 16 are as follows:

| Cell A16 | Enter 1 for the first customer |
| Cell B16 | Simulate the interarrival time for customer 1 (uniform distribution) =$B$4+RAND()*($B$5−$B$4) |
| Cell C16 | Compute the arrival time for customer 1 =B16 |
| Cell D16 | Compute the start time for customer 1 =C16 |
| Cell E16 | Compute the wait time for customer 1 =D16−C16 |
| Cell F16 | Simulate the service time for customer 1 (normal distribution) =NORMINV(RAND(),$B$8,$B$9) |
| Cell G16 | Compute the completion time for customer 1 =D16+F16 |
| Cell H16 | Compute the time in the system for customer 1 =G16−C16 |

Simulation information for the second customer appears in row 17 of the spreadsheet. The cell formulas for row 17 are as follows:

| Cell A17 | Enter 2 for the second customer |
| Cell B17 | Simulate the interarrival time for customer 2 (uniform distribution) =$B$4+RAND()*($B$5−$B$4) |
| Cell C17 | Compute the arrival time for customer 2 =C16+B17 |
| Cell D17 | Compute the start time for customer 2 =IF(C17>G16,C17,G16) |
| Cell E17 | Compute the wait time for customer 2 =D17-C17 |
| Cell F17 | Simulate the service time for customer 2 (normal distribution) =NORMINV(RAND(),$B$8,$B$9) |
| Cell G17 | Compute the completion time for customer 2 =D17+F17 |
| Cell H17 | Compute the time in the system for customer 2 =G17−C17 |

Cells A17:H17 can be copied to cells A1015:H1015 in order to provide the 1000 customer simulation.

Ultimately, summary statistics will be collected in order to describe the results of 1000 customers. Before collecting the summary statistics, let us point out that most simulation studies of dynamic systems focus on the operation of the system during its long-run or steady-state operation. To ensure that the effect of start-up conditions are not included in

**Figure 13.20    SPREADSHEET SIMULATION OF THE HAMMONDSPORT SAVINGS BANK WITH ONE ATM**

| | A | B | C | D | E | F | G | H |
|---|---|---|---|---|---|---|---|---|
| 1 | **Hammondsport Savings Bank with One ATM** | | | | | | | |
| 2 | | | | | | | | |
| 3 | **Interarrival Times (Uniform Distribution)** | | | | | | | |
| 4 | Smallest Value | 0 | | | | | | |
| 5 | Largest Value | 5 | | | | | | |
| 6 | | | | | | | | |
| 7 | **Service Times (Normal Distribution)** | | | | | | | |
| 8 | Mean | 2 | | | | | | |
| 9 | Standard Dev | 0.5 | | | | | | |
| 10 | | | | | | | | |
| 11 | | | | | | | | |
| 12 | **Simulation** | | | | | | | |
| 13 | | | | | | | | |
| 14 | | Interarrival | Arrival | Service | Wait | Service | Completion | Time |
| 15 | Customer | Time | Time | Start Time | Time | Time | Time | in System |
| 16 | 1 | 1.4 | 1.4 | 1.4 | 0.0 | 2.3 | 3.7 | 2.3 |
| 17 | 2 | 1.3 | 2.7 | 3.7 | 1.0 | 1.5 | 5.2 | 2.5 |
| 18 | 3 | 4.9 | 7.6 | 7.6 | 0.0 | 2.2 | 9.8 | 2.2 |
| 19 | 4 | 3.5 | 11.1 | 11.1 | 0.0 | 2.5 | 13.6 | 2.5 |
| 20 | 5 | 0.7 | 11.8 | 13.6 | 1.8 | 1.8 | 15.4 | 3.6 |
| 1011 | 996 | 0.5 | 2496.8 | 2498.1 | 1.3 | 0.6 | 2498.7 | 1.9 |
| 1012 | 997 | 0.2 | 2497.0 | 2498.7 | 1.7 | 2.0 | 2500.7 | 3.7 |
| 1013 | 998 | 2.7 | 2499.7 | 2500.7 | 1.0 | 1.9 | 2502.5 | 2.8 |
| 1014 | 999 | 3.7 | 2503.4 | 2503.4 | 0.0 | 2.5 | 2505.8 | 2.5 |
| 1015 | 1000 | 4.1 | 2507.4 | 2507.4 | 0.0 | 1.9 | 2509.3 | 1.9 |
| 1016 | | | | | | | | |
| 1017 | | **Summary Statistics** | | | | | | |
| 1018 | | Number Waiting | | | 549 | | | |
| 1019 | | Probability of Waiting | | | 0.6100 | | | |
| 1020 | | Average Wait Time | | | 1.59 | | | |
| 1021 | | Maximum Wait Time | | | 13.5 | | | |
| 1022 | | Utilization of ATM | | | 0.7860 | | | |
| 1023 | | Number Waiting > 1 Min | | | 393 | | | |
| 1024 | | Probability of Waiting > 1 Min | | | 0.4367 | | | |

the steady-state calculations, a dynamic simulation model is usually run for a specified period without collecting any data about the operation of the system. The length of the startup period can vary depending on the application. For the Hammondsport Savings Bank ATM simulation, we treated the results for the first 100 customers as the start-up period. The simulation information for customer 100 appears in row 115 of the spreadsheet. Cell G115 shows that the completion time for the 100th customer is 247.8. Thus the length of the start-up period is 247.8 minutes.

Summary statistics are collected for the next 900 customers corresponding to rows 116 to 1015 of the spreadsheet. The following Excel formulas provided the summary statistics.

Cell E1018   Number of customers who had to wait (i.e., wait time > 0) =COUNTIF(E116:E1015,">0")

Cell E1019   Probability of waiting =E1018/900

Cell E1020   The average wait time =AVERAGE(E116:E1015)

Cell E1021   The maximum wait time =MAX(E116:E1015)

Cell E1022   The utilization of the ATM[4] =SUM(F116:F1015)/(G1015−G115)

Cell E1023   The number of customers who had to wait more than 1 minute =COUNTIF(E116:E1015,">1")

Cell E1024   Probability of waiting more than 1 minute =E1023/900

---

[4] The proportion of time the ATM is in use is equal to the sum of the 900 customer service times in column F divided by the total elapsed time required for the 900 customers to complete service. This total elapsed time is the difference between the completion time of customer 1000 and the completion time of customer 100.

# PHARMACIA & UPJOHN, INC.*

## BRIDGEWATER, NEW JERSEY

The companies that make up Pharmacia & Upjohn have been helping people live longer and healthier for more than 140 years. In all, more than 20 companies from Europe and the United States have merged to create one of the world's largest pharmaceutical groups. The merger between Pharmacia (1911) and Upjohn (1886) to form the Pharmacia & Upjohn Company occurred in 1995.

### Management Science

The management science function is part of the Management Information and Office Services organization and offers a high-quality, professional problem-solving service to any part of the corporation. The mission of the group is to provide decision-making support for the company's customers, strategies, and priorities by using quantitative techniques to solve business problems and exploit business opportunities in a cost-effective manner. The primary areas of application are problem definition and analysis, modeling and simulation, capacity planning, resource allocation, scheduling, and project management.

### A Computer Simulation Application

Demand for one long-standing product had remained stable for several years at a level easily satisfied by the company's manufacturing facility. However, changes in market conditions caused an increase in demand to a level beyond the capacity of the current facility. In the discussion that follows, we describe a simulation study successfully undertaken to determine the most cost-effective means of increasing production to meet the new level of demand.

*The authors are indebted to Dr. David B. Magerlein, Dr. James M. Magerlein, and Mr. Michael J. Goodrich of Pharmacia & Upjohn for providing this application.

The production process is shown in Figure 13.21. It consists of three independent subprocesses: raw material processing, bulk processing, and spent material reprocessing. Raw material processing takes purchased material as input and transforms it into material that can be used in bulk processing. Bulk processing (shown within the dashed line in Figure 13.21), which involves initial processing, assay, and final processing, converts the raw materials into a finished product. The key step occurs when an assay of the initial bulk processing output or intermediate is performed to determine whether the lot is ready for final processing. If the assay is acceptable, the lot proceeds to final processing and completion. If the assay is not acceptable, the intermediate is returned to initial bulk processing and several steps are repeated. The new intermediate material, which is input during the repeat processing, is obtained by reprocessing one of the spent materials generated during a prior initial bulk processing.

Each time the initial bulk process is run, a quantity of spent material is generated for possible reprocessing. Although the primary use of the reprocessed material is as input for repeat bulk processing, it also can be used as a replacement for the original raw material at the start of the bulk processing. Because the cost of the reprocessed material is significantly less than the cost of new raw material, using as much reprocessed material as possible is beneficial.

A simulation model of the production process was developed, and these questions were addressed:

1. What is the maximum throughput of the existing facility?
2. How can the production process be modified to increase the throughput of the existing facility?

---

**Figure 13.21    A PRODUCTION PROCESS**

3.  How much equipment (tanks and centrifuges) must be added to the current facility to increase the capacity to meet the forecasted demand?
4.  How should the reprocessed spent material be used to minimize the total production cost?
5.  If a new facility is required, what is the optimal size and configuration?

The scope of the simulation model included the raw material and bulk- and spent-material processes already defined. The model was built in a modular flexible manner that allowed for the evaluation of resource levels within the facility, staffing levels and hours, changes in process times or equipment usage, changes in lot size, and/or yield changes. The logic of the process flow served as the core of the model and was developed in collaboration with the lead operators and supervisors of the production area. Because a good logical model is the key to good simulation results, a significant amount of time was spent defining the logic of the process flow. The model development process provided a secondary benefit in that production personnel got to review and evaluate the process as they explained it.

The computer simulation model has been used on several occasions over the past two years. Simulation results have assisted management in addressing capacity, resource allocation, and operating policy issues. Each time a request to evaluate an issue is made, a detailed experimental design is developed that defines the alternatives to be evaluated. The appropriate simulation runs are made, the results are evaluated and presented to pro-

duction management and personnel, and follow-up actions defined.

The computer simulation model was developed using the SLAMSYSTEM® Version 3.0 simulation language from the Pritsker Corporation. All simulation runs were made on a personal computer.

## Benefits of the Simulation Model

The ongoing investigation of the production process using computer simulation has resulted in numerous benefits to the company, including the following:

1.  Optimizing the use of reprocessed spent material to replace fresh raw material. Total material costs were reduced by approximately $3 million per year.
2.  Demonstrating that the current facility, with some operating policy improvements, was large enough to satisfy the increased demand for the next several years. Expansion to a new facility was not necessary.
3.  Determining the impact on facility throughput from alternative process changes. Numerous potential changes were investigated. The simulation model predicted how each change would affect total facility throughput. One change was identified that would increase throughput beyond what was needed for the 5-year forecasted demand.
4.  Determining appropriate staffing levels within the facility. The model determined the number of

operators that will be required as the production level increases in the future. This forecast ensures that the proper number of operators will be trained by the time they are needed.

5. Determining the required size and configuration for a new facility. Although the current facility was found adequate to meet demand, the model still allowed management to determine the cost required to build a new facility.

The final actions taken based on the simulation results included alterations in policies for using reprocessed spent material, priority implementation of the process change that most impacted increasing facility throughput, establishment of appropriate staffing levels, and cost minimization because the expense of building a new or expanded facility was avoided.

## Questions

1. Briefly describe the production operation.
2. What was the primary reason for conducting a study of this operation?
3. Describe some of the factors that had to be included in the simulation model.
4. What were the advantages of simulation?

# 14

## DECISION ANALYSIS

**CONTENTS**

Decision analysis can be used to determine an optimal strategy when a decision maker is faced with several decision alternatives and an uncertain or risk-filled pattern of future events. For example, the manager of a retail business with seasonal clothing products would like to order a large quantity of a particular product if demand for the product will be high. Conversely, the manager would like to order a much smaller quantity if demand for the product will be low. Unfortunately, seasonal clothing products require the manager to make an order quantity decision and place an order with the supplier before demand is known. In fact, the actual demand for the product will not be known until the product has been placed into the store and customers have had the opportunity to purchase it. The selection of the best order quantity when the manager is faced with an uncertain demand is a problem suited for decision analysis.

We begin the study of decision analysis by considering problems having reasonably few decision alternatives and reasonably few possible future events. We introduce the concept of a payoff table to provide a structure for a decision problem and to illustrate the fundamentals of decision analysis. We then introduce decision trees as a way to structure more complex decision problems. Ultimately, we show how an analysis of a decision tree will identify an optimal decision strategy for a problem.

## 14.1    STRUCTURING THE DECISION PROBLEM

Pittsburgh Development Corporation (PDC) has purchased land for a luxury, riverfront condominium complex. The site provides a spectacular view of downtown Pittsburgh and the Golden Triangle where the Allegheny and Monongahela rivers meet to form the Ohio River. The individual condominium units will be priced from \$300,000 to \$1,200,000, depending on the floor the unit is located on, the square footage of the unit, and optional features such as fireplaces and large balconies.

The company has preliminary architectural drawings for three different project sizes: 6 floors with 30 units, 12 floors with 60 units, and 18 floors with 90 units. The financial success of the project will depend heavily on the decision that PDC makes regarding the size of the condominium project. Let us consider how decision analysis can help PDC determine which size project to develop.

The first step in the decision analysis approach is to identify the decision alternatives that are being considered. PDC has three alternatives:

$d_1$ = a small condominium complex with 6 floors and 30 units

$d_2$ = a medium condominium complex with 12 floors and 60 units

$d_3$ = a large condominium complex with 18 floors and 90 units

A key factor in selecting one of these decision alternatives involves management's assessment of the demand for the condominiums.

When asked about possible market acceptance of the condominium project, management viewed the possible acceptance of the project as an all-or-nothing situation. That is, management believes that market acceptance will be one of two possibilities: high market acceptance of the project and hence a substantial demand for the condominiums, or low market acceptance of the project and hence a limited demand for the condominiums. Although management can exercise some influence over market acceptance with advertising, the high prices for the units mean that demand will likely depend on a variety of other factors over which PDC will have no control.

In decision analysis, events that may occur but which the decision maker cannot control are referred to as **states of nature.** The list of possible states of nature includes everything that can happen, and individual states of nature are defined so that exactly one will occur. For the PDC condominium project, the two states of nature are

$s_1$ = high market acceptance and hence a substantial demand for the units

$s_2$ = low market acceptance and hence a limited demand for the units

## Payoff Tables

Given the three decision alternatives and the two states of nature, which condominium size should PDC select? To answer this question, PDC will need information on the profit associated with each combination of a decision alternative and a state of nature. For example, what profit would PDC realize if it constructs a large condominium complex ($d_3$) and market acceptance turns out to be high ($s_1$)? But what would happen to the profit if PDC constructs a large condominium complex ($d_3$) and market acceptance turns out to be low ($s_2$)? In decision analysis, we refer to the outcome that results from a specific decision alternative and the occurrence of a particular state of nature as a **payoff.** A table showing the payoffs for all combinations of the decision alternatives and states of nature is a **payoff table.**

Using the best information available, management has estimated the payoffs, or profits, for the PDC condominium project. These estimates, with profits expressed in millions of dollars, are presented in Table 14.1. In general, entries in a payoff table can be stated in terms of profit, cost, time, distance, or any other measure of output that may be appropriate for the situation being analyzed. We will refer to the payoff associated with decision alternative $i$ and state of nature $j$ as $V_{ij}$. For example, Table 14.1 shows that $V_{31} = 20$, indicating that a \$20 million profit is anticipated if the large complex is constructed ($d_3$) and a high market acceptance ($s_1$) occurs. However, $V_{32} = -9$ shows an anticipated loss of \$9 million if the large complex is constructed ($d_3$) and a low market acceptance ($s_2$) occurs.

## Decision Trees

A **decision tree** provides a graphical representation of the decision-making process. Figure 14.1 presents a decision tree for the PDC problem. Note that the decision tree shows the natural or logical progression that will occur over time. First, PDC must make a decision regarding the size of the condominium complex ($d_1$, $d_2$, or $d_3$). Then, after the decision is implemented, either state of nature $s_1$ or $s_2$ will occur. The number at each end point of the tree indicates the payoff associated with a particular sequence. For example the topmost payoff of 8 indicates that an \$8 million profit is anticipated if PDC constructs a small

| Table 14.1 | PAYOFF TABLE FOR THE PDC CONDOMINIUM PROJECT (PAYOFFS IN \$ MILLION) |

| Decision Alternative | High Acceptance $s_1$ | Low Acceptance $s_2$ |
|---|---|---|
| Small complex, $d_1$ | 8 | 7 |
| Medium complex, $d_2$ | 14 | 5 |
| Large complex, $d_3$ | 20 | -9 |

condominium complex ($d_1$) and market acceptance turns out to be high ($s_1$). The next payoff of 7 indicates an anticipated profit of $7 million if PDC constructs a small condominium complex ($d_1$) and market acceptance turns out to be low ($s_2$). Thus, the decision tree shows graphically the sequences of decision alternatives and states of nature that provide the six possible outcomes and payoffs for PDC.

If you have a payoff table, you can develop a decision tree. Try Problem 1(a).

We refer to an intersection or junction point of the decision tree as a **node** and the arc or connector between nodes as a **branch**. Figure 14.1 shows the PDC decision tree with the nodes numbered 1–4. When the branches *leaving* a node are decision branches, we refer to the node as a *decision node* and represent it by a square. Similarly, when the branches leaving a node are state-of-nature branches, we refer to the node as a *state-of-nature node* and represent it by a circle. Hence, node 1 is a decision node, whereas nodes 2, 3, and 4 are state-of-nature nodes.

The identification of the decision alternatives, the states of nature, and the payoff associated with each decision alternative and state-of-nature combination are the first three steps in the decision-analysis process. We now turn to this question: How can the decision maker best utilize the information presented in the payoff table or the decision tree to arrive at a decision? Several approaches may be used.

---

| N O T E S *and Comments* | 1. Experts in problem solving agree that the first step in solving a complex problem is to decompose it into a series of smaller subproblems. Decision trees provide a useful way to show how the problem can be decomposed and the sequential nature of the decision process.<br><br>2. People often view the same problem from different perspectives. Thus, the discussion regarding the development of a decision tree may provide additional insight about the problem. |
| --- | --- |

---

**Figure 14.1    DECISION TREE FOR THE PDC CONDOMINIUM PROJECT (PAYOFFS IN $ MILLION)**

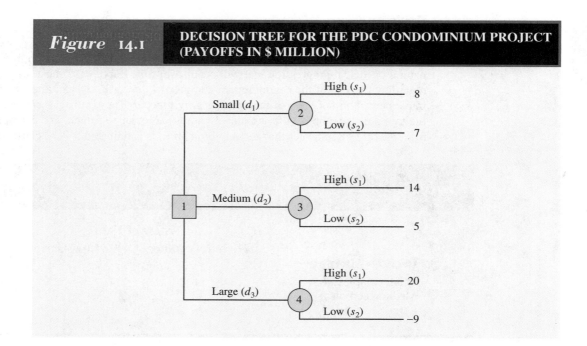

............................................................................................../  /.............

## I4.2    DECISION MAKING WITHOUT PROBABILITIES

Many people think of a good decision as one in which the outcome is good. However, in some instances, a good, well-thought-out decision may still lead to a bad or undesirable outcome.

In this section we consider approaches to decision making that do not require knowledge of the probabilities of the states of nature. These approaches are appropriate in situations in which the decision maker has little confidence in the ability to assess the probabilities of the various states of nature, or in which a simple best- and worst-case analysis of the states of nature is desirable. Because different approaches sometimes lead to different decision recommendations, the decision maker needs to understand the approaches available and then select the specific approach that, according to the decision maker's judgment, is the most appropriate.

### Optimistic Approach

The **optimistic approach** evaluates each decision alternative in terms of the *best* payoff that can occur. The decision alternative that is recommended is the one that provides the best possible payoff. For a problem in which maximum profit is desired, as in the PDC problem, the optimistic approach would lead the decision maker to choose the alternative corresponding to the largest profit. For problems involving minimization, this approach leads to choosing the alternative with the smallest payoff.

For a maximization problem, the optimistic approach often is referred to as the *maximax* approach; for a minimization problem, the corresponding terminology is *minimim*.

To illustrate the optimistic approach, we use it to develop a recommendation for the PDC problem. First, we determine the maximum payoff for each decision alternative; then we select the decision alternative that provides the overall maximum payoff. These steps systematically identify the decision alternative that provides the largest possible profit. Table 14.2 illustrates these steps.

Since 20, corresponding to $d_3$, is the largest payoff, the decision to construct the large condominium complex is the recommended decision alternative using the optimistic approach.

### Conservative Approach

The **conservative approach** evaluates each decision alternative in terms of the *worst* payoff that can occur. The decision alternative recommended is the one that provides the best of the worst possible payoffs. For a problem in which the output measure is profit, as in the PDC problem, the conservative approach would lead the decision maker to choose the alternative that maximizes the minimum possible profit that could be obtained. For problems involving minimization, this approach identifies the alternative that will minimize the maximum payoff.

For a maximization problem, the conservative approach is often referred to as the *maximin* approach; for a minimization problem, the corresponding terminology is *minimax*.

To illustrate the conservative approach, we use it to develop a recommendation for the PDC problem. First, we identify the minimum payoff for each of the decision alternatives; then we select the decision alternative that maximizes the minimum payoff. Table 14.3 illustrates these steps for the PDC problem.

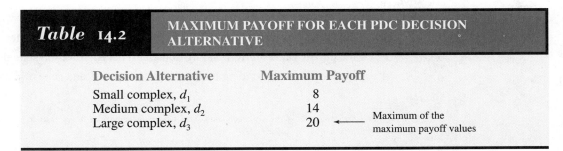

| *Table* I4.2 | MAXIMUM PAYOFF FOR EACH PDC DECISION ALTERNATIVE | |
|---|---|---|
| **Decision Alternative** | **Maximum Payoff** | |
| Small complex, $d_1$ | 8 | |
| Medium complex, $d_2$ | 14 | |
| Large complex, $d_3$ | 20 | ← Maximum of the maximum payoff values |

| Table 14.3 | MINIMUM PAYOFF FOR EACH PDC DECISION ALTERNATIVE |
|---|---|

| Decision Alternative | Minimum Payoff | |
|---|---|---|
| Small complex, $d_1$ | 7 | ← Maximum of the minimum payoff values |
| Medium complex, $d_2$ | 5 | |
| Large complex, $d_3$ | −9 | |

Because 7, corresponding to $d_1$, yields the maximum of the minimum payoffs, the decision alternative of a small condominium complex is recommended. This decision approach is considered conservative because it identifies the worst possible payoffs and then recommends the decision alternative that avoids the possibility of extremely "bad" payoffs. In the conservative approach, PDC is guaranteed a profit of at least $7 million. Although PDC may make more, it *cannot* make less than $7 million.

## Minimax Regret Approach

**Minimax regret** is an approach to decision making that is neither purely optimistic nor purely conservative. Let us illustrate the minimax regret approach by showing how it can be used to select a decision alternative for the PDC problem.

Suppose that the PDC constructs a small condominium complex ($d_1$) and market acceptance turns out to be high ($s_1$). Table 14.1 shows that the resulting profit for PDC would be $8 million. However, we now know that the high acceptance state of nature ($s_1$) has occurred, so we realize that the decision to construct a large condominium complex ($d_3$), yielding a profit of $20 million, would have been the best decision. The difference between the payoff for the best decision alternative ($20 million) and the payoff for the decision to construct a small condominium complex ($8 million) is the **opportunity loss,** or **regret,** associated with decision alternative $d_1$ when state of nature $s_1$ occurs; thus, for this case, the opportunity loss or regret is $20 million − $8 million = $12 million. Similarly, if PDC makes the decision to construct a medium condominium complex ($d_2$) and the high acceptance state of nature ($s_1$) occurs, the opportunity loss, or regret, associated with $d_2$ would be $20 million − $14 million = $6 million.

In general the following expression represents the opportunity loss, or regret.

$$R_{ij} = |V_j^* - V_{ij}| \tag{14.1}$$

where

$R_{ij}$ = the regret associated with decision alternative $d_i$ and state of nature $s_j$

$V_j^*$ = the payoff value[1] corresponding to the best decision for the state of nature $s_j$

$V_{ij}$ = the payoff corresponding to decision alternative $d_i$ and state of nature $s_j$

---

[1] In maximization problems, $V_j^*$ will be the largest entry in column $j$ of the payoff table. In minimization problems, $V_j^*$ will be the smallest entry in column $j$ of the payoff table.

Note the role of the absolute value in equation (14.1). That is, for minimization problems, the best payoff, $V_j^*$, is the smallest entry in column $j$. Because this value always is less than or equal to $V_{ij}$, the absolute value of the difference between $V_j^*$ and $V_{ij}$ ensures that the regret is always the magnitude of the difference.

Using equation (14.1) and the payoffs in Table 14.1, we can compute the regret associated with each combination of decision alternative $d_i$ and state of nature $s_j$. Since the PDC problem is a maximization problem, $V_j^*$ will be the largest entry in column $j$ of the payoff table. Thus, to compute the regret, we simply subtract each entry in a column from the largest entry in the column. Table 14.4 shows the opportunity loss, or regret, table for the PDC problem.

The next step in applying the minimax regret approach is to list the maximum regret for each decision alternative; Table 14.5 shows the results for the PDC problem. Selecting the decision alternative with the *minimum* of the *maximum* regret values—hence, the name *minimax regret*—yields the minimax regret decision. For the PDC problem, the alternative to construct the medium condominium complex, with a corresponding maximum regret of $6 million, is the recommended minimax regret decision.

Note that the three approaches discussed in this section provide different recommendations, which in itself isn't bad. It simply reflects the difference in decision-making philosophies that underlie the various approaches. Ultimately, the decision maker will have to choose the most appropriate approach and then make the final decision accordingly. The main criticism of the approaches discussed in this section is that they do not consider any information about the probabilities of the various states of nature. In the next section we discuss an approach that utilizes probability information in selecting a decision alternative.

For practice in developing a decision recommendation using the optimistic, conservative, and minimax regret approaches, try Problem 1(b).

**Table 14.4 — OPPORTUNITY LOSS, OR REGRET, TABLE FOR THE PDC CONDOMINIUM PROJECT ($ MILLION)**

|  | State of Nature | |
|---|---|---|
|  | High Acceptance | Low Acceptance |
| Decision Alternative | $s_1$ | $s_2$ |
| Small complex, $d_1$ | 12 | 0 |
| Medium complex, $d_2$ | 6 | 2 |
| Large complex, $d_3$ | 0 | 16 |

**Table 14.5 — MAXIMUM REGRET FOR EACH PDC DECISION ALTERNATIVE**

| Decision Alternative | Maximum Regret |
|---|---|
| Small complex $d_1$ | 12 |
| Medium complex, $d_2$ | 6 ← Minimum of the maximum regret |
| Large complex, $d_3$ | 16 |

....................................................................................../  /.............

**14.3     DECISION MAKING WITH PROBABILITIES**

In many decision-making situations, we can obtain probability estimates for the states of nature. When such probabilities are available, we can use the **expected value approach** to identify the best decision alternative. Let us first define the expected value of a decision alternative and then apply it to the PDC problem.

Let

$$N = \text{the number of states of nature}$$
$$P(s_j) = \text{the probability of state of nature } s_j$$

Since one and only one of the $N$ states of nature can occur, the probabilities must satisfy two conditions:

$$P(s_j) \geq 0 \qquad \text{for all states of nature} \tag{14.2}$$

$$\sum_{j=1}^{N} P(s_j) = P(s_1) + P(s_2) + \cdots + P(s_N) = 1 \tag{14.3}$$

The **expected value (EV)** of decision alternative $d_i$ is defined as follows.

$$EV(d_i) = \sum_{j=1}^{N} P(s_j)V_{ij} \tag{14.4}$$

In words, the expected value of a decision alternative is the sum of weighted payoffs for the decision alternative. The weight for a payoff is the probability of the associated state of nature and therefore the probability that the payoff will occur. Let us return to the PDC problem to see how the expected value approach can be applied.

PDC is optimistic about the potential for the luxury high-rise condominium complex. Suppose that this optimism provides an initial subjective probability assessment of 0.8 that market acceptance will be high ($s_1$) and a corresponding probability of 0.2 that market acceptance will be low ($s_2$). Thus, $P(s_1) = 0.8$ and $P(s_2) = 0.2$. Using the payoff values in Table 14.1 and equation (14.4), we compute the expected value for each of the three decision alternatives as follows:

$$EV(d_1) = 0.8(8) + 0.2(7) = 7.8$$
$$EV(d_2) = 0.8(14) + 0.2(5) = 12.2$$
$$EV(d_3) = 0.8(20) + 0.2(-9) = 14.2$$

Thus, using the expected value approach, we find that the large condominium complex, with an expected value of $14.2 million, is the recommended decision.

The calculations required to identify the decision alternative with the best expected value can be conveniently carried out on a decision tree. Figure 14.2 shows the decision tree for the PDC problem with state-of-nature branch probabilities. Working backward through the decision tree, we first compute the expected value at each state-of-nature node. That is, at each state-of-nature node, we weight each possible payoff by its chance of occurrence. By doing so, we obtain the expected values for nodes 2, 3, and 4, as shown in Figure 14.3.

Can you now use the expected value approach to develop a decision recommendation? Try Problem 5.

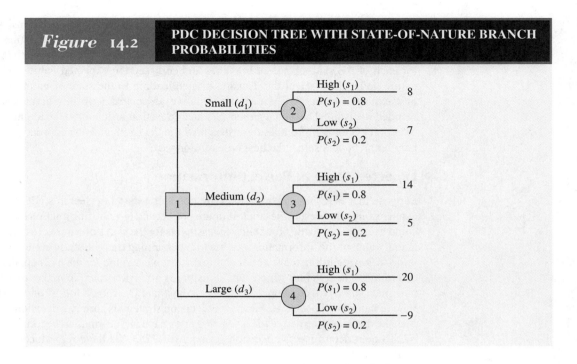

**Figure 14.2    PDC DECISION TREE WITH STATE-OF-NATURE BRANCH PROBABILITIES**

Because the decision maker controls the branch leaving decision node 1 and because we are trying to maximize the expected profit, the best decision branch at node 1 is $d_3$. Thus, the decision tree analysis leads to a recommendation of $d_3$ with an expected value of $14.2 million. Note that this recommendation is also obtained with the expected value approach in conjunction with the payoff table.

Other decision problems may be substantially more complex than the PDC problem, but if a reasonable number of decision alternatives and states of nature are present, you can

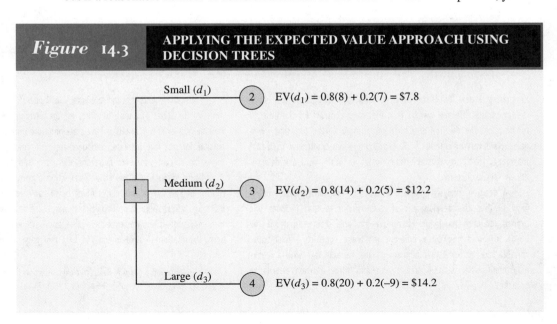

**Figure 14.3    APPLYING THE EXPECTED VALUE APPROACH USING DECISION TREES**

use the decision tree approach outlined here. First, draw a decision tree consisting of decision and state-of-nature nodes and branches that describe the sequential nature of the problem. If you use the expected value approach, the next step is to determine the probabilities for each of the state-of-nature branches and compute the expected value at each state-of-nature node. Then select the decision branch leading to the state-of-nature node with the best expected value. The decision alternative associated with this branch is the recommended decision. The Management Science in Action article on decision analysis and the selection of home mortgages describes how the decision analysis approach can be used to help home buyers select the best type of mortgage.

## Expected Value of Perfect Information

Suppose that PDC has the opportunity to conduct a market research study that would help evaluate buyer interest in the condominium project and provide information that management could use to improve the probability assessments for the states of nature. To determine the potential value of this information, we begin by assuming that the study could provide *perfect information* regarding the states of nature; that is, we assume for the moment that PDC could determine with certainty which state of nature is going to occur. To make use of this perfect information, we will develop a decision strategy that PDC should follow once it knows which state of nature will occur. As we show, a decision strategy is simply a decision rule that specifies the decision alternative to be selected after the new information becomes available.

To help determine the decision strategy for PDC, we have reproduced PDC's payoff table as Table 14.6. Note that, if PDC knew for sure that state of nature $s_1$ would occur, the best decision alternative would be $d_3$, with a payoff of $20 million. Similarly, if PDC knew for sure that state of nature $s_2$ would occur, the best decision alternative would be $d_1$, with a payoff of $7 million. Thus, we can state PDC's optimal decision strategy based on perfect information as follows:

$$\text{If } s_1, \text{ select } d_3.$$
$$\text{If } s_2, \text{ select } d_1.$$

# MANAGEMENT SCIENCE IN ACTION

## DECISION ANALYSIS AND THE SELECTION OF HOME MORTGAGES*

Purchasing a new home can be a stressful experience, especially when it may commit the new owners to a mortgage contract for the next 20 to 30 years. The decision is further complicated by the fact that mortgages have varying interest rates that range from traditional fixed-rate mortgages (FRM) to adjustable-rate mortgages (ARM) with a wide variety of special features.

A decision analysis approach to selecting the best type of mortgage involves the development of a decision tree that includes one branch for each mortgage alternative available. For example, if the buyer is considering three different mortgage contracts—fixed rate, variable rate with a 3-year adjustment, and variable rate with a 5-year adjustment—the decision tree begins with three decision alternative branches.

The future events that indicate what can happen to interest rates over time are the states of nature branches for the decision tree. For instance, variable-rate mortgage branches have state-of-nature branches that indicate possible interest rate increases and decreases. The complete decision tree shows the outcomes for each mortgage alternative and its associated cost.

Using decision analysis criteria reflecting a conservative or an optimistic perspective, a prospective home buyer can select a recommended mortgage alternative. If probability estimates are available for the future mortgage rates, the expected value approach will use the probability information to recommend the best mortgage alternative.

*Robert E. Luna, and Richard A. Reid, "Mortgage Selection Using a Decision Tree Approach," *Interfaces* 16, no. 3 (May–June 1986): 73–81.

| Table 14.6 | PAYOFF TABLE FOR THE PDC CONDOMINIUM PROJECT ($ MILLION) | |
|---|---|---|
| | **State of Nature** | |
| | **High Acceptance** | **Low Acceptance** |
| **Decision Alternative** | $s_1$ | $s_2$ |
| Small complex, $d_1$ | 8 | 7 |
| Medium complex, $d_2$ | 14 | 5 |
| Large complex, $d_3$ | 20 | -9 |

What is the expected value for this decision strategy? To compute the expected value with perfect information, we return to the original probability estimates for the states of nature: $P(s_1) = 0.8$, and $P(s_2) = 0.2$. Based on these probabilities, there is a 0.8 probability that the perfect information will indicate state of nature $s_1$. In this case, the resulting decision alternative $d_3$ will provide a \$20 million profit. Similarly, with a 0.2 probability for state of nature $s_2$, the resulting decision alternative $d_1$ will provide a \$7 million profit. Thus, from equation (14.4), the expected value of the decision strategy that uses perfect information is

$$0.8(20) + 0.2(7) = 17.4$$

We refer to the expected value of \$17.4 million as the *expected value with perfect information* (EVwPI).

Earlier in this section we showed that the recommended decision using the expected value approach is decision alternative $d_3$, with an expected value of \$14.2 million. Because this decision recommendation and expected value computation were made without the benefit of perfect information, \$14.2 million is referred to as the *expected value without perfect information* (EVwoPI).

The expected value with perfect information is \$17.4 million, and the expected value without perfect information is \$14.2; therefore, the expected value of the perfect information (EVPI) is \$17.4 − \$14.2 = \$3.2 million. In other words, \$3.2 million represents the additional expected value that can be obtained if perfect information were available about the states of nature.

For practice in determining the expected value of perfect information, try Problem 12.

Generally speaking, a market research study will not provide "perfect" information; however, if the market research study is a good one, the information gathered might be worth a sizable portion of the \$3.2 million. Given the EVPI of \$3.2 million, PDC should seriously consider the market survey as a way to obtain more information about the states of nature.

In general, the **expected value of perfect information** is computed as follows:

$$EVPI = |EVwPI - EVwoPI|$$

where

$$EVPI = \text{expected value of perfect information}$$
$$EVwPI = \text{expected value } with \text{ perfect information about the states of nature}$$
$$EVwoPI = \text{expected value } without \text{ perfect information about the states of nature}$$

Note the role of the absolute value in equation (14.5). That is, for minimization problems the expected value with perfect information is always less than or equal to the expected value without perfect information. In this case, EVPI is the magnitude of the difference between EVwPI and EVwoPI, or the absolute value of the difference as shown in equation (14.5).

| N O T E S *and Comments* | We restate the *opportunity loss,* or *regret,* table for the PDC problem (see Table 14.4) as follows. |

|  | State of Nature | |
| --- | --- | --- |
|  | **High Acceptance** | **Low Acceptance** |
| **Decision Alternative** | $s_1$ | $s_2$ |
| Small complex, $d_1$ | 12 | 0 |
| Medium complex, $d_2$ | 6 | 2 |
| Large complex, $d_3$ | 0 | 16 |

Using $P(s_1)$, $P(s_2)$, and the opportunity loss values, we can compute the *expected opportunity loss* (EOL) for each decision alternative. With $P(s_1) = 0.8$ and $P(s_2) = 0.2$, the expected opportunity loss for each of the three decision alternatives is

$$EOL(d_1) = 0.8(12) + 0.2(0) = 9.6$$
$$EOL(d_2) = 0.8(6) + 0.2(2)\ = 5.2$$
$$EOL(d_3) = 0.8(0) + 0.2(16) = 3.2$$

Regardless of whether the decision analysis involves maximization or minimization, the *minimum* expected opportunity loss always provides the best decision alternative. Thus, with $EOL(d_3) = 3.2$, $d_3$ is the recommended decision. In addition, the minimum expected opportunity loss always is *equal to the expected value of perfect information.* That is, EOL(best decision) = EVPI; for the PDC problem, this value is $3.2 million.

## 14.4  SENSITIVITY ANALYSIS

In this section we consider how changes in the probability estimates for the states of nature affect or alter the recommended decision alternative. The study of the effect of such changes is referred to as **sensitivity analysis.**

One approach to sensitivity analysis is to consider different probabilities for the states of nature and recompute the expected value for each decision alternative. Repeating this computation for several different probabilities, we can begin to learn how changes in the probabilities for the states of nature affect the recommended decision. For example, in the PDC problem, suppose that the probability of high acceptance is reduced to 0.2 and that the probability of low acceptance is increased to 0.8. Using $P(s_1) = 0.2$, $P(s_2) = 0.8$. With equation (14.4), we obtain the expected value for each decision alternative:

$$EV(d_1) = 0.2(8) + 0.8(7) = 7.2$$
$$EV(d_2) = 0.2(14) + 0.8(5) = 6.8$$
$$EV(d_3) = 0.2(20) + 0.8(-9) = -3.2$$

Thus, with these probabilities the recommended decision alternative is to construct a small condominium complex ($d_1$), with an expected value of $7.2 million. The probability of high acceptance is only 0.2, so constructing the large condominium complex ($d_3$) is the least preferred alternative, with an expected value or loss of $3.2 million.

Thus, when the probability of high acceptance is large, PDC should build the large complex; when the probability of high acceptance is small, PDC should build the small complex. Obviously, we could continue to modify the probabilities of the states of nature and learn even more about how changes in the probabilities affect the recommended decision alternative. The only drawback to this approach is the numerous calculations required to evaluate the effect of several possible changes in the state-of-nature probabilities.

For the special case of two states of nature, a graphical procedure substantially eases the sensitivity analysis computations. To demonstrate this procedure, we let $p$ denote the probability of state of nature $s_1$; that is, $P(s_1) = p$. With only two states of nature in the PDC problem, the probability of state of nature $s_2$ is

$$P(s_2) = 1 - P(s_1) = 1 - p$$

Using equation (14.4) and the payoff values in Table 14.1, we determine the expected value for decision alternative $d_1$ as follows:

$$
\begin{aligned}
EV(d_1) &= P(s_1)(8) + P(s_2)(7) \\
&= p(8) + (1 - p)(7) \\
&= 8p + 7 - 7p = p + 7
\end{aligned}
\tag{14.6}
$$

Repeating the expected value computations for decision alternatives $d_2$ and $d_3$, we obtain expressions for the expected value of each decision alternative as a function of $p$:

$$EV(d_2) = 9p + 5 \tag{14.7}$$
$$EV(d_3) = 29p - 9 \tag{14.8}$$

Thus, we have developed three equations that show the expected value of the three decision alternatives as a function of the probability of state of nature $s_1$.

We continue by developing a graph with values of $p$ on the horizontal axis and the associated EVs on the vertical axis. Because equations (14.6), (14.7), and (14.8) are linear equations, the graph of each equation is a straight line. For each equation, then, we can obtain the line by identifying two points that satisfy the equation and drawing a line through the points. For instance, if we let $p = 0$ in equation (14.6), $EV(d_1) = 7$. Then, letting $p = 1$, $EV(d_1) = 8$. Connecting these two points, $(0, 7)$ and $(1, 8)$, provides the line labeled $EV(d_1)$ in Figure 14.4. Similarly, we obtain the lines labeled $EV(d_2)$ and $EV(d_3)$; these lines are the graphs of equations (14.7) and (14.8), respectively.

Figure 14.4 shows how the recommended decision changes as $p$, the probability of the high acceptance state of nature ($s_1$), changes. Note that for small values of $p$, decision alternative $d_1$ (small complex) provides the largest expected value and is thus the recommended decision. When the value of $p$ increases to a certain point, decision alternative $d_2$ (medium complex) provides the largest expected value and is the recommended decision. Finally, for large values of $p$, decision alternative $d_3$ (large complex) becomes the recommended decision.

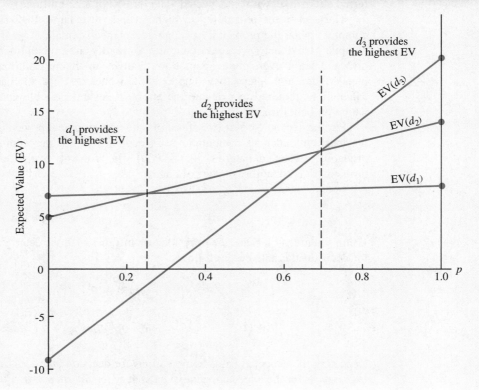

**Figure 14.4 EXPECTED VALUE FOR THE PDC DECISION ALTERNATIVES AS A FUNCTION OF $p$**

The value of $p$ for which the expected values of $d_1$ and $d_2$ are equal is the value of $p$ corresponding to the intersection of the $EV(d_1)$ and the $EV(d_2)$ lines. To determine this value, we set $EV(d_1) = EV(d_2)$ and solve for the value of $p$:

$$p + 7 = 9p + 5$$
$$8p = 2$$
$$p = \frac{2}{8} = 0.25$$

Hence, whenever $p = 0.25$, decision alternatives $d_1$ and $d_2$ provide the same expected value. Repeating this calculation for the value of $p$ corresponding to the intersection of the $EV(d_2)$ and $EV(d_3)$ lines we obtain $p = 0.70$.

Using Figure 14.4, we can conclude that decision alternative $d_1$ provides the largest expected value for $p \leq 0.25$, decision alternative $d_2$ provides the largest expected value for $0.25 \leq p \leq 0.70$, and decision alternative $d_3$ provides the largest expected value for $p \geq 0.70$. Since $p$ is simply the probability of state of nature $s_1$ and $(1 - p)$ is the probability of state of nature $s_2$, we now have the sensitivity analysis information that tells us how changes in the state-of-nature probabilities affect the recommended decision alternative.

Sensitivity analysis can assist management in deciding whether they should invest more time and money to obtain more accurate probability estimates.

The benefit of performing sensitivity analysis is that it can provide a better perspective on management's original judgement regarding the state-of-nature probabilities. Management originally estimated the probability of high customer acceptance as $P(s_1) = 0.8$. As a result, decision alternative $d_3$ was recommended. After carrying out the sensitivity analysis, we can now tell management that as long as $P(s_1) > 0.70$, the $d_3$ decision alternative remains optimal.

Graphical sensitivity analysis determines how changes in the probability estimates affect the recommended decision. Try Problem 8.

The graphical sensitivity analysis procedure just described for the PDC problem applies only to decision analysis problems with two states of nature. However, sensitivity analysis also is important in problems with more than two states of nature. In these cases, a spreadsheet or computer software package can be used to assist with the computations. Basically, we return to the approach of testing a variety of likely changes for the state-of-nature probabilities. A spreadsheet or software package is helpful in making the necessary expected value computations and providing the decision alternative recommendations with a minimum of time and effort.

## 14.5 DECISION ANALYSIS WITH SAMPLE INFORMATION

In applying the expected value approach, we have shown how probability information about the states of nature affects the expected value calculations and thus the decision recommendation. Frequently, decision makers have preliminary or **prior probability** estimates for the state of nature that are the best probability values available. However, to make the best possible decision, the decision maker may want to seek additional information about the states of nature. This new information can be used to revise or update the prior probabilities so that the final decision is based on more accurate probability estimates for the states of nature. Most often, additional information is obtained through experiments designed to provide **sample information** about the states of nature. Raw material sampling, product testing, and market research studies are examples of experiments that may enable management to revise or update the state-of-nature probabilities. These *revised* probabilities are called **posterior probabilities.**

Let us return to the PDC problem and assume that management is considering a six-month market research study designed to evaluate market acceptance of the PDC condominium project. Management anticipates that the market research study will provide one of the following two results:

1. Favorable report: A significant number of the individuals contacted express interest in purchasing a PDC condominium.
2. Unfavorable report: Very few of the individuals contacted express interest in purchasing a PDC condominium.

By introducing the possibility of conducting a market research study, the PDC problem has become more complex. First, PDC's management must decide whether the market research should be conducted. If it is conducted, PDC's management must be prepared to make a decision about the size of the condominium project if the market research report is favorable and possibly a different decision about the size of the condominium project if the market research report is unfavorable. The decision tree in Figure 14.5 shows this PDC decision problem. The squares are *decision nodes* and the circles are *probability nodes*. At each decision node, the branch of the tree that is taken is based on the decision made. At each probability node, the branch of the tree that is taken is based on probability or chance. For example, decision node 1 shows that PDC must first make the decision of whether to

**Figure** 14.5    **THE PDC DECISION TREE INCLUDING THE MARKET RESEARCH STUDY**

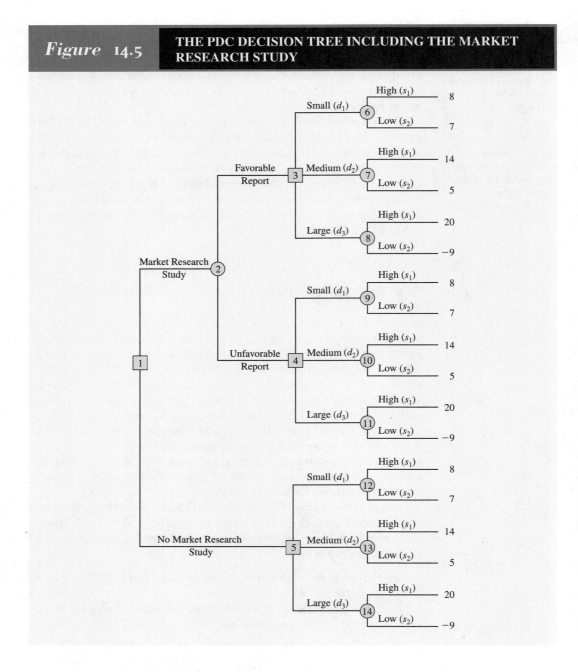

conduct the market research study. If the market research study is undertaken, probability node 2 indicates that both the favorable report branch and the unfavorable report branch are not under PDC's control and will be determined by chance. Node 3 is a decision node, indicating that PDC must make the decision to construct the small, medium, or large complex if the market research report is favorable. Node 4 is a decision node showing that PDC must make the decision to construct the small, medium, or large complex if the market research report is unfavorable. Node 5 is a decision node indicating that PDC must make the decision to construct the small, medium, or large complex if the market research is not undertaken. Nodes 6 to 14 are probability nodes indicating that the high acceptance or low acceptance state-of-nature branches will be determined by chance.

At this point, the analysis of the decision tree requires that we know the branch probabilities corresponding to all probability nodes. PDC estimates the following branch probabilities.

If the market research study is undertaken

$$P(\text{Favorable report}) = 0.77$$
$$P(\text{Unfavorable report}) = 0.23$$

If the market research report is favorable

$$P(\text{High acceptance given a Favorable report}) = 0.94$$
$$P(\text{Low acceptance given a Favorable report}) = 0.06$$

If the market research report is unfavorable

$$P(\text{High acceptance given an Unfavorable report}) = 0.35$$
$$P(\text{Low acceptance given an Unfavorable report}) = 0.65$$

If the market research report is not undertaken

$$P(\text{High acceptance}) = 0.80$$
$$P(\text{Low acceptance}) = 0.20$$

The branch probabilities are shown on the decision tree in Figure 14.6.

The approach used to determine the optimal decision strategy is based on a backward pass through the decision tree using the following steps:

1. At a probability node, compute the expected value at the node by multiplying the payoff at the end of each branch by the corresponding branch probabilities.
2. At a decision node, select the decision branch that leads to the best expected value. This expected value becomes the expected value at the decision node.

Starting the backward pass calculations by computing the expected values at probability nodes 6 to 16 provides the following results.

$$
\begin{aligned}
EV(\text{Node 6}) \ &= 0.94(8) \ + 0.06(7) \ \ &= \ \ 7.94 \\
EV(\text{Node 7}) \ &= 0.94(14) + 0.06(5) \ \ &= 13.46 \\
EV(\text{Node 8}) \ &= 0.94(20) + 0.06(-9) &= 18.26 \\
EV(\text{Node 9}) \ &= 0.35(8) \ + 0.65(7) \ \ &= \ \ 7.35 \\
EV(\text{Node 10}) &= 0.35(14) + 0.65(5) \ \ &= \ \ 8.15 \\
EV(\text{Node 11}) &= 0.35(20) + 0.65(-9) &= \ \ 1.15 \\
EV(\text{Node 12}) &= 0.80(8) \ + 0.20(7) \ \ &= \ \ 7.80 \\
EV(\text{Node 13}) &= 0.80(14) + 0.20(5) \ \ &= 12.20 \\
EV(\text{Node 14}) &= 0.80(20) + 0.20(-9) &= 14.20
\end{aligned}
$$

Next move to decision nodes 3, 4, and 5. For each of these nodes, we select the decision alternative branch that leads to the best expected value. For example, at node 3 we have the

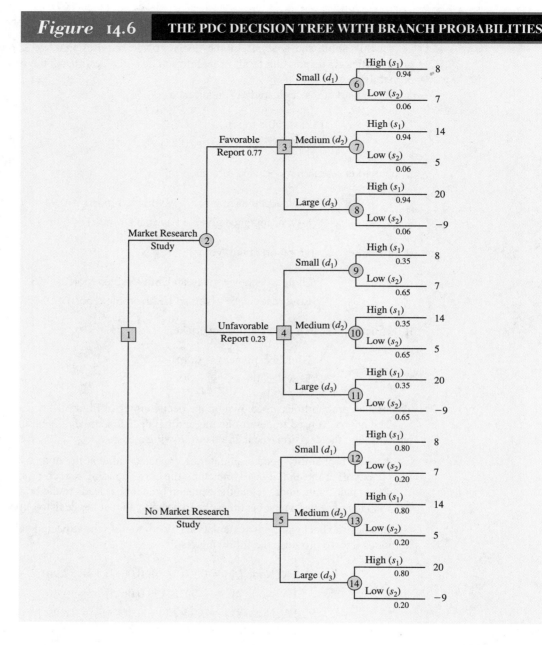

*Figure* 14.6    THE PDC DECISION TREE WITH BRANCH PROBABILITIES

choice of the small complex branch with EV(Node 6) = 7.94, the medium complex branch with EV(Node 7) = 13.46, and the large complex branch with EV(Node 8) = 18.26. Thus, we select the large complex decision alternative branch and the expected value at node 3 becomes EV(Node 3) = 18.26.

For node 4, we select the best expected value from nodes 9, 10, and 11. The best decision alternative is the medium complex branch which provides EV(Node 4) = 8.15. For node 5, we select the best expected value from nodes 12, 13, and 14. The best decision alternative is the large complex branch which provides EV(Node 5) = 14.20.

The expected value at probability node 2 can now be computed as follows:

$$EV(\text{Node 2}) = 0.77EV(\text{Node 3}) + 0.23EV(\text{Node 4})$$
$$= 0.77(18.26) + 0.23(8.15) = 15.93$$

Finally, the decision can be made at decision node 1 by selecting the best expected values from nodes 2 and 5. This action leads to the decision alternative to conduct the market research study, which provides an overall expected value of 15.93.

The optimal decision for PDC is to conduct the market research study and then carry out the following decision strategy:

### Decision Strategy

If the market research is favorable, construct the large condominium complex.

If the market research is unfavorable, construct the medium condominium complex.

Problem 14 will test your ability to develop an optimal decision strategy.

The analysis of the PDC decision tree describes the methods that can be used to analyze any decision problem. First, draw a decision tree consisting of decision and probability nodes and branches that describe the sequential nature of the problem. Determine the probabilities for all probability branches. Then, by working backward through the tree, compute expected values at all probability nodes and select the best decision branch at all decision nodes. The sequence of optimal decision branches determines the optimal decision strategy for the problem. The Management Science in Action article on drug testing for student athletes describes how Santa Clara University used decision analysis to make a decision regarding whether to implement a drug testing program for student athletes.

### Expected Value of Sample Information

In the PDC problem, the market research study is the sample information that provides the optimal decision strategy. The expected value associated with the market research study is $15.93. In Section 14.3 we showed that the best expected value if the market research study is *not* undertaken is $14.20. Thus, we can conclude that the difference,

# MANAGEMENT SCIENCE IN ACTION

## DECISION ANALYSIS AND DRUG TESTING FOR STUDENT ATHLETES*

The athletic governing board of Santa Clara University considered whether to implement a drug-testing program for the university's intercollegiate athletes. The decision analysis framework contains two decision alternatives: implement a drug-testing program and do not implement a drug-testing program. Each student athlete is either a drug user or not a drug user, so these two possibilities are considered to be the states of nature for the problem.

If the drug-testing program is implemented, student athletes will be required to take a drug-screening test. Results of the test will be either positive (test indicates a potential drug user) or negative (test does not indicate a potential drug user). The test outcomes are considered to be the sample information in the decision problem. If the test result

is negative, no follow-up action will be taken. However, if the test result is positive, follow-up action will be taken to determine whether the student athlete actually is a drug user. The payoffs include the cost of not identifying a drug user and the cost of falsely identifying a nonuser.

Decision analysis showed that if the test result is positive, a reasonably high probability still exists that the student athlete is not a drug user. The cost and other problems associated with this type of misleading test result were considered significant. Consequently, the athletic governing board decided not to implement the drug-testing program.

*Charles D. Feinstein, "Deciding Whether to Test Student Athletes for Drug Use," *Interfaces* 20, no. 3 (May–June 1990): 80–87.

$15.93 - $14.20 = $1.73, is the **expected value of sample information.** In other words, conducting the market research study adds $1.73 million to the PDC expected value. In general, the expected value of sample information is as follows:

$$EVSI = |EVwSI - EVwoSI| \qquad (14.9)$$

where

$\quad\quad EVSI$ = expected value of sample information

$\quad\quad EVwSI$ = expected value *with* sample information about the states of nature

$\quad\quad EVwoSI$ = expected value *without* sample information about the states of nature

Note the role of the absolute value in equation (14.9). That is, for minimization problems the expected value with sample information always is less than or equal to the expected value without sample information. In this case, EVSI is the magnitude of the difference between EVwSI and EVwoSI; thus, by taking the absolute value of the difference as shown in equation (14.9), we can handle both the maximization and minimization cases with one equation.

### Efficiency of Sample Information

In Section 14.3 we showed that the expected value of perfect information (EVPI) for the PDC problem is $3.2 million. We never anticipated that the market research report would obtain perfect information, but we can use an **efficiency** measure to express the value of the market research information. With perfect information having an efficiency rating of 100%, the efficiency rating E for sample information is computed as follows.

$$E = \frac{EVSI}{EVPI} \times 100 \qquad (14.10)$$

For the PDC problem,

$$E = \frac{1.73}{3.2} \times 100 = 54.1\%$$

In other words, the information from the market research study is 54.1% as efficient as perfect information.

Low efficiency ratings for sample information might lead the decision maker to look for other types of information. However, high efficiency ratings indicate that the sample information is almost as good as perfect information and that additional sources of information would not yield significantly better results.

## 14.6  COMPUTING BRANCH PROBABILITIES

In Section 14.5 the branch probabilities for the PDC decision tree probability nodes were specified in the problem description. No computations were required to determine these probabilities. In this section we show how **Bayes Theorem,** a topic that is covered in most introductory courses on probability, can be used to compute the branch probabilities for decision trees.

The PDC decision tree is shown again in Figure 14.7. Let

$$F = \text{Favorable market research report}$$
$$U = \text{Unfavorable market research report}$$
$$s_1 = \text{High acceptance (state of nature 1)}$$
$$s_2 = \text{Low acceptance (state of nature 2)}$$

At probability node 2, we need to know the branch probabilities $P(F)$ and $P(U)$. At probability nodes 6, 7, and 8, we need to know the branch probabilities $P(s_1 \mid F)$, the probability

## Figure 14.7    THE PDC DECISION TREE

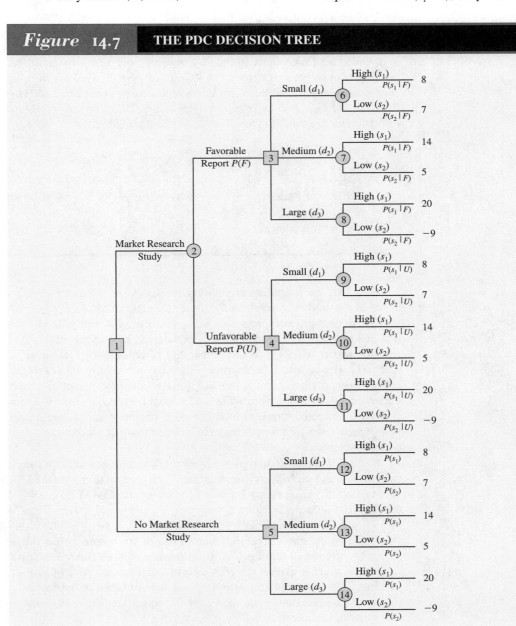

of state of nature 1 given a favorable market research report, and $P(s_2 \mid F)$, the probability of state of nature 2 given a favorable market research report. $P(s_1 \mid F)$ and $P(s_2 \mid F)$ are referred to as **conditional probabilities.** At probability nodes 9, 10, and 11, we need to know the branch probabilities $P(s_1 \mid U)$ and $P(s_2 \mid U)$; note that these are also conditional probabilities, denoting the probabilities of the two states of nature *given* that the market research report is unfavorable. Finally at probability nodes 12, 13, and 14, we need the probabilities for the states of nature, $P(s_1)$ and $P(s_2)$, if the market research study is not undertaken.

In making the probability computations, we need to know PDC's best estimates of the probabilities for the two states of nature, $P(s_1)$ and $P(s_2)$; these are the prior probabilities as discussed earlier. In addition, we must know the conditional probability of the market research outcomes (the sample information) *given* each state of nature. For example, we need to know the conditional probability of a favorable market research report given that the state of nature is high acceptance of the PDC project; note that this conditional probability of $F$ given state of nature $s_1$ is written $P(F \mid s_1)$. To carry out the probability calculations, we will need conditional probabilities for all sample outcomes given all states of nature, that is, $P(F \mid s_1)$, $P(F \mid s_2)$, $P(U \mid s_1)$ and $P(U \mid s_2)$. In the PDC problem, we assume that the following estimates are available for these conditional probabilities.

|  | Market Research | |
| --- | --- | --- |
| State of Nature | Favorable, $F$ | Unfavorable, $U$ |
| High acceptance, $s_1$ | $P(F \mid s_1) = 0.90$ | $P(U \mid s_1) = 0.10$ |
| Low acceptance, $s_2$ | $P(F \mid s_2) = 0.25$ | $P(U \mid s_2) = 0.75$ |

Note that the preceding probability estimates provide a reasonable degree of confidence in the market research study. If the true state of nature is $s_1$, the probability of a favorable market research report is 0.90, and the probability of an unfavorable market research report is 0.10. If the true state of nature is $s_2$, the probability of a favorable market research report is 0.25, and the probability of an unfavorable market research report is 0.75. The reason for a 0.25 probability of a potentially misleading favorable market research report for state of nature $s_2$ is that when some potential buyers first hear about the new condominium project, their enthusiasm may lead them to overstate their real interest in it. A potential buyer's initial favorable response can change quickly to a "no thank you" when later faced with the reality of signing a purchase contract and making a down payment.

In the following discussion, we present a tabular approach as a convenient method for carrying out the probability computations. The computations for the PDC problem based on a favorable market research report ($F$) are summarized in Table 14.7. The steps used to develop this table are as follows.

Step 1   In column 1 enter the states of nature. In column 2 enter the *prior probabilities* for the states of nature. In column 3 enter the *conditional probabilities* of a favorable market research report ($F$) given each state of nature.

Step 2   In column 4 compute the **joint probabilities** by multiplying the prior probability values in column 2 by the corresponding conditional probability values in column 3.

Step 3  Sum the joint probabilities in column 4 to obtain the probability of a favorable market research report, $P(F)$.

Step 4  Divide each joint probability in column 4 by $P(F) = 0.77$ to obtain the revised or *posterior probabilities*, $P(s_1 \mid F)$ and $P(s_2 \mid F)$.

Table 14.7 shows that the probability of obtaining a favorable market research report is $P(F) = 0.77$. In addition, $P(s_1 \mid F) = 0.94$ and $P(s_2 \mid F) = 0.06$. In particular, note that favorable market research report will prompt a revised or posterior probability of 0.94 that the market acceptance of the condominium will be high, $s_1$.

The tabular probability computation procedure must be repeated for each possible sample information outcome. Thus, Table 14.8 shows the computations of the branch probabilities of the PDC problem based on an unfavorable market research report. Note that the probability of obtaining an unfavorable market research report is $P(U) = 0.23$. If an unfavorable report is obtained, the posterior probability of a high market acceptance, $s_1$, is 0.35 and of a low market acceptance, $s_2$, is 0.65. The branch probabilities from Table 14.7 and 14.8 were shown on the PDC decision tree in Figure 14.6.

The previous discussion shows an underlying relationship between the probabilities of the various probability branches in a decision tree. To assume different prior probabilities, $P(s_1)$ and $P(s_2)$, without determining how these changes would alter $P(F)$ and $P(U)$, as well as the posterior probabilities $P(s_1 \mid F)$, $P(s_2 \mid F)$, $P(s_1 \mid U)$ and $P(s_2 \mid U)$ would be inappropriate. Fortunately, a spreadsheet can be helpful in making the computations required to update these probabilities.

Problem 22 asks you to compute the posterior probabilities.

### Table 14.7  BRANCH PROBABILITIES FOR THE PDC CONDOMINIUM PROJECT BASED ON A FAVORABLE MARKET RESEARCH REPORT

| States of Nature $s_j$ | Prior Probabilities $P(s_j)$ | Conditional Probabilities $P(F \mid s_j)$ | Joint Probabilities $P(F \cap s_j)$ | Posterior Probabilities $P(s_j \mid F)$ |
|---|---|---|---|---|
| $s_1$ | 0.8 | 0.90 | 0.72 | 0.94 |
| $s_2$ | 0.2 | 0.25 | 0.05 | 0.06 |
|  |  |  | $P(F) = 0.77$ |  |

### Table 14.8  BRANCH PROBABILITIES FOR THE PDC CONDOMINIUM PROJECT BASED ON AN UNFAVORABLE MARKET RESEARCH REPORT

| States of Nature $s_j$ | Prior Probabilities $P(s_j)$ | Conditional Probabilities $P(U \mid s_j)$ | Joint Probabilities $P(U \cap s_j)$ | Posterior Probabilities $P(s_j \mid U)$ |
|---|---|---|---|---|
| $s_1$ | 0.8 | 0.10 | 0.08 | 0.35 |
| $s_2$ | 0.2 | 0.75 | 0.15 | 0.65 |
|  |  |  | $P(U) = 0.23$ |  |

## 14.7   UTILITY AND DECISION MAKING

In the previous section of this chapter we expressed the payoffs in terms of monetary values. When probability information was available about the states of nature, we recommended selecting the decision alternative with the best expected monetary value. However, in some situations the decision alternative with the best expected monetary value may not be the most desirable decision.

By the most desirable decision we mean the one that is preferred by the decision maker after taking into account not only monetary value, but also other factors such as the risk associated with the outcomes. Examples of situations in which selecting the decision alternative with the best expected monetary value may not lead to the selection of the most preferred decision are numerous. One such example is the decision to buy house insurance. Clearly, buying insurance for a house does not provide a higher expected monetary value than not buying such insurance. Otherwise, insurance companies could not pay expenses and make a profit. Similarly, many people buy tickets for state lotteries even though the expected monetary value of such a decision is negative.

Should we conclude that persons or businesses that buy insurance or participate in lotteries do so because they are unable to determine which decision alternative leads to the best expected monetary value? On the contrary, we take the view that in these cases monetary value is not the sole measure of the true worth of the outcome to the decision maker.

We will see that in cases where expected monetary value does not lead to the most preferred decision alternative, expressing the value (or worth) of an outcome in terms of its *utility* will permit the use of *expected utility* to identify the most desirable decision.

### The Meaning of Utility

**Utility** is a measure of the total worth of a particular outcome; it reflects the decision maker's attitude toward a collection of factors such as profit, loss, and risk. As an example of a case where utility can help in selecting the best decision alternative, let us consider the problem faced by Swofford, Inc., a relatively small real estate investment firm located in Atlanta, Georgia. Swofford currently has two investment opportunities, which require approximately the same cash outlay. The cash requirements necessary prohibit Swofford from making more than one investment at this time. Consequently, three possible decision alternatives may be considered.

The three decision alternatives, denoted by $d_1$, $d_2$, and $d_3$, are as follows:

$$d_1 = \text{make investment A}$$
$$d_2 = \text{make investment B}$$
$$d_3 = \text{do not invest}$$

The monetary payoffs associated with the investment opportunities depend largely on what happens to the real estate market during the next 6 months. Real estate prices will go up, remain stable, or go down. Thus, the states of nature, denoted by $s_1$, $s_2$, and $s_3$, are as follows:

$$s_1 = \text{real estate prices go up}$$
$$s_2 = \text{real estate prices remain stable}$$
$$s_3 = \text{real estate prices go down}$$

Using the best information available, Swofford has estimated the profits or payoffs associated with each decision alternative and state-of-nature combination. The resulting payoff table is shown in Table 14.9.

The best estimate of the probability that prices will go up is 0.3, the best estimate of the probability that prices will remain stable is 0.5, and the best estimate of the probability that real estate prices will go down is 0.2. Thus, the expected values for the three decision alternatives are

$$EV(d_1) = 0.3(\$30,000) + 0.5(\$20,000) + 0.2(-\$50,000) = \$9,000$$
$$EV(d_2) = 0.3(\$50,000) + 0.5(-\$20,000) + 0.2(-\$30,000) = -\$1,000$$
$$EV(d_3) = 0.3(\$0) + 0.5(\$0) + 0.2(\$0) = \$0$$

Using the expected value approach, the optimal decision is to select investment A, with an expected monetary value of $9000. Is this really the best decision alternative? Let us consider some other relevant factors that relate to Swofford's capability for absorbing the $50,000 loss if investment A is made and real estate prices go down.

It turns out that Swofford's financial position is very weak. This fact was partly reflected in Swofford's ability to undertake, at most, one investment at the current time. More important, however, the firm's president feels that if the next investment results in substantial losses, Swofford's future will be in jeopardy. Although the expected value approach leads to a recommendation for $d_1$, do you think this is the decision the firm's president would prefer? We suspect that $d_2$ or $d_3$ would be selected to avoid the possibility of incurring a $50,000 loss. In fact, it is reasonable to believe that if a loss as great as even $30,000 could drive Swofford out of business, the president would select $d_3$, feeling that both investment A and investment B are too risky for Swofford's current financial position.

The way we resolve Swofford's dilemma is first to determine Swofford's utility for the various monetary outcomes. Recall that the utility of any outcome is the total worth of that outcome, taking into account the risks and payoffs involved. If the utilities for the various outcomes are assessed correctly, then the decision alternative with the highest expected utility is the most preferred or best alternative.

## Developing Utilities for Payoffs

The procedure we will use to establish utility values for the payoffs requires that we first assign a utility value to the best and worst possible payoffs in the decision situation. Any values will work as long as the utility assigned to the best payoff is greater than the utility assigned to the worst payoff. In Swofford's case, Table 14.9 shows that $50,000 is the best

**Table 14.9**    PAYOFF TABLE FOR SWOFFORD, INC. (PROFIT IN $)

| Decision Alternative | State of Nature | | |
| | Prices Up $s_1$ | Prices Stable $s_2$ | Prices Down $s_3$ |
| --- | --- | --- | --- |
| Investment A, $d_1$ | 30,000 | 20,000 | −50,000 |
| Investment B, $d_2$ | 50,000 | −20,000 | −30,000 |
| Do not invest, $d_3$ | 0 | 0 | 0 |

payoff and $-\$50,000$ is the worst payoff. Suppose, then, that we arbitrarily make the following assignments of these two payoffs:

$$\text{Utility of } -\$50,000 = U(-\$50,000) = 0$$
$$\text{Utility of } \quad \$50,000 = U(\$50,000) \quad = 10$$

Now let us see how we can determine the utility associated with every other payoff.

Consider the process of establishing the utility of a payoff of $30,000. First, we ask Swofford's president to state a preference between a guaranteed $30,000 payoff and the opportunity to engage in the following **lottery,** or bet:

Lottery: Swofford obtains a payoff of $50,000 with probability $p$
and a payoff of $-\$50,000$ with probability $(1 - p)$.

If $p$ is very close to 1, Swofford's president would prefer the lottery to the certain payoff of $30,000 since the firm would virtually guarantee itself a payoff of $50,000. On the other hand, if $p$ is very close to 0, the president would clearly prefer the guarantee of $30,000. In any event, as $p$ changes continuously from 0 to 1, the preference for the guaranteed payoff of $30,000 will change at some point into a preference for the lottery. At the change point, the president is indifferent between the guaranteed payoff of $30,000 and the lottery. For example, let us assume that when $p = 0.95$, the president is indifferent between the certain payoff of $30,000 and the lottery. Given this value of $p$, we can compute the utility of a $30,000 payoff as follows:

$$U(\$30,000) = pU(\$50,000) + (1 - p)U(-\$50,000)$$
$$= 0.95(10) + (0.05)(0)$$
$$= 9.5$$

Obviously, if we had started with a different assignment of utilities for payoffs of $50,000 and $-\$50,000$, we would have ended up with a different utility for $30,000. Hence, we must conclude that the utility assigned to each payoff is not unique, but is relative to the initial choice of utilities for the best and worst payoffs. We will discuss this factor further at the end of this section. For now, however, we will continue to use a value of 10 for the utility of $50,000 and a value of 0 for the utility of $-\$50,000$.

Before computing the utility for the other payoffs, let us consider the significance of assigning a utility of 9.5 to a payoff of $30,000. Clearly, when $p = 0.95$, the expected value of the lottery is

$$EV(\text{lottery}) = 0.95(\$50,000) + 0.05(-\$50,000)$$
$$= \$47,500 - \$2,500$$
$$= \$45,000$$

We see that although the expected value of the lottery when $p = 0.95$ is $45,000, Swofford's president would just as soon take a guaranteed payoff of $30,000 and thus take a conservative, or risk-avoiding, viewpoint. That is, the president would rather have $30,000 for certain than risk anything greater than a 5% chance of incurring a loss of $50,000. One can view the difference between the EV of $45,000 for the lottery and the $30,000 guaranteed payoff as the risk premium that the president would be willing to pay to avoid the 5% chance of losing $50,000.

To compute the utility associated with a payoff of $-\$20,000$, we must ask Swofford's president to state a preference between a guaranteed $-\$20,000$ payoff and the opportunity to engage in the following lottery.

Lottery: Swofford obtains a payoff of $50,000 with probability $p$
and a payoff of $-\$50,000$ with probability $(1 - p)$.

Note that this is exactly the same lottery we used to establish the utility of a payoff of $30,000. In fact, this lottery will be used to establish the utility for any monetary value in the Swofford payoff table. Using this lottery, then, we must ask the president to state the value of $p$ that provides an indifference between a guaranteed payoff of $-\$20,000$ and the lottery. For example, we might begin by asking the president to choose between a certain loss of $20,000 and the lottery with a payoff of $50,000 with probability $p = 0.90$ and a payoff of $-\$50,000$ with probability $(1 - p) = 0.10$. What answer do you think we would get? Surely, with this high probability of obtaining a payoff of $50,000, the president would elect the lottery. Next, we might ask if $p = 0.85$ would result in indifference between the loss of $20,000 for certain and the lottery. Again, the president might tell us that the lottery would be preferred. Suppose that we continue in this fashion until we get to $p = 0.55$, where we find that with this value of $p$, the president is indifferent between the payoff of $-\$20,000$ and the lottery. That is, for any value of $p$ less than 0.55, the president would rather take a loss of $20,000 for certain than risk the potential loss of $50,000 with the lottery; for any value of $p$ above 0.55, the president would elect the lottery. Thus, the utility assigned to a payoff of $-\$20,000$ is

$$U(-\$20,000) = pU(50,000) + (1 - p)U(-\$50,000)$$
$$= 0.55(10) + 0.45(0)$$
$$= 5.5$$

Again, let us examine the significance of this assignment as compared with the expected value approach. When $p = 0.55$, the expected value of the lottery is

$$EV(\text{lottery}) = 0.55(\$50,000) + 0.45(-\$50,000)$$
$$= \$27,500 - \$22,500$$
$$= \$5,000$$

Thus, the president would just as soon absorb a loss of $20,000 for certain as take the lottery, even though the expected value of the lottery is $5000. Once again we see the conservative, or risk-avoiding, point of view of Swofford's president.

In the two preceding examples where we computed the utility for a specific monetary payoff, $M$, we first found the probability $p$ where the decision maker was indifferent between a guaranteed payoff of $M$ and a lottery with a payoff of $50,000 with probability $p$ and $-\$50,000$ with probability $(1 - p)$. The utility of $M$ was then computed as

$$U(M) = pU(\$50,000) + (1 - p)U(-\$50,000)$$
$$= p(10) + (1 - p)0$$
$$= 10p$$

Using the above procedure, utility values for the rest of the payoffs in Swofford's problem were developed. The results are presented in Table 14.10.

Now that we have determined the utility value of each of the possible monetary values, we can write the original payoff table in terms of utility values. Table 14.11 shows the utility for the various outcomes in the Swofford problem. The notation we will use for the entries in the utility table is $U_{ij}$, which denotes the utility associated with decision alternative $d_i$ and state of nature $s_j$. Using this notation, we see that $U_{23}, = 4.0$.

| Table 14.10 | UTILITY OF MONETARY PAYOFFS FOR THE SWOFFORD, INC., PROBLEM |
|---|---|

| Monetary Value | Indifference Value of $p$ | Utility Value |
|---|---|---|
| $ 50,000 | Does not apply | 10.0 |
| 30,000 | 0.95 | 9.5 |
| 20,000 | 0.90 | 9.0 |
| 0 | 0.75 | 7.5 |
| −20,000 | 0.55 | 5.5 |
| −30,000 | 0.40 | 4.0 |
| −50,000 | Does not apply | 0.0 |

| Table 14.11 | UTILITY TABLE FOR SWOFFORD, INC., PROBLEM |
|---|---|

| | State of Nature | | |
|---|---|---|---|
| **Decision Alternative** | **Prices Up** $s_1$ | **Prices Stable** $s_2$ | **Prices Down** $s_3$ |
| Investment A, $d_1$ | 9.5 | 9.0 | 0.0 |
| Investment B, $d_2$ | 10.0 | 5.5 | 4.0 |
| Do not invest, $d_3$ | 7.5 | 7.5 | 7.5 |

### The Expected Utility Approach

We can now apply the expected value computations introduced in Section 14.3 to the pay-offs in Table 14.11 in order to select an optimal decision alternative for Swofford, Inc. However, because utility values represent such a special case of expected value, we will refer to the expected value when applied to utility values as the *expected utility* (EU). In this way, we will avoid any possible confusion between the expected value for the original payoff table and the expected value for the payoff table consisting of *utility values*. Thus, the **expected utility approach** requires the analyst to compute the expected utility for each decision alternative and then select the alternative yielding the best expected utility. If there are $N$ possible states of nature, the expected utility of a decision alternative $d_i$ is given by

$$\text{EU}(d_i) = \sum_{j=1}^{N} P(s_j)U_{ij} \tag{14.11}$$

The expected utility for each of the decision alternatives in the Swofford problem is computed as follows:

$$\text{EU}(d_1) = 0.3(9.5) + 0.5(9.0) + 0.2(0) = 7.35$$
$$\text{EU}(d_2) = 0.3(10) + 0.5(5.5) + 0.2(4.0) = 6.55$$
$$\text{EU}(d_3) = 0.3(7.5) + 0.5(7.5) + 0.2(7.5) = 7.50$$

Problem 28 asks you to use the expected utility approach to determine the optimal decision.

We see that the optimal decision using the expected utility approach is $d_3$, do not invest. The ranking of alternatives according to the president's utility assignments and the associated monetary value is as follows:

| Ranking of Decision Alternatives | Expected Utility | Expected Monetary Value |
|---|---|---|
| Do not invest | 7.50 | $ 0 |
| Investment A | 7.35 | 9000 |
| Investment B | 6.55 | $-1000$ |

Note that whereas investment A had the highest expected monetary value of $9000, the analysis indicates that Swofford should decline this investment. The rationale behind not selecting Investment A is that the 0.2 probability of a $50,000 loss was considered by Swofford's president to involve a serious risk. The seriousness of this risk and its associated impact on the company were not adequately reflected by the expected monetary value of investment A. It was necessary to assess the utility for each payoff to adequately take this risk into account.

Unfortunately, the determination of the appropriate utilities is not a trivial task. As we have seen, measuring utility requires a degree of subjectivity on the part of the decision maker, and different decision makers will have different utility functions. This aspect of utility often causes decision makers to feel uncomfortable about using the expected utility approach. However, if we encounter a decision situation in which we are convinced monetary value is not the only relevant measure of performance, utility analysis should be considered.

## NOTES and Comments

1. In the Swofford problem, we used a utility of 10 for the largest possible payoff and 0 for the smallest. Had we chosen 1 for the utility of the largest payoff and 0 for the utility of the smallest, the utility for any monetary value $M$ would have been the value of $p$ at which the decision maker was indifferent between a certain payoff of $M$ and a lottery in which the best payoff is obtained with probability of $p$ and the worst payoff is obtained with probability of $(1 - p)$. Thus the utility for any monetary value would have been equal to the probability of earning the highest payoff. Often, this choice is made because of the ease in computation. We chose not to do so to emphasize the distinction between the utility values and the indifference probabilities for the lottery.

2. Generally, when the payoffs for a particular decision-making problem fall into a reasonable range—the best is not too good and the worst is not too bad—decision makers tend to express preferences in agreement with the expected monetary value approach. Thus, as a guideline we suggest asking the decision maker to consider the best and worst possible payoffs for a problem and assess their reasonableness. If the decision maker believes they are in the reasonable range, the expected monetary value criterion can be used. However, if the payoffs appear unreasonably large or unreasonably small and if the decision maker feels monetary values do not adequately reflect the true preferences for the payoffs, a utility analysis of the problem should be considered.

······················································································/ /··············

## SUMMARY

In this chapter we showed how decision analysis can be used to solve problems with reasonably few decision alternatives and reasonably few states of nature. The goal of decision analysis is to identify the best decision alternative in the face of uncertain or risk-filled future events known as *states of nature.*

We presented three approaches—optimistic, conservative, and minimax regret—for decision making without probabilities. When probability information about the states of nature was available, we used the expected value approach to determine the best decision alternative. In Section 14.5, we introduced the use of sample information to develop an optimal decision strategy. This approach results in a more complex decision problem that can be solved by using a decision tree. A decision tree approach is general and can be used to solve a wide variety of decision analysis problems.

In Section 14.6, we pointed out that probabilities on decision tree branches can be interrelated such that changes in some of the branch probabilities may alter other branch probabilities. We presented a tabular computational procedure that could be used to compute the branch probabilities.

In the last section, we suggested that the expected utility approach should be used in situations in which monetary value is not the only relevant measure of performance. Unlike monetary value, utility is a measure of the total worth of an outcome resulting from the choice of a decision alternative and the occurrence of a state of nature. As such, utility takes into account the decision maker's attitude toward the profit, loss, and risk associated with an outcome. In the examples, we have seen how the use of utility analysis can lead to decision recommendations that differ from those that would be selected using the expected monetary value approach.

······················································································/ /··············

## GLOSSARY

**States of nature**  Uncontrollable future events that affect the payoff associated with a decision alternative.

**Payoff**  An outcome measure such as profit, cost, or time. Each combination of a decision alternative and a state of nature has an associated payoff.

**Payoff table**  A tabular representation of the payoffs for a decision problem.

**Decision tree**  A graphical representation of the decision problem that shows the sequential nature of the decision-making process.

**Node**  An intersection or junction point of a decision tree.

**Branch**  A line or arc connecting nodes of a decision tree.

**Optimistic approach**  An approach to choosing a decision alternative without using probabilities. For a maximization problem, it leads to choosing the decision alternative corresponding to the largest payoff; for a minimization problem, it leads to choosing the decision alternative corresponding to the smallest payoff.

**Conservative approach**  An approach to choosing a decision alternative without using probabilities. For a maximization problem, it leads to choosing the decision alternative that maximizes the minimum payoff; for a minimization problem, it leads to choosing the decision alternative that minimizes the maximum payoff.

**Minimax regret approach**  An approach to choosing a decision alternative without using probabilities. For each alternative, the maximum regret is computed. This approach leads to choosing the decision alternative that minimizes the maximum regret.

**Opportunity loss, or regret**  The amount of loss (lower profit or higher cost) from not making the best decision for each state of nature.

**Expected value approach**  An approach to choosing a decision alternative that is based on the expected value of each decision alternative. The recommended decision alternative is the one that provides the best expected value.

**Expected value (EV)**  For a decision alternative, it is the weighted average of the payoffs. The weights are the state-of-nature probabilities.

**Expected value of perfect information (EVPI)**  The expected value of information that would tell the decision maker exactly which state of nature is going to occur (i.e., perfect information).

**Sensitivity analysis**  The study of how changes in the probability estimates for the states of nature affect the recommended decision alternative.

**Prior probabilities**  The probabilities of the states of nature prior to obtaining sample information.

**Sample information**  New information obtained through research or experimentation that enables an updating or revision of the state-of-nature probabilities.

**Posterior (revised) probabilities**  The probabilities of the states of nature after revising the prior probabilities based on sample information.

**Expected value of sample information (EVSI)**  The difference between the expected value of an optimal strategy based on sample information and the "best" expected value without any sample information.

**Efficiency**  The ratio of EVSI to EVPI; perfect information is 100% efficient.

**Bayes theorem**  A probability expression that enables the use of sample information to revise prior probabilities.

**Conditional probabilities**  The probabilities of the sample information, given an assumed state of nature.

**Joint probabilities**  The probabilities of both sample information and a particular state of nature occurring simultaneously.

**Utility**  A measure of the total worth of an outcome reflecting a decision maker's attitude toward considerations such as profit and loss, and intangibles such as risk.

**Lottery**  A hypothetical investment alternative with a probability $p$ of obtaining the best possible payoff and a probability of $(1 - p)$ of obtaining the worst possible payoff.

**Expected utility approach**  An approach that considers the expected utility for each decision alternative and then selects the decision alternative yielding the highest expected utility.

## PROBLEMS

**1.** The following payoff table shows profit for a decision analysis problem with two decisions and three states of nature.
   **a.** Construct a decision tree for this problem.
   **b.** If the decision maker knows nothing about the probabilities of the three states of nature, what is the recommended decision using the optimistic, conservative, and minimax regret approaches?

|  | State of Nature | | |
|---|---|---|---|
| **Decision Alternative** | $s_1$ | $s_2$ | $s_3$ |
| $d_1$ | 250 | 100 | 25 |
| $d_2$ | 100 | 100 | 75 |

**2.** Suppose that a decision maker faced with four decision alternatives and four states of nature develops the following profit payoff table.

|  | State of Nature | | | |
|---|---|---|---|---|
| **Decision Alternative** | $s_1$ | $s_2$ | $s_3$ | $s_4$ |
| $d_1$ | 14 | 9 | 10 | 5 |
| $d_2$ | 11 | 10 | 8 | 7 |
| $d_3$ | 9 | 10 | 10 | 11 |
| $d_4$ | 8 | 10 | 11 | 13 |

   **a.** If the decision maker knows nothing about the probabilities of the four states of nature, what is the recommended decision using the optimistic, conservative, and minimax regret approaches?
   **b.** Which approach do you prefer? Explain. Is establishing the most appropriate approach before analyzing the problem important for the decision maker? Explain.
   **c.** Assume that the payoff table provides *cost* rather than profit payoffs. What is the recommended decision using the optimistic, conservative, and minimax regret approaches?

**3.** Southland Corporation's decision to produce a new line of recreational products has resulted in the need to construct either a small plant or a large plant. The selection of plant size depends on how the marketplace reacts to the new product line. To conduct an analysis, marketing management has decided to view the possible long-run demand as either low, medium, or high. The following payoff table shows the projected profit in millions of dollars:

|  | Long-Run Demand | | |
|---|---|---|---|
| **Decision Alternative** | **Low** | **Medium** | **High** |
| Small plant | 150 | 200 | 200 |
| Large plant | 50 | 200 | 500 |

a.  Construct a decision tree for this problem.
b.  Recommend a decision based on the use of the optimistic, conservative, and minimax regret approaches.

4. Investment Advisors, Inc., has three investment strategies under consideration. Profits from the strategies will depend on what happens to the prime interest rate over the next three months. Payoffs (in thousand of dollars) are shown.

|  | State of Nature | | |
|---|---|---|---|
|  | Rate Decrease | No Change | Rate Increase |
| Decision Alternative | $s_1$ | $s_2$ | $s_3$ |
| Strategy $d_1$ | 50 | 70 | 40 |
| Strategy $d_2$ | 55 | 35 | 80 |
| Strategy $d_3$ | 15 | 60 | 70 |

What investment strategy would you recommend based on the use of the optimistic, pessimistic, and minimax regret approaches?

5. The following profit payoff table was presented in Problem 1. Suppose that the decision maker has obtained the probability estimates: $P(s_1) = 0.65$, $P(s_2) = 0.15$, and $P(s_3) = 0.20$. Use the expected value approach to determine the optimal decision.

**SELF TEST**

|  | State of Nature | | |
|---|---|---|---|
| Decision Alternative | $s_1$ | $s_2$ | $s_3$ |
| $d_1$ | 250 | 100 | 25 |
| $d_2$ | 100 | 100 | 75 |

6. The profit payoff table presented in Problem 2 is repeated here.

|  | State of Nature | | | |
|---|---|---|---|---|
| Decision Alternative | $s_1$ | $s_2$ | $s_3$ | $s_4$ |
| $d_1$ | 14 | 9 | 10 | 5 |
| $d_2$ | 11 | 10 | 8 | 7 |
| $d_3$ | 9 | 10 | 10 | 11 |
| $d_4$ | 8 | 10 | 11 | 13 |

Suppose that the decision maker obtains information that enables the following probability estimates to be made: $P(s_1) = 0.5$, $P(s_2) = 0.2$, $P(s_3) = 0.2$, and $P(s_4) = 0.1$.
a.  Use the expected value approach to determine the optimal decision.
b.  Now assume that the entries in the payoff table are costs; use the expected value approach to determine the optimal decision.

7. Hudson Corporation is considering three options for managing its data processing operation: continuing with its own staff, hiring an outside vendor to do the managing (referred to as *outsourcing*), or using a combination of its own staff and an outside vendor. The cost of the operation depends on future demand. The annual cost of each decision alternative and state of nature (in $000s) is as follows.

| | State of Nature | | |
|---|---|---|---|
| | **High Demand** | **Medium Demand** | **Low Demand** |
| **Decision Alternative** | $s_1$ | $s_2$ | $s_3$ |
| Own staff, $d_1$ | 650 | 650 | 600 |
| Vendor, $d_2$ | 900 | 600 | 300 |
| Combination, $d_3$ | 800 | 650 | 500 |

If the demand probabilities are 0.2, 0.5, and 0.3, which decision alternative will minimize the expected cost of the data processing operation? What is the expected annual cost associated with that recommendation?

**SELF TEST**

8. The following payoff table shows the profit for a decision problem with two states of nature and two decision alternatives.

| | State of Nature | |
|---|---|---|
| **Decision Alternative** | $s_1$ | $s_2$ |
| $d_1$ | 10 | 1 |
| $d_2$ | 4 | 3 |

Use graphical sensitivity analysis to determine the range of probabilities of state of nature $s_1$ for which each of the decision alternatives has the largest expected value.

9. The following payoff table shows the profit for a decision problem with two states of nature and three decision alternatives.

| | State of Nature | |
|---|---|---|
| **Decision Alternative** | $s_1$ | $s_2$ |
| $d_1$ | 80 | 50 |
| $d_2$ | 65 | 85 |
| $d_3$ | 30 | 100 |

Use graphical sensitivity analysis to determine the range of values for the probability of state of nature $s_1$ for which each of the decision alternatives is best.

10. Political Systems, Inc., is a new firm specializing in information services such as surveys and data analysis for individuals running for political office. The firm is opening its headquarters in Chicago and is considering three office locations, which differ in cost due to square footage and office equipment requirements. The profit projections shown (in thousands of dollars) for each location were based on both high demand and low demand states of nature.

| | State of Nature | |
|---|---|---|
| **Decision Alternative** | **High Demand,** $s_1$ | **Low Demand,** $s_2$ |
| Location A | 200 | −20 |
| Location B | 120 | 10 |
| Location C | 100 | 60 |

a.  Initially, management is uncomfortable stating probabilities for the states of nature. Let $p$ denote the probability of the high demand state of nature. What does graphical sensitivity analysis tell management about location preferences? Can any location be dropped from consideration? Why or why not?

b.  After further review, management estimated the probability of a high demand at 0.65. Based on the results in part (a), which location should be selected? What is the expected value associated with that decision?

11.  Six months ago, Reynold's Properties purchased an option to buy a tract of land that has the potential of becoming desirable commercial property. Currently, another real estate investment firm has offered to purchase Reynold's option. If Reynold's sells its option, it will experience a $250,000 profit. On the other hand, if Reynold's keeps the option, the success of the project depends upon what happens to the real estate market over the next year. In the worst case, Reynold's could lose $1.5 million, while in the best case Reynold's could have a $4 million profit. The decision alternatives, states of nature, and payoffs in $ millions are as follows:

| | State of Nature | | |
|---|---|---|---|
| **Decision Alternative** | **Market Down** | **Market Steady** | **Market Up** |
| Sell option | 0.25 | 0.25 | 0.25 |
| Keep option | −1.50 | 1.00 | 4.00 |

a.  If Reynold's managers believe that the probabilities of the real estate market being down, steady, and up are 0.6, 0.3, and 0.1, respectively, what decision alternative is recommended? What is the expected value of this recommendation?

b.  Suppose that the three probabilities are revised to 0.5, 0.3, and 0.2. What should Reynold's do? Repeat this question if the three probabilities are revised to 0.4, 0.4, and 0.2. What do the results suggest about Reynold's decision?

c.  Suppose that after further consideration, Reynold's managers conclude that 0.1 is a realistic probability of the market being up. What would the probability of the market being down have to be for the sell option to be the recommended decision alternative? Would this information be helpful in making a final decision regarding whether to sell or keep the option? Explain.

12.  The following profit payoff table was presented in Problems 1 and 5.

SELF TEST

| | State of Nature | | |
|---|---|---|---|
| **Decision Alternative** | $s_1$ | $s_2$ | $s_3$ |
| $d_1$ | 250 | 100 | 25 |
| $d_2$ | 100 | 100 | 75 |

The probabilities for the states of nature are: $P(s_1) = 0.65$, $P(s_2) = 0.15$, and $P(s_3) = 0.20$.
a. What is the optimal decision strategy if perfect information were available?
b. What is the expected value for the decision strategy developed in part (a)?
c. Using the expected value approach, what is the recommended decision? What is its expected value?
d. What is the expected value of perfect information?

13. The following profit payoff table was presented in Problems 2 and 6.

| Decision Alternative | State of Nature | | | |
|---|---|---|---|---|
| | $s_1$ | $s_2$ | $s_3$ | $s_4$ |
| $d_1$ | 14 | 9 | 10 | 5 |
| $d_2$ | 11 | 10 | 8 | 7 |
| $d_3$ | 9 | 10 | 10 | 11 |
| $d_4$ | 8 | 10 | 11 | 13 |

The probabilities are $P(s_1) = 0.5$, $P(s_2) = 0.2$, $P(s_3) = 0.2$, and $P(s_4) = 0.1$.
a. What is the optimal decision strategy if perfect information were available?
b. What is the expected value for the decision strategy developed in part (a)?
c. Using the expected value approach, what is the recommended decision? What is its expected value? What is the value of perfect information?

**SELF TEST**

14. Consider a variation of the PDC decision tree shown in Figure 14.6. The company must first decide whether to undertake the market research study. If the market research study is conducted, the outcome will either be favorable ($F$) or unfavorable ($U$). Assume that there are only two decision alternatives $d_1$ and $d_2$ and two states of nature $s_1$ and $s_2$. The payoff table showing profit is as follows:

| Decision Alternative | State of Nature | |
|---|---|---|
| | $s_1$ | $s_2$ |
| $d_1$ | 100 | 300 |
| $d_2$ | 400 | 200 |

a. Show the decision tree.
b. Using the following probabilities, what is the optimal decision strategy?

$P(F) = 0.56$     $P(s_1 \mid F) = 0.57$     $P(s_1 \mid U) = 0.18$     $P(s_1) = 0.40$

$P(U) = 0.44$     $P(s_2 \mid F) = 0.43$     $P(s_2 \mid U) = 0.82$     $P(s_2) = 0.60$

15. A real estate investor has the opportunity to purchase land that is currently zoned residential. If the county board approves a request to rezone the property as commercial within the next year, the investor will be able to lease the land to a large discount firm that wants to open a new store on the property. However, if the zoning change is not approved, the in-

vestor will have to sell the property at a loss. Profits (in $000s) are shown in the following payoff table.

| | State of Nature | |
|---|---|---|
| | Rezoning Approved | Rezoning Not Approved |
| Decision Alternative | $s_1$ | $s_2$ |
| Purchase, $d_1$ | 600 | −200 |
| Do not purchase, $d_2$ | 0 | 0 |

a. If the probability that the rezoning will be approved is 0.5, what decision is recommended? What is the expected profit?

b. The investor can purchase an option to buy the land. Under the option, the investor maintains the rights to purchase the land anytime during the next 3 months while learning more about possible resistance to the rezoning proposal from area residents. Probabilities are as follows.

$$\text{Let } H = \text{High resistance to rezoning}$$
$$L = \text{Low resistance to rezoning}$$

$$P(H) = 0.55 \quad P(s_1 \mid H) = 0.18 \quad P(s_2 \mid H) = 0.82$$
$$P(L) = 0.45 \quad P(s_1 \mid L) = 0.89 \quad P(s_2 \mid L) = 0.11$$

What is the optimal decision strategy if the investor uses the option period to learn more about the resistance from area residents before making the purchase decision?

c. If the option will cost the investor an additional $10,000, should the investor purchase the option? Why or why not? What is the maximum that the investor should be willing to pay for the option?

16. McHuffter Condominiums, Inc., of Pensacola, Florida, recently purchased land near the Gulf of Mexico and is attempting to determine the size of the condominium development it should build. It is considering three sizes of developments: small, $d_1$; medium, $d_2$; and large, $d_3$. At the same time, an uncertain economy makes ascertaining the demand for the new condominiums difficult. McHuffter's management realizes that a large development followed by low demand could be very costly to the company. However, if McHuffter makes a conservative small-development decision and then finds a high demand, the firm's profits will be lower than they might have been. With the three levels of demand—low, medium, and high—McHuffter's management has prepared the following profit (in $000s) payoff table.

| | State of Nature | | |
|---|---|---|---|
| Decision Alternatives | Low, $s_1$ | Medium, $s_2$ | High, $s_3$ |
| Small Condo, $d_1$ | 400 | 400 | 400 |
| Medium Condo, $d_2$ | 100 | 600 | 600 |
| Large Condo, $d_3$ | −300 | 300 | 900 |

The probabilities for the states of nature are $P(s_1) = 0.20$, $P(s_2) = 0.35$, and $P(s_3) = 0.45$. Suppose that before making a final decision, McHuffter is considering conducting a survey to help evaluate the demand for the new condominium development. The survey report is anticipated to indicate one of three levels of demand: weak ($W$), average ($A$), or strong ($S$). The relevant probabilities are as follows:

| | | | |
|---|---|---|---|
| $P(W) = 0.30$ | $P(s_1 \mid W) = 0.39$ | $P(s_1 \mid A) = 0.16$ | $P(s_1 \mid S) = 0.06$ |
| $P(A) = 0.38$ | $P(s_2 \mid W) = 0.46$ | $P(s_2 \mid A) = 0.37$ | $P(s_2 \mid S) = 0.22$ |
| $P(S) = 0.32$ | $P(s_3 \mid W) = 0.15$ | $P(s_3 \mid A) = 0.47$ | $P(s_3 \mid S) = 0.72$ |

a. Construct a decision tree for this problem.
b. What is the recommended decision if the survey is not undertaken? What is the expected value?
c. What is the expected value of perfect information?
d. What is McHuffter's optimal decision strategy?
e. What is the expected value of the survey information?
f. What is the efficiency of the survey information?

17. Hale's TV Productions is considering producing a pilot for a comedy series at a major television network. The network may decide to reject the series, but it may also decide to purchase the rights to the series for either one or two years. At this point in time, Hale may either produce the pilot and wait for the network's decision or transfer the rights for the pilot and series to a competitor for $100,000. Hale's decision alternatives and profits (in thousands of dollars) are as follows:

| | State of Nature | | |
|---|---|---|---|
| **Decision Alternative** | **Reject, $s_1$** | **1 Year, $s_2$** | **2 Years, $s_3$** |
| Produce Pilot, $d_1$ | −100 | 50 | 150 |
| Sell to Competitor, $d_2$ | 100 | 100 | 100 |

The probabilities for the states of nature are $P(s_1) = 0.20$, $P(s_2) = 0.30$, and $P(s_3) = 0.50$. For a consulting fee of $5,000, an agency will review the plans for the comedy series and indicate the overall chances of a favorable network reaction to the series. Assume that the agency review will result in a favorable ($F$) or an unfavorable ($U$) review and that the following probabilities are relevant.

| | | |
|---|---|---|
| $P(F) = 0.69$ | $P(s_1 \mid F) = 0.09$ | $P(s_1 \mid U) = 0.45$ |
| $P(U) = 0.31$ | $P(s_2 \mid F) = 0.26$ | $P(s_2 \mid U) = 0.39$ |
| | $P(s_3 \mid F) = 0.65$ | $P(s_3 \mid U) = 0.16$ |

a. Construct a decision tree for this problem.
b. What is the recommended decision if the agency opinion is not used? What is the expected value?
c. What is the expected value of perfect information?
d. What is Hale's optimal decision strategy assuming the agency's information is used?
e. What is the expected value of the agency's information?
f. Is the agency's information worth the $5,000 fee? What is the maximum that Hale should be willing to pay for the information?
g. What is the recommended decision?

18.  Martin's Service Station is considering entering the snowplowing business for the coming win-
     ter season. Martin can purchase either a snowplow blade attachment for the station's pick-up
     truck or a new heavy-duty snowplow truck. Martin has analyzed the situation and believes that
     either alternative would be a profitable investment if the snowfall is heavy. Smaller profits
     would result if the snowfall is moderate, and losses would result if the snowfall is light. The fol-
     lowing profits have been determined.

| | State of Nature | | |
| Decision Alternatives | Heavy, $s_1$ | Moderate, $s_2$ | Light, $s_3$ |
| --- | --- | --- | --- |
| Blade Attachment, $d_1$ | 3500 | 1000 | −1500 |
| New Snowplow, $d_2$ | 7000 | 2000 | −9000 |

The probabilities for the states of nature are $P(s_1) = 0.4$, $P(s_2) = 0.3$, and $P(s_3) = 0.3$. Suppose
that Martin decides to wait until September before making a final decision. Estimates of the
probabilities associate with a normal ($N$) or unreasonably cold ($U$) September are as follows:

$$P(N) = 0.80 \qquad P(s_1 \mid N) = 0.35 \qquad P(s_1 \mid U) = 0.62$$
$$P(U) = 0.20 \qquad P(s_2 \mid N) = 0.30 \qquad P(s_2 \mid U) = 0.31$$
$$P(s_3 \mid N) = 0.35 \qquad P(s_3 \mid U) = 0.07$$

a.  Construct a decision tree for this problem.
b.  What is the recommended decision if Martin does not wait until September? What is the
    expected value?
c.  What is the expected value of perfect information?
d.  What is Martin's optimal decision strategy if the decision is not made until the September
    weather is determined? What is the expected value of this decision strategy?

19.  Joseph Software, Inc. (JSI), has been investigating the possibility of developing a grammar-
     and-style checker for use on microcomputers. Based on its experience with other software
     projects, JSI estimates that the total cost to develop a prototype is $200,000. If the performance
     of the prototype is somewhat better than existing software, referred to as a *moderate success,*
     JSI believes that it could sell the rights to the software to a large software developer for
     $600,000. If the performance of the prototype is significantly better than existing software, re-
     ferred to as a *major success,* JSI believes that it can sell the software for $1.2 million. How-
     ever, if the performance of the prototype does not exceed the performance of existing software,
     referred to as a *failure,* JSI will not be able to sell the software and hence will lose all its devel-
     opment costs.
     a.  If the best estimates of the states of nature are $P$(failure) $= 0.70$, $P$(moderate suc-
         cess) $= 0.20$, and $P$(major success) $= 0.10$, what should JSI do if it uses the expected
         value approach?
     b.  Suppose that JSI can hire an independent consultant to review its ideas for the new soft-
         ware. For a fee of $20,000, the consultant will make a recommendation as to whether JSI
         should develop a prototype.

         Let $D$ = recommendation to develop the prototype
         $N$ = recommendation to not develop the prototype
         $s_1$ = failure
         $s_2$ = moderate success
         $s_3$ = major success

Based on experience with this consultant, JSI has assigned the following probabilities:

$$P(D) = 0.35 \qquad P(s_1 \mid D) = 0.40 \qquad P(s_1 \mid N) = 0.86$$
$$P(N) = 0.65 \qquad P(s_2 \mid D) = 0.34 \qquad P(s_2 \mid N) = 0.12$$
$$P(s_3 \mid D) = 0.26 \qquad P(s_3 \mid N) = 0.02$$

Should JSI hire the consultant? Explain.

c. What is the optimal strategy?

20. Milford Trucking Company of Chicago has requests to haul two shipments, one to St. Louis and one to Detroit. Because of a scheduling problem, Milford will be able to accept only one of these assignments. The St. Louis customer has guaranteed a return shipment, but the Detroit customer has not. Thus, if Milford accepts the Detroit shipment and cannot find a Detroit–Chicago return shipment, the truck will return to Chicago empty. The payoff table showing profit is as follows.

| Shipment | Return Shipment from Detroit $s_1$ | No Return Shipment from Detroit $s_2$ |
|---|---|---|
| St. Louis, $d_1$ | 2000 | 2000 |
| Detroit, $d_2$ | 2500 | 1000 |

a. If the probability of a Detroit return shipment is 0.4, what should Milford do?
b. What is the expected value of perfect information that would tell Milford Trucking whether Detroit has a return shipment?
c. Milford can telephone a Detroit truck dispatch center and determine whether the general Detroit shipping activity is busy ($B$) or slow ($S$). If shipping activity is busy, the chances of obtaining a return shipment will increase. Suppose that the relevant probabilities are

$$P(B) = 0.42 \qquad P(s_1 \mid B) = 0.57 \qquad P(s_1 \mid S) = 0.28$$
$$P(S) = 0.58 \qquad P(s_2 \mid B) = 0.43 \qquad P(s_2 \mid S) = 0.72$$

What should Milford do?

21. Lawson's Department Store faces a buying decision for a seasonal product for which demand can be high, medium, and low. The purchaser for Lawson's can order 1, 2, or 3 lots of the product before the season begins but cannot reorder later. Profit projections (in $000s) are shown.

| | State of Nature | | |
|---|---|---|---|
| Decision Alternative | High Demand $s_1$ | Medium Demand $s_2$ | Low Demand $s_3$ |
| Order 1 lot, $d_1$ | 60 | 60 | 50 |
| Order 2 lots, $d_2$ | 80 | 80 | 30 |
| Order 3 lots, $d_3$ | 100 | 70 | 10 |

a.  If the prior probabilities for the three states of nature are 0.3, 0.3, and 0.4, respectively, what is the recommended order quantity?

b.  At each preseason sales meeting, the vice-president of sales provides a personal opinion regarding potential demand for this product. Because of the vice-president's enthusiasm and optimistic nature, the predictions of market conditions have always been either "excellent" (E) or "very good" (V). Probabilities are as follows. What is the optimal decision strategy?

$$P(E) = 0.70 \qquad P(s_1 \mid E) = 0.34 \qquad P(s_1 \mid V) = 0.20$$
$$P(V) = 0.30 \qquad P(s_2 \mid E) = 0.32 \qquad P(s_2 \mid V) = 0.26$$
$$\qquad\qquad\qquad P(s_3 \mid E) = 0.34 \qquad P(s_3 \mid V) = 0.54$$

c.  Use the efficiency of sample information and discuss whether the firm should consider a consulting expert who could provide independent forecasts of market conditions for the product.

22.  Suppose that you are given a decision situation with three possible states of nature: $s_1$, $s_2$, and $s_3$. The prior probabilities are $P(s_1) = 0.2$, $P(s_2) = 0.5$, and $P(s_3) = 0.3$. With sample information $I$, $P(I \mid s_1) = 0.1$, $P(I \mid s_2) = 0.05$, and $P(I \mid s_3) = 0.2$. Compute the revised or posterior probabilities: $P(s_1 \mid I)$, $P(s_2 \mid I)$, and $P(s_3 \mid I)$.

**SELF TEST**

23.  In the following profit payoff table for a decision problem with two states of nature and three decision alternatives, the prior probabilities, for $s_1$ and $s_2$ are $P(s_1) = 0.8$ and $P(s_2) = 0.2$.

|  | State of Nature | |
|---|---|---|
| **Decision Alternative** | $s_1$ | $s_2$ |
| $d_1$ | 15 | 10 |
| $d_2$ | 10 | 12 |
| $d_3$ | 8 | 20 |

a.  What is the optimal decision?

b.  Find the EVPI.

c.  Suppose that sample information $I$ is obtained, with $P(I \mid s_1) = 0.2$, $P(I \mid s_2) = 0.75$. Find the posterior probabilities $P(s_1 \mid I)$ and $P(s_2 \mid I)$. Recommend a decision alternative based on these probabilities.

24.  To save on expenses, Rona and Jerry agreed to form a carpool for traveling to and from work. Rona preferred to use the somewhat longer but more consistent Queen City Avenue. Although Jerry preferred the quicker expressway, he agreed with Rona that they should take Queen City Avenue if the expressway had a traffic jam. The following payoff table provides the one-way times estimate in minutes for traveling to or from work.

|  | State of Nature | |
|---|---|---|
|  | **Expressway Open** | **Expressway Jammed** |
| **Decision Alternative** | $s_1$ | $s_2$ |
| Queen City Avenue, $d_1$ | 30 | 30 |
| Expressway, $d_2$ | 25 | 45 |

Based on their experience with traffic problems, Rona and Jerry agreed on a 0.15 probability that the expressway would be jammed.

In addition, they agreed that weather seemed to affect the traffic conditions on the expressway. Let

$$C = \text{clear}$$
$$O = \text{overcast}$$
$$R = \text{rain}$$

The following conditional probabilities apply.

| | | |
|---|---|---|
| $P(C \mid s_1) = 0.8$ | $P(O \mid s_1) = 0.2$ | $P(R \mid s_1) = 0.0$ |
| $P(C \mid s_2) = 0.1$ | $P(O \mid s_2) = 0.3$ | $P(R \mid s_2) = 0.6$ |

a. Use the Bayes' probability revision procedure to compute the probability of each weather condition and the conditional probability of the expressway open $s_1$ or jammed $s_2$ given each weather condition.
b. Show the decision tree for this problem.
c. What is the optimal decision strategy and what is the expected travel time?

25. The Gorman Manufacturing Company must decide whether to manufacture a component part at its Milan, Michigan, plant or purchase the component part from a supplier. The resulting profit is dependent upon the demand for the product. The following payoff table shows the projected profit (in $000s).

| | State of Nature | | |
|---|---|---|---|
| | **Low Demand** | **Medium Demand** | **High Demand** |
| **Decision Alternative** | $s_1$ | $s_2$ | $s_3$ |
| Manufacture, $d_1$ | −20 | 40 | 100 |
| Purchase, $d_2$ | 10 | 45 | 70 |

The state-of-nature probabilities are $P(s_1) = 0.35$, $P(s_2) = 0.35$, and $P(s_3) = 0.30$.
a. Use a decision tree to recommend a decision.
b. Use EVPI to determine whether Gorman should attempt to obtain a better estimate of demand.
c. A test market study of the potential demand for the product is expected to report either a favorable ($F$) or unfavorable ($U$) condition. The relevant conditional probabilities are as follows:

| | |
|---|---|
| $P(F \mid s_1) = 0.10$ | $P(U \mid s_1) = 0.90$ |
| $P(F \mid s_2) = 0.40$ | $P(U \mid s_2) = 0.60$ |
| $P(F \mid s_3) = 0.60$ | $P(U \mid s_3) = 0.40$ |

What is the probability that the market research report will be favorable?
d. What is Gorman's optimal decision strategy?
e. What is the expected value of the market research information?
f. What is the efficiency of the information?

26. Three decision makers have assessed utilities for the following decision problem (payoff in dollars).

**SELF TEST**

| Decision Alternative | State of Nature | | |
|---|---|---|---|
| | $s_1$ | $s_2$ | $s_3$ |
| $d_1$ | 20 | 50 | -20 |
| $d_2$ | 80 | 100 | -100 |

The indifference probabilities are as follows.

| Payoff | Indifference Probability ($p$) | | |
|---|---|---|---|
| | Risk Avoider | Risk Taker | Risk Neutral |
| 100 | 1.00 | 1.00 | 1.00 |
| 80 | 0.95 | 0.70 | 0.90 |
| 50 | 0.90 | 0.60 | 0.75 |
| 20 | 0.70 | 0.45 | 0.60 |
| -20 | 0.50 | 0.25 | 0.40 |
| -100 | 0.00 | 0.00 | 0.00 |

For the payoff of 20, what is the premium that the risk avoider will pay to avoid risk? What is the premium that the risk taker will pay to have the opportunity of the high payoff?

27. In Problem 26, if $P(s_1) = 0.25$, $P(s_2) = 0.50$, and $P(s_3) = 0.25$, find a recommended decision for each of the three decision makers. Note that for the same decision problem, different utilities can lead to different decisions.

28. A firm has three investment alternatives. The payoff table (in $000s) and associated probabilities are as follows:

**SELF TEST**

| Investment | Economic Condition | | |
|---|---|---|---|
| | Up | Stable | Down |
| $d_1$ | 100 | 25 | 0 |
| $d_2$ | 75 | 50 | 25 |
| $d_3$ | 50 | 50 | 50 |
| Probabilities | 0.40 | 0.30 | 0.30 |

a.  Using the expected value approach, which decision is preferred?
b.  For the lottery having a payoff of $100,000 with probability $p$ and $0 with probability $(1 - p)$, two decision makers expressed the following indifference probabilities:

| Profit | Indifference Probability ($p$) | |
|---|---|---|
| | Decision Maker A | Decision Maker B |
| $75,000 | 0.80 | 0.60 |
| 50,000 | 0.60 | 0.30 |
| 25,000 | 0.30 | 0.15 |

Find the most preferred decision for each decision maker using the expected utility approach.
c.  Why don't decision makers A and B select the same decision alternative?

29. In a certain state lottery, a lottery ticket costs $2. In terms of the decision to purchase or not to purchase a lottery ticket, suppose the following payoff table (in $) applies:

|  | State of Nature | |
| --- | --- | --- |
|  | Win | Lose |
| Decision Alternative | $s_1$ | $s_2$ |
| Purchase lottery ticket, $d_1$ | 300,000 | −2 |
| Do not purchase lottery ticket, $d_2$ | 0 | 0 |

   a. If a realistic estimate of the chances of winning are 1 in 250,000, use the expected value approach to recommend a decision.
   b. If a particular decision maker assigns an indifference probability of 0.000001 to the $0 payoff, would this individual purchase a lottery ticket? Use expected utility to justify your answer.

30. Alexander Industries is considering purchasing an insurance policy for its new office building in St. Louis. The policy has an annual cost of $10,000. If Alexander Industries does not purchase the insurance and minor fire damage occurs to the office building, a cost of $100,000 is anticipated; the cost if major or total destruction occurs is $200,000. The payoff table in ($), including the state-of-nature probabilities, is as follows:

|  | Damage | | |
| --- | --- | --- | --- |
|  | None | Minor | Major |
| Decision Alternative | $s_1$ | $s_2$ | $s_3$ |
| Purchase insurance, $d_1$ | 10,000 | 10,000 | 10,000 |
| Do not purchase insurance, $d_2$ | 0 | 100,000 | 200,000 |
| Probabilities | 0.96 | 0.03 | 0.01 |

   a. Using the expected value approach, what decision do you recommend?
   b. What lottery would you use to assess utilities? (Note that since the data are costs, the best payoff is $0.)
   c. Assume we found the following indifference probabilities for the lottery defined in part (b):

| Cost | Indifference Probability ($p$) |
| --- | --- |
| $ 10,000 | 0.99 |
| 100,000 | 0.60 |

   What decision would you recommend?
   d. Do you favor using expected value or expected utility for this decision problem? Why?

31. Suppose that the point spread for a particular sporting event is 10 points and that with this spread you are convinced you would have a 0.6 probability of winning a bet on your team. However, the local bookie will accept only a $1000 bet. Assuming that such bets are legal, would you bet

on your team? (Disregard any commission charged by the bookie.) Remember that *you* must pay losses out of your own pocket. Your payoff table (in $) is as follows:

|  | State of Nature | |
|---|---|---|
|  | **You Win** | **You Lose** |
| **Decision Alternative** | $s_1$ | $s_2$ |
| Bet, $d_1$ | 1000 | $-1000$ |
| Don't bet, $d_2$ | 0 | 0 |

a.   What decision does the expected value approach recommend?
b.   What is *your* indifference probability for the $0 payoff? (While this determination is not easy, be as realistic as possible. Remember, this calculation is required if we are to do an analysis that reflects your attitude toward risk.)
c.   What decision would you make based on the expected utility approach?
d.   Would other individuals assess the same utility values you do? Explain.
e.   If your decision in part (c) was to place the bet, repeat the analysis, assuming a minimum bet of $10,000.

32.   There are two different routes for traveling between two cities. Route A normally takes 60 minutes, while route B normally takes 45 minutes. If traffic problems are encountered on route A, the travel time increases to 70 minutes; traffic problems on route B increase travel time to 90 minutes. The probability of the delay is 0.2 for route A and 0.3 for route B.
a.   Using the expected value approach, what is the recommended route?
b.   If utilities are to be assigned to the travel times, what is the appropriate lottery? Note that the smaller times should reflect higher utilities.
c.   Using the lottery of part (b), assume the decision maker expresses indifference probabilities of

$$p = 0.8 \quad \text{for 60 minutes}$$
$$p = 0.6 \quad \text{for 70 minutes}$$

What route should this decision maker select?

33.   A new product has the following profit projections and associated probabilities:

| Profit | Probability |
|---|---|
| 150,000 | 0.10 |
| 100,000 | 0.25 |
| 50,000 | 0.20 |
| 0 | 0.15 |
| $-50,000$ | 0.20 |
| $-100,000$ | 0.10 |

a.   Use the expected value approach to make the decision of whether to market the new product.
b.   Because of the high dollar values involved, especially the possibility of a $100,000 loss, the marketing vice-president has expressed some concern about the use of the expected

value approach. As a consequence, if a utility analysis is performed, what is the appropriate lottery? Assume the following indifference probabilities are assigned:

| Profit | Indifference Probability ($p$) |
|---|---|
| $100,000 | 0.95 |
| 50,000 | 0.70 |
| 0 | 0.50 |
| −50,000 | 0.25 |

   c. Use expected utility to make a recommended decision.
   d. Should the decision maker feel comfortable with the final decision recommended by the analysis?

34. A Las Vegas roulette wheel has 38 different numerical values. If an individual bets on one number and wins, the payoff is 35 to 1.
   a. Show a payoff table for a $10 bet on one number using decision alternatives of bet and do not bet.
   b. What is the recommended decision using the expected value approach?
   c. What range of utility values would a decision maker have to assign to the $0 payoff to have expected utility justify his or her decision to place the $10 bet?

## Case Problem    PROPERTY PURCHASE STRATEGY

Glenn Foreman, president of Oceanview Development Corporation, is considering submitting a bid to purchase property that will be sold by sealed bid at a county tax foreclosure. Glenn's initial judgment is to submit a bid of $5 million. Based on his experience, Glenn estimates that a bid of $5 million will have a 0.2 probability of being the highest bid and securing the property for Oceanview. The current date is June 1. Sealed bids for the property must be submitted by August 15. The winning bid will be announced on September 1.

If Oceanview submits the highest bid and obtains the property, the firm plans to build and sell a complex of luxury condominiums. However, a complicating factor is that the property is currently zoned for single-family residences only. Glenn believes that a referendum could be placed on the voting ballot in time for the November election. Passage of the referendum would change the zoning of the property and permit construction of the condominiums.

The sealed-bid procedure requires the bid to be submitted with a certified check for 10% of the amount bid. If the bid is rejected, the deposit is refunded. If the bid is accepted, the deposit is the down payment for the property. However, if the bid is accepted and the bidder does not follow through with the purchase and meet the remainder of the financial obligation within six months, the deposit will be forfeited. In this case, the county will offer the property to the next highest bidder.

To determine whether Oceanview should submit the $5 million bid, Glenn has done some preliminary analysis. This preliminary work provided an estimate of 0.3 for the probability that the referendum for a zoning change will be approved and resulted in the following estimates of the costs and revenues that will be incurred if the condominiums are built.

**Cost and Revenue Estimates**

| | |
|---|---|
| Revenue from condominium sales | $15,000,000 |
| Cost | |
| Property | $5,000,000 |
| Construction expenses | $8,000,000 |

If Oceanview obtains the property and the zoning change is rejected in November, Glenn believes that the best option would be for the firm not to complete the purchase of the property. In this case, Oceanview would forfeit the 10% deposit that accompanied the bid.

Because the likelihood that the zoning referendum will be approved is such an important factor in the decision process, Glenn has suggested that the firm hire a market research service to conduct a survey of voters. The survey would provide a better estimate of the likelihood that the referendum for a zoning change would be approved. The market research firm that Oceanview Development has worked with in the past has agreed to do the study for $15,000. The results of the study will be available August 1, so that Oceanview will have this information before the August 15 bid deadline. The results of the survey will be either a prediction that the zoning change will be approved or a prediction that the zoning change will be rejected. After considering the record of the market research service in previous studies conducted for Oceanview, Glenn has developed the following probability estimates concerning the accuracy of the market research information.

$$P(A \mid s_1) = 0.9 \qquad P(N \mid s_1) = 0.1$$
$$P(A \mid s_2) = 0.2 \qquad P(N \mid s_2) = 0.8$$

where

$A$ = prediction of zoning change approval

$N$ = prediction that zoning change will not be approved

$s_1$ = the zoning change is approved by the voters

$s_2$ = the zoning change is rejected by the voters

## Managerial Report

Perform an analysis of the problem facing the Oceanview Development Corporation, and prepare a report that summarizes your findings and recommendations. Include the following items in your report:

1. A decision tree that shows the logical sequence of the decision problem
2. A recommendation regarding what Oceanview should do if the market research information is not available
3. A decision strategy that Oceanview should follow if the market research is conducted
4. A recommendation as to whether Oceanview should employ the market research firm, along with the value of the information provided by the market research firm. Include the details of your analysis as an appendix to your report.

............................................................................................................../ /..............

## Appendix 14.1    DECISION ANALYSIS WITH SPREADSHEETS

A spreadsheet provides a convenient way to perform the basic decision analysis computations. A spreadsheet may be designed for any of the decision analysis approaches described in this chapter. We will demonstrate use of the spreadsheet in decision analysis by solving the PDC condominium problem using the expected value approach.

### The Expected Value Approach

This spreadsheet solution is shown in Figure 14.8. The payoff table with appropriate headings is placed into cell A3 through cell C8. In addition, the probabilities for the two states of nature are placed in cells B9 and C9. The Excel formulas that provide the calculations and optimal solution recommendation are as follows:

Cell D6    Compute the expected value for each decision alternative
=SUMPRODUCT($B$9:$C$9,B6:C6)    (Copy D6 to D7:D8)
Cell D11    Compute the maximum expected value
=MAX(D6:D8)
Cell E6    Determine which decision alternative is the recommended
=IF(D6=$D$11,A6,"")    (Copy E6 to E7:E8)

As Figure 14.8 shows, the expected value approach recommends the larger complex decision alternative with a maximum expected value of 14.2.

The only change required to convert the spreadsheet in Figure 14.8 into a minimization analysis is to change the formula in cell D11 to =MIN(D6:D8). With this change, the decision alternative with the minimum expected value will be shown in column E.

### Computation of Branch Probabilities

Spreadsheets can be used to compute the branch probabilities for a decision tree as discussed in Section 14.6. A spreadsheet used to compute the branch probabilities for the PDC problem is shown in Figure 14.9. The prior probabilities are entered into cells B5 and B6.

**Figure 14.8    SPREADSHEET SOLUTION FOR THE PDC PROBLEM USING THE EXPECTED VALUE APPROACH**

|   | A | B | C | D | E |
|---|---|---|---|---|---|
| 1 | **PDC Problem - Expected Value Approach** | | | | |
| 2 | | | | | |
| 3 | **Payoff Table** | | | | |
| 4 | | **State of Nature** | | **Expected** | **Recommended** |
| 5 | **Decision Alternative** | High acceptance | Low acceptance | **Value** | **Decision** |
| 6 | Small complex | 8 | 7 | 7.8 | |
| 7 | Medium complex | 14 | 5 | 12.2 | |
| 8 | Large complex | 20 | -9 | 14.2 | Large complex |
| 9 | **Probability** | 0.8 | 0.2 | | |
| 10 | | | | | |
| 11 | **Maximum Expected Value** | | | 14.2 | |

| | SPREADSHEET SOLUTION FOR THE PDC PROBLEM |
|---|---|
| Figure 14.9 | PROBABILITY CALCULATIONS |

| | A | B | C | D | E |
|---|---|---|---|---|---|
| 1 | **PDC Problem - Bayes' Probability Calculations** | | | | |
| 2 | | | | | |
| 3 | | Prior | | | |
| 4 | **States of Nature** | Probabilities | | | |
| 5 | High Acceptance | 0.8 | | | |
| 6 | Low Acceptance | 0.2 | | | |
| 7 | | | | | |
| 8 | **Conditional Probabilities** | | | | |
| 9 | | Market Research | | | |
| 10 | If State of Nature Is | Favorable | Unfavorable | | |
| 11 | High Acceptance | 0.90 | 0.10 | | |
| 12 | Low Acceptance | 0.25 | 0.75 | | |
| 13 | | | | | |
| 14 | | | | | |
| 15 | **Market Research Favorable (F)** | | | | |
| 16 | | Prior | Conditional | Joint | Posterior |
| 17 | State of Nature | Probabilities | Probabilities | Probabilities | Probabilities |
| 18 | High Acceptance | 0.8 | 0.90 | 0.72 | 0.94 |
| 19 | Low Acceptance | 0.2 | 0.25 | 0.05 | 0.06 |
| 20 | | | | P(F) = | 0.77 |
| 21 | | | | | |
| 22 | | | | | |
| 23 | **Market Research Unfavorable (U)** | | | | |
| 24 | | Prior | Conditional | Joint | Posterior |
| 25 | State of Nature | Probabilities | Probabilities | Probabilities | Probabilities |
| 26 | High Acceptance | 0.8 | 0.10 | 0.08 | 0.35 |
| 27 | Low Acceptance | 0.2 | 0.75 | 0.15 | 0.65 |
| 28 | | | | P(U) = | 0.23 |

The four conditional probabilities are entered into cells B11, B12, C11, and C12. The following cell formulas perform the probability calculations for the PDC problem based on a favorable market research report, shown previously in Table 14.7.

Cells B18 and B19   Enter the prior probabilities
                    =B5
                    =B6
Cells C18 and C19   Enter the conditional probabilities for a favorable market research report
                    =B11
                    =B12
Cells D18 and D19   Compute the joint probabilities
                    =B18*C18
                    =B19*C19

|  |  |
|---|---|
| Cell D20 | Compute the probability of a favorable market research report<br>=SUM(D18:D19) |
| Cells E18 and E19 | Compute the posterior probabilities for each state of nature<br>=D18/D20<br>=D19/D20 |

The same logic was used to perform the probability calculations based on an unfavorable market research report shown in cells B23:E28.

# OHIO EDISON COMPANY*

## AKRON, OHIO

Ohio Edison Company is an operating company of FirstEnergy Corporation. Ohio Edison and its subsidiary, Pennsylvania Power Company, provide electrical service to more than one million customers in central and northeastern Ohio and western Pennsylvania. Most of this electricity is generated by coal-fired power plants. To meet evolving air-quality standards, Ohio Edison replaced existing particulate control equipment at most of its generating plants with more efficient equipment. The combination of this program to upgrade air-quality control equipment with the continuing need to construct new generating plants to meet future power requirements resulted in a large capital investment program.

Management science activities at Ohio Edison are distributed throughout the company rather than centralized in a specific department, and are more or less evenly divided among the following areas: fossil and nuclear fuel planning, environmental studies, capacity planning, large equipment evaluation, and corporate planning. Applications include decision analysis, optimal ordering strategies, computer modeling, and simulation.

## A Decision Analysis Application

The flue gas emitted by coal-fired power plants contains small ash particles and sulfur dioxide ($SO_2$). Federal and state regulatory agencies have established emission limits for both particulates and sulfur dioxide. In the late 1970s, Ohio Edison developed a plan to comply with new air-quality standards at one of its largest power plants. This plant, which consists of seven coal-fired

units (most of which were constructed in the 1960s), constitutes about one-third of the generating capacity of Ohio Edison and its subsidiary company. Although all units were initially constructed with particulate emission control equipment, that equipment was no longer capable of meeting new particulate emission requirements.

A decision had already been made to burn low-sulfur coal in four of the smaller units (units 1–4) at the plant in order to meet $SO_2$ emission standards. Fabric filters were to be installed on these units to control particulate emissions. Fabric filters, also known as baghouses, use thousands of fabric bags to filter out the particulates; they function in much the same way as a household vacuum cleaner.

It was considered likely, although not certain, that the three larger units (units 5–7) at this plant would burn medium- to high-sulfur coal. A method of controlling particulate emissions at these units had not yet been selected. Preliminary studies narrowed the particulate control equipment choice to a decision between fabric filters and electrostatic precipitators (which remove particulates suspended in the flue gas by passing the flue gas through a strong electric field). This decision was affected by a number of uncertainties, including the following:

- Uncertainty in the way some air-quality laws and regulations might be interpreted
- Potential requirements that either low-sulfur coal or high-sulfur Ohio coal (or neither) be burned in units 5–7
- Potential future changes to air quality laws and regulations
- An overall plant reliability improvement program already under way at this plant

*The authors are indebted to Thomas J. Madden and M. S. Hyrnick of Ohio Edison Company, Akron, Ohio, for providing this application.

- The outcome of this program itself, which would affect the operating costs of whichever pollution control technology was installed in these units
- Uncertain construction costs of the equipment, particularly since limited space at the plant site made it necessary to install the equipment on a massive bridge deck over a four-lane highway immediately adjacent to the power plant
- Uncertain costs associated with replacing the electrical power required to operate the particulate control equipment
- Various other factors, including potential accidents and chronic operating problems that could increase the costs of operating the generating units (the degree to which each of these factors could affect operating costs varied with the choice of technology and with the sulfur content of the coal)

## Particulate Control Decision

The air-quality program involved a choice between two types of particulate control equipment (fabric filters and electrostatic precipitators) for units 5–7. Because of the complexity of the problem, the high degree of uncertainty associated with factors affecting the decision, and the importance (because of potential reliability and cost impact on Ohio Edison) of the choice, decision analysis was used in the selection process.

The decision measure used to evaluate the outcomes of the particulate technology decision analysis was the annual revenue requirements for the three large units over their remaining lifetime. Revenue requirements are the monies that would have to be collected from the utility customers to recover costs resulting from the decision. They include not only direct costs but also the cost of capital and return on investment.

A decision tree was constructed to represent the particulate control decision and its uncertainties and costs. A simplified version of this decision tree is shown in Figure 14.10. The decision and state-of-nature nodes are indicated. Note that to conserve space, a type of shorthand notation is used. The coal sulfur content state-of-nature node should actually be located at the end of each branch of the capital cost state-of-nature node, as the dashed lines indicate. Each state-of-nature node actually represents several probabilistic cost models or submodels. The total revenue requirements are the sum of the revenue requirements for capital and operating costs. Costs associated with these models were obtained from

engineering calculations or estimates. Probabilities were obtained from existing data or the subjective assessments of knowledgeable persons.

## Results

A decision tree similar to that shown in Figure 14.10 was used to generate cumulative probability distributions for the annual revenue requirements outcomes calculated for each of the two particulate control alternatives. Careful study of these results led to the following conclusions:

- The expected value of annual revenue requirements for the electrostatic precipitator technology was approximately $1 million lower than that for the fabric filters.
- The fabric filter alternative had a higher upside risk—that is, a higher probability of high revenue requirements—than did the precipitator alternative.
- The precipitator technology had nearly an 80% probability of lower annual revenue requirements than the fabric filters.
- Although the capital cost of the fabric filter equipment (the cost of installing the equipment) was lower than for the precipitator, this cost was more than offset by the higher operating costs associated with the fabric filter.

These results led Ohio Edison to select the electrostatic precipitator technology for the generating units in question. Had the decision analysis not been performed, the particulate control decision might have been based chiefly on capital cost, a decision measure that would have favored the fabric filter equipment. Decision analysis offers a means for effectively analyzing the uncertainties involved in a decision. Because of this analysis, the use of decision analysis methodology in this application resulted in a decision that yielded both lower expected revenue requirements and lower risk.

## Questions

1. Why was decision analysis used in the selection of particulate control equipment for units 5, 6, and 7?
2. List the decision alternatives for the decision analysis problem developed by Ohio Edison.
3. What were the benefits of using decision analysis in this application?

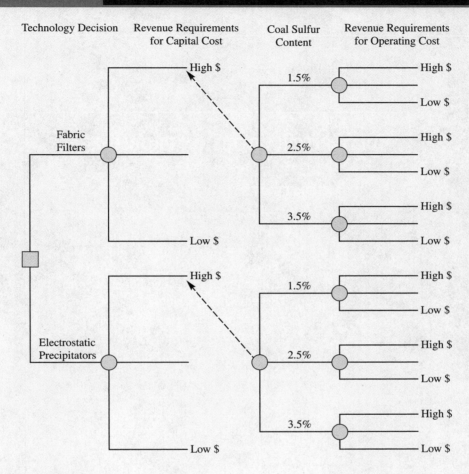

**Figure 14.10    SIMPLIFIED PARTICULATE CONTROL EQUIPMENT DECISION TREE**

# 15

# MULTICRITERIA DECISION PROBLEMS

## CONTENTS

In previous chapters we have shown how a variety of management science methods can help managers make better decisions. Whenever we desired an optimal solution, we utilized a single criterion (e.g., maximize profit, minimize cost, minimize time). In this chapter we discuss techniques that are appropriate for situations in which the decision maker needs to consider multiple criteria in arriving at the overall best decision. For example, consider a company involved in selecting a location for a new manufacturing plant. The cost of land and construction may vary from location to location, so one criterion in selecting the best site could be the cost involved in building the plant; if cost were the sole criterion of interest, management would simply select the location that minimizes land cost plus construction cost. Before making any decision, however, management might also want to consider additional criteria such as the availability of transportation from the plant to the firm's distribution centers, the attractiveness of the proposed location in terms of hiring and retaining employees, energy costs at the proposed site, and state and local taxes. In such situations the complexity of the problem increases because one location may be more desirable in terms of one criterion and less desirable in terms of one or more of the other criteria.

To introduce the topic of multicriteria decision making, we consider a technique referred to as *goal programming*. This technique has been developed to handle multiple criteria situations within the general framework of linear programming. We next consider a *scoring model* as a relatively easy way to identify the best decision alternative for a multicriteria problem. Finally, we introduce a method known as the *analytical hierarchy process (AHP),* which allows the user to make pairwise comparisons among the criteria and a series of pairwise comparisons among the decision alternatives in order to arrive at a prioritized ranking of the decision alternatives.

## I5.I   GOAL PROGRAMMING: FORMULATION AND GRAPHICAL SOLUTION

To illustrate the goal programming approach to multicriteria decision problems, let us consider a problem facing Nicolo Investment Advisors. A client has $80,000 to invest and, as an initial strategy, would like the investment portfolio restricted to two stocks:

| Stock | Price/Share | Estimated Annual Return/Share | Risk Index/Share |
|---|---|---|---|
| U.S. Oil | $25 | $3 | 0.50 |
| Hub Properties | $50 | $5 | 0.25 |

U.S. Oil, which has a return of $3 on a $25 share price, provides an annual rate of return of 12%, whereas Hub Properties provides an annual rate of return of 10%. The risk index per share, 0.50 for U.S. Oil and 0.25 for Hub Properties, is a rating Nicolo has assigned to measure the relative risk of the two investments. Higher risk index values imply greater risk; hence, Nicolo has judged U.S. Oil to be the riskier investment. By specifying a maximum portfolio risk index, Nicolo will avoid placing too much of the portfolio in high-risk investments.

To illustrate how to use the risk index per share to measure the total portfolio risk, suppose that Nicolo chooses a portfolio that invests all $80,000 in U.S. Oil, the higher risk, but higher return, investment. Nicolo could purchase $80,000/$25 = 3200 shares of U.S. Oil, and the portfolio would have a risk index of 3200(0.50) = 1600. Conversely, if Nicolo purchases no shares of either stock, the portfolio will have no risk, but also no return. Thus, the portfolio risk index will vary from 0 (least risk) to 1600 (most risk).

Nicolo's client would like to avoid a high-risk portfolio; thus, investing all funds in U.S. Oil would not be desirable. However, the client agreed that an acceptable level of risk would correspond to portfolios with a maximum total risk index of 700. Thus, considering only risk, one *goal* is to find a portfolio with a risk index of 700 or less.

Another goal of the client is to obtain an annual return of at least $9000. This goal can be achieved with a portfolio consisting of 2000 shares of U.S. Oil (at a cost of 2000($25) = $50,000) and 600 shares of Hub Properties (at a cost of 600($50) = $30,000); the annual return in this case would be 2000($3) + 600($5) = $9000. Note, however, that the portfolio risk index for this investment strategy would be 2000(0.50) + 600(0.25) = 1150; thus, this portfolio achieves the annual return goal but does not satisfy the portfolio risk index goal.

Thus, the portfolio selection problem is a multicriteria decision problem involving two conflicting goals: one dealing with risk and one dealing with annual return. The goal programming approach was developed precisely for this kind of problem. Goal programming can be used to identify a portfolio that comes closest to achieving both goals. Before applying the methodology, the client must determine which, if either, goal is more important.

Suppose that the client's top-priority goal is to restrict the risk; that is, keeping the portfolio risk index at 700 or less is so important that the client is not willing to trade the achievement of this goal for any amount of an increase in annual return. But, as long as the portfolio risk index does not exceed 700, the client seeks the best possible return. Based on this statement of priorities, the goals for the problem are as follows:

### Primary Goal (Priority Level 1)

**Goal 1:**    Find a portfolio that has a risk index of 700 or less.

### Secondary Goal (Priority Level 2)

**Goal 2:**    Find a portfolio that will provide an annual return of at least $9000.

The primary goal is called a *priority level 1 goal,* and the secondary goal is called a *priority level 2 goal.* In goal programming terminology, these are called **preemptive priorities** because the decision maker is not willing to sacrifice any amount of achievement of the priority level 1 goal for the lower priority goal. The portfolio risk index of 700 is the **target value** for the priority level 1 (primary) goal, and the annual return of $9000 is the target value for the priority level 2 (secondary) goal. The difficulty in finding a solution that will achieve these goals is that only $80,000 is available for investment.

*In goal programming with preemptive priorities, we never permit trade-offs between higher and lower level goals.*

### Developing the Constraints and the Goal Equations

We begin by defining the decision variables:

$$x_1 = \text{number of shares of U.S. Oil purchased}$$
$$x_2 = \text{number of shares of Hub Properties purchased}$$

Constraints for goal programming problems are handled in the same way as in an ordinary linear programming problem. In the Nicolo Investment Advisors problem, one constraint corresponds to the funds available. Because each share of U.S. Oil costs \$25 and each share of Hub Properties costs \$50, the constraint representing the funds available is

$$25x_1 + 50x_2 \leq 80,000$$

To complete the formulation of the model, we must develop a **goal equation** for each goal. Let us begin by writing the goal equation for the primary goal. Each share of U.S. Oil has a risk index of 0.50 and each share of Hub Properties has a risk index of 0.25, therefore the portfolio risk index is $0.50x_1 + 0.25x_2$. Depending on the values of $x_1$ and $x_2$, the portfolio risk index may be less than, equal to, or greater than the target value of 700. To represent these possibilities mathematically, we create the goal equation

$$0.50x_1 + 0.25x_2 = 700 + d_1^+ - d_1^-$$

where

$d_1^+$ = the amount by which the portfolio risk index exceeds the target
   value of 700

$d_1^-$ = the amount by which the portfolio risk index is less than the target
   value of 700

To achieve a goal exactly, the two deviation variables must both equal zero.

In goal programming, $d_1^+$ and $d_1^-$ are called **deviation variables.** The purpose of deviation variables is to allow for the possibility of not meeting the target value exactly. Consider, for example, a portfolio that consists of $x_1$ = 2000 shares of U.S. Oil and $x_2$ = 0 shares of Hub Properties. The portfolio risk index is $0.50(2000) + 0.25(0) = 1000$. In this case, $d_1^+ = 300$ reflects the fact that the portfolio risk index exceeds the target value by 300 units; note also that since $d_1^+$ is greater than zero, the value of $d_1^-$ must be zero. For a portfolio consisting of $x_1$ = 0 shares of U.S. Oil and $x_2$ = 1000 shares of Hub Properties, the portfolio risk index would be $0.50(0) + 0.25(1000) = 250$. In this case, $d_1^- = 450$ and $d_1^+ = 0$, indicating that the solution provides a portfolio risk index of 450 less than the target value of 700.

In general, the letter $d$ is used for deviation variables in a goal programming model. A superscript of plus $(+)$ or minus $(-)$ is used to indicate whether the variable corresponds to a positive or negative deviation from the target value. If we bring the deviation variables to the left-hand side, we can rewrite the goal equation for the primary goal as

$$0.50x_1 + 0.25x_2 - d_1^+ + d_1^- = 700$$

Note that the value on the right-hand side of the goal equation is the target value for the goal. The left-hand side of the goal equation consists of two parts:

1.  A function that defines the amount of goal achievement in terms of the decision variables (e.g., $0.50x_1 + 0.25x_2$)
2.  Deviation variables representing the difference between the target value for the goal and the level achieved

To develop a goal equation for the secondary goal, we begin by writing a function representing the annual return for the investment:

$$\text{Annual return} = 3x_1 + 5x_2$$

Then we define two deviation variables that represent the amount of over- or under-achievement of the goal. Doing so, we obtain

$d_2^+$ = the amount by which the annual return for the portfolio is greater than the target value of \$9000

$d_1^-$ = the amount by which the annual return for the portfolio is less than the target value of \$9000

Using these two deviation variables, we write the goal equation for goal 2 as

$$3x_1 + 5x_2 = 9000 + d_2^+ - d_2^-$$

or

$$3x_1 + 5x_2 - d_2^+ + d_2^- = 9000$$

This step completes the development of the goal equations and the constraints for the Nicolo portfolio problem. We are now ready to develop an appropriate objective function for the problem.

### Developing an Objective Function with Preemptive Priorities

The objective function in a goal programming model calls for minimizing a function of the deviation variables. In the portfolio selection problem, the most important goal, denoted $P_1$, is to find a portfolio with a risk index of 700 or less. This problem has only two goals, and the client is unwilling to accept a portfolio risk index greater than 700 to achieve the secondary annual return goal. Therefore, the secondary goal is denoted $P_2$. As we stated previously, these goal priorities are referred to as preemptive priorities because the satisfaction of a higher level goal cannot be traded for the satisfaction of a lower level goal.

Goal programming problems with preemptive priorities are solved by treating priority level 1 goals ($P_1$) first in an objective function. The idea is to start by finding a solution that comes closest to satisfying the priority level 1 goals. This solution is then modified by solving a problem with an objective function involving only priority level 2 goals ($P_2$); however, revisions in the solution are permitted only if they do not hinder achievement of the $P_1$ goals. In general, solving a goal programming problem with preemptive priorities involves solving a sequence of linear programs with different objective functions; $P_1$ goals are considered first, $P_2$ goals second, $P_3$ goals third, and so on. At each stage of the procedure, a revision in the solution is permitted only if it causes no reduction in the achievement of a higher priority goal.

We must solve one linear program for each priority level.

The number of linear programs that we must solve in sequence to develop the solution to a goal programming problem is determined by the number of priority levels. One linear program must be solved for each priority level. We will call the first linear program solved the priority level 1 problem, the second linear program solved the priority level 2 problem, and so on. Each linear program is obtained from the one at the next higher level by changing the objective function and adding a constraint.

We first formulate the objective function for the priority level 1 problem. The client has stated that the portfolio risk index should not exceed 700. Is underachieving the target value of 700 a concern? Clearly, the answer is no because portfolio risk index values of less than 700 correspond to less risk. Is overachieving the target value of 700 a concern? The answer is yes because portfolios with a risk index greater than 700 correspond to unacceptable levels of risk. Thus, the objective function corresponding to the priority level 1 linear program should minimize the value of $d_1^+$.

The goal equations and the funds available constraint have already been developed. Thus, the priority level 1 linear program can now be stated.

### $P_1$ Problem

$$\text{Min} \quad d_1^+$$

s.t.

$$
\begin{aligned}
25x_1 + 50x_2 && \leq 80{,}000 \quad &\text{Funds available} \\
0.50x_1 + 0.25x_2 - d_1^+ + d_1^- && = 700 \quad &P_1 \text{ goal} \\
3x_1 + 5x_2 \quad - d_2^+ + d_2^- &= 9000 \quad &P_2 \text{ goal} \\
x_1, x_2, d_1^+, d_1^-, d_2^+, d_2^- \geq 0
\end{aligned}
$$

## The Graphical Solution Procedure

One approach that can often be used to solve a difficult problem is to break the problem into two or more smaller or easier problems. The linear programming procedure we use to solve the goal programming problem is based on this approach.

The graphical solution procedure for goal programming is similar to that for linear programming presented in Chapter 2. The only difference is that the procedure for goal programming involves a separate solution for each priority level. Recall that the linear programming graphical solution procedure uses a graph to display the values for the decision variables. Because the decision variables are nonnegative, we consider only that portion of the graph where $x_1 \geq 0$ and $x_2 \geq 0$. Recall also that every point on the graph is called a *solution point*.

We begin the graphical solution procedure for the Nicolo Investment problem by identifying all solution points that satisfy the available funds constraint:

$$25x_1 + 50x_2 \leq 80{,}000$$

The shaded region in Figure 15.1, feasible portfolios, consists of all points that satisfy this constraint—that is, values of $x_1$ and $x_2$ for which $25x_1 + 50x_2 \leq 80{,}000$.

The objective for the priority level 1 linear program is to minimize $d_1^+$, the amount by which the portfolio index exceeds the target value of 700. Recall that the $P_1$ goal equation is

$$0.50x_1 + 0.25x_2 - d_1^+ + d_1^- = 700$$

When the $P_1$ goal is met exactly, $d_1^+ = 0$ and $d_1^- = 0$; the goal equation then reduces to $0.50x_1 + 0.25x_2 = 700$. Figure 15.2 shows the graph of this equation; the shaded region identifies all solution points that satisfy the available funds constraint and also result in the value of $d_1^+ = 0$. Thus, the shaded region contains all the feasible solution points that achieve the priority level 1 goal.

At this point, we have solved the priority level 1 problem. Note that alternative optimal solutions are possible; in fact, all solution points in the shaded region in Figure 15.2 maintain a portfolio risk index of 700 or less, and hence $d_1^+ = 0$.

The priority level 2 goal for the Nicolo Investment problem is to find a portfolio that will provide an annual return of at least $9000. Is overachieving the target value of $9000 a concern? Clearly, the answer is no because portfolios with an annual return of more than $9000 correspond to higher returns. Is underachieving the target value of $9000 a concern? The answer is yes because portfolios with an annual return of less than $9000 are not acceptable to the client. Thus, the objective function corresponding to the priority level 2 linear program should minimize the value of $d_2^-$. However, because goal 2 is a secondary goal, the solution to the priority level 2 linear program must not degrade the optimal solution to the priority level 1 problem. Thus, the priority level 2 linear program can now be stated.

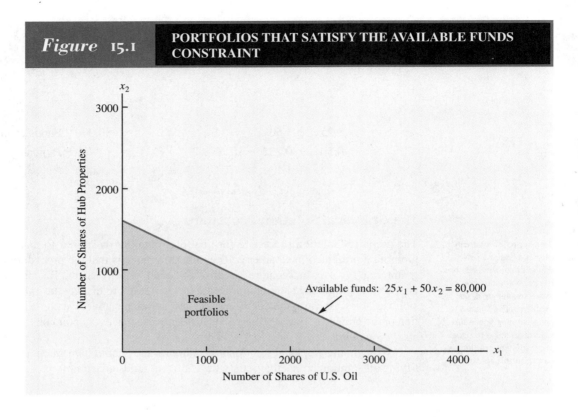

**Figure 15.1    PORTFOLIOS THAT SATISFY THE AVAILABLE FUNDS CONSTRAINT**

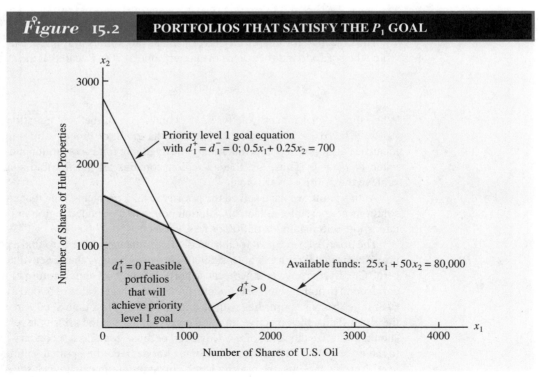

**Figure 15.2    PORTFOLIOS THAT SATISFY THE $P_1$ GOAL**

**$P_2$ Problem**

Min        $d_2^-$

s.t.

$$
\begin{array}{llll}
25x_1 + & 50x_2 & & \leq 80{,}000 & \text{Funds available} \\
0.50x_1 + & 0.25x_2 - d_1^+ + d_1^- & & = \quad 700 & P_1 \text{ goal} \\
3x_1 + & 5x_2 & - d_2^+ + d_2^- = & 9000 & P_2 \text{ goal} \\
& d_1^+ & = & 0 & \text{Maintain achievement} \\
& & & & \text{of } P_1 \text{ goal}
\end{array}
$$

$$x_1, x_2, d_1^+, d_1^-, d_2^+, d_2^- \geq 0$$

Note that the priority level 2 linear program differs from the priority level 1 linear program in two ways. The objective function involves minimizing the amount by which the portfolio annual return underachieves the level 2 goal, and another constraint has been added to ensure that no amount of achievement of the priority level 1 goal is sacrificed.

Let us now continue the graphical solution procedure. The goal equation for the priority level 2 goal is

$$3x_1 + 5x_2 - d_2^+ + d_2^- = 9000$$

When both $d_2^+$ and $d_2^-$ equal zero, this equation reduces to $3x_1 + 5x_2 = 9000$; we show the graph with this equation in Figure 15.3.

At this stage, we cannot consider any solution point that will degrade the achievement of the priority level 1 goal. Figure 15.3 shows that no solution points will achieve the

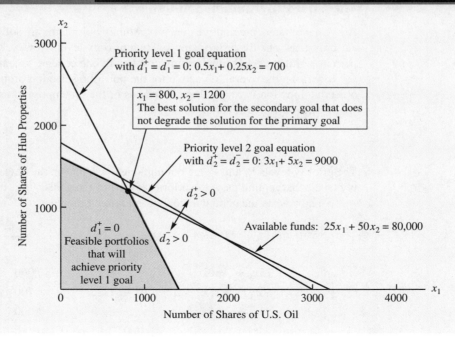

**Figure 15.3    BEST SOLUTION WITH RESPECT TO BOTH GOALS (SOLUTION TO $P_2$ PROBLEM)**

Priority level 1 goal equation with $d_1^+ = d_1^- = 0$: $0.5x_1 + 0.25x_2 = 700$

$x_1 = 800, x_2 = 1200$
The best solution for the secondary goal that does not degrade the solution for the primary goal

Priority level 2 goal equation with $d_2^+ = d_2^- = 0$: $3x_1 + 5x_2 = 9000$

$d_2^+ > 0$

$d_1^+ = 0$
Feasible portfolios that will achieve priority level 1 goal

$d_2^- > 0$

Available funds: $25x_1 + 50x_2 = 80{,}000$

Number of Shares of Hub Properties

Number of Shares of U.S. Oil

priority level 2 goal and maintain the values we were able to achieve for the priority level 1 goal. In fact, the best solution that can be obtained when considering the priority level 2 goal is given by the point ($x_1 = 800$, $x_2 = 1200$); in other words, this point comes the closest to satisfying the priority level 2 goal from among those solutions satisfying the priority level 1 goal. Since the annual return corresponding to this solution point is $3(800) + $5(1200) = $8400$, identifying a portfolio that will satisfy both the priority level 1 and the priority level 2 goals is impossible. In fact, the best solution underachieves goal 2 by $d_2^- = \$9000 - \$8400 = \$600$.

Thus, the goal programming solution for the Nicolo Investment problem recommends that the $80,000 available for investment be used to purchase 800 shares of U.S. Oil and 1200 shares of Hub Properties. Note that the priority level 1 goal of a portfolio risk index of 700 or less has been achieved. However, the priority level 2 goal of at least a $9000 annual return is not achievable. The annual return for the recommended portfolio is $8400.

In summary, the graphical solution procedure for goal programming involves the following steps.

1. Identify the feasible solution points that satisfy the problem constraints.
2. Identify all feasible solutions that achieve the highest-priority goal; if no feasible solutions will achieve the highest priority goal, identify the solution(s) that comes closest to achieving it.
3. Move down one priority level, and determine the "best" solution possible without sacrificing any achievement of higher priority goals.
4. Repeat step 3 until all priority levels have been considered.

*Problem 2 will test your ability to formulate a goal programming model and use the graphical solution procedure to obtain a solution.*

Although the graphical solution procedure is a convenient method for solving goal programming problems involving two decision variables, the solution of larger problems requires a computer-aided approach. In Section 15.2 we illustrate how to use a computer software package to solve more complex goal programming problems.

## The Goal Programming Model

As we have stated, preemptive goal programming problems are solved as a sequence of linear programs: one linear program for each priority level. However, having a notation that permits writing a goal programming problem in one concise statement is helpful.

In writing the overall objective for the portfolio selection problem, we must write the objective function in a way that reminds us of the preemptive priorities. We can do so by writing the objective function as

$$\text{Min } P_1(d_1^+) + P_2(d_2^-)$$

The priority levels $P_1$ and $P_2$ are not numerical weights on the deviation variables, but simply labels that remind us of the priority levels for the goals.

We now write the complete goal programming model as

$$
\begin{aligned}
\text{Min} \quad & P_1(d_1^+) + P_2(d_2^-) \\
\text{s.t.} \quad & \\
& 25x_1 + 50x_2 && \leq 80{,}000 && \text{Funds available} \\
& 0.50x_1 + 0.25x_2 - d_1^+ + d_1^- && = 700 && P_1 \text{ goal} \\
& 3x_1 + 5x_2 - d_2^+ + d_2^- && = 9000 && P_2 \text{ goal} \\
& x_1, x_2, d_1^+, d_1^-, d_2^+, d_2^- \geq 0
\end{aligned}
$$

With the exception of the $P_1$ and $P_2$ priority levels in the objective function, this model is a linear programming model. The solution of this linear program involves solving a sequence of linear programs involving goals at decreasing priority levels.

We now summarize the procedure used to develop a goal programming model.

1. Identify the goals and any constraints that reflect resource capacities or other restrictions that may prevent achievement of the goals.
2. Determine the priority level of each goal; goals with priority level $P_1$ are most important, those with priority level $P_2$ are next most important, and so on.
3. Define the decision variables.
4. Formulate the constraints in the usual linear programming fashion.
5. For each goal, develop a goal equation, with the right-hand side specifying the target value for the goal. Deviation variables $d_i^+$ and $d_i^-$ are included in each goal equation to reflect the possible deviations above or below the target value.
6. Write the objective function in terms of minimizing a prioritized function of the deviation variables.

---

### N O T E S
### *and Comments*

1. The constraints in the general goal programming model are of two types: goal equations and ordinary linear programming constraints. Some analysts call the goal equations *goal constraints* and the ordinary linear programming constraints *system constraints*.
2. You might think of the general goal programming model as having "hard" and "soft" constraints. The hard constraints are the ordinary linear programming constraints that cannot be violated. The soft constraints are the ones resulting from the goal equations. Soft constraints can be violated but with a penalty for doing so. The penalty is reflected by the coefficient of the deviation variable in the objective function. In Section 15.2 we illustrate this point with a problem that has a coefficient of 2 for one of the deviation variables.
3. Note that the constraint added in moving from the linear programming problem at one priority level to the linear programming problem at the next lower priority level becomes a hard constraint. No amount of achievement of a higher priority goal may be sacrificed to achieve a lower priority goal.

---

## 15.2    GOAL PROGRAMMING: SOLVING MORE COMPLEX PROBLEMS

In Section 15.1 we formulated and solved a goal programming model that involved one priority level 1 goal and one priority level 2 goal. In this section we show how to formulate and solve goal programming models that involve multiple goals within the same priority level. Although computer programs have been specially developed to solve goal programming models, these programs are not as readily available as general purpose linear programming software packages. Thus, the computer solution procedure outlined in this section develops a solution to a goal programming model by solving a sequence of linear programming models with a general purpose linear programming software package.

## The Suncoast Office Supplies Problem

The management of Suncoast Office Supplies establishes monthly goals, or quotas, for the types of customers contacted. For the next 4 weeks, Suncoast's customer contact strategy calls for the salesforce, which consists of four salespeople, to make 200 contacts with customers who have previously purchased supplies from the firm. In addition, the strategy calls for 120 contacts of new customers. The purpose of this latter goal is to ensure that the salesforce is continuing to investigate new sources of sales.

Making allowances for travel and waiting time, as well as for demonstration and direct sales time, Suncoast has allocated 2 hours of sales force effort to each contact of a previous customer. New customer contacts tend to take longer and require 3 hours per contact. Normally, each salesperson works 40 hours per week, or 160 hours over the 4-week planning horizon; under a normal work schedule, the four salespeople will have $4(160) = 640$ hours of salesforce time available for customer contacts.

Management is willing to use some overtime, if needed, but is also willing to accept a solution that uses less than the scheduled 640 hours available. However, management wants both overtime and underutilization of the workforce limited to no more than 40 hours over the 4-week period. Thus, in terms of overtime, management's goal is to use no more than $640 + 40 = 680$ hours of salesforce time; and in terms of labor utilization, management's goal is to use at least $640 - 40 = 600$ hours of salesforce time.

In addition to the customer contact goals, Suncoast has established a goal regarding sales volume. Based on its experience, Suncoast estimates that each previous customer contacted will generate $250 of sales and that each new customer contacted will generate $125 of sales. Management wants to generate sales revenue of at least $70,000 for the next month.

Given Suncoast's small salesforce and the short time frame involved, management has decided that the overtime goal and the labor utilization goal are both priority level 1 goals. Management also concluded that the $70,000 sales revenue goal should be a priority level 2 goal and that the two customer contact goals should be priority level 3 goals. Based on these priorities, we can now summarize the goals.

### Priority Level 1 Goals

**Goal 1:**  Do not use any more than 680 hours of sales force time.

**Goal 2:**  Do not use any less than 600 hours of sales force time.

### Priority Level 2 Goal

**Goal 3:**  Generate sales revenue of at least $70,000.

### Priority Level 3 Goals

**Goal 4:**  Call on at least 200 previous customers.

**Goal 5:**  Call on at least 120 new customers.

## Formulating the Goal Equations

Next, we must define the decision variables whose values will be used to determine whether we are able to achieve the goals. Let

$$x_1 = \text{the number of previous customers contacted}$$
$$x_2 = \text{the number of new customers contacted}$$

Using these decision variables and appropriate deviation variables, we can develop a goal equation for each goal. The procedure used parallels the approach introduced in the preceding section. A summary of the results obtained is shown for each goal.

**Goal 1**

$$2x_1 + 3x_2 - d_1^+ + d_1^- = 680$$

where

$d_1^+$ = the amount by which the number of hours used by the salesforce is greater than the target value of 680 hours

$d_1^-$ = the amount by which the number of hours used by the salesforce is less than the target value of 680 hours

**Goal 2**

$$2x_1 + 3x_2 - d_2^+ + d_2^- = 600$$

where

$d_2^+$ = the amount by which the number of hours used by the salesforce is greater than the target value of 600 hours

$d_2^-$ = the amount by which the number of hours used by the salesforce is less than the target value of 600 hours

**Goal 3**

$$250x_1 + 125x_2 - d_3^+ + d_3^- = 70{,}000$$

where

$d_3^+$ = the amount by which the sales revenue is greater than the target value of \$70,000

$d_3^-$ = the amount by which the sales revenue is less than the target value of \$70,000

**Goal 4**

$$x_1 - d_4^+ + d_4^- = 200$$

where

$d_4^+$ = the amount by which the number of previous customer contacts is greater than the target value of 200 previous customer contacts

$d_4^-$ = the amount by which the number of previous customer contacts is less than the target value of 200 previous customer contacts

**Goal 5**

$$x_2 - d_5^+ + d_5^- = 120$$

where

$d_5^+$ = the amount by which the number of new customer contacts is greater than the target value of 120 new customer contacts

$d_5^-$ = the amount by which the number of new customer contacts is less than the target value of 120 new customer contacts

## Formulating the Objective Function

To develop the objective function for the Suncoast Office Supplies problem, we begin by considering the priority level 1 goals. When considering goal 1, if $d_1^+ = 0$, we will have found a solution that uses no more than 680 hours of salesforce time. Because solutions for which $d_1^+$ is greater than zero represent overtime beyond the desired level, the objective function should minimize the value of $d_1^+$. When considering goal 2, if $d_2^- = 0$, we will have found a solution that uses *at least* 600 hours of salesforce time. If $d_2^-$ is greater than zero, however, labor utilization will not have reached the acceptable level. Thus, the objective function for the priority level 1 goals should minimize the value of $d_2^-$. Because both priority level 1 goals are equally important, the objective function for the priority level 1 problem is

$$\text{Min } d_1^+ + d_2^-$$

In considering the priority level 2 goal, we note that management wants to achieve sales revenues of at least $70,000. If $d_3^- = 0$, Suncoast will achieve revenues of *at least* $70,000, and if $d_3^- > 0$, revenues of less than $70,000 will be obtained. Thus, the objective function for the priority level 2 problem is

$$\text{Min } d_3^-$$

Next, we consider what the objective function must be for the priority level 3 problem. When considering goal 4, if $d_4^- = 0$, we will have found a solution with *at least* 200 previous customer contacts; however, if $d_4^- > 0$, we will have underachieved the goal of contacting at least 200 previous customers. Thus, for goal 4 the objective is to minimize $d_4^-$. When considering goal 5, if $d_5^- = 0$, we will have found a solution with *at least* 120 new customer contacts; however, if $d_5^- > 0$, we will have underachieved the goal of contacting at least 120 new customers. Thus, for goal 5 the objective is to minimize $d_5^-$. If both goals 4 and 5 are equal in importance, the objective function for the priority level 3 problem would be

$$\text{Min } d_4^- + d_5^-$$

However, suppose that management believes that generating new customers is vital to the long-run success of the firm and that goal 5 should be weighted more than goal 4. If management believes that goal 5 is twice as important as goal 4, the objective function for the priority level 3 problem would be

$$\text{Min } d_4^- + 2d_5^-$$

Combining the objective functions for all three priority levels, we obtain the overall objective function for the Suncoast Office Supplies problem:

$$\text{Min } P_1(d_1^+) + P_1(d_2^-) + P_2(d_3^-) + P_3(d_4^-) + P_3(2 d_5^-)$$

As we indicated previously, $P_1$, $P_2$, and $P_3$ are simply labels that remind us that goals 1 and 2 are the priority level 1 goals, goal 3 is the priority level 2 goal, and goals 4 and 5 are the priority level 3 goals. We can now write the complete goal programming model for the Suncoast Office Supplies problem as follows:

$$\text{Min} \quad P_1(d_1^+) + P_1(d_2^-) + P_2(d_3^-) + P_3(d_4^-) + P_3(2 d_5^-)$$

s.t.

$$
\begin{array}{llll}
2x_1 + & 3x_2 - d_1^+ + d_1^- & = & 680 \quad \text{Goal 1} \\
2x_1 + & 3x_2 \quad\quad - d_2^+ + d_2^- & = & 600 \quad \text{Goal 2} \\
250x_1 + & 125x_2 \quad\quad - d_3^+ + d_3^- & = & 70{,}000 \quad \text{Goal 3} \\
x_1 \quad\quad & - d_4^+ + d_4^- & = & 200 \quad \text{Goal 4} \\
& x_2 \quad\quad - d_5^+ + d_5^- = & & 120 \quad \text{Goal 5}
\end{array}
$$

$$x_1, x_2, d_1^+, d_1^-, d_2^+, d_2^-, d_3^+, d_3^-, d_4^+, d_4^-, d_5^+, d_5^- \geq 0$$

## Computer Solution

The following computer procedure develops a solution to a goal programming model by solving a sequence of linear programming problems. The first problem comprises all the constraints and all the goal equations for the complete goal programming model; however, the objective function for this problem involves only the $P_1$ priority level goals. Again, we refer to this problem as the $P_1$ problem.

Whatever the solution to the $P_1$ problem, a $P_2$ problem is formed by adding a constraint to the $P_1$ model that ensures that subsequent problems will not degrade the solution obtained for the $P_1$ problem. The objective function for the priority level 2 problem takes into consideration only the $P_2$ goals. We continue the process until we have considered all priority levels. We illustrate the procedure for the Suncoast Office Supplies problem using the linear programming module of The Management Scientist software package.

To solve the Suncoast Office Supplies problem, we begin by solving the $P_1$ problem:

$$\text{Min} \quad d_1^+ + d_2^-$$

s.t.

$$
\begin{array}{llll}
2x_1 + & 3x_2 - d_1^+ + d_1^- & = & 680 \quad \text{Goal 1} \\
2x_1 + & 3x_2 \quad\quad - d_2^+ + d_2^- & = & 600 \quad \text{Goal 2} \\
250x_1 + & 125x_2 \quad\quad - d_3^+ + d_3^- & = & 70{,}000 \quad \text{Goal 3} \\
x_1 \quad\quad & - d_4^+ + d_4^- & = & 200 \quad \text{Goal 4} \\
& x_2 \quad\quad - d_5^+ + d_5^- = & & 120 \quad \text{Goal 5}
\end{array}
$$

$$x_1, x_2, d_1^+, d_1^-, d_2^+, d_2^-, d_3^+, d_3^-, d_4^+, d_4^-, d_5^+, d_5^- \geq 0$$

In Figure 15.4 we show The Management Scientist solution for this linear program. Note that D1PLUS refers to $d_1^+$, D2MINUS refers to $d_2^-$, D1MINUS refers to $d_1^-$, and so on. The solution shows $x_1 = 250$ previous customer contacts and $x_2 = 60$ new customer contacts. Because D1PLUS = 0 and D2MINUS = 0, we see that the solution achieves both goals 1 and 2. Alternatively, the value of the objective function is 0, confirming that both priority level 1 goals have been achieved. Next, we consider goal 3, the priority level 2 goal, which is to minimize D3MINUS. The solution in Figure 15.4 shows that

| | |
|---|---|
| **Figure** 15.4 | **THE MANAGEMENT SCIENTIST SOLUTION OF THE $P_1$ PROBLEM** |

```
Objective Function Value = 0.000

        Variable              Value           Reduced Costs
     --------------        -----------      --------------------
        D1PLUS                0.000               1.000
        D2MINUS               0.000               1.000
          X1                250.000               0.000
          X2                 60.000               0.000
        D1MINUS               0.000               0.000
        D2PLUS               80.000               0.000
        D3PLUS                0.000               0.000
        D3MINUS               0.000               0.000
        D4PLUS               50.000               0.000
        D4MINUS               0.000               0.000
        D5PLUS                0.000               0.000
        D5MINUS              60.000               0.000
```

D3MINUS = 0. Thus, the solution of $x_1$ = 250 previous customer contacts and $x_2$ = 60 new customer contacts also achieves goal 3, the priority level 2 goal, which is to generate a sales revenue of at least $70,000. The fact that D3PLUS = 0 indicates that the current solution satisfies goal 3 exactly at $70,000. Finally, the solution in Figure 15.4 shows D4PLUS = 50 and D5MINUS = 60. These values tell us that goal 4 of the priority level 3 goals is overachieved by 50 previous customers, but that goal 5 is underachieved by 60 new customers. As this point, both the priority level 1 and 2 goals have been achieved, but we need to solve another linear program to determine whether a solution can be identified that will satisfy both of the priority level 3 goals. Therefore, we go directly to the $P_3$ problem.

The linear programming model for the $P_3$ problem is a modification of the linear programming model for the $P_1$ problem. Specifically, the objective function for the $P_3$ problem is expressed in terms of the priority level 3 goals. Thus, the $P_3$ problem objective function becomes minimize D4MINUS + 2D5MINUS. The original five constraints of the $P_1$ problem appear in the $P_3$ problem. However, two additional constraints must be added to insure that the solution to the $P_3$ problem continues to satisfy the priority level 1 and priority level 2 goals. Thus, we add the priority level 1 constraint D1PLUS + D2MINUS = 0 and the priority level 2 constraint D3MINUS = 0. Making these modifications to the $P_1$ problem, we obtain the solution to the $P_3$ problem shown in Figure 15.5.

Referring to Figure 15.5, we see the objective function value of 120 indicates that the priority level 3 goals cannot be achieved. Since D5MINUS = 60, the optimal solution of $x_1$ = 250 and $x_2$ = 60 results in 60 fewer new customer contacts than desired. However, the fact that we have solved the $P_3$ problem tells us the goal programming solution comes as close as possible to satisfying priority level 3 goals given the achievement of both the priority level 1 and 2 goals. Because all priority levels have been considered, the solution procedure is finished. The optimal solution for Suncoast is to contact 250 previous customers and 60 new customers. Although this solution will not achieve management's goal of contacting at least 120 new customers, it does achieve each of the other goals specified. If management isn't happy with this solution, a different set of priorities could be considered. Management must keep in mind, however, that in any situation involving multiple goals at different priority levels, rarely will all the goals be achieved with existing resources.

| Figure 15.5 | THE MANAGEMENT SCIENTIST SOLUTION OF THE $P_3$ PROBLEM |
|---|---|

Objective Function Value = 120.000

| Variable | Value | Reduced Costs |
|---|---|---|
| D1PLUS | 0.000 | 0.000 |
| D2MINUS | 0.000 | 1.000 |
| X1 | 250.000 | 0.000 |
| X2 | 60.000 | 0.000 |
| D1MINUS | 0.000 | 1.000 |
| D2PLUS | 80.000 | 0.000 |
| D3PLUS | 0.000 | 0.008 |
| D3MINUS | 0.000 | 0.000 |
| D4PLUS | 50.000 | 0.000 |
| D4MINUS | 0.000 | 1.000 |
| D5PLUS | 0.000 | 2.000 |
| D5MINUS | 60.000 | 0.000 |

**NOTES and Comments**

1. Not all goal programming problems involve multiple priority levels. For problems with one priority level, only one linear program needs to be solved to obtain the goal programming solution. The analyst simply minimizes the weighted deviations from the goals. Trade-offs are permitted among the goals because they are all at the same priority level.

2. The goal programming approach can be used when the analyst is confronted with an infeasible solution to an ordinary linear program. Reformulating some constraints as goal equations with deviation variables allows a solution that minimizes the weighted sum of the deviation variables. Often, this approach will suggest a reasonable solution.

3. The approach that we used to solve goal programming problems with multiple priority levels is to solve a sequence of linear programs. These linear programs are closely related so that complete reformulation and solution are not necessary. By changing the objective function and adding a constraint, we can go from one linear program to the next.

## 15.3    SCORING MODELS

A scoring model is a relatively quick and easy way to identify the best decision alternative for a multicriteria decision problem. We will demonstrate the use of a scoring model for a job selection application.

Assume that a graduating college student with a double major in finance and accounting has received job offers for the following three positions:

- A financial analyst for an investment firm located in Chicago
- An accountant for a manufacturing firm located in Denver
- An auditor for a CPA firm located in Houston

When asked about which job is preferred, the student made the following comments: "The financial analyst position in Chicago provides the best opportunity for my long-run career advancement. However, I would prefer living in Denver rather than in Chicago or Houston. On the other hand, I liked the management style and philosophy at the Houston CPA firm the best." The student's statement points out that this example is clearly a multi-criteria decision problem. Considering only the *long-run career advancement* criterion, the financial analyst position in Chicago is the preferred decision alternative. Considering only the *location* criterion, the best decision alternative is the accountant position in Denver. Finally, considering only the *management style* criterion, the best alternative is the auditor position with the CPA firm in Houston. For most individuals, a multicriteria decision problem that requires a trade-off among the several criteria is difficult to solve. In this section, we describe how a **scoring model** can assist in analyzing a multicriteria decision problem and help identify the preferred decision alternative.

The steps required to develop a scoring model are as follows:

Step 1 Develop a list of the criteria to be considered. The criteria are the factors that the decision maker considers relevant for evaluating each decision alternative.

Step 2 Assign a weight to each criterion that describes the criterion's relative importance. Let

$$w_i = \text{the weight for criterion } i$$

Step 3 Assign a rating for each criterion that shows how well each decision alternative satisfies the criterion. Let

$$r_{ij} = \text{the rating for criterion } i \text{ and decision alternative } j$$

Step 4 Compute the score for each decision alternative. Let

$$S_j = \text{score for decision alternative } j$$

The equation used to compute $S_j$ is as follows:

$$S_j = \sum_i w_i r_{ij} \tag{15.1}$$

Step 5 Order the decision alternatives from the highest score to the lowest score to provide the scoring model's ranking of the decision alternatives. The decision alternative with the highest score is the recommended decision alternative.

> A scoring model enables a decision maker to identify the criteria and indicate the weight or importance of each criterion.

Let us return to the multicriteria job-selection problem the graduating student was facing and illustrate the use of a scoring model to assist in the decision-making process. In carrying out Step 1 of the scoring model procedure, the student listed seven criteria as important factors in the decision-making process. These criteria are as follows:

- Career advancement
- Location
- Management style
- Salary
- Prestige
- Job security
- Enjoyment of the work

In Step 2, a weight is assigned to each criterion to indicate the criterions relative importance in the decision-making process. For example, using the following five-point scale, this question would be posed for the career advancement criterion:

Relative to the other criteria you are considering, how important is career advancement?

| Importance | Weight |
|---|---|
| Very important | 5 |
| Somewhat important | 4 |
| Average importance | 3 |
| Somewhat unimportant | 2 |
| Very unimportant | 1 |

By repeating this question for each of the seven criteria, the student provided the criterion weights shown in Table 15.1. Using this table, we see that career advancement and enjoyment of the work are the two most important criteria, each receiving a weight of 5. The management style and job security criteria are both considered somewhat important, and thus each received a weight of 4. Location and salary are considered average in importance, each receiving a weight of 3. Finally, because prestige is considered to be somewhat unimportant, it received a weight of 2.

The weights shown in Table 15.1 are subjective values provided by the student. A different student would most likely choose to weight the criteria differently. One of the key advantages of a scoring model is that it uses the subjective weights that most closely reflect the preferences of the individual decision maker.

In Step 3, each decision alternative is rated in terms of how well it satisfies each criterion. For example, using a nine-point scale, the specific question for the "financial analyst in Chicago" alternative and the career advancement criterion would be as follows:

To what extent does the financial analyst position in Chicago satisfy your career advancement criterion?

| Level of Satisfaction | Rating |
|---|---|
| Extremely high | 9 |
| Very high | 8 |
| High | 7 |
| Slightly high | 6 |
| Average | 5 |
| Slightly low | 4 |
| Low | 3 |
| Very low | 2 |
| Extremely low | 1 |

A score of 8 on this question would indicate that the student believes the financial analyst position would be rated "very high" in terms of satisfying the career advancement criterion.

This scoring process must be completed for each combination of decision alternative and decision criterion. Because seven decision criteria and three decision alternatives need to be considered, $7 \times 3 = 21$ ratings must be provided. Table 15.2 summarizes the student's responses. Scanning this table provides some insights about how the student rates each

| Table 15.1 | WEIGHTS FOR THE SEVEN JOB SELECTION CRITERIA | |
|---|---|---|

| Criterion | Importance | Weight ($w_i$) |
|---|---|---|
| Career advancement | Very important | 5 |
| Location | Average importance | 3 |
| Management style | Somewhat important | 4 |
| Salary | Average importance | 3 |
| Prestige | Somewhat unimportant | 2 |
| Job security | Somewhat important | 4 |
| Enjoyment of the work | Very important | 5 |

decision criterion and decision alternative combination. For example, a rating of 9, corresponding to an extremely high level of satisfaction, only appears for the management style criterion and the auditor position in Houston. Thus, considering all combinations, the student rates the auditor position in Houston as the very best in terms of satisfying the management criterion. The lowest rating in the table is a 3 that appears for the location criterion and the financial analyst position in Chicago. This rating indicates that Chicago is rated "low" in terms of satisfying the student's location criterion. Other insights and interpretations are possible, but the question at this point is how does a scoring model use the data in Tables 15.1 and 15.2 to identify the best overall decision alternative.

Step 4 of the procedure shows that equation (15.1) is used to compute the score for each decision alternative. The data in Table 15.1 provide the weight for each criterion ($w_i$) and the data in Table 15.2 provide the ratings of each decision alternative for each criterion ($r_{ij}$). Thus for decision alternative 1, the score for the financial analyst position in Chicago is

$$S_1 = \sum_i w_i \, r_{i1} = 5(8) + 3(3) + 4(5) + 3(6) + 2(7) + 4(4) + 5(8) = 157$$

By comparing the scores for each criterion, a decision maker can learn why a particular decision alternative has the highest score.

The scores for the other decision alternatives are computed in the same manner. The computations are summarized in Table 15.3.

From Table 15.3, we see that the highest score of 167 corresponds to the accountant position in Denver. Thus, the accountant position in Denver is the recommended decision

| Table 15.2 | RATINGS FOR EACH DECISION CRITERIA AND EACH DECISION ALTERNATIVE COMBINATION | | |
|---|---|---|---|

| | Decision Alternative | | |
|---|---|---|---|
| Criterion | Financial Analyst Chicago | Accountant Denver | Auditor Houston |
| Career Advancement | 8 | 6 | 4 |
| Location | 3 | 8 | 7 |
| Management style | 5 | 6 | 9 |
| Salary | 6 | 7 | 5 |
| Prestige | 7 | 5 | 4 |
| Job security | 4 | 7 | 6 |
| Enjoyment of the work | 8 | 6 | 5 |

| Table 15.3 | COMPUTATION OF SCORES FOR THE THREE DECISION ALTERNATIVES | | | | | | |
|---|---|---|---|---|---|---|---|
| | | **Decision Alternative** | | | | | |
| | | **Financial Analyst Chicago** | | **Accountant Denver** | | **Auditor Houston** | |
| | **Weight** | **Rating** | **Score** | **Rating** | **Score** | **Rating** | **Score** |
| **Criterion** | $w_i$ | $r_{i1}$ | $w_i r_{i1}$ | $r_{i2}$ | $w_i r_{i2}$ | $r_{i3}$ | $w_i r_{i3}$ |
| Career advancement | 5 | 8 | 40 | 6 | 30 | 4 | 20 |
| Location | 3 | 3 | 9 | 8 | 24 | 7 | 21 |
| Management style | 4 | 5 | 20 | 6 | 24 | 9 | 36 |
| Salary | 3 | 6 | 18 | 7 | 21 | 5 | 15 |
| Prestige | 2 | 7 | 14 | 5 | 10 | 4 | 8 |
| Job security | 4 | 4 | 16 | 7 | 28 | 6 | 24 |
| Enjoyment of the work | 5 | 8 | 40 | 6 | 30 | 5 | 25 |
| Score | | | 157 | | 167 | | 149 |

alternative. The financial analyst position in Chicago, with a score of 157, is ranked second, and the auditor position in Houston, with a score of 149, is ranked third.

## 15.4   THE ANALYTIC HIERARCHY PROCESS

The **analytic hierarchy process (AHP),** developed by Thomas L. Saaty,[1] is designed to solve complex multicriteria decision problems. AHP requires the decision maker to provide judgments about the relative importance of each criterion and then specify a preference for each decision alternative using each criterion. The output of AHP is a prioritized ranking of the decision alternatives based on the overall preferences expressed by the decision maker.

To introduce AHP, we consider a car purchasing decision problem faced by Diane Payne. After a preliminary analysis of the makes and models of several used cars, Diane has narrowed her list of decision alternatives to three cars: a Honda Accord, a Saturn, and a Chevrolet Cavalier. Table 15.4 summarizes the information Diane has collected about these cars.

Diane decided that the following criteria were relevant for her car-selection decision process:

- Price
- Miles per gallon (MPG)
- Comfort
- Style

Data regarding the Price and MPG are provided in Table 15.4. However, measures of the Comfort and Style cannot be specified so directly. Diane will need to consider factors such as the car's interior, type of audio system, ease of entry, seat adjustments, and driver visibility in order to determine the comfort level of each car. The style criterion will have to be based on Diane's subjective evaluation of the color and the general appearance of each car.

---

[1] T. L. Saaty, *The Analytic Hierarchy Process* (New York: McGraw-Hill, 1988).

| Table 15.4 | INFORMATION FOR THE CAR SELECTION PROBLEM | | |
|---|---|---|---|
| | Decision Alternative | | |
| **Characteristics** | **Accord** | **Saturn** | **Cavalier** |
| Price | $13,100 | $11,200 | $9500 |
| Color | Black | Red | Blue |
| Miles per gallon | 19 | 23 | 28 |
| Interior | Deluxe | Above Average | Standard |
| Body type | 4-door midsize | 2-door sport | 2-door compact |
| Sound system | AM/FM, tape, CD | AM/FM | AM/FM |

Even when a criterion such as price can be as easily measured, subjectivity becomes an issue whenever a decision maker indicates his or her personal preference for the decision alternatives based on price. For instance, the price of the Accord ($13,100) is $3600 more than the price of the Cavalier ($9500). The $3600 difference might represent a great deal of money to one person, but not much of a difference to another person. Thus, whether the Accord is considered "extremely more expensive" than the Cavalier or perhaps only "moderately more expensive" than the Cavalier depends upon the financial status and the subjective opinion of the person making the comparison. An advantage of AHP is that it can handle situations in which the unique subjective judgments of the individual decision maker constitute an important part of the decision-making process.

> AHP allows a decision maker to express personal preferences and subjective judgments about the various aspects of a multicriteria problem.

### Developing the Hierarchy

The first step in AHP is to develop a graphical representation of the problem in terms of the overall goal, the criteria to be used, and the decision alternatives. Such a graph depicts the **hierarchy** for the problem. Figure 15.6 shows the hierarchy for the car selection problem. Note that the first level of the hierarchy shows that the overall goal is to select the best car. At the second level, the four criteria (Price, MPG, Comfort, and Style) each contribute to the achievement of the overall goal. Finally, at the third level, each decision alternative—Accord, Saturn, and Cavalier—contributes to each criterion in a unique way.

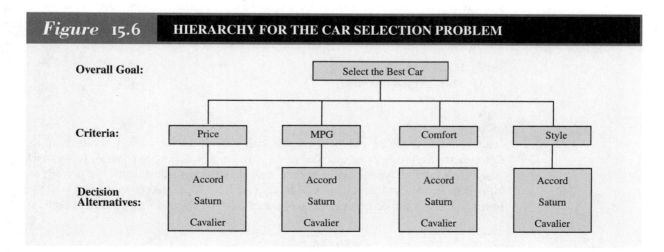

**Figure 15.6     HIERARCHY FOR THE CAR SELECTION PROBLEM**

Using AHP, the decision maker specifies judgments about the relative importance of each of the four criteria in terms of its contribution to the achievement of the overall goal. At the next level, the decision maker indicates a preference for each decision alternative based on each criterion. A mathematical process is used to synthesize the information on the relative importance of the criteria and the preferences for the decision alternatives to provide an overall priority ranking of the decision alternatives. In the car selection problem, AHP will use Diane's personal preferences to provide a priority ranking of the three cars in terms of how well each car meets the overall goal of being the *best* car.

## 15.5    ESTABLISHING PRIORITIES USING AHP

In this section we show how AHP uses pairwise comparisons expressed by the decision maker to establish priorities for the criteria and priorities for the decision alternatives based on each criterion. Using the car selection example, we show how AHP determines priorities for each of the following:

1.  How the four criteria contribute to the overall goal of selecting the best car
2.  How the three cars compare using the Price criterion
3.  How the three cars compare using the MPG criterion
4.  How the three cars compare using the Comfort criterion
5.  How the three cars compare using the Style criterion

In the following discussion, we demonstrate how to establish priorities for the four criteria in terms of how each contributes to the overall goal of selecting the best car. The priorities of the three cars using each criterion can be determined similarly.

### Pairwise Comparisons

Pairwise comparisons form the fundamental building blocks of AHP. In establishing the priorities for the four criteria, AHP will require Diane to state how important each criterion is relative to each other criterion when the criteria are compared two at a time (pairwise). That is, with the four criteria (Price, MPG, Comfort, and Style) Diane must make the following pairwise comparisons:

> Price compared to MPG
>
> Price compared to Comfort
>
> Price compared to Style
>
> MPG compared to Comfort
>
> MPG compared to Style
>
> Comfort compared to Style

In each comparison, Diane must select the more important criterion and then express a judgment of how much more important the selected criterion is.

For example, in the Price-MPG pairwise comparison, assume that Diane indicates that Price is more important than MPG. To measure how much more important Price is compared to MPG, AHP uses scale with values from 1 to 9. Table 15.5 shows how the decision maker's verbal description of the relative importance between the two criteria are converted into a numerical rating. In the car selection example, suppose that Diane states that Price is "moderately more important" than MPG. In this case, a numerical rating of 3 is assigned to

| Table 15.5 | COMPARISON SCALE FOR THE IMPORTANCE OF CRITERIA USING AHP |
|---|---|

| Verbal Judgment | Numerical Rating |
|---|---|
| Extremely more important | 9 |
| | 8 |
| Very strongly more important | 7 |
| | 6 |
| Strongly more important | 5 |
| | 4 |
| Moderately more important | 3 |
| | 2 |
| Equally important | 1 |

the Price-MPG pairwise comparison. Using Table 15.5, we see "strongly more important" receives a numerical rating of 5 while "very strongly more important" receives a numerical rating of 7. Intermediate judgments such as "strongly to very strongly more important" are possible and would receive a numerical rating of 6.

Table 15.6 provides a summary of the six pairwise comparisons Diane provided for the car selection problem. Using the information in this table, Diane has specified that

Price is moderately more important than MPG

Price is equally to moderately more important than Comfort

Price is equally to moderately more important than Style

Comfort is moderately to strongly more important than MPG

Style is moderately to strongly more important than MPG

Style is equally to moderately more important than Comfort

AHP uses the numerical ratings from the pairwise comparisons to establish a priority or importance measure for each criterion.

As shown, the flexibility of AHP can accommodate the unique preferences of each individual decision maker. First, the choice of the criteria that are considered can vary depending upon the decision maker. Not everyone would agree that Price, MPG, Comfort, and Style are the only criteria to be considered in a car selection problem. Perhaps you would

| Table 15.6 | SUMMARY OF DIANE PAYNE'S PAIRWISE COMPARISONS OF THE FOUR CRITERIA FOR THE CAR SELECTION PROBLEM |
|---|---|

| Pairwise Comparison | More Important Criterion | How Much More Important | Numerical Rating |
|---|---|---|---|
| Price-MPG | Price | Moderately | 3 |
| Price-Comfort | Price | Equally to moderately | 2 |
| Price-Style | Price | Equally to moderately | 2 |
| MPG-Comfort | Comfort | Moderately to strongly | 4 |
| MPG-Style | Style | Moderately to strongly | 4 |
| Comfort-Style | Style | Equally to moderately | 2 |

want to add safety, resale value, and/or other criteria if you were making the car selection decision. AHP can accommodate any set of criteria specified by the decision maker. Of course, if additional criteria are added, more pairwise comparisons will be necessary. In addition, if you agree with Diane that Price, MPG, Comfort, and Style are the four criteria to use, you would probably disagree with her as to the relative importance of the criteria. Using the format of Table 15.6, you could provide your own assessment of the importance of each pairwise comparison, and AHP would adjust the numerical ratings to reflect your personal preferences.

## The Pairwise Comparison Matrix

To determine the priorities for the four criteria, we need to construct a matrix of the pairwise comparison ratings provided in Table 15.6. Using the four criteria, the **pairwise comparison matrix** will consist of four rows and four columns as shown here:

|         | Price | MPG | Comfort | Style |
|---------|-------|-----|---------|-------|
| Price   |       |     |         |       |
| MPG     |       |     |         |       |
| Comfort |       |     |         |       |
| Style   |       |     |         |       |

Each of the numerical ratings in Table 15.6 must be entered into the pairwise comparison matrix. To illustrate how this is done, consider the numerical rating of 3 for the Price-MPG pairwise comparison. Table 15.6 shows that for this pairwise comparison that Price is the most important criterion. Thus, we must enter a 3 into the row label Price and the column labeled MPG in the pairwise comparison matrix. In general, the entries in the column labeled Most Important Criterion in Table 15.6 indicate which row of the pairwise comparison matrix the numerical rating must be placed in. As another illustration, consider the MPG-Comfort pairwise comparison. Table 15.6 shows that Comfort is the most important criterion for this pairwise comparison and that the numerical rating is 4. Thus, we enter a 4 into the row labeled Comfort and into the column labeled MPG. Following this procedure for the other pairwise comparisons shown in Table 15.6, we obtain the following pairwise comparison matrix.

|         | Price | MPG | Comfort | Style |
|---------|-------|-----|---------|-------|
| Price   |       | 3   | 2       | 2     |
| MPG     |       |     |         |       |
| Comfort |       | 4   |         |       |
| Style   |       | 4   | 2       |       |

Because the diagonal elements are comparing each criterion to itself, the diagonal elements of the pairwise comparison matrix are always equal to 1. For example, if Price is compared to Price, the verbal judgment would be "equally important" with a rating of 1; thus, a 1 would be placed into the row labeled Price and into the column labeled Price in the pairwise comparison matrix. At this point, the pairwise comparison matrix appears as follows:

|         | Price | MPG | Comfort | Style |
|---------|-------|-----|---------|-------|
| Price   | 1     | 3   | 2       | 2     |
| MPG     |       | 1   |         |       |
| Comfort |       | 4   | 1       |       |
| Style   |       | 4   | 2       | 1     |

All that remains is to complete the entries for the remaining cells of the matrix. To illustrate how these values are obtained, consider the numerical rating of 3 for the Price-MPG pairwise comparison. This rating implies that the MPG-Price pairwise comparison should have a rating of $\frac{1}{3}$. That is, since Diane has already indicated Price is moderately more important than MPG (a rating of 3), we can infer that a pairwise comparison of MPG relative to Price should be $\frac{1}{3}$. Similarly, since the Comfort-MPG pairwise comparison has a rating of 4, the MPG-Comfort pairwise comparison would be $\frac{1}{4}$. Thus the complete pairwise comparison matrix for the car selection criteria is as follows:

|         | Price          | MPG | Comfort        | Style          |
|---------|----------------|-----|----------------|----------------|
| Price   | 1              | 3   | 2              | 2              |
| MPG     | $\frac{1}{3}$  | 1   | $\frac{1}{4}$  | $\frac{1}{4}$  |
| Comfort | $\frac{1}{2}$  | 4   | 1              | $\frac{1}{2}$  |
| Style   | $\frac{1}{2}$  | 4   | 2              | 1              |

## Synthesization

Using the pairwise comparison matrix, we can now calculate the priority of each criterion in terms of its contribution to the overall goal of selecting the best car. This aspect of AHP is referred to as **synthesization.** The exact mathematical procedure required to perform synthesization is beyond the scope of this text. However, the following three-step procedure provides a good approximation of the synthesization results.

1. Sum the values in each column of the pairwise comparison matrix.
2. Divide each element in the pairwise comparison matrix by its column total; the resulting matrix is referred to as the **normalized pairwise comparison matrix.**
3. Compute the average of the elements in each row of the normalized pairwise comparison matrix; these averages provide the priorities for the criteria.

To show how the synthesization process works, we carry out this three-step procedure for the criteria pairwise comparison matrix.

Step 1  Sum the values in each column

| | Price | MPG | Comfort | Style |
|---|---|---|---|---|
| Price | 1 | 3 | 2 | 2 |
| MPG | ⅓ | 1 | ¼ | ¼ |
| Comfort | ½ | 4 | 1 | ½ |
| Style | ½ | 4 | 2 | 1 |
| Sum | 2.333 | 12.000 | 5.250 | 3.750 |

Step 2  Divide each element of the matrix by its column total

| | Price | MPG | Comfort | Style |
|---|---|---|---|---|
| Price | 0.429 | 0.250 | 0.381 | 0.533 |
| MPG | 0.143 | 0.083 | 0.048 | 0.067 |
| Comfort | 0.214 | 0.333 | 0.190 | 0.133 |
| Style | 0.214 | 0.333 | 0.381 | 0.267 |

Step 3  Average the elements in each row to determine the priority of each criterion

| | Price | MPG | Comfort | Style | Priority |
|---|---|---|---|---|---|
| Price | 0.429 | 0.250 | 0.381 | 0.533 | 0.398 |
| MPG | 0.143 | 0.083 | 0.048 | 0.067 | 0.085 |
| Comfort | 0.214 | 0.333 | 0.190 | 0.133 | 0.218 |
| Style | 0.214 | 0.333 | 0.381 | 0.267 | 0.299 |

The AHP synthesization procedure has provided the priority of each criterion in terms of its contribution to the overall goal of selecting the best car. Thus, using Diane's pairwise comparisons provided in Table 15.6, AHP has determined that Price with a priority of 0.398 is the most important criterion in the car selection process. Style with a priority of 0.299 ranks second in importance and is closely followed by Comfort with a priority of 0.218. MPG is the least important criterion with a priority of 0.085.

## Consistency

A key step in AHP is the making of several pairwise comparisons as previously described. An important consideration in this process is the **consistency** of the pairwise judgments provided by the decision maker. For example, if criterion A compared to criterion B has a numerical rating of 3 and if criterion B compared to criterion C has a numerical rating of 2, perfect consistency of criterion A compared to criterion C would have a numerical rating of $3 \times 2 = 6$. If the A to C numerical rating assigned by the decision maker was 4 or 5, some inconsistency would exist among the pairwise comparison.

With numerous pairwise comparisons, perfect consistency is difficult to achieve. In fact, some degree of inconsistency can be expected to exist in almost any set of pairwise comparisons. To handle the consistency issue, AHP provides a method for measuring the degree of consistency among the pairwise comparisons provided by the decision maker. If the degree of consistency is unacceptable, the decision maker should review and revise the pairwise comparisons before proceeding with the AHP analysis.

AHP provides a measure of the consistency for the pairwise comparisons by computing a **consistency ratio.** This ratio is designed in such a way that a value *greater than* 0.10 indicates an inconsistency in the pairwise judgments. Thus, if the consistency ratio is 0.10 or less, the consistency of the pairwise comparisons is considered reasonable, and the AHP process can continue with the synthesization computations.

Although the exact mathematical computation of the consistency ratio is beyond the scope of this text, an approximation of the ratio can be obtained with little difficulty. The step-by-step procedure for estimating the consistency ratio for the criteria of the car selection problem follows.

> A consistency ratio greater than 0.10 indicates inconsistency in the pairwise comparisons. In such cases, the decision maker should review the pairwise comparisons before proceeding.

Step 1  Multiply each value in the first column of the pairwise comparison matrix by the priority of the first item; multiply each value in the second column of the pairwise comparison matrix by the priority of the second item; continue this process for all columns of the pairwise comparison matrix. Sum the values across the rows to obtain a vector of values labeled "weighted sum." This computation for the car selection problem is as follows:

$$0.398 \begin{bmatrix} 1 \\ \frac{1}{3} \\ \frac{1}{2} \\ \frac{1}{2} \end{bmatrix} + 0.085 \begin{bmatrix} 3 \\ 1 \\ 4 \\ 4 \end{bmatrix} + 0.218 \begin{bmatrix} 2 \\ \frac{1}{4} \\ 1 \\ 2 \end{bmatrix} + 0.299 \begin{bmatrix} 2 \\ \frac{1}{4} \\ \frac{1}{2} \\ 1 \end{bmatrix} =$$

$$\begin{bmatrix} 0.398 \\ 0.133 \\ 0.199 \\ 0.199 \end{bmatrix} + \begin{bmatrix} 0.255 \\ 0.085 \\ 0.340 \\ 0.340 \end{bmatrix} + \begin{bmatrix} 0.436 \\ 0.054 \\ 0.218 \\ 0.436 \end{bmatrix} + \begin{bmatrix} 0.598 \\ 0.075 \\ 0.149 \\ 0.299 \end{bmatrix} = \begin{bmatrix} 1.687 \\ 0.347 \\ 0.907 \\ 1.274 \end{bmatrix}$$

Step 2  Divide the elements of the weighted sum vector obtained in Step 1 by the corresponding priority for each criterion.

$$\text{Price} \quad \frac{1.687}{0.398} = 4.236$$

$$\text{MPG} \quad \frac{0.347}{0.085} = 4.077$$

$$\text{Comfort} \quad \frac{0.907}{0.218} = 4.163$$

$$\text{Style} \quad \frac{1.274}{0.299} = 4.264$$

**Step 3** Compute the average of the values found in step 2; this average is denoted $\lambda_{max}$.

$$\lambda_{max} = \frac{(4.236 + 4.077 + 4.163 + 4.264)}{4} = 4.185$$

**Step 4** Compute the consistency index (CI) as follows:

$$CI = \frac{\lambda_{max} - n}{n - 1}$$

where $n$ is the number of items being compared. Thus, we have

$$CI = \frac{4.185 - 4}{4 - 1} = 0.0616$$

**Step 5** Compute the consistency ratio, which is defined as

$$CR = \frac{CI}{RI}$$

where RI is the consistency index of a *randomly* generated pairwise comparison matrix. The value of RI depends on the number of items being compared and is given as follows:

| $n$ | 3 | 4 | 5 | 6 | 7 | 8 |
|---|---|---|---|---|---|---|
| **RI** | 0.58 | 0.90 | 1.12 | 1.24 | 1.32 | 1.41 |

Thus, for the car selection problem with $n = 4$ criteria, we have RI = 0.90 and a consistency ratio

$$CR = \frac{0.0616}{0.90} = 0.068$$

Problem 16 will give you practice with the synthesization calculations and determining the consistency ratio.

As mentioned previously, a consistency ratio of 0.10 or less is considered acceptable. Since the pairwise comparisons for the car selection criteria show CR = 0.068, we can conclude that the degree of consistency in the pairwise comparisons is acceptable.

## Other Pairwise Comparisons for the Car Selection Problem

Continuing with the AHP analysis of the car selection problem, we need to use the pairwise comparison procedure to determine the priorities for the three cars using each of the criteria: Price, MPG, Comfort, and Style. Determining these priorities requires Diane to express pairwise comparison preferences for the cars using each criterion one at a time. For example, using the price criterion, Diane must make the following pairwise comparisons:

> the Accord compared to the Saturn
> 
> the Accord compared to the Cavalier
> 
> the Saturn compared to the Cavalier

In each comparison, Diane must select the more preferred car and then express a judgment of how much more preferred the selected car is.

For example, using the Price as the basis for comparison, assume that Diane considers the Accord-Saturn pairwise comparison and indicates that the less expensive Saturn is more preferred. Table 15.7 shows how AHP uses Diane's verbal description of the preference between the Accord and Saturn to determine a numerical rating of the preference. For example, suppose that Diane states that based on Price, the Saturn is "moderately more preferred" to the Accord. Thus, using the Price criterion, a numerical rating of 3 is assigned to the Saturn row and Accord column of the pairwise comparison matrix.

Table 15.8 shows the summary of the car pairwise comparisons that Diane provided for each criterion of the car selection problem. Using this table and referring to selected pairwise comparison entries, we see that Diane has stated the following preferences:

In terms of Price, the Cavalier is moderately to strongly more preferred than the Accord.

In terms of the MPG, the Cavalier is moderately more preferred than the Saturn.

In terms of Comfort, the Accord is very strongly to extremely more preferred than the Cavalier.

In terms of Style, the Saturn is moderately more preferred than the Accord.

| *Table* 15.7 | PAIRWISE COMPARISON SCALE FOR THE PREFERENCE OF DECISION ALTERNATIVES USING AHP |
|---|---|

| Verbal Judgment | Numerical Rating |
|---|---|
| Extremely preferred | 9 |
| | 8 |
| Very strongly preferred | 7 |
| | 6 |
| Strongly preferred | 5 |
| | 4 |
| Moderately preferred | 3 |
| | 2 |
| Equally preferred | 1 |

| *Table* 15.8 | PAIRWISE COMPARISON MATRIXES SHOWING PREFERENCES FOR THE CARS USING EACH CRITERION |
|---|---|

**Price**

| | Accord | Saturn | Cavalier |
|---|---|---|---|
| Accord | 1 | $\frac{1}{3}$ | $\frac{1}{4}$ |
| Saturn | 3 | 1 | $\frac{1}{2}$ |
| Cavalier | 4 | 2 | 1 |

**MPG**

| | Accord | Saturn | Cavalier |
|---|---|---|---|
| Accord | 1 | $\frac{1}{4}$ | $\frac{1}{6}$ |
| Saturn | 4 | 1 | $\frac{1}{3}$ |
| Cavalier | 6 | 3 | 1 |

**Comfort**

| | Accord | Saturn | Cavalier |
|---|---|---|---|
| Accord | 1 | 2 | 8 |
| Saturn | $\frac{1}{2}$ | 1 | 6 |
| Cavalier | $\frac{1}{8}$ | $\frac{1}{6}$ | 1 |

**Style**

| | Accord | Saturn | Cavalier |
|---|---|---|---|
| Accord | 1 | $\frac{1}{3}$ | 4 |
| Saturn | 3 | 1 | 7 |
| Cavalier | $\frac{1}{4}$ | $\frac{1}{7}$ | 1 |

Using the pairwise comparison matrixes in Table 15.8, many other insights may be gained about the preferences Diana has expressed for the cars. However, at this point, AHP continues by synthesizing each of the four pairwise comparison matrixes in Table 15.8 in order to determine the priority of each car using each criterion. A synthesization is conducted for each pairwise comparison matrix using the three-step procedure described previously for the criteria pairwise comparison matrix. Four synthesization computations provide the four sets of priorities shown in Table 15.9. Using this table, we see that the Cavalier is the preferred alternative based on Price (0.557), the Cavalier is the preferred alternative based on MPG (0.639), the Accord is the preferred alternative based on Comfort (0.593), and the Saturn is the preferred alternative based on Style (0.656). At this point, no car is the clear, overall best. The next section shows how to combine the priorities for the criteria and the priorities in Table 15.9 to develop an overall priority ranking for the three cars.

Practice setting up a pairwise comparison matrix and determine whether judgments are consistent by working problem 20.

| *Table* 15.9 | PRIORITIES FOR EACH CAR USING EACH CRITERION | | | |
|---|---|---|---|---|
| | Criterion | | | |
| | Price | MPG | Comfort | Style |
| Accord | 0.123 | 0.087 | 0.593 | 0.265 |
| Saturn | 0.320 | 0.274 | 0.341 | 0.656 |
| Cavalier | 0.557 | 0.639 | 0.065 | 0.080 |

## 15.6    USING AHP TO DEVELOP AN OVERALL PRIORITY RANKING

In Section 15.5, we used Diane's pairwise comparisons of the four criteria to develop the priorities of 0.398 for Price, 0.085 for MPG, 0.281 for Comfort, and 0.299 for Style. We now want to use these priorities and the priorities shown in Table 15.9 to develop an overall priority ranking for the three cars.

The procedure used to compute the overall priority is to weight each car's priority shown in Table 15.9 by the corresponding criterion priority. For example, the Price criterion has a priority of 0.398, and the Accord has a priority of 0.123 in terms of the Price criterion. Thus, $0.398 \times 0.123 = 0.049$ is the priority value of the Accord based on the Price criterion. To obtain the overall priority of the Accord, we need to make similar computations for the MPG, Comfort, and Style criteria and then add the values to obtain the overall priority. This calculation is as follows:

**Overall Priority of the Accord:**

$$0.398(0.123) + 0.085(0.087) + 0.218(0.593) + 0.299(0.265) = 0.265$$

Repeating this calculation for the Saturn and the Cavalier, we obtain the following results:

**Overall Priority of the Saturn:**

$$0.398(0.32) + 0.085(0.274) + 0.218(0.341) + 0.299(0.656) = 0.421$$

**Overall Priority of the Cavalier:**

$$0.398(0.557) + 0.085(0.639) + 0.218(0.065) + 0.299(0.080) = 0.314$$

Ranking these priorities, we have the AHP ranking of the decision alternatives:

| Car | Priority |
|---|---|
| 1. Saturn | 0.421 |
| 2. Cavalier | 0.314 |
| 3. Accord | 0.265 |

These results provide a basis for Diane to make a decision regarding the purchase of a car. As long as Diane believes that her judgments regarding the importance of the criteria and her preferences for the cars using each criterion are valid, the AHP priorities show that the Saturn is preferred. In addition to the recommendation of the Saturn as the best car, the AHP analysis has helped Diane gain a better understanding of the trade-offs in the decision-making process and a clearer understanding of why the Saturn is the AHP recommended alternative.

*Work problem 24 and determine the AHP priorities for the two decision alternatives.*

**N O T E S**
**and Comments**

1. The scoring model in Section 15.3 used the following equation to compute the overall score of a decision alternative.

$$S_j = \sum_i w_i r_{ij}$$

where

$w_i$ = the weight for criterion $i$

$r_{ij}$ = the rating for criterion $i$ and decision alternative $j$

In Section 15.5 AHP used the same calculation to determine the overall priority of each decision alternative. The difference between the two approaches is that the scoring model required the decision maker to estimate the values of $w_i$ and $r_{ij}$ directly. AHP used synthesization to compute the criterion priorities $w_i$ and the decision alternative priorities $r_{ij}$ based on the pairwise comparison information provided by the decision maker.

2. The software package Expert Choice® marketed by Decision Support Software provides a user-friendly procedure for implementing AHP on a personal computer. Expert Choice will take the decision maker through the pairwise comparison process in a step-by-step manner. Once the decision maker has responded to the pairwise comparison prompts, Expert Choice will automatically construct the pairwise comparison matrix, conduct the synthesization calculations, and present the overall priorities. Expert Choice is a software package that should warrant consideration by a decision maker who anticipates solving a variety of multicriteria decision problems.

·················································································/  /···········

# SUMMARY

In this chapter we used goal programming to solve problems with multiple goals within the linear programming framework. We showed that the goal programming model contains one or more goal equations and an objective function designed to minimize deviations from the goals. In situations where resource capacities or other restrictions affect the achievement of the goals, the model will contain constraints that are formulated and treated in the same manner as constraints in an ordinary linear programming model.

In goal programming problems with preemptive priorities, priority level 1 goals are treated first in an objective function to identify a solution that will best satisfy these goals. This solution is then revised by considering an objective function involving only the priority level 2 goals; solution modifications are considered only if they do not degrade the solution obtained for the priority level 1 goals. This process continues until all priority levels have been considered.

We showed how a variation of the linear programming graphical solution procedure can be used to solve goal programming problems with two decision variables. Specialized goal programming computer packages are available for solving the general goal programming problem, but such computer codes are not as readily available as are general purpose linear programming computer packages. As a result, we showed how the linear programming module of The Management Scientist software package can be used to solve a goal programming problem.

We then presented a scoring model as a quick and relatively easy way to identify the most desired decision alternative in a multicriteria problem. The decision maker provides a subjective weight indicating the importance of each criterion. Then the decision maker rates each decision alternative in terms of how well it satisfies each criterion. The end result is a score for each decision alternative that indicates the preference for the decision alternative considering all criteria.

We also presented an approach to multicriteria decision making called the *analytic hierarchy process (AHP)*. We showed that a key part of AHP is the development of judgments concerning the relative importance of, or preference for, the elements being compared. A consistency ratio is computed to determine the degree of consistency exhibited by the decision maker in making the pairwise comparisons. Values of the consistency ratio less than or equal to 0.10 are considered acceptable.

Once the set of all pairwise comparisons has been developed, a process referred to as synthesization is used to determine the priorities for the elements being compared. The final step of the analytic hierarchy process involves multiplying the priority levels established for the decision alternatives relative to each criterion by the priority levels reflecting the importance of the criteria themselves; the sum of these products over all the criteria provides the overall priority level for each decision alternative.

·················································································/  /···········

# GLOSSARY

**Goal programming**  A linear programming approach to multicriteria decision problems whereby the objective function is designed to minimize the deviations from goals.

**Preemptive priorities**  Priorities assigned to goals that ensure that the satisfaction of a higher level goal cannot be traded for the satisfaction of a lower level goal.

**Target value** A value specified in the statement of the goal. Based on the context of the problem, management will want the solution to the goal programming problem to result in a value for the goal that is less than, equal to, or greater than the target value.

**Goal equation** An equation whose right-hand side is the target value for the goal; the left-hand side of the goal equation consists of (1) a function representing the level of achievement and (2) deviation variables representing the difference between the target value for the goal and the level achieved.

**Deviation variables** Variables that are added to the goal equation to allow the solution to deviate from the goal's target value.

**Scoring model** An approach to multicriteria decision making that requires the user to assign weights to each criterion that describes the criterion's relative importance and to assign a rating that shows how well each decision alternative satisfies each criterion. The output is a score for each decision alternative.

**Analytic hierarchy process (AHP)** An approach to multicriteria decision making based on pairwise comparisons for elements in a hierarchy.

**Hierarchy** A diagram that shows the levels of a problem in terms of the overall goal, the criteria, and the decision alternatives.

**Pairwise comparison matrix** A matrix that consists of the preference, or relative importance, ratings provided during a series of pairwise comparisons.

**Synthesization** A mathematical process that uses the preference or relative importance values in the pairwise comparison matrix to develop priorities.

**Normalized pairwise comparison matrix** The matrix obtained by dividing each element of the pairwise comparison matrix by its column total. This matrix is computed as an intermediate step in the synthesization of priorities.

**Consistency** A concept developed to assess the quality of the judgments made during a series of pairwise comparisons. It is a measure of the internal consistency of these comparisons.

**Consistency ratio** A numerical measure of the degree of consistency in a series of pairwise comparisons. Values less than or equal to 0.10 are considered reasonable.

## PROBLEMS

1. The RMC Corporation blends three raw materials to produce two products: a fuel additive and a solvent base. Each ton of fuel additive is a mixture of 2/5 ton of material 1 and 3/5 ton of material 3. A ton of solvent base is a mixture of 1/2 ton of material 1, 1/5 ton of material 2, and 3/10 ton of material 3. RMC's production is constrained by a limited availability of the three raw materials. For the current production period, RMC has the following quantities of each raw material: material 1, 20 tons; material 2, 5 tons; material 3, 21 tons. Management wants to achieve the following $P_1$ priority level goals.

   **Goal 1:** Produce at least 30 tons of fuel additive.

   **Goal 2:** Produce at least 15 tons of solvent base.

   Assume there are no other goals.
   a. Is it possible for management to achieve both $P_1$ level goals given the constraints on the amounts of each material available? Explain.
   b. Treating the amounts of each material available as constraints, formulate a goal programming model to determine the optimal product mix. Assume that both $P_1$ priority level goals are equally important to management.

c.  Use the graphical goal programming procedure to solve the model formulated in part (b).

d.  If goal 1 is twice as important as goal 2, what is the optimal product mix?

2.  DJS Investment Services must develop an investment portfolio for a new client. As an initial investment strategy, the new client would like to restrict the portfolio to a mix of two stocks:

| Stock | Price/Share | Estimated Annual Return (%) |
|---|---|---|
| AGA Products | $ 50 | 6 |
| Key Oil | 100 | 10 |

The client has $50,000 to invest and has established the following two investment goals.

*Priority Level 1 Goal*

**Goal 1:**  Obtain an annual return of at least 9%.

*Priority Level 2 Goal*

**Goal 2:**  Limit the investment in Key Oil, the riskier investment, to no more than 60% of the total investment.

a.  Formulate a goal programming model for the DJS Investment problem.

b.  Use the graphical goal programming procedure to obtain a solution.

3.  The L. Young & Sons Manufacturing Company produces two products, which have the following profit and resource requirement characteristics.

| Characteristic | Product 1 | Product 2 |
|---|---|---|
| Profit/unit | $4 | $2 |
| Dept. A hours/unit | 1 | 1 |
| Dept. B hours/unit | 2 | 5 |

Last month's production schedule used 350 hours of labor in department A and 1000 hours of labor in department B.

Young's management has been experiencing workforce morale and labor union problems during the past 6 months because of monthly departmental work load fluctuations. New hiring, layoffs, and interdepartmental transfers have been common because the firm has not attempted to stabilize workload requirements.

Management would like to develop a production schedule for the coming month that will achieve the following goals.

**Goal 1:**  Use 350 hours of labor in department A.

**Goal 2:**  Use 1000 hours of labor in department B.

**Goal 3:**  Earn a profit of at least $1300.

a.  Formulate a goal programming model for this problem, assuming that goals 1 and 2 are $P_1$ level goals and goal 3 is a $P_2$ level goal; assume that goals 1 and 2 are equally important.

b.  Solve the model formulated in part (a) using the graphical goal programming procedure.

c.  Suppose that the firm ignores the workload fluctuations and considers the 350 hours in department A and the 1000 hours in department B as the maximum available. Formulate and solve a linear programming problem to maximize profit subject to these constraints.

d. Compare the solutions obtained in parts (b) and (c). Discuss which approach you favor, and why.

e. Reconsider part (a) assuming that the priority level 1 goal is goal 3 and the priority level 2 goals are goals 1 and 2; as before, assume that goals 1 and 2 are equally important. Solve this revised problem using the graphical goal programming procedure and compare your solution to the one obtained for the original problem.

4. Industrial Chemicals produces two adhesives used in the manufacturing process for airplanes. The two adhesives, which have different bonding strengths, require different amounts of production time: the IC-100 adhesive requires 20 minutes of production time per gallon of finished product, and the IC-200 adhesive uses 30 minutes of production time per gallon. Both products use 1 pound of a highly perishable resin for each gallon of finished product. There are 300 pounds of the resin in inventory, and more can be obtained if necessary. However, because of the shelf life of the material, any amount not used in the next 2 weeks will be discarded.

   The firm has existing orders for 100 gallons of IC-100 and 120 gallons of IC-200. Under normal conditions, the production process operates 8 hours per day, 5 days per week. Management wants to schedule production for the next 2 weeks to achieve the following goals.

   *Priority Level 1 Goals*

   **Goal 1:** Avoid underutilization of the production process.

   **Goal 2:** Avoid overtime in excess of 20 hours for the 2 weeks.

   *Priority Level 2 Goals*

   **Goal 3:** Satisfy existing orders for the IC-100 adhesive; that is, produce at least 100 gallons of IC-100.

   **Goal 4:** Satisfy existing orders for the IC-200 adhesive; that is, produce at least 120 gallons of IC-200.

   *Priority Level 3 Goal*

   **Goal 5:** Use all the available resin.

   a. Formulate a goal programming model for the Industrial Chemicals problem. Assume that both priority level 1 goals and that both priority level 2 goals are equally important.

   b. Use the graphical goal programming procedure to develop a solution for the model formulated in part (a).

5. Reconsider the RMC data presented in Problem 1. Assume that the two $P_1$ priority level goals remain the same and that both goals are equally important to management. Suppose that management has learned that additional amounts of material 3 can be obtained from another RMC plant. Although management wants to obtain a solution that satisfies their production goals using the 21 tons of material 3 currently available, it is willing to consider using additional amounts of material 3 from the other plant. With this new goal as a $P_2$ priority level goal, the problem goals can now be restated.

   *Priority Level 1 Goals*

   **Goal 1:** Produce at least 30 tons of fuel additive.

   **Goal 2:** Produce at least 15 tons of solvent base.

   *Priority Level 2 Goal*

   **Goal 3:** Use no more than 21 tons of material 3.

   a. Treat the amounts of materials 1 and 2 available as problem constraints and formulate a goal programming model for this problem.

   b. Use the goal programming computer procedure illustrated in Section 15.2 to solve the model formulated in part (a).

   c. How many tons of material 3 need to be obtained from RMC's other plant?

6. Michigan Motors Corporation (MMC) has just introduced a new luxury touring sedan. As part of its promotional campaign, the marketing department has decided to send personalized invitations to test drive the new sedan to two target groups: (1) current owners of an MMC luxury automobile and (2) owners of luxury cars manufactured by one of MMC's competitors. The cost of sending a personalized invitation to each customer is estimated to be $1 per letter. Based on previous experience with this type of advertising, MMC estimates that 25% of the customers contacted from group 1 and 10% of the customers contacted from group 2 will test drive the new sedan. As part of this campaign, MMC has set the following goals.

   Goal 1:  Get at least 10,000 customers from group 1 to test drive the new sedan.

   Goal 2:  Get at least 5000 customers from group 2 to test drive the new sedan.

   Goal 3:  Limit the expense of sending out the invitations to $70,000.

   Assume that goals 1 and 2 are $P_1$ priority level goals and that goal 3 is a $P_2$ priority level goal.
   a.  Suppose that goals 1 and 2 are equally important; formulate a goal programming model of the MMC problem.
   b.  Use the goal programming computer procedure illustrated in Section 15.2 to solve the model formulated in part (a).
   c.  If management believes that contacting customers from group 2 is twice as important as contacting customers from group 1, what should MMC do?

7. A committee in charge of promoting a Ladies Professional Golf Association tournament is trying to determine how best to advertise the event during the 2 weeks prior to the tournament. The committee obtained the following information about the three advertising media they are considering using.

| Category | Audience Reached Per Advertisement | Cost Per Advertisement | Maximum Number of Advertisements |
|---|---|---|---|
| TV | 200,000 | $2500 | 10 |
| Radio | 50,000 | $ 400 | 15 |
| Newspaper | 100,000 | $ 500 | 20 |

The last column in this table shows the maximum number of advertisements that can be run during the next 2 weeks; these values should be treated as constraints. The committee has established the following goals for the campaign.

*Priority Level 1 Goal*

Goal 1:  Reach at least 4 million people.

*Priority Level 2 Goal*

Goal 2:  The number of television advertisements should be at least 30% of the total number of advertisements.

*Priority Level 3 Goal*

Goal 3:  The number of radio advertisements should not exceed 20% of the total number of advertisements.

*Priority Level 4 Goal*

Goal 4:  Limit the total amount spent for advertising to $20,000.

   a.  Formulate a goal programming model for this problem.
   b.  Use the goal programming computer procedure illustrated in Section 15.2 to solve the model formulated in part (a).

8. Morley Company is attempting to determine the best location for a new machine in an existing layout of three machines. The existing machines are located at the following $x_1$, $x_2$ coordinates on the shop floor.

$$\text{Machine 1:} \quad x_1 = 1, x_2 = 7$$
$$\text{Machine 2:} \quad x_1 = 5, x_2 = 9$$
$$\text{Machine 3:} \quad x_1 = 6, x_2 = 2$$

a. Develop a goal programming model that can be solved to minimize the total distance of the new machine from the three existing machines. The distance is to be measured rectangularly. For example, if the location of the new machine is $(x_1 = 3, x_2 = 5)$, it is considered to be a distance of $|3 - 1| + |5 - 7| = 2 + 2 = 4$ from machine 1. *Hint:* In the goal programming formulation, let

$x_1$ = first coordinate of the new machine location

$x_2$ = second coordinate of the new machine location

$d_i^+$ = amount by which the $x_1$ coordinate of the new machine exceeds the $x_1$ coordinate of machine $i$ ($i = 1, 2, 3$)

$d_i^-$ = amount by which the $x_1$ coordinate of machine $i$ exceeds the $x_1$ coordinate of the new machine ($i = 1, 2, 3$)

$e_i^+$ = amount by which the $x_2$ coordinate of the new machine exceeds the $x_2$ coordinate of machine $i$ ($i = 1, 2, 3$)

$e_i^-$ = amount by which the $x_2$ coordinate of machine $i$ exceeds the $x_2$ coordinate of the new machine ($i = 1, 2, 3$)

b. What is the optimal location for the new machine?

**SELF TEST**

9. One advantage of using the multicriteria decision-making methods presented in this chapter is that the criteria weights and the decision alternative ratings may be modified to reflect the unique interests and preferences of each individual decision maker. For example, assume that another graduating college student had the same three job offers described in Section 15.3. This student provided the following scoring model information. Rank the overall preference for the three positions. Which position is recommended?

|  |  | Ratings |  |  |
| --- | --- | --- | --- | --- |
| Criteria | Weight | Analyst Chicago | Accountant Denver | Auditor Houston |
| Career advancement | 5 | 7 | 4 | 4 |
| Location | 2 | 5 | 6 | 4 |
| Management style | 5 | 6 | 5 | 7 |
| Salary | 4 | 7 | 8 | 4 |
| Prestige | 4 | 8 | 5 | 6 |
| Job security | 2 | 4 | 5 | 8 |
| Enjoyment of the work | 4 | 7 | 5 | 5 |

10. The Kenyon Manufacturing Company is interested in selecting the best location for a new plant. After a detailed study of ten sites, the three location finalists are Georgetown, Kentucky; Marysville, Ohio; and Clarksville, Tennessee. The Kenyon management team provided the following data on location criteria, criteria importance, and location ratings. Use a scoring model to determine the best location for the new plant.

| Criteria | Weight | Ratings Georgetown, Kentucky | Marysville, Ohio | Clarksville, Tennessee |
|---|---|---|---|---|
| Land cost | 4 | 7 | 4 | 5 |
| Labor cost | 3 | 6 | 5 | 8 |
| Labor availability | 5 | 7 | 8 | 6 |
| Construction cost | 4 | 6 | 7 | 5 |
| Transportation | 3 | 5 | 7 | 4 |
| Access to customers | 5 | 6 | 8 | 5 |
| Long-range goals | 4 | 7 | 6 | 5 |

11. The Davis family of Atlanta, Georgia, is planning its annual summer vacation. Three vacation locations along with criteria weights and location ratings follow. What is the recommended vacation location?

| Criteria | Weight | Ratings Myrtle Beach, South Carolina | Smoky Mountains | Branson, Missouri |
|---|---|---|---|---|
| Travel distance | 2 | 5 | 7 | 3 |
| Vacation cost | 5 | 5 | 6 | 4 |
| Entertainment available | 3 | 7 | 4 | 8 |
| Outdoor activities | 2 | 9 | 6 | 5 |
| Unique experience | 4 | 6 | 7 | 8 |
| Family fun | 5 | 8 | 7 | 7 |

12. A high school senior is considering attending one of the following four colleges or universities. Eight criteria, criteria weights, and school ratings are also shown. What is the recommended choice?

| Criteria | Weight | Ratings Midwestern University | State College at Newport | Handover College | Tecumseh State |
|---|---|---|---|---|---|
| School prestige | 3 | 8 | 6 | 7 | 5 |
| Number of students | 4 | 3 | 5 | 8 | 7 |
| Average class size | 5 | 4 | 5 | 8 | 7 |
| Cost | 5 | 5 | 8 | 3 | 6 |
| Distance from home | 2 | 7 | 8 | 7 | 6 |
| Sports program | 4 | 9 | 5 | 4 | 6 |
| Housing desirability | 4 | 6 | 5 | 7 | 6 |
| Beauty of campus | 3 | 5 | 3 | 8 | 5 |

13. Mr. and Mrs. Brinkley are interested in purchasing condominium property in Naples, Florida. The three most preferred condominiums are listed along with criteria weights and rating information. Which condominium is preferred?

|  | | Ratings | | |
| Criteria | Weight | Park Shore | The Terrace | Gulf View |
|---|---|---|---|---|
| Cost | 5 | 5 | 6 | 5 |
| Location | 4 | 7 | 4 | 9 |
| Appearance | 5 | 7 | 4 | 7 |
| Parking | 2 | 5 | 8 | 5 |
| Floor plan | 4 | 8 | 7 | 5 |
| Swimming pool | 1 | 7 | 2 | 3 |
| View | 3 | 5 | 4 | 9 |
| Kitchen | 4 | 8 | 7 | 6 |
| Closet space | 3 | 6 | 8 | 4 |

14. Clark and Julie Anderson are interested in purchasing a new boat and have limited their choice to one of three boats manufactured by Sea Ray, Inc.: the 220 Bowrider, the 230 Overnighter, and the 240 Sundancer. The Bowrider weights 3100 pounds, has no overnight capability, and has a price of $28,500. The 230 Overnighter weights 4300 pounds, has a reasonable overnight capability, and has a price of $37,500. The 240 Sundancer weights 4500 pounds, has an excellent overnight capability (kitchen, bath, and bed), and has a price of $48,200. The Andersons provided the scoring model information separately as shown here.

**Clark Anderson**

|  | | Ratings | | |
| Criteria | Weight | 220 Bowrider | 230 Overnighter | 240 Sundancer |
|---|---|---|---|---|
| Cost | 5 | 8 | 5 | 3 |
| Overnight capability | 3 | 2 | 6 | 9 |
| Kitchen/bath facilities | 2 | 1 | 4 | 7 |
| Appearance | 5 | 7 | 7 | 6 |
| Engine/speed | 5 | 6 | 8 | 4 |
| Towing/handling | 4 | 8 | 5 | 2 |
| Maintenance | 4 | 7 | 5 | 3 |
| Resale value | 3 | 7 | 5 | 6 |

**Julie Anderson**

|  | | Ratings | | |
| Criteria | Weight | 220 Bowrider | 230 Overnighter | 240 Sundancer |
|---|---|---|---|---|
| Cost | 3 | 7 | 6 | 5 |
| Overnight capability | 5 | 1 | 6 | 8 |
| Kitchen/bath facilities | 5 | 1 | 3 | 7 |
| Appearance | 4 | 5 | 7 | 7 |
| Engine/speed | 2 | 4 | 5 | 3 |
| Towing/handling | 2 | 8 | 6 | 2 |
| Maintenance | 1 | 6 | 5 | 4 |
| Resale value | 2 | 5 | 6 | 6 |

       a.    Which boat does Clark Anderson prefer?

       b.    Which boat does Julie Anderson prefer?

15.    Use the pairwise comparison matrix for the price criterion shown in Table 15.8 to verify that the priorities after synthesization are 0.123, 0.320, and 0.557. Compute the consistency ratio and comment on its acceptability.

**SELF TEST**

16.    Use the pairwise comparison matrix for the style criterion as shown in Table 15.8 to verify that the priorities after synthesization are 0.265, 0.656, and 0.080. Compute the consistency ratio and comment on its acceptability.

17.    Dan Joseph was considering entering one of two graduate schools of business to pursue studies for an MBA degree. When asked how he compared the two schools with respect to reputation, he responded that he preferred school A strongly to very strongly to school B.

       a.    Set up the pairwise comparison matrix for this problem.

       b.    Determine the priorities for the two schools relative to this criterion.

18.    An organization was investigating relocating its corporate headquarters to one of three possible cities. The following pairwise comparison matrix shows the president's judgments regarding the desirability for the three cities.

|        | City 1 | City 2 | City 3 |
|--------|--------|--------|--------|
| City 1 | 1      | 5      | 7      |
| City 2 | ⅕      | 1      | 3      |
| City 3 | ⅐      | ⅓      | 1      |

       a.    Determine the priorities for the three cities.

       b.    Is the president consistent in terms of the judgments provided? Explain.

19.    The following pairwise comparison matrix contains the judgments of an individual regarding the fairness of two proposed tax programs, A and B.

|   | A   | B   |
|---|-----|-----|
| A | 1   | 3   |
| B | ⅓   | 1   |

       a.    Determine the priorities for the two programs.

       b.    Are the individual's judgments consistent? Explain.

20.    Asked to compare three soft drinks with respect to flavor, an individual stated that

            A is moderately more preferable than B,

            A is equally to moderately more preferable than C, and

            B is strongly more preferable than C.

       a.    Set up the pairwise comparison matrix for this problem.

       b.    Determine the priorities for the soft drinks with respect to the flavor criterion.

       c.    Compute the consistency ratio. Are the individual's judgments consistent? Explain.

21.    Refer to Problem 20. Suppose that the individual had stated the following judgments instead of those given in Problem 20.

             A is strongly more preferable than C.

             B is equally to moderately more preferable than A.

             B is strongly more preferable than C.

Answer parts (a), (b), and (c) as stated in Problem 20.

22. The national sales director for Jones Office Supplies needs to determine the best location for the next national sales meeting. Three locations have been proposed: Dallas, San Francisco, and New York. One criterion considered important in the decision is the desirability of the location in terms of restaurants, entertainment, and so on. The national sales manager made the following judgments with regard to this criterion.

> New York is very strongly more preferred than Dallas.
>
> New York is moderately more preferred than San Francisco.
>
> San Francisco is moderately to strongly more preferred than Dallas.

    a. Set up the pairwise comparison matrix for this problem.
    b. Determine the priorities for the desirability criterion.
    c. Compute the consistency ratio. Are the sales manager's judgments consistent? Explain.

23. A study comparing four personal computers resulted in the following pairwise comparison matrix for the performance criterion.

|   | 1 | 2 | 3 | 4 |
|---|---|---|---|---|
| 1 | 1 | 3 | 7 | $\frac{1}{3}$ |
| 2 | $\frac{1}{3}$ | 1 | 4 | $\frac{1}{4}$ |
| 3 | $\frac{1}{7}$ | $\frac{1}{4}$ | 1 | $\frac{1}{6}$ |
| 4 | 3 | 4 | 6 | 1 |

    a. Determine the priorities for the four computers relative to the performance criterion.
    b. Compute the consistency ratio. Are the judgments regarding performance consistent? Explain.

**SELF TEST**

24. An individual was interested in determining which of two stocks to invest in, Central Computing Company (CCC) or Software Research, Inc. (SRI). The criteria thought to be most relevant in making the decision are the potential yield of the stock and the risk associated with the investment. The pairwise comparison matrixes for this problem are

| Criterion | Yield | Risk |
|---|---|---|
| Yield | 1 | 2 |
| Risk | $\frac{1}{2}$ | 1 |

| Yield | CCC | SRI |
|---|---|---|
| CCC | 1 | 3 |
| SRI | $\frac{1}{3}$ | 1 |

| Risk | CCC | SRI |
|---|---|---|
| CCC | 1 | $\frac{1}{2}$ |
| SRI | 2 | 1 |

    a. Compute the priorities for each pairwise comparison matrix.
    b. Determine the overall priority for the two investments, CCC and SRI. Which investment is preferred based on yield and risk?

25. The vice-president of Harling Equipment needs to select a new director of marketing. The two possible candidates are Bill Jacobs and Sue Martin, and the criteria thought to be most relevant in the selection are leadership ability (L), personal skills (P), and administrative skills (A). The following pairwise comparison matrixes were obtained.

|  | Criterion | | |
|---|---|---|---|
|  | **L** | **P** | **A** |
| **L** | 1 | $\frac{1}{3}$ | $\frac{1}{4}$ |
| **P** | 3 | 1 | 2 |
| **A** | 4 | $\frac{1}{2}$ | 1 |

|  | Leadership | |
|---|---|---|
|  | **Jacobs** | **Martin** |
| **Jacobs** | 1 | 4 |
| **Martin** | $\frac{1}{4}$ | 1 |

|  | Personal | |
|---|---|---|
|  | **Jacobs** | **Martin** |
| **Jacobs** | 1 | $\frac{1}{3}$ |
| **Martin** | 3 | 1 |

|  | Administrative | |
|---|---|---|
|  | **Jacobs** | **Martin** |
| **Jacobs** | 1 | 2 |
| **Martin** | $\frac{1}{2}$ | 1 |

a.  Compute the priorities for each pairwise comparison matrix.

b.  Determine an overall priority for each candidate. Which candidate is preferred?

26.  A woman considering the purchase of a custom sound stereo system for her car looked at three different systems (A, B, and C) that varied in terms of price, sound quality, and FM reception. The following pairwise comparison matrices were developed.

|  | Criterion | | |
|---|---|---|---|
|  | **Price** | **Sound** | **Reception** |
| **Price** | 1 | 3 | 4 |
| **Sound** | $\frac{1}{3}$ | 1 | 3 |
| **Reception** | $\frac{1}{4}$ | $\frac{1}{3}$ | 1 |

|  | Price | | |
|---|---|---|---|
|  | **A** | **B** | **C** |
| **A** | 1 | 4 | 2 |
| **B** | $\frac{1}{4}$ | 1 | $\frac{1}{3}$ |
| **C** | $\frac{1}{2}$ | 3 | 1 |

|  | Sound | | |
|---|---|---|---|
|  | **A** | **B** | **C** |
| **A** | 1 | $\frac{1}{2}$ | $\frac{1}{4}$ |
| **B** | 2 | 1 | $\frac{1}{3}$ |
| **C** | 4 | 3 | 1 |

|  | Reception | | |
|---|---|---|---|
|  | **A** | **B** | **C** |
| **A** | 1 | 4 | 2 |
| **B** | $\frac{1}{4}$ | 1 | 1 |
| **C** | $\frac{1}{2}$ | 1 | 1 |

a.  Compute the priorities for each pairwise comparison matrix.

b.  Determine an overall priority for each system. Which stereo system is preferred?

## Case Problem    PRODUCTION SCHEDULING

EZ Trailers, Inc., manufactures a variety of general purpose trailers, including a complete line of boat trailers. Two of their best-selling boat trailers are the EZ-190 and the EZ-250. The EZ-190 is designed for boats up to 19 feet in length, and the EZ-250 can be used for boats up to 25 feet in length.

EZ Trailers would like to schedule production for the next two months for these two models. Each unit of the EZ-190 requires 4 hours of production time, and each unit of the EZ-250 uses 6 hours of production time. The following orders have been received for March and April.

| Model | March | April |
|-------|-------|-------|
| EZ-190 | 800 | 600 |
| EZ-250 | 1100 | 1200 |

The ending inventory from February was 200 units of the EZ-190 and 300 units of the EZ-250. The total number of hours of production time used in February was 6300 hours.

The management of EZ Trailers is concerned about being able to satisfy existing orders for the EZ-250 for both March and April. In fact, it believes that this goal is the most important one that a production schedule should meet. Next in importance is satisfying existing orders for the EZ-190. In addition, management doesn't want to implement any production schedule that would involve significant labor fluctuations from month to month. In this regard, its goal is to develop a production schedule that would limit fluctuations in labor hours used to a maximum of 1000 hours from one month to the next.

## Managerial Report

Perform an analysis of EZ Trailers's production scheduling problem, and prepare a report for EZ's president that summarizes your findings. Include a discussion and analysis of the following items in your report.

1. The production schedule that best achieves the goals as specified by management.
2. Suppose that EZ Trailers's storage facilities would accommodate only a maximum of 300 trailers in any one month. What effect would this have on the production schedule?
3. Suppose that EZ Trailers can store only a maximum of 300 trailers in any one month. In addition, suppose management would like to have an ending inventory in April of at least 100 units of each model. What effect would both changes have on the production schedule?
4. What changes would occur in the production schedule if the labor fluctuation goal was the highest priority goal?

## Appendix 15.1   SCORING MODELS WITH SPREADSHEETS

A spreadsheet provides an efficient way to analyze a multicriteria decision problem that can be described by a scoring model. We will use the job selection application from Section 15.3 to demonstrate this procedure.

A spreadsheet for the job selection scoring model is shown in Figure 15.7. The criteria weights are placed into cells B6 to B12. The ratings for each criterion and decision alternative are entered into cells C6 to E12.

**Figure 15.7    SPREADSHEET FOR THE JOB SELECTION SCORING MODEL**

|    | A | B | C | D | E |
|----|---|---|---|---|---|
| 1  | **Job Selection Scoring Model** | | | | |
| 2  | | | | | |
| 3  | | | | **Ratings** | |
| 4  | | | **Analyst** | **Accountant** | **Auditor** |
| 5  | **Criteria** | **Weight** | **Chicago** | **Denver** | **Houston** |
| 6  | Career Advancement | 5 | 8 | 6 | 4 |
| 7  | Location | 3 | 3 | 8 | 7 |
| 8  | Management Style | 4 | 5 | 6 | 9 |
| 9  | Salary | 3 | 6 | 7 | 5 |
| 10 | Prestige | 2 | 7 | 5 | 4 |
| 11 | Job Security | 4 | 4 | 7 | 6 |
| 12 | Enjoy the Work | 5 | 8 | 6 | 5 |
| 13 | | | | | |
| 14 | | | | | |
| 15 | **Scoring Calculations** | | | | |
| 16 | | | **Analyst** | **Accountant** | **Auditor** |
| 17 | **Criteria** | | **Chicago** | **Denver** | **Houston** |
| 18 | Career Advancement | | 40 | 30 | 20 |
| 19 | Location | | 9 | 24 | 21 |
| 20 | Management Style | | 20 | 24 | 36 |
| 21 | Salary | | 18 | 21 | 15 |
| 22 | Prestige | | 14 | 10 | 8 |
| 23 | Job Security | | 16 | 28 | 24 |
| 24 | Enjoy the Work | | 40 | 30 | 25 |
| 25 | | | | | |
| 26 | **Score** | | 157 | 167 | 149 |

The calculations used to compute the score for each decision alternative are shown in the bottom portion of the spreadsheet. The calculation for cell C18 is provided by the cell formula

$$=\$B6*C6$$

This cell formula can be copied from cell C18 to cells C18:E24 to provide the results shown in rows 18 to 24. The score for the financial analyst position in Chicago is found by placing the following formula in cell C26:

$$=SUM(C18:C24)$$

Copying cell C26 to cells D26:E26 provides the scores for the accountant in Denver and the auditor in Houston positions.

# FORECASTING

## CONTENTS

An essential aspect of managing any organization is planning for the future. Indeed, the long-run success of an organization is closely related to how well management is able to anticipate the future and develop appropriate strategies. Good judgment, intuition, and an awareness of the state of the economy may give a manager a rough idea or "feeling" of what is likely to happen in the future. However, converting this feeling into a number that can be used as next quarter's sales volume or next year's raw material cost per unit often is difficult. The purpose of this chapter is to introduce several **forecasting** methods.

Suppose that we have been asked to provide quarterly forecasts of the sales volume for a particular product during the coming year. Production schedules, raw material purchasing plans, inventory policies, and sales quotas will be affected by the quarterly forecasts that we provide. Consequently, poor forecasts may result in increased costs for the firm. How should we go about providing the quarterly sales volume forecasts?

We will certainly want to review the actual sales data for the product in previous periods. Using these historical data, we can identify the general level of sales and any trend such as an increase or decrease in sales volume over time. A further review of the data might reveal a seasonal pattern such as peak sales occurring in the third quarter of each year and sales volume bottoming out during the first quarter. By reviewing historical data, we can often develop a better understanding of the pattern of past sales, leading to better predictions of future sales for the product.

The historical sales data form a time series. A **time series** is a set of observations of a variable measured at successive points in time or over successive periods of time. In this chapter we introduce several procedures for analyzing time series. The objective of such analyses is to provide good **forecasts** or predictions of future values of the time series.

Forecasting methods can be classified as quantitative or qualitative. Quantitative forecasting methods can be used when (1) past information about the variable being forecast is available, (2) the information can be quantified, and (3) a reasonable assumption is that the pattern of the past will continue into the future. In such cases, a forecast can be developed using a time series method or a causal method.

If the historical data are restricted to past values of the variable that we are trying to forecast, the forecasting procedure is called a *time series method*. The objective of time series methods is to discover a pattern in the historical data and then extrapolate this pattern into the future; the forecast is based solely on past values of the variable that we are trying to forecast and/or on past forecast errors. In this chapter we discuss three time series methods: smoothing (moving averages, weighted moving averages, and exponential smoothing), trend projection, and trend projection adjusted for seasonal influence.

Causal forecasting methods are based on the assumption that the variable we are trying to forecast exhibits a cause-effect relationship with one or more other variables. In this chapter we discuss the use of regression analysis as a causal forecasting method. For instance, the sales volume for many products is influenced by advertising expenditures, so regression analysis may be used to develop an equation showing how these two variables are related. Then, once the advertising budget has been set for the next period, we could substitute this value into the equation to develop a prediction or forecast of the sales volume for that period. Note that if a time series method had been used to develop the forecast, advertising expenditures would not even have been considered; that is, a time series method would have based the forecast solely on past sales.

Qualitative methods generally involve the use of expert judgment to develop forecasts. For instance, a panel of experts might develop a consensus forecast of the prime rate for a year from now. An advantage of qualitative procedures is that they can be applied when the information on the variable being forecast cannot be quantified and when historical data either are not applicable or available. Figure 16.1 provides an overview of the types of forecasting methods.

---

Most companies can forecast total demand for all products, as a group, with errors of less than 5%. However, forecasting demand for individual products may result in significantly higher errors.

A forecast is simply a *prediction* of what will happen in the future. Managers must learn to accept the fact that, regardless of the technique used, they will not be able to develop perfect forecasts.

**Figure 16.1**    AN OVERVIEW OF FORECASTING METHODS

## 16.1    THE COMPONENTS OF A TIME SERIES

The pattern or behavior of the data in a time series has several components. The usual assumption is that four separate components—trend, cyclical, seasonal, and irregular—combine to provide specific values for the time series. Let us look more closely at each of these components.

### Trend Component

In time series analysis, the measurements may be taken every hour, day, week, month, or year, or at any other regular interval. Although time series data generally exhibit random fluctuations, the time series may still show gradual shifts or movements to relatively higher or lower values over a longer period of time. The gradual shifting of the time series is referred to as the **trend** in the time series; this shifting or trend is usually the result of long-term factors such as changes in the population, demographic characteristics of the population, technology, and consumer preferences.

For example, a manufacturer of photographic equipment may observe substantial month-to-month variability in the number of cameras sold. However, in reviewing sales over the past 10 to 15 years, this manufacturer may note a gradual increase in the annual sales volume. Suppose that the sales volume was approximately 1700 cameras per month in 1989, 2300 cameras per month in 1994, and 2500 cameras per month in 1999. Although actual month-to-month sales volumes may vary substantially, this gradual growth in sales shows an upward trend for the time series. Figure 16.2 shows a straight line that may be a good approximation of the trend in camera sales. Although the trend for camera sales appears to be linear and increasing over time, sometimes the trend in a time series can be described better by some other pattern.

Figure 16.3 shows some other possible time series trend patterns. Part (a) shows a nonlinear trend; in this case, the time series shows little growth initially, then a period of rapid

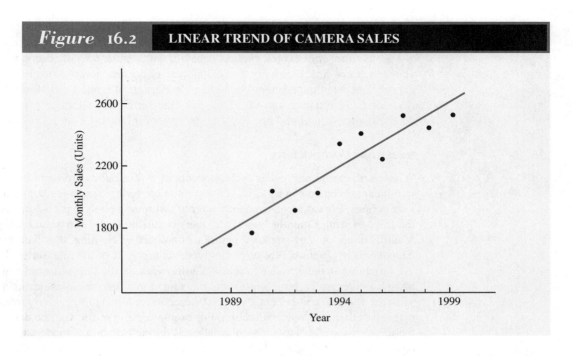

**Figure 16.2    LINEAR TREND OF CAMERA SALES**

**Figure 16.3    EXAMPLES OF SOME POSSIBLE TIME SERIES TREND PATTERNS**

(a) Nonlinear trend    (b) Linear decreasing trend    (c) No trend

growth, and finally a leveling off. This trend pattern might be a good approximation of sales for a product from introduction through a growth period and into a period of market saturation. The linear decreasing trend in part (b) is useful for time series displaying a steady decline over time. The horizontal line in part (c) represents a time series that has no consistent increase or decrease over time and thus no trend.

## Cyclical Component

Although a time series may exhibit a trend over long periods of time, all future values of the time series will not fall exactly on the trend line. In fact, time series often show alternating sequences of points below and above the trend line. Any recurring sequence of points above and below the trend line lasting more than one year can be attributed to the **cyclical**

**component** of the time series. Figure 16.4 shows the graph of a time series with an obvious cyclical component. The observations are taken at intervals of one year.

Many time series exhibit cyclical behavior with regular runs of observations below and above the trend line. Generally, this component of the time series is due to multiyear cyclical movements in the economy. For example, periods of modest inflation followed by periods of rapid inflation can lead to many time series that alternate below and above a generally increasing trend line (e.g., a time series for housing costs).

## Seasonal Component

Whereas the trend and cyclical components of a time series are identified by analyzing multiyear movements in historical data, many time series show a regular pattern over one-year periods. For example, a manufacturer of swimming pools expects low sales activity in the fall and winter months, with peak sales occurring in the spring and summer months. Manufacturers of snow removal equipment and heavy clothing, however, expect just the opposite yearly pattern. Not surprisingly, the component of the time series that represents the variability in the data due to seasonal influences is called the **seasonal component.** Although we generally think of seasonal movement in a time series as occurring within one year, the seasonal component also may be used to represent any regularly repeating pattern that is less than one year in duration. For example, daily traffic volume data show within-the-day "seasonal" behavior, with peak levels during rush hours, moderate flow during the rest of the day, and light flow from midnight to early morning.

## Irregular Component

The **irregular component** of the time series is the residual or "catchall" factor that includes deviations of actual time series values from those expected given the effects of the trend, cyclical, and seasonal components. It accounts for the random variability in the time series. The irregular component is caused by the short-term, unanticipated, and nonrecurring factors that affect the time series. Because this component accounts for the random variability in the time series, it is unpredictable. We cannot attempt to predict its impact on the time series.

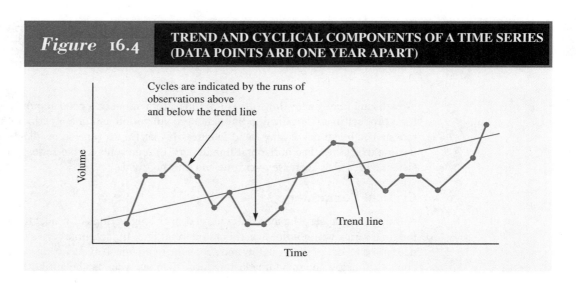

**Figure 16.4**   **TREND AND CYCLICAL COMPONENTS OF A TIME SERIES (DATA POINTS ARE ONE YEAR APART)**

## 16.2    USING SMOOTHING METHODS IN FORECASTING

Many manufacturing environments require forecasts for thousands of items weekly or monthly. Thus, in choosing a forecasting technique, simplicity and ease of use are important criteria. The data requirements for the techniques in this section are minimal, and the techniques are easy to use and understand.

In this section we discuss three forecasting methods: moving averages, weighted moving averages, and exponential smoothing. The objective of each of these methods is to "smooth out" the random fluctuations caused by the irregular component of the time series. Therefore, they are referred to as *smoothing methods*. Smoothing methods are appropriate for a stable time series—that is, one that exhibits no significant trend, cyclical, or seasonal effects—because they adapt well to changes in the level of the time series. However, without modification, they do not work as well when a significant trend and/or seasonal variation are present.

Smoothing methods are easy to use and generally provide a high level of accuracy for short-range forecasts such as a forecast for the next time period. One of the methods, exponential smoothing, has minimal data requirements and thus is a good method to use when forecasts are required for large numbers of items.

### Moving Averages

The **moving averages** method uses the average of the *most recent n* data values in the time series as the forecast for the next period. Mathematically,

$$\text{Moving average} = \frac{\sum(\text{most recent } n \text{ data values})}{n} \tag{16.1}$$

The term *moving* indicates that, as a new observation becomes available for the time series, it replaces the oldest observation in equation (16.1), and a new average is computed. As a result, the average will change, or move, as new observations become available.

To illustrate the moving averages method, consider the 12 weeks of data presented in Table 16.1 and Figure 16.5. These data show the number of gallons of gasoline sold by a gasoline distributor in Bennington, Vermont, over the past 12 weeks. Figure 16.5 indicates that, although random variability is present, the time series appears to be stable over time. Thus, the smoothing methods of this section are applicable.

| *Table* 16.1 | GASOLINE SALES TIME SERIES |
|---|---|
| **Week** | **Sales (000s of gallons)** |
| 1 | 17 |
| 2 | 21 |
| 3 | 19 |
| 4 | 23 |
| 5 | 18 |
| 6 | 16 |
| 7 | 20 |
| 8 | 18 |
| 9 | 22 |
| 10 | 20 |
| 11 | 15 |
| 12 | 22 |

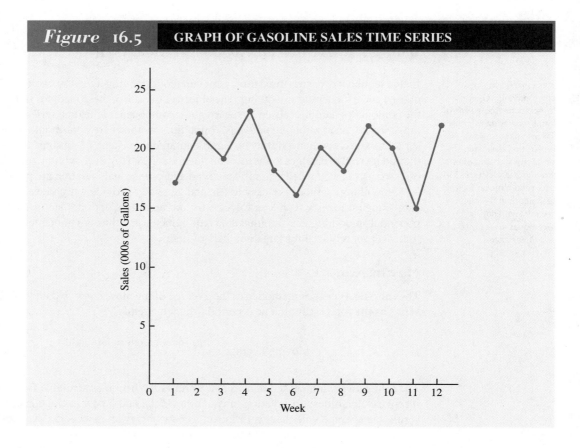

*Figure* 16.5     GRAPH OF GASOLINE SALES TIME SERIES

To use moving averages to forecast gasoline sales, we must first select the number of data values to be included in the moving average. For example, let us compute forecasts using a 3-week moving average. The moving average calculation for the first 3 weeks of the gasoline sales time series is

$$\text{Moving average (weeks 1–3)} = \frac{17 + 21 + 19}{3} = 19$$

We then use this moving average value as the forecast for week 4. The actual value observed in week 4 is 23, so the forecast error in week 4 is $23 - 19 = 4$. In general, the error associated with a forecast is the difference between the observed value of the time series and the forecast.

The calculation for the second 3-week moving average is

$$\text{Moving average (weeks 2–4)} = \frac{21 + 19 + 23}{3} = 21$$

*Try Problem 1 for practice in using moving averages to compute a forecast.*

Hence, the forecast for week 5 is 21, and the error associated with this forecast is $18 - 21 = -3$. Thus, the forecast error may be positive or negative, depending on whether the forecast is too low or too high. A complete summary of the 3-week moving average calculations for the gasoline sales time series is shown in Table 16.2.

| Table 16.2 | SUMMARY OF 3-WEEK MOVING AVERAGE CALCULATIONS | | | |
|---|---|---|---|---|
| Week | Time Series Value | Moving Average Forecast | Forecast Error | Squared Forecast Error |
| 1 | 17 | | | |
| 2 | 21 | | | |
| 3 | 19 | | | |
| 4 | 23 | 19 | 4 | 16 |
| 5 | 18 | 21 | −3 | 9 |
| 6 | 16 | 20 | −4 | 16 |
| 7 | 20 | 19 | 1 | 1 |
| 8 | 18 | 18 | 0 | 0 |
| 9 | 22 | 18 | 4 | 16 |
| 10 | 20 | 20 | 0 | 0 |
| 11 | 15 | 20 | −5 | 25 |
| 12 | 22 | 19 | 3 | 9 |
| | | Totals | 0 | 92 |

To forecast gasoline sales for week 13 using a 3-month moving average, we need to compute the average of sales for weeks 10, 11, and 12. The calculation for this moving average is

$$\text{Moving average (weeks 10–12)} = \frac{20 + 15 + 22}{3} = 19$$

Hence, the forecast for week 13 is 19, or 19,000 gallons of gasoline. Figure 16.6 shows a graph of the original time series and the 3-week moving average forecasts.

**Forecast Accuracy.**    An important consideration in selecting a forecasting method is the accuracy of the forecast. Clearly, we want forecast errors to be small. The last two columns of Table 16.2, which contain the forecast errors and the forecast errors squared, can be used to develop measures of forecast accuracy.

For the gasoline sales time series, we can use the last column of Table 16.2 to compute the average of the sum of the squared errors. Doing so, we obtain

$$\text{Average of the sum of squared errors} = \frac{92}{9} = 10.22$$

This average of the sum of squared errors is commonly referred to as the **mean squared error (MSE).** The MSE is an often-used measure of the accuracy of a forecasting method and is the one we use in this chapter.

As we indicated previously, to use the moving averages method, we must first select the number of data values to be included in the moving average. Not surprisingly, for a

Problem 2 will test your ability to use MSE as a measure of forecast accuracy.

particular time series, different lengths of moving averages will affect the accuracy of the forecast. One possible approach to choosing the number of values to be included is to use trial and error to identify the length that minimizes the MSE. Then, if we assume that the length that is best for the past will also be best for the future, we would forecast the

**Figure 16.6** GRAPH OF GASOLINE SALES TIME SERIES AND 3-WEEK MOVING AVERAGE FORECASTS

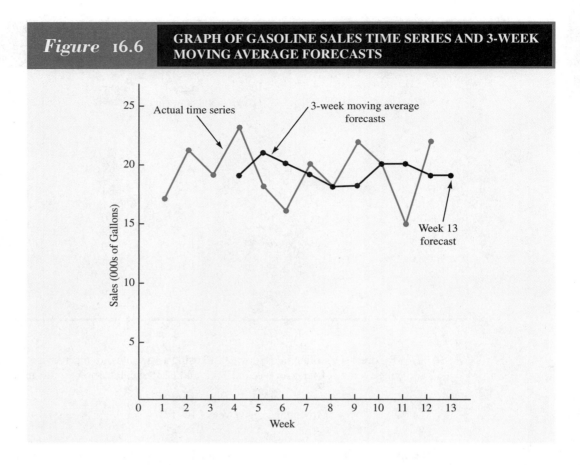

next value in the time series using the number of data values that minimized the MSE for the historical time series.

## Weighted Moving Averages

In the moving averages method, each observation in the calculation receives the same weight. One variation, known as **weighted moving averages,** involves selecting different weights for each data value and then computing a weighted average of the most recent $n$ data values as the forecast. In most cases, the most recent observation receives the most weight, and the weight decreases for older data values. For example, we can use the gasoline sales time series to illustrate the computation of a weighted 3-week moving average, with the most recent observation receiving a weight three times as great as that given the oldest observation, and the next oldest observation receiving a weight twice as great as the oldest. For week 4 the computation is

$$\text{Weighted moving averages forecast for week 4} = \frac{3}{6}(19) + \frac{2}{6}(21) + \frac{1}{6}(17) = 19.33$$

Note that for the weighted moving average the sum of the weights is equal to 1. Actually, this condition was also true for the simple moving average: Each weight was $\frac{1}{3}$. However, recall that the simple or unweighted moving average provided a forecast of 19.

**Forecast Accuracy.**    To use the weighted moving averages method, we must first select the number of data values to be included in the weighted moving average and then choose weights for each of the data values. In general, if we believe that the recent past is a better predictor of the future than the distant past, larger weights should be given to the more recent observations. However, when the time series is highly variable, selecting approximately equal weights for each data value may be best. Note that the only requirement in selecting the weights is that their sum must equal 1. To determine whether one particular combination of data values and weights provides a more accurate forecast than another combination, we will continue to use the MSE criterion as the measure of forecast accuracy. That is, if we assume that the combination that is best for the past will also be best for the future, we would use the combination of data values and weights that minimized MSE for the historical time series to forecast the next value in the time series.

## Exponential Smoothing

Exponential smoothing is simple and has few data requirements. Thus, it is an inexpensive, useful approach for firms that make many forecasts each period.

**Exponential smoothing** uses a weighted average of past time series values as the forecast; it is a special case of the weighted moving averages method in which we select only one weight—the weight for the most recent observation. The weights for the other data values are automatically computed and get smaller and smaller as the observations move farther into the past. The basic exponential smoothing model is:

$$F_{t+1} = \alpha Y_t + (1 - \alpha)F_t \qquad (16.2)$$

where

$$F_{t+1} = \text{forecast of the time series for period } t + 1$$
$$Y_t = \text{actual value of the time series in period } t$$
$$F_t = \text{forecast of the time series for period } t$$
$$\alpha = \text{smoothing constant } (0 \leq \alpha \leq 1)$$

Equation (16.2) shows that the forecast for period $t + 1$ is a weighted average of the actual value in period $t$ and the forecast for period $t$; note in particular that the weight given to the actual value in period $t$ is $\alpha$ and that the weight given to the forecast in period $t$ is $1 - \alpha$. We can demonstrate that the exponential smoothing forecast for any period also is a weighted average of *all the previous actual values* for the time series with a time series consisting of three periods of data: $Y_1$, $Y_2$, and $Y_3$. To start the calculations, we let $F_1$ equal the actual value of the time series in period 1; that is, $F_1 = Y_1$. Hence, the forecast for period 2

$$F_2 = \alpha Y_1 + (1 - \alpha)F_1$$
$$= \alpha Y_1 + (1 - \alpha)Y_1$$
$$= Y_1$$

Thus, the exponential smoothing forecast for period 2 is equal to the actual value of the time series in period 1.

The forecast for period 3 is

$$F_3 = \alpha Y_2 + (1 - \alpha)F_2 = \alpha Y_2 + (1 - \alpha)Y_1$$

Finally, substituting this expression for $F_3$ in the expression for $F_4$, we obtain

$$F_4 = \alpha Y_3 + (1 - \alpha)F_3$$
$$= \alpha Y_3 + (1 - \alpha)[\alpha Y_2 + (1 - \alpha)Y_1]$$
$$= \alpha Y_3 + \alpha(1 - \alpha)Y_2 + (1 - \alpha)^2 Y_1$$

Hence, $F_4$ is a weighted average of the first three time series values. The sum of the coefficients, or weights, for $Y_1$, $Y_2$, and $Y_3$ equals 1. A similar argument can be made to show that, in general, any forecast $F_{t+1}$ is a weighted average of all the previous time series values.

Despite the fact that exponential smoothing provides a forecast that is a weighted average of all past observations, all the past data do not need to be saved in order to compute the forecast for the next period. In fact, once the **smoothing constant** $\alpha$ has been selected, only two pieces of information are required to compute the forecast. Equation (16.2) shows that with a given $\alpha$ we can compute the forecast for period $t + 1$ simply by knowing the actual and forecast time series values for period $t$—that is, $Y_t$ and $F_t$.

To illustrate the exponential smoothing approach to forecasting, consider the gasoline sales time series presented previously in Table 16.1 and Figure 16.5. As indicated, the exponential smoothing forecast for period 2 is equal to the actual value of the time series in period 1. Thus, with $Y_1 = 17$, we set $F_2 = 17$ to get the exponential smoothing computations started. From the time series data in Table 16.1, we find an actual time series value in period 2 of $Y_2 = 21$. Thus, period 2 has a forecast error of $21 - 17 = 4$.

Continuing with the exponential smoothing computations, using a smoothing constant of $\alpha = 0.2$, provides the forecast for period 3:

$$F_3 = 0.2Y_2 + 0.8F_2 = 0.2(21) + 0.8(17) = 17.8$$

Once the actual time series value in period 3, $Y_3 = 19$, is known, we can generate a forecast for period 4:

$$F_4 = 0.2Y_3 + 0.8F_3 = 0.2(19) + 0.8(17.8) = 18.04$$

By continuing the exponential smoothing calculations, we can determine the weekly forecast values and the corresponding weekly forecast errors, as shown in Table 16.3. Note that we have not shown an exponential smoothing forecast or the forecast error for period 1 because no forecast was made. For week 12, we have $Y_{12} = 22$ and $F_{12} = 18.48$. Can we use this information to generate a forecast for week 13 before the actual value of week 13 becomes known? Using the exponential smoothing model, we have

$$F_{13} = 0.2Y_{12} + 0.8F_{12} = 0.2(22) + 0.8(18.48) = 19.18$$

Thus, the exponential smoothing forecast of the amount sold in week 13 is 19.18, or 19,180 gallons of gasoline. With this forecast, the firm can make plans and decisions accordingly. The accuracy of the forecast will not be known until the end of week 13.

Figure 16.7 shows the plot of the actual and the forecast values from Table 16.3. Note in particular how the forecasts "smooth out" the irregular fluctuations in the time series.

**Forecast Accuracy.** In the preceding exponential smoothing calculations, we used a smoothing constant of $\alpha = 0.2$. Although any value of $\alpha$ between 0 and 1 is acceptable,

Can you now use
exponential smoothing to
develop forecasts? Try
Problem 4.

| Table 16.3 | SUMMARY OF THE EXPONENTIAL SMOOTHING FORECASTS AND FORECAST ERRORS FOR GASOLINE SALES WITH SMOOTHING CONSTANT $\alpha = 0.2$ |
| --- | --- |

| Week ($t$) | Time Series Value ($Y_t$) | Exponential Smoothing Forecast ($F_t$) | Forecast Error ($Y_t - F_t$) |
| --- | --- | --- | --- |
| 1 | 17 | | |
| 2 | 21 | 17.00 | 4.00 |
| 3 | 19 | 17.80 | 1.20 |
| 4 | 23 | 18.04 | 4.96 |
| 5 | 18 | 19.03 | −1.03 |
| 6 | 16 | 18.83 | −2.83 |
| 7 | 20 | 18.26 | 1.74 |
| 8 | 18 | 18.61 | −0.61 |
| 9 | 22 | 18.49 | 3.51 |
| 10 | 20 | 19.19 | 0.81 |
| 11 | 15 | 19.35 | −4.35 |
| 12 | 22 | 18.48 | 3.52 |

| Figure 16.7 | GRAPH OF ACTUAL AND FORECAST GASOLINE SALES TIME SERIES WITH SMOOTHING CONSTANT $\alpha = 0.2$ |
| --- | --- |

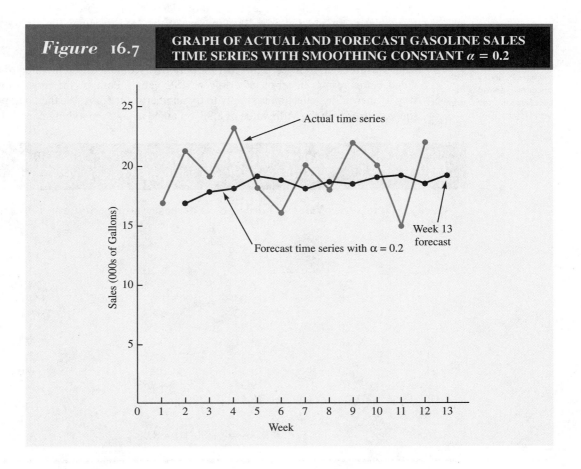

some values will yield better forecasts than others. Insight into choosing a good value for $\alpha$ can be obtained by rewriting the basic exponential smoothing model as follows:

$$F_{t+1} = \alpha Y_t + (1 - \alpha)F_t \qquad (16.3)$$
$$= \alpha Y_t + F_t - \alpha F_t$$
$$= \underbrace{F_t}_{\substack{\text{Forecast} \\ \text{in period } t}} + \alpha \underbrace{(Y_t - F_t)}_{\substack{\text{Forecast error} \\ \text{in period } t}}$$

Thus, the new forecast $F_{t+1}$ is equal to the previous forecast $F_t$ plus an adjustment, which is $\alpha$ times the most recent forecast error, $Y_t - F_t$. That is, the forecast in period $t + 1$ is obtained by adjusting the forecast in period $t$ by a fraction of the forecast error. If the time series contains substantial random variability, a small value of the smoothing constant is preferred. The reason for this choice is that, because much of the forecast error is due to random variability, we do not want to overreact and adjust the forecasts too quickly. For a time series with relatively little random variability, larger values of the smoothing constant have the advantage of quickly adjusting the forecasts when forecasting errors occur and therefore allowing the forecast to react faster to changing conditions.

The criterion we use to determine a desirable value for the smoothing constant $\alpha$ is the same as the criterion we proposed earlier for determining the number of periods of data to include in the moving averages calculation. That is, we choose the value of $\alpha$ that minimizes the mean squared error. A summary of the MSE calculations for the exponential smoothing forecast of gasoline sales with $\alpha = 0.2$ is shown in Table 16.4. Note that there is one less squared error term than the number of periods of data because we had no past values with which to make a forecast for period 1. Would a different value of $\alpha$ have provided better results in terms of a lower MSE value? Perhaps the most straightforward way to answer this question is simply to try another value for $\alpha$. We then compare its mean squared error with the MSE value of 8.98, obtained using a smoothing constant of $\alpha = 0.2$.

*Problem 5 asks you to determine whether moving averages or exponential smoothing provides the best forecasts for a given set of data.*

| *Table* 16.4 | MEAN SQUARED ERROR COMPUTATIONS FOR FORECASTING GASOLINE SALES WITH $\alpha = 0.2$ | | |
|---|---|---|---|
| **Week** ($t$) | **Time Series Value** ($Y_t$) | **Forecast** ($F_t$) | **Forecast Error** ($Y_t - F_t$) | **Squared Forecast Error** ($(Y_t - F_t)^2$) |

| Week ($t$) | Time Series Value ($Y_t$) | Forecast ($F_t$) | Forecast Error ($Y_t - F_t$) | Squared Forecast Error ($(Y_t - F_t)^2$) |
|---|---|---|---|---|
| 1 | 17 | | | |
| 2 | 21 | 17.00 | 4.00 | 16.00 |
| 3 | 19 | 17.80 | 1.20 | 1.44 |
| 4 | 23 | 18.04 | 4.96 | 24.60 |
| 5 | 18 | 19.03 | $-1.03$ | 1.06 |
| 6 | 16 | 18.83 | $-2.83$ | 8.01 |
| 7 | 20 | 18.26 | 1.74 | 3.03 |
| 8 | 18 | 18.61 | $-0.61$ | 0.37 |
| 9 | 22 | 18.49 | 3.51 | 12.32 |
| 10 | 20 | 18.49 | 0.81 | 0.66 |
| 11 | 15 | 19.35 | $-4.35$ | 18.92 |
| 12 | 22 | 18.48 | 3.52 | 12.39 |
| | | | Total | 98.80 |

$$\text{MSE} = 98.80/11 = 8.98$$

The exponential smoothing results with $\alpha = 0.3$ are shown in Table 16.5. With MSE = 9.35, a smoothing constant of $\alpha = 0.3$ results in less forecast accuracy than a smoothing constant of $\alpha = 0.2$. Thus, we would be inclined to use the original smoothing constant of 0.2. Using a trial-and-error calculation with other values of $\alpha$, we can find a "good" value for the smoothing constant. This value can be used in the exponential smoothing model to provide forecasts for the future. At a later date, after new time series observations have been obtained, we analyze the newly collected time series data to determine whether the smoothing constant should be revised to provide better forecasting results.

| Table 16.5 | MEAN SQUARED ERROR COMPUTATIONS FOR FORECASTING GASOLINE SALES WITH $\alpha = 0.3$ | | | |
|---|---|---|---|---|
| Week $(t)$ | Time Series Value $(Y_t)$ | Forecast $(F_t)$ | Forecast Error $(Y_t - F_t)$ | Squared Forecast Error $(Y_t - F_t)^2$ |
| 1 | 17 | | | |
| 2 | 21 | 17.00 | 4.00 | 16.00 |
| 3 | 19 | 18.20 | 0.80 | 0.64 |
| 4 | 23 | 18.44 | 4.56 | 20.79 |
| 5 | 18 | 19.81 | −1.81 | 3.28 |
| 6 | 16 | 19.27 | −3.27 | 10.69 |
| 7 | 20 | 18.29 | 1.71 | 2.92 |
| 8 | 18 | 18.80 | −0.80 | 0.64 |
| 9 | 22 | 18.56 | 3.44 | 11.83 |
| 10 | 20 | 19.59 | 0.41 | 0.17 |
| 11 | 15 | 19.71 | −4.71 | 22.18 |
| 12 | 22 | 18.30 | 3.70 | 13.69 |
| | | | Total | 102.83 |

$$\text{MSE} = 102.83/11 = 9.35$$

## NOTES and Comments

1. Another commonly used measure of forecast accuracy is the **mean absolute deviation (MAD).** This measure is simply the average of the absolute values of all the forecast errors. Using the errors given in Table 16.2, we obtain

$$\text{MAD} = \frac{4 + 3 + 4 + 1 + 0 + 4 + 0 + 5 + 3}{9} = 2.67$$

One major difference between the MSE and the MAD is that the MSE measure is influenced much more by large forecast errors than by small errors (for the MSE measure the errors are squared). The selection of the best measure of forecasting accuracy is not a simple matter. Indeed, forecasting experts often disagree as to which measure should be used. We use the MSE measure in this chapter.

2. Spreadsheet packages are an effective aid in choosing a good value of $\alpha$ for exponential smoothing and selecting weights for the weighted moving averages method. With the time series data and the forecasting formulas in the spreadsheets, you can experiment with different values of $\alpha$ (or moving average weights) and choose the value(s) providing the smallest MSE or MAD. In the chapter appendix, we show how this can be done.

............................................................................................./  /............

## 16.3   USING TREND PROJECTION IN FORECASTING

In this section we show how to forecast the values of a time series that exhibits a long-term linear trend. The type of time series for which the trend projection method is applicable shows a consistent increase or decrease over time; it is not stable so the smoothing methods described in the preceding section are not applicable.

Consider the time series for bicycle sales of a particular manufacturer over the past 10 years, as shown in Table 16.6 and Figure 16.8. Note that 21,600 bicycles were sold in year 1; 22,900 were sold in year 2; and so on. In year 10, the most recent year, 31,400 bicycles were sold. Although Figure 16.8 shows some up-and-down movement over the past 10 years, the time series for the number of bicycles sold seems to have an overall increasing or upward trend.

We do not want the trend component of a time series to follow each and every "up" and "down" movement. Rather, the trend component should reflect the gradual shifting—in this case, growth—of the time series values. After we view the time series data in Table 16.6 and the graph in Figure 16.8, we might agree that a linear trend as shown in Figure 16.9 provides a reasonable description of the long-run movement in the series.

We use the bicycle sales data to illustrate the calculations involved in applying regression analysis to identify a linear trend. For a linear trend, the estimated sales volume expressed as a function of time is

$$T_t = b_0 + b_1 t \tag{16.4}$$

where

$T_t =$ trend value for bicycle sales in period $t$

$b_0 =$ intercept of the trend line

$b_1 =$ slope of the trend line

---

**Table 16.6     BICYCLE SALES TIME SERIES**

| Year (t) | Sales (000s) ($Y_t$) |
|:---:|:---:|
| 1 | 21.6 |
| 2 | 22.9 |
| 3 | 25.5 |
| 4 | 21.9 |
| 5 | 23.9 |
| 6 | 27.5 |
| 7 | 31.5 |
| 8 | 29.7 |
| 9 | 28.6 |
| 10 | 31.4 |

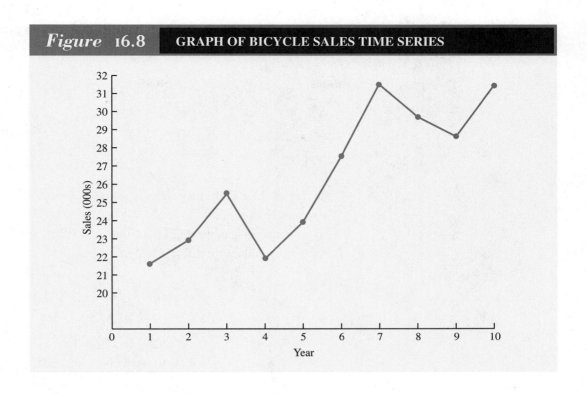

**Figure 16.8    GRAPH OF BICYCLE SALES TIME SERIES**

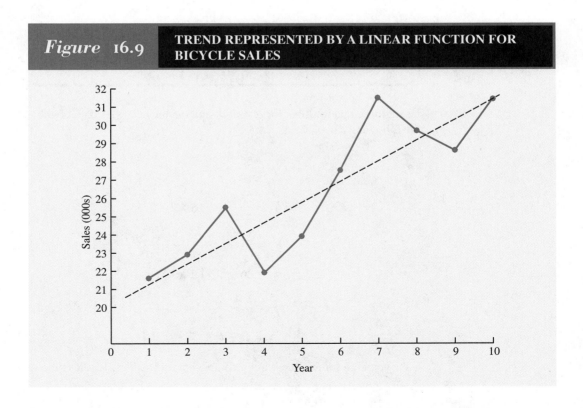

**Figure 16.9    TREND REPRESENTED BY A LINEAR FUNCTION FOR BICYCLE SALES**

Note that, for the time series on bicycle sales, $t = 1$ corresponds to the oldest time series value and $t = 10$ corresponds to the most recent time series value. Formulas for computing $b_1$ and $b_0$ are:

$$b_1 = \frac{\sum tY_t - (\sum t \sum Y_t)/n}{\sum t^2 - (\sum t)^2/n}$$  (16.5)

$$b_0 = \bar{Y} - b_1\bar{t}$$  (16.6)

where

$Y_t$ = actual value of the time series in period $t$

$n$ = number of periods

$\bar{Y}$ = average value of the time series; that is, $\bar{Y} = \sum Y_t/n$

$\bar{t}$ = average value of $t$; that is, $\bar{t} = \sum t/n$

| $t$ | $Y_t$ | $tY_t$ | $t^2$ |
|---|---|---|---|
| 1 | 21.6 | 21.6 | 1 |
| 2 | 22.9 | 45.8 | 4 |
| 3 | 25.5 | 76.5 | 9 |
| 4 | 21.9 | 87.6 | 16 |
| 5 | 23.9 | 119.5 | 25 |
| 6 | 27.5 | 165.0 | 36 |
| 7 | 31.5 | 220.5 | 49 |
| 8 | 29.7 | 237.6 | 64 |
| 9 | 28.6 | 257.4 | 81 |
| 10 | 31.4 | 314.0 | 100 |
| Totals 55 | 264.5 | 1545.5 | 385 |

Using these relationships for $b_0$ and $b_1$ and the bicycle sales data of Table 16.6, we obtain the following calculations.

$$\bar{t} = \frac{55}{10} = 5.5$$

$$\bar{Y} = \frac{264.5}{10} = 26.45$$

$$b_1 = \frac{1545.5 - (55)(264.5)/10}{385 - (55)^2/10} = 1.10$$

$$b_0 = 26.45 - 1.10(5.5) = 20.4$$

Therefore,

$$T_t = 20.4 + 1.1t$$  (16.7)

is the equation for the linear trend component for the bicycle sales time series.

Try Problem 14 for practice in developing the equation for the linear trend component of a time series.

The slope of 1.1 in the trend equation indicates that over the past 10 years the firm has experienced an average growth in sales of about 1100 units per year. If we assume that the past 10-year trend in sales is a good indicator for the future, we can use equation (16.7) to project the trend component of the time series. For example, substituting $t = 11$ into equation (16.7) yields next year's trend projection, $T_{11}$:

$$T_{11} = 20.4 + 1.1(11) = 32.5$$

Thus the trend component yields a sales forecast of 32,500 bicycles for next year.

We can also use the trend line to forecast sales farther into the future. For instance, using equation (16.7), we develop forecasts for an additional 2 and 3 years into the future as follows:

$$T_{12} = 20.4 + 1.1(12) = 33.6$$
$$T_{13} = 20.4 + 1.1(13) = 34.7$$

The use of a linear function to model the trend is common. However, as we discussed earlier, sometimes time series exhibit a curvilinear (nonlinear) trend similar to those shown in Figure 16.10. More advanced texts discuss how to develop models for these more complex relationships.

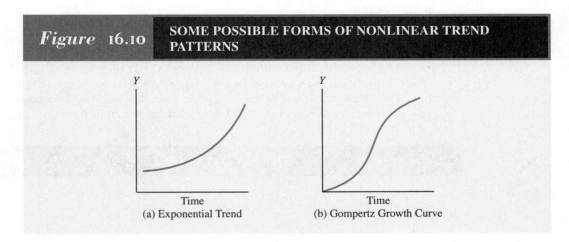

**Figure 16.10    SOME POSSIBLE FORMS OF NONLINEAR TREND PATTERNS**

(a) Exponential Trend    (b) Gompertz Growth Curve

## 16.4    USING TREND AND SEASONAL COMPONENTS IN FORECASTING

We have shown how to forecast the values of a time series that has a trend component. In this section we extend the discussion by showing how to forecast the values of a time series that has both trend and seasonal components.

Many situations in business and economics involve period-to-period comparisons. For instance, we might be interested to learn that unemployment is up 2% compared to last month, steel production is up 5% over last month, or that the production of electric power is down 3% from the previous month. Care must be exercised in using such information, however, because whenever a seasonal influence is present, such comparisons usually are not especially meaningful. For instance, the fact that electric power consumption is down by 3% from August to September might be only the seasonal effect associated with a decrease in the use of air conditioning and not because of a long-term decline in the use of electric power. Indeed, after adjusting for the seasonal effect, we might even find that the use of electric power has increased.

Removing the seasonal effect from a time series is known as *deseasonalizing the time series*. After we do so, period-to-period comparisons are more meaningful and can help identify whether a trend exists. The approach we take in this section is appropriate in situations when only seasonal effects are present or in situations when both seasonal and trend components are present. The first step is to compute seasonal indexes and use them to deseasonalize the data. Then, if a trend is apparent in the deseasonalized data, we use regression analysis on the deseasonalized data to estimate the trend.

### The Multiplicative Model

In addition to a trend component $T$ and a seasonal component $S$, we assume that the time series also has an irregular component $I$. The irregular component accounts for the random effects in the time series that cannot be explained by the trend and seasonal components. Using $T_t$, $S_t$, and $I_t$ to identify the trend, seasonal, and irregular components at time $t$, we assume that the actual time series value, denoted by $Y_t$, can be described by the **multiplicative time series model**

$$Y_t = T_t \times S_t \times I_t \tag{16.8}$$

In this model, $T_t$ is the trend measured in units of the item being forecast. However, the $S_t$ and $I_t$ components are measured in relative terms, with values above 1.00 indicating effects above the trend, and values below 1.00 indicating effects below the trend.

We illustrate the use of the multiplicative model with trend, seasonal, and irregular components by working with the quarterly data presented in Table 16.7 and Figure 16.11.

| *Table* 16.7 | QUARTERLY DATA FOR TELEVISION SET SALES | |
|---|---|---|

| Year | Quarter | Sales (000s) |
|---|---|---|
| 1 | 1 | 4.8 |
|   | 2 | 4.1 |
|   | 3 | 6.0 |
|   | 4 | 6.5 |
| 2 | 1 | 5.8 |
|   | 2 | 5.2 |
|   | 3 | 6.8 |
|   | 4 | 7.4 |
| 3 | 1 | 6.0 |
|   | 2 | 5.6 |
|   | 3 | 7.5 |
|   | 4 | 7.8 |
| 4 | 1 | 6.3 |
|   | 2 | 5.9 |
|   | 3 | 8.0 |
|   | 4 | 8.4 |

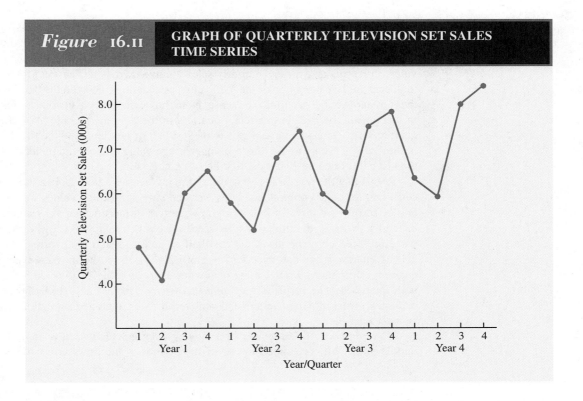

**Figure 16.11** — **GRAPH OF QUARTERLY TELEVISION SET SALES TIME SERIES**

These data show television set sales (in thousands of units) for a particular manufacturer over the past 4 years. We begin by showing how to identify the seasonal component of the time series.

## Calculating the Seasonal Indexes

Figure 16.11 indicates that sales are lowest in the second quarter of each year, followed by higher sales levels in quarters 3 and 4. Thus, we conclude that a seasonal pattern exists for television set sales. We begin the computational procedure used to identify each quarter's seasonal influence by computing a moving average to isolate the combined seasonal and irregular components, $S_t$ and $I_t$.

To do so, we use 1 year of data in each calculation. Because we are working with a quarterly series, we use four data values in each moving average. The moving average calculation for the first 4 quarters of the television set sales data is

$$\text{First moving average} = \frac{4.8 + 4.1 + 6.0 + 6.5}{4} = \frac{21.4}{4} = 5.35$$

Note that the moving average calculation for the first 4 quarters yields the average quarterly sales over year 1 of the time series. Continuing the moving average calculation, we next add the 5.8 value for the first quarter of year 2 and drop the 4.8 for the first quarter of year 1. Thus, the second moving average is

$$\text{Second moving average} = \frac{4.1 + 6.0 + 6.5 + 5.8}{4} = \frac{22.4}{4} = 5.6$$

Similarly, the third moving average calculation is $(6.0 + 6.5 + 5.8 + 5.2)/4 = 5.875$.

Before we proceed with the moving average calculations for the entire time series, we return to the first moving average calculation, which resulted in a value of 5.35. The 5.35 value represents an average quarterly sales volume (across all seasons) for year 1. As we look back at the calculation of the 5.35 value, associating 5.35 with the "middle" quarter of the moving average group makes sense. Note, however, that we encounter some difficulty in identifying the middle quarter; 4 quarters in the moving average allow for no middle quarter. The 5.35 value corresponds to the last half of quarter 2 and the first half of quarter 3. Similarly, if we go to the next moving average value of 5.60, the middle corresponds to the last half of quarter 3 and the first half of quarter 4.

Recall that the reason for computing moving averages is to isolate the combined seasonal and irregular components. However, the moving average values we have computed do not correspond directly to the original quarters of the time series. We can resolve this difficulty by using the midpoints between successive moving average values. For example, since 5.35 corresponds to the first half of quarter 3 and 5.60 corresponds to the last half of quarter 3, we can use $(5.35 + 5.60)/2 = 5.475$ as the moving average value for quarter 3. Similarly, we associate a moving average value of $(5.60 + 5.875)/2 = 5.738$ with quarter 4. The result is a *centered moving average*. Table 16.8 shows a complete summary of the moving average and centered moving average calculations for the television set sales data.

If the number of data points in a moving average calculation is an odd number, the middle point will correspond to one of the periods in the time series. In such cases, we

| Table 16.8 | CENTERED MOVING AVERAGE CALCULATIONS FOR THE TELEVISION SET SALES TIME SERIES | | | |
|---|---|---|---|---|
| Year | Quarter | Sales (000s) | 4-Quarter Moving Average | Centered Moving Average |
| 1 | 1 | 4.8 | | |
| | 2 | 4.1 | | |
| | 3 | 6.0 | 5.350 | 5.475 |
| | 4 | 6.5 | 5.600 | 5.738 |
| 2 | 1 | 5.8 | 5.875 | 5.975 |
| | 2 | 5.2 | 6.075 | 6.188 |
| | 3 | 6.8 | 6.300 | 6.325 |
| | 4 | 7.4 | 6.350 | 6.400 |
| 3 | 1 | 6.0 | 6.450 | 6.538 |
| | 2 | 5.6 | 6.625 | 6.675 |
| | 3 | 7.5 | 6.725 | 6.763 |
| | 4 | 7.8 | 6.800 | 6.838 |
| 4 | 1 | 6.3 | 6.875 | 6.938 |
| | 2 | 5.9 | 7.000 | 7.075 |
| | 3 | 8.0 | 7.150 | |
| | 4 | 8.4 | | |

would not have to center the moving average values to correspond to a particular time period, as we did in the calculations in Table 16.8.

What do the centered moving averages in Table 16.8 tell us about this time series? Figure 16.12 shows plots of the actual time series values and the corresponding centered moving average. Note particularly how the centered moving average values tend to "smooth out" both the seasonal and irregular fluctuations in the time series. The moving average values computed for 4 quarters of data do not include the fluctuations due to seasonal influences because the seasonal effect has been averaged out. Each point in the centered moving average represents what the value of the time series would be without seasonal or irregular influences.

By dividing each time series observation by the corresponding centered moving average value, we can identify the seasonal-irregular effect in the time series. For example, the third quarter of year 1 shows 6.0/5.475 = 1.096 as the combined seasonal-irregular component. Table 16.9 summarizes the resulting seasonal-irregular values for the entire time series.

Consider the third quarter. The results from years 1, 2, and 3 show third-quarter values of 1.096, 1.075, and 1.109, respectively. Thus, in all cases the seasonal-irregular component appears to have an above average influence in the third quarter. The fluctuations over the 3 years can be attributed to the irregular component, so we can average the computed values to eliminate the irregular influence and obtain an estimate of the third-quarter seasonal influence:

$$\text{Seasonal effect of third quarter} = \frac{1.096 + 1.075 + 1.109}{3} = 1.09$$

**Figure 16.12    GRAPH OF QUARTERLY TELEVISION SET SALES TIME SERIES AND CENTERED MOVING AVERAGE**

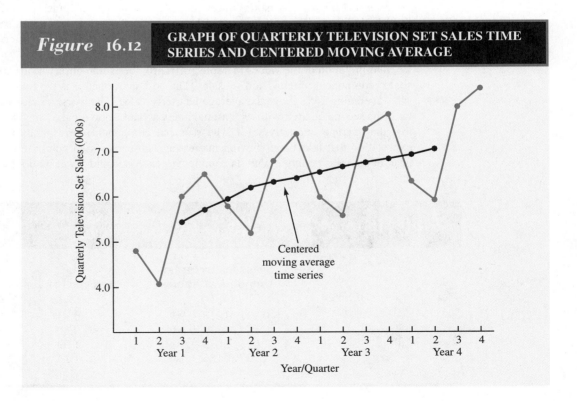

| Table 16.9 | | SEASONAL-IRREGULAR VALUES FOR THE TELEVISION SET SALES TIME SERIES | | |
|---|---|---|---|---|

| Year | Quarter | Sales (000s) | Centered Moving Average | Seasonal-Irregular Value |
|---|---|---|---|---|
| 1 | 1 | 4.8 | | |
| | 2 | 4.1 | | |
| | 3 | 6.0 | 5.475 | 1.096 |
| | 4 | 6.5 | 5.738 | 1.133 |
| 2 | 1 | 5.8 | 5.975 | 0.971 |
| | 2 | 5.2 | 6.188 | 0.840 |
| | 3 | 6.8 | 6.325 | 1.075 |
| | 4 | 7.4 | 6.400 | 1.156 |
| 3 | 1 | 6.0 | 6.538 | 0.918 |
| | 2 | 5.6 | 6.675 | 0.839 |
| | 3 | 7.5 | 6.763 | 1.109 |
| | 4 | 7.8 | 6.838 | 1.141 |
| 4 | 1 | 6.3 | 6.938 | 0.908 |
| | 2 | 5.9 | 7.075 | 0.834 |
| | 3 | 8.0 | | |
| | 4 | 8.4 | | |

We refer to 1.09 as the **seasonal index** for the third quarter. In Table 16.10 we summarize the calculations involved in computing the seasonal indexes for the television set sales time series. Thus, the seasonal indexes for all 4 quarters are: quarter 1, 0.93; quarter 2, 0.84; quarter 3, 1.09; and quarter 4, 1.14.

Interpretation of the values in Table 16.10 provides some observations about the "seasonal" component in television set sales. The best sales quarter is the fourth quarter, with sales averaging 14% above the average quarterly value. The worst, or slowest, sales quarter is the second quarter, with its seasonal index at 0.84, showing the sales average 16% below the average quarterly sales. The seasonal component corresponds to the intuitive expectation that television viewing interest and thus television purchase patterns tend to peak in the fourth quarter, with its coming winter season and fewer outdoor activities. The

| Table 16.10 | SEASONAL INDEX CALCULATIONS FOR THE TELEVISION SET SALES TIME SERIES | |
|---|---|---|

| Quarter | Seasonal-Irregular Component Values $(S_t I_t)$ | Seasonal Index $(S_t)$ |
|---|---|---|
| 1 | 0.971, 0.918, 0.908 | 0.93 |
| 2 | 0.840, 0.839, 0.834 | 0.84 |
| 3 | 1.096, 1.075, 1.109 | 1.09 |
| 4 | 1.133, 1.156, 1.141 | 1.14 |

Can you now compute and
interpret seasonal indexes
for a time series? Try
Problem 25.

low second-quarter sales reflect the reduced television interest resulting from the spring and presummer activities of the potential customers.

One final adjustment may be necessary in obtaining the seasonal indexes. The multiplicative model requires that the average seasonal index equal 1.00, so the sum of the four seasonal indexes in Table 16.10 must equal 4.00. In other words, the seasonal effects must even out over the year. The average of the seasonal indexes in our example is equal to 1.00, and hence, this type of adjustment is not necessary. In other cases, a slight adjustment may be necessary. To make the adjustment, multiply each seasonal index by the number of seasons divided by the sum of the unadjusted seasonal indexes. For instance, for quarterly data, multiply each seasonal index by 4/(sum of the unadjusted seasonal indexes). Some of the problems at the end of the chapter require this adjustment.

### Deseasonalizing the Time Series

With deseasonalized data,
comparing sales in
successive periods makes
sense. With data that have
not been deseasonalized,
relevant comparisons can
often be made between
sales in the current period
and sales in the same
period one year ago.

The purpose of finding seasonal indexes is to remove the seasonal effects from a time series. This process is referred to as *deseasonalizing* the time series. Economic time series adjusted for seasonal variations (**deseasonalized time series**) are reported in the *Survey of Current Business, The Wall Street Journal,* and *Business Week.* Using the notation of the multiplicative model, we have

$$Y_t = T_t \times S_t \times I_t$$

By dividing each time series observation by the corresponding seasonal index, we remove the effect of season from the time series. The deseasonalized time series for television set sales is summarized in Table 16.11. A graph of the deseasonalized television set sales time series is shown in Figure 16.13.

| *Table* 16.11 | | DESEASONALIZED VALUES FOR THE TELEVISION SET SALES TIME SERIES | | |
|---|---|---|---|---|
| Year | Quarter | Sales (000s) $(Y_t)$ | Seasonal Index $(S_t)$ | Deseasonalized Sales $(Y_t/S_t = T_t I_t)$ |
| 1 | 1 | 4.8 | 0.93 | 5.16 |
|   | 2 | 4.1 | 0.84 | 4.88 |
|   | 3 | 6.0 | 1.09 | 5.50 |
|   | 4 | 6.5 | 1.14 | 5.70 |
| 2 | 1 | 5.8 | 0.93 | 6.24 |
|   | 2 | 5.2 | 0.84 | 6.19 |
|   | 3 | 6.8 | 1.09 | 6.24 |
|   | 4 | 7.4 | 1.14 | 6.49 |
| 3 | 1 | 6.0 | 0.93 | 6.45 |
|   | 2 | 5.6 | 0.84 | 6.67 |
|   | 3 | 7.5 | 1.09 | 6.88 |
|   | 4 | 7.8 | 1.14 | 6.84 |
| 4 | 1 | 6.3 | 0.93 | 6.77 |
|   | 2 | 5.9 | 0.84 | 7.02 |
|   | 3 | 8.0 | 1.09 | 7.34 |
|   | 4 | 8.4 | 1.14 | 7.37 |

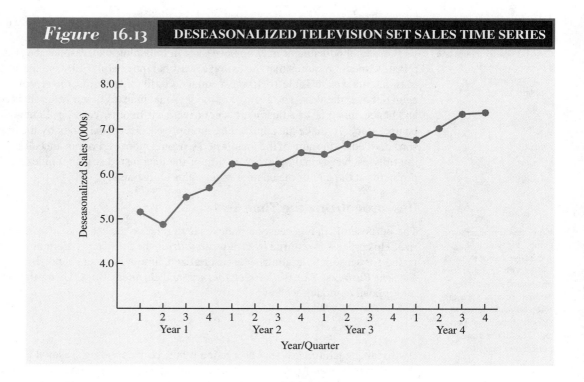

*Figure* 16.13      DESEASONALIZED TELEVISION SET SALES TIME SERIES

## Using the Deseasonalized Time Series to Identify Trend

Although the graph in Figure 16.13 shows some up-and-down movement over the past 16 quarters, the time series seems to have an upward linear trend. To identify this trend, we use the same procedure as in the preceding section; in this case, the data used are quarterly deseasonalized sales values. Thus, for a linear trend, the estimated sales volume expressed as a function of time is

$$T_t = b_0 + b_1 t$$

where

$$T_t = \text{trend value for television set sales in period } t$$
$$b_0 = \text{intercept of the trend line}$$
$$b_0 = \text{slope of the trend line}$$

As before, $t = 1$ corresponds to the time of the first observation for the time series, $t = 2$ corresponds to the time of the second observation, and so on. Thus, for the deseasonalized television set sales time series, $t = 1$ corresponds to the first deseasonalized quarterly sales value and $t = 16$ corresponds to the most recent deseasonalized quarterly sales value. The formulas for computing the values of $b_0$ and $b_1$ again are

$$b_1 = \frac{\sum t Y_t - (\sum t \sum Y_t)/n}{\sum t^2 - (\sum t)^2/n} \quad \text{and} \quad b_0 = \bar{Y} - b_1 \bar{t}$$

Note, however, that $Y_t$ now refers to the deseasonalized time series value at time $t$ and not to the actual value of the time series. Using the given relationships for $b_0$ and $b_1$ and the deseasonalized sales data of Table 16.11, we make the following calculations.

| $t$ | $Y_t$ (deseasonalized) | $tY_t$ | $t^2$ |
|---|---|---|---|
| 1 | 5.16 | 5.16 | 1 |
| 2 | 4.88 | 9.76 | 4 |
| 3 | 5.50 | 16.50 | 9 |
| 4 | 5.70 | 22.80 | 16 |
| 5 | 6.24 | 31.20 | 25 |
| 6 | 6.19 | 37.14 | 36 |
| 7 | 6.24 | 43.68 | 49 |
| 8 | 6.49 | 51.92 | 64 |
| 9 | 6.45 | 58.05 | 81 |
| 10 | 6.67 | 66.70 | 100 |
| 11 | 6.88 | 75.68 | 121 |
| 12 | 6.84 | 82.08 | 144 |
| 13 | 6.77 | 88.01 | 169 |
| 14 | 7.02 | 98.28 | 196 |
| 15 | 7.34 | 110.10 | 225 |
| 16 | 7.37 | 117.92 | 256 |
| Totals  136 | 101.74 | 914.98 | 1496 |

$$\bar{t} = \frac{136}{16} = 8.5$$

$$\bar{Y} = \frac{101.74}{16} = 6.359$$

$$b_1 = \frac{914.98 - (136)(101.74)/16}{1496 - (136)^2/16} = 0.148$$

$$b_0 = 6.359 - 0.148(8.5) = 5.101$$

Therefore,

$$T_t = 5.101 + 0.148t$$

is the equation for the linear trend component of the time series.

The slope of 0.148 indicates that over the past 16 quarters the firm has experienced an average deseasonalized growth in sales of about 148 sets per quarter. If we assume that the past 16-quarter trend in sales data is a reasonably good indicator of the future, we can use this equation to project the trend component of the time series for future quarters. For example, substituting $t = 17$ into the equation yields next quarter's trend projection, $T_{17}$:

$$T_{17} = 5.101 + 0.148(17) = 7.617$$

Thus, the trend component yields a sales forecast of 7617 television sets for the next quarter. Similarly, the trend component produces sales forecasts of 7765, 7913, and 8061 television sets in quarters 18, 19, and 20, respectively.

## Seasonal Adjustments

The final step in developing the forecast when both trend and seasonal components are present is to use the seasonal index to adjust the trend projection. Returning to the television set sales example, we have a trend projection for the next 4 quarters. Now we must adjust the forecast for the seasonal effect. The seasonal index for the first quarter of year 5 ($t = 17$) is 0.93, so we obtain the quarterly forecast by multiplying the forecast based on trend ($T_{17} = 7617$) times the seasonal index (0.93). Thus, the forecast for the next quarter is $7617(0.93) = 7084$. Table 16.12 shows the quarterly forecast for quarters 17–20. The forecasts show the high-volume fourth quarter with a 9190-unit forecast and the low-volume second quarter with a 6523-unit forecast.

## Models Based on Monthly Data

In the preceding television set sales example we used quarterly data to illustrate the computation of seasonal indexes. However, many businesses use monthly rather than quarterly forecasts. In such cases, the procedures introduced in this section can be applied with minor modifications. First, a 12-month moving average replaces the 4-quarter moving average; second, 12 monthly seasonal indexes, rather than the 4 quarterly indexes, must be computed. Other than these changes, the computational and forecasting procedures are identical.

## Cyclical Component

Mathematically, the multiplicative model of equation (16.8) can be expanded to include a cyclical component as follows:

$$Y_t = T_t \times C_t \times S_t \times I_t \qquad (16.9)$$

The seasonal component is attributable to multiyear cycles in the time series. It is analogous to the seasonal component but over a longer period of time. However, because of the length of time involved, obtaining enough relevant data to estimate the cyclical component often is difficult. Another difficulty is that the length of cycles usually varies. We leave further discussion of the cyclical component to texts on forecasting methods.

**Table 16.12 — QUARTERLY FORECASTS FOR THE TELEVISION SET SALES TIME SERIES**

| Year | Quarter | Trend Forecast | Seasonal Index (see Table 16.10) | Quarterly Forecast |
|---|---|---|---|---|
| 5 | 1 | 7617 | 0.93 | $(7617)(0.93) = 7084$ |
|   | 2 | 7765 | 0.84 | $(7765)(0.84) = 6523$ |
|   | 3 | 7913 | 1.09 | $(7913)(1.09) = 8625$ |
|   | 4 | 8061 | 1.14 | $(8061)(1.14) = 9190$ |

## 16.5    USING REGRESSION ANALYSIS IN FORECASTING

**Regression analysis** is a statistical technique that can be used to develop a mathematical equation showing how variables are related. In regression terminology, the variable that is being predicted is called the *dependent* or *response* variable. The variable or variables being used to predict the value of the dependent variable are called the *independent* or *predictor* variables. Regression analysis involving one independent variable and one dependent variable for which the relationship between the variables is approximated by a straight line is called *simple linear regression*. Regression analysis involving two or more independent variables is called *multiple regression analysis*. In Section 16.3 we utilized simple linear regression to fit a linear trend to the bicycle sales time series. Recall that we developed a linear equation relating bicycle sales to the time period. The number of bicycles sold isn't actually causally related to time; instead, time is a surrogate for variables to which the number of bicycles sold is actually related but which are either unknown or too difficult or costly to measure. Thus, the use of regression analysis for trend projection is not a causal forecasting method because only past values of sales, the variable being forecast, were used.

When we use regression analysis to relate the variable that we want to forecast to other variables that are supposed to influence or explain that variable, it becomes a causal forecasting method. The Management Science in Action: Spare Parts Forecasting at American Airlines explains why that company uses regression analysis as a causal forecasting method to estimate the demand for spare parts.

### Using Regression Analysis As a Causal Forecasting Method

To illustrate how regression analysis is used as a causal forecasting method, we consider the sales forecasting problem faced by Armand's Pizza Parlors, a chain of Italian restaurants doing business in a five-state area. The most successful locations have been near college campuses. The managers believe that quarterly sales for these restaurants (denoted by $y$) are related positively to the size of the student population (denoted by $x$); that

## MANAGEMENT SCIENCE IN ACTION

### SPARE PARTS FORECASTING AT AMERICAN AIRLINES*

American Airlines developed the Rotables Allocation and Planning System (RAPS) to provide demand forecasts for spare parts, assist in allocating spare parts to airports, and calculate the availability level of each spare part. The demand forecasting module of RAPS provides monthly demand forecasts for more than 5000 parts, ranging from coffee makers to landing gears. The average price for parts covered by RAPS is approximately $5000.

Prior to RAPS, American Airlines used time series methodology to forecast spare parts demand. The time series methodology was slow to respond to external factors such as changes in aircraft utilization and major fleet expansions. To correct for these deficiencies, the forecasting component of RAPS involves the use of regression analysis "to establish a relationship between monthly part removals and various functions of monthly flying hours." The RAPS system generates the monthly demand forecasts in less than an hour.

Nearly all the parts covered by the RAPS system are essential to the operation of an aircraft. A part shortage can even result in cancellation of a flight, so the cost can be substantial. The materials management group at American Airlines estimated "that using RAPS has provided a one-time savings of $7 million and recurring annual savings of nearly $1 million."

*Mark J. Tedone, "Repairable Part Management," *Interfaces* 19, No. 4 (July—August 1989): 61–68.

is, restaurants near campuses with a large population tend to generate more sales than those located near campuses with a small population. Using regression analysis we can develop an equation showing how the dependent variable $y$ is related the independent variable $x$. This equation can then be used to forecast quarterly sales for restaurants located near college campuses given the size of the student population.

In situations where time series data are not available, regression analysis can still be used to develop a forecast. For instance, suppose that management wanted to forecast sales for a new restaurant they were considering opening near a college campus. Since no historical data are available on sales for a new restaurant, Armand cannot use time series data to develop the forecast. But, as we will now illustrate, regression analysis can still be used to forecast quarterly sales.

To develop the equation relating quarterly sales and the size of the student population, Armand's collected data from a sample of 10 of its restaurants located near college campuses. These data are summarized in Table 16.13. For example, restaurant 1, with $y = 58$ and $x = 2$, had \$58,000 in quarterly sales and is located near a campus with 2000 students. Figure 16.14 shows graphically the data presented in Table 16.13. The size of the student population is shown on the horizontal axis, with quarterly sales shown on the vertical axis. This type of graph is called a *scatter diagram*. Usually the independent variable is plotted on the horizontal axis, and the dependent variable is plotted on the vertical axis. The advantage of a scatter diagram is that it provides an overview of the data and enables us to draw preliminary conclusions about a possible relationship between the variables.

What preliminary conclusions can we draw from Figure 16.14? Sales appear to be higher at campuses with larger student populations. Also, it appears that the relationship between the two variables can be approximated by a straight line; indeed, there appears to be a positive relationship between $x$ and $y$. In Figure 16.15 we have drawn a straight line through the data that appears to provide a good linear approximation of the relationship between the variables. Observe that the relationship isn't perfect. Indeed, few, if any, of the data fall exactly on the line. However, if we can develop the mathematical expression for this line, we may be able to use it to forecast the value of $y$ corresponding to each possible value of $x$. The resulting equation of the line is called the *estimated regression equation*.

| *Table* 16.13 | DATA ON QUARTERLY SALES AND STUDENT POPULATION FOR 10 RESTAURANTS | |
|---|---|---|
| Restaurant | $y$ = Quarterly Sales ($000s) | $x$ = Student Population (000s) |
| 1 | 58 | 2 |
| 2 | 105 | 6 |
| 3 | 88 | 8 |
| 4 | 118 | 8 |
| 5 | 117 | 12 |
| 6 | 137 | 16 |
| 7 | 157 | 20 |
| 8 | 169 | 20 |
| 9 | 149 | 22 |
| 10 | 202 | 26 |

**Figure 16.14**    SCATTER DIAGRAM OF QUARTERLY SALES VERSUS STUDENT POPULATION

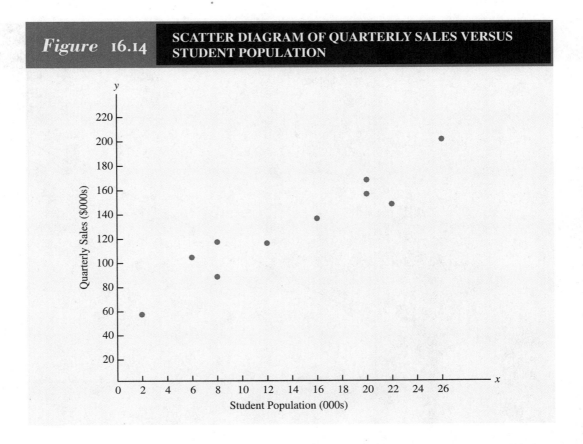

Using the least-squares method of estimation, we develop the estimated regression equation

$$\hat{y} = b_0 + b_1 x \tag{16.10}$$

where

$\hat{y}$ = estimated value of the dependent variable (quarterly sales)

$b_0$ = intercept of the estimated regression equation

$b_1$ = slope of the estimated regression equation

$x$ = value of the independent variable (student population)

We use the sample data and the following expression to compute the intercept $b_0$ and slope $b_1$:

$$b_1 = \frac{\sum x_i y_i - (\sum x_i \sum y_i)/n}{\sum x_i^2 - (\sum x_i)^2/n} \tag{16.11}$$

$$b_0 = \bar{y} - b_1 \bar{x} \tag{16.12}$$

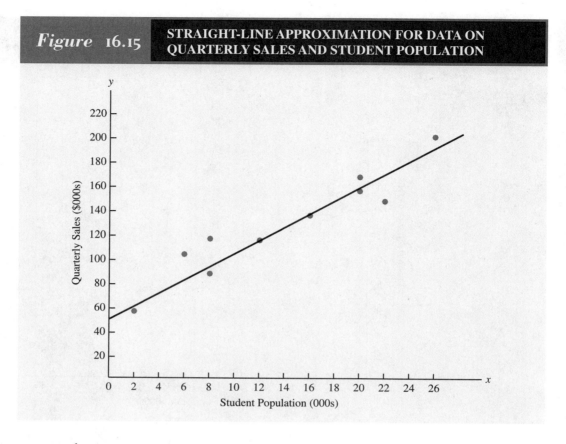

**Figure 16.15**  STRAIGHT-LINE APPROXIMATION FOR DATA ON QUARTERLY SALES AND STUDENT POPULATION

where

$x_i$ = value of the independent variable for the $i$th observation

$y_i$ = value of the dependent variable for the $i$th observation

$\bar{x}$ = mean value for the independent variable

$\bar{y}$ = mean value for the dependent variable

$n$ = total number of observations

Some of the calculations necessary to develop the least-squares estimated regression equation for the data on student population and quarterly sales are shown in Table 16.14. Our example contains 10 restaurants or observations; hence $n = 10$. Using equations (16.11) and (16.12), we can now compute the slope and intercept of the estimated regression equation. We calculate the slope $b_1$ as follows:

$$b_1 = \frac{\sum x_i y_i - (\sum x_i \sum y_i)/n}{\sum x_i^2 - (\sum x_i)^2/n}$$

$$= \frac{21{,}040 - (140)(1300)/10}{2528 - (140)^2/10}$$

$$= \frac{2840}{568}$$

$$= 5$$

| Table 16.14 | CALCULATIONS FOR THE LEAST-SQUARES ESTIMATED REGRESSION EQUATION FOR ARMAND'S PIZZA PARLORS |
| --- | --- |

| Restaurant ($i$) | $y_i$ | $x_i$ | $x_i y_i$ | $x_i^2$ |
| --- | --- | --- | --- | --- |
| 1 | 58 | 2 | 116 | 4 |
| 2 | 105 | 6 | 630 | 36 |
| 3 | 88 | 8 | 704 | 64 |
| 4 | 118 | 8 | 944 | 64 |
| 5 | 117 | 12 | 1,404 | 144 |
| 6 | 137 | 16 | 2,192 | 256 |
| 7 | 157 | 20 | 3,140 | 400 |
| 8 | 169 | 20 | 3,380 | 400 |
| 9 | 149 | 22 | 3,278 | 484 |
| 10 | 202 | 26 | 5,252 | 676 |
| Totals | 1300 | 140 | 21,040 | 2528 |

We then calculate the intercept $b_0$ as follows:

$$\bar{x} = \frac{\sum x_i}{n} = \frac{140}{10} = 14$$

$$\bar{y} = \frac{\sum y_i}{n} = \frac{1300}{10} = 130$$

$$b_0 = \bar{y} - b_1\bar{x}$$
$$= 130 - 5(14)$$
$$= 60$$

Thus, the estimated regression equation found by using the method of least squares is

$$\hat{y} = 60 + 5x$$

We show the graph of this equation in Figure 16.16.

The slope of the estimated regression equation ($b_1 = 5$) is positive, implying that, as student population increases, quarterly sales increase. In fact, we can conclude (because sales are measured in thousands of dollars and student population in thousands) that an increase in the student population of 1000 is associated with an increase of $5000 in expected quarterly sales; that is, quarterly sales are expected to increase by $5 per student.

If we believe that the least-squares estimated regression equation adequately describes the relationship between $x$ and $y$, using the estimated regression equation to forecast the value of $y$ for a given value of $x$ seems reasonable. For example, if we wanted to forecast quarterly sales for a new restaurant to be located near a campus with 16,000 students, we would compute

$$\hat{y} = 60 + 5(16)$$
$$= 140$$

Practice using regression analysis to develop a forecast by working Problem 33.

Hence, we would forecast quarterly sales of $140,000 per year.

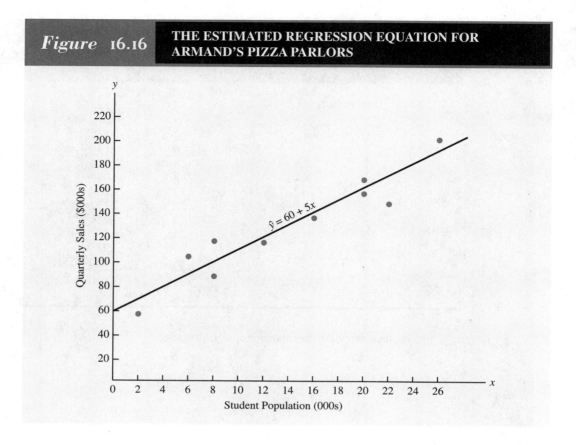

**Figure 16.16** THE ESTIMATED REGRESSION EQUATION FOR ARMAND'S PIZZA PARLORS

The sales forecasting problem facing Armand's Pizza Parlors illustrates how simple linear regression analysis can be used to develop forecasts when time series data are not available. Multiple regression analysis also can be applied in these situations if additional data for other independent variables are available. For example, suppose that the management of Armand's Pizza Parlors, also believes that the number of competitors near the college campus is related to quarterly sales. Intuitively, management believes that restaurants located near campuses where there are fewer competitors generate more sales revenue than those located near campuses where there are more competitors. With additional data, multiple regression analysis could be used to develop an equation relating quarterly sales to the size of the student population and the number of competitors.

## Using Regression Analysis with Time Series Data

In Section 16.3 we fit a linear trend to the bicycle sales time series to show how simple linear regression analysis can be used to forecast future values of a time series when past values of the time series are available. Recall that for this problem the annual sales in year $t$ was treated as the dependent variable and the year $t$ was treated as the independent variable. The inherent complexity of most real-world problems necessitates the consideration of more than one independent variable to predict the dependent variable. We now consider how multiple regression analysis is used to develop forecasts when time series data are available.

To use multiple regression analysis, we need a sample of observations for the dependent variable and all the independent variables. In time series analysis, the $n$ periods of time series data provide a sample of $n$ observations for each variable. To describe the wide variety of regression-based models that can be developed, we use the following notation:

$$Y_t = \text{actual value of the time series in period } t$$
$$x_{1t} = \text{value of independent variable 1 in period } t$$
$$x_{2t} = \text{value of independent variable 2 in period } t$$
$$\cdot$$
$$\cdot$$
$$\cdot$$
$$x_{kt} = \text{value of independent variable } k \text{ in period } t$$

The $n$ periods of data necessary to develop the estimated regression equation would appear as follows.

| Period | Time Series $(Y_t)$ | Value of Independent Variables $x_{1t}$ | $x_{2t}$ | $x_{3t}$ | $\cdot\ \cdot\ \cdot$ | $x_{kt}$ |
|--------|---------------------|------------------------------------------|----------|----------|------------------------|----------|
| 1 | $Y_1$ | $x_{11}$ | $x_{21}$ | $x_{31}$ | $\cdot\ \cdot\ \cdot$ | $x_{k1}$ |
| 2 | $Y_2$ | $x_{12}$ | $x_{22}$ | $x_{32}$ | $\cdot\ \cdot\ \cdot$ | $x_{k2}$ |
| $\cdot$ | $\cdot$ | $\cdot$ | $\cdot$ | $\cdot$ | $\cdot\ \cdot\ \cdot$ | $\cdot$ |
| $\cdot$ | $\cdot$ | $\cdot$ | $\cdot$ | $\cdot$ | $\cdot\ \cdot\ \cdot$ | $\cdot$ |
| $\cdot$ | $\cdot$ | $\cdot$ | $\cdot$ | $\cdot$ | $\cdot\ \cdot\ \cdot$ | $\cdot$ |
| $n$ | $Y_n$ | $x_{1n}$ | $x_{2n}$ | $x_{3n}$ | $\cdot\ \cdot\ \cdot$ | $x_{kn}$ |

As you might imagine, a number of choices can be made when selecting the independent variables in a forecasting model. One possible choice is simply time. We made this choice in Section 16.3 when we estimated the trend of the time series using a linear function of the independent variable time. Letting

$$x_{1t} = t$$

we obtain an estimated regression equation of the form

$$\hat{Y}_t = b_0 + b_1 t$$

where $\hat{Y}_t$ is the estimate of the time series value $Y_t$ and where $b_0$ and $b_1$ are the estimated regression coefficients. In a more complex model, additional terms could be added corresponding to time raised to other powers. For example, if

$$x_{2t} = t^2 \quad \text{and} \quad x_{3t} = t^3$$

the estimated regression equation would become

$$\hat{Y}_t = b_0 + b_1 x_{1t} + b_2 x_{2t} + b_3 x_{3t}$$
$$= b_0 + b_1 t + b_2 t^2 + b_3 t^3$$

Note that this model provides a forecast of a time series with curvilinear characteristics over time.

Other regression-based forecasting models involve the use of a mixture of economic and demographic independent variables. For example, in forecasting the sale of refrigerators, we might select independent variables such as

$x_{1t}$ = price in period $t$

$x_{2t}$ = total industry sales in period $t - 1$

$x_{3t}$ = number of building permits for new houses in period $t - 1$

$x_{4t}$ = population forecast for period $t$

$x_{5t}$ = advertising budget for period $t$

According to the usual multiple regression procedure, an estimated regression equation with five independent variables would be used to develop forecasts in this case.

Whether a regression approach provides a good forecast depends largely on how well we are able to identify and obtain data for independent variables that are closely related to the time series. Generally, during the development of an estimated regression equation, we will want to consider many possible sets of independent variables. Thus, part of the regression analysis procedure should focus on the selection of the set of independent variables that provides the best forecasting model.

In the chapter introduction we stated that **causal forecasting methods** utilized time series related to the one being forecast in an effort to explain better the cause of a time series' behavior. Regression analysis is the tool most often used in developing causal models. The related time series become the independent variables, and the time series being forecast is the dependent variable.

Another type of regression-based forecasting model occurs whenever all the independent variables are previous values of the *same* time series. For example, if the time series values are denoted $Y_1, Y_2, \ldots, Y_n$, we might try to find an estimated regression equation relating $Y_t$ to the most recent time series values, $Y_{t-1}, Y_{t-2}$, and so on. For instance, if we use the actual values of the time series for the three most recent periods as independent variables, the estimated regression equation would be

$$\hat{Y}_t = b_0 + b_1 Y_{t-1} + b_2 Y_{t-2} + b_3 Y_{t-3}$$

Regression models such as this one in which the independent variables are previous values of the time series are referred to as **autoregressive models.**

Finally, another regression-based forecasting approach is one that incorporates a mixture of the independent variables previously discussed. For example, we might select a combination of time variables, some economic/demographic variables, and some previous values of the time series variable itself.

Spyros Makridakis, a noted forecasting expert, has conducted research showing that simple techniques usually outperform more complex procedures for short-term forecasting. Using a more sophisticated and expensive procedure will not guarantee better forecasts.

## 16.6   QUALITATIVE APPROACHES TO FORECASTING

In the preceding sections we discussed several types of quantitative forecasting methods. Most of these techniques require historical data on the variable of interest, so they cannot be applied when no historical data are available. Furthermore, even when such data are available, a significant change in environmental conditions affecting the time series may make the use of past data questionable in predicting future values of the time series. For ex-

If historical data are not available, managers may use a qualitative technique to develop forecasts. But the cost of using qualitative techniques can be high because of the time commitment required from the people involved.

Empirical evidence and theoretical arguments suggest that between 5 and 20 experts should be used in judgmental forecasting.

ample, a government-imposed gasoline rationing program would raise questions about the validity of a gasoline sales forecast based on historical data. Qualitative forecasting techniques offer an alternative in these and other cases.

## Delphi Method

One of the most commonly used qualitative forecasting techniques is the **Delphi method.** This technique, originally developed by a research group at the Rand Corporation, attempts to develop forecasts through "group consensus." In its usual application, the members of a panel of experts—all of whom are physically separated from and unknown to each other—are asked to respond to a series of questionnaires. The responses from the first questionnaire are tabulated and used to prepare a second questionnaire that contains information and opinions of the entire group. Each respondent is then asked to reconsider and possibly revise his or her previous response in light of the group information provided. This process continues until the coordinator feels that some degree of consensus has been reached. The goal of the Delphi method is not to produce a single answer as output, but instead to produce a relatively narrow spread of opinions within which the majority of experts concur.

## Expert Judgment

Qualitative forecasts often are based on the judgment of a single expert or represent the consensus of a group of experts. For example, each year a group of experts at Merrill Lynch gather to forecast the level of the Dow Jones Industrial Average and the prime rate for the next year. In doing so, the experts individually consider information that they believe will influence the stock market and interest rates; then they combine their conclusions into a forecast. No formal model is used, and no two experts are likely to consider the same information in the same way.

Expert judgment is a forecasting method that is often recommended when conditions in the past are not likely to hold in the future. Even though no formal quantitative model is used, expert judgment has provided good forecasts in many situations. The Management Science in Action: The *Business Week* Industry Outlook shows that the magazine provides a good one-year forecast of industry prospects.

## MANAGEMENT SCIENCE IN ACTION

### THE *BUSINESS WEEK* INDUSTRY OUTLOOK*

The *Business Week* industry outlook survey is a qualitative approach to forecasting based on expert judgment. It combines information from hundreds of interviews with industry leaders with the expertise of the magazine's editors who have followed the industries daily to provide a judgment on the prospects for the next year. Steven Schnaars and Iris Mohr conducted a study to evaluate the accuracy of the *Business Week* forecasts for five industries (autos, steel, chemicals, computers, and energy) over a nine-year period (1978–1986).

Schnaars and Mohr evaluated *Business Week*'s approach in terms of its ability to predict correctly the general direction for the industry

(getting better or getting worse) and the accuracy of specific forecasts (e.g., sales and profit). They found that "nearly 80 percent of the outlooks correctly foresaw the overall direction in which the industry would move in the coming year." And, when comparing the *Business Week* forecast with a naive forecast of no change in the coming year, the *Business Week* forecast clearly was better. The authors conclude that judgmental forecasting can work well for forecasting the general direction of change.

*Steven P. Schnaars, and Iris Mohr, "The Accuracy of *Business Week*'s Industry Outlook Survey," *Interfaces* 18, No. 5 (September–October 1988): 31–38.

### Scenario Writing

The qualitative procedure referred to as **scenario writing** consists of developing a conceptual scenario of the future based on a well-defined set of assumptions. Different sets of assumptions lead to different scenarios. The job of the decision maker is to decide how likely each scenario is and then to make decisions accordingly.

### Intuitive Approaches

*Subjective,* or *intuitive qualitative approaches* are based on the ability of the human mind to process a variety of information that, in most cases, is difficult to quantify. These techniques are often used in group work, wherein a committee or panel seeks to develop new ideas or solve complex problems through a series of "brainstorming sessions." In such sessions, individuals are freed from the usual group restrictions of peer pressure and criticism because they can present any idea or opinion without regard to its relevancy and, even more importantly, without fear of criticism.

## SUMMARY

In this chapter we discussed how forecasts can be developed to help management develop appropriate strategies for the future. We began by defining a time series as a set of observations on a variable measured at successive points in time or over successive periods of time. A time series may involve four separate components: trend, seasonal, irregular, and cyclical. By isolating these components and measuring their apparent effects, future values of the time series can be forecast.

Quantitative forecasting methods include time series methods and causal methods. A time series method is appropriate when the historical data are restricted to past values of the variable being forecast. The three time series methods discussed in the chapter are smoothing (moving averages, weighted moving averages, and exponential smoothing), trend projection, and trend projection adjusted for seasonal influence.

Smoothing methods are appropriate for a stable time series, that is, one that exhibits no significant trend, cyclical, or seasonal effects. The moving averages approach consists of computing an average of past values and then using this average as the forecast for the next period. The weighted moving averages method allows for the possibility of unequal weights for the data; thus, the moving averages method is a special case of the weighted moving averages method in which all the weights are equal. Exponential smoothing also is a special case of the weighted moving averages method involving only one parameter: the weight for the most recent observation.

When a time series consists of random fluctuations around a long-term trend line, a linear equation may be used to estimate the trend. When seasonal effects are present, seasonal indexes can be computed and used to deseasonalize the data and to develop forecasts. When both seasonal and long-term trend effects are present, a trend line is fitted to the deseasonalized data; the seasonal indexes are then used to adjust the trend projections.

Causal forecasting methods are based on the assumption that the variable being forecast exhibits a cause-effect relationship with one or more other variables. A causal forecasting method is one that relates the variable being forecast to other variables that are thought to influence or explain it. Regression analysis is a causal forecasting method that can be used to develop forecasts when time series data are not available.

Qualitative forecasting methods may be used when little or no historical data are available. Qualitative forecasting methods also are considered most appropriate when the historical pattern of the time series is not expected to continue into the future.

## GLOSSARY

**Time series**  A set of observations measured at successive points in time or over successive periods of time.

**Forecast**  A projection or prediction of future values of a time series.

**Trend**  The long-run shift or movement in the time series observable over several periods of data.

**Cyclical component**  The component of the time series model that results in periodic above-trend and below-trend behavior of the time series lasting more than one year.

**Seasonal component**  The component of the time series model that shows a periodic pattern over one year or less.

**Irregular component**  The component of the time series model that reflects the random variation of the actual time series values beyond what can be explained by the trend, cyclical, and seasonal components.

**Moving averages**  A method of forecasting or smoothing a time series by averaging each successive group of data points.

**Mean squared error (MSE)**  An approach to measuring the accuracy of a forecasting model. This measure is the average of the sum of the squared differences between the actual time series values and the forecasted values.

**Weighted moving averages**  A method of forecasting or smoothing a time series by computing a weighted average of past time series values. The sum of the weights must equal 1.

**Exponential smoothing**  A forecasting technique that uses a weighted average of past time series values to arrive at smoothed time series values that can be used as forecasts.

**Smoothing constant**  A parameter of the exponential smoothing model that provides the weight given to the most recent time series value in the calculation of the forecast.

**Mean absolute deviation (MAD)**  A measure of forecast accuracy. The average of the absolute values of the forecast errors.

**Multiplicative time series model**  A model that assumes that the separate components of the time series can be multiplied together to identify the actual time series value. When the four components of trend, cyclical, seasonal, and irregular are assumed present, we obtain $Y_t = T_t \times C_t \times S_t \times I_t$. When cyclical effects are not modeled, we obtain $Y_t = T_t \times S_t \times I_t$.

**Seasonal index**  A measure of the seasonal effect on a time series. A seasonal index above 1 indicates a positive effect, a seasonal index of 1 indicates no seasonal effect, and a seasonal index less than 1 indicates a negative effect.

**Deseasonalized time series**  A time series that has had the effect of season removed by dividing each original time series observation by the corresponding seasonal index.

**Regression analysis**  A statistical technique that can be used to develop a mathematical equation showing how variables are related.

**Causal forecasting methods** Forecasting methods that relate a time series to other variables that are believed to explain or cause its behavior.

**Autoregressive model** A time series model that uses a regression relationship based on historical time series values to predict the future time series values.

**Delphi method** A qualitative forecasting method that obtains forecasts through group consensus.

**Scenario writing** A qualitative forecasting method that consists of developing a conceptual scenario of the future based on a well-defined set of assumptions.

## PROBLEMS

1. Corporate Triple A Bond interest rates for 12 consecutive months are 9.5, 9.3, 9.4, 9.6, 9.8, 9.7, 9.8, 10.5, 9.9, 9.7, 9.6, and 9.6.
   a. Develop 3- and 4-month moving averages for this time series. Which moving average provides the better forecasts? Explain.
   b. What is the moving average forecast for the next month?

2. Refer to the gasoline sales time series data in Table 16.1.
   a. Compute 4- and 5-week moving averages for the time series.
   b. Compute the MSE for the 4- and 5-week moving average forecasts.
   c. What appears to be the best number of weeks of past data to use in the moving average computation? Remember that the MSE for the 3-week moving average is 10.22.

3. Refer again to the gasoline sales time series data in Table 16.1.
   a. Use a weight of ½ for the most recent observation, ⅓ for the second most recent, and ⅙ for the third most recent to compute a 3-week weighted moving average for the time series.
   b. Compute the MSE for the weighted moving average in part (a). Do you prefer this weighted moving average to the unweighted moving average? Remember that the MSE for the unweighted moving average is 10.22.
   c. Suppose that you are allowed to choose any weights as long as they sum to 1. Could you always find a set of weights that would make the MSE smaller for a weighted moving average than for an unweighted moving average? Why or why not?

4. Use the gasoline sales time series data from Table 16.1 to show the exponential smoothing forecasts using $\alpha = 0.1$. Using the mean squared error criterion, would you prefer a smoothing constant of $\alpha = 0.1$ or $\alpha = 0.2$?

5. For the Hawkins Company, the monthly percentages of all shipments that were received on time over the past 12 months are 80, 82, 84, 83, 83, 84, 85, 84, 82, 83, 84, and 83.
   a. Compare a 3-month moving average forecast with an exponential smoothing forecast for $\alpha = 0.2$. Which provides the better forecasts?
   b. What is the forecast for next month?

6. With a smoothing constant of $\alpha = 0.2$, equation (16.2) shows that the forecast for the 13th week of the gasoline sales data from Table 16.1 is given by $F_{13} = 0.2Y_{12} + 0.8F_{12}$. However, the forecast for week 12 is given by $F_{12} = 0.2Y_{11} + 0.8F_{11}$. Thus, we could combine these two results to write the forecast for the 13th week as

$$F_{13} = 0.2Y_{12} + 0.8(0.2Y_{11} + 0.8F_{11}) = 0.2Y_{12} + 0.16Y_{11} + 0.64F_{11}$$

   a. Make use of the fact that $F_{11} = 0.2Y_{10} + 0.8F_{10}$ (and similarly for $F_{10}$ and $F_9$) and continue to expand the expression for $F_{13}$ until you have written it in terms of the past data values $Y_{12}, Y_{11}, Y_{10}, Y_9$, and $Y_8$, and the forecast for period 8.

b.  Refer to the coefficients or weights for the past data values $Y_{12}$, $Y_{11}$, $Y_{10}$, $Y_9$, and $Y_8$; what observation can you make about how exponential smoothing weights past data values in arriving at new forecasts? Compare this weighting pattern with the weighting pattern of the moving averages method.

7.  Alabama building contracts for a 12-month period (in millions of dollars) are 240, 350, 230, 260, 280, 320, 220, 310, 240, 310, 240, and 230.
    a.  Compare a 3-month moving average forecast with an exponential smoothing forecast using $\alpha = 0.2$. Which provides the better forecasts?
    b.  What is the forecast for the next month?

8.  Moving averages often are used to identify movements in stock prices. Weekly closing prices (in dollars per share) for Toys "R" Us for September 22, 1997, through December 8, 1997, follow (Prudential Securities, Inc.).

| Week | Price ($) | Week | Price ($) |
|---|---|---|---|
| September 22 | $34\frac{7}{8}$ | November 3 | $33\frac{5}{8}$ |
| September 29 | $35\frac{5}{8}$ | November 10 | $35\frac{1}{16}$ |
| October 6 | $34\frac{11}{16}$ | November 17 | $34\frac{1}{16}$ |
| October 13 | $33\frac{9}{16}$ | November 24 | $34\frac{1}{8}$ |
| October 20 | $32\frac{5}{8}$ | December 1 | $33\frac{1}{4}$ |
| October 27 | 34 | December 8 | $32\frac{1}{16}$ |

a.  Use a three-month moving average to smooth the time series. Forecast the closing price for December 15, 1997.
b.  Use a three-month weighted moving average to smooth the time series. Use a weight of .4 for the most recent period, .4 for the next period back, and .2 for the third period back. Forecast the closing price for December 15, 1997.
c.  Use exponential smoothing with a smoothing constant of $\alpha = .35$ to smooth the time series. Forecast the closing price for December 15, 1997.
d.  Which of the three methods do you prefer? Why?

9.  The following data represent 15 quarters of manufacturing capacity utilization (in percentages).

| Quarter/Year | Utilization | Quarter/Year | Utilization |
|---|---|---|---|
| 1/1996 | 82.5 | 1/1998 | 78.8 |
| 2/1996 | 81.3 | 2/1998 | 78.7 |
| 3/1996 | 81.3 | 3/1998 | 78.4 |
| 4/1996 | 79.0 | 4/1998 | 80.0 |
| 1/1997 | 76.6 | 1/1999 | 80.7 |
| 2/1997 | 78.0 | 2/1999 | 80.7 |
| 3/1997 | 78.4 | 3/1999 | 80.8 |
| 4/1997 | 78.0 | | |

a.  Compute 3- and 4-quarter moving averages for this time series. Which moving average provides the better forecast for the fourth quarter of 1999?
b.  Use smoothing constants of $\alpha = 0.4$ and $\alpha = 0.5$ to develop forecasts for the fourth quarter of 1999. Which smoothing constant provides the better forecast?
c.  Based on the analyses in parts (a) and (b), which method—moving averages or exponential smoothing—provides the better forecast? Explain.

10. The Federal Election Commission maintains data showing the voting age population, the number of registered voters, and the turnout for federal elections. The following table shows the national voter turnout as a percentage of the voting age population from 1972 to 1996. (*The Wall Street Journal Almanac,* 1998)

| Year | % Turnout |
|------|-----------|
| 1972 | 55 |
| 1974 | 38 |
| 1976 | 54 |
| 1978 | 37 |
| 1980 | 53 |
| 1982 | 40 |
| 1984 | 53 |
| 1986 | 36 |
| 1988 | 50 |
| 1990 | 37 |
| 1992 | 55 |
| 1994 | 39 |
| 1996 | 49 |

a. Use exponential smoothing to forecast this time series. Consider smoothing constants of $\alpha = .1$ and .2. What value of the smoothing constant provides the best forecast?
b. What is the forecast of the percentage turnout in 1998?

11. The percentage of individual investors' portfolios committed to stock depends on the state of the economy. As of April 1997, a typical portfolio consisted of cash (19%), stocks (30%), stock funds (37%), bonds (8%), and bond funds (6%) (*AAII Journal,* June 1997). The following table reports the percentage of stocks in a typical portfolio in nine quarters from 1995 to 1997.

| Quarter | Stock % |
|---------|---------|
| 1st—1995 | 29.8 |
| 2nd—1995 | 31.0 |
| 3rd—1995 | 29.9 |
| 4th—1995 | 30.1 |
| 1st—1996 | 32.2 |
| 2nd—1996 | 31.5 |
| 3rd—1996 | 32.0 |
| 4th—1996 | 31.9 |
| 1st—1997 | 30.0 |

a. Use exponential smoothing to forecast this time series. Consider smoothing constants of $\alpha = .2, .3,$ and .4. What value of the smoothing constant provides the best forecast?
b. What is the forecast of the percentage of assets committed to stocks for the second quarter of 1997?

12. United Dairies, Inc., supplies milk to several independent grocers throughout Dade County, Florida. Management wants to develop a forecast of the number of half-gallons of milk sold per week. Sales data (in units) for the past 12 weeks are as follows.

| Week | Sales | Week | Sales |
|------|-------|------|-------|
| 1 | 2750 | 7 | 3300 |
| 2 | 3100 | 8 | 3100 |
| 3 | 3250 | 9 | 2950 |
| 4 | 2800 | 10 | 3000 |
| 5 | 2900 | 11 | 3200 |
| 6 | 3050 | 12 | 3150 |

Use exponential smoothing, with $\alpha = 0.4$, to develop a forecast of demand for week 13.

13. Ten weeks of data on the Commodity Futures Index are 7.35, 7.40, 7.55, 7.56, 7.60, 7.52, 7.52, 7.70, 7.62, and 7.55.
   a. Compute the exponential smoothing values for $\alpha = 0.2$.
   b. Compute the exponential smoothing values for $\alpha = 0.3$.
   c. Which exponential smoothing model provides the better forecasts? Forecast week 11.

14. The enrollment data (000s) for a state college for the past 6 years are shown.

| Year | 1 | 2 | 3 | 4 | 5 | 6 |
|------|------|------|------|------|------|------|
| Enrollment | 20.5 | 20.2 | 19.5 | 19.0 | 19.1 | 18.8 |

Develop the equation for the linear trend component for this time series. Comment on what is happening to enrollment at this institution.

15. Automobile sales at B. J. Scott Motors, Inc., provided the following 10-year time series.

| Year | Sales | Year | Sales |
|------|-------|------|-------|
| 1 | 400 | 6 | 260 |
| 2 | 390 | 7 | 300 |
| 3 | 320 | 8 | 320 |
| 4 | 340 | 9 | 340 |
| 5 | 270 | 10 | 370 |

Plot the time series, and comment on the appropriateness of a linear trend. What type of functional form would be best for the trend pattern of this time series?

16. The president of a small manufacturing firm has been concerned about the continual growth in manufacturing costs over the past several years. The following is a time series of the cost per unit (in dollars) for the firm's leading product over the past 8 years.

| Year | Cost Per Unit | Year | Cost Per Unit |
|------|---------------|------|---------------|
| 1 | 20.00 | 5 | 26.60 |
| 2 | 24.50 | 6 | 30.00 |
| 3 | 28.20 | 7 | 31.00 |
| 4 | 27.50 | 8 | 36.00 |

   a. Graph this time series. Does a linear trend appear?
   b. Develop the equation for the linear trend component for the time series. What is the average cost increase per year?

17. In the late 1990s many firms began downsizing in order to reduce their costs. One of the results of these cost-cutting measures has been a decline in the percentage of private-industry jobs that are managerial. The following data show the percentage of females who are managers from 1990 to 1995 (*The Wall Street Journal Almanac,* 1998).

| Year | 1990 | 1991 | 1992 | 1993 | 1994 | 1995 |
|------|------|------|------|------|------|------|
| **Percentage** | 7.45 | 7.53 | 7.52 | 7.65 | 7.62 | 7.73 |

    a. Develop a linear trend equation for this time series.
    b. Use the trend equation to estimate the percentage of females who are managers for 1996 and 1997.

18. ACT Networks, Inc., develops, markets, manufactures, and sells integrated wide-area network access products. The following are annual sales data from 1992 to 1997 (*Stock Investor Pro,* American Association of Individual Investors, August 31, 1997).

| Year | Sales ($millions) |
|------|-------------------|
| 1992 | 5.4 |
| 1993 | 6.2 |
| 1994 | 12.7 |
| 1995 | 20.6 |
| 1996 | 28.4 |
| 1997 | 44.9 |

    a. Develop a linear trend equation for this time series.
    b. What is the firm's average increase in sales per year?
    c. Use the trend equation to forecast sales for 1998.

19. The following data show the time series of the most recent quarterly capital expenditures (in billions of dollars) for the 1000 largest manufacturing firms: 24, 25, 23, 24, 22, 26, 28, 31, 29, 32, 37, and 42.
    a. Develop a linear trend equation for the time series.
    b. Graph the time series and the linear trend equation.
    c. What appears to be happening to capital expenditures? What is the forecast 1 year, or 4 quarters, into the future?

20. The Costello Music Company has been in business for 5 years. During that time, the sale of electric organs has grown from 12 units in the first year to 76 units in the most recent year. Fred Costello, the firm's owner, wants to develop a forecast of organ sales for the coming year based on the historical data shown.

| Year | 1 | 2 | 3 | 4 | 5 |
|------|---|---|---|---|---|
| **Sales** | 12 | 28 | 34 | 50 | 76 |

    a. Graph this time series. Does a linear trend appear?
    b. Develop the equation for the linear trend component for the time series. What is the average increase in sales per year for the firm?

21. Hudson Marine has been an authorized dealer for C&D marine radios for the past 7 years. The number of radios sold each year is shown.

| Year | 1 | 2 | 3 | 4 | 5 | 6 | 7 |
|------|---|---|---|---|---|---|---|
| **Number Sold** | 35 | 50 | 75 | 90 | 105 | 110 | 130 |

a. Graph this time series. Does a linear trend appear?
b. Develop the equation for the linear trend component for the time series.
c. Use the linear trend developed in part (b) to prepare a forecast for sales in year 8.

22. The Motion Picture Association of America (MPAA) collects data that show the cost of making movies for MPAA members, including Disney, Paramount, Universal, Warner Brothers, MGM, Fox, Sony, and Turner. The following data show the average production costs (in $000s) from 1985 to 1996 for MPAA members (*The Wall Street Journal Almanac,* 1998).

| Year | Average Production Costs ($000s) |
|------|----------------------------------|
| 1985 | $16,779 |
| 1986 | $17,455 |
| 1987 | $20,051 |
| 1988 | $18,061 |
| 1989 | $23,454 |
| 1990 | $26,783 |
| 1991 | $26,136 |
| 1992 | $28,858 |
| 1993 | $29,910 |
| 1994 | $34,288 |
| 1995 | $36,370 |
| 1996 | $39,836 |

a. Plot the time series and comment on the appropriateness of a linear trend.
b. Develop the equation for the linear trend component for this time series.
c. What is the average increase in production costs that MPAA members have been experiencing per year?
d. Use the trend equation to forecast the average production costs in 1997 and 1998.

23. The Garden Avenue Seven sells tapes of its musical performances. The following data show sales for the past 18 months. The group's manager wants an accurate method for forecasting future sales.

| Month | Sales | Month | Sales | Month | Sales |
|-------|-------|-------|-------|-------|-------|
| 1 | 293 | 7 | 381 | 13 | 549 |
| 2 | 283 | 8 | 431 | 14 | 544 |
| 3 | 322 | 9 | 424 | 15 | 601 |
| 4 | 355 | 10 | 433 | 16 | 587 |
| 5 | 346 | 11 | 470 | 17 | 644 |
| 6 | 379 | 12 | 481 | 18 | 660 |

a. Use exponential smoothing, with $\alpha = 0.3$, 0.4, and 0.5. Which value of $\alpha$ provides the best forecasts?
b. Use trend projection to provide a forecast. What is the value of MSE?
c. Which method of forecasting would you recommend to the manager? Why?

24. The Mayfair Department Store in Davenport, Iowa, is trying to determine the amount of sales lost while it was shut down because of the summer 1993 floods. Sales data for January–June 1993 are shown.

| Month | Sales ($000s) |
|---|---|
| January | 185.72 |
| February | 167.84 |
| March | 205.11 |
| April | 210.36 |
| May | 255.57 |
| June | 261.19 |

a. Use exponential smoothing, with $\alpha = 0.4$, to develop a forecast for July and August. (Hint: Use the forecast for July as the actual sales in July in developing the August forecast.) Comment on the use of exponential smoothing for forecasts more than one period into the future.

b. Use trend projection to forecast sales for July and August.

c. Mayfair's insurance company has proposed a settlement based on lost sales of $240,000 in July and August. Is this amount fair? If not, what amount would you counter with?

**SELF TEST**

25. The quarterly sales data (number of copies sold) for a college textbook over the past 3 years are as follows.

| Quarter | Year 1 | Year 2 | Year 3 |
|---|---|---|---|
| 1 | 1690 | 1800 | 1850 |
| 2 | 940 | 900 | 1100 |
| 3 | 2625 | 2900 | 2930 |
| 4 | 2500 | 2360 | 2615 |

a. Show the 4-quarter moving average values for this time series. Plot both the original time series and the moving averages on the same graph.

b. Compute seasonal indexes for the 4 quarters.

c. When does the textbook publisher experience the largest seasonal index? Does this result appear to be reasonable? Explain.

26. Identify the monthly seasonal indexes for the following 3 years of expenses for a 6-unit apartment house in southern Florida. Use a 12-month moving average calculation.

| Month | Year 1 | Year 2 | Year 3 |
|---|---|---|---|
| January | 170 | 180 | 195 |
| February | 180 | 205 | 210 |
| March | 205 | 215 | 230 |
| April | 230 | 245 | 280 |
| May | 240 | 265 | 290 |
| June | 315 | 330 | 390 |
| July | 360 | 400 | 420 |
| August | 290 | 335 | 330 |
| September | 240 | 260 | 290 |
| October | 240 | 270 | 295 |
| November | 230 | 255 | 280 |
| December | 195 | 220 | 250 |

27. Air pollution control specialists in southern California monitor the amount of ozone, carbon dioxide, and nitrogen dioxide in the air on an hourly basis. The hourly time series data exhibit seasonality, with the levels of pollutants showing similar patterns over the hours in the day. On

July 15, 16, and 17, the observed levels of nitrogen dioxide in a city's downtown area for the 12 hours from 6:00 A.M. to 6:00 P.M. were as follows.

**July 15**   25   28   35   50   60   60   40   35   30   25   25   20
**July 16**   28   30   35   48   60   65   50   40   35   25   20   20
**July 17**   35   42   45   70   72   75   60   45   40   25   25   25

  a. Identify the hourly seasonal indexes for the 12-hourly daily readings.
  b. Based on the seasonal indexes in part (a), the trend equation developed for the deseasonalized data is $T_t = 32.983 + 0.3922t$. Use the trend component only to develop forecasts for the 12 hours for July 18.
  c. Use the seasonal indexes from part (a) to adjust the trend forecasts in part (b).

28. Refer to Problem 21. Suppose that the following are the quarterly sales data for the past 7 years.

| Year | Quarter 1 | Quarter 2 | Quarter 3 | Quarter 4 | Total Sales |
|---|---|---|---|---|---|
| 1 | 6 | 15 | 10 | 4 | 35 |
| 2 | 10 | 18 | 15 | 7 | 50 |
| 3 | 14 | 26 | 23 | 12 | 75 |
| 4 | 19 | 28 | 25 | 18 | 90 |
| 5 | 22 | 34 | 28 | 21 | 105 |
| 6 | 24 | 36 | 30 | 20 | 110 |
| 7 | 28 | 40 | 35 | 27 | 130 |

  a. Show the 4-quarter moving average values for this time series. Plot both the original time series and the moving averages on the same graph.
  b. Compute the seasonal indexes for the 4 quarters.
  c. When does Hudson Marine experience the largest seasonal effect? Does this result seem reasonable? Explain.

29. Consider the Costello Music Company scenario presented in Problem 20 and the following quarterly sales data.

| Year | Quarter 1 | Quarter 2 | Quarter 3 | Quarter 4 | Total Yearly Sales |
|---|---|---|---|---|---|
| 1 | 4 | 2 | 1 | 5 | 12 |
| 2 | 6 | 4 | 4 | 14 | 28 |
| 3 | 10 | 3 | 5 | 16 | 34 |
| 4 | 12 | 9 | 7 | 22 | 50 |
| 5 | 18 | 10 | 13 | 35 | 76 |

  a. Compute the seasonal indexes for the 4 quarters.
  b. When does Costello Music experience the largest seasonal effect? Does this result appear to be reasonable? Explain.

30. Refer to the Hudson Marine data in Problem 28.
  a. Deseasonalize the data, and use the deseasonalized time series to identify the trend.
  b. Use the results of part (a) to develop a quarterly forecast for next year based on trend.
  c. Use the seasonal indexes developed in Problem 28 to adjust the forecasts developed in part (b) to account for the effect of season.

**31.** Consider the Costello Music Company time series in Problem 29.
     **a.** Deseasonalize the data, and use the deseasonalized time series to identify the trend.
     **b.** Use the results of part (a) to develop a quarterly forecast for next year based on trend.
     **c.** Use the seasonal indexes developed in Problem 29 to adjust the forecasts developed in part (b) to account for seasonal effects.

**32.** Electric power consumption is measured in kilowatt-hours (kWh). The local utility company has an interrupt program, whereby commercial customers who participate receive favorable rates but must agree to cut back consumption if the utility requests them to do so. Timko Products cut back consumption at 12:00 noon Thursday. To assess the savings, the utility must estimate Timko's usage without the interrupt. The period of interrupted service was from noon to 8:00 P.M. Data on electric consumption for the past 72 hours is available.

| Time Period | Monday | Tuesday | Wednesday | Thursday |
|---|---|---|---|---|
| 12–4 A.M. | — | 19,281 | 31,209 | 27,330 |
| 4–8 A.M. | — | 33,195 | 37,014 | 32,715 |
| 8–12 noon | — | 99,516 | 119,968 | 152,465 |
| 12–4 P.M. | 124,299 | 123,666 | 156,033 | |
| 4–8 P.M. | 113,545 | 111,717 | 128,889 | |
| 8–12 midnight | 41,300 | 48,112 | 73,923 | |

     **a.** Is there a seasonal effect over the 24-hour period? Compute seasonal indexes for the six 4-hour periods.
     **b.** Use trend adjusted for seasonal factors to estimate Timko's normal usage over the period of interrupted service.

**33.** Eddie's Restaurants collected the following data on the relationship between advertising and sales at a sample of five restaurants.

| Advertising Expenditures ($000s) | 1.0 | 4.0 | 6.0 | 10.0 | 14.0 |
|---|---|---|---|---|---|
| Sales ($000s) | 19.0 | 44.0 | 40.0 | 52.0 | 53.0 |

     **a.** Let $x$ represent advertising expenditures and $y$ represent sales. Use the method of least squares to develop a straight-line approximation of the relationship between the two variables.
     **b.** Use the equation developed in part (a) to forecast sales for an advertising expenditure of $8000.

**34.** The management of a chain of fast-food restaurants wants to investigate the relationship between the daily sales volume (in dollars) of a company restaurant and the number of competitor restaurants within a 1-mile radius. The following data have been collected.

| Number of Competitors Within 1 Mile | Sales |
|---|---|
| 1 | 3600 |
| 1 | 3300 |
| 2 | 3100 |
| 3 | 2900 |
| 3 | 2700 |
| 4 | 2500 |
| 5 | 2300 |
| 5 | 2000 |

     **a.** Develop the least-squares estimated regression equation that relates daily sales volume to the number of competitor restaurants within a 1-mile radius.

b. Use the estimated regression equation developed in part (a) to forecast the daily sales volume for a particular company restaurant that has four competitors within a 1-mile radius.

35. The supervisor of a manufacturing process believed that assembly-line speed (in feet/minute) affected the number of defective parts found during on-line inspection. To test this theory, management had the same batch of parts inspected visually at a variety of line speeds. The following data were collected.

| Line Speed | Number of Defective Parts Found |
|---|---|
| 20 | 21 |
| 20 | 19 |
| 40 | 15 |
| 30 | 16 |
| 60 | 14 |
| 40 | 17 |

a. Develop the estimated regression equation that relates line speed to the number of defective parts found.
b. Use the equation developed in part (a) to forecast the number of defective parts found for a line speed of 50 feet per minute.

## Case Problem    FORECASTING SALES

The Vintage Restaurant is located on Captiva Island, a resort community near Fort Meyers, Florida. The restaurant, which is owned and operated by Karen Payne, has just completed its third year of operation. During this time, Karen has sought to establish a reputation for the restaurant as a high-quality dining establishment that specializes in fresh seafood. The efforts made by Karen and her staff have proven successful, and her restaurant has become one of the best and fastest-growing restaurants on the island.

Karen has concluded that, to plan better for the growth of the restaurant in the future, she needs to develop a system that will enable her to forecast food and beverage sales by month for up to 1 year in advance. Karen has the following data on total food and beverage sales for the 3 years of operation.

### Food and Beverage Sales for the Vintage Restaurant ($000s)

| Month | First Year | Second Year | Third Year |
|---|---|---|---|
| January | 242 | 263 | 282 |
| February | 235 | 238 | 255 |
| March | 232 | 247 | 265 |
| April | 178 | 193 | 205 |
| May | 184 | 193 | 210 |
| June | 140 | 149 | 160 |
| July | 145 | 157 | 166 |
| August | 152 | 161 | 174 |
| September | 110 | 122 | 126 |
| October | 130 | 130 | 148 |
| November | 152 | 167 | 173 |
| December | 206 | 230 | 235 |

## Managerial Report

Perform an analysis of the sales data for the Vintage Restaurant. Prepare a report for Karen that summarizes your findings, forecasts, and recommendations. Include the following:

1.  A graph of the time series.
2.  An analysis of the seasonality of the data. Indicate the seasonal indexes for each month, and comment on the high seasonal and low seasonal sales months. Do the seasonal indexes make intuitive sense? Discuss.
3.  Forecast sales for January through December of the fourth year.
4.  Assume that January sales for the fourth year turned out to be $295,000. What was your forecast error? If this error is large, Karen may be puzzled about the difference between your forecast and the actual sales value. What can you do to resolve her uncertainty in the forecasting procedure?
5.  Recommendations as to when the system that you have developed should be updated to account for new sales data that will occur.
6.  Include detailed calculations of your analysis in the appendix of your report.

····································································································/  /············

## Case Problem     FORECASTING LOST SALES

The Carlson Department Store suffered heavy damage when a hurricane struck on August 31, 1996. The store was closed for four months (September 1996 through December 1996), and Carlson is now involved in a dispute with its insurance company concerning the amount of lost sales during the time the store was closed. Two key issues must be resolved: (1) the amount of sales Carlson would have made if the hurricane had not struck; and (2) whether Carlson is entitled to any compensation for excess sales from increased business activity after the storm. More than $8 billion in federal disaster relief and insurance money came into the county, resulting in increased sales at department stores and numerous other businesses.

Table 16.15 shows the sales data for the 48 months preceding the storm. The U.S. Department of Commerce also has published total sales for the 48 months preceding the storm

| *Table* 16.15 | SALES FOR CARLSON DEPARTMENT STORE, SEPTEMBER 1992 THROUGH AUGUST 1996 | | | | |
|---|---|---|---|---|---|
| Month | 1992 | 1993 | 1994 | 1995 | 1996 |
| Jan. | | 1.45 | 2.31 | 2.31 | 2.56 |
| Feb. | | 1.80 | 1.89 | 1.99 | 2.28 |
| Mar. | | 2.03 | 2.02 | 2.42 | 2.69 |
| Apr. | | 1.99 | 2.23 | 2.45 | 2.48 |
| May | | 2.32 | 2.39 | 2.57 | 2.73 |
| June | | 2.20 | 2.14 | 2.42 | 2.37 |
| July | | 2.13 | 2.27 | 2.40 | 2.31 |
| Aug. | | 2.43 | 2.21 | 2.50 | 2.23 |
| Sept. | 1.71 | 1.90 | 1.89 | 2.09 | |
| Oct. | 1.90 | 2.13 | 2.29 | 2.54 | |
| Nov. | 2.74 | 2.56 | 2.83 | 2.97 | |
| Dec. | 4.20 | 4.16 | 4.04 | 4.35 | |

for all department stores in the county, as well as the total sales in the county for the 4 months the Carlson Department Store was closed. Table 16.16 shows these data. Management has asked you to analyze these data and develop estimates of the lost sales at the Carlson Department Store for the months of September through December 1996. Management also has asked you to determine whether a case can be made for excess storm-related sales during the same period. If such a case can be made, Carlson is entitled to compensation for excess sales it would have earned in addition to ordinary sales.

## Managerial Report

Prepare a report for the management of the Carlson Department store that summarizes your findings, forecasts, and recommendations. Include the following.

1. An estimate of sales had there been no hurricane.
2. An estimate of countywide department store sales had there been no hurricane.
3. Use the countywide actual department stores sales for September through December 1996 and the estimate in part (2) to make a case for or against excess storm-related sales.
4. An estimate of lost sales for the Carlson Department Store for September through December 1996.

| Month | 1992 | 1993 | 1994 | 1995 | 1996 |
|---|---|---|---|---|---|
| Jan. | | 46.8 | 46.8 | 43.8 | 48.0 |
| Feb. | | 48.0 | 48.6 | 45.6 | 51.6 |
| Mar. | | 60.0 | 59.4 | 57.6 | 57.6 |
| Apr. | | 57.6 | 58.2 | 53.4 | 58.2 |
| May | | 61.8 | 60.6 | 56.4 | 60.0 |
| June | | 58.2 | 55.2 | 52.8 | 57.0 |
| July | | 56.4 | 51.0 | 54.0 | 57.6 |
| Aug. | | 63.0 | 58.8 | 60.6 | 61.8 |
| Sept. | 55.8 | 57.6 | 49.8 | 47.4 | 69.0 |
| Oct. | 56.4 | 53.4 | 54.6 | 54.6 | 75.0 |
| Nov. | 71.4 | 71.4 | 65.4 | 67.8 | 85.2 |
| Dec. | 117.6 | 114.0 | 102.0 | 100.2 | 121.8 |

Table 16.16 DEPARTMENT STORE SALES FOR THE COUNTY, SEPTEMBER 1992 THROUGH DECEMBER 1996

## Appendix 16.1   SPREADSHEETS FOR FORECASTING

In this appendix we show how Excel can be used to develop forecasts using three forecasting methods: moving averages, exponential smoothing, and trend projection.

### Moving Averages

To show how Excel can be used to develop forecasts using the moving averages method, we will develop a forecast for the gasoline sales time series in Table 16.1 and Figure 16.5.

We assume that the user has entered the sales data for the 12 weeks into worksheet rows 1 through 12 of column A. The following steps can be used to produce a three-week moving average.

Step 1  Select the **Tools** pull-down menu
Step 2  Select the **Data Analysis** option
Step 3  When the Data Analysis Tools dialog box appears, choose **Moving Average**
Step 4  When the Moving Average dialog box appears:
    Enter A1:A12 in the **Input Range** box
    Enter 3 in the **Interval** box
    Enter B1 in the **Output Range** box
    Select **OK**

The three-week moving average forecasts will appear in column B of the worksheet. Note that forecasts for periods of other length can be computed easily by entering a different value in the Interval box.

## Exponential Smoothing

To show how Excel can be used for exponential smoothing, we again develop a forecast for the gasoline sales time series in Table 16.1 and Figure 16.5. We assume that the user has entered the sales data for the 12 weeks into worksheet rows 1 through 12 of column A and that the smoothing constant is $\alpha = 0.2$. The following steps can be used to produce a forecast.

Step 1  Select the **Tools** pull-down menu
Step 1  Select the **Data Analysis** option
Step 3  When the Data Analysis Tools dialog box appears, choose **Exponential Smoothing**
Step 4  When the Exponential Smoothing dialog box appears:
    Enter A1:A12 in the **Input Range** box
    Enter 0.8 in the **Damping factor** box
    Enter B1 in the **Output Range** box
    Select **OK**

The exponential smoothing forecasts will appear in column B of the worksheet. Note that the value we entered in the Damping factor box is $1 - \alpha$; forecasts for other smoothing constants can be computed easily by entering a different value for $1 - \alpha$ in the Damping factor box.

## Trend Projection

To show how Excel can be used for trend projection, we develop a forecast for the bicycle sales time series in Table 16.6 and Figure 16.8. We assume that the user has entered the year (1–10) for each observation into worksheet rows 1 through 10 of column A and the sales values into worksheet rows 1 through 10 of column B. The following steps can be used to produce a forecast for year 11 by trend projection.

Step 1  Select an empty cell in the worksheet
Step 2  Select the **Insert** pull-down menu

Step 3 Choose the **Function** option
Step 4 When the Paste Function dialog box appears:
Choose **Statistical** in the Function Category box
Choose **Forecast** in the Function Name box
Select **OK**
Step 5 When the Forecast dialog box appears:
Enter 11 in the **x** box
Enter B1:B10 in the **Known y's** box
Enter A1:A10 in the **Known x's** box
Select **OK**

The forecast for year 11, in this case 32.5, will appear in the cell selected in Step 1.

# MANAGEMENT SCIENCE IN PRACTICE

# THE CINCINNATI GAS & ELECTRIC COMPANY*

## CINCINNATI, OHIO

The Cincinnati Gas Light and Coke Company was chartered by the state of Ohio on April 3, 1837. Under this charter, the company manufactured gas by distillation of coal and sold it for lighting purposes. During the last quarter of the nineteenth century, the company successfully marketed gas for lighting, heating, and cooking and as fuel for gas engines.

In 1901 the Cincinnati Gas Light and Coke Company and the Cincinnati Electric Light Company merged to form The Cincinnati Gas & Electric Company (CG&E). This new company was able to shift from manufactured gas to natural gas and adopt the rapidly emerging technologies in generating and distributing electricity. CG&E operated as a subsidiary of the Columbia Gas Electric Company from 1909 until 1944.

In 1994, CG&E merged with Public Service of Indiana to form Cinergy Corporation. Today, CG&E is a subsidiary of Cinergy serving approximately 440,000 gas customers and 720,000 electric customers. The company's service area covers approximately 3000 square miles in and around the Greater Cincinnati area.

## Forecasting at CG&E

As in any modern company, forecasting at CG&E is an integral part of operating and managing the business. Depending on the decision to be made, the forecasting techniques used range from judgment and graphical trend projections to sophisticated multiple regression models.

Forecasting in the utility industry offers some unique perspectives. Because electricity cannot take the form of finished-goods or in-process inventories, this product must be generated to meet the instantaneous requirements of the customers. Electrical shortages are not just lost sales, but "brownouts" or "blackouts." This situation places an unusual burden on the utility forecaster. On the positive side, the demand for energy and the sale of energy are more predictable than for many other products. Also, unlike the situation in a multiproduct firm, a great amount of forecasting effort and expertise can be concentrated on the two products: gas and electricity.

## Forecasting Electric Energy and Peak Loads

The two types of forecasts discussed in this section are the long-range forecasts of electric peak load and electric energy. The largest observed electric demand for any given period, such as an hour, a day, a month, or a year, is defined as the peak load. The cumulative amount of energy generated and used over the period of an hour is referred to as electric energy.

Until the mid-1970s the seasonal patterns of both electric energy and electric peak load were very regular; the time series for both of these exhibited a fairly steady exponential growth. Business cycles had little noticeable effect on either. Perhaps the most serious shift in the behavior of these time series came from the increasing installation of air conditioning units in the Greater Cincinnati area, which caused an accelerated growth in the trend component and also in the relative magnitude of the summer peaks. Nevertheless, the two time series remained regular and generally quite predictable.

Trend projection was the most popular method used to forecast electric energy and electric peak load. The forecast accuracy was quite acceptable and even enviable when compared to forecast errors experienced in other industries.

*The authors are indebted to Dr. Richard Evans, The Cincinnati Gas & Electric Company, Cincinnati, Ohio, for providing this application.

## A New Era in Forecasting

In the mid-1970s a variety of actions by the government, the off-and-on energy shortages, and price signals to the consumer began to affect the consumption of electric energy. The behavior of the peak load and electric energy time series became less predictable, and a simple trend projection forecasting model was no longer adequate. As a result, a special forecasting model—referred to as an econometric model—was developed by CG&E to better account for the behavior of these time series.

The purpose of the econometric model is to forecast the annual energy consumption by residential, commercial, and industrial classes of service. These forecasts are then used to develop forecasts of summer and winter peak loads. First, energy consumption in the industrial and commercial classes is forecast. For an assumed level of economic activity, the projection of electric energy is made along with a forecast of employment in the area. The employment forecast is converted to a forecast of adult population through the use of unemployment rates and labor force participation rates. Household forecasts are then developed through the use of demographic statistics on the average number of persons per household. The resulting forecast of households is used as an indicator of residential customers.

At this point, a comparison is made with the demographic projections for the area population. The differences between the residential customers forecast and the population forecast are reconciled to produce the final forecast of residential customers. This forecast becomes the principal independent variable in forecasting residential electric energy.

Summer and winter peak loads are then forecast by applying class peak contribution factors to the energy forecasts. The contributions that each class makes toward the peak are summed to establish the peak forecast.

A number of economic and demographic time series are used in the construction of this econometric model.

Simply speaking, the entire forecasting system is a compilation of several statistically verified multiple regression equations.

### Impact and Value of the Forecasts

The forecast of the annual electric peak load guides the timing decisions for constructing future generating units, and the financial impact of these decisions is great. For example, a large generating unit built by the company cost nearly $600 million, and the interest rate on a recent first mortgage bond was 16%. At this rate, annual interest costs would be nearly $100 million. Obviously, a timing decision that leads to having the unit available no sooner than necessary is crucial.

The energy forecasts are important in other ways also. For example, purchases of coal as fuel for the generating units are based on the forecast levels of energy needed. The revenue from the electric operations of the company is determined from forecasted sales, which in turn enters into the planning of rate changes and external financing. These planning and decision-making processes are among the most important management activities in the company. It is imperative that the decision makers have the best forecast information available to assist them in arriving at these decisions.

### Questions

1. Describe some of the unique perspectives associated with forecasting in the utility industry as compared with other industries.
2. What type of forecasting procedure was used by CG&E into the mid-1970s? What necessitated a change?
3. Briefly describe CG&E's current approach to forecasting.
4. What are the benefits of accurate forecasts for CG&E?

# 17

# MARKOV PROCESSES

## CONTENTS

Markov process models are useful in studying the evolution of systems over repeated trials. The repeated trials are often successive time periods where the state of the system in any particular period cannot be determined with certainty. Rather, transition probabilities are used to describe the manner in which the system makes transitions from one period to the next. Hence, we are interested in the probability of the system being in a particular state at a given time period.

Markov process models have been used to describe the probability that a machine that is functioning in one period will continue to function or will break down in the next period. They have also been used to describe the probability that a consumer purchasing brand A in one period will purchase brand B in the next period. In this chapter we present a marketing application that involves an analysis of the store-switching behavior of supermarket customers. As a second illustration, we consider an accounting application that is concerned with the transitioning of accounts receivable dollars to different account-aging categories.

Since an in-depth treatment of Markov processes is beyond the scope of this text, the analysis in both illustrations is restricted to situations consisting of a finite number of states, the transition probabilities remain constant over time, and the probability of being in a particular state at any one time period depends only on the state in the immediately preceding time period. Such Markov processes are referred to as *Markov chains with stationary transition probabilities.*

## 17.1    MARKET SHARE ANALYSIS

Suppose we are interested in analyzing the market share and customer loyalty for Murphy's Foodliner and Ashley's Supermarket, the only two grocery stores in a small town. We focus on the sequence of shopping trips of one customer, and assume that the customer makes one shopping trip each week to either Murphy's Foodliner or Ashley's Supermarket, but not both.

Using the terminology of Markov processes, we refer to the weekly periods or shopping trips as the **trials of the process.** Thus, at each trial, the customer will shop at either Murphy's Foodliner or Ashley's Supermarket. The particular store selected in a given week is referred to as the **state of the system** in that period. Since the customer has two shopping alternatives at each trial, we say the system has two states, and since the number of states is finite, we can identify each state as follows:

State 1.  The customer shops at Murphy's Foodliner
State 2.  The customer shops at Ashley's Supermarket

If we say the system is in state 1 at trial 3, we are simply saying that the customer shops at Murphy's during the third weekly shopping period.

As we continue the shopping trip process into the future, we cannot say for certain where the customer will shop during a given week or trial. In fact, we realize that during any given week, the customer may be either a Murphy's customer or an Ashley's customer. However, using a Markov process model, we will be able to compute the probability that the customer shops at each store during any period. For example, we may find a 0.6 probability that the customer will shop at Murphy's during a particular week and a 0.4 probability that the customer will shop at Ashley's.

To determine the probabilities of the various states occurring at successive trials of the Markov process, we need information on the probability that a customer remains with the same store or switches to the competing store as the process continues from trial to trial or week to week.

Suppose that, as part of a market research study, we collect data from 100 shoppers over a 10-week period. Suppose further that these data show each customer's weekly shopping trip pattern in terms of the sequence of visits to Murphy's and Ashley's. To develop a Markov process model for the sequence of weekly shopping trips, we need to express the probability of selecting each store (state) in a given period solely in terms of the store (state) that was selected during the previous period. In reviewing the data, suppose that we find that of all customers who shopped at Murphy's in a given week, 90% shopped at Murphy's the following week while 10% switched to Ashley's. Suppose that similar data for the customers who shopped at Ashley's in a given week show that 80% shopped at Ashley's the following week while 20% switched to Murphy's. Probabilities based on these data are shown in Table 17.1. Because these probabilities indicate that a customer moves, or makes a transition, from a state in a given period to each state in the following period, these probabilities are called **transition probabilities.**

An important property of the table of transition probabilities is that the sum of the probabilities in each row is 1; each row of the table provides a probability distribution. For example, a customer who shops at Murphy's one week must shop at either Murphy's or Ashley's the next week. The entries in row 1 give the probabilities associated with each of these events. The 0.9 and 0.8 probabilities in Table 17.1 can be interpreted as measures of store loyalty in that they indicate the probability of a repeat visit to the same store. Similarly, the 0.1 and 0.2 probabilities are measures of the store-switching characteristics of the customers.

In developing a Markov process model for this problem, we are assuming that the transition probabilities will be the same for any customer and that the transition probabilities will not change over time.

*The chapter appendix contains a review of matrix notation and operations.*

Note that Table 17.1 has one row and one column for each state of the system. We will use the symbol $p_{ij}$ to represent the transition probabilities and the symbol $P$ to represent the matrix of transition probabilities; that is,

$$p_{ij} = \text{probability of making a transition from state } i \text{ in a given period to state } j \text{ in the next period}$$

For the supermarket problem, we have

*A quick check for a valid matrix of transition probabilities is to make sure the sum of the probabilities in each row equals 1.*

$$P = \begin{bmatrix} p_{11} & p_{12} \\ p_{21} & p_{22} \end{bmatrix} = \begin{bmatrix} 0.9 & 0.1 \\ 0.2 & 0.8 \end{bmatrix}$$

Using the matrix of transition probabilities, we can now determine the probability that a customer will be a Murphy's customer or an Ashley's customer at some period in the future. Let us begin by assuming that we have a customer whose last weekly shopping trip was to Murphy's. What is the probability that this customer will shop at Murphy's on the next weekly shopping trip, period 1? In other words, what is the probability that the system will be in state 1 after the first transition? The matrix of transition probabilities indicates that this probability is $p_{11} = 0.9$.

Now let us consider the state of the system in period 2. A useful way of depicting what can happen on the second weekly shopping trip is to draw a tree diagram of the possible

| Table 17.1 | TRANSITION PROBABILITIES FOR MURPHY'S AND ASHLEY'S GROCERY SALES | |
|---|---|---|
| **Current Weekly Shopping Period** | **Next Weekly Shopping Period** | |
| | **Murphy's Foodliner** | **Ashley's Supermarket** |
| Murphy's Foodliner | 0.9 | 0.1 |
| Ashley's Supermarket | 0.2 | 0.8 |

outcomes (see Figure 17.1). Using this tree diagram, we see that the probability that the customer shops at Murphy's during both the first and the second weeks is (0.9)(0.9) = 0.81. Also, note that the probability of the customer switching to Ashley's on the first trip and then switching back to Murphy's on the second trip is (0.1)(0.2) = 0.02. Because these options are the only two ways that the customer can be in state 1 (shopping at Murphy's) during the second period, the probability of the system being in state 1 during the second period

| Figure 17.1 | TREE DIAGRAM DEPICTING TWO WEEKLY SHOPPING TRIPS OF A CUSTOMER WHO SHOPPED LAST AT MURPHY'S |
|---|---|

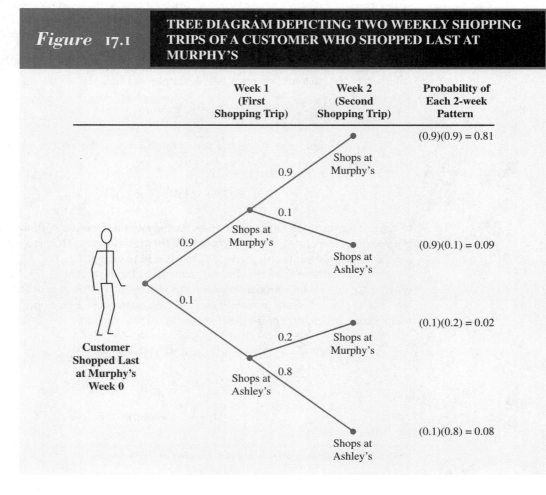

is $0.81 + 0.02 = 0.83$. Similarly, the probability of the system being in state 2 during the second period is $0.09 + 0.08 = 0.17$.

As desirable as the tree diagram approach may be from an intuitive point of view, it becomes cumbersome when we want to extend the analysis to three or more periods. Fortunately, we have an easier way to calculate the probabilities of the system being in state 1 or state 2 for any subsequent period. First, we introduce a notation that will allow us to represent these probabilities for any given period. Let

$$\pi_i(n) = \text{probability that the system is in state } i \text{ in period } n$$

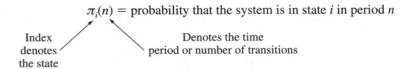

Index denotes the state

Denotes the time period or number of transitions

For example, $\pi_1(1)$ denotes the probability of the system being in state 1 in period 1, while $\pi_2(1)$ denotes the probability of the system being in state 2 in period 1. Since $\pi_i(n)$ is the probability that the system is in state $i$ in period $n$, this probability is referred to as a **state probability.**

The terms $\pi_1(0)$ and $\pi_2(0)$ will denote the probability of the system being in state 1 or state 2 at some initial or starting period. Week 0 represents the most recent period, when we are beginning the analysis of a Markov process. If we set $\pi_1(0) = 1$ and $\pi_2(0) = 0$, we are saying that as an initial condition the customer shopped last week at Murphy's; alternatively, if we set $\pi_1(0) = 0$ and $\pi_2(0) = 1$, we would be starting the system with a customer who shopped last week at Ashley's. In the tree diagram of Figure 17.1, we consider the situation where the customer shopped last at Murphy's. Thus,

$$[\pi_1(0) \quad \pi_2(0)] = [1 \quad 0]$$

is a vector that represents the initial state probabilities of the system. In general, we use the notation

$$\Pi(n) = [\pi_1(n) \quad \pi_2(n)]$$

to denote the vector of state probabilities for the system in period $n$. In the example, $\Pi(1)$ is a vector representing the state probabilities for the first week, $\Pi(2)$ is a vector representing the state probabilities for the second week, and so on.

Using this notation, we can find the state probabilities for period $n + 1$ by simply multiplying the known state probabilities for period $n$ by the transition probability matrix. Using the vector of state probabilities and the matrix of transition probabilities, the multiplication[1] can be expressed as follows:

$$\Pi(\text{next period}) = \Pi(\text{current period})P$$

or

$$\Pi(n + 1) = \Pi(n)P \tag{17.1}$$

---

[1]Appendix 17.1 provides the step-by-step procedure for vector and matrix multiplication.

Beginning with the system in state 1 at period 0, we have $\Pi(0) = [1\ 0]$. We can compute the state probabilities for period 1 as follows:

$$\Pi(1) = \Pi(0)P$$

or

$$[\pi_1(1)\quad \pi_2(1)] = [\pi_1(0)\quad \pi_2(0)]\begin{bmatrix} p_{11} & p_{12} \\ p_{21} & p_{22} \end{bmatrix}$$

$$= [1\quad 0]\begin{bmatrix} 0.9 & 0.1 \\ 0.2 & 0.8 \end{bmatrix}$$

$$= [0.9\quad 0.1]$$

The state probabilities $\pi_1(1) = 0.9$ and $\pi_2(1) = 0.1$ are the probabilities that a customer who shopped at Murphy's during week 0 will shop at Murphy's or at Ashley's during week 1.

Using equation (17.1), we can compute the state probabilities for the second week as follows:

$$\Pi(2) = \Pi(1)P$$

or

$$[\pi_1(2)\quad \pi_2(2)] = [\pi_1(1)\quad \pi_2(1)]\begin{bmatrix} p_{11} & p_{12} \\ p_{21} & p_{22} \end{bmatrix}$$

$$= [0.9\quad 0.1]\begin{bmatrix} 0.9 & 0.1 \\ 0.2 & 0.8 \end{bmatrix}$$

$$= [0.83\quad 0.17]$$

We see that the probability of shopping at Murphy's during the second week is 0.83, while the probability of shopping at Ashley's during the second week is 0.17. These same results were previously obtained using the tree diagram of Figure 17.1. By continuing to apply equation (17.1), we can compute the state probabilities for any future period; that is,

$$\Pi(3) = \Pi(2)P$$
$$\Pi(4) = \Pi(3)P$$
$$\vdots \qquad \vdots$$
$$\Pi(n + 1) = \Pi(n)P$$

Table 17.2 shows the result of carrying out these calculations for ten periods.

The vectors $\Pi(1)$, $\Pi(2)$, $\Pi(3)$, . . . contain the probabilities that a customer who started out as a Murphy customer will be in state 1 or state 2 in the first period, the second period, the third period, and so on. In Table 17.2 we see that after a few periods these probabilities do not change much from one period to the next.

If we had started with 1000 Murphy customers—that is, 1000 consumers who last shopped at Murphy's—our analysis indicates that during the fifth weekly shopping period, 723 would be customers of Murphy's, and 277 would be customers of Ashley's. Moreover,

| Table 17.2 | STATE PROBABILITIES FOR FUTURE PERIODS BEGINNING INITIALLY WITH A MURPHY'S CUSTOMER | | | | | | | | | | |
|---|---|---|---|---|---|---|---|---|---|---|---|

| State Probability | Period ($n$) | | | | | | | | | | |
|---|---|---|---|---|---|---|---|---|---|---|---|
| | 0 | 1 | 2 | 3 | 4 | 5 | 6 | 7 | 8 | 9 | 10 |
| $\pi_1(n)$ | 1 | 0.9 | 0.83 | 0.781 | 0.747 | 0.723 | 0.706 | 0.694 | 0.686 | 0.680 | 0.676 |
| $\pi_2(n)$ | 0 | 0.1 | 0.17 | 0.219 | 0.253 | 0.277 | 0.294 | 0.306 | 0.314 | 0.320 | 0.324 |

during the tenth weekly shopping period, 676 would be customers of Murphy's, and 324 would be customers of Ashley's.

Now let us repeat the analysis, but this time we will begin the process with a customer who shopped last at Ashley's. Thus,

$$\Pi(0) = [\pi_1(0) \quad \pi_2(0)] = [0 \quad 1]$$

Using equation (17.1), the probability of the system being in state 1 or state 2 in period 1 is given by

$$\Pi(1) = \Pi(0)P$$

or

$$[\pi_1(1) \quad \pi_2(1)] = [\pi_1(0) \quad \pi_2(0)]\begin{bmatrix} p_{11} & p_{12} \\ p_{21} & p_{22} \end{bmatrix}$$

$$= [0 \quad 1]\begin{bmatrix} 0.9 & 0.1 \\ 0.2 & 0.8 \end{bmatrix}$$

$$= [0.2 \quad 0.8]$$

Proceeding as before, we can calculate subsequent state probabilities. Doing so, we obtain the results shown in Table 17.3.

In the fifth shopping period, the probability that the customer will be shopping at Murphy's is 0.555, and the probability that the customer will be shopping at Ashley's is 0.445. In the tenth period, the probability that a customer will be shopping at Murphy's is 0.648, and the probability that a customer will be shopping at Ashley's is 0.352.

| Table 17.3 | STATE PROBABILITIES FOR FUTURE PERIODS BEGINNING INITIALLY WITH AN ASHLEY'S CUSTOMER | | | | | | | | | | |
|---|---|---|---|---|---|---|---|---|---|---|---|

| State Probability | Period ($n$) | | | | | | | | | | |
|---|---|---|---|---|---|---|---|---|---|---|---|
| | 0 | 1 | 2 | 3 | 4 | 5 | 6 | 7 | 8 | 9 | 10 |
| $\pi_1(n)$ | 0 | 0.2 | 0.34 | 0.438 | 0.507 | 0.555 | 0.589 | 0.612 | 0.628 | 0.640 | 0.648 |
| $\pi_2(n)$ | 1 | 0.8 | 0.66 | 0.562 | 0.493 | 0.445 | 0.411 | 0.388 | 0.372 | 0.360 | 0.352 |

As we continue the Markov process, we find that the probability of the system being in a particular state after a large number of periods is independent of the beginning state of the system. The probabilities that we approach after a large number of transitions are referred to as the **steady-state probabilities.** We shall denote the steady-state probability for state 1 with the symbol $\pi_1$ and the steady-state probability for state 2 with the symbol $\pi_2$. In other words, in the steady-state case, we simply omit the period designation from $\pi_i(n)$ because it is no longer necessary.

Analyses of Tables 17.2 and 17.3 indicate that as $n$ gets larger, the difference between the state probabilities for the $n$th period and the $(n + 1)$th period becomes increasingly smaller. This analysis leads us to the conclusion that as $n$ gets large, the state probabilities at the $(n + 1)$th period are very close to those at the $n$th period. This observation provides the basis of a simple method for computing the steady-state probabilities without having to actually carry out a large number of calculations.

In general, we know from equation (17.1) that

$$[\pi_1(n + 1) \quad \pi_2(n + 1)] = [\pi_1(n) \quad \pi_2(n)]\begin{bmatrix} p_{11} & p_{12} \\ p_{21} & p_{22} \end{bmatrix}$$

Because for sufficiently large $n$ the difference between $\Pi(n + 1)$ and $\Pi(n)$ is negligible, we see that in the steady state $\pi_1(n + 1) = \pi_1(n) = \pi_1$, and $\pi_2(n + 1) = \pi_2(n) = \pi_2$. Thus, we have

$$[\pi_1 \quad \pi_2] = [\pi_1 \quad \pi_2]\begin{bmatrix} p_{11} & p_{12} \\ p_{21} & p_{22} \end{bmatrix}$$

$$= [\pi_1 \quad \pi_2]\begin{bmatrix} 0.9 & 0.1 \\ 0.2 & 0.8 \end{bmatrix}$$

After carrying out the multiplications, we obtain

$$\pi_1 = 0.9\pi_1 + 0.2\pi_2 \tag{17.2}$$

and

$$\pi_2 = 0.1\pi_1 + 0.8\pi_2 \tag{17.3}$$

However, we also know the steady-state probabilities must sum to 1 with

$$\pi_1 + \pi_2 = 1 \tag{17.4}$$

Using equation (17.4) to solve for $\pi_2$ and substituting the result in equation (17.2), we obtain

$$\pi_1 = 0.9\pi_1 + 0.2(1 - \pi_1)$$
$$\pi_1 = 0.9\pi_1 + 0.2 - 0.2\pi_1$$
$$\pi_1 - 0.7\pi_1 = 0.2$$
$$0.3\pi_1 = 0.2$$
$$\pi_1 = \tfrac{2}{3}$$

Then, using equation (17.4), we can conclude that $\pi_2 = 1 - \pi_1 = \frac{1}{3}$. Thus, using equations (17.2) and (17.4), we can solve for the steady-state probabilities directly. You can check for yourself that we could have obtained the same result using equations (17.3) and (17.4).[2]

Thus, if we have 1000 customers in the system, the Markov process model tells us that in the long run, with steady-state probabilities $\pi_1 = \frac{2}{3}$ and $\pi_2 = \frac{1}{3}$, $\frac{2}{3}(1000) = 667$ customers will be Murphy's and $\frac{1}{3}(1000) = 333$ customers will be Ashley's. The steady-state probabilities can be interpreted as the market shares for the two stores.

Market share information is often quite valuable in decision making. For example, suppose Ashley's Supermarket is contemplating an advertising campaign to attract more of Murphy's customers to its store. Let us suppose further that Ashley's believes this promotional strategy will increase the probability of a Murphy's customer switching to Ashley's from 0.10 to 0.15. The revised transition probabilities are given in Table 17.4.

Given the new transition probabilities, we can modify equations (17.2) and (17.4) to solve for the new steady-state probabilities or market shares. Thus, we obtain

$$\pi_1 = 0.85\pi_1 + 0.20\pi_2$$

Substituting $\pi_2 = 1 - \pi_1$ from equation (17.4), we have

$$\pi_1 = 0.85\pi_1 + 0.20(1 - \pi_1)$$
$$\pi_1 = 0.85\pi_1 + 0.20 - 0.20\pi_1$$
$$\pi_1 - 0.65\pi_1 = 0.20$$
$$0.35\pi_1 = 0.20$$
$$\pi_1 = 0.57$$

and

$$\pi_2 = 1 - 0.57 = 0.43$$

Can you now compute the steady-state probabilities for Markov processes with two states? Problem 3 provides an application.

With three states, the steady-state probabilities are found by solving three equations for the three unknown steady-state probabilities. Try Problem 7 as a slightly more difficult problem involving three states.

We see that the proposed promotional strategy will increase Ashley's market share from $\pi_2 = 0.33$ to $\pi_2 = 0.43$. Suppose that the total market consists of 6000 customers per week. The new promotional strategy will increase the number of customers doing their weekly

| *Table* 17.4 | REVISED TRANSITION PROBABILITIES FOR MURPHY'S AND ASHLEY'S GROCERY STORES | |
|---|---|---|
| **Current Weekly Shopping Period** | **Next Weekly Shopping Period** | |
| | **Murphy's Foodliner** | **Ashley's Supermarket** |
| Murphy's Foodliner | 0.85 | 0.15 |
| Ashley's Supermarket | 0.20 | 0.80 |

[2] Even though equations (17.2) and (17.3) provide two equations and two unknowns, we must include equation (17.4) when solving for $\pi_1$ and $\pi_2$ to ensure that the sum of steady-state probabilities will equal 1.

Other examples of Markov processes include the promotion of managers to various positions within an organization, the migration of people into and out of various regions of the country, and the progression of students through the years of college, including eventually dropping out or graduating.

shopping at Ashley's from 2000 to 2580. If the average weekly profit per customer is $10, the proposed promotional strategy can be expected to increase Ashley's profits by $5800 per week. If the cost of the promotional campaign is less than $5800 per week, Ashley should consider implementing the strategy.

This example demonstrates how a Markov analysis of a firm's market share can be useful in decision making. Suppose that instead of trying to attract customers from Murphy's Foodliner, Ashley's directed a promotional effort at increasing the loyalty of its own customers. In this case, $p_{22}$ would increase, and $p_{21}$ would decrease. Once we knew the amount of the change, we could calculate new steady-state probabilities and compute the impact on profits.

## N O T E S
## and Comments

1. The Markov processes presented in this section have what is called the *memoryless property:* the current state of the system together with the transition probabilities contains all the information necessary to predict the future behavior of the system. The prior states of the system do not have to be considered. Such Markov processes are considered first-order Markov processes. Higher-order Markov processes are ones in which future states of the system depend on two or more previous states.

2. Analysis of a Markov process model is not intended to optimize any particular aspect of a system. Rather, the analysis predicts or describes the future and steady-state behavior of the system. For instance, in the grocery store example, the analysis of the steady-state behavior provided a forecast or prediction of the market shares for the two competitors. In other applications, quantitative analysts have extended the study of Markov processes to what are called *Markov decision processes.* In these models, decisions can be made at each period that affect the transition probabilities and hence influence the future behavior of the system. Markov decision processes have been used in analyzing machine breakdown and maintenance operations, planning the movement of patients in hospitals, developing inspection strategies, determining newspaper subscription duration, and analyzing equipment replacement.

## 17.2 ACCOUNTS RECEIVABLE ANALYSIS

An accounting application in which Markov processes have produced useful results involves the estimation of the allowance for doubtful accounts receivable. This allowance is an estimate of the amount of accounts receivable that will ultimately prove to be uncollectible (i.e., bad debts).

Let us consider the accounts receivable situation for Heidman's Department Store. Heidman's has two aging categories for its accounts receivable: (1) accounts that are classified as 0–30 days old and (2) accounts that are classified as 31–90 days old. If any portion of an account balance exceeds 90 days, that portion is written off as a bad debt. Heidman's follows the procedure of aging the total balance in any customer's account according to the oldest unpaid bill. For example, suppose that one customer's account balance on September 30 is as follows:

| Date of Purchase | Amount Charged |
|---|---|
| August 15 | $25 |
| September 18 | 10 |
| September 28 | 50 |
| Total | $85 |

An aging of accounts receivable on September 30 would assign the total balance of $85 to the 31–90-day category because the oldest unpaid bill of August 15 is 46 days old. Let us assume that one week later, October 7, the customer pays the August 15 bill of $25. The remaining total balance of $60 would now be placed in the 0–30-day category since the oldest unpaid amount, corresponding to the September 18 purchase, is less than 31 days old. This method of aging accounts receivable is called the *total balance method* because the total account balance is placed in the age category corresponding to the oldest unpaid amount.

Note that under the total balance method of aging accounts receivable, dollars appearing in a 31–90-day category at one point in time may appear in a 0–30-day category at a later point in time. In the preceding example, this movement between categories was true for $60 of September billings, which shifted from a 31–90-day to a 0–30-day category after the August bill had been paid.

Let us assume that on December 31 Heidman's shows a total of $3000 in its accounts receivable and that the firm's management would like an estimate of how much of the $3000 will eventually be collected and how much will eventually result in bad debts. The estimated amount of bad debts will appear as an allowance for doubtful accounts in the year-ending financial statements.

Let us see how we can view the accounts receivable operation as a Markov process. First, concentrate on what happens to *one* dollar currently in accounts receivable. As the firm continues to operate into the future, we can consider each week as a trial of a Markov process with a dollar existing in one of the following states of the system:

State 1. Paid category
State 2. Bad debt category
State 3. 0–30-day category
State 4. 31–90-day category

Thus, we can track the week-by-week status of one dollar by using a Markov analysis to identify the state of the system at a particular week or period.

Using a Markov process model with the preceding states, we define the transition probabilities as follows:

$p_{ij}$ = probability of a dollar in state $i$ in one week moving to state $j$ in the next week

Based on historical transitions of accounts receivable dollars, the following matrix of transition probabilities, $P$, has been developed for Heidman's Department Store:

$$P = \begin{bmatrix} p_{11} & p_{12} & p_{13} & p_{14} \\ p_{21} & p_{22} & p_{23} & p_{24} \\ p_{31} & p_{32} & p_{33} & p_{34} \\ p_{41} & p_{42} & p_{43} & p_{44} \end{bmatrix} = \begin{bmatrix} 1.0 & 0.0 & 0.0 & 0.0 \\ 0.0 & 1.0 & 0.0 & 0.0 \\ 0.4 & 0.0 & 0.3 & 0.3 \\ 0.4 & 0.2 & 0.3 & 0.1 \end{bmatrix}$$

Note that the probability of a dollar in the 0–30-day category (state 3) moving to the paid category (state 1) in the next period is 0.4. Also, this dollar has a 0.3 probability it will remain in the 0–30-day category (state 3) one week later, and a 0.3 probability that it will be in the 31–90-day category (state 4) one week later. Note also that a dollar in a 0–30-day account cannot make the transition to a bad debt (state 2) in one week.

When absorbing states are present, each row of the transition matrix corresponding to an absorbing state will have a single 1 and all other probabilities will be 0.

An important property of the Markov process model for Heidman's accounts receivable situation is the presence of *absorbing states.* For example, once a dollar makes a transition to state 1, the paid state, the probability of making a transition to any other state is zero. Similarly, once a dollar is in state 2, the bad debt state, the probability of a transition to any other state is zero. Thus, once a dollar reaches state 1 or state 2, the system will remain in this state indefinitely. We can conclude that all accounts receivable dollars will eventually be absorbed into either the paid or the bad debt state, and hence the name **absorbing state.**

## The Fundamental Matrix and Associated Calculations

Whenever a Markov process has absorbing states, we do not compute steady-state probabilities because each unit ultimately ends up in one of the absorbing states. With absorbing states present, we are interested in knowing the probability that a unit will end up in each of the absorbing states. For the Heidman's Department Store problem, we want to know the probability that a dollar currently in the 0–30-day age category will end up paid (absorbing state 1) as well as the probability that a dollar in this age category will end up a bad debt (absorbing state 2). We also want to know these absorbing-state probabilities for dollar currently in the 31–90-day age category.

The computation of the absorbing-state probabilities requires the determination and use of what is called a **fundamental matrix.** The mathematical logic underlying the fundamental matrix is beyond the scope of this text. However, as we show, the fundamental matrix is derived from the matrix of transition probabilities and is relatively easy to compute for Markov processes with a small number of states. In the following example, we show the computation of the fundamental matrix and the determination of the absorbing-state probabilities for Heidman's Department Store.

We begin the computations by partitioning the matrix of transition probabilities into the following four parts:

$$P = \left[ \begin{array}{cc|cc} 1.0 & 0.0 & 0.0 & 0.0 \\ 0.0 & 1.0 & 0.0 & 0.0 \\ \hline 0.4 & 0.0 & 0.3 & 0.3 \\ 0.4 & 0.2 & 0.3 & 0.1 \end{array} \right] = \left[ \begin{array}{cc|cc} 1.0 & 0.0 & 0.0 & 0.0 \\ 0.0 & 1.0 & 0.0 & 0.0 \\ \hline & R & & Q \end{array} \right]$$

where

$$R = \begin{bmatrix} 0.4 & 0.0 \\ 0.4 & 0.2 \end{bmatrix} \qquad Q = \begin{bmatrix} 0.3 & 0.3 \\ 0.3 & 0.1 \end{bmatrix}$$

A matrix $N$, called a *fundamental matrix,* can be calculated using the following formula:

$$N = (I - Q)^{-1} \qquad (17.5)$$

where $I$ is an identity matrix with 1s on the main diagonal and 0s elsewhere. The superscript $-1$ is used to indicate the inverse of the matrix $(I - Q)$. In Appendix 17.1 we present formulas for finding the inverse of a matrix with two rows and two columns.

Before proceeding, we note that to use equation (17.5), the identity matrix $I$ must be chosen such that it has the *same size or dimensionality* as the matrix $Q$. In our example problem, $Q$ has two rows and two columns, so we must choose

$$I = \begin{bmatrix} 1.0 & 0.0 \\ 0.0 & 1.0 \end{bmatrix}$$

Let us now continue with the example problem by computing the fundamental matrix.

$$I - Q = \begin{bmatrix} 1.0 & 0.0 \\ 0.0 & 1.0 \end{bmatrix} - \begin{bmatrix} 0.3 & 0.3 \\ 0.3 & 0.1 \end{bmatrix}$$
$$= \begin{bmatrix} 0.7 & -0.3 \\ -0.3 & 0.9 \end{bmatrix}$$

and (see Appendix 17.1)

$$N = (I - Q)^{-1} = \begin{bmatrix} 1.67 & 0.56 \\ 0.56 & 1.30 \end{bmatrix}$$

If we multiply the fundamental matrix $N$ times the $R$ portion of the $P$ matrix, we obtain the probabilities that accounts receivable dollars initially in states 3 or 4 will eventually reach each of the absorbing states. The multiplication of $N$ times $R$ for the Heidman's Department Store problem provides the following results (again, see Appendix 17.1 for the steps of this matrix multiplication):

$$NR = \begin{bmatrix} 1.67 & 0.56 \\ 0.56 & 1.30 \end{bmatrix}\begin{bmatrix} 0.4 & 0.0 \\ 0.4 & 0.2 \end{bmatrix} = \begin{bmatrix} 0.89 & 0.11 \\ 0.74 & 0.26 \end{bmatrix}$$

The first row of the product $NR$ is the probability that a dollar in the 0–30-day age category will end up in each absorbing state. Thus, we see a 0.89 probability that a dollar in the 0–30-day category will eventually be paid and a 0.11 probability that it will become a bad debt. Similarly, the second row shows the probabilities associated with a dollar in the 31–90-day category; that is, a dollar in the 31–90-day category has a 0.74 probability of eventually being paid and a 0.26 probability of proving to be uncollectible. Using this information, we can predict the amount of money that will be paid and the amount that will be lost as bad debts.

## Establishing the Allowance for Doubtful Accounts

Let $B$ represent a two-element vector that contains the current accounts receivable balances in the 0–30-day and the 31–90-day categories; that is,

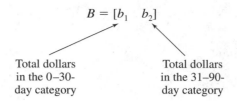

$$B = [b_1 \quad b_2]$$

Total dollars in the 0–30-day category

Total dollars in the 31–90-day category

Suppose that the December 31 balance of accounts receivable for Heidman's shows $1000 in the 0–30-day category (state 3) and $2000 in the 31–90-day category (state 4).

$$B = [1000 \quad 2000]$$

We can multiply $B$ times $NR$ to determine how much of the $3000 will be collected and how much will be lost. For example

$$BNR = [1000 \quad 2000] \begin{bmatrix} 0.89 & 0.11 \\ 0.74 & 0.26 \end{bmatrix}$$

$$= [2370 \quad 630]$$

Thus, we see that $2370 of the accounts receivable balances will be collected and $630 will be written off as a bad debt expense. Based on this analysis, the accounting department would set up an allowance for doubtful accounts of $630.

The matrix multiplication of $BNR$ is simply a convenient way of computing the eventual collections and bad debts of the accounts receivable. Recall that the $NR$ matrix showed a 0.89 probability of collecting dollars in the 0–30-day category and a 0.74 probability of collecting dollars in the 31–90-day category. Thus, as was shown by the $BNR$ calculation, we expect to collect a total of $(1000)0.89 + (2000)0.74 = 890 + 1480 = \$2370$.

Suppose that on the basis of the previous analysis Heidman's would like to investigate the possibility of reducing the amount of bad debts. Recall that the analysis indicated that a 0.11 probability or 11% of the amount in the 0–30-day age category and 26% of the amount in the 31–90-day age category will prove to be uncollectible. Let us assume that Heidman's is considering instituting a new credit policy involving a discount for prompt payment.

Management believes that the policy under consideration will increase the probability of a transition from the 0–30-day age category to the paid category and decrease the probability of a transition from the 0–30-day to the 31–90-day age category. Let us assume that a careful study of the effects of this new policy leads management to conclude that the following transition matrix would be applicable:

$$P = \begin{bmatrix} 1.0 & 0.0 & | & 0.0 & 0.0 \\ 0.0 & 1.0 & | & 0.0 & 0.0 \\ - & - & - & - & - \\ 0.6 & 0.0 & | & 0.3 & 0.1 \\ 0.4 & 0.2 & | & 0.3 & 0.1 \end{bmatrix}$$

We see that the probability of a dollar in the 0–30-day age category making a transition to the paid category in the next period has increased to 0.6 and that the probability of a dollar in the 0–30-day age category making a transition to the 31–90-day category has decreased to 0.1. To determine the effect of these changes on bad debt expense, we must calculate $N$, $NR$, and $BNR$. We begin by using equation (17.5) to calculate the fundamental matrix $N$:

$$N = (I - Q)^{-1} = \left\{ \begin{bmatrix} 1.0 & 0.0 \\ 0.0 & 1.0 \end{bmatrix} - \begin{bmatrix} 0.3 & 0.1 \\ 0.3 & 0.1 \end{bmatrix} \right\}^{-1}$$

$$= \begin{bmatrix} 0.7 & -0.1 \\ -0.3 & 0.9 \end{bmatrix}^{-1}$$

$$= \begin{bmatrix} 1.5 & 0.17 \\ 0.5 & 1.17 \end{bmatrix}$$

By multiplying $N$ times $R$, we obtain the new probabilities that the dollars in each age category will end up in the two absorbing states:

$$NR = \begin{bmatrix} 1.5 & 0.17 \\ 0.5 & 1.17 \end{bmatrix} \begin{bmatrix} 0.6 & 0.0 \\ 0.4 & 0.2 \end{bmatrix}$$

$$= \begin{bmatrix} 0.97 & 0.03 \\ 0.77 & 0.23 \end{bmatrix}$$

We see that with the new credit policy we would expect only 3% of the funds in the 0–30-day age category and 23% of the funds in the 31–90-day age category to prove to be uncollectible. If, as before, we assume a current balance of $1000 in the 0–30-day age category and $2000 in the 31–90-day age category, we can calculate the total amount of accounts receivable that will end up in the two absorbing states by multiplying $B$ times $NR$. We obtain

$$BNR = \begin{bmatrix} 1000 & 2000 \end{bmatrix} \begin{bmatrix} 0.97 & 0.03 \\ 0.77 & 0.23 \end{bmatrix}$$

$$= \begin{bmatrix} 2510 & 490 \end{bmatrix}$$

Problem 11, which provides a variation of Heidman's Department Store problem, will give you practice in analyzing Markov processes with absorbing states.

Thus, the new credit policy shows a bad debt expense of $490. Under the previous credit policy, we found the bad debt expense to be $630. Thus, a savings of $630 − $490 = $140 could be expected as a result of the new credit policy. Given the total accounts receivable balance of $3000, this savings represents a 4.7% reduction in bad debt expense. After considering the costs involved, management can evaluate the economics of adopting the new credit policy. If the cost, including discounts, is less than 4.7% of the accounts receivable balance, we would expect the new policy to lead to increased profits for Heidman's Department Store.

········································································································/  /············

## SUMMARY

In this chapter we have presented Markov process models as well as examples of their application. We saw that a Markov analysis could provide helpful decision-making information about a situation that involves a sequence of repeated trials with a finite number of possible states on each trial. A primary objective is obtaining information about the probability of each state after a large number of transitions or time periods.

A market share application showed the computational procedure for determining the steady-state probabilities that could be interpreted as market shares for two competing supermarkets. In an accounts receivable application, we introduced the notion of absorbing states; for the two absorbing states, referred to as the paid and bad debt categories, we showed how to determine the percentage of an accounts receivable balance that would be absorbed in each of these states.

## GLOSSARY

**Trials of the process**  The events that trigger transitions of the system from one state to another. In many applications, successive time periods represent the trials of the process.

**State of the system**  The condition of the system at any particular trial or time period.

**Transition probability**  Given the system is in state $i$ during one period, the transition probability $p_{ij}$ is the probability that the system will be in state $j$ during the next period.

**State probability**  The probability that the system will be in any particular state. (That is, $\pi_i(n)$ is the probability of the system being in state $i$ in period $n$.)

**Steady-state probability**  The probability that the system will be in any particular state after a large number of transitions. Once steady state has been reached, the state probabilities do not change from period to period.

**Absorbing state**  A state is said to be absorbing if the probability of making a transition out of that state is zero. Thus, once the system has made a transition into an absorbing state, it will remain there.

**Fundamental matrix**  A matrix necessary for the computation of probabilities associated with absorbing states of a Markov process.

## PROBLEMS

1. In the market share analysis of Section 17.1, suppose that we are considering the Markov process associated with the shopping trips of one customer, but we do not know where the customer shopped during the last week. Thus, we might assume a 0.5 probability that the customer shopped at Murphy's and a 0.5 probability that the customer shopped at Ashley's at period 0; that is, $\pi_1(0) = 0.5$ and $\pi_2(0) = 0.5$. Given these initial state probabilities, develop a table similar to Table 17.2 showing the probability of each state in future periods. What do you observe about the long-run probabilities of each state?

2. Management of the New Fangled Softdrink Company believes that the probability of a customer purchasing Red Pop or the company's major competition, Super Cola, is based on the customer's most recent purchase. Suppose that the following transition probabilities are appropriate:

|  | To | |
| --- | --- | --- |
| **From** | **Red Pop** | **Super Cola** |
| Red Pop | 0.9 | 0.1 |
| Super Cola | 0.1 | 0.9 |

a. Show the two-period tree diagram for a customer who last purchased Red Pop. What is the probability that this customer purchases Red Pop on the second purchase?
b. What is the long-run market share for each of these two products?
c. A Red Pop advertising campaign is being planned to increase the probability of attracting Super Cola customers. Management believes that the new campaign will increase to 0.15 the probability of a customer switching from Super Cola to Red Pop. What is the projected effect of the advertising campaign on the market shares?

3.  The computer center at Rockbottom University has been experiencing computer downtime. Let us assume that the trials of an associated Markov process are defined as one-hour periods and that the probability of the system being in a running state or a down state is based on the state of the system in the previous period. Historical data show the following transition probabilities:

|  | To | |
|---|---|---|
| **From** | **Running** | **Down** |
| Running | 0.90 | 0.10 |
| Down | 0.30 | 0.70 |

a.  If the system is initially running, what is the probability of the system being down in the next hour of operation?
b.  What are the steady-state probabilities of the system being in the running state and in the down state?

4.  One cause of the downtime in Problem 3 was traced to a specific piece of computer hardware. Management believes that switching to a different hardware component will result in the following transition probabilities:

|  | To | |
|---|---|---|
| **From** | **Running** | **Down** |
| Running | 0.95 | 0.05 |
| Down | 0.60 | 0.40 |

a.  What are the steady-state probabilities of the system being in the running and down states?
b.  If the cost of the system being down for any period is estimated to be $500 (including lost profits for time down and maintenance), what is the breakeven cost for the new hardware component on a time-period basis?

5.  A major traffic problem in the Greater Cincinnati area involves traffic attempting to cross the Ohio River from Cincinnati to Kentucky using Interstate I-75. Let us assume that the probability of no traffic delay in one period, given no traffic delay in the preceding period, is 0.85 and that the probability of finding a traffic delay in one period, given a delay in the preceding period, is 0.75. Traffic is classified as having either a delay or a no-delay state, and the period considered is 30 minutes.
a.  Assume that you are a motorist entering the traffic system and receive a radio report of a traffic delay, what is the probability that for the next 60 minutes (two time periods) the system will be in the delay state? Note that this result is the probability of being in the delay state for two consecutive periods.
b.  What is the probability that in the long run the traffic will not be in the delay state?
c.  An important assumption of the Markov process models presented in this chapter has been the constant or stationary transition probabilities as the system operates in the future. Do you believe this assumption should be questioned for this traffic problem? Explain.

6.  Data collected from selected major metropolitan areas in the eastern United States show that 2% of individuals living within the city limits move to the suburbs during a 1-year period while 1% of individuals living in the suburbs move to the city during a 1-year period. Answer the following questions assuming that this process is modeled by a Markov process with two states: city and suburbs.

a. Prepare the matrix of transition probabilities.
b. Compute the steady-state probabilities.
c. In a particular metropolitan area, 40% of the population live in the city, and 60% of the population live in the suburbs. What population changes do your steady-state probabilities project for this metropolitan area?

7. Assume that a third grocery store, Quick Stop Groceries, enters the market share and customer loyalty situation described in Section 17.1. Quick Stop Groceries is smaller than either Murphy's Foodliner or Ashley's Supermarket. However, Quick Stop's convenience with faster service and gasoline for automobiles can be expected to attract some customers who currently make weekly shopping visits to either Murphy's or Ashley's. Assume that the transition probabilities are as follows:

|  | To | | |
| --- | --- | --- | --- |
| **From** | **Murphy's** | **Ashley's** | **Quick Stop** |
| Murphy's Foodliner | 0.85 | 0.10 | 0.05 |
| Ashley's Supermarket | 0.20 | 0.75 | 0.05 |
| Quick Stop Groceries | 0.15 | 0.10 | 0.75 |

a. Compute the steady-state probabilities for this three-state Markov process.
b. What market share will Quick Stop obtain?
c. With 1000 customers, the original two-state Markov process in Section 17.1 projected 667 weekly customer trips to Murphy's Foodliner and 333 weekly customer trips to Ashley's Supermarket. What impact will Quick Stop have on the customer visits at Murphy's and Ashley's? Explain.

8. The purchase patterns for two brands of toothpaste can be expressed as a Markov process with the following transition probabilities:

|  | To | |
| --- | --- | --- |
| **From** | **Special B** | **MDA** |
| Special B | 0.90 | 0.10 |
| MDA | 0.05 | 0.95 |

a. Which brand appears to have the most loyal customers? Explain.
b. What are the projected market shares for the two brands?

9. Suppose that in Problem 8 a new toothpaste brand enters the market such that the following transition probabilities exist:

|  | To | | |
| --- | --- | --- | --- |
| **From** | **Special B** | **MDA** | **T-White** |
| Special B | 0.80 | 0.10 | 0.10 |
| MDA | 0.05 | 0.75 | 0.20 |
| T-White | 0.40 | 0.30 | 0.30 |

What are the new long-run market shares? Which brand will suffer most from the introduction of the new brand of toothpaste?

10. Given the following transition matrix with states 1 and 2 as absorbing states, what is the probability that units in states 3 and 4 end up in each of the absorbing states?

$$P = \begin{bmatrix} 1.0 & 0.0 & 0.0 & 0.0 \\ 0.0 & 1.0 & 0.0 & 0.0 \\ 0.2 & 0.1 & 0.4 & 0.3 \\ 0.2 & 0.2 & 0.1 & 0.5 \end{bmatrix}$$

**SELF TEST**

11. In the Heidman's Department Store problem of Section 17.2, suppose that the following transition matrix is appropriate:

$$P = \begin{bmatrix} 1.0 & 0.0 & 0.0 & 0.0 \\ 0.0 & 1.0 & 0.0 & 0.0 \\ 0.5 & 0.0 & 0.25 & 0.25 \\ 0.5 & 0.2 & 0.05 & 0.25 \end{bmatrix}$$

If Heidman's has $4000 in the 0–30-day category and $5000 in the 31–90-day category, what is your estimate of the amount of bad debts the company will experience?

12. The KLM Christmas Tree Farm owns a plot of land with 5000 evergreen trees. Each year KLM allows retailers of Christmas trees to select and cut trees for sale to individual customers. KLM protects small trees (usually less than 4 feet tall) so that they will be available for sale in future years. Currently 1500 trees are classified as protected trees, while the remaining 3500 are available for cutting. However, even though a tree is available for cutting in a given year, it may not be selected for cutting until future years. While most trees not cut in a given year live until the next year, some diseased trees are lost every year.

In viewing the KLM Christmas tree operation as a Markov process with yearly periods, we define the following four states:

State 1. Cut and sold
State 2. Lost to disease
State 3. Too small for cutting
State 4. Available for cutting but not cut and sold

The following transition matrix is appropriate:

$$P = \begin{bmatrix} 1.0 & 0.0 & 0.0 & 0.0 \\ 0.0 & 1.0 & 0.0 & 0.0 \\ 0.1 & 0.2 & 0.5 & 0.2 \\ 0.4 & 0.1 & 0.0 & 0.5 \end{bmatrix}$$

How many of the farm's 5000 trees will be sold eventually, and how many will be lost?

13. A large corporation has collected data on the reasons both middle managers and senior managers leave the company. Some managers eventually retire, but others leave the company prior to retirement for personal reasons including more attractive positions with other firms. Assume that the following matrix of one-year transition probabilities applies with the four states of the Markov process being retirement, leaves prior to retirement for personal reasons, stays as a middle manager, stays as a senior manager.

| | Retirement | Leaves—Personal | Middle Manager | Senior Manager |
|---|---|---|---|---|
| Retirement | 1.00 | 0.00 | 0.00 | 0.00 |
| Leaves—Personal | 0.00 | 1.00 | 0.00 | 0.00 |
| Middle Manager | 0.03 | 0.07 | 0.80 | 0.10 |
| Senior Manager | 0.08 | 0.01 | 0.03 | 0.88 |

   a.  What states are considered absorbing states? Why?
   b.  Interpret the transition probabilities for the middle managers.
   c.  Interpret the transition probabilities for the senior managers.
   d.  What percentage of the current middle managers will eventually retire from the company? What percentage will leave the company for personal reasons?
   e.  The company currently has 920 managers: 640 middle managers and 280 senior managers. How many of these managers will eventually retire from the company? How many will leave the company for personal reasons?

14. Data for the progression of college students at a particular college are summarized in the following matrix of transition probabilities.

|  | Graduate | Dropout | Freshman | Sophomore | Junior | Senior |
|---|---|---|---|---|---|---|
| Graduate | 1.00 | 0.00 | 0.00 | 0.00 | 0.00 | 0.00 |
| Dropout | 0.00 | 1.00 | 0.00 | 0.00 | 0.00 | 0.00 |
| Freshman | 0.00 | 0.20 | 0.15 | 0.65 | 0.00 | 0.00 |
| Sophomore | 0.00 | 0.15 | 0.00 | 0.10 | 0.75 | 0.00 |
| Junior | 0.00 | 0.10 | 0.00 | 0.00 | 0.05 | 0.85 |
| Senior | 0.90 | 0.05 | 0.00 | 0.00 | 0.00 | 0.05 |

   a.  What states are absorbing states?
   b.  Interpret the transition probabilities for a sophomore.
   c.  Use The Management Scientist software package to compute the probabilities that a sophomore will graduate and that a sophomore will drop out.
   d.  In an address to the incoming class of 600 freshmen, the dean asks the students to look around the auditorium and realize that about 50% of the freshmen present today will not make it to graduation day. Does your Markov process analysis support the dean's statement? Explain.
   e.  Currently, the college has 600 freshmen, 520 sophomores, 460 juniors, and 420 seniors. What percentage of the 2000 students attending the college will eventually graduate?

## Appendix 17.1    MATRIX NOTATION AND OPERATIONS

### Matrix Notation

A *matrix* is a rectangular arrangement of numbers. For example, consider the following matrix that we have named $D$:

$$D = \begin{bmatrix} 1 & 3 & 2 \\ 0 & 4 & 5 \end{bmatrix}$$

The matrix $D$ is said to consist of six elements, where each element of $D$ is a number. To identify a particular element of a matrix, we have to specify its location. Therefore, we introduce the concepts of rows and columns.

All elements across some horizontal line in a matrix are said to be in a row of the matrix. For example, elements 1, 3, and 2 in $D$ are in the first row, and elements 0. 4, and 5 are in the second row. By convention, we refer to the top row as row 1, the second row from the top as row 2, and so on.

All elements along some vertical line are said to be in a column of the matrix. Elements 1 and 0 in $D$ are elements in the first column, elements 3 and 4 are elements of the second column, and elements 2 and 5 are elements of the third column. By convention, we refer to the leftmost column as column 1, the next column to the right as column 2, and so on.

We can identify a particular element in a matrix by specifying its row and column position. For example, the element in row 1 and column 2 of $D$ is the number 3. This position is written as

$$d_{12} = 3$$

In general, we use the following notation to refer to the specific elements of $D$:

$$d_{ij} = \text{element located in the } i\text{th row and } j\text{th column of } D$$

We always use capital letters for the names of matrixes and the corresponding lowercase letters with two subscripts to denote the elements.

The *size* of a matrix is the number of rows and columns in the matrix and is written as the number of rows $\times$ the number of columns. Thus, the size of $D$ is $2 \times 3$.

Frequently we will encounter matrixes that have only one row or one column. For example,

$$G = \begin{bmatrix} 6 \\ 4 \\ 2 \\ 3 \end{bmatrix}$$

is a matrix that has only one column. Whenever a matrix has only one column, we call the matrix a *column vector*. In a similar manner, any matrix that has only one row is called a *row vector*. Using our previous notation for the elements of a matrix, we would refer to specific elements in $G$ by writing $g_{ij}$. However, since $G$ has only one column, the column position is unimportant, and we need only specify the row the element of interest is in. That is, instead of referring to elements in a vector using $g_{ij}$, we specify only one subscript, which denotes the position of the element in the vector. For example,

$$g_1 = 6 \qquad g_2 = 4 \qquad g_3 = 2 \qquad g_4 = 3$$

## Matrix Operations

**Matrix Transpose.**    The transpose of a matrix is formed by making the rows in the original matrix the columns in the transpose matrix, and by making the columns in the original matrix the rows in the transpose matrix. For example, the transpose of the matrix

$$D = \begin{bmatrix} 1 & 3 & 2 \\ 0 & 4 & 5 \end{bmatrix}$$

is

$$D^t = \begin{bmatrix} 1 & 0 \\ 3 & 4 \\ 2 & 5 \end{bmatrix}$$

Note that we use the superscript $t$ to denote the transpose of a matrix.

**Matrix Multiplication.**   We demonstrate how to perform two types of matrix multiplication: (1) multiplying two vectors and (2) multiplying a matrix times a matrix.

The product of a row vector of size $1 \times n$ times a column vector of size $n \times 1$ is the number obtained by multiplying the first element in the row vector times the first element in the column vector, the second element in the row vector times the second element in the column vector, and continuing on through the last element in the row vector times the last element in the column vector, and then summing the products. Suppose, for example, that we wanted to multiply the row vector $H$ times the column vector $G$, where

$$H = [2 \quad 1 \quad 5 \quad 0] \text{ and } G = \begin{bmatrix} 6 \\ 4 \\ 2 \\ 3 \end{bmatrix}$$

The product $HG$, referred to as a vector product, is given by

$$HG = 2(6) + 1(4) + 5(2) + 0(3) = 26$$

The product of a matrix of size $p \times n$ and a matrix of size $n \times m$ is a new matrix of size $p \times m$. The element in the $i$th row and $j$th column of the new matrix is given by the vector product of the $i$th row of the $p \times n$ matrix times the $j$th column of the $n \times m$ matrix. Suppose, for example, that we want to multiply $D$ times $A$, where

$$D = \begin{bmatrix} 1 & 3 & 2 \\ 0 & 4 & 5 \end{bmatrix} \quad A = \begin{bmatrix} 1 & 3 & 5 \\ 2 & 0 & 4 \\ 1 & 5 & 2 \end{bmatrix}$$

Let $C = DA$ denote the product of $D$ times $A$. The element in row 1 and column 1 of $C$ is given by the vector product of the first row of $D$ times the first column of $A$. Thus

$$c_{11} = [1 \quad 3 \quad 2] \begin{bmatrix} 1 \\ 2 \\ 1 \end{bmatrix} = 1(1) + 3(2) + 2(1) = 9$$

The element in row 2 and column 1 of $C$ is given by the vector product of the second row of $D$ times the first column of $A$. Thus,

$$c_{21} = [0 \quad 4 \quad 5] \begin{bmatrix} 1 \\ 2 \\ 1 \end{bmatrix} = 0(1) + 4(2) + 5(1) = 13$$

Calculating the remaining elements of $C$ in a similar fashion, we obtain

$$C = \begin{bmatrix} 9 & 13 & 21 \\ 13 & 25 & 26 \end{bmatrix}$$

Clearly, the product of a matrix and a vector is just a special case of multiplying a matrix times a matrix. For example, the product of a matrix of size $m \times n$ and a vector of size

$n \times 1$ is a new vector of size $m \times 1$. The element in the $i$th position of the new vector is given by the vector product of the $i$th row of the $m \times n$ matrix times the $n \times 1$ column vector. Suppose, for example, that we want to multiply $D$ times $K$, where

$$D = \begin{bmatrix} 1 & 3 & 2 \\ 0 & 4 & 5 \end{bmatrix} \quad K = \begin{bmatrix} 1 \\ 4 \\ 2 \end{bmatrix}$$

The first element of $DK$ is given by the vector product of the first row of $D$ times $K$. Thus,

$$\begin{bmatrix} 1 & 3 & 2 \end{bmatrix} \begin{bmatrix} 1 \\ 4 \\ 2 \end{bmatrix} = 1(1) + 3(4) + 2(2) = 17$$

The second element of $DK$ is given by the vector product of the second row of $D$ and $K$. Thus,

$$\begin{bmatrix} 0 & 4 & 5 \end{bmatrix} \begin{bmatrix} 1 \\ 4 \\ 2 \end{bmatrix} = 0(1) + 4(4) + 5(2) = 26$$

Hence, we see that the product of the matrix $D$ times the vector $K$ is given by

$$DK = \begin{bmatrix} 1 & 3 & 2 \\ 0 & 4 & 5 \end{bmatrix} \begin{bmatrix} 1 \\ 4 \\ 2 \end{bmatrix} = \begin{bmatrix} 17 \\ 26 \end{bmatrix}$$

Can any two matrixes be multiplied? The answer is no. To multiply two matrixes, the number of the columns in the first matrix must equal the number of rows in the second. If this property is satisfied, the matrixes are said to *conform for multiplication*. Thus, in our example, $D$ and $K$ could be multiplied because $D$ had three columns and $K$ had three rows.

**Matrix Inverse.**   The inverse of a matrix $A$ is another matrix, denoted $A^{-1}$, such that $A^{-1}A = I$ and $AA^{-1} = I$. The inverse of any square matrix $A$ consisting of two rows and two columns is computed as follows:

$$A = \begin{bmatrix} a_{11} & a_{12} \\ a_{21} & a_{22} \end{bmatrix}$$

$$A^{-1} = \begin{bmatrix} a_{22}/d & -a_{12}/d \\ -a_{21}/d & a_{11}/d \end{bmatrix}$$

where $d = a_{11}a_{22} - a_{21}a_{12}$ is the determinant of the $2 \times 2$ matrix $A$. For example, if

$$A = \begin{bmatrix} 0.7 & -0.3 \\ -0.3 & 0.9 \end{bmatrix}$$

then

$$d = (0.7)(0.9) - (-0.3)(-0.3) = 0.54$$

and

$$A^{-1} = \begin{bmatrix} 0.9/0.54 & 0.3/0.54 \\ 0.3/0.54 & 0.7/0.54 \end{bmatrix} = \begin{bmatrix} 1.67 & 0.56 \\ 0.56 & 1.30 \end{bmatrix}$$

# U.S. GENERAL ACCOUNTING OFFICE*

## WASHINGTON, D.C.

The U.S. General Accounting Office (GAO) is an independent, nonpolitical audit organization in the legislative branch of the federal government. The GAO was created by the Budget and Accounting Act of 1921 and has three basic purposes:

1. To assist Congress, its committees, and its members in carrying out their legislative and oversight responsibilities, consistent with its role as an independent, nonpolitical agency.
2. To audit and evaluate the programs, activities, and financial operations of federal departments and agencies and to make recommendations toward more efficient and effective operations.
3. To carry out financial control and other functions with respect to federal government programs and operations including accounting, legal, and claims settlement work.

GAO evaluators, in fulfilling the main role in the GAO, determine the effectiveness of existing or proposed federal programs and the efficiency, economy, legality, and effectiveness with which federal agencies carry out their responsibilities. These evaluations culminate in reports to the Congress and to the heads of federal departments and agencies. Such reports typically include recommendations to Congress concerning the need for enabling or remedial legislation and suggestions to agencies concerning the need for changes in programs or operations to improve their economy, efficiency, and effectiveness.

GAO evaluators analyze policies and practices and the use of resources within and among federal programs,

identify problem areas and deficiencies in meeting program goals, develop and analyze alternative solutions to problems of program execution, and develop and recommend changes to enable the programs to better conform to congressional goals and legislative intent. To effectively carry out their duties, evaluators must be proficient in interviewing, data processing, records review, legislative research, quantitative methods, and statistical analysis techniques.

## Impact of Services on the Well-being of Older People

GAO evaluators obtained data from a random sample of noninstitutionalized persons aged 65 and older living in Cleveland, Ohio. The health conditions of the sampled individuals in the 65- to 69-year-old groups were defined by the following three states:

- **Best.** Individual able to perform 13 identified activities of daily living without help.
- **Next best.** Individual able to perform the same 13 activities but required help for at least one activity.
- **Worst.** Individual unable to perform the same 13 activities even with help.

Using a 2-year period, GAO evaluators developed estimates of the year-to-year transition probabilities of individuals in the 65- to 69-year-old group. These estimates were then used to develop a transition probability matrix such as shown in the following table. Note that a death state has been added as an absorbing state.

Using the transition probabilities, a Markov process analysis can be used to determine the state probabilities for any number of periods (years) into the future. To ver-

*The authors are indebted to Bill Ammann, U.S. General Accounting Office, Washington, D.C., for providing this application.

Chapter 17 Markov Processes header

| Current Year Condition | Following Year Condition | | | |
|---|---|---|---|---|
| | **Best** | **Next Best** | **Worst** | **Death** |
| Best | $p_{11}$ | $p_{12}$ | $p_{13}$ | $p_{14}$ |
| Next Best | $p_{21}$ | $p_{22}$ | $p_{23}$ | $p_{24}$ |
| Worst | $p_{31}$ | $p_{32}$ | $p_{33}$ | $p_{34}$ |
| Death | 0 | 0 | 0 | 1 |

ify the appropriateness of the Markov process model, GAO evaluators used the transition probabilities to determine the state probabilities for the 65- to 69-year-old age group 5 years into the future. The resulting state probabilities were compared with the health states of individuals in a known 70- to 74-year-old age group. No statistically significant difference occurred between the probabilities provided by the model and the actual state probabilities of the 70- to 74-year-old group.

## Estimating the Likely Effects of Health Care Programs

The individuals in the original study were subdivided into two groups: those receiving appropriate health care and those not receiving appropriate health care. For the purpose of the study, a person was classified as receiving appropriate health care if the person was taking medication and/or treatment for each illness present and if the person was receiving help to perform each of the 13 activities of daily living as specifically needed. As a result, GAO evaluators developed two matrixes of transition probabilities: one for individuals receiving appropriate health care and one for individuals not receiving appropriate health care.

For any individuals not receiving appropriate help, the kind of additional help needed was determined, and the cost of that help was estimated. Then those persons were artificially aged using the transition probabilities to establish the likely benefits in terms of improved health states for the individuals. Over a 20-year period, a net savings occurred for the health care program provided all other factors remained equal. That is, the increased cost to provide sufficient appropriate help to all persons was eventually offset by individuals either improving their health state or by not spending as much time in a worse state. Although benefits of health care are often proclaimed theoretically, the Markov process model provided evidence that indicated benefits would be achieved with the health care program.

This type of Markov analysis was also conducted for economic, social, and life view status as well as for the health status. In some instances, the Markov model showed that additional help and/or programs did not result in net savings over time.

## Questions

1. Suppose the transition probabilities in the table were as follows:

$$\begin{bmatrix} 0.80 & 0.10 & 0.06 & 0.04 \\ 0.05 & 0.75 & 0.15 & 0.05 \\ 0.00 & 0.05 & 0.75 & 0.20 \\ 0.00 & 0.00 & 0.00 & 1.00 \end{bmatrix}$$

   Assume that a particular city has 1000 individuals in the best state, 2000 in the next best state, and 500 in the worst state. Estimate how many of each of these individuals will be in each state 2 years from now.

2. How might health care programs affect the matrix of transition probabilities in Question 1? What effect would you expect to see in the distribution of individuals across the four states 2 years from now?

# 18

## DYNAMIC PROGRAMMING

### CONTENTS

**Dynamic programming** is an approach to problem solving that decomposes a large problem that may be difficult to solve into a number of smaller problems that are usually much easier to solve. Moreover, the dynamic programming approach allows us to break up a large problem in such a way that once all the smaller problems have been solved, we have an optimal solution to the large problem. We shall see that each of the smaller problems is identified with a stage of the dynamic programming solution procedure. As a consequence, the technique has been applied to decision problems that are multistage in nature. Often, multiple stages are created because a sequence of decisions must be made over time. For example, a problem of determining an optimal decision over a 1-year horizon might be broken into 12 smaller stages, where each stage requires an optimal decision over a 1-month horizon. In most cases, each of these smaller problems cannot be considered to be completely independent of the others, and it is here that dynamic programming is helpful. Let us begin by showing how to solve a shortest-route problem using dynamic programming.

## 18.1    A SHORTEST-ROUTE PROBLEM

In Chapter 9 we studied a labeling algorithm for solving the shortest-route problem. Let us now illustrate the dynamic programming approach by using it to solve a shortest-route problem. Consider the network presented in Figure 18.1. Assuming that the numbers above each arc denote the direct distance in miles between two nodes, find the shortest route from node 1 to node 10.

Before attempting to solve this problem, let us note an important characteristic of shortest-route problems. This characteristic is actually a restatement of Richard Bellman's famous **principle of optimality** as it applies to the shortest-route problem.[1]

---

**The Principle of Optimality**

If a particular node is on the optimal route, then the shortest path from that node to the end is also on the optimal route.

---

The dynamic programming approach to the shortest-route problem essentially involves treating each node as if it were on the optimal route and making calculations accordingly. In doing so, we will work backward by starting at the terminal node, node 10, and calculating the shortest route from each node to node 10 until we reach the origin, node 1. At this point, we will have solved the original problem of finding the shortest route from node 1 to node 10.

As we stated in the introduction to this chapter, dynamic programming decomposes the original problem into a number of smaller problems that are much easier to solve. In the shortest-route problem for the network in Figure 18.1, the smaller problems that we will create define a four-stage dynamic programming problem. The first stage begins with nodes that are exactly one arc away from the destination, and ends at the destination node. Note from Figure 18.1 that only nodes 8 and 9 are exactly one arc away from node 10. In dynamic programming terminology, nodes 8 and 9 are considered to be the input nodes for stage 1, and node 10 is considered to be the output node for stage 1.

---

[1] S. Dreyfus, *Dynamic Programming and the Calculus of Variations* (New York: Academic Press, 1965).

**Figure 18.1    NETWORK FOR THE SHORTEST-ROUTE PROBLEM**

The second stage begins with all nodes that are exactly two arcs away from the destination and ends with all nodes that are exactly one arc away. Hence, nodes 5, 6, and 7 are the input nodes for stage 2, and nodes 8 and 9 are the output nodes for stage 2. Note that the output nodes for stage 2 are the input nodes for stage 1. The input nodes for the third-stage problem are all nodes that are exactly three arcs away from the destination—that is, nodes 2, 3, and 4. The output nodes for stage 3, all of which are one arc closer to the destination, are nodes 5, 6, and 7. Finally, the input node for stage 4 is node 1, and the output nodes are 2, 3, and 4. The decision problem we shall want to solve at each stage is, Which arc is best to travel over in moving from each particular input node to an output node? Let us consider the stage 1 problem.

We arbitrarily begin the stage 1 calculations with node 9. Because only one way affords travel from node 9 to node 10, this route is obviously shortest and requires us to travel a distance of 2 miles. Similarly, only one path goes from node 8 to node 10. The shortest route from node 8 to the end is thus the length of that route, or 5 miles. The stage 1 decision problem is solved. For each input node, we have identified an optimal decision—that is, the best arc to travel over to reach the output node. The stage 1 results are summarized here:

| | Stage 1 | |
|---|---|---|
| Input Node | Arc (decision) | Shortest Distance to Node 10 |
| 8 | 8–10 | 5 |
| 9 | 9–10 | 2 |

To begin the solution to the stage 2 problem, we move to node 7. (We could have selected node 5 or 6; the order of the nodes selected at any stage is arbitrary.) Two arcs leave node 7 and are connected to input nodes for stage 1: arc 7–8, which has a length of 8 miles, and arc 7–9, which has a length of 10 miles. If we select arc 7–8, we will have a distance from node 7 to node 10 of 13 miles; i.e., the length of arc 7–8, 8 miles, plus the shortest distance to node 10 from node 8, 5 miles. Thus, the decision to select arc 7–8 has a total associated distance of 8 + 5 = 13 miles. With a distance of 10 miles for arc 7–9 and stage 1 results showing a distance of 2 miles from node 9 to node 10, the decision to select arc 7–9 has an associated distance of 10 + 2 = 12 miles. Thus, given we are at node 7, we should select arc 7–9 because it is on the path that will reach node 10 in the shortest distance (12 miles). By performing similar calculations for nodes 5 and 6, we can generate the following stage 2 results:

| | | Stage 2 | |
|---|---|---|---|
| Input Node | Arc (decision) | Output Node | Shortest Distance to Node 10 |
| 5 | 5–8 | 8 | 8 |
| 6 | 6–9 | 9 | 7 |
| 7 | 7–9 | 9 | 12 |

In Figure 18.2 the number in the square by each node considered so far indicates the length of the shortest route from that node to the end. We have completed the solution to the first two subproblems (stages 1 and 2). We now know the shortest route from nodes 5, 6, 7, 8, and 9 to node 10.

To begin the third stage, let us start with node 2. Note that three arcs connect node 2 to the stage 2 input nodes. Thus, to find the shortest route from node 2 to node 10, we must make three calculations. If we select arc 2–7 and then follow the shortest route to the end, we will have a distance of 11 + 12 = 23 miles. Similarly, selecting arc 2–6 requires 12 + 7 = 19 miles, and selecting arc 2–5 requires 13 + 8 = 21 miles. Thus, the shortest route from node 2 to node 10 is 19 miles, which indicates that arc 2–6 is the best decision, given that we are at node 2. Similarly, we find that the shortest route from node 3 to node 10 is given by Min {4 + 12, 10 + 7, 6 + 8} = 14; the shortest route from node 4 to node

## Figure 18.2   INTERMEDIATE SOLUTION TO THE SHORTEST-ROUTE PROBLEM USING DYNAMIC PROGRAMMING

10 is given by Min $\{14 + 7, 12 + 8\} = 20$. We complete the stage 3 calculations with the following results:

| | | Stage 3 | |
|---|---|---|---|
| Input Node | Arc (decision) | Output Node | Shortest Distance to Node 10 |
| 2 | 2–6 | 6 | 19 |
| 3 | 3–5 | 5 | 14 |
| 4 | 4–5 | 5 | 20 |

In solving the stage 4 subproblem, we find that the shortest route from node 1 to node 10 is given by Min $\{1 + 19, 5 + 14, 2 + 20\} = 19$. Thus, the optimal decision at stage 4 is the selection of arc 1–3. By moving through the network from stage 4 to stage 3 to stage 2 to stage 1, we can identify the best decision at each stage and therefore the shortest route from node 1 to node 10.

| Stage | Arc (decision) |
|---|---|
| 4 | 1–3 |
| 3 | 3–5 |
| 2 | 5–8 |
| 1 | 8–10 |

Thus, the shortest route is through nodes 1–3–5–8–10 with a distance of $5 + 6 + 3 + 5 = 19$ miles.

Note how the calculations at each successive stage make use of the calculations at prior stages. This characteristic is an important part of the dynamic programming procedure. Figure 18.3 illustrates the final network calculations. Note that in working back through the stages we have now determined the shortest route from every node to node 10.

Dynamic programming, while enumerating or evaluating several paths at each stage, does not require us to enumerate all possible paths from node 1 to node 10. Returning to the stage 4 calculations, we consider three alternatives for leaving node 1. The complete route associated with each of these alternatives is presented as follows:

| Arc Alternatives at Node 1 | Complete Path to Node 10 | Distance | |
|---|---|---|---|
| 1–2 | 1–2–6–9–10 | 20 | |
| 1–3 | 1–3–5–8–10 | 19 | ←— Selected as best |
| 1–4 | 1–4–5–8–10 | 22 | |

Try Problem 2, part (a), for practice solving a shortest-route problem using dynamic programming.

When you realize that there are a total of 16 alternate routes from node 1 to node 10, you can see that dynamic programming has provided substantial computational savings over a total enumeration of all possible solutions.

The fact that we did not have to evaluate all the paths at each stage as we moved backward from node 10 to node 1 is illustrative of the power of dynamic programming. Using

| Figure 18.3 | FINAL SOLUTION TO THE SHORTEST-ROUTE PROBLEM USING DYNAMIC PROGRAMMING |

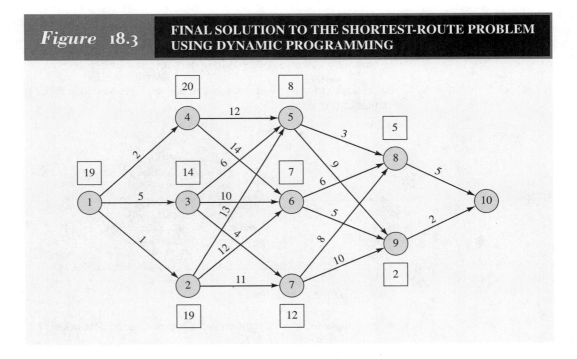

dynamic programming, we need only make a small fraction of the number of calculations that would be required using total enumeration. If the example network had been larger, the computational savings provided by dynamic programming would have been even greater.

## 18.2    DYNAMIC PROGRAMMING NOTATION

Perhaps one of the most difficult aspects of learning to apply dynamic programming involves understanding the notation. The notation we will use is the same as that used by Nemhauser[2] and is fairly standard.

The **stages** of a dynamic programming solution procedure are formed by decomposing the original problem into a number of subproblems. Associated with each subproblem is a stage in the dynamic programming solution procedure. For example, the shortest-route problem introduced in the preceding section was solved using a four-stage dynamic programming solution procedure. We had four stages because we decomposed the original problem into the following four subproblems:

1. **Stage 1 Problem:** Where should we go from nodes 8 and 9 so that we will reach node 10 along the shortest route?
2. **Stage 2 Problem:** Using the results of stage 1, where should we go from nodes 5, 6, and 7 so that we will reach node 10 along the shortest route?

---

[2] G. L. Nemhauser, *Introduction to Dynamic Programming* (New York: Wiley, 1966).

3. **Stage 3 Problem:** Using the results of stage 2, where should we go from nodes 2, 3, and 4 so that we will reach node 10 along the shortest route?

4. **Stage 4 Problem:** Using the results of stage 3, where should we go from node 1 so that we will reach node 10 along the shortest route?

Let us look closely at what occurs at the stage 2 problem. Consider the following representation of this stage:

Using dynamic programming notation, we define

$x_2$ = input to stage 2; represents the location in the network at the beginning of stage 2 (node 5, 6, or 7).

$d_2$ = decision variable at stage 2 (the arc selected to move to stage 1).

$x_1$ = output for stage 2; represents the location in the network at the end of stage 2 (node 8 or 9).

Using this notation, the stage 2 problem can be represented as follows:

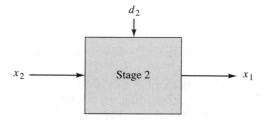

Recall that using dynamic programming to solve the shortest-route problem, we worked backward through the stages, beginning at node 10. When we reached stage 2, we did not know $x_2$ because the stage 3 problem had not yet been solved. The approach used was to consider *all* alternatives for the input $x_2$. Then we determined the best decision $d_2$ for each of the inputs $x_2$. Later, when we moved forward through the system to recover the optimal sequence of decisions, we saw that the stage 3 decision provided a specific $x_2$, node 5, and from our previous analysis we knew the best decision ($d_2$) to make as we continued on to stage 1.

Let us consider a general dynamic programming problem with $N$ stages and adopt the following general notation:

$$x_n = \text{input to stage } n \text{ (output from stage } n + 1)$$
$$d_n = \text{decision variable at stage } n$$

The general $N$-stage problem is decomposed as follows:

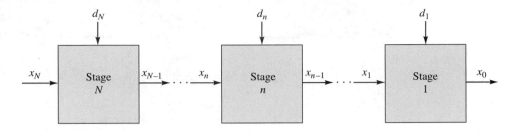

The four-stage shortest-route problem can be represented as follows:

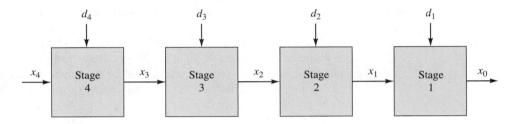

The values of the input and output variables $x_4$, $x_3$, $x_2$, $x_1$, and $x_0$ are important because they join the four subproblems together. At any stage, we will ultimately need to know the input $x_n$ to make the best decision $d_n$. These $x_n$ variables can be thought of as defining the *state* or condition of the system as we move from stage to stage. Accordingly, these variables are referred to as the **state variables** of the problem. In the shortest-route problem, the state variables represented the location in the network at each stage (i.e., a particular node).

At stage 2 of the shortest-route problem, we considered the input $x_2$ and made the decision $d_2$ that would provide the shortest distance to the destination. The output $x_1$ was based on a combination of the input and the decision; that is, $x_1$ was a function of $x_2$ and $d_2$. In dynamic programming notation, we write:

$$x_1 = t_2(x_2, d_2)$$

where $t_2(x_2, d_2)$ is the function that determines the stage 2 output. Since $t_2(x_2, d_2)$ is the function that "transforms" the input to the stage into the output, this function is referred to as the **stage transformation function.** The general expression for the stage transformation function is

$$x_{n-1} = t_n(x_n, d_n)$$

The mathematical form of the stage transformation function is dependent on the particular dynamic programming problem. In the shortest-route problem, the transformation function was based on a tabular calculation. For example, Table 18.1 shows the stage transformation function $t_2(x_2, d_2)$ for stage 2. The possible values of $d_2$ are the arcs selected in the body of the table.

Each stage also has a return associated with it. In the shortest-route problem, the return was the arc distance traveled in moving from an input node to an output node. For example,

| | STAGE TRANSFORMATION $x_1 = t_2(x_2, d_2)$ FOR STAGE 2 WITH THE VALUE OF $x_1$ CORRESPONDING TO EACH VALUE OF $x_2$ |
|---|---|
| **Table 18.1** | |

| | $x_1$ Output State | |
|---|---|---|
| $x_2$ Input State | 8 | 9 |
| 5 | 5–8 | 5–9 |
| 6 | 6–8 | 6–9 |
| 7 | 7–8 | 7–9 |

if node 7 were the input state for stage 2 and we selected arc 7–9 as $d_2$, the return for that stage would be the arc length, 10 miles. The return at a stage, which may be thought of as the payoff or value for a stage, is represented by the general notation $r_n(x_n, d_n)$.

Using the stage transformation function and the **return function,** the shortest-route problem can be shown as follows.

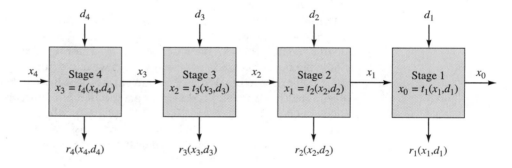

If we view a system or a process as consisting of $N$ stages, we can represent a dynamic programming formulation as follows:

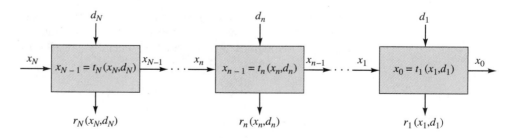

Each of the rectangles in the diagram represents a stage in the process. As indicated, each stage has two inputs: the state variable and the decision variable. Each stage also has two outputs: a new value for the state variable and a return for the stage. The new value for the state variable is determined as a function of the inputs using $t_n(x_n, d_n)$. The value of the return for a stage is also determined as a function of the inputs using $r_n(x_n, d_n)$.

*The optimal total return depends only on the state variable.*

In addition, we will use the notation $f_n(x_n)$ to represent the optimal total return from stage $n$ and all remaining stages, given an input of $x_n$ to stage $n$. For example, in the shortest-route problem, $f_2(x_2)$ represents the optimal total return (i.e., the minimum distance) from stage 2 and all remaining stages, given an input of $x_2$ to stage 2. Thus, we see from Figure 18.3 that $f_2(x_2 = \text{node } 5) = 8$, $f_2(x_2 = \text{node } 6) = 7$, and $f_2(x_2 = \text{node } 7) = 12$. These values are the ones indicated in the squares at nodes 5, 6, and 7.

## NOTES and Comments

1. The primary advantage of dynamic programming is its "divide and conquer" solution strategy. Using dynamic programming, a large, complex problem can be divided into a sequence of smaller interrelated problems. By solving the smaller problems sequentially, the optimal solution to the larger problem is found. Dynamic programming is a general approach to problem solving; it is not a specific technique such as linear programming, which can be applied in the same fashion to a variety of problems. Although some characteristics are common to all dynamic programming problems, each application requires some degree of creativity, insight, and expertise to recognize how the larger problems can be broken into a sequence of interrelated smaller problems.

2. Dynamic programming has been applied to a wide variety of problems including inventory control, production scheduling, capital budgeting, resource allocation, equipment replacement and maintenance. In many of these applications, periods such as days, weeks, and months provide the sequence of interrelated stages for the larger multiperiod problem.

## 18.3   THE KNAPSACK PROBLEM

The basic idea of the **knapsack problem** is that there are $N$ different types of items that can be put into a knapsack. Each item has a certain weight associated with it as well as a value. The problem is to determine how many units of each item to place in the knapsack to maximize the total value. A constraint is placed on the maximum weight permissible.

To provide a practical application of the knapsack problem, consider a manager of a manufacturing operation who must make a biweekly selection of jobs from each of 4 categories to process during the following 2-week period. A list showing the number of jobs waiting to be processed is presented in Table 18.2. The estimated time required for completion and the value rating associated with each job are also shown.

The value rating assigned to each job category is a subjective score assigned by the manager. A scale from 1 to 20 is used to measure the value of each job, where 1 represents jobs of the least value, and 20 represents jobs of most value. The value of a job depends on such things as expected profit, length of time the job has been waiting to be processed, priority, and so on. In this situation, we would like to select certain jobs during the next 2 weeks such that all the jobs selected can be processed within 10 working days and the total value of the jobs selected is maximized. In knapsack problem terminology, we are in essence selecting the best jobs for the 2-week (10 working days) knapsack, where the knapsack has a capacity equal to the 10-day production capacity. Let us formulate and solve this problem using dynamic programming.

| Table 18.2 | JOB DATA FOR THE MANUFACTURING OPERATION | | |
|---|---|---|---|
| Job Category | Number of Jobs to Be Processed | Estimated Completion Time Per Job (days) | Value Rating Per Job |
| 1 | 4 | 1 | 2 |
| 2 | 3 | 3 | 8 |
| 3 | 2 | 4 | 11 |
| 4 | 2 | 7 | 20 |

This problem can be formulated as a dynamic programming problem involving four stages. At stage 1, we must decide how many jobs from category 1 to process; at stage 2, we must decide how many jobs from category 2 to process; and so on. Thus, we let

$d_n$ = number of jobs processed from category $n$ (decision variable at stage $n$)

$x_n$ = number of days of processing time remaining at the beginning of stage $n$ (state variable for stage $n$)

Thus, with a 2-week production period, $x_4 = 10$ represents the total number of days available for processing jobs. The stage transformation functions are as follows:

Stage 4  $x_3 = t_4(x_4, d_4) = x_4 - 7d_4$
Stage 3  $x_2 = t_3(x_3, d_3) = x_3 - 4d_3$
Stage 2  $x_1 = t_2(x_2, d_2) = x_2 - 3d_2$
Stage 1  $x_0 = t_1(x_1, d_1) = x_1 - 1d_1$

The return at each stage is based on the value rating of the associated job category and the number of jobs selected from that category. The return functions are as follows:

Stage 4  $r_4(x_4, d_4) = 20d_4$
Stage 3  $r_3(x_3, d_3) = 11d_3$
Stage 2  $r_2(x_2, d_2) = \phantom{0}8d_2$
Stage 1  $r_1(x_1, d_1) = \phantom{0}2d_1$

Figure 18.4 shows a schematic of the problem.

As with the shortest-route problem in Section 18.1, we will apply a backward solution procedure; that is, we will begin by assuming that decisions have already been made for stages 4, 3, and 2 and that the final decision remains (how many jobs from category 1 to select at stage 1). A restatement of the principle of optimality can be made in terms of this problem. That is, regardless of whatever decisions have been made at previous stages, if the decision at stage $n$ is to be part of an optimal overall strategy, the decision made at stage $n$ must necessarily be optimal for all remaining stages.

Let us set up a table that will help us calculate the optimal decisions for stage 1.

Stage 1    Note that stage 1's input ($x_1$), the number of days of processing time available at stage 1, is unknown because we have not yet identified the decisions at the previous stages. Therefore, in our analysis at stage 1, we will have to consider all possible values of $x_1$ and identify the best decision $d_1$ for each case; $f_1(x_1)$ will be the total return after decision $d_1$ is made. The possible values of $x_1$ and the associated $d_1$ and $f_1(x_1)$ values are as follows:

| $x_1$ | $d_1^*$ | $f_1(x_1)$ |
|-------|---------|------------|
| 0 | 0 | 0 |
| 1 | 1 | 2 |
| 2 | 2 | 4 |
| 3 | 3 | 6 |
| 4 | 4 | 8 |
| 5 | 4 | 8 |
| 6 | 4 | 8 |
| 7 | 4 | 8 |
| 8 | 4 | 8 |
| 9 | 4 | 8 |
| 10 | 4 | 8 |

The $d_1^*$ column gives the optimal values of $d_1$ corresponding to a particular value of $x_1$, where $x_1$ can range from 0 to 10. The specific value of $x_1$ will depend on how much processing time has been used by the jobs in the other categories selected in stages 2, 3, and 4. Since each stage 1 job requires 1 day of processing time and has a positive return of 2 per job, we always select as many jobs at this stage as possible. The number of category 1 jobs selected will depend on the processing time available, but cannot exceed four.

Recall that $f_1(x_1)$ represents the value of the optimal total return from stage 1 and all remaining stages, given an input of $x_1$ to stage 1. Therefore, $f_1(x_1) = 2x_1$ for values of $x_1 \leq 4$, and $f_1(x_1) = 8$ for values of $x_1 > 4$. The optimization of stage 1 is accomplished. We now move on to stage 2 and carry out the optimization at that stage.

**Stage 2**  Again, we will use a table to help identify the optimal decision. Since stage 2's input $(x_2)$, is unknown, we have to consider all possible values from 0 to 10. Also, we have to consider all possible values of $d_2$ (i.e., 0, 1, 2, or 3). The entries under the heading $r_2(x_2, d_2) + f_1(x_1)$ represent the total return that will be forthcoming from the final two stages, given the input of $x_2$ and the decision

**Figure 18.4**  **DYNAMIC PROGRAMMING FORMULATION OF THE JOB SELECTION PROBLEM**

of $d_2$. For example, if stage 2 were entered with $x_2 = 7$ days of processing time remaining, and if a decision were made to select two jobs from category 2 (i.e., $d_2 = 2$), the total return for stages 1 and 2 would be 18.

| $d_2$ | $r_2(x_2, d_2) + f_1(x_1)$ | | | | | | $x_1 = t_2(x_2, d_2^*)$ | |
| $x_2$ | 0 | 1 | 2 | 3 | $d_2^*$ | $f_2(x_2)$ | $= x_2 - 3d_2^*$ |
|---|---|---|---|---|---|---|---|
| 0 | ⓪ | — | — | — | 0 | 0 | 0 |
| 1 | ② | — | — | — | 0 | 2 | 1 |
| 2 | ④ | — | — | — | 0 | 4 | 2 |
| 3 | 6 | ⑧ | — | — | 1 | 8 | 0 |
| 4 | 8 | ⑩ | — | — | 1 | 10 | 1 |
| 5 | 8 | ⑫ | — | — | 1 | 12 | 2 |
| 6 | 8 | 14 | ⑯ | — | 2 | 16 | 0 |
| 7 | 8 | 16 | ⑱ | — | 2 | 18 | 1 |
| 8 | 8 | 16 | ⑳ | — | 2 | 20 | 2 |
| 9 | 8 | 16 | 22 | ㉔ | 3 | 24 | 0 |
| 10 | 8 | 16 | 24 | ㉖ | 3 | 26 | 1 |

The return for stage 2 would be $r_2(x_2, d_2) = 8d_2 = 8(2) = 16$, and with $x_2 = 7$ and $d_2 = 2$, we would have $x_1 = x_2 - 3d_2 = 7 - 6 = 1$. From the previous table, we see that the optimal return from stage 1 with $x_1 = 1$ is $f_1(1) = 2$. Thus, the total return corresponding to $x_2 = 7$ and $d_2 = 2$ is given by $r_2(7,2) + f_1(1) = 16 + 2 = 18$. Similarly, with $x_2 = 5$, and $d_2 = 1$, we get $r_2(5,1) + f_1(2) = 8 + 4 = 12$. Note that some combinations of $x_2$ and $d_2$ are not feasible. For example, with $x_2 = 2$ days, $d_2 = 1$ is infeasible because category 2 jobs each require 3 days to process. The infeasible solutions are indicated by a dash.

After all the total returns in the rectangle have been calculated, we can determine an optimal decision at this stage for each possible value of the input or state variable $x_2$. For example, if $x_2 = 9$, we can select one of four possible values for $d_2$: 0, 1, 2, or 3. Clearly $d_3 = 3$ with a value of 24 yields the maximum total return for the last two stages. Therefore, we record this value in the $d_2^*$ column. For additional emphasis, we circle the element inside the rectangle corresponding to the optimal return. The optimal total return, given that we are in state $x_2 = 9$ and must pass through two more stages, is thus 24, and we record this value in the $f_2(x_2)$ column. Given that we enter stage 2 with $x_2 = 9$ and make the optimal decision there of $d_2^* = 3$, we will enter stage 1 with $x_1 = t_2(9, 3) = x_2 - 3d_2 = 9 - 3(3) = 0$. This value is recorded in the last column in the table. We can now go on to stage 3.

Stage 3   The table we construct here is much the same as for stage 2. The entries under the heading $r_3(x_3, d_3) + f_2(x_2)$ represent the total return over stages 3, 2, and 1 for all possible inputs $x_3$ and all possible decisions $d_3$.

| $d_3$ | $r_3(x_3, d_3) + f_2(x_2)$ | | | | | $x_2 = t_3(x_3, d_3^*)$ |
|---|---|---|---|---|---|---|
| $x_3$ | 0 | 1 | 2 | $d_3^*$ | $f_3(x_3)$ | $= x_3 - 4d_3^*$ |
| 0 | ⓪ | — | — | 0 | 0 | 0 |
| 1 | ② | — | — | 0 | 2 | 1 |
| 2 | ④ | — | — | 0 | 4 | 2 |
| 3 | ⑧ | — | — | 0 | 8 | 3 |
| 4 | 10 | ⑪ | — | 1 | 11 | 0 |
| 5 | 12 | ⑬ | — | 1 | 13 | 1 |
| 6 | ⑯ | 15 | — | 0 | 16 | 6 |
| 7 | 18 | ⑲ | — | 1 | 19 | 3 |
| 8 | 20 | 21 | ㉒ | 2 | 22 | 0 |
| 9 | ㉔ | 23 | ㉔ | 0,2 | 24 | 9,1 |
| 10 | 26 | ㉗ | 26 | 1 | 27 | 6 |

Some features of interest appear in this table that were not present at stage 2. We note that if the state variable $x_3 = 9$, then two possible decisions will lead to an optimal total return from stages 1, 2, and 3; that is, we may elect to process no jobs from category 3, in which case, we will obtain no return from stage 3, but will enter stage 2 with $x_2 = 9$. Since $f_2(9) = 24$, the selection of $d_3 = 0$ would result in a total return of 24. However, a selection of $d_3 = 2$ also leads to a total return of 24. We obtain a return of $11(d_3) = 11(2) = 22$ for stage 3 and a return of 2 for the remaining two stages since $x_2 = 1$. To show the available alternative optimal solutions at this stage, we have placed two entries in the $d_3^*$ and $x_2 = t_3(x_3, d_3^*)$ columns. The other entries in this table are calculated in the same manner as at stage 2. Let us now move on to the last stage.

Stage 4  We know that 10 days are available in the planning period; therefore, the input to stage 4 is $x_4 = 10$. Thus, we have to consider only one row in the table, corresponding to stage 4.

| $d_4$ | $r_4(x_4, d_4) + f_3(x_3)$ | | | | $x_3 = t_4(x_4, d_4^*)$ |
|---|---|---|---|---|---|
| $x_4$ | 0 | 1 | $d_4^*$ | $f_4(x_4)$ | $= 10 - 7d_4^*$ |
| 10 | 27 | ㉘ | 1 | 28 | 3 |

The optimal decision, given $x_4 = 10$, is $d_4^* = 1$.

We have completed the dynamic programming solution of this problem. To identify the overall optimal solution, we must now trace back through the tables, beginning at stage 4, the last stage considered. The optimal decision at stage 4 is $d_4^* = 1$. Thus, $x_3 = 10 - 7d_4^* = 3$, and we enter stage 3 with 3 days available for processing. With $x_3 = 3$, we see that the best decision at stage 3 is $d_3^* = 0$. Thus, we enter stage 2 with $x_2 = 3$. The optimal decision at stage 2 with $x_2 = 3$ is $d_2^* = 1$, resulting in $x_1 = 0$. Finally, the decision at stage 1 must be $d_1^* = 0$. The optimal strategy for the manufacturing operation is as follows:

| Decision | Return |
|---|---|
| $d_1^* = 0$ | 0 |
| $d_2^* = 1$ | 8 |
| $d_3^* = 0$ | 0 |
| $d_4^* = 1$ | 20 |
| Total | 28 |

We should schedule one job from category 2 and one job from category 4 for processing over the next 10 days.

Another advantage of the dynamic programming approach can now be illustrated. Suppose we wanted to schedule the jobs to be processed over an 8-day period only. We can solve this new problem simply by making a recalculation at stage 4. The new stage 4 table would appear as follows:

| $d_4$ $\backslash$ $x_4$ | $r_4(x_4, d_4) + f_3(x_3)$ | | | $d_4^*$ | $f_4(x_4)$ | $x_3 = t_4(x_4, d_4^*)$ $= 8 - 7d_4^*$ |
|---|---|---|---|---|---|---|
| | 0 | 1 | | | | |
| 8 | ㉒ | ㉒ | | 0,1 | 22 | 8,1 |

Actually, we are testing the sensitivity of the optimal solution to a change in the total number of days available for processing. We have here the case of alternative optimal solutions. One solution can be found by setting $d_4^* = 0$ and tracing through the tables. Doing so, we obtain the following:

| Decision | Return |
|---|---|
| $d_1^* = 0$ | 0 |
| $d_2^* = 0$ | 0 |
| $d_3^* = 2$ | 22 |
| $d_4^* = 0$ | 0 |
| Total | 22 |

A second optimal solution can be found by setting $d_4^* = 1$ and tracing back through the tables. Doing so, we obtain another solution (which has exactly the same total return):

| Decision | Return |
|---|---|
| $d_1^* = 1$ | 2 |
| $d_2^* = 0$ | 0 |
| $d_3^* = 0$ | 0 |
| $d_4^* = 1$ | 20 |
| Total | 22 |

Can you now solve a knapsack problem using dynamic programming? Try Problem 3.

From the shortest-route and the knapsack examples you should be familiar with the stage-by-stage solution procedure of dynamic programming. In the next section we show how dynamic programming can be used to solve a production and inventory control problem.

. . . . . . . . . . . . . . . . . . . . . . . . . . . . . . . . . . . . . . . . . . . . . . . . . . . . . . . . . . . . . . . . . . . . . . . . . . . . . . . . . . . . . . . . . . . . . . . . . . . . . . . . . . . . . . . . . . . . . . . . . ./  /. . . . . . . . . . . .

## 18.4    A PRODUCTION AND INVENTORY CONTROL PROBLEM

Suppose we have developed forecasts of the demand for a particular product over several periods and we would like to decide on a production quantity for each of the periods so that demand can be satisfied at a minimum cost. Two costs need to be considered: production costs and holding costs. We will assume that one production setup will be made each period; thus, setup costs will be constant. As a result, setup costs are not considered in the analysis.

We will allow the production and holding costs to vary across periods. This provision makes the model more flexible since it also allows for the possibility of using different facilities for production and storage in different periods. Production and storage capacity constraints, which may vary across periods, will be included in the model. We adopt the following notation:

$N$ = number of periods (stages in the dynamic programming formulation)

$D_n$ = demand during stage $n$; $n = 1, 2, \ldots, N$

$x_n$ = a state variable representing the amount of inventory on hand at the beginning of stage $n$; $n = 1, 2, \ldots, N$

$d_n$ = production quantity for stage $n$; $n = 1, 2, \ldots, N$

$P_n$ = production capacity in stage $n$; $n = 1, 2, \ldots, N$

$W_n$ = storage capacity at the end of stage $n$; $n = 1, 2, \ldots, N$

$C_n$ = production cost per unit in stage $n$; $n = 1, 2, \ldots, N$

$H_n$ = holding cost per unit of ending inventory for stage $n$; $n = 1, 2, \ldots, N$

We will develop the dynamic programming solution for a problem covering 3 months of operation. The data for the problem are presented in Table 18.3. We can think of each month as a stage in a dynamic programming formulation. Figure 18.5 shows a schematic of such a formulation. Note that the beginning inventory in January is one unit.

| *Table* 18.3 | PRODUCTION AND INVENTORY CONTROL PROBLEM DATA | | | | |
|---|---|---|---|---|---|
| | | Capacity | | Cost Per Unit | |
| Month | Demand | Production | Storage | Production | Holding |
| January | 2 | 3 | 2 | $175 | $30 |
| February | 3 | 2 | 3 | 150 | 30 |
| March | 3 | 3 | 2 | 200 | 40 |
| | The beginning inventory for January is one unit. | | | | |

**Figure 18.5     PRODUCTION AND INVENTORY CONTROL PROBLEM AS A THREE-STAGE DYNAMIC PROGRAMMING PROBLEM**

In Figure 18.5 we have numbered the periods backward; that is, stage 1 corresponds to March, stage 2 corresponds to February, and stage 3 corresponds to January. The stage transformation functions take the form of ending inventory = beginning inventory + production − demand. Thus, we have

$$x_3 = 1$$
$$x_2 = x_3 + d_3 - D_3 = x_3 + d_3 - 2$$
$$x_1 = x_2 + d_2 - D_2 = x_2 + d_2 - 3$$
$$x_0 = x_1 + d_1 - D_1 = x_1 + d_1 - 3$$

The return functions for each stage represent the sum of production and holding costs for the month. For example, in stage 1 (March), $r_1(x_1, d_1) = 200d_1 + 40(x_1 + d_1 - 3)$ represents the total production and holding costs for the period. The production costs are $200 per unit, and the holding costs are $40 per unit of ending inventory. The other return functions are

$$r_2(x_2, d_2) = 150d_2 + 30(x_2 + d_2 - 3) \qquad \text{Stage 2, February}$$
$$r_3(x_3, d_3) = 175d_3 + 30(x_3 + d_3 - 2) \qquad \text{Stage 3, January}$$

This problem is particularly interesting because three constraints must be satisfied at each stage as we perform the optimization procedure. The first constraint is that the ending inventory must be less than or equal to the warehouse capacity. Mathematically, we have

$$x_n + d_n - D_n \le W_n$$

or

$$x_n + d_n \le W_n + D_n \tag{18.1}$$

The second constraint is that the production level in each period may not exceed the production capacity. Mathematically, we have

$$d_n \le P_n \tag{18.2}$$

In order to satisfy demand, the third constraint is that the beginning inventory plus production must be greater than or equal to demand. Mathematically, this constraint can be written as

$$x_n + d_n \geq D_n \qquad (18.3)$$

Let us now begin the stagewise solution procedure. At each stage, we want to minimize $r_n(x_n, d_n) + f_{n-1}(x_{n-1})$ subject to the constraints given by equations (18.1), (18.2), and (18.3).

Stage 1  The stage 1 problem is as follows:

$$\text{Min} \quad r_1(x_1, d_1) = 200d_1 + 40(x_1 + d_1 - 3)$$

s.t.

$$x_1 + d_1 \leq 5 \quad \text{Warehouse constraint}$$
$$d_1 \leq 3 \quad \text{Production constraint}$$
$$x_1 + d_1 \geq 3 \quad \text{Satisfy demand constraint}$$

Combining terms in the objective function, we can rewrite the problem:

$$\text{Min} \quad r_1(x_1, d_1) = 240d_1 + 40x_1 - 120$$

s.t.

$$x_1 + d_1 \leq 5$$
$$d_1 \leq 3$$
$$x_1 + d_1 \geq 3$$

Following the tabular approach we adopted in Section 18.3, we will consider all possible inputs to stage 1 ($x_1$) and make the corresponding minimum-cost decision. Since we are attempting to minimize cost, we will want the decision variable $d_1$ to be as small as possible and still satisfy the demand constraint. Thus, the table for stage 1 is as follows:

Now let us proceed to stage 2.

Stage 2

$$\text{Min} \quad r_2(x_2, d_2) + f_1(x_1) = 150d_2 + 30(x_2 + d_2 - 3) + f_1(x_1)$$
$$= 180d_2 + 30x_2 - 90 + f_1(x_1)$$

s.t.

$$x_2 + d_2 \leq 6$$
$$d_2 \leq 2$$
$$x_2 + d_2 \geq 3$$

The stage 2 calculations are summarized in the following table:

| $d_2$ | $r_2(x_2, d_2) + f_1(x_1)$ | | | Production capacity of 2 for stage 2 | | |
|---|---|---|---|---|---|---|
| $x_2$ | 0 | 1 | 2 | $d_2^*$ | $f_2(x_2)$ | $x_1 = x_2 + d_2^* - 3$ |
| 0 | — | — | — | — | $M$ | — |
| 1 | — | — | (900) | 2 | 900 | 0 |
| 2 | — | 750 | (730) | 2 | 730 | 1 |

↑
Warehouse
capacity of 2
from stage 3

Check demand constraint $x_2 + d_2 \geq 3$ for
each $x_2$, $d_2$ combination
($-$indicates an infeasible solution)

The detailed calculations for $r_2(x_2, d_2) + f_1(x_1)$ when $x_2 = 1$ and $d_2 = 2$ are as follows:

$$r_2(1,2) + f_1(0) = 180(2) + 30(1) - 90 + 600 = 900$$

For $r_2(x_2, d_2) + f_1(x_1)$ when $x_2 = 2$ and $d_2 = 1$, we have

$$r_2(2,1) + f_1(0) = 180(1) + 30(2) - 90 + 600 = 750$$

For $x_2 = 2$ and $d_2 = 2$, we have

$$r_2(2,2) + f_1(1) = 180(2) + 30(2) - 90 + 400 = 730$$

Note that an arbitrarily high cost $M$ is assigned to the $f_2(x_2)$ column for $x_2 = 0$. Because an input of 0 to stage 2 does not provide a feasible solution, the $M$ cost associated with the $x_2 = 0$ input will prevent $x_2 = 0$ from occurring in the optimal solution.

Stage 3

$$\text{Min} \quad r_3(x_3, d_3) + f_2(x_2) = 175d_3 + 30(x_3 + d_3 - 2) + f_2(x_2)$$
$$= 205d_3 + 30x_3 - 60 + f_2(x_2)$$

s.t.

$$x_3 + d_3 \leq 4$$
$$d_3 \leq 3$$
$$x_3 + d_3 \geq 2$$

With $x_3 = 1$ already defined by the beginning inventory level, the table for stage 3 becomes

| $x_3$ | $d_3$ 0 | 1 | 2 | 3 | $d_3^*$ | $f_3(x_3)$ | $x_2 = x_3 + d_3^* - 2$ |
|---|---|---|---|---|---|---|---|
| 1 | — | $M$ | ⬭1280 | 1315 | 2 | 1280 | 1 |

*(column header: $r_3(x_3, d_3) + f_2(x_2)$ spanning 0–3; arrow to "Production capacity of 3 at stage 3")*

Try Problem 10 for practice using dynamic programming to solve a production and inventory control problem.

Thus, we find that the total cost associated with the optimal production and inventory policy is $1280. To find the optimal decisions and inventory levels for each period, we trace back through each stage and identify $x_n$ and $d_n^*$ as we go. Table 18.4 summarizes the optimal production and inventory policy.

**Table 18.4    OPTIMAL PRODUCTION AND INVENTORY CONTROL POLICY**

| Month | Beginning Inventory | Production | Production Cost | Ending Inventory | Holding Cost | Total Monthly Cost |
|---|---|---|---|---|---|---|
| January | 1 | 2 | $ 350 | 1 | $30 | $ 380 |
| February | 1 | 2 | 300 | 0 | 0 | 300 |
| March | 0 | 3 | 600 | 0 | 0 | 600 |
| | | Totals | $1250 | | $30 | $1280 |

**NOTES and Comments**

1. With dynamic programming, as with other management science techniques, the computer can be a valuable computational aid. However, because dynamic programming is a general approach with stage decision problems differing substantially from application to application, no one algorithm or computer software package is available for solving dynamic programs. Some software packages exist for specific types of problems; however, most new applications of dynamic programming will require specially designed software if a computer solution is to be obtained.

2. The introductory illustrations of dynamic programming presented in this chapter are deterministic and involve a finite number of decision alternatives and a finite number of stages. For problems such as these, computations can be organized and carried out in a tabular form. With this structure, the optimization problem at each stage can usually be solved by total enumeration of all possible outcomes. More complex dynamic programming models may include probabilistic components, continuous decision variables, and/or an infinite number of stages. In cases where the optimization problem at each stage involves continuous decision variables, linear programming or calculus-based procedures may be needed to obtain an optimal solution.

..................................................................................../  /............

## SUMMARY

Dynamic programming is an attractive approach to problem solving when it is possible to break a large problem up into interrelated smaller problems. The solution procedure then proceeds recursively, solving one of the smaller problems at each stage. Dynamic programming is not a specific algorithm, but rather an approach to problem solving. Thus, the recursive optimization may be carried out differently for different problems. In any case, it is almost always easier to solve a series of smaller problems than one large one. Through this process, dynamic programming obtains its power.

..................................................................................../  /............

## GLOSSARY

**Dynamic programming** An approach to problem solving that permits decomposing a large problem that may be difficult to solve into a number of interrelated smaller problems that are usually easier to solve.

**Principle of optimality** Regardless of the decisions that have been made at the previous stages, if the decision made at stage $n$ is to be part of an overall optimal solution, the decision made at stage $n$ must be optimal for all remaining stages.

**Stages** When a large problem is decomposed into a number of subproblems, the dynamic programming solution approach creates a stage to correspond to each of the subproblems.

**State variables $x_n$ and $x_{n-1}$** An input state variable $x_n$ and an output state variable $x_{n-1}$ together define the condition of the process at the beginning and end of stage $n$.

**Decision variable $d_n$** A variable representing the possible decisions that can be made at stage $n$.

**Stage transformation function $t_n(x_n, d_n)$** The rule or equation that relates the output state variable $x_{n-1}$ for stage $n$ to the input state variable $x_n$ and the decision variable $d_n$.

**Return function $r_n(x_n, d_n)$** A value (such as profit or loss) associated with making decision $d_n$ at stage $n$ for a specific value of the input state variable $x_n$.

**Knapsack problem** Finding the number of $N$ items, each of which has a different weight and value, that can be placed in a knapsack with limited weight capacity so as to maximize the total value of the items placed in the knapsack.

..................................................................................../  /............

## PROBLEMS

1. In Section 18.1 we solved a shortest-route problem using dynamic programming. Find the optimal solution to this problem by total enumeration; that is, list all 16 possible routes from the origin, node 1, to the destination, node 10, and pick the one with the smallest value. Explain why dynamic programming results in fewer computations for this problem.

2. Consider the following network. The numbers above each arc represent the distance between the connected nodes.

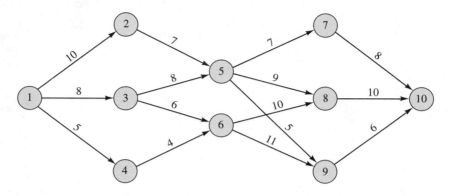

a. Find the shortest route from node 1 to node 10 using dynamic programming.
b. What is the shortest route from node 4 to node 10?
c. Enumerate all possible routes from node 1 to node 10. Explain how dynamic programming has reduced the number of computations to fewer than the number required by total enumeration.

3. A charter pilot has additional capacity for 2000 pounds of cargo on a flight from Dallas to Seattle. A transport company has four types of cargo in Dallas to be delivered to Seattle. The number of units of each cargo type, the weight per unit, and the delivery fee per unit are shown.

| Cargo Type | Units Available | Weight Per Unit (100 pounds) | Delivery Fee ($100) |
|---|---|---|---|
| 1 | 2 | 8 | 22 |
| 2 | 2 | 5 | 12 |
| 3 | 4 | 3 | 7 |
| 4 | 3 | 2 | 3 |

a. Use dynamic programming to find how many units of each cargo type the pilot should contract to deliver.
b. Suppose the pilot agrees to take another passenger and the additional cargo capacity is reduced to 1800 pounds. How does your recommendation change?

4. A firm has just hired eight new employees and would like to determine how to allocate their time to four activities. The firm has prepared the following table, which gives the estimated profit for each activity as a function of the number of new employees allocated to it:

| Activities | 0 | 1 | 2 | 3 | 4 | 5 | 6 | 7 | 8 |
|---|---|---|---|---|---|---|---|---|---|
| 1 | 22 | 30 | 37 | 44 | 49 | 54 | 58 | 60 | 61 |
| 2 | 30 | 40 | 48 | 55 | 59 | 62 | 64 | 66 | 67 |
| 3 | 46 | 52 | 56 | 59 | 62 | 65 | 67 | 68 | 69 |
| 4 | 5 | 22 | 36 | 48 | 52 | 55 | 58 | 60 | 61 |

Number of New Employees

    **a.** Use dynamic programming to determine the optimal allocation of new employees to the activities.

    **b.** Suppose only six new employees were hired. Which activities would you assign to these employees?

5. A sawmill receives logs in 20-foot lengths, cuts them to smaller lengths, and then sells these smaller lengths to a number of manufacturing companies. The company has orders for the following lengths:

$$l_1 = \phantom{1}3 \text{ ft}$$
$$l_2 = \phantom{1}7 \text{ ft}$$
$$l_3 = 11 \text{ ft}$$
$$l_4 = 16 \text{ ft}$$

The sawmill currently has an inventory of 2000 logs in 20-foot lengths and would like to select a cutting pattern that will maximize the profit made on this inventory. Assuming the sawmill has sufficient orders available, its problem becomes one of determining the cutting pattern that will maximize profits. The per-unit profit for each of the smaller lengths is as follows:

| Length (feet) | 3 | 7 | 11 | 16 |
|---|---|---|---|---|
| Profit ($) | 1 | 3 | 5 | 8 |

Any cutting pattern is permissible as long as

$$3d_1 + 7d_2 + 11d_3 + 16d_4 \leq 20$$

where $d_i$ is the number of pieces of length $l_i$ cut, $i = 1, 2, 3, 4$.

    **a.** Set up a dynamic programming model of this problem, and solve it. What are your decision variables? What is your state variable?

    **b.** Explain briefly how this model can be extended to find the best cutting pattern in cases where the overall length $l$ can be cut into $N$ lengths, $l_1, l_2, \ldots, l_N$.

6. A large manufacturing company has a well-developed management training program. Each trainee is expected to complete a four-phase program, but at each phase of the training program a trainee may be given a number of different assignments. The following assignments are available with their estimated completion times in months at each phase of the program.

| Phase I | Phase II | Phase III | Phase IV |
|---|---|---|---|
| A–13 | E–3 | H–12 | L–10 |
| B–10 | F–6 | I–6 | M–5 |
| C–20 | G–5 | J–7 | N–13 |
| D–17 | | K–10 | |

Assignments made at subsequent phases depend on the previous assignment. For example, a trainee who completes assignment A at phase I may only go on to assignment F or G at phase II—that is, a precedence relationship exists for each assignment.

| Assignment | Feasible Succeeding Assignments | Assignment | Feasible Succeeding Assignments |
|:---:|:---:|:---:|:---:|
| A | F, G | H | L, M |
| B | F | I | L, M |
| C | G | J | M, N |
| D | E, G | K | N |
| E | H, I, J, K | L | Finish |
| F | H, K | M | Finish |
| G | J, K | N | Finish |

a.  The company would like to determine the sequence of assignments that will minimize the time in the training program. Formulate and solve this problem as a dynamic programming problem. (*Hint:* Develop a network representation of the problem where each node represents completion of an activity.)

b.  If a trainee has just completed assignment F and would like to complete the remainder of the training program in the shortest possible time, which assignment should be chosen next?

7.  Crazy Robin, the owner of a small chain of Robin Hood Sporting Goods stores in Des Moines and Cedar Rapids, Iowa, has just purchased a new supply of 500 dozen top-line golf balls. Because she was willing to purchase the entire amount of a production overrun, Robin was able to buy the golf balls at one-half the usual price.

   Three of Robin's stores do a good business in the sale of golf equipment and supplies, and, as a result, Robin has decided to retail the balls at these three stores. Thus, Robin is faced with the problem of determining how many dozen balls to allocate to each store. The following estimates show the expected profit from allocating 100, 200, 300, 400, or 500 dozen to each store:

| | Number of Dozens of Golf Balls | | | | |
|:---:|:---:|:---:|:---:|:---:|:---:|
| Store | 100 | 200 | 300 | 400 | 500 |
| 1 | $600 | $1100 | $1550 | $1700 | $1800 |
| 2 | 500 | 1200 | 1700 | 2000 | 2100 |
| 3 | 550 | 1100 | 1500 | 1850 | 1950 |

Assuming the lots cannot be broken into any sizes smaller than 100 dozen each, how many dozen golf balls should Crazy Robin send to each store?

8.  The Max X. Posure Advertising Agency is conducting a 10-day advertising campaign for a local department store. The agency has determined that the most effective campaign would possibly include placing ads in four media: daily newspaper, Sunday newspaper, radio, and television. A total of $8000 has been made available for this campaign, and the agency would like to distribute this budget in $1000 increments across the media in such a fashion that an advertising exposure index is maximized. Research conducted by the agency permits the following estimates to be made of the exposure per each $1000 expenditure in each of the media.

| Media | **Thousands of Dollars Spent** | | | | | | | |
|---|---|---|---|---|---|---|---|---|
| | **1** | **2** | **3** | **4** | **5** | **6** | **7** | **8** |
| Daily newspaper | 24 | 37 | 46 | 59 | 72 | 80 | 82 | 82 |
| Sunday newspaper | 15 | 55 | 70 | 75 | 90 | 95 | 95 | 95 |
| Radio | 20 | 30 | 45 | 55 | 60 | 62 | 63 | 63 |
| Television | 20 | 40 | 55 | 65 | 70 | 70 | 70 | 70 |

a. How much should the agency spend on each medium to maximize the department store's exposure?

b. How would your answer change if only $6000 were budgeted?

c. How would your answers in parts (a) and (b) change if television were not considered as one of the media?

9. Suppose we have a three-stage process where the yield for each stage is a function of the decision made. In mathematical notation, we may state our problem as follows:

$$\text{Max} \quad r_1(d_1) + r_2(d_2) + r_3(d_3)$$

s.t.

$$d_1 + d_2 + d_3 \leq 1000$$

The possible values the decision variables may take on at each stage and the corresponding returns are as follows:

| **Stage 1** | | **Stage 2** | | **Stage 3** | |
|---|---|---|---|---|---|
| $d_1$ | $r_1(d_1)$ | $d_2$ | $r_2(d_2)$ | $d_3$ | $r_3(d_3)$ |
| 0 | 0 | 100 | 120 | 100 | 175 |
| 100 | 110 | 300 | 400 | 500 | 700 |
| 200 | 300 | 500 | 650 | | |
| 300 | 400 | 600 | 700 | | |
| 400 | 425 | 800 | 975 | | |

a. Use total enumeration to list all feasible sequences of decisions for this problem. Which one is optimal (i.e., maximizes $r_1(d_1) + r_2(d_2) + r_3(d_3)$)?

b. Use dynamic programming to solve this problem.

10. Recall the production and inventory control problem of Section 18.4. Mills Manufacturing Company has just such a production and inventory control problem for an armature the company manufactures as a component for a generator. The available data for the next 3-month planning period are as follows:

**SELF TEST**

| Month | Demand | **Capacity** | | **Cost Per Unit** | |
|---|---|---|---|---|---|
| | | Production | Warehouse | Production | Holding |
| 1 | 20 | 30 | 40 | $2.00 | $0.30 |
| 2 | 30 | 20 | 30 | 1.50 | 0.30 |
| 3 | 30 | 30 | 20 | 2.00 | 0.20 |

Use dynamic programming to find the optimal production quantities and inventory levels in each period for the Mills Manufacturing Company. Assume an inventory of 10 units on hand at the beginning of month 1 and production runs are completed in multiples of 10 units (i.e., 10, 20, or 30 units).

11. A chemical processing plant is considering introducing a new product. However, before making a final decision, management has requested that you provide estimates of profits associated with different process designs. The general flow process is represented:

Raw material is fed into a heater at the rate of 4500 pounds per week. The heated material is then routed to a reactor where a portion of the raw material is converted to pure product. A separator then withdraws the finished product for sale. The unconverted material is discarded as waste.

Profit considerations are to be based on a 2-year payback period on investments; that is, all capital expenditures must be recovered in 2 years (100 weeks). All calculations will be based on weekly operations. Raw material costs are expected to stay fixed at $1 per pound, and it has been forecast that the finished product will sell for $6 per pound.

It is your responsibility to determine the process design that will yield maximum profit per week. You and your co-workers have collected the following preliminary data.

One heater with an initial cost of $12,000 is being considered at stage 3. Two temperatures, 700°F and 800°F, are feasible. The operating costs for the heater depend directly on the temperature to be attained. These costs are as follows:

**Operating Costs at Stage 3**

| | Decisions at Stage 3 | |
| --- | --- | --- |
| Input $x_3$ | 700°F | 800°F |
| 4500 lb | $280/week | $380/week |

Stage 3's output $x_2$, which is also the input to stage 2, may be expressed as 4500 pounds of raw material heated to either 700°F or 800°F. One of the decisions you must make is to what temperature the raw material should be heated.

A reactor, which can operate with either of two catalysts, C1 or C2, is to be used for stage 2. The initial cost of this reactor is $50,000. The operating costs of this reactor are independent of the input $x_2$ and depend only on the catalyst selected. The costs of the catalysts are included in the operating costs. The output will be expressed in pounds of converted (or pure) material. The percentage of material converted depends on the incoming temperature and the catalyst used. The following tables summarize the pertinent information. Thus, a second decision you must make is to specify which catalyst should be used.

**Percent Conversion**

| | Decisions at Stage 2 | |
| --- | --- | --- |
| $x_2$ | C1 | C2 |
| (4500 lb, 700°F) | 20 | 40 |
| (4500 lb, 800°F) | 40 | 60 |

**Operating Costs Decision at Stage 2**

| C1 | C2 |
| --- | --- |
| $450/week | $650/week |

One of two separators, S1 or S2, will be purchased for stage 1. The S1 separator has an initial cost of $20,000 and a weekly operating cost of $0.10 per pound of pure product to be separated. Comparatively, S2 has an initial cost of $5000 and a weekly operating cost of $0.20. Included in these operating costs is the expense of discarding the unconverted raw material as waste.

Develop a dynamic programming model for this problem. What is your recommendation for the best temperature for the heater? The best catalyst to use with the reactor? The best separator to purchase? What is the maximum weekly profit?

# U.S. ENVIRONMENTAL PROTECTION AGENCY*

## WASHINGTON, D.C.

The U.S. Environmental Protection Agency (EPA) is an independent agency of the executive branch of the federal government. Fifteen components of five executive departments and independent agencies were consolidated to form the EPA on December 2, 1970, under Reorganization Plan No. 3 by President Nixon. Today, the EPA administers comprehensive environmental protection laws related to the following areas:

- Water pollution control, water quality, and drinking water
- Air pollution and radiation
- Pesticides and toxic substances
- Solid and hazardous waste, including emergency spill response and Superfund site remediation

Program offices for each of these media support the EPA administrator through policy development, standards and criteria development, and support and evaluation of regional activities. The ten regional offices implement and enforce standards, conduct monitoring and surveillance programs, and provide technical and financial assistance to state and local governments.

Functional activities at EPA headquarters, which transcend all media, include planning and management, enforcement, and research and development. Management science techniques are used extensively in the experimental design of research studies, providing quality assurance of monitoring surveys and enforcement actions, as well as environmental modeling and simulation studies to evaluate the cost effectiveness of alternative environmental policies, regulations, and control technologies.

*The authors are indebted to John Convery, Environmental Protection Agency, for providing this application.

The EPA's Office of Research and Development serves as the primary source of scientific and technical support to the agency's operating programs and regional offices by conducting in-house and extramural research at 14 locations throughout the country. Research activities focus on analytical methods, development and quality assurance, environmental processes and effects research, health effects research, and environmental engineering. Environmental modeling is conducted for all media at many of these research locations. The Office of Research and Development maintains a Center for Water Quality Modeling at its laboratory in Athens, Georgia. The following dynamic programming application was developed by the Municipal Environmental Research Laboratory in Cincinnati, Ohio, as part of an effort to evaluate the usefulness of seasonal discharge permits in reducing the cost of wastewater treatment while maintaining water quality.

## Water-Quality Management Program

The EPA administers programs designed to maintain acceptable water-quality conditions for rivers and streams throughout the United States. To guard against polluted rivers and streams, the government requires companies to obtain a discharge permit from federal or state authorities before any form of pollutants can be discharged into a body of water. These permits specifically notify each discharger as to the amount of legally dischargeable waste that can be placed in the river or stream. The discharge limits are determined by ensuring that water-quality criteria are met even in unusually dry seasons when the river or stream has a critically low flow condition. Most often, this condition is based on the lowest flow recorded over the past ten years. Ensuring that water quality is maintained under the low-flow conditions provides a high degree of reliability that the water-quality criteria can be maintained throughout the year.

At different seasons of the year, water will flow at different rates in the various rivers and streams. With these seasonal variations, seasonal discharge permits can be issued that allow different discharge limits at the different times of the year. As a result, companies can take advantage of higher stream flow rates to reduce treatment requirements and to lower the discharge treatment costs. A goal of the EPA is to establish seasonal discharge limits that enable lower treatment costs while maintaining water-quality standards at a prescribed level of reliability.

## A Dynamic Programming Model for Seasonal Discharge Limits

A dynamic programming model has been formulated for establishing the allowable waste discharge load during the various seasons of the year. The periods or stages of the model correspond to different seasons considered during the year, with a separate stage for each season. The return function at each stage is the cost of the treatment for waste discharged during that stage. The decision variable at each stage is the design stream flow for the body of water receiving the waste. Once the design stream flow has been established, an allowable waste discharge and its associated treatment cost can be determined. The design stream flow decisions at each stage interact to determine the overall reliability that the annual water-quality conditions will be maintained. In this regard, the decision variable choice at any one stage, or period, is affected by the decision variable choices at the other stages.

The probability of no water-quality violations over the entire year is the product of the seasonal probabilities of no violations. To maintain reliability standards, the probability of no violation during the year must exceed a certain value. Suppose we let $P_j(q_j)$ represent the probability of no violation during season $j$ when the design stream flow is $q_j$. Then the probability of no water-quality violation over the entire year is given by

$$\prod_{j=1}^{N} P_j(q_j) = \text{probability of no violation}$$

where $N$ is the number of seasons during the year.

The reliability requirement is satisfied when this probability is sufficiently high. Suppose $\alpha$ is the minimal acceptable probability. The water-quality constraint is then

$$\prod_{j=1}^{N} P_j(q_j) \geq \alpha$$

By taking the logarithm of both sides, this constraint can be written as

$$\sum_{j=1}^{N} \log P_j(q_j) \geq \log \alpha$$

The state variable at stage $j$ is then defined to be

$$s_j = \sum_{k=1}^{j} P_k(q_k)$$

The design stream flows (the decision variables) are chosen to minimize treatment cost subject to requirements that the allowable waste discharge be within given limits and that the state variable ensure sufficient reliability of no water-quality violations.

The solution to the model provides the design stream flows for each seasonal period. These stream flows combine with the water-quality criterion to establish the seasonal waste discharge load. With the return function measuring treatment cost, the model obtains the minimum-cost solution that will maintain the EPA water-quality standards.

## Questions

1. Suppose each of the four seasons has a probability of a water-quality violation of 0.01, 0.05, 0.02, and 0.01, respectively. What is the probability of no water-quality violation over the entire year?

2. Let $P_j$ = the probability of no water-quality violation in season $j$. Suppose there are three seasons. Write a constraint specifying that the minimal acceptable probability of no violation over the three seasons is 0.90.

# Appendixes

Developments in computer technology have been a major factor in making management science techniques available to decision makers. A software package called *The Management Scientist* has been prepared to accompany this text. Version 5.0 is now available for Windows 95, Windows 98, and Windows NT operating systems. This software can be used to solve problems in the text as well as small-scale problems encountered in practice. Using The Management Scientist will give you an understanding and appreciation of the role of the computer in applying management science to decision problems.

The Management Scientist contains twelve modules, or programs, that will enable you to solve problems in the following areas:

| | |
|---|---|
| Chapter 2–6 | Linear programming |
| Chapter 7 | Transportation and assignment |
| Chapter 8 | Integer linear programming |
| Chapter 9 | Shortest route and minimal spanning tree |
| Chapter 10 | PERT/CPM |
| Chapter 11 | Inventory models |
| Chapter 12 | Waiting line models |
| Chapter 14 | Decision analysis |
| Chapter 16 | Forecasting |
| Chatper 17 | Markov processes |

Use of The Management Scientist with the text is optional. Occasionally, we insert a figure in the text that shows the output The Management Scientist provides for a problem. However, familiarity with the use of the software is not necessary to understand the figure and the text material. The remainder of this appendix provides an overview of the features and the use of the software.

## Selecting a Module

After starting The Management Scientist, you will encounter the module selection screen as shown in Figure A.1. The choices provide access to the 12 modules. Simply click the desired module and select OK to load the requested module into the computer's memory.

## The File Menu

After a module is loaded, you will need to click the File menu to begin working with a problem. The File menu provides the following options.

**New**   Select this option to begin a new problem. Dialog boxes and input templates will guide you through the data input process.

**Open**   Select this option to retrieve a problem that has been previously saved. When the problem is selected it will be displayed on the screen so that you can verify the problem is the one you want to solve.

**Figure A.1**    MODULE SELECTION SCREEN FOR THE MANAGEMENT SCIENTIST

Select A Module

○  1. Linear Programming               ○   7. PERT/CPM
○  2. Transportation                   ○   8. Inventory
○  3. Assignment                       ○   9. Waiting Lines
○  4. Integer Linear Programming       ○  10. Decision Analysis
○  5. Shortest Route                   ○  11. Forecasting
○  6. Minimal Spanning Tree            ○  12. Markov Processes

OK

**Save**    Once a new problem has been entered, you may want to save it for future use or modification. The Save option will guide you through the naming and saving process. If you create a folder named Problems, the Open and Save options will take you automatically to the Problems folder.

**Change Modules**    This option returns control to the screen in Figure A.1 and another module may be selected.

**Exit**    This option will exit The Management Scientist.

### The Edit Menu

After a new problem has been solved, you may want to make one or more modifications to the problem before resolving. The Edit menu provides the option to display the problem and then make revisions in the problem before solving or saving. In the linear and integer programming modules, the Edit menu also has options to change the problem size by adding or deleting variables and adding or deleting constraints. Similar options to change the problem size are provided in the Edit menu of the transportation and assignment modules.

### The Solution Menu

The Solution menu provides two options.

**Solve**    This option solves the current problem and displays the solution on the screen.

**Print Solution**    Once the solution is on the screen, the Solution menu has the Print Solution option, which sends the solution to a printer or to a text file. If the text file option is used, the file can be accessed later by a word processor so that the solution output may be displayed as part of a solution report.

### Advice about Data Input

Any time a new problem is selected, the appropriate module will provide dialog boxes and forms for describing the features of the problem and for entering data. When using The Management Scientist, you may find the following data input suggestions helpful.

1. Do not enter commas (,) with your input data. For example, the value 104,000 should be entered with the six digits: 104000.
2. Do not enter the dollar sign ($) for profit or cost data. For example, a cost of $20.00 should be entered as 20.
3. Do not enter the percent sign (%) if percentage is requested. For example, 25% should be entered as 25, not 25% or .25.
4. Occasionally, a model may be formulated with fractional values such as $\frac{1}{4}$, $\frac{2}{3}$, $\frac{5}{6}$, and so on. The data input for The Management Scientist must be in decimal form. The fraction $\frac{1}{4}$ can be entered as .25. However, fractions such as $\frac{2}{3}$ and $\frac{5}{6}$ have repeating decimal forms. In these cases, we recommend the convention of rounding to five places such as .66667 and .83333.
5. Finally, we recommend that in general you attempt to scale extremely large input data so that smaller numbers may be input and operated on by the computer. For example, costs such as $2,500,000 may be scaled to 2.5 with the understanding that the data used in the problem reflect millions of dollars.

# APPENDIX B  AREAS FOR THE STANDARD NORMAL DISTRIBUTION

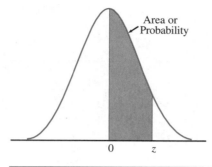

Area or Probability

Entries in the following table give the area under the curve between the mean and $z$ standard deviations above the mean. For example, for $z = 1.25$ the area under the curve between the mean and $z$ is 0.3944.

| z | 0.00 | 0.01 | 0.02 | 0.03 | 0.04 | 0.05 | 0.06 | 0.07 | 0.08 | 0.09 |
|---|---|---|---|---|---|---|---|---|---|---|
| 0.0 | 0.0000 | 0.0040 | 0.0080 | 0.0120 | 0.0160 | 0.0199 | 0.0239 | 0.0279 | 0.0319 | 0.0359 |
| 0.1 | 0.0398 | 0.0438 | 0.0478 | 0.0517 | 0.0557 | 0.0596 | 0.0636 | 0.0675 | 0.0714 | 0.0753 |
| 0.2 | 0.0793 | 0.0832 | 0.0871 | 0.0910 | 0.0948 | 0.0987 | 0.1026 | 0.1064 | 0.1103 | 0.1141 |
| 0.3 | 0.1179 | 0.1217 | 0.1255 | 0.1293 | 0.1331 | 0.1368 | 0.1406 | 0.1443 | 0.1480 | 0.1517 |
| 0.4 | 0.1554 | 0.1591 | 0.1628 | 0.1664 | 0.1700 | 0.1736 | 0.1772 | 0.1808 | 0.1844 | 0.1879 |
| 0.5 | 0.1915 | 0.1950 | 0.1985 | 0.2019 | 0.2054 | 0.2088 | 0.2123 | 0.2157 | 0.2190 | 0.2224 |
| 0.6 | 0.2257 | 0.2291 | 0.2324 | 0.2357 | 0.2389 | 0.2422 | 0.2454 | 0.2486 | 0.2518 | 0.2549 |
| 0.7 | 0.2580 | 0.2612 | 0.2642 | 0.2673 | 0.2704 | 0.2734 | 0.2764 | 0.2794 | 0.2823 | 0.2852 |
| 0.8 | 0.2881 | 0.2910 | 0.2939 | 0.2967 | 0.2995 | 0.3023 | 0.3051 | 0.3078 | 0.3106 | 0.3133 |
| 0.9 | 0.3159 | 0.3186 | 0.3212 | 0.3238 | 0.3264 | 0.3289 | 0.3315 | 0.3340 | 0.3365 | 0.3389 |
| 1.0 | 0.3413 | 0.3438 | 0.3461 | 0.3485 | 0.3508 | 0.3531 | 0.3554 | 0.3577 | 0.3599 | 0.3621 |
| 1.1 | 0.3643 | 0.3665 | 0.3686 | 0.3708 | 0.3729 | 0.3749 | 0.3770 | 0.3790 | 0.3810 | 0.3830 |
| 1.2 | 0.3849 | 0.3869 | 0.3888 | 0.3907 | 0.3925 | 0.3944 | 0.3962 | 0.3980 | 0.3997 | 0.4015 |
| 1.3 | 0.4032 | 0.4049 | 0.4066 | 0.4082 | 0.4099 | 0.4115 | 0.4131 | 0.4147 | 0.4162 | 0.4177 |
| 1.4 | 0.4192 | 0.4207 | 0.4222 | 0.4236 | 0.4251 | 0.4265 | 0.4279 | 0.4292 | 0.4306 | 0.4319 |
| 1.5 | 0.4332 | 0.4345 | 0.4357 | 0.4370 | 0.4382 | 0.4394 | 0.4406 | 0.4418 | 0.4429 | 0.4441 |
| 1.6 | 0.4452 | 0.4463 | 0.4474 | 0.4484 | 0.4495 | 0.4505 | 0.4515 | 0.4525 | 0.4535 | 0.4545 |
| 1.7 | 0.4554 | 0.4564 | 0.4573 | 0.4582 | 0.4591 | 0.4599 | 0.4608 | 0.4616 | 0.4625 | 0.4633 |
| 1.8 | 0.4641 | 0.4649 | 0.4656 | 0.4664 | 0.4671 | 0.4678 | 0.4686 | 0.4693 | 0.4699 | 0.4706 |
| 1.9 | 0.4713 | 0.4719 | 0.4726 | 0.4732 | 0.4738 | 0.4744 | 0.4750 | 0.4756 | 0.4761 | 0.4767 |
| 2.0 | 0.4772 | 0.4778 | 0.4783 | 0.4788 | 0.4793 | 0.4798 | 0.4803 | 0.4808 | 0.4812 | 0.4817 |
| 2.1 | 0.4821 | 0.4826 | 0.4830 | 0.4834 | 0.4838 | 0.4842 | 0.4846 | 0.4850 | 0.4854 | 0.4857 |
| 2.2 | 0.4861 | 0.4864 | 0.4868 | 0.4871 | 0.4875 | 0.4878 | 0.4881 | 0.4884 | 0.4887 | 0.4890 |
| 2.3 | 0.4893 | 0.4896 | 0.4898 | 0.4901 | 0.4904 | 0.4906 | 0.4909 | 0.4911 | 0.4913 | 0.4916 |
| 2.4 | 0.4918 | 0.4920 | 0.4922 | 0.4925 | 0.4927 | 0.4929 | 0.4931 | 0.4932 | 0.4934 | 0.4936 |
| 2.5 | 0.4938 | 0.4940 | 0.4941 | 0.4943 | 0.4945 | 0.4946 | 0.4948 | 0.4949 | 0.4951 | 0.4952 |
| 2.6 | 0.4953 | 0.4955 | 0.4956 | 0.4957 | 0.4959 | 0.4960 | 0.4961 | 0.4962 | 0.4963 | 0.4964 |
| 2.7 | 0.4965 | 0.4966 | 0.4967 | 0.4968 | 0.4969 | 0.4970 | 0.4971 | 0.4972 | 0.4973 | 0.4974 |
| 2.8 | 0.4974 | 0.4975 | 0.4976 | 0.4977 | 0.4977 | 0.4978 | 0.4979 | 0.4979 | 0.4980 | 0.4981 |
| 2.9 | 0.4981 | 0.4982 | 0.4982 | 0.4983 | 0.4984 | 0.4984 | 0.4985 | 0.4985 | 0.4986 | 0.4986 |
| 3.0 | 0.4986 | 0.4987 | 0.4987 | 0.4988 | 0.4988 | 0.4989 | 0.4989 | 0.4989 | 0.4990 | 0.4990 |

| $\lambda$ | $e^{-\lambda}$ | $\lambda$ | $e^{-\lambda}$ | $\lambda$ | $e^{-\lambda}$ |
|------|--------|------|--------|-------|----------|
| 0.05 | 0.9512 | 2.05 | 0.1287 | 4.05 | 0.0174 |
| 0.10 | 0.9048 | 2.10 | 0.1225 | 4.10 | 0.0166 |
| 0.15 | 0.8607 | 2.15 | 0.1165 | 4.15 | 0.0158 |
| 0.20 | 0.8187 | 2.20 | 0.1108 | 4.20 | 0.0150 |
| 0.25 | 0.7788 | 2.25 | 0.1054 | 4.25 | 0.0143 |
| 0.30 | 0.7408 | 2.30 | 0.1003 | 4.30 | 0.0136 |
| 0.35 | 0.7047 | 2.35 | 0.0954 | 4.35 | 0.0129 |
| 0.40 | 0.6703 | 2.40 | 0.0907 | 4.40 | 0.0123 |
| 0.45 | 0.6376 | 2.45 | 0.0863 | 4.45 | 0.0117 |
| 0.50 | 0.6065 | 2.50 | 0.0821 | 4.50 | 0.0111 |
| 0.55 | 0.5769 | 2.55 | 0.0781 | 4.55 | 0.0106 |
| 0.60 | 0.5488 | 2.60 | 0.0743 | 4.60 | 0.0101 |
| 0.65 | 0.5220 | 2.65 | 0.0707 | 4.65 | 0.0096 |
| 0.70 | 0.4966 | 2.70 | 0.0672 | 4.70 | 0.0091 |
| 0.75 | 0.4724 | 2.75 | 0.0639 | 4.75 | 0.0087 |
| 0.80 | 0.4493 | 2.80 | 0.0608 | 4.80 | 0.0082 |
| 0.85 | 0.4274 | 2.85 | 0.0578 | 4.85 | 0.0078 |
| 0.90 | 0.4066 | 2.90 | 0.0550 | 4.90 | 0.0074 |
| 0.95 | 0.3867 | 2.95 | 0.0523 | 4.95 | 0.0071 |
| 1.00 | 0.3679 | 3.00 | 0.0498 | 5.00 | 0.0067 |
| 1.05 | 0.3499 | 3.05 | 0.0474 | 5.05 | 0.0064 |
| 1.10 | 0.3329 | 3.10 | 0.0450 | 5.10 | 0.0061 |
| 1.15 | 0.3166 | 3.15 | 0.0429 | 5.15 | 0.0058 |
| 1.20 | 0.3012 | 3.20 | 0.0408 | 5.20 | 0.0055 |
| 1.25 | 0.2865 | 3.25 | 0.0388 | 5.25 | 0.0052 |
| 1.30 | 0.2725 | 3.30 | 0.0369 | 5.30 | 0.0050 |
| 1.35 | 0.2592 | 3.35 | 0.0351 | 5.35 | 0.0047 |
| 1.40 | 0.2466 | 3.40 | 0.0334 | 5.40 | 0.0045 |
| 1.45 | 0.2346 | 3.45 | 0.0317 | 5.45 | 0.0043 |
| 1.50 | 0.2231 | 3.50 | 0.0302 | 5.50 | 0.0041 |
| 1.55 | 0.2122 | 3.55 | 0.0287 | 5.55 | 0.0039 |
| 1.60 | 0.2019 | 3.60 | 0.0273 | 5.60 | 0.0037 |
| 1.65 | 0.1920 | 3.65 | 0.0260 | 5.65 | 0.0035 |
| 1.70 | 0.1827 | 3.70 | 0.0247 | 5.70 | 0.0033 |
| 1.75 | 0.1738 | 3.75 | 0.0235 | 5.75 | 0.0032 |
| 1.80 | 0.1653 | 3.80 | 0.0224 | 5.80 | 0.0030 |
| 1.85 | 0.1572 | 3.85 | 0.0213 | 5.85 | 0.0029 |
| 1.90 | 0.1496 | 3.90 | 0.0202 | 5.90 | 0.0027 |
| 1.95 | 0.1423 | 3.95 | 0.0193 | 5.95 | 0.0026 |
| 2.00 | 0.1353 | 4.00 | 0.0183 | 6.00 | 0.0025 |
|      |        |      |        | 7.00 | 0.0009 |
|      |        |      |        | 8.00 | 0.000335 |
|      |        |      |        | 9.00 | 0.000123 |
|      |        |      |        | 10.00 | 0.000045 |

# Chapter 1   Introduction

Churchman, C. W., R. L. Ackoff, and E. L. Arnoff. *Introduction to Operations Research.* Wiley, 1957.

Leon, Linda, Z. Przasnyski, and K. C. Seal. "Spreadsheets and OR/MS Models: An End-User Perspective," *Interfaces* (March–April 1996).

Powell, S. G. "Innovative Approaches to Management Science," *OR/MS Today* (October 1996).

Savage, S. "Weighing the Pros and Cons of Decision Technology and Spreadsheets," *OR/MS Today* (February 1997).

Winston, W. L. "The Teachers' Forum: Management Science with Spreadsheets for MBAs at Indiana University," *Interfaces* (March–April 1996).

# Chapters 2 to 8   Linear Programming, Transportation, Assignment, Transshipment, and Integer Programming Problems

Bazarra, M. S., J. J. Jarvis, and H. D. Sherali. *Linear Programming and Network Flows,* 2d ed. Wiley, 1990.

Carino, H. F., and C. H. Le Noir, Jr. "Optimizing Wood Procurement in Cabinet Manufacturing," *Interfaces* (March–April 1988): 10–19.

Dantzig, G. B. *Linear Programming and Extensions.* Princeton University Press, 1963.

Geoffrion, A., and G. Graves. "Better Distribution Planning with Computer Models," *Harvard Business Review* (July–August 1976).

Greenberg, H. J. "How to Analyze the Results of Linear Programs—Part 1: Preliminaries," *Interfaces* 23, no. 4 (July–August 1993): 56–67.

Greenberg, H. J. "How to Analyze the Results of Linear Programs—Part 2: Price Interpretation," *Interfaces* 23, no. 5 (September–October 1993): 97–114.

Greenberg, H. J. "How to Analyze the Results of Linear Programs—Part 3: Infeasibility Diagnosis," *Interfaces* 23, no. 6 (November–December 1993): 120–139.

Nemhauser, G. L. and L. A. Wolsey. *Integer and Combinatorial Optimization.* Wiley, 1988.

Sherman, H. D. "Hospital Efficiency Measurement and Evaluation," *Medical Care* 22, no. 10 (October 1984): 922–938.

Winston, W. L. *Operations Research: Applications and Algorithms,* 3d ed. Duxbury Press, 1994.

# Chapter 9   Network Models

Bazaraa, M. S., J. J. Jarvis, and H. D. Sherali. *Linear Programming and Network Flows,* 2d ed. Wiley, 1990.

Evans, J. R., and E. Minieka. *Optimization Algorithms for Networks and Graphs,* 2d ed. Marcel Dekker, 1992.

Ford, L. R., and D. R. Fulkerson. *Flows and Networks.* Princeton University Press, 1962.

Glover, F., and D. Klingman. "Network Applications in Industry and Government," *AIIE Transactions* (December 1977).

Jensen, P. A., and W. J. Barnes. *Network Flow Programming.* Krieger, 1987.

# Chapter 10   Project Scheduling: PERT/CPM

Moder, J. J., C. R. Phillips, and E. W. Davis. *Project Management with CPM, PERT and Precedence Diagramming,* 3d ed. Blitz, 1995.

Wasil, E. A., and A. A. Assad. "Project Management on the PC: Software, Applications, and Trends," *Interfaces,* 18, no. 2 (March–April 1988): 75–84.

Wiest, J., and F. Levy. *Management Guide to PERT-CPM,* 2d ed. Prentice-Hall, 1977.

# Chapter 11   Inventory Models

Fogarty, D. W., J. H. Blackstone, and T. R. Hoffman. *Production and Inventory Management,* 2d ed. South-Western, 1990.

Hillier, F., and G. J. Lieberman. *Introduction to Operations Research,* 6th ed. McGraw-Hill, 1995.

Narasimhan, S. L., D. W. McLeavey, and P. B. Lington. *Production Planning and Inventory Control,* 2d ed. Prentice Hall, 1995.

Orlicky, J., and G. W. Plossi. *Orlicky's Material Requirements Planning.* McGraw-Hill, 1994.

Vollmann, T. E., W. L. Berry, and D. C. Whybark. *Manufacturing Planning and Control Systems,* 4th ed. McGraw-Hill, 1997.

# Chapter 12   Waiting Lines

Bunday, B. D. *An Introduction to Queueing Theory.* Wiley, 1996.

Gross, D., and C. M. Harris. *Fundamentals of Queueing Theory,* 3d ed. Wiley, 1997.

Hall, R. W. *Queueing Methods: For Service and Manufacturing.* Prentice-Hall, 1991.

Hillier, F., and G. J. Lieberman. *Introduction to Operations Research,* 6th ed. McGraw-Hill, 1995.

Kao, E. P. C. *An Introduction to Stochastic Processes.* Duxbury, 1996.

Saaty, T. *Elements of Queueing with Applications.* Dover, 1983.

## Chapter 13    Simulation

Banks, J., J. S. Carson, and B. L. Nelson. *Discrete-Event System Simulation,* 2d ed. Prentice-Hall, 1995.

Fishwick, P. A. *Simulation Model Design and Execution: Building Digital Worlds.* Prentice-Hall, 1995.

Harrell, C. R., and K. Tumau. *Simulation Made Easy: A Manager's Guide.* Institute of Industrial Engineers, 1996.

Kelton, W. D., R. P. Sadowski, and D. A. Sadowski. *Simulation with Anema.* McGraw-Hill, 1998.

Law, A. M., and W. D. Kelton. *Simulation Modeling and Analysis,* 2d ed. McGraw-Hill, 1991.

Pidd, M. *Computer Simulation in Management Science,* 4th ed. Wiley, 1998.

Thesen, A., and L. E. Travis. *Simulation for Decision Making.* Wadsworth, 1992.

## Chapter 14    Decision Analysis

Berger, J. O., *Statistical Decision Theory and Bayesian Analysis,* 2d ed. Springer-Verlag, 1985.

Chernoff, H. and L. E. Moses. *Elementary Decision Theory.* Dover, 1987.

Goodwin, P. and G. Wright. *Decision Analysis for Management Judgment.* Wiley, 1997.

Gregory, G. *Decision Analysis.* Plenum, 1988.

Pratt, J. W., H. Raiffa, and R. Schlaiter. *Introduction to Statistical Decision Theory.* MIT Press, 1995.

Raiffa, H. *Decision Analysis.* McGraw-Hill, 1997.

Schlaiter, R. *Analysis of Decisions Under Uncertainty.* Krieger, 1978.

## Chapter 15    Multicriteria Decision Problems

Dyer, J. S. "A Clarification of Remarks on the Analytic Hierarchy Process," *Management Science* 36, no. 3 (March 1990): 274–275.

Dyer, J. S. "Remarks on the Analytic Hierarchy Process," *Management Science* 36, no. 3 (March 1990): 249–258.

Harker, P. T., and L. G. Vargas. "The Theory of Ratio Scale Estimation: Saaty's Analytic Hierarchy Process," *Management Science* 33, no. 11 (November 1987): 1383–1403.

Harker, P. T., and L. G. Vargas. "Reply to Remarks on the Analytic Hierarchy Process by J. S. Dyer," *Management Science* 36, no. 3 (March 1990): 269–273.

Ignizio, J. *Introduction to Linear Goal Programming.* Sage, 1986.

Keeney, R. L., and H. Raiffa. *Decisions with Multiple Objectives: Preferences and Value Tradeoffs.* Cambridge, 1993.

Saaty, T. *Decision Making for Leaders: The Analytic Hierarchy Process for Decisions in a Complex World,* 3d ed. RWS, 1995.

Saaty, T., and L. Vargas. *Fundamentals of Decision Making and Priority Theory with the Analytic Hierarchy Process.* RWS, 1994.

Saaty, T. *Multicriteria Decision Making,* 2d ed. RWS, 1996.

Saaty, T. L. "An Exposition of the AHP in Reply to the Paper Remarks on the Analytic Hierarchy Process," *Management Science* 36, no. 3 (March 1990): 259–268.

Saaty, T. L. "Rank Generation, Preservation, and Reversal in the Analytic Hierarchy Decision Process," *Decision Sciences* 18 (1987): 157–177.

Winkler, R. L. "Decision Modeling and Rational Choice: AHP and Utility Theory," *Management Science* 36, no. 3 (March 1990): 247–248.

## Chapter 16    Forecasting

Bowerman, B. L., and R. T. O'Connell. *Forecasting and Time Series: An Applied Approach,* 3d ed. Duxbury, 1993.

Box, G. E. P., G. M. Jenkins, and G. C. Reinsel. *Time Series Analysis: Forecasting and Control,* 3d ed. Prentice-Hall, 1994.

Hanke, J. E., and A. G. Reitsch. *Business Forecasting,* 6th ed. Prentice-Hall, 1998.

Makridakis, S. G., S. C. Wheelwright, and R. J. Hyndman. *Forecasting: Methods and Applications,* 3d ed. Wiley, 1997.

Wilson, J. H., and B. Keating. *Business Forecasting,* 3d ed. Irwin, 1998.

## Chapter 17    Markov Processes

Bharucha-Reid, A. T. *Elements of the Theory of Markov Processes and Their Applications.* Dover, 1997.

Bhat, U. N., *Elements of Applied Stochastic Processes,* 2d ed. Wiley, 1984.

Filar, J. A. and K. Vrieze. *Competitive Markov Decision Processes.* Springer-Verlag, 1996.

Norris, J. *Markov Chains.* Cambridge, 1997.

## Chapter 18    Dynamic Programming

Bellman, R. E. *Dynamic Programming and Modern Control.* Academic Press, 1966.

Bertsekas, D. P. *Dynamic Programming and Optimal Control,* vol. 1 and 2. Athena Scientific, 1995.

Dreyfus, S. E., *The Art and Theory of Dynamic Programming.* Academic Press, 1977.

Nemhauser, G. L. *Introduction to Dynamic Programming.* Wiley, 1966.

## Chapter 1

**2.** Methodological developments based on research advances in computer technology.

**4.** The problem is large, complex, important, new, and repetitive

**6.** Iconic—scale model of a new building
Analog—barometer
Mathematical—inventory cost equation

**8. a.** Max $10x + 5y$
s.t.
$$5x + 2y \le 40$$
$$x \ge 0, y \ge 0$$

**b.** Controllable inputs: $x$ and $y$
Uncontrollable inputs: profit, labor-hours per unit, and total labor-hours available

**d.** $x = 0, y = 20$, profit $= \$100$

**10.** If $a = 3$, $x = 13\frac{1}{3}$ and profit $= \$133$
If $a = 4$, $x = 10$ and profit $= \$100$
If $a = 5$, $x = 8$ and profit $= \$80$
If $a = 6$, $x = 6\frac{2}{3}$ and profit $= \$67$

**12.** A deterministic model with $d =$ distance, $m =$ miles per gallon, and $c =$ cost per gallon, where total cost $= (2d/m)c$

**14.** Quicker to formulate, easier to solve, and/or more easily understood

**16. a.** 4706
**b.** Loss $12,000
**c.** $23
**d.** $11,800

**18. a.** Max $6x + 4y$
**b.** $50x + 30y \le 80,000$
$50x \qquad \le 50,000$
$\qquad 30y \le 45,000$

## Chapter 2

**6.** $-\frac{7}{10}, -\frac{3}{2}, \frac{4}{7}$

**10.** $x_1 = \frac{12}{7}, x_2 = \frac{15}{7}$, Value of optimal solution $= \frac{69}{7}$

**12. a.** $x_1 = 3, x_2 = 1.5$, Value of optimal solution $= 13.5$
**b.** $x_1 = 0, x_2 = 3$, Value of optimal solution $= 18$
**c.** four: (0, 0), (4, 0), (3, 1.5), and (0.3)

**14. a.** Feasible region consists of a line segment
**b.** (5, 1) and (2, 4)
**c.** $x_1 = 2, x_2 = 4$

**16. a.** $S = 300, D = 420$, Value of optimal solution $= 10,560$
**b.** $S = 708, D = 0$, Value of optimal solution $= 14,160$
**c.** Sewing constraint is redundant; optimal solution is still $S = 540, D = 252$

**20. b.** $x_1 = \frac{20}{3}, x_2 = \frac{8}{3}$, Value of optimal solution $= 30\frac{2}{3}$
**c.** $s_1 = \frac{28}{3}, s_2 = 0, s_3 = 0$

**22. a.** Max $5R + 8C$
s.t.
$$1R + \tfrac{3}{2}C \le 900$$
$$\tfrac{1}{2}R + \tfrac{1}{3}C \le 300$$
$$\tfrac{1}{8}R + \tfrac{1}{4}C \le 100$$
$$R, C \ge 0$$

**b.** $R = 500, C = 150$
**c.** $3700
**d.** 725, 300, 100
**e.** 175, 0, 0

**24. a.** Max $50N + 80R$
s.t.
$$N + R = 1000$$
$$N \qquad \ge 250$$
$$R \ge 250$$
$$N - 2R \ge 0$$
$$N, R \ge 0$$

**b.** $N = 666.67, R = 333.33$, Audience exposure $= 60,000$

**26. a.** Max $1W + 1.25M$
s.t.
$$5W + 7M \le 4480$$
$$3W + 1M \le 2080$$
$$2W + 2M \le 1600$$
$$W, M \ge 0$$

**d.** $W = 560, M = 240$, Profit $= 860$

**28. a.** Max $15E + 18C$
s.t.
$$40E + 25C \le 50,000$$
$$40E \qquad \ge 15,000$$
$$25C \ge 10,000$$
$$25C \le 25,000$$
$$E, C \ge 0$$

**c.** (375, 400); (1000, 400); (625, 1000); (375, 1000)
**d.** $E = 625, C = 1000$
Total return $= \$27,375$

**30.**

| Extreme Points | Objective Function Value | Surplus Demand | Surplus Total Production | Slack Processing Time |
|---|---|---|---|---|
| (250, 100) | 800 | 125 | — | — |
| (125, 225) | 925 | — | — | 125 |
| (125, 350) | 1300 | — | 125 | — |

**32. b.** $(4, 1)$, $(21/4, 9/4)$
    **c.** $x_1 = 4$, $x_2 = 1$

**34. a.** Min    $10,000T + 8,000P$
    s.t.

$$T \geq 8$$
$$P \geq 10$$
$$T + P \geq 25$$
$$3T + 2P \leq 84$$

    **c.** $(15, 10)$; $(21.33, 10)$; $(8, 30)$; $(8, 17)$
    **d.** $T = 8$, $P = 17$,
         Total cost = \$216,000

**36. a.** Min    $2.5A + 2B$
    s.t.

$$2A + 1.5B \geq 1.7$$
$$2A + 3B \leq 2.8$$
$$4A + 3B \leq 3.6$$
$$A + B = 1$$
$$A, B \geq 0$$

    **b.** $A = 0.6$, $B = 0.4$, Cost = \$0.022
    **c.** $0.1, 0.4, 0, 0$
    **d.** \$0.176

**38.** $P_1 = 30$, $P_2 = 25$, Cost = \$55

**40.** Infeasibility

**42. a.** $x_1 = 30/16$, $x_2 = 30/16$, Value of optimal solution = $60/16$
    **b.** $x_1 = 0$, $x_2 = 3$, Value of optimal solution = 6
    **c.** Max $x_1 + 5/3 x_2$

**44. a.** 180, 20
    **b.** Alternative optimal solutions
    **c.** 120, 80

**46.** No feasible solution

**48. a.** No feasible region
    **b.** Need an additional 1.5 tons of material 3.

**50.** $M = 65.45$, $R = 261.82$, Profit = \$45,818

**52.** $S = 384$, $O = 80$

**54. a.** Max    $160M_1 + 345M_2$
    s.t.

$$M_1 + M_2 \leq 15$$
$$M_2 \leq 10$$
$$M_1 \geq 5$$
$$M_2 \geq 5$$
$$40M_1 + 50M_2 \leq 1000$$
$$M_1, M_2 \geq 0$$

    **b.** $M_1 = 12.5$, $M_2 = 10$

## Chapter 3

**2.** New optimal solution is $F = 100/3$ and $S = 40/3$
    Dual price for the material 3 constraint is \$44.44

**4.** 1.5, 0

**6.** $-0.333, -0.333, 0$

**8. a.** $x_1 = 9$, $x_2 = 4$
    **b.** 0, 0.0769

**10. a.** $x_1 = 0$, $x_2 = 10$, Value = 100
    **b.** No change

**12. a.** 4 to 12 and 3.33 to 10
    **c.** 725 to No Upper Limit; 133.33 to 400; 75 to 135
    **d.** \$560

**14. a.** More than \$7.00
    **b.** More than \$3.50
    **c.** None

**16. a.** $S = 4000$; $M = 10,000$; Total risk = 62,000
    **b.** 3.75 to No Upper Limit and No Lower Limit to 6.4
    **c.** \$60,000
    **d.** 5%
    **e.** 0.057 risk units
    **f.** 5.7%

**18. a.** 0, 25, 125, 0; Value = 525.0
    **b.** A and C
    **c.** B; 425 hours
    **d.** Yes

**20. a.** 7.30, 0, 1.89; Value = 139.73
    **b.** Two and three
    **c.** $0, -3.41, -4.43$
    **d.** Decrease the right-hand side of constraint three from 20 to 19

**22. a.** All Pro: 1000; College: 200; High School: 0
    **b.** Sewing and minimum All Pro production requirement
    **c.** 4000 minutes of unused cutting and dyeing time; all the sewing time is being used; 5200 minutes of unused inspection and packaging time; only the minimum number of the All Pro model is being produced
    **d.** No Lower Limit to 5; 5 to No Upper Limit; No Lower Limit to 4

**24. a.** Max   $0.07H + 0.12P + 0.09A$
s.t.

$$H + P + A = 1{,}000{,}000$$
$$0.6H - 0.4P - 0.4A \geq 0$$
$$P - 0.6A \leq 0$$
$$H, P, A \geq 0$$

**b.** $H = \$400{,}000$, $P = \$225{,}000$, $A = \$375{,}000$
Total annual return $= \$88{,}750$
Annual percentage return $= 8.875\%$

**c.** No change

**d.** Increase of $890

**e.** Increase of $312.50 or 0.031%

**26. a.** Min   $30L + 25D + 18S$
s.t.

$$L + D + S = 100$$
$$0.6L - 0.4D \geq 0$$
$$-0.15L - 0.15D + 0.85S \geq 0$$
$$-0.25L - 0.25D + S \leq 0$$
$$L \leq 50$$
$$L, D, S \geq 0$$

**b.** $L = 48$, $D = 72$, $S = 30$
Total cost $= \$3780$

**c.** No change

**d.** No change

**28. a.** 333.3, 0, 833.3; Risk $= 14{,}666.7$; Return $= 18{,}000$ or 9%

**b.** 1000, 0, 0, 2500; Risk $= 18{,}000$; Return $= 22{,}000$ or 11%

**c.** $4000

**30. a.**

|  | Manufacture | Purchase |
|---|---|---|
| Base | 3750 | 1250 |
| Cartridge | 5000 | 0 |
| Handle | 3750 | 1250 |

**b.** A and B

**c.**

|  | Manufacture | Purchase |
|---|---|---|
| Base | 2500 | 2500 |
| Cartridge | 5000 | 0 |
| Handle | 5000 | 0 |

**32. b.** $G = 120{,}000$; $S = 30{,}000$; $M = 150{,}000$

**c.** 0.15 to 0.60; No Lower Limit to 0.122; 0.02 to 0.20

**d.** 4668

**e.** $G = 48{,}000$; $S = 192{,}000$; $M = 60{,}000$

**f.** The client's risk index and the amount of funds available

**34. a.** $L = 3$, $N = 7$, $W = 5$, $S = 5$

**b.** Each additional minute of broadcast time increases cost by $100

**c.** If local coverage is increased by 1 minute, total cost will increase by $100

**d.** If the time devoted to local and national news is increased by 1 minute, total cost will increase by $100

**e.** Increasing the sports by one minute will have no effect because the dual price is 0

# Chapter 4

**2. a.** $x_1 = 77.89$, $x_2 = 63.16$, $\$3284.21$

**b.** Department A $15.79; Department B $47.37

**c.** $x_1 = 87.21$, $x_2 = 65.12$, $\$3341.34$
Department A 10 hours; Department B 3.2 hours

**4. a.** $x_1 = 500$, $x_2 = 300$, $x_3 = 200$, $\$550$

**b.** $0.55

**c.** Aroma, 75; Taste 84.4

**d.** $0.60

**6.** 50 units of product 1; 0 units of product 2; 300 hours department A; 600 hours department B

**8.** Schedule 19 officers as follows:
3 begin at 8:00 A.M.; 3 begin at noon; 7 begin at 4:00 P.M.; 4 begin at midnight, 2 begin at 4:00 A.M.

**10.**

| Product | Modern Line | Old Line |
|---|---|---|
| 1 | 500 | 0 |
| 2 | 300 | 400 |

Cost $= \$3850$

**12. a.** Purchase 5000 bases

**b.** Same solution with objective function increased by $80

**c.** Yes; Total cost $= \$24{,}293.33$; $FCP = 1333$ and $FCM = 1667$

**14. b.**

| Quarter | Production | Ending Inventory |
|---|---|---|
| 1 | 4000 | 2100 |
| 2 | 3000 | 1100 |
| 3 | 2000 | 100 |
| 4 | 1900 | 500 |

**16.** $x_i$ = number of 10-inch rolls processed by cutting alternative $i$

**a.** $x_1 = 0$, $x_2 = 125$, $x_3 = 500$, $x_4 = 1500$, $x_5 = 0$, $x_6 = 0$, $x_7 = 0$; 2125 rolls with waste of 750 inches

**b.** 2500 rolls with no waste; however, 1½-inch size is overproduced by 3000 units

**18. a.** 5 super, 2 regular, and 3 econotankers
**b.** Total cost $583,000; monthly operating cost $4650

**20.** Produce 10,250 units in March, 10,250 units in April, and 12,000 units in May

**22.** 5, 515, 887 sq. in. of waste
machine 3: 492 minutes

**24.** Investment strategy: 45.8% of A and 100% of B
Objective function = $4340.40
Savings/Loan Schedule

|  | Period | | | |
|---|---|---|---|---|
|  | **1** | **2** | **3** | **4** |
| Savings | 242.11 | — | — | 341.04 |
| Funds from loan | — | 200.00 | 127.58 | — |

**26. b.** Solution does not indicate that General Hospital is relatively inefficient
**c.** General Hospital

**28. c.** No; E = 1 indicates that the amount of resources used by Hospital E are required to produce the outputs of Hospital E
**d.** Hospital E

# Chapter 5

**2. a.** Max  $x_1 + 2x_2$
s.t.
$$x_1 + 5x_2 + s_1 \qquad = 10$$
$$2x_1 + 6x_2 \qquad + s_2 = 16$$
$$x_1, x_2, s_1, s_2 \geq 0$$

**b.** 2

**c.** $x_1 = 0, x_2 = 0, s_1 = 10, s_2 = 16$; feasible
$x_1 = 0, x_2 = 2, s_1 = 0, s_2 = 4$; feasible
$x_1 = 0, x_2 = 8/3, s_1 = -10/3, s_2 = 0$; not feasible
$x_1 = 10, x_2 = 0, s_1 = 0, s_2 = -4$; not feasible
$x_1 = 8, x_2 = 0, s_1 = 2, s_2 = 0$; feasible
$x_1 = 5, x_2 = 1, s_1 = 0, s_2 = 0$; feasible

**d.** $x_1 = 8, x_2 = 0$; Value = 8

**4. a.** Max  $60x_1 + 90x_2$
s.t.
$$15x_1 + 45x_2 + s_1 \qquad = 90$$
$$5x_1 + 5x_2 \qquad + s_2 = 20$$
$$x_1, x_2, s_1, s_2 \geq 0$$

**b.**

| $x_1$ | $x_2$ | $s_1$ | $s_2$ | |
|---|---|---|---|---|
| 60 | 90 | 0 | 0 | |
| 15 | 45 | 1 | 0 | 90 |
| 5 | 5 | 0 | 1 | 20 |

**6. a.**

| $z_j$ | 0 | 0 | 0 | 0 | 0 | 0 | 0 |
|---|---|---|---|---|---|---|---|
| $c_j - z_j$ | 5 | 20 | 25 | 0 | 0 | 0 | |

**b.** Max  $5x_1 + 20x_2 + 25x_3 + 0s_1 + 0s_2 + 0s_3$
s.t.
$$2x_1 + 1x_2 \qquad\qquad + 1s_1 \qquad\qquad = 40$$
$$2x_2 + 1x_3 \qquad\qquad + 1s_2 \qquad = 30$$
$$3x_1 \qquad - \tfrac{1}{2}x_3 \qquad\qquad\qquad + 1s_3 = 15$$
$$x_1, x_2, x_3, s_1, s_2, s_3 \geq 0$$

**c.** $s_1, s_2, s_3$; it is the origin
**d.** 0
**e.** $x_3$ enters, $s_2$ leaves
**f.** 30, 750
**g.** $x_1 = 10, s_1 = 20$
$x_2 = 0, s_2 = 0$, Value = 800
$x_3 = 30, s_3 = 0$

**8. a.** $x_1 = 540, x_2 = 252$
**b.** $7668
**c.** 630, 480, 708, 117
**d.** 0, 120, 0, 18

**10.** $x_2 = 250, x_3 = 150, s_2 = 4000$
Value = 4850

**12.** A = 0, B = 0, C = $33\tfrac{1}{3}$; Profit = 500

**14. a.** $x_1 = 0, x_2 = 50, x_3 = 75$; Profit = $210
**c.** Grade B grapes and labor

**16.**
Max  $-4x_1 - 5x_2 - 3x_3 + 0s_1 + 0s_2 + 0s_4 - Ma_1 - Ma_2 - Ma_3$
s.t.
$$4x_1 \qquad + 2x_3 - 1s_1 \qquad\qquad + 1a_1 \qquad\qquad = 20$$
$$-1x_2 + 1x_3 \qquad - 1s_2 \qquad\qquad + 1a_2 \qquad = 8$$
$$-1x_1 + 2x_2 \qquad\qquad\qquad\qquad\qquad + 1a_3 = 5$$
$$2x_1 + 1x_2 + 1x_3 \qquad\qquad + 1s_4 \qquad\qquad = 12$$
$$x_1, x_2, x_3, s_1, s_2, s_4, a_1, a_2, a_3 \geq 0$$

**18.** $x_2 = 60, x_3 = 60, s_3 = 20$; Value = 2040

**20.** 2400 boxes of 33 gallon bags
Profit = $480

**22.** $x_1 = 480, x_4 = 480, x_6 = 800$; Value = 46,400

**24.** Alternative optimal solution: $x_1 = 4, x_2 = 4$
$x_1 = 8, x_2 = 0$

**26.** Alternative optimal solution: $x_1 = 4, x_2 = 0, x_3 = 0$
$x_1 = 0, x_2 = 0, x_3 = 8$

**28.** Infeasible

**30. a.** Infeasible solution; not enough sewing time
**b.** Alternative optimal solutions: $x_1 = 1000$, $x_2 = 0$, $x_3 = 250$ or $x_1 = 1000, x_2 = 200, x_3 = 0$
Profit = $4000

# Chapter 6

2. a. $31.25 \le c_2 \le 83.33$
   b. $-43.33 \le c_{s_2} \le 8.75$
   c. $c_{s_3} \le {}^{26}\!/_5$
   d. Variables do not change; Value = $1920

4. a. $100 \le b_1 \le 150$
   b. $40 \le b_2 \le 60$
   c. $b_3 \le 110$

6. a. $6.3 \le c_1 \le 13.5$
   b. $6^2\!/_3 \le c_2 \le 14^2\!/_7$
   c. Variables do not change; Value = $7164
   d. Below $6^2\!/_3$ or above $14^2\!/_7$
   e. $x_1 = 300$, $x_2 = 420$; Value = $9300

8. a. $x_1 = 5220/11$, $x_2 = 3852/11$; Value = 86,868/11
   b. No, $s_1$ would enter the basis

10. a. Increase in profit
    b. No

12. a. $14 \le b_1 \le 21\frac{1}{2}$
    b. $4 \le b_2$
    c. $18\frac{3}{4} \le b_3 \le 30$
    d. Dual price = 400/9; Range: $18\frac{3}{4} \le b_3 \le 30$

14. a. $400/3 \le b_1 \le 800$
    b. $275 \le b_2$
    c. $275/2 \le b_3 \le 625$

16. a. $x_1 = 4000$, $x_2 = 10,000$; Total risk = 62,000
    b. Increase it by 2.167 per unit
    c. $48,000 \le b_2 \le 102,000$
    d. $x_1 = 5667$, $x_2 = 9167$; Total risk = 72,833
    e. Variables do not change; Total risk = 66,000

18. Max $\quad 5u_1 + 5u_2 + 24u_3$
    s.t.
    $$15u_1 + 4u_2 + 12u_3 \le 2800$$
    $$15u_1 + 8u_2 \qquad \le 6000$$
    $$u_1 \qquad + 8u_3 \le 1200$$
    $$u_1, u_2, u_3 \ge 0$$

20. a. Max $\quad 30u_1 + 20u_2 + 80u_3$
    s.t.
    $$u_1 \qquad + \quad u_3 \le 1$$
    $$u_2 + 2u_3 \le 1$$
    $$u_1, u_2, u_3 \ge 0$$
    b. $x_1 = 30$, $x_2 = 25$
    c. Reduce cost by $0.50

22. a. Max $\quad 10x_1 + 5x_2$
    s.t.
    $$x_1 \qquad \ge 20$$
    $$x_2 \ge 20$$
    $$x_1 \qquad \le 100$$
    $$x_2 \le 100$$
    $$3x_1 + \quad x_2 \le 175$$
    $$x_1, x_2 \ge 0$$

   b. Min $\quad -20u_1 - 20u_2 + 100u_3 + 100u_4 + 175u_5$
      s.t.
      $$-u_1 \qquad + \quad u_3 \qquad + \quad 3u_5 \ge 10$$
      $$- \quad u_2 \qquad + \quad u_4 + \quad u_5 \ge 5$$
      $$u_1, u_2, u_3, u_4, u_5 \ge 0$$
      Solution: $u_4 = {}^5\!/_3$, $u_5 = {}^{10}\!/_3$

   c. $x_1 = 25$, $x_2 = 100$; commission = $750

24. Check both constraints with $x_1 = 10$, $x_2 = 30$, $x_3 = 15$
    Both constraints are satisfied; solution remains optimal

# Chapter 7

2. a. Min $\quad 14x_{11} + 9x_{12} + 7x_{13} + 8x_{21} + 10x_{22} + 5x_{23}$
   s.t.
   $$x_{11} + \quad x_{12} + \quad x_{13} \qquad \le 30$$
   $$x_{21} + x_{22} \quad + x_{23} \le 20$$
   $$x_{11} \qquad + \quad x_{21} \qquad = 25$$
   $$x_{12} \qquad + \quad x_{22} \qquad = 15$$
   $$x_{13} \qquad + \quad x_{23} = 10$$
   $$x_{11}, x_{12}, x_{13}, x_{21}, x_{22}, x_{23} \ge 0$$
   b. $x_{11} = 5$, $x_{12} = 15$, $x_{13} = 10$, $x_{21} = 20$

4. b. $x_{12} = 300$, $x_{21} = 100$, $x_{22} = 100$, $x_{23} = 300$, $x_{31} = 100$
   Cost = 10,400

6. b. Seattle–Denver       4000;   Seattle–Los Angeles    5000;
      Columbus–Mobile       4000;   New York–Pittsburgh    3000;
      New York–Mobile       1000;   New York–Los Angeles 1000;
      New York–Washington 3000
      Cost = $150,000
   c. Seattle–Denver       4000;   Seattle–Los Angeles    5000;
      Columbus–Mobile       5000;   New York–Pittsburgh    4000;
      New York–Los Angeles 1000;   New York–Washington 3000
      Cost actually decreases by $9000

8. Clifton–$D_2$   4000;   Clifton–$D_4$   1000;
   Danville–$D_1$   2000;   Danville–$D_4$   1000
   Customer 2 has a shortfall of 1000; customer 3's demand
   is not satisfied

10. 1–A 300; 1–C 1200; 2–A 1200; 3–A 500; 3–B 500

12. b. Jackson–2, Ellis–1, Smith–3; Total completion time = 64

14. b. Bostock–Southwest, Miller–Northwest

16. b. Toy–2, auto parts–4, housewares–3 video–1; Profit = 61

18. a. Plano: Kansas City, Dallas
      Flagstaff: Los Angeles
      Springfield: Chicago, Columbus, Atlanta
      Boulder: Newark, Denver
      Total Cost = $216,000
   b. Nashville not used
   c. Columbus switched from Springfield to Nashville
      Total cost = $227,000

20. A to MS, B to Ph.D., C to MBA, D to undergrad
    Maximum total rating = 3.3

**22. a.**

| | | | Supplier | | | |
|---|---|---|---|---|---|---|
| Division | 1 | 2 | 3 | 4 | 5 | 6 |
| 1 | 614 | 660 | 534 | 680 | 590 | 630 |
| 2 | 603 | 639 | 702 | 693 | 693 | 630 |
| 3 | 865 | 830 | 775 | 850 | 900 | 930 |
| 4 | 532 | 553 | 511 | 581 | 595 | 553 |
| 5 | 720 | 648 | 684 | 693 | 657 | 747 |

**b.** Optimal Solution:

| | |
|---|---|
| Supplier 1—Division 2 | $603 |
| Supplier 2—Division 5 | 648 |
| Supplier 3—Division 3 | 775 |
| Supplier 5—Division 1 | 590 |
| Supplier 6—Division 4 | 553 |
| Total | $3169 |

**24. c.** $x_{14} = 320$, $x_{25} = 600$, $x_{47} = 300$, $x_{49} = 20$, $x_{56} = 300$, $x_{58} = 300$, $x_{39} = 380$
Cost = $11,220

**26. c.** Optimal Solution:

| Variable | Value | Variable | Value |
|---|---|---|---|
| $x_{13}$ | 50 | $x_{36}$ | 0 |
| $x_{14}$ | 250 | $x_{37}$ | 150 |
| $x_{23}$ | 100 | $x_{45}$ | 150 |
| $x_{24}$ | 0 | $x_{46}$ | 100 |
| $x_{35}$ | 0 | $x_{47}$ | 0 |

Objective function = 4300

**28.**

| Optimal Solution | Units Shipped | Cost |
|---|---|---|
| Muncie–Cincinnati | 1 | 6 |
| Cincinnati–Concord | 3 | 84 |
| Brazil–Louisville | 6 | 18 |
| Louisville–Macon | 2 | 88 |
| Louisville–Greenwood | 4 | 136 |
| Xenia–Cincinnati | 5 | 15 |
| Cincinnati–Chatham | 3 | 72 |
| Total | | 419 |

Two rail cars must be held at Muncie until a buyer is found

**32. c.** Regular month 1: 275; overtime month 1: 25; inventory end of month 1: 150

Regular month 2: 200; overtime month 2: 50; inventory end of month 2: 150
Regular month 3: 100; overtime month 3: 50; inventory end of month 3: 0

**34. a.** San Jose–Los Angeles 100; Las Vegas–Los Angeles 100; Las Vegas–San Diego 200; Tucson–San Francisco 300
Cost = $7800
**b.** Initial solution is optimal
**c.** San Jose–San Francisco 100; Las Vegas–Los Angeles 200; Las Vegas–San Diego 100; Tucson–San Francisco 200; Tuscon–San Diego 100
Cost = $7800
**d.** San Jose–San Francisco 100; Las Vegas–Los Angeles 200; Las Vegas–San Francisco 100; Tucson–San Francisco 100; Tuscon–San Diego 200
Cost = $8000

**36.** See Problem 4

**40.** See Problem 12

**42.** Terry 2; Carle 3; McClymonds 1; Higley unassigned
Time = 26 days

**44.** Toy–2; auto–4; housewares–3; video–1

# Chapter 8

**2. b.** $x_1 = 1.43$, $x_2 = 4.29$; Value = 41.47
Rounded: $x_1 = 1$, $x_2 = 4$; Value = 37
**c.** $x_1 = 0$, $x_2 = 5$; Value = 40
Not the same

**4. a.** $x_1 = 3.67$, $x_2 = 0$; Value = 36.7
Rounded: $x_1 = 3$, $x_2 = 0$; Value = 30
Lower bound = 30; Upper bound = 36.7
**b.** $x_1 = 3$, $x_2 = 2$; Value = 36
**c.** Alternative optimal solutions: $x_1 = 0$, $x_2 = 5$
$x_1 = 2$, $x_2 = 4$

**6. b.** $x_1 = 1.96$, $x_2 = 5.48$; Value = 7.44
Rounded: $x_1 = 1.96$, $x_2 = 5$; Value = 6.96
Lower bound = 6.96; Upper bound = 7.44
**c.** $x_1 = 1.29$, $x_2 = 6$; Value = 7.29

**8. a.** $x_3 = 1$, $x_4 = 1$, $x_6 = 1$; Value = 17,500
**b.** Add $x_1 + x_2 \leq 1$
**c.** Add $x_3 - x_4 = 0$

**10. b.** Choose locations B and E

**12. a.** $P \leq 15 + 15Y_P$
$D \leq 15 + 15Y_D$
$J \leq 15 + 15Y_J$
$Y_P + Y_D + Y_J \leq 1$
**b.** $P = 15$, $D = 15$, $J = 30$
$Y_P = 0$, $Y_D = 0$, $Y_J = 1$; Value = 50

14. **b.** Modernize plants 1 and 3 or plants 4 and 5
    **d.** Modernize plants 1 and 3

16. **b.** Use all part-time employees
    Bring on as follows: 9:00 A.M.–6, 11:00 A.M.–2, 12:00 noon–6, 1:00 P.M.–1, 3:00 P.M.–6
    Cost = $672
    **c.** Same as in part (b)
    **d.** New solution is to bring on 1 full-time employee at 9:00 A.M., 4 more at 11:00 A.M. and part-time employees as follows:
    9:00 A.M.–5, 12:00 noon–5, and 3:00 P.M.–2

18. **a.** New objective function: Min $25x_1 + 40x_2 + 40x_3 + 40x_4 + 25x_5$
    **b.** $x_4 = x_5 = 1$; modernize the Ohio and California plants
    **c.** Add the constraint $x_2 + x_3 = 1$
    **d.** $x_1 = x_3 = 1$

20. $x_1 + x_2 + x_3 = 3y_1 + 5y_2 + 7y_3$
    $y_1 + y_2 + y_3 = 1$

# Chapter 9

2.

| Node | Shortest Route from Node 7 | Distance |
|------|----------------------------|----------|
| 1 | 7–6–5–3–1 | 22 |
| 2 | 7–4 –2 | 11 |
| 3 | 7–6 –5–3 | 12 |
| 4 | 7–4 | 5 |
| 5 | 7–5–6 | 8 |
| 6 | 7–6 | 6 |

4. 1–4–5–6–8; distance = 10

6.

| Node | Shortest Route from Node C | Distance |
|------|----------------------------|----------|
| 1 | C–1 | 35 |
| 2 | C–2 | 20 |
| 3 | C–3 | 20 |
| 4 | C–4 | 30 |
| 5 | C–3–5 | 55 |
| 6 | C–3–6 | 50 |
| 7 | C–3–8–7 | 100 |
| 8 | C–3–8 | 80 |
| 9 | C–4 –10–9 | 85 |
| 10 | C–4 –10 | 70 |

8. 1–2–8–10–11

10. 1–6, 6–7, 7–8, 7–10, 10–9, 9– 4, 9–3, 3–2, 4 –5, 7–11, 8–13, 14 –15, 15–12, 14 –13
    Total = 37

12. 1–2, 2–5, 5–6, 6–3, 6–8, 3– 4, 8–7
    Total length = 2900 feet

14. 1– 4, 2–3, 3– 4, 4–5, 4–6, 6–7, 7–8, 8–9, 9–11, 11–10
    Minimum length = 28 miles

16. Maximal flow = 11,000 vehicles per hour

18. **a.** 10 hours; 10,000 gallons per hour
    **b.** 11.1 hours; flow reduced to 9000 gallons per hour

20. Maximal flow = 23 gallons/minute
    From steps 2 and 5, we see that the total flow from 3 to 5 must be 5 gallons/minute

# Chapter 10

2.

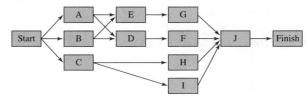

4. **a.** A–D–G
   **b.** No; Time = 15 months

6. **a.** A–D–F–H
   **b.** 22 weeks
   **c.** No, it is a critical activity
   **d.** Yes, 2 weeks
   **e.** ES = 3, LS = 4, EF = 10, LF = 11

8. **b.** B–C–E–F–H
   **d.** Yes, time = 49 weeks

10. **a.**

| Activity | Time | Variance |
|----------|------|----------|
| A | 5.00 | 0.11 |
| B | 9.00 | 0.11 |
| C | 8.00 | 0.44 |
| D | 8.83 | 0.25 |
| E | 7.17 | 0.25 |
| F | 6.00 | 0.11 |

**b.** 23.83, 0.47

12. **a.** A–D–H–I
    **b.** 25.66 days
    **c.** 0.2578

14. **a.** A–D–F–G
    **b.** 1.5 days
    **c.** 29.5, 2.36
    **d.** 0.6293

16. a.

| E(T) | Variance |
|---|---|
| 16 | 3.92 |
| 13 | 2.03 |
| 10 | 1.27 |

 b. 0.9783, approximately 1.00, approxmiately 1.00

18. c. A–B–D–G–H–I, 14.17 weeks
 d. 0.0951, yes

20. b. Crash B(1 week), D(2 weeks), E(1 week), F(1 week), G(1 week)
 Total cost = $2427
 c. All activities are critical

22. b. Crash C(1 day) and E(1 day)
 c. $9300

24. c. A–B–C–F, 31 weeks
 d. Crash A(2 weeks), B(2 weeks), C(1 week), D(1 week), E(1 week)
 e. All activities are critical
 f. $112,500

# Chapter 11

2. $164.32 for each; Total cost = $328.64

4. a. 1095.45
 b. 240
 c. 22.82 days
 d. $273.86 for each; Total cost = $547.72

6. a. 15.95
 b. $2106
 c. 15.04
 d. 16.62 days

8. $Q^* = 11.73$, use 12
 5 classes per year
 $225,200

10. $Q^* = 1414.21$
 $T = 28.28$ days
 Production runs of 7.07 days

12. $Q^* = 1000$; Total cost = $1200
 Yes, the change saves $300 per year

14. New $Q^* = 4509$

16. 135.55; $r = dm - S$; less than

18. 64, 24.44

20. $Q^* = 100$; Total cost = $3,601.50

22. $Q^* = 300$; Savings = $480

24. a. 500
 b. 580.4

26. a. 397
 b. 0.70
 c. 489, 0.35

28. a. 440
 b. 0.60
 c. 710
 d. $c_u = $17$

30. a. 13.68 (14)
 b. 17.83 (18)
 c. 2, $10; 6, $30

32. a. 31.62
 b. 19.86 (20); 0.2108
 c. 5, $15

34. a. 243
 b. 93, $54.87
 c. 613
 d. 163, $96.17
 e. Yes, added cost only $41.30 per year
 f. Yes, added cost would be $4130 per year

36. a. 40
 b. 62.25; 7.9
 c. 54
 d. 36

38. Engines           10
 Air cleaners      7
 Filter housings   2

40. Base assemblies        13
 Wheel subassemblies   9
 Tires                 4

# Chapter 12

2. a. 0.4512
 b. 0.6988
 c. 0.3012

4. 0.3333, 0.2222, 0.1481, 0.0988, 0.1976

6. a. 0.3333
 b. 1.3333
 c. 0.1111 days (53.3 minutes)
 d. 0.6667

8. 0.20, 3.2, 4, 3.2, 4, 0.80
 Slightly poorer service

10. a. New: 0.3333, 1.3333, 2, 0.6667, 1, 0.6667
 Experienced: 0.50, 0.50, 1, 0.25, 0.50, 0.50
 b. New $74; experienced $50; hire experienced

12. a. 0.25, 2.25, 3, 0.15 hours, 0.20 hours, 0.75
 b. The service needs improvement

14. a. 8
 b. 0.3750

c. 1.0417
d. 12.5 minutes
e. 0.6250
f. Need to add a second consultant

16. a. 0.50
    b. 0.50
    c. 0.10 hours (6 minutes)
    d. 0.20 hours (12 minutes)
    e. Yes, $W_q$ = 6 minutes is most likely acceptable for a marina.

18. a. 0.5385
    b. 0.0593
    c. 0.0099 hours (0.59 minutes)
    d. 0.1099 hours (6.59 minutes)
    e. 0.1385

20. a. 0.2360, 0.1771, 1.5771, 0.0126 hours, 0.1126 hours
    b. $P$(wait) = 0.2024 for a 3-channel system

22.

| Characteristic | A | B | C |
|---|---|---|---|
| a. $P_0$ | 0.2000 | 0.5000 | 0.4286 |
| b. $L_q$ | 3.2000 | 0.5000 | 0.1524 |
| c. $L$ | 4.0000 | 1.0000 | 0.9524 |
| d. $W_q$ | 0.1333 | 0.0208 | 0.0063 |
| e. $W$ | 0.1667 | 0.0417 | 0.0397 |
| f. $P_w$ | 0.8000 | 0.5000 | 0.2286 |

The two-channel System C provides the best service.

24. a. 0.0466, 0.05
    b. 1.4
    c. 11:00 A.M.

26. a. 0.2668, 10 minutes, 0.6667
    b. 0.0667, 7 minutes, 0.4669
    c. $25.33; $33.34; one-channel

28. a. 10, 9.6
    b. Design A with $\mu$ = 10
    c. 0.05, 0.01
    d. A: 0.5, 0.3125, 0.8125, 0.0625, 0.1625, 0.5
       B: 0.4792, 0.2857, 0.8065, 0.0571, 0.1613, 0.5208
    e. Design B has slightly less waiting time

30. a. 0.1460, 0.3066, 0.3220, 0.2254
    b. 0.2254
    c. 1.6267
    d. 4; 0.1499

32. a. 31.03%
    b. 27.59%
    c. 0.2759, 0.1092, 0.0351
    d. 3, 10.92%

34. a. 0.4790
    b. 0.3110
    c. 0.8321

d. 2.9854 minutes
e. 7.9854 minutes
f. 95.8 minutes; 35.8 minutes
g. Yes, assistants spend too much time waiting at the copier

## Chapter 13

2. a. Profit = $(50 - c)x - 30{,}000$
   b. 6000, −22,200, 41,400
   c. Helps estimate probability of loss

4. a. 0.00–0.08, 0.08–0.20, 0.20–0.48, 0.48–0.72, 0.72–0.86, 0.86–0.96, 0.96–1.00
   b. 2, 5, 2, 3, 3, 2, 4, 2, 1, 1, 2
   c. 24 units

6. a. 0.00–0.83, 0.83–0.89, 0.89–0.94, 0.94–0.96, 0.96–0.98, 0.98–0.99, 0.99–1.00
   b. 4 claims paid; Total = $22,000

8. a. Atlanta wins each game if random number is in interval 0.00–0.60, 0.00–0.55, 0.00–0.48, 0.00–0.45, 0.00–0.48, 0.00–0.55, 0.00–0.50.
   b. Atlanta wins games 1, 2, 4, and 6
      Atlanta wins series 4 to 2
   c. Repeat many times; record % of Atlanta wins

10. a. 0.00–0.40 for Yes; 0.40–1.00 for No
       If Yes, 0.00–0.30, 0.30–0.60, 0.60–1.00
       If No, 0.00–0.50, 0.50–0.90, 0.90–1.00
    b. Uncertain, definitely yes, definitely no
    c. Repeat many times; record % of definitely yes

12. a. $7, $3, $12
    b. Purchase: 0.00–0.25, 0.25–0.70, 0.70–1.00
       Labor: 0.00–0.10, 0.10–0.35, 0.35–0.70, 0.70–1.00
       Transportation: 0.00–0.75, 0.75–1.00
    c. $5
    d. $7
    e. Provide probability profit less than $5/unit

14. a. Most simulations between $5500 and $6500
    b. Most simulations between 0.24 and 0.30
    c. Project is too risky

16. Most simulations between 6 and 16 still working; 11 is the expected number

18. a. Most simulations between 0.60 and 0.65
    b. $775,000 roughly 0.82; $785,000 roughly 0.88
       Select $775,000

20. a. Results vary with each simulation run
       Approximate results: 50,000 provided $230,000
                            60,000 provided $190,000
                            70,000 less than $100,000
    b. Recommend 50,000 units
    c. Roughly 0.75

22. Very poor operation; some customers wait 30 minutes or more

# Chapter 14

**2. a.** Optimistic: $d_1$
Conservative: $d_3$
Minimax regret: $d_3$
**c.** Optimistic: $d_1$
Conservative: $d_2$ or $d_3$
Minimax regret: $d_2$

**4.** Optimistic: $d_2$
Conservative: $d_1$
Minimax regret: $d_2$

**6. a.** $d_1$
**b.** $d_4$

**8.** If $P(s_1) < 0.25\ d_2$
If $P(s_1) = 0.25$, $d_1$ or $d_2$
If $P(s_1) > 0.25\ d_1$

**10. a.** If $p > 0.44$, location A; if $p < 0.44$, location C
**b.** Location A because $0.65 > 0.44$

**12. a.** If $s_1$, then $d_1$; if $s_2$, then $d_1$ or $d_2$; if $s_3$, then $d_2$
**b.** 192.5
**c.** $d_1$; 182.5
**d.** 10

**14. b.** If favorable, $d_2$
If unfavorable, $d_1$
EV = 292

**16. b.** $d_2$, 500
**c.** 195
**d.** If weak, then $d_2$; if average, then $d_2$; if strong, then $d_3$
**e.** 41.8
**f.** 21%

**18. b.** $d_1$, 1250
**c.** 1700
**d.** If N, $d_1$
If U, $d_2$; 1666

**20. a.** $d_1$, 2000
**b.** 200
**c.** $d_1$, 2000; don't call

**22.** 0.1915, 0.2381, 0.5714

**24. a.** 0.695, 0.215, 0.090
0.98, 0.02
0.79, 0.21
0.00, 1.00
**c.** If C, Expressway
If O, Expressway
If R, Queen City
26.6 minutes

**26.** $20, $30

**28. a.** $d_2$; EV$(d_2) = 52.5$
**b.** A—$d_3$; 6.0
B—$d_1$; 4.45
**c.** Different attitudes toward risk

**30. a.** $d_2$; EV$(d_2) = \$5,000$
**b.** $p$ = probability of a $0 cost
$1 - p$ = probability of a $200,000 cost
**c.** $d_1$; EV$(d_1) = 9.9$
**d.** Expected utility approach

**32. a.** Route B; EV = 58.5
**b.** $p$ = probability of a 45-minute travel time
$1 - p$ = probability of a 90-minute travel time
**c.** Route A: EV = 7.6; risk-avoider strategy

**34. a.**

|  | Win | Lose |
|---|---|---|
| Bet | 350 | −10 |
| Do not bet | 0 | 0 |

**b.** $d_2$
**c.** Between 0 and 0.26

# Chapter 15

**2. a.** Min $\quad P_1(d_1^-) + P_2(d_2^+)$
s.t.
$$
\begin{aligned}
50x_1 + 100x_2 &\leq 50{,}000 \\
3x_1 + 10x_2 - d_1^+ + d_1^- &= 4500 \\
x_2 - d_2^+ + d_2^- &= 300 \\
x_1, x_2, d_1^+, d_1^-, d_2^+, d_2^- &\geq 0
\end{aligned}
$$
**b.** $x_1 = 250$, $x_2 = 375$

**4. a.** Min $\quad P_1(d_1^-) + P_1(d_2^+) + P_2(d_3^-) + P_2(d_4^-) + P_3(d_5^-)$
s.t.
$$
\begin{aligned}
20x_1 + 30x_2 - d_1^+ + d_1^- &= 1800 \\
20x_1 + 30x_2 - d_2^+ + d_2^- &= 6000 \\
x_1 \qquad - d_3^+ + d_3^- &= 100 \\
x_2 - d_4^+ + d_4^- &= 120 \\
x_1 + x_2 \quad - d_5^+ + d_5^- &= 300 \\
x_1, x_2, \text{ all deviation variables} &\geq 0
\end{aligned}
$$
**b.** $x_1 = 120$, $x_2 = 120$

**6. a.** Let $x_1$ = number of letters mailed to group 1 customers
$x_2$ = number of letters mailed to group 2 customers
Min $\quad P_1(d_1^-) + P_1(d_2^-) + P_2(d_3^+)$
s.t.
$$
\begin{aligned}
x_1 \qquad - d_1^+ + d_1^- &= 40{,}000 \\
x_2 - d_2^+ + d_2^- &= 50{,}000 \\
x_1 + x_2 - d_3^+ + d_3^- &= 70{,}000 \\
x_1, x_2, \text{ all deviation variables} &\geq 0
\end{aligned}
$$
**b.** $x_1 = 40{,}000$, $x_2 = 50{,}000$
**c.** Optimal solution does not change

8. **a.** Min $d_1^- + d_1^+ + e_1^- + e_1^+ + d_2^- + d_2^+ + e_2^- +$
$e_2^+ + d_3^- + d_3^+ + e_3^- + e_3^+$
s.t.
$$x_1 \qquad + d_1^- - d_1^+ = 1$$
$$x_2 + e_1^- - e_1^+ = 7$$
$$x_1 \qquad + d_2^- - d_2^+ = 5$$
$$x_2 + e_2^- - e_2^+ = 9$$
$$x_1 \qquad + d_3^- - d_3^+ = 6$$
$$x_2 + e_3^- - e_3^+ = 2$$
all variables $\geq 0$

   **b.** $x_1 = 5, x_2 = 7$

10. 178, 184, 151
Marysville

12. 170, 168, 190, 183
Handover College

14. **a.** 220 Bowrider (194)
   **b.** 240 Sundancer (144)

16. CR = 0.028, acceptable

18. **a.** 0.724, 0.193, 0.083
   **b.** CR = 0.057, yes

20. **a.**

|   | A | B | C |
|---|---|---|---|
| A | 1 | 3 | 2 |
| B | ⅓ | 1 | 5 |
| C | ½ | ⅕ | 1 |

   **b.** 0.503, 0.348, 0.148
   **c.** CR = 0.415, no

22. **a.**

|   | D | S | N |
|---|---|---|---|
| D | 1 | ¼ | ⅐ |
| S | 4 | 1 | ⅓ |
| N | 7 | 3 | 1 |

   **b.** 0.080, 0.265, 0.656
   **c.** Since CR = 0.028, yes

24. **a.** Criterion: 0.667, 0.033
     Yield: 0.750, 0.250
     Risk: 0.333, 0.667
   **b.** CCC, 0.611; SRI, 0.389
     CCC is preferred

26. **a.** Criterion: 0.608, 0.272, 0.120
     Price: 0.557, 0.123, 0.320
     Sound: 0.137, 0.239, 0.623
     Reception: 0.579, 0.187, 0.046
   **b.** 0.446, 0.162, 0.392
     System A is preferred

# Chapter 16

2. **a.**

| Week | 4-Week | 5-Week |
|------|--------|--------|
| 10 | 19.00 | 18.80 |
| 11 | 20.00 | 19.20 |
| 12 | 18.75 | 19.00 |

   **b.** 9.65, 7.41
   **c.** 5-week

4. Weeks 10, 11, and 12: 18.48, 18.63, 18.27
MSE = 9.25; $\alpha = 0.2$ is better

6. **b.** The more recent data receive the greater weight or importance in determining the forecast

8. **a.** 33.1458
   **b.** 32.9500
   **c.** 33.2187
   **d.** Exponential smoothing; it has the smallest MSE (1.24)

10. **a.** $\alpha = 0.2$
   **b.** 46.1

12. 3117.01

14. $T_t = 20.7466 - 0.3514t$
Enrollment appears to be decreasing by an average of 351 students per year

16. **a.** Linear trend appears to be reasonable
   **b.** $T_t = 19.993 + 1.774t$
     Average cost increase of $1.77 per unit per year

18. **a.** $T_t = -7.5 + 7.7714t$
   **b.** 7.7714($M) per year
   **c.** 46.9

20. **a.** A linear trend appears to exist
   **b.** $T_t = -5 + 15t$
     Average increase in sales is 15 units per year

22. **a.** A linear trend appears to be appropriate
   **b.** $T_t = 12,899.98 + 2092.066$
   **c.** $2,092,066
   **d.** $40,096,838 and $42,188,904

24. **a.** Forecast for July is 236.97; forecast for August is 236.97
   **b.** Forecast for July is 278.88; forecast for August is 297.33
   **c.** Not fair; it does not account for upward trend in sales

26. 0.707, 0.777, 0.827, 0.966, 1.016, 1.305, 1.494, 1.225, 0.976, 0.986, 0.936, 0.787

28. **a.** Selected centered moving averages for $t = 5, 10, 15,$ and 20 are 11.125, 18.125, 22.875, and 27.000
   **b.** 0.899, 1.362, 1.118, 0.621
   **d.** Quarter 2, prior to summer boating season

30. a. $T_t = 6.329 + 1.055t$
    b. 36.92, 37.98, 39.03, 40.09
    c. 33.23, 51.65, 43.71, 24.86

32. a. Yes, there is a seasonal effect; seasonal indexes are 1.696, 1.458, 0.711, 0.326, 0.448, 1.362
    b. Forecast for 12–4 is 166,761.13; forecast for 4–8 is 146,052.99

34. a. $T_t = 37.666 - 3.222t$
    b. $3444

## Chapter 17

2. a. 0.82
   b. $\pi_1 = 0.5, \pi_2 = 0.5$
   c. $\pi_1 = 0.6, \pi_2 = 0.4$

4. a. $\pi_1 = 0.92, \pi_2 = 0.08$
   b. $85

6. a.

|  | City | Suburbs |
|---|---|---|
| **City** | 0.98 | 0.02 |
| **Suburbs** | 0.01 | 0.99 |

   b. $\pi_1 = 0.333, \pi_2 = 0.667$
   c. City will decrease from 40% to 33%; suburbs will increase from 60% to 67%

8. a. MDA
   b. $\pi = \frac{1}{3}, \pi_2 = \frac{2}{3}$

10. $3 - 1(0.59), 4 - 1(0.52)$

12. 3580 will be sold eventually; 1420 will be lost

14. a. Graduate and drop out
    b. $P$(Drop out) = 0.15, $P$(Sophomore) = 0.10, $P$(Junior) = 0.75

c. 0.706, 0.294
d. Yes; $P$(Graduate) = 0.54
   $P$(Drop out) = 0.46
e. 1479 (74%) will graduate

## Chapter 18

2. a. 1–4–6–9–10
   b. 4–6–9–10
   c.

| Route | Value | Route | Value |
|---|---|---|---|
| (1–2–5–7–10) | 32 | (1–3–6–8–10) | 34 |
| (1–2–5–8–10) | 36 | (1–3–6–9–10) | 31 |
| (1–2–5–9–10) | 28 | (1–4–6–8–10) | 29 |
| (1–3–5–7–10) | 31 | (1–4–6–9–10) | 26 |
| (1–3–5–8–10) | 35 |  |  |
| (1–3–5–9–10) | 27 |  |  |

4. a. Alternative optimal solutions: value = 186
   Solution 1: A1–3, A2–2, A3–0, A4–3
   Solution 2: A1–2, A2–3, A3–0, A4–3
   b. A1–1, A2–2, A3–0, A4–3

6. a. A–G–J–M
   b. Choose H

8. a. Daily News–1, Sunday news–3, radio–1, TV-3; Max exposure = 169
   b. 1, 2, 1, 2; Max exposure = 139
   c. For part (a): 2, 3, 3; Max exposure = 152
      For part (b): 2, 3, 1; Max exposure = 127

10. Monthly production: 20, 20, 30

# APPENDIX F   SOLUTIONS TO SELF-TEST PROBLEMS

## Chapter 1

4. A quantitative approach should be considered because the problem is large, complex, important, new, and repetitive

8. **a.** Max   $10x + 5y$
    s.t.    $5x + 2y \le 40$
            $x \ge 0, y \ge 0$
   **b.** Controllable inputs: $x$ and $y$
      Uncontrollable inputs: profit (10,5), labor-hours (5,2) and labor-hour availability (40)
   **c.** See Figure 1.8c
   **d.** $x = 0, y = 20$; Profit = $100
      (Solution by trial and error)

15. **a.** $TC = 1000 + 30x$
   **b.** $P = 40x - (1000 + 30x) = 10x - 1000$
   **c.** Break even when $P = 0$
      Thus $10x - 1000 = 0$
      $$10x = 1000$$
      $$x = 100$$

## Chapter 2

1. Parts (a), (b), and (e) are acceptable linear programming relationships

Part (c) is not acceptable because of $-2x_2^2$
Part (d) is not acceptable because of $3\sqrt{x_1}$
Part (f) is not acceptable because of $1x_1x_2$
Parts (c), (d), and (f) could not be found in a linear programming model because they have the above non-linear terms

2. **a.**

**b.**

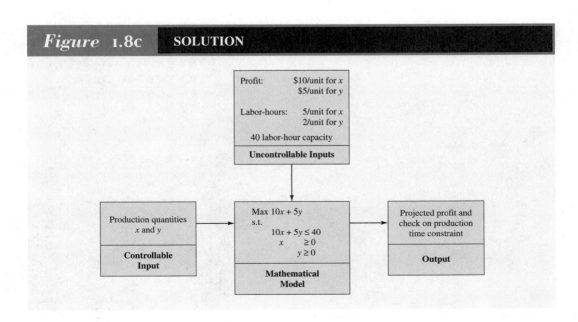

**Figure 1.8c**    SOLUTION

A-21

**c.**

**6.** For $7x_1 + 10x_2$, slope $= -7/10$
For $6x_1 + 4x_2$, slope $= -6/4 = -3/2$
For $-4x_1 + 7x_2$, slope $= -4/7$

**7.**

**10.**

$$
\begin{array}{rcll}
x_1 + 2x_2 &=& 6 & (1) \\
5x_1 + 3x_2 &=& 15 & (2) \\
5x_1 + 10x_2 &=& 30 & (3)
\end{array}
$$
Equation (1) times 5:

Equation (2) minus equation (3):     $-7x_2 = -15$
                                       $x_2 = 15/7$
From equation (1):     $x_1 = 6 - 2(15/7)$
                       $= 6 - 30/7 = 12/7$

**14. a.**

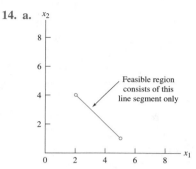

**b.** The extreme points are (5,1) and (2,4)

**c.**

**18.** Max   $5x_1 + 2x_2 + 8x_3 + 0s_1 + 0s_2 + 0s_3$
s.t.

$$
\begin{array}{rcll}
1x_1 - 2x_2 + \tfrac{1}{2}x_3 + 1s_1 &=& 420 \\
2x_1 + 3x_2 - 1x_3 \qquad\; + 1s_2 &=& 610 \\
6x_1 - 1x_2 + 3x_3 \qquad\qquad + 1s_3 &=& 125
\end{array}
$$
$x_1, x_2, x_3, s_1, s_2, s_3 \geq 0$

**22. a.** Let $R$ = number of units of regular model
$C$ = number of units of catcher's model

Max   $5R + 8C$

$$
\begin{array}{rll}
1R + \tfrac{3}{2}C \leq 900 & \text{Cutting and sewing} \\
\tfrac{1}{2}R + \tfrac{1}{3}C \leq 300 & \text{Finishing} \\
\tfrac{1}{8}R + \tfrac{1}{4}C \leq 100 & \text{Packaging and shipping}
\end{array}
$$
$R, C \geq 0$

**b.**

c.  $5(500) + 8(150) = \$3,700$
d.  C & S      $1(500) + \frac{3}{2}(150) = 725$
    F          $\frac{1}{2}(500) + \frac{1}{3}(150) = 300$
    P & S      $\frac{1}{8}(500) + \frac{1}{4}(150) = 100$

e.

| Department | Capacity | Usage | Slack |
|---|---|---|---|
| Cutting and sewing | 900 | 725 | 175 hours |
| Finishing | 300 | 300 | 0 hours |
| Packaging and shipping | 100 | 100 | 0 hours |

29.

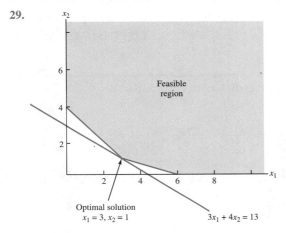

Optimal solution
$x_1 = 3, x_2 = 1$          $3x_1 + 4x_2 = 13$

Objective function value = 13

32. a.

(21/4, 9/4)

(4, 1)

b.  There are two extreme points

$$x_1 = 4 \qquad x_1 = 21/4$$
$$x_2 = 1 \qquad x_2 = 9/4$$

c.  The optimal solution (see part (a)) is $x_1 = 4, x_2 = 1$

33. a.  Min   $6x_1 + 4x_2 + 0s_1 + 0s_2 + 0s_3$
    s.t.
$$2x_1 + 1x_2 - s_1 \qquad\qquad = 12$$
$$1x_1 + 1x_2 \qquad - s_2 \qquad = 10$$
$$1x_2 \qquad\qquad + s_3 = 4$$
$$x_1, x_2, s_1, s_2, s_3 \geq 0$$

b.  The optimal solution is $x_1 = 6, x_2 = 4$
c.  $s_1 = 4, s_2 = 0, s_3 = 0$

40.

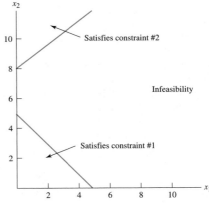

Satisfies constraint #2

Infeasibility

Satisfies constraint #1

41.

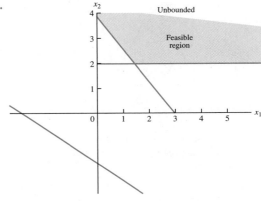

Unbounded

Feasible region

# Chapter 3

3. a.

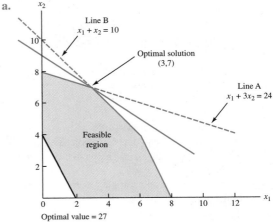

Line B
$x_1 + x_2 = 10$

Optimal solution
(3,7)

Line A
$x_1 + 3x_2 = 24$

Feasible region

Optimal value = 27

b.  Slope of line B = $-1$
    Slope of line A = $-\frac{1}{3}$
    Let $C_1$ = objective function coefficient of $x_1$
        $C_2$ = objective function coefficient of $x_2$
    $-1 \leq -C_1/3 \leq -\frac{1}{3}$
    $1 \geq C_1/3 \quad C_1/3 \geq \frac{1}{3}$
    $C_1 \leq 3 \qquad C_1 \geq 1$
    Range: $1 \leq C_1 \leq 3$

c. $-1 \leq -2/C_2 \leq -\frac{1}{3}$
  $1 \geq 2/C_2 \quad 2/C_2 \geq \frac{1}{3}$
  $C_2 \geq 2 \qquad C_2 \leq 6$
  Range: $2 \leq C_2 \leq 6$

d. Since this change leaves $C_1$ in its range of optimality, the same solution ($x_1 = 3, x_2 = 7$) is optimal

e. This change moves $C_2$ outside its range of optimality; the new optimal solution is

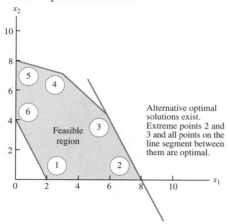

Alternative optimal solutions exist.
Extreme points 2 and 3 and all points on the line segment between them are optimal.

Alternative optimal solutions exist; extreme points 2 and 3 and all points on the line segment between them are optimal

4. By making a small increase in the right-hand side of constraint 1 and resolving, we find a dual price of 1.5 for the constraint. Thus, the objective function will improve at the rate of 1.5 per unit increase in the right-hand side. Because constraint 2 is not binding, its dual price is zero.

11. a. Regular glove = 500; Catcher's mitt = 150; Value = 3700
   b. The finishing, packaging, and shipping constraints are binding; there is no slack
   c. Cutting and sewing = 0
      Finishing = 3
      Packaging and shipping = 28
      Additional finishing time is worth $3 per unit, and additional packaging and shipping time is worth $28 per unit
   d. In the packaging and shipping department, each additional hour is worth $28

12. a. 4 to 12
       3.33 to 10
    b. As long as the profit contribution for the regular glove is between $4.00 and $12.00, the current solution is optimal. As long as the profit contribution for the catcher's mitt stays between $3.33 and $10.00, the current solution is optimal. The optimal solution is not sensitive to small changes in the profit contributions for the gloves.

c. The dual prices for the resources are applicable over the following ranges.

| Constraint | Range of Feasibility |
|---|---|
| Cutting and sewing | 725 to No Upper Limit |
| Finishing | 133.33 to 400 |
| Packaging and shipping | 75 to 135 |

d. Amount of increase = (28)(20) = $560

16. a. S = 4000, M = 10,000, Total risk = 62,000
    b.

| Variable | Range of Optimality |
|---|---|
| S | 3.75 to No Upper Limit |
| M | No Lower Limit to 6.4 |

c. 5(4000) + 4(10,000) = $60,000
d. 60,000 / 1,200,000 = 0.05 or 5%
e. 0.057 risk units
f. 0.057(100) = 5.7%

18. a. $x_1 = 0; x_2 = 25; x_3 = 125; x_4 = 0$
       Value of solution = 525.0
    b. The constraints on machine A and machine C hours are binding
    c. Machine B has 425 hours of excess capacity
    d. Yes, the allowable increase is only 0.05

19. a.

| Variable | Range of Optimality |
|---|---|
| $x_1$ | No Lower Limit to 4.05 |
| $x_2$ | 5.923 to 9 |
| $x_3$ | 2 to 12 |
| $x_4$ | No Lower Limit to 4.5 |

b. There is no lower limit on the allowable decrease for the objective function coefficient of $x_1$; thus the percentage decrease is 0%.

$$1.5/3 + 1/3.5 = 0.79$$

The accumulated percentage of allowable increases and decreases is 79%. Since this is less than 100%, the optimal solution will not change.

c.

| Constraint | Range of Feasibility |
|---|---|
| Machine A hours | 133.33 to 800 |
| Machine B hours | 275 to No Upper Limit |
| Machine C hours | 137.5 to 825 |

d. Yes, because that is outside the range of feasibility.

# Chapter 4

**1. a.** Let $x_1$ = number of television advertisements
$x_2$ = number of radio advertisements
$x_3$ = number of newspaper advertisements

Max   $100,000x_1 + 18,000x_2 + 40,000x_3$
s.t.

$$2000x_1 + 300x_2 + 600x_3 \leq 18,200 \text{ Budget}$$
$$x_1 \leq 10 \text{ Max TV}$$
$$x_2 \leq 20 \text{ Max radio}$$
$$x_3 \leq 10 \text{ Max news}$$
$$-0.5x_1 + 0.5x_2 - 0.5x_3 \leq 0 \text{ Max 50\% radio}$$
$$0.9x_1 - 0.1x_2 - 0.1x_3 \geq 0 \text{ Min 10\% TV}$$
$$x_1, x_2, x_3 \geq 0$$

| | Budget $ |
|---|---|
| Solution:  $x_1 = 4$ | $ 8000 |
| $x_2 = 14$ | 4200 |
| $x_3 = 10$ | 6000 |
| | $18,200 |

Audience = 1,052,000

**b.** The dual price for the budget constraint is 51.30. Thus, a $100 increase in the budget should provide an increase in audience coverage of approximately 5130. The range of feasibility for the right-hand side of the budget constraint will show that this interpretation is correct.

**9. a.** Decision variables A, P, M, H, and G represent the fraction or proportion of the total investment in each alternative

Max   $0.073A + 0.103P + 0.064M + 0.075H + 0.045G$
s.t.

$$A + P + M + H + G = 1$$
$$0.5A + 0.5P - 0.5M - 0.5H \leq 0$$
$$-0.5A - 0.5P + 0.5M + 0.5H \leq 0$$
$$- 0.25M - 0.25H + G \geq 0$$
$$-0.6A + 0.4P \leq 0$$
$$A, P, M, H, G \geq 0$$

Objective function = 0.079; $A = 0.178$; $P = 0.267$; $M = 0.000$; $H = 0.444$; $G = 0.111$

**b.** Multiplying $A, P, M, H,$ and $G$ by the $100,000 invested provides the following

| | |
|---|---|
| Atlantic Oil | $ 17,800 |
| Pacific Oil | 26,700 |
| Huber Steel | 44,400 |
| Government Bonds | 11,100 |
| | $100,000 |

**c.** $0.079(\$100,000) = \$7900$

**d.** The marginal rate of return is 0.079

**12. a.** The only change is in the objective function with the price per unit for the number of bases purchased (BP) lowered from 0.60 to 0.55. The solution for the new model provides an objective function value of $24,276.67, which is an overall savings of $166,66 compared to the previous solution. Janders will now purchase all 5000 bases from the supplier. In addition, Janders will increase the manufacturing of financial cartridges from 667 to 2333 units to take advantage of the manufacturing capacity freed by the fact that the company no longer needs to manufacture bases.

**b.** By referring to the computer solution in Figure 4.5, we can answer the question without modifying and resolving the original problem. The range of optimality for the objective function coefficient for TTP is No Lower Limit to $0.875. Because the price increase to $0.82 is within the range, the manufacturing and purchasing plan will not change. However, Janders purchases 2000 Technician tops. Thus, the price increase from $0.78 to $0.82 per unit will add $0.04(2000) = $80 to the total cost.

**c.** The only change in the original problem is to reduce the objective function coefficient for overtime (OT) premium from $9 to $2 per hour. This change enables Janders to use all 50 hours of overtime for manufacturing. The total cost is further reduced to $24,293, but the company still needs purchases of 1333 financial cartridges (FCP), 3000 financial tops (FTP), and 2000 technician tops (TTP). The overtime is used to increase the manufacturing of financial cartridges (FCM) from 667 to 1667 units.

**15.** Let $x_{11}$ = gallons of crude 1 used to produce regular
$x_{12}$ = gallons of crude 1 used to produce high octane
$x_{21}$ = gallons of crude 2 used to produce regular
$x_{22}$ = gallons of crude 2 used to produce high octane

Min   $0.10x_{11} + 0.10x_{12} + 0.15x_{21} + 0.15x_{22}$
s.t.

Each gallon of regular must have at least 40% A

$x_{11} + x_{21}$ = amount of regular produced
$0.4(x_{11} + x_{21})$ = amount of A required for regular
$0.2x_{11} + 0.50x_{21}$ = amount of A in $(x_{11} + x_{21})$ gallons of regular gas
$\therefore 0.2x_{11} + 0.50x_{21} \geq 0.4x_{11} + 0.40x_{21}$
$\therefore -0.2x_{11} + 0.10x_{21} \geq 0$

Each gallon of high octane can have at most 50% B

$x_{12} + x_{22}$ = amount high octane
$0.5(x_{12} + x_{22})$ = amount of B required for high octane
$0.60x_{12} + 0.30x_{22}$ = amount of B in $(x_{12} + x_{22})$ gallons of high octane
$\therefore 0.60x_{12} + 0.30x_{22} \leq 0.5x_{12} + 0.5x_{22}$
$\therefore 0.1x_{12} - 0.2x_{22} \leq 0$
$$x_{11} + x_{21} \geq 800,000$$
$$x_{12} + x_{22} \geq 500,000$$
$$x_{11}, x_{12}, x_{21}, x_{22} \geq 0$$

Optimal solution: $x_{11} = 266,667, x_{12} = 333,333, x_{21} = 533,333,$
$x_{22} = 166,667$
Cost = $165,000

**19. a.** Let $x_{11}$ = amount of men's model in month 1

$x_{21}$ = amount of women's model in month 1

$x_{12}$ = amount of men's model in month 2

$x_{22}$ = amount of women's model in month 2

$s_{11}$ = inventory of men's model at end of month 1

$s_{21}$ = inventory of women's model at end of month 1

$s_{12}$ = inventory of men's model at end of month 2

$s_{22}$ = inventory of women's model at end of month 2

Min $120x_{11} + 90x_{21} + 120x_{12} + 90x_{22} + 2.4s_{11} + 1.8s_{21} + 2.4s_{12} + 1.8s_{22}$

s.t.

$$\left.\begin{array}{l} x_{11} - \quad\quad s_{11} = 130 \\ x_{21} - \quad\quad s_{21} = \ 95 \\ s_{11} + x_{12} - s_{12} = 200 \\ s_{21} + x_{22} - s_{22} = 150 \end{array}\right\} \text{Satisfy demand}$$

$$\left.\begin{array}{l} s_{12} \geq 25 \\ \\ s_{22} \geq 25 \end{array}\right\} \text{Ending inventory requirement}$$

Labor-hours: Men's $2.0 + 1.5 = 3.5$

Women's $1.6 + 1.0 = 2.6$

$$\left.\begin{array}{l} 3.5x_{11} + 2.6x_{21} \geq \ 900 \\ 3.5x_{11} + 2.6x_{21} \leq 1100 \\ 3.5x_{11} + 2.6x_{21} - 3.5x_{12} - 2.6x_{22} \leq 100 \\ -3.5x_{11} - 2.6x_{21} + 3.5x_{12} + 2.6x_{22} \leq 100 \end{array}\right\} \text{Labor smoothing}$$

$x_{11}, x_{12}, x_{21}, x_{22}, s_{11}, s_{12}, s_{21}, s_{22} \geq 0$

Solution: $x_{11} = 193; x_{21} = 95; x_{12} = 162; x_{22} = 175$

Total cost = $67,156

Inventory levels: $s_{11} = 63; s_{12} = 25; s_{21} = 0; s_{22} = 25$

Labor levels: Previous     1000 hours

           Month 1     922.25 hours

           Month 2    1022.25 hours

**b.** To accommodate the new policy, the right-hand sides of the four labor-smoothing constraints must be changed to 950, 1050, 50, and 50, respectively. The new total cost is $67,175.

# Chapter 5

**1. a.** With $x_1 = 0$, we have

$$\begin{array}{ll} x_2 \quad\quad = 6 & (1) \\ 4x_2 + x_3 = 12 & (2) \end{array}$$

From (1), we have $x_2 = 6$; substituting for $x_2$ in (2) yields

$$4(6) + x_3 = 12$$
$$x_3 = 12 - 24 = -12$$

Basic solution: $x_1 = 0, x_2 = 6, x_3 = -12$

**b.** With $x_2 = 0$, we have

$$\begin{array}{ll} 3x_1 \quad\quad = 6 & (3) \\ 2x_1 + x_3 = 12 & (4) \end{array}$$

From (3), we find $x_1 = 2$; substituting for $x_1$ in (4) yields

$$2(2) + x_3 = 12$$
$$x_3 = 12 - 4 = 8$$

Basic solution: $x_1 = 2, x_2 = 0, x_3 = 8$

**c.** With $x_3 = 0$, we have

$$\begin{array}{ll} 3x_1 + \ x_2 = \ 6 & (5) \\ 2x_1 + 4x_2 = 12 & (6) \end{array}$$

Multiplying (6) by $\frac{3}{2}$ and subtracting from (5) yields

$$\begin{array}{r} 3x_1 + \ x_2 = 6 \\ -(3x_1 + 6x_2) = -18 \\ \hline -5x_2 = -12 \\ x_2 = {}^{12}\!/_5 \end{array}$$

Substituting $x_2 = {}^{12}\!/_5$ into (5) yields

$$3x_1 + {}^{12}\!/_5 = 6$$
$$3x_1 = {}^{18}\!/_5$$
$$x_1 = {}^{6}\!/_5$$

Basic solution: $x_1 = {}^{6}\!/_5, x_2 = {}^{12}\!/_5, x_3 = 0$

**d.** The basic solutions found in parts (b) and (c) are basic feasible solutions. The one in part (a) is not because $x_3 = -12$.

**4. a.** Standard form:

Max   $60x_1 + 90x_2$

s.t.

$$\begin{array}{l} 15x_1 + 45x_2 + s_1 \quad\quad = 90 \\ 5x_1 + \ 5x_2 \quad\quad + s_2 = 20 \\ x_1, x_2, s_1, s_2 \geq 0 \end{array}$$

**b.** Partial initial simple tableau:

|  | $x_1$ | $x_2$ | $s_1$ | $s_2$ |  |
|---|---|---|---|---|---|
|  | 60 | 90 | 0 | 0 |  |
|  | 15 | 45 | 1 | 0 | 90 |
|  | 5 | 5 | 0 | 1 | 20 |

**5. a.** Initial tableau:

|  |  | $x_1$ | $x_2$ | $s_1$ | $s_2$ |  |
|---|---|---|---|---|---|---|
| *Basis* | $c_B$ | 5 | 9 | 0 | 0 |  |
| $s_1$ | 0 | 10 | 9 | 1 | 0 | 90 |
| $s_2$ | 0 | -5 | 3 | 0 | 1 | 15 |
| $z_j$ |  | 0 | 0 | 0 | 0 | 0 |
| $c_j - z_j$ |  | 5 | 9 | 0 | 0 |  |

**b.** We would introduce $x_2$ at the first iteration

**c.** Max   $5x_1 + 9x_2$

s.t.

$$\begin{array}{l} 10x_1 + 9x_2 \leq 90 \\ -5x_1 + 3x_2 \leq 15 \\ x_1, x_2 \geq 0 \end{array}$$

**15.** Max   $4x_1 + 2x_2 - 3x_3 + 5x_4 + 0s_1 - Ma_1 + 0s_2 - Ma_3$

s.t.

$$\begin{array}{l} 2x_1 - 1x_2 + 1x_3 + 2x_4 - 1s_1 + 1a_1 \quad\quad\quad\quad = 50 \\ 3x_1 \quad\quad - 1x_3 + 2x_4 \quad\quad\quad\quad + 1s_2 \quad\quad = 80 \\ 1x_1 + 1x_2 \quad\quad + 1x_4 \quad\quad\quad\quad\quad\quad + 1a_3 = 60 \\ x_1, x_2, x_3, x_4, s_1, s_2, a_1, a_3 \geq 0 \end{array}$$

**17.** Converting to a max problem and solving using the simplex method, the final simplex tableau is

| Basis | $c_B$ | $x_1$ $-3$ | $x_2$ $-4$ | $x_3$ $-8$ | $s_1$ $0$ | $s_2$ $0$ | |
|---|---|---|---|---|---|---|---|
| $x_1$ | $-3$ | 1 | 0 | $-1$ | $-\frac{1}{4}$ | $\frac{1}{8}$ | 1 |
| $x_2$ | $-4$ | 0 | 1 | 2 | 0 | $-\frac{1}{4}$ | 4 |
| $z_j$ | | $-3$ | $-4$ | $-5$ | $\frac{3}{4}$ | $\frac{5}{8}$ | $-19$ |
| $c_j - z_j$ | | 0 | 0 | $-3$ | $-\frac{3}{4}$ | $-\frac{5}{8}$ | |

23. Final simplex tableau:

| Basis | $c_B$ | $x_1$ $4$ | $x_2$ $8$ | $s_1$ $0$ | $s_2$ $0$ | $a_2$ $-M$ | |
|---|---|---|---|---|---|---|---|
| $x_2$ | $8$ | 1 | 1 | $\frac{1}{2}$ | 0 | 0 | 5 |
| $a_2$ | $-M$ | $-2$ | 0 | $-\frac{1}{2}$ | $-1$ | 1 | 3 |
| $z_j$ | | $8+2M$ | 8 | $4+M/2$ | $+M$ | $-M$ | $40-3M$ |
| $c_j - z_j$ | | $-4-2M$ | 0 | $-4-M/2$ | $-M$ | 0 | |

Infeasible; optimal solution condition is reached with the artificial variable $a_2$ still in the solution

24. Alternative optimal solutions:

| Basis | $c_B$ | $x_1$ $-3$ | $x_2$ $-3$ | $s_1$ $0$ | $s_2$ $0$ | $s_3$ $0$ | |
|---|---|---|---|---|---|---|---|
| $s_2$ | $0$ | 0 | 0 | $-\frac{4}{3}$ | 1 | $\frac{1}{6}$ | 4 |
| $x_1$ | $-3$ | 1 | 0 | $-\frac{2}{3}$ | 0 | $\frac{1}{12}$ | 4 |
| $x_2$ | $-3$ | 0 | 1 | $\frac{2}{3}$ | 0 | $-\frac{1}{3}$ | 4 |
| $z_j$ | | $-3$ | $-3$ | 0 | 0 | $\frac{3}{4}$ | $-24$ |
| $c_j - z_j$ | | 0 | 0 | 0 | 0 | $-\frac{3}{4}$ | |

$$\uparrow$$

Indicates alternative optimal solutions exist:
$$x_1 = 4, x_2 = 4, z = 24$$
$$x_1 = 8, x_2 = 0, z = 24$$

25. Unbounded solution:

| Basis | $c_B$ | $x_1$ $1$ | $x_2$ $1$ | $s_1$ $0$ | $s_2$ $0$ | $s_3$ $0$ | |
|---|---|---|---|---|---|---|---|
| $s_3$ | $0$ | $\frac{8}{3}$ | 0 | $-\frac{1}{3}$ | 0 | 1 | 4 |
| $s_2$ | $0$ | 4 | 0 | $-1$ | 1 | 0 | 36 |
| $x_2$ | $1$ | $\frac{4}{3}$ | 1 | $-\frac{1}{6}$ | 0 | 0 | 4 |
| $z_j$ | | $\frac{4}{3}$ | 1 | $-\frac{1}{6}$ | 0 | 0 | 4 |
| $c_j - z_j$ | | $-\frac{1}{3}$ | 0 | $\frac{1}{6}$ | 0 | 0 | |

$$\uparrow$$

Incoming column

# Chapter 6

1. a. Recomputing the $c_j - z_j$ values for the nonbasic variables with $c_1$ as the coefficient of $x_1$ leads to the following inequalities that must be satisfied:

For $x_2$, we get no inequality because of the zero in the $x_2$ column for the row in which $x_1$ is a basic variable
For $s_1$, we get

$$0 + 4 - c_1 \leq 0$$
$$c_1 \geq 4$$

For $s_2$, we get

$$0 - 12 + 2c_1 \leq 0$$
$$2c_1 \leq 12$$
$$c_1 \leq 6$$
$$\text{Range: } 4 \leq c_1 \leq 6$$

b. Because $x_2$ is nonbasic, we have

$$c_2 \leq 8$$

c. Because $s_1$ is nonbasic, we have

$$c_{s_1} \leq 1$$

3. a. It is the $z_j$ value for $s_1$; dual price = 1
   b. It is the $z_j$ value for $s_2$; dual price = 2
   c. It is the $z_j$ value for $s_3$; dual price = 0
   d. $$s_3 = 80 + 5(-2) = 70$$
      $$x_3 = 30 + 5(-1) = 25$$
      $$x_1 = 20 + 5(1) = 25$$
      $$\text{Value} = 220 + 5(1) = 225$$
   e. $$s_3 = 80 - 10(-2) = 100$$
      $$x_3 = 30 - 10(-1) = 40$$
      $$x_1 = 20 - 10(1) = 10$$
      $$\text{Value} = 220 - 10(1) = 210$$

4. a. $80 + \Delta b_1(-2) \geq 0 \qquad \Delta b_1 \leq 40$
      $30 + \Delta b_1(-1) \geq 0 \qquad \Delta b_1 \leq 30$
      $20 + \Delta b_1(1) \geq 0 \qquad \Delta b_1 \geq -20$
      $$-20 \leq \Delta b_1 \leq 30$$
      $$100 \leq b_1 \leq 150$$
   b. $80 + \Delta b_2(7) \geq 0 \qquad \Delta b_2 \geq -80/7$
      $30 + \Delta b_2(3) \geq 0 \qquad \Delta b_2 \geq -10$
      $20 + \Delta b_2(-2) \geq 0 \qquad \Delta b_2 \leq 10$
      $$-10 \leq \Delta b_2 \leq 10$$
      $$40 \leq b_2 \leq 60$$
   c. $80 - \Delta b_3(1) \geq 0 \rightarrow \Delta b_3 \leq 80$
      $30 - \Delta b_3(0) \geq 0$
      $20 - \Delta b_3(0) \geq 0$
      $$\Delta b_3 \leq 80$$
      $$b_3 \leq 110$$

17. a. The dual is given by:

   Min $550u_1 + 700u_2 + 200u_3$
   s.t.
   $$\begin{aligned}
   1.5u_1 + 4u_2 + 2u_3 &\geq 4 \\
   2u_1 + 1u_2 + 3u_3 &\geq 6 \\
   4u_1 + 2u_2 + 1u_3 &\geq 3 \\
   3u_1 + 1u_2 + 2u_3 &\geq 1 \\
   u_1, u_2, u_3 &\geq 0
   \end{aligned}$$

   b. Optimal solution: $u_1 = 3/10$; $u_2 = 0$, $u_3 = 54/30$
   The $z_j$ values for the four surplus variables of the dual show $x_1 = 0$, $x_2 = 25$, $x_3 = 125$, and $x_4 = 0$

**c.** Because $u_1 = 3/10$, $u_2 = 0$, and $u_3 = 54/30$, machines A and C ($u_j > 0$) are operating at capacity; machine C is the priority machine since each hour is worth 54/30

**18.** The dual is given by

Max $5u_1 + 5u_2 + 24u_3$

s.t.

$$15u_1 + 4u_2 + 12u_3 \leq 2800$$
$$15u_1 + 8u_2 \qquad \leq 6000$$
$$u_1 \qquad + 8u_3 \leq 1200$$
$$u_1, u_2, u_3 \geq 0$$

**19.** The canonical form is

Max $3x_1 + x_2 + 5x_3 + 3x_4$

s.t.

$$3x_1 + 1x_2 + 2x_3 \qquad \leq 30$$
$$-3x_1 - 1x_2 - 2x_3 \qquad \leq -30$$
$$-2x_1 - 1x_2 - 3x_3 - x_4 \leq -15$$
$$2x_2 \qquad + 3x_4 \leq 25$$
$$x_1, x_2, x_3, x_4 \geq 0$$

The dual is

Min $30u_1' - 30u_1'' - 15u_2 + 25u_3$

s.t.

$$3u_1' - 3u_1'' - 2u_2 \qquad \geq 3$$
$$u_1' - u_1'' - u_2 + 2u_3 \geq 1$$
$$2u_1' - 2u_1'' - 3u_2 \qquad \geq 5$$
$$- u_2 + 3u_3 \geq 3$$
$$u_1', u_1'', u_2, u_3 \geq 0$$

## Chapter 7

**1.**

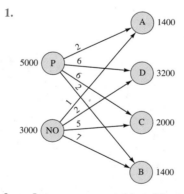

**2. a.** Let $x_{11}$ = amount shipped from Jefferson City to Des Moines

$x_{12}$ = amount shipped from Jefferson City to Kansas City

$\vdots$

$x_{23}$ = amount shipped from Omaha to St. Louis

Min $14x_{11} + 9x_{12} + 7x_{13} + 8x_{21} + 10x_{22} + 5x_{23}$

s.t.

$$x_{11} + x_{12} + x_{13} \qquad \leq 30$$

$$x_{21} + x_{22} + x_{23} \leq 20$$
$$x_{11} \qquad + x_{21} \qquad = 25$$
$$x_{12} \qquad + x_{22} \qquad = 15$$
$$x_{13} \qquad + x_{23} = 10$$
$$x_{11}, x_{12}, x_{13}, x_{21}, x_{22}, x_{23} \geq 0$$

**b.**

| Optimal Solution | Amount | Cost |
|---|---|---|
| Jefferson City–Des Moines | 5 | 70 |
| Jefferson City–Kansas City | 15 | 135 |
| Jefferson City–St. Louis | 10 | 70 |
| Omaha–Des Moines | 20 | 160 |
| | Total | 435 |

**8.** The network model, the linear programming formulation and the optimal solution are shown. Note that the third constraint corresponds to the dummy origin; the variables $x_{31}$, $x_{32}$, $x_{33}$, and $x_{34}$ are the amounts shipped out of the dummy origin and do not appear in the objective function since they are given a coefficient of zero.

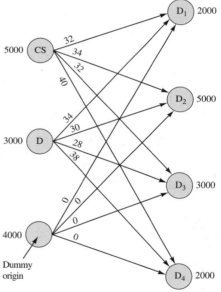

Max $32x_{11} + 34x_{12} + 32x_{13} + 40x_{14} + 34x_{21} + 30x_{22} + 28x_{23} + 38x_{24}$

s.t.

$$x_{11} + x_{12} + x_{13} + x_{14} \qquad \leq 5000$$
$$x_{21} + x_{22} + x_{23} + x_{24} \qquad \leq 3000$$
$$x_{31} + x_{32} + x_{33} + x_{34} \leq 4000$$
$$x_{11} \qquad + x_{21} \qquad + x_{31} \qquad = 2000$$
$$x_{12} \qquad + x_{22} \qquad + x_{32} \qquad = 5000$$
$$x_{13} \qquad + x_{23} \qquad + x_{33} \qquad = 3000$$
$$x_{14} \qquad + x_{24} \qquad + x_{34} = 2000$$
$$x_{ij} \geq 0 \qquad \text{for all } i, j$$

| Optimal Solution | Units | Cost |
|---|---|---|
| Clifton Springs–$D_2$ | 4000 | $136,000 |
| Clifton Springs–$D_4$ | 1000 | 40,000 |
| Danville–$D_1$ | 2000 | 68,000 |
| Danville–$D_4$ | 1000 | 38,000 |
| | Total | $282,000 |

Customer 2 demand has a shortfall of 1000; customer 3 demand of 3000 is not satisfied

**12. a.**

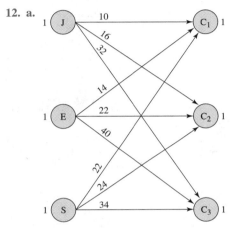

**b.**

$$\text{Min} \quad 10x_{11} + 16x_{12} + 32x_{13} + 14x_{21} + 22x_{22} + 40x_{23} + 22x_{31} + 24x_{32} + 34x_{33}$$

s.t.

$$
\begin{aligned}
x_{11} + x_{12} + x_{13} &\leq 1 \\
x_{21} + x_{22} + x_{23} &\leq 1 \\
x_{31} + x_{32} + x_{33} &\leq 1 \\
x_{11} + x_{21} + x_{31} &= 1 \\
x_{12} + x_{22} + x_{32} &= 1 \\
x_{13} + x_{23} + x_{33} &= 1 \\
x_{ij} &\geq 0 \text{ for all } i, j
\end{aligned}
$$

Solution $x_{12} = 1$, $x_{21} = 1$, $x_{33} = 1$; total completion time = 64

**23. a.**

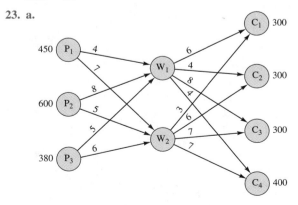

**b.**

$$
\begin{aligned}
\text{Min} \quad & 4x_{14} + 7x_{15} + 8x_{24} + 5x_{25} + 5x_{34} + 6x_{35} + 6x_{46} + 4x_{47} \\
& + 8x_{48} + 4x_{49} + 3x_{56} + 6x_{57} + 7x_{58} + 7x_{59} + x_{14} + x_{15} \leq 450 \\
& \qquad\qquad\qquad\qquad\qquad\qquad\qquad\qquad\qquad\qquad x_{24} + x_{25} \leq 600 \\
& \qquad\qquad\qquad\qquad\qquad\qquad\qquad\qquad\qquad\qquad x_{34} + x_{35} \leq 380 \\
& -x_{14} - x_{24} - x_{34} + x_{46} + x_{47} + x_{48} + x_{49} = 0 \\
& -x_{15} - x_{25} - x_{35} + x_{56} + x_{57} + x_{58} + x_{59} = 0 \\
& \qquad\qquad\qquad\qquad\qquad\qquad x_{46} + x_{56} = 300 \\
& \qquad\qquad\qquad\qquad\qquad\qquad x_{47} + x_{57} = 300 \\
& \qquad\qquad\qquad\qquad\qquad\qquad x_{48} + x_{58} = 300 \\
& \qquad\qquad\qquad\qquad\qquad\qquad x_{49} + x_{59} = 300
\end{aligned}
$$

**c.**

| | Warehouse | |
|---|---|---|
| **Plant** | **1** | **2** |
| 1 | 450 | — |
| 2 | — | 600 |
| 3 | 250 | — |

Total cost = $11,850

| | Customer | | | |
|---|---|---|---|---|
| **Warehouse** | **1** | **2** | **3** | **4** |
| 1 | — | 300 | — | 400 |
| 2 | 300 | — | 300 | — |

**34. a.** An initial solution is

| | Los Angeles | San Francisco | San Diego |
|---|---|---|---|
| San Jose | 4 / 100 | 10 | 6 |
| Las Vegas | 8 / 100 | 16 | 6 / 200 |
| Tucson | 14 | 18 / 300 | 10 |

Total cost = $7800

**b.** Note that the initial solution is degenerate because only 4 cells are occupied; a zero is assigned to the cell in row 3 and column 1 so that the row and column indexes can be computed.

**Transportation tableau (top left):**

| $u_i$ | $v_j$ = 4 | $v_j$ = 8 | $v_j$ = 2 |
|---|---|---|---|
| 0 | 4 / 100 | 10 / (2) | 6 / (4) |
| 4 | 8 / 100 | 16 / (4) | 6 / 200 |
| 10 | 14 / 0 | 18 / 300 | 10 / (−2) |

Cell in row 3 and column 3 is identified as an incoming cell; however, 0 units can be added to this cell. Initial solution remains optimal.

**c.**

| | |
|---|---|
| San Jose–San Francisco: | 100 |
| Las Vegas–Los Angeles: | 200 |
| Las Vegas–San Diego: | 100 |
| Tucson–San Francisco: | 200 |
| Tucson–San Diego | 100 |
| Total Cost = $7800 | |

Note that this total cost is the same as for part (a); thus, we have alternative optimal solution

**d.** The final transportation tableau is shown; the total transportation cost is $8000, an increase of $200 over the solution to part (a)

| $u_i$ | $v_j$ = 2 | $v_j$ = 10 | $v_j$ = 2 | |
|---|---|---|---|---|
| 0 | 4 / (2) | 10 / 100 | 6 / (4) | 100 |
| 6 | 8 / 200 | 16 / 100 | M / (M−8) | 300 |
| 8 | 14 / (4) | 18 / 100 | 10 / 200 | 300 |
| | 200 | 300 | 200 | 700 |

**40.** Subtract 10 from row 1, 14 from row 2, and 22 from row 3 to obtain:

| | 1 | 2 | 3 |
|---|---|---|---|
| Jackson | 0 | 6 | 22 |
| Ellis | 0 | 8 | 26 |
| Smith | 0 | 2 | 12 |

Subtract 0 from column 1, 2 from column 2, and 12 from column 3 to obtain:

| | 1 | 2 | 3 |
|---|---|---|---|
| Jackson | 0 | (4) | 10 |
| Ellis | 0 | 6 | 14 |
| Smith | 0 | 0 | 0 |

Two lines cover the zeros; the minimum unlined element is 4; Step 3 yields:

| | 1 | 2 | 3 |
|---|---|---|---|
| Jackson | 0 | [0] | 6 |
| Ellis | [0] | 2 | 10 |
| Smith | 0 | 0 | [0] |

Optimal solution: Jackson–2
Ellis–1
Smith–3
Time requirement is 64 days

**43.** We start with the opportunity loss matrix:

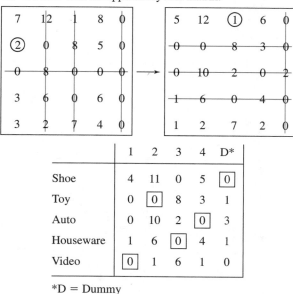

|  | 1 | 2 | 3 | 4 | D* |
|---|---|---|---|---|---|
| Shoe | 4 | 11 | 0 | 5 | [0] |
| Toy | 0 | [0] | 8 | 3 | 1 |
| Auto | 0 | 10 | 2 | [0] | 3 |
| Houseware | 1 | 6 | [0] | 4 | 1 |
| Video | [0] | 1 | 6 | 1 | 0 |

*D = Dummy

| | Optimal Solution | Profit |
|---|---|---|
| Toy | 2 | 18 |
| Auto | 4 | 16 |
| Houseware | 3 | 13 |
| Video | 1 | 14 |
| | Total | 61 |

# Chapter 8

**2. a.**

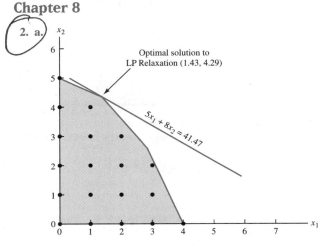

Optimal solution to LP Relaxation (1.43, 4.29)

$5x_1 + 8x_2 = 41.47$

**b.** The optimal solution to the LP Relaxation is given by $x_1 = 1.43$, $x_2 = 4.29$ with an objective function value of 41.47. Rounding down gives the feasible integer solution $x_1 = 1$, $x_2 = 4$; its value is 37

**c.**

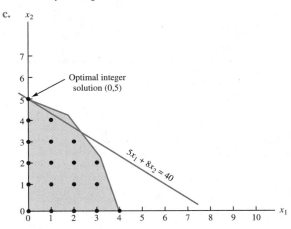

Optimal integer solution (0,5)

$5x_1 + 8x_2 = 40$

The optimal solution is given by $x_1 = 0$, $x_2 = 5$; its value is 40. It is not the same solution as found by rounding down; it provides a 3-unit increase in the value of the objective function

**5. a.** The feasible mixed-integer solutions are indicated by the boldface vertical lines in the graph

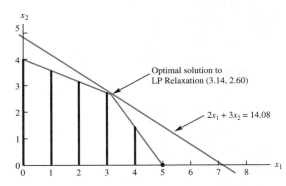

Optimal solution to LP Relaxation (3.14, 2.60)

$2x_1 + 3x_2 = 14.08$

**b.** The optimal solution to the LP Relaxation is given by $x_1 = 3.14$, $x_2 = 2.60$; its value is 14.08
Rounding down the value of $x_1$ to find a feasible mixed-integer solution yields $x_1 = 3$, $x_2 = 2.60$ with a value of 13.8; this solution is clearly not optimal; with $x_1 = 3$, $x_2$ can be made larger without violating the constraints

**c.** The optimal solution to the MILP is given by $x_1 = 3$, $x_2 = 2.67$; its value is 14 as shown in the following figure

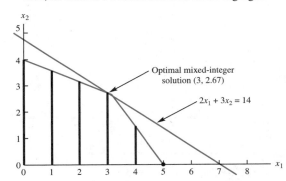

Optimal mixed-integer solution (3, 2.67)

$2x_1 + 3x_2 = 14$

**7. a.** $x_1 + x_3 + x_5 + x_6 = 2$
**b.** $x_3 - x_5 = 0$
**c.** $x_1 + x_4 = 1$
**d.** $x_4 \leq x_1$
$x_4 \leq x_3$
**e.** $x_4 \leq x_1$
$x_4 \leq x_3$
$x_4 \geq x_1 + x_3 - 1$

**13. a.** Add the following multiple-choice constraint to the problem
$y_2 + y_2 = 1$
New optimal Solution: $y_1 = 1$, $y_3 = 1$, $x_{12} = 10$, $x_{31} = 30$, $x_{52} = 10$, $x_{53} = 20$
Value = 940

**b.** Because one plant is already located in St. Louis, it is only necessary to add the following constraint to the model
$y_3 + y_4 \leq 1$
New Optimal Solution: $y_4 = 1$, $x_{42} = 20$, $x_{43} = 20$, $x_{51} = 30$
Value = 860

# Chapter 9

**1.**

| Node | Shortest Route from Node 1 | Distance |
|------|------|------|
| 2 | 1–2 | 7 |
| 3 | 1–3 | 9 |
| 4 | 1–2–5–6–4 | 17 |
| 5 | 1–2–5 | 12 |
| 6 | 1–2–5–6 | 14 |
| 7 | 1–2–5–6–7 | 17 |

**10.**

| Connect | Distant |
|------|------|
| 1–6 | 2 |
| 6–7 | 3 |
| 7–8 | 1 |
| 7–10 | 2 |
| 10–9 | 3 |
| 9–4 | 2 |
| 9–3 | 3 |
| 3–2 | 1 |
| 4–5 | 3 |
| 7–11 | 4 |
| 8–13 | 4 |
| 14–15 | 2 |
| 15–12 | 3 |
| 14–13 | 4 |
| Total | 37 |

**15.**

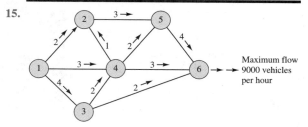

Maximum flow 9000 vehicles per hour

# Chapter 10

**3.**

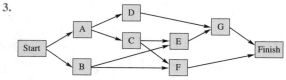

**6. a.** Crital path: A–D–F–H
**b.** 22 weeks
**c.** No, it is a critical activity
**d.** Yes, 2 weeks
**e.** Schedule for activity E:

| | |
|------|------|
| Earliest start | 3 |
| Latest start | 4 |
| Earliest finish | 10 |
| Latest finish | 11 |

**10. a.**

| Activity | Optimistic | Most Probable | Pessimistic | Expected Times | Variance |
|------|------|------|------|------|------|
| A | 4 | 5.0 | 6 | 5.00 | 0.11 |
| B | 8 | 9.0 | 10 | 9.00 | 0.11 |
| C | 7 | 7.5 | 11 | 8.00 | 0.44 |
| D | 7 | 9.0 | 10 | 8.83 | 0.25 |
| E | 6 | 7.0 | 9 | 7.17 | 0.25 |
| F | 5 | 6.0 | 7 | 6.00 | 0.11 |

**b.** Critical activities: B–D–F
Expected project completion time: $9.00 + 8.83 + 6.00 = 23.83$
Variance of projection completion time: $0.11 + 0.25 + 0.11 = 0.47$

**13.**

| Activity | Expected Time | Variance |
|------|------|------|
| A | 5 | 0.11 |
| B | 3 | 0.03 |
| C | 7 | 0.11 |
| D | 6 | 0.44 |
| E | 7 | 0.44 |
| F | 3 | 0.11 |
| G | 10 | 0.44 |
| H | 8 | 1.78 |

From Problem 6, A–D–F–H is the critical path, so
$E(T) = 5 + 6 + 3 + 8 = 22$
$\sigma^2 = 0.11 + 0.44 + 0.11 + 1.78 = 2.44$
$$z = \frac{\text{Time} - E(T)}{\sigma} = \frac{\text{Time} - 22}{\sqrt{2.44}}$$

**a.** Time = 21:　　　　$z = -0.64$　　　Area 0.2389
　　$P(21 \text{ weeks}) = 0.500 - 0.2389 = 0.2611$

**b.** Time = 22:　　　　$z = 0$　　　Area 0.0000
　　$P(22 \text{ weeks}) = 0.5000$

**c.** Time = 25:　　　　$z = +1.92$　　　Area 0.4726
　　$P(25 \text{ weeks}) = 0.5000 + 0.4726 = 0.9726$

**21. a.**

| Activity | Earliest Start | Latest Start | Earliest Finish | Latest Finish | Slack | Critical Activity |
|---|---|---|---|---|---|---|
| A | 0 | 0 | 3 | 3 | 0 | Yes |
| B | 0 | 1 | 2 | 3 | 1 | |
| C | 3 | 3 | 8 | 8 | 0 | Yes |
| D | 2 | 3 | 7 | 8 | 1 | |
| E | 8 | 8 | 14 | 14 | 0 | Yes |
| F | 8 | 10 | 10 | 12 | 2 | |
| G | 10 | 12 | 12 | 14 | 2 | |

Critical Path: A–C–E
Project completion time $= t_A + t_C + t_E = 3 + 5 + 6 = $ 14 days
**b.** Total cost = $8400

**22. a.**

| Activity | Max Crash Days | Crash Cost/Day |
|---|---|---|
| A | 1 | 600 |
| B | 1 | 700 |
| C | 2 | 400 |
| D | 2 | 400 |
| E | 2 | 500 |
| F | 1 | 400 |
| G | 1 | 500 |

Min  $600Y_A + 700Y_B + 400Y_C + 400Y_D + 500Y_E + 400Y_F + 400Y_G$
s.t.

$$X_A + \quad Y_A \geq 3$$
$$X_B + \quad Y_B \geq 2$$
$$-X_A + X_C + Y_C \geq 5$$
$$-X_B + X_D + Y_D \geq 5$$
$$-X_C + X_E + Y_E \geq 6$$
$$-X_D + X_E + Y_E \geq 6$$
$$-X_C + X_F + Y_F \geq 2$$
$$-X_D + X_F + Y_F \geq 2$$
$$-X_F + X_G + Y_G \geq 2$$
$$-X_E + X_{FIN} \geq 0$$
$$-X_G + X_{FIN} \geq 0$$
$$X_{FIN} \leq 12$$
$$Y_A \leq 1$$
$$Y_B \leq 1$$
$$Y_C \leq 2$$
$$Y_D \leq 2$$
$$Y_E \leq 2$$
$$Y_F \leq 1$$
$$Y_G \leq 1$$
All $X, Y \geq 0$

**b.** Solution of the linear programming model in part (a) shows

| Activity | Crash | Crashing Cost |
|---|---|---|
| C | 1 day | $400 |
| E | 1 day | 500 |
| | Total | $900 |

**c.** Total cost = Normal cost + Crashing cost
= $8400 + $900 = $9300

## Chapter 11

**1. a.** $Q^* = \sqrt{\dfrac{2DC_0}{C_h}} = \sqrt{\dfrac{2(3600)(20)}{0.25(3)}} = 438.18$

**b.** $r = dm = \dfrac{3600}{250}(5) = 72$

**c.** $T = \dfrac{250Q^*}{D} = \dfrac{250(438.18)}{3600} = 30.43$ days

**d.** $TC = \dfrac{1}{2}QC_h + \dfrac{D}{Q}C_0$

$= \dfrac{1}{2}(438.18)(0.25)(3) + \dfrac{3600}{438.18}(20) = \$328.63$

**13. a.** $Q^* = \sqrt{\dfrac{2DC_0}{(1 - D/P)C_h}}$

$= \sqrt{\dfrac{2(7200)(150)}{(1 - 7200/25,000)(0.18)(14.50)}} = 1078.12$

**b.** Number of production runs $= \dfrac{D}{Q^*} = \dfrac{7200}{1078.12} = 6.68$

**c.** $T = \dfrac{250Q}{D} = \dfrac{250(1078.12)}{7200} = 37.43$ days

**d.** Production run length $= \dfrac{Q}{P/250}$

$= \dfrac{1078.12}{25,000/250} = 10.78$ days

**e.** Maximum inventory $= \left(1 - \dfrac{D}{P}\right)Q$

$= \left(1 - \dfrac{7200}{25,000}\right)(1078.12)$

$= 767.62$

**f.** Holding cost $= \dfrac{1}{2}\left(1 - \dfrac{D}{P}\right)QC_h$

$= \dfrac{1}{2}\left(1 - \dfrac{7200}{25,000}\right)(1078.12)(0.18)(14.50)$

$= \$1001.74$

$$\text{Ordering cost} = \frac{D}{Q}C_0 = \frac{7200}{1078.12}(150) = \$1001.74$$

$$\text{Total cost} = \$2003.48$$

**g.** $r = dm = \left(\dfrac{D}{250}\right)m = \dfrac{7200}{250}(15) = 432$

**15. a.** $Q^* = \sqrt{\dfrac{2DC_0}{C_h}\left(\dfrac{C_h + C_b}{C_b}\right)}$

$\phantom{15. a. Q^*} = \sqrt{\dfrac{2(12,000)(25)}{0.50}\left(\dfrac{0.50 + 5}{0.50}\right)} = 1148.91$

**b.** $S^* = Q^*\left(\dfrac{C_h}{C_h + C_b}\right) = 1148.91\left(\dfrac{0.50}{0.50 + 5}\right) = 104.45$

**c.** Max inventory $= Q^* - S^* = 1044.46$

**d.** $T = \dfrac{250Q^*}{D} = \dfrac{250(1148.91)}{12,000} = 23.94$ days

**e.**   Holding $= \dfrac{(Q - S)^2}{2Q}C_h = \$237.38$

$\phantom{e.}$ Ordering $= \dfrac{D}{Q}C_0 = 261.12$

$\phantom{e.}$ Backorder $= \dfrac{S^2}{2Q}C_b = 23.74$

$\phantom{e.}$ Total cost $= \$522.24$

The total cost for the EOQ model in Problem 4 was \$547.72; allowing backorders reduces the total cost.

**21.**   $Q = \sqrt{\dfrac{2DC_0}{C_h}}$

$\phantom{21.} Q_1 = \sqrt{\dfrac{2(500)(40)}{0.20(10)}} = 141.42$

$\phantom{21.} Q_2 = \sqrt{\dfrac{2(500)(40)}{0.20(9.7)}} = 143.59$

Because $Q_1$ is over its limit of 99 units, $Q_1$ cannot be optimal (see Problem 23); use $Q_2 = 143.59$ as the optimal order quantity.

$\text{Total cost} = \dfrac{1}{2}QC_h + \dfrac{D}{Q}C_0 + DC$

$\phantom{\text{Total cost}} = 139.28 + 139.28 + 4850.00 = \$5128.56$

**25. a.**     $c_o = 80 - 50 = 30$

$\phantom{25. a.} c_u = 125 - 80 = 45$

$\phantom{25. a.} P(D \le Q^*) = \dfrac{c_u}{c_u + c_o} = \dfrac{45}{45 + 30} = 0.60$

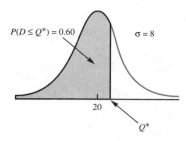

$P(D \le Q^*) = 0.60$      $\sigma = 8$

For an area of 0.60 below $Q^*$, $z = 0.25$
$Q^* = 20 + 0.25(8) = 22$

**b.** $P(\text{Sell all}) = P(D \ge Q^*) = 1 - 0.60 = 0.40$

**29. a.** $r = dm = (200/250)15 = 12$

**b.** $\dfrac{D}{Q} = \dfrac{200}{25} = 8$ orders/year

The limit of 1 stockout per year means that
$P(\text{Stockout/ cycle}) = 1/8 = 0.125$

$\sigma = 2.5$

$P(\text{Stockout}) = 0.125$

For area in tail $= 0.125$, $z = 1.15$
$$z = \frac{r - 12}{2.5} = 1.15$$
or
$$r = 12 + 1.15(2.5) = 14.875 \approx 15$$

**c.** Safety stock $= 3$ units
Added cost $= 3(\$5) = \$15$/year

**33. a.** $1/52 = 0.0192$

**b.** $M = \mu + z\sigma = 60 + 2.07(12) = 85$

**c.** $M = 35 + (0.9808)(85 - 35) = 84$

**37.** Quantity of snowblowers to be produced:

| | |
|---|---:|
| Quantity of snowblowers to be produced: | 5000 |
| Gross requirements, engines: | 5000 |
| Engines in inventory: | 2000 |
| Net requirements, engines: | 3000 |
| Gross requirements, air cleaners: | 3000 |
| Air cleaners in inventory: | 1500 |
| Net requirements, air cleaners: | 1500 |
| Gross requirements, filter housings: | 1500 |
| Filter housings in inventory: | 1000 |
| Net requirements, filter housing: | 500 |

## Chapter 12

**5. a.** $P_0 = 1 - \dfrac{\lambda}{\mu} = 1 - \dfrac{10}{12} = 0.1667$

b. $L_q = \dfrac{\lambda^2}{\mu(\mu - \lambda)} = \dfrac{10^2}{12(12 - 10)} = 4.1667$

c. $W_q = \dfrac{L_q}{\lambda} = 0.4167$ hour (25 minutes)

d. $W = W_q + \dfrac{1}{\mu} = 0.5$ hour (30 minutes)

e. $P_w = \dfrac{\lambda}{\mu} = \dfrac{10}{12} = 0.8333$

**11. a.**  $\lambda = 2.5;$  $\mu = \dfrac{60}{10} = 6$ customers per hour

$L_q = \dfrac{\lambda^2}{\mu(\mu - \lambda)} = \dfrac{(2.5)^2}{6(6 - 2.5)} = 0.2976$

$L = L_q + \dfrac{\lambda}{\mu} = 0.7143$

$W_q = \dfrac{L_q}{\lambda} = 0.1190$ hours (7.14 minutes)

$W = W_q + \dfrac{1}{\mu} = 0.2857$ hours

$P_w = \dfrac{\lambda}{\mu} = \dfrac{2.5}{6} = 0.4167$

b. No; $W_q = 7.14$ minutes; firm should increase the mean service rate $(\mu)$ for the consultant or hire a second consultant

c.  $\mu = \dfrac{60}{8} = 7.5$ customers per hour

$L_q = \dfrac{\lambda^2}{\mu(\mu - \lambda)} = \dfrac{(2.5)^2}{7.5(7.5 - 2.5)} = 0.1667$

$W_q = \dfrac{L_q}{\lambda} = 0.0667$ hour (4 minutes)

The service goal is being met

**19. a.** $k = 2; \lambda/\mu = 14/10 = 1.4; P_0 = 0.1765$

b. $L_q = \dfrac{(\lambda/\mu)^2 \lambda\mu}{1!(2\mu - \lambda)^2} P_0 = \dfrac{(1.4)^2(14)(10)}{(20 - 14)^2}(0.1765)$

$= 1.3451$

$L = L_q + \dfrac{\lambda}{\mu} = 1.3451 + \dfrac{14}{10} = 2.7451$

c. $W_q = \dfrac{L_q}{\lambda} = \dfrac{1.3453}{14} = 0.961$ hours (5.77 min.)

d. $W = W_q + \dfrac{1}{\mu} = 0.0961 + \dfrac{1}{10}$

$= 0.1961$ hours (11.77 min.)

e. $P_0 = 0.1765$

$P_1 = \dfrac{(\lambda/\mu)^1}{1!} P_0 = \dfrac{14}{10}(0.1765) = 0.2470$

$P(\text{wait}) = P(n \geq 2) = 1 - P(n \leq 1)$
$= 1 - 0.4235 = 0.5765$

**21.** From Problem 11, a service time of 8 minutes has $\mu = 60/8 = 7.5$

$L_q = \dfrac{\lambda^2}{\mu(\mu - \lambda)} = \dfrac{(2.5)^2}{7.5(7.5 - 2.5)} = 0.1667$

$L = L_q + \dfrac{\lambda}{\mu} = 0.50$

Total cost = $25L + $16
$= 25(0.50) + 16 = $28.50$
Two channels: $\lambda = 2.5; \mu = 60/10 = 6$
Using equation (12.11) and $P_0 = 0.6552$, we get

$L_q = \dfrac{(\lambda/\mu)^2 \lambda\mu}{1!(2\mu - \lambda)^2} P_0 = 0.0189$

$L = L_q + \dfrac{\lambda}{\mu} = 0.4356$

Total cost = $25(0.4356) + 2(16) = $42.89$
Use one consultant with an 8-minute service time

**25.** $\lambda = 4, W = 10$ minutes
a. $\mu = \frac{1}{2} = 0.5$
b. $W_q = W - 1/\mu = 10 - 1/0.5 = 8$ minutes
c. $L = \lambda W = 4(10) = 40$

**27. a.** $\frac{2}{8}$ hours $= 0.25$ per hour
b. $1/3.2$ hours $= 0.3125$ per hour
c. $L_q = \dfrac{\lambda^2\sigma^2 + (\lambda/\mu)^2}{2(1 - \lambda/\mu)}$

$= \dfrac{(0.25)^2(2)^2 + (0.25/0.3125)^2}{2(1 - 0.25/0.3125)} = 2.225$

d. $W_q = \dfrac{L_q}{\lambda} = \dfrac{2.225}{0.25} = 8.9$ hours

e. $W = W_q + \dfrac{1}{\mu} = 8.9 + \dfrac{1}{0.3125} = 12.1$ hours

f. Same as $P_w = \dfrac{\lambda}{\mu} = \dfrac{0.25}{0.3125} = 0.80$
80% of the time the welder is busy

**30. a.** $\lambda = 42; \mu = 20$

| $i$ | $(\lambda/\mu)^i/i!$ |
|---|---|
| 0 | 1.0000 |
| 1 | 2.1000 |
| 2 | 2.2050 |
| 3 | 1.5435 |
| Total | 6.8485 |

| $j$ | $P_j$ | |
|---|---|---|
| 0 | 1/6.8485 | = 0.1460 |
| 1 | 2.1/6.8485 | = 0.3066 |
| 2 | 2.2050/6.8485 | = 0.3220 |
| 3 | 1.5435/6.8485 | = 0.2254 |
| | | 1.0000 |

b. 0.2254

c. $L = \lambda/\mu(1 - P_k) = 42/20(1 - 0.2254) = 1.6267$

d. Four lines will be necessary; the probability of denied access is 0.1499

34. $N = 5$;   $\lambda = 0.025$;   $\mu = 0.20$;   $\lambda/\mu = 0.125$

a.

| $n$ | $\dfrac{N!}{(N-n)!}\left(\dfrac{\lambda}{\mu}\right)^n$ |
|---|---|
| 0 | 1.0000 |
| 1 | 0.6250 |
| 2 | 0.3125 |
| 3 | 0.1172 |
| 4 | 0.0293 |
| 5 | 0.0037 |
| Total | 2.0877 |

$P_0 = 1/2.0877 = 0.4790$

b. $L_q = N - \left(\dfrac{\lambda + \mu}{\lambda}\right)(1 - P_0)$

$= 5 - \left(\dfrac{0.225}{0.025}\right)(1 - 0.4790) = 0.3110$

c. $L = L_q + (1 - P_0) = 0.3110 + (1 - 0.4790)$
$= 0.8321$

d. $W_q = \dfrac{L_q}{(N - L)\lambda} = \dfrac{0.3110}{(5 - 0.8321)(0.025)}$
$= 2.9854$ minutes

e. $W = W_q + \dfrac{1}{\mu} = 2.9854 + \dfrac{1}{0.20} = 7.9854$ minutes

f. Trips/day = (8 hours)(60 minutes/hour)($\lambda$)
$= (8)(60)(0.025) = 12$ trips
Time at copier: $12 \times 7.9854 = 95.8$ minutes/day
Wait time at copier: $12 \times 2.9854 = 35.8$ minutes/day

g. Yes, five assistants $\times$ 35.8 = 179 minutes (3 hours/day), so 3 hours per day are lost to waiting
$(35.8/480)(100) = 7.5\%$ of each assistant's day is spent waiting for the copier

## Chapter 13

2. a. $c$ = variable cost per unit
$x$ = demand
Profit = $(50 - c)x - 30,000$

b. Base: Profit = $(50 - 20)1200 - 30,000 = 6,000$
Worst: Profit = $(50 - 24)300 - 30,000 = -22,200$
Best: Profit = $(50 - 16)2100 - 30,000 = 41,400$

c. Simulation will be helpful in estimating the probability of a loss

5. a.

| Stock Price Change | Interval |
|---|---|
| $-2$ | 0.00 but less than 0.05 |
| $-1$ | 0.05 but less than 0.15 |
| 0 | 0.15 but less than 0.40 |
| $+1$ | 0.40 but less than 0.60 |
| $+2$ | 0.60 but less than 0.80 |
| $+3$ | 0.80 but less than 0.90 |
| $+4$ | 0.90 but less than 1.00 |

b. Beginning price $39
0.1091 indicates $-1$ change; $38
0.9407 indicates $+4$ change; $42
0.1941 indicates 0 change; $42
0.8083 indicates $+3$ change; $45 (ending price)

9. a. Base-case based on most likely;
Time = $6 + 5 + 14 + 8 = 33$ weeks
Worst: Time = $8 + 7 + 18 + 10 = 43$ weeks
Best: Time = $5 + 3 + 10 + 8 = 26$ weeks

b. 0.1778 for A: 5 weeks
0.9617 for B: 7 weeks
0.6849 for C: 14 weeks
0.4503 for D: 8 weeks; Total = 24 weeks

c. Simulation will provide an estimate of the probability of 35 weeks or less

14. Selected cell formulas for the spreadsheet shown in Figure S13.14 are as follows:

| Cell | Formula |
|---|---|
| B13 | =$C$7+RAND()*($C$8-$C$7) |
| C13 | =NORMINV(RAND(),$G$7,$G$8) |
| D13 | =($C$3-B13)*C13-$C$4 |

a. The mean profit should be approximately $6,000. Simulation results will vary with most simulations having a mean profit between $5,500 and $6,500.

b. 120 to 150 of the 500 simulation trials should show a loss. Thus, the probability of a loss should be between 0.24 and 0.30.

c. This project appears too risky.

18. Selected cell formulas for the spreadsheet shown in Figures S13.18 are as follows:

| Cell | Formula |
|---|---|
| B11 | =$C$4 + RAND()*($C$5-$C$4) |
| C11 | =NORMINV(RAND(),$H$4,$H$5) |
| D11 | =MAX(B11:C11) |
| G11 | =COUNTIF(D11:D1010,"<750") |
| H11 | =G11/COUNT(D11:D1010) |

a. $750,000 should win roughly 600 to 650 of the 1000 times. The probability of winning the bid should be between 0.60 and 0.65.

b. The probability of $775,000 winning should be roughly 0.82, and the probability of $785,000 winning

| Figure S13.14 | SPREADSHEET FOR THE MADEIRA MANUFACTURING COMPANY |
|---|---|

| | A | B | C | D | E | F | G |
|---|---|---|---|---|---|---|---|
| 1 | Madeira Manufacturing Company | | | | | | |
| 2 | | | | | | | |
| 3 | Selling Price Per Unit | | $50 | | | | |
| 4 | Fixed Cost | | $30,000 | | | | |
| 5 | | | | | | | |
| 6 | Variable Cost (Uniform Distribution) | | | | Demand (Normal Distribution) | | |
| 7 | Smallest Value | | $16 | | Mean | | 1200 |
| 8 | Largest Value | | $24 | | Standard Deviation | | 300 |
| 9 | | | | | | | |
| 10 | Simulation Trials | | | | | | |
| 11 | | Variable | | | | | |
| 12 | Trial | Cost Per Unit | Demand | Profit | | | |
| 13 | 1 | $17.81 | 788 | ($4,631) | | | |
| 14 | 2 | $18.86 | 1078 | $3,580 | | | |

should be roughly 0.88. A contractor's bid of $775,000 is recommended.

## Chapter 14

**1. a.**

**b.**

| Decision | Maximum Profit | Minimum Profit |
|---|---|---|
| $d_1$ | 250 | 25 |
| $d_2$ | 100 | 75 |

Optimistic approach: Select $d_1$
Conservative approach: Select $d_2$

***Regret or opportunity loss table:***

| Decision | $s_1$ | $s_2$ | $s_3$ |
|---|---|---|---|
| $d_1$ | 0 | 0 | 50 |
| $d_2$ | 150 | 0 | 0 |

Maximum regret: 50 for $d_1$ and 150 for $d_2$; select $d_1$

**5.** $EV(d_1) = 0.65(250) + 0.15(100) + 0.20(25) = 182.5$
$EV(d_2) = 0.65(100) + 0.15(100) + 0.20(75) = 95$
The optimal decision is $d_1$

**8.** $EV(d_1) = p(10) + (1 - p)(1) = 9p + 1$
$EV(d_2) = p(4) + (1 - p)(3) = 1p + 3$

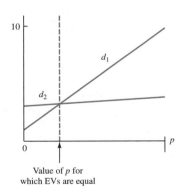

Value of $p$ for
which EVs are equal

$9p + 1 = 1p + 3$ and hence $p = 0.25$
At $P(s_1) = 0.25$, $EV(d_1) = EV(d_2) = 3.25$
If $P(s_1) < 0.25$, $EV(d_2)$ is greater.
If $P(s_1) > 0.25$, $EV(d_1)$ is greater.

**12. a.** If $s_1$, then $d_1$; if $s_2$, then $d_1$ or $d_2$; if $s_3$, then $d_2$
   **b.** EVwPI = $0.65(250) + 0.15(100) + 0.20(75) = 192.5$
   **c.** From the solution to Problem 5, we know that $EV(d_1) = 182.5$ and $EV(d_2) = 95$; thus, recommended decision is $d_1$; hence, EVwoPI = 182.5
   **d.** EVPI = EVwPI − EVwoPI = 192.5 − 182.5 = 10

## Figure S13.18  SPREADSHEET FOR THE CONTRACTOR BIDDING

|    | A | B | C | D | E | F | G | H |
|----|---|---|---|---|---|---|---|---|
| 1 | Contractor Bidding | | | | | | | |
| 2 | | | | | | | | |
| 3 | Contractor A (Uniform Distribution) | | | | | Contractor B (Normal Distribution) | | |
| 4 | Smallest Value | | $600 | | | Mean | | $700 |
| 5 | Largest Value | | $800 | | | Standard Deviation | | $50 |
| 6 | | | | | | | | |
| 7 | | | | | | | | |
| 8 | Simulation | | | | | Results | | |
| 9 | | Contractor | Contractor | Highest | | Contractor's | Number | Probability |
| 10 | Trial | A's Bid | B's Bid | Bid | | Bid | of Wins | of Winning |
| 11 | 1 | $673.4 | $719.8 | $719.8 | | 750 | 629 | 0.629 |
| 12 | 2 | $756.9 | $654.8 | $756.9 | | 775 | 824 | 0.824 |
| 13 | 3 | $705.5 | $791.1 | $791.1 | | 785 | 887 | 0.887 |
| 14 | 4 | $638.0 | $677.1 | $677.1 | | | | |

**14. a.**

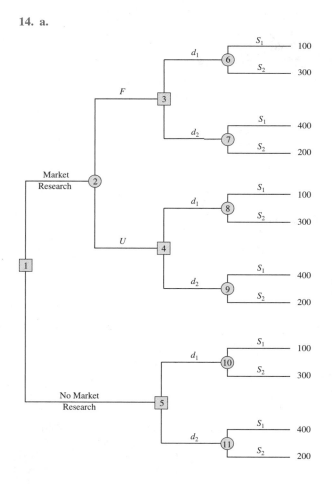

**b.** EV(node 6) = 0.57(100) + 0.43(300) = 186
EV(node 7) = 0.57(400) + 0.43(200) = 314
EV(node 8) = 0.18(100) + 0.82(300) = 264
EV(node 9) = 0.18(400) + 0.82(200) = 236
EV(node 10) = 0.40(100) + 0.60(300) = 220
EV(node 11) = 0.40(400) + 0.60(200) = 280
EV(node 3) = max(186,314) = 314 $d_2$
EV(node 4) = max(264,236) = 264 $d_1$
EV(node 5) = max(220,280) = 280 $d_2$
EV(node 2) = 0.56(314) + 0.44(264) = 292
EV(node 1) = max(292,280) = 292
Conduct Market Research,
If $F$, $d_2$; If $U$, $d_1$

**22.**

| State of Nature | $P(s_j)$ | $P(I/s_j)$ | $P(I \cap s_j)$ | $P(s_j/I)$ |
|---|---|---|---|---|
| $s_1$ | 0.2 | 0.10 | 0.020 | 0.1905 |
| $s_2$ | 0.5 | 0.05 | 0.025 | 0.2381 |
| $s_3$ | 0.3 | 0.20 | 0.060 | 0.5714 |
| | 1.0 | | $P(I) = 0.105$ | 1.0000 |

**26.** Risk-avoider, at $20 payoff $p = 0.70$
EV(Lottery) = 0.70(100) + 0.30(−100) = $40
Will Pay 40 − 20 = $20
Risk-taker, at $20 payoff $p = 0.45$
EV(Lottery) = 0.45(100) + 0.55(−100) = −$10
Will Pay 20 − (−10) = $30

**28. a.** $EV(d_1) = 0.40(100) + 0.30(25) + 0.30(0) = 47.5$
$EV(d_2) = 0.40(75) + 0.30(50) + 0.30(25) = 52.5 \Big\} d_2$
$EV(d_3) = 0.40(50) + 0.30(50) + 0.30(50) = 50.0$

**b.** Using utilities

| Decision Maker A | Decision Maker B |
|---|---|
| $EU(d_1) = 4.9$ | $EU(d_1) = 4.45$ Best |
| $EU(d_2) = 5.9$ | $EU(d_2) = 3.75$ |
| $EU(d_3) = 6.0$ Best | $EU(d_3) = 3.00$ |

**c.** Difference in attitude toward risk; decision maker A tends to avoid risk, whereas decision maker B tends to take a risk for the opportunity of a large payoff

# Chapter 15

**2. a.** Let $x_1$ = number of shares of AGA Products purchased
$x_2$ = number of shares of Key Oil purchased
To obtain an annual return of exactly 9%:

$$0.06(50)x_1 + 0.10(100)x_2 = 0.09(50,000)$$
$$3x_1 + 10x_2 = 4500$$

To have exactly 60% of the total investment in Key Oil:

$$100x_2 = 0.60(50,000)$$
$$x_2 = 300$$

Therefore, we can write the goal programming model as follows:

Min $P_1(d_1^-) + P_2(d_2^+)$
s.t.

$$
\begin{aligned}
50x_1 + 100x_2 &\le 50,000 \quad \text{Funds available} \\
3x_1 + 10x_2 - d_1^+ + d_1^- &= 4,500 \quad P_1 \text{ goal} \\
x_2 - d_2^+ + d_2^- &= 300 \quad P_2 \text{ goal} \\
x_1, x_2, d_1^+, d_1^-, d_2^+, d_2^- &\ge 0
\end{aligned}
$$

**b.** In the following graphical solution, $x_1 = 250$ and $x_2 = 375$

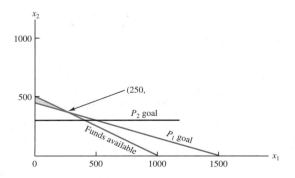

**9.** Scoring Calculations

| Criteria | Analyst Chicago | Accountant Denver | Auditor Houston |
|---|---|---|---|
| Career advancement | 35 | 20 | 20 |
| Location | 10 | 12 | 8 |
| Management | 30 | 25 | 35 |
| Salary | 28 | 32 | 16 |
| Prestige | 32 | 20 | 24 |
| Job security | 8 | 10 | 16 |
| Enjoyment of the work | 28 | 20 | 20 |
| Totals | 171 | 139 | 139 |

The analyst position in Chicago is recommended.

**16.** Step 1: Column totals are $^{17}\!/_4$, $^{31}\!/_{21}$, and 12
Step 2:

| Style | Accord | Saturn | Cavalier |
|---|---|---|---|
| Accord | $^4\!/_{17}$ | $^7\!/_{31}$ | $^4\!/_{12}$ |
| Saturn | $^{12}\!/_{17}$ | $^{21}\!/_{31}$ | $^7\!/_{12}$ |
| Cavalier | $^1\!/_{17}$ | $^3\!/_{31}$ | $^1\!/_{12}$ |

Step 3:

| Style | Accord | Saturn | Cavalier | Row Average |
|---|---|---|---|---|
| Accord | 0.235 | 0.226 | 0.333 | 0.265 |
| Saturn | 0.706 | 0.677 | 0.583 | 0.656 |
| Cavalier | 0.059 | 0.097 | 0.083 | 0.080 |

Consistency Ratio
Step 1:

$$0.265\begin{bmatrix}1\\3\\ \frac14\end{bmatrix} + 0.656\begin{bmatrix}\frac13\\1\\ \frac17\end{bmatrix} + 0.080\begin{bmatrix}4\\7\\1\end{bmatrix}$$

$$\begin{bmatrix}0.265\\0.795\\0.066\end{bmatrix} + \begin{bmatrix}0.219\\0.656\\0.094\end{bmatrix} + \begin{bmatrix}0.320\\0.560\\0.080\end{bmatrix} = \begin{bmatrix}0.802\\2.007\\0.239\end{bmatrix}$$

Step 2: 0.802/0.265 = 3.028
2.007/0.656 = 3.062
0.239/0.080 = 3.007
Step 3: $\lambda_{max}$ = (3.028 + 3.062 + 3.002)/3 = 3.032
Step 4: CI = (3.032 − 3)/2 = 0.016
Step 5: CR = 0.016/0.58 = 0.028
Because CR = 0.028 is less than 0.10, the degree of consistency exhibited in the pairwise comparison matrix for style is acceptable

20. a.

| Flavor | A | B | C |
|--------|-----|-----|-----|
| A | 1 | 3 | 2 |
| B | 1/3 | 1 | 5 |
| C | 1/2 | 1/5 | 1 |

b. Step 1: Column totals are $11/6$, $21/5$, and 8
Step 2:

| Flavor | A | B | C |
|--------|-------|-------|-----|
| A | 6/11 | 15/21 | 2/8 |
| B | 2/11 | 5/21 | 5/8 |
| C | 3/11 | 1/21 | 1/8 |

Step 3:

| Flavor | A | B | C | Row Average |
|--------|-------|-------|-------|-------------|
| A | 0.545 | 0.714 | 0.250 | 0.503 |
| B | 0.182 | 0.238 | 0.625 | 0.348 |
| C | 0.273 | 0.048 | 0.125 | 0.148 |

c. Step 1:

$$0.503 \begin{bmatrix} 1 \\ 1/3 \\ 1/2 \end{bmatrix} + 0.348 \begin{bmatrix} 3 \\ 1 \\ 1/5 \end{bmatrix} + 0.148 \begin{bmatrix} 2 \\ 5 \\ 1 \end{bmatrix}$$

$$\begin{bmatrix} 0.503 \\ 0.168 \\ 0.252 \end{bmatrix} + \begin{bmatrix} 1.044 \\ 0.348 \\ 0.070 \end{bmatrix} + \begin{bmatrix} 0.296 \\ 0.740 \\ 0.148 \end{bmatrix} = \begin{bmatrix} 1.845 \\ 1.258 \\ 0.470 \end{bmatrix}$$

Step 2: $1.845/0.503 = 3.668$
$1.258/0.348 = 3.615$
$0.470/0.148 = 3.123$
Step 3: $\lambda_{max} = (3.668 + 3.615 + 3.123)/3 = 3.469$
Step 4: CI $= (3.469 - 3)/2 = 0.235$
Step 5: CR $= 0.235/0.58 = 0.415$
Because CR $= 0.415$ is greater than 0.10, the individual's judgments are not consistent.

24. Criteria: Yield and Risk
Step 1: Column totals are 1.5 and 3
Step 2:

|  | Yield | Risk | Priority |
|------|-------|-------|----------|
| Yield | 0.667 | 0.667 | 0.667 |
| Risk | 0.333 | 0.333 | 0.333 |

With only 2 criteria, CR $= 0$; no need to compute CR
Preceding calculations for Yield and Risk provide

| Stocks | Yield Priority | Risk Priority |
|--------|----------------|---------------|
| CCC | 0.750 | 0.333 |
| SRI | 0.250 | 0.667 |

Overall Priorities:
CCC $0.667(0.750) + 0.333(0.333) = 0.611$
SRI $0.667(0.250) + 0.333(0.667) = 0.387$
CCC is preferred

# Chapter 16

1. a.

| Month | Time-Series Value | 3-Month Moving Average Forecast | (Error)² | 4-Month Moving Average Forecast | (Error)² |
|-------|-------|-------|-------|-------|-------|
| 1 | 9.5 | | | | |
| 2 | 9.3 | | | | |
| 3 | 9.4 | | | | |
| 4 | 9.6 | 9.40 | 0.04 | | |
| 5 | 9.8 | 9.43 | 0.14 | 9.45 | 0.12 |
| 6 | 9.7 | 9.60 | 0.01 | 9.53 | 0.03 |
| 7 | 9.8 | 9.70 | 0.01 | 9.63 | 0.03 |
| 8 | 10.5 | 9.77 | 0.53 | 9.73 | 0.59 |
| 9 | 9.9 | 10.00 | 0.01 | 9.95 | 0.00 |
| 10 | 9.7 | 10.07 | 0.14 | 9.98 | 0.08 |
| 11 | 9.6 | 10.03 | 0.18 | 9.97 | 0.14 |
| 12 | 9.6 | 9.73 | 0.02 | 9.92 | 0.10 |
| | | Totals | 1.08 | | 1.09 |

MSE(3-month) $= 1.08/9 = 0.12$
MSE(4-month) $= 1.09/8 = 0.14$
Use a 3-month moving average.
b. Forecast $= (9.7 + 9.6 + 9.6)/3 = 9.63$

2. a.

| Week | Time-Series Value | 4-Week Moving Average Forecast | (Error)² | 5-Week Moving Average Forecast | (Error)² |
|------|-------|-------|-------|-------|-------|
| 1 | 17 | | | | |
| 2 | 21 | | | | |
| 3 | 19 | | | | |
| 4 | 23 | | | | |
| 5 | 18 | 20.00 | 4.00 | | |
| 6 | 16 | 20.25 | 18.06 | 19.60 | 12.96 |
| 7 | 20 | 19.00 | 1.00 | 19.40 | 0.36 |
| 8 | 18 | 19.25 | 1.56 | 19.20 | 1.44 |
| 9 | 22 | 18.00 | 16.00 | 19.00 | 9.00 |
| 10 | 20 | 19.00 | 1.00 | 18.80 | 1.44 |
| 11 | 15 | 20.00 | 25.00 | 19.20 | 17.64 |
| 12 | 22 | 18.75 | 10.56 | 19.00 | 9.00 |
| | | Totals | 77.18 | | 51.84 |

**b.** MSE(4-week) = 77.18/8 = 9.65
MSE(5-week) = 51.84/7 = 7.41

**c.** For the limited data provided, the 5-week moving average provides the smallest MSE

**4.**

| Week | Time-Series Value | Forecast | Error | $(Error)^2$ |
|------|------|------|------|------|
| 1 | 17 | | | |
| 2 | 21 | 17.00 | 4.00 | 16.00 |
| 3 | 19 | 17.40 | 1.60 | 2.56 |
| 4 | 23 | 17.56 | 5.44 | 29.59 |
| 5 | 18 | 18.10 | −0.10 | 0.01 |
| 6 | 16 | 18.09 | −2.09 | 4.37 |
| 7 | 20 | 17.88 | 2.12 | 4.49 |
| 8 | 18 | 18.10 | −0.10 | 0.01 |
| 9 | 22 | 18.09 | 3.91 | 15.29 |
| 10 | 20 | 18.48 | 1.52 | 2.31 |
| 11 | 15 | 18.63 | −3.63 | 13.18 |
| 12 | 22 | 18.27 | 3.73 | 13.91 |
| | | | Total | 101.72 |

MSE = 101.72/11 = 9.25
$\alpha = 0.2$ provided a lower MSE; therefore $\alpha = 0.2$ is better than $\alpha = 0.1$

**5. a.**

| Month | $Y_t$ | 3-Month Moving Averages Forecast | $(Error)^2$ | $\alpha = 2$ Forecast | $(Error)^2$ |
|------|------|------|------|------|------|
| 1 | 80 | | | | |
| 2 | 82 | | | 80.00 | 4.00 |
| 3 | 84 | | | 80.40 | 12.96 |
| 4 | 83 | 82.00 | 1.00 | 81.12 | 3.53 |
| 5 | 83 | 83.00 | 0.00 | 81.50 | 2.25 |
| 6 | 84 | 83.33 | 0.45 | 81.80 | 4.84 |
| 7 | 85 | 83.33 | 2.79 | 82.24 | 7.62 |
| 8 | 84 | 84.00 | 0.00 | 82.79 | 1.46 |
| 9 | 82 | 84.33 | 5.43 | 83.03 | 1.06 |
| 10 | 83 | 83.67 | 0.45 | 82.83 | 0.03 |
| 11 | 84 | 83.00 | 1.00 | 82.86 | 1.30 |
| 12 | 83 | 83.00 | 0.00 | 83.09 | 0.01 |
| | | Totals 11.12 | | | 39.06 |

MSE(3-month) = 11.12/9 = 1.24
MSE($\alpha = 0.2$) = 39.06/11 = 3.55
Use a 3-month moving average
**b.** (83 + 84 + 83)/3 = 83.3

**14.** $\sum t = 21; \sum t^2 = 91; \sum Y_t = 117.1;$
$\sum tY_t = 403.7; n = 6$

$$b_1 = \frac{\sum tY_t - (\sum t \sum Y_t)/n}{\sum t^2 - (\sum t)^2/n}$$

$$= \frac{403.7 - (21)(117.1)/6}{91 - (21)^2/6}$$

$$= -0.3514$$

$b_0 = \bar{Y} - b_1\bar{t} = 19.5167 - (-.3514)(3.5) = 20.7466$
$T_t = 20.7466 - 0.3514t$
Conclusion: Enrollment appears to be decreasing by an average of approximately 351 students per year

**25. a.** Four-quarter moving averages beginning with
(1690 + 940 + 2625 + 2500)/4 = 1938.75
Other moving averages are

| | |
|------|------|
| 1966.25 | 2002.50 |
| 1956.25 | 2052.50 |
| 2025.00 | 2060.00 |
| 1990.00 | 2123.75 |

**b.**

| Quarter | Seasonal-Irregular Component Values | | Seasonal Index | Adjusted Seasonal Index |
|------|------|------|------|------|
| 1 | 0.904 | 0.900 | 0.9020 | 0.900 |
| 2 | 0.448 | 0.526 | 0.4970 | 0.486 |
| 3 | 1.344 | 1.453 | 1.3985 | 1.396 |
| 4 | 1.275 | 1.164 | 1.2195 | 1.217 |
| | | | Total 4.0070 | |

**c.** The largest seasonal effect is in the third quarter, which corresponds to the back-to-school demand during July, August, and September of each year.

**33.** Note: Adjustment for seasonal index = 4.000/4.007 = 0.9983
**a.**

| Restaurant (i) | $x_i$ | $y_i$ | $x_iy_i$ | $x_i^2$ |
|------|------|------|------|------|
| 1 | 1 | 19 | 19 | 1 |
| 2 | 4 | 44 | 176 | 16 |
| 3 | 6 | 40 | 240 | 36 |
| 4 | 10 | 52 | 520 | 100 |
| 5 | 14 | 53 | 742 | 196 |
| Totals | 35 | 208 | 1697 | 349 |

$$\bar{x} = \frac{35}{5} = 7$$

$$\bar{y} = \frac{208}{5} = 41.6$$

$$b_1 = \frac{\sum x_i y_i - (\sum x_i \sum y_i)/n}{\sum x_i^2 - (\sum x_i)^2/n}$$

$$= \frac{1697 - (35)(208)/5}{349 - (35)^2/5}$$

$$= \frac{241}{104} = 2.317$$

$b_0 = \bar{y} - b_1\bar{x} = 41.6 - 2.317(7) = 25.381$

$\hat{y} = 25.381 + 2.317x$

b. $\hat{y} = 25.381 + 2.317(8) = 43.917$ or $\$43,917$

## Chapter 17

3. a. 0.10 as given by the transition probability

b. $\pi_1 = 0.90\pi_1 + 0.30\pi_2$     (1)

  $\pi_2 = 0.10\pi_1 + 0.70\pi_2$     (2)

  $\pi_1 + \pi_1 = 1$     (3)

  Using (1) and (3),

    $0.10\pi_1 - 0.30\pi_2 = 0$

    $0.10\pi_1 - 0.30(1 - \pi_1) = 0$

    $0.10\pi_1 - 0.30 + 0.30\pi_1 = 0$

          $0.40\pi_1 = 0.30$

              $\pi_1 = 0.75$

     $\pi_2 = (1 - \pi_1) = 0.25$

7. a. $\pi_1 = 0.85\pi_1 + 0.20\pi_2 + 0.15\pi_3$   (1)

  $\pi_2 = 0.10\pi_1 + 0.75\pi_2 + 0.10\pi_3$   (2)

  $\pi_3 = 0.05\pi_1 + 0.05\pi_2 + 0.75\pi_3$   (3)

  $\pi_1 + \pi_2 + \pi_3 = 1$   (4)

  Using (1), (2), and (4) provides three equations with three unknowns; solving provides $\pi_1 = 0.548$, $\pi_2 = 0.286$, and $\pi_3 = 0.166$

b. 16.6% as given by $\pi_3$

c. Quick Stop should take

    $667 - 0.548(1000) = 119$ Murphy's customers

   and $333 - 0.286(1000) = \underline{\phantom{0}47}$ Ashley's customers

           Total  166 Quick Stop customers

  It will take customers from Murphy and Ashley.

11. $I = \begin{bmatrix} 1 & 0 \\ 0 & 1 \end{bmatrix}$    $Q = \begin{bmatrix} 0.25 & 0.25 \\ 0.25 & 0.25 \end{bmatrix}$

$(I - Q) = \begin{bmatrix} 0.75 & -0.25 \\ -0.05 & 0.75 \end{bmatrix}$

$N = (I - Q)^{-1} = \begin{bmatrix} 1.3636 & 0.4545 \\ 0.0909 & 1.3636 \end{bmatrix}$

$NR = \begin{bmatrix} 1.3636 & 0.4545 \\ 0.0909 & 1.3636 \end{bmatrix} \begin{bmatrix} 0.5 & 0.0 \\ 0.5 & 0.2 \end{bmatrix} = \begin{bmatrix} 0.909 & 0.091 \\ 0.727 & 0.273 \end{bmatrix}$

$BNR = \begin{bmatrix} 4000 & 5000 \end{bmatrix} \begin{bmatrix} 0.909 & 0.091 \\ 0.727 & 0.273 \end{bmatrix} = \begin{bmatrix} 7271 & 1729 \end{bmatrix}$

Estimate $\$1729$ in bad debts

## Chapter 18

2. a. The numbers in the squares above each node represent the shortest route from the node to node 10

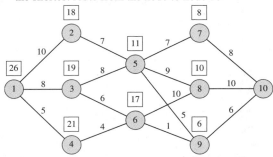

The shortest route is given by the sequence of nodes (1–4–6–9–10)

b. The shortest route from node 4 to node 10 is given by (4–6–9–10)

c.

| Route | Value | Route | Value |
|---|---|---|---|
| (1–2–5–7–10) | 32 | (1–3–6–8–10) | 34 |
| (1–2–5–8–10) | 36 | (1–3–6–9–10) | 31 |
| (1–2–5–9–10) | 28 | (1–4–6–8–10) | 29 |
| (1–3–5–7–10) | 31 | (1–4–6–9–10) | 26 |
| (1–3–5–8–10) | 35 | | |
| (1–3–5–9–10) | 27 | | |

3. Use four stages (one for each type of cargo); let the state variable represent the amount of cargo space remaining

a. In hundreds of pounds, we have up to 20 units of capacity available

**Stage 1 (Cargo Type 1):**

| $x_1$ | 0 | 1 | 2 | $d_1^*$ | $f_1(x_1)$ | $x_0$ |
|---|---|---|---|---|---|---|
| 0–7 | 0 | — | — | 0 | 0 | 0–7 |
| 8–15 | 0 | 22 | — | 1 | 22 | 0–7 |
| 16–20 | 0 | 22 | 44 | 2 | 44 | 0–4 |

**Stage 2 (Cargo Type 2):**

| $x_2$ | 0 | 1 | 2 | $d_2^*$ | $f_2(x_2)$ | $x_1$ |
|---|---|---|---|---|---|---|
| 0–4 | 0 | — | — | 0 | 0 | 0–4 |
| 5–7 | 0 | 12 | — | 1 | 12 | 0–2 |
| 8–9 | 22 | 12 | — | 0 | 22 | 8–9 |
| 10–12 | 22 | 12 | 24 | 2 | 24 | 0–2 |
| 13–15 | 22 | 34 | 24 | 1 | 34 | 8–10 |
| 16–17 | 44 | 34 | 24 | 0 | 44 | 16–17 |
| 18–20 | 44 | 34 | 46 | 2 | 46 | 8–10 |

**Stage 3 (Cargo Type 3):**

| $x_3$ | 0 | 1 | 2 | 3 | 4 | $d_3^*$ | $f_3(x_3)$ | $x_2$ |
|---|---|---|---|---|---|---|---|---|
| 0–2 | 0 | — | — | — | — | 0 | 0 | 0–2 |
| 3–4 | 0 | 7 | — | — | — | 1 | 7 | 0–1 |
| 5 | 12 | 7 | — | — | — | 0 | 12 | 5 |
| 6–7 | 12 | 7 | 14 | — | — | 2 | 14 | 0–1 |
| 8 | 22 | 19 | 14 | — | — | 0 | 22 | 8 |
| 9 | 22 | 19 | 14 | 21 | — | 0 | 22 | 9 |
| 10 | 24 | 19 | 14 | 21 | — | 0 | 24 | 10 |
| 11 | 24 | 29 | 26 | 21 | — | 1 | 29 | 8 |
| 12 | 24 | 29 | 26 | 21 | 28 | 1 | 29 | 9 |
| 13 | 34 | 31 | 26 | 21 | 28 | 0 | 34 | 13 |
| 14–15 | 34 | 31 | 36 | 33 | 28 | 2 | 36 | 8–9 |
| 16 | 44 | 41 | 38 | 33 | 28 | 0 | 44 | 16 |
| 17 | 44 | 41 | 38 | 43 | 40 | 0 | 44 | 17 |
| 18 | 46 | 41 | 38 | 43 | 40 | 0 | 46 | 18 |
| 19 | 46 | 51 | 48 | 45 | 40 | 1 | 51 | 16 |
| 20 | 46 | 51 | 48 | 45 | 50 | 1 | 51 | 17 |

**Stage 4 (Cargo Type 4):**

| $x_4$ | 0 | 1 | 2 | 3 | $d_4^*$ | $f_4(x_4)$ | $x_3$ |
|---|---|---|---|---|---|---|---|
| 20 | 51 | 49 | 50 | 45 | 0 | 51 | 20 |

Tracing back through the tables, we find

| Stage | State Variable Entering | Optimal Decision | State Variable Leaving |
|---|---|---|---|
| 4 | 20 | 0 | 20 |
| 3 | 20 | 1 | 17 |
| 2 | 17 | 0 | 17 |
| 1 | 17 | 2 | 1 |

Load 1 unit of cargo type 3 and 2 units of cargo type 1 for a total return of $5100

b. Only the calculations for stage 4 need to be repeated; the entering value for the state variable is 18

| $x_4$ | 0 | 1 | 2 | 3 | $d_4^*$ | $f_4(x_4)$ | $x_3$ |
|---|---|---|---|---|---|---|---|
| 18 | 46 | 47 | 42 | 38 | 1 | 47 | 16 |

Optimal solution: $d_4 = 1$, $d_3 = 0$, $d_2 = 0$, $d_1 = 2$
Value = 47

10. The optimal production schedule is as follows:

| Month | Beginning Inventory | Production | Ending Inventory |
|---|---|---|---|
| 1 | 10 | 20 | 10 |
| 2 | 10 | 20 | 0 |
| 3 | 0 | 30 | 0 |

LINDO (Linear, INteractive, and Discrete Optimizer) was developed by Linus E. Schrage at the University of Chicago; it is available in Command-line and Windows (Windows 3.1®, Windows NT®, or Windows 95®) versions. In this appendix we describe how to use the Windows version by entering and solving the Par, Inc., problem introduced in Chapter 2. Since LINDO requires decimal rather than fractional data values, we restate the complete mathematical model for the Par, Inc., problem with decimal coefficients:

$$
\begin{array}{lrll}
\text{Max } 10S & + & 9D \\
\text{s.t.} \\
0.7S & + & 1D \leq 630 & \text{Cutting and dyeing} \\
0.5S & + & 0.83333D \leq 600 & \text{Sewing} \\
1S & + & 0.66667D \leq 708 & \text{Finishing} \\
0.1S & + & 0.25D \leq 135 & \text{Inspection and packaging} \\
& S,D \geq 0
\end{array}
$$

When you start LINDO, two windows are immediately displayed. The outer window labeled "LINDO" contains all the command menus and the command toolbar. The smaller window labeled "<untitled>" is the model window. This window is used to enter and edit the linear programming model that you want to solve. The first item you must enter into the model window is the objective function. Thus, for the Par, Inc., problem, type MAX 10S + 9D. To indicate that the objective function has been completely entered and that the model constraints will follow, press the enter key and type the words SUBJECT TO (or just the letters ST). Next, after pressing the enter key to move to a new line, enter the first Par, Inc., constraint by typing 0.7S + 1D < 630. Note that LINDO interprets the < symbol as ≤. Then, after pressing the enter key, enter the second constraint by typing 0.5S + 0.83333D < 600. Press the enter key again and type the third constraint, 1S + 0.66667D < 708. Then, press the enter key and type the fourth and final constraint, 0.1S + 0.25D < 135. Finally, after pressing the enter key, type END to signal LINDO that the model input is complete. If you make an error entering the model, you can correct it at any time by simply positioning the cursor where you made the error and typing the necessary corrections.

To solve the problem that you have just entered, you must select the Solve command from the Solve menu, or press the Solve button on the LINDO toolbar. If LINDO does not find any errors in the model input, it will begin to solve the model, When the solver is finished, LINDO will ask whether you want to do sensitivity and range analysis. If you select the "YES" button and close the Status Window, LINDO displays the complete solution to the Par, Inc., problem on a new window titled "Reports Window." The output that appears in the Reports Window is shown in Figure G.1.

The first section of the output shown in Figure G.1 is self-explanatory. For example, after rounding, we see that the optimal solution is $S = 540$ and $D = 252$, and that the value of the objective function at the optimal solution is 7668. After displaying the values of the slack variables and the dual prices, LINDO displays the ranges on the objective function coefficients and the right sides of the constraints.

Consider the information provided under the computer output heading OBJ COEFFI-CIENT RANGES. Variable $S$, with a current profit coefficient of 10, has an allowable increase of 3.5 and an allowable decrease of 3.7. Adding 3.5 to and subtracting 3.7 from the current coefficient of 10 provides the range of optimality for $C_S$:

$$6.3 \leq C_S \leq 13.5$$

Similarly, the range of optimality for $C_D$ is

$$6.67 \leq C_D \leq 14.29$$

The information under the heading RIGHT HAND SIDE RANGES permits computing the range of feasibility for each right-hand side. Simply subtract the allowable decrease from the current value to get the lower limit, and add the allowable increase to the current value to get the upper limit. Doing so, we obtain

| Constraint | Min RHS | Max RHS |
|---|---|---|
| Cutting and dyeing | 495.6 | 682.4 |
| Sewing | 480.0 | No upper limit |
| Finishing | 580.0 | 900.0 |
| Inspection and packaging | 117.0 | No upper limit |

```
          OBJECTIVE FUNCTION VALUE

     1)       7667.994

 VARIABLE         VALUE        REDUCED COST
     S         539.998413        0.000000
     D         252.001114        0.000000

    ROW     SLACK OR SURPLUS     DUAL PRICES
     2)        0.000000          4.374956
     3)      120.000717          0.000000
     4)        0.000000          6.937531
     5)       17.999882          0.000000

NO. ITERATIONS=        2

                        OBJ COEFFICIENT RANGES
 VARIABLE       CURRENT        ALLOWABLE        ALLOWABLE
                COEF           INCREASE         DECREASE
     S         10.000000       3.499932         3.700000
     D          9.000000       5.285714         2.333300

                        RIGHTHAND SIDE RANGES
    ROW         CURRENT        ALLOWABLE        ALLOWABLE
                RHS            INCREASE         DECREASE
     2         630.000000      52.363155        134.400009
     3         600.000000      INFINITY         120.000717
     4         708.000000      192.000000       127.998589
     5         135.000000      INFINITY         17.999882
```